श्रीमद्भागवतम्

SRIMAD BHAGAVATA

VOLUME II

श्रीमद्भागवतम्

SRIMAD BHAGAVATA

THE HOLY BOOK OF GOD

Translated by

SWAMI TAPASYANANDA

VOLUME II

SKANDHAS V-IX

SRI RAMAKRISHNA MATH

MADRAS-600 004 INDIA

Published by
Adhyaksha
Sri Ramakrishna Math
Mylapore, Chennai-4

First Edition, August 1981
Ninth print, July 2021
1000 copies

ISBN: 978-81-7883-833-5 (Paperback)

Printed in India at
Sri Ramakrishna Math Printing Press
Mylapore, Chennai-4

CONTENTS

SKANDHA V

SKANDHA VI

SKANDHA VIII

Srimad Bhagavata Mahapurana
Skandha Five
PROLOGUE

The fifth Skandha of the Bhagavata has twenty six chapters, which contain six hundred and sixty eight passages in verse and prose. A considerable portion of the text is in prose.

According to tradition the topic treated in it is Sthiti, also called Sthana, which forms the third of the topics of discourse in a Mahapurana. Sthiti is described as 'the augmentation of the Lord's scheme' (II. 10.4). What is actually given under this head in the fifth Skandha is a schematic description of the universe (Brahmanda), including a detailed plan of the surface of the earth. These worlds form the residences of living beings of various kinds.

In another enumeration of the themes of the Puranas, the third item is referred to as Vritti (livelihood), and it is described as: 'For living beings that move, motionless objects and other moving beings form the Vritti or source of livelihood. For man, Vritti is what provides him with sustenance as given by Nature, or what is procured out of desire, or what is ordained by the scriptures' (XII.7.13). Since residence and livelihood form the most important aspects of maintenance or 'augmentation of the Lord's scheme', all these words have practically the same connotation.

As we had occasion to state earlier, many subjects that do not come under the main theme are discussed in the loose literary scheme of the Puranas. So in this Skandha of twenty six chapters, the first fifteen deal with the rule of several pious kings descended from Swāyambhuva Manu. The doings of Manu Swāyambhuva's son Uttānapāda and his successors up to Prāchinabarhis have been described in an earlier Skandha, namely the fourth. Here the history of Priyavrata, another son of the Manu, and his successors is treated. Naturally disposed to asceticism, Priyavrata renounced the world under Narada's instruction, but was brought back to take up the duties of kingship by Brahma, who taught him the way to be in the world while being not of it. He is famous for having given the earth's surface its peculiar geographical features which the Pauranikas describe as the seven Dweepas or continents, with Jambu Dweepa as the central region, surrounded by seven oceans in concentric circles around intervening land belts that form the other Dweepas. These encircling seas are described as the ruts formed by Priyavrata's chariot wheels as he circled the universe following the chariot of the sun. More details about the continents and the oceans are given hereafter in this essay. It is difficult to make out any meaning for the theory of ocean being formed by the rut of a chariot. The Purana is itself aware of the obvious incredibility of it, and says that it was possible for him because of the might of the Lord that manifested through him on account of his devotion and austerities.

Priyavrata's son was Agnidhra, a very pious and noble ruler, who finally succumbed to the charms of an Apsara female. His son was Nābhi, a great and devout ruler, to whom Mahavishnu announced at a Yajna that He would incarnate Himself as his son. The son so born was Rishabha, one of the greatest among the Rajarshis. The object of this incarnation was to set an example of an ideal householder and of a Paramahamsa. He had several sons, of whom nine became the Nava-yogis, famous for their spiritual attainment. They figure in the 11th Skandha. All others except Bharata took to Vedic study and became Brahmanas. Rishabha, on retirement from the duties of State, took to the life of a Paramahamsa to be an exemplar of extreme asceticism. His achievements and teachings are given in three chapters, from the fourth to the sixth. It is noteworthy that Jains also consider him to be one of their spiritual Masters (Tirthankaras).

The most famous of Rishabha's sons was Bharata, who succeeded him to the throne. His impact on the country was so great that the land, which was known earlier as Ajanābhavarsha, came to be called Bhāratavarsha after him. Besides being a great ruler, he was a great devotee who took to asceticism in later life. We get an elaborate account of how attachment to a fawn brought on him re-birth as a deer and afterwards again as a man with full enlightenment, how he came to be known as Jadabharata, and how he delivered a great discourse on devotion to king Rahūgana—all these are graphically described in chapters seven to fourteen. These form some of the most attractive and instructive chapters of this Skandha. This section closes with the fifteenth chapter where we get accounts of Bharata's successors up to Gaya, a very worthy king.

From the sixteenth chapter to the end of the Skandha, eleven chapters are devoted to what looks like a schematic description of the universe. The geography and astronomy of the descriptions may look queer and fantastic to us who are conversant with the discoveries of modern science. But we should not labour under the impression that the object of these writers is to teach us geography and astronomy. It is clearly stated at the beginning of the section that these descriptions are given in order to impress on man that this universe is the gross form of the Lord, and that by meditating on it and by being impressed by its wonderful uniqueness and by the might and wisdom revealed in it, one's mind is helped to grasp the subtle, the spiritual Essence that gives substantiality to the universe. God, who is otherwise some imaginary extra-cosmic being, becomes the real of the real, the ultimate reality, when He is conceived as the support of what is most real and concrete to us. Just as an image or a Yantra (a ceremonial design) becomes a symbol for worship, an aid for grasping the immaterial Spirit, the whole universe too can be used for such a purpose with great effect by a man endowed with faith. The description is absolutely schematic but idealistic too. It is poetical not prosaic; and often poetry can convey to us the essence of things more powerfully than dull and verbose prose. What is required for meditation is not the so-called exact factualness of description, but it must be powerful, stimulating and suggestive enough to generate a vivid and convincing experience of this Divine might and mystery, wisdom and beauty, transcendence and accessibility. Those to whom this outlook appears appealing can profitably study these descriptions of the earth and the universe. Others may do well to skip them.

From chapter sixteen to the twentieth, the surface of the earth and its geographical features are described. The surface of the earth, which is in the form of a lotus leaf, consists of seven Dweepas (continents or islands) arranged in the form of concentric circles round the central land mass called the Jambu Dweepa, each Dweepa being separated from those on both sides by moat-like encircling oceans also numbering seven. The name of these continents are as follows: the central one, Jambu Dweepa surrounded by salt sea; next Plaksha Dweepa surrounded by an ocean of cane juice; next Salmali Dweepa surrounded by an ocean of liquor; next Kusa Dweepa surrounded by the sea of clarified butter; next Krauncha Dweepa surrounded by milky sea; next Saka Dweepa surrounded by a sea of curds; and next Pushkara Dweepa surrounded by an ocean of fresh water. Through the middle of the Pushkara Dweepa encircles the great mountain Mānasottara, ten thousand Yojanas in height. Along the top of the mountain travels the sun facing the earth and giving light to the earth and the regions above.

Beyond that fresh water sea at a distance equal to that between Meru at the centre of the earth and Mānasottara on its circumference, runs the Lokāloka mountain encircling the whole earth. Beyond that mountain the sun's rays do not go and it is pitch dark. This mountain is called Lokāloka because it is the barrier between the sun and the unseeable regions.

Various details of the physical features and peculiarities of these regions or Varshas are given. Here it will suffice to give only one. They are inhabited by men much superior to us in physical and mental endowments. But they can only enjoy their beneficial Karmas, they cannot generate new ones for which they have to be born in Bhārata in Jambu Dweepa. They also cannot attain liberation.

Before these other Dweepas are described, the Text gives a detailed description of the central one, the Jambu Dweepa in four chapters (16 to 19) because Bhāratavarsha, our own region, is situated in it. A few details of it are given below. Jambu Dweepa is the central land mass amidst the seven oceans and the intervening land belts lying in concentric circles. It has got in its centre Mount Mahameru of huge dimensions, serving as the central axis for the world and the pivot to which the axle-tree of the sun's chariot is attached, as in an oil mill, enabling the sun to rotate round the world along the top of the Mānasottara mountain. With Meru as the central and pivotal range, there are three mountain ranges to the north and three to the south, running from shore to shore of the encircling salt ocean, and dividing this circular surface of the Dweepa into seven sectors. In the central sector, to the east and the west are two mountain ranges, other than those already described, linking the proximate mountain ranges to the north and the south, and thereby dividing the central sector into three. Thus there are on the whole nine sectors in the Jambu Dweepa separated by mountain ranges as boundaries. The central sector lying around Mahāmeru is Ilāvrita. To the north of it are the divisions known as the Ramyaka, Hiranmaya, and Kuru. To the south stand Harivarsha, Kimpurushavarsha, and Bhāratavarsha. To the east and the west of Ilāvrita are the divisions Ketumāla and Bhadrāswa. In all these nine regions Mahavishnu is worshipped in His various aspects by leading devotees. All these regions except Bhāratavarsha are quasi-Paradisaic where men only enjoy the good results of their Karma as in heaven. Only in Bhāratavarsha (India), over which Nara-Narayana preside, men can acquire Karma, and suffer the good and evil fruits of it in other regions. They have to be born again in Bhāratavarsha to acquire new merits by performing Karma. Above all it is only here that the Jiva can strive successfully for Moksha. So even the celestials long to be born as men in Bhāratavarsha.

The earth has six heavenly regions above it, these being Bhuvarloka, Svarloka, Maharloka, Janaloka, Tapoloka, and Brahmaloka. Below the earth there are subterranean regions—Atala, Vitala, Sutala, Rasātala, Talātala, Mahātala, and Pātāla. Underneath Pātāla is Ananta (Infinity), also called Sankarshana (the power holding material nature on to the Spirit), who is one of the four manifestations (Vyuha) of Mahavishnu. And above the Brahmaloka all the constellations are conceived as clustering round Dhruva, supported by him from above, in what is called the Sisumara Chakra or Crocodile Formation. Such is the schematic plan of the universe drawn before a devout worshipper, not so much to teach him geography or astronomy, as to give him a cosmic picture of the universe, formulating it as the physical body of the Divine. By such meditation on the gross form, when he is led into its subtle spiritual essence as a real entity, he would not feel that the subtle is something purely imaginary, but that it is *Satyasya satyam*—the truth of the true.

In the concluding chapter of the Skandha we get descriptions of Naraka, usually translated as hell but really connoting purgatory. For, the purpose of the sufferings inflicted in the purgatory is not mere punishment but purification of the Jiva. There are today wise jurists who plead that hardened criminals should be received with chocolates and potent drinks rather than with imprisonment or hanging. But unlike these wise men, the Pauranikas thought that suffering has in itself the power of softening and purifying a man, just as cruelty and iniquity in themselves harden and brutalise him. The Jiva on whom punishments are inflicted is thereby purified through sufferings, and he gets another chance of self-improvement and spiritual development. Many of these punishments described are quite gruesome, and people may doubt their factualness with considerable justification. It is pointed out in Kapilopadesa that even here on earth men undergo sufferings not much less gruesome. Why could it not be then elsewhere also?

In these days the tendency of people, even of those who accept and follow religious teachings, is to disbelieve in Naraka. But this unfashionable theory has one great virtue. If the main content of the theory, that iniquities done now will surely boomerang or come back to their perpetrators as sufferings in future, is accepted by men in general, this world would have been a better place. The deterrent nature of punishment cannot be overlooked in spite of the fashionable jurists who decry it. Suffering has got a purifying effect on man.

श्रीमद्भागवतम्

पञ्चमः स्कन्धः अथ प्रथमोऽध्यायः

राजोवाच

प्रियव्रतो भागवत आत्मारामः कथं मुने। गृहेऽरमत यन्मूलः कर्मबन्धः पराभवः ॥ 1॥
न नूनं मुक्तसङ्गानां तादृशानां द्विजर्षभ। गृहेष्वभिनिवेशोऽयं पुंसां भवितुमर्हति ॥ 2॥
महतां खलु विप्रर्षे उत्तमश्लोकपादयोः। छायानिर्वृतचित्तानां न कुटुम्बे स्पृहामतिः ॥ 3॥
संशयोऽयं महान् ब्रह्मन् दारागारसुतादिषु। सक्तस्य यत्सिद्धिरभूत् कृष्णे च मतिरच्युता ॥ 4॥

श्रीशुक उवाच

बाढमुक्तं भगवत उत्तमश्लोकस्य श्रीमच्चरणारविन्दमकरन्दरस आवेशितचेतसो भागवतपरमहंस-
दयितकथां किञ्चिदन्तरायविहितां स्वां शिवतमां पदवीं न प्रायेण हिन्वन्ति ॥ 5॥ यर्हि वाव ह राजन्
स राजपुत्रः प्रियव्रतः परमभागवतो नारदस्य चरणोपसेवयाञ्जसावगतपरमार्थसतत्त्वो ब्रह्मसत्रेण
दीक्षिष्यमाणोऽवनितलपरिपालनायाम्नातप्रवरगुणगणैकान्तभाजनतया स्वपित्रोपामन्त्रितो भगवति
वासुदेव एवाव्यवधानसमाधियोगेन समावेशितसकलकारकक्रियाकलापो नैवाभ्यनन्दद्यद्यपि तद-

Skandha V : Chapter 1
THE STORY OF PRIYAVRATA

Combination of worldly and spiritual Pursuits: Example of Priyavrata (1-19)

Rajah Parikshit said: **1.** O revered sage! Priyavrata was a great devotee ever revelling in the Atman. Why did he then take to the life of a householder, which causes the bondage of Karma and the forfeiture of spiritual awareness? **2.** Also, it is not possible for persons like him, who are established in the Atman, to feel attached to the home. **3.** O wise one! In those who experience the bliss arising from the reflection of the Lord's feet in their hearts, the desire for a family of their own can never arise. **4.** I have a grave doubt how one attached to one's own life, house and children happened to have firm and deep-rooted devotion to Krishna at the same time.

Sri Suka said: **5.** What you have said is correct in a way. But it can happen that a devotee, though his mind is deeply immersed in imbibing the nectar of the Lord's lotus-feet, is for a short time obstructed in his devotional life by his Prarabdha. But in such a case, he does not abandon the exalted ways of the Lord's devotees like taking delight in hearing and chanting the Lord's name and excellences. **6.** O King! Instructed by the sage Narada, Priyavrata had attained to the knowledge of the Atman, and had resolved to worship the Lord through a Brahmasatra consisting in the continuous concentration of the mind on Him. But being possessed of all those qualities required for the kingship and administration of the country, he was called upon by his father to take up such responsibilities. A father's command is, of course, never to be disobeyed. But yet Priyavrata, whose mind and senses had been completely dedicated to the Lord in the course of his practice

प्रत्याम्नातव्यं तदधिकरण आत्मनोऽन्यस्मादसतोऽपि पराभवमन्वीक्षमाणः ॥6॥ अथ ह भगवानादिदेव एतस्य गुणविसर्गस्य परिबृंहणानुध्यानव्यवसितसकलजगदभिप्राय आत्मयोनिरखिलनिगमनिजगण-परिवेष्टितः स्वभवनादवततार ॥7॥ स तत्र तत्र गगनतल उडुपतिरिव विमानावलिभिरनुपथममर-परिवृढैरभिपूज्यमानः पथि पथि च वरूथशः सिद्धगन्धर्वसाध्यचारणमुनिगणैरुपगीयमानो गन्धमादन-द्रोणीमवभासयन्नुपससर्प ॥8॥ तत्र ह वा एनं देवर्षिर्हंसयानेन पितरं भगवन्तं हिरण्यगर्भमुपलभमानः सहसैवोत्थायार्हणेन स पितापुत्राभ्यामवहिताञ्जलिरुपतस्थे ॥9॥ भगवानपि भारत तदुपनीतार्हणः सूक्तवाकेनातितरामुदितगुणगणावतारसुजयः प्रियव्रतमादिपुरुषस्तं सदयहासावलोक इति होवाच ॥10॥

श्रीभगवानुवाच

निबोध तातेदमृतं ब्रवीमि मासूयितुं देवमर्हस्यप्रमेयम्।
वयं भवस्ते तत एष महर्षिर्वहाम सर्वे विवशा यस्य दिष्टम् ॥11॥
न तस्य कश्चित्तपसा विद्यया वा न योगवीर्येण मनीषया वा।
नैवार्थधर्मैः परतः स्वतो वा कृतं विहन्तुं तनुभृद्विभूयात् ॥12॥
भवाय नाशाय च कर्म कर्तुं शोकाय मोहाय सदा भयाय।
सुखाय दुःखाय च देहयोगमव्यक्तदिष्टं जनताङ्ग धत्ते ॥13॥

of continuous and concentrated absorption in Samadhi, did not like to accept his father's order, fearing that application to matters of State, though belonging only to the category of appearances, was none the less likely to distract him from the spiritual path.

Brahma's Advice on the above Theme

7. Just then appeared Brahma, the first of the divinities, who was ever thinking of the ways and means whereby the interest of created beings could be promoted and was for this purpose always keeping himself in the know of the requirements of all beings. He was accompanied by a host of Devas and a large number of his own followers. **8.** Like the moon in the sky, Brahma moved, worshipped on the way by great Devas travelling in their aerial vehicles, and hymned by hosts of celestial beings and artistes like Siddhas, Gandharvas, Sādhyas, Chāranas and Munis. Finally, illumining the whole valley of Mount Gandhamādana, he reached the place where Priyavrata was staying with Narada. **9.** Seeing his omniscient father's arrival on his swan-vehicle, Narada arose from his seat along with the son and the father (i.e. Priyavrata and his father Swāyambhuva Manu), worshipped him and sang his praise. **10.** O scion of the Bharata clan! Accepting the worship of Narada, and smiling in a kindly manner at the hymn of praise recounting his attributes and works, he said as follows, addressing Priyavrata:

Brahma said: **11.** I am telling you the truth. Listen to me. No one can transgress the supreme and immeasurable Being. All of us, including I, Rudra, your father the Manu, and this sage your teacher—all are without freedom. We all carry out the will of that Supreme Being. **12.** No embodied being can counteract His will by austerity, meditation, Yogic power, intellectual skill, or worldly power. Neither with the help of others nor by oneself alone can one do so. **13.** Man takes on the body given to him by that mysterious Power for the very purpose of undergoing the experiences it subjects him to—birth, death, work, bereavement, grief, infatuation, fear, happiness, misery

यद्वाचि तन्त्या गुणकर्मदामभिः सुदुस्तरैर्वत्स वय सुयोजिताः ।
सर्वे वहामो बलिमीश्वराय प्रोता नसीव द्विपदे चतुष्पदः ॥14॥
ईशाभिसृष्टं ह्यवरुन्ध्महेऽङ्ग दुःखं सुखं वा गुणकर्मसङ्गात् ।
आस्थाय तत्तद्यदयुङ्क्त नाथश्चक्षुष्मतान्धा इव नीयमानाः ॥15॥
मुक्तोऽपि तावद्बिभृयात्स्वदेहमारब्धमश्नन्नभिमानशून्यः ।
यथानुभूतं प्रतियातनिद्रः किं त्वन्यदेहाय गुणान्न वृङ्क्ते ॥16॥
भयं प्रमत्तस्य वनेष्वपि स्याद्यतः स आस्ते सहषट्सपत्नः ।
जितेन्द्रियस्यात्मरतेर्बुधस्य गृहाश्रमः किं नु करोत्यवद्यम् ॥17॥
यः षट्सपत्नान् विजिगीषमाणो गृहेषु निर्विश्य यतेत पूर्वम् ।
अत्येति दुर्गाश्रित ऊर्जितारीन् क्षीणेषु कामं विचरेद्विपश्चित् ॥18॥
त्वं त्वब्जनाभाङ्घ्रिसरोजकोशदुर्गाश्रितो निर्जितषट्सपत्नः ।
भुङ्क्ष्वेह भोगान् पुरुषातिदिष्टान् विमुक्तसङ्गः प्रकृतिं भजस्व ॥19॥

श्रीशुक उवाच

इति समभिहितो महाभागवतो भगवतस्त्रिभुवनगुरोरनुशासनमात्मनो लघुतयावनतशिरोधरो

etc. **14.** We all offer our tribute of works as offerings to Him as cattle pulled by their nose strings do to their masters. The Veda consisting of sounds is the cable to which we all are tied with the smaller but stronger strings of the three Gunas of Prakriti and works springing from them. He controls and directs us with this rope, as their owners do their draught animals. **15.** O dear one! We are like a blind man, directed entirely by another with eyes. The Lord gives us each a body according to our eligibility through our nature and Karma, and with that we undergo the sufferings and enjoyments He awards us. **16.** Even a liberated man has to undergo the results of Karma that have become operative, and for this he has to continue his bodily existence without any ego-sense, undergoing enjoyments and sufferings just as he undergoes in a dream. But impressions and qualities causative of future births do not accrue to him. **17.** A heedless man without any control over the senses, is subject to the fear of spiritual degradation, even if he resides in a forest. For wherever he goes, the six enemies in the shape of the six senses accompany him. But, for an enlightened man with control over the senses and absorption in the Atman, what harm can the household life do? **18.** Whoever wants to conquer the six enemies in the form of the six senses, should try to overcome them step by step remaining in the home, experiencing unprohibited enjoyments with discrimination. A king overcomes his powerful enemies remaining within a fortress. When the enemy has been weakened, one can be within the fortress or outside it. So too can be a man of discrimination. **19.** You have conquered the sixfold enemy, with His lotus feet as your strong and secure fortress. So you can without fear enjoy here what the Lord has assigned to you, and afterwards you can abandon everything and be merged in the Atman.

Priyavrata assumes Rulership (20-29)

Sri Suka said: **20.** Being told so, the great devotee Priyavrata, considering that this was the commandment of the Supreme Master of all the worlds to a devotee so

बाढमिति सबहुमानमुवाह ॥20॥ भगवानपि मनुना यथावदुपकल्पितापचितिः प्रियव्रत-
नारदयोरविषममभिसमीक्षमाणयोरात्मसमवस्थानमवाङ्मनसं क्षयमव्यवहृतं प्रवर्तयन्नगमत् ॥21॥

मनुरपि परेणैवं प्रतिसन्धितमनोरथः सुरर्षिवरानुमतेनात्मजमखिलधरामण्डलस्थितिगुप्तय आस्थाप्य
स्वयमतिविषमविषयविषजलाशयाशाया उपरराम ॥22॥ इति ह वाव स जगतीपतिरीश्वरेच्छया-
धिनिवेशितकर्माधिकारोऽखिलजगद्बन्धध्वंसनपरानुभावस्य भगवत आदिपुरुषस्याङ्घ्रियुगलानवरत-
ध्यानानुभावेन परिरन्धितकषायाशयोऽवदातोऽपि मानवर्धनो महतां महीतलमनुशशास ॥23॥
अथ च दुहितरं प्रजापतेर्विश्वकर्मण उपयेमे बर्हिष्मतीं नाम तस्यामु ह वाव आत्मजानात्मसमानशीलगुण-
कर्मरूपवीर्योदारान्दश भावयाम्बभूव कन्यां च यवीयसीमूर्जस्वतीं नाम ॥24॥ आग्नीध्रेध्मजिह्व-
यज्ञबाहुमहावीरहिरण्यरेतोघृतपृष्ठसवनमेधातिथिवीतिहोत्रकवय इति सर्व एवाग्निनामानः ॥25॥ एतेषां
कविर्महावीरः सवन इति त्रय आसन्नूर्ध्वरेतसस्त आत्मविद्यायामर्भभावादारभ्य कृतपरिचयाः पारमहंस्य-
मेवाश्रममभजन् ॥26॥ तस्मिन्नु ह वा उपशमशीलाः परमर्षयः सकलजीवनिकायावासस्य भगवतो
वासुदेवस्य भीतानां शरणभूतस्य श्रीमच्चरणारविन्दाविरतस्मरणाविगलितपरमभक्तियोगानुभावेन
परिभावितान्तर्हृदयाधिगते भगवति सर्वेषां भूतानामात्मभूते प्रत्यगात्मन्येवात्मनस्तादात्म्यमविशेषेण

small and humble like himself, agreed to do as ordered, showing due respect and regard for Brahma. **21.** The Manu then worshipped Brahma and did proper honour to him. Neither Narada nor Priyavrata felt any disappointment in their mind that the mission of Brahma had obstructed their spiritual programme. Even as they gazed on, Brahma departed to his transcendental realm of Satyaloka, contemplating on the Supreme Lord who is beyond word and thought, who is uninvolved in deeds, and who is one's central support.

22. By Brahma's mission the Manu Swāyambhuva had his heart's desire accomplished. So with Narada's permission, he enthroned his son Priyavrata for the protection of the whole earth, and then retired from the poisonous attachments of worldly life. **23.** Thus by the will of the Lord, Priyavrata assumed the powers and duties of State, though he was free from all desires and impurities of mind through constant contemplation of the Supreme Being who destroys the bondage of His devotees. It was only to honour the command of a great personage that he took up the reins of government, and not from any personal ambition or desire for power and position. **24.** He then married Barhishmati, the daughter of Prajapati Viswakarma. He begot by her ten sons equal to him in qualities like good manners, goodness of nature, energy, personality, prowess, generosity etc. Younger to these was also born a daughter named Ūrjaswati.

25. All his ten sons had synonyms of Agni as their names, which ran as follows: Agnidhra, Idhmajihva, Yajnabāhu, Mahāvira, Hiranyaretas, Ghritaprishta, Savana, Medhādithi, Vītihotra, and Kavi. **26.** Of those, three, namely Kavi, Mahāvira, and Savana, were devoted to the contemplation of the Atman from their very boyhood, and adopted the way of life of the Paramahamsas. **27.** These great spiritual personages were established in supreme peace. By the practice of loving devotion characterised by the unbroken remembrance and contemplation of the Lord, their heart became purified enough to have in it the constant presence of Sri Vāsudeva, who is the dwelling place of all beings and the shelter of those who want to get out of transmigratory existence. They attained to oneness with Him who is the

समीयुः ॥27॥ अन्यस्यामपि जायायां त्रयः पुत्रा आसन्नुत्तमस्तामसो रैवत इति मन्वन्तराधिपतयः ॥28॥
एवमुपशमायनेषु स्वतनयेष्वथ जगतीपतिर्जगतीमर्बुदान्येकादश परिवत्सराणामव्याहताखिल-
पुरुषकारसारसम्भृतदोर्दण्डयुगलापीडितमौर्वीगुणस्तनितविरमितधर्मप्रतिपक्षो बर्हिष्मत्याश्चानुदिनमेध-
मानप्रमोदप्रसरणयौषिण्यव्रीडाप्रमुषितहासावलोकरुचिरक्ष्वेल्यादिभिः पराभूयमानविवेक इवानवबुध्यमान
इव महामना बुभुजे ॥29॥ यावदवभासयति सुरगिरिमनुपरिक्रामन् भगवानादित्यो वसुधातलमर्धेनैव
प्रतपत्यर्धेनावच्छादयति तदा हि भगवदुपासनोपचितातिपुरुषप्रभावस्तदनभिनन्दन् समजवेन रथेन
ज्योतिर्मयेन रजनीमपि दिनं करिष्यामीति सप्तकृत्वस्तरणिमनुपर्यक्रामद् द्वितीय इव पतङ्गः ॥30॥
ये वा उ ह तद्रथचरणनेमिकृतपरिखातास्ते सप्त सिन्धव आसन् यत एव कृताः सप्त भुवो द्वीपाः
॥31॥ जम्बूप्लक्षशाल्मलिकुशक्रौञ्चशाकपुष्करसंज्ञास्तेषां परिमाणं पूर्वस्मात्पूर्वस्मादुत्तर उत्तरो
यथासंख्यं द्विगुणमानेन बहिः समन्तत उपक्लृप्ताः ॥32॥ क्षारोदेक्षुरसोदसुरोदघृतोदक्षीरोददधि-
मण्डोदशुद्धोदाः सप्त जलधयः सप्त द्वीपपरिखा इवाभ्यन्तरद्वीपसमाना एकैकश्येन यथानुपूर्वं
सप्तस्वपि बहिर्द्वीपेषु पृथक् परित उपकल्पितास्तेषु जम्ब्वादिषु बर्हिष्मतीपतिरनुव्रतानात्मजाना-

Atman of all and the indweller in everything. **28.** By another wife he had three sons named Uttama, Tamasa, and Raivata who became the third, fourth and fifth Manus respectively. **29.** While some of his sons took to exhaustive spiritual pursuits, he ruled over the earth for eleven crores of years. During that period he put down all forces of Adharma by the mere twang of his bow string drawn by his long arms, whose power there was none anywhere to withstand or oppose. And simultaneously putting on the appearance of an ordinary worldly man without any knowledge of the Self, he also enjoyed the delights of the company of his wife Barhishmati, who evinced increasing delight on seeing him, who got up from her seat always to honour him, who exhibited her amorous charms to him and who displayed also a coyness that put a check on unrestrained laughter, passionate looks, and words of apparent ridicule as expression of love.

Emergence of the Dweepas (30-35)

30. The power he possessed by the Lord's grace was so unique that he was equal to the sun both in splendour and in speed. The sun, who circles the Mount Meru, renders one half of the earth bright at a time, while the other half he leaves dark. Now king Priyavrata, in order to overcome this handicap and make even night bright like daytime, got into a chariot as speedy and brilliant as the sun's, and circumambulated Mount Meru seven times along the course of the sun, following him. This he could achieve only because of the extraordinary powers he derived by the worship of the Lord. **31.** The seven oceans are but the ruts caused by the wheels of Priyavrata's chariot, and they lie as concentric circles dividing the surface of the earth into seven Dweepas (islands or continents) consisting of the land belts between them. **32.** These Dweepas are: Jambudweepa, Plakshadweepa, Salmalidweepa, Kusadweepa, Kraunchadweepa, Sakadweepa and Pushkaradweepa. In size each outer one is double the size of the one inner to it. They encircle the oceans that divide them in the order mentioned below. **33.** Around the Dweepas, functioning as moats to them, are these seven oceans of salt water, sugarcane juice, liquor, ghee, milk, curds and pure water. Lying around the Dweepas, each

ग्नीध्रेध्मजिह्वयज्ञबाहुहिरण्यरेतोघृतपृष्ठमेधातिथिवीतिहोत्रसंज्ञान् यथासंख्येनैकैकस्मिन्नेकमेवाधिपतिं विदधे ॥33॥ दुहितरं चोर्जस्वतीं नामोशनसे प्रायच्छद्यस्यामासीद् देवयानी नाम काव्यसुता ॥34॥

नैवंविधः पुरुषकार उरुक्रमस्य पुंसां तदङ्घ्रिरजसा जितषड्गुणानाम् ।
चित्रं विदूरविगतः सकृदाददीत यन्नामधेयमधुना स जहाति बन्धम् ॥35॥

स एवमपरिमितबलपराक्रम एकदा तु देवर्षिचरणानुशयनानुपतितगुणविसर्गसंसर्गेणानिर्वृतमिवात्मानं मन्यमान आत्मनिर्वेद इदमाह ॥36॥ अहो असाध्वनुष्ठितं यदभिनिवेशितोऽहमिन्द्रियैरविद्यारचितविषमविषयान्धकूपे तदलमलममुष्या वनिताया विनोदमृगं मां धिग्धिगिति गर्हयाञ्चकार ॥37॥ परदेवताप्रसादाधिगतात्मप्रत्यवमर्शेनानुप्रवृत्तेभ्यः पुत्रेभ्य इमां यथादायं विभज्य भुक्तभोगां च महिषीं मृतकमिव सहमहाविभूतिमपहाय स्वयं निहितनिर्वेदो हृदि गृहीतहरिविहारानुभावो भगवतो नारदस्य पदवीं पुनरेवानुससार ॥38॥

तस्य ह वा एते श्लोकाः—

प्रियव्रतकृतं कर्म को नु कुर्याद्विनेश्वरम् । यो नेमिनिम्नैरकरोच्छायां घ्नन् सप्त वारिधीन् ॥
भूसंस्थानं कृतं येन सरिद्गिरिवनादिभिः । सीमा च भूतनिर्वृत्यै द्वीपे द्वीपे विभागशः ॥40॥

one of these oceans is equal in size to the Dweepa it surrounds. In each of these seven Dweepas, Priyavrata installed a son of his. **34.** He gave his daughter Ūrjaswati in marriage to Maharshi Sukra. Of this marriage was born a famous daughter Devayāni. **35.** All this power and capacity are no matter for wonder in the case of such a great devotee of the Lord as he, who has conquered all the senses by worshipping Him. For the Lord's unique power is such that even a man of low birth without any special qualifications overcomes the bondage of Samsara, if he but once utters His name with deep faith.

Priyavrata's Renunciation (36-41)

36. The king with limitless strength and courage once felt that he had been deprived of the bliss of communion with the Atman by the intervention of these kingly duties while he was undergoing spiritual disciplines under the great divine sage Narada. He said to himself: **37.** Alas! I have committed a blunder. I have allowed myself to be pushed by the senses into the abandoned well of worldly life with its attachments and darkness of ignorance. So enough of these sensuous enjoyments. Fie upon me who have degraded myself into a play-animal of women—thus did he criticise himself. **38.** By the grace of the Supreme Lord discriminative power dawned on him. Urged by the powerful spirit of renunciation, he gave away the kingdom to his children and abandoned the immense power and wealth of royalty as also his wife who had provided him with enjoyment in life, as if all these were but rotting carcases. Endowed with the unique potency derived from constant remembrance of Sri Hari's glories, he once again resorted to Sri Narada's advice to adopt the life of renunciation.

39. There are the following verses in praise of him: Except the Supreme Lord, who can do those wonderful deeds which Priyavrata performed! He dispelled the darkness of night, and made the seven oceans with the rims of the wheels of his chariot. **40.** Priyavrata made separate regions for habitation in the world by dividing it into continents (Dweepas), with each continent having rivers, moun-

भौमं दिव्यं मानुषं च महित्वं कर्मयोगजम् । यश्चक्रे निरयौपम्यं पुरुषानुजनप्रियः ॥41॥

इति श्रीमद्भागवते महापुराणे पारमहंस्यां संहितायां पञ्चमस्कन्धे प्रियव्रतविजये प्रथमोऽध्यायः ॥1॥

tains, forests etc., for their prosperity. **41.** Dear as he was to all devotees, he finally attained to that acme of renunciation which made him realise every form of worldly felicity, whether it be human or divine, to be no better than the life of hell.

अथ द्वितीयोऽध्यायः

श्रीशुक उवाच

एवं पितरि सम्प्रवृत्ते तदनुशासने वर्तमान आग्नीध्रो जम्बूद्वीपौकसः प्रजा औरसवद्धर्मा-
वेक्षमाणः पर्यगोपायत् ॥1॥ स च कदाचित्पितृलोककामः सुरवरवनिताक्रीडाचलद्रोण्यां भगवन्तं
विश्वसृजां पतिमाभृतपरिचर्योपकरण आत्मैकाग्र्येण तपस्व्याराधयाम्बभूव ॥2॥ तदुपलभ्य भगवाना-
दिपुरुषः सदसि गायन्तीं पूर्वचित्तिं नामाप्सरसमभियापयामास ॥3॥ सा च तदाश्रमोपवनमति-
रमणीयं विविधनिबिडविटपिविटपनिकरसंश्लिष्टपुरटलतारूढस्थलविहङ्गममिथुनैः प्रोच्यमानश्रुतिभिः
प्रतिबोध्यमानसलिलकुक्कुटकारण्डवकलहंसादिभिर्विचित्रमुपकूजितामलजलाशयकमलाकरमुपबभ्राम ।4॥
तस्याः सुललितगमनपदविन्यासगतिविलासायाश्चानुपदं खणखणायमानरुचिरचरणाभरणस्वन-
मुपाकर्ण्य नरदेवकुमारः समाधियोगेनामीलितनयननलिनमुकुलयुगलमीषद्विकचय्य व्यचष्ट ॥5॥
तामेवाविदूरे मधुकरीमिव सुमनस उपजिघ्रन्तीं दिविजमनुजमनोनयनाह्लाददुघैर्गतिविहारव्रीडा-
विनयावलोकसुस्वराक्षरावयवैर्मनसि नृणां कुसुमायुधस्य विदधतीं विवरं निजमुखविगलितामृतासव-

Skandha V : Chapter 2

THE STORY OF AGNIDHRA

Agnidhra meeting Apsaras (1-6)

Sri Suka said: **1.** After Priyavrata's final attainment, his son Agnidhra, following the traditions of his father, ruled over the inhabitants of Jambudweepa in accordance with the rules of Dharma, as a father looks after his own children. **2.** Once, desiring offspring, he performed austerities in the valleys of Mandara Mountain, where celestial damsels generally went for recreation. Collecting all ingredients of worship, he worshipped Brahma there with great devotion and concentration. **3.** Knowing this, Brahma sent to the place where the king was staying, a songstress of his court, an Apsara woman named Pūrvachitti, **4.** She went to Priyavrata's Ashrama and wandered about in its precincts. There, on the golden creepers closely embraced by the branches and foliage of the dense growth of trees, were perched Kokila pairs whose warblings in the early mornings awakened water birds like Kukkutas, Kārandakas and Hamsas, which in turn began to give out their delightful chirping sounds, as they hovered over the lake full of blooming lotuses. **5.** As the Apsara woman moved about in that grove, the measured move-

सहासभाषणामोदमदान्धमधुकरनिकरोपरोधेन द्रुतपदविन्यासेन वल्गुस्पन्दनस्तनकलशकबरभाररशनां
देवीं तदवलोकनेन विवृतावसरस्य भगवतो मकरध्वजस्य वशमुपनीतो जडवदिति होवाच ॥6॥

का त्वं चिकीर्षसि च किं मुनिवर्य शैले मायासि कापि भगवत्परदेवतायाः ।
विज्ये बिभर्षि धनुषी सुहृदात्मनोऽर्थे किं वा मृगान् मृगयसे विपिने प्रमत्तान् ॥ 7॥
बाणाविमौ भगवतः शतपत्रपत्रौ शान्तावपुङ्खरुचिरावतितिग्मदन्तौ ।
कस्मै युयुङ्क्षसि वने विचरन्न विद्मः क्षेमाय नो जडधियां तव विक्रमोऽस्तु ॥ 8॥
शिष्या इमे भगवतः परितः पठन्ति गायन्ति साम सरहस्यमजस्रमीशम् ।
युष्मच्छिखाविलुलिताः सुमनोऽभिवृष्टीः सर्वे भजन्त्यृषिगणा इव वेदशाखाः ॥ 9॥
वाचं परं चरणपञ्जरतित्तिरीणां ब्रह्मन्नरूपमुखरां शृणवाम तुभ्यम् ।
लब्धा कदम्बरुचिरङ्कविटङ्कबिम्बे यस्यामलातपरिधिः क्व च वल्कलं ते ॥10॥

ments of her steps caused her anklets to produce a ringing sound, which, entering the ears of the King, made him open a little his lotus-bud-like eyes that had till then remained closed in the practice of Samadhi. **6.** Before him he saw the attractive form of the Apsara woman. Like the bees hovering about, she was moving from flower to flower enjoying their smell. Her gait, her playful attitudes, her look mingled with shyness and modesty, her sweet voice, and her physical features, all seemed to be capable of making a big opening on the heart-walls of humanity for Cupid to gain entrance. The speech of her smiling lips emitted not only honeyed words but a sweet smell which attracted such a large number of honey-bees that she had to take several quick steps which made her high breasts throb and her locks and wearing cloth undulate. On the prince opening his eyes, her sight became the occasion for invincible Cupid to overpower him and make him speak to the woman as follows like a senseless fool:

Love Prattle of Agnidhra (7-16)

7. May I know who you are, good lady? Are you a great sage come to this mountain side for some great purpose? Are you Maya, the alluring power of the Lord? O friend, (referring to her eyebrows) are you carrying these stringless bows, your arching eyebrows, for your own protection? Or are you in search of some heedless prey like me with plenty of animal spirits? **8.** Moving about in this forest, at whom are you aiming these shafts of your side-long glances, having those lotus-like eyes for their feathers, having their speed gentled by the rolling of the eyeballs, and equipped with arrow heads, sharp and well-shaped but devoid of shafts? I do not understand at whom you are aiming them. But, pray, let this brave expedition of yours be for the welfare of a love-lorn and stupefied fellow like me. **9.** These honey beetles hovering round your fragrant flower of a face are, as it were, your disciples, learning the Sāma-chants of their humming sound from you. All are collecting the flowers fallen from your locks, as Rishis collect and preserve the Vedic recensions. **10.** From the anklets adorning your feet, I hear the murmuring sound of the precious gems within –a sound that is clear but without any speaker. For these charming hips of yours, wherefrom did you get this glorious complexion of Kadamba flowers? Over it I find an encircling band of fire – your girdle; (confusing the colour of the cloth with the bodily part), but where is

किं सम्भृतं रुचिरयोर्द्विज शृङ्गयोस्ते मध्ये कृशो वहसि यत्र दृशिः श्रिता मे ।
पङ्कोऽरुणः सुरभिरात्मविषाण ईदृग् येनाश्रमं सुभग मे सुरभीकरोषि ॥11॥
लोकं प्रदर्शय सुहृत्तम तावकं मे यत्रत्य इत्थमुरसावयवावपूर्वौ ।
अस्मद्विधस्य मनउन्नयनौ बिभर्ति बह्वद्भुतं सरसराससुधादि वक्त्रे ॥12॥
का वाऽऽत्मवृत्तिरदनाद्धविरङ्ग वाति विष्णोः कलास्यनिमिषोन्मकरौ च कर्णौ ।
उद्विग्नमीनयुगलं द्विजपङ्क्तिशोचिरासन्नभृङ्गनिकरं सर उन्मुखं ते ॥13॥
योऽसौ त्वया करसरोजहतः पतङ्गो दिक्षु भ्रमन् भ्रमत एजयतेऽक्षिणी मे ।
मुक्तं न ते स्मरसि वक्रजटावरूथं कष्टोऽनिलो हरति लम्पट एष नीवीम् ॥14॥
रूपं तपोधन तपश्चरतां तपोघ्नं ह्येतत्तु केन तपसा भवतोपलब्धम् ।
चर्तुं तपोऽर्हसि मया सह मित्र मह्यं किं वा प्रसीदति स वै भवभावनो मे ॥15॥
न त्वां त्यजामि दयितं द्विजदेवदत्तं यस्मिन्मनो दृगपि नो न वियाति लग्नम् ।
मां चारुशृङ्ग्यर्हसि नेतुमनुव्रतं ते चित्तं यतः प्रतिसरन्तु शिवाः सचिव्यः ॥16॥

श्रीशुक उवाच

इति ललनानुनयातिविशारदो ग्राम्यवैदग्ध्यया परिभाषया तां विबुधवधूं विबुधमतिरधि-

the cloth around your waist? **11.** With what precious stuff have you filled those two cornucopias on your chest! But for their weight, your slender waist would not bend like this. My eyes have got glued to them. Crimson coloured, fragrant and matchless unguents smeared over them are flooding my hermitage with their fragrance. **12.** Show me, friend, that country of yours where people have such magnificent breasts as astound and agitate the minds of love-lorn men like us, and possess faces with such playful expressions, sweet words and honeyed lips. **13.** Dear one! On what does your body thrive? Is it Havis, the sacrificial food of the celestials? For your mouth seems to emit the fragrance of Havis. You seem to be an aspect of Mahavishnu, for like His ear-rings, yours too have fish-marked emblem and a lustre that does not fade. Your face is like a lake, the black and unsteady eyeballs being the swimming fish; your pearl-white teeth, the flight of birds; and your curly frontal locks, the honey bees hovering about that lake. **14.** This play ball, struck by your delicate hand, bounces about in different directions, drawing my eyes to its movements. Absorbed in the ball play, how is it that you fail to notice that your curly locks have got dishevelled, or that this voluptuous fellow, the wind, is removing your wearing cloth! **15.** O austere one! What kind of austerity gave you this form that can disturb the austere vow of any ascetic? Friend! It is befitting that for my sake you perform austerities with me. Would the great creator who wants to multiply his creations be gracious to me in this respect? **16.** I am not going to leave you, who have been gifted to me by Brahma. My mind and my eyes have got stuck to you, and they refuse to come away. O beauty! Take me also, your obedient servant, wherever your mind takes you. May the ladies in attendance on you be also pleased to follow me!

Agnidhra's Story Concluded (17-23)

17. Thus did that intelligent Agnidhra, skilled in winning the confidence of women, honour and please that Apsara woman by words that were highly attractive to

सभाजयामास ॥17॥ सा च ततस्तस्य वीरयूथपतेर्बुद्धिशीलरूपवयःश्रियौदार्येण पराक्षिप्तमनास्तेन सहायुतायुतपरिवत्सरोपलक्षणं कालं जम्बूद्वीपपतिना भौमस्वर्गभोगान् बुभुजे ॥18॥ तस्यामु ह वा आत्मजान् स राजवर आग्नीध्रो नाभिकिम्पुरुषहरिवर्षेलावृतरम्यकहिरण्मयकुरुभद्राश्वकेतुमालसंज्ञान्नव पुत्रानजनयत् ॥19॥

सा सूत्वाथ सुतान्नवानुवत्सरं गृह एवापहाय पूर्वचित्तिर्भूय एवाजं देवमुपतस्थे ॥20॥ आग्नीध्रसुतास्ते मातुरनुग्रहादौत्पत्तिकेनैव संहननबलोपेताः पित्रा विभक्ता आत्मतुल्यनामानि यथाभागं जम्बूद्वीपवर्षाणि बुभुजुः ॥21॥ आग्नीध्रो राजातृप्तः कामानामप्सरसमेवानुदिनमधिमन्यमानस्तस्याः सलोकतां श्रुतिभिरवारुन्ध यत्र पितरो मादयन्ते ॥22॥ सम्परेते पितरि नव भ्रातरो मेरुदुहितॄर्मेरुदेवीं प्रतिरूपामुग्रदंष्ट्रीं लतां रम्यां श्यामां नारीं भद्रां देववीतिमितिसंज्ञा नवोदवहन् ॥23॥

इति श्रीमद्भागवते महापुराणे पारमहंस्यां संहितायां पञ्चमस्कन्धे आग्नीध्रवर्णनं नाम द्वितीयोऽध्यायः ॥2॥

lascivious persons. **18.** That Apsara woman too, being strongly fascinated by the king's intelligence, manners, form, youth, splendour, generosity and other virtues, got engrossed in him, and spent many divine years with him, the ruler of Jambudweepa, in enjoyments which, though earthly, were equal to those of heaven itself. **19.** King Agnidhra begot by her nine sons: Nābhi, Kimpurusha, Harivarsha, Ilāvrita, Ramyaka, Hiranmaya, Kuru, Bhadrāswa and Ketumāla. **20.** Pūrvachitti gave birth to these nine, in so many years, and then leaving them with the king at the palace, went away to rejoin the court of Brahma. **21.** All the sons of Agnidhra inherited from their mother healthy bodies and great abilities, and were appointed by their father to rule over the nine regions of Jambudweepa that came to be known after their respective names. **22.** King Agnidhra was not, however, satisfied with the enjoyments he had with the Apsara woman. So constantly thinking of her, and performing Vedic rituals for fulfilment of desires, he in the end attained to the world of Apsaras and joined her. In that realm, the Pitris live joyfully. **23.** After the death of the king, the nine sons married the nine daughters of Meru, their names being Merudevi, Pratirūpa, Ugradamshtri, Latā, Ramyā, Syāma, Nāri, Bhadrā, and Devavītī.

अथ तृतीयोऽध्यायः

श्रीशुक उवाच

नाभिरपत्यकामोऽप्रजया मेरुदेव्या भगवन्तं यज्ञपुरुषमवहितात्मायजत ॥1॥ तस्य ह वाव श्रद्धया विशुद्धभावेन यजतः प्रवर्ग्येषु प्रचरत्सु द्रव्यदेशकालमन्त्रर्त्विग्दक्षिणाविधानयोगोपपत्त्या दुर-

Skandha V : Chapter 3

THE STORY OF NĀBHI

Lord's Revelation at Nābhi's Yajna (1-3)

Sri Suka said: **1.** Nābhi, the eldest son of Agnidhra, desirous of a son, worshipped Sri Hari, the Lord of Yajnas, with great concentration of mind, along with his wife Merudevi. **2.** He performed a Yajna in invocation of Mahavishnu with utmost faith and purity. Though the Lord is unattainable by any of the ela-

धिगमोऽपि भगवान् भागवतवात्सल्यतया सुप्रतीक आत्मानमपराजितं निजजनाभिप्रेतार्थविधित्सया गृहीतहृदयो हृदयङ्गमं मनोनयनानन्दनावयवाभिराममाविश्चकार ॥2॥ अथ ह तमाविष्कृतभुज-युगलद्वयं हिरण्मयं पुरुषविशेषं कपिशकौशेयाम्बरधरमुरसि विलसच्छ्रीवत्सललामं दरवरवनरुहवन-मालाच्छूर्यमृतमणिगदादिभिरुपलक्षितं स्फुटकिरणप्रवरमुकुटकुण्डलकटककटिसूत्रहारकेयूरनूपुराद्यङ्ग-भूषणविभूषितमृत्विक्सदस्यगृहपतयोऽधना इवोत्तमधनमुपलभ्य सबहुमानमर्हणेनावनतशीर्षाण उप-तस्थुः ॥3॥

ऋत्विज ऊचुः

अर्हसि मुहुरर्हत्तमार्हणमस्माकमनुपथानां नमो नम इत्येतावत्सदुपशिक्षितं कोऽर्हति पुमान् प्रकृतिगुणव्यतिकरमतिरनीश ईश्वरस्य परस्य प्रकृतिपुरुषयोरर्वाक्तनाभिर्नामरूपाकृतिभी रूपनिरूपणम् ॥4॥ सकलजननिकायवृजिननिरसनशिवतमप्रवरगुणगणैकदेशकथनादृते ॥5॥ परिजनानुरागविरचित-शबलसंशब्दसलिलसितकिसलयतुलसिकादूर्वाङ्कुरैरपि सम्भृतया सपर्यया किल परम परितुष्यसि ॥6॥ अथानयापि न भवत इज्ययोरुभारभरया समुचितमर्थमिहोपलभामहे ॥7॥ आत्मन

borate requisites of the Yajna like ingredients, proper time and place, Mantras, sacrificial priests, sacrificial gifts, correct procedures of rituals etc., He none the less revealed Himself out of His parental love for devotees, while the rite called Pravargya was being performed. He revealed Himself with his shining form, which no one can experience unless He vouchsafes it, which thrills the senses with its beauty and brings joy and peace to the mind. **3.** His divine form was four-armed, luminous, dressed in golden yellow cloth, and adorned with the Srivatsa mark, floral wreath and the gem Kaustubha. He was sporting in his arms insignias and weapons like conch, lotus, discus, mace etc., and he was wearing various kinds of ornaments and decorations of gold studded with precious stones like diadem, ear ornaments, girdle, pearl necklaces, bracelets and anklets. All the people there —the master of the sacrifice, the sacrificial priests and the assembled devotees—stood in adoration with heads bowing down, as penniless men would before a treasure trove.

Hymn of sacrificial Priests (4-15)

The sacrificial priests said: **4.** O Worshipful One! Though Thou art in Thyself full and self-satisfied, it behoves Thee to accept the devout adoration of Thy humble servants. Salutation to Thee again and again. To salute Thee and adore Thee in this way is all that we have been taught by great men. We cannot do more than this. For we are engrossed with worldly objects that are the products of Prakriti, and therefore devoid of the higher powers of the mind to grasp Thy unique glory. Placed as we are, how can we praise Thy form and attributes that are above Prakriti, with our notions of name, form and attributes vitiated by the limitations of our world-bound minds? **5.** All that we can do is to make vague references to Thy unique and auspicious attributes which eradicate the sinful tendencies of those who approach Thee. **6.** O Exalted One! Thou art the Most High, above the descriptive power of our minds, yet Thou art delighted with the prayer of devotees whose voice becomes indistinct and tremulous with emotion, and who make offerings of water, leaves, Tulasi, tender grass etc. with devotion. **7.** If it is without devotion, we know that even a Yajna like this with abounding offerings and numerous rites is of no interest to Thee. **8.**

एवानुसवनमञ्जसाव्यतिरेकेण बोभूयमानाशेषपुरुषार्थस्वरूपस्य किन्तु नाथाशिष आशासानानामेतद-
भिसंराधनमात्रं भवितुमर्हति ॥8॥ तद्यथा बालिशानां स्वयमात्मनः श्रेयः परमविदुषां परमपरम-
पुरुष प्रकर्षकरुणया स्वमहिमानं चापवर्गाख्यमुपकल्पयिष्यन् स्वयं नापचित एवेतरवदिहोपलक्षितः
॥9॥ अथायमेव वरो ह्यर्हत्तम यर्हि बर्हिषि राजर्षेर्वरदर्षभो भवान्निजपुरुषेक्षणविषय आसीत् ॥10॥

असङ्गनिशितज्ञानानलविधूताशेषमलानां भवत्स्वभावानामात्मारामाणां मुनीनामनवरतपरि-
गुणितगुणगणपरममङ्गलायनगुणगणकथनोऽसि ॥11॥ अथ कथञ्चित्स्खलनक्षुत्पतनजृम्भणदुरवस्थाना-
दिषु विवशानां नः स्मरणाय ज्वरमरणदशायामपि सकलकश्मलनिरसनानि तव गुणकृतनामधेयानि
वचनगोचराणि भवन्तु ॥12॥

किञ्चायं राजर्षिरपत्यकामः प्रजां भवादृशीमाशासान ईश्वरमाशिषां स्वर्गापवर्गयोरपि
भवन्तमुपधावति प्रजायामर्थप्रत्ययो धनदमिवाधनः फलीकरणम् ॥13॥ को वा इह तेऽपराजितो-
ऽपराजितया माययानवसितपदव्यानावृतमतिर्विषयविषरयानावृतप्रकृतिरनुपासितमहच्चरणः ॥14॥ यदु
ह वाव तव पुनरदभ्रकर्तरिह समाहूतस्तत्रार्थधियां मन्दानां नस्तद्यद्देवहेलनं देवदेवार्हसि साम्येन
सर्वान् प्रतिबोढुमविदुषाम् ॥15॥

In truth, to Thee who art in Thyself the summation of the highest values that the human mind can conceive—of what value these Yajnas and their offerings can be? Lord! This is only a way of worship sanctioned to us who are moved by desires and their fulfilment, as we are not capable of higher forms of worship. **9.** O Supreme Being! For the sake of ignorant and foolish people like us, who do not know what is ultimately good for us, Thou, out of Thy boundless grace and with a resolve to bestow on us liberation, which is Thy highest glory and blessing, hast appeared before us like a common person, even without being invoked by us. **10.** O Worshipful One! This is indeed the greatest of blessings we have got that in this Yajna of King Nābhi, Thou, the master of all boons, hast been pleased to appear before the eyes of men. **11.** O Lord! Thou art the centre of infinite graces and sportive manifestations which are praised and sung about by sages, whose impurities have all been burnt up by the fire of renunciation augmented by knowledge, and who, being delighted in the Self alone, are of the same nature as Thyself. **12.** May Thy divine names, descriptive of Thy attributes and capable of erasing all sins, engage our speech at all times of difficulty—be it injury, fall, lassitude, distress, fever and other ailments or death itself. **13.** Besides, here is this Rajarshi who looks upon the birth of a son for himself as the supreme end of his life. He is approaching Thee for the attainment of this trivial object of getting a son equal to Thee in all respects, even though such a prayer before Thee, the Supreme Being, who can bestow all worldly good and liberation, is as ridiculous as the prayer of a poor man for some chaff before a great king. **14.** Excepting those who have served holy men and gained their grace, who is there that is not overcome by Thy invincible Maya? Who is there whose intellect is not clouded by that power of unknown origin? Who is there whose nature is not transformed by the poisonous influence of sense objects? **15.** O Lord, Thou who art ever engaged in works of cosmic significance! Pardon us for having invoked Thee here for such a small fulfilment as progeny. Dull-witted and ignorant as we are, we consider such attain-

श्रीशुक उवाच

इति निगदेनाभिष्टूयमानो भगवाननिमिषर्षभो वर्षधराभिवादिताभिवन्दितचरणः सदयमिदमाह ॥16॥

श्रीभगवानुवाच

अहो बताहमृषयो भवद्भिरवितथगीर्भिर्वरमसुलभमभियाचितो यदमुष्यात्मजो मया सदृशो भूयादिति ममाहमेवाभिरूपः कैवल्यादथापि ब्रह्मवादो न मृषा भवितुमर्हति ममैव हि मुखं यद् द्विजदेवकुलम् ॥17॥ तत आग्नीध्रीयेंऽशकलयावतरिष्याम्यात्मतुल्यमनुपलभमानः ॥18॥

श्रीशुक उवाच

इति निशामयन्त्या मेरुदेव्याः पतिमभिधायान्तर्दधे भगवान् ॥19॥ बर्हिषि तस्मिन्नेव विष्णुदत्त भगवान् परमर्षिभिः प्रसादितो नाभेः प्रियचिकीर्षया तदवरोधायने मेरुदेव्यां धर्मान् दर्शयितुकामो वातरशनानां श्रमणानामृषीणामूर्ध्वमन्थिनां शुक्लया तनुवावततार ॥20॥

इति श्रीमद्भागवते महापुराणे पारमहंस्यां संहितायां पञ्चमस्कन्धे नाभिचरिते ऋषभावतारो नाम तृतीयोऽध्यायः ॥3॥

ments as the be-all and end-all of existence. It behoves Thee, the even-sighted, to pardon us for our failings.

Announcement of Incarnation (16-20)

Sri Suka said: **16.** Being thus praised and worshipped by the sacrificial priests who had themselves been honoured by the king, the Lord said as follows mercifully: *Sri Bhagavan said:* **17.** 'O great Rishis! The boon you have asked of Me, that he, the king, should have a son equal to Me, is one that is almost impossible to realise. For as I am the one without a second, there can never be one equal to Me. Yet you are devoted to truth, and the words of such masters of the Veda should not go in vain. For, they are veritably My mouth. **18.** So, since there is none equal to Me, I shall Myself be born with a part of Myself, as the son of this Nābhi, the son of Agnidhra.' **19.** Announcing this to Nābhi in the hearing of his wife Merudevi, the Lord disappeared from sight. **20.** O Parikshit! Thus propitiated in the Yajna by the Rishis, the Lord, in order to bless Nābhi, was born of Merudevi in the inner apartment of the king's palace with a form that was constituted of pure Sattva. The object of His incarnation was to make known to the world the ways of life of ascetics who are celibates for life (Nityabrahmacharins) and who wear no cloth except the quarters (Digambaras).

अथ चतुर्थोऽध्यायः

श्रीशुक उवाच

अथ ह तमुत्पत्त्यैवाभिव्यज्यमानभगवल्लक्षणं साम्योपशमवैराग्यैश्वर्यमहाविभूतिभिरनुदिनमेधमाना-
नुभावं प्रकृतयः प्रजा ब्राह्मणा देवताश्चावनितलसमवनायातितरां जगृधुः ॥1॥ तस्य ह वा इत्थं
वर्ष्मणा वरीयसा बृहच्छ्लोकेन चौजसा बलेन श्रिया यशसा वीर्यशौर्याभ्यां च पिता ऋषभ इतीदं
नाम चकार ॥2॥ तस्य हीन्द्रः स्पर्धमानो भगवान् वर्षे न ववर्ष तदवधार्य भगवानृषभदेवो योगेश्वरः
प्रहस्यात्मयोगमायया स्ववर्षमजनाभं नामाभ्यवर्षत् ॥3॥ नाभिस्तु यथाभिलषितं सुप्रजास्त्वम-
वरुध्यातिप्रमोदभरविह्वलो गद्गदाक्षरया गिरा स्वैरं गृहीतनरलोकसधर्मं भगवन्तं पुराणपुरुषं
मायाविलसितमतिर्वत्स तातेति सानुरागमुपलालयन् परां निर्वृतिमुपगतः ॥4॥ विदितानुरागमापौर-
प्रकृति जनपदो राजा नाभिरात्मजं समयसेतुरक्षायामभिषिच्य ब्राह्मणेषूपनिधाय सह मेरुदेव्या
विशालायां प्रसन्ननिपुणेन तपसा समाधियोगेन नरनारायणाख्यं भगवन्तं वासुदेवमुपासीनः कालेन
तन्महिमानमवाप ॥5॥

यस्य ह पाण्डवेय श्लोकावुदाहरन्ति—

को नु तत्कर्म राजर्षेर्नाभेरन्वाचरेत्पुमान्। अपत्यतामगाद्यस्य हरिः शुद्धेन कर्मणा ॥ 6॥
ब्रह्मण्योऽन्यः कुतो नाभेर्विप्रा मङ्गलपूजिताः। यस्य बर्हिषि यज्ञेशं दर्शयामासुरोजसा ॥ 7॥

Skandha V : Chapter 4

THE STORY OF RISHABHA

Rishabha's Installation (1-7)

Sri Suka said: **1.** The son of Nābhi had at his birth itself the marks of Vajra, Ankusa etc., the unique emblems of Mahavishnu, on the under-surface of his feet. Equanimity, peace, non-attachment, splendour, and many-sided virtues, all combined in him to make him an extraordinarily powerful personality. So the ministers, the subjects, the Brahmanas and the Devas were all eager to have him installed as king. **2.** His father gave him the name Rishabha, signifying the numerous blessed qualities like his striking personality, impressiveness, strength, fame, power, courage etc., which have been the topic of compositions by many a bard. **3.** Once, out of jealousy, Indra did not send rain to his land known as Ajanābha. Smiling at this, Rishabha, by the application of his extraordinary Yogic power, generated rain.

4. Overjoyed on obtaining a worthy son according to his heart, and overcome with the attachment of parental affection for him, Nābhi addressed him with a broken voice as 'O darling! O beloved one!' etc., although that son was none other than the Supreme Being who had assumed human form. **5.** On knowing of the great confidence and love of the people and the ministers for his son Rishabha, Nābhi installed him as king for the protection of law and order in the land, and himself, with Merudevi, went to Badaryāshrama where he adored Vāsudeva manifest as Nara-Narayana through Samadhi and austerities calculated to bring peace to the mind, and gradually attained Mukti. **6-7.** Hear, O Parikshit, two verses on the greatness of Nābhi: 'Who can imitate the great actions of Nābhi whose pure worship pleased Hari so much that He became

अथ ह भगवानृषभदेवः स्ववर्षं कर्मक्षेत्रमनुमन्यमानः प्रदर्शितगुरुकुलवासो लब्धवरैर्गुरुभिरनुज्ञातो गृहमेधिनां धर्माननुशिक्षमाणो जयन्त्यामिन्द्रदत्तायामुभयलक्षणं कर्म समाम्नायाम्नातमभियुञ्जन्नात्मजानामात्मसमानानां शतं जनयामास ॥8॥ येषां खलु महायोगी भरतो ज्येष्ठः श्रेष्ठगुण आसीद्येनेदं वर्षं भारतमिति व्यपदिशन्ति ॥9॥ तमनु कुशावर्त इलावर्तो ब्रह्मावर्तो मलयः केतुर्भद्रसेन इन्द्रस्पृग्विदर्भः कीकट इति नव नवतिप्रधानाः ॥10॥

कविर्हरिरन्तरिक्षः प्रबुद्धः पिप्पलायनः । आविर्होत्रोऽथ द्रुमिलश्चमसः करभाजनः ॥11॥

इति भागवतधर्मदर्शना नव महाभागवतास्तेषां सुचरितं भगवन्महिमोपबृंहितं वसुदेवनारदसंवादमुपशमायनमुपरिष्टाद्वर्णयिष्यामः ॥12॥ यवीयांस एकाशीतिर्जायन्तेयाः पितुरादेशकरा महाशालीना महाश्रोत्रिया यज्ञशीलाः कर्मविशुद्धा ब्राह्मणा बभूवुः ॥13॥

भगवानृषभसंज्ञ आत्मतन्त्रः स्वयं नित्यनिवृत्तानर्थपरम्परः केवलानन्दानुभव ईश्वर एव विपरीतवत्कर्माण्यारभमाणः कालेनानुगतं धर्ममाचरणेनोपशिक्षयन्नतद्विदां सम उपशान्तो मैत्रः कारुणिको धर्मार्थयशःप्रजानन्दामृतावरोधेन गृहेषु लोकं नियमयत् ॥14॥ यद्यच्छीर्षण्याचरितं तत्तदनुवर्तते लोकः ॥15॥ यद्यपि स्वविदितं सकलधर्मं ब्राह्मं गुह्यं ब्राह्मणैर्दर्शितमार्गेण सामादिभिरुपायै-

his son? Where is another man so devoted to holy men as Nābhi, to whose vision the holy men, pleased with respectful worship and offerings of Dakshina, brought the Supreme Being Himself?'

Rishabha's holy Family (8-13)

8. Bhagavan Rishabha, realising that the region of his advent was a place dominated by Vedic rituals, adopted the life of a religious student under a teacher of the Vedas, and after pleasing the teacher with gifts, came back home with his blessings. He adopted the householder's station of life in order to teach the world about the duties of that Order, observed all the ceremonials and duties laid down in the scriptures, married a girl named Jayanti given to him by Indra, and begot by her a hundred sons equal to himself in all respects. **9.** Of all these sons, Bharata was the eldest and the noblest. This Ajanābha Varsha came to be known after him as Bhāratavarsha. **10.** Next to him, the eldest, nine other sons—Kusāvarta, Ilāvarta, Brahmāvarta, Malaya, Ketu, Bhadrasena, Indrasprik, Vidharbha and Kīkata—were elder to the remaining ninety. **11-12.** Among these ninety, another nine—Kavi, Hari, Antarīksha, Pippalāyana, Āvirhotra, Drumila, Chamasa and Karabhājana—became great devotees and teachers of the Bhakti cult. Their life and teachings, spreading the message of peace and love, and revealing the glory of the Supreme Being, is dealt with elsewhere (in the 11th Skandha) in the form of a conversation between Vasudeva and Narada. **13.** The remaining eighty one of the brothers, who were humble in nature, learned in the Vedas, adepts in sacrificial rites, and extremely pure through their observances, became Brahmanas according to their father's instruction.

Rishabha as ideal Householder (14-19)

14-15. Though ever established in the Atman, ever transcending the unholy and unspiritual influences of the world, perfect in self-mastery, and filled with bliss, he behaved otherwise just like a man of the world. In order to teach the duties of the householder's life, which people had forgotten and given up in course of time, he observed all the rites and ceremonials of the householder, and ever unattached, peaceful, helpful and bene-

जेनतामनुशशास ॥16॥ द्रव्यदेशकालवयःश्रद्धर्त्विग्विविधोद्देशोपचितैः सर्वैरपि क्रतुभिर्यथोपदेशं शतकृत्व इयाज ॥17॥ भगवतर्षभेण परिरक्ष्यमाण एतस्मिन् वर्षे न कश्चन पुरुषो वाञ्छत्यविद्यमानमिवात्मनोऽन्यस्मात्कथञ्चन किमपि कर्हिचिदवेक्षते भर्तर्यनुसवनं विजृम्भितस्नेहातिशयमन्तरेण ॥18॥ स कदाचिदटमानो भगवानृषभो ब्रह्मावर्तगतो ब्रह्मर्षिप्रवरसभायां प्रजानां निशामयन्तीनामात्मजानवहितात्मनः प्रश्रयप्रणयभरसुयन्त्रितानप्युपशिक्षयन्निति होवाच ॥19॥

इति श्रीमद्भागवते महापुराणे पारमहंस्यां संहितायां पञ्चमस्कन्धे चतुर्थोऽध्यायः ॥4॥

ficent, he directed the world's attention to the idea that household life is a field not for mere undisciplined enjoyments, but for the acquisition of Dharma, wealth, good name, progeny and spiritual attainment. For, ordinary people usually follow the example set by noble ones. **16.** Though he was well versed in the Vedic lore that shed light on all aspects of Dharma, he none the less followed the rules of statecraft like conciliation and others, as directed by his Brahmana advisers. **17**. He adored the Supreme Being by performing a hundred Yajnas, perfect from the points of view of ingredients, place, time, age, faith, officiating priests and the various deities. **18**. In this land under Rishabha's rule, every one had sufficient to live upon, and therefore looked upon others' properties as non-existent like a sky-flower. Their only desire was for more and more of love for the great lord and master ruling over them. **19**. Once while moving about the country, Rishabha was in Brahmāvarta. There in an assembly of sages, where a large audience was present to listen to him, Rishabha delivered a sermon especially to teach his sons, though they were endowed with self-control, humility, affection and discipline in all matters of life.

अथ पञ्चमोऽध्यायः

ऋषभ उवाच

नायं देहो देहभाजां नृलोके कष्टान् कामानर्हते विड्भुजां ये।
तपो दिव्यं पुत्रका येन सत्त्वं शुद्ध्येद्यस्माद् ब्रह्मसौख्यं त्वनन्तम् ॥ 1॥
महत्सेवां द्वारमाहुर्विमुक्तेस्तमोद्वारं योषितां सङ्गिसङ्गम्।
महान्तस्ते समचित्ताः प्रशान्ता विमन्यवः सुहृदः साधवो ये ॥ 2॥

Skandha V : Chapter 5

RISHABHA'S SERMON AND AFTER

Rishabha's Sermon: Aim of Life (1-3)

Rishabha said: **1.** O children! The sacred human body that you have got in the world is not meant to be utilised for sensuous enjoyments as by low creatures, who too get such enjoyments through the filth they consume. It is to be used for the observance of austerity with noble spiritual ends. By such austerity the mind becomes pure, enabling one to attain to the bliss of Brahman. **2.** The association with holy ones is the door for entrance to the realm of liberation. And the entrance

ये वा मयीशे कृतसौहृदार्था जनेषु देहम्भरवार्तिकेषु ।
गृहेषु जायात्मजरातिमत्सु न प्रीतियुक्ता यावदर्थाश्च लोके ॥ 3॥
नूनं प्रमत्तः कुरुते विकर्म यदिन्द्रियप्रीतय आपृणोति ।
न साधु मन्ये यत आत्मनोऽयमसन्नपि क्लेशद आस देहः ॥ 4॥
पराभवस्तावदबोधजातो यावन्न जिज्ञासत आत्मतत्त्वम् ।
यावत्क्रियास्तावदिदं मनो वै कर्मात्मकं येन शरीरबन्धः ॥ 5॥
एवं मनः कर्मवशं प्रयुङ्क्ते अविद्ययाऽऽत्मन्युपधीयमाने ।
प्रीतिर्न यावन्मयि वासुदेवे न मुच्यते देहयोगेन तावत् ॥ 6॥
यदा न पश्यत्ययथागुणेहां स्वार्थे प्रमत्तः सहसा विपश्चित् ।
गतस्मृतिर्विन्दति तत्र तापानासाद्य मैथुन्यमगारमज्ञः ॥ 7॥
पुंसः स्त्रिया मिथुनीभावमेतं तयोर्मिथो हृदयग्रन्थिमाहुः ।
अथो गृहक्षेत्रसुताप्तवित्तैर्जनस्य मोहोऽयमहं ममेति ॥ 8॥

to hell (spiritual degradation) consists in association with worldly-minded men who are intensely attached to women. Holy men are those who are even-sighted, peaceful, unperturbed, friendly to all, and endowed with all good qualities. **3.** Or holy men are those who consider the intense attraction they have for Me as their noblest attainment in life, who have no attachment to worldly-minded people, nor to wife, children, properties etc., and who are satisfied with that much of requirements as are enough to live on.

Spiritual Degradation (4-9)

4. Whoever struggles to satisfy the senses is bound to be morally and spiritually lethargic and do many evil deeds. I find no meaning in men doing again and again those very kind of Karmas which have brought into existence this body which, besides being short-lived and ephemeral, is the cause of all sufferings now. The repetition of these Karmas is bound to cause new embodiments and more sufferings. **5.** So long as man does not make an earnest enquiry about the Spirit within, so long will he, out of ignorance, be debarring the dawn of spiritual consciousness in him. So long as he works for selfish attainments, so long will his mind be inclined only towards such actions (and not for spiritual enquiry). And for such body-centred men given to selfish actions, embodiments are caused again and again. **6.** When ignorance clouds the mind, it is enslaved by the impressions of actions done earlier. So long as the mind does not develop attraction and love for Me, Vāsudeva, so long release from embodiment is out of question. **7.** As long as man, heedless of life's purpose, fails to perceive that the actions of his body-mind are not of the Atman, the spiritual Self, he will be completely oblivious of his spiritual nature and behave like an ignorant person, a merely body-centred being, seeking delight in the sex-dominated life of the household but suffering from its endless woes. **8.** The union of man with woman is spoken of by great men as a new knot in their heart, added to the already existing knot of I-sense. For, from that springs the terrible infatuation causing the extension of the sense of identification, consisting in the sense of 'mine-ness', with regard to house, property, son, friend, money and so on.

यदा मनोहृदयग्रन्थिरस्य कर्मानुबद्धो दृढ आश्लथेत।
तदा जनः सम्परिवर्ततेऽस्मान्मुक्तः परं यात्यतिहाय हेतुम् ॥ 9॥
हंसे गुरौ मयि भक्त्यानुवृत्त्या वितृष्णया द्वन्द्वतितिक्षया च।
सर्वत्र जन्तोर्व्यसनावगत्या जिज्ञासया तपसेहानिवृत्त्या ॥10॥
मत्कर्मभिर्मत्कथया च नित्यं मद्देवसङ्गाद् गुणकीर्तनान्मे।
निर्वैरसाम्योपशमेन पुत्रा जिहासया देहगेहात्मबुद्धेः ॥11॥
अध्यात्मयोगेन विविक्तसेवया प्राणेन्द्रियात्माभिजयेन सध्र्यक्।
सच्छ्रद्धया ब्रह्मचर्येण शश्वद् असम्प्रमादेन यमेन वाचाम् ॥12॥
सर्वत्र मद्भावविचक्षणेन ज्ञानेन विज्ञानविराजितेन।
योगेन धृत्युद्यमसत्त्वयुक्तो लिङ्गं व्यपोहेत्कुशलोऽहमाख्यम् ॥13॥
कर्माशयं हृदयग्रन्थिबन्धमविद्ययाऽऽसादितमप्रमत्तः।
अनेन योगेन यथोपदेशं सम्यग्व्यपोह्योपरमेत योगात् ॥14॥
पुत्रांश्च शिष्यांश्च नृपो गुरुर्वा मल्लोककामो मदनुग्रहार्थः।
इत्थं विमन्युरनुशिष्यादतज्ज्ञान्न योजयेत्कर्मसु कर्ममूढान्।
कं योजयन्मनुजोऽर्थं लभेत निपातयन्नष्टदृशं हि गर्ते ॥15॥

9. This knot of the heart, the I-sense (Ahankara), which is the result of tendencies created by past actions, is therefore identical with the mind. So if man is to be totally free from the bondage of sex, his mind, free from all modifications, should be dissolved in the category superior to it. Then man becomes free from the cause of bondage, namely, ignorance.

The Means of Upliftment (10-20)

10. The means to be adopted by one who wants to break this knot of the heart are as follows: Devotion to, and service of, an enlightened Guru who is only Myself; renunciation; equanimity in suffering and enjoyment; the constant remembrance that suffering is there in any attainment in this world or in the hereafter; intelligent reflection on the true nature of all experiences; abandonment of works for personal gains; austerity; **11.** Dedication of works to Me; hearing the recitals of My divine actions every day; contact with great devotees having Me as their object of adoration; singing about My excellences; non-entertainment of animosity to any one; equanimity; tranquillity; cultivation of intense desire to get over identification with home and one's own body; **12.** Study of scriptures; living in solitude; conquest of the senses and the vital energy; strong faith; celibacy; vigilance; restraint of speech; **13.** The knowledge and insight to see My presence in everything; practice of Samadhi; cultivation of equanimity; firmness, perseverance and discrimination. By practising all these, an earnest aspirant can get over the knot of the I-sense. **14.** After one has, by the instruction of the teacher and the careful practice of the above disciplines, completely overcome the knot of the heart (the I-sense), which is born of ignorance and forms the seat of tendencies leading to works, one can give up all practices of Yoga. (For once the I-sense or self-centredness, is shattered, Sadhana by conscious effort becomes redundant.) **15.** These instructions should be given by a father to a son, a teacher to a disciple, and a king to a subject, if they wish to

लोकः स्वयं श्रेयसि नष्टदृष्टिर्योऽर्थान् समीहेत निकामकामः ।
अन्योन्यवैरः सुखलेशहेतोरनन्तदुःखं च न वेद मूढः ।।16।।
कस्तं स्वयं तदभिज्ञो विपश्चिद् अविद्यायामन्तरे वर्तमानम् ।
दृष्ट्वा पुनस्तं सघृणः कुबुद्धिं प्रयोजयेदुत्पथगं यथान्धम् ।।17।।
गुरुर्न स स्यात्स्वजनो न स स्यात्पिता न स स्याज्जननी न सा स्यात् ।
दैवं न तत्स्यान्न पतिश्च स स्यान्न मोचयेद्यः समुपेतमृत्युम् ।।18।।
इदं शरीरं मम दुर्विभाव्यं सत्त्वं हि मे हृदयं यत्र धर्मः ।
पृष्ठे कृतो मे यदधर्म आराद् अतो हि मामृषभं प्राहुरार्याः ।।19।।
तस्माद्भवन्तो हृदयेन जाताः सर्वे महीयांसममुं सनाभम् ।
अक्लिष्टबुद्ध्या भरतं भजध्वं शुश्रूषणं तद्भरणं प्रजानाम् ।।20।।
भूतेषु वीरुद्भ्य उदुत्तमा ये सरीसृपास्तेषु सबोधनिष्ठाः ।
ततो मनुष्याः प्रमथास्ततोऽपि गन्धर्वसिद्धा विबुधानुगा ये ।।21।।

attain to My state or aspire for My grace. It should be done patiently without getting annoyed even when they are found unreceptive. They should not be allowed to get more and more involved in works for sensuous gratifications with which their discriminative faculty is already dulled. What gain can a teacher have by confirming such men, already blinded spiritually for want of discrimination, in their involvement in this whirlpool of Samsara by prompting them to works and rituals for worldly advantages?

16. The ignorant men of the world without a proper awareness of their ultimate good, acquire objects of enjoyment out of their intense desire for them. In mutual competition for these petty objects of enjoyment, they quarrel and fight among themselves and suffer misery without end. **17.** No wise person, who knows what is good for man and is endowed with a kindly disposition, would, on seeing another man steeped in ignorance and perverted in intelligence, encourage him to persist in the wrong path he is following, even as he would not do so with a blind man going towards a pit. **18.** One who would not save another from the path to death, on which the latter has entered, cannot be called one's Guru if he is the Guru, one's relative if he is a relative, one's father if he is the father, one's mother if she is the mother, one's deity if he is the deity, one's husband if he is the husband. **19.** This body of mine is of an inexplicable nature, as it cannot be accounted for by Karma. My mind is dominated by Sattva quality, by virtue of which devotion to God flourishes in it and Adharma finds no place, as it has been left far behind. So wise men call me Rishabha (the best among one's kind). **20.** Hence all of you, who have sprung from my heart, serve without any reservations Bharata, your brother, who is adorable for his excellences. Serving him is equal to looking after the subjects.

Greatness of Holy Men (21-27)

21. Among objects that have existence, plants with life are superior to lifeless things like stock and stone. Among living objects, moving beings like animals with consciousness are superior to plants. Among creatures with consciousness, man is superior. Higher than man are astral beings; higher than these are beings like

देवासुरेभ्यो मघवत्प्रधाना दक्षादयो ब्रह्मसुतास्तु तेषाम् ।
भवः परः सोऽथ विरिञ्चवीर्यः स मत्परोऽहं द्विजदेवदेवः ॥22॥
न ब्राह्मणैस्तुलये भूतमन्यत्पश्यामि विप्राः किमतः परंतु ।
यस्मिन्नृभिः प्रहुतं श्रद्धयाहमश्नामि कामं न तथाग्निहोत्रे ॥23॥
धृता तनूरुशती मे पुराणी येनेह सत्त्वं परमं पवित्रम् ।
शमो दमः सत्यमनुग्रहश्च तपस्तितिक्षानुभवश्च यत्र ॥24॥
मत्तोऽप्यनन्तात्परतः परस्मात्स्वर्गापवर्गाधिपतेर्न किञ्चित् ।
येषां किमु स्यादितरेण तेषामकिञ्चनानां मयि भक्तिभाजाम् ॥25॥
सर्वाणि मद्धिष्ण्यतया भवद्भिश्चराणि भूतानि सुता ध्रुवाणि ।
सम्भावितव्यानि पदे पदे वो विविक्तदृग्भिस्तदुहार्हणं मे ॥26॥
मनोवचोदृक्करणेहितस्य साक्षात्कृतं मे परिबर्हणं हि ।
विना पुमान् येन महाविमोहात्कृतान्तपाशान्न विमोक्तुमीशेत् ॥27॥

श्रीशुक उवाच

एवमनुशास्यात्मजान् स्वयमनुशिष्टानपि लोकानुशासनार्थं महानुभावः परमसुहृद्भगवानृषभापदेश उपशमशीलानामुपरतकर्मणां महामुनीनां भक्तिज्ञानवैराग्यलक्षणं पारमहंस्यधर्ममुपशिक्षमाणः

Gandharvas, Siddhas and Kinnaras. **22.** Greater than Siddhas and Kinnaras are the Asuras; greater than they are the Devas with Indra at their head. Greater than these are the sons of Brahma, the Prajapatis. Among the sons of Brahma, Rudra is the greatest; greater than Rudra is Brahma who is My devotee (i.e. of Mahavishnu). And I am the devotee of holy men. **23.** I do not consider any one to be equal to a holy man. I do not find any one higher. What food men offer Me through holy men with faith and devotion, that I accept wholeheartedly—not so even what is offered in fire at the Agnihotra. **24.** In this world it is the holy man who holds within himself my primeval and most worshipful form, the Veda. I do not find any one equal to the holy man in whom the supremely pure qualities of Sattva, control of mind, control of the senses, austerity, forbearance, truth, benevolence towards all, and realisation are present. **25.** These supreme devotees who have nothing to call their own, do not pray for any personal advantage even from Me, the Infinite and the Absolute Being, and the grantor of heavenly enjoyments and liberation. Why will they then seek small perishable worldly advantages? **26.** Seeing that all things, moving and unmoving, are ensouled by Me, you must salute them every moment with sincere feeling. This indeed is My real worship. **27.** The true meaning of all that man does by mind, speech, sight and his other instruments of knowledge and actions is only My adoration. Without this kind of worship of Me, man will not be able to rid himself from the noose of Yama, which consists in the great infatuation of looking upon the body as the spirit.

Rishabha as an Avadhuta (28-35)

Sri Suka said: **28.** Though his sons knew all the above teachings in a way, he made his sermon in order that the world at large might understand this doctrine. After this, Rishabha, the friend of all, desired to teach and demonstrate to the world the Dharma of the Paramaham-

स्वतनयशतज्येष्ठं परमभागवतं भगवज्जनपरायणं भरतं धरणिपालनायाभिषिच्य स्वयं भवन
एवोर्वरितशरीरमात्रपरिग्रह उन्मत्त इव गगनपरिधानः प्रकीर्णकेश आत्मन्यारोपिताहवनीयो ब्रह्मा-
वर्तात्प्रवव्राज ॥28॥ जडान्धमूकबधिरपिशाचोन्मादकवदवधूतवेषोऽभिभाष्यमाणोऽपि जनानां गृहीत-
मौनव्रतस्तूष्णीं बभूव ॥29॥ तत्र तत्र पुरग्रामाकरखेटवाटखर्वटशिबिरव्रजघोषसार्थगिरिवनाश्रमा-
दिष्वनुपथमवनिचरापसदैः परिभूयमानो मक्षिकाभिरिव वनगजस्तर्जनताडनावमेहनष्ठीवनग्रावशकृद्रजः-
प्रक्षेपपूतिवातदुरुक्तैस्तदविगणयन्नेवासत्संस्थान एतस्मिन् देहोपलक्षणे सदपदेश उभयानुभवस्वरूपेण
स्वमहिमावस्थानेनासमारोपिताहंममाभिमानत्वादविखण्डितमनाः पृथिवीमेकचरः परिबभ्राम ॥30॥
अतिसुकुमारकरचरणोरःस्थलविपुलबाह्वंसगलवदनाद्यवयवविन्यासः प्रकृतिसुन्दरस्वभावहाससुमुखो
नवनलिनदलायमानशिशिरताराारुणायतनयनरुचिरः सदृशसुभगकपोलकर्णकण्ठनासो विगूढस्मितवदन-
महोत्सवेन पुरवनितानां मनसि कुसुमशरासनमुपदधानः परागवलम्बमानकुटिलजटिलकपिशकेशभूरि-
भारोऽवधूतमलिननिजशरीरेण ग्रहगृहीत इवादृश्यत ॥31॥
यर्हि वाव स भगवान् लोकमिमं योगस्याद्धा प्रतीपमिवाचक्षाणस्तत्प्रतिक्रियाकर्म बीभत्सितमिति

sas characterised by repose in the Self, renunciation of actions, devotion, knowledge and dispassion. He, therefore, installed in succession to him as the ruler of the country, his eldest son Bharata, who was himself of a highly devotional temperament, and who was devoted to the servants of the Lord and dependent on them in all matters. Then he left his residence, taking with him nothing but the body. He was thenceforth like one inebriated, completely nude, and having dishevelled hair. Withdrawing into his heart the sacrificial fires like the Āhavanīya maintained by him, he took to the life of a Sannyasin and wandered away from his country, the Brahmāvarta. **29.** In the midst of men he appeared from time to time as a senseless man, blind man, dumb man, deaf man, a ghoul or a drunkard. In such repulsive attires, he was found to remain silent, not answering even any one's questions. **30.** He travelled through towns, villages, military cantonments, cow-pens, cowherd settlements, travellers' shelters, mountains, forests and hermitages. All along the way, as an elephant in rut is pestered by flies, evil men persecuted him by threatening, beating, urinating on him, spitting on him, throwing stones, cowdung and dust at him, and insulting and abusing him. Being firmly established in the knowledge of the real and the unreal, and in the conviction that one was nothing but the Universal Spirit, he had no identification with the body, which for men in ignorance is the most real entity, but was for him unreal. So none of these persecutions disturbed him, and he travelled all over the world alone, his mind merged in the Atman. **31.** By nature he was endowed with very handsome and well-proportioned hands, legs, chest, arms, shoulders, neck and face. His face always shone with a natural smile. His eyes were long and red like a lotus petal, having pupils that assuaged the grief of men. The parts of the face, like the ears, eyes, cheeks, neck and nose were all well-proportioned and symmetrical. The veiled smile on his lips always attracted the interest of women. This handsome form of his now presented the appearance of a ghoul with dishevelled hair, dirty and unwashed, owing to lack of body consciousness. **32.** Rishabha realised from the persecutions of ignorant people that society was hostile to the practice of Yoga. To retaliate against the persecutors would be still worse. So he

व्रतमाजगरमास्थितः शयान एवाश्नाति पिबति खादत्यवमेहति हदति स्म चेष्टमान उच्चरित आदिग्धोद्देशः ॥32॥ तस्य ह यः पुरीषसुरभिसौगन्ध्यवायुस्तं देशं दशयोजनं समन्तात्सुरभिं चकार ॥33॥ एवं गोमृगकाकचर्यया व्रजंस्तिष्ठन्नासीनः शयानः काकमृगगोचरितः पिबति खादत्यवमेहति स्म ॥34॥ इति नानायोगचर्याचरणो भगवान् कैवल्यपतिर्ऋषभोऽविरतपरममहानन्दानुभव आत्मनि सर्वेषां भूतानामात्मभूते भगवति वासुदेव आत्मनोऽव्यवधानानन्तरोदरभावेन सिद्धसमस्तार्थपरिपूर्णो योगैश्वर्याणि वैहायसमनोजवान्तर्धानपरकायप्रवेशदूरग्रहणादीनि यदृच्छयोपगतानि नाञ्जसा नृप हृदयेनाभ्यनन्दत् ॥35॥

इति श्रीमद्भागवते महापुराणे पारमहंस्यां संहितायां पञ्चमस्कन्धे ऋषभदेवानुचरिते पञ्चमोऽध्यायः ॥5॥

gave up the habit of moving about and adopted what is called Ajagaravritti, the way of life of a python which remains at a spot without going for food anywhere. He laid himself in one place, took his food there, performed the functions of excretion there, stretched himself there and rolled in the faecal matter, and got himself covered with it. **33.** His excreta, however, were so fragrant that the atmosphere up to ten Yojanas was filled with its sweet smell. **34.** Similarly he followed also the ways of a cow, deer, even of crow—walking, sitting, eating and drinking and excreting like all those creatures. **35.** Bhagavan Rishabha then practised various forms of Yogic discipline, experienced the unbroken bliss of the Spirit, and attained to the sense of oneness with the all-pervading Being. In the course of it, various Yogic powers like movement through the sky, speed like that of mind, power of disappearance, entrance into another body, clairaudience etc., came to him automatically without his striving, but he rejected them all.

अथ षष्ठोऽध्यायः

राजोवाच

न नूनं भगव आत्मारामाणां योगसमीरितज्ञानावभर्जितकर्मबीजानामैश्वर्याणि पुनः क्लेशदानि भवितुमर्हन्ति यदृच्छयोपगतानि ॥1॥

ऋषिरुवाच

सत्यमुक्तं किन्त्विह वा एकेन मनसोऽद्धा विश्रम्भमनवस्थानस्य शठकिरात इव सङ्गच्छन्ते ॥2॥ तथा चोक्तम्–

Skandha V : Chapter 6

RISHABHA'S END

Wanderings at Kutakadri (1-8)

The Rajah Parikshit said: **1.** O great one! In the case of those who are established in the Atman, they have already burnt the seeds of Karma in the fire of Yoga. How can the powers of Yoga that have come to them automatically, prove to be a bondage to them? Why did then Rishabha refuse to accept them?

Sri Suka said: **2.** What you say is true in a way. But though the mind has been controlled, it cannot be trusted too much. The best of Yogis do not do so, knowing its fickleness and untrustworthiness, just as a determined hunter would not trust a

न कुर्यात्कर्हिचित्सख्यं मनसि ह्यनवस्थिते। यद्विश्रम्भाच्चिराच्चीर्णं चस्कन्द तप ऐश्वरम् 3॥
नित्यं ददाति कामस्य छिद्रं तमनु येऽरयः। योगिनः कृतमैत्रस्य पत्युर्जायेव पुंश्चली ॥ 4॥
कामो मन्युर्मदो लोभः शोकमोहभयादयः। कर्मबन्धश्च यन्मूलः स्वीकुर्यात्को नु तद् बुधः 5॥

अथैवमखिललोकपालललामोऽपि विलक्षणैर्जडवदवधूतवेषभाषाचरितैरविलक्षितभगवत्प्रभावो
योगिनां साम्परायविधिमनुशिक्षयन् स्वकलेवरं जिहासुरात्मन्यात्मानमसंव्यवहितमनर्थान्तरभावेना-
न्वीक्षमाण उपरतानुवृत्तिरुपरराम ॥6॥ तस्य ह वा एवं मुक्तलिङ्गस्य भगवत ऋषभस्य योग-
मायावासनया देह इमां जगतीमभिमानाभासेन संक्रममाणः कोङ्कवेङ्ककुटकान्दक्षिणकर्णाटकान् देशान्
यदृच्छयोपगतः कुटकाचलोपवन आस्यकृताश्मकवल उन्माद इव मुक्तमूर्धजोऽसंवीत एव विचचार
॥7॥ अथ समीरवेगविधूतवेणुविकर्षणजातोग्रदावानलस्तद्वनमालेलिहानः सह तेन ददाह ॥8॥

यस्य किलानुचरितमुपाकर्ण्य कोङ्कवेङ्ककुटकानां राजार्हन्नामोपशिक्ष्य कलावधर्म उत्कृष्यमाणे
भवितव्येन विमोहितः स्वधर्मपथमकुतोभयमपहाय कुपथपाखण्डमसमञ्जसं निजमनीषया मन्दः
सम्प्रवर्तयिष्यते ॥9॥ येन ह वाव कलौ मनुजापसदा देवमायामोहिताः स्वविधिनियोगशौच-

captured animal with any freedom. **3.** So it is said: Do not compromise with the fickle mind. For, by doing so, even very powerful personages have lost all their spiritual powers. **4.** A Yogi who trusts his mind too much is like a husband who does so in regard to an unfaithful wife. The fickle mind might betray him into the hands of his enemies like lust and its allies, just as the faithless wife might betray her husband by colluding with a lover. **5.** Can any man of true discrimination put full trust in the mind in the belief that it has come under his control—the mind which is the root cause of all dangerous passions like lust, anger, pride, greed, sorrow, infatuation, fear, and the bondage of Karma?

6. Thus, though he was the king of kings, he veiled his divine nature from vulgar eyes by assuming the attitude of a senseless man in dress, language and conduct. Next, in order to show how great Yogis abandon their body, he established himself in the perpetual consciousness of the Atman by recognising the indivisibility of the Atman into the seer and the seen, and thus overcoming even the modicum of tendencies he had assumed for the blessing of the world. **7.** Without connection with even the Lingasarīra, (subtle body), by the mere remaining momentum left of the impulsion given by Yogamaya, his body travelled all over the land, and reached the region of Konka, Venkata, and Kutaka included in Dakshina Karnataka. There he travelled in the forest at the foot of the mountain known as Kutakādri like a ghoul—with the mouth filled with stones, hair dishevelled, and stark naked. **8.** Once a forest fire broke out there by the mutual rubbing of bamboos in a strong wind. The whole forest, along with his holy body, was burnt in that fire.

Significance of his Life (9-19)

9. In the evil age of Kali, Arha, the king of Konka, Venkata and Kutaka, happening to hear about the doings of Rishabha that transcended the conduct of all the Ashramas, would interpret it, owing to the influence of his own evil deeds of the past, as connected with a school of atheism. Abandoning his own faith and the way of life leading to the state of fearlessness, he would preach this atheistic gospel, the product of his own evil brain, among his subjects. **10.** Hearing the preaching of this king, evil-minded men of the Kali

चारित्रविहीना देवहेलनान्यपव्रतानि निजनिजेच्छया गृह्णाना अस्नानानाचमनाशौचकेशोल्लुञ्चनादीनि कलिनाधर्मबहुलेनोपहतधियो ब्रह्मब्राह्मणयज्ञपुरुषलोकविदूषकाः प्रायेण भविष्यन्ति ॥१०॥ ते च ह्यर्वाक्तनया निजलोकयात्रयान्धपरम्परयाऽऽश्वस्तास्तमस्यन्धे स्वयमेव प्रपतिष्यन्ति ॥११॥

अयमवतारो रजसोपप्लुतकैवल्योपशिक्षणार्थः ॥१२॥ तस्यानुगुणान् श्लोकान् गायन्ति –

अहो भुवः सप्तसमुद्रवत्या द्वीपेषु वर्षेष्वधिपुण्यमेतत् ।
गायन्ति यत्रत्यजना मुरारेः कर्माणि भद्राण्यवतारवन्ति ॥१३॥
अहो नु वंशो यशसावदातः प्रैयव्रतो यत्र पुमान् पुराणः ।
कृतावतारः पुरुषः स आद्यः चचार धर्मं यदकर्महेतुम् ॥१४॥
को न्वस्य काष्ठामपरोऽनुगच्छेन्मनोरथेनाप्यभवस्य योगी ।
यो योगमायाः स्पृहयत्युदस्ता ह्यसत्तया येन कृतप्रयत्नाः ॥१५॥

इति ह स्म सकलवेदलोकदेवब्राह्मणगवां परमगुरोर्भगवत ऋषभाख्यस्य विशुद्धाचरितमीरितं पुंसां समस्तदुश्चरिताभिहरणं परममहामङ्गलायनमिदमनुश्रद्धयोपचितयानुशृणोत्याश्रावयति वावहितो भगवति तस्मिन् वासुदेव एकान्ततो भक्तिरनयोरपि समनुवर्तते ॥१६॥ यस्यामेव कवय आत्मानमविरतं विविधवृजिनसंसारपरितापोपतप्यमानमनुसवनं स्नापयन्तस्तयैव परया निर्वृत्या ह्यपवर्ग-

age, would abandon the rules of conduct laid down in the Vedas for the purification of the body and mind; transgress the Deities presented in the Vedas; prefer mean forms of worship concocted by their evil brains; give up purificatory rites like bath, Achamana etc.; adopt the practice of plucking the hairs on the head; and refuse to accept the Veda, the custodians of the Veda and the God that the Veda reveals. **11.** They would find satisfaction in following superstitious practices fabricated by their own brains and without any Vedic support. In the end they would fall into utter darkness.

12. But then is Rishabha's Avatara a cause of evil! What is its purpose? So it is said: The purpose of Rishabha's incarnation was to show people dominated by Rajas that ritualism for enjoyments here and hereafter is not the primary teaching of the Veda, but that it consists in renunciation, knowledge and devotion which bring enlightenment to the spirit. **13.** There are the following verses on this subject: 'Among the seven continents of this earth surrounded by seven seas, Bhāratavarsha is the most holy;

here people enthusiastically sing about the Lord's incarnations and His sportive actions. **14.** The line of Priyavrata is famous for its holy traditions. For it is in that line that the Supreme Being took his birth and demonstrated the Dharma of one seeking liberation. **15.** Which Yogi can even in his imagination follow this path followed by Rishabha? All Yogis only try to obtain a little of those psychic powers which Rishabha Deva threw away as dirt.' **16.** This account of Rishabha, which reveals the greatness of, and truth about, the Vedas, the higher worlds, Devas, holy men and spiritual duties, has the power to remove all sins, and is the source of everything auspicious, spiritual and good. Whoever hears this or makes others hear it, with a mind devoted and concentrated, will attain to higher and higher stages of devotion to Him, who is self-effulgent and the support of all.

17. The wise men, finding their spirit suffering from the heat of sins pertaining to the life of Samsara—the miseries arising from physical and supra-mundane

मात्यन्तिकं परमपुरुषार्थमपि स्वयमासादितं नो एवाद्रियन्ते भगवदीयत्वेनैव परिसमाप्तसर्वार्थाः ॥17॥

राजन् पतिर्गुरुरलं भवतां यदूनां दैवं प्रियः कुलपतिः क्व च किङ्करो वः ।
अस्त्वेवमङ्ग भगवान् भजतां मुकुन्दो मुक्तिं ददाति कर्हिचित्स्म न भक्तियोगम् 18॥
नित्यानुभूतनिजलाभनिवृत्ततृष्णः श्रेयस्यतद्रचनया चिरसुप्तबुद्धेः ।
लोकस्य यः करुणयाभयमात्मलोकमाख्यान्नमो भगवते ऋषभाय तस्मै ॥19॥

इति श्रीमद्भागवते महापुराणे पारमहंस्यां संहितायां पञ्चमस्कन्धे ऋषभदेवानुचरिते षष्ठोऽध्यायः ॥6॥

causes—try to assuage themselves from that heat by bathing in the nectar of God-love. The bliss arising from the devotional experience is such that they reject even Moksha, considered the highest value open to a Jiva, which comes automatically to them as a result of their Bhakti discipline. Rather than getting merged in Him, they prefer to continue in the core of Bhakti-experience—the consciousness that they are the Lord's own. **18.** O King! The Lord Krishna is the master, teacher, visible deity and leader for you, the Pandavas and the Yadus. Nay, he has ever been your servant, acting as a messenger and a charioteer. So be it. He grants Mukti (liberation) to those who worship Him, but seldom Bhakti, that intense loving devotion (which makes God Himself a servant of the devotee). **19.** Salutation to that Lord Rishabha—to that exalted being who, on account of his constant consciousness of the inherent bliss of the Atman, was absolutely indifferent to every thing else; to that exalted being who out of his mercy declared the truth of the Atman, the one refuge from all fears, to men caught up in the sleep of body-consciousness and utterly oblivious of their own ultimate good.

अथ सप्तमोऽध्यायः

श्रीशुक उवाच

भरतस्तु महाभागवतो यदा भगवतावनितलपरिपालनाय संचिन्तितस्तदनुशासनपरः पञ्चजनीं विश्वरूपदुहितरमुपयेमे ॥1॥ तस्यामु ह वा आत्मजान् कार्त्स्न्येनानुरूपानात्मनः पञ्च जनयामास भूतादिरिव भूतसूक्ष्माणि ॥2॥ सुमतिं राष्ट्रभृतं सुदर्शनमावरणं धूम्रकेतुमिति । अजनाभं नामैतद्वर्षं भारतमिति यत आरभ्य व्यपदिशन्ति ॥3॥

स बहुविन्महीपतिः पितृपितामहवदुरुवत्सलतया स्वे स्वे कर्मणि वर्तमानाः प्रजाः स्वधर्मम-

Skandha V : Chapter 7

THE STORY OF BHARATA

Bharata's Rule (1-7)

Sri Suka said: **1.** On his father resolving to instal him as ruler, the pious Bharata made himself ready for his duties, and first married Panchajani, the daughter of Viswarupa. **2.** By her he begot five issue, just as out of Bhutadi (or the Ahankara) the five Bhuta-sukshmas (or subtle elements) come out. **3.** These five sons were Sumati, Rāshtrabhrit, Sudarsana, Āvarana and Dhūmraketu. It was from the time of Bharata's rule that the land, known till then as Ajanābhavarsha, came to be

नुवर्तमानः पर्यपालयत् ॥4॥ ईजे च भगवन्तं यज्ञक्रतुरूपं क्रतुभिरुच्चावचैः श्रद्धयाऽऽहृताग्निहोत्र-
दर्शपूर्णमासचातुर्मास्यपशुसोमानां प्रकृतिविकृतिभिरनुसवनं चातुर्होत्रविधिना ॥5॥ सम्प्रचरत्सु नाना-
यागेषु विरचिताङ्गक्रियेष्वपूर्वं यत्तत्क्रियाफलं धर्माख्यं परे ब्रह्मणि यज्ञपुरुषे सर्वदेवतालिङ्गानां
मन्त्राणामर्थनियामकतया साक्षात्कर्तरि परदेवतायां भगवति वासुदेव एव भावयमान आत्मनैपुण्य-
मृदितकषायो हविःष्वध्वर्युभिर्गृह्यमाणेषु स यजमानो यज्ञभाजो देवांस्तान् पुरुषावयवेष्वभ्यध्यायत्
॥6॥ एवं कर्मविशुद्धचा विशुद्धसत्त्वस्यान्तर्हृदयाकाशशरीरे ब्रह्मणि भगवति वासुदेवे महापुरुष-
रूपोपलक्षणे श्रीवत्सकौस्तुभवनमालारिदरगदादिभिरुपलक्षिते निजपुरुषहृल्लिखितेनात्मनि पुरुषरूपेण
विरोचमान उच्चैस्तरां भक्तिरनुदिनमेधमानरयाजायत ॥7॥

एवं वर्षायुतसहस्रपर्यन्तावसितकर्मनिर्वाणावसरोऽधिभुज्यमानं स्वतनयेभ्यो रिक्थं पितृपैतामहं
यथादायं विभज्य स्वयं सकलसम्पन्निकेतात्स्वनिकेतात् पुलहाश्रमं प्रवव्राज ॥8॥ यत्र ह वाव
भगवान् हरिरद्यापि तत्रत्यानां निजजनानां वात्सल्येन सन्निधाप्यत इच्छारूपेण ॥9॥ यत्राश्रम-
पदान्युभयतोनाभिभिर्दृषच्चक्रैश्चक्रनदी नाम सरित्प्रवरा सर्वतः पवित्रीकरोति ॥10॥

तस्मिन् वाव किल स एकलः पुलहाश्रमोपवने विविधकुसुमकिसलयतुलसिकाम्बुभिः कन्दमूल-
फलोपहारैश्च समीहमानो भगवत आराधनं विविक्त उपरतविषयाभिलाष उपभृतोपशमः परां

called Bhāratavarsha. **4.** That learned king, following the example of his illustrious father and grandfather, observed his Swadharma, and ruled over his subjects with great affection for them, encouraging them to follow their Swadharma. **5.** The Lord is of the form of Yajna and Kratu—the two forms of sacrifice without and with the installation of the sacrificial post. He is to be worshipped by these two forms of sacrifice. With great faith, he performed, according to his capacity and at proper times, many sacrifices like Agnihotra, Chāturmāsya, Pasubandha and Somayāga in their elaborate and abridged forms. **6.** When the various Yajnas, with their many subsidiary rites, were being performed, Bharata, the master of the Yajnas, offered all the fruits accruing from them to Vāsudeva, who is Parabrahman, who is of the form of Yajna, who is the controller of the Vedic Mantras and the Deities invoked thereby, and who is the ultimate doer and master of all works. **7.** Powerful currents of Bhakti developed in the heart of Bharata, which was purified by the above-mentioned worship through works (Yajnas), and there shone in it the form of the Lord Vāsudeva in all the splendour of His supreme majesty with the marks of Srivatsa, Kaustubha, Vanamala, conch, discus, mace and other paraphernalia, as revealed in the hearts of other great devotees like Narada.

Bharata's Life at Pulahāshrama (8-14)

8. After he ruled for a crore of years, he felt he had completed his allotted period of active life. So he divided his ancestral kingdom and wealth among his sons, and abandoning his luxurious palace, went away as a wandering ascetic to the Pulahāshrama, a famous place of worship of Sri Hari. **9.** In that place Sri Hari, out of love for His devotees, manifests to their vision in various attractive forms. **10.** That place is purified by the river Chakranadi (Gandaki), wherein one gets Mahavishnu's holy emblem Sālagrāma, which has cavities with symbolic designs on both sides. **11.** Abandoning all desires from the heart, alone, peaceful and blissful at heart, he stayed there in a thinly wooded locality, continuously wor-

निर्वृतिमवाप ॥11॥ तयेत्थमविरतपुरुषपरिचर्यया भगवति प्रवर्धमानानुरागभरद्रुतहृदयशैथिल्यः प्रहर्ष-वेगेनात्मन्युद्भिद्यमानरोमपुलककुलक औत्कण्ठ्यप्रवृत्तप्रणयबाष्पनिरुद्धावलोकनयन एवं निजरमणारुण-चरणारविन्दानुध्यानपरिचितभक्तियोगेन परिप्लुतपरमाह्लादगम्भीरहृदयह्रदावगाढधिषणस्तामपि क्रियमाणां भगवत्सपर्यां न सस्मार ॥12॥ इत्थं धृतभगवद्व्रत ऐणेयाजिनवाससानुसवनाभिषेकार्द्रकपिश-कुटिलजटाकलापेन च विरोचमानः सूर्यर्चा भगवन्तं हिरण्मयं पुरुषमुज्जिहाने सूर्यमण्डलेऽभ्युपतिष्ठ-न्नेतदु होवाच ॥13॥

परोरजः सवितुर्जातवेदो देवस्य भर्गो मनसेदं जजान।
सुरेतसादः पुनराविश्य चष्टे हंसं गृध्राणं नृषद्रिङ्गिरामिमः ॥14॥

इति श्रीमद्भागवते महापुराणे पारमहंस्यां संहितायां पञ्चमस्कन्धे भरतचरिते भगवत्परिचर्यायां सप्तमोऽध्यायः ॥7॥

shipping Sri Hari with flowers, leaves, Tulasi, water and food offerings consisting of tubers, roots and fruits. **12.** By the daily adoration of Sri Hari in this way, the sentiment of devotion grew so strong in him as to melt his heart. The massive bliss he experienced within expressed itself as horripilation all over the body. Anxious longing blinded him with profuse tears. His intellect got submerged in the lake of his heart filled with the joy of devotional experience generated by the constant contemplation of the ruby red feet of his most beloved Lord. **13.** Disciplining himself in devotional practices, he wore a dress of deer skin. Impressive with his curly matted hair, turned tawny and wet by constant bath at times of worship, he stood before the brilliant rising sun at dawn invoking him as Suryanarayana with the following Rik, descriptive of his glory: **14.** 'We seek refuge in that Splendrous Puissance that is Surya-Narayana (the Lord manifest as the Sun-deity), untouched by Rajas and bestowing the fruits of the Karmas of all—the Puissance that projects the universe, indwells it and protects the Jiva pursuing his desires—with that Puissance we seek refuge for the proper direction of our understanding.'

अथाष्टमोऽध्यायः

श्रीशुक उवाच

एकदा तु महानद्यां कृताभिषेकनैयमिकावश्यको ब्रह्माक्षरमभिगृणानो मुहूर्तत्रयमुदकान्त उपविवेश ॥1॥ तत्र तदा राजन् हरिणी पिपासया जलाशयाभ्याशमेकैवोपजगाम ॥2॥ तया पेपीयमान उदके तावदेवाविदूरेण नदतो मृगपतेरुन्नादो लोकभयंकर उदपतत् ॥3॥ तमुपश्रुत्य

Skandha V : Chapter 8

STORY OF BHARATA: THE DEER EPISODE

Bharata getting a fawn (1-7)

Sri Suka said: **1.** One day, Bharata, after finishing his ablutions and his daily rites, sat on the bank of the river for about three Muhurtas uttering the Pranava (Om). **2.** O King! Just then a solitary doe approached the river bank to quench her thirst. **3.** While she was drinking water, the terrifying roar of a lion was

सा मृगवधूः प्रकृतिविक्लवा चकितनिरीक्षणा सुतरामपि हरिभयाभिनिवेशव्यग्रहृदया पारिप्लवदृष्टि-
रगततृषा भयात्सहसैवोच्चक्राम ॥4॥

तस्या उत्पतन्त्या अन्तर्वत्न्या उरुभयावगलितो योनिनिर्गतो गर्भः स्रोतसि निपपात ॥5॥
तत्प्रसवोत्सर्पणभयखेदातुरा स्वगणेन वियुज्यमाना कस्याञ्चिद्दर्यां कृष्णसारसती निपपाताथ च
ममार ॥6॥

तं त्वेणकुणकं कृपणं स्रोतसानूह्यमानमभिवीक्ष्यापविद्धं बन्धुरिवानुकम्पया राजर्षिर्भरत आदाय
मृतमातरमित्याश्रमपदमनयत् ॥7॥ तस्य ह वा एणकुणक उच्चैरेतस्मिन् कृतनिजाभिमानस्याहरह-
स्तत्पोषणपालनलालनप्रीणनानुध्यानेनात्मनियमाः सहयमाः पुरुषपरिचर्यादय एकैकशः कति-
पयेनाहर्गणेन वियुज्यमानाः किल सर्व एवोदवसन् ॥8॥ अहो बतायं हरिणकुणकः कृपण ईश्वर-
रथचरणपरिभ्रमणरयेण स्वगणसुहृद्बन्धुभ्यः परिवर्जितः शरणं च मोपसादितो मामेव मातापितरौ
भ्रातृज्ञातीन् यौथिकांश्चैवोपेयाय नान्यं कञ्चन वेद मय्यतिविस्रब्धश्चात एव मया मत्परायणस्य
पोषणपालनप्रीणनलालनमनसूयुनानुष्ठेयं शरण्योपेक्षादोषविदुषा ॥9॥ नूनं ह्यार्याः साधव उपशम-
शीलाः कृपणसुहृद एवंविधार्थे स्वार्थानपि गुरुतरानुपेक्षन्ते ॥10॥

इति कृतानुषङ्ग आसनशयनाटनस्थानाशनादिषु सह मृगजहुना स्नेहानुबद्धहृदय आसीत् ॥11॥
कुशकुसुमसमित्पलाशफलमूलोदकान्याहरिष्यमाणो वृकसालावृकादिभ्यो भयमाशंसमानो यदा सह

heard from the neighbourhood. **4.** The timid doe of tremulous glances was frightened beyond measure by that roar, and while still in the act of drinking, sprang to the other shore with a wild and distracted look in her eyes. **5.** Being big with young, she delivered, even while springing, due to the shock that fear generated, and the young one thereupon fell into the current of the river. **6.** Fear, delivery, the act of springing, separation from the flock—the cumulative effect of all these circumstances distressed her so much that she fell down dead in a cave on the other side. **7.** The Rajarshi Bharata saw that forlorn and endangered calf of the deer being swept down by the current of the river. Overcome with pity for the motherless new-born, he caught it and brought it to his Ashrama.

Bharata's Attachment to Fawn (8-25)

8. The Rajarshi was now possessed by the idea that the fawn was his own and consequently got infatuated with it. Daily he fed it, fattened it, protected it from enemies, fondled it, and in every way tried to please it. In proportion to the increase of his interest in it, his zeal in his devotional practices declined until he gave them up totally sometime after. **9.** He thought: 'Alas! The swift-moving action of the Wheel of Time has separated this poor fawn from his parents and his flock, and it has taken refuge with me as his father, mother, brother, relative and friend. Putting his trust entirely in me, he knows none else. So even at the expense of my own interest, I am bound to protect, nourish, fondle and in every way look after the interests of this calf of a deer, knowing as I do the sin of abandoning one who has sought refuge. **10.** Many a worshipful person who followed the path of peace and service of the afflicted, has, for the sake of such work, abandoned his own self-interest in important matters.' **11.** In this way getting infatuated with the fawn, he always came to be accompanied by it while sitting, lying, walking, standing or eating. **12.** Fearing that it might be attacked by dogs or wolves, he took it also

हरिणकुणकेन वनं समाविशति ॥12॥ पथिषु च मुग्धभावेन तत्र तत्र विषक्तमतिप्रणयभरहृदयः कार्पण्यात्स्कन्धेनोद्वहति एवमुत्सङ्ग उरसि चाधायोपलालयन्मुदं परमामवाप ॥13॥ क्रियायां निर्वर्त्यमानायामन्तरालेऽप्युत्थायोत्थाय यदैनमभिचक्षीत तर्हि वाव स वर्षपतिः प्रकृतिस्थेन मनसा तस्मा आशिष आशास्ते स्वस्ति स्ताद्वत्स ते सर्वत इति ॥14॥

अन्यदा भृशमुद्विग्नमना नष्टद्रविण इव कृपणः सकरुणमतितर्षेण हरिणकुणकविरहविह्वल-हृदयसंतापस्तमेवानुशोचन् किल कश्मलं महदभिरम्भित इति होवाच ॥15॥ अपि बत स वै कृपण एणबालको मृतहरिणीसुतोऽहो ममानार्यस्य शठकिरातमतेरकृतसुकृतस्य कृतविस्रम्भ आत्म-प्रत्ययेन तदविगणयन् सुजन इवागमिष्यति ॥16॥ अपि क्षेमेणास्मिन्नाश्रमोपवने शष्पाणि चरन्तं देवगुप्तं द्रक्ष्यामि ॥17॥ अपि च न वृकः सालावृकोऽन्यतमो वा नैकचर एकचरो वा भक्षयति ॥18॥ निम्लोचति ह भगवान् सकलजगत्क्षेमोदयस्त्रय्यात्माद्यापि मम न मृगवधून्यास आगच्छति ॥19॥ अपिस्विदकृतसुकृतमागत्य मां सुखयिष्यति हरिणराजकुमारो विविधरुचिरदर्शनीयनिजमृग-दारकविनोदैरसन्तोषं स्वानामपनुदन् ॥20॥ क्ष्वेलिकायां मां मृषा समाधिनाऽऽमीलितदृशं प्रेम-संरम्भेण चकितचकित आगत्य पृषदपरुषविषाणाग्रेण लुठति ॥21॥ आसादितहविषि बर्हिषि दूषिते मयोपालब्धो भीतभीतः सपद्युपरतरास ऋषिकुमारवदवहितकरणकलाप आस्ते ॥22॥

किं वा अरे आचरितं तपस्तपस्विन्यानया यदियमवनिः सविनयकृष्णसारतनयतनुतरसुभग-

with him whenever he went out to collect grass, flower, fuel, leaves, fruits, roots and water. **13.** Whenever it stopped on the way interested in something or other, he took it on his shoulders, or lap, or embraced it, and enjoyed intense delight in doing so. **14.** Even when he was engaged in worship, he would now and then get up and have a look at the fawn to assure himself that it was safe, and would pronounce his blessings on it, saying: 'May you live safe without any danger befalling you!' **15.** If for a time it could not be seen nearby, he would become grief-stricken like one who has lost his all. Owing to the intensity of his attachment to it, he felt heart-broken at its absence, and bemoaning over its fate repeatedly, he would in the most pitiable way say to himself: **16.** 'Ah! Would this pitiable young deer, orphaned of its mother doe, come back at all to me, trusting me to be a good man out of its own innocence, overlooking the perversities of a luckless fellow like myself, cruel and mean like a hunter? **17.** Shall I ever see it, thanks to the protecting hand of the Lord, browsing somewhere in the woodlands of this Ashrama! **18.** I hope it has not been eaten up by any predatory creature, a wild dog or a wolf, moving about singly or in herds. **19.** Sun, the universal benefactor and the repository of the Vedas, is about to set, and the fawn, a treasure deposited with me for safe custody by that doe, has not yet returned. **20.** Will that gem of a fawn come back to my unlucky self and delight his own folk with its childish frolics? **21.** As it plays about and I sit there with my eyes half-closed in fake Samadhi, it approaches me in a mood of love-quarrel for not participating in its play, and in order to know whether I am really in Samadhi, prods me with the tip of his horn soft like water, with a show of great hesitation and fright. **22.** When he pulls away the grass where Havis (sacrificial offerings for Devas) is arranged, and I happen to take him to task for the same, then like any boy of the hermitage, he withdraws from

शिवतमाखरखुरपदपङ्क्तिभिर्द्रविणविधुरातुरस्य कृपणस्य मम द्रविणपदवीं सूचयन्त्यात्मान च सर्वतः कृतकौतुकं द्विजानां स्वर्गापवर्गकामानां देवयजनं करोति ॥23॥ अपिस्विदसौ भगवानुडुपतिरेनं मृगपतिभयान्मृतमातरं मृगबालकं स्वाश्रमपरिभ्रष्टमनुकम्पया कृपणजनवत्सलः परिपाति ॥24॥ किं वाऽऽत्मजविश्लेषज्वरदवदहनशिखाभिरुपतप्यमानहृदयस्थलनलिनीकं मामुपसृतमृगीतनयं शिशिरशान्तानुरागगुणितनिजवदनसलिलामृतमयगभस्तिभिः स्वधयतीति च ॥25॥

एवमघटमानमनोरथाकुलहृदयो मृगदारकाभासेन स्वारब्धकर्मणा योगारम्भणतो विभ्रंशितः स योगतापसो भगवदाराधनलक्षणाच्च कथमितरथा जात्यन्तर एणकुणक आसङ्गः साक्षान्निःश्रेयसप्रतिपक्षतया प्राक्परित्यक्तदुस्त्यजहृदयाभिजातस्य तस्यैवमन्तरायविहतयोगारम्भणस्य राजर्षेर्भरतस्य तावन्मृगार्भकपोषणपालनप्रीणनलालनानुषङ्गेणाविगणयत आत्मानमहिरिवाखुबिलं दुरतिक्रमः कालः करालरभस आपद्यत ॥26॥ तदानीमपि पार्श्ववर्तिनमात्मजमिवानुशोचन्तमभिवीक्षमाणो मृग एवाभिनिवेशितमना विसृज्य लोकमिमं सह मृगेण कलेवरं मृतमनु न मृतजन्मानुस्मृतिरितरवन्मृग-

all play and remains motionless with all his limbs controlled. **23.** What great austerities must this land have done to deserve this good fortune of being marked with the tiny and beautiful hoof-prints of this young black buck (Krishnasara)! For, these hoof-prints, besides cheering me with the prospect of tracing the whereabouts of their owner, make this land a suitable holy place for the performance of all sacred rites by those who seek heavenly felicity and worldly welfare.'

24. Referring to the mark of the deer found in the disc of the rising moon, he would say: 'Is it that the moon has taken for protection this poor motherless fawn, seeing that it has now strayed away from the precincts of this Ashrama? **25.** The loss of this fawn, which is like a son to me, is scorching the land-lotus of my heart like a forest fire. Are you, O moon, intending to quench that heat by the cool and refreshing water from your face, augmented by the sight of my condition, as I go about pitiably in search of my young deer!'

Dire Consequence of Attachment (26-27)

26. Thus distressed by vague and baseless fears, the Rajarshi was led to stray away completely from his practice of Yoga, austerities, and the worship of the Supreme Lord by his own Prarabdha Karma (destiny) in the shape of a deer calf. How can it be attributed to anything else? In the case of one like this Rajarshi, who had abandoned even his sons, considering them to be an obstacle in the spiritual quest, what other explanation can be given for this strange phenomenon of obsession with a deer calf, which did not belong even to the human species? Thus the Rajarshi Bharata happened to slide away from the path of Yoga, and engage himself, completely absorbed, in the protection, feeding, fondling etc., of the fawn, devoid of all thoughts regarding the Atman. Just then the hour that is inevitable for every one, that of death, approached him with irresistible pace, just like a serpent gliding towards a rat in its hole. **27.** Even at the moment of death, he was looking at the fawn by his side, as if it were a son in mourning sitting beside him; and he left his body and the deer behind, with his mind firmly fixed on the latter. Though his old body was dead, his consciousness of the experiences of that birth was not lost. Following the fate of an ordinary man under such circumstances, he was born as

शरीरमवाप ॥27॥ तत्रापि ह वा आत्मनो मृगत्वकारणं भगवदाराधनसमीहानुभावेनानुस्मृत्य
भृशमनुतप्यमान आह ॥28॥ अहो कष्टं भ्रष्टोऽहमात्मवतामनुपथाद्यद्विमुक्तसमस्तसङ्गस्य विविक्त-
पुण्यारण्यशरणस्यात्मवत आत्मनि सर्वेषामात्मनां भगवति वासुदेवे तदनुश्रवणमननसङ्कीर्तनाराधना-
नुस्मरणाभियोगेनाशून्यसकलयामेन कालेन समावेशितं समाहितं कार्त्स्न्येन मनस्तत्तु पुनर्ममाबुधस्या-
रान्मृगसुतमनु परिसुस्राव ॥29॥

इत्येवं निगूढनिर्वेदो विसृज्य मृगीं मातरं पुनर्भगवत्क्षेत्रमुपशमशीलमुनिगणदयितं शालग्रामं
पुलस्त्यपुलहाश्रमं कालञ्जरात्प्रत्याजगाम ॥30॥ तस्मिन्नपि कालं प्रतीक्षमाणः सङ्गाच्च भृशमुद्विग्न
आत्मसहचरः शुष्कपर्णतृणवीरुधा वर्तमानो मृगत्वनिमित्तावसानमेव गणयन्मृगशरीरं तीर्थोदक-
क्लिन्नमुत्ससर्ज ॥31॥

इति श्रीमद्भागवते महापुराणे पारमहंस्यां संहितायां पञ्चमस्कन्धे भरतचरितेऽष्टमोऽध्यायः ॥8॥

a deer in the next life; but he retained the memory of the past birth.

His Redemption (28-31)

28. Thanks to the power of his adoration of the Supreme Lord, he remembered even in the deer body the cause of his birth in such a frame, and said to himself with an anguished mind: **29.** 'Alas! Alas! What a pity that I have fallen from the ways of the spiritually accomplished! My mind was completely offered at the feet of the Lord, and not a bit of my time was wasted in any occupation other than the thought of the Lord. Residing in the solitude of a holy forest Ashrama after abandoning all attachments of life, my mind was entirely fixed on Him, the Lord of all and the soul of all souls. Completely absorbed in the devotional disciplines of hearing, praising, remembering and worshipping, and in unbroken contemplation, not a minute was spent in vain purposes. But alas! the fool that I was, my mind in the end went too far after that deer with the disastrous consequences that have followed.' **30.** Unknown to all, the Bharata-deer was thus full of renunciation within. Therefore, he left his mother doe and his place of birth in the Kalanjara mountains and migrated to the spot where stood the Ashramas of Pulastya and Pulaha, which had an abundance of palm trees, and which was dear to holy men because of the manifest presence of the Divine. **31.** Then keeping himself aloot from the company of others out of fear of the consequences, and moving about alone, feeding on dry leaves, grass, roots etc., and biding the exhaustion of the Prarabdha Karma that had brought him to this strait, he awaited the dawn of his last day. And at last when it came, he abandoned his deer body in the holy waters of the river there.

अथ नवमोऽध्यायः

श्रीशुक उवाच

अथ कस्यचिद् द्विजवरस्याङ्गिरः प्रवरस्य शमदमतपःस्वाध्यायाध्ययनत्यागसन्तोषतितिक्षाप्रश्रय-
विद्यानसूयात्मज्ञानानन्दयुक्तस्यात्मसदृशश्रुतशीलाचाररूपौदार्यगुणा नव सोदर्या अङ्गजा बभूवुर्मिथुनं
च यवीयस्यां भार्यायाम् ॥1॥ यस्तु तत्र पुमांस्तं परमभागवतं राजर्षिप्रवरं भरतमुत्सृष्टमृगशरीरं
चरमशरीरेण विप्रत्वं गतमाहुः ॥2॥ तत्रापि स्वजनसङ्गाच्च भृशमुद्विजमानो भगवतः कर्मबन्ध-
विध्वंसनश्रवणस्मरणगुणविवरणचरणारविन्दयुगलं मनसा विदधदात्मनः प्रतिघातमाशङ्कमानो
भगवदनुग्रहेणानुस्मृतस्वपूर्वजन्मावलिरात्मानमुन्मत्तजडान्धबधिरस्वरूपेण दर्शयामास लोकस्य ॥3॥
तस्यापि ह वा आत्मजस्य विप्रः पुत्रस्नेहानुबद्धमना आसमावर्तनात् संस्कारान् यथोपदेशं विदधान
उपनीतस्य च पुनः शौचाचमनादीन् कर्मनियमाननभिप्रेतानपि समशिक्षयदनुशिष्टेन हि भाव्यं
पितुः पुत्रेणेति ॥4॥ स चापि तदुह पितृसन्निधावेवासध्रीचीनमिव स्म करोति छन्दांस्यध्यापयिष्यन्
सह व्याहृतिभिः सप्रणवशिरस्त्रिपदीं सावित्रीं ग्रैष्मवासन्तिकान्मासानधीयानमप्यसमवेतरूपं
ग्राहयामास ॥5॥

Skandha V : Chapter 9

STORY OF BHARATA: SACRIFICE TO BHADRAKALI

Bharata's new Birth (1-7)

Sri Suka said: **1.** There was a Brahmana born in the Gotra of Angiras noted for such qualities as control of the mind and the senses, austerity, Vedic study, Vedic teaching, generosity, joyous temperament, forbearance, humility, knowledge of Vedic rituals, absence of envy, knowledge of the Atman as distinguished from the body, and bliss of Atman-consciousness. He had two wives, by the first of whom he had nine sons, all noted for their exemplary conduct, knowledge of the Vedas, handsome appearance, generosity and such other qualities as he himself possessed. By the second wife he had twins, a boy and a girl. **2.** It is said that the second wife's son was Bharata reborn after his death as a deer, the assumption of this Brahmana body constituting his final birth.

3. But even in this birth he was found to be very allergic to the company of his relatives. He was always mentally contemplating on the Lord's feet through hearing, remembering and recounting His excellences which destroy one's bondage of Karma. Ever remembering the experiences of his past birth through the Lord's grace, he was constantly vigilant against new obstacles, and in order to dissociate himself from the company of others, he put on the air of an inebriated man, a senseless man, and a man without sight or hearing.

4. Eager that his son should excel him in virtue, his father decided to put him through all the preparatory disciplines that a Brahmana should undergo up to Samavartana (the ceremony marking the end of education). He first had his Upanayana performed, and tried to teach him various purificatory rites like Achamana, in spite of his being a senseless boy. **5.** But Bharata performed all these rites in an indifferent manner even in the father's presence, so that the father might soon give him up as hopeless. With the idea of teaching him the Vedas, the father first instructed him in the Gayatri Mantra

एवं स्वतनुज आत्मन्यनुरागावेशितचित्तः शौचाध्ययनव्रतनियमगुर्वनलशुश्रूषणाद्यौपकुर्वाणककर्माण्यनभियुक्तान्यपि समनुशिष्टेन भाव्यमित्यसदाग्रहः पुत्रमनुशास्य स्वयं तावदनधिगतमनोरथः कालेनाप्रमत्तेन स्वयं गृह एव प्रमत्त उपसंहृतः ॥6॥ अथ यवीयसी द्विजसती स्वगर्भजातं मिथुनं सपत्न्या उपन्यस्य स्वयमनुसंस्थया पतिलोकमगात् ॥7॥

पितर्युपरते भ्रातर एनमतत्प्रभावविदस्त्रय्यां विद्यायामेव पर्यवसितमतयो न परविद्यायां जडमतिरिति भ्रातुरनुशासननिरबन्धान्न्यवृत्सन्त ॥8॥ स च प्राकृतैर्द्विपदपशुभिरुन्मत्तजडबधिरेत्यभिभाष्यमाणो यदा तदनुरूपाणि प्रभाषते कर्माणि च स कार्यमाणः परेच्छया करोति विष्टितो वेतनतो वा याच्ञया यदृच्छया वोपसादितमल्पं बहु मृष्टं कदन्नं वाभ्यवहरति परं नेन्द्रियप्रीतिनिमित्तम् । नित्यनिवृत्तनिमित्तस्वसिद्धविशुद्धानुभवानन्दस्वात्मलाभाधिगमः सुखदुःखयोर्द्वन्द्वनिमित्तयोरसम्भावितदेहाभिमानः ॥9॥ शीतोष्णवातवर्षेषु वृष इवानावृताङ्गः पीनः संहननाङ्गः स्थण्डिलसंवेशनानुन्मर्दनामज्जनरजसा महामणिरिवानभिव्यक्तब्रह्मवर्चसः कुपटावृतकटिरुपवीतेनोरुमषिणा द्विजातिरिति

combined with the Vyahritis and the Pranava. But even after four months' teaching, the boy could not recite them with proper intonation. **6.** The father had deep affection for his son, who is to be looked upon by a father as a replica of one's own self. He therefore wrongly thought that it was his duty to teach his son, even against his will, all the duties of the Brahmacharin like purificatory rites, Vedic study, observance of vows, disciplines of life, service of teacher, performance of Homa (fire worship) etc. He tried his best to do so, but failed. So years passed by, with the father unaware of its passage on account of his engrossment in household affairs. But ever-vigilant Time soon swallowed him up in death. **7.** Thereupon the second wife of the Brahmana entrusted her two children to the elder wife, and herself accompanied her husband in death.

His strange Conduct (8-11)

8. After the father's death, the brothers who had only the theoretical knowledge of the Vedas but no spiritual realisation, thought that it was of no use to educate a senseless fellow like their brother and soon desisted from attempts in that direction, without any inkling of his spiritual worth.

9. When vulgar men, who were no better than two-legged animals, called him a madcap or idiot or dumb and deaf fellow, he behaved accordingly, and when they forced him to act in any way, he did so also. He subsisted on whatever he got by chance, or by begging, or by working for wages, or by what he was given for doing forced labour. Whatever he got, whether it was small or large in quantity, whether it was well-cooked or ill-cooked, he ate it for the mere sustenance of the body and not for placating the sense of taste. But he always remained in the intuitive bliss of Atman that was natural to him and did not depend on any extraneous cause or stimulation for its inducement. Enjoyment and suffering, honour and dishonour, which are only matters affecting the body, were never attributed by him to the Atman, his real nature. **10.** In heat and cold, in rain and wind, he moved about like an ox without anything to protect the body. By giving up bath and cleaning of the body, and by the practice of lying on the bare ground, his well-built and muscular frame was covered with a thick layer of dirt, through which his Brahmic lustre was very dimly visible like the luminosity of an unpolished gem. Wearing a dirty cloth

ब्रह्मबन्धुरिति संज्ञयातज्ज्ञजनावमतो विचचार ॥10॥ यदा तु परत आहारं कर्मवेतनत ईहमानः स्वभ्रातृभिरपि केदारकर्मणि निरूपितस्तदपि करोति किन्तु न समं विषमं न्यूनमधिकमिति वेद कणपिण्याकफलीकरणकुल्माषस्थालीपुरीषादीन्यप्यमृतवदभ्यवहरति ॥11॥

अथ कदाचित्कश्चिद् वृषलपतिर्भद्रकाल्यै पुरुषपशुमालभतापत्यकामः ॥12॥ तस्य ह दैवमुक्तस्य पशोः पदवीं तदनुचराः परिधावन्तो निशि निशीथसमये तमसाऽऽवृतायामनधिगतपशव आकस्मिकेन विधिना केदारान् वीरासनेन मृगवराहादिभ्यः संरक्षमाणमङ्गिरःप्रवरसुतमपश्यन् ॥13॥ अथ त एनमनवद्यलक्षणमवमृश्य भर्तृकर्मनिष्पत्तिं मन्यमाना बद्ध्वा रशनया चण्डिकागृहमुपनिन्युर्मुदा विकसितवदनाः ॥14॥

अथ पणयस्तं स्वविधिनाभिषिच्याहतेन वाससाऽऽच्छाद्य भूषणालेपस्रक्तिलकादिभिरुपस्कृतं भुक्तवन्तं धूपदीपमाल्यलाजकिसलयाङ्कुरफलोपहारोपेतया वैशससंस्थया महता गीतस्तुतिमृदङ्ग-पणवघोषेण च पुरुषपशुं भद्रकाल्याः पुरत उपवेशयामासुः ॥15॥ अथ वृषलराजपणिः पुरुषपशोर-सृगासवेन देवीं भद्रकालीं यक्ष्यमाणस्तदभिमन्त्रितमसिमतिकरालनिशितमुपाददे ॥16॥

इति तेषां वृषलानां रजस्तमःप्रकृतीनां धनमदरजउत्सिक्तमनसां भगवत्कलावीरकुलं कदर्थी-

and a soiled Yajnopavita, he moved about here and there, mocked by the vulgar folk as the madcap Brahmana. **11.** When he consented to do work in exchange for food, he would be engaged even by his brothers to level fields with earth and other similar works. While doing such work, he was not aware of what he did—whether he had levelled the ground or whether he had heaped up earth helter-skelter, whether he had filled up the place or whether more earth was required to do so. Whatever they gave him, be it rice flour, oil-cake, chaff, spoilt pulses, or charred food—he ate up everything as if it were nectar.

Sacrifice to Bhadrakali (12-20)

12. Now at that time a chieftain of a tribe of brigands resolved to perform a human sacrifice to Bhadrakali in order to have a male issue. **13.** The sacrificial human-beast he had secured managed to run away from his custody. So his men ran hither and thither in the darkness of that midnight in search of that victim. Unable to find him anywhere, they at last came across this scion of the Gotra of Angiras (i.e. Jada-Bharata, or Bharata in the role of a dullard), sitting solemnly in a shed in the fields, guarding them from the depradations of deer, wild boars and other animals. **14.** On seeing him of well-developed body, their face bloomed in the satisfaction that a proper victim had been obtained to complete their master's rites, and so tying him up with ropes, led him to the temple of Bhadrakali. **15.** The priests there, in accordance with the rules of their Abhichara ritual, bathed and decorated this human victim with new cloth, unguents, Tilaka, garlands etc., and fed him. Then amidst the sound of tom-toms, drums and songs, he was made to sit before the image of Bhadrakali, where the various ingredients for the rites like light, incense, garlands, flowers, tender leaves, fried grains, buds, fruits etc., were arranged. **16.** The low-born priest, who officiated for the chieftain of the thieves, resolving to worship Bhadrakali by offering the human victim's blood as drink, took up the sharp sacrificial sword, uttering proper Mantras.

17. These low-born men of the tribe of theives were by nature endowed with

कृत्योत्पथेन स्वैरं विहरतां हिंसाविहाराणां कर्मातिदारुणं यद्ब्रह्मभूतस्य साक्षाद्ब्रह्मर्षिसुतस्य निर्वैरस्य
सर्वभूतसुहृदः सूनायामप्यननुमतमालम्भनं तदुपलभ्य ब्रह्मतेजसातिदुर्विषहेण दन्दह्यमानेन वपुषा
सहसोच्चचाट सैव देवी भद्रकाली ॥17॥ भृशममर्षरोषावेशरभसविलसितभ्रुकुटिविटपकुटिलदंष्ट्रा-
रुणेक्षणाटोपातिभयानकवदना हन्तुकामेवेदं महाट्टहासमतिसंरम्भेण विमुञ्चन्ती तत उत्पत्य पापीयसां
दुष्टानां तेनैवासिना विवृक्णशीर्ष्णां गलात्स्रवन्तमसृगासवमत्युष्णं सह गणेन निपीयातिपानमद-
विह्वलोच्चैस्तरां स्वपार्षदैः सह जगौ ननर्त च विजहार च शिरःकन्दुकलीलया ॥18॥ एवमेव
खलु महदभिचारातिक्रमः कार्त्स्न्येनात्मने फलति ॥19॥ न वा एतद्विष्णुदत्त महदद्भुतं यदसम्भ्रमः
स्वशिरश्छेदन आपतितेऽपि विमुक्तदेहाद्यात्मभावसुदृढहृदयग्रन्थीनां सर्वसत्त्वसुहृदात्मनां निर्वैराणां
साक्षाद्भगवतानिमिषारिवरायुधेनाप्रमत्तेन तैस्तैर्भावैः परिरक्ष्यमाणानां तत्पादमूलमकुतश्चिद्भयमुप-
सृतानां भागवतपरमहंसानाम् ॥20॥

इति श्रीमद्भागवते महापुराणे पारमहंस्यां संहितायां पञ्चमस्कन्धे जडभरतचरिते नवमोऽध्यायः ॥9॥

Tamas and Rajas. Due to the inordinate pride that wealth brought, they had abandoned the royal road of worship of Mahavishnu and were given to a licentious life and indulgence in slaughter unguided by any moral code. For, even though some sacrificial rites have been laid down for men of fierce nature when they are threatened by some dangerous situations, what these ruffians were now about to do was a transgression of an extremely cruel nature. The sacrifice of a great man who had become one with Brahman, who was the scion of a great and holy family, who was beyond all antagonism, and who was the friend of all—was an act of unpardonable and intolerable cruelty. The divine prowess (Brahma-tejas) emanating from that extraordinary victim began to burn up Bhadrakali herself, and so she emerged suddenly from the image. **18.** The Devi was fierce to look at. Her eye-brows were arching with unbearable anger and remorse at the heinous act that was contemplated. With her curved fangs, red eyes and fierce look, she stepped out with a terrific roar, as if she were going to destroy everything. Taking up the same sacrificial sword, she cut off the heads of all those miscreants, drank their blood, and intoxicated with that drink, played foot-ball with their heads and danced and sang with her attendants. **19.** Though these people were the worshippers of Bhadrakali, this sad end for them was but legitimate. For, cruel rites performed to endanger great men, are always bound to boomerang on the performer himself. **20.** O King Parikshit! Do not consider it a wonder or anything unusual that Bharata was unperturbed even when his head was about to be cut off. He had abandoned the identification of the self with the body, and thus cut asunder that powerful knot of the heart. Persons like him are moved by universal love and friendship. Residing as the indweller in all, the Lord himself is ever vigilant in protecting such devotees from all dangers with His discus that is the wheel of Time.

अथ दशमोऽध्यायः

श्रीशुक उवाच

अथ सिन्धुसौवीरपते रहूगणस्य व्रजत इक्षुमत्यास्तटे तत्कुलपतिना शिबिकावाहपुरुषान्वेषणसमये दैवेनोपसादितः स द्विजवर उपलब्ध एष पीवा युवा संहननाङ्गो गोखरवद् धुरं वोढुमलमिति पूर्वविष्टिगृहीतैः सह गृहीतः प्रसभमतदर्ह उवाह शिबिकां स महानुभावः ॥1॥

यदा हि द्विजवरस्येषुमात्रावलोकानुगतेर्न समाहिता पुरुषगतिस्तदा विषमगतां स्वशिबिकां रहूगण उपधार्य पुरुषानधिवहत आह हे वोढारः साध्वतिक्रमत किमिति विषममुह्यते यानमिति ॥2॥

अथ त ईश्वरवचः सोपालम्भमुपाकर्ण्योपायतुरीयाच्छङ्कितमनसस्तं विज्ञापयाम्बभूवुः ॥3॥

न वयं नरदेव प्रमत्ता भवन्नियमानुपथाः साध्वेव वहामः। अयमधुनैव नियुक्तोऽपि न द्रुतं व्रजति नानेन सह वोढुमु ह वयं पारयाम इति ॥4॥

सांसर्गिको दोष एव नूनमेकस्यापि सर्वेषां सांसर्गिकाणां भवितुमर्हतीति निश्चित्य निशम्य कृपणवचो राजा रहूगण उपासितवृद्धोऽपि निसर्गेण बलात्कृत ईषदुत्थितमन्युरविस्पष्टब्रह्मतेजसं जातवेदसमिव रजसाऽऽवृतमतिराह ॥5॥ अहो कष्टं भ्रातर्व्यक्तमुरु परिश्रान्तो दीर्घमध्वानमेक एव ऊहिवान् सुचिरं नातिपीवा न संहननाङ्गो जरसा चोपद्रुतो भवान् सखे नो एवापर एते सङ्घट्टिन

Skandha V : Chapter 10

STORY OF BHARATA: MEETING WITH RAHŪGANA

Bharata as Palanquin Bearer (1-6)

Sri Suka said: **1.** Rahūgana, the king of Sindhu and Sauvira, was once travelling in a palanquin to the Ashrama of Kapila. When the party of the king was on the banks of the river Ikshumati, their captain felt the need for some more palanquin bearers. While he was searching for one, this exalted personage Bharata arrived at the spot, guided as it were by his destiny. Finding him young, well-built and strong, the captain felt that he could bear weight like a bullock or mule. So he compelled him to join the party of bearers he had collected earlier by force, although a great man like him did not deserve such treatment. **2.** The newly recruited bearer was found walking slow, surveying the path up to three feet (the length of an arrow) carefully in order to avoid trampling over living creatures. The pace of the palanquin bearers therefore began to vary, and King Rahūgana, who was inside the palanquin, got vexed with its unsteady movements. So he exclaimed to the bearers: 'O bearers! Walk properly, all moving at an equal speed. Why are you not bearing the vehicle in the correct way?' **3.** Hearing their master's words of displeasure, they told him as follows, afraid of punishment: **4.** 'O our Lord and King! We are not careless. Obedient to your order, we are carrying the palanquin the proper way. But this new bearer, though he has only just now joined the team, is not walking fast enough. It will be impossible to carry the palanquin with him in the team.'

5. 'The defect of one in a company is likely to affect the work of all who have to work with him'—concluding so and moved by the words of the distressed palanquin bearers, King Raghūgana, though he had served great devotees, none the less got somewhat angry at the new

इति बहुविप्रलब्धोऽप्यविद्यया रचितद्रव्यगुणकर्माशयस्वचरमकलेवरेऽवस्तुनि संस्थानविशेषेऽहं ममेत्यनध्यारोपितमिथ्याप्रत्ययो ब्रह्मभूतस्तूष्णीं शिबिकां पूर्ववदुवाह ॥6॥

अथ पुनः स्वशिबिकायां विषमगतायां प्रकुपित उवाच रहूगणः किमिदमरे त्वं जीवन्मृतो मां कदर्थीकृत्य भर्तृशासनमतिचरसि प्रमत्तस्य च ते करोमि चिकित्सां दण्डपाणिरिव जनताया यथा प्रकृतिं स्वां भजिष्यस इति ॥7॥

एवं बह्वबद्धमपि भाषमाणं नरदेवाभिमानं रजसा तमसानुविद्धेन मदेन तिरस्कृताशेष-भगवत्प्रियनिकेतं पण्डितमानिनं स भगवान् ब्राह्मणो ब्रह्मभूतः सर्वभूतसुहृदात्मा योगेश्वरचर्यायां नातिव्युत्पन्नमतिं स्मयमान इव विगतस्मय इदमाह ॥8॥

ब्राह्मण उवाच

त्वयोदितं व्यक्तमविप्रलब्धं भर्तुः स मे स्याद्यदि वीर भारः ।
गन्तुर्यदि स्यादधिगम्यमध्वा पीवेति राशौ न विदां प्रवादः ॥ 9॥
स्थौल्यं कार्श्यं व्याधय आधयश्च क्षुत्तृड् भयं कलिरिच्छा जरा च ।
निद्रा रतिर्मन्युरहंमदः शुचो देहेन जातस्य हि मे न सन्ति ॥10॥

bearer owing to the assertion of past tendencies. Overcome by Rajoguna, and unable to recognise, under his external garb, the Brahmic lustre of Bharata, as of live cinders covered by ashes, Rahūgana said to him in a tone of ridicule. **6.** 'O brother! You are very tired, aren't you? For, you have indeed been bearing the palanquin single-handed for such a long distance! Is'nt it so? Moreover you are not so well-built and strong. Besides, it seems you are also very old. But all your fellow bearers are not like that.' Though ridiculed in this way, Bharata continued to walk as before without uttering a single word in reply. For in this, his last birth, he had become one with Brahman without any sense of indentification with this last body of his, which is a combination of elements brought about by Avidya and which has no substantial reality.

Bharata's Reply as a wise Man (7-13)

7. Finding that the palanquin was still irregular in its movement, Rahūgana became extremely angry and exclaimed: 'O Sirrah! You a living corpse (Jivan-mrita)! Are you belittling me, your master, and violating my command? As Yama gives to heedless people, I shall give you, fellow, a radical treatment, which will restore you to your original state.' **8.** Thus the king, out of pride born of his royal status and learning, and out of the promptings of the qualities of passion and dullness, spoke many such stupid things to that holy man without understanding the ways of great spiritual personages. Not in the least perturbed by all that, Bharata the bearer who had realised his unity with Brahman and attained to universal love, said to him smiling, as if mocking at the ignorance of the Rajah, but really out of his extreme humility.

Bharata said: **9.** O bold one! Your ridicule has relevance provided there is a thing called weight for one to bear, provided there is a destination for the traveller to reach, and provided there is corpulence for the Jiva to be carried. Wise men, however, do not assent to such a proposition. (As weight, body, distance etc., are all the effects of Maya and therefore false, and as I am the Spirit and not the body, your words of ridicule become pointless.) **10.** Corpulence, leanness, disease, hunger, thirst, fear, quarrel, desire, old age, sleep, attachment, anger, pride,

जीवन्मृतत्वं नियमेन राजन् आद्यन्तवद्यद्विकृतस्य दृष्टम् ।
स्वस्वाम्यभावो ध्रुव ईड्य यत्र तर्ह्युच्यतेऽसौ विधिकृत्ययोगः ॥11॥
विशेषबुद्धेर्विवरं मनाक् च पश्याम यन्न व्यवहारतोऽन्यत् ।
क ईश्वरस्तत्र किमीशितव्यं तथापि राजन् करवाम किं ते ॥12॥
उन्मत्तमत्तजडवत्स्वसंस्थां गतस्य मे वीर चिकित्सितेन ।
अर्थः कियान् भवता शिक्षितेन स्तब्धप्रमत्तस्य च पिष्टपेषः ॥13॥

श्रीशुक उवाच

एतावदनुवादपरिभाषया प्रत्युदीर्य मुनिवर उपशमशील उपरतानात्म्यनिमित्त उपभोगेन कर्मारब्धं व्यपनयन् राजयानमपि तथोवाह ॥14॥ स चापि पाण्डवेय सिन्धुसौवीरपतिस्तत्त्वजिज्ञासायां सम्यक्श्रद्धयाधिकृताधिकारस्तद्धृदयग्रन्थिमोचनं द्विजवच आश्रुत्य बहुयोगग्रन्थसम्मतं त्वरयावरुह्य शिरसा पादमूलमुपसृतः क्षमापयन् विगतनृपदेवस्मय उवाच ॥15॥

कस्त्वं निगूढश्चरसि द्विजानां बिभर्षि सूत्रं कतमोऽवधूतः ।
कस्यासि कुत्रत्य इहापि कस्मात् क्षेमाय नश्चेदसि नोत शुक्लः ॥16॥

grief etc., are all true only in regard to one born with a body, but not to me who am the Atman. **11.** O King! The state of being a living corpse (Jivanmrita) is not a characteristic special to me; it applies to everything that is an effect. For everything that is an effect, is subject to birth and death, to a beginning and to an end. As for the charge of violating your command, O worshipful one, it would have been true if the relation between master and servant were permanent. (But it is not. By a change of fortune the master can become the servant, and the servant, the master.) **12.** Except for the worldly convention, I find no reason for the distinction between master and servant. Who is the master and who is the servant? Still if you feel you are the king, you order me what I am to do. **13.** O brave king! If my behaviour as a madcap or a dunce is the result of my establishment in my nature as the Atman, what change can your punishment effect in me? So also if I am really a confirmed lunatic or a dunce, your attempt at reforming me by punishment will be like powdering a powdered stuff once again.

Rahūgana discovers Bharata (14-25)

Sri Suka said: **14.** Having thus made a non-controversial reply, that sage, who was full of peace and who was no longer identifying himself with the body, continued to carry the palanquin of the king as before, in order to exhaust his Prarabdha Karma. **15.** O descendent of the Pandavas! At this stage, the mind of Rahūgana, the king of Sindhu and Sauvira, was filled with faith, and he derived the fitness to enquire about the Supreme Truth. Hearing the words of Bharata, based on scriptural texts and powerful enough to cut the knot of egotism (Ahankara), Rahūgana gave up his pride of being a king, and hurriedly coming down from the palanquin, prostrated himself before that great one and said: **16.** 'Who are you travelling incognito in this form? Among the famous ascetics like Dattatreya and others, who could you possibly be? You bear the holy thread indicating that you are a Brahmana: Whose son are you? Which is your place? How do you happen to be here? Am I to understand that you are Mahavishnu's incarnation Kapila himself come here to

नाहं विशङ्के सुरराजवज्रान्न त्र्यक्षशूलान्न यमस्य दण्डात् ।
नाग्न्यर्कसोमानिलवित्तपास्त्राच्छङ्के भृशं ब्रह्मकुलावमानात् ॥17॥
तद् ब्रूह्यसङ्गो जडवन्निगूढविज्ञानवीर्यो विचरस्यपारः ।
वचांसि योगग्रथितानि साधो न नः क्षमन्ते मनसापि भेत्तुम् ॥18॥
अहं च योगेश्वरमात्मतत्त्वविदां मुनीनां परमं गुरुं वै ।
प्रष्टुं प्रवृत्तः किमिहारणं तत् साक्षाद्धरिं ज्ञानकलावतीर्णम् ॥19॥
स वै भवांल्लोकनिरीक्षणार्थमव्यक्तलिङ्गो विचरत्यपिस्वित् ।
योगेश्वराणां गतिमन्धबुद्धिः कथं विचक्षीत गृहानुबन्धः ॥20॥
दृष्टः श्रमः कर्मत आत्मनो वै भर्तुर्गन्तुर्भवतश्चानुमन्ये ।
यथासतोदानयनाद्यभावात् समूल इष्टो व्यवहारमार्गः ॥21॥
स्थाल्यग्नितापात्पयसोऽभितापस्तत्तापतस्तण्डुलगर्भरन्धिः ।
देहेन्द्रियास्वाशयसन्निकर्षात् तत्संसृतिः पुरुषस्यानुरोधात् ॥22॥
शास्ताभिगोप्ता नृपतिः प्रजानां यः किङ्करो वै न पिनष्टि पिष्टम् ।
स्वधर्ममाराधनमच्युतस्य यदीहमानो विजहात्यघौघम् ॥23॥

bless us? **17.** I fear not the thunderbolt of Indra, nor the trident of Rudra, nor the rod of Yama, nor the weapons of any of the divinities like Agni, Surya, Chandra, Vayu and Kubera. But I am terribly afraid of the consequences of insulting an illumined personage belonging to a great and holy family. **18.** Therefore, please tell me all about yourself. I feel that you are really one possessed of unfathomable knowledge, hiding your spiritual power and enlightenment, and going about incognito like a dunce. For, your words convey the meaning of Yoga Sastras and are too profound for our minds to grasp. **19.** I am myself on my way to the Muni Kapila, the Incarnation of Mahavishnu, the teacher of all wise men and an embodiment of Yoga, to learn from him what constitutes the refuge for man in this transmigratory existence. **20.** It may be that you are that very Kapila going about incognito to see the condition of the world. How can a person tied to the household and without any spiritual enlightenment understand the ways of master Yogis like you? **21.** [In criticism of your denial of exhaustion etc., to your body, I reply:] By doing various administrative and military duties, I really feel tired. So I can guess that you too will feel exhausted by walking, carrying a load. This practical aspect of life based on actual experience, I accept as a fact. To deny it, will be like denying the existence of pots with which watering is being done. **22.** In cooking, the heat applied to the pot penetrates to the water in it; that heat affects not only the surface of the rice in it, but the very core of the grains. In the same way, owing to their mutual contact, the experiences of the body pass on through the inner layers of senses, Pranas and mind to the Atman. So the experience of Samsara by the Atman has to be accepted as real. **23.** In answer to the criticism of the master and servant relationship, I reply: Though the master and servant relationship is temporal and artificial, when a man becomes a king, he becomes the ruler and protector of others. If one accepts the idea that in discharging his duties, a ruler is only carrying out the will of God, the objection

तन्मे भवान्नरदेवाभिमानमदेन तुच्छीकृतसत्तमस्य ।
कृषीष्ट मैत्रीदृशमार्तबन्धो यथा तरे सदवध्यानमंहः ॥24॥
न विक्रिया विश्वसुहृत्सखस्य साम्येन वीताभिमतेस्तवापि ।
महद्विमानात् स्वकृताद्धि मादृङ् नङ्क्ष्यत्यदूरादपि शूलपाणिः ॥25॥

इति श्रीमद्भागवते महापुराणे पारमहंस्यां संहितायां पञ्चमस्कन्धे दशमोऽध्यायः ॥10॥

of pounding the already pounded stuff, does not arise in regard to his corrective acts for changing even the incorrigible. For, whoever performs the worship of the Lord through Swadharma, is freed from all sins. **24.** Regarding my offence of slighting a great man, I seek pardon of you. Out of your goodwill, deign to order things in such a way that I incur no sin. **25.** It may be said that you are not affected or perturbed by adoration or insult, as you are established in the attitude of universal friendship, even-mindedness towards all, and non-identification with the body. But still an offender like me, even if he were as powerful as Sri Parameswara, is bound to perish in consequence.'

अथैकादशोऽध्यायः

ब्राह्मण उवाच

अकोविदः कोविदवादवादान् वदस्यथो नातिविदां वरिष्ठः ।
न सूरयो हि व्यवहारमेनं तत्त्वावमर्शेन सहामनन्ति ॥ 1॥
तथैव राजन्नुरुगार्हमेधवितानविद्योरुविजृम्भितेषु ।
न वेदवादेषु हि तत्त्ववादः प्रायेण शुद्धो नु चकास्ति साधुः ॥ 2॥
न तस्य तत्त्वग्रहणाय साक्षाद्वरीयसीरपि वाचः समासन् ।
स्वप्ने निरुक्त्या गृहमेधिसौख्यं न यस्य हेयानुमितं स्वयं स्यात् ॥ 3॥

Skandha V : Chapter 11

STORY OF BHARATA: INSTRUCTION TO RAHŪGANA

Phenomenal Nature of the World (1-3)

The Brahmana (Bharata) said: **1.** Though you are in spiritual ignorance, you try to speak like a man of unfailing knowledge, which however you are not. For, a really knowing one will not take this relative existence with its differences of master, servant etc., as a proved fact in determining what is real. As it is found to be merely temporal on reflection, they call it 'an attribution of the thoughtless'. But, as you take it all as real, you are not the best among thinkers. **2.** Not only the world and its relation, but even the Vedic teaching dealing with Karma, belongs to the realm of falsity for a thinker. O King! In the highly eulogistic Vedic passages dealing with rituals relevant to the householder's life, there will not generally be any discussion on the truth of the Atman which is based in purity and righteousness. **3.** A person who is not able to grasp the phenomenality and worthlessness of the happiness of waking life, by applying the analogy of dream expe-

यावन्मनो रजसा पूरुषस्य सत्त्वेन वा तमसा वानुरुद्धम् ।
चेतोभिराकूतिभिरातनोति निरङ्कुशं कुशलं चेतरं वा ॥ 4॥
स वासनात्मा विषयोपरक्तो गुणप्रवाहो विकृतः षोडशात्मा ।
बिभ्रत्पृथङ्नामभि रूपभेदमन्तर्बहिष्ट्वं च पुरैस्तनोति ॥ 5॥
दुःखं सुखं व्यतिरिक्तं च तीव्रं कालोपपन्नं फलमाव्यनक्ति ।
आलिङ्ग्य मायारचितान्तरात्मा स्वदेहिनं संसृतिचक्रकूटः ॥ 6॥
तावानयं व्यवहारः सदाविः क्षेत्रज्ञसाक्ष्यो भवति स्थूलसूक्ष्मः ।
तस्मान्मनो लिङ्गमदो वदन्ति गुणागुणत्वस्य परावरस्य ॥ 7॥
गुणानुरक्तं व्यसनाय जन्तोः क्षेमाय नैर्गुण्यमथो मनः स्यात् ।
यथा प्रदीपो घृतवर्तिमश्नन् शिखाः सधूमा भजति ह्यन्यदा स्वम् ।
पदं तथा गुणकर्मानुबद्धं वृत्तीर्मनः श्रयतेऽन्यत्र तत्त्वम् ॥ 8॥
एकादशासन्मनसो हि वृत्तय आकूतयः पञ्च धियोऽभिमानः ।
मात्राणि कर्माणि पुरं च तासां वदन्ति हैकादश वीर भूमीः ॥ 9॥

riences, will not be able to arrive at the truth even from the great teachings of the Vedanta.

Mind as Cause of Samsara (4-7)

4. As long as a man's mind is dominated by any of the three Gunas of Prakriti, Sattva, Rajas and Tamas, so long it will be uncontrollable. It will constantly engage the organs of knowledge and action in producing meritorious and demeritorious works. **5.** The mind, a bundle of tendencies, is the principal of the sixteen categories. It is prone to go to sense objects. The Gunas of Prakriti move it here and there, and also shape it into various modes of desire and other passions. Investing the Jiva with various forms as Devas, men, animals etc., it generates all these differences of high and low based on these forms. **6.** The mind has been created by Maya as the manifesting field of the Atman. It is the entity responsible for keeping the Jiva in the transmigratory cycle. For, holding the Atman in close embrace, it brings on him enjoyment, suffering and infatuation in accordance with the inevitable process of time. **7.** So long as there is ignorance, this world of practical life, with its gross and subtle conditions consisting of waking, dream and sleep states, persists as an object of experience before the embodied being. Therefore, the mind is said to be the cause of the Jiva's bondage and of his liberation from the Gunas, as also for his birth in high and low situations.

The Modes of the Mind (8-11)

8. The mind that is attached to sense objects causes miseries, and when it is free from such attachments, it leads to liberation. A wick light in contact with ghee gives light and smoke. Otherwise it remains in its pristine condition. So also the mind caught up amidst sense objects and actions, takes up the form of Vrittis or modes. When it is not so modified, it dwells in Truth. **9.** The modes (Vrittis) of the mind are said to be eleven, these being five in the form of actions, five of knowledge, and one in the form of I-sense. The five organs of action become the basis of active modes; the five organs of knowledge, of knowledge modes; and the body,

गन्धाकृतिस्पर्शरसश्रवांसि विसर्गरत्यर्त्यभिजल्पशिल्पाः ।
एकादशं स्वीकरणं ममेति शय्यामहं द्वादशमेक आहुः ॥10॥
द्रव्यस्वभावाशयकर्मकालैरेकादशामी मनसो विकाराः ।
सहस्रशः शतशः कोटिशश्च क्षेत्रज्ञतो न मिथो न स्वतः स्युः ॥11॥
क्षेत्रज्ञ एता मनसो विभूतीर्जीवस्य मायारचितस्य नित्याः ।
आविर्हिताः क्वापि तिरोहिताश्च शुद्धो विचष्टे ह्यविशुद्धकर्तुः ॥12॥
क्षेत्रज्ञ आत्मा पुरुषः पुराणः साक्षात्स्वयंज्योतिरजः परेशः ।
नारायणो भगवान् वासुदेवः स्वमाययाऽऽत्मन्यवधीयमानः ॥13॥
यथानिलः स्थावरजङ्गमानामात्मस्वरूपेण निविष्ट ईशेत् ।
एवं परो भगवान् वासुदेवः क्षेत्रज्ञ आत्मेदमनुप्रविष्टः ॥14॥
न यावदेतां तनुभृन्नरेन्द्र विधूय मायां वयुनोदयेन ।
विमुक्तसङ्गो जितषट्सपत्नो वेदात्मतत्त्वं भ्रमतीह तावत् ॥15॥
न यावदेतन्मन आत्मलिङ्गं संसारतापावपनं जनस्य ।
यच्छोकमोहामयरागलोभवैरानुबन्धं ममतां विधत्ते ॥16॥

of I-sense. **10.** The eleven modes for the functioning of the mind are: the five organs of knowledge like smell, sight, touch, taste and sound; the five organs of action like excretion, sex enjoyment, walking, speaking and handling. The sense of 'mine' is the eleventh mode. Some speak of the sense of 'I' with reference to the body, the base in which the Jiva dwells, as the twelfth mode. **11.** By the influence of factors like Nature, purification, unseen forces and Time, these eleven modes of the mind may take a hundred, a thousand or a crore of shapes. They cannot, however, do so either by themselves or by mutual influence. It is born of the limitless power of the Lord, the Kshetrajna (the Lord as the knower of the field).

The Kshetrajna (12-17)

12. These movements of the mind caused by the power of Maya, which result in actions that do not in any way contribute to the purification of the mind, appear always in the states of waking and dream, and disappear completely in sleep. Kshetrajna, the ever pure and unaffected Spirit, merely witnesses these movements of the mind. **13.** The Kshetrajna is the all-pervading Spirit, the indweller of all, the cause of all causes, the self-conscious effulgence, the birthless, the god of all Divinities, the director of all Jivas, the possessor of the sixfold excellence, and the support of all Jivas. He dwells as Controller in all Jivas by His Maya. **14.** Just as the vital energy permeates everything, moving and unmoving, and controls them from within, in the same way the Supreme Lord Vāsudeva, the Kshetrajna, permeates and controls all beings. **15.** The Jiva is bound to move about in this transmigratory existence so long as he does not realise himself to be the Atman through enlightenment. For this he has, O King, first of all to become non-attached through the discharge of all his duties as offerings to the Lord and to control his six enemies constituted of the six infirmities (lust, anger, greed, intense longings, pride and jealousy). **16.** The mind, which functions as the limiting adjunct of the Spirit, is the veritable field yielding a bumper harvest of the ills of

भ्रातृव्यमेनं तददभ्रवीर्यमुपेक्षयाध्येधितमप्रमत्तः ।
गुरोर्हरेश्चरणोपासनास्त्रो जहि व्यलीकं स्वयमात्ममोषम् ॥17॥

इति श्रीमद्भागवते महापुराणे पारमहंस्यां संहितायां पञ्चमस्कन्धे ब्राह्मणरहूगणसंवादे एकादशोऽध्यायः ॥11॥

transmigratory life. Until one understands this, one will be involved in the transmigratory cycle. The mind generates sorrow, suffering, infatuation, diseases, attachments, desires, enmity and the sense of possession regarding objects. **17.** This mind is like a strong enemy grown very powerful because of negligence. It may ultimately be a mere appearance, but it has none the less hidden the Atman from view. Kill him with the arrow of service to the feet of Sri Hari, the Teacher who gives enlightenment. Be extremely vigilant in this matter.

अथ द्वादशोऽध्यायः

रहूगण उवाच

नमो नमः कारणविग्रहाय स्वरूपतुच्छीकृतविग्रहाय ।
नमोऽवधूत द्विजबन्धुलिङ्गनिगूढनित्यानुभवाय तुभ्यम् ॥ 1॥
ज्वरामयार्तस्य यथागदं सत् निदाघदग्धस्य यथा हिमाम्भः ।
कुदेहमानाहिविदष्टदृष्टेः ब्रह्मन् वचस्तेऽमृतमौषधं मे ॥ 2॥
तस्माद्भवन्तं मम संशयार्थं प्रक्ष्यामि पश्चादधुना सुबोधम् ।
अध्यात्मयोगग्रथितं तवोक्तमाख्याहि कौतूहलचेतसो मे ॥ 3॥
यदाह योगेश्वर दृश्यमानं क्रियाफलं सद्व्यवहारमूलम् ।
न ह्यञ्जसा तत्त्वविमर्शनाय भवानमुष्मिन् भ्रमते मनो मे ॥ 4॥

Skandha V : Chapter 12

STORY OF BHARATA: INSTRUCTION TO RAHŪGANA (CONT.)

Analysis of objective World (1-10)

Rahūgana said: **1.** O Supreme Yogin! Salutations to thee who hast taken a body for the good of mankind. Salutations to thee who hast devalued the body as worthless because of thy being steeped in thy inherent bliss. Salutations again to one whose constant intuitive knowledge is masked under the form of a degraded Brahmana. **2.** O enlightened one! Just as a potent medicine is to a man suffering from high fever, just as cold water is to one burnt by the heat of summer, so your words have been a rejuvenating ambrosia to me who have been deprived of true insight by the powerful poison from the bite of the cobra of body-consciousness. **3.** On the doubts I have in respect of these matters, I shall question you afterwards. But now be pleased to expound to me your words of spiritual import in a manner that is easily understandable to me. **4.** O great Yogin! You have stated that the actually felt, and therefore the unerased, fatigue and its cause, namely, bearing the palanquin, are all only provisionally spoken about, and have no place in determining the nature of Truth—this is a statement which causes confusion in my mind.

ब्राह्मण उवाच

अयं जनो नाम चलन् पृथिव्यां यः पार्थिवः पार्थिव कस्य हेतोः ।
तस्यापि चाङ्घ्र्योरधि गुल्फजङ्घाजानूरुमध्योरशिरोधरांसाः ॥ 5॥
अंसेऽधि दार्वी शिबिका च यस्यां सौवीरराजेत्यपदेश आस्ते ।
यस्मिन् भवान् रूढनिजाभिमानो राजास्मि सिन्धुष्विति दुर्मदान्धः ॥ 6॥
शोच्यानिमांस्त्वमधिकष्टदीनान् विष्टया निगृह्णन्निरनुग्रहोऽसि ।
जनस्य गोप्तास्मि विकत्थमानो न शोभसे वृद्धसभासु धृष्टः ॥ 7॥
यदा क्षितावेव चराचरस्य विदाम निष्ठां प्रभवं च नित्यम् ।
तन्नामतोऽन्यद् व्यवहारमूलं निरूप्यतां सत् क्रिययानुमेयम् ॥ 8॥
एवं निरुक्तं क्षितिशब्दवृत्तमसन्निधानात्परमाणवो ये ।
अविद्यया मनसा कल्पितास्ते येषां समूहेन कृतो विशेषः ॥ 9॥
एवं कृशं स्थूलमणुर्बृहद्यद् असच्च सज्जीवमजीवमन्यत् ।
द्रव्यस्वभावाशयकालकर्मनाम्नाजयावेहि कृतं द्वितीयम् ॥10॥
ज्ञानं विशुद्धं परमार्थमेकमनन्तरं त्वबहिर्ब्रह्म सत्यम् ।
प्रत्यक् प्रशान्तं भगवच्छब्दसंज्ञं यद्वासुदेवं कवयो वदन्ति ॥11॥

The Brahmana (Bharata) said: **5.** O King! The being called man, who bears body, is only a moving lump of earth, an effect brought out of earth, by some unknown causes. That body in truth is constituted of a number of limbs—feet, ankles, foreleg, knees, thighs, waist, chest, neck, shoulders, head etc.—arranged one above the other. (Apart from these limbs, we do not see any entity of whom they are parts or limbs. Where then is the person to suffer from exhaustion?) **6.** On the shoulders of these bearers is a mass of wood called palanquin. In that is seated another lump—a mere lump of earth but called the king of Sauvira. With that lump of clay seated within the palanquin, you have the firm identification, 'It is I', and you have besides that, the arrogant notion that the 'I' spoken of here is the king of Sindhu. **7.** You who are making these poor and pitiable palanquin bearers do forced labour without any, or adequate, payment, are an extremely cruel person. Therefore your false boast that you are the 'protector' of the people, will not command respect in an assembly of wise men. **8.** When we know that all these beings originate and dissolve in the element earth, what reality other than the earth need we infer as the person—a mere conventional word assumed from considerations of practical life? **9.** Even what is called the earth cannot exist apart from its components, the imperceptible atoms, which are mere mental constructs of men who, in their ignorance, seek to explain this substance earth as an assemblage of these assumed particles. (Ultimately they and everything else have their basis only in the cosmic power of the Lord.) **10.** In this way everything of this world of multiplicity spoken of as subtle or gross, small or big, cause or effect, living or inert, is all the creation of the Cosmic Power (Aja) of the Supreme Being, called differently by different philosophers as substance, Nature, tendencies, Time and Karma.

How Enlightenment comes (11-16)

11. The ultimate Truth is what the sages call Vāsudeva, (the support of all) and

रहूगणैतत्तपसा न याति न चेज्यया निर्वपणाद् गृहाद्वा ।
नच्छन्दसा नैव जलाग्निसूर्यैर्विना महत्पादरजोऽभिषेकम् ॥12॥
यत्रोत्तमश्लोकगुणानुवादः प्रस्तूयते ग्राम्यकथाविघातः ।
निषेव्यमाणोऽनुदिनं मुमुक्षोर्मतिं सतीं यच्छति वासुदेवे ॥13॥
अहं पुरा भरतो नाम राजा विमुक्तदृष्टश्रुतसङ्गबन्धः ।
आराधनं भगवत ईहमानो मृगोऽभवं मृगसङ्गाद्धतार्थः ॥14॥
सा मां स्मृतिर्मृगदेहेऽपि वीर कृष्णार्चनप्रभवा नो जहाति ।
अथो अहं जनसङ्गादसङ्गो विशङ्कमानोऽविवृतश्चरामि ॥15॥
तस्मान्नरोऽसङ्गसुसङ्गजातज्ञानासिनेहैव विवृक्णमोहः ।
हरिं तदीहाकथनश्रुताभ्यां लब्धस्मृतिर्यात्यतिपारमध्वनः ॥16॥

इति श्रीमद्भागवते महापुराणे पारमहंस्यां संहितायां पञ्चमस्कन्धे ब्राह्मणरहूगणसंवादे द्वादशोऽध्यायः ॥12॥

the Bhagavan (the possessor of all divine majesties). He is described variously as knowledge, absolute purity, the real existence, the one without a second, the one without an inside and outside, Brahman, the all-inclusive, the peaceful etc. **12.** Without bathing oneself in the dust of holy men's feet, this enlightenment cannot be had, O Rahūgana, merely through various disciplines like austerity, sacrifices, charitable gifts of food and the like, by domestic duties, by Vedic study, or worship of various deities. **13.** In the company of holy men there will be continuous discourses on the excellences of the Lord, thus completely eschewing all chances of talks on worldly matters. When aspirants imbibe it through their ears every day, their mind gets that highly coveted tendency to flow towards Vāsudeva. **14.** I was in an earlier birth a king named Bharata who abandoned attachment for everything in this world and the next, and took to the exclusive worship of the Divine. But due to my Prarabdha, I got attached to a deer and as a result had a spiritual downfall. In my next birth I became a deer. **15.** But, O King, the memory of my devotional past did not desert me even when embodied as a deer, because of the power gained by the worship of Krishna. So I am very suspicious about the evil consequences of contact with others, and I have, therefore, been trying to move about in obscurity, without attachment for anything. **16.** With the sword of knowledge obtained by spiritually fruitful association with holy men, one should cut off one's infatuation for the world. By adoring Hari through the hearing and recital of texts dealing with His glories and excellences, one gains the spiritual consciousness that one is the Atman and not the body, and attains to Sri Hari, who is the goal of the aspirant, beyond the limits of transmigratory existence.

अथ त्रयोदशोऽध्यायः

ब्राह्मण उवाच

दुरत्ययेऽध्वन्यजया निवेशितो रजस्तमःसत्त्वविभक्तकर्मदृक् ।
स एष सार्थोऽर्थपरः परिभ्रमन् भवाटवीं याति न शर्म विन्दति ।। 1।।
यस्यामिमे षण्णरदेव दस्यवः सार्थं विलुम्पन्ति कुनायकं बलात् ।
गोमायवो यत्र हरन्ति सार्थिकं प्रमत्तमाविश्य यथोरणं वृकाः ।। 2।।
प्रभूतवीरुत्तृणगुल्मगह्वरे कठोरदंशैर्मशकैरुपद्रुतः ।
क्वचित्तु गन्धर्वपुरं प्रपश्यति क्वचित्क्वचिच्चाशुरयोल्मुकग्रहम् ।। 3।।
निवासतोयद्रविणात्मबुद्धिस्ततस्ततो धावति भो अटव्याम् ।
क्वचिच्च वात्योत्थितपांसुधूम्रा दिशो न जानाति रजस्वलाक्षः ।। 4।।
अदृश्यझिल्लीस्वनकर्णशूल उलूकवाग्भिर्व्यथितान्तरात्मा ।
अपुण्यवृक्षान् श्रयते क्षुधार्दितो मरीचितोयान्यभिधावति क्वचित् ।। 5।।
क्वचिद्वितोयाः सरितोऽभियाति परस्परं चालषते निरन्धः ।
आसाद्य दावं क्वचिदग्नितप्तो निर्विद्यते क्व च यक्षैर्हृतासुः ।। 6।।

Skandha V : Chapter 13

STORY OF BHARATA: THE FOREST OF SAMSARA

The Forest of Samsara (1-13)

The Brahmana (Bharata) said: **1.** The Jivas, pushed into the path of Samsara by the Lord's Maya, consider that their duty consists in following the various ways of work dictated by the Gunas of Sattva, Rajas and Tamas, and enter into various forms of activities in the hope of getting happiness. Just like merchants who out of greed for wealth sometimes enter into forests, so the Jiva enters into this forest of Samsara in quest of happiness, but he obtains none. **2.** O King! In this forest a band of six brigands, the five organs of knowledge headed by an extremely evil-minded leader, the corrupted intellect, attack these travellers and rob them of their possessions. There are jackals in it which often carry away the heedless travellers, as wolves snatch away kids. **3.** They are troubled there by paths impenetrable because of the thick growth of creepers and grass and by the attack of fierce forest flies and mosquitoes. Here and there they see castles in the air and the light emitted by evil spirits that fly like meteors. **4.** With the mind naturally set on house, property, wealth etc., the Jiva wanders in this forest of Samsara. Sometimes when the winds raise the dust and blind his eyes, it is not possible for him to see the directions, filled as they are with thick clouds of dust. **5.** Distressed by the ear-piercing sound of crickets, and frightened by the ominous hoots of owls, he goes and takes shelter, hungry and forlorn, under some poisonous trees. To quench his thirst, he goes after some mirage in the desert. **6.** Sometimes he falls into dried up rivers without any water. Sometimes for want of food he has to beg of relatives. Sometimes he is scorched in forest fires. Sometimes Yakshas squeeze out his vital energy. **7.** Sometimes he is put to great sorrow

शूरैर्हृतस्वः क्व च निर्विण्णचेताः शोचन् विमुह्यन्नुपयाति कश्मलम् ।
क्वचिच्च गन्धर्वपुरं प्रविष्टः प्रमोदते निर्वृतवन्मुहूर्तम् ।। 7।।
चलन् क्वचित्कण्टकशर्कराङ्घ्रिर्नगारुरुक्षुर्विमना इवास्ते ।
पदे पदेऽभ्यन्तरवह्निनार्दितः कौटुम्बिकः क्रुध्यति वै जनाय ।। 8।।
क्वचिन्निगीर्णोऽजगराहिना जनो नावैति किञ्चिद्विपिनेऽपविद्धः ।
दष्टः स्म शेते क्व च दन्दशूकैरन्धोऽन्धकूपे पतितस्तमिस्रे ।। 9।।
कर्हि स्म चित्क्षुद्ररसान् विचिन्वंस्तन्मक्षिकाभिर्व्यथितो विमानः ।
तत्रातिकृच्छ्रात्प्रतिलब्धमानो बलाद्विलुम्पन्त्यथ तं ततोऽन्ये ।।10।।
क्वचिच्च शीतातपवातवर्षप्रतिक्रियां कर्तुमनीश आस्ते ।
क्वचिन्मिथो विपणन् यच्च किञ्चिद्विद्वेषमृच्छत्युत वित्तशाठ्यात् 11।।
क्वचित्क्वचित्क्षीणधनस्तु तस्मिन् शय्यासनस्थानविहारहीनः ।
याचन् परादप्रतिलब्धकामः पारक्यदृष्टिर्लभतेऽवमानम् ।।12।।
अन्योन्यवित्तव्यतिषङ्गवृद्धवैरानुबन्धो विवहन्मिथश्च ।
अध्वन्यमुष्मिन्नुरुकृच्छ्रवित्तबाधोपसर्गैर्विहरन् विपन्नः ।।13।।
तांस्तान् विपन्नान् स हि तत्र तत्र विहाय जातं परिगृह्य सार्थः ।
आवर्ततेऽद्यापि न कश्चिदत्र वीराध्वनः पारमुपैति योगम् ।।14।।

because of powerful men robbing away his wealth. Sometimes he faints owing to intense sorrow and infatuation. Sometimes he enters into a castle in the air and for a short time enjoys its imaginary bliss. **8.** Sometimes in attempting to surmount inaccessible mountains, he is frustrated by his feet getting lacerated by stones and thorns, and he sinks into the depths of disappointment. Often the householder falls foul on his wife and others in the family when food is not supplied in time and he is tormented by hunger. **9.** Now and then, caught in the grip of the python of sleep in a forest, he remains as if he is a dead body. Often blinded by desires, he falls into the dark pit of infatuation wherein he is bitten by the fierce serpents of evil men. **10.** Sometimes in quest of the degrading sweet of forbidden sex, he comes into conflict with its custodian bees, and even if he attains to it by dint of great efforts, it is soon snatched away by more powerful people, and from them by still others yet more powerful. **11.** Sometimes he is unable to protect himself against life's distressing circumstances of cold, heat, storm, and rain. Sometimes on questions of exchange of wealth and commodities, he comes into conflict with others. **12.** Often reduced to poverty by loss in business, he may not be able to provide himself with house, furniture, or vehicles. He then looks with eager eyes at others' possessions, and begs for help only to receive insults from them. **13.** Though quarrelling and on inimical terms with others in money matters, he compromises when worldly relationships like marriage become necessary. Thus engrossed in this path of worldly life, with its difficulties, loss of wealth, antagonisms etc., they are reduced ultimately to a dazed state in which one is as good as dead.

Caravan of merry Travellers (14-20)

14. O King! In this company of travel-

मनस्विनो निर्जितदिग्गजेन्द्रा ममेति सर्वे भुवि बद्धवैराः ।
मृधे शयीरन्न तु तद्व्रजन्ति यन्न्यस्तदण्डो गतवैरोऽभियाति ।।15।।
प्रसज्जति क्वापि लताभुजाश्रयस्तदाश्रयाव्यक्तपदद्विजस्पृहः ।
क्वचित्कदाचिद्धरिचक्रतस्त्रसन् सख्यं विधत्ते बककङ्कगृध्रैः ।।16।।
तैर्वञ्चितो हंसकुलं समाविशन्न रोचयन् शीलमुपैति वानरान् ।
तज्जातिरासेन सुनिर्वृतेन्द्रियः परस्परोद्वीक्षणविस्मृतावधिः ।।17।।
द्रुमेषु रंस्यन् सुतदारवत्सलो व्यवायदीनो विवशः स्वबन्धने ।
क्वचित्प्रमादाद्गिरिकन्दरे पतन् वल्लीं गृहीत्वा गजभीत आस्थितः 18।।
अतः कथञ्चित्स विमुक्त आपदः पुनश्च सार्थं प्रविशत्यरिन्दम ।
अध्वन्यमुष्मिन्नजया निवेशितो भ्रमञ्जनोऽद्यापि न वेद कश्चन ।।19।।
रहूगण त्वमपि ह्यध्वनोऽस्य संन्यस्तदण्डः कृतभूतमैत्रः ।
असज्जितात्मा हरिसेवया शितं ज्ञानासिमादाय तरातिपारम् ।।20।।

lers, whoever dies in the course of travel, they leave them there, and whoever is newly born, they take him and proceed with their endless journey. None of them have till this day come back to the place they started from, nor are they able to reach their goal beyond the frontiers of the forest. On the other hand, they go round and round aimlessly. **15.** The brave kings who take pride in conquering all the surrounding country, making territory the bone of contention, cultivate animosity among themselves, fight, and die on the field of battle. They do not reach the goal which holy men who have abandoned hatred and cruelty attain. **16.** Sometimes they are supported wholly by the creeper of women's arms, and they delight in, and are bound by, the chirpings of the fledgelings of babies in that cluster of creepers. Sometimes, on being frightened by the lions of death, they take shelter with the treacherous cranes, kites and vultures of atheistic philosophers. **17.** Disappointed with them, they resort to the Swans of holy men, but as they find their company disagreeable, they go in the company of the monkeys of vulgar men. Delighting in the sportive enjoyments characteristic of monkeys, they spend time thoughtlessly looking at each other's faces, oblivious even of the threatening death. **18.** Delighting in the bowery tree of the home, caught up in family affection, surfeited with sexual enjoyments, and unable in any way to release themselves from these entanglements, they fall down one day due to heedlessness from the tree into a mountain ravine where they hang precariously on creepers of fatal ailments, shivering from the sight of elephants, the forms of death, roaming about. **19.** O King! If for the time being they are freed from danger, they go again to that caravan of marching people. Being set on this road of Samsara by the Lord's Maya, beyond wandering about in that path, man does not know the Supreme Being who is the ultimate meaning of all these experiences. **20.** O Rahūgana! You too have been put on this path. Therefore, abandoning oppression of all creatures, practising universal love, and eschewing all worldly attachments, take up the sword of Jnana sharpened by the worship of Sri Hari, and go beyond this path.

Rahūgana's Redemption (21-26)

राजोवाच

अहो नृजन्माखिलजन्मशोभनं किं जन्मभिस्त्वपरैरप्यमुष्मिन् ।
न यद्धृषीकेशयशःकृतात्मनां महात्मनां वः प्रचुरः समागमः ॥21॥
न ह्यद्भुतं त्वच्चरणाब्जरेणुभिर्हतांहसो भक्तिरधोक्षजेऽमला ।
मौहूर्तिकाद्यस्य समागमाच्च मे दुस्तर्कमूलोऽपहतोऽविवेकः ॥22॥
नमो महद्भ्योऽस्तु नमः शिशुभ्यो नमो युवभ्यो नम आ वटुभ्यः ।
ये ब्राह्मणा गामवधूतलिङ्गाश्चरन्ति तेभ्यः शिवमस्तु राज्ञाम् ॥23॥

श्रीशुक उवाच

इत्येवमुत्तरामातः स वै ब्रह्मर्षिसुतः सिन्धुपतय आत्मसतत्त्वं विगणयतः परानुभावः परमकारुणिकतयोपदिश्य रहूगणेन सकरुणमभिवन्दितचरण आपूर्णार्णव इव निभृतकरणोर्म्याशयो धरणिमिमां विचचार ॥24॥ सौवीरपतिरपि सुजनसमवगतपरमात्मसतत्त्व आत्मन्यविद्याध्यारोपितां च देहात्ममतिं विससर्ज । एवं हि नृप भगवदाश्रिताश्रितानुभावः ॥25॥

राजोवाच

यो ह वा इह बहुविदा महाभागवत त्वयाभिहितः परोक्षेण वचसा जीवलोकभवाध्वा स ह्यार्यमनीषया कल्पितविषयो नाञ्जसाव्युत्पन्नलोकसमधिगमः । अथ तदेवैतद्दुरवगमं समवेतानुकल्पेन निर्दिश्यतामिति ॥26॥

इति श्रीमद्भागवते महापुराणे पारमहंस्यां संहितायां पञ्चमस्कन्धे त्रयोदशोऽध्यायः ॥13॥

Rahūgana said: **21.** This human birth is indeed the most glorious of all births. Of what use is embodiment in Swarga and other heavenly spheres? For one cannot have there the frequent opportunity of contact with holy men like you who have attained to the highest spiritual fulfilment through devotion to Sri Hari. **22.** It is quite easy to understand that in the mind of one who has been freed from all sinful tendencies by the contact of your feet, devotion to the Lord will be generated at once. For, even by a minute's contact with you, my tendency for argumentation born of sheer ignorance has departed. **23.** Salutations to the great ones! Salutations to infants! Salutations to the Youth! Salutations to Brahmacharins! Salutations to those knowers of Brahman who move about in the world as Avadhūtas! May good sense and good fortune dawn on kings like me!

Sri Suka said: **24.** O Parikshit! Thus, though insulted by Rahūgana at first, that great sage, out of his limitless compassion, instructed the king in the knowledge of the Supreme Being. Then worshipped by Rahūgana, the sage with his mind and senses absolutely unruffled like the unagitated surface of a calm sea, proceeded again to move about in the country. **25.** Rahūgana, the king of the Sauviras, having gained the knowledge of the Atman through his contact with that great sage, abandoned the ignorance-born identification of the body with the Atman. Such are the benefits that accrue from association with devotees who have taken refuge in the Lord.

Rajah Parikshit said: **26.** O paragon of devotees! What you have said before in an allegorical language about the Road of Samsara, is intelligible only to well-instructed people. Ignorant men cannot grasp it with ease. Therefore, please elaborate the allegory on this difficult subject, showing the corresponding meaning of all the figures used.

अथ चतुर्दशोऽध्यायः

स होवाच

य एष देहात्ममानिनां सत्त्वादिगुणविशेषविकल्पितकुशलाकुशलसमवहारविनिर्मितविविध-
देहावलिभिर्वियोगसंयोगाद्यनादिसंसारानुभवस्य द्वारभूतेन षडिन्द्रियवर्गेण तस्मिन्दुर्गाध्ववदसुगमे-
ऽध्वन्यापतित ईश्वरस्य भगवतो विष्णोर्वशवर्तिन्या मायया जीवलोकोऽयं यथा वणिक्सार्थोऽर्थपरः
स्वदेहनिष्पादितकर्मानुभवः श्मशानवदशिवतमायां संसाराटव्यां गतो नाद्यापि विफलबहु-
प्रतियोगेहस्तत्तापोपशमनीं हरिगुरुचरणारविन्दमधुकरानुपदवीमवरुन्धे यस्यामु ह वा एते
षडिन्द्रियनामानः कर्मणा दस्यव एव ते ॥1॥ तद्यथा पुरुषस्य धनं यत्किञ्चिद्धर्मौपयिकं
बहुकृच्छ्राधिगतं साक्षात्परमपुरुषाराधनलक्षणो योऽसौ धर्मस्तं तु साम्पराय उदाहरन्ति । तद्धर्म्यं
धनं दर्शनस्पर्शनश्रवणास्वादनावघ्राणसङ्कल्पव्यवसायगृहग्राम्योपभोगेन कुनाथस्याजितात्मनो यथा
सार्थस्य विलुम्पन्ति ॥2॥ अथ च यत्र कौटुम्बिका दारापत्यादयो नाम्ना कर्मणा वृकसृगाला
एवानिच्छतोऽपि कदर्यस्य कुटुम्बिन उरणकवत्संरक्ष्यमाणं मिषतोऽपि हरन्ति ॥3॥ यथा ह्यनुवत्सरं

Skandha V : Chapter 14

STORY OF BHARATA: FOREST OF SAMSARA EXPLAINED

Explanation of Allegory (1-41)

Sri Suka said: **1.** By the operation of the forces of Prakriti known as Sattva, Rajas and Tamas, the Jivas, who mistakenly identify themselves with the body, get repeated embodiments according to their Karmas, which are either meritorious, demeritorious or mixed. The six senses of man are the prime factors for the Jiva's involvement in Samsara, or transmigratory cycle, with its never-ending experiences of births and deaths. It is the infinitely powerful Maya, the will of the Lord, that has pushed the Jiva into this path of Samsara full of perils and difficulties. For the enjoyment of the fruits of their actions the Jivas have been put on this path in the forest of Samsara which is as impure and weird as a cremation ground. But in spite of this, they persist in their travel through that forest like greedy merchants in quest of wealth. They continue to perform selfish actions, however difficult that may be, and prolong their involvement in Samsara indefinitely, in place of cutting it short by following the foot-steps of holy ones who are absorbed in the bliss of the Lord's lotus-feet. The six senses of man are the robbers that attack him in the forest.

2. The wealth of man is really meant for the adoration of the Lord and for charitable and religious purposes that promote his higher evolution in the hereafter. But the mind and the five organs of knowledge, which are like six brigands, rob away that wealth by attracting it to mean sensuous enjoyments that could be derived through sight, hearing, touch, taste, smell, imagination etc., as robbers do with the wealth of merchants who are badly led and who are careless about their safety. Know these six senses to be the brigands of the forest of Samsara.

3. In that forest of Samsara there are members of one's family known as wife, children etc. Though known by such names indicating closeness, they are the wolves of the forest who, much against

**कृष्यमाणमप्यदग्धबीजं क्षेत्रं पुनरेवावपनकाले गुल्मतृणवीरुद्भिर्गह्वरमिव भवत्येवमेव गृहाश्रमः कर्मक्षेत्रं
यस्मिन्न हि कर्माण्युत्सीदन्ति यदयं कामकरण्ड एष आवसथः ॥4॥**

**तत्र गतो दंशमशकसमापसदैर्मनुजैः शलभशकुन्ततस्करमूषकादिभिरुपरुध्यमानबहिःप्राणः
क्वचित्परिवर्तमानोऽस्मिन्नध्वन्यविद्याकामकर्मभिरुपरक्तमनसानुपपन्नार्थं नरलोकं गन्धर्वनगरमुपपन्नमिति
मिथ्यादृष्टिरनुपश्यति ॥5॥ तत्र च क्वचिदातपोदकनिभान् विषयानुपधावति पानभोजनव्यवायादि-
व्यसनलोलुपः ॥6॥ क्वचिच्चाशेषदोषनिषदनं पुरीषविशेषं तद्वर्णगुणनिर्मितमतिः सुवर्णमुपा-
दित्सत्यग्निकामकातर इवोल्मुकपिशाचम् ॥7॥ अथ कदाचिन्निवासपानीयद्रविणाद्यनेकात्मोपजीव-
नाभिनिवेश एतस्यां संसाराटव्यामितस्ततः परिधावति ॥8॥ क्वचिच्च वात्यौपम्यया
प्रमदयाऽऽरोहमारोपितस्तत्कालरजसा रजनीभूत इवासाधुमर्यादो रजस्वलाक्षोऽपि दिग्देवता
अतिरजस्वलमतिर्न विजानाति ॥9॥ क्वचित्सकृदवगतविषयवैतथ्यः स्वयं पराभिध्यानेन
विभ्रंशितस्मृतिस्तयैव मरीचितोयप्रायांस्तानेवाभिधावति ॥10॥ क्वचिदुलूकझिल्लीस्वनवदतिपरुष-**

the will of the miserly householder, demand and deprive him of his strongly guarded wealth as wolves carry away young kids from a flock of sheep.

4. Though a field is ploughed every year, it is found covered with creepers and grass when new sowing operations start; for the seeds of the old plants have been present in it. Even so, the household is the field of Karma, and works never end there because of the presence of these seeds in the shape of desires and tendencies. It is as in the case of a box in which camphor is kept. Even if the substance is removed, the smell persists. (Know this to be the vegetation covering the path of Samsara.)

5. The traveller on the road of Samsara is attacked even without any purpose by evil men as mosquitoes and flies do, and he is deprived of his wealth by insects, birds, rats and thieves. Prompted by ignorance, desire, and tendency for work, he moves about in this world of men, attributing substance and value to it, which in truth is as illusory as a castle in the air.

6. Sometimes infatuated with sense enjoyments, which to a discerning mind are ephemeral like mirage, the Jiva gets engrossed with eating, drinking and mating.

7. Sometimes he comes across gold, the source of all evils. Prompted by Rajas, which is of the same colour as gold, he goes to take it. But the pursuit of the bright metal only brings on him all-round trouble, just as in the case of a man who, distressed by intense cold, runs towards a flaming devil.

8. Sometimes the Jiva is in dire want of a dwelling place, food and drink, wealth and other objects of enjoyment, and wanders about everywhere in quest of them in the forest of Samsara.

9. Sometimes he gets entangled with women who are like a dusty whirlwind that completely blinds his eye of discrimination. With all power of discrimination erased, he allows himself to be petted and fondled in the lap of women, and as a consequence all his lowest animal propensities based in Tamas are let loose. Ridden with lust and totally blinded by desire, he even forgets the presence of Devas that stand always as witnesses to the actions of men.

10. Sometimes he may realise the vanity of sensuous life and its enjoyments, yet being deprived of the memory of his spiritual nature by the overpowering bodily consciousness, he runs after those very same mirage-like sensuous fulfilments as before.

रभसाटोपं प्रत्यक्षं परोक्षं वा रिपुराजकुलनिर्भर्त्सितेनातिव्यथितकर्णमूलहृदयः ॥11॥ स यदा
दुग्धपूर्वसुकृतस्तदा कारस्करकाकतुण्डाद्यपुण्यद्रुमलताविषोदपानवदुभयार्थशून्यद्रविणान् जीवन्मृतान्
स्वयं जीवन्म्रियमाण उपधावति ॥12॥ एकदासत्प्रसङ्गान्निकृतमतिर्व्युदकस्रोतःस्खलनवदुभयतोऽपि-
दुःखदं पाखण्डमभियाति ॥13॥ यदा तु परबाधयान्ध आत्मने नोपनमति तदा हि पितृपुत्रबर्हिष्मतः
पितृपुत्रान् वा स खलु भक्षयति ॥14॥ क्वचिदासाद्य गृहं दाववत्प्रियार्थविधुरमसुखोदर्कं शोकाग्निना
दह्यमानो भृशं निर्वेदमुपगच्छति ॥15॥ क्वचित्कालविषमितराजकुलरक्षसापहृतप्रियतमधनासुः
प्रमृतक इव विगतजीवलक्षण आस्ते ॥16॥ कदाचिन्मनोरथोपगतपितृपितामहाद्यसत्सदिति
स्वप्ननिर्वृतिलक्षणमनुभवति ॥17॥ क्वचिद् गृहाश्रमकर्मचोदनातिभरगिरिमारुरुक्षमाणो लोकव्यसन-
कर्षितमनाः कण्टकशर्कराक्षेत्रं प्रविशन्निव सीदति ॥18॥ क्वचिच्च दुःसहेन कायाभ्यन्तरवह्निना
गृहीतसारः स्वकुटुम्बाय क्रुध्यति ॥19॥ स एव पुनर्निद्राजगरगृहीतोऽन्धे तमसि मग्नः शून्यारण्य
इव शेते नान्यत्किञ्चन वेद शव इवापविद्धः ॥20॥

11. The direct and indirect threats of kings and enemies are what have been described as the harsh hoots of owls and shrill screeches of crickets, causing as much unpleasantness to the heart as to the ear.

12. When the results of a Jiva's good works are exhausted and he is without any means of livelihood, he becomes the dependant of other worldly men who are wealthy but none the less deserve only to be called the 'living-dead', for the wealth of these pitiable men, owing to misuse, is a menace to themselves in this world and fails to secure any good for them in the hereafter. These are described as poisonous trees, creepers and wells, which serve no useful purpose to anyone.

13. Sometimes through unholy associations, he is lured into atheistic sects which are like waterless rivers. Just as a person falling into them only hurts himself, these atheistic religions only bring suffering to the Jiva in this world and the next.

14. When a man is not able to gain his livelihood even by oppressing others, he turns towards his father and mother and even to distant relatives to dispossess them by asserting his right to their belongings.

15. Sometimes due to want of food and other necessaries, he undergoes intense and increasing sufferings in his home like one caught in a forest fire and is thrown into utter despair and depression.

16. The Yakshas who are supposed to steal away the vital energy of man, are the kings who, in adverse times like war and invasions, deprive a man of his whole wealth, dear to him as life itself, and leave him practically a lifeless corpse.

17. Sometimes he enters into the realms of fancy and thinks of the days of his ancestors like father and grandfather, and seems to get some relaxation as in a dream experience.

18. The mountain he tries to cross is the performance of the various rites and duties he has to accomplish in the household life. Like one trying to cross over a mountain, he gets hurt and exhausted by walking over stones and thorns, and finally gives up all efforts and sits quietly in a place in utter frustration.

19. Sometimes tormented and exhausted by unbearable hunger, he seeks compensation by losing his temper at his wife.

20. The python gripping him is sleep, absorbed in which he afterwards lives like a dead body in the darkness of Tamas,

कदाचिद्भग्नमानदंष्ट्रो दुर्जनदन्दशूकैरलब्धनिद्राक्षणो व्यथितहृदयेनानुक्षीयमाणविज्ञानोऽन्धकूपे-
ऽन्धवत्पतति ॥21॥ कर्हि स्म चित्काममधुलवान् विचिन्वन् यदा परदारपरद्रव्याण्यवरुन्धानो
राज्ञा स्वामिभिर्वा निहतः पतत्यपारे निरये ॥22॥ अथ च तस्मादुभयथापि हि कर्मास्मिन्नात्मनः
संसारावपनमुदाहरन्ति ॥23॥ मुक्तस्ततो यदि बन्धाद्देवदत्त उपाच्छिनत्ति तस्मादपि विष्णुमित्र
इत्यनवस्थितिः ॥24॥ क्वचिच्च शीतवाताद्यनेकाधिदैविकभौतिकात्मीयानां दशानां प्रतिनिवारणे-
ऽकल्पो दुरन्तचिन्तया विषण्ण आस्ते ॥25॥ क्वचिन्मिथो व्यवहरन् यत्किञ्चिद्धनमन्येभ्यो वा
काकिणिकामात्रमप्यपहरन् यत्किञ्चिद्वा विद्वेषमेति वित्तशाठ्यात् ॥26॥ अध्वन्यमुष्मिन्निम
उपसर्गास्तथा सुखदुःखरागद्वेषभयाभिमानप्रमादोन्मादशोकमोहलोभमात्सर्येर्ष्यावमानक्षुत्पिपासाधि-
व्याधिजन्मजरामरणादयः ॥27॥ क्वापि देवमायया स्त्रिया भुजलतोपगूढः प्रस्कन्नविवेकविज्ञानो
यद्विहारगृहारम्भाकुलहृदयस्तदाश्रयावसक्तसुतदुहितृकलत्रभाषितावलोकविचेष्टितापहृतहृदय आत्मान-
मजितात्मापारेऽन्धे तमसि प्रहिणोति ॥28॥ कदाचिदीश्वरस्य भगवतो विष्णोश्चक्रात्परमाण्वादि-
द्विपरार्धापवर्गकालोपलक्षणात्परिवर्तितेन वयसा रंहसा हरत आब्रह्मतृणस्तम्बादीनां भूतानाम-

abandoned by all in a lonely forest.

21. Evil men are the fierce serpents who attack and shatter his molars that stand for self-respect. The shock caused thereby deprives him of sleep and his power of correct judgement. Like a blind man fallen into a disused well, he welters in stupefying sorrow.

22. At times owing to his hankering for the honey of vulgar enjoyments, he runs after other people's women and wealth, only to be killed by their masters or the ruling king. He suffers the torment of abysmal hell as a consequence.

23. Hence great men say that self-centred action prompted by desires is the fertile field of sufferings in this world and the next.

24. Perhaps he is now free from the trammels of poverty because of some wealth that has come to him. Immediately one Devadatta robs him of that, and a Vishnudatta, in turn, deprives Devadatta of it. Thus wealth flies from hand to hand unendingly.

25. Sometimes unable to protect himself from various natural visitations like storms, cold etc., and from sufferings originating in mental and psychical disturbances, he loses himself in the sorrow of worrying thoughts that have no end.

26. Sometimes in the course of financial dealings with others, man tries to deceive his opposite numbers of at least a little of their wealth, leading thereby to mutual hatred and quarrel.

27. In this path of Samsara, there are, besides the above, innumerable other travails and hindrances like joy, sorrow, attachments, aversions, fear, pride, heedlessness, mental derangement, sorrow, infatuation, greed, jealousy, insult, hunger, thirst, diseases, worries, birth, old age and death.

28. Sometimes the ignorant Jiva, caught in the embrace of the creeper-like arms of a woman, who is nothing but the embodiment of the Lord's deluding power, becomes devoid of discriminative power. He is in mad pursuit of a home to live in with her. There he becomes completely taken up with the sweet words and loving relationship of the inhabitants of that home, namely, wife, sons, daughters etc., and sinks into the dense depth of ignorance.

29. Man becomes conscious of the relentless movement of the Lord's des-

निमिषतो मिषतां वित्रस्तहृदयस्तमेवेश्वरं कालचक्रनिजायुधं साक्षाद्भगवन्तं यज्ञपुरुषमनादृत्य
पाखण्डदेवताः कङ्कगृध्रबककवटप्राया आर्यसमयपरिहृताः साङ्केत्येनाभिधत्ते ॥29॥ यदा पाखण्डिभि-
रात्मवञ्चितैस्तैरुरु वञ्चितो ब्रह्मकुलं समावसंस्तेषां शीलमुपनयनादिश्रौतस्मार्तकर्मानुष्ठानेन
भगवतो यज्ञपुरुषस्याराधनमेव तदरोचयन् शूद्रकुलं भजते निगमाचारेऽशुद्धितो यस्य मिथुनीभावः
कुटुम्बभरणं यथा वानरजातेः ॥30॥ तत्रापि निरवरोधः स्वैरेण विहरन्नतिकृपणबुद्धिरन्योन्यमुख-
निरीक्षणादिना ग्राम्यकर्मणैव विस्मृतकालावधिः ॥31॥ क्वचिद् द्रुमवदैहिकार्थेषु गृहेषु रंस्यन्
यथा वानरः सुतदारवत्सलो व्यवायक्षणः ॥32॥

एवमध्वन्यवरुन्धानो मृत्युगजभयात्तमसि गिरिकन्दरप्राये ॥33॥ क्वचिच्छीतवाताद्यनेकदैविक-
भौतिकात्मीयानां दुःखानां प्रतिनिवारणेऽकल्पो दुरन्तविषयविषण्ण आस्ते ॥34॥ क्वचिन्मिथो
व्यवहरन् यत्किञ्चिद्धनमुपयाति वित्तशाठ्येन ॥35॥ क्वचित्क्षीणधनः शय्यासनाशनाद्युपभोगविहीनो
यावदप्रतिलब्धमनोरथोपगतादानेऽवसितमतिस्ततस्ततोऽवमानादीनि जनादभिलभते ॥36॥ एवं

tructive wheel of Time when he notices before his very eyes its irresistible movement, embracing a period extending from a moment to the Dviparardha and swallowing up all creatures from a blade of grass to Brahma through the stages of birth, childhood, youth, old age and death. Though frightened by it, he does not go for shelter to the Supreme Lord Mahavishnu, the Lord of all Yajnas and the holder of the wheel of Time, but discarding Him seeks shelter in false deities preached by atheistic and heretical teachers resembling deceptive cranes, crows and vultures—deities and teachings that have no sanction of the authentic scriptures and traditions, but are the mere concoctions of heretics.

30. When they realise that they have been totally misled by these self-deluded heretics, they resort to the community of holy men. Soon, their way of life, consisting in the performance of all the scripture-ordained duties like Upanayana and the rest as an offering unto the Lord, ceases to please them, and they then associate with groups of vulgar folk, who, being devoid of the Vedic purificatory observances and disciplines, live the life of monkeys, with sex enjoyments and family care as the sole concerns in life.

31. There, unrestrained by any scriptural injunctions and guided by instincts alone, persons of such a pitiable outlook spend their life in vulgar enjoyments, their time being wholly taken up with men and women gazing at each other's face. Engrossed in these preoccupations they forget even the approach of death.

32. At times like a monkey on the branches of a tree, a worldly minded man lives merrily in the home, which is only a place of vulgar enjoyments, and spends his days in extreme attachment for his wife and children and in sexual frivolities.

33. Caught in the way of Samsara, he is now frightened by the sight of the elephant of death, and falls into the dark mountain cavern of disease.

34. Unable to stand physical inclemencies like heat and cold, as well as mental worries and psychical unrest he is subjected to utmost misery.

35. Bent on making money, he acquires some wealth through business transactions with others, adopting even unfair means.

36. When all his wealth is exhausted and he is in great need of the necessaries of life like home, food, clothing etc., he tries to get these from others through

वित्तव्यतिषङ्गविवृद्धवैरानुबन्धोऽपि पूर्ववासनया मिथ उद्वहत्यथापवहति ।।37।। एतस्मिन् संसारा-
ध्वनि नानाक्लेशोपसर्गबाधित आपन्नविपन्नो यत्र यस्तमु ह वावेतरस्तत्र विसृज्य जातं जातमुपादाय
शोचन्मुह्यन् बिभ्यद्विवदन् क्रन्दन् संहृष्यन् गायन्नह्यमानः साधुवर्जितो नैवावर्ततेऽद्यापि यत आरब्ध
एष नरलोकसार्थो यमध्वनः पारमुपदिशन्ति ।।38।। यदिदं योगानुशासनं न वा एतदवरुन्धते यन्न्यस्त-
दण्डा मुनय उपशमशीला उपरतात्मानः समवगच्छन्ति ।।39।। यदपि दिगिभजयिनो यज्विनो
ये वै राजर्षयः किं तु परं मृधे शयीरन्नस्यामेव ममेयमिति कृतवैरानुबन्धायां विसृज्य स्वयमुपसंहृताः
।।40।। कर्मवल्लीमवलम्ब्य तत आपदः कथञ्चिन्नरकाद्विमुक्तः पुनरप्येवं संसाराध्वनि वर्तमानो
नरलोकसार्थमुपयाति एवमुपरि गतोऽपि ।।41।।

तस्येदमुपगायन्ति –

आर्षभस्येह राजर्षेर्मनसापि महात्मनः । नानुवर्त्मार्हति नृपो मक्षिकेव गरुत्मतः ।।42।।
यो दुस्त्यजान्दारसुतान् सुहृद्राज्यं हृदिस्पृशः । जहौ युवैव मलवदुत्तमश्लोकलालसः ।।43।।
यो दुस्त्यजान् क्षितिसुतस्वजनार्थदारान् प्रार्थ्यां श्रियं सुरवरैः सदयावलोकाम् ।
नैच्छन्नृपस्तदुचितं महतां मधुद्विट्सेवानुरक्तमनसामभवोऽपि फल्गुः ।।44।।

deception. Being exposed, he has to stand the insults heaped on him by their owners.

37. Though thus inimical to others because of greed for wealth, he none the less, owing to his long-cultivated habit, enters into marriage alliances with those very people, only to break them very soon.

38. In the course of their travel along the path of Samsara, facing various dangers and obstacles, the men who die are left behind, and others walk on with those who are born in the meantime. They trudge on, sorrowing, bungling, fearing, arguing, crying, singing, and dying. But they never turn towards or reach their source, the Lord, from whom this caravan started; only a few devotees do so.

39. They never attain to Jnana and Bhakti, the fruits of spiritual striving, which holy men established in universal love, self-control and peace gain.

40. Even great kings who are world conquerors and far-famed for the great Yajnas they have performed, do not attain to it. For, being at bitter feud with others owing to their intense sense of possessiveness, they in the end abandon those very possessions and lie dead in the field of battle.

41. Holding on to the creeper of Prarabdha they may get release from the hell into which they are consigned, but they soon return, only to join that band of travellers on the road of Samsara once again. The same is the fate of the denizens of higher worlds like that of Indra.

The unique greatness of Bharata has been sung as follows by the ancients:

Greatness of Bharata (42-46)

42. A fly cannot emulate the flight of Garuda. Even so no other king has found it possible even mentally to emulate the example of the great Rajarshi Bharata, the son of Rishabha. **43.** Who can follow that exalted example of the one who, even as a youth, was overcome by such intense love of the Lord that he could easily abandon like filth all worldly loves—wife, children, friends, kingdom and the like which usually bind the human mind fast, making it impossible for it to give them up. **44.** It is no wonder that this great king was able to abandon what others find it so difficult to do—kingdom,

यज्ञाय धर्मपतये विधिनैपुणाय योगाय सांख्यशिरसे प्रकृतीश्वराय।
नारायणाय हरये नम इत्युदारं हास्यन्मृगत्वमपि यः समुदाजहार ॥45॥

य इदं भागवतसभाजितावदातगुणकर्मणो राजर्षेर्भरतस्यानुचरितं स्वस्त्ययनमायुष्यं धन्यं यशस्यं स्वर्ग्यापवर्ग्यं वानुश्रृणोत्याख्यास्यत्यभिनन्दति च सर्वा एवाशिष आत्मन आशास्ते न काञ्चन परत इति ॥46॥

इति श्रीमद्भागवते महापुराणे पारमहंस्यां संहितायां पञ्चमस्कन्धे भरतोपाख्याने पारोक्ष्यविवरणं नाम चतुर्दशोऽध्यायः ॥14॥

sons, wife, relatives, wealth and even the solicitations of Srī, the goddess of good fortune, for a mere look from whom even divinities are praying. For, those who are engrossed with the delight of the Lord's service look upon as trifle even Moksha, considered the highest blessing for an embodied being (Jiva). **45.** Such renunciation is befitting so great a soul as Bharata who, even while abandoning the deer form, went on ardently adoring the Lord, saying: 'Salutations to Yajna! Salutations to the One awarding the results of Yajna! Salutations to the One established in Dharma! Salutations to the One attainable by Yoga! Salutations to the One whose essence is Knowledge! Salutations to the One who controls Prakriti! Salutations to the One who is the indweller of all beings! Salutations to Sri Hari!'

46. Whoever hears, recites, or studies with faith and devotion this holy account which records the excellences of the great Rajarshi Bharata who is respected and sung about by great devotees, and which confers on its votary longevity, wealth, fame, heaven, and liberation—all the wants of such a person are supplied by the Indwelling Self; he requires no external aid.

अथ पञ्चदशोऽध्यायः

श्रीशुक उवाच

भरतस्यात्मजः सुमतिर्नामाभिहितो यमु ह वाव केचित्पाखण्डिन ऋषभपदवीमनुवर्तमानं चानार्या अवेदसमाम्नातां देवतां स्वमनीषया पापीयस्या कलौ कल्पयिष्यन्ति ॥1॥ तस्माद् वृद्धसेनायां देवताजिन्नाम पुत्रोऽभवत् ॥2॥ अथासुर्यां तत्तनयो देवद्युम्नस्ततो धेनुमत्यां सुतः परमेष्ठी तस्य सुवर्चलायां प्रतीह उपजातः ॥3॥ य आत्मविद्यामाख्याय स्वयं संशुद्धो महापुरुषमनुसस्मार ॥4॥

Skandha V : Chapter 15

THE LINE OF BHARATA

Successors of Bharata (1-6)

1. Bharata's son was Sumati. Finding him following Rishabha's way of life, some low-born heretics of the Kaliyuga will deify him as a non-Vedic Deity, as dictated by their perverted intellect. **2.** He had as son Devatājit, born of Vriddhasena. **3.** Afterwards Devatājit had by his wife Āsuri, a son named Devadyumna. He begot by his wife Dhenumati a son named Parameshthi, who in turn had by Suvarcha a son Pratīha. **4.** Pratīha taught the knowledge of the Atman to many.

प्रतीहात्सुवर्चलायां प्रतिहर्त्रादयस्त्रय आसन्निज्याकोविदाः सूनवःप्रतिहर्तुः स्तुत्यामजभूमानावजनिषाताम्
॥5॥ भूम्न ऋषिकुल्यायामुद्गीथस्ततः प्रस्तावो देवकुल्यायां प्रस्तावान्नियुत्सायां हृदयज आसीद्वि-
भुर्विभोरत्यां च पृथुषेणस्तस्मान्नक्त आकूत्यां जज्ञे नक्ताद्द्रुतिपुत्रो गयो राजर्षिप्रवर उदारश्रवा
अजायत साक्षाद्भगवतो विष्णोर्जगद्रिरक्षिषया गृहीतसत्त्वस्य कलाऽऽत्मवत्त्वादिलक्षणेन महापुरुषतां
प्राप्तः ॥6॥ स वै स्वधर्मेण प्रजापालनपोषणप्रीणनोपलालनानुशासनलक्षणेनेज्यादिना च भगवति
महापुरुषे परावरे ब्रह्मणि सर्वात्मनार्पितपरमार्थलक्षणेन ब्रह्मविच्चरणानुसेवयाऽऽपादितभगवद्भक्ति-
योगेन चाभीक्ष्णशः परिभावितातिशुद्धमतिरुपरतानात्म्य आत्मनि स्वयमुपलभ्यमानब्रह्मात्मानुभवोऽपि
निरभिमान एवावनिमजूगुपत् ॥7॥ तस्येमां गाथां पाण्डवेय पुराविद उपगायन्ति ॥8॥

गयं नृपः कः प्रतियाति कर्मभिर्यज्वाभिमानी बहुविद्धर्मगोप्ता ।
समागतश्रीः सदसस्पतिः सतां सत्सेवकोऽन्यो भगवत्कलामृते ॥ 9॥
यमभ्यषिञ्चन् परया मुदा सतीः सत्याशिषो दक्षकन्याः सरिद्भिः ।
यस्य प्रजानां दुदुहे धराऽऽशिषो निराशिषो गुणवत्सस्नुतोधाः ॥10॥

Being a person of highly purified mind, he had the realisation of the Supreme Being.

5. Pratīha had by his wife Suvarchala three sons—Pratiharta, Prastota and Udgāta. All of them were adepts in the performance of Vedic sacrifices. Pratiharta had two sons named Aja and Bhūma by his wife Stuti. **6.** Bhūma had by his wife Rishikulya, Udgītha; he by Devakula, Prastāva; he by Niyutsa, Vibhu; he by Rati, Prithushena; Prithushena by his wife Ākuti, Nakta; and Nakta by Druti, Gaya. This famous Gaya was the incarnation of a part of Mahavishnu, and he came to be recognised as a high-souled and saintly personage.

Greatness of King Gaya (7-16)

7. He performed all his duties, like governing the country, working for prosperity, pleasing others, showing kindness, awarding punishments etc., as a whole-hearted and genuine worship of the supreme, omnipotent and all-pervading Being. By such discharge of Swadharma, by the performance of many Yajnas, and by service to illumined personages of great holiness, he attained to true devotion and purification of mind, by virtue of which he was freed from the identification of the Self with the body. In his mind therefore the Supreme Being shone as the Self. So he was able to govern the country without an iota of egotism. **8.** O offspring of the Pandus! Great men have sung about him as follows in the past:

9. Who else except Gaya, a partial incarnation of the Lord, has done so many Yajnas, has been so high-minded, intelligent and all-knowing, has maintained the standards of Dharma so well in the country, has been a master of such plenty, has received such universal acceptance as the head of all gatherings of the virtuous, and has gained such reputation as the servant of holy men! **10.** He on whom the noble and virtuous ladies, the daughters of Daksha, poured the holy waters at the time of coronation in great joy; that desireless one to whose subjects the earth, assuming the shape of a cow, yielded from her udder, under the influence of the calf of his virtues, all desirable things they were in need of—where is the man capable of following the foot-

छन्दांस्यकामस्य च यस्य कामान् दुदूहुराजह्रुरथो बलिं नृपाः ।
प्रत्यञ्चिता युधि धर्मेण विप्रा यदाशिषां षष्ठमंशं परेत्य ।।11।।
यस्याध्वरे भगवानध्वरात्मा मघोनि माद्यत्युरुसोमपीथे ।
श्रद्धाविशुद्धाचलभक्तियोगसमर्पितेज्याफलमाजहार ।।12।।
यत्प्रीणनाद्बर्हिषि देवतिर्यङ्मनुष्यवीरुत्तृणमाविरिञ्चात् ।
प्रीयेत सद्यः स विश्वजीवः प्रीतः स्वयं प्रीतिमगाद्गयस्य ।।13।।

गयाद्गयन्त्यां चित्ररथः सुगतिरवरोधन इति त्रयः पुत्रा बभूवुश्चित्ररथादूर्णायां सम्राडजनिष्ट
।।14।। तत उत्कलायां मरीचिर्मरीचेर्बिन्दुमत्यां बिन्दुमानुदपद्यत तस्मात्सरघायां मधुर्नामाभवन्मधोः
सुमनसि वीरव्रतस्ततो भोजायां मन्थुप्रमन्थू जज्ञाते मन्थोः सत्यायां भौवनस्ततो दूषणायां
त्वष्टाजनिष्ट त्वष्टुर्विरोचनायां विरजो विरजस्य शतजित्प्रवरं पुत्रशतं कन्या च विषूच्यां किल
जातम् ।।15।।

तत्रायं श्लोकः –

प्रैयव्रतं वंशमिमं विरजश्चरमोद्भवः । अकरोदत्यलं कीर्त्या विष्णुः सुरगणं यथा ।।16।।

इति श्रीमद्भागवते महापुराणे पारमहंस्यां संहितायां पञ्चमस्कन्धे प्रियव्रतवंशानुकीर्तनं नाम पञ्चदशोऽध्यायः ।।15।।

steps of that Gaya? **11.** He who, though free from all desires, had all his wants fulfilled by the Vedic sacrifices; to whom all kings offered one sixth of their revenue as tribute, being 'worshipped in battle with his sharp arrows; to whom the Brahmanas, being worshipped through his rule of the land according to the principles of Dharma, yielded in the hereafter a sixth of their merits—where is the man capable of following the footsteps of that Gaya? **12.** He in whose Yajna Indra got intoxicated by drinking Soma whereupon the Lord, who is the soul of Yajna, Himself accepted the fruits of Yajna offered to Him with faith, purity and unwavering devotion—where is the man that can follow in the footsteps of that Gaya? **13.** He, to whom the Lord, the soul of the worlds—by pleasing whom through sacrifice all creatures from Brahma down to Devas, men, animals and vegetation are pleased—became so propitious that He out of His own accord manifestly expressed His immense satisfaction—who is the man that can follow the example of that Gaya?

14. By his wife Gayanti, Gaya had three sons—Chitraratha, Sugati, and Avarodha. Chitraratha had by his wife Ūrna a son named Samrāt. **15.** Samrāt had by his wife Utkala a son named Marīchi; he by Bindumati, Bindumān; he by Saragha, Madhu; he by Sumanas, Vīravrata; he by Bhoja, Manthu and Pramanthu; Manthu by Satyā, Bhauvana; he by Dūshanā, Tvashta; he by Virochanā, Viraja; he by Vishūchi, a hundred sons headed by Satajit, and a daughter. **16.** There is a famous saying about this: Viraja, the last in the line of Priyavrata, rendered that line glorious as Mahavishnu did the Devas.

PLAN OF THE EARTH

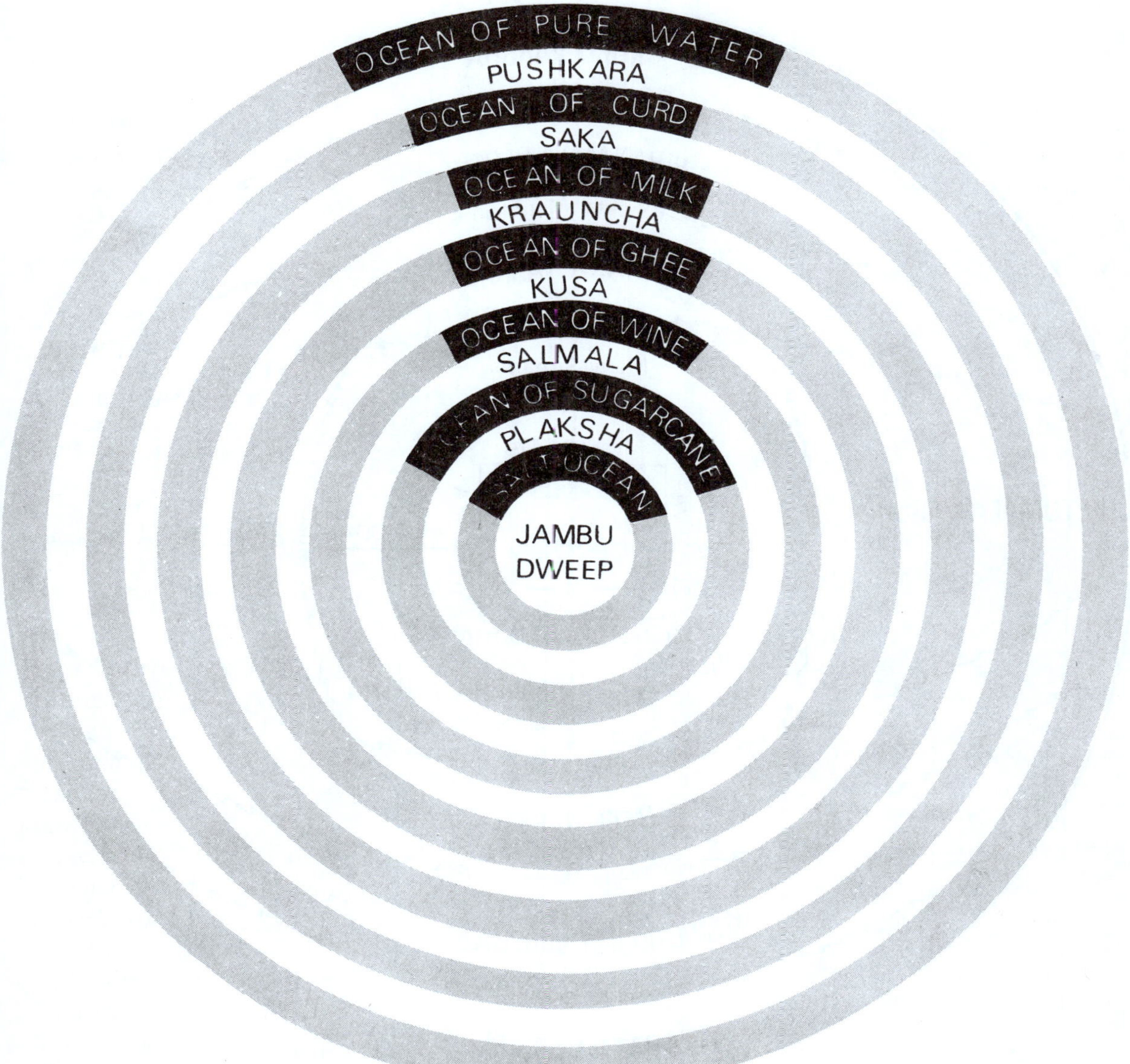

PLAN OF JAMBU DWEEP

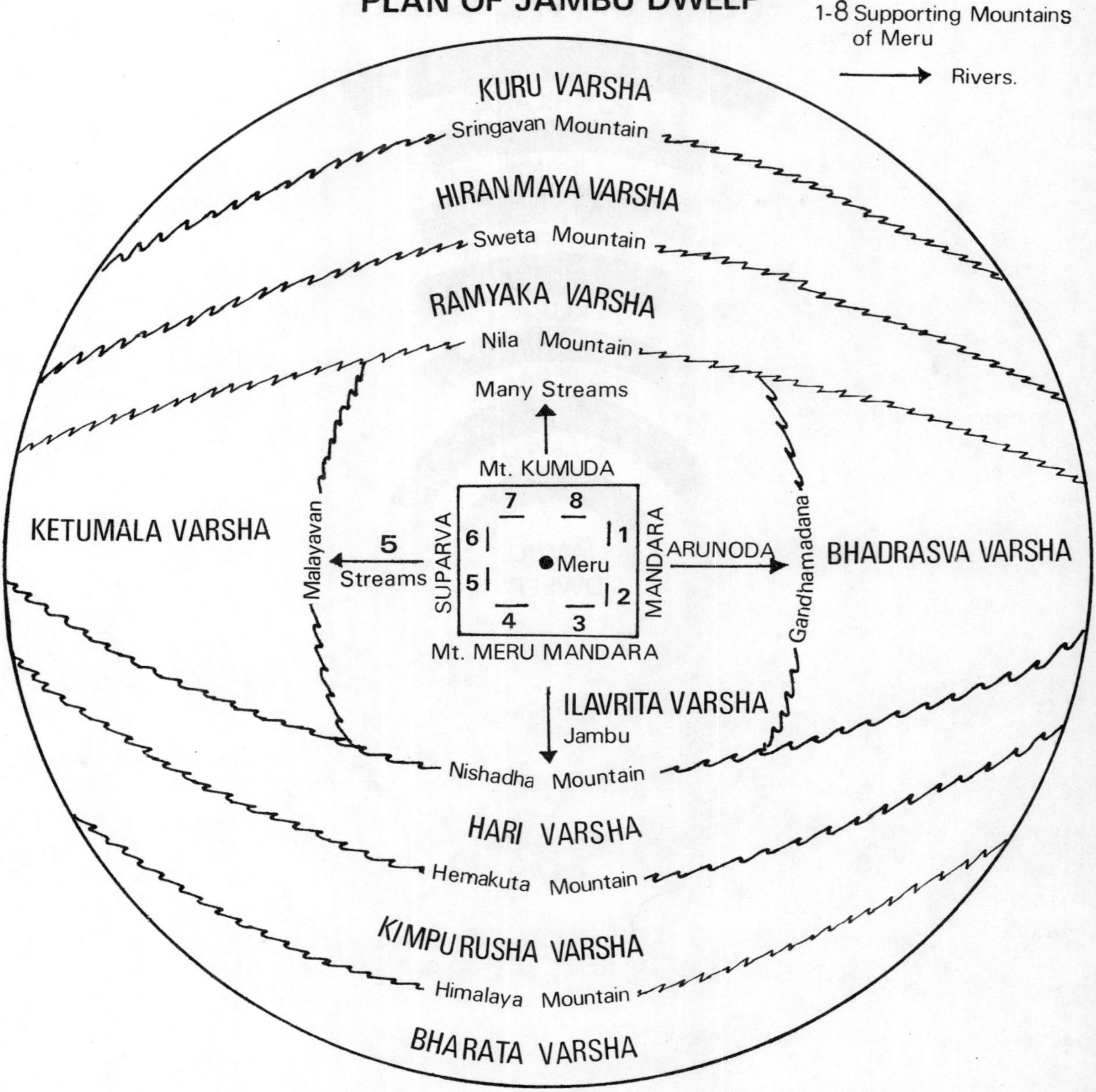

अथ षोडशोऽध्यायः

राजोवाच

उक्तस्त्वया भूमण्डलायामविशेषो यावदादित्यस्तपति यत्र चासौ ज्योतिषां गणैश्चन्द्रमा वा सह दृश्यते ॥1॥ तत्रापि प्रियव्रतरथचरणपरिखातैः सप्तभिः सप्त सिन्धव उपक्लृप्ता यत एतस्याः सप्तद्वीपविशेषविकल्पस्त्वया भगवन् खलु सूचित एतदेवाखिलमहं मानतो लक्षणतश्च सर्वं विजिज्ञासामि ॥2॥ भगवतो गुणमये स्थूलरूप आवेशितं मनो ह्यगुणेऽपि सूक्ष्मतम आत्मज्योतिषि परे ब्रह्मणि भगवति वासुदेवाख्ये क्षममावेशितुं तदु हैतद्गुरोऽर्हस्यनुवर्णयितुमिति ॥3॥

ऋषिरुवाच

न वै महाराज भगवतो मायागुणविभूतेः काष्ठां मनसा वचसा वाधिगन्तुमलं विबुधायुषापि पुरुषस्तस्मात्प्राधान्येनैव भूगोलकविशेषं नामरूपमानलक्षणतो व्याख्यास्यामः ॥4॥ यो वायं द्वीपः कुवलयकमलकोशाभ्यन्तरकोशो नियुतयोजनविशालः समवर्तुलो यथा पुष्करपत्रम् ॥5॥ यस्मिन्नव वर्षाणि नवयोजनसहस्रायामान्यष्टभिर्मर्यादागिरिभिः सुविभक्तानि भवन्ति ॥6॥ एषां मध्ये इलावृतं नामाभ्यन्तरवर्षं यस्य नाभ्यामवस्थितः सर्वतः सौवर्णः कुलगिरिराजो मेरुर्द्वीपायामसमुन्नाहः कर्णिकाभूतः कुवलयकमलस्य मूर्धनि द्वात्रिंशत्सहस्रयोजनविततो मूले षोडशसहस्रं

Skandha V : Chapter 16

GEOGRAPHICAL REFLECTIONS

Query about Dimensions (1-3)

Rajah Parikshit said: **1.** You have already described to me the terrestrial region as extending all round up to where the light of the sun reaches, and above where the moon is visible along with the stars. **2.** Then you indicated in brief that the seven oceans were created by the ruts formed by the wheels of emperor Priya-vrata's chariot as he went round Mount Mahameru, and that these oceans demarcate the seven Dweepas (continents or islands) on the earth. I would like to know all about these matters, including the dimensions and other features of these continents. **3.** For, if the mind is drawn to the external world constituted of Prakriti as the gross body of the Lord, then it can concentrate easily on His transcendental spiritual aspect beyond Prakriti, which is extremely subtle, which is of the nature of conscious luminosity, and which is known by the name of Vāsudeva. Hence, O master, kindly describe them.

Jambudweepa and its Divisions (4-6)

Sri Suka said: **4.** O Great King! No one can comprehend by thought or describe by speech even in a thousand divine years the extent and mystery of the evolution of the Lord's power known as His Maya, in this world of Becoming. Therefore I shall give a brief description only of the globe earth in respect of its location, size, and characteristics. **5.** In the innermost cavity of the lotus-like body called the earth, there is a continent which is a lakh of Yojanas in extent. It is called Jambudweepa and is of the round shape of a lotus leaf. **6.** In that Jambudweepa, there are nine regions or divisions (Varshas), each extending over nine thousand Yojanas and demarcated by eight mountain ranges as natural boundaries.

तावतान्तर्भूम्यां प्रविष्टः ॥7॥ उत्तरोत्तरेणेलावृतं नीलः श्वेतः शृङ्गवानिति त्रयो रम्यकहिरण्मय-
कुरूणां वर्षाणां मर्यादागिरयः प्रागायता उभयतः क्षारोदावधयो द्विसहस्रपृथव एकैकशः
पूर्वस्मात्पूर्वस्मादुत्तर उत्तरो दशांशाधिकांशेन दैर्घ्य एव ह्रसन्ति ॥8॥
एवं दक्षिणेनेलावृतं निषधो हेमकूटो हिमालय इति प्रागायता यथा नीलादयोऽयुतयोजनोत्सेधा
हरिवर्षकिम्पुरुषभारतानां यथासंख्यम् ॥9॥ तथैवेलावृतमपरेण पूर्वेण च माल्यवद्गन्धमादनावा-
नीलनिषधायतौ द्विसहस्रं पप्रथतुः केतुमालभद्राश्वयोः सीमानं विदधाते ॥10॥ मन्दरो मेरुमन्दरः
सुपार्श्वः कुमुद इत्ययुतयोजनविस्तारोन्नाहा मेरोश्चतुर्दिशमवष्टम्भगिरय उपक्लृप्ताः ॥11॥ चतुर्ष्वेतेषु
चूतजम्बूकदम्बन्यग्रोधाश्चत्वारः पादपप्रवराः पर्वतकेतव इवाधिसहस्रयोजनोन्नाहास्तावद्विटपविततयः
शतयोजनपरिणाहाः ॥12॥
ह्रदाश्चत्वारः पयोमध्विक्षुरसमृष्टजला यदुपस्पर्शिन उपदेवगणा योगैश्वर्याणि स्वाभाविकानि
भरतर्षभ धारयन्ति ॥13॥ देवोद्यानानि च भवन्ति चत्वारि नन्दनं चैत्ररथं वैभ्राजकं सर्वतो-

Illāvrita: Its Four Regions (7-10)

7. In the centre of Jambudweepa is the region known a Ilāvrita, which is the most interior of all regions. In the middle of Ilāvrita is situated Mahameru, the king of the mighty mountains. This golden mountain, is like a central pistil to the earth-lotus. A lakh of Yojanas in height, measuring thirty-two thousand Yojanas at the top, and sixteen thousand at the foot, its bottom penetrates to a depth of sixteen thousand Yojanas into the earth. **8.** North of Ilāvrita are three mountains, Nīla, Sveta, and Sringavān, standing in the order stated. They form the boundaries demarcating the three regions (Varshas)—Ramyaka, Hiranmaya, and Kuru respectively. These mountains run east to west, touching the salt ocean on both ends. All of them are two thousand Yojanas in width, but in length each one at the back is about a tenth less than the one immediately in front of it. **9.** South of Ilāvrita are three mountains as in the north. These are Nishādha, Hemakūta and Himālaya, which too like the mountain Nīla and others mentioned before, run east to west and have a height of ten thousand Yojanas. They demarcate the boundaries of regions known as Harivarsha, Kimpurushavarsha and Bhāratavarsha respectively. **10.** To the west and the east of Ilāvrata are the mountains Mālyavān and Gandhamādana. Lengthwise they touch Mount Nīla in the north and Mount Nishādha in the south. They are two thousand Yojanas in their width. They are the boundaries of the regions known as Ketumālā and Bhadrāsva.

Its Mountains and Rivers (11-25)

11. There are four mountains, Mandara, Merumandara, Supārsva and Kumuda, each ten thousand Yojanas in height and width, standing on the four sides of Meru as its embankments. **12.** On these four mountains looking like the towers of victory, there are four trees—a mango tree, a wood apple tree (Jambu), a Kadamba tree and a banyan tree respectively. They are one thousand one hundred Yojanas in height with branches of equal size. Each of them has a girth of one hundred Yojanas. **13.** O scion of the Bharata race! There are on these four mountains four lakes filled with milk, honey, sugarcane juice and pure water respectively. The demigods like Siddhas, Sādhyas and others who drink these waters become naturally endowed with Yogic powers. **14.** Situated on the moun-

भद्रमिति ।।14।। येष्वमरपरिवृढाः सहसुरललनाललामयूथपतय उपदेवगणैरुपगीयमानमहिमानः किल विहरन्ति ।।15।।

मन्दरोत्सङ्ग एकादशशतयोजनोत्तुङ्गदेवचूतशिरसो गिरिशिखरस्थूलानि फलान्यमृतकल्पानि पतन्ति ।।16।। तेषां विशीर्यमाणानामतिमधुरसुरभिसुगन्धिबहुलारुणरसोदेनारुणोदा नाम नदी मन्दरगिरिशिखरान्निपतन्ती पूर्वेणेलावृतमुपप्लावयति ।।17।। यदुपजोषणाद्भवान्या अनुचरीणां पुण्यजनवधूनामवयवस्पर्शसुगन्धवातो दशयोजनं समन्तादनुवासयति ।।18।। एवं जम्बूफलानामत्युच्चनिपातविशीर्णानामनस्थिप्रायाणामिभकायनिभानां रसेन जम्बू नाम नदी मेरुमन्दरशिखरादयुतयोजनादवनितले निपतन्ती दक्षिणेनात्मानं यावदिलावृतमुपस्यन्दयति ।।19।। तावदुभयोरपि रोधसोर्या मृत्तिका तद्रसेनानुविध्यमाना वाय्वर्कसंयोगविपाकेन सदामरलोकाभरणं जाम्बूनदं नाम सुवर्णं भवति ।।20।। यदु ह वाव विबुधादयः सह युवतिभिर्मुकुटकटककटिसूत्राद्याभरणरूपेण खलु धारयन्ति ।।21।।

यस्तु महाकदम्बः सुपार्श्वनिरूढो यास्तस्य कोटरेभ्यो विनिःसृताः पञ्चायामपरिणाहाः पञ्च मधुधाराः सुपार्श्वशिखरात्पतन्त्योऽपरेणात्मानमिलावृतमनुमोदयन्ति ।।22।। या ह्युपयुञ्जानानां मुखनिर्वासितो वायुः समन्ताच्छतयोजनमनुवासयति ।।23।।

एवं कुमुदनिरूढो यः शतवल्शो नाम वटस्तस्य स्कन्धेभ्यो नीचीनाः पयोदधिमधुघृतगुडान्नाद्य-

tains are four celestial gardens—Nandana, Chaitraratha, Vaibhrājika and Sarvatobhadra. **15.** In these gardens Deva chiefs sport with handsome Deva women, and the Gandharvas sing their praise. **16.** On the top of the Mandara mountain is a heavenly mango tree, one thousand and one hundred Yojanas in height. Luscious mangoes, sweet like the immortal drink Amrita, and equal to mountain peaks in size, fall from it. **17.** The pure, sweet and fragrant juice of reddish hue of these mangoes, crushed by the fall from the top, has formed into the famous river Arunoda, which flows down from the peaks of the Mandara mountain and waters the eastern side of Ilāvrita. **18.** Drinking the waters of that river, the Yaksha women who attend on Sri Parvati have developed such bodily aroma that the atmosphere there for about ten Yojanas is rendered fragrant by the breeze contacting their bodies. **19.** In the same way from the ten thousand Yojana high peaks of Mount Merumandara flows the well-known river Jambu whose waters are formed by the juice of the elephant-sized Jambu fruits with but tiny seeds, falling from the great height of that tree at the top of the mountain. It waters the southern portions of Ilāvrita. **20.** The earth on both sides of the river, soaked by the waters of it and acted upon by air and sunlight, gets converted into the brand of gold called Jāmbūnada, which forms the material for the ornaments of the Devas. **21.** The celestials and their women wear ornaments like diadems, bangles and girdles made of this metal. **22.** From the cavities of the great Kadamba tree at the top of the mountain Supārsva flow five streams of honey, each five fathoms in width. These, flowing down from the mountain, water the western side of Ilāvrita, making the whole place fragrant. **23.** The breath coming from the mouth of people who drink those sweet waters can render a hundred Yojanas in the neighbourhood fragrant. **24.** In the same way on the Mount Kumuda is the banyan tree called Satavalsa. From its branches flow rivers that bring

म्बरशय्यासनाभरणादयः सर्व एव कामदुघा नदाः कुमुदाग्रात्पतन्तस्तमुत्तरेणेलावृतमुपयोजयन्ति
॥24॥ यानुपजुषाणानां न कदाचिदपि प्रजानां वलीपलितक्लमस्वेददौर्गन्ध्यजरामयमृत्युशीतोष्ण-
वैवर्ण्योपसर्गादयस्तापविशेषा भवन्ति यावज्जीवं सुखं निरतिशयमेव ॥25॥

कुरङ्गकुररकुसुम्भवैकङ्कत्रिकूटशिशिरपतङ्गरुचकनिषधशिनीवासकपिलशङ्खवैदूर्यजारुधिहंसर्षभनाग-
कालञ्जरनारदादयो विंशतिगिरयो मेरोः कर्णिकाया इव केसरभूता मूलदेशे परित उपक्लृप्ताः
॥26॥ जठरदेवकूटौ मेरुं पूर्वेणाष्टादशयोजनसहस्रमुदगायतौ द्विसहस्रं पृथुतुङ्गौ भवतः । एवमपरेण
पवनपारियात्रौ दक्षिणेन कैलासकरवीरौ प्रागायतावेवमुत्तरतस्त्रिशृङ्गमकरावष्टभिरेतैः परिस्तृतो-
ऽग्निरिव परितश्चकास्ति काञ्चनगिरिः ॥27॥ मेरोर्मूर्धनि भगवत आत्मयोनेर्मध्यत उपक्लृप्तां
पुरीमयुतयोजनसाहस्रीं समचतुरस्रां शातकौम्भीं वदन्ति ॥28॥ तामनु परितो लोकपालानामष्टानां
यथादिशं यथारूपं तुरीयमानेन पुरोऽष्टावुपक्लृप्ताः ॥29॥

इति श्रीमद्भागवते महापुराणे पारमहंस्यां संहितायां पञ्चमस्कन्धे भुवनकोशवर्णनं नाम षोडशोऽध्यायः ॥16॥

milk, curd, honey, ghee, molasses, food stuffs, clothes, beddings, seats, ornaments, and all other desirable things. They wash the northern side of Ilāvrita. **25.** Those who drink those waters will be free from infirmities like wrinkles, grey hair, exhaustion, perspiration, bad odours, disease, premature death, distress from heat and cold, loss of complexion etc. They will live a happy life.

Mountains surrounding Meru (26-29)

26. Kuranga, Kurara, Kusumbha, Vaikanka, Trikūta, Sisira, Patanga, Ruchaka, Nishadha, Sinīvāsa, Kapila, Sankha, Vaidūrya, Jārudhi, Hamsa, Rishabha, Nāga, Kālanjara, Nārada, Ādi—these are twenty foot-hills which, like filaments encircling the style of a lotus, stand round the base of Mahameru, as ordained by the Creator. **27.** To the east of the Meru, stretching eighteen thousand Yojanas from north to south, are two mountains Jathara and Devakūta by name, with a height and a width of two thousand Yojanas. In the same way on the west of Meru are two other mountains, Pavana and Pāriyātra. Running east-west on the southern side of Meru are the two mountains Kailāsa and Karavīra. On the north stand two other mountains Trisringa and Makara. Thus surrounded by eight mountains, the golden Meru shines like a well-kindled sacred fire. **28.** It is said by authoritative sources that in the centre of the top of Meru there is the golden city of Lord Brahma the self-created one, in the shape of a square, covering ten million Yojanas. **29.** Surrounding it are located the eight cities of the Lokapalas (guardian deities of the quarters), each two thousand five hundred Yojanas in extent, and appropriate to each of them in direction and colour.

अथ सप्तदशोऽध्यायः

श्रीशुक उवाच

तत्र भगवतः साक्षाद्यज्ञलिङ्गस्य विष्णोर्विक्रमतो वामपादाङ्गुष्ठनखनिर्भिन्नोर्ध्वाण्डकटाह-
विवरेणान्तः प्रविष्टा या बाह्यजलधारातच्चरणपङ्कजावनेजनारुणकिञ्जल्कोपरञ्जिताखिलजगद-
घमलापहोपस्पर्शनामला साक्षाद्भगवत्पदीत्यनुपलक्षितवचोऽभिधीयमानातिमहता कालेन युगसहस्रोप-
लक्षणेन दिवो मूर्धन्यवततार यत्तद्विष्णुपदमाहुः ॥1॥ यत्र ह वाव वीरव्रत औत्तानपादिः
परमभागवतोऽस्मत्कुलदेवताचरणारविन्दोदकमिति यामनुसवनमुत्कृष्यमाणभगवद्भक्तियोगेन
दृढं क्लिद्यमानान्तर्हृदय औत्कण्ठ्यविवशामीलितलोचनयुगलकुड्मलविगलितामलबाष्पकलया-
भिव्यज्यमानरोमपुलककुलकोऽधुनापि परमादरेण शिरसा बिभर्ति ॥2॥

ततः सप्त ऋषयस्तत्प्रभावाभिज्ञा यां ननु तपस आत्यन्तिकी सिद्धिरेतावती भगवति
सर्वात्मनि वासुदेवेऽनुपरतभक्तियोगलाभेनैवोपेक्षितान्यार्थात्मगतयो मुक्तिमिवागतां मुमुक्षव इव
सबहुमानमद्यापि जटाजूटैरुद्वहन्ति ॥3॥ ततोऽनेकसहस्रकोटिविमानानीकसंकुलदेवयानेनाव-
तरन्तीन्दुमण्डलमावार्य ब्रह्मसदने निपतति ॥4॥

Skandha V : Chapter 17

DEVOTIONAL LIFE IN ILĀVRITA

Ganga's Descent (1-4)

Sri Suka said: **1.** Mahavishnu was incarnated as Vamana in order to take back the whole of the universe from Mahabali, under the guise of asking for a gift of three feet of earth. While measuring with His feet, He pressed His left toe on the dome of the Cosmic Shell, creating a hole in it. Through that hole a current of water from the beyond, flowed down to the lower regions washing the feet of the Lord. As it washed the lotus-feet of the Lord and carried the pollen of saffron from His holy feet, it acquired the efficiency to eradicate the sins of men by its contact but itself never becoming impure, and came to be known by the significant name Bhagavatpādi. In the course of a thousand Yugas, it fell on the top of the heavens well-known as Vishnupada. **2.** This Vishnupada is the Realm of Dhruva, the son of Uttānapāda, the great devotee of the Lord. With horripilations all over, and with a heart melting in devotion generated by the thought that it is the water with which his Lord's feet have been washed, and with tears rushing from his lotus-bud-like and half-closed eyes, that great devotee Dhruva is even today bathing his head in that water. **3.** There are the Saptarshis who consider the fairest fruit of all austere observances to consist in having unwavering devotion to the Lord and as a consequence reject all other attainments including Mukti. Even they consider the Ganga so sacred that they devoutly bear the waters of it in their matted locks, just as aspirants of Mukti gladly embrace that state when it is within their reach. **4.** After descending through the heavenly path dotted with vast numbers of aerial mansions of the celestials, and moistening the orb of the moon, it descends on the top of Mahameru, the abode of Brahma.

Ganga branching into Four (5-10)

तत्र चतुर्धा भिद्यमाना चतुर्भिर्नामभिश्चतुर्दिशमभिस्पन्दन्ती नदनदीपतिमेवाभिनिविशति सीतालकनन्दा चक्षुर्भद्रेति ॥5॥ सीता तु ब्रह्मसदनात्केसराचलादिगिरिशिखरेभ्योऽधोऽधः प्रस्रवन्ती गन्धमादनमूर्धसु पतित्वान्तरेण भद्राश्ववर्षं प्राच्यां दिशि क्षारसमुद्रमभिप्रविशति ॥6॥ एवं माल्यवच्छिखरान्निष्पतन्ती ततोऽनुपरतवेगा केतुमालमभि चक्षुः प्रतीच्यां दिशि सरित्पतिं प्रविशति ॥7॥ भद्रा चोत्तरतो मेरुशिरसो निपतिता गिरिशिखराद्गिरिशिखरमतिहाय शृङ्गवतः शृङ्गादवस्यन्दमाना उत्तरांस्तु कुरूनभित उदीच्यां दिशि जलधिमभिप्रविशति ॥8॥ तथैवालकनन्दा दक्षिणेन ब्रह्मसदनाद्बहूनि गिरिकूटान्यतिक्रम्य हेमकूटाद्धैमकूटान्यतिरभसतररंहसा लुठयन्ती भारतमभि वर्षं दक्षिणस्यां दिशि जलधिमभिप्रविशति यस्यां स्नानार्थं चागच्छतः पुंसः पदे पदेऽश्वमेधराजसूयादीनां फलं न दुर्लभमिति ॥9॥ अन्ये च नदा नद्यश्च वर्षे वर्षे सन्ति बहुशो मेर्वादिगिरिदुहितरः शतशः ॥10॥

तत्रापि भारतमेव वर्षं कर्मक्षेत्रमन्यान्यष्ट वर्षाणि स्वर्गिणां पुण्यशेषोपभोगस्थानानि भौमानि स्वर्गपदानि व्यपदिशन्ति ॥11॥ एषु पुरुषाणामयुतपुरुषायुर्वर्षाणां देवकल्पानां नागायुतप्राणानां वज्रसंहननबलवयोमोदप्रमुदितमहासौरतमिथुनव्यवायापवर्गवर्षधृतैकगर्भकलत्राणां तत्र तु त्रेतायुगसमः

5. There dividing into four streams, Sīta, Alakananda, Chakshu and Bhadrā, it flows through the four regions into the sea. **6.** Of these Sīta, starting from Brahma's abode and passing through the tops of the mountains that stand as filaments in the centre of the earth-lotus, falls down to the top of the mountain Gandhamādana. It then flows east through the middle of the region Bhadrāsva and falls into the salt ocean on the east. **7.** In the same way the branch river Chakshu, falling from the top of Mount Mālyavān, flows swiftly in the direction of the region Ketumala, and into the western sea. **8.** The branch river Bhadrā, too, flowing down from Mahameru through different mountain tops below and passing from one mountain to another, finally descends from the top of Sringavān into the Uttara Kuru region, and flowing northwards, reaches the northern sea. **9.** In the same way the river Alakananda flowing down from the abode of Brahma by the southern side, and passing through several mountains reaches the mountain Hemakūta, from where it flows very rapidly through mountain peaks in the direction of Bhāratavarsha and joins the southern sea. One who comes for a bath in that Alakananda, easily gets the fruits of Asvamedha and Rajasuya at every step he takes towards the holy river. So holy it is! **10.** Besides these, there are innumerable other rivers, big and small, originating from mountains like Meru and flowing through each and every one of these regions.

Uniqueness of Bhāratavarsha (11-13)

11. Of all these Varshas (regions), Bhāratavarsha alone is the field of Karma, or the place where a Jiva can acquire merit and demerit by work. The other eight Varshas, are places where Jivas who have almost completed their merits in enjoyment in Swarga (heaven), come to reap the effects of their residuary meritorious deeds. **12.** The conditions of the inhabitants of those regions are like those in Tretayuga. They have a life-span of a ten thousand years; they have adamant-like bodies, unfailing youth, strength, and joyous temperament. They and their wives have extraordinarily high sexual potency which enables them to

कालो वर्तते ॥12॥ यत्र ह देवपतयः स्वैः स्वैर्गणनायकैर्विहितमहार्हणाः सर्वर्तुकुसुमस्तबकफल-
किसलयश्रियाऽऽनम्यमानविटपलताविटपिभिरुपशुम्भमानरुचिरकाननाश्रमायतनवर्षगिरिद्रोणीषु तथा
चामलजलाशयेषु विकचविविधनववनरुहामोदमुदितराजहंसजलकुक्कुटकारण्डवसारसचक्रवाकादिभि-
र्मधुकरनिकराकृतिभिरुपकूजितेषु जलक्रीडादिभिर्विचित्रविनोदैः सुललितसुरसुन्दरीणां काम-
कलिलविलासहासलीलावलोकाकृष्टमनोदृष्टयः स्वैरं विहरन्ति ॥13॥

नवस्वपि वर्षेषु भगवान्नारायणो महापुरुषः पुरुषाणां तदनुग्रहायात्मतत्त्वव्यूहेनात्मनाद्यापि
सन्निधीयते ॥14॥ इलावृते तु भगवान् भव एक एव पुमान्न ह्यन्यस्तत्रापरो निर्विशति भवान्याः
शापनिमित्तज्ञो यत्प्रवेक्ष्यतः स्त्रीभावस्तत्पश्चाद्वक्ष्यामि ॥15॥ भवानीनाथैः स्त्रीगणार्बुदसहस्रैरवरुध्यमानो
भगवतश्चतुर्मूर्तेर्महापुरुषस्य तुरीयां तामसीं मूर्तिं प्रकृतिमात्मनः सङ्कर्षणसंज्ञामात्मसमाधिरूपेण
सन्निधाप्यैतदभिगृणन् भव उपधावति ॥16॥

श्रीभगवानुवाच

ॐ नमो भगवते महापुरुषाय सर्वगुणसंख्यानायानन्तायाव्यक्ताय नम इति ॥17॥

भजे भजन्यारणपादपङ्कजं भगस्य कृत्स्नस्य परं परायणम् ।
भक्तेष्वलं भावितभूतभावनं भवापहं त्वा भवभावमीश्वरम् ॥18॥

have protracted sexual enjoyment all through their life, disturbed by the birth of only one issue towards the end of their life-span. **13.** In these Varshas leading Devas are honoured with grand receptions by the chiefs of their votaries. There are retreats and sanctuaries with an abundance of trees whose branches are bending in all seasons alike with their loads of leaves, flowers and fruits. In the valleys of the mountains of these regions are lakes of pure water inhabited by numerous water birds like swans, water-fowls, cranes, Kārandavas and Chakravākas. These birds as well as honey-bees, inebriated and delighted with the fragrance of freshly blown lotus flowers in the lakes, fill the atmosphere with their delightful warblings. The leading celestials engage themselves in water-sports in these lakes with their women of ravishing beauty augmented by the stimulation of love expressed through their excited looks, smiles and sportive dispositions.

Sankarshana Worship in Ilāvrita (14-24)

14. In all these nine Varshas (regions) Bhagavan Narayana is even today manifested in different forms in order to bless the inhabitants of those regions. **15.** In the Ilāvrita there is Sri Parameswara. He is the only male there. Because of the curse of Devi Bhavani, anyone entering there will become a woman. So no man ever enters there. The reason for this will be explained elsewhere (in the ninth Skandha). **16.** There Siva together with his consort Bhavani and surrounded by the countless number of women attendants of the latter, meditates upon and establishes in his heart the Lord Sankarshana, the fourth of the Vyuhas (Emanations) of the Mahapurusha, the Supreme Being, embodying His power of destruction, which is also his (Siva's) own source. He recites the following Mantra and prays:

17. Om! Salutations to the Lord, the Supreme Being, who is the support and manifester of the whole objective world constituted of the Gunas without Himself being affected by it, who has no limitations of space and time, who is beyond all individuality, and who has the eightfold power in its fullness. **18.** O Worshipful

न यस्य मायागुणचित्तवृत्तिभिर्निरीक्षतो ह्यण्वपि दृष्टिरज्यते ।
ईशे यथा नोऽजितमन्युरंहसां कस्तं न मन्येत जिगीषुरात्मनः ॥19॥
असद्दृशो यः प्रतिभाति मायया क्षीबेव मध्वासवताम्रलोचनः ।
न नागवध्वोऽर्हण ईशिरे ह्रिया यत्पादयोः स्पर्शनधर्षितेन्द्रियाः ॥20॥
यमाहुरस्य स्थितिजन्मसंयमं त्रिभिर्विहीनं यमनन्तमृषयः ।
न वेद सिद्धार्थमिव क्वचित्स्थितं भूमण्डलं मूर्धसहस्रधामसु ॥21॥
यस्याद्य आसीद् गुणविग्रहो महान् विज्ञानधिष्ण्यो भगवानजः किल ।
यत्सम्भवोऽहं त्रिवृता स्वतेजसा वैकारिकं तामसमैन्द्रियं सृजे ॥22॥
एते वयं यस्य वशे महात्मनः स्थिताः शकुन्ता इव सूत्रयन्त्रिताः ।
महानहं वैकृततामसेन्द्रियाः सृजाम सर्वे यदनुग्रहादिदम् ॥23॥
यन्निर्मितां कर्ह्यपि कर्मपर्वणीं मायां जनोऽयं गुणसर्गमोहितः ।
न वेद निस्तारणयोगमञ्जसा तस्मै नमस्ते विलयोदयात्मने ॥24॥

इति श्रीमद्भागवते महापुराणे पारमहंस्यां संहितायां पञ्चमस्कन्धे सप्तदशोऽध्यायः ॥17॥

One! Adoration to Thee! Thou alone art endowed with all Bhagas or divine majesties. Though the cause of all, Thou dost manifest specially through Thy devotees. Thou causest bondage to persons without devotion, while Thou breakest that of devotees. Thou art the one at whose lotus-feet everyone can take refuge. **19.** Though controlling and directing the whole of this manifested universe as its witness, Thou art not in the least affected by the modes of ignorance and the passions resulting from them unlike us who are perturbed by anger and other passions. Who is the man that feels the urge for freedom from enslavement, attachments and passions, and yet will not worship Thee, that Supreme Being, who art unaffected in the least by Maya?

20. He who out of His mysterious power, appears to the ignorant as one inebriated and having eyes reddened like those of a person under intoxicants; He who is so charming that the serpent-wives in attendance are overwhelmed with bashfulness on contacting His feet; **21.** He who is the ultimate source of creation, preservation and destruction of the worlds, and who, being beyond all these three, is called Ananta (the unlimited); who feels unconcerned with the burden of the earth resting somewhere on his numerous hoods as if it were a mere mustard seed; **22.** He who first manifested a form for Himself based on the Sattva quality under the name Mahattattva, known also as Brahma, from whom I was born (as non-separate from Vāsudeva) with the function of creation based on the three types of Ahankara—Sattvika, Rajasika and Tamasika; **23.** He by whose grace we, the Mahattattva, Ahankara, Devas and Bhutas, carry on the work of creation, being directed in that work as birds are by the person holding them by the string; **24.** By the infatuating power of whose Maya the world gets entangled in external manifestations of Nature and the ego-centred actions springing from them, without knowing the way to overcome that infatuation—to that Being, the source of the functions of creation and dissolution of the universe, we offer our salutations!

अथाष्टादशोऽध्यायः

श्रीशुक उवाच

तथा च भद्रश्रवा नाम धर्मसुतस्तत्कुलपतयः पुरुषा भद्राश्ववर्षे साक्षाद्भगवतो वासुदेवस्य प्रियां तनुं धर्ममयीं हयशीर्षाभिधानां परमेण समाधिना संनिधाप्येदमभिगृणन्त उपधावन्ति ॥1॥

भद्रश्रवस ऊचुः

ॐ नमो भगवते धर्मायात्मविशोधनाय नम इति ॥2॥
अहो विचित्रं भगवद्विचेष्टितं घ्नन्तं जनोऽयं हि मिषन्न पश्यति ।
ध्यायन्नसद्यर्हि विकर्म सेवितुं निर्हृत्य पुत्रं पितरं जिजीविषति ॥ 3॥
वदन्ति विश्वं कवयः स्म नश्वरं पश्यन्ति चाध्यात्मविदो विपश्चितः ।
तथापि मुह्यन्ति तवाज मायया सुविस्मितं कृत्यमजं नतोऽस्मि तम् ॥ 4॥
विश्वोद्भवस्थाननिरोधकर्म ते ह्यकर्तुरङ्गीकृतमप्यपावृतः ।
युक्तं न चित्रं त्वयि कार्यकारणे सर्वात्मनि व्यतिरिक्ते च वस्तुतः ॥ 5॥
वेदान् युगान्ते तमसा तिरस्कृतान् रसातलाद्यो नृतुरङ्गविग्रहः ।
प्रत्याददे वै कवयेऽभियाचते तस्मै नमस्तेऽवितथेहिताय इति ॥ 6॥

Skandha V : Chapter 18

WORSHIP OF THE LORD IN THE VARIOUS VARSHAS

Hayagrīva in Bhadrāswa (1-6)

Sri Suka said: **1.** In the Bhadrāswavarsha, the son of Dharma named Bhadrasravas along with his chiefs, worships with deep devotion and concentration the spiritual form of Vāsudeva known as Hayagrīva. They invoke Him with the following hymn:

Bhadrasravas says: **2.** Om! Salutations to the Lord, the embodiment of Dharma and the grantor of purity of heart to his votaries! **3.** Wonderful indeed is the Lord's play! See how even while witnessing the death of others on all sides, man fails to recognise that death would visit him too! See how, even immediately after the funeral rites of their fathers and sons, men are eager to possess their wealth and ready to indulge in any mean action that would help them enjoy the trivial pleasures of the world! **4.** Wise men speak of the world as impermanent, and men of spiritual insight realise it as such. Yet people at large blindly take it as permanent under the infatuation of Thy Yogamaya—this, indeed, is a surprising play of Thine. **5.** Though Thou art the pure spirit, untainted and actionless, the scriptures accept Thee as the cause of the manifestation, sustentation and dissolution of the worlds. In Thee, who art both the cause and the effect (the creator and the created), who art the essence of all but yet dost transcend them in fact, this harmony of contradictions is nothing strange considering Thy power Yogamaya. **6.** At the end of the Kalpa, when the forces of ignorance represented by Sankhāsura hid the Veda in the nether worlds, Thou didst embody Thyself as Hayagrīva, with the head of a horse and the body of a man, lift them up from the nether worlds and bestow them on Brahma, who was eagerly seeking it from Thee. My salutations to Thee of unfailing

हरिवर्षे चापि भगवान्नरहरिरूपेणास्ते तद्रूपग्रहणनिमित्तमुत्तरत्राभिधास्ये तद्दयितं रूपं महापुरुषगुणभाजनो महाभागवतो दैत्यदानवकुलतीर्थीकरणशीलाचरितः प्रह्लादोऽव्यवधानानन्य-भक्तियोगेन सह तद्वर्षपुरुषैरुपास्ते इदं चोदाहरति ॥७॥ ॐ नमो भगवते नरसिंहाय नमस्तेजस्तेजसे आविराविर्भव वज्रनख वज्रदंष्ट्र कर्माशयान् रन्धय रन्धय तमो ग्रस ग्रस ॐ स्वाहा । अभयम-भयमात्मनि भूयिष्ठा ॐ क्ष्रौम् ॥८॥

स्वस्त्यस्तु विश्वस्य खलः प्रसीदतां ध्यायन्तु भूतानि शिवं मिथो धिया ।
मनश्च भद्रं भजतादधोक्षजे आवेश्यतां नो मतिरप्यहैतुकी ॥ ९॥
मागारदारात्मजवित्तबन्धुषु सङ्गो यदि स्याद्भगवत्प्रियेषु नः ।
यः प्राणवृत्त्या परितुष्ट आत्मवान् सिद्ध्यत्यदूरान्न तथेन्द्रियप्रियः ॥१०॥
यत्सङ्गलब्धं निजवीर्यवैभवं तीर्थं मुहुः संस्पृशतां हि मानसम् ।
हरत्यजोऽन्तः श्रुतिभिर्गतोऽङ्गजं को वै न सेवेत मुकुन्दविक्रमम् ॥११॥
यस्यास्ति भक्तिर्भगवत्यकिञ्चना सर्वैर्गुणैस्तत्र समासते सुराः ।
हरावभक्तस्य कुतो महद्गुणा मनोरथेनासति धावतो बहिः ॥१२॥

resolution!

Narasimha in Harivarsha (7-14)

7. In the region known as Harivarsha, the Lord is manifest as Narasimha. Why he did so, is described elsewhere (Skandha VII). There Prahlada, whose birth and life among the Asuras sanctified that race, meditates on that charming form with unwavering and concentrated devotion along with all his followers. He addresses the following hymn beginning with this Mantra:

8. Our salutations to the Lord Krishna —to Him who is the Light of all lights! Manifest Thyself before us, O Lord, with Thy powerful teeth and claws! Burn up in us all impressions born of Karma! Consume away the darkness of ignorance in us! The Atman is our refuge! The Atman is our refuge! Om Kshraum! **9.** May all the worlds be happy! May the wicked men attain to purity and peace! Let all people pray for mutual peace! May their minds be at peace! And may our minds too, along with all others, attain to that state of spontaneous flow towards the Lord, free from the promptings of all worldly desires. **10.** May we be free from attachment to house, wife, sons, wealth, and relatives! If we are to be attached to any, let it be to the devotees of the Lord. For the man who is free from worldly attachments, who is satisfied with bare subsistence, and who is self-controlled, does attain soon to spiritual realisation, but not so those engrossed in properties and sense enjoyments. **11.** In the company of holy men, an aspirant naturally happens to hear about the Lord's excellences, and by virtue of the communion the devotees thus establish with Him through the sense of hearing, He verily enters into their hearts and rids them of the very tendencies that lead to sinful actions. Repeated dips in holy waters can remove only the dirt of the body and fructified sin but not the tendencies that prompt one to sinful acts. Who is the right-minded man that would, under the circumstances, abstain from listening to the Lord's excellences? **12.** All the Deities along with all virtues attend upon him who has whole-hearted and motiveless devotion to the Lord. But a person who is always moving amidst the

हरिर्हि साक्षाद्भगवान् शरीरिणामात्मा झषाणामिव तोयमीप्सितम् ।
हित्वा महांस्तं यदि सज्जते गृहे तदा महत्त्वं वयसा दम्पतीनाम् ।।13।।
तस्माद्रजोरागविषादमन्युमानस्पृहाभयदैन्याधिमूलम् ।
हित्वा गृहं संसृतिचक्रवालं नृसिंहपादं भजताकुतोभयमिति ।।14।।

केतुमालेऽपि भगवान् कामदेवस्वरूपेण लक्ष्म्याः प्रियचिकीर्षया प्रजापतेर्दुहितॄणां पुत्राणां तद्वर्षपतीनां पुरुषायुषाहोरात्रपरिसंख्यानानां यासां गर्भा महापुरुषमहास्त्रतेजसोद्वेजितमनसां विध्वस्ता व्यसवः संवत्सरान्ते विनिपतन्ति ।।15।। अतीव सुललितगतिविलासविलसितरुचिरहासलेशावलोक-लीलया किञ्चिदुत्तम्भितसुन्दरभ्रूमण्डलसुभगवदनारविन्दश्रिया रमां रमयन्निन्द्रियाणि रमयते ।।16।। तद्भगवतो मायामयं रूपं परमसमाधियोगेन रमा देवी संवत्सरस्य रात्रिषु प्रजापतेर्दुहितृभिरुपेताहःसु च तद्भर्तृभिरुपास्ते इदं चोदाहरति ।।17।। ॐ ह्रां ह्रीं ह्रूं ॐ नमो भगवते हृषीकेशाय सर्वगुण-विशेषैर्विलक्षितात्मने आकूतीनां चित्तीनां चेतसां विशेषाणां चाधिपतये षोडशकलाय छन्दोमयायान्न-मयायामृतमयाय सर्वमयाय सहसे ओजसे बलाय कान्ताय कामाय नमस्ते उभयत्र भूयात् ।।18।।

objects of the senses and has no longing for the Lord—how can he be endowed with any great virtue as benevolence, enlightenment, renunciation and the like? **13.** Just as water is what sustains the life of the fish, so is the Bhagavan, Sri Hari, the very sustenance of all embodied beings. Nothing should therefore be dearer to them than He. If men who are forgetful of this and are attached to their homes, relatives and possessions, are none the less called great because of their worldly position—such estimation of them is a mere convention, just as in regard to a married couple it is a convention to consider the elder partner, the husband, as superior merely because of his age. **14.** Therefore abandon the worldly life—the sphere of the repetitive experience of life and death, and the source of all miseries arising from restlessness, attachments, anxieties, anger, desire, pride, fear, sickness, and worries, and let man take shelter at the feet of Nrisimha, where he will find a veritable haven of peace and security.

Kāmadeva in Ketumāla (15-23)

15. In the region (Varsha) called Ketumāla the Lord manifests as Kāmadeva (Cupid) in order to please Lakshmi Devi and also the thirty six thousand daughters and sons of the Prajapati (Samvatsara), who is the master of that Varsha. The deities identifying themselves with nights are the daughters, and those with days are the sons. The pregnancy of these daughters get aborted before a year, because of the fierce puissance of the discus of the Lord. **16.** There the Lord sports, by delighting Ramā by His graceful and sportive movements, by His attractive smile and looks, and by His most charming face whose eyebrows are slightly raised as he playfully glances at the surroundings. **17.** There Ramā adores the enchanting form of the Lord through concentrated meditation and worship, along with the daughters of Prajapati at nights, and with his sons during the day. The following are the Mantras and hymn with which she invokes the Lord:

18. Om, Hrām, Hrīm, Hrūm! Salutations to Thee both within and without! O Lord of all divine majesties! Thou controller of the senses of all! The one indicated as their transcendent source by all impressive manifestations of virtue! Thou the Lord of all worship, knowledge, spiritual aspirations and their fulfilments!

स्त्रियो व्रतैस्त्वा हृषिकेश्वरं स्वतो ह्याराध्य लोके पतिमाशासतेऽन्यम् ।
तासां न ते वै परिपान्त्यपत्यं प्रियं धनायूंषि यतोऽस्वतन्त्राः ॥19॥
स वै पतिः स्यादकुतोभयः स्वयं समन्ततः पाति भयातुरं जनम् ।
स एक एवेतरथा मिथो भयं नैवात्मलाभादधि मन्यते परम् ॥20॥
या तस्य ते पादसरोरुहार्हणं निकामयेत्साखिलकामलम्पटा ।
तदेव रासीप्सितमीप्सितोऽर्चितो यद्भग्नयाच्ञा भगवन् प्रतप्यते ॥21॥
मत्प्राप्तयेऽजेशसुरासुरादयस्तप्यन्त उग्रं तप ऐन्द्रियेधियः ।
ऋते भवत्पादपरायणान्न मां विन्दन्त्यहं त्वद्धृदया यतोऽजित ॥22॥
स त्वं ममाप्यच्युत शीर्ष्णि वन्दितं कराम्बुजं यत्त्वदधायि सात्वताम् ।
बिभर्षि मां लक्ष्म वरेण्य मायया क ईश्वरस्येहितमूहितुं विभुरिति ॥23॥

रम्यके च भगवतः प्रियतमं मात्स्यमवताररूपं तद्वर्षपुरुषस्य मनोः प्राक्प्रदर्शितं स इदानीमपि

Thou the one endowed with sixteen parts! Thou the one who has assumed the form of all Vedic metres, of all objects of enjoyment, of all bliss, of all that exists, of all strength in the world, and of all beauty seen therein! **19.** In this world women adore Thee, the master of all the senses, by the practice of austerities and other disciplines with the desire that they might get worthy husbands. But they little realise that these husbands, their coveted masters, whom they seek in distinction from Thee, are not able to save their dear children, their wealth and their life; for they are themselves limited beings, with no freedom for themselves. Unlike them, I, Lakshmi, adore as my husband the eternal and omnipotent Bhagavan Mahavishnu. **20.** He is the real master (husband) who, himself fearless, saves the fear-stricken people from all fears. The one free from all fears is Thyself. For Thou, being the one all-comprehending existence with no second entity outside of Thee, has nothing to gain except what Thyself art. Nor hast Thou any to be afraid of, being the sole existence, unlike the various divinities who have necessarily to be afraid of their compeers. **21.** That woman who desires for nothing but the service of Thy feet, has all her longings fulfilled. She becomes indeed a reveller in all desires! To those who worship Thee with particular worldly desires (like obtaining a worthy husband), Thou dost indeed grant those desires; but, O Lord, they will have cause to grieve afterwards when the effects of those particular boons are exhausted. **22.** For attaining me (Srī or the goddess of wealth and good fortune) even Brahma, Siva, Devas and Asuras perform difficult austerities with their minds set on material prosperity. But, O Lord, my heart is entirely given over to Thee, and I care not for any except those who are devoted to Thy feet. **23.** O Imperishable one! Deign to place on my head the lotus-palm of Thine as an act of blessing, as Thou dost on the heads of Thy devotees. Thou worshipful one! Thou hast certainly given me a place on Thy chest as an emblem of Thine, but Thou has not yet blessed me placing Thy hand on my head. Who, indeed, can fathom the depth of the intentions behind the play enacted by Thy Yogamaya?

Cosmic Fish in Ramyaka (24-28)

24. In the region called Ramyakavarsha, Manu Vaivaswata, to whom in his previous birth as Satyavrata the Lord revealed His form as the Fish, is even

महता भक्तियोगेनाराधयतीदं चोदाहरति ॥24॥ ॐ नमो भगवते मुख्यतमाय नमः सत्त्वाय प्राणायौजसे सहसे बलाय महामत्स्याय नम इति ॥25॥

अन्तर्बहिश्चाखिललोकपालकैरदृष्टरूपो विचरस्युरुस्वनः ।
स ईश्वरस्त्वं य इदं वशेऽनयन्नाम्ना यथा दारुमयीं नरः स्त्रियम् ॥26॥
यं लोकपालाः किल मत्सरज्वरा हित्वा यतन्तोऽपि पृथक् समेत्य च ।
पातुं न शेकुर्द्विपदश्चतुष्पदः सरीसृपं स्थाणु यदत्र दृश्यते ॥27॥
भवान् युगान्तार्णव ऊर्मिमालिनि क्षोणीमिमामोषधिवीरुधां निधिम् ।
मया सहोरु क्रमतेऽज ओजसा तस्मै जगत्प्राणगणात्मने नम इति ॥28॥

हिरण्मयेऽपि भगवान् निवसति कूर्मतनुं बिभ्राणस्तस्य तत्प्रियतमां तनुमर्यमा सह वर्षपुरुषैः पितृगणाधिपतिरुपधावति मन्त्रमिमं चानुजपति ॥29॥ ॐ नमो भगवते अकूपाराय सर्वसत्त्वगुण-विशेषणायानुपलक्षितस्थानाय नमो वर्ष्मणे नमो भूम्ने नमो नमोऽवस्थानाय नमस्ते ॥30॥

यद्रूपमेतन्निजमाययार्पितमर्थस्वरूपं बहुरूपरूपितम् ।
संख्या न यस्यास्त्ययथोपलम्भनात्तस्मै नमस्तेऽव्यपदेशरूपिणे ॥31॥
जरायुजं स्वेदजमण्डजोद्भिदं चराचरं देवर्षिपितृभूतमैन्द्रियम् ।
द्यौः खं क्षितिः शैलसरित्समुद्रद्वीपग्रहर्क्षेत्यभिधेय एकः ॥32॥

today adoring Him in that form, repeating the following Mantra and hymn:

25. Om! Salutations to the Divine Fish, the Supreme Lord and the greatest of all beings, the embodiment of pure Sattva, the master of life, energy and strength in the body, senses and the mind of all beings! Salutation again! **26.** Unseen even by the presiding deities either within or without the universe, Thou art sporting in the worlds giving out the mighty voice of the Vedas to reveal Thy unseen presence. Just as in a puppet show, a man manipulates a wooden doll of a woman's form by means of strings, so dost Thou, the Lord of all, control and regulate this universe by the string of names (Vedic injunctions). **27.** Vain was the attempt of the presiding deities at the governance of the universe consisting of countless beings and inert substances, when they attempted to do so severally and collectively in a spirit of competition and in forgetfulness of Thee. **28.** In the wave-tossed ocean flooding everything at the end of the cycle, Thou, O Lord, didst as the Incarnate Fish, speed away in that flood with me in the boat-shaped earth, the seat of countless trees and vegetation.

Cosmic Tortoise in Hiranmaya (29-33)

29. In the region known as Hiranmayavarsha the Lord manifests as the Cosmic Tortoise. Thus Aryama, the head of the Pitris (manes), worships Him along with other devotees, repeating the following Mantra and hymn:

30. Om! Salutations to Thee, the tortoise shaped! Thou art the embodiment of pure, unsullied Sattva-guna; Thy source has never been traced by any one. Time limits Thee not. Thy presence is everywhere, and everything is contained in Thee. Om! Salutations! **31.** This world of multiplicity projected by Thy Maya as a factually perceived universe, is verily Thy form. It is seen as a countless multiplicity, because it is viewed apart from Thee. Salutations to Thy indescribable forms!

32. All this universe consisting of creatures born of the womb, sweat, egg and

यस्मिन्नसंख्येयविशेषनामरूपाकृतौ कविभिः कल्पितेयम् ।
संख्या यया तत्त्वदृशापनीयते तस्मै नमः सांख्यनिदर्शनाय ते इति ॥33॥

उत्तरेषु च कुरुषु भगवान् यज्ञपुरुषः कृतवराहरूप आस्ते तं तु देवी हैषा भूः सह कुरुभिरस्खलितभक्तियोगेनोपधावति इमां च परमामुपनिषदमावर्तयति ॥34॥ ॐ नमो भगवते मन्त्रतत्त्वलिङ्गाय यज्ञक्रतवे महाध्वरावयवाय महापुरुषाय नमः कर्मशुक्लाय त्रियुगाय नमस्ते ॥35॥

यस्य स्वरूपं कवयो विपश्चितो गुणेषु दारुष्विव जातवेदसम् ।
मथ्नन्ति मथ्ना मनसा दिदृक्षवो गूढं क्रियार्थैर्नम ईरितात्मने ॥36॥
द्रव्यक्रियाहेत्वयनेशकर्तृभिर्मायागुणैर्वस्तुनिरीक्षितात्मने ।
अन्वीक्षयाङ्गातिशयात्मबुद्धिभिर्निरस्तमायाकृतये नमो नमः ॥37॥
करोति विश्वस्थितिसंयमोदयं यस्येप्सितं नेप्सितमीक्षितुर्गुणैः ।
माया यथायो भ्रमते तदाश्रयं ग्राव्णो नमस्ते गुणकर्मसाक्षिणे ॥38॥

earth; all entities described as moving and unmoving—Devas, Rishis, Pitris, elements, senses, firmament, space, sky, earth, mountains, rivers, oceans, continents, planets, and stars—all these form one unity in Thee. **33.** The countless forms, names and attributes into which Thou hast manifested through Yogamaya have been classified into twenty-four categories by great philosophers. But even this perception of the many as separate existences is effaced when spiritual insight reveals their unity in Thee. Om! Salutations to Thee revealed by unitive understanding.

Cosmic Boar in Uttarakuru (34-39)

34. In Uttarakuruvarsha the Yajna-embodied Lord, manifests in the form of the Cosmic Boar. Along with the devotees there, Mother Earth adores Him with great devotion and continuously repeats the following Mantra:

35. Om! Salutation to the Lord, the Great Being, who is understood through Mantras, whose form consists in Yajnas and Kratus, whose limbs are the great Adhvaras (sacrifices), who effects purification through rituals, and who is manifest in the three Yugas! **36.** Thy form, figuratively conceived in rituals and their fruits, is brought out by intelligent philosophers and devotees by applying their minds to Thy truth hidden in the body-mind phenomenon, just as ritualists churn out the fire latent in the firesticks by striking one stick against another. Salutations to Thee who thus manifestest Thyself to the aspirants! **37.** The truth of Thy being is at first indicated by, and next investigated through, the manifestation of Thy Power (Maya) as the various aspects of Nature like sense objects, senses and the rest. But this power-manifestation of Thine is rejected and Thy transcendent being intuited by sages whose intelligence has become restrained and concentrated through the practice of self-control and discrimination. Salutation to Thee! **38.** Though Thyself devoid of any desire, Thou out of Thy mercy for the Jivas, assumest the desire to create, without any involvement, and as in the presence of a magnet a piece of iron becomes activised and performs various movements, even so in Thy presence, Maya, Thy power of manifestation, functions, creating, preserving and dissolving the universe. Salutations to Thee the uninvolved witness of the cosmic process!

प्रमथ्य दैत्यं प्रतिवारणं मृधे यो मां रसाया जगदादिसूकरः ।
कृत्वाग्रदंष्ट्रे निरगादुदन्वतः क्रीडन्निवेभः प्रणतास्मि तं विभुमिति ॥39॥

इति श्रीमद्भागवते महापुराणे पारमहंस्यां संहितायां पञ्चमस्कन्धे भुवनकोशवर्णनं नामाष्टादशोऽध्यायः ॥18॥

39. Having destroyed Thy enemy, the elephant-like Asura (Hiranyāksha) in battle, and lifting me upon Thy tusk, Thou in Thy manifestation as the Cosmic Boar, didst come out of the waters like a sporting elephant. My salutations to Thee, the all-pervading Being and the Lord of all!

अथैकोनविंशोऽध्यायः

श्रीशुक उवाच

किंपुरुषे वर्षे भगवन्तमादिपुरुषं लक्ष्मणाग्रजं सीताभिरामं रामं तच्चरणसन्निकर्षाभिरतः परमभागवतो हनुमान् सह किम्पुरुषैरविरतभक्तिरुपास्ते ॥1॥ आर्ष्टिषेणेन सह गन्धर्वैरनुगीयमानां परमकल्याणीं भर्तृभगवत्कथां समुपशृणोति स्वयं चेदं गायति ॥2॥ ॐ नमो भगवते उत्तमश्लोकाय नम आर्यलक्षणशीलव्रताय नम उपशिक्षितात्मन उपासितलोकाय नमः साधुवादनिकषणाय नमो ब्रह्मण्यदेवाय महापुरुषाय महाराजाय नम इति ॥3॥

यत्तद्विशुद्धानुभवमात्रमेकं स्वतेजसा ध्वस्तगुणव्यवस्थम् ।
प्रत्यक् प्रशान्तं सुधियोपलम्भनं ह्यनामरूपं निरहं प्रपद्ये ॥ 4॥
मर्त्यावतारस्त्विह मर्त्यशिक्षणं रक्षोवधायैव न केवलं विभोः ।
कुतोऽन्यथा स्याद्रमतः स्व आत्मनः सीताकृतानि व्यसनानीश्वरस्य ॥ 5॥

Skandha V : Chapter 19

WORSHIP IN KIMPURUSHA AND BHĀRATAVARSHAS

Worship in Kimpurushavarsha (1-8)

Sri Suka said: **1.** In Kimpurushavarsha the worshipful Lord, the Primeval Person, is unceasingly adored as Sri Ramachandra, the brother of Lakshmana and the husband of Sita, by His great devotee and servant, Hanuman, along with all the devotees of that Varsha. **2.** Listening to the musical and sweet rendering of his Master's story by the Gandharvas headed by sage Arshtishena, he hymns as follows:

3. Om! Salutations to Thee, the possessor of all divine majesties and of taintless fame! Salutations to Thee, the possessor of supreme nobility of form and character! Salutations to Thee of absolute self-control but following the way of a human being so as to set an example to the world! Salutations to Thee who art the touchstone for testing nobility and greatness everywhere! Salutations to Thee, the lover of all holy men! Salutations to Thee, the great one possessing royal majesty! **4.** I take shelter in Him who is pure awareness, who is the one without a second, who transcends matter and its modifications by His spiritual glory, who is all-pervading, who is all-peace, who is without the limitations of name, form, or individuality, and who is intuited by the purified mind. **5.** Thy incarnation as a

न वै स आत्माऽऽत्मवतां सुहृत्तमः सक्तस्त्रिलोक्यां भगवान् वासुदेवः ।
न स्त्रीकृतं कश्मलमश्नुवीत न लक्ष्मणं चापि विहातुमर्हति ॥ 6॥
न जन्म नूनं महतो न सौभगं न वाङ् न बुद्धिर्नाकृतिस्तोषहेतुः ।
तैर्यद्विसृष्टानपि नो वनौकसश्चकार सख्ये बत लक्ष्मणाग्रजः ॥ 7॥
सुरोऽसुरो वाप्यथ वानरो नरः सर्वात्मना यः सुकृतज्ञमुत्तमम् ।
भजेत रामं मनुजाकृतिं हरिं य उत्तराननयत्कोसलान्दिवमिति ॥ 8॥

भारतेऽपि वर्षे भगवान् नरनारायणाख्य आकल्पान्तमुपचितधर्मज्ञानवैराग्यैश्वर्योपशमोपरमात्मोप-
लम्भनमनुग्रहायात्मवतामनुकम्पया तपोऽव्यक्तगतिश्चरति ॥9॥ तं भगवान् नारदो वर्णाश्रमवतीभि-
र्भारतीभिः प्रजाभिर्भगवत्प्रोक्ताभ्यां सांख्ययोगाभ्यां भगवदनुभावोपवर्णनं सावर्णेरुपदेक्ष्यमाणः
परमभक्तिभावेनोपसरति इदं चाभिगृणाति ॥10॥ ॐ नमो भगवते उपशमशीलायोपरतानात्म्याय
नमोऽकिञ्चनवित्ताय ऋषिऋषभाय नरनारायणाय परमहंसपरमगुरवे आत्मारामाधिपतये नमो नम
इति ॥11॥

human being is for teaching men and not merely for the destruction of Rakshasas. Otherwise how can the sorrow of separation from Sita affect Thee, who art ever absorbed in Thy inherent bliss? **6.** Thou, Vāsudeva, who art the Lord of all and the soul and the dear one of self-controlled ones, has no attachment to anything in the universe. How then could Thou be moved by infatuation for Sita and how could Thou think of abandoning Lakshmana? (It was only just for teaching that too much of personal love and too much of adherence to the letter of the law are self-defeating in their effect.) **7.** Neither nobility nor birth, nor great beauty of form, nor proficiency in speech, nor intelligence can make any one dear to Thee. Otherwise how couldst Thou have united Thyself in friendship with us, mere inhabitants of the forests devoid of all those qualifications? **8.** Let one be a Sura (Deva) or an Asura (demon), a Vanara (monkey) or a Nara (man). What matters is that he should with his whole heart worship Rama, who is none but Hari embodied as man, who is pleased with the least good performed, and who gave salvation to all the inhabitants of Kosala.

Worship in Bhāratavarsha
(9-15)

9. In the Bhāratavarsha, the Lord, assuming simultaneously the twin form of the worshipful Nara-Narayana, moves about unknown to any one. For the blessing of pious men out of mercy, he will live till the end of the Kalpa revealing the true nature of the Atman through a life of austerity characterised by the highest morality, enlightenment, renunciation, power, self-control and freedom from egoism. **10.** There along with the pious inhabitants of Bhārata, who follow the Varnasrama social system, the worshipful Narada, who had resolved to instruct Manu Sāvarni in the doctrines of the Pāncharātra as also in Sastras like Samkhya and Yoga revealed by the Lord, worships Him devoutly and repeats the following Mantra:

11. Om! Salutations again and again to the Lord Nara-Narayana, the peaceful, the egoless, the wealth of the possessionless, the noblest among Rishis, the teacher of the Paramahamsas, the best among the self-absorbed ones! *He also sings:* **12**. Though Thou art the creator of the worlds, Thou art not bound by Thy

गायति चेदम् –

कर्तास्य सर्गादिषु यो न बध्यते न हन्यते देहगतोऽपि दैहिकैः ।
द्रष्टुर्न दृग्यस्य गुणैर्विदूष्यते तस्मै नमोऽसक्तविविक्तसाक्षिणे ॥12॥
इदं हि योगेश्वर योगनैपुणं हिरण्यगर्भो भगवान् जगाद यत् ।
यदन्तकाले त्वयि निर्गुणे मनो भक्त्या दधीतोज्झितदुष्कलेवरः ॥13॥
यथैहिकामुष्मिककामलम्पटः सुतेषु दारेषु धनेषु चिन्तयन् ।
शङ्केत विद्वान् कुकलेवरात्ययाद्यस्तस्य यत्नः श्रम एव केवलम् ॥14॥
तन्नः प्रभो त्वं कुकलेवरार्पितां त्वन्माययाहंममतामधोक्षज ।
भिन्द्याम येनाशु वयं सुदुर्भिदां विधेहि योगं त्वयि नः स्वभावमिति ॥15॥

भारतेऽप्यस्मिन् वर्षे सरिच्छैलाः सन्ति बहवो मलयो मङ्गलप्रस्थो मैनाकस्त्रिकूट ऋषभः कुटकः कोल्लकः सह्यो देवगिरिर्ऋष्यमूकः श्रीशैलो वेङ्कटो महेन्द्रो वारिधारो विन्ध्यः शुक्तिमानृक्षगिरिः पारियात्रो द्रोणश्चित्रकूटो गोवर्धनो रैवतकः ककुभो नीलो गोकामुख इन्द्रकीलः कामगिरिरिति चान्ये च शतसहस्रशः शैलास्तेषां नितम्बप्रभवा नदा नद्यश्च सन्त्यसंख्याताः ॥16॥ एतासामपो भारत्यः प्रजा नामभिरेव पुनन्तीनामात्मना चोपस्पृशन्ति ॥17॥ चन्द्रवसा ताम्रपर्णी अवटोदा कृतमाला वैहायसी कावेरी वेणी पयस्विनी शर्करावर्ता तुङ्गभद्रा कृष्णा वेण्या भीमरथी गोदावरी

creative activity. Though residing in a body, Thy spiritual splendour is not in the least suppressed by bodily infirmities. Though the witness of everything, the world of objects consisting in the effects of Prakriti do not affect Thee. Salutations to the unattached, to the uninvolved, to the witness! **13.** O Lord of Yogins! The skill in Yoga described by Brahma consists in the capacity to abandon at the time of death all attachments to the perishable body and concentrate the mind on Thee, who art above the modifications of Prakriti (Nirguna). **14.** If a learned man, too, is afraid of giving up this miserable body, just like worldly men with countless desires and attachments for wife, children and wealth, then all his efforts at gaining knowledge can only be called a thankless task, an exercise in futility. **15.** Therefore, O Lord, bestow on us that form of loving devotion exclusively directed towards Thee, by virtue of which we can cut asunder this intense and irremediable attachment to this debased thing of a body, generated by Thy Maya through a sense of identification with it.

Physical Features of Bhārata (16-18)

16. In Bhāratavarsha there are numerous mountains and rivers. A list of them is as follows: Malaya, Mangalaprastha, Maināka, Trikūta, Rishabha, Kutaka, Kollaka, Sahya, Devagiri, Rishyamūka. Srisaila, Venkata, Mahendra, Vāridhāra, Vindhya, Suktimān, Rikshagiri, Pāriyātra, Drona, Chitrakūta, Govardhana, Raivataka, Kukubha, Nīla, Gokāmukha, Indrakīla, Kāmagiri etc. Besides these, there are numerous other mountains, and there are several rivers too having their source in these mountains. **17.** The people of Bhārata take their bath in these rivers which are so holy that even their names are capable of purifying a person.

18. The names of the great rivers of Bhārata are as follows: Chandravasā, Tāmraparni, Avatoda, Kritamāla, Vaihāyasi, Kāveri, Veni, Payasvini, Sarkarāvarta, Tungabhadra, Krishna, Venyā, Bhīmarathi, Godāvari, Nirvindhya, Payoshni,

निर्विन्ध्या पयोष्णी तापी रेवा सुरसा नर्मदा चर्मण्वती सिन्धुरन्धः शोणश्च नदौ महानदी वेदस्मृति-र्ऋषिकुल्या त्रिसामा कौशिकी मन्दाकिनी यमुना सरस्वती दृषद्वती गोमती सरयू रोधस्वती सप्तवती सुषोमा शतद्रूश्चन्द्रभागा मरुद्वृधा वितस्ता असिक्नी विश्वेति महानद्यः ॥18॥ अस्मिन्नेव वर्षे पुरुषैर्लब्धजन्मभिः शुक्ललोहितकृष्णवर्णेन स्वारब्धेन कर्मणा दिव्यमानुषनारकगतयो बह्व्य आत्मन आनुपूर्व्येण सर्वा ह्येव सर्वेषां विधीयन्ते यथावर्णविधानमपवर्गश्चापि भवति ॥19॥ योऽसौ भगवति सर्वभूतात्मन्यनात्म्येऽनिरुक्तेऽनिलयने परमात्मनि वासुदेवेऽनन्यनिमित्तभक्तियोगलक्षणो नानागतिनिमित्ताविद्याग्रन्थिरन्धनद्वारेण यदा हि महापुरुषपुरुषप्रसङ्गः ॥20॥

एतदेव हि देवा गायन्ति—

अहो अमीषां किमकारि शोभनं प्रसन्न एषां स्विदुत स्वयं हरिः ।
यैर्जन्म लब्धं नृषु भारताजिरे मुकुन्दसेवौपयिकं स्पृहा हि नः ॥21॥
किं दुष्करैर्नः क्रतुभिस्तपोव्रतैर्दानादिभिर्वा द्युजयेन फल्गुना ।
न यत्र नारायणपादपङ्कजस्मृतिः प्रमुष्टातिशयेन्द्रियोत्सवात् ॥22॥
कल्पायुषां स्थानजयात्पुनर्भवात् क्षणायुषां भारतभूजयो वरम् ।
क्षणेन मर्त्येन कृतं मनस्विनः संन्यस्य संयान्त्यभयं पदं हरेः ॥23॥

Tāpi, Reva, Surasa, Narmada, Charmanvati, Sindhu, Andham, Sonam, Mahānadi, Vedasmriti, Rishikulya, Trisāma, Kausiki, Mandākini, Yamuna, Saraswati, Drishadvati, Gomati, Sarayu, Rodhaswati, Saptavati, Sushoma, Satadru, Chandrabhāga, Marudvridha, Vitasta, Asikni and Visva.

Glory of Bhāratavarsha (19-31)

19. For men born in this Bhāratavarsha, there are three prospects open—the world of the Devas, the world of men, and the region of purgatory—according as their works are dictated by the qualities of Sattva, Rajas or Tamas. Following the disciplines of Varnasrama, all progress from stage to stage and attain Mukti. **20.** When close association with holy men is established, then, through the severing of the constricting knot of ignorance, there arises in the heart of man spiritual freedom consisting in the desire-free and single-minded devotion to the Supreme Being who is the Soul of all souls, who is free from all passions, who is beyond the power of words to describe, who is His own support as also the support of all beings and who is the transcendent Spirit.

21. So the Devas sing as follows about the greatness of birth in Bhāratavarsha: Is it because the auspicious acts done by them are of such transcendent merit, or is it because Sri Hari has bestowed on them His unconditioned grace, that these Jivas have obtained a birth in Bhāratavarsha, where conditions are propitious for the practice of devotion to Sri Hari? Would that we too obtain such birth in Bhārata! **22.** Of what use are the hard and difficult observances like Yajnas, austerities, vows and charitable works by virtue of which we have attained to these ephemeral heavenly regions? For, the minds of beings in these regions are without the capacity to entertain devotional sentiments towards Narayana, and even in those who have something of it, such devotional tendencies are quickly effaced by the preponderance of sensuous enjoyments here. **23.** Far more covetable is birth in Bhārata, in spite of the life-span there being short, than embodiment in those heavenly re-

न यत्र वैकुण्ठकथासुधापगा न साधवो भागवतास्तदाश्रयाः ।
न यत्र यज्ञेशमखा महोत्सवाः सुरेशलोकोऽपि न वै स सेव्यताम् ॥24॥
प्राप्ता नृजातिं त्विह ये च जन्तवो ज्ञानक्रियाद्रव्यकलापसम्भृताम् ।
न वै यतेरन्नपुनर्भवाय ते भूयो वनौका इव यान्ति बन्धनम् ॥25॥
यैः श्रद्धया बर्हिषि भागशो हविर्निरुप्तमिष्टं विधिमन्त्रवस्तुतः ।
एकः पृथङ्नामभिराहुतो मुदा गृह्णाति पूर्णः स्वयमाशिषां प्रभुः ॥26॥
सत्यं दिशत्यर्थितमर्थितो नृणां नैवार्थदो यत्पुनरर्थिता यतः ।
स्वयं विधत्ते भजतामनिच्छतामिच्छापिधानं निजपादपल्लवम् ॥27॥
यद्यत्र नः स्वर्गसुखावशेषितं स्विष्टस्य सूक्तस्य कृतस्य शोभनम् ।
तेनाजनाभे स्मृतिमज्जन्म नः स्याद् वर्षे हरिर्यद्भजतां शं तनोति ॥28॥

श्रीशुक उवाच

जम्बूद्वीपस्य च राजन्नुपद्वीपानष्टौ हैक उपदिशन्ति सगरात्मजैरश्वान्वेषण इमां महीं परितो निखनद्भिरुपकल्पितान् ॥29॥ तद्यथा स्वर्णप्रस्थश्चन्द्रशुक्ल आवर्तनो रमणको मन्दरहरिणः

gions where life extends to eons. For, striving with a human body, wise men overcome and abandon the bondage of Karma easily and attain to the eternal state of Hari. **24.** Where flows not the continuous narration of divine excellences, where exist not holy men devoted wholeheartedly to the Lord, where prevails not the practice of divine worship attended with grand celebrations—avoid such places, even if they be the heaven of Indra. **25.** Even after obtaining embodiment in the human body, which offers all the necessary facilities for the attainment of enlightenment and devotion, if a man fails to strive for spiritual freedom, he is like a bird which remains entrapped even when the way of escape is open to it. **26.** There devout men of Bhārata engaged in scripture-ordained rites make offerings in the sacrificial fire, observing the ritualistic rules and uttering the proper Mantras in invocation of various deities. Though called under different names all these deities are none but Thyself, and so it is Thyself alone, the perfect one and the bestower of the rewards of all worship, that accepts all these offerings. **27.** To such devotees praying to Thee for worldly fulfilments, their prayers are indeed granted by Thee. But such gifts do not represent Thy real blessing. For, not satisfied with what has been got, more prayers for further fulfilments continue from these recipients afterwards. But on those who seek no boon of any kind, Thou, of Thy own accord, bestowest a place at Thy feet which have the power to give them that ultimate fulfilment which eradicates all desires from their hearts. **28.** If any more meritorious deeds remain in store for us after these enjoyments in heaven, may we, by virtue of these, be born in the blessed Ajanābhavarsha (an earlier name of Bhāratavarsha) with our minds devoted to Thee. For, on those who practise devotion in this region, Thou dost bestow Thy grace.

Sri Suka said: **29.** O King! Some say that there are eight minor islands in Jambudweepa. These came into existence when the sons of Sagara dug the earth while going about in search of the horse in connection with their father's sacrifice. **30.** These are Svarnaprastha, Chandrasukla, Āvartana, Ramanaka, Mandara-

पाञ्चजन्यः सिंहलो लङ्केति ॥30॥ एवं तव भारतोत्तम जम्बूद्वीपवर्षविभागो यथोपदेशमुपवर्णित इति ॥31॥

इति श्रीमद्भागवते महापुराणे पारमहंस्यां संहितायां पञ्चमस्कन्धे जम्बूद्वीपवर्णनं नामैकोनविंशोऽध्यायः ॥19॥

harina, Pānchajanya, Simhala and Lanka. **31.** O Thou the best of the clan of Bhāratas! I have given you an account of Jambudweepa and its divisions according to the instruction I have received.

अथ विंशोऽध्यायः

श्रीशुक उवाच

अतः परं प्लक्षादीनां प्रमाणलक्षणसंस्थानतो वर्षविभाग उपवर्ण्यते ॥1॥ जम्बूद्वीपोऽयं यावत्प्रमाणविस्तारस्तावता क्षारोदधिना परिवेष्टितो यथा मेरुर्जम्ब्वाख्येन लवणोदधिरपि ततो द्विगुणविशालेन प्लक्षाख्येन परिक्षिप्तो यथा परिखा बाह्योपवनेन । प्लक्षो जम्बूप्रमाणो द्वीपाख्याकरो हिरण्मय उत्थितो यत्राग्निरुपास्ते सप्तजिह्वस्तस्याधिपतिः प्रियव्रतात्मज इध्मजिह्वः स्वं द्वीपं सप्तवर्षाणि विभज्य सप्तवर्षनामभ्य आत्मजेभ्य आकलय्य स्वयमात्मयोगेनोपरराम ॥2॥ शिवं यवसं सुभद्रं शान्तं क्षेमममृतमभयमिति वर्षाणि तेषु गिरयो नद्यश्च सप्तैवाभिज्ञाताः ॥3॥ मणिकूटो वज्रकूट इन्द्रसेनो ज्योतिष्मान् सुपर्णो हिरण्यष्ठीवो मेघमाल इति सेतुशैलाः । अरुणा नृम्णाऽऽङ्गिरसी सावित्री सुप्रभाता ऋतम्भरा इति महानद्यः । यासां जलोपस्पर्शनविधूतरजस्तमसो हंसपतङ्गोर्ध्वायनसत्याङ्गसंज्ञाश्चत्वारो वर्णाः सहस्रायुषो विबुधोपमसन्दर्शनप्रजननाः स्वर्गद्वारं त्रय्या विद्यया भगवन्तं त्रयीमयं सूर्यमात्मानं यजन्ते ॥4॥

Skandha V : Chapter 20

THE SIX DWEEPAS AND THE LOKĀLOKA

Plaksha and its Features (1-6)

Sri Suka said: **1.** Now will be described the other six Dweepas (continents or islands) beginning with Plaksha, with details about their division, area, characteristics and positions. **2.** Just as Mahameru is surrounded by Jambudweepa, so is Jambudweepa surrounded by the salt water ocean equal in area to the Dweepa itself. Plakshadweepa, double in extent, encircles this salt ocean, just as a belt of woodland surrounds a moat. There stands on it a Plaksha tree, a lakh of Yojanas in extent and golden in colour, giving its name to the Dweepa just as Jambudweepa got its name from the Jambu tree on it. The Lord in the form of a Fire with seven tongues (flames) is present there. Idhmajihva, the son of Priyavrata, was once its king. He divided it into seven Varshas (regions), allotting these to his seven sons who had names identical with these Varshas. He eventually took to a contemplative life for the attainment of Moksha. **3.** Siva, Yavasa, Subhadra, Sānta, Kshema, Amrita, Abhaya—these are the seven Varshas. On them there are seven well-known mountains and rivers. **4.** The names of the mountains are: Manikūta, Vajrakūta, Indrasena, Jyotishmān, Suparna, Hiranyashtīva and Meghamāla.

The rivers are: Aruna, Nrimna,

प्रत्नस्य विष्णो रूपं यत्सत्यस्यर्तस्य ब्रह्मणः । अमृतस्य च मृत्योश्च सूर्यमात्मानमीमहीति ॥ 5॥

प्लक्षादिषु पञ्चसु पुरुषाणामायुरिन्द्रियमोजः सहो बलं बुद्धिर्विक्रम इति च सर्वेषामौत्पत्तिकी सिद्धिरविशेषेण वर्तते ॥6॥

प्लक्षः स्वसमानेनेक्षुरसोदेनावृतो यथा तथा द्वीपोऽपि शाल्मलो द्विगुणविशालः समानेन सुरोदेनावृतः परिवृङ्क्ते ॥7॥ यत्र ह वै शाल्मली प्लक्षायामा यस्यां वाव किल निलयमाहुर्भगवतश्छन्दःस्तुतः पतत्त्रिराजस्य सा द्वीपहूतये उपलक्ष्यते ॥8॥ तद्द्वीपाधिपतिः प्रियव्रतात्मजो यज्ञबाहुः स्वसुतेभ्यः सप्तभ्यस्तन्नामानि सप्तवर्षाणि व्यभजत्सुरोचनं सौमनस्यं रमणकं देववर्षं पारिभद्रमाप्यायनमविज्ञातमिति ॥9॥ तेषु वर्षाद्रयो नद्यश्च सप्तैवाभिज्ञाताः स्वरसः शतशृङ्गो वामदेवः कुन्दो मुकुन्दः पुष्पवर्षः सहस्रश्रुतिरिति । अनुमतिः सिनीवाली सरस्वती कुहू रजनी नन्दा राकेति ॥10॥ तद्वर्षपुरुषाः श्रुतधरवीर्यधरवसुन्धरेषन्धरसंज्ञा भगवन्तं वेदमयं सोममात्मानं वेदेन यजन्ते ॥11॥ स्वगोभिः पितृदेवेभ्यो विभजन् कृष्णशुक्लयोः । प्रजानां सर्वासां राजान्धः सोमो न आस्त्विति 12॥

Āngirasi, Sāvitri, Suprabhāta, Ritambhara and Satyambhara. Purified from the influence of Rajas and Tamas by drinking the water of these rivers, the people of those Varshas divided into four communities—Hamsa, Patanga, Ūrdhvāyana and Satyānga—live for a life-span of a thousand years. They are like the Devas in being devoid of perspiration and in their way of procreation. They worship the Lord as Surya-Narayana, the saviour and embodiment of the Vedas, with Vedic Mantras. **5.** 'I salute Surya-Narayana, the manifestation of the eternal being Mahavishnu, the basis of all Dharma in its practical and theoretical aspect, as also of immortality and destruction.' **6.** In all the five Dweepas beginning with Plaksha people are naturally alike in the endowment of longevity, sense-power, mental strength, physical power, intelligence, courage etc.

Sālmala and its Features (7-12)

7. Plakshadweepa is encircled by the sea of sugarcane juice of the same width as that Dweepa itself. Beyond that sea and double its width lies the encircling Sālmaladweepa, which in turn is encircled by the sea of liquor equal to it in width. **8.** It is called Sālmaladweepa, because on it stands the tree called Sālmala (silk cotton), equal in size to the Plaksha tree in the Plakshadweepa. Great men say that seated on this tree Garuda is singing the glory of Mahavishnu through the Vedic chant. **9.** The king of this Dweepa is Priyavrata's son, Yajnabāhu. He divided this land into seven Varshas (regions) among his seven sons. The names of these Varshas, which are identical with those of their rulers, are as follows: Surochana, Soumanasya, Ramanaka, Devavarsha, Pāribhadra, Āpyāyana and Avijnāta. **10.** The important mountains in these regions are called Svarasa, Satasringa, Vāmadeva, Kunda, Mukunda, Pushpavarsha and Sahasrasruti, and the names of the rivers are Anumati, Sinīvāli, Saraswati, Kuhu, Rajani, Nanda and Rāka. **11.** Their four types of inhabitants known as Srutadhara, Vīryadhara, Vasundhara and Īshandhara, perform sacrifices to the Supreme Being, who has taken the form of the Veda and the Soma. **12.** They pray: 'Soma bestows by his rays food on Pitris during the dark fortnight and on the Devas in the bright fortnight. May that Soma, the Raja, be propitious to us his subjects!

एवं सुरोदाद्बहिस्तद्द्विगुणः समानेनावृतो घृतोदेन यथापूर्वः कुशद्वीपो यस्मिन् कुशस्तम्बो
देवकृतस्तद्द्वीपाख्याकरो ज्वलन इवापरः स्वशष्परोचिषा दिशो विराजयति ॥13॥ तद्द्वीपपतिः
प्रैयव्रतो राजन् हिरण्यरेतो नाम स्वं द्वीपं सप्तभ्यः स्वपुत्रेभ्यो यथाभागं विभज्य स्वयं तप आतिष्ठत
वसुवसुदानदृढरुचिनाभिगुप्तस्तुत्यव्रतविविक्तवामदेवनामभ्यः ॥14॥ तेषां वर्षेषु सीमागिरयो नद्यश्चा-
भिज्ञाताः सप्त सप्तैव चक्रश्चतुःशृङ्गः कपिलश्चित्रकूटो देवानीक ऊर्ध्वरोमा द्रविण इति रसकुल्या
मधुकुल्या मित्रविन्दा श्रुतविन्दा देवगर्भा घृतच्युता मन्त्रमालेति ॥15॥ यासां पयोभिः कुशद्वीपौकसः
कुशलकोविदाभियुक्तकुलकसंज्ञा भगवन्तं जातवेदसरूपिणं कर्मकौशलेन यजन्ते ॥16॥
परस्य ब्रह्मणः साक्षाज्जातवेदोऽसि हव्यवाट्। देवानां पुरुषाङ्गानां यज्ञेन पुरुषं यजेति ॥17॥

तथा घृतोदाद्बहिः क्रौञ्चद्वीपो द्विगुणः स्वमानेन क्षीरोदेन परित उपक्लृप्तो वृतो यथा
कुशद्वीपो घृतोदेन यस्मिन् क्रौञ्चो नाम पर्वतराजो द्वीपनामनिर्वर्तक आस्ते ॥18॥ योऽसौ गुहप्रहरणो-
न्मथितनितम्बकुञ्जोऽपि क्षीरोदेनासिच्यमानो भगवता वरुणेनाभिगुप्तो विभयो बभूव ॥19॥
तस्मिन्नपि प्रैयव्रतो घृतपृष्ठो नामाधिपतिः स्वे द्वीपे वर्षाणि सप्त विभज्य तेषु पुत्रनामसु सप्त

Kusadweepa and its Features (13-17)

13. Like the above Dweepas, the Kusadweepa extends beyond the liquor ocean, encircling it and having double its width. It is surrounded by the ocean of ghee equal to itself in dimension. Its name Kusadweepa is derived from a pillar of Kusa grass created by the Lord Himself, which emits heatless but brilliant rays as of fire, and illumines the quarters. **14.** O King! The son of Priyavrata named Hiranyaretas was the king of that Dweepa. He divided it into seven regions which he named after his seven sons and awarded them to those seven sons according to their names, and then departed for spending his time in meditation on the Lord. The names of these are: Vasu, Vasudāna, Dridharuchi, Nābhigupta, Stutyavrata, Vivikta, and Vāmadeva. **15.** In these regions there are seven boundary mountains, Chakra, Chatussringa, Kapila, Chitrakūta, Devanīka, Ūrdhvaroma and Dravina, as also seven important rivers, Rasakulya, Madhukulya, Mitravinda, Srutavinda, Devagarbha, Ghritachyuta and Mantramāla. **16.** There are four classes of inhabitants there—Kusala, Kovida, Abhiyukta, and Kulaka—who, being purified by the waters of the aforesaid rivers, worship the Lord manifest there in the form of fire, with rituals offered therein without egotism or expectation. They pray: **17.** 'O Fire! Thou art the carrier of the offerings to the Supreme Being. By making offerings to the Deities, who are only parts of the Supreme Being, one is making offerings to the whole, i.e. to the Supreme Being Himself.'

Kraunch and its Features (18-23)

18. Beyond the ocean of ghee, is the Kraunchadweepa double its extent and surrounded in turn by an ocean of milk equal to the Dweepa in area, even as the Kusadweepa is encircled by the ocean of ghee. On it stands the king of mountains Krauncha, from which the continent derives its name. **19.** Though its rocky middle region and its arbours had been pounded by the weapon of Guha, it was saved through the protection of Varuna and of the waves of the milk ocean washing its foot.

20. Ghritaprishta, one of the sons of Priyavrata, was the ruler of it. He divided it into seven regions, giving the names of his seven sons to them, and assigned each to the son of that name.

रिक्थादान् वर्षपान्निवेश्य स्वयं भगवान् भगवतः परमकल्याणयशस आत्मभूतस्य हरेश्चरणारविन्द-
मुपजगाम ॥20॥ आमो मधुरुहो मेघपृष्ठः सुधामा भ्राजिष्ठो लोहितार्णो वनस्पतिरिति घृतपृष्ठ-
सुतास्तेषां वर्षगिरयः सप्त सप्तैव नद्यश्चाभिख्याताः शुक्लो वर्धमानो भोजन उपबर्हिणो नन्दो
नन्दनः सर्वतोभद्र इति अभया अमृतौघा आर्यका तीर्थवती वृत्तिरूपवती पवित्रवती शुक्लेति ॥21॥
यासामम्भः पवित्रममलमुपयुञ्जानाः पुरुषऋषभद्रविणदेवकसंज्ञा वर्षपुरुषा आपोमयं देवमपां
पूर्णेनाञ्जलिना यजन्ते ॥22॥

आपः पुरुषवीर्याः स्थ पुनन्तीर्भूर्भुवः सुवः । ता नः पुनीतामीवघ्नीः स्पृशतामात्मना भुव इति ॥23॥

एवं पुरस्तात्क्षीरोदात्परित उपवेशितः शाकद्वीपो द्वात्रिंशल्लक्षयोजनायामः समानेन च
दधिमण्डोदेन परीतो यस्मिन् शाको नाम महीरुहः स्वक्षेत्रव्यपदेशको यस्य ह महासुरभिगन्धस्तं
द्वीपमनुवासयति ॥24॥ तस्यापि प्रैयव्रत एवाधिपतिर्नाम्ना मेधातिथिः सोऽपि विभज्य सप्त वर्षाणि
पुत्रनामानि तेषु स्वात्मजान् पुरोजवमनोजवपवमानधूम्रानीकचित्ररेफबहुरूपविश्वधारसंज्ञान्निधाप्या-
धिपतीन् स्वयं भगवत्यनन्त आवेशितमतिस्तपोवनं प्रविवेश ॥25॥ एतेषां वर्षमर्यादागिरयो नद्यश्च
सप्त सप्तैव ईशान उरुशृङ्गो बलभद्रः शतकेसरः सहस्रस्रोतो देवपालो महानस इति अनघाऽऽयुर्दा
उभयस्पृष्टिरपराजिता पञ्चपदी सहस्रस्रुतिर्निजधृतिरिति ॥26॥ तद्वर्षपुरुषा ऋतव्रतसत्यव्रतदान-

After that, he retired, attained to enlightenment, and sought shelter at the feet of Sri Hari, the auspicious, the soul of all. **21.** The names of those sons of Ghritaprishta and of the regions they rule over are: Āma, Madhuruha, Meghaprishtha, Sudhāma, Bhrājishtha, Lohitārna and Vanaspati. The seven mountains of these regions are: Sukla, Vardhamāna, Bhojana, Upabarhina, Nanda, Nandana and Sarvatobhadra. And the seven rivers are: Abhaya, Amritougha, Āryaka, Tīrthavati, Vrittirūpavati, Pavitravati and Sukla. **22.** Purified by the waters of these rivers, the four kinds of people inhabiting it, known as Purusha, Rishabha, Dravina and Devaka, worship Him as water, with offerings of water filled in their cupped palms. They recite: **23.** 'O pure waters! You have derived power from the Almighty Himself. You purify the three worlds. By nature you possess the power to eradicate the result of sins. May you purify our bodies by your contact!'

Sāka and its Features (24-28)

24. Beyond the milk ocean, surrounding it by a width of thirty two lakhs of Yojanas, is the Sākadweepa, which in turn is surrounded by a sea of curds of equal width. This Dweepa is so called because of a Sāka tree standing on it. The sweet smell it emits makes the whole continent fragrant. **25.** The ruler of it Medhātidhi, a son of Priyavrata, divided it into seven regions, each with the name of each of his sons, and put them as rulers of regions bearing their respective names. He then went as an ascetic to the forest to devote his mind entirely to concentrate on the Supreme Being who is beyond the limitation of time and space. The names of those regions are: Purojava, Manojava, Pavamāna, Dhūmranīka, Chitrarepha, Bahurūpa and Viswadhāra. **26.** The boundary mountains in these regions are seven—these being Īsāna, Urusringa, Balabhadra, Satakesara, Sahasrasrotas, Devapāla and Mahānasa. The seven main rivers of the region are Anagha, Āyurda, Ubhayasprishti, Aparājita, Panchapadi, Sahasrasruti and Nijadhriti. **27.** Ritavrata, Satyavrata, Dānavrata, Anu-

व्रतानुव्रतनामानो भगवन्तं वाय्वात्मकं प्राणायामविधूतरजस्तमसः परमसमाधिना यजन्ते ॥27॥
अन्तः प्रविश्य भूतानि यो बिभर्त्यात्मकेतुभिः । अन्तर्यामीश्वरः साक्षात्पातु नो यद्वशे स्फुटम् 28॥
एवमेव दधिमण्डोदात्परतः पुष्करद्वीपस्ततो द्विगुणायामः समन्तत उपकल्पितः समासेन
स्वादूदकेन समुद्रेण बहिरावृता यस्मिन् बृहत्पुष्करं ज्वलनशिखामलकनकपत्रायुतायुतं भगवतः
कमलासनस्याध्यासनं परिकल्पितम् ॥29॥ तद्द्वीपमध्ये मानसोत्तरनामैक एवार्वाचीनपराचीनवर्षयो-
र्मर्यादाचलोऽयुतयोजनोच्छ्रायायामो यत्र तु चतसृषु दिक्षु चत्वारि पुराणि लोकपालानामिन्द्रादीनां
यदुपरिष्टात्सूर्यरथस्य मेरुं परिभ्रमतः संवत्सरात्मकं चक्रं देवानामहोरात्राभ्यां परिभ्रमति ॥30॥
तद्द्वीपस्याप्यधिपतिः प्रैयव्रतो वीतिहोत्रो नामैतस्यात्मजौ रमणकधातकिनामानौ वर्षपती नियुज्य
स स्वयं पूर्वजवद्भगवत्कर्मशील एवास्ते ॥31॥ तद्वर्षपुरुषा भगवन्तं ब्रह्मरूपिणं सकर्मकेण कर्मणा-
ऽऽराधयन्तीदं चोदाहरन्ति ॥32॥
यत्तत्कर्ममयं लिङ्गं ब्रह्मलिङ्गं जनोऽर्चयेत् । एकान्तमद्वयं शान्तं तस्मै भगवते नम इति 33॥

vrata—these are the four types of people inhabiting it. They destroy the element of Rajas and Tamas in themselves through Pranayama. Thus purified, they meditate on the Supreme Being as Vayu (air) and adore Him through Samadhi. **28.** They pray: 'He who, having entered into the innermost core of all beings, sustains them with Prana, a symbol indicating His existence behind it—may that inner pervader and the unquestioned Lord of all protect us. It is indeed clear that the world functions under the control of His manifestation as Prana.'

Pushkara and its Features (29-33)

29. Beyond the curd ocean, is the Pushkaradweepa, in extent double that of the curd ocean. It is surrounded by an ocean of pure water equal to the Dweepa in dimension. There is in it a lotus flower (Pushkara) with innumerable thousands of petals shining like flames. This lotus has been assigned as the seat of Brahma (who is worshipped by the inhabitants of the Dweepa). **30.** In the middle of that Dweepa there is only one mountain named Mānasottara, which marks the boundary of the only two Varshas into which this Dweepa is divided. This mountain is ten thousand Yojanas in height and in length. On its four sides the cities of the four protecting deities of the four quarters including Indra are situated. Along the top of that mountain, the sun traverses his course around the Mahameru in his chariot, whose one rotation around Mahameru constitutes one year, consisting of Uttarayana and Dakshinayana, the day and the night of the Devas. **31.** Its ruler Vītihotra, also a son of Priyavrata, divided the Dweepa into two Varshas for his two sons, Ramanaka and Dhātaki, and retired to engage himself in devotional practices following the footsteps of his precursors. **32.** The people there worship the Supreme Being as Brahma with rites conducive to the attainment of Brahmaloka. They repeat the following Mantra: **33.** 'Salutations to Thee, O Brahma, the object of people's worship, who represents the highest goal that Karma can take one to; who is the manifestation of Brahman, the Supreme Being, and a symbol indicative of Him; who is one with the Supreme Being though he has assumed separation for the purpose of creation; and who is all peace.

Lokāloka Mountain (34-46)

ऋषिरुवाच

ततः परस्ताल्लोकालोकनामाचलो लोकालोकयोरन्तराले परित उपक्षिप्तः ॥34॥ यावन्मानसोत्तरमेर्वोरन्तरं तावती भूमिः काञ्चन्यन्याऽऽदर्शतलोपमा यस्यां प्रहितः पदार्थो न कथञ्चित्पुनः प्रत्युपलभ्यते तस्मात्सर्वसत्त्वपरिहृताऽऽसीत् ॥35॥ लोकालोक इति समाख्या यदनेनाचलेन लोकालोकस्यान्तर्वर्तिनावस्थाप्यते ॥36॥ स लोकत्रयान्ते परित ईश्वरेण विहितो यस्मात्सूर्यादीनां ध्रुवापवर्गाणां ज्योतिर्गणानां गभस्तयोऽर्वाचीनांस्त्रींल्लोकानावितन्वाना न कदाचित्पराचीना भवितुमुत्सहन्ते तावदुन्नहनायामः ॥37॥

एतावांल्लोकविन्यासो मानलक्षणसंस्थाभिर्विचिन्तितः कविभिः स तु पञ्चाशात्कोटिगणितस्य भूगोलस्य तुरीयभागोऽयं लोकालोकाचलः ॥38॥ तदुपरिष्टाच्चतसृष्वाशास्वात्मयोनिनाखिलजगद्गुरुणाधिनिवेशिता ये द्विरदपतय ऋषभः पुष्करचूडो वामनोऽपराजित इति सकललोकस्थितिहेतवः ॥39॥ तेषां स्वविभूतीनां लोकपालानां च विविधवीर्योपबृंहणाय भगवान् परममहापुरुषो महाविभूतिपतिरन्तर्याम्यात्मनो विशुद्धसत्त्वं धर्मज्ञानवैराग्यैश्वर्याद्यष्टमहासिद्ध्युपलक्षणं विष्वक्सेनादिभिः स्वपार्षदप्रवरैः परिवारितो निजवरायुधोपशोभितैर्निजभुजदण्डैः संधारयमाणस्तस्मिन् गिरिवरे समन्तात्सकललोकस्वस्तय आस्ते ॥40॥ आकल्पमेवं वेषं गत एष भगवानात्मयोगमायया

Sri Suka said: **34.** Beyond that ocean of fresh water is the famous mountain Lokāloka, which stands as an encircling wall between the regions having sunlight and those without it. **35.** There is between Lokāloka and the fresh water sea a land equal in extent to the distance between the Mānasottara mountain (forming the outer ring of the Dweepas) and the Meru (the centre). Beyond that is another region, golden and shining like a mirror. Nothing put in it can return, as it will get dissolved. So it is without any living being. **36.** As the mountain stands between Loka (seen worlds) and Aloka (worlds that cannot be seen), it gained the name of Lokāloka. **37.** This Lokāloka is the boundary mountain placed by the Creator beyond and around as the limit of the three worlds. These three worlds are lighted by the sun's rays. Neither the light of the sun nor that of any luminary up to Dhruva (the pole star) can go beyond the top of this mountain. It is so high and extensive. **38.** This much is the conclusion of wise men about the earth—its disposition, size, characteristics, position etc. Fifty crores of Yojana is the extent of the earth. The Lokāloka mountain is a fourth of it, i.e twelve and a half crores of Yojanas. **39.** The Self-born one, the Lord and master of all, has for the stability of the universe placed on the four sides of the Lokāloka mountain four elephants known as the Elephants of the Quarters. They are Rishabha, Pushkarachūda, Vāmana and Aparājita. **40.** For encouraging and imparting power to these, and to the guardian lords of the worlds (Lokapalas), who are His glories, the Supreme Lord—the indweller of all and the source and spring of all majesties and powers—reveals all over that mountain His one divine form of Suddhasattva, endowed with excellences like virtue, knowledge, dispassion, lordliness, the eight-fold powers etc., as also with many arms holding conch, discus, etc. and surrounded by his followers like Vishvaksena. **41.** It is only by way of sport, for the protection of the worlds and the Jivas inhabiting them, that He has assumed this form with the mysterious power of His Yogamaya. **42.** In giving the measurement of the Loka or the

विरचितविविधलोकयात्रागोपीथायेत्यर्थः ॥41॥ योऽन्तर्विस्तार एतेन ह्यलोकपरिमाणं च व्याख्यातं यद्बहिर्लोकालोकाचलात् । ततः परस्ताद्योगेश्वरगतिं विशुद्धामुदाहरन्ति ॥42॥

अण्डमध्यगतः सूर्यो द्यावाभूम्योर्यदन्तरम् । सूर्याण्डगोलयोर्मध्ये कोटयः स्युः पञ्चविंशतिः ॥

मृतेऽण्ड एष एतस्मिन् यदभूत्ततो मार्तण्ड इति व्यपदेशः ।

हिरण्यगर्भ इति यद्धिरण्याण्डसमुद्भवः ॥44॥

सूर्येण हि विभज्यन्ते दिशः खं द्यौर्मही भिदा । स्वर्गापवर्गौ नरका रसौकांसि च सर्वशः ॥45॥

देवतिर्यङ्मनुष्याणां सरीसृपसवीरुधाम् । सर्वजीवनिकायानां सूर्य आत्मा दृगीश्वरः ॥46॥

इति श्रीमद्भागवते महापुराणे पारमहंस्यां संहितायां पञ्चमस्कन्धे भुवनकोशवर्णने समुद्रवर्षसन्निवेशपरिमाणलक्षणो विंशोऽध्यायः ॥20॥

area within the enclosure of the Lokāloka mountain, the area of the Aloka outside it has also been given; for they are the same. (From the Meru to the Lokāloka mountain the distance is thirty seven and a half crores of Yojanas. The same is the extent of Aloka or the region beyond Loka.) Great men say that this is the holy regions of the Masters of Yoga. **43.** The middle of the cosmic shell, which is also midway between the earth below and the heaven above, is the region of the sun. The distance between the sun and the heaven, and of the sun and the earth is alike twenty-five crores of Yojanas. **44.** For having entered (as the Viratpurusha) this lifeless cosmic shell (*mrite ande*), the sun is called Mārtānda. He is also called Hiranyagarbha, because he was generated in the luminous shell. **45.** It is on the basis of the sun that all these divisions and distinctions connected with the quarters, sky, heaven, earth, regions of enjoyment, regions of liberation, hells, the various worlds etc., are made. **46.** He is to be meditated upon thus: 'This Surya-Narayana is the soul and the presiding deity of the organ of sight of all beings—celestials, men, animals, reptiles, vegetation and all living creatures.'

अथैकविंशोऽध्यायः

श्रीशुक उवाच

एतावानेव भूवलयस्य सन्निवेशः प्रमाणलक्षणतो व्याख्यातः ॥1॥ एतेन हि दिवो मण्डलमानं तद्विद उपदिशन्ति यथा द्विदलयोर्निष्पावादीनां ते अन्तरेणान्तरिक्षं तदुभयसन्धितम् ॥2॥ यन्मध्यगतो

Skandha V : Chapter 21
THE COURSE OF THE SUN

Uttarayana and Dakshinayana (1-6)

Sri Suka said: **1.** Now we have described the location, extent, characteristic etc., of the earth. **2.** By the description of the extent of the earth as fifty crores of Yojanas, the extent of (Dyo) heaven has also been described. It is just as in the case of plants having leaves in pairs, one covering the other; for the heaven (Dyo) above covers the earth below. The regions intermediate between the earth and the heaven is the Antariksha, the intervening atmospheric region. **3.** In the

भगवांस्तपताम्पतिस्तपन आतपेन त्रिलोकीं प्रतपत्यवभासयत्यात्मभासा स एष उदगयनदक्षिणायनवैषुवतसंज्ञाभिर्मान्द्यशैघ्र्यसमानाभिर्गतिभिरारोहणावरोहणसमानस्थानेषु यथासवनमभिपद्यमानो मकरादिषु राशिष्वहोरात्राणि दीर्घह्रस्वसमानानि विधत्ते ॥3॥ यदा मेषतुलयोर्वर्तते तदाहोरात्राणि समानानि भवन्ति यदा वृषभादिषु पञ्चसु च राशिषु चरति तदाहान्येव वर्धन्ते ह्रसति च मासि मास्येकैका घटिका रात्रिषु ॥4॥ यदा वृश्चिकादिषु पञ्चसु वर्तते तदाहोरात्राणि विपर्ययाणि भवन्ति ॥5॥ यावद्दक्षिणायनमहानि वर्धन्ते यावदुदगयनं रात्रयः ॥6॥

एवं नव कोटय एकपञ्चाशल्लक्षाणि योजनानां मानसोत्तरगिरिपरिवर्तनस्योपदिशन्ति तस्मिन्नैन्द्रीं पुरीं पूर्वस्मान्मेरोर्देवधानीं नाम दक्षिणतो याम्यां संयमनीं नाम पश्चाद्वारुणीं निम्लोचनीं नाम उत्तरतः सौम्यां विभावरीं नाम तासूदयमध्याह्नास्तमयनिशीथानीति भूतानां प्रवृत्तिनिवृत्तिनिमित्तानि समयविशेषेण मेरोश्चतुर्दिशम् ॥7॥ तत्रत्यानां दिवसमध्यंगत एव सदाऽऽदित्यस्तपति सव्येनाचलं दक्षिणेन करोति ॥8॥ यत्रोदेति तस्य ह समानसूत्रनिपाते निम्लोचति यत्र क्वचन स्यन्देनाभितपति तस्य हैष समानसूत्रनिपाते प्रस्वापयति तत्र गतं न पश्यन्ति ये तं समनुपश्येरन् ॥9॥

middle of the Antariksha is located the sun, the brightest of all the luminaries, heating and illumining the three regions—the earth, the middle region (Antariksha) and heaven (Dyo). He has three movements, accelerated, retarded, and even, which are called Uttarayana (the northern declination or the summer solstice), Dakshinayana (the southern declination or winter solstice), and Vaishuvata (across the equator at the equinoxes.) In the course of these movements he is in high, low and in middle positions. While he passes onward through his sign of the Zodiac Makara (Capricornus), the days are lengthened and nights shortened, and vice versa when he goes in the opposite direction towards Karkataka (Cancer). They are equal when he is in the middle. **4.** When the sun moves through Mesha (Aries) and Tula (Libra), the days and nights are equal in length. When he moves from Vrishabha (Taurus) through the five succeeding Rasis (signs), the day is longer and the night becomes shorter every month by about one Ghatika (twenty four minutes). **5.** When the sun moves from Vrischika (Scorpio) through the succeeding five Rasis, the days become shorter and nights longer. **6.** Until Dakshinayana starts, day time grows longer, and until Uttarayana starts nights grow longer.

Sun's Course on Mānasottara (7-12)

7. For the sun to go thus once round the universe along the top of Mānasottara mountain, he has to traverse nine crores and fifty one lakhs of Yojanas, according to wise men. On the Mānasottara mountain towards the eastern direction of Meru stands Devadhāni or the city of Indra; towards the south, Yama's city known as Samyamani; towards the west, Varuna's city Nimlochani; and towards the north, Vibhāvari, the city of Soma. In these regions in the four directions of Meru, sun-rise, midday, sun-set and midnight occur one after the other each in succession, thus enabling people to regulate their time for work, rest, prayers etc. **8.** But to the inhabitants of Meru, it is always perpetual midday. Though the sun moves in an easterly direction, keeping Meru to the left, it appears as keeping Meru to the right because of the movement of the whole system of the luminuous bodies (as explained in passage 2 of chapter 22) **9.** The sun rises and sets in opposite directions. At one point he

यदा चैन्द्रद्याः पुर्याः प्रचलते पञ्चदशघटिकाभिर्याम्यां सपादकोटिद्वयं योजनानां सार्धद्वादश-
लक्षाणि साधिकानि चोपयाति ॥10॥ एवं ततो वारुणीं सौम्यामैन्द्रीं च पुनस्तथान्ये च ग्रहाः
सोमादयो नक्षत्रैः सह ज्योतिश्चक्रे समभ्युद्यन्ति सह वा निम्लोचन्ति ॥11॥ एवं मुहूर्तेन चतुस्त्रिंश-
ल्लक्षयोजनान्यष्टशताधिकानि सौरो रथस्त्रयीमयोऽसौ चतसृषु परिवर्तते पुरीषु ॥12॥

यस्यैकं चक्रं द्वादशारं षण्नेमि त्रिणाभि संवत्सरात्मकं समामनन्ति तस्याक्षो मेरोर्मूर्धनि
कृतो मानसोत्तरे कृतेतरभागो यत्र प्रोतं रविरथचक्रं तैलयन्त्रचक्रवद् भ्रमन्मानसोत्तरगिरौ परिभ्रमति
॥13॥ तस्मिन्नक्षे कृतमूलो द्वितीयोऽक्षस्तुर्यमानेन सम्मितस्तैलयन्त्राक्षवद् ध्रुवे कृतोपरिभागः ॥14॥

रथनीडस्तु षट्त्रिंशल्लक्षयोजनायतस्तत्तुरीयभागविशालस्तावान् रविरथयुगो यत्र हयाश्छन्दो-
नामानः सप्तारुणयोजिता वहन्ति देवमादित्यम् ॥15॥ पुरस्तात्सवितुररुणः पश्चाच्च नियुक्तः सौत्ये
कर्मणि किलास्ते ॥16॥ तथा वालखिल्या ऋषयोऽङ्गुष्ठपर्वमात्राः षष्टिसहस्राणि पुरतः सूर्यं सूक्त-
वाकाय नियुक्ताः संस्तुवन्ति ॥17॥ तथान्ये च ऋषयो गन्धर्वाप्सरसो नागा ग्रामण्यो यातुधाना

causes perspiration by his heat at midday; when he reaches the opposite point, it is midnight causing deep sleep, and he is then absolutely invisible. **10.** After the sun starts from the city of Indra in the east, he travels two crores and thirty seven and a half lakhs of Yojanas within fifteen Ghatikas before he reaches the city of Yama in the south. Afterwards it takes him the same distance and time to reach the cities of Varuna in the west and from there to that of Soma in the North, and from there back to Indra's city. **11.** The moon and the other planets rise and set with the other stars. The rising and the setting of the sun also take place along with those of the stars, but as the latter is invisible, the above statement is made. **12.** Thus the Veda-embodied chariot of the sun, travelling at the rate of thirty-four lakhs and eight hundred Yojanas per Muhurta, travels through these four cities.

The Chariot of the Sun (13-19)

13. Great men have described the chariot of the sun thus: The year is its single wheel. The wheel has twelve spokes constituted of twelve months. It has a rim with six segments in the form of the six seasons. The three Chaturmasyas (a third of a year) constitute the three pieces with which its hub is made. Its axle-tree has one of its ends established on the top of Mahameru and the other end in Mānasottara mountain. The wheel of the chariot of the sun, being linked with this axle, moves round along the Mānasottara mountain like the single wheel of an oil press. **14.** There is another axle, connected with the first, like the axle-tree of an oil mill. It is one-fourth the length of the first (i.e thirty nine lakh thirty seven thousand and five hundred Yojanas). While its lower end is connected with the first axle, the other is connected with the Dhruvamandala (pole-star) above. **15.** The seating space in the sun's chariot is thirty six lakh Yojanas in length and about a fourth of it in breadth. The yoke for tying the horses is also of the same length. Aruna, the charioteer, attaches to it the seven Vedic metres, Gayatri, Ushnik, Anushtup, Brihati, Trishtup, Pangti, and Sogati as the horses of the chariot, which carries Surya-Narayana. **16.** Aruna, though seated in front of the chariot, faces the sun while working as the charioteer. **17.** A host of sixty thousand Rishis of the size of a thumb known as Valakhilyas, stand before the sun and invoke him with hymns. **18.** Besides these

देवा इत्येकैकशो गणाः सप्त चतुर्दश मासि मासि भगवन्तं सूर्यमात्मानं नानानामानं पृथङ्नानानामानः पृथक्कर्मभिर्द्वन्द्वश उपासते ॥18॥ लक्षोत्तरं सार्धनवकोटियोजनपरिमण्डलं भूवलयस्य क्षणेन सगव्यूत्युत्तरं द्विसहस्रयोजनानि स भुङ्क्ते ॥19॥

इति श्रीमद्भागवते महापुराणे पारमहंस्यां संहितायां पञ्चमस्कन्धे ज्योतिश्चक्रसूर्यरथमण्डलवर्णनं नामैकविंशोऽध्यायः ॥21॥

Valakhilyas, there are fourteen others, forming seven Ganas or groups of two, attending on him. These groups are Rishis, Gandharvas, Apsaras, Nāgas, Grāmanis, Yātudhānas and Devas. They bear different names and change every month. They attend upon Surya-Narayana, each Gana of two serving him in its own particular way. **19.** The circumference round the earth sphere (measured along the top of the Mānasottara mountain in Pushkaradweepa, the outermost of all Dweepas) traversed by the sun is nine crores and fifty lakhs of Yojanas. He traverses this at the rate of two thousand Yojanas and two Krosas every Kshana (4/5 of a second).

अथ द्वाविंशोऽध्यायः

राजोवाच

यदेतद्भगवत आदित्यस्य मेरुं ध्रुवं च प्रदक्षिणेन परिक्रामतो राशीनामभिमुखं प्रचलितं चाप्रदक्षिणं भगवतोपवर्णितममुष्य वयं कथमनुमिमीमहीति ॥1॥

स होवाच

यथा कुलालचक्रेण भ्रमता सह भ्रमतां तदाश्रयाणां पिपीलिकादीनां गतिरन्यैव प्रदेशान्तरेष्वप्युपलभ्यमानत्वादेवं नक्षत्रराशिभिरुपलक्षितेन कालचक्रेण ध्रुवं मेरुं च प्रदक्षिणेन परिधावता सह परिधावमानानां तदाश्रयाणां सूर्यादीनां ग्रहाणां गतिरन्यैव नक्षत्रान्तरे राश्यन्तरे चोपलभ्यमानत्वात् ॥2॥ स एष भगवानादिपुरुष एव साक्षान्नारायणो लोकानां स्वस्तय आत्मानं त्रयीमयं कर्मविशुद्धि-

Skandha V : Chapter 22

THE MOVEMENT OF THE SUN AND THE PLANETS

Reverse Movement of the Sun (1-2)

Rajah Parikshit said: **1.** You have stated that the sun appears to circle keeping Mahameru and the Dhruva to the right, but that it actually travels facing the Rasis (signs of the zodiac) and keeping Meru to the left. Being contradictory, I am not able to understand this.

Sri Suka said: **2.** We see that while a potter's wheel is moving in one direction, the ants on the wheel can move in an opposite direction. There is no contradiction in it. In the same way the wheel of Time along with all the stars and Rasis (constellations and signs of the zodiac) moves in one direction, while the sun and planets on the wheel make independent movement in an opposite direction along the wheel. There is no contradiction in it. This peculiarity of movement can be seen in stars and Rasis also.

Surya-Narayana (3-7)

3. It is Narayana—the origin of all, the quest of the Vedas and of those who

निमित्तं कविभिरपि च वेदेन विजिज्ञास्यमानो द्वादशधा विभज्य षट्सु वसन्तादिष्वृतुषु यथोपजोषमृतुगुणान् विदधाति ॥3॥ तमेतमिह पुरुषास्त्रय्या विद्यया वर्णाश्रमाचारानुपथा उच्चावचैः कर्मभिराम्नातैर्योगवितानैश्च श्रद्धया यजन्तोऽञ्जसा श्रेयः समधिगच्छन्ति ॥4॥ अथ स एष आत्मा लोकानां द्यावापृथिव्योरन्तरेण नभोवलयस्य कालचक्रगतो द्वादश मासान् भुङ्क्ते राशिसंज्ञान् संवत्सरावयवान् मासः पक्षद्वयं दिवा नक्तं चेति सपादर्क्षद्वयमुपदिशन्ति यावता षष्ठमंशं भुञ्जीत स वै ऋतुरित्युपदिश्यते संवत्सरावयवः ॥5॥

अथ च यावतार्धेन नभोवीथ्यां प्रचरति तं कालमयनमाचक्षते ॥6॥ अथ च यावन्नभोमण्डलं सह द्यावापृथिव्योर्मण्डलाभ्यां कार्त्स्न्येन स ह भुञ्जीत तं कालं संवत्सरं परिवत्सरमिडावत्सरमनुवत्सरं वत्सरमिति भानोर्मान्द्यशैघ्र्यसमगतिभिः समामनन्ति ॥7॥

एवं चन्द्रमा अर्कगभस्तिभ्य उपरिष्टाल्लक्षयोजनत उपलभ्यमानोऽर्कस्य संवत्सरभुक्तिं पक्षाभ्यां मासभुक्तिं सपादर्क्षाभ्यां दिनेनैव पक्षभुक्तिमग्रचारी द्रुततरगमनो भुङ्क्ते ॥8॥ अथ चापूर्यमाणाभिश्च कलाभिरमराणां क्षीयमाणाभिश्च कलाभिः पितॄणामहोरात्राणि पूर्वपक्षापरपक्षाभ्यां वितन्वानः सर्वजीवनिवहप्राणो जीवश्चैकमेकं नक्षत्रं त्रिंशता मुहूर्तैर्भुङ्क्ते ॥9॥ य एष षोडशकलः पुरुषो

know the Vedas—that has taken the form of Surya-Narayana for the purification of all Vedic rites. For the welfare of the worlds He has divided his form into twelve, which is experienced as the six seasons giving diverse experiences to Jivas according to their Karma. **4.** Those who follow the way of life laid down by Varnasrama Dharma, adore him with faith and devotion through various rites and meditations laid down in the Vedas, and attain to spiritual development easily. **5.** Sun, the inner soul of everything, travelling along the wheel of Time through the intermediary region between the earth and the heaven, creates the twelve limbs of the year known as months by their zodiacal signs. The month is divided into two fortnights according to the reckoning based on the moon. For the Pitris this is a day and a night. When the sun experiences one-sixth of a year, that is called a Ritu (season). **6.** When the sun completes half of his course in the sky i.e., passes through the six Rasis, that is called an Ayana. **7.** The time taken by the sun to traverse the whole of the firmament of the intermediary region i.e., the twelve Rasis, is known differently, according to the reckoning of the speed of his movement as quick, slow or medium, as Samvatsara, Parivatsara, Idavatsara, Anuvatsara and Vatsara in different systems of calculations.

The Moon and its Movements (8-10)

8. The moon, who is more than a lakh of Yojanas above the sun, and moving with accelerated motion before the sun, covers the distance of the sun's round for one year in two fortnights; for one month in two and a quarter days; and for a fortnight in one day. **9.** The waxing and waning of the moon, signifying the bright and the dark fortnights, constitute the day and the night for the Devas and the reverse for the Pitris. The moon gives food and energy to all, as he helps the growth of cereals. The moon passes through each constellation (Nakshatra) in thirty Muhurtas. **10.** The worshipful moon has sixteen digits. He is thought-formed, food-formed, and bliss-formed. He is also the all-formed, because he satisfies the hunger, the life-principle, in all beings—Devas, Pitris, men, animals,

भगवान् मनोमयोऽन्नमयोऽमृतमयो देवपितृमनुष्यभूतपशुपक्षिसरीसृपवीरुधां प्राणाप्यायनशील-
त्वात्सर्वमय इति वर्णयन्ति ॥10॥

तत उपरिष्टात्त्रिलक्षयोजनतो नक्षत्राणि मेरुं दक्षिणेनैव कालायन ईश्वरयोजितानि
सहाभिजिताष्टाविंशतिः ॥11॥ तत उपरिष्टादुशना द्विलक्षयोजनत उपलभ्यते पुरतः पश्चात्सहैव
वार्कस्य शैघ्र्यमान्द्यसाम्याभिर्गतिभिरर्कवच्चरति लोकानां नित्यदानुकूल एव प्रायेण वर्षयंश्चारेणा-
नुमीयते स वृष्टिविष्टम्भग्रहोपशमनः ॥12॥

उशनसा बुधो व्याख्यातस्तत उपरिष्टाद् द्विलक्षयोजनतो बुधः सोमसुत उपलभ्यमानः
प्रायेण शुभकृद्यदार्काद् व्यतिरिच्येत तदातिवाताभ्रप्रायानावृष्ट्यादिभयमाशंसते ॥13॥ अथ ऊर्ध्वम-
ङ्गारकोऽपि योजनलक्षद्वितय उपलभ्यमानस्त्रिभिस्त्रिभिः पक्षैरेकैकशो राशीन् द्वादशानुभुङ्क्ते यदि
न वक्रेणाभिवर्तते प्रायेणाशुभग्रहोऽघशंसः ॥14॥ तत उपरिष्टाद् द्विलक्षयोजनान्तरगतो भगवान्
बृहस्पतिरेकैकस्मिन् राशौ परिवत्सरं परिवत्सरं चरति यदि न वक्रः स्यात्प्रायेणा-
नुकूलो ब्राह्मणकुलस्य ॥15॥

तत उपरिष्टाद्योजनलक्षद्वयात्प्रतीयमानः शनैश्चर एकैकस्मिन् राशौ त्रिंशन्मासान् विलम्बमानः
सर्वानेवानुपर्येति तावद्भिरनुवत्सरैः प्रायेण हि सर्वेषामशान्तिकरः ॥16॥ तत उत्तरस्मादृषय
एकादशलक्षयोजनान्तर उपलभ्यन्ते य एव लोकानां शमनुभावयन्तो भगवतो विष्णोर्यत्परमं पदं
प्रदक्षिणं प्रक्रमन्ति ॥17॥

इति श्रीमद्भागवते महापुराणे पारमहंस्यां संहितायां पञ्चमस्कन्धे ज्योतिश्चक्रवर्णने द्वाविंशोऽध्यायः ॥22॥

birds, serpents, trees, creepers etc. For, all cereals that provide food for all beings grow due to his light.

Constellations (11-17)

11. Three lakhs of Yojanas above the moon there are twenty eight Nakshatras (constellations) including Abhijit, fixed to the Wheel of time, and going round the Mahameru keeping always to the left. **12.** Two lakhs of Yojanas further from this, Sukra or Usanas (Venus) is seen. His movements resemble those of the sun, and by his accelerated, retarded and even movements he is sometimes in advance of the sun, sometimes behind him, and sometimes along with him. He is always favourable to living beings. By his movement he brings rain, and from this it has to be inferred that he inhibits the evil influence of planets that retard rain. **13.** Two and a half lakh Yojanas beyond Sukra is Budha (Mercury), the son of Soma. Much of what is said of Sukra is applicable to him. He has beneficial influence on creatures. But when he goes far away from the sun, he creates storms, heavy clouds without rain and other undesirable phenomena. **14.** Next, two and a half lakhs of Yojanas above, is the planet Mars (Angāraka). When he is not in retrograde motion, he traverses each of the twelve signs of the zodiac (Rasi) in three fortnights. He is generally a force of evil and is inauspicious. **15.** Higher still by two lakhs of Yojanas, is Brihaspati (Jupiter). When he is not subject to retrograde movement, he travels through each Rasi in the course of a year. He is a favourable planet. **16.** At a distance of two lakhs of Yojanas from there, Sani (Saturn) is seen. He takes thirty months to pass through each Rasi, and requires several years to cover all the Rasis. He is an evil planet. **17.** Eleven lakhs of Yojanas higher still, the Saptarshis (the Great Bear) move round the Dhruva, the abode of the Lord, working for the welfare of all creation.

अथ त्रयोविंशोऽध्यायः

श्रीशुक उवाच

अथ तस्मात्परतस्त्रयोदशलक्षयोजनान्तरतो यत्तद्विष्णोः परमं पदमभिवदन्ति यत्र ह महाभागवतो ध्रुव औत्तानपादिरग्निनेन्द्रेण प्रजापतिना कश्यपेन धर्मेण च समकालयुग्भिः सबहुमानं दक्षिणतः क्रियमाण इदानीमपि कल्पजीविनामाजीव्य उपास्ते तस्येहानुभाव उपवर्णितः ॥1॥ स हि सर्वेषां ज्योतिर्गणानां ग्रहनक्षत्रादीनामनिमिषेणाव्यक्तरंहसा भगवता कालेन भ्राम्यमाणानां स्थाणुरिवावष्टम्भ ईश्वरेण विहितः शश्वदवभासते ॥2॥ यथा मेढीस्तम्भ आक्रमणपशवः संयोजितास्त्रिभिस्त्रिभिः सवनैर्यथास्थानं मण्डलानि चरन्त्येवं भगणा ग्रहादय एतस्मिन्नन्तर्बहिर्योगेन कालचक्र आयोजिता ध्रुवमेवावलम्ब्य वायुनोदीर्यमाणा आकल्पान्तं परिचङ्क्रमन्ति नभसि यथा मेघाः श्येनादयो वायुवशाः कर्मसारथयः परिवर्तन्ते एवं ज्योतिर्गणाः प्रकृतिपुरुषसंयोगानुगृहीताः कर्मनिर्मितगतयो भुवि न पतन्ति ॥3॥

केचनैतज्ज्योतिरनीकं शिशुमारसंस्थानेन भगवतो वासुदेवस्य योगधारणायामनुवर्णयन्ति ॥4॥ यस्य पुच्छाग्रेऽवाक्शिरसः कुण्डलीभूतदेहस्य ध्रुव उपकल्पितस्तस्य लाङ्गूले प्रजापतिरग्निरिन्द्रो धर्म इति पुच्छमूले धाता विधाता च कट्यां सप्तर्षयः । तस्य दक्षिणावर्तकुण्डलीभूतशरीरस्य

Skandha V : Chapter 23

DHRUVA THE POLE STAR

Dhruva the Pivot of the Universe (1-3)

Sri Suka said: **1.** Thirteen lakhs of Yojanas above the region of Saptarshis, is the realm of Dhruva, very dear to the Supreme Being. There Dhruva, the son of Uttānapāda, stays, and out of respect for him Agni, Indra, Kasyapa Prajapati and Dharma circumambulate keeping him to their right. He stays till the end of the Kalpa doing good to all beings. His story has been described earlier (in the fourth Skandha). **2.** The sphere of Dhruva shines, established as it were by the will of the Lord as a central post for supporting the movements of the numerous planets, constellations and other luminaries that are moving round and round by the impulsion of Time, the vigilant, the matchlessly swift and the omnipotent manifestation of the Lord Himself. **3.** Just as on the threshing floor oxen are tied to a central pole and made to go round and round in three circles in three fixed radii, so are all the constellations and planets fixed to the Pole Star Dhruva and made to go round and round him till the end of the Kalpa, driven by the power of Wind. Just as clouds and birds do not fall down, from the sky, thanks to the wind and their own movement, so also these luminaries, who are meritorious Jivas, are sustained in the sky by their Karma, without being allowed to fall down.

Sisumāra Form of the Lord (4-9)

4. Some describe this assemblage of luminaries as a formation in the shape of an alligator (Sisumāra) manifested and sustained by the Yogic power of the Divine Vāsudeva. **5.** The alligator is suspended with tail above and the head down in a curved position. At the tip of the tail is Dhruva. On the body of the tail are located Prajapati Kasyapa, Agni, Indra, and Dharma; towards the junction of the tail with the body is Dhātā and Vidhātā; on the waist, the Seven Rishis; on the

यान्युदगयनानि दक्षिणपार्श्वे तु नक्षत्राण्युपकल्पयन्ति दक्षिणायनानि तु सव्ये । यथा शिशुमारस्य कुण्डलाभोगसंनिवेशस्य पार्श्वयोरुभयोरप्यवयवाः समसंख्या भवन्ति । पृष्ठे त्वजवीथी आकाशगङ्गा चोदरतः ॥5॥ पुनर्वसुपुष्यौ दक्षिणवामयोः श्रोण्योरार्द्राश्लेषे च दक्षिणवामयोः पश्चिमयोः पादयोरभिजिदुत्तराषाढे दक्षिणवामयोर्नासिकयोर्यथासंख्यं श्रवणपूर्वाषाढे दक्षिणवामयोर्लोचनयोर्धनिष्ठा मूलं च दक्षिणवामयोः कर्णयोर्मघादीन्यष्ट नक्षत्राणि दक्षिणायनानि वामपार्श्ववङ्क्रिषु युञ्जीत तथैव मृगशीर्षादीन्युदगयनानि दक्षिणपार्श्ववङ्क्रिषु प्रातिलोम्येन प्रयुञ्जीत शतभिषाज्येष्ठे स्कन्धयोर्दक्षिणवामयोर्न्यसेत् ॥6॥ उत्तराहनावगस्तिरधराहनौ यमो मुखेषु चाङ्गारकः शनैश्चर उपस्थे बृहस्पतिः ककुदि वक्षस्यादित्यो हृदये नारायणो मनसि चन्द्रो नाभ्यामुशना स्तनयोरश्विनौ बुधः प्राणापानयो राहुर्गले केतवः सर्वाङ्गेषु रोमसु सर्वे तारागणाः ॥7॥

एतदु हैव भगवतो विष्णोः सर्वदेवतामयं रूपमहरहः सन्ध्यायां प्रयतो वाग्यतो निरीक्षमाण उपतिष्ठेत नमो ज्योतिर्लोकाय कालायनायानिमिषां पतये महापुरुषायाभिधीमहीति ॥8॥

ग्रहर्क्षतारामयमाधिदैविकं पापापहं मन्त्रकृतां त्रिकालम् ।
नमस्यतः स्मरतो वा त्रिकालं नश्येत तत्कालजमाशु पापम् ॥9॥

इति श्रीमद्भागवते महापुराणे पारमहंस्यां संहितायां पञ्चमस्कन्धे शिशुमारसंस्थावर्णनं नाम त्रयोविंशोऽध्यायः ॥23॥

right side, bending towards the right, the fourteen Uttarayana Nakshatras from Abhijit to Punarvasu; and on the left side, the fourteen Dakshinayana Nakshatras, from Pushya to Uttarāshādha. Just as the ribs on both sides of the alligator are equal, so are on each side of that curved formation, fourteen Nakshatras. On its back are the constellations called Ajavīthi, and on the under surface is Ākāsa-Ganga. **6.** The constellations on the left and the right are located as follows: on the right and left loins are Punarvasu and Pushya; Ārdra and Āslesha are on the right and left hind legs; Abhijit and Uttarāshādha are on the right and left nostrils; Sravana and Pūrvāshādha are at the right and left eyes; Dhanishthā and Mūla are at the right and left ears. The eight constellations from Magha onwards, marking the southern course of the sun, are on the ribs at the left side: the other eight ones from Mrigasīrsha, marking the northern course, are on the ribs at the right side in the reverse order. The remaining Satabhishak and Jyeshthā are at the right and left shoulders. **7.** Further, at the upper jaw is located Agastya, and Yama at the lower; Mars (Angāraka) at the mouth, and Saturn (Sani) at the penis; Jupiter (Brihaspati) at the hump at the back of the throat, and the sun (Āditya) at the chest; Narayana at the heart, and the moon (Chandra) in the mind; Venus (Sukra) at the navel, and Aswini Kumaras at the nipples; Mercury (Budha) in the outgoing and incoming breaths, and Rāhu at the throat. Comets (Ketu) are to be placed all over the body, while the other galaxies are to be located in the hairs on the body.

8. Every day at nightfall one should sit silently gazing at the above described form of Mahavishnu including in it all the Divinities, and with great concentration pray: 'I meditate on the Supreme Person, who is the master of all Divinities, who is of the form of the Wheel of Time, and who is the support of all the luminous constellations.' **9.** Whoever meditates on, and makes obeisance to, this divine form of the Lord (known as Sisumāra), constituted of all planets, stars and constellations uttering the above mentioned

Mantra during the three junction periods (Sandhya) of the day, will be freed from the effects of all the sins committed that day.

अथ चतुर्विंशोऽध्यायः

श्रीशुक उवाच

अधस्तात्सवितुर्योजनायुते स्वर्भानुर्नक्षत्रवच्चरतीत्येके योऽसावमरत्वं ग्रहत्वं चालभत भगवदनुकम्पया स्वयमसुरापसदः सैंहिकेयो ह्यतदर्हस्तस्य तात जन्मकर्माणि चोपरिष्टाद्वक्ष्यामः ॥1॥ यददस्तरणेर्मण्डलं प्रतपतस्तद्विस्तरतो योजनायुतमाचक्षते द्वादशसहस्रं सोमस्य त्रयोदशसहस्रं राहोर्यः पर्वणि तद्व्यवधानकृद्वैरानुबन्धः सूर्याचन्द्रमसावभिधावति ॥2॥ तन्निशम्योभयत्रापि भगवता प्रयुक्तं सुदर्शनं नाम भागवतं दयितमस्त्रं तत्तेजसा दुर्विषहं मुहुः परिवर्तमानमभ्यवस्थितो मुहूर्तमुद्विजमानश्चकितहृदय आरादेव निवर्तते तदुपरागमिति वदन्ति लोकाः ॥3॥

ततोऽधस्तात्सिद्धचारणविद्याधराणां सदनानि तावन्मात्र एव ॥4॥ ततोऽधस्ताद्यक्षरक्षःपिशाचप्रेतभूतगणानां विहाराजिरमन्तरिक्षं यावद्वायुः प्रवाति यावन्मेघा उपलभ्यन्ते ॥5॥ ततोऽधस्ताच्छतयोजनान्तर इयं पृथिवी यावद्धंसभासश्येनसुपर्णादयः पतत्त्रिप्रवरा उत्पतन्तीति ॥6॥

Skandha V : Chapter 24

THE NETHER REGIONS

Rāhu (1-3)

Sri Suka said: **1.** Some say that ten thousand Yojanas below the sun there is a body called Rāhu, which moves like a constellation. He is in reality a perverse Asura, being the son of the Asura woman Simhika. Though undeserving, he got the status of a Deva and of a planet by the mercy of the Lord. How this happened will be described later (in Skandha VIII). **2.** It is said that the burning body of the sun is ten thousand Yojanas in diameter, that of the moon twelve thousand Yojanas, and that of Rāhu thirteen thousand Yojanas. Rahu happened to thrust himself between the sun and the moon at the time of the distribution of Amrita, hiding his identity as an Asura. But the sun and the moon exposed him, and for this reason he has been maintaining enmity with these two luminaries and rushing forward to consume them during the times of eclipse. **3.** Seeing this, the Lord would release his favourite discus Sudarsana for the protection of his devotees, and Rāhu, frightened by the sight of the irresistible discus whirling before him, would stand looking at it for a time from a distance and then retreat, trembling with fear. There is only this confrontation and no swallowing (*grahana*), as people speak of it.

Region of Siddhas etc. (4-6)

4. Ten thousand Yojanas below Rāhu is the region of the Siddhas, Chāranas and Vidyādharas. **5.** Below that up to where clouds are seen and powerful winds blow, is the Antariksha (upper air), forming the playground of Yakshas, Rakshasas, Pisachas, Pretas, elementals, and the like, **6.** A hundred Yojanas below that lies the earth, its sphere extending up to the heights reached by great birds like swans, eagles, hawks, Garuda etc.

उपवर्णितं भूमेर्यथासन्निवेशावस्थानमवनेरप्यधस्तात्सप्त भूविवरा एकैकशो योजनायुतान्तरेणायाम-
विस्तारेणोपक्लृप्ता अतलं वितलं सुतलं तलातलं महातलं रसातलं पातालमिति ॥7॥
एतेषु हि बिलस्वर्गेषु स्वर्गादप्यधिककामभोगैश्वर्यानन्दभूतिविभूतिभिः सुसमृद्धभवनोद्याना-
क्रीडविहारेषु दैत्यदानवकाद्रवेया नित्यप्रमुदितानुरक्तकलत्रापत्यबन्धुसुहृदनुचरा गृहपतय ईश्वराद-
प्यप्रतिहतकामा मायाविनोदा निवसन्ति ॥8॥ येषु महाराज मयेन मायाविना विनिर्मिताः
पुरो नानामणिप्रवरप्रवेकविरचितविचित्रभवनप्राकारगोपुरसभाचैत्यचत्वरायतनादिभिर्नागासुर-
मिथुनपारावतशुकसारिकाकीर्णकृत्रिमभूमिभिर्विवरेश्वरगृहोत्तमैः समलङ्कृताश्चकासति ॥9॥
उद्यानानि चातितरां मनइन्द्रियानन्दिभिः कुसुमफलस्तबकसुभगकिसलयावनतरुचिरविटपविटपिनां
लताङ्गालिङ्गितानां श्रीभिः समिथुनविविधविहङ्गमजलाशयानाममलजलपूर्णानां झषकुलोल्लङ्घन-
क्षुभितनीरनीरजकुमुदकुवलयकह्लारनीलोत्पललोहितशतपत्रादिवनेषु कृतनिकेतनानामेकविहारा-
कुलमधुरविविधस्वनादिभिरिन्द्रियोत्सवैरमरलोकश्रियमतिशयितानि ॥10॥ यत्र ह वाव न भयम-
होरात्रादिभिः कालविभागैरुपलक्ष्यते ॥11॥ यत्र हि महाहिप्रवरशिरोमणयः सर्वं तमः प्रबाधन्ते
॥12॥ न वा एतेषु वसतां दिव्यौषधिरसरसायनान्नपानस्नानादिभिराधयो व्याधयो वलीपलितजरादयश्च
देहवैवर्ण्यदौर्गन्ध्यस्वेदक्लमग्लानिरिति वयोऽवस्थाश्च भवन्ति ॥13॥ न हि तेषां कल्याणानां प्रभवति

Six subterranean Regions (7-15)

7. The position and features of the earth have already been described. Now below the earth, each separated by ten thousand Yojanas from the other, are the seven subterranean regions—Atala, Vitala, Sutala, Talātala, Mahātala, Rasātala and Pātāla. **8.** Here Daityas, Danavas, Sarpas etc., live in great joy with families, friends and followers in conditions that provide more enjoyments than heaven. Here abound houses, gardens and places for sports and recreation. Without interference from even Iswara, they live a life of enjoyment in their households. They possess great magical powers. **9.** O King! In these subterranean regions, Maya, the architect of great magical powers, has built cities with wonderful houses studded all over with precious stones, and having walls, frontal towers, council halls, temples, courtyards etc. The houses of the leading inhabitants there are full of occupants of both sexes of Asuras and Nagas, besides singing birds like cuckoos and parrots. **10.** The gardens there, more attractive than those of heaven itself, are full of trees whose branches are bending low with the load of bunches of fruits and flowers and tender leaves. The attractiveness of the place is further enhanced by beautiful birds in pairs and by lakes of pure water in which fish leap about creating a stir in their placid waters. The lakes are covered with various aquatic flowers like lotuses, lilies, Kalharas, blue lotuses, red lotuses and lotuses with a hundred petals, on which settle sweet warblers of the sky. **11.** As there is no daylight there, the inhabitants are not disturbed by alternating day and night. **12.** The luminous gems on the hoods of the huge serpents dispel the darkness of the region. **13.** Due to the effect of the various kinds of miraculous herbs, juices, elixirs, foods and drinks they take, the inhabitants there are free from worries and disease, from perspiration, bad odours and exhaustion, as also from signs of old age like wrinkles, grey hairs and change of complexion. They are always full of spirit and enthusiasm. **14.** There is no death for these fortunate beings except from

कुतश्चन मृत्युर्विना भगवत्तेजसश्चक्रापदेशात् ॥14॥ यस्मिन् प्रविष्टेऽसुरवधूनां प्रायः पुंसवनानि भयादेव स्रवन्ति पतन्ति च ॥15॥

अथातले मयपुत्रोऽसुरो बलो निवसति येन ह वा इह सृष्टाः षण्णवतिर्मायाः काश्चनाद्यापि मायाविनो धारयन्ति यस्य च जृम्भमाणस्य मुखतस्त्रयः स्त्रीगणा उदपद्यन्त स्वैरिण्यः कामिन्यः पुंश्चल्य इति या वै विलायनं प्रविष्टं पुरुषं रसेन हाटकाख्येन साधयित्वा स्वविलासावलोकनानुराग-स्मितसंलापोपगूहनादिभिः स्वैरं किल रमयन्ति यस्मिन्नुपयुक्ते पुरुष ईश्वरोऽहं सिद्धोऽहमित्ययुत-महागजबलमात्मानमभिमन्यमानः कत्थते मदान्ध इव ॥16॥

ततोऽधस्ताद्वितले हरो भगवान् हाटकेश्वरः स्वपार्षदभूतगणावृतः प्रजापतिसर्गोपबृंहणाय भवो भवान्या सह मिथुनीभूत आस्ते यतः प्रवृत्ता सरित्प्रवरा हाटकी नाम भवयोर्वीर्येण यत्र चित्रभानु-र्मातरिश्वना समिध्यमान ओजसा पिबति तन्निष्ठ्यूतं हाटकाख्यं सुवर्णं भूषणेनासुरेन्द्रावरोधेषु पुरुषाः सह पुरुषीभिर्धारयन्ति ॥17॥

ततोऽधस्तात्सुतले उदारश्रवाः पुण्यश्लोको विरोचनात्मजो बलिर्भगवता महेन्द्रस्य प्रियं चिकीर्षमाणेनादितेर्लब्धकायो भूत्वा वटुवामनरूपेण पराक्षिप्तलोकत्रयो भगवदनुकम्पयैव पुनः प्रवेशित इन्द्रादिष्वविद्यमानया सुसमृद्धया श्रियाभिजुष्टः स्वधर्मेणाराधयंस्तमेव भगवन्तमाराधनीयम-

the Sudarsana discus of Mahavishnu. **15.** When the discus enters these regions, the pregnancies of the Asura females abort out of fear.

Atala and its Specialities (16-17)

16. In Atala, lives the Asura Bala, the son of Maya. He formulated the ninety-six forms of magical devices. Some of them are still in use among magicians. As Bala yawned, out of his mouth came three types of women known as Svairini, Kāmini and Pumschali. Svairini is one who mates only with one's class. Kāmini is one who mates with anybody, and Pumschali is the most promiscuous among these. A person conveyed to this subterranean heaven is received by these women. They make him drink an elixir called Hātaka to enhance his sexual potency, and delight him with their amorous looks, talks, laughter and embraces. Owing to the extraordinary potency of the elixir, he experiences within himself the strength of a thousand elephants, and in the intoxication and elation of it, declares himself to be all-mighty and all-perfect.

17. In the still lower region called Vitala, Sri Parameswara, accompanied by his consort Parvati and surrounded by his host of Bhutas, has manifested as Hātakeswara in order to help Brahma in the work of augmenting the creation. Out of the virility flowing from their union is formed the river Hātaki. Agni absorbs it, prompted by Vayu (wind), and then spits it out in the form of a golden stuff called Hātaka, with which are made the ornaments worn by Asura chiefs and their womenfolk inhabiting those regions.

Sutala and Mahabali (18-27)

18. Below that is the region called Sutala, where the great one Mahabali, noted for his generosity, lives. In order to help Indra, Lord Mahavishnu was born in Aditi as Vāmana and took away the mastery of the worlds from Mahabali by a stratagem. But out of His grace He sent Bali to Sutala where he lives in the midst of splendour, to which even Indra is a stranger. But in the midst of it all Mahabali continues to worship the Supreme

पगतसाध्वस आस्तेऽधुनापि ॥18॥ नो एवैतत्साक्षात्कारो भूमिदानस्य यत्तद्भगवत्यशेषजीवनिकायानां जीवभूतात्मभूते परमात्मनि वासुदेवे तीर्थतमे पात्र उपपन्ने परया श्रद्धया परमादरसमाहितमनसा सम्प्रतिपादितस्य साक्षादपवर्गद्वारस्य यद्बिलनिलयैश्वर्यम् ॥19॥ यस्य ह वाव क्षुतपतनप्रस्खलनादिषु विवशः सकृन्नामाभिगृणन् पुरुषः कर्मबन्धनमञ्जसा विधुनोति यस्य हैव प्रतिबाधनं मुमुक्षवोऽन्यथैवोपलभन्ते ॥20॥ तद्भक्तानामात्मवतां सर्वेषामात्मन्यात्मद आत्मतयैव ॥21॥ न वै भगवान्नूनममुष्यानुजग्राह यदुत पुनरात्मानुस्मृतिमोषणं मायामयभोगैश्वर्यमेवातनुतेति ॥22॥ यत्तद्भगवतानधिगतान्योपायेन याच्ञाच्छलेनापहृतस्वशरीरावशेषितलोकत्रयो वरुणपाशैश्च सम्प्रतिमुक्तो गिरिदर्यां चापविद्ध इति होवाच ॥23॥ नूनं बतायं भगवानर्थेषु न निष्णातो योऽसाविन्द्रो यस्य सचिवो मन्त्राय वृत एकान्ततो बृहस्पतिस्तमतिहाय स्वयमुपेन्द्रेणात्मानमयाचतात्मनश्चाशिषो नो एव तद्दास्यमतिगम्भीरवयसः कालस्य मन्वन्तरपरिवृत्तं कियल्लोकत्रयमिदम् ॥24॥ यस्यानुदास्यमे-

Being by the discharge of his ordained duties as an offering unto Him.

19. This attainment of Sutala cannot be considered a direct result or reward for offering the world to the Lord. For, such a petty worldly fulfilment like the attainment of this subterranean heaven can never be an adequate reward for making an offering of this whole world with firm faith (Sraddha), readiness and concentration, to that Supreme Being Vāsudeva—the soul of all Jivas, the inner pervader, the controller of everything—when he presented himself before Bali as a worthy seeker of a favour. Such a whole-hearted adoration of the Lord should have brought on Bali the bliss of Moksha itself, not the paltry reward of a subterranean heaven. **20-21.** By uttering His name once even with a feeling of distress while yawning, falling, or sustaining an injury, a man overcomes the bondage of Karma, an attainment for which aspirants following the disciplines of Samkhya and Yoga put themselves to endless troubles and difficulties. For making a true devotional and dedicated offering of the whole world to such an exalted Divinity who bestows Himself as also reveals Himself as one's own Self to all great devotees and men of enlightenment—such a worthless thing as the attainment of the joy of this subterranean heaven is an absolutely incompatible reward. **22.** The attainment of prosperity and facilities for enjoyment cannot even be considered a blessing in the case of a devotee; for prosperity is likely to make one forgetful of the Lord. So Mahabali's attainment of the subterranean heaven of Sutala should be attributed to his Prarabdha. **23.** Finding no other way, the Lord in this incarnation as Vāmana adopted the stratagem of begging and thereby deprived Mahabali of all his possessions. Mahabali was then bound with the Varuna noose and shut up in a mountain cell. Even then he says as follows without any dismay: **24.** 'Indra and his trusted adviser Brihaspati are persons with little understanding of what constitutes the highest value of life. Abandoning Him, the Lord, who is the highest end for man to attain, they have utilised Him to get back from me such petty things as the world and its riches. They did not pray for being admitted as His servants. How insignificant is the lordship of these three worlds lasting for the duration of a Manvantara (about 71 Chaturyugas) before infinite Time which is awe-inspiring to contemplate! **25.** My grandfather Prahlada, after his father Hiranyakasipu's death, was offered by the Lord the whole of his patrimony which he

वास्मत्पितामहः किल वव्रे न तु स्वपित्र्यं यदुताकुतोभयं पदं दीयमानं भगवतः परमिति भगवतोपरते खलु स्वपितरि ॥25॥ तस्य महानुभावस्यानुपथममृजितकषायः को वास्मद्विधः परिहीणभगवदनुग्रह उपजिगमिषतीति ॥26॥ तस्यानुचरितमुपरिष्टाद्विस्तरिष्यते यस्य भगवान् स्वयमखिलजगद्गुरुर्नारायणो द्वारि गदापाणिरवतिष्ठते निजजनानुकम्पितहृदयो येनाङ्गुष्ठेन पदा दशकन्धरो योजनायुतायुतं दिग्विजय उच्चाटितः ॥27॥

ततोऽधस्तात्तलातले मयो नाम दानवेन्द्रस्त्रिपुराधिपतिर्भगवता पुरारिणा त्रिलोकीशं चिकीर्षुणा निर्दग्धस्वपुरत्रयस्तत्प्रसादाल्लब्धपदो मायाविनामाचार्यो महादेवेन परिरक्षितो विगतसुदर्शनभयो महीयते ॥28॥

ततोऽधस्तान्महातले काद्रवेयाणां सर्पाणां नैकशिरसां क्रोधवशो नाम गणः कुहकतक्षककालियसुषेणादिप्रधाना महाभोगवन्तः पतत्त्रिराजाधिपतेः पुरुषवाहादनवरतमुद्विजमानाः स्वकलत्रापत्यसुहृत्कुटुम्बसङ्गेन क्वचित्प्रमत्ता विहरन्ति ॥29॥

ततोऽधस्ताद्रसातले दैतेया दानवाः पणयो नाम निवातकवचाः कालेया हिरण्यपुरवासिन इति विबुधप्रत्यनीका उत्पत्त्या महौजसो महासाहसिनो भगवतः सकललोकानुभावस्य हरेरेव तेजसा प्रतिहतबलावलेपा बिलेशया इव वसन्ति ये वै सरमयेन्द्रदूत्या वाग्भिर्मन्त्रवर्णाभिरिन्द्राद् बिभ्यति ॥30॥

could enjoy without fear of any rival, but he did not accept it, as those positions and riches would be disparate from the Lord. He sought only the privilege of being His servant. He is indeed a fortunate person! **26.** It is impossible for persons like me, whose tendencies for worldly enjoyments have not been effaced and who have not received the Lord's grace, to think or dream of following the example of that great personage.' **27.** Later on (in the eighth Skandha) will be told the story of Mahabali, at whose gate the Lord, overcome by His passionate love for devotees, remains armed with a mace as a gate keeper, in which capacity He threw the ten-headed Ravana several thousand Yojanas away with a flick of his toe when that Rakshasa approached the realm of Mahabali to challenge him in the course of his march of conquest over the whole universe.

Talātala and Mahātala (28-29)

28. Below Sutala is Talātala presided over by the famous Asura, Maya, the master of the triune city. For the good of the world Sri Parameswara burnt his city, but later, being blessed by Him, Maya was given a place in Talātala. He is the prime teacher of all who specialise in magical arts. Being protected by Sri Parameswara, he lives without fear of even the Sudarsana.

29. Lower even than Talātala is the region called Mahātala which is inhabited by a tribe of many-headed serpents, children of Kadru, known for their special trait of anger. Kuhaka, Takshaka, Kāliya and Sushena are some of the leaders of these huge-bodied serpents. They spend their time sometimes in dread of Garuda, the divine vehicle of Mahavishnu, and at other times delighting in the company of their family and friends.

Rasātala (30)

30. In Rasātala, the region still lower, dwell the offspring of Diti and Danu who are known as Panis and divided into three tribes of Asuras—the Nivātakavachas, and Kāleyas and the inhabitants of Hiranyapura. They are a very powerful

ततोऽधस्तात्पाताले नागलोकपतयो वासुकिप्रमुखाः शङ्खकुलिकमहाशङ्खश्वेतधनञ्जयधृतराष्ट्रशङ्ख-चूडकम्बलाश्वतरदेवदत्तादयो महाभोगिनो महामर्षा निवसन्ति येषामु ह वै पञ्चसप्तदशशतसहस्र-शीर्षाणां फणासु विरचिता महामणयो रोचिष्णवः पातालविवरतिमिरनिकरं स्वरोचिषा विधमन्ति ॥31॥

इति श्रीमद्भागवते महापुराणे पारमहंस्यां संहितायां पञ्चमस्कन्धे राह्वादिस्थितिबिलस्वर्गमर्यादानिरूपणं नाम चतुर्विंशोऽध्यायः ॥24॥

and daring species who have an inherent enmity to the Devas. Their will for domination being suppressed by the might of the Lord's Sudarsana, they live like serpents in Rasātala. They are frightened by the power of the Vedic chants uttered by Indra's messenger Sarama in the guise of a bitch.

Pātāla (31)

31. Lower still is Pātāla, which great serpents of a ferocious nature inhabit. The names of the leading ones among them are: Vāsuki, Sankha, Kulika, Mahāsankha, Sveta, Dhananjaya, Dhritarashtra, Sankhachūda, Kambala, Asvatara and Devadatta. They have hoods varying in number from five to seven, ten, hundred, and thousand. The precious stones on the hoods of these serpents illumine the whole of Pātāla, completely eradicating the darkness of the region.

अथ पञ्चविंशोऽध्यायः

श्रीशुक उवाच

तस्य मूलदेशे त्रिंशद्योजनसहस्रान्तर आस्ते या वै कला भगवतस्तामसी समाख्यातानन्त इति सात्वतीया द्रष्टृदृश्ययोः सङ्कर्षणमहमित्यभिमानलक्षणं यं सङ्कर्षणमित्याचक्षते ॥1॥

यस्येदं क्षितिमण्डलं भगवतोऽनन्तमूर्तेः सहस्रशिरस एकस्मिन्नेव शीर्षणि ध्रियमाणं सिद्धार्थ इव लक्ष्यते ॥2॥ यस्य ह वा इदं कालेनोपसञ्जिहीर्षतोऽमर्षविरचितरुचिरभ्रमद्भ्रुवोरन्तरेण साङ्कर्षणो नाम रुद्र एकादशव्यूहस्त्र्यक्षस्त्रिशिखं शूलमुत्तम्भयन्नुदतिष्ठत् ॥3॥ यस्याङ्घ्रिकमलयुगलारुण-

Skandha V : Chapter 25

THE LORD AS ANANTA OR SANKARSHANA

Sphere of Ananta (1-6)

Sri Suka said: **1.** Thirty thousand Yojanas below Pātāla, the Tamasika aspect of the Lord resides under the name of Ananta, the Endless One. The followers of the Vaishnava Tantras, in their adoration of the Lord as His four Vyuhas, describe that Ananta as the power that makes the Drashta, the seer or the subject (the spirit), feel identified with the Drisya, the seen or the object (body, senses etc.), under the sense of 'I'. They therefore call him Sankarshana, the unifier. **2.** Resting on a single one of his thousand hoods, this whole universe looks like a small mustard seed. **3.** At the close of the cycles when he desires to dissolve the worlds, there comes out of the middle of his handsome brows, now quivering in an angry frown, the three-eyed Rudra in his elevenfold aspect, known as "Sankarshana's progeny", flourishing a trident in his hands. **4.** At his feet, having ruby-like

विशदनखमणिषण्डमण्डलेष्वहिपतयः सह सात्वतर्षभैरेकान्तभक्तियोगेनावनमन्तः स्ववदनानि परिस्फुरत्कुण्डलप्रभामण्डितगण्डस्थलान्यतिमनोहराणि प्रमुदितमनसः खलु विलोकयन्ति ॥4॥ यस्यैव हि नागराजकुमार्य आशिष आशासानाश्चार्वङ्गवलयविलसितविशदविपुलधवलसुभगरुचिरभुजरजतस्तम्भेष्वगुरुचन्दनकुङ्कुमपङ्कानुलेपेनावलिम्पमानास्तदभिमर्शनोन्मथितहृदयमकरध्वजावेशरुचिरललितस्मितास्तदनुरागमदमुदितमदविघूर्णितारुणकरुणावलोकनयनवदनारविन्दं सव्रीडं किल विलोकयन्ति ॥5॥ स एव भगवाननन्तोऽनन्तगुणार्णव आदिदेव उपसंहृतामर्षरोषवेगो लोकानां स्वस्तय आस्ते ॥6॥

ध्यायमानः सुरासुरोरगसिद्धगन्धर्वविद्याधरमुनिगणैरनवरतमदमुदितविकृतविह्वललोचनः सुललितमुखरिकामृतेनाप्यायमानः स्वपार्षदविबुधयूथपतीनपरिम्लानरागनवतुलसिकामोदमध्वासवेन माद्यन्मधुकरव्रातमधुरगीतश्रियं वैजयन्तीं स्वां वनमालां नीलवासा एककुण्डलो हलककुदि कृतसुभगसुन्दरभुजो भगवान् माहेन्द्रो वारणेन्द्र इव काञ्चनीं कक्षामुदारलीलो बिभर्ति ॥7॥

य एष एवमनुश्रुतो ध्यायमानो मुमुक्षूणामनादिकालकर्मवासनाग्रथितमविद्यामयं हृदयग्रन्थिं सत्त्वरजस्तमोमयमन्तर्हृदयं गत आशु निर्भिनत्ति तस्यानुभावान् भगवान् स्वायम्भुवो नारदः सह तुम्बुरुणा सभायां ब्रह्मणः संश्लोकयामास ॥8॥

nails, great devotees and leading serpents are bowing down with single-minded devotion and are delighted to look at each other's faces beaming with joy and illumined by the reflection of the golden ear-rings on their shining cheeks. **5.** Young serpent damsels of great beauty, desirous of his blessings, are applying unguents made of sandal paste, saffron and other fragrant ingredients on the long, fair and extremely charming arms of Sankarshana. The contact with his arms, which are like silver pillars, generate in these damsels a wave of amorous sentiments, which make them smile delightfully with a touch of bashfulness and look at the face of Sankarshana which shines with his eyes of slightly reddish tinge blooming with the satisfaction of love and rolling with intoxication. **6.** That worshipful Deity, who is none but the Infinite of countless attributes and powers, having controlled his impatient and choleric disposition, is now in the mood of affording protection to the whole world.

Meditation on Sankarshana (7-8)

7. Sankarshana is thus described for purposes of meditation: Having eyes elated, tremulous, and overflowing with the bliss of inebriation; delighting his attendants and the adoring Devas by his nectarine speech; wearing an unfading floral wreath of Vaijayanti over which bees hover and hum with intoxication caused by the drinking of flower-nectar flavoured with the fragrance of holy Tulasi leaves; presenting, with that floral wreath, the appearance of Indra's celestial elephant Airavata with a golden chain round his neck; dressed with a wearing cloth and upper cloth of bluish tinge; having only one ear ornament; resting his beautiful hands on his weapon called Hala; engaged in the sport of fulfilling the prayer of His votaries—such is the form of Sankarshana adored and meditated upon by Devas, Asuras, Siddhas, Nāgas, Gandharvas, Vidyādharas and Munis. **8.** If an aspirant after Moksha hears and meditates on Sankarshana in this way, the Lord will penetrate into the heart of that devotee and cut asunder the knot of egoity, which is generated by Karmas and their tendencies lasting from time without beginning, which is of the form of ignorance,

उत्पत्तिस्थितिलयहेतवोऽस्य कल्पाः सत्त्वाद्याः प्रकृतिगुणा यदीक्षयाऽऽसन् ।
यद्रूपं ध्रुवमकृतं यदेकमात्मन्नानाधात्कथमु ह वेद तस्य वर्त्म ।। 9।।
मूर्ति नः पुरुकृपया बभार सत्त्वं संशुद्धं सदसदिदं विभाति यत्र ।
यल्लीलां मृगपतिराददेऽनवद्यामादातुं स्वजनमनांस्युदारवीर्यः ।।10।।
यन्नाम श्रुतमनुकीर्तयेदकस्मादार्तो वा यदि पतितः प्रलम्भनाद्वा ।
हन्त्यंहः सपदि नृणामशेषमन्यं कं शेषाद्भगवत आश्रयेन्मुमुक्षुः ।।11।।
मूर्धन्यर्पितमणुवत्सहस्रमूर्ध्नो भूगोलं सगिरिसरित्समुद्रसत्त्वम् ।
आनन्त्यादनिमितविक्रमस्य भूम्नः को वीर्याण्यधिगणयेत्सहस्रजिह्वः ।।12।।
एवंप्रभावो भगवाननन्तो दुरन्तवीर्योरुगुणानुभावः ।
मूले रसायाः स्थित आत्मतन्त्रो यो लीलया क्ष्मां स्थितये बिभर्ति ।।13।।

एता ह्येवेह नृभिरुपगन्तव्या गतयो यथाकर्मविनिर्मिता यथोपदेशमनुवर्णिताः कामान् कामयमानैः ।।14।। एतावतीर्हि राजन् पुंसः प्रवृत्तिलक्षणस्य धर्मस्य विपाकगतय उच्चावचा विसदृशा यथाप्रश्नं व्याचख्ये किमन्यत्कथयाम इति ।।15।।

इति श्रीमद्भागवते महापुराणे पारमहंस्यां संहितायां पञ्चमस्कन्धे भूविवरविध्युपवर्णनं नाम पञ्चविंशोऽध्यायः ।।25।।

and which is constituted of Sattva, Rajas and Tamas, the qualities of Prakriti. About the greatness of Sankarshana the sage Narada along with Tumburu sings as follows in the assembly of Brahma:

Narada praises Sankarshana (9-15)

9. He by whose look Sattva and the other Gunas of Prakriti become competent to perform their functions of creation, preservation and dissolution, whose form is eternal without beginning or end, who though one, created the many in, and by, Himself—how can any one understand the ultimate truth about Him! **10.** He, in whom this creation in its subtle and gross aspects manifests, has assumed this form of Suddhasattva out of His infinite mercy towards all creatures. In order to attract the mind of the Jivas to Him, He, the Master of all and the omnipotent Being, has performed in His incarnations numerous sportive deeds that are flawless and heroic like those of a lion. **11.** He, by uttering whose name out of suffering or out of repentance for degradation, or by way of fun or even without any cause, man is able to overcome the effects of all sins—to whom except to that worshipful Sesha should a man aspiring for liberation go for shelter? **12.** Even a being with a thousand tongues cannot fully describe the greatness of Ādisesha of unlimited prowess, who on one of his thousand hoods sustains like a minute particle the mighty earth sphere with all its mountains, rivers, land and seas. **13.** This Ananta of unlimited powers and of countless auspicious qualities remains at the base of the earth sphere. He who has no support other than Himself, remains sustaining the earth in a sportive manner for the good of all living beings.

(Sri Suka concluded.) **14.** According to the teachings I have received, I have described to you all these spheres which men can attain to as a result of the ritualistic and other actions they perform with desires for their fruits. **15. O King!** These are the high and low attainments through Dharma of the nature of Pravritti (self-centred action). In reply to your question I have described all these. What else do you want to know?

अथ षड्विंशोऽध्यायः

राजोवाच

महर्ष एतद्वैचित्र्यं लोकस्य कथमिति ॥1॥

ऋषिरुवाच

त्रिगुणत्वात्कर्तुः श्रद्धया कर्मगतयः पृथग्विधाः सर्वा एव सर्वस्य तारतम्येन भवन्ति ॥2॥ अथेदानीं प्रतिषिद्धलक्षणस्याधर्मस्य तथैव कर्तुः श्रद्धाया वैसादृश्यात्कर्मफलं विसदृशं भवति या ह्यनाद्यविद्यया कृतकामानां तत्परिणामलक्षणाः सृतयः सहस्रशः प्रवृत्तास्तासां प्राचुर्येणानुवर्णयिष्यामः ॥3॥

राजोवाच

नरका नाम भगवन् किं देशविशेषा अथवा बहिस्त्रिलोक्या आहोस्विदन्तराल इति ॥4॥

ऋषिरुवाच

अन्तराल एव त्रिजगत्यास्तु दिशि दक्षिणस्यामधस्ताद्भूमेरुपरिष्टाच्च जलाद्यस्यामग्निष्वात्तादयः पितृगणा दिशि स्वानां गोत्राणां परमेण समाधिना सत्या एवाशिष आशासाना निवसन्ति ॥5॥ यत्र ह वाव भगवान् पितृराजो वैवस्वतः स्वविषयं प्रापितेषु स्वपुरुषैर्जन्तुषु सम्परेतेषु यथाकर्मावद्यं दोषमेवानुल्लङ्घितभगवच्छासनः सगणो दमं धारयति ॥6॥ तत्र हैके नरकानेकविंशतिं गणयन्ति

Skandha V : Chapter 26

DESCRIPTION OF PURGATORIES

Question on Purgatories (1-6)

Rajah Parikshit said: **1.** O great sage! How has this diversity of enjoyments and sufferings come in this world?

Sri Suka said: **2.** It is because of the differences in the Sraddha (faith) of the actor that differences in the fruits of action occur. Generally it can be said that Sattva, Rajas and Tamas generate actions that bring merit, merit-cum-demerit and demerit respectively. But the Sraddha of man can cause variations even in the fruits of actions of a similar nature prompted by these. **3.** As there are variations also in the nature of prohibited actions and in the Sraddha of people doing them, there are diversities in the fruits of such actions. I shall describe some features of the destiny that awaits people who do evil actions, dictated by their intense and virulent desire-nature. To describe it exhaustively is impossible.

The Rajah said: **4.** O respected one! Where is purgatory (Naraka)? Is it a region in the earth itself or is it outside the three Lokas (worlds), or is it somewhere within the three Lokas but outside the earth?

Sri Suka said: **5.** It is within the three Lokas itself—towards the south, at a lower level from the earth and above the water. There, Agnishwāttas and other groups of Pitris live working for the welfare of their progeny on earth, through prayer and meditation. **6.** There Yama, the Lord of all Pitris, lives inflicting corrective punishments on the souls of the dead whom his emissaries fetch, without in any way violating the commandments of Sri Hari and in accordance with the effects of the evil deeds they have committed.

अथ तांस्ते राजन्नामरूपलक्षणतोऽनुक्रमिष्यामस्तामिस्रोऽन्धतामिस्रो रौरवो महारौरवः कुम्भीपाकः कालसूत्रमसिपत्रवनं सूकरमुखमन्धकूपः कृमिभोजनः सन्दंशस्तप्तसूर्मिर्वज्रकण्टकशाल्मली वैतरणी पूयोदःप्राणरोधो विशसनं लालाभक्षः सारमेयादनमवीचिरयःपानमिति ॥ किञ्च क्षारकर्दमो रक्षोगणभोजनः शूलप्रोतो दन्दशूकोऽवटनिरोधनः पर्यावर्तनः सूचीमुखमित्यष्टाविंशतिर्नरका विविधयातनाभूमयः ॥7॥

तत्र यस्तु परवित्तापत्यकलत्राण्यपहरति स हि कालपाशबद्धो यमपुरुषैरतिभयानकैस्तामिस्रे नरके बलान्निपात्यते अनशनानुदपानदण्डताडनसन्तर्जनादिभिर्यातनाभिर्यात्यमानो जन्तुर्यत्र कश्मलमासादित एकदैव मूर्च्छामुपयाति तामिस्रप्राये ॥8॥ एवमेवान्धतामिस्रे यस्तु वञ्चयित्वा पुरुषं दारादीनुपयुङ्क्ते यत्र शरीरी निपात्यमानो यातनास्थो वेदनया नष्टमतिर्नष्टदृष्टिश्च भवति यथा वनस्पतिर्वृश्च्यमानमूलस्तस्मादन्धतामिस्रं तमुपदिशन्ति ॥9॥

यस्त्विह वा एतदहमिति ममेदमिति भूतद्रोहेण केवलं स्वकुटुम्बमेवानुदिनं प्रपुष्णाति स तदिह विहाय स्वयमेव तदशुभेन रौरवे निपतति ॥10॥ ये त्विह यथैवामुना विहिंसिता जन्तवः परत्र यमयातनामुपगतं त एव रुरवो भूत्वा तथा तमेव विहिंसन्ति तस्माद्रौरवमित्याहू रुरुरिति सर्पादतिक्रूरसत्त्वस्यापदेशः ॥11॥ एवमेव महारौरवो यत्र निपतितं पुरुषं क्रव्यादा नाम रुरवस्तं क्रव्येण घातयन्ति यः केवलं देहम्भरः ॥12॥

The Twenty-one Purgatories (7-37)

7. Some speak of these purgatories as being twenty-one in number. I shall describe them to you with their names, their features etc. They are: Tāmisra, Andhatāmisra, Raurava, Mahāraurava, Kumbhīpāka, Kālasūtra, Asipatravana, Sūkaramukha, Andhakūpa, Krimibhojana, Sandamsa, Taptasūrmi, Vajrakantaka-sālmali, Vaitarani, Pūyoda, Prānarodha, Visasana, Lālābhaksha, Sārameyādana, Avīchi and Ayah-pāna. Besides these twenty-one, there are seven more of them where Jivas suffer the consequences of heinous sins. These are: Kshārakardama, Rakshoganabhojana, Sūlaprota, Dandasūka, Avatanirodhana, Paryāvartana and Sūchīmukha. Thus the purgatories are twenty-eight, where sinners are subjected to sufferings for their purification.

8. Among these, Tāmisra is the place where persons who deprive others of their wealth, son, wife etc., are bound and thrown by force by fierce-looking emissaries of Yama. They are starved, frightened, beaten and in other ways punished in that utterly dark region until they become unconscious. **9.** He who deceives a husband and enjoys his wife is put into Andhatāmisra. Suffering from the fierce tortures of that place, the sinner loses his senses and his sight, and falls like a tree that has been cut. That is why this purgatory is called Andhatāmisra. **10.** He who, looking upon his body as the self, has been persecuting other creatures for the prosperity of himself and his family, will have to leave that body and that family here, and he will be hurled into the Raurava automatically, due to the effects of his own sins. **11.** All those creatures who had been oppressed and killed by this kind of a sinner will appear as the fierce animals called Rurus which are more ferocious than serpents, and torture the sinner by biting. For this reason this particular purgatory is called Raurava. **12.** He who perpetrates Adharma and is solely concerned with filling his own stomach by any means falls into the purgatory called Mahā-

यस्त्विह वा उग्रः पशून् पक्षिणो वा प्राणत उपरन्धयति तमपकरुणं पुरुषादैरपि विगर्हितममुत्र
यमानुचराः कुम्भीपाके तप्ततैले उपरन्धयन्ति ॥13॥ यस्त्विह पितृविप्रब्रह्मध्रुक् स कालसूत्रसंज्ञके
नरके अयुतयोजनपरिमण्डले ताम्रमये तप्तखले उपर्यधस्तादग्न्यर्काभ्यामतितप्यमानेऽभिनिवेशितः
क्षुत्पिपासाभ्यां च दह्यमानान्तर्बहिःशरीर आस्ते शेते चेष्टतेऽवतिष्ठति परिधावति च यावन्ति
पशुरोमाणि तावद्वर्षसहस्राणि ॥14॥

यस्त्विह वै निजवेदपथादनापद्यपगतः पाखण्डं चोपगतस्तमसिपत्रवनं प्रवेश्य कशया प्रहरन्ति
तत्र हासावितस्ततो धावमान उभयतोधारैस्तालवनासिपत्रैश्छिद्यमानसर्वाङ्गो हा हतोऽस्मीति परमया
वेदनया मूर्च्छितः पदे पदे निपतति स्वधर्महा पाखण्डानुगतं फलं भुङ्क्ते ॥15॥

यस्त्विह वै राजा राजपुरुषो वा अदण्ड्ये दण्डं प्रणयति ब्राह्मणे वा शरीरदण्डं
स पापीयान्नरकेऽमुत्र सूकरमुखे निपतति तत्रातिबलैर्विनिष्पिष्यमाणावयवो यथैवेहेक्षुखण्ड आर्तस्वरेण
स्वनयन् क्वचिन्मूर्च्छितः कश्मलमुपगतो यथैवेहादृष्टदोषा उपरुद्धाः ॥16॥

यस्त्विह वै भूतानामीश्वरोपकल्पितवृत्तीनामविविक्तपरव्यथानां स्वयं पुरुषोपकल्पितवृत्ति-
र्विविक्तपरव्यथो व्यथामाचरति स परत्रान्धकूपे तदभिद्रोहेण निपतति तत्र हासौ तैर्जन्तुभिः
पशुमृगपक्षिसरीसृपैर्मशकयूकामत्कुणमक्षिकादिभिर्ये के चाभिद्रुग्धास्तैः सर्वतोऽभिद्रुह्यमाणस्तमसि
विहतनिद्रानिर्वृतिरलब्धावस्थानः परिक्रामति यथा कुशरीरे जीवः ॥17॥

raurava and is eaten up by the type of Rurus called Kravyādas (flesh-eaters). **13.** Those heartlessly cruel fellows who cook birds and animals alive—a practice detested even by Rakshasas—are put into the purgatory called Kumbhīpāka, where they are fried in boiling oil. **14.** Whoever commits atrocities against parents, holy men and the Vedas are consigned to the purgatory known as Kālasūtra. It is a place of ten thousand Yojanas of burning copper sheet, heated from above by the sun and from below by fire. Heated within by want of food and drink, and outside by the burning metal, the sinner sometimes sits, sometimes lies, sometimes walks and sometimes runs hither and thither in utter distress for as many years as there are hairs on an animal's body. **15.** Those who abandon their Dharma based on the Vedas even without the threat of any danger or compulsion, and join sects of atheistic philosophers, are consigned to the purgatory called Asipatravana. There they are whipped and made to run about in a forest full of trees with sword-like leaves which lacerate their bodies as they pass through their midst. Crying out of terrible pain, they swoon at every step. **16.** If a king or an officer under him punishes innocent people, he goes to the purgatory called Sūkaramukha. There are powerful emissaries of Yama there with faces resembling those of pigs. The sinners are thus subjected to attack by them as a sugarcane field by elephants. With bodies broken, they swoon, just like the innocent persons they had tortured. **17.** God has given different forms of livelihood to different creatures. Some of these may go against the interest of man. But man should not retaliate against these creatures for two reasons. They are not endowed with the capacity to know that they are doing injury to man; and next, man knows that they will be injured if he retaliates. A person who injures lower creations for selfish purposes goes to the purgatory called Andhakūpa and there he will have to live in a low type of body, attacked by the creatures he had injured. In darkness, without sleep, and restless, he will have to drag on a wretched

यस्त्विह वा असंविभज्याश्नाति यत्किञ्चनोपनतमनिर्मितपञ्चयज्ञो वायससंस्तुतः स परत्र कृमिभोजने नरकाधमे निपतति तत्र शतसहस्रयोजने कृमिकुण्डे कृमिभूतः स्वयं कृमिभिरेव भक्ष्यमाणः कृमिभोजनो यावत्तदप्रत्ताप्रहुतादोऽनिर्वेशमात्मानं यातयते ॥18॥ यस्त्विह वै स्तेयेन बलाद्वा हिरण्यरत्नादीनि ब्राह्मणस्य वापहरत्यन्यस्य वानापदि पुरुषस्तममुत्र राजन् यमपुरुषा अयस्मयैरग्निपिण्डैः सन्दंशैस्त्वचि निष्कुषन्ति ॥19॥ यस्त्विह वा अगम्यां स्त्रियमगम्यं वा पुरुषं योषिदभिगच्छति तावमुत्र कशया ताडयन्तस्तिग्मया सूर्म्या लोहमय्या पुरुषमालिङ्गयन्ति स्त्रियं च पुरुषरूपया सूर्म्या ॥20॥ यस्त्विह वै सर्वाभिगमस्तममुत्र निरये वर्तमानं वज्रकण्टकशाल्मलीमारोप्य निष्कर्षन्ति ॥21॥

ये त्विह वै राजन्या राजपुरुषा वा अपाखण्डा धर्मसेतून् भिन्दन्ति ते सम्परेत्य वैतरण्यां निपतन्ति भिन्नमर्यादास्तस्यां निरयपरिखाभूतायां नद्यां यादोगणैरितस्ततो भक्ष्यमाणा आत्मना न वियुज्यमानाश्चासुभिरुह्यमानाः स्वाघेन कर्मपाकमनुस्मरन्तो विण्मूत्रपूयशोणितकेशनखास्थिमेदोमांसवसावाहिन्यामुपतप्यन्ते ॥22॥ ये त्विह वै वृषलीपतयो नष्टशौचाचारनियमास्त्यक्तलज्जाः पशुचर्यां चरन्ति ते चापि प्रेत्य पूयविण्मूत्रश्लेष्ममलापूर्णार्णवे निपतन्ति तदेवातिबीभत्सितमश्नन्ति ॥23॥ ये त्विह वै श्वगर्दभपतयो ब्राह्मणादयो मृगयाविहारा अतीर्थे च मृगान्निघ्नन्ति तानपि सम्परेतांल्लक्ष्यभूतान् यमपुरुषा इषुभिर्विध्यन्ति ॥24॥

ये त्विह वै दाम्भिका दम्भयज्ञेषु पशून् विशसन्ति तानमुष्मिंल्लोके वैशसे नरके पतितान्निरयपतयो यातयित्वा विशसन्ति ॥25॥ यस्त्विह वै सवर्णां भार्यां द्विजो रेतः पाययति

existence. **18.** He who eats food alone like a crow, without doing the Pancha-mahayajnas and without sharing his food with others, falls into the purgatory called Krimibhojana, which is a lakh of Yojanas in length. There he gets the form of a worm and himself eats worms, and is eaten by big worms until his sin is expiated.

19. Whoever steals or takes by force the properties of a holy man or takes away the wealth of others even when no imminent danger threatens him, is scorched in Yama's realm with heated iron spikes. **20.** Men and women who enter into prohibited sex relationship out of lust, are whipped in Yamaloka by the emissaries of Yama, and made to embrace red-hot metal effigies of the opposite sex. **21.** Men who out of lust seek intercourse with animals are taken to the purgatory known as Vajrakantaka-sālmali and are tortured by being dragged through the branches of trees having thorns like adamantine spikes. **22.** Kings, their officers and men of status claiming themselves to be the followers of the Vedas but who disregard all rules of morality and good conduct, fall after death into Vaitarani, a river that flows like a moat around the region of the purgatory. They are partly eaten up by many fierce creatures living in it. Still living and remembering their sins, they float about in the river whose water consists of filthy fluids like blood, pus, urine, faeces, flesh, fat etc. **23.** Those who live in concubinage with unchaste women, and indulge in unrestricted sensuous life abandoning rules of purity, good conduct, law, sense of shame—they too will fall into this Vaitarani, full of faeces, urine, phlegm etc., and be forced to subsist on the filthy stuff. **24.** Brahmanas who keep dogs and asses, who go about hunting, and who kill prohibited animals, are shot at by Yama's emissaries with sharp arrows and wounded all over. **25.** Those who organise fake Yajnas for mere show and strangle animals in it, those degenerate men go after death to the purgatory known as Vaisasa, and are similarly strangled by Yama's men. **26.** A

काममोहितस्तं पापकृतममुत्र रेतःकुल्यायां पातयित्वा रेतः सम्पाययन्ति ।।26।। ये त्विह वै दस्यवोऽग्निदा गरदा ग्रामान् सार्थान् वा विलुम्पन्ति राजानो राजभटा वा तांश्चापि हि परेत्य यमदूता वज्रदंष्ट्राः श्वानः सप्तशतानि विंशतिश्च सरभसं खादन्ति ।।27।।

यस्त्विह वा अनृतं वदति साक्ष्ये द्रव्यविनिमये दाने वा कथञ्चित्स वै प्रेत्य नरकेऽवीचिमत्यधःशिरा निरवकाशे योजनशतोच्छ्रायाद्गिरिमूर्ध्नः सम्पात्यते यत्र जलमिव स्थलमश्मपृष्ठमवभासते तदवीचिमत्तिलशो विशीर्यमाणशरीरो न म्रियमाणः पुनरारोपितो निपतति ।।28।।

यस्त्विह वै विप्रो राजन्यो वैश्यो वा सोमपीथस्तत्कलत्रं वा सुरां व्रतस्थोऽपि वा पिबति प्रमादतस्तेषां निरयं नीतानामुरसि पदाऽऽक्रम्यास्ये वह्निना द्रवमाणं कार्ष्णायसं निषिञ्चन्ति ।।29।। अथ च यस्त्विह वा आत्मसम्भावनेन स्वयमधमो जन्मतपोविद्याचारवर्णाश्रमवतो वरीयसो न बहु मन्येत स मृतक एव मृत्वा क्षारकर्दमे निरयेऽवाक्शिरा निपातितो दुरन्ता यातना ह्यश्नुते ।।30।।

ये त्विह वै पुरुषाः पुरुषमेधेन यजन्ते याश्च स्त्रियो नृपशून् खादन्ति तांश्च ते पशव इव निहता यमसदने यातयन्तो रक्षोगणाः सौनिका इव स्वधितिनावदायासृक् पिबन्ति नृत्यन्ति च गायन्ति च हृष्यमाणा यथेह पुरुषादाः ।।31।। ये त्विह वा अनागसोऽरण्ये ग्रामे वा वैश्रम्भकैरुपसृतानुपविश्रम्भय्य जिजीविषून् शूलसूत्रादिषूपप्रोतान् क्रीडनकतया यातयन्ति तेऽपि च प्रेत्य यमयातनासु शूलादिषु प्रोतात्मानः क्षुत्तृड्भ्यां चाभिहताः कङ्कवटादिभिश्चेतस्ततस्तिग्मतुण्डैराहन्यमाना आत्मशमलं स्मरन्ति ।।32।।

sexual pervert who subjects women to abnormal sexual practices is taken to the purgatory known as Retahkulya and then forced to live on semen. **27.** Kings and their soldiers who behave like brigands, burning villages, poisoning water and perpetrating similar atrocities against men, find themselves after death in the purgatory known as Sārameyadāna where they are attacked and torn to shreds by a pack of seven hundred and twenty dogs. **28.** Whoever tells lies and behaves dishonestly in bearing witness, in financial transactions and in making charitable gifts, he is taken after death to the purgatory known as Avīchimat where he is hurled headlong from mountain tops a hundred Yojanas high. He falls on the ground that looks from above as a watery surface, but is in reality a flat rocky slab. Falling on it he is shattered to pieces. Yet he does not die. He becomes alive to be thrown down again from the mountain top. **29.** If a Brahmana or his wife or any one observing a sacred vow drinks liquor, and so also if any Kshatriya or Vaisya drinks the juice of Soma plant, they are led to the purgatory where the emissaries of Yama, trampling on their chest, pour molten metal into their mouth. **30.** A degraded man, who pretends himself to be very eminent, and insults men who are wise, virtuous, austere and adhering to scripture-ordained ways of life, is taken to the purgatory called Kshārakardama. There he is dropped from above headlong and suffers miseries without end. **31.** Men who use human beings as sacrificial beasts for propitiating evil deities and women who eat the flesh of such human victims, are attacked in the purgatory by goblins who are none other than the human beings they slaughtered. Like butchers they cut them up, drink their blood, and perform wild dances, as these persons had done on earth at their sacrificial festivals. **32.** There are persons who entice innocent creatures living in villages and forests, generate confidence in them, and get them near and then put

ये त्विह वै भूतान्युद्वेजयन्ति नरा उल्बणस्वभावा यथा दन्दशूकास्तेऽपि प्रेत्य नरके दन्द-
शूकाख्ये निपतन्ति यत्र नृप दन्दशूकाः पञ्चमुखाः सप्तमुखा उपसृत्य ग्रसन्ति यथा बिलेशयान् ।।33।।
ये त्विह वा अन्धावटकुसूलगुहादिषु भूतानि निरुन्धन्ति तथामुत्र तेष्वेवोपवेश्य सगरेण वह्निना
धूमेन निरुन्धन्ति ।।34।। यस्त्विह वा अतिथीनभ्यागतान् वा गृहपतिरसकृदुपगतमन्युर्दिधक्षुरिव
पापेन चक्षुषा निरीक्षते तस्य चापि निरये पापदृष्टेरक्षिणी वज्रतुण्डा गृध्राः कङ्ककाकवटादयः
प्रसह्योरुबलादुत्पाटयन्ति ।।35।।

यस्त्विह वा आढ्याभिमतिरहङ्कृतिस्तिर्यक्प्रेक्षणः सर्वतोऽभिविशङ्की अर्थव्ययनाशचिन्तया
परिशुष्यमाणहृदयवदनो निर्वृतिमनवगतो ग्रह इवार्थमभिरक्षति स चापि प्रेत्य तदुत्पादनोत्कर्षण-
संरक्षणशमलग्रहः सूचीमुखे नरके निपतति यत्र ह वित्तग्रहं पापपुरुषं धर्मराजपुरुषा वायका इव
सर्वतोऽङ्गेषु सूत्रैः परिवयन्ति ।।36।।

एवंविधा नरका यमालये सन्ति शतशः सहस्रशस्तेषु सर्वेषु च सर्व एवाधर्मवर्तिनो ये
केचिदिहोदिता अनुदिताश्चावनिपते पर्यायेण विशन्ति तथैव धर्मानुवर्तिन इतरत्र इह तु पुनर्भवे
त उभयशेषाभ्यां निविशन्ति ।।37।।

निवृत्तिलक्षणमार्ग आदावेव व्याख्यातः ।। एतावानेवाण्डकोशो यश्चतुर्दशधा पुराणेषु विकल्पित
उपगीयते यत्तद्भगवतो नारायणस्य साक्षान्महापुरुषस्य स्थविष्ठं रूपमात्ममायागुणमयमनुर्वणितमादृतः

them on sharp spears or entrap them in nooses, and subject them to various tortures for the mere fun of it and enjoy the sight. Such torturers are put on spears in the purgatory and vultures and other birds of prey tear out their flesh. **33.** Extremely cruel men who terrorise creatures like serpents, fall into the purgatory called Dantasūka where they are swallowed like rats by serpents having five or seven hoods. **34.** Those who suffocate living beings by burying them in pits or shutting them up in garrets, caves etc., are treated similarly in the purgatory. They are shut up in similar places and smoked with poisonous stuff. **35.** A householder who looks with extreme annoyance at guests known or unknown, as if to burn them up, that sinful man's eyes will be pecked at and pulled by the vultures and crows of the purgatory. **36.** There are men who are suspicious of every one and every thing, because of a false consciousness of their own superiority over others on account of their wealth or position. Always afraid of losing their wealth, they sit tight over it like a guardian spirit, gloomy, hapless and without any trace of joy in their heart. Such misers, who have taken infinite pains to earn, augment and conserve wealth, will go to the purgatory known as Sūchīmukha. All over their body, stitches of the type that tailors make, are put by the servants of Yama.

37. Besides these, there are several other terrible hells in the realm of Yama. Just as persons who have lived a life of virtue go to heavens, sinners of the type mentioned here and others go to these hells for suffering for their sinful acts. Both the inheritors of heaven and of hell after having enjoyed or suffered for the actions they have done, return to the earth with their residuary Karma for fresh embodiment.

The Purpose of those Descriptions (38-40)

38. This is what is called the way of Pravritti (works with self-centred motives). The way of Nivritti (salvation through renunciation) has already been taught in the second Skandha. Here we have described all the fourteen worlds

पठति शृणोति श्रावयति स उपगेयं भगवतः परमात्मनोऽग्राह्यमपि श्रद्धाभक्तिविशुद्धबुद्धिर्वेद ।।38।।
श्रुत्वा स्थूलं तथा सूक्ष्मं रूपं भगवतो यतिः । स्थूले निर्जितमात्मानं शनैः सूक्ष्मं धिया नयेदिति 39।।
भूद्वीपवर्षसरिदद्रिनभःसमुद्रपातालदिङ्नरकभागणलोकसंस्था ।
गीता मया तव नृपाद्भुतमीश्वरस्य स्थूलं वपुः सकलजीवनिकायधाम ।।40।।

इति श्रीमद्भागवते महापुराणे वैयासिक्यामष्टादशसाहस्र्यां पारमहंस्यां संहितायां पञ्चमस्कन्धे नरकानुवर्णनं नाम षड्विंशोऽध्यायः ।।26।।

इति पञ्चमः स्कन्धः समाप्तः
हरिः ॐ तत्सत्

which are included in what the Puranas call the Brahmānda (the cosmic shell). This much is the description of the gross body of the Supreme constituted of His inherent spiritual power. Whoever hears, recites or studies it with faith and devotion, he will attain the purity of mind by virtue of his Sraddha and Bhakti, and will come to understand the subtle form of the Lord which is beyond the grasp of the senses. **39.** The rule is that the aspirant should hear about both the gross and subtle forms of the Lord. Then after attaining concentration on the gross form, he should gradually draw his mind towards the subtle form. **40.** O King! I have now finished describing to you the wonderful gross body of the Lord, which is the residence of all living beings, and which consists of all gross entities—the terrestrial sphere, the Dweepas and Varshas with their rivers, mountains, skies and oceans, the fourteen worlds from Satyaloka to Pātāla, the quarters, the purgatories and the galaxies.

END OF THE FIFTH SKANDHA

Skandha Six

PROLOGUE

The sixth Skandha consists of nineteen chapters with a total number of 849 verses. The main topic dealt with in it is called *Poshana*, which is described as *Tadanugraha*—His redemptive acts (II. 10.4) Probably *Poshana* can be brought under the still wider concept of *Raksha*, stated as the fourth topic in another list of subjects dealt with in the Puranas. (XII.7.9-10). *Raksha* is described as the Lord's sportive manifestations in different ages among various species of beings as brute creation, men, Rishis and Devas. One of the important purposes of all incarnations is to save man from Samsara, and that is nothing but redemption. But *Poshana* also connotes unconditioned grace, by which even the apparently most undeserving are saved. In the sixth Skandha two such cases are discussed—the instances of Ajamila the confirmed sinner, and of Indra in distress on account of his own sins in killing Viswarupa and Vritra.

The first three chapters are devoted to the Ajāmila episode. Originally a very pious person, Ajāmila took to a life of sin due to evil association. On his deathbed, overcome by fear at the sight of Yama's emissaries, he unconsciously takes the Lord's name, and he is saved thereby. How such an unworthy sinner is saved for merely taking the Lord's name once, and that, even without having Him in mind, is a mystery which could be solved only if one accepts the Bhagavata theory of the inherent power and holiness of the Divine name. The point is discussed in the relevant chapter of the Text and in the footnote we have added there.

Preparatory to the story of Vritra, the Text then takes up the line of Daksha, the son of Prachetasas, and his descendants in chapters five to eight. In that line was Twashta, the son of Aditi and Kasyapa, and his son was Viswarupa, a person of great occult powers. Though he had, because of parental connections, some sympathy with the cause of the Asuras, Indra was forced to take him as his Acharya (Priest), as Brihaspati, his permanent Acharya, had left him, piqued by Indra's insolent behaviour. Viswarupa equipped Indra with Narayana-kavacha, which helped Indra to gain great victories over the Asuras. But in spite of this, on coming to know of Viswarupa's sympathy for the Asuras, Indra murdered him in cold blood.

In the subsequent chapters, from the ninth to thirteenth, the story of Vritra is narrated. Viswarupa's father Twashta was infuriated at Indra's conduct, and out of his sacrificial fire he created a ferocious fiend-like being called Vritra, under whose lead the Asuras again came to dominate over the Devas. Indra was now advised to forge the thunderbolt weapon with the bones of the sage Dadhīchi, a holy man with great occult powers. As an act of great self-sacrifice for the good of others, Dadhīchi yielded his bones, with which the thunderbolt weapon was forged, and Vritra was killed with it in a very destructive battle between the Devas and the Asuras.

The fight between Indra and Vritra reveals the grandeur of the character of Vritra in contrast to his ferocious appearance. In the course of the fight with Indra we find Vritra delivering a profound philosophical discourse to Indra and addressing a most appealing prayer to the Lord. A line from that hymn is worth quoting. It runs: "As a fledgeling eagerly awaits its mother's arrival, as a hungry calf longs for its mother's udder, as a faithful wife anxiously awaits the return of her long-separated husband—so does, O Lotus-eyed One, my mind yearn for and expectantly await Thee" (VI.11.26.). This is perhaps the most poetic and one of the most fervent of the many prayers and hymns we get in the *Bhagavata*.

The devotionally oriented character of Vritra, who was externally a ferocious fiend, makes King Parikshit ask for an explanation of this mystery; and in answer Suka narrates the previous history of Vritra in chapters fourteen to seventeen. It is a long story abounding in devotional sentiment. Vritra in a previous birth was a pious king called Chitraketu who was childless and who, after performing many sacrifices, obtained an issue by the grace of the Lord. But the child was poisoned by its jealous step-mothers. This had the effect of driving Chitraketu to a life of devotion and austerity. He got the vision of his Chosen Ideal Sankarshana by whose grace he became a Gandharva leader, singing the praise of the Lord at the head of a party of celestial singers and moving from one part of the universe to another. Once, on his visit to Kailasa, he passed some derogatory remarks on Uma and Parameswara, which brought on him a curse from the Devi to be demoted to inferior birth. It was after this that he got embodiment as Vritra from the sacrificial fire of Twashta and was commissioned to destroy Indra. Though his form was terrific, his mind, swayed by his devotional past, was full of spiritual aspiration and divine love. Hence his strange conduct on the field of battle when he was engaged in mortal combat with Indra. These ten chapters dealing with Vritra and Chitraketu abound in thrilling narratives and highly evocative hymns.

In the last two chapters, the 19th and the 20th, is described how Diti's efforts to have an issue who would be able to destroy Indra was foiled by Indra himself, and how he converted his would-be antagonists, the Maruts, into his friends. The rules for undergoing the vow called Payovrata, observed by Diti as conducive to the fulfilment of one's desires, are described in the 19th chapter.

The Ajāmila story and the purification of Indra from the sin of Brahmahatya in the Vritra episode, form the main subject matter of this Skandha, and through the thrilling narratives, philosophical discourses and devotional hymns contained therein, is described how God's grace works in unforeseen ways, and how the highest devotion is sometimes discovered even in unexpected quarters.

श्रीमद्भागवतम्

षष्टः स्कन्धः अथ प्रथमोऽध्यायः

राजोवाच

निवृत्तिमार्गः कथित आदौ भगवता यथा। क्रमयोगोपलब्धेन ब्रह्मणा यदसंसृतिः ॥ 1॥
प्रवृत्तिलक्षणश्चैव त्रैगुण्यविषयो मुने। योऽसावलीनप्रकृतेर्गुणसर्गः पुनः पुनः ॥ 2॥
अधर्मलक्षणा नाना नरकाश्चानुवर्णिताः। मन्वन्तरश्च व्याख्यात आद्यः स्वायम्भुवो यतः ॥
प्रियव्रतोत्तानपदोर्वंशस्तच्चरितानि च। द्वीपवर्षसमुद्राद्रिनद्युद्यानवनस्पतीन् ॥ 4॥
धरामण्डलसंस्थानं भागलक्षणमानतः। ज्योतिषां विवराणां च यथेदमसृजद् विभुः 5॥
अधुनेह महाभाग यथैव नरकान्नरः। नानोग्रयातनान्नेयात्तन्मे व्याख्यातुमर्हसि ॥ 6॥

श्रीशुक उवाच

न चेदिहैवापचितिं यथांहसः कृतस्य कुर्यान्मनउक्तिपाणिभिः।
ध्रुवं स वै प्रेत्य नरकानुपैति ये कीर्तिता मे भवतस्तिग्मयातनाः ॥ 7॥
तस्मात्पुरैवाश्विह पापनिष्कृतौ यतेत मृत्योरविपद्यताऽऽत्मना।
दोषस्य दृष्ट्वा गुरुलाघवं यथा भिषक् चिकित्सेत रुजां निदानवित् ॥ 8॥

Skandha VI : Chapter 1

AJĀMILA EPISODE: AJĀMILA'S SINFUL LIFE

Sin and how to overcome it (1-19)

Rajah Parikshit said: **1.** You, worshipful Sir, have at first expounded the means for emancipation from transmigratory existence, following the method of gradual release. It consists in practising divine communion through different disciplines and attaining to Brahma's realm, and from there attaining release from embodied existence at the time of the Pralaya along with Brahma himself. **2.** You have also described the life of involvement in Samsara—how, driven by the forces of Karma, the Jiva is born repeatedly in different spheres, all of which are constituted of the evolutes of the three Gunas of Prakriti. **3.** The various purgatories which await evil-doers, were described, besides Manvantaras, the period of rule of the Manus, the first of whom was Swāyambhuva. (See footnote in the Prologue to the 4th Skandha.) **4.** Descriptions of the dynasties of Uttānapāda and Priyavrata, as well as accounts of continents, regions, oceans, mountains, rivers, gardens and forests were given. **5.** Besides, you have already discoursed to me on subjects like the divisions, characteristics, and dimensions of the earth, the galaxies, the heavens, and the nether worlds, and all other regions. **6.** Now it behoves you, O holy one, to explain how man can save himself from the sufferings of the purgatory described by you.

Sri Suka said: **7.** Unless a man does expiations even here in this world for the sins he has committed by his mind, speech and organs, he is sure to undergo the fierce sufferings of the purgatories I described to you. **8.** Therefore, long before death, sufficiently early in life, when the mind and the body have not become decrepit, man should do expiations for

राजोवाच

दृष्टश्रुताभ्यां यत्पापं जानन्नप्यात्मनोऽहितम् । करोति भूयो विवशः प्रायश्चित्तमथो कथम् 9॥
क्वचिन्निवर्ततेऽभद्रात् क्वचिच्चरति तत्पुनः । प्रायश्चित्तमतोऽपार्थं मन्ये कुञ्जरशौचवत् ॥10॥

श्रीशुक उवाच

कर्मणा कर्मनिर्हारो न ह्यात्यन्तिक इष्यते । अविद्वदधिकारित्वात् प्रायश्चित्तं विमर्शनम् 11॥
नाश्नतः पथ्यमेवान्नं व्याधयोऽभिभवन्ति हि । एवं नियमकृद्राजन् शनैः क्षेमाय कल्पते ॥12॥
तपसा ब्रह्मचर्येण शमेन च दमेन च । त्यागेन सत्यशौचाभ्यां यमेन नियमेन च ॥13॥
देहवाग्बुद्धिजं धीरा धर्मज्ञाः श्रद्धयान्विताः । क्षिपन्त्यघं महदपि वेणुगुल्ममिवानलः ॥14॥
केचित्केवलया भक्त्या वासुदेवपरायणाः । अघं धुन्वन्ति कार्त्स्न्येन नीहारमिव भास्करः 15
न तथा ह्यघवान् राजन् पूयेत तपआदिभिः । यथा कृष्णार्पितप्राणस्तत्पूरुषनिषेवया ॥16॥
सध्रीचीनो ह्ययं लोके पन्थाः क्षेमोऽकुतोभयः । सुशीलाः साधवो यत्र नारायणपरायणाः ॥17॥
प्रायश्चित्तानि चीर्णानि नारायणपराङ्मुखम् । न निष्पुनन्ति राजेन्द्र सुराकुम्भमिवापगाः 18॥

whatever sins he had done, according to their seriousness, just as a physician skilled in diagnosis treats diseases with remedies appropriate to the prevailing condition.

The Rajah said: **9.** Even after understanding from experience and instruction that something is sinful, men are found to commit the same sin in spite of themselves. Of what use then are these expiations? (They are not able to erase the sinful tendency.) **10.** For some time man may abstain from sin, but a little later, he indulges in it in spite of expiations. I therefore feel that expiations are useless, like bathing and cleaning an elephant whose habit it is to spray dust on its back always.

Sri Suka said: **11.** Avidya (ignorance) is the ultimate source of all Karma, including expiations. Expiations can therefore wash off only the effects of particular sinful acts, but not the tendency to commit them, so long as ignorance, their source, persists. (This can be ultimately effaced only by the knowledge of God.) **12.** A man who is on wholesome diet does not fall ill. In the same way, O King, one who practises spiritual disciplines gradually attains purification of mind and, through that, the knowledge of God. **13-14.** By means of austerity, celibacy, control of the mind, control of the senses, charity, practice of virtues like kindness, truth etc., and of disciplines like Japa, worship etc., a man of righteousness and faith overcomes even great sins committed by body, words and mind, just as a fire destroys a grove of reeds. **15.** There are some rare persons who, endowed with intense and unadulterated devotion, resign themselves completely to Vāsudeva and thereby eradicate sin utterly like the sun dissipating mist. **16.** The purification effected by austerity and other disciplines is not so complete as by dedication of all one's faculties to Krishna, achieved through the service of His devotees. **17.** This path of devotion, which is without any risk and which is comparatively easy to practise, is the best suited for men in general. For, those who follow this path can draw on the support of great devotees who are extremely devoted to Narayana and are disposed to help others. **18.** O King! The expiations performed by men who are not devoted to Narayana fail to cleanse them entirely,

सकृन्मनः कृष्णपदारविन्दयोर्निवेशितं तद्गुणरागि यैरिह ।
न ते यमं पाशभृतश्च तद्भटान् स्वप्नेऽपि पश्यन्ति हि चीर्णनिष्कृताः ।।19।।

अत्र चोदाहरन्तीममितिहासं पुरातनम् । दूतानां विष्णुयमयोः संवादस्तं निबोध मे ।।20।।
कान्यकुब्जे द्विजः कश्चिद् दासीपतिरजामिलः । नाम्ना नष्टसदाचारो दास्याः संसर्गदूषितः 21।।
वन्द्यक्षकैतवैश्चौर्यैर्गर्हितां वृत्तिमास्थितः । बिभ्रत्कुटुम्बमशुचिर्यातयामास देहिनः ।।22।।
एवं निवसतस्तस्य लालयानस्य तत्सुतान् । कालोऽत्यगान्महान् राजन्नष्टाशीत्यायुषः समाः ।।
तस्य प्रवयसः पुत्रा दश तेषां तु योऽवमः । बालो नारायणो नाम्ना पित्रोश्च दयितो भृशम् ।।
स बद्धहृदयस्तस्मिन्नर्भके कलभाषिणि । निरीक्षमाणस्तल्लीलां मुमुदे जरठो भृशम् ।।25।।
भुञ्जानः प्रपिबन् खादन् बालकस्नेहयन्त्रितः । भोजयन् पाययन्मूढो न वेदागतमन्तकम् ।।26।।
स एवं वर्तमानोऽज्ञो मृत्युकाल उपस्थिते । मतिं चकार तनये बाले नारायणाह्वये ।।27।।
स पाशहस्तांस्त्रीन् दृष्ट्वा पुरुषान् भृशदारुणान् । वक्रतुण्डानूर्ध्वरोम्ण आत्मानं नेतुमागतान् ।28।।
दूरे क्रीडनकासक्तं पुत्रं नारायणाह्वयम् । प्लावितेन स्वरेणोच्चैराजुहावाकुलेन्द्रियः ।।29।।
निशम्य म्रियमाणस्य ब्रुवतो हरिकीर्तनम् । भर्तुर्नाम महाराज पार्षदाः सहसाऽपतन् ।।30।।
विकर्षतोऽन्तर्हृदयाद् दासीपतिमजामिलम् । यमप्रेष्यान् विष्णुदूता वारयामासुरोजसा ।।31।।

like water, a liquor pot. **19.** If a man, with a feeling of passionate attachment, unites his mind with Krishna's feet even once, he will not see Yama or his emissaries with noose in hand, even in dream.

Sinner Ajāmila on his Death-bed (20-36)

20. This is illustrated by an ancient traditional account of a conversation between the emissaries of Yama and of Vishnu. Hear it from me. **21.** In the city of Kānyakubja there was a Brahmana named Ajāmila who had a harlot as his concubine. Corrupted by association with her, he abandoned the scriptural regulations binding the life of a Brahmana. **22.** He adopted for the support of himself and his family such heinous means as highway robbery, gambling, cheating, stealing and the like, and lived a life of corruption and of cruelty to living beings. **23.** Absorbed in fondling the children of that woman, he spent a major part of his life until he was eighty-eight. **24.** The old man had ten sons, of whom Narayana, the youngest, was very dear to his parents. **25.** The most joyous occupation for that old man was to watch the pranks of that sweetly prattling child, to whom he was so deeply attached. **26.** Feeding the child along with himself, making him eat and drink with himself, that foolish man failed to notice the approach of the god of death, completely dominated as he was by his attachment to the child.

27. While spending his time thus, his last days approached. Still that man of little understanding continued to bestow his whole mind on his child Narayana. **28-29.** When the time of death came, he saw before him three fierce beings, the emissaries of Yama, with curved faces and with erect hair and with ropes in hand, come to fetch him. On seeing them he was struck with fear, and cried aloud to his boy Narayana, who was playing at some distance away from there. **30.** Hearing the dying man's cry, invoking the sacred name of Sri Hari, the emissaries of Mahavishnu hurried to his side. **31.** These emissaries of Vishnu forcibly disengaged the attendants of Yama, who were already pulling out the soul from the heart of that degenerate servant-maid's para-

ऊचुर्निषेधितास्तांस्ते वैवस्वतपुरःसराः। के यूयं प्रतिषेद्धारो धर्मराजस्य शासनम् ॥32॥
कस्य वा कुत आयाताः कस्मादस्य निषेधथ। किं देवा उपदेवा वा यूयं किं सिद्धसत्तमाः ॥33॥
सर्वे पद्मपलाशाक्षाः पीतकौशेयवाससः। किरीटिनः कुण्डलिनो लसत्पुष्करमालिनः ॥34॥
सर्वे च नूत्नवयसः सर्वे चारुचतुर्भुजाः। धनुर्निषङ्गासिगदाशङ्खचक्राम्बुजश्रियः ॥35॥
दिशो वितिमिरालोकाः कुर्वन्तः स्वेन रोचिषा। किमर्थं धर्मपालस्य किङ्करान्नो निषेधथ ॥36॥

श्रीशुक उवाच

इत्युक्ते यमदूतैस्तैर्वासुदेवोक्तकारिणः। तान् प्रत्यूचुः प्रहस्येदं मेघनिर्ह्रादया गिरा ॥37॥

विष्णुदूता ऊचुः

यूयं वै धर्मराजस्य यदि निर्देशकारिणः। ब्रूत धर्मस्य नस्तत्त्वं यच्च धर्मस्य लक्षणम् ॥38॥
कथंस्विद्ध्रियते दण्डःकिं वास्य स्थानमीप्सितम्। दण्डयाःकिं कारिणःसर्वे आहोस्वित्कतिचिन्नृणाम्

यमदूता ऊचुः

वेदप्रणिहितो धर्मो ह्यधर्मस्तद्विपर्ययः। वेदो नारायणः साक्षात्स्वयम्भूरिति शुश्रुम ॥40॥
येन स्वधाम्न्यमी भावा रजःसत्त्वतमोमयाः। गुणनामक्रियारूपैर्विभाव्यन्ते यथातथम् ॥41॥
सूर्योऽग्निः खं मरुद्गावः सोमः सन्ध्याहनी दिशः। कं कुः कालो धर्म इति ह्येते दैह्यस्य साक्षिणः 42॥
एतैरधर्मो विज्ञातः स्थानं दण्डस्य युज्यते। सर्वे कर्मानुरोधेन दण्डमर्हन्ति कारिणः ॥43॥

mour. **32.** When so obstructed, the attendants of Yama, the son of Vivaswān, said: 'Who are you to go counter to the order of Yama, the Lord of Dharma? **33.** Whose servants are you? Where are you coming from? Why do you obstruct our taking away this man? Are you celestials or demigods or Siddha chiefs? **34-36.** All of you have eyes like lotus petals, are dressed in yellow silk, have diadems and earpendents, and are wearing beautiful lotus garlands. You all look young, and are endowed with four arms and equipped with bow, quiver, sword, mace, conch, discus, and play-lotus. By your lustre, you are illumining the surroundings. Why are you obstructing us, the attendants of Dharmaraja, the god of justice, in the discharge of our duties?'

Sin, Expiation and Purgatory (37-55)

Sri Suka said: **37.** When the attendants of Yama said like this, the emissaries of Vishnu smiled and replied in words that sounded like thunder. *The emissaries of Vishnu said:* **38.** 'If you are the emissaries of Dharmaraja, then you would be able to tell us what the essence of Dharma is and what its signs are. **39.** You should also be able to inform us how you are going to inflict punishment, what punishments you would be inflicting, what kind of people are liable for punishment, and whether it would be inflicted on all or on some only.'

The attendants of Yama replied: **40.** Dharma is what is ordained in the Veda. What is prohibited in the Veda is Adharma. The self-originated Veda is Narayana Himself, having emerged with His breath. **41.** Narayana is He who creates in Himself creatures out of the qualities of Sattva, Rajas and Tamas, characterised by distinctions of forms, names and actions. **42.** Sun, fire, sky, air, the senses, moon, Sandhya, daytime, night, quarters, water, earth, time, Dharma—these are the witnesses of all actions of man. **43.** They testify to man's evil actions. A man found guilty of evil deeds is a fit subject for punishment. All men who engage themselves in evil actions are liable to punishment according to the nature of their

सम्भवन्ति हि भद्राणि विपरीतानि चानघाः । कारिणां गुणसङ्गोऽस्ति देहवान्न ह्यकर्मकृत् ॥44॥
येन यावान् यथाधर्मो धर्मो वेह समीहितः । स एव तत्फलं भुङ्क्ते तथा तावदमुत्र वै ॥45॥
यथेह देवप्रवरास्त्रैविध्यमुपलभ्यते । भूतेषु गुणवैचित्र्यात्तथान्यत्रानुमीयते ॥46॥
वर्तमानोऽन्ययोः कालो गुणाभिज्ञापको यथा । एवं जन्मान्ययोरेतद्धर्माधर्मनिदर्शनम् ॥47॥
मनसैव पुरे देवः पूर्वरूपं विपश्यति । अनुमीमांसतेऽपूर्वं मनसा भगवानजः ॥48॥
यथाज्ञस्तमसा युक्त उपास्ते व्यक्तमेव हि । न वेद पूर्वमपरं नष्टजन्मस्मृतिस्तथा ॥49॥
पञ्चभिः कुरुते स्वार्थान् पञ्च वेदाथ पञ्चभिः । एकस्तु षोडशेन त्रीन् स्वयं सप्तदशोऽश्नुते ॥50॥
तदेतत् षोडशकलं लिङ्गं शक्तित्रयं महत् । धत्तेऽनुसंसृतिं पुंसि हर्षशोकभयार्तिदाम् ॥51॥
देह्यज्ञोऽजितषड्वर्गो नेच्छन् कर्माणि कार्यते । कोशकार इवात्मानं कर्मणाऽऽच्छाद्य मुह्यति 52॥
न हि कश्चित्क्षणमपि जातु तिष्ठत्यकर्मकृत् । कार्यते ह्यवशः कर्म गुणैः स्वाभाविकैर्बलात् 53॥

works. **44.** O holy ones! All works produce a mixture of good and bad effects. These accrue to the worker, because he has attachment for works and their fruits. And no man with a body can absolutely abstain from work. **45.** Whoever has performed Dharma and Adharma, and to the extent he has done them, in proportion to it he enjoys and suffers in the life hereafter. **46.** O noble celestials! Just as in this world men have happiness or misery or happiness-cum-misery because of the operation of the three Gunas of Prakriti, it can be presumed that the same happens to them hereafter as well. **47.** Just as from the current season, say spring, we can infer the nature of the past and the future spring seasons, so also the present birth is a pointer regarding the Dharma and Adharma of a Jiva in his past and future births.

48. The worshipful Yama, Brahma-like in wisdom, can even while remaining in his realm 'Samyamani' understand, through the power of his mind, all the previous history of a dying individual, and decide what kind of purgatory should be awarded to him, and what kind of future birth he should have. **49.** Just as a person, caught in the darkness of ignorance that overtakes him in the dream state, regards the dream ego alone as himself and not his body of the waking state, so also man thinks of his present body as himself in complete forgetfulness of the other bodies he had in earlier births. **50.** The ten senses, inclusive of five of knowledge and five of action, the five Pranas and the mind, constitute the sixteen adjuncts of the Jiva, the seventeenth category being the Jiva himself. Though distinct from all the other categories, he, the Jiva, enjoys through the sixteenth category (the mind), the experiences gathered by the three —the organs of action, the senses and the mind. **51.** The Linga Sarira (subtle body), which is beginningless in origin and is constituted of the above-mentioned sixteen adjuncts born of the three Gunas of Prakriti, involves the Jiva in the endless flux of Samsara, bringing on him various experiences such as joy, fear, sorrow and sufferings. **52.** The Jiva who has not yet conquered the senses is forced to perform Karma even if he does not like it. Like a silk worm, the Jiva covers himself with the cocoon of Karma with no means to get out. **53.** No one can remain without Karma even for a minute. Compelled by natural impulses like desire, greed, anger etc., which are born of the Gunas of

लब्ध्वा निमित्तमव्यक्तं व्यक्ताव्यक्तं भवत्युत । यथायोनि यथाबीजं स्वभावेन बलीयसा ॥54॥
एष प्रकृतिसङ्गेन पुरुषस्य विपर्ययः । आसीत् स एव नचिरादीशसङ्गाद्विलीयते ॥55॥
अयं हि श्रुतसम्पन्नः शीलवृत्तगुणालयः । धृतव्रतो मृदुर्दान्तः सत्यवान्मन्त्रविच्छुचिः ॥56॥
गुर्वग्न्यतिथिवृद्धानां शुश्रूषुर्निरहङ्कृतः । सर्वभूतसुहृत्साधुर्मितवागनसूयकः ॥57॥
एकदासौ वनं यातः पितृसन्देशकृद् द्विजः । आदाय तत आवृत्तः फलपुष्पसमित्कुशान् ॥58॥
ददर्श कामिनं कञ्चिच्छूद्रं सह भुजिष्यया । पीत्वा च मधु मैरेयं मदाघूर्णितनेत्रया ॥59॥
मत्तया विश्लथन्नीव्या व्यपेतं निरपत्रपम् । क्रीडन्तमनु गायन्तं हसन्तमनयान्तिके ॥60॥
दृष्ट्वा तां कामलिप्तेन बाहुना परिरम्भिताम् । जगाम हृच्छयवशं सहसैव विमोहितः ॥61॥
स्तम्भयन्नात्मनाऽऽत्मानं यावत्सत्त्वं यथाश्रुतम् । न शशाक समाधातुं मनो मदनवेपितम् ।
तन्निमित्तस्मरव्याजग्रहग्रस्तो विचेतनः । तामेव मनसा ध्यायन् स्वधर्माद्विरराम ह ॥63॥
तामेव तोषयामास पित्र्येणार्थेन यावता । ग्राम्यैर्मनोरमैः कामैः प्रसीदेत यथा तथा ॥64॥

Prakriti and its evolutes, all men are compelled to work. **54.** Driven by the force of tendencies provided by the store of his past actions, the Jiva gets a gross and a subtle body resembling the man and the woman through whom he has got embodiment. **55.** This transformation of the condition of the Jiva from his pristine nature into a transmigrating individual is due to his association with Prakriti (Nature), but it will soon come to an end if he develops intense devotion to the Supreme Lord.

Ajāmila's previous History (56-68)

56. This Ajāmila was originally a man learned in scriptures, virtuous, pure-hearted, possessed of an exemplary character and conduct, given to austere living, tender-hearted, established in sense control, devoted to truth, and learned in Mantras. **57.** He was also devoted to the service of the teacher, the sacred fire, guests and elders, besides being prideless, friendly and helpful to all, moderate in speech, and devoid of jealousy and allied vices.

58. Once this Brahmana, as directed by his father, went to the adjoining woodland to collect flowers, fruits, sacrificial firewood, Kusa grass etc., and after gathering all these, he was returning home. **59-60.** On the way back he saw an extremely lascivious man in the company of a harlot, whose eyes were rolling under the influence of a liquor brewed from rice. He saw nearby this man engaging himself in amorous preoccupations with that intoxicated woman, whose clothes had fallen off in her inebriated state. Shamelessly, without any consideration for good conduct, the man was laughing and singing to her tune. **61.** Seeing the man embracing her with his arms anointed with sexually exciting unguents, the Brahmana was completely carried away by an outburst of passion and became enslaved to Cupid.

62. Though he tried his best to restrain himself, using the power of his will and scriptural understanding, all his efforts were of no avail, and his mind was powerfully stirred by Cupid. **63.** Possessed by that evil spirit in the shape of Cupid with the sight of that woman as the occasion, he lost even the memory of his past holy life, and began to spend his time in constant absorption in her thought, abandoning all his sacred and secular duties. **64.** Whatever property he had got from his father, he utilised to please her through vulgar and exciting indulgences according

विप्रां स्वभार्यामप्रौढां कुले महति लम्भिताम् । विससर्जाचिरात्पापः स्वैरिण्यापाङ्गविद्धधीः ॥
यतस्ततश्चोपनिन्ये न्यायतोऽन्यायतो धनम् । बभारास्याः कुटुम्बिन्याः कुटुम्बं मन्दधीरयम् ॥
यदसौ शास्त्रमुल्लङ्घ्य स्वैरचार्यार्यगर्हितः । अवर्तत चिरं कालमघायुरशुचिर्मलात् ॥67॥
तत एनं दण्डपाणेः सकाशं कृतकिल्बिषम् । नेष्यामोऽकृतनिर्वेशं यत्र दण्डेन शुद्धयति ॥68॥

इति श्रीमद्भागवते महापुराणे पारमहंस्यां संहितायां षष्ठस्कन्धेऽजामिलोपाख्याने प्रथमोऽध्यायः ॥1॥

to her liking. **65.** With his good senses shattered by the weapon of that harlot's sidelong glances, he before long abandoned his young wife of tender years, hailing from a very respectable Brahmana family and married to him according to Vedic rites. **66.** This stupid man brought his concubine wealth from here and there, having earned it by means fair and foul, and somehow maintained her family. **67-68.** He spent a long time living the unrestricted life of a libertine, throwing all the Vedic injunctions to the winds, eating the harlot's impure food, and indulging in sins and ways of life condemned by all respectable people. Nor has he done any atonement or expiation for the sins he committed. So we are taking him to the realm of Yama, the holder of the rod of punishment, so that he may be purified in the purgatory.

अथ द्वितीयोऽध्यायः

श्रीशुक उवाच

एवं ते भगवद्दूता यमदूताभिभाषितम् । उपधार्याथ तान् राजन् प्रत्याहुर्नयकोविदाः ॥ 1॥

विष्णुदूता ऊचुः

अहो कष्टं धर्मदृशामधर्मः स्पृशते सभाम् । यत्रादण्डचेष्वपापेषु दण्डो यैर्ध्रियते वृथा ॥ 2॥
प्रजानां पितरो ये च शास्तारः साधवः समाः । यदि स्यात्तेषु वैषम्यं कं यान्ति शरणं प्रजाः ॥ 3॥
यद्यदाचरति श्रेयानितरस्तत्तदीहते । स यत्प्रमाणं कुरुते लोकस्तदनुवर्तते ॥ 4॥
यस्याङ्के शिर आधाय लोकः स्वपिति निर्वृतः । स्वयं धर्ममधर्मं वा न हि वेद यथा पशुः ॥ 5॥
स कथं न्यर्पितात्मानं कृतमैत्रमचेतनम् । विश्रम्भणीयो भूतानां सघृणो द्रोग्धुमर्हति ॥ 6॥

Skandha VI : Chapter 2

AJĀMILA EPISODE: HIS REDEMPTION

The Power of the Lord's Name (1-19)

Sri Suka said: **1.** O King! The emissaries of Vishnu, who were experts in scriptures and in sound reasoning, said as follows in reply to Yama's attendants.

Vishnu's attendants said: **2.** Alas! Sin accrues to an assembly of judges who are expected to know the righteous law, if they inflict punishment on innocent people undeserving of it. **3.** If the even-sighted and holy personages who are expected to be both the protecting fathers and the punishing disciplinarians turn out to be partial, where can ordinary people get relief from injustice? **4.** Whatever men of position accepted as leaders do, that is followed by others too; the standards set by such leading men become examples for others to follow. **5-6.** Men at large are by nature

अयं हि कृतनिर्वेशो जन्मकोट्यंहसामपि । यद् व्याजहार विवशो नाम स्वस्त्ययनं हरेः 7॥
एतेनैव ह्यघोनोऽस्य कृतं स्यादघनिष्कृतम् । यदा नारायणायेति जगाद चतुरक्षरम् ॥ 8॥
स्तेनः सुरापो मित्रध्रुग्ब्रह्महा गुरुतल्पगः । स्त्रीराजपितृगोहन्ता ये च पातकिनोऽपरे ॥ 9॥
सर्वेषामप्यघवतामिदमेव सुनिष्कृतम् । नामव्याहरणं विष्णोर्यतस्तद्विषया मतिः ॥10॥
न निष्कृतैरुदितैर्ब्रह्मवादिभिस्तथा विशुद्ध्यत्यघवान् व्रतादिभिः ।
यथा हरेर्नामपदैरुदाहृतैस्तदुत्तमश्लोकगुणोपलम्भकम् ॥11॥
नैकान्तिकं तद्धि कृतेऽपि निष्कृते मनः पुनर्धावति चेदसत्पथे ।
तत्कर्मनिर्हारमभीप्सतां हरेर्गुणानुवादः खलु सत्त्वभावनः ॥12॥
अथैनं मापनयत कृताशेषाघनिष्कृतम् । यदसौ भगवन्नाम म्रियमाणः समग्रहीत् ॥13॥
साङ्केत्यं पारिहास्यं वा स्तोभं हेलनमेव वा । वैकुण्ठनामग्रहणमशेषाघहरं विदुः ॥14॥
पतितः स्खलितो भग्नः संदष्टस्तप्त आहतः । हरिरित्यवशेनाह पुमान्नार्हति यातनाम् ॥15॥

like animals, without an understanding of what is Dharma and what is Adharma, what is right and what is wrong. The administrators of law, sacred and secular, are like persons in whose laps these ignorant men lay their head and sleep carefree. If these leaders are faithful and have in them an atom of love and fair play, how can they go against the interest and welfare of those ignorant men who have reposed such confidence in them? **7.** This man has already done expiation for his sins not only of this life but of his innumerable past ones. For though it be in a fit of helplessness, he has been uttering the name of the Lord, which is not only a sin-destroying power but also the harbinger of everything good and auspicious. **8.** 'O Narayana come!', by merely uttering this name of the Lord with four syllables, the expiation of the sins of this heinous sinner has been accomplished. **9-10.** A man might be a thief, a drunkard, a traitor, a murderer, a violator of the sanctity of the Guru's bed, or a killer of a woman, king, father or cow—for these and whatever other types of sins he might have committed, the utterance of Vishnu's name is the best expiation. Besides, by uttering His name, the Lord's attention is drawn to the person seeking protection. **11.** The sinful man is not as much purified by the austere practices prescribed in the form of expiations by Vedic scholars, as he is by repeating His names; for the former only removes the sins, but the name not only does this but effects the positive purification of the heart by arousing the consciousness of the Lord's attributes. **12.** If after certain observances the mind still runs on the sinful path, those observances cannot be called expiations in an ultimate sense. So for those who desire the total eradication of the sinful tendency, there is nothing like the Lord's names extolling His attributes. They purify the mind by destroying even sinful tendencies.

13. So, as this man has already done expiation for all his sins, do not carry him along the path of evil doers. For, at the time when death was imminent, he uttered the Lord's name in fullness. **14.** According to the conviction of great men, the utterance of the Lord's name by itself purifies men of their sins, whether the utterance is made casually by way of calling some one by that name, or in jest, or for improvising, for the completion of lines in recitals, or even in an attitude of disregard. **15.** If anyone utters 'Hari', be it while falling down or stumbling, being wounded or bitten by snake, in the deli-

गुरूणां च लघूनां च गुरूणि च लघूनि च । प्रायश्चित्तानि पापानां ज्ञात्वोक्तानि महर्षिभिः ॥
तैस्तान्यघानि पूयन्ते तपोदानजपादिभिः । नाधर्मजं तद्धृदयं तदपीशाङ्घ्रिसेवया ॥17॥
अज्ञानादथवा ज्ञानादुत्तमश्लोकनाम यत् । सङ्कीर्तितमघं पुंसो दहेदेधो यथानलः ॥18॥
यथागदं वीर्यतममुपयुक्तं यदृच्छया । अजानतोऽप्यात्मगुणं कुर्यान्मन्त्रोऽप्युदाहृतः ॥

श्रीशुक उवाच

त एवं सुविनिर्णीय धर्मं भागवतं नृप । तं याम्यपाशान्निर्मुच्य विप्रं मृत्योरमूमुचन् 20॥
इति प्रत्युदिता याम्या दूता यात्वा यमान्तिके । यमराज्ञे यथा सर्वमाचचक्षुररिन्दम ॥21॥
द्विजः पाशाद्विनिर्मुक्तो गतभीः प्रकृतिं गतः । ववन्दे शिरसा विष्णोः किङ्करान् दर्शनोत्सवः 22॥

rium of fever or while beaten—he deserves not the tortures of the purgatory. **16.** Sages have laid down expiations easy or severe in nature, according to the lightness or seriousness of sins committed. **17.** Austerity, charity, Japa and such other disciplines efface only the effects of sins, but not the heart, the source from which they spring. Even that source, the sinful tendency, is effaced by the service of the Lord's feet. **18.** As a fire burns up a heap of fuel, the name of the Lord of holy fame, chanted whether with knowledge of its greatness or without it, destroys the sins of man. **19.** O King! A powerful medicine taken in even casually benefits a man, though he may be unaware of its potency. The same is the case with a Mantra, the Lord's name.[1]

Ajāmila's Repentance (20-38)

Sri Suka said: **20.** O King! With this firm and unequivocal statement of the law of devotional life, these emissaries of Vishnu released the Brahmana from the noose of Yama's attendants and saved him from death for the time being. **21.** O heroic King! The attendants of Yama, thus obstructed in their work, returned to Yama's realm and reported to him everything as it happened. **22.** And Ajāmila, the Brahmana, thus released from Yama's noose, was now free from fear. He recovered his nature and he made pros-

[1] The justification given for Ajāmila's rescue from punishment is that he took the name of Vishnu at the time of death in utter fear and helplessness. That he had in mind only his son when he uttered 'Narayana', does not detract from the saving power of the Divine Name, according to the Bhagavata doctrine. It is contended that just as a potent medicine has its effect on a man swallowing it irrespective of his knowledge or ignorance of its potency, or of his attitude towards it, the Divine Name exerts its inherent saving power on one who utters it. It attracts the Lord's attention to the utterer. Besides, its power being inherent, its effectiveness is not dependent on any extraneous factor. This uncompromising Bhagavata doctrine of the complete objective efficacy of the Name, without any reference to the knowledge, faith or attitude of the utterer, may be a great hurdle to a rational devotee. He may be prepared to accept its claim as an Arthavāda—a eulogy or exaggeration to prompt people to the devotional path with the thought that if the Name could even save a man like Ajāmila by casual utterance, how much more effective would it indeed be in the case of good men calling on God in faith and sincerity!

There is an implication of this kind in VI.2.49 coming hereafter, but some of the commentators of the *Bhagavata* hold that this doctrine is not a eulogy or exaggeration, but a real truth, and any doubt on this is only a sign of lack of faith in, and understanding of, the greatness of God and His Divine Name. Such a doubting attitude is technically called Nāmāparādha or offence to the sanctity of the Divine Name, and is considered highly sinful. There are, however, some commentators who seek to reconcile the points of view of reason and of faith in regard to the power of the Name by holding that the word *Vivasa*, 'in helplessness and supplication', used in the text to refer to Ajāmila's attitude at the time of death, indicates that the thought of the Supreme Being as his only Saviour must have come to his mind at the moment. Another point to be remembered is that Ajāmila was, according to the *Bhagavata* text, leading a holy life before he took to sinful ways, and that is pointed out as the justification for the sacred name of God with saving power coming to his mind, be it by chance, at what was going to be his last moment. Besides, Ajāmila survived this incident, and lived for some time more, reconverted to the ways of holy living that he had once abandoned.

तं विवक्षुमभिप्रेत्य महापुरुषकिङ्कराः । सहसा पश्यतस्तस्य तत्रान्तर्दधिरेऽनघ ॥23॥
अजामिलोऽप्यथाकर्ण्य दूतानां यमकृष्णयोः । धर्मं भागवतं शुद्धं त्रैविद्यं च गुणाश्रयम् ॥24॥
भक्तिमान् भगवत्याशु माहात्म्यश्रवणाद्धरेः । अनुतापो महानासीत्स्मरतोऽशुभमात्मनः ॥25॥
अहो मे परमं कष्टमभूदविजितात्मनः । येन विप्लावितं ब्रह्म वृषल्यां जायताऽऽत्मना ॥26॥
धिङ्मां विगर्हितं सद्भिर्दुष्कृतं कुलकज्जलम् । हित्वा बालां सतीं योऽहं सुरापामसतीमगाम् 27॥
वृद्धावनाथौ पितरौ नान्यबन्धू तपस्विनौ । अहो मयाधुना त्यक्तावकृतज्ञेन नीचवत् ॥28॥
सोऽहं व्यक्तं पतिष्यामि नरके भृशदारुणे । धर्मघ्नाः कामिनो यत्र विन्दन्ति यमयातनाः 29॥
किमिदं स्वप्न आहोस्वित्साक्षाद् दृष्टमिहाद्भुतम् क्व याता अद्य ते ये मां व्यकर्षन् पाशपाणयः 30॥
अथ ते क्व गताः सिद्धाश्चत्वारश्चारुदर्शनाः । व्यमोचयन्नीयमानं बद्ध्वा पाशैरधो भुवः ॥31॥
अथापि मे दुर्भगस्य विबुधोत्तमदर्शने । भवितव्यं मङ्गलेन येनात्मा मे प्रसीदति ॥32॥
अन्यथा म्रियमाणस्य नाशुचेर्वृषलीपतेः । वैकुण्ठनाम ग्रहणं जिह्वा वक्तुमिहार्हति ॥33॥
क्व चाहं कितवः पापो ब्रह्मघ्नो निरपत्रपः । क्व च नारायणेत्येतद्भगवन्नाम मङ्गलम् ॥34॥
सोऽहं तथा यतिष्यामि यतचित्तेन्द्रियानिलः । यथा न भूय आत्मानमन्धे तमसि मज्जये ॥35॥

tration to the emissaries of Vishnu with a heart overflowing with joy. **23.** He wanted to speak to those servants of the Supreme Person, Mahavishnu, but without giving him an opportunity, they disappeared suddenly even as he looked on.

24-25. From the conversation between the emissaries of Yama and of the Supreme Being Mahavishnu, Ajāmila had a comparative understanding of the Vedic Dharma expounded by Yama's attendants as applicable to those whose life is based on the three Gunas of Prakriti, and of the immaculate path of devotion based upon the pure love of the Lord, for which Vishnu's emissaries stood. Hearing about the supreme excellences of the Lord, he became filled with divine love at once. He also became extremely repentant of his past sinful life. **26.** He thought: 'Alas! Great has been my mistake through lack of control over the senses. My birth as a Brahmana has gone to waste because of my consorting with a harlot. **27.** Fie upon me, a blot on my class! I am despicable in the eyes of good men for having abandoned my very young and devoted wife and gone after a harlot given to drinking! **28.** Alas! The degenerate and ungrateful fellow that I am, I deserted my old, helpless and sorrowing parents whose only son I am! **29.** I, a sinful wretch, am sure to be consigned to the purgatory where unrighteous and sensuous sinners undergo terrible sufferings for their purification. **30.** Is all that I saw a mere dream, or is it a miracle witnessed in the waking state? Where have they gone—those who were tying me up with ropes in hand? **31.** And where have those four attractive and angelic beings too gone, who got me released from being bound and led down to some nether region? **32.** Though I am an unfortunate man, there must have been a modicum of auspicious Karma to my credit inasmuch as I had the good fortune of meeting those celestial personages. By their meeting, my mind has become very peaceful. **33.** Otherwise, the tongue of a paramour of a harlot like myself could not have had the power to utter the name of the Lord of Vaikuntha while facing imminent death. **34.** Where am I, a shameless, sinful cheat who has no hesitation to kill even holy men—and where is the auspicious name of the worshipful Lord Narayana! **35.** So I, who have passed through all these experiences, shall

विमुच्य तमिमं बन्धमविद्याकामकर्मजम् । सर्वभूतसुहृच्छान्तो मैत्रः करुण आत्मवान् ॥36॥
मोचये ग्रस्तमात्मानं योषिन्मय्याऽऽत्ममायया । विक्रीडितो ययैवाहं क्रीडामृग इवाधमः ॥37॥
ममाहमिति देहादौ हित्वामिथ्यार्थधीर्मतिम् । धास्ये मनो भगवति शुद्धं तत्कीर्तनादिभिः ॥38॥

श्रीशुक उवाच

इति जातसुनिर्वेदः क्षणसङ्गेन साधुषु । गङ्गाद्वारमुपेयाय मुक्तसर्वानुबन्धनः ॥39॥
स तस्मिन्देवसदन आसीनो योगमाश्रितः । प्रत्याहृतेन्द्रियग्रामो युयोज मन आत्मनि ॥40॥
ततो गुणेभ्य आत्मानं वियुज्यात्मसमाधिना । युयुजे भगवद्धाम्नि ब्रह्मण्यनुभवात्मनि ॥41॥
यर्ह्युपारतधीस्तस्मिन्नद्राक्षीत्पुरुषान् पुरः । उपलभ्योपलब्धान् प्रागवन्दे शिरसा द्विजः 42॥
हित्वा कलेवरं तीर्थे गङ्गायां दर्शनादनु । सद्यः स्वरूपं जगृहे भगवत्पार्श्ववर्तिनाम् ॥43॥
साकं विहायसा विप्रो महापुरुषकिङ्करैः । हैमं विमानमारुह्य ययौ यत्र श्रियः पतिः ॥44॥
एवं स विप्लावितसर्वधर्मा दास्याः पतिः पतितो गर्ह्यकर्मणा ।
निपात्यमानो निरये हतव्रतः सद्यो विमुक्तो भगवन्नाम गृह्णन् ॥45॥

hereafter strive not to fall into this darkness of blinding ignorance, by practising the control of the senses, mind and vital energies. **36.** Releasing myself from this bondage born of ignorance, desire and of actions undertaken for fulfilling them, I shall lead a life of self-control, peacefulness, benevolence, and friendliness to all alike. **37.** I shall soon liberate my spirit from thraldom to the Lord's infatuating power in the shape of a woman, who used this wretch of a fellow as her pet play-animal dancing to her tunes. **38.** Abandoning the sense of 'I' and 'mine' with regard to the body and withdrawing my mind from the fleeting objects of the world, I shall fix my mind on the worshipful Lord by purifying it by devotional practices like chanting His name and extolling His deeds and excellences.

Liberation of Ajāmila (39-49)

Sri Suka said: **39-40.** By contact with holy men for a few minutes, Ajāmila was filled with disgust for worldly life. Abandoning all worldly attachments and entanglements, he went to the sacred spot called the Doorway to Hari (Haridwāra). In that holy spot he gave himself up to the practice of the Yoga of devotion to Hari. With all the senses ingathered into the mind, he united that concentrated mind on the Atman, the innermost essence in all. **41.** By such concentration he disentangled the Atman, the individual self, from identification with the body, the product of the Gunas of Prakriti. Then he united that liberated Self with the intuitively experienced Brahman, who is the worshipful Lord Himself. **42.** When all his mental modifications had subsided, he saw before him those emissaries of Mahavishnu who had appeared to him earlier. Recognising their identity, the Brahmana prostrated himself before them in salutation. **43.** After their vision, he consigned his physical body into the sacred Ganga, and immediately got a body similar to that possessed by those celestial beings. **44.** Ascending a golden aerial car with those celestials, that Brahmana went through ethereal regions to the Realm of Mahavishnu, the Lord of Srī.

45. By uttering the Lord's name even once, this Ajāmila—a libertine, who broke all the laws of Dharma, a harlot's paramour, a fallen man who discarded all vows and codes of good conduct, a sure candidate for purgatory—even he be-

नातः परं कर्मनिबन्धकृन्तनं मुमुक्षतां तीर्थपदानुकीर्तनात् ।
न यत्पुनः कर्मसु सज्जते मनो रजस्तमोभ्यां कलिलं ततोऽन्यथा ॥46॥
य एवं परमं गुह्यमितिहासमघापहम् । शृणुयाच्छ्रद्धया युक्तो यश्च भक्त्यानुकीर्तयेत् ॥47॥
न वै स नरकं याति नेक्षितो यमकिङ्करैः । यद्यप्यमङ्गलो मर्त्यो विष्णुलोके महीयते ॥48॥
म्रियमाणो हरेर्नाम गृणन् पुत्रोपचारितम् । अजामिलोऽप्यगाद्धाम किं पुनः श्रद्धया गृणन् ॥

इति श्रीमद्भागवते महापुराणे पारमहंस्यां संहितायां षष्ठस्कन्धेऽजामिलोपाख्याने द्वितीयोऽध्यायः ॥2॥

came liberated at once. **46.** Therefore, for those who aspire for liberation, there is nothing so effective as the chanting of the Lord's name for destroying the bad impressions of past actions and purifying the mind. For, once love of God is developed, the mind never goes after self-centred actions for fulfilment of desires; otherwise, the mind will be contaminated by the qualities of Rajas and Tamas. **47-48.** Whoever hears or recites with faith and devotion this traditional account of Ajāmila and his redemption, noted for its spiritual worth and its sin-effacing capacity, will never be cast into the purgatory, nor will the attendants of Yama even look at him. Whatever demerits he might have, he will gain a high place in the realm of Vishnu. **49.** Though Ajāmila had called the name of Hari at the time of death, intending to summon his son Narayana, still he attained to the Realm of Mahavishnu, because he uttered the sacred name of the Lord—Narayana. It is then needless to describe the glorious result of uttering the name of Hari with faith and devotion.[1]

[1] This verse indicates that, unlike some of its commentators, the *Bhagavata* is not intolerant of the view that takes this episode as a eulogy, as indicated in the preceding verses, though its sympathy is more with literalism. It should, however, be carefully noted that the intention of the *Bhagavata* text in stressing the unqualified holiness of the Name is not to encourage wrong doing in the hope of effecting easy expiation through uttering the Divine Name afterwards, knowingly or unknowingly. It is firmly held by the Vaishnava thinkers that nothing can be a more unpardonable insult to the Name (*Nāmāparādha*) than entertaining such a light attitude towards the Name as to consider it a cheap remedy available at one's choice, and to sin in anticipation. Remembrance of God's Name at death takes place only in the case of men whose lives have had a devotional trend. Or, Ajāmila's is an exceptional case, probably an instance of Divine Grace. It also highlights the unqualified greatness of the Name even in a purely objective sense. In pure grace there can be no law or regulatory principle as in justice. Or, as is stated by Ajāmila himself in a later verse, his good deeds in a previous birth might have been the cause of this unexpected good fortune. In this view grace is tempered with justice.

In these two verses the *Bhagavata* seems to prefer the acceptance of the power of the Name as such, though it is tolerant of the view that considers the claim to be a eulogy. But it has to be noted that what Ajāmila got by taking the Name in desperation was the prospect of Mukti but not Bhakti. For the question remains: In the light of the Ajāmila episode, what is the need of long and sustained devotional practice? This question is implied in VI.3.23-24. The commentator Sridhara answers this question by saying that sinful tendencies of the mind as distinguished from sins, will be eliminated only by the long practice of devotional disciplines. Only then will Divine Love as deep-rooted and unshakable sentiment of the heart be generated. According to the Bhakti Sastra, Mukti or liberation is not the highest gift of God to man; Bhakti is His highest gift. It is therefore called the fifth Purushartha (end to be realised). In verse V.6.18 the Lord says that He gives Mukti to some, but Bhakti very rarely. The superiority of Bhakti over Mukti is emphasised in several places in this Text. See Prologue, Vol. III, pp. 15-16. It is said that merely by dying at Kasi one obtains Mukti. So also Mukti may be had by uttering the Divine Name at the time of death. But Bhakti is generated only through constant practice of devotional disciplines and the attainment thereby of not merely expiation from sin but effacement of sinful tendency itself.

अथ तृतीयोऽध्यायः

राजोवाच

निशम्य देवः स्वभटोपवर्णितं प्रत्याह किं तान् प्रति धर्मराजः ।
एवं हताज्ञो विहतान्मुरारेर्नैदेशिकैर्यस्य वशे जनोऽयम् ॥ 1॥
यमस्य देवस्य न दण्डभङ्गः कुतश्चनर्षे श्रुतपूर्व आसीत् ।
एतन्मुने वृश्चति लोकसंशयं न हि त्वदन्य इति मे विनिश्चितम् ॥ 2॥

श्रीशुक उवाच

भगवत्पुरुषै राजन् याम्याः प्रतिहतोद्यमाः । पतिं विज्ञापयामासुर्यमं संयमनीपतिम् ॥ 3॥

यमदूता ऊचुः

कति सन्तीह शास्तारो जीवलोकस्य वै प्रभो । त्रैविध्यं कुर्वतः कर्म फलाभिव्यक्तिहेतवः ॥ 4॥
यदि स्युर्बहवो लोके शास्तारो दण्डधारिणः । कस्य स्यातां न वा कस्य मृत्युश्चामृतमेव वा 5॥
किन्तु शास्तृबहुत्वे स्याद्बहूनामिह कर्मिणाम् । शास्तृत्वमुपचारो हि यथा मण्डलवर्तिनाम् 6॥
अतस्त्वमेको भूतानां सेश्वराणामधीश्वरः । शास्ता दण्डधरो नृणां शुभाशुभविवेचनः ॥ 7॥
तस्य ते विहतो दण्डो न लोके वर्ततेऽधुना । चतुर्भिरद्भुतैः सिद्धैराज्ञा ते विप्रलम्भिता ॥ 8॥

Skandha VI : Chapter 3

AJĀMILA EPISODE: SANCTITY OF DIVINE NAME

Attendants' Report to Yama (1-10)

Rajah Parikshit said: **1.** On hearing the report of his attendants about the obstruction caused to their work by the emissaries of Mahavishnu, to whose control the whole world is subject, what did Yama, the Lord of Righteousness, reply, having had to suffer this rebuff? **2.** O great Rishi! Never have we heard that Yama's order on punishment has ever met with obstruction. This is a doubt which all would have, and there is none but you to clarify it.

Sri Suka said: **3.** O King! The attendants of Yama informed their master residing at Samyamani of their discomfiture. *The Attendants of Yama said:* **4.** 'O Master! How many are there in this universe as enforcers of the moral law awarding the fruits of action to living beings, according as they are Sattvika (predominently good), Rajasika (with a tilt to evil) and Tamasika (positively evil)? **5.** If there are many as the enforcers of the moral law, it can be that some get their deserts and some do not, and there will be utter confusion in the awarding of the fruits of Karma. **6.** If a multiplicity of enforcers is accepted as required for the large numbers to be dealt with, these enforcers will be rulers by courtesy only like feudatory chieftains. Unless there is an overlord, a single system of law cannot be enforced uniformly. **7.** So you are the one with sway over all men and their rulers—the one endowed with power to distinguish between the sins and the merits of individuals, and enforce the moral law by giving punishments to those who deserve them. **8.** That authority of yours for enforcement of due punishments no longer prevails in the world; for it has now been violated by four celestials of wonderful

नीयमानं तवादेशादस्माभिर्यातनागृहान्। व्यमोचयन् पातकिनं छित्त्वा पाशान् प्रसह्य ते ॥
तांस्ते वेदितुमिच्छामो यदि नो मन्यसे क्षमम्। नारायणेत्यभिहिते मा भैरित्यायर्युद्रुतम् ॥10॥

श्रीशुक उवाच

इति देवः स आपृष्टः प्रजासंयमनो यमः। प्रीतः स्वदूतान् प्रत्याह स्मरन् पादाम्बुजं हरेः 11॥

यम उवाच

परो मदन्यो जगतस्तस्थुषश्च ओतं प्रोतं पटवद्यत्र विश्वम्।
यदंशतोऽस्य स्थितिजन्मनाशा नस्योतवद्यस्य वशे च लोकः ॥12॥
यो नामभिर्वाचि जनान्निजायां बध्नाति तन्त्यामिव दामभिर्गाः।
यस्मै बलिं त इमे नामकर्मनिबन्धबद्धाश्चकिता वहन्ति ॥13॥
अहं महेन्द्रो निर्ऋतिः प्रचेताः सोमोऽग्निरीशः पवनोऽर्को विरिञ्चः।
आदित्यविश्वे वसवोऽथ साध्या मरुद्गणा रुद्रगणाः ससिद्धाः ॥14॥
अन्ये च ये विश्वसृजोऽमरेशा भृग्वादयोऽस्पृष्टरजस्तमस्काः।
यस्येहितं न विदुः स्पृष्टमायाः सत्त्वप्रधाना अपि किं ततोऽन्ये ॥15॥
यं वै न गोभिर्मनसासुभिर्वा हृदा गिरा वासुभृतो विचक्षते।
आत्मानमन्तर्हृदि सन्तमात्मनां चक्षुर्यथैवाकृतयस्ततः परम् ॥16॥

appearance. **9.** By your order we were bringing a great sinner to the purgatory when these celestials cut the rope we had tied him with and released him by force. **10.** If you think it fit, we would like to hear about them from your holiness himself. As soon as the sinner uttered 'Narayana,' these celestials appeared on the scene, saying: 'Do not be afraid.'

The Supremacy of Sri Hari (11-18)

Sri Suka said: **11.** Pleased to hear this submission, Yama the divinity for enforcing the moral law over all men, thought of Sri Hari's feet, and said smiling to his attendants.

Yama said: **12.** Different from me, there is an overlord for this world with its moving and unmoving beings. In Him all this world is spread as a piece of cloth is on the warp and woof. From a particle of Him are born Brahma, Vishnu and Maheswara who create, sustain and dissolve the universe. The whole is held by Him as an ox is by its nose-string. **13.** By the words of His Vedic revelation, He holds men as cattle are held by a big rope, to which they are attached with small halters. All men, bound by these strings of Vedic regulations laying down duties, are tendering offerings to Him in fear by the discharge of their duties, sacred and secular. **14-15.** Myself, Indra, Nirriti, Varuna, Chandra, Agni, Īsa, Vāyu, Sūrya, Brahma, the sons of Aditi, the Viswedevas, the eight Vasus, the Sādhyas, the hosts of Maruts, Rudras and Siddhas, besides the Prajapatis, chiefs of celestials and leading Maharshis like Bhrigu—all these are without the dominance of Rajas and Tamas, and are very largely possessed of Sattva. Still, infatuated by the Lord's Yogamaya, they are not able to understand His intentions or His sportive disposition. Then what to speak of others! **16.** Neither by the organs of knowledge, nor by mind, nor by Prana, nor by Chitta, nor by word can He be comprehended, as He resides in the heart of creatures as the Witnessing Spirit, distinct from these faculties and their objects, just as forms and colours cannot see the eye that reveals them.

तस्यात्मतन्त्रस्य हरेरधीशितुः परस्य मायाधिपतेर्महात्मनः ।
प्रायेण दूता इह वै मनोहराश्चरन्ति तद्रूपगुणस्वभावाः ॥17॥
भूतानि विष्णोः सुरपूजितानि दुर्दर्शलिङ्गानि महाद्भुतानि ।
रक्षन्ति तद्भक्तिमतः परेभ्यो मत्तश्च मर्त्यानथ सर्वतश्च ॥18॥
धर्मं तु साक्षाद्भगवत्प्रणीतं न वै विदुर्ऋषयो नापि देवाः ।
न सिद्धमुख्या असुरा मनुष्याः कुतश्च विद्याधरचारणादयः ॥19॥
स्वयम्भूर्नारदः शम्भुः कुमारः कपिलो मनुः । प्रह्लादो जनको भीष्मो बलिर्वैयासकिर्वयम् 20॥
द्वादशैते विजानीमो धर्मं भागवतं भटाः । गुह्यं विशुद्धं दुर्बोधं यं ज्ञात्वामृतमश्नुते ॥21॥
एतावानेव लोकेऽस्मिन् पुंसां धर्मः परः स्मृतः । भक्तियोगो भगवति तन्नामग्रहणादिभिः ॥22॥
नामोच्चारणमाहात्म्यं हरेः पश्यत पुत्रकाः । अजामिलोऽपि येनैव मृत्युपाशादमुच्यत ॥23॥
एतावतालमघनिर्हरणाय पुंसां सङ्कीर्तनं भगवतो गुणकर्मनाम्नाम् ।
विक्रुश्य पुत्रमघवान् यदजामिलोऽपि नारायणेति म्रियमाण इयाय मुक्तिम् ॥24॥

17. Generally the emissaries of the Supreme Being Hari, the independent and transcendent Master of Maya and the Lord of all, move about everywhere in the world. They are enchanting in appearance and bear the impress of His form and attributes. **18.** These emissaries of Vishnu, who are adored by all including the celestials, whose wonderful form is beyond the ken of others, afford protection to the Lord's devotees from enemies and from all fears, including that from myself, the god of Death.

The Glory of the Divine Name (19-30)

19. The Bhagavata Dharma, is the Dharma par excellence given by the Lord Himself. The Rishis know it not, the celestials know it not, Siddhas know it not—what to speak then of men, Asuras, Chāranas and Vidyādharas! **20-21.** O my boys! There are only twelve persons who know this Dharma proclaimed by the Lord which is esoteric, pure, difficult to grasp and potent enough to confer immortality. These twelve are Brahma, Narada, Parameswara, Sanatkumara, Kapila, Swāyambhuva Manu, Prahlada, Janaka, Bhishma, Mahābali, Sri Suka, and myself.

22. That Dharma briefly stated is as follows: It is the view of great men that the highest duty of man born in this world is to attain devotion to the Lord through disciplines like the chanting of His Name. **23.** O dear ones! See the greatness and power of the utterance of the Lord's Name. By that alone (without any previous practice of devotional sentiment), Ajāmila the sinner obtained release from the noose of death. **24.** The recital of the Lord's name, attributes and actions with faith and devotion as a long-standing spiritual practice is not needed for mere expiation of sins. For even without that, by merely shouting the name 'Narayana' when faced with death, with only his own son in view, even the sinner Ajāmila obtained Mukti, freedom from the effects of sin. So even the Lord's name alone, uttered without any knowledge or devotion, constitutes adequate expiation. (But what is the use then of regular devotional practices like chanting the divine name with faith and love? It consists in this: Such practice alone can efface all evil tendencies as contrasted with the effects of sinful actions, and generate deep-rooted loving devotion, Premabhakti, which is a higher consummation than mere

प्रायेण वेद तदिदं न महाजनोऽयं देव्या विमोहितमतिर्बत माययालम् ।
त्रय्यां जडीकृतमतिर्मधुपुष्पितायां वैतानिके महति कर्मणि युज्यमानः ॥25॥
एवं विमृश्य सुधियो भगवत्यनन्ते सर्वात्मना विदधते खलु भावयोगम् ।
ते मे न दण्डमर्हन्त्यथ यद्यमीषां स्यात् पातकं तदपि हन्त्युरुगायवादः ॥26॥
ते देवसिद्धपरिगीतपवित्रगाथा ये साधवः समदृशो भगवत्प्रपन्नाः ।
तान् नोपसीदत हरेर्गदयाभिगुप्तान् नैषां वयं न च वयः प्रभवाम दण्डे ॥27॥
तानानयध्वमसतो विमुखान् मुकुन्दपादारविन्दमकरन्दरसादजस्रम् ।
निष्किञ्चनैः परमहंसकुलै रसज्ञैर्जुष्टाद् गृहे निरयवर्त्मनि बद्धतृष्णान् ॥28॥
जिह्वा न वक्ति भगवद्गुणनामधेयं चेतश्च न स्मरति तच्चरणारविन्दम् ।
कृष्णाय नो नमति यच्छिर एकदापि तानानयध्वमसतोऽकृतविष्णुकृत्यान् ॥29॥
तत् क्षम्यतां स भगवान् पुरुषः पुराणो नारायणः स्वपुरुषैर्यदसत्कृतं नः ।
स्वानामहो न विदुषां रचिताञ्जलीनां क्षान्तिर्गरीयसि नमः पुरुषाय भूम्ने ॥30॥
तस्मात् सङ्कीर्तनं विष्णोर्जगन्मङ्गलमंहसाम् । महतामपि कौरव्य विद्धयैकान्तिकनिष्कृतिम् 31॥

effacement of sin, or even Mukti.)

25. Why then have great sages laid down the elaborate expiatory rites in place of announcing this easily performed discipline? The answer is this: The so-called great men, with their minds infatuated by the Lord's Maya (delusive power), with their intelligence rendered dull by the sweet and flowery Vedic texts offering promises of attractive rewards and heavenly felicities, and with their attention fixed on elaborate Vedic rites for the achievements of such ends, are not generally aware of this saving gospel of devotion. **26.** Therefore, after due deliberation, let all men practise whole-hearted devotion to the worshipful Lord, the Infinite Being, the indweller in all. Such devotees do not come within the scope of our corrective punishment. Even if they have sins, they are all dispelled by taking the name of the Lord. **27.** The holy personages, whose sanctifying doings are followed by even Devas and Siddhas, whose attention is always on the all-pervading Lord, and who have taken refuge in Him, are always protected by His mace. Do not approach them. Neither we, Divinities, nor Time can inflict any punishment on them. **28.** Bring here to this purgatory such evil Jivas as are averse to taste the nectar of the lotus-feet of the Lord, which is constantly consumed by all-renouncing ascetics. Bring Jivas who are intensely attached to home life which leads them to sinful ways deserving the punishment of purgatory. **29.** Bring here such Jivas as those whose tongue never utter even once the names of the Lord declaring His excellences, whose minds never remember the Lord's feet, and whose head never bows down to the Lord, and who never perform any of the devotional rites connected with the worship of Vishnu. **30.** Whatever wrong we, his ignorant and humbly saluting servants have done—may it be pardoned by the worshipful Lord, the most ancient, the indweller of everything. In the most powerful, forbearance is an ornament. Salutations to the Supreme Being!

Exhortation to take the Divine Name (31-35)

Sri Suka said: **31.** Therefore, O scion of the Kuru clan, know that the chanting

शृण्वतां गृणतां वीर्याण्युद्दामानि हरेर्मुहुः। यथा सुजातया भक्त्या शुद्ध्येन्नात्मा व्रतादिभिः ॥
कृष्णाङ्घ्रिपद्ममधुलिण् न पुनर्विसृष्टमायागुणेषु रमते वृजिनावहेषु।
अन्यस्तु कामहत आत्मरजः प्रमार्ष्टुमीहेत कर्म यत एव रजः पुनः स्यात् ॥33॥
इत्थं स्वभर्तृगदितं भगवन्महित्वं संस्मृत्य विस्मितधियो यमकिङ्कारास्ते।
नैवाच्युताश्रयजनं प्रतिशङ्कमाना द्रष्टुं च बिभ्यति ततः प्रभृति स्म राजन् ॥34॥
इतिहासमिमं गुह्यं भगवान् कुम्भसम्भवः। कथयामास मलय आसीनो हरिमर्चयन् ॥35॥

इति श्रीमद्भागवते महापुराणे पारमहंस्यां संहितायां षष्ठस्कन्धे यमपुरुषसंवादे तृतीयोऽध्यायः ॥3॥

of the Lord's name with faith and devotion is the ultimate and sure expiation for even the greatest of sins. **32.** No vow or austerity purifies the heart of man so effectively as devotion engendered easily by hearing and uttering the names of Sri Hari denoting His sanctifying deeds and excellences. **33.** One who has imbibed the nectar of Krishna's lotus feet would not thereafter hanker after those sin-generating worldly values that have been once rejected. But the one who has not sought refuge in the Lord and is full of desires in the mind, performs Karmas of an expiatory nature for eradicating his sins, but in the course of doing them, he may commit fresh sins. **34.** Those attendants of Yama were wonder-struck to hear and ponder over what their master said to them about the greatness of the worshipful Lord. Thenceforth, O King, they became afraid of even looking at devotees who have taken refuge at the feet of the Lord. **35.** This ancient tradition about Ajāmila, unknown to men at large, was narrated by the worshipful Agastya, the pot-born sage, who stays on the Malaya mountain worshipping Sri Hari.

अथ चतुर्थोऽध्यायः

राजोवाच

देवासुरनृणां सर्गो नागानां मृगपक्षिणाम्। सामासिकस्त्वया प्रोक्तो यस्तु स्वायम्भुवेऽन्तरे ॥
तस्यैव व्यासमिच्छामि ज्ञातुं ते भगवन् यथा। अनुसर्गं यया शक्त्या ससर्ज भगवान् परः ॥ 2॥

सूत उवाच

इति सम्प्रश्नमाकर्ण्य राजर्षेर्बादरायणिः। प्रतिनन्द्य महायोगी जगाद मुनिसत्तमाः ॥ 3॥

Skandha VI : Chapter 4

BLESSING BESTOWED ON DAKSHA

The Prachetasas and the War on Trees (1-15)

Rajah Parikshit said: **1-2.** You gave a brief account of the creation of Devas, Asuras, men, serpents, animals, birds etc., during the rule of the Manu Swāyambhuva. O worshipful one! I wish to hear from you about the elaboration of this creative activity. By what powers of his and in what all ways did Brahma continue his subsequent creative work?

Suta said: **3.** Hearing this question of the pious king, the great Rishi Suka con-

श्रीशुक उवाच

यदा प्रचेतसः पुत्रा दश प्राचीनबर्हिषः। अन्तःसमुद्रादुन्मग्ना ददृशुर्गां द्रुमैर्वृताम् ॥ 4॥
द्रुमेभ्यः क्रुध्यमानास्ते तपोदीपितमन्यवः। मुखतो वायुमग्निं च ससृजुस्तद्दिधक्षया ॥ 5॥
ताभ्यां निर्दह्यमानांस्तानुपलभ्य कुरूद्वह। राजोवाच महान् सोमो मन्युं प्रशमयन्निव ॥ 6॥
मा द्रुमेभ्यो महाभागा दीनेभ्यो द्रोग्धुमर्हथ। विवर्धयिषवो यूयं प्रजानां पतयः स्मृताः ॥ 7॥
अहो प्रजापतिपतिर्भगवान् हरिरव्ययः। वनस्पतीनोषधीश्च ससर्जोर्जमिषं विभुः ॥ 8॥
अन्नं चराणामचरा ह्यपदः पादचारिणाम्। अहस्ता हस्तयुक्तानां द्विपदां च चतुष्पदः ॥ 9॥
यूयं च पित्रान्वादिष्टा देवदेवेन चानघाः। प्रजासर्गाय हि कथं वृक्षान् निर्दग्धुमर्हथ ॥10॥
आतिष्ठत सतां मार्गं कोपं यच्छत दीपितम्। पित्रा पितामहेनापि जुष्टं वः प्रपितामहैः ॥11॥
तोकानां पितरौ बन्धू दृशः पक्ष्म स्त्रियाः पतिः। पतिः प्रजानां भिक्षूणां गृह्यज्ञानां बुधः सुहृत् 12॥
अन्तर्देहेषु भूतानामात्माऽऽस्ते हरिरीश्वरः। सर्वं तद्धिष्ण्यमीक्षध्वमेवं वस्तोषितो ह्यसौ ॥13॥
यः समुत्पतितं देह आकाशान्मन्युमुल्बणम्। आत्मजिज्ञासया यच्छेत् स गुणानतिवर्तते ॥14॥

gratulated him.

Sri Suka said: **4-5.** When the ten Prachetasas, the sons of Prachinabarhis, emerged from the sea, they found the earth all covered over by a thick growth of trees. Annoyed at this, their anger flamed up against that thick growth of trees that was obstructing all movements. Their austerities had given them the power to burn everything in the fire of their anger. In order to burn up the trees, they brought out fire and wind from their faces. **6.** Seeing that the combination of fire and wind was rapidly consuming the forests, the moon-deity came forward to assauge the anger of the Prachetasas. **7.** He said: 'O high-souled ones! It behoves you not to destroy the poor trees in this way. Your mission is to protect your subjects and work for the prosperity of all, including the trees. **8.** The Eternal Being, the worshipful Hari, who is the Brahma too, brought into existence trees, herbs and other vegetation to provide food offerings to the manes and the Devas. **9.** For the moving, the unmoving objects provide food. For creatures moving on feet, those without feet (i.e. which move less fast) are the food. For those with arms, the armless ones become food. And for those with two feet, the four-footed creatures become food. So for you, this destruction of forests is an act of wanton annihilation serving no purpose. **10.** O sinless ones! You have been commissioned by your father as also by the Lord of all to multiply the species. How can you then indulge in this destruction of trees which are very useful for man? **11.** Following the path of virtue in the footsteps of your father, grandfather and other ancestors, try to control your flaming anger. **12.** Of children, parents are the supporters; of eye, the eyelid; of women, their husbands; of Sannyasins, the householders; of the ignorant, the learned; and of the subjects, their rulers the Prajapatis. You being the rulers of all including the trees, it behoves you not to destroy them. **13.** In the hearts of all beings resides the Lord who is the all-pervading Spirit and master of all. Therefore view all beings as His tabernacle. Then the Lord will be pleased with you. **14.** Whoever is able to control by means of reflection on the Self, the fierce anger that suddenly overtakes the mind like a bolt from the blue, he alone overcomes

अलं दग्धैर्द्रुमैर्दीनैः खिलानां शिवमस्तु वः । वार्क्षी ह्येषा वरा कन्या पत्नीत्वे प्रतिगृह्यताम् ॥
इत्यामन्त्र्य वरारोहां कन्यामाप्सरसीं नृप । सोमो राजा ययौ दत्त्वा ते धर्मेणोपयेमिरे ॥16॥
तेभ्यस्तस्यां समभवद्दक्षः प्राचेतसः किल । यस्य प्रजाविसर्गेण लोका आपूरितास्त्रयः ॥17॥
यथा ससर्ज भूतानि दक्षो दुहितृवत्सलः । रेतसा मनसा चैव तन्ममावहितः शृणु ॥18॥
मनसैवासृजत्पूर्वं प्रजापतिरिमाः प्रजाः । देवासुरमनुष्यादीन् नभस्थलजलौकसः ॥19॥
तमबृंहितमालोक्य प्रजासर्गं प्रजापतिः । विन्ध्यपादानुपव्रज्य सोऽचरद् दुष्करं तपः ॥20॥
तत्राघमर्षणं नाम तीर्थं पापहरं परम् । उपस्पृश्यानुसवनं तपसातोषयद्धरिम् ॥21॥
अस्तौषीद्धंसगुह्येन भगवन्तमधोक्षजम् । तुभ्यं तदभिधास्यामि कस्यातुष्यद् यतो हरिः ॥

प्रजापतिरुवाच

नमः परायावितथानुभूतये गुणत्रयाभासनिमित्तबन्धवे ।
अदृष्टधाम्ने गुणतत्त्वबुद्धिभिर्निवृत्तमानाय दधे स्वयम्भुवे ॥23॥
न यस्य सख्यं पुरुषोऽवैति सख्युः सखा वसन् संवसतः पुरेऽस्मिन् ।
गुणो यथा गुणिनो व्यक्तदृष्टेस्तस्मै महेशाय नमस्करोमि ॥24॥

the forces of Nature. **15.** Enough of burning trees, who are most pitiable because they cannot retaliate! May the remaining trees and you prosper! Accept this noble girl, the daughter of the trees, as your wife, and make peace with them.'

Daksha, Son of Prachetasas (16-22)

(Sri Suka continued:) **16.** O King! The moon-deity, after saying this much, presented that noble daughter of the trees, born of an Apsaras named Amlocha, to the Prachetasas brothers, and departed. Then they married her according to proper rites. **17.** By them she had a son known as Daksha, the son of Prachetasas. The three worlds were populated by his procreative activity. **18.** Hear from me how Daksha, who was very loving to his daughters, multiplied the species both by insemination and by the mind. **19.** At first he created by his mental effort alone numerous creatures like celestials, Asuras, men and other creatures, inhabiting the higher worlds, the earth and water. **20.** Seeing that with this kind of creative process there was no satisfactory progress of creation, Daksha went to the Vindhya mountains and engaged himself in austere practices of great severity. **21.** Then he took bath during the three Sandhyas of the day—at sunrise, mid-day and sunset in the holy lake of Aghamarshana and sought to please Hari by his austerities. **22.** He extolled the worshipful Lord, who is not perceived by the senses, with a hymn known as Hamsaguhya, which pleased the Lord very much. I shall transmit it to you.

Hamsaguhya-stotra (23-34)

The Prajapati Daksha said: **23.** Salutations to the Supreme Being whose experience is Truth abiding, who is the sustainer of both Maya and the Jiva, whose glorious presence is not felt by people with intelligence overpowered by longing for material fulfilments, who transcends all the ordinary means of knowledge but is intuited as Self-effulgent Consciousness. **24.** Just as the object of a sense, though in intimate contact with that sense, does not perceive that sense as the sense perceives the object, even so the Supreme Being, the friend and lover of the Jiva, is present with the Jiva in the same body, but the Jiva knows Him not, the universal

देहोऽसवोऽक्षा मनवो भूतमात्रा नात्मानमन्यं च विदुः परं यत् ।
सर्वं पुमान् वेद गुणांश्च तज्ज्ञो न वेद सर्वज्ञमनन्तमीडे ॥25॥
यदोपरामो मनसो नामरूपरूपस्य दृष्टस्मृतिसम्प्रमोषात् ।
य ईयते केवलया स्वसंस्थया हंसाय तस्मै शुचिसद्मने नमः ॥26॥
मनीषिणोऽन्तर्हृदि सन्निवेशितं स्वशक्तिभिर्नवभिश्च त्रिवृद्भिः ।
वह्निं यथा दारुणि पाञ्चदश्यं मनीषया निष्कर्षन्ति गूढम् ॥27॥
स वै ममाशेषविशेषमायानिषेधनिर्वाणसुखानुभूतिः ।
स सर्वनामा स च विश्वरूपः प्रसीदतामनिरुक्तात्मशक्तिः ॥28॥
यद् यन्निरुक्तं वचसा निरूपितं धियाक्षभिर्वा मनसा वोत यस्य ।
मा भूत् स्वरूपं गुणरूपं हि तत्तत् स वै गुणापायविसर्गलक्षणः ॥29॥
यस्मिन् यतो येन च यस्य यस्मै यद् यो यथा कुरुते कार्यते च ।
परावरेषां परमं प्राक् प्रसिद्धं तद् ब्रह्म तद्धेतुरनन्यदेकम् ॥30॥
यच्छक्तयो वदतां वादिनां वै विवादसंवादभुवो भवन्ति ।
कुर्वन्ति चैषां मुहुरात्ममोहं तस्मै नमोऽनन्तगुणाय भूम्ने ॥31॥

witness, and His love. To that Supreme Being my salutation. **25.** The physical body, Pranas (vital energy), mind, gross elements and subtle elements, being aspects of unconscious Prakriti, are not naturally conscious of themselves or of the senses which grasp them or of the presiding deities. But the Jiva who makes them all externally conscious, is aware of them all and their source, the Gunas of Prakriti. Still the Jiva is not aware of the knower of all, the Ultimate Knower who is the support of the Jiva himself. May I offer my words of praise to that Supreme Being! **26.** Salutations to Thee who shinest in Thy pristine state in a mind that has attained to extreme purity by the subsidence of all perception and memory and the consequent arresting of the mental modifications that objectify names and forms or take shape as external objects. **27.** Though Thou art covered up by Thy powers manifesting as the various categories—as the Prakriti with its three Gunas, Mahattattva, Ahankara, Manas, and the five Tanmantras—wise men separate and grasp Thee through discriminative intelligence as existing in the heart, just as the celestial fire lodged in the sacrificial fuel is ignited and brought into manifestation through the fifteen sacred Mantras. **28.** Thou art the transcendent Spirit ever steeped in eternal bliss, negating the diversities of relative existence produced by Maya. But being the possesor of the innate power Maya that baffles all definitions, Thou art also all manifested beings having names and forms. May that Sri Hari be propitious unto me. **29.** Whatever is described by words and understood by the intellect, whatever is grasped by the senses and imagined by the mind—that is not Thy pristine nature. They are all the expressions of Thy power Maya with its three Gunas, from whose work of creation, preservation and dissolution Thy being is indirectly cognised. **30.** Whatever that is manifest as high and low, as objects, instruments, agents, actions etc., Thou didst exist before them transcending them as the unitary non-dual Brahman, the Cause of all causes. **31.** Salutations to Thee with countless attributes, whose inscrutable Power causes self-forgetfulness and delusion in those

अस्तीति नास्तीति च वस्तुनिष्ठयोरेकस्थयोर्भिन्नविरुद्धधर्मयोः ।
अवेक्षितं किञ्चन योगसांख्ययोः समं परं ह्यनुकूलं बृहत् तत् ॥32॥
योऽनुग्रहार्थं भजतां पादमूलमनामरूपो भगवाननन्तः ।
नामानि रूपाणि च जन्मकर्मभिर्भेजे स मह्यं परमः प्रसीदतु ॥33॥
यः प्राकृतैर्ज्ञानपथैर्जनानां यथाशयं देहगतो विभाति ।
यथानिलः पार्थिवमाश्रितो गुणं स ईश्वरो मे कुरुतान्मनोरथम् ॥34॥

श्रीशुक उवाच

इति स्तुतः संस्तुवतः स तस्मिन्नघमर्षणे । आविरासीत्कुरुश्रेष्ठ भगवान् भक्तवत्सलः ॥35॥
कृतपादः सुपर्णांसे प्रलम्बाष्टमहाभुजः । चक्रशङ्खासिचर्मेषुधनुःपाशगदाधरः ॥36॥
पीतवासा घनश्यामः प्रसन्नवदनेक्षणः । वनमालानिवीताङ्गो लसच्छ्रीवत्सकौस्तुभः ॥37॥
महाकिरीटकटकः स्फुरन्मकरकुण्डलः । काञ्च्यङ्गुलीयवलयनूपुराङ्गदभूषितः ॥38॥
त्रैलोक्यमोहनं रूपं बिभ्रत् त्रिभुवनेश्वरः । वृतो नारदनन्दाद्यैः पार्षदैः सुरयूथपैः ॥39॥
स्तूयमानोऽनुगायद्भिः सिद्धगन्धर्वचारणैः । रूपं तन्महदाश्चर्यं विचक्ष्यागतसाध्वसः ॥40॥

controversialists to whom that Power forms the topic of argument and counter-argument. **32.** Viewing Thee as their common ground, the Yoga (the school of devotion) and the Samkhya (the school of knowledge) claim absolute truth for their respective views but speak of Thee in divided and contradictory ways—the one positively as Personal Being with all auspicious attributes and a form, and the other negatively, denying all these and describing Thee as 'not this, not this.' Thou art that transcendent and Infinite Being, favourable to both these views alike. (What are called contradictions cease to be so in Thee, the Infinite Being who art both the Personal Deity and the Impersonal Absolute.) **33.** May that Infinite Being, the worshipful Lord, who transcends name and form, but manifests Himself under many forms of Suddha-sattva and under countless names as Deities and Incarnations, and performs various sportive actions for the blessing of the devotees—may He be propitious unto Me. **34.** May He, the Lord of all, who, like the air that takes the smell of whatever it is in contact with, assumes the forms of Deities as conceived by even various crude cults according to the tendencies of the votaries—may He be propitious to me and grant my prayers.

Lord's Appearance and Blessing (35-54)

Sri Suka said: **35.** Hymned in this way at the holy lake of Aghamarshana, the worshipful Lord, who loves his devotees, appeared before Daksha who extolled Him with deep faith and fervour. **36-39.** He appeared seated on the shoulders of Garuda. He had eight powerful arms, sporting His discus, conch, sword, shield, arrow, bow, cord, and mace. Blue like a rain cloud, clad in yellow cloth, serene in expression, and luminous with Srivatsa mark and the Kaustubha jewel, he appeared framed in a wreath of wild flowers and leaves. He was adorned with a great crown, bracelets, gleaming ear ornaments, girdle, rings, anklets, and armlets. Assuming a form impressive enough to dumbfound the three worlds of which He was the Lord, He appeared surrounded by sages and attendants like Narada, Nanda and other celestials. **40.** At the sight of this rare and wonderful form, followed by the hymning choir of Siddhas, Chāranas and Gandhar-

ननाम दण्डवद् भूमौ प्रहृष्टात्मा प्रजापतिः। न किञ्चनोदीरयितुमशकत् तीव्रया मुदा।
आपूरितमनोद्वारैर्ह्रदिन्य इव निर्झरैः ॥41॥
तं तथावनतं भक्तं प्रजाकामं प्रजापतिम्। चित्तज्ञः सर्वभूतानामिदमाह जनार्दनः ॥42॥

श्रीभगवानुवाच

प्राचेतस महाभाग संसिद्धस्तपसा भवान्। यच्छ्रद्धया मत्परया मयि भावं परं गतः ॥43॥
प्रीतोऽहं ते प्रजानाथ यत्तेऽस्योद्बृंहणं तपः। ममैष कामो भूतानां यद्भूयासुर्विभूतयः ॥44॥
ब्रह्मा भवो भवन्तश्च मनवो विबुधेश्वराः। विभूतयो मम ह्येता भूतानां भूतिहेतवः ॥45॥
तपो मे हृदयं ब्रह्मंस्तनुर्विद्या क्रियाऽऽकृतिः। अङ्गानि क्रतवो जाता धर्म आत्मासवः सुराः 46॥
अहमेवासमेवाग्रे नान्यत् किञ्चान्तरं बहिः। संज्ञानमात्रमव्यक्तं प्रसुप्तमिव विश्वतः ॥47॥
मय्यनन्तगुणेऽनन्ते गुणतो गुणविग्रहः। यदाऽऽसीत्तत एवाद्यः स्वयम्भूः समभूदजः ॥48॥
स वै यदा महादेवो मम वीर्योपबृंहितः। मेने खिलमिवात्मानमुद्यतः सर्गकर्मणि ॥49॥
अथ मेऽभिहितो देवस्तपोऽतप्यत दारुणम्। नव विश्वसृजो युष्मान् येनादावसृजद्विभुः ॥50॥
एषा पञ्चजनस्याङ्ग दुहिता वै प्रजापतेः। असिक्नी नाम पत्नीत्वे प्रजेश प्रतिगृह्यताम् 51॥

vas, the Prajapati Daksha was awestruck. **41.** With a mind overflowing with joy, he made a full prostration to the Lord, falling before him like a stick. For a time he was not able to speak anything, as his mind was like a lake filled with the water of mountain-torrents flowing into it. **42.** The Lord Hari, who knows the heart of all, now said as follows to that saluting Prajapati desirous of progeny:

The worshipful Lord said: **43.** O son of Prachetasas! O noble one! You have become perfect by your austerity. For, your intense faith and devotion to Me has generated supreme love of Me in you. **44.** O protector of men! I am much pleased with your austere practices, because they are meant for the good of the world. It is My wish that prosperity attends on all beings. **45.** Brahma, Bhava, Manus and you Prajapatis, are all expressions of My power for working for the prosperity and advancement of all beings. **46.** O learned one! My heart is Tapas, consisting in the practice of inward concentration. My body is Vidya, consisting in the repetition of the sacred Mantra in the proper way with all their auxiliaries. My form is Kriya, the performance of the daily and occasional rites. The sacrificial rites (Kratus) are my limbs. Dharma consisting in the Apurva or the efficiency-potential of sacrifice is my mind. And the Devas receiving sacrificial offerings are my vital energy (Prana). **47.** At first I alone was, Pure Consciousness, transcending relations, devoid of within and without, and unmanifested. Nothing else there was. It was as if everything were in slumber. **48.** When in Me, the immeasurable and of infinite attributes, My Power Maya brought out My cosmic body (the Brahmanda), simultaneously Brahma, the original being and self-born one, also came into existence. **49.** Though the first of Divinities, and though fortified by My prowess, Brahma still felt weak when he started the work of creation. **50.** Afterwards that Divinity, as instructed by Me, performed Tapas (inward concentration) of an intense nature. Becoming all-powerful by such Tapas, he first brought out you, the nine Prajapatis, into existence to aid in the work of creation. **51.** You, who are anxious to have progeny, may accept this woman, Asikni, daughter of another Prajapati Panchajana

मिथुनव्यवायधर्मस्त्वं प्रजासर्गमिमं पुनः। मिथुनव्यवायधर्मिण्यां भूरिशो भावयिष्यसि 52॥
त्वत्तोऽधस्तात् प्रजाः सर्वा मिथुनीभूय मायया। मदीयया भविष्यन्ति हरिष्यन्ति च मे बलिम् 53॥

श्रीशुक उवाच

इत्युक्त्वा मिषतस्तस्य भगवान् विश्वभावनः। स्वप्नोपलब्धार्थ इव तत्रैवान्तर्दधे हरिः ॥54॥

इति श्रीमद्भागवते महापुराणे पारमहंस्यां संहितायां षष्ठस्कन्धे चतुर्थोऽध्यायः ॥4॥

as your wife. **52.** By following the law of sexual intercourse with her, who is also desirous of the same, you will be bringing forth numerous progeny. **53.** The generations that are to come after you will all consort with women prompted by My Maya, and offer Me service.

Sri Suka said: **54.** Saying so, even as Daksha was locking on, Sri Hari, the worshipful Lord and protector of the worlds, disappeared like a phenomenon perceived in a dream.

अथ पञ्चमोऽध्यायः

श्रीशुक उवाच

तस्यां स पाञ्चजन्यां वै विष्णुमायोपबृंहितः। हर्यश्वसंज्ञानयुतं पुत्रानजनयद् विभुः ॥ 1॥
अपृथग्धर्मशीलास्ते सर्वे दाक्षायणा नृप। पित्रा प्रोक्ताः प्रजासर्गे प्रतीचीं प्रययुर्दिशम् ॥ 2॥
तत्र नारायणसरस्तीर्थं सिन्धुसमुद्रयोः। सङ्गमो यत्र सुमहन्मुनिसिद्धनिषेवितम् ॥ 3॥
तदुपस्पर्शनादेव विनिर्धूतमलाशयाः। धर्मे पारमहंस्ये च प्रोत्पन्नमतयोऽप्युत ॥ 4॥
तेपिरे तप एवोग्रं पित्रादेशेन यन्त्रिताः। प्रजाविवृद्धये यत्तान् देवर्षिस्तान् ददर्श ह ॥ 5॥
उवाच चाथ हर्यश्वाः कथं स्रक्ष्यथ वै प्रजाः। अदृष्ट्वान्तं भुवो यूयं बालिशा बत पालकाः ॥ 6॥

Skandha VI : Chapter 5

NARADA AND THE SONS OF DAKSHA

Riddle posed by Narada (1-9)

Sri Suka said: **1.** Overpowered by Mahavishnu's Maya, the powerful Daksha begot ten thousand sons, known as Haryaswas, by his wife Asikni, the daughter of Panchajana. **2.** These ten thousand sons of Daksha behaved and thought like one man. Asked by their father to multiply the species, they went in a westerly direction to perform Tapas and gain the blessing of the Lord. **3.** At about the place where the river Sindhu joins the sea there is a holy spot called Narayanasaras (in Kutch), which is the resort of many sages and ascetics. **4.** By bathing in the holy waters of the place, all the impurities in the minds of Daksha's sons were effaced, and they became confirmed in the ideal of renunciation, which is the way of the Paramahamsas. **5.** Obedient to their father's direction, they practised extremely rigorous austerities. Narada, the divine sage, happened to see them at that stage when, even after attaining to great purity of mind, they were still preparing themselves for the propagation of the species.

Narada said to them: **6.** O Haryaswas! Though you are rulers of men, you seem to be simpletons. Alas! Without wit-

तथैकपुरुषं राष्ट्रं बिलं चादृष्टनिर्गमम्। बहुरूपां स्त्रियं चापि पुमांसं पुंश्चलीपतिम्॥ 7॥
नदीमुभयतोवाहां पञ्चपञ्चाद्भुतं गृहम्। क्वचिद्धंसं चित्रकथं क्षौरपव्यं स्वयंभ्रमिम्॥ 8॥
कथं स्वपितुरादेशमविद्वांसो विपश्चितः। अनुरूपमविज्ञाय अहो सर्गं करिष्यथ॥ 9॥

श्रीशुक उवाच

तन्निशम्याथ हर्यश्वा औत्पत्तिकमनीषया। वाचः कूटं तु देवर्षेः स्वयं विममृशुर्धिया॥10॥
भूः क्षेत्रं जीवसंज्ञं यदनादि निजबन्धनम्। अदृष्ट्वा तस्य निर्वाणं किमसत्कर्मभिर्भवेत्॥11॥
एक एवेश्वरस्तुर्यो भगवान् स्वाश्रयः परः। तमदृष्ट्वाभवं पुंसः किमसत्कर्मभिर्भवेत्॥12॥
पुमान् नैवैति यद् गत्वा बिलस्वर्गं गतो यथा। प्रत्यग्धामाविद इह किमसत्कर्मभिर्भवेत्॥13॥
नानारूपाऽऽत्मनो बुद्धिः स्वैरिणीव गुणान्विता। तन्निष्ठामगतस्येह किमसत्कर्मभिर्भवेत्॥14॥
तत्सङ्गभ्रंशितैश्वर्यं संसरन्तं कुभार्यवत्। तद्गतीरबुधस्येह किमसत्कर्मभिर्भवेत्॥15॥

nessing the end of the earth, how are you going to procreate issue? **7.** Without knowing the kingdom with a single inhabitant, the cave from which there is no exit, the woman with many forms, and the paramour of a harlot—how are you going to procreate issue? **8.** Without knowing the river that flows both ways, the unique house built of twenty-five substances, the swan which has a wonderful history, and the self-revolving structure built of material sharp and hard as diamond—how are you going to procreate issue? **9.** And without a proper understanding of the meaning of your farsighted father's command, suited to your capacity, how are you going to engage yourself in the work of multiplying the species?

The Riddle explained (10-22)

Sri Suka said: **10.** The Haryaswas reflected on the words of the divine sage, enigmatic but deep in implications, with the help of their own natural intelligence and came to the following conclusion about it: **11.** The subtle body (the Linga-sarira), which is the limiting adjunct causing bondage to the Jiva from beginningless time, is the earth referred to in the riddle. In place of hastening the dissolution of this binding adjunct of a subtle body, of what use is involvement in desire-prompted actions which only go to strengthen that bondage? **12.** The sole inhabitant of the country referred to is the transcendent and the worshipful Lord of all, who is described as the Fourth beyond the three states, the one without a second and depending on none but Himself. Without striving to attain to Him, of what use is the pursuit of these desire-prompted actions that are not offered to Him.

13. One has to gain the knowledge of the Light within (the self-conscious spiritual essence permeating everything), understanding which one does not come back to the transmigratory world, even like one who has gone to the Bilaswarga, or the heaven of the nether world. Without achieving that, of what use is the pursuit of desire-prompted actions giving trivial joys? (This is with reference to the cave without exit.) **14.** The woman of the riddle is man's Buddhi, the understanding. Attracted by the objects of the world, the products of the Gunas of Prakriti, it moves from one fancy to another like a seductive woman, wearing many make-ups. In place of eradicating this tendency of one's understanding through the practice of discrimination, of what use is the pursuit of desire-prompted actions giving trivial joys? **15.** Like a man married to a harlot, an unenlightened Jiva yoked to an impure

सृष्टयप्ययकरीं मायां वेलाकूलान्तवेगिताम् । मत्तस्य तामविज्ञस्य किमसत्कर्मभिर्भवेत् ॥16॥
पञ्चविंशतितत्त्वानां पुरुषोऽद्भुतदर्पणम् । अध्यात्ममबुधस्येह किमसत्कर्मभिर्भवेत् ॥17॥
ऐश्वरं शास्त्रमुत्सृज्य बन्धमोक्षानुदर्शनम् । विविक्तपदमज्ञाय किमसत्कर्मभिर्भवेत् ॥18॥
कालचक्रं भ्रमिस्तीक्ष्णं सर्वं निष्कर्षयज्जगत् । स्वतन्त्रमबुधस्येह किमसत्कर्मभिर्भवेत् ॥19॥
शास्त्रस्य पितुरादेशं यो न वेद निवर्तकम् । कथं तदनुरूपाय गुणविश्रम्भ्युपक्रमेत् ॥20॥
इति व्यवसिता राजन् हर्यश्वा एकचेतसः । प्रययुस्तं परिक्रम्य पन्थानमनिवर्तनम् ॥21॥
स्वरब्रह्मणि निर्भातहृषीकेशपदाम्बुजे । अखण्डं चित्तमावेश्य लोकाननुचरन्मुनिः ॥22॥
नाशं निशम्य पुत्राणां नारदाच्छीलशालिनाम् । अन्वतप्यत कः शोचन् सुप्रजास्त्वं शुचां पदम् 23॥
स भूयः पाञ्चजन्यायामजेन परिसान्त्वितः । पुत्रानजनयद् दक्षः शबलाश्वान् सहस्रशः ॥24॥

mind is dragged by it to goals of sufferings and enjoyments, oblivious of his (Jiva's) real nature as the pure and the unaffected Atman. Instead of seeking the spiritual identity of the Jiva, of what use for him is this pursuit of desire-prompted actions giving trivial joys? **16.** The river flowing in both directions is Maya consisting of the two processes of creation and dissolution which constitute the movement of the same force in contrary directions, just like a river at its estuary, agitated by opposite currents. In place of cultivating an awareness of this contrary process of life and death in which one's own body and the world are by force involved, of what use is the thoughtless pursuit of desire-prompted actions giving only trivial joys? **17.** For the body which is constituted of the twenty-five categories of Prakriti, the Spirit or the Purusha is the support giving a unity. The Purusha is the mirror of self-consciousness by identification with which the body-mind becomes a self-conscious entity. In place of understanding that indwelling Purusha, the support of this wonderful house of a body, of what use is the pursuit of desire-prompted actions giving trivial joys? **18.** Abandoning the study of the scriptures that clarify the distinction between the states of bondage and freedom, between the conscious and unconscious entities, and which deal with the knowledge of the Supreme Being, of what use is the pursuit of desire-prompted actions yielding trivial joys? **19.** Without understanding this sharp wheel of Time, which revolves with unimpeded speed destroying all the worlds, of what use is the pursuit of desire-prompted actions giving trivial joys? **20** Without knowing the Scripture, which is man's well-wisher like a father, and its teachings, which have renunciation as their goal, how can a man, devoting himself to worldly values alone, obtain freedom from the transmigratory cycle?

21. O King! Haryaswas, who always thought alike, accepted the teachings of the sage unanimously. They circumambulated him, and departed to take to the life of renunciation and devotion from which there is no return to worldly life. **22.** And Narada continued his wanderings all over the world, concentrating his mind on the lotus feet of the Lord that dawned within while he sang about His excellences.

Daksha's second Set of Progeny (23-33)

23. Hearing about the loss of his excellent sons to himself and family because of Narada's interference, Daksha was overpowered by sorrow and grieved over it for a long time. To have good children can, in this way, be a cause of sorrow also. **24.** Comforted and consoled by Brahma,

तेऽपि पित्रा समादिष्टाः प्रजासर्गे धृतव्रताः । नारायणसरो जग्मुर्यत्र सिद्धाः स्वपूर्वजाः ॥25॥
तदुपस्पर्शनादेव विनिर्धूतमलाशयाः । जपन्तो ब्रह्म परमं तेपुस्तेऽत्र महत् तपः ॥26॥
अब्भक्षाः कतिचिन्मासान् कतिचिद्वायुभोजनाः । आराधयन् मन्त्रमिममभ्यस्यन्त इडस्पतिम् 27॥
ॐ नमो नारायणाय पुरुषाय महात्मने । विशुद्धसत्त्वधिष्ण्याय महाहंसाय धीमहि ॥28॥
इति तानपि राजेन्द्र प्रतिसर्गधियो मुनिः । उपेत्य नारदः प्राह वाचःकूटानि पूर्ववत् ॥29॥
दाक्षायणाः संश्रृणुत गदतो निगमं मम । अन्विच्छतानुपदवीं भ्रातॄणां भ्रातृवत्सलाः 30॥
भ्रातॄणां प्रायणं भ्राता योऽनुतिष्ठति धर्मवित् । स पुण्यबन्धुः पुरुषो मरुद्भिः सह मोदते ॥31॥
एतावदुक्त्वा प्रययौ नारदोऽमोघदर्शनः । तेऽपि चान्वगमन्मार्गं भ्रातॄणामेव मारिष ॥32॥
सध्रीचीनं प्रतीचीनं परस्यानुपथं गताः । नाद्यापि ते निवर्तन्ते पश्चिमा यामिनीरिव ॥33॥
एतस्मिन् काल उत्पातान् बहून् पश्यन् प्रजापतिः । पूर्ववन्नारदकृतं पुत्रनाशमुपाश्रृणोत् ॥34॥
चुक्रोध नारदायासौ पुत्रशोकविमूर्च्छितः । देवर्षिमुपलभ्याह रोषाद्विस्फुरिताधरः ॥35॥

दक्ष उवाच

अहो असाधो साधूनां साधुलिङ्गेन नस्त्वया । असाध्वकार्यर्भकाणां भिक्षोर्मार्गः प्रदर्शितः 36॥

Daksha again begot several thousand children, known as Sabalaswas, by his wife Asikni, the daughter of Panchajana. **25.** Commissioned by their father to multiply the species, and vowed to observe rigorous austerities, they went to the same Narayanasaras, where their elder brothers attained to spiritual perfection. **26.** Attaining purity of mind by bathing in those holy waters, they performed severe austerities uttering a great Mantra. **27.** For some months they lived on water alone. Next for some months they took in air alone. Uttering the following Mantra, they meditated on Mahavishnu, the Master and Lord of all masters: **28.** 'Om! Salutations to Narayana, the resort of all liberated souls, the pervader of everything, the perfect being, the form reflected in all pure hearts, and the spirit untouched and uncontaminated by anything.'

29. Approaching them, whose mind was set on procreation, the sage Narada, as before, spoke to them in words with enigmatic meaning. **30.** He said: 'O sons of Daksha, beloved of your brothers! Hear my advice. Follow the footsteps of your brothers. **31.** A brother, who knows righteous conduct and follows the noble path chalked out by his brother, gains merits in this world and rejoices in the hereafter with the deities known as Maruts noted for their intimate fraternity.' **32.** O King! Saying this much, Narada, whose company is unfailing in its effect, moved on. And these Sabalaswas, too, followed the footsteps of their elder brothers. **33.** Thus placed on the track towards the Lord, which is the blessing that comes on an inward-looking mind, they went forward without turning back, like nights that have passed away.

Daksha's Curse on Narada (34-44)

34. The Prajapati Daksha began to see many omens portending evil. Soon he came to know of the loss of his sons on account of Narada's repeated mischief. **35.** Stunned by grief at the loss of his sons, he became violently angry at Narada. With his lips quivering in anger, he said as follows to Narada who then happened to arrive at the spot. *Daksha said:* **36.** 'O hypocrite who has put on the garb of a pious man! You have perpetrated a great atrocity against us who have been

ऋणैस्त्रिभिरमुक्तानाममीमांसितकर्मणाम् । विघातः श्रेयसः पाप लोकयोरुभयोः कृतः ॥37॥
एवं त्वं निरनुक्रोशो बालानां मतिभिद्धरेः । पार्षदमध्ये चरसि यशोहा निरपत्रपः ॥38॥
ननु भागवता नित्यं भूतानुग्रहकातराः । ऋते त्वां सौहृदघ्नं वै वैरङ्करमवैरिणाम् ॥39॥
नेत्थं पुंसां विरागः स्यात् त्वया केवलिना मृषा । मन्यसे यद्युपशमं स्नेहपाशनिकृन्तनम् ॥40॥
नानुभूय न जानाति पुमान् विषयतीक्ष्णताम् । निर्विद्येत स्वयं तस्मान्न तथा भिन्नधीः परैः ॥41॥
यन्नस्त्वं कर्मसन्धानां साधूनां गृहमेधिनाम् । कृतवानसि दुर्मर्षं विप्रियं तव मर्षितम् ॥42॥
तन्तुकृन्तन यन्नस्त्वमभद्रमचरः पुनः । तस्माल्लोकेषु ते मूढ न भवेद् भ्रमतः पदम् ॥43॥

श्रीशुक उवाच

प्रतिजग्राह तद्बाढं नारदः साधुसम्मतः । एतावान् साधुवादो हि तितिक्षेतेश्वरः स्वयम् 44॥

इति श्रीमद्भागवते महापुराणे पारमहंस्यां संहितायां षष्ठस्कन्धे नारदशापो नाम पञ्चमोऽध्यायः ॥5॥

following the path of pious men. You have converted my children into begging mendicants. **37.** O sinful one! You have marred the future of these children in this world and in the hereafter. For one has to discharge one's three debts—to the Rishis by Vedic study, to the Devas by Yajnas, and to the ancestors by begetting progeny. These sons of mine have not discharged these, nor have they made any study of the ritualistic code. One who takes to the life of Sannyasa without discharging all these duties, loses this world and the next. You have reduced my sons to this fate. **38.** You are unfit to move among the devotees of the Lord—you whose hobby it is to confuse the minds of youngsters, you who are merciless and shameless, who form a blemish on the reputation of Sri Hari whom you profess to serve. **39.** Except you, whose occupation consists in making friends into mutual enemies and thus destroying harmonious relationship among people, the Bhagavatas (devotees of the Lord Vishnu) are generally very particular to be a blessing to the people. **40.** You seem to think that mere passivity will enable people to cut off all these bonds of love with the near and the dear ones. It cannot; only renunciation (Vairagya) can. And this renunciation will not be generated in the mind of anyone by the tactics of a pseudo-ascetic like you, having only the form of a Paramahamsa, but not his knowledge. Men have to pass through the discipline of Karma to acquire renunciation. **41.** Without actual experience, man will not understand the ephemerality of worldly joys and the intensity of suffering. Through experience of them alone can man turn away from them and become a true renouncer. He does not become so by the confusion of thought created by the instigation of others. **42.** You did an unpardonable offence to us, devoted ritualists following the path of rectitude and the ways of a householder's life. Still we put up with your mischief once. **43.** But, O snapper of the thread of our lineage! You have done it again, depriving us of progeny to continue our lines. For that you shall suffer without any permanent place to stay; you shall be always wandering about in the worlds.'

Sri Suka said: **44.** Narada, universally respected as a holy man (Sadhu), received this curse of Daksha without any reaction. Forbearance even when one has power to retaliate is the sign of a real Sadhu.

अथ षष्ठोऽध्यायः

श्रीशुक उवाच

ततः प्राचेतसोऽसिक्न्यामनुनीतः स्वयम्भुवा । षष्टिं सञ्जनयामास दुहितॄः पितृवत्सलाः ॥ 1॥
दश धर्माय कायेन्दोर्द्विषट् त्रिणव दत्तवान् । भूताङ्गिरःकृशाश्वेभ्यो द्वे द्वे तार्क्ष्याय चापराः 2॥
नामधेयान्यमूषां त्वं सापत्यानां च मे शृणु । यासां प्रसूतिप्रसवैर्लोका आपूरितास्त्रयः ॥ 3॥
भानुर्लम्बा ककुब्जामिर्विश्वा साध्या मरुत्वती । वसुर्मुहूर्ता सङ्कल्पा धर्मपत्न्यः सुतान् शृणु ॥ 4॥
भानोस्तु देवऋषभ इन्द्रसेनस्ततो नृप । विद्योत आसील्लम्बायास्ततश्च स्तनयित्नवः 5॥
ककुभः सङ्कटस्तस्य कीकटस्तनयो यतः । भुवो दुर्गाणि जामेयः स्वर्गो नन्दिस्ततोऽभवत् 6॥
विश्वेदेवास्तु विश्वाया अप्रजांस्तान् प्रचक्षते । साध्यो गणस्तु साध्याया अर्थसिद्धिस्तु तत्सुतः ॥
मरुत्वांश्च जयन्तश्च मरुत्वत्यां बभूवतुः । जयन्तो वासुदेवांश उपेन्द्र इति यं विदुः ॥ 8॥
मौहूर्तिका देवगणा मुहूर्तायाश्च जज्ञिरे । ये वै फलं प्रयच्छन्ति भूतानां स्वस्वकालजम् 9॥
सङ्कल्पायाश्च सङ्कल्पः कामः सङ्कल्पजः स्मृतः । वसवोऽष्टौ वसोः पुत्रास्तेषां नामानि मे शृणु 10॥
द्रोणः प्राणो ध्रुवोऽर्कोऽग्निर्दोषो वसुर्विभावसुः । द्रोणस्याभिमतेः पत्न्या हर्षशोकभयादयः ॥11॥

Skandha VI : Chapter 6

THE LINE OF DAKSHA'S DAUGHTERS

Daksha's Daughters (1-10)

Sri Suka said: **1.** Afterwards under the loving persuasion of Brahma, Daksha, the son of Prachetasas, begot by his wife Asikni, sixty daughters, who were very much devoted to their parents. **2.** He gave these daughters in marriage as follows: ten to Dharma, thirteen to Kasyapa Prajapati, twenty seven to Chandra, two each to Bhūta, Angiras and Krisāsva, and the remaining four again to Kasyapa who is also called Tārkshya. **3.** I shall now give the names of these daughters and their offspring, whose progeny gradually filled the three worlds. **4.** Bhānu, Lambā, Kakubh, Jāmi, Visvā, Sādhyā, Marutvatī, Vasu, Muhūrtā, Sankalpā—these ten were the wives of Dharma. Hear the names of their offspring.

5. Bhānu's son was Devarshabha; his son, Indrasena. Lambā's son was known as Vidyota, from whom were born Stanayitnus, the presiding deities of clouds. **6.** Kakubha's son was Sankata, and his son, Kītaka. Kītaka's issue were the deities presiding over fortresses of the earth. Of Jāmi was born Svarga, and of him, Nandi. **7.** Viswā's sons were Viswedevas. These had no issue according to the traditions of wise men. Sādhyā's sons were those known under the group name of Sādhyas. Their son was Arthasiddhi. **8.** Of Marutvatī two sons named Marutvan and Jayanta were born. Jayanta was a partial manifestation of Vāsudeva, and was known also as Upendra. **9.** Muhūrtā's issue were known under the group name of Mauhūrtikas. They distribute the fruits of actions to living beings at proper times. They preside over the thirty Muhūrtas (each of 48 minutes duration) into which the day is divided. **10.** The son of Sankalpā was Sankalpa, the deity presiding over manifestation, and his son was Kāma. The sons of Vasu formed the group of eight Vasus.

The Vasus and their Issue (11-16)

11. The names of these eight Vasus were

प्राणस्योर्जस्वती भार्या सह आयुः पुरोजवः । ध्रुवस्य भार्या धरणिरसूत विविधाः पुरः ॥12॥
अर्कस्य वासना भार्या पुत्रास्तर्षादयः स्मृताः । अग्नेर्भार्या वसोर्धारा पुत्रा द्रविणकादयः ॥13॥
स्कन्दश्च कृत्तिकापुत्रो ये विशाखादयस्ततः । दोषस्य शर्वरीपुत्रः शिशुमारो हरेः कलाः ॥14॥
वसोराङ्गिरसीपुत्रो विश्वकर्मा कृतीपतिः । ततो मनुश्चाक्षुषोऽभूद् विश्वे साध्या मनोः सुताः ॥
विभावसोरसूतोषा व्युष्टं रोचिषमातपम् । पञ्चयामोऽथ भूतानि येन जाग्रति कर्मसु ॥16॥
सरूपासूत भूतस्य भार्या रुद्रांश्च कोटिशः । रैवतोऽजो भवो भीमो वाम उग्रो वृषाकपिः ॥17॥
अजैकपादहिर्बुध्न्यो बहुरूपो महानिति । रुद्रस्य पार्षदाश्चान्ये घोरा भूतविनायकाः ॥18॥
प्रजापतेरङ्गिरसः स्वधा पत्नी पितॄनथ । अथर्वाङ्गिरसं वेदं पुत्रत्वे चाकरोत् सती ॥19॥
कृशाश्वोऽर्चिषि भार्यायां धूम्रकेशमजीजनत् । धिषणायां वेदशिरो देवलं वयुनं मनुम् ॥20॥
तार्क्ष्यस्य विनता कद्रूः पतङ्गी यामिनीति च । पतङ्ग्यसूत पतगान् यामिनी शलभानथ ॥21॥
सुपर्णासूत गरुडं साक्षाद् यज्ञेशवाहनम् । सूर्यसूतमनूरुं च कद्रूर्नागाननेकशः ॥22॥
कृत्तिकादीनि नक्षत्राणीन्दोः पत्न्यस्तु भारत । दक्षशापात् सोऽनपत्यस्तासु यक्ष्मग्रहार्दितः ॥23॥

Drona, Prāna, Dhruva, Arka, Agni, Dosha, Vasu and Vibhāvasu. Of these, Drona had Abhimati for wife, by whom he had Harsha, Soka and Bhaya as sons. **12.** Prāna's wife was Ūrjaswati by whom he had three sons, Saha, Āyu, and Purojava. The wife of Dhruva was Dharanī who bore him as progeny the deities presiding over various cities and towns. **13.** The wife of Arka was Vāsanā; Tarsha and others were her children. The wife of Agni was Vasordhārā. Dravinaka and others were her sons. **14.** Skanda was Agni's son by Krittikā. Skanda's sons were Visākha and others. Dosha's wife was Sarvarī. Her son Sisumāra was a part of Hari. **15.** Vasu's wife was Āngirasī, and they had as their son Viswakarma who became the architect of the celestials. Viswakarma's son by his wife Ākriti was Chākshusha who became a famous Manu of that name. The Devas known as Viswas and Sadhyas are the sons of Chākshusha Manu. **16.** Vibhāvasu's wife was Usha who had three sons, Vyushta, Rochis, Ātapa. Ātapa had a son who was the presiding deity of the day, with five periods known as Yāmas. He is therefore called Panchayāma, and all creatures are prompted to action by that deity.

Rudras, Pitris etc. (17-24)

17-18. Bhūta had two wives. Of these Sarūpā gave birth to innumerable Rudras, of which the eleven principal ones were Raivata, Aja, Bhava, Bhīma, Vāma, Ugra, Vrishākapi, Ajaikapāt, Ahirbudhnya, Bahurūpa and Mahān. From the second wife of Bhūta were born the fierce attendants of Rudra known as Vināyakas and Pretas. **19.** The Prajapati Angiras had two wives. Of these, the one known as Swadhā gave birth to Pitris. The other wife Satī had a son named Atharvāngiras presiding over the fourth Veda. **20.** Krisāswa had two wives named Archis and Dhishanā, of whom the first had as son Dhūmrakesa, and the second, Vedasiras, Devala, Vayuna and Manu. **21-22.** Tārkshya (known also as Kasyapa) had four wives known as Vinatā, Kadrū, Patangī and Yāminī. Of these Patangī brought forth the birds (Patangas); Yāminī, the locusts; Vinatā (also called Suparnā), the vehicle of Mahavishnu known as Garuda, and Aruna, the charioteer of the sun-deity; and Kadrū, serpents. **23.** The wives of Chandra or Soma (Moon-deity) were the twenty seven Nakshatras (constellations)

पुनः प्रसाद्य तं सोमः कला लेभे क्षये दिताः ।
शृणु नामानि लोकानां मातॄणां शंकराणि च 24॥
अथ कश्यपपत्नीनां यत्प्रसूतमिदं जगत् ।
अदितिर्दितिर्दनुः काष्ठा अरिष्टा सुरसा इला 25॥
मुनिः क्रोधवशा ताम्रा सुरभिः सरसा तिमिः ।
तिमेर्यादोगणा आसन् श्वापदाः सरमासुताः 26॥
सुरभेर्महिषा गावो ये चान्ये द्विशफा नृप ।
ताम्रायाः श्येनगृध्राद्या मुनेरप्सरसां गणाः ॥27॥
दन्दशूकादयः सर्पा राजन् क्रोधवशात्मजाः ।
इलाया भूरुहाः सर्वे यातुधानाश्च सौरसाः ॥28॥
अरिष्टायाश्च गन्धर्वाः काष्ठाया द्विशफेतराः ।
सुता दनोरेकषष्टिस्तेषां प्राधानिकान् शृणु 29॥
द्विमूर्धा शम्बरोऽरिष्टो हयग्रीवो विभावसुः ।
अयोमुखः शङ्कुशिराः स्वर्भानुः कपिलोऽरुणः 30॥
पुलोमा वृषपर्वा च एकचक्रोऽनुतापनः ।
धूम्रकेशो विरूपाक्षो विप्रचित्तिश्च दुर्जयः ॥31॥
स्वर्भानोः सुप्रभां कन्यामुवाह नमुचिः किल ।
वृषपर्वणस्तु शर्मिष्ठां ययातिर्नाहुषो बली ॥32॥
वैश्वानरसुता याश्च चतस्रश्चारुदर्शनाः ।
उपदानवी हयशिरा पुलोमा कालका तथा ॥33॥
उपदानवीं हिरण्याक्षः क्रतुर्हयशिरां नृप ।
पुलोमां कालकां च द्वे वैश्वानरसुते तु कः ॥34॥
उपयेमेऽथ भगवान् कश्यपो ब्रह्मचोदितः ।
पौलोमाः कालकेयाश्च दानवा युद्धशालिनः ॥35॥
तयोः षष्टिसहस्राणि यज्ञघ्नांस्ते पितुः पिता ।
जघान स्वर्गतो राजन्नेक इन्द्रप्रियङ्करः ॥36॥

beginning with Krittika. But Chandra had no issue by his wives, because his father-in-law, Daksha Prajapati, cursed him to be a consumptive patient as punishment for his neglect of all his wives except Rohinī, of whom he was inordinately fond. **24.** By propitiating Daksha afterwards, Soma got back the digits that he lost during the dark fortnight. Now hear about the auspicious names of Kasyapa's wives.

Prajapati Kasyapa's Line (25-37)

25-26. The world got filled with the issue of Kasyapa's wives. Thirteen in number, their names are: Aditi, Diti, Danu, Kāshthā, Arishtā, Surasā, Ilā, Muni, Krodhavasā, Tāmrā, Surabhi, Saramā and Timi. All aquatic creatures were the offspring of Timi; and all wild animals, of Saramā. **27.** O King! All buffaloes, cows, and other two-hoofed animals were born of Surabhi, while all birds like kites, vultures etc. were the issue of Tāmrā. The Apsaras were born of Muni. **28.** Krodhavasā's children were the terrible poisonous snakes. The vegetable kingdom formed the offspring of Ilā; and Yātudhānas (Rakshasas) of Surasā. **29.** The Gandharvas were the offspring of Arishtā; and all the single-hoofed animals like horses, of Kāshthā. Danu had sixty one issue. Hear the names of the important ones among them. **30-31.** These were Dwimūrdhā, Sambara, Arishta, Hayagrīva, Vibhāvasu, Ayomukha, Sankusiras, Swarbhānu, Kapila, Aruna, Pulomā, Vrishaparvā, Ekachakra, Anutāpana, Dhūmrakesa, Virūpāksha, Viprachitti and Durjaya. **32.** From among the above, Swarbhānu's daughter Suprabhā was married by Namuchi; and Vrishaparvā's daughter Sarmishthā by the powerful Yayāti, the son of Nahusha. **33.** One of the sons of Danu known as Vaiswānara had Upadānavī, Hayasirā, Pulomā, and Kālakā as daughters noted for their beauty. **34.** O King! Of these Upadānavī was married by Hiranyāksha, and Hayasirā by Kratu, while the other daughters Pulomā and Kālakā became the wives of Kasyapa Prajapati. **35-36.** Kasyapa married these two according to the direction of Brahma. From these marriages were born two clans of powerful and warlike Danavas well-known as Paulomas and Kālakeyas (known also as Nivātakavachas), num-

विप्रचित्तिः सिंहिकायां शतं चैकमजीजनत्। राहुज्येष्ठं केतुशतं ग्रहत्वं य उपागतः ॥37॥
अथातः श्रूयतां वंशो योऽदितेरनुपूर्वशः। यत्र नारायणो देवः स्वांशेनावतरद्विभुः ॥38॥
विवस्वानर्यमा पूषा त्वष्टाथ सविता भगः। धाता विधाता वरुणो मित्रः शक्रः उरुक्रमः 39॥
विवस्वतः श्राद्धदेवं संज्ञासूयत वै मनुम्। मिथुनं च महाभागा यमं देवं यमीं तथा।
सैव भूत्वाथ वडवा नासत्यौ सुषुवे भुवि ॥40॥
छाया शनैश्चरं लेभे सावर्णिं च मनुं ततः। कन्यां च तपतीं या वै वव्रे संवरणं पतिम् ॥41॥
अर्यम्णो मातृका पत्नी तयोश्चर्षणयः सुताः। यत्र वै मानुषी जातिर्ब्रह्मणा चोपकल्पिता ॥42॥
पूषानपत्यः पिष्टादो भग्नदन्तोऽभवत्पुरा। योऽसौ दक्षाय कुपितं जहास विवृतद्विजः ॥43॥
त्वष्टुर्दैत्यानुजा भार्या रचना नाम कन्यका। संनिवेशस्तयोर्जज्ञे विश्वरूपश्च वीर्यवान् ॥44॥
तं वव्रिरे सुरगणाः स्वस्रीयं द्विषतामपि। विमतेन परित्यक्ता गुरुणाऽऽङ्गिरसेन यत् ॥45॥

इति श्रीमद्भागवते महापुराणे पारमहंस्यां संहितायां षष्ठस्कन्धे षष्ठोऽध्यायः ॥6॥

bering sixty thousand. Your grandfather Arjuna, O King, destroyed single-handed the whole lot of them, desecrators of sacrifices, and thereby became very dear to Indra. **37.** The Danava named Viprachitti begot by Simhikā, Rāhu and a hundred other sons known by the collective name of Ketus. Rahu became a planet (*graha*).

Aditi and her Issue (38-45)

38. Next hear the enumeration of the famous line originating from Aditi. The all-powerful Lord Narayana incarnated in that line with a part of His. **39.** Aditi had twelve sons named Vivaswān, Aryamā, Pūshā, Tvashtā, Savitā, Bhaga, Dhātā, Vidhātā, Varuna, Mitra, Sakra and Urukrama (Vāmana). **40.** O pious one! Vivaswān begot by his wife Samjnā a Manu named Srāddha Deva (known also as Vaivasvata), and the twins—a male Yama and a female Yamī. Afterwards taking the form of a mare on earth, the same Samjnā bore him the twin-born Aswinidevas, also known as Nāsatyas. **41.** Afterwards Samjnā became Chhāyā and bore Vivaswan three issue—Sani, Manu Sāvarni, and a daughter Tapatī who chose Samvarana as her husband. **42.** The wife of Aryamā was Mātrikā. They had as issue a group called Charshanīs, who were endowed with powers of introspection (or knowledge of Karma and Moksha). Brahma modelled human species on them. **43.** Pūshā had no issue. He was toothless and had to subsist on rice flour. He laughed at Rudra showing his teeth when the latter was incensed by Daksha. This was what led to the loss of his teeth. **44.** Tvashtā had for his wife Rachanā, a younger sister of the Daityas. By her was born Viswarupa and Sannivesa of great puissance. **45.** When Brihaspati, smarting under an insult, abandoned his priestly services to the Devas, they adopted this Viswarupa as their priest, even though he was the nephew of their enemies, the Daityas.

1

अथ सप्तमोऽध्यायः

राजोवाच

कस्य हेतोः परित्यक्ता आचार्येणात्मनः सुराः । एतदाचक्ष्व भगवञ्छिष्याणामक्रमं गुरौ ॥ 1॥

श्रीशुक उवाच

इन्द्रस्त्रिभुवनैश्वर्यमदोल्लङ्घितसत्पथः । मरुद्भिर्वसुभी रुद्रैरादित्यैर्ऋभुभिर्नृप ॥ 2॥
विश्वेदेवैश्च साध्यैश्च नासत्याभ्यां परिश्रितः । सिद्धचारणगन्धर्वैर्मुनिभिर्ब्रह्मवादिभिः ॥ 3॥
विद्याधराप्सरोभिश्च किन्नरैः पतगोरगैः । निषेव्यमाणो मघवान् स्तूयमानश्च भारत ॥ 4॥
उपगीयमानो ललितमास्थानाध्यासनाश्रितः । पाण्डुरेणातपत्रेण चन्द्रमण्डलचारुणा ॥ 5॥
युक्तश्चान्यैः पारमेष्ठचैश्चामरव्यजनादिभिः । विराजमानः पौलोम्या सहार्धासनया भृशम् 6॥
स यदा परमाचार्यं देवानामात्मनश्च ह । नाभ्यनन्दत सम्प्राप्तं प्रत्युत्थानासनादिभिः 7॥
वाचस्पतिं मुनिवरं सुरासुरनमस्कृतम् । नोच्चचालासनादिन्द्रः पश्यन्नपि सभागतम् 8॥
ततो निर्गत्य सहसा कविराङ्गिरसः प्रभुः । आययौ स्वगृहं तूष्णीं विद्वान् श्रीमदविक्रियाम् 9॥
तर्ह्येव प्रतिबुद्ध्येन्द्रो गुरुहेलनमात्मनः । गर्हयामास सदसि स्वयमात्मानमात्मना ॥10॥
अहो बत ममासाधु कृतं वै दभ्रबुद्धिना । यन्मयैश्वर्यमत्तेन गुरुः सदसि कात्कृतः ॥11॥

Skandha VI : Chapter 7
INDRA'S DOWNFALL

Indra's Insults to Brihaspati (1-9)

Rajah Parikshit said: **1.** For what reason did Brihaspati, the Acharya of the Devas, abandon them, his disciples? What was the offence on the part of the disciples that made him do so? Please explain this to me, O all-knowing one!

Sri Suka said: **2-9.** O King! Indra was one day sitting on his throne, with his consort Paulomi sharing half of it. He was sitting inflated with pride born of his mastery over the resources of the three worlds, forgetting even the bounds of courteous conduct. He was sitting in audience, surrounded by his retinue consisting of the forty-nine Maruts, eight Vasus, the Rudras, Ādityas, Ribhus, Visvedevas, Sādhyas and Aswinidevas; and he was being attended on and extolled by Siddhas, Chāranas, Gandharvas, Rishis, Vidyādharas, Apsaras, Kinnaras, Patagas and Sarpas. While he was thus sitting on his throne with his consort Paulomi, having the white moon-like ceremonial umbrella held above and other royal insignia like Chamara (fly-whisk) waving, Brihaspati, the Guru of all the Devas and of (Indra) himself, entered the audience hall. But Indra did not rise up or offer a seat by way of honouring that sage who was universally respected by celestials, Asuras and all others. Thereupon, seeing that Indra did not move even an inch from his seat in spite of observing him, that all-powerful sage came out of the assembly hall immediately, and understanding how Indra was swollen with pride due to his prosperity, returned home without uttering a word.

Indra's belated Regret (10-19)

10. Immediately after, Indra realized his offence of having insulted the Guru, and began to criticise himself in that assembly for the same. **11.** He said. 'Alas! I have

को गृध्येत् पण्डितो लक्ष्मीं त्रिविष्टपपतेरपि । ययाहमासुरं भावं नीतोऽद्य विबुधेश्वरः ॥12॥
ये पारमेष्ठ्यं धिषणमधितिष्ठन् न कञ्चन । प्रत्युत्तिष्ठेदिति ब्रूयुर्धर्मं ते न परं विदुः ॥13॥
तेषां कुपथदेष्टॄणां पततां तमसि ह्यधः । ये श्रद्दध्युर्वचस्ते वै मज्जन्त्यश्मप्लवा इव ॥14॥
अथाहममराचार्यमगाधधिषणं द्विजम् । प्रसादयिष्ये निशठः शीर्ष्णा तच्चरणं स्पृशन् 15॥
एवं चिन्तयतस्तस्य मघोनो भगवान् गृहात् । बृहस्पतिर्गतोऽदृष्टां गतिमध्यात्ममायया ॥16॥
गुरोर्नाधिगतः संज्ञां परीक्षन् भगवान् स्वराट् । ध्यायन् धिया सुरैर्युक्तः शर्म नालभतात्मनः 17॥
तच्छ्रुत्वैवासुराः सर्व आश्रित्यौशनसं मतम् । देवान् प्रत्युद्यमं चक्रुर्दुर्मदा आततायिनः ॥18॥
तैर्विसृष्टेषुभिस्तीक्ष्णैर्निर्भिन्नाङ्गोरुबाहवः । ब्रह्माणं शरणं जग्मुः सहेन्द्रा नतकन्धराः ॥19॥
तांस्तथाभ्यर्दितान् वीक्ष्य भगवानात्मभूरजः । कृपया परया देव उवाच परिसान्त्वयन् ॥20॥

ब्रह्मोवाच

अहो बत सुरश्रेष्ठा ह्यभद्रं वः कृतं महत् । ब्रह्मिष्ठं ब्राह्मणं दान्तमैश्वर्यान्नाभ्यनन्दत ॥21॥
तस्यायमनयस्यासीत् परेभ्यो वः पराभवः । प्रक्षीणेभ्यः स्ववैरिभ्यः समृद्धानां च यत्सुराः 22॥
मघवन् द्विषतः पश्य प्रक्षीणान् गुर्वतिक्रमात् । सम्प्रत्युपचितान् भूयः काव्यमाराध्य भक्तितः ।
आददीरन् निलयनं ममापि भृगुदेवताः ॥23॥

done a great wrong. Dull-witted and puffed up with the pride of wealth, I have insulted my Guru openly in this assembly. **12.** Whoever possessed of true wisdom and learning would desire to have this kind of affluence derived from the rulership of all the three worlds (as I have), if it were to lead to such disastrous results? For, though I am the head of the Devas noted for their gentle nature, affluence has made me behave like an Asura. **13.** Those who explain away this offence by saying that a king sitting in audience on his throne need not rise up to honour anyone, do not know anything about the highest duty. **14.** Those who follow the teaching of these people, who, themselves steeped in ignorance, give such perverse advice to others, will sink down instantly to their destruction like men trying to cross the sea on a slab of stone, mistaking it to be a boat. **15.** So without any obstinacy or reservation, I am going to placate that learned teacher of the Devas by touching his feet with my head.'

16. While Indra was thinking in this way, the worshipful Brihaspati, using his extraordinary psychic power, disappeared from that place. **17.** Even after much reflection within himself and consultations with other celestials, Indra was not able to find out the whereabouts of the teacher Brihaspati. He was much worried on this account. **18.** Coming to know about this situation, arrogant Asuras, advised by their teacher Sukra, took up arms and started a fight with the Devas. **19.** Severely wounded all over their bodies with the sharp arrows of the Asuras, the Devas headed by Indra took shelter at the feet of Brahma in all humility.

Brahma's Advice (20-25)

20. Seeing the Devas in distress, Brahma, who had his origin from the Supreme Being, was all pity for them and spoke consolingly. *Brahma said:* **21.** 'O leader of the celestials! You have indeed done a great wrong. Alas! Infatuated with pride of wealth, you failed to show proper regard to a holy man like Brihaspati, who has conquered the senses and is established in Brahman. **22.** O celestials! It is as a result of this offence of yours that in spite of being powerful you have had to suffer this defeat from a weak enemy. **23.** O

त्रिविष्टपं किं गणयन्त्यभेद्यमन्त्रा भृगूणामनुशिक्षितार्थाः ।
न विप्रगोविन्दगवीश्वराणां भवन्त्यभद्राणि नरेश्वराणाम् ॥24॥
तद्विश्वरूपं भजताशु विप्रं तपस्विनं त्वाष्ट्रमथात्मवन्तम् ।
सभाजितोऽर्थान् स विधास्यते वो यदि क्षमिष्यध्वमुतास्य कर्म ॥25॥

श्रीशुक उवाच

त एवमुदिता राजन् ब्रह्मणा विगतज्वराः । ऋषिं त्वाष्ट्रमुपव्रज्य परिष्वज्येदमब्रुवन् ॥26॥

देवा ऊचुः

वयं तेऽतिथयः प्राप्ता आश्रमं भद्रमस्तु ते । कामः सम्पाद्यतां तात पितॄणां समयोचितः 27॥
पुत्राणां हि परो धर्मः पितृशुश्रूषणं सताम् । अपि पुत्रवतां ब्रह्मन् किमुत ब्रह्मचारिणाम् 28॥
आचार्यो ब्रह्मणो मूर्तिः पिता मूर्तिः प्रजापतेः । भ्राता मरुत्पतेर्मूर्तिर्माता साक्षात् क्षितेस्तनुः 29॥
दयाया भगिनी मूर्तिर्धर्मस्यात्मातिथिः स्वयम् । अग्नेरभ्यागतो मूर्तिः सर्वभूतानि चात्मनः ॥30॥
तस्मात् पितॄणामार्तानामार्तिं परपराभवम् । तपसापनयंस्तात सन्देशं कर्तुमर्हसि ॥31॥
वृणीमहे त्वोपाध्यायं ब्रह्मिष्ठं ब्राह्मणं गुरुम् । यथाञ्जसा विजेष्यामः सपत्नांस्तव तेजसा 32॥
न गर्हयन्ति ह्यर्थेषु यविष्ठाङ्घ्र्यभिवादनम् । छन्दोभ्योऽन्यत्र न ब्रह्मन् वयो ज्यैष्ठ्यस्य कारणम्

Indra! Look at your enemies, the Asuras. They were once weak because of their spurning their Guru, Sukra. Now because they have propitiated him by service, they have again grown in power and wealth. Devoted as they are now to Bhrigu (Sukra), they might now take over even my state. **24.** When they are so powerful, because of the guidance they get from Sukra and the strength instilled into them by Mantras, the heaven of Indra is quite easy for them to take over. Calamities do not overtake kings who are devoted to the Lord and to holy men, and are kind to all creatures. **25.** So go soon to Viswarupa, the son of Tvashta, who is a Brahmana of great austerity and insight and try to please him. Overlooking his leanings to the side of the Asuras due to his Karma, if you please him and get him on your side, he will fulfil your objective.'

Indra's Mission to Viswarupa (26-40)

Sri Suka said: **26.** O King! Instructed in this way by Brahma, the Devas were relieved of their sorrow. They went to Tvashta's son, Viswarupa, embraced him, and said as follows. *The Devas said:* **27.** 'We have come to your Ashrama as your guests. May you be happy! Dear one! There is one favour we seek of you out of our present need. It behoves you to fulfil the same like a son. **28.** Service of their parents continues to be the highest duty of men even after they have children of their own. It is still more so of persons who are unmarried. **29.** The Acharya is a replica of Brahma; the father, of Prajapati; the brother, of Indra; and the mother, of the Earth-deity. **30.** The sister is a replica of Daya (mercy). A guest is the very embodiment of Dharma, a visiting traveller is a form of Fire; and all creatures are expressions of the Lord. **31.** Therefore, it behoves you, who are like a son to us, to help us overcome, by virtue of your austerity and by proper advice, the difficulties we now face on account of our defeat at the hands of our enemies. **32.** We desire to choose you, a wise and enlightened personage, as our teacher so that by your power we may overcome our enemies without any difficulty. **33.** On serious occasions, there is no impropriety in an

ऋषिरुवाच

अभ्यर्थितः सुरगणैः पौरोहित्ये महातपाः । स विश्वरूपस्तानाह प्रसन्नः श्लक्ष्णया गिरा ॥34॥

विश्वरूप उवाच

विगर्हितं धर्मशीलैर्ब्रह्मवर्च उपव्ययम् । कथं नु मद्विधो नाथा लोकेशैरभियाचितम् ।
प्रत्याख्यास्यति तच्छिष्यः स एव स्वार्थ उच्यते ॥35॥
अकिञ्चनानां हि धनं शिलोञ्छनं तेनेह निर्वर्तितसाधुसत्क्रियः ।
कथं विगर्ह्यं नु करोम्यधीश्वराः पौरोधसं हृष्यति येन दुर्मतिः ॥36॥
तथापि न प्रतिब्रूयां गुरुभिः प्रार्थितं कियत् । भवतां प्रार्थितं सर्वं प्राणैरर्थैश्च साधये ॥37॥

श्रीशुक उवाच

तेभ्य एवं प्रतिश्रुत्य विश्वरूपो महातपाः । पौरोहित्यं वृतश्चक्रे परमेण समाधिना ॥38॥
सुरद्विषां श्रियं गुप्तामौशनस्यापि विद्यया । आच्छिद्यादान्महेन्द्राय वैष्णव्या विद्यया विभुः ॥
यया गुप्तः सहस्राक्षो जिग्येऽसुरचमूर्विभुः । तां प्राह स महेन्द्राय विश्वरूप उदारधीः ॥40॥

इति श्रीमद्भागवते महापुराणे पारमहंस्यां संहितायां षष्ठस्कन्धे सप्तमोऽध्यायः ॥7॥

elder person prostrating at the feet of one younger. O learned one! One's knowledge of the Veda is the real mark of one's superiority, and not mere age.'

Sri Suka said: **34.** That Viswarupa of great austerity, being thus implored by the delegation of Devas, replied to them, highly pleased, in sweet words. *Viswarupa said:* **35.** 'Priestly office, which ends in the wastage of one's spiritual power, is deprecated by people who know the sacred laws. But how can I, who am like a disciple to you, the masters of the worlds, refuse a request made by you? In the fulfilment of the wants of a preceptor or master lies the fulfilment of the life of a pupil or a servant. **36.** Regarding those who have taken the vow of poverty and non-possession and practise exclusive devotion to the Lord, their only income consists in the fallen grains that they collect from the fields and streets. O Lord of the three worlds! How can I, who am now discharging the noble duties of a householder's life with the sacred materials collected in this way, take to the ignoble profession of a priest? **37.** Still I am not going to refuse your request. After all, what a trifle you, my superiors, are asking for! I shall devote all my resources, including my life, for the achievement of your purpose.'

Sri Suka said: **38.** On being thus chosen by the Devas, Viswarupa, famous for all his great austerity, offered his services to them as their priest. He thenceforth discharged his priestly duties with wholehearted attention. **39.** By the power derived through meditation on Vishnu (through the practice of Narayana-kavacha), he deprived the Asuras of their good fortune safeguarded by Sukra's occult practices, and transferred it to Indra. **40.** The high-minded Viswarupa imparted to Indra this meditation known as the Narayana-kavacha (the armour of psychic potency relating to Narayana). Protected by it, Indra of a thousand eyes, easily overcame the armies of the Asuras.

अथाष्टमोऽध्यायः

राजोवाच

यया गुप्तः सहस्राक्षः सवाहान् रिपुसैनिकान् । क्रीडन्निव विनिर्जित्य त्रिलोक्या बुभुजे श्रियम् 1॥
भगवंस्तन्ममाख्याहि वर्म नारायणात्मकम् । यथाऽऽततायिनः शत्रून् येन गुप्तोऽजयन्मृधे 2॥

श्रीशुक उवाच

वृतः पुरोहितस्त्वाष्ट्रो महेन्द्रायानुपृच्छते । नारायणाख्यं वर्माह तदिहैकमनाः शृणु ॥ 3॥

विश्वरूप उवाच

धौताङ्घ्रिपाणिराचम्य सपवित्र उदङ्मुखः । कृतस्वाङ्गकरन्यासो मन्त्राभ्यां वाग्यतः शुचिः ॥
नारायणमयं वर्म सन्नह्येद् भय आगते । पादयोर्जानुनोरूर्वोरुदरे हृद्यथोरसि ॥ 5॥
मुखे शिरस्यानुपूर्व्यादोङ्कारादीनि विन्यसेत् । ॐ नमो नारायणायेति विपर्ययमथापि वा ॥ 6॥
करन्यासं ततः कुर्याद् द्वादशाक्षरविद्यया । प्रणवादियकारान्तमङ्गुल्यङ्गुष्ठपर्वसु ॥ 7॥
न्यसेद्धृदय ओङ्कारं विकारमनु मूर्धनि । षकारं तु भ्रुवोर्मध्ये णकारं शिखया दिशेत् ॥ 8॥

Skandha VI : Chapter 8

IMPARTING OF NARAYANA-KAVACHA TO INDRA

Meditation on Narayana-kavacha (1-11)

The Rajah said: **1-2.** It behoves you to tell me what that occult armour of Mantras called Narayana-kavacha is, protected by which Indra was able to conquer as easily as in play, enemies who were equipped with all vehicles and weapons and wrest from them the suzerainty over the three worlds. You ought to explain how under its protection Indra could conquer his well-armed enemies.

Sri Suka said: **3.** After choosing Viswarupa, the son of Tvashta as priest, Indra asked him to impart to him the Narayana-kavacha and Viswarupa did so. Now listen attentively to what he said.

Viswarupa said: **4-6.** The Narayana-kavacha should be repeated and meditated upon when one is faced with a dangerous situation. Washing hands and feet, doing Achamana (sipping water ceremonially), and putting on the Pavitra (the grass ring), a person should sit facing the north with a pure mind and controlled speech. With the two Mantras, the eight-syllabled and the twelve-syllabled, he should perform Anganyasa and Karanyasa before he meditates on Narayana-kavacha. In the Anganyasa, the eight syllabled Mantra '*Om Namo Narayanaya*' should be spread over the body by the touch of the fingers, along with the repetition of each of the syllables, in their order on the eight parts of the body—feet, knee, thigh, abdomen, heart, chest, face and head. Utterance of each syllable should be prefaced and followed by the sound Om. Or the order of the parts touched and the syllables uttered may be reversed also. **7.** In Karanyasa the twelve-syllabled Mantra '*Om Namo Bhagavate Vāsudevaya*' should be spread by touching the fingers and the phalanges of the thumbs in due order, uttering the syllables of the Mantra from the Pranava to *ya* in their order with each touch. Each syllable should be prefaced and ended with the utterance of Om. **8.** Next he should do Nyasa of the Mantra '*Om Vishnave namah*'. The syllable *Om* should be placed on the heart; *vi* on the head; *sh* between the brows; *na* at the tuft.

वेकारं नेत्रयोर्युञ्ज्यान्नकारं सर्वसन्धिषु । मकारमस्त्रमुद्दिश्य मन्त्रमूर्तिर्भवेद् बुधः ॥ 9॥
सविसर्गं फडन्तं तत् सर्वदिक्षु विनिर्दिशेत् । ॐ विष्णवे नम इति ॥10॥
आत्मानं परमं ध्यायेद् ध्येयं षट्शक्तिभिर्युतम् । विद्यातेजस्तपोमूर्तिमिमं मन्त्रमुदाहरेत् ॥11॥

ॐ हरिर्विदध्यान्मम सर्वरक्षां न्यस्ताङ्घ्रिपद्मः पतगेन्द्रपृष्ठे ।
दरारिचर्मासिगदेषुचापपाशान् दधानोऽष्टगुणोऽष्टबाहुः ॥12॥
जलेषु मां रक्षतु मत्स्यमूर्तिर्यादोगणेभ्यो वरुणस्य पाशात् ।
स्थलेषु मायावटुवामनोऽव्यात् त्रिविक्रमः खेऽवतु विश्वरूपः ॥13॥
दुर्गेष्वटव्याजिमुखादिषु प्रभुः पायान्नृसिंहोऽसुरयूथपारिः ।
विमुञ्चतो यस्य महाट्टहासं दिशो विनेदुर्न्यपतंश्च गर्भाः ॥14॥
रक्षत्वसौ माध्वनि यज्ञकल्पः स्वदंष्ट्रयोन्नीतधरो वराहः ।
रामोऽद्रिकूटेष्वथ विप्रवासे सलक्ष्मणोऽव्याद् भरताग्रजोऽस्मान् ॥15॥
मामुग्रधर्मादखिलात् प्रमादान्नारायणः पातु नरश्च हासात् ।
दत्तस्त्वयोगादथ योगनाथः पायाद् गुणेशः कपिलः कर्मबन्धात् ॥16॥
सनत्कुमारोऽवतु कामदेवाद्धयशीर्षा मां पथि देवहेलनात् ।
देवर्षिवर्यः पुरुषार्चनान्तरात् कूर्मो हरिर्मां निरयादशेषात् ॥17॥

9. The syllable *ve* should be placed in the eyes; *na* in all the joints; and *ma* meditated upon as a powerful weapon (*Astra*) representing the Deity of the Mantra, with whom the worshipper should get identified. **10.** Then using *Visarga* with *ma* and adding *phat* to the sound, he should utter the formula *mah astrāya phat* and project it in all directions, snapping the thumb and middle finger together in each of the directions to ward off evil spirits. **11.** One should then meditate on the Supreme Being, the one object fit for meditation by all, possessed of all His powers like lordship (*aiswarya*) and having the form of consciousness, energy and austerity. He should then repeat the following Mantra constituting the Narayana-kavacha:

Narayana-kavacha Mantra (12-34)

12. Om! May Hari—who is seated on Garuda, who is endowed with eight powers, who has eight arms, and who holds in them His eight weapons — conch, discus, shield, sword, mace, arrow, bow and rope—ensure my protection in every way. **13.** In the water may He protect me as the Great Fish from Varuna's weapons. In the land let Him protect me as the mystic Dwarf. In the sky may His universe-encompassing Trivikrama form protect me. **14.** In danger zones like the battle front, the forest and the like, may He protect me as the Man-lion, the destroyer of Asura hosts, whose terrific roars pierced the quarters and caused the foetus in (Asura) females to abort. **15.** In my travels may the Divine Boar, whose body represents sacrifice and who lifted the earth on His tusks, protect me. On the top of mountains may Rama with the axe protect me. During sojourn in foreign lands, may Rama, the elder brother of Bharata, along with Lakshmana, protect me. **16.** May Narayana protect me from the destructive incantations of enemies as also from my own listlessness. May Nara save me from pride. May Datta, the master of Yoga, save me from fall from the path of Yoga. May Kapila, the master of the Gunas of Prakriti, save me from the bondage of matter. **17.** May Sanat-

धन्वन्तरिर्भगवान् पात्वपथ्याद् द्वन्द्वाद् भयादृषभो निर्जितात्मा ।
यज्ञश्च लोकादवताज्जनान्ताद् बलो गणात् क्रोधवशादहीन्द्रः ॥18॥
द्वैपायनो भगवानप्रबोधाद् बुद्धस्तु पाखण्डगणात् प्रमादात् ।
कल्किः कलेः कालमलात्प्रपातु धर्मावनायोरुकृतावतारः ॥19॥
मां केशवो गदया प्रातरव्याद् गोविन्द आसङ्गवमात्तवेणुः ।
नारायणः प्राह्ण उदात्तशक्तिर्मध्यन्दिने विष्णुररीन्द्रपाणिः ॥20॥
देवोऽपराह्णे मधुहोग्रधन्वा सायं त्रिधामावतु माधवो माम् ।
दोषे हृषीकेश उतार्धरात्रे निशीथ एकोऽवतु पद्मनाभः ॥21॥
श्रीवत्सधामापररात्र ईशः प्रत्यूष ईशोऽसिधरो जनार्दनः ।
दामोदरोऽव्यादनुसन्ध्यं प्रभाते विश्वेश्वरो भगवान् कालमूर्तिः ॥22॥
चक्रं युगान्तानलतिग्मनेमि भ्रमत् समन्ताद् भगवत्प्रयुक्तम् ।
दन्दग्धि दन्दग्ध्यरिसैन्यमाशु कक्षं यथा वातसखो हुताशः ॥23॥
गदेऽशनिस्पर्शनविस्फुलिङ्गे निष्पिण्ढि निष्पिण्ढ्यजितप्रियासि ।
कूष्माण्डवैनायकयक्षरक्षोभूतग्रहांश्चूर्णय चूर्णयारीन् ॥24॥

kumara save me from the influence of Cupid. May Hayagrīva save me from the folly of offering insult to Divinities. May the great Devarshi Narada safeguard me from showing negligence in the worship of the Supreme Being. May Hari as the Divine Tortoise save me from conduct leading to hell. **18.** May the worshipful Dhanvantari protect me from unwholesome food. May Rishabha Deva, noted for his conquest of the senses, save me from the miseries arising from the pairs of opposites. May Yajna protect me from the scandalous criticisms of men. May Balabhadra protect me from the attacks of the populace; and Ādisesha, the king of the serpents, from the fear of deadly serpents known as Krodhavasas. **19.** May the worshipful Dvaipāyana save me from ignorance. May the Buddha save me from atheism and indolence. May Kalki, come as a powerful incarnation for the protection of Dharma, save me from the evils of the age of Kali. **20.** May Kesava protect me with his mace at daybreak *(prātah)*. May Govinda with flute protect me during the second watch of the day (*āsangava*). May Narayana assuming all his powers protect Me during forenoon (*prāhnah*). May Vishnu with the discus in hand protect me during the noon (*mādhyandina*). **21.** May Madhusudana armed with his powerful bow protect me in the afternoon (*aparāhnah*). May Mādhava, who has become the Trinity, protect me in the evening (*sāyam*). May Hrishikesa protect me in the first watch of the night (*pradosha*). May Padmanābha protect me both in the second watch of the night and at midnight. **22.** May the Lord with the Srivatsa mark on his chest protect me during the watch following midnight. In the pre-dawn watch may Janārdana wielding the sword protect me. May Dāmodara protect me during the Sandhyas (junction periods of day and night) and may Visweswara, the embodiment of Time, protect me at dawn. **23.** May the sharp-edged discus Sudarsana, fiercely destructive like the fire of cosmic dissolution, and speeding anywhere on being released by the Lord, burn up, burn up, the enemy forces as dry grass by fire. **24.** O mace, Thou the favourite weapon of the Lord

त्वं यातुधानप्रमथप्रेतमातृपिशाचविप्रग्रहघोरदृष्टीन् ।
दरेन्द्र विद्रावय कृष्णपूरितो भीमस्वनोऽरेर्हृदयानि कम्पयन् ॥25॥
त्वं तिग्मधारासिवरारिसैन्यमीशप्रयुक्तो मम छिन्धि छिन्धि ।
चक्षूंषि चर्मञ्छतचन्द्र छादय द्विषामघोनां हर पापचक्षुषाम् ॥26॥

यन्नो भयं ग्रहेभ्योऽभूत् केतुभ्यो नृभ्य एव च । सरीसृपेभ्यो दंष्ट्रिभ्यो भूतेभ्योंऽहोभ्य एव वा 27॥
सर्वाण्येतानि भगवन्नामरूपास्त्रकीर्तनात् । प्रयान्तु संक्षयं सद्यो ये नः श्रेयःप्रतीपकाः ॥28॥
गरुडो भगवान् स्तोत्रस्तोभश्छन्दोमयः प्रभुः । रक्षत्वशेषकृच्छ्रेभ्यो विष्वक्सेनः स्वनामभिः 29॥
सर्वापद्भ्यो हरेर्नामरूपयानायुधानि नः । बुद्धीन्द्रियमनःप्राणान् पान्तु पार्षदभूषणाः 30॥
यथा हि भगवानेव वस्तुतः सदसच्च यत् । सत्येनानेन नः सर्वे यान्तु नाशमुपद्रवाः ॥31॥
यथैकात्म्यानुभावानां विकल्परहितः स्वयम् । भूषणायुधलिङ्गाख्या धत्ते शक्तीः स्वमायया 32॥
तेनैव सत्यमानेन सर्वज्ञो भगवान्हरिः । पातु सर्वैः स्वरूपैर्नः सदा सर्वत्र सर्वगः ॥33॥

विदिक्षु दिक्षूर्ध्वमधः समन्तादन्तर्बहिर्भगवान् नारसिंहः ।
प्रहापयंल्लोकभयं स्वनेन स्वतेजसा ग्रस्तसमस्ततेजाः ॥34॥

मघवन्निदमाख्यातं वर्म नारायणात्मकम् । विजेष्यस्यञ्जसा येन दंशितोऽसुरयूथपान् 35॥

emitting fire and having the impact of the thunderbolt! May you pound, pound all evil forces like the Kūshmāndas, Yakshas, Rakshasas, Vināyakas, Bhūtas and Pretas! Smash, smash all enemies to smithereens! **25.** O the famous conch Pānchajanya! Blown by the Lord, frighten, frighten and drive away by your terrific sound all evil influences like Rakshasas, Pramathas, Pretas, Matris, Pisāchas, and Brahmarāksasas. **26.** O sharp-edged sword, (Nandaka) used by the Lord! Cut to pieces, cut to pieces the ranks of my enemies! O shield with the mark of a hundred moons! Cover the eyes of sinful enemies! Blind them who have evil eyes! **27-28.** Whatever beings and influences there are, causing us fears and standing in the way of our progress—be they planets, comets, men, serpents, wild animals, Bhūtas or one's own sins—may they all disperse and be destroyed, O Lord, by Thy name, form and weapons! **29.** May the worshipful Garuda, the all-powerful, the embodiment of Veda and the object of adoration by Sāma chants, protect us! May Vishwaksena, protect us in all difficult situations by the power of his name! **30.** May Hari's name, form, vehicles, weapons and chief attendants give protection to us, our intellect, senses, mind and Pranas! **31.** If the truth is that the worshipful Lord alone is all existence, gross and subtle, may all troubles and difficulties of ours be dissolved by the power of that Truth! **32.** Though the Lord is without any differentiation for those who are experiencing the unity of all existence, still by His Yogamaya (which is His free will) He assumes various powers, forms, weapons and adornments. **33.** It being the truth that He is the substance in every thing, may He, the all-powerful and the all-knowing One, protect us always and everywhere presenting Himself in forms appropriate to the situation. **34.** May the Lord as Nrisimha (Man-lion) protect us, above, below and around, on four sides and in the four corners, within and without, by driving away all causes of fear by his roars and by extinguishing the powers of all others by his unmatched puissance.

Narayana-kavacha and a Yogi (35-42)

35. O Indra! I have now imparted to you that psychic armour called Narayana-

एतद् धारयमाणस्तु यं यं पश्यति चक्षुषा । पदा वा संस्पृशेत् सद्यः साध्वसात् स विमुच्यते ॥
न कुतश्चिद्भयं तस्य विद्यां धारयतो भवेत् । राजदस्युग्रहादिभ्यो व्याघ्रादिभ्यश्च कर्हिचित् ॥
इमां विद्यां पुरा कश्चित् कौशिको धारयन् द्विजः । योगधारणया स्वाङ्गं जहौ स मरुधन्वनि ॥38॥
तस्योपरि विमानेन गन्धर्वपतिरेकदा । ययौ चित्ररथः स्त्रीभिर्वृतो यत्र द्विजक्षयः 39॥
गगनान्न्यपतत् सद्यः सविमानो ह्यवाक्शिराः । स वालखिल्यवचनादस्थीन्यादाय विस्मितः ।
प्रास्य प्राचीसरस्वत्यां स्नात्वा धाम स्वमन्वगात् ॥40॥

श्रीशुक उवाच

य इदं शृणुयात् काले यो धारयति चादृतः । तं नमस्यन्ति भूतानि मुच्यते सर्वतो भयात् ॥41॥
एतां विद्यामधिगतो विश्वरूपाच्छतक्रतुः । त्रैलोक्यलक्ष्मीं बुभुजे विनिर्जित्य मृधेऽसुरान् 42॥

इति श्रीमद्भागवते महापुराणे पारमहंस्यां संहितायां षष्ठस्कन्धे नारायणवर्मकथनं नामाष्टमोऽध्यायः ॥8॥

kavacha. Protected by it, you can easily conquer all the leaders of the Asuras. **36.** Wearing this, if you look at or touch with your foot any one, that man will at once be rid of all fear. **37.** He who protects Himself with this armour has nothing to fear from kings, thieves, planets, or wild animals like tigers. **38.** Once a Brahmana of Kausika's lineage invoked this Mantra in a desert without any water to do purificatory rites, and by the application of the Yogic technique, left the body then and there. **39.** Over that region where this Brahmana left his body, Chitraratha, a leader of the Gandharvas, once passed in his aerial car surrounded by many Gandharva women. **40.** As he passed over the spot, the vehicle was upturned, and all the occupants came down topsy-turvy to the ground. On the advice of the saints known as the Balakhilyas, Chitraratha collected the bones of the dead Yogi, consigned them to the Saraswati where the river flows eastwards, took his bath in it, and went home.

Sri Suka said: **41.** Whoever hears this or meditates upon this with full faith, he receives the homage of all living beings. He is freed from all kinds of fear. **42.** Having obtained the knowledge of this meditation from Viswarupa, Indra obtained victory over the Asuras, and became the master of the resources of all the three worlds.

अथ नवमोऽध्यायः

श्रीशुक उवाच

तस्यासन् विश्वरूपस्य शिरांसि त्रीणि भारत । सोमपीथं सुरापीथमन्नादमिति शुश्रुम ॥ 1॥
स वै बर्हिषि देवेभ्यो भागं प्रत्यक्षमुच्चकैः । अवदद् यस्य पितरो देवाः सप्रश्रयं नृप ॥ 2॥

Skandha VI : Chapter 9

THE APPEARANCE OF VRITRA

Viswarupa's Slaughter (1-10)

Sri Suka said: **1.** We have heard that this Viswarupa had three heads, through each of which he consumed each of the three—Soma, liquor and food. **2.** O King! Viswarupa, whose father was a Deva, always made offerings to Devas with

स एव हि ददौ भागं परोक्षमसुरान् प्रति । यजमानोऽवहद् भागं मातृस्नेहवशानुगः ॥ 3॥
तद् देवहेलनं तस्य धर्मालीकं सुरेश्वरः । आलक्ष्य तरसा भीतस्तच्छीर्षाण्यच्छिनद् रुषा ॥
सोमपीथं तु यत्तस्य शिर आसीत् कपिञ्जलः । कलविङ्कः सुरापीथमन्नादं यत् स तित्तिरिः ॥ 5॥
ब्रह्महत्यामञ्जलिना जग्राह यदपीश्वरः । संवत्सरान्ते तदघं भूतानां स विशुद्धये ।
भूम्यम्बुद्रुमयोषिद्भ्यश्चतुर्धा व्यभजद्धरिः ॥ 6॥
भूमिस्तुरीयं जग्राह खातपूरवरेण वै । ईरिणं ब्रह्महत्याया रूपं भूमौ प्रदृश्यते ॥ 7॥
तुर्यं छेदविरोहेण वरेण जगृहुर्द्रुमाः । तेषां निर्यासरूपेण ब्रह्महत्या प्रदृश्यते ॥ 8॥
शश्वत् कामवरेणांहस्तुरीयं जगृहुः स्त्रियः । रजोरूपेण तास्वंहो मासि मासि प्रदृश्यते ॥ 9॥
द्रव्यभूयोवरेणापस्तुरीयं जगृहुर्मलम् । तासु बुद्बुदफेनाभ्यां दृष्टं तद्धरति क्षिपन् ॥10॥
हतपुत्रस्ततस्त्वष्टा जुहावेन्द्राय शत्रवे । इन्द्रशत्रो विवर्धस्व मा चिरं जहि विद्विषम् ॥11॥
अथान्वाहार्यपचनादुत्थितो घोरदर्शनः । कृतान्त इव लोकानां युगान्तसमये यथा ॥12॥

humility and loud utterances of the Mantra. **3.** But drawn by affection for his mother, who came from the ranks of the Asuras, he secretly gave a part of the offerings to the Asuras too, whenever he sacrificed to the Devas. **4.** Indra was aghast at this unrighteous deception practised on the celestials, and in great anger cut off Viswarupa's heads. **5.** The head that drank the Soma became *Kapinjala* (black cock); that which took liquor became *Kalavinga* (sparrow); and that which consumed food became *Tittiri* (partridge). **6.** By this act Indra, though a powerful personage, had to incur the sin of Brahmahatya (the killing of a holy man). At the end of a year, in order to rid himself of it, he transferred and partitioned that sin among the four, namely, the earth, water, trees and women. **7.** One fourth portion of it was accepted by the earth in return for the boon that any pit dug on the ground will be naturally filled up. The deserts seen on the surface of the earth are the effect of that sin inherited by the earth. So in such desert regions the study of the Veda and performance of sacrifices are prohibited. **8.** The trees accepted another fourth portion of the sin for the boon that their branches would grow again even if clipped. What is seen as exudation in trees when cut, is the sinful expression of Brahmahatya. **9.** Women received the third quarter of the sin, accepting as boon that there will be no obstruction to their love-life even in pregnancy. That sin expresses in them through the monthly menstrual flow. **19.** Water received the remaining fourth of the sin on being given the boon that its addition to anything will swell its bulk. The bubbles and foam seen in water constitute that sin. So people take water only after removing the dirty portions that represent this sin.

Vritra's Appearance (11-20)

11. Now Tvashta, the father of the slaughtered Viswarupa, was grief-stricken by the death of his son, and he began a sacrificial rite in order to produce a person powerful enough to kill Indra. 'O enemy of Indra! Grow into mighty proportions, and slay the enemy soon!', so prayed Tvashta. **12.** Thereupon from the sacrificial fire known as the Dakshinagni, a terrific being came out. Like the all-consuming form of Death appearing at the time of the total destruction of the Pralaya, a being emerged from the Dakshinagni.

विष्वग्विवर्धमानं तमिषुमात्रं दिने दिने । दग्धशैलप्रतीकाशं सन्ध्याभ्रानीकवर्चसम् ॥13॥
तप्तताम्रशिखाश्मश्रुं मध्याह्नार्कोग्रलोचनम् ॥14॥
देदीप्यमाने त्रिशिखे शूल आरोप्य रोदसी । नृत्यन्तमुन्नदन्तं च चालयन्तं पदा महीम् ॥15॥
दरीगम्भीरवक्त्रेण पिबता च नभस्तलम् । लिहता जिह्वयर्क्षाणि ग्रसता भुवनत्रयम् ॥16॥
महता रौद्रदंष्ट्रेण जृम्भमाणं मुहुर्मुहुः । वित्रस्ता दुद्रुवुर्लोका वीक्ष्य सर्वे दिशो दश ॥17॥
येनावृता इमे लोकास्तमसा त्वाष्ट्रमूर्तिना । स वै वृत्र इति प्रोक्तः पापः परमदारुणः ॥18॥
तं निजघ्नुरभिद्रुत्य सगणा विबुधर्षभाः । स्वैः स्वैर्दिव्यास्त्रशस्त्रौघैः सोऽग्रसत् तानि कृत्स्नशः
ततस्ते विस्मिताः सर्वे विषण्णा ग्रस्ततेजसः । प्रत्यञ्चमादिपुरुषमुपतस्थुः समाहिताः ॥20॥

देवा ऊचुः

वाय्वम्बराग्न्यप्क्षितयस्त्रिलोका ब्रह्मादयो ये वयमुद्विजन्तः ।
हराम यस्मै बलिमन्तकोऽसौ बिभेति यस्मादरणं ततो नः ॥21॥
अविस्मितं तं परिपूर्णकामं स्वेनैव लाभेन समं प्रशान्तम् ।
विनोपसर्पत्यपरं हि बालिशः श्वलाङ्गुलेनातितितर्ति सिन्धुम् ॥22॥
यस्योरुशृङ्गे जगतीं स्वनावं मनुर्यथाऽऽबध्य ततार दुर्गम् ।
स एव नस्त्वाष्ट्रभयाद् दुरन्तात् त्राताऽऽश्रितान् वारिचरोऽपि नूनम् 23॥

13-17. Every day the all-round growth of his body was equal to the dimension of a bow. His complexion was black like that of a mountain burnt by forest fire mingled with the glow of a cloud at sunset. The hair on his head and his face looked like heated copper, while his fierce eyes resembled the midday sun. He was wildly dancing to the accompaniment of tumultuous roars and earth-shaking treads, holding an uplifted trident with three dazzling points, as if he were lifting up heaven and earth impaled on it. Every one fled away as he stood yawning, exposing the extensive cavern of his mouth, with the terrible and protruding tongue, as if he were going to lick the stars and drink up the sky, and swallow the three worlds. **18.** That extremely cruel and sinful being came to be known as Vritra, because he, the offspring of Tvashta's Mantra, was the very embodiment of Tamas covering the world with the darkness emanating from him. **19.** On seeing him, the Devas with all their following rushed at him and struck him with their divine weapons, but Vritra swallowed up all those weapons. **20.** The Devas who were stunned at this, found simultaneously that they had lost their puissance. Overcome with grief, they became introspective, and prayed to the Supreme Being as follows:

The Devas in Praise of Mahavishnu (21-30)

The Devas said: **21.** Time which swallows everything is the dread of us all—the five elements like air, sky, fire, water and earth, the worlds formed by their combination, Brahma who directs the process, and we his subordinates. In Him, who is the dread even of that Time, we seek refuge. **22.** He indeed is a simpleton who seeks the shelter of others, leaving aside Him, the unconditioned, the self-satisfied, the passionless Being. He who does so is a fool like the one trying to cross the ocean with the aid of a dog's tail. **23.** Thou the great Fish on whose antenna Manu Vaivaswata tied his boat of the earth, and thus overcame the great danger caused by the universal flood—

पुरा स्वयंभूरपि संयमाम्भस्युदीर्णवातोर्मिरवैः कराले।
एकोऽरविन्दात् पतितस्ततार तस्माद् भयाद् येन स नोऽस्तु पारः ॥24॥
य एक ईशो निजमायया नः ससर्ज येनानुसृजाम विश्वम्।
वयं न यस्यापि पुरः समीहतः पश्याम लिङ्गं पृथगीशमानिनः ॥25॥
यो नः सपत्नैर्भृशमर्द्यमानान्देवर्षितिर्यङ्नृषु नित्य एव।
कृतावतारस्तनुभिः स्वमायया कृत्वाऽऽत्मसात्पाति युगे युगे च ॥26॥
तमेव देवं वयमात्मदैवतं परं प्रधानं पुरुषं विश्वमन्यम्।
व्रजाम सर्वे शरणं शरण्यं स्वानां स नो धास्यति शं महात्मा ॥27॥

श्रीशुक उवाच

इति तेषां महाराज सुराणामुपतिष्ठताम्। प्रतीच्यां दिश्यभूदाविः शङ्खचक्रगदाधरः ॥28॥
आत्मतुल्यैः षोडशभिर्विना श्रीवत्सकौस्तुभौ। पर्युपासितमुन्निद्रशरदम्बुरुहेक्षणम् ॥29॥
दृष्ट्वा तमवनौ सर्व ईक्षणाह्लादविक्लवाः। दण्डवत् पतिता राजञ्छनैरुत्थाय तुष्टुवुः ॥30॥

देवा ऊचुः

नमस्ते यज्ञवीर्याय वयसे उत ते नमः। नमस्ते ह्यस्तचक्राय नमः सुपुरुहूतये ॥31॥
यत् ते गतीनां तिसृणामीशितुः परमं पदम्। नार्वाचीनो विसर्गस्य धातर्वेदितुमर्हति ॥32॥

may Thou save us, Thy dependants, from the fear facing us in the form of Vritra. **24.** In the beginning of creation Brahma found himself falling from his solitary situation in Thy navel-lotus amidst the limitless expanse of cosmic waters rendered all the more forbidding by the furious winds that raged over it. May He, who saved him in that dire situation, be our saviour too. **25.** He the one Lord of all, who out of His Maya brought us into existence to carry on the creative activity by His blessing; He who *even without us,* has all through been the creator of everything, though unperceived by us on account of our infatuated feeling of being mighty Lords; **26.** He who saves us, His own people, whenever we are under the threat of enemies, by becoming incarnate among Devas, Rishis, men and lower creatures, in spite of His being the Eternal One; **27.** He who presents Himself as our Chosen Deity in different aspects though He is the Supreme Cause, who is both the Purusha and the Prakriti, who is transcendent though manifest as the world—in Him we seek shelter. May He, the Supreme Being, do what is auspicious unto us!

Sri Suka said: **28.** O King! As the Devas recited their hymn, the Lord sporting the conch and the discus in hand, manifested Himself in their heart (or in the western direction). **29-30.** Seeing Him with eyes resembling the petals of an autumnal lotus, accompanied by his sixteen close associates who were exactly like Him except that they had no Kaustubha and Srivatsa, all the Devas were overcome with bliss, and fell before Him in prostration like so many rods.

Hymn of the Devas (31-45)

The Devas said: **31.** Salutations to Him whose prowess is displayed through Yajna conferring heavenly felicity! Salutations to Him who is also the destroyer of everything as Time! Salutations to Him who releases the discus Sudarsana against the transgressors of the sacred law! Salutations to Him who has many names indicative of His attributes! **32.** O Creator!

ॐ नमस्तेऽस्तु भगवन्नारायण वासुदेवादिपुरुष महापुरुष महानुभाव परममङ्गल परमकल्याण परमकारुणिक केवल जगदाधार लोकैकनाथ सर्वेश्वर लक्ष्मीनाथ परमहंसपरिव्राजकैः परमेणात्म-योगसमाधिना परिभावितपरिस्फुटपारमहंस्यधर्मेणोद्घाटिततमःकपाटद्वारे चित्तेऽपावृत आत्मलोके स्वयमुपलब्धनिजसुखानुभवो भवान् ॥33॥ दुरवबोध इव तवायं विहारयोगो यदशरणोऽशरीर इदमनवेक्षितास्मत्समवाय आत्मनैवाविक्रियमाणेन सगुणमगुणः सृजसि पासि हरसि ॥34॥ अथ तत्र भवान् किं देवदत्तवदिह गुणविसर्गपतितः पारतन्त्र्येण स्वकृतकुशलाकुशलं फलमुपाददात्याहो-स्विदात्माराम उपशमशीलः समञ्जसदर्शन उदास्त इति ह वाव न विदामः ॥35॥ न हि विरोध उभयं भगवत्यपरिगणितगुणगणे ईश्वरेऽनवगाह्यमाहात्म्येऽर्वाचीनविकल्पवितर्कविचारप्रमाणाभास-कुतर्कशास्त्रकलिलान्तःकरणाश्रयदुरवग्रहवादिनां विवादानवसर उपरतसमस्तमायामये केवल एवात्ममायामन्तर्धाय को न्वर्थो दुर्घट इव भवति स्वरूपद्वयाभावात् ॥36॥ समविषममतीनां मतमनुसरसि यथा रज्जुखण्डः सर्पादिधियाम् ॥37॥ स एव हि पुनः सर्ववस्तुनि वस्तुस्वरूपः

Thou hast brought into existence the three realms—the heavenly regions, the earth and the nether worlds. Thy Supreme State, which transcends all these, is beyond the understanding of all of us who are subsequent to Thy creative will which brought us into existence. Only Thy grace can help us know it. **33.** Om! Salutations to Thee Bhagavan; to Thee Narayana the indweller of all; to Thee Vāsudeva the support of all; to Thee the source of self-effulgent self-consciousness; to Thee the original Being; to Thee the Supreme Person; to Thee the home of all greatness, auspiciousness, goodness and mercy; to Thee the pure Being and the pure Witness; to Thee the basis of the whole world phenomenon, its master and its director; to Thee the Lord of Lakshmī; to Thee the pristine Consciousness-Bliss that shines in the heart of the Paramahamsas from whom every trace of ignorance has vanished by the service of Thy sacred feet with intense concentration derived by long practice. **34.** It looks as if this, Thy cosmic play, will ever remain inscrutable. For without any aid, without a body, without anyone to assist, Thou, who art both with attributes and without, dost create, preserve and dissolve this universe undergoing no change or transformation in Thyself in the process. **35.** It is a mystery beyond our understanding—whether Thou art, like the Jiva, involved in the evolutionary process of Prakriti, dependant on external factors and subject to the good and evil fruits of one's own actions; or whether Thou art only the witness of the whole cosmic process, abiding in Thy own bliss, actionless and over-seeing. **36.** In the Bhagavan, the Supreme Lord, possessed of inscrutable greatness and inexhaustible glories, these alternatives are not contradictions. Thou art beyond the understanding capacity of the modern controversialists whose minds have been made turbid by a system of sophistry based on false authorities, on mere guess work, and on false arguments. When Thy Maya ceases to function, everything subsides and Thou alone art. And when Thy Maya is functioning, what is there impossible for her to achieve? In transcendence and world manifestation, there are no two beings, Thou alone being both, without suffering any diminution of Thy nature or entity. **37.** According to the nature of the minds perceiving, whether they are poised in equanimity, or agitated, Thou doth manifest differently, as a piece of rope is manifested to different people as a snake, a garland or a streak of water. **38.** He

सर्वेश्वरः सकलजगत्कारणकारणभूतः सर्वप्रत्यगात्मत्वात् सर्वगुणाभासोपलक्षित एक एव पर्यवशेषितः
॥38॥ अथ ह वाव तव महिमामृतरससमुद्रविप्रुषा सकृदवलीढया स्वमनसि निष्यन्दमानानवरतसुखेन
विस्मारितदृष्टश्रुतविषयसुखलेशाभासाः परमभागवता एकान्तिनो भगवति सर्वभूतप्रियसुहृदि
सर्वात्मनि नितरां निरन्तरं निर्वृतमनसः कथमु ह वा एते मधुमथन पुनः स्वार्थकुशला ह्यात्मप्रिय-
सुहृदः साधवस्त्वच्चरणाम्बुजानुसेवां विसृजन्ति न यत्र पुनरयं संसारपर्यावर्तः ॥39॥ त्रिभुवनात्मभवन
त्रिविक्रम त्रिनयन त्रिलोकमनोहरानुभाव तवैव विभूतयो दितिजदनुजादयश्चापि तेषामनुपक्रम-
समयोऽयमिति स्वात्ममायया सुरनरमृगमिश्रितजलचराकृतिभिर्यथापराधं दण्डं दण्डधर दधर्थ एवमे-
नमपि भगवञ्जहि त्वाष्ट्रमुत यदि मन्यसे ॥40॥ अस्माकं तावकानां तव नतानां तत ततामह
तव चरणनलिनयुगलध्यानानुबद्धहृदयनिगडानां स्वलिङ्गविवरणेनात्मसात्कृतानामनुकम्पानुरञ्जित-
विशदरुचिरशिशिरस्मितावलोकेन विगलितमधुरमुखरसामृतकलया चान्तस्तापमनघार्हसि शमयितुम्
॥41॥ अथ भगवंस्तवास्माभिरखिलजगदुत्पत्तिस्थितिलयनिमित्तायमानदिव्यमायाविनोदस्य सकल-
जीवनिकायानामन्तर्हृदयेषु बहिरपि च ब्रह्मप्रत्यगात्मस्वरूपेण प्रधानरूपेण च यथादेशकालदेहा-
वस्थानविशेषं तदुपादानोपलम्भकतयानुभवतः सर्वप्रत्ययसाक्षिण आकाशशरीरस्य साक्षात् परब्रह्मणः
परमात्मनः कियानिह वा अर्थविशेषो विज्ञापनीयः स्याद् विस्फुलिङ्गादिभिरिव हिरण्यरेतसः ॥42॥

alone is the Truth in all beings. He is the Lord of all, and is the ultimate cause out of which all materials and agents of creation have sprung. By His indwelling, the whole world is in manifestation and stands as a pointer to His existence. He alone remains when everything dissolves in dissolution. **39.** How can these whole-hearted devotees of Thine—who have become oblivious of the pseudo-joys provided by the sensuous objects of this and the higher worlds on account of the constant flow of bliss produced in their minds by the contact of a single spray from the nectarine ocean of Thy glory, and whose minds have attained to the peace that is in Thee, the soul of all beings—how, O destroyer of Madhu, can such holy men devoted to truth, having Thee as their only friend and dear one, and ever wakeful in their quest of Thee as the highest goal of their life, how can they forget the service of Thy lotus feet, attaining which there is no return to this transmigratory life? **40.** O Thou the soul and resident of the three worlds! Thou the measurer of the three worlds by three strides! Thou the director of the three worlds! Thou the bestower of joy on the three worlds! Though the Asuras, the sons of Diti, too are manifestations of Thy glory, the present not being the time for their ascendancy, Thou didst suppress the Asuras by assuming, through Thy Yogamaya, various forms in Thy incarnations among Devas, men, sub-human species and aquatic creatures, and punished them according to their offences. In the same way, deign to destroy this son of Tvashta too, if it pleases Thee to do so. **41.** O Father! O Grandsire! We, Thy dependants, Thy votaries, have our hearts chained to Thy lotus feet through constant contemplation. By granting Thy vision, Thou hast made us Thy own. And now deign to assuage the intense grief gnawing our hearts by casting on us Thy looks lit up with a loving and sympathetic smile and accompanied by the sweet and continuous flow of Thy nectarine speech. **42.** O Lord! Creation, preservation and dissolution of the universe form Thy sport with Thy Yogamaya. Within all beings Thou art present as Brahman and as the indwelling

अत एव स्वयं तदुपकल्पयास्माकं भगवतः परमगुरोस्तव चरणशतपलाशच्छायां विविधवृजिनसंसार-परिश्रमोपशमनीमुपसृतानां वयं यत्कामेनोपसादिताः ॥43॥

अथो ईश जहि त्वाष्ट्रं ग्रसन्तं भुवनत्रयम् । ग्रस्तानि येन नः कृष्ण तेजांस्यस्त्रायुधानि च 44॥

हंसाय दह्रनिलयाय निरीक्षकाय कृष्णाय मृष्टयशसे निरुपक्रमाय ।
सत्संग्रहाय भवपान्थनिजाश्रमाप्तावन्ते परीष्टगतये हरये नमस्ते ॥45॥

श्रीशुक उवाच

अथैवमीडितो राजन् सादरं त्रिदशैर्हरिः । स्वमुपस्थानमाकर्ण्य प्राह तानभिनन्दितः ॥46॥

श्रीभगवानुवाच

प्रीतोऽहं वः सुरश्रेष्ठा मदुपस्थानविद्यया । आत्मैश्वर्यस्मृतिः पुंसां भक्तिश्चैव यया मयि 47॥
किं दुरापं मयि प्रीते तथापि विबुधर्षभाः । मय्येकान्तमतिर्नान्यन्मत्तो वाञ्छति तत्त्ववित् ॥
न वेद कृपणः श्रेय आत्मनो गुणवस्तुदृक् । तस्य तानिच्छतो यच्छेद् यदि सोऽपि तथाविधः ॥
स्वयं निःश्रेयसं विद्वान् न वक्त्यज्ञाय कर्म हि । न राति रोगिणोऽपथ्यं वाञ्छतो हि भिषक्तमः 50
मघवन् यात भद्रं वो दध्यञ्चमृषिसत्तमम् । विद्याव्रततपःसारं गात्रं याचत माचिरम् ॥51॥

Self, and outside as Nature (Prakriti). And according to the requirements of time, region and embodiment, Thou, as their material cause and revealer, art the witness of every experience of theirs, without being attached in the least, like the sky. To Thee, the Supreme Being and the Supreme Self who thus knows the hearts of all—what are we to represent, we who are standing before Thee like sparks before a conflagration? **43.** Therefore deign to know, by Thy insight into the hearts of all, the objects with which we have come to see Thee, seeking shelter at Thy feet which save beings from the travails of transmigratory existence! **44.** O Lord! Deign to destroy this Vritra, the son of Tvashta, who is consuming the three worlds. He has consumed our prowess, along with our weapons. **45.** Salutations to Hari—the eternally pure, the resident in the sky of the heart, the witness, the existence-knowlege-bliss, the sun of undimmed fame, the eternal being, the one grasped by holy men as their support, and the divine goal which all beings involved in the travails of Samsara ultimately reach.

Thunderbolt Weapon of Indra (46-55)

Sri Suka said: **46.** Sri Hari was propitiated by the fervent hymn addressed to Him by the Devas, and He said to them highly pleased. *The Lord said:* **47.** 'O leading celestials! I am pleased with you for having expressed the truth about My nature through your hymn. From your hymn people will get an idea of my attributes and prowess, and their mind will be filled with devotion for Me. **48.** O great celestials! What is there difficult to attain if I am propitious! But a whole-hearted devotee, a knower of the Truth, hankers for nothing else but Me. **49.** One who is involved with the sense objects is pitiable because he does not understand his own real good. Those who long for petty objects and those who grant it, are both to be pitied. **50.** One who knows what constitutes the Supreme Good of man, never induces the ignorant man to the path of desire-prompted Karmas. A good physician will never allow his patient to take unwholesome food even if the patient likes to do so. **51.** Indra! May good befall you!

स वा अधिगतो दध्यङ्ङश्विभ्यां ब्रह्म निष्कलम् । यद्वा अश्वशिरो नाम तयोरमरतां व्यधात् ॥52॥
दध्यङ्ङाथर्वणस्त्वष्ट्रे वर्माभेद्यं मदात्मकम् । विश्वरूपाय यत् प्रादात् त्वष्टा यत् त्वमधास्ततः ॥
युष्मभ्यं याचितोऽश्विभ्यां धर्मज्ञोऽङ्गानि दास्यति । ततस्तैरायुधश्रेष्ठो विश्वकर्मविनिर्मितः ।
येन वृत्रशिरो हर्ता मत्तेजउपबृंहितः ॥54॥
तस्मिन् विनिहते यूयं तेजोऽस्त्रायुधसम्पदः । भूयः प्राप्स्यथ भद्रं वो न हिंसन्ति च मत्परान् 55॥

इति श्रीमद्भागवते महापुराणे पारमहंस्यां संहितायां षष्ठस्कन्धे नवमोऽध्यायः ॥9॥

Approach the great Rishi Dadhīchi (Dadhyang). Beg of him to give you his body, which has been fortified by meditation, vows and austere practices. **52.** The sage Dadhīchi is a great knower of Brahman, the partless Infinite. He taught the meditation on Brahman known as Aswasiras to Aswinidevas, which gained for them the status of immortals. **53.** The Maharshi Dadhīchi, who is an expert in Atharvana Veda, gave instruction on this unbreakable psychic armour known as Narayana-kavacha, which is ensouled by Me, to Tvashta, who in turn gave it to his son Viswarupa, from whom you have acquired it. **54.** Sage Dadhīchi is a knower of the rules of Dharma. If you make a request to him through the Aswinidevas, his disciples, he will certainly give you his limbs, out of which Viswakarma can make a unique divine weapon. **55.** With that weapon of thunderbolt, augmented by My power, you will be able to cut off the head of Vritra. And when Vritra is dead, you will recover your prowess, missiles, weapons, wealth and everything.'

अथ दशमोऽध्यायः

श्रीशुक उवाच

इन्द्रमेवं समादिश्य भगवान् विश्वभावनः । पश्यतामनिमेषाणां तत्रैवान्तर्दधे हरिः ॥ 1॥
तथाभियाचितो देवैर्ऋषिराथर्वणो महान् । मोदमान उवाचेदं प्रहसन्निव भारत ॥ 2॥
अपि वृन्दारका यूयं न जानीथ शरीरिणाम् । संस्थायां यस्त्वभिद्रोहो दुःसहश्चेतनापहः ॥ 3॥
जिजीविषूणां जीवानामात्मा प्रेष्ठ इहेप्सितः । क उत्सहेत तं दातुं भिक्षमाणाय विष्णवे ॥ 4॥

देवा ऊचुः

किं नु तद् दुस्त्यजं ब्रह्मन् पुंसां भूतानुकम्पिनाम् । भवद्विधानां महतां पुण्यश्लोकेड्यकर्मणाम् ॥ 5॥

Skandha VI : Chapter 10

DEVAS IN CONFRONTATION WITH VRITRA

Devas approaching Dadhīchi (1-10)

1. Hari, the cause of this whole universe, now disappeared from the sight of the celestials, after having advised Indra as above. **2.** When the Devas approached the great sage Dadhīchi, an expert in Atharvana Veda, and requested him as instructed, he looked pleased and replied jestingly as follows: **3.** 'O celestials! Are you not aware of the intensely paralysing fear that human beings have for death? **4.** Jivas, in whom love of life is instinctive, cling to this dear body with passionate attachment.' *The Devas replied:* **5.** 'O great one! For personages like you,

ननु स्वार्थपरो लोको न वेद परसङ्कटम्। यदि वेद न याचेत नेति नाह यदीश्वरः ॥ 6॥

ऋषिरुवाच

धर्मं वः श्रोतुकामेन यूयं मे प्रत्युदाहृताः। एष वः प्रियमात्मानं त्यजन्तं संत्यजाम्यहम् 7॥

योऽध्रुवेणात्मना नाथा न धर्मं न यशः पुमान्। ईहेत भूतदयया स शोच्यः स्थावरैरपि ॥ 8॥

एतावानव्ययो धर्मः पुण्यश्लोकैरुपासितः। यो भूतशोकहर्षाभ्यामात्मा शोचति हृष्यति 9॥

अहो दैन्यमहो कष्टं पारक्यैः क्षणभङ्गुरैः। यन्नोपकुर्यादस्वार्थैर्मर्त्यः स्वज्ञातिविग्रहैः ॥10॥

श्रीशुक उवाच

एवं कृतव्यवसितो दध्यङ्ङाथर्वणस्तनुम्। परे भगवति ब्रह्मण्यात्मानं सन्नयञ्जहौ ॥11॥

यताक्षासुमनोबुद्धिस्तत्त्वदृग् ध्वस्तबन्धनः। आस्थितः परमं योगं न देहं बुबुधे गतम् ॥12॥

अथेन्द्रो वज्रमुद्यम्य निर्मितं विश्वकर्मणा। मुनेः शुक्तिभिरुत्सिक्तो भगवत्तेजसान्वितः ॥13॥

वृतो देवगणैः सर्वैर्गजेन्द्रोपर्यशोभत। स्तूयमानो मुनिगणैस्त्रैलोक्यं हर्षयन्निव ॥14॥

वृत्रमभ्यद्रवच्छेत्तुमसुरानीकयूथपैः। पर्यस्तमोजसा राजन् क्रुद्धो रुद्र इवान्तकम् 15॥

ततः सुराणामसुरै रणः परमदारुणः। त्रेतामुखे नर्मदायामभवत् प्रथमे युगे ॥16॥

greatly reputed for holiness, for the nobility of your actions, and for your universal love, what is there too difficult to give away as gift! **6.** Men who are interested only in their own well-being never understand the sufferings of others. If they did, they would never beg in this way as we are doing. And one who has the resources and the inclination to make a gift, would never refuse to oblige.'

The Rishi said: **7.** I refused your request at first in order to hear from you what is Dharma (the right course). I shall now give up for your sake, this body which one has to give up one day or the other. **8.** O Devas! Those who do not strive for fame and attainment of merit through the sacrifice of this impermanent body out of one's love of living beings, are liable to be looked upon with pity even by inanimate objects. **9.** The eternal path of virtue followed by men famous for their holiness consists in their feeling sorrow for the sorrows of others, and joy for their joys. **10.** It is indeed a tragedy, it is indeed a pity, that man fails to do good to his fellow beings with this body, which is ever threatened with death and is bound to be food for dogs, and with his wealth, children and other resources which are transient and intrinsically worthless.

Making of the Thunderbolt Weapon (11-14)

Sri Suka said: **11.** Resolving thus, Dadhīchi united his spirit with the Supreme Lord, the Parabrahman, and thereby left his body dead. **12.** With the senses, Pranas, mind and intellect controlled, and with his consciousness concentrated exclusively on the Reality, he broke all bonds through Supreme Yoga and left his body, without even being aware of his passing away. **13-14.** Next Viswakarma made the thunderbolt weapon with the bones of the great Rishi, and Indra, endowed with the power of the Lord, took it up. Armed with it, and seated on his elephant Airavata, he shone amidst celestials and Rishis, who sang his praise, expressing the joy of all the three worlds.

Confrontation of Indra with Vritra (15-33)

15. Like Rudra rushing at Antaka, the god of death, Indra now charged violently at Vritra, who was surrounded by his army of Asuras, in order to bring about his destruction. **16.** A fierce battle now

रुद्रैर्वसुभिरादित्यैरश्विभ्यां पितृवह्निभिः। मरुद्भिर्ऋभुभिः साध्यैर्विश्वेदेवैर्मरुत्पतिम् 17॥
दृष्ट्वा वज्रधरं शक्रं रोचमानं स्वया श्रिया। नामृष्यन्नसुरा राजन् मृधे वृत्रपुरःसराः ॥18॥
नमुचिः शम्बरोऽनर्वा द्विमूर्धा ऋषभोऽम्बरः। हयग्रीवः शङ्कुशिरा विप्रचित्तिरयोमुखः ॥19॥
पुलोमा वृषपर्वा च प्रहेतिर्हेतिरुत्कलः। दैतेया दानवा यक्षा रक्षांसि च सहस्रशः ॥20॥
सुमालिमालिप्रमुखाः कार्तस्वरपरिच्छदाः। प्रतिषिध्येन्द्रसेनाग्रं मृत्योरपि दुरासदम् ॥21॥
अभ्यर्दयन्नसम्भ्रान्ताः सिंहनादेन दुर्मदाः। गदाभिः परिघैर्बाणैः प्रासमुद्गरतोमरैः ॥22॥
शूलैः परश्वधैः खड्गैः शतघ्नीभिर्भुशुण्डिभिः। सर्वतोऽवाकिरन् शस्त्रैरस्त्रैश्च विबुधर्षभान् 23॥
न तेऽदृश्यन्त संछन्नाः शरजालैः समन्ततः। पुङ्खानुपुङ्खपतितैर्ज्योतींषीव नभोघनैः ॥24॥
न ते शस्त्रास्त्रवर्षौघा ह्यासेदुः सुरसैनिकान्। छिन्नाः सिद्धपथे देवैर्लघुहस्तैः सहस्रधा ॥25॥
अथ क्षीणास्त्रशस्त्रौघा गिरिश्रृङ्गद्रुमोपलैः। अभ्यवर्षन् सुरबलं चिच्छिदुस्तांश्च पूर्ववत् ॥26॥

तानक्षतान् स्वस्तिमतो निशाम्य शस्त्रास्त्रपूगैरथ वृत्रनाथाः।
द्रुमैर्दृषद्भिर्विविधाद्रिश्रृङ्गैरविक्षतांस्तत्रसुरिन्द्रसैनिकान् ॥27॥
सर्वे प्रयासा अभवन् विमोघाः कृताः कृता देवगणेषु दैत्यैः।
कृष्णानुकूलेषु यथा महत्सु क्षुद्रैः प्रयुक्ता रुशती रूक्षवाचः ॥28॥

took place between the Devas and the Asuras on the banks of the Narmada at the beginning of Tretayuga of the first Chatur-yuga (the period of four Yugas) of the present (Vaivaswata) Manvantara. **17-18.** Great was the wrath of Vritra and of the other Asuras at the sight of the luminous form of Indra, the Lord of Maruts, accompanied by the Rudras, Vasus, the Ādityas, Aswinidevas, Pitris, Maruts, Ribhus, Siddhas and Viswedevas. **19-22.** The army of the Asuras consisted of leaders like Namuchi, Sambara, Anarva, Dvimūrdha, Rishabha, Ambara, Hayagrīva, Sankusiras, Viprachitti, Ayomukha, Puloma, Vrishaparva, Praheti, Heti, Utkala, Māli and Sumāli, and a huge host of other Asuras, Yakshas and Rakshasas. That Asura host adorned with various decorations, unperturbed and raising fierce war cries, caused great distress in the ranks of the formidable force of the Devas by their steady and fearless charges with their weapons like mace, clubs, arrows, Prāsas, hammers and Tomaras. **23.** They rained on those Deva chiefs volleys of weapons like tridents, battle axes, swords, Sataghnīs and Bhusundis. **24.** Covered by the vast number of arrows shot in such quick succession that each arrow touched the back end of the one in front, the Devas looked like the moon and the other celestial luminaries hidden by the gathering clouds in the sky. **25.** But the expert archers on the side of the Devas shattered the volley of arrows into bits even before it had reached their side. **26.** When all their arrows and other weapons were exhausted, the Asuras began to shower hillocks, trees and boulders at the Devas, who pulverised them in no time as they did with the weapons. **27.** Great fear seized the Asuras, the followers of Vritra, when they saw that not even a scratch was caused on the bodies of the Devas by all the weapons, hillocks, trees, boulders etc., darted at them. **28.** Just like the vulgar and harsh words used by silly men at high-souled spiritual personages, all attacks that the Asuras directed at the Devas recoiled ineffectively.

ते स्वप्रयासं वितथं निरीक्ष्य हरावभक्ता हतयुद्धदर्पाः ।
पलायनायाजिमुखे विसृज्य पतिं मनस्ते दधुरात्तसाराः ॥29॥
वृत्रोऽसुरांस्ताननुगान् मनस्वी प्रधावतः प्रेक्ष्य बभाष एतत् ।
पलायितं प्रेक्ष्य बलं च भग्नं भयेन तीव्रेण विहस्य वीरः ॥30॥
कालोपपन्नां रुचिरां मनस्विनामुवाच वाचं पुरुषप्रवीरः ।
हे विप्रचित्ते नमुचे पुलोमन् मयानर्वञ्छम्बर मे श‍ृणुध्वम् ॥31॥
जातस्य मृत्युर्ध्रुव एष सर्वतः प्रतिक्रिया यस्य न चेह क्लृप्ता ।
लोको यशश्चाथ ततो यदि ह्यमुं को नाम मृत्युं न वृणीत युक्तम् ॥32॥
द्वौ सम्मताविह मृत्यू दुरापौ यद् ब्रह्मसन्धारणया जितासुः ।
कलेवरं योगरतो विजह्याद् यदग्रणीर्वीरशयेऽनिवृत्तः ॥33॥

इति श्रीमद्भागवते महापुराणे पारमहंस्यां संहितायां षष्ठस्कन्धे इन्द्रवृत्रासुरयुद्धवर्णनं नाम दशमोऽध्यायः ॥10॥

29. The ungodly Asuras who had no faith in Hari, now found that all their previous strength was absorbed by their enemies. Their lust for battle therefore subsided, and they got ready to run away from the leader and the battle-field, finding that all their struggle was in vain. **30.** The courageous and intelligent Vritra, on finding his defeated and terror-stricken followers ready to take to their heels, smiled and addressed them **31.** Vritra addressed his men in words appropriate to the occasion and sweet to the ears of heroes: 'O Viprachitti, Namuchi, Puloma, Maya, Anarva and Sambara! Hear me. **32.** Death is sure and certain for one born as a mortal. There is no remedy laid down for it in any text. That being the case, who could not covet a death that would bring reputation in this life and happiness in the next? **33.** There are two types of death approved by the wise, but difficult to have —one being the exit from the body with the Pranas controlled and the mind in equipoise and concentrated on Brahman, and the other, death in the field of battle without taking even a foot back from the enemy.'

अथैकादशोऽध्यायः

श्रीशुक उवाच

त एवं शंसतो धर्मं वचः पत्युरचेतसः । नैवागृह्णन् भयत्रस्ताः पलायनपरा नृप ॥ 1॥
विशीर्यमाणां पृतनामासुरीमसुरर्षभः । कालानुकूलैस्त्रिदशैः काल्यमानामनाथवत् 2॥
दृष्ट्वातप्यत संक्रुद्ध इन्द्रशत्रुरमर्षितः । तान्निवार्यौजसा राजन्निर्भर्त्स्येदमुवाच ह ॥ 3॥

Skandha VI : Chapter 11

EXCELLENCE OF VRITRA

Vritra's Charge (1-12)

Sri Suka said: **1.** The frightened and dispirited Asuras who were on the point of flight refused to be moved by the words of right conduct spoken by their master. **2-3.** O King! Finding his army in complete disarray, fleeing leaderless under the attacks of the Devas and the adverse influence of Time, Vritra became desperate

किं व उच्चरितैर्मातुर्धावद्भिः पृष्ठतो हतैः। न हि भीतवधः श्लाघ्यो न स्वर्ग्यः शूरमानिनाम् ॥
यदि वः प्रधने श्रद्धा सारं वा क्षुल्लका हृदि। अग्रे तिष्ठत मात्रं मे न चेद् ग्राम्यसुखे स्पृहा ॥ 5॥
एवं सुरगणान् क्रुद्धो भीषयन् वपुषा रिपून्। व्यनदत् सुमहाप्राणो येन लोका विचेतसः ॥ 6॥
तेन देवगणाः सर्वे वृत्रविस्फोटनेन वै। निपतुर्मूर्च्छिता भूमौ यथैवाशनिना हताः ॥ 7॥

ममर्द पद्भ्यां सुरसैन्यमातुरं निमीलिताक्षं रणरङ्गदुर्मदः।
गां कम्पयन्नुद्यतशूल ओजसा नालं वनं यूथपतिर्यथोन्मदः ॥ 8॥
विलोक्य तं वज्रधरोऽत्यमर्षितः स्वशत्रवेऽभिद्रवते महागदाम्।
चिक्षेप तामापततीं सुदुःसहां जग्राह वामेन करेण लीलया ॥ 9॥
स इन्द्रशत्रुः कुपितो भृशं तया महेन्द्रवाहं गदयोग्रविक्रमः।
जघान कुम्भस्थल उन्नदन् मृधे तत्कर्म सर्वे समपूजयन् नृप ॥10॥
ऐरावतो वृत्रगदाभिमृष्टो विघूर्णितोऽद्रिः कुलिशाहतो यथा।
अपासरद्भिन्नमुखः सहेन्द्रो मुञ्चन्नसृक् सप्तधनुर्नृशार्तः ॥11॥
न सन्नवाहाय विषण्णचेतसे प्रायुङ्क्त भूयः स गदां महात्मा।
इन्द्रोऽमृतस्यन्दिकराभिमर्शवीतव्यथक्षतवाहोऽवतस्थे ॥12॥
स तं नृपेन्द्राहवकाम्यया रिपुं वज्रायुधं भ्रातृहणं विलोक्य।
स्मरंश्च तत्कर्म नृशंसमंहः शोकेन मोहेन हसञ्जगाद ॥13॥

with grief and anger, and railed at the Devas thus: **4.** 'Of what avail for you is this pursuit and slaughter of these fleeing Asuras, who have proved to be the very dirt secreted by their mothers! For those who claim to be heroes, slaughter of a flying enemy contributes neither to fame here nor to their welfare hereafter. **5.** O mean cowards! Dare to stand before me for a moment if you are really warlike and courageous, and provided you have also had all your pre-death worldly cravings fulfilled.'

6. The powerful Vritra thus frightened the Devas by his fierce form and his terrific roar which shook and paralysed the whole world. **7.** Like men struck by lightning, the Devas fell down unconscious by the stunning effect of Vritra's roar. **8.** As an elephant in rut tramples over groves of reeds, so did the irresistible Vritra dance and trample over the stunned bodies of Devas, with his trident held aloft in hand, and causing tremors on the earth by his powerful strides. **9.** Seeing Vritra thus attacking his forces and charging at himself, the enraged Indra threw his powerful mace at him. But Vritra caught it with his left hand as in play, with utmost contempt. **10.** Fierce and courageous as he was, Vritra struck the elephant of Indra on his forehead with his mace—a feat, for which, O King, both friend and foe alike acclaimed him. **11.** With Indra seated on him, his elephant Airavata when thus struck with the mace, receded by a distance of seven bow-lengths, his face shattered and bleeding profusely like a mountain hit by lightning. **12.** The chivalrous Vritra, on seeing Indra discomfited and his mount disabled, did not strike again with his mace. In the meantime Indra, by the touch of his nectar-raining palms, healed and resuscitated Airavata, and stood ready for fight.

Vritra's Challenge (13-18)

13. O King! Vritra on seeing Indra, the cruel-hearted enemy responsible for the murder of his brother Viswarupa, standing ready for battle, said as follows, with a

वृत्र उवाच

दिष्टया भवान् मे समवस्थितो रिपुर्यो ब्रह्महा गुरुहा भ्रातृहा च ।
दिष्टयानृणोऽद्याहमसत्तम त्वया मच्छूलनिर्भिन्नदृषद्धृदाचिरात् ॥14॥
यो नोऽग्रजस्यात्मविदो द्विजातेर्गुरोरपापस्य च दीक्षितस्य ।
विश्रभ्य खड्गेन शिरांस्यवृश्चत् पशोरिवाकरुणः स्वर्गकामः ॥15॥
ह्रीश्रीदयाकीर्तिभिरुज्झितं त्वां स्वकर्मणा पुरुषादैश्च गर्ह्यम् ।
कृच्छ्रेण मच्छूलविभिन्नदेहमस्पृष्टवह्निं समदन्ति गृध्राः ॥16॥
अन्येऽनु ये त्वेह नृशंसमज्ञा ये ह्युद्यतास्त्राः प्रहरन्ति मह्यम् ।
तैर्भूतनाथान् सगणान् निशातत्रिशूलनिर्भिन्नगलैर्यजामि ॥17॥
अथो हरे मे कुलिशेन वीर हर्ता प्रमथ्यैव शिरो यदीह ।
तत्रानृणो भूतबलिं विधाय मनस्विनां पादरजः प्रपत्स्ये ॥18॥
सुरेश कस्मान्न हिनोषि वज्रं पुरः स्थिते वैरिणि मय्यमोघम् ।।
मा संशयिष्ठा न गदेव वज्रं स्यान्निष्फलं कृपणार्थेव याच्ञा ॥19॥
नन्वेष वज्रस्तव शक्र तेजसा हरेर्दधीचेस्तपसा च तेजितः ।
तेनैव शत्रुं जहि विष्णुयन्त्रितो यतो हरिर्विजयः श्रीर्गुणास्ततः ॥20॥

mock laughter in a mood of grief and amazement at the enormity of Indra's sin. *Vritra said:* **14.** 'It is indeed a piece of great good fortune that you, who are guilty of the slaughter of one so holy as my brother and a Guru of yours to boot, should stand before me for battle. O evil genius! I shall be freed from the debt I owe to my brother, when today your stony heart is pierced with my trident. **15.** Just as a heaven-seeking ritualist decapitates a sacrificial animal, you, practising a confidence trick, mercilessly cut off the heads of my brother, who was at once a holy man, your teacher, a sinless person, an observer of vows and a knower of the Atman. **16.** Devoid, as you are, of modesty, grace, kindness and a good name—the abomination of even cannibals—you shall, with your body pierced easily by my trident, soon lie uncremated on the battlefield for vultures to tear open and consume. **17.** And whoever there be ignorantly following your cruel-hearted self and showering weapons on me, their bodies too, with heads chopped off with my sharp trident, shall be made an offering to the lords of elementals and their following. **18.** But, O Indra, if, however, it is I whose head happens to be chopped off with your thunderbolt weapon, then I would thereby be freeing myself from the bondage of Karma and attaining to the realm of the heroes, after having offered my body as food to the birds and the beasts.'

Vritra's Devotion to the Lord (19-27)

19. (*Vritra continued:*) 'O Indra! Why do you hesitate to strike me, who am standing before you, with your unfailing thunderbolt? Doubt not that it will be ineffective like the mace you used to strike with before, even as the prayer for favours addressed to a miserly person. **20.** This thunderbolt weapon, O Indra, has been powered by the energy of Mahavishnu and the austerity of the Rishi Dadhīchi. Commissioned as you are by Mahavishnu Himself, destroy me, your enemy, even now with that thunderbolt weapon. Wherever Hari is, there victory follows,

अहं समाधाय मनो यथाऽऽह सङ्कर्षणस्तच्चरणारविन्दे ।
त्वद्वज्ररंहोलुलितग्राम्यपाशो गतिं मुनेर्याम्यपविद्धलोकः ॥21॥
पुंसां किलैकान्तधियां स्वकानां याः सम्पदो दिवि भूमौ रसायाम् ।
न राति यद् द्वेष उद्वेग आधिर्मदः कलिर्व्यसनं संप्रयासः ॥22॥
त्रैवर्गिकायासविघातमस्मत्पतिर्विधत्ते पुरुषस्य शक्र ।
ततोऽनुमेयो भगवत्प्रसादो यो दुर्लभोऽकिञ्चनगोचरोऽन्यैः ॥23॥
अहं हरे तव पादैकमूलदासानुदासो भवितास्मि भूयः ।
मनः स्मरेतासुपतेर्गुणांस्ते गृणीत वाक् कर्म करोतु कायः ॥24॥
न नाकपृष्ठं न च पारमेष्ठ्यं न सार्वभौमं न रसाधिपत्यम् ।
न योगसिद्धीरपुनर्भवं वा समञ्जस त्वा विरहय्य काङ्क्षे ॥25॥
अजातपक्षा इव मातरं खगाः स्तन्यं यथा वत्सतराः क्षुधार्ताः ।
प्रियं प्रियेव व्युषितं विषण्णा मनोऽरविन्दाक्ष दिदृक्षते त्वाम् ॥26॥
ममोत्तमश्लोकजनेषु सख्यं संसारचक्रे भ्रमतः स्वकर्मभिः ।
त्वन्माययाऽऽत्मात्मजदारगेहेष्वासक्तचित्तस्य न नाथ भूयात् ॥27॥

इति श्रीमद्भागवते महापुराणे पारमहंस्यां संहितायां षष्ठस्कन्धे वृत्रस्येन्द्रोपदेशो नामैकादशोऽध्यायः ॥11॥

and prosperity and virtues too. **21.** As my Chosen Deity Sankarshana has commanded me, I shall hold my concentrated mind at His lotus feet, and with all the bonds of my body-generating Karma (Prarabdha) cut asunder with your thunderbolt weapon when you destroy my body, I shall go the way of all saintly contemplatives. **22.** The Lord does not generally grant the riches and felicities of the heavenly realm, or of the earth, or of Rasātala, to his servants who have whole-hearted devotion to Him. For where wealth is, there also thrive animosity, fear, worry, pride, quarrels, grief and tiresome toil. **23.** O Indra! Our Lord and Master, the Supreme Being, causes obstruction to the efforts made by devotees for the attainment of heaven, prosperity and enjoyments (Dharma, Artha and Kama) in order to divert them to the path of devotion. From such obstruction one should infer the operation of the Lord's grace on his all-renouncing devotees, a favour that the others of little devotion can never obtain. **24.** O Hari! May I be born in successive births as the servant of Thy servants who have Thee as their sole support in life. May my mind ever contemplate on the attributes pertaining to Thee, the master of my life-breath! And may my words be always devoted to the description of Thy glories, and my body, to Thy service. **25.** O Thou the home of all auspiciousness! I do not aspire for the state of the creator Brahma, or for the sovereignty of Rasatala, or for the Yogic powers, or even for the state of freedom from Samsara, if the attainment of these means separation from Thee. **26.** As fledglings eagerly await their mother's return, as hungry calves long for their dam's udder, and as a faithful wife anxiously awaits the return of her long-separated husband—so does my mind, O lotus-eyed one, yearn for, and wait in eager expectation of, Thy blessed vision. **27.** To me who am tossed about on this wheel of transmigratory existence, may there be opportunities of intimate relationship with the devotees of Him of holy fame! And may I have nothing to do with those whose minds are bound by Thy Yogamaya to body, children, wife, house and the like.'

अथ द्वादशोऽध्यायः

ऋषिरुवाच

एवं जिहासुर्नृप देहमाजौ मृत्युं वरं विजयान्मन्यमानः ।
शूलं प्रगृह्याभ्यपतत् सुरेन्द्रं यथा महापुरुषं कैटभोऽप्सु ॥ 1॥
ततो युगान्ताग्निकठोरजिह्वमाविध्य शूलं तरसासुरेन्द्रः ।
क्षिप्त्वा महेन्द्राय विनद्य वीरो हतोऽसि पापेति रुषा जगाद ॥ 2॥
ख आपतत् तद् विचलद्ग्रहोल्कवन्निरीक्ष्य दुष्प्रेक्ष्यमजातविक्लवः ।
वज्रेण वज्री शतपर्वणाच्छिनद् भुजं च तस्योरगराजभोगम् ॥ 3॥
छिन्नैकबाहुः परिघेण वृत्रः संरब्ध आसाद्य गृहीतवज्रम् ।
हनौ तताडेन्द्रमथामरेभं वज्रं च हस्तान्न्यपतन्मघोनः ॥ 4॥
वृत्रस्य कर्मातिमहाद्भुतं तत् सुरासुराश्चारणसिद्धसङ्घाः ।
अपूजयंस्तत् पुरुहूतसङ्कटं निरीक्ष्य हाहेति विचुक्रुशुर्भृशम् ॥ 5॥
इन्द्रो न वज्रं जगृहे विलज्जितश्च्युतं स्वहस्तादरिसन्निधौ पुनः ।
तमाह वृत्रो हर आत्तवज्रो जहि स्वशत्रुं न विषादकालः ॥ 6॥
युयुत्सतां कुत्रचिदाततायिनां जयः सदैकत्र न वै परात्मनाम् ।
विनैकमुत्पत्तिलयस्थितीश्वरं सर्वज्ञमाद्यं पुरुषं सनातनम् ॥ 7॥

Skandha VI : Chapter 12
DESTRUCTION OF VRITRA

Further Fight with Vritra (1-5)

Sri Suka said: **1.** O King! Resolved in this way to embrace death in battle rather than to court victory as the more meritorious course, Vritra rushed at Indra with his trident in hand, just as the Asura Kaitabha charged at Mahavishnu from the waters of cosmic dissolution. **2.** The heroic Vritra, whirled powerfully his trident whose tip was as fiercely brilliant as the fire of cosmic dissolution, and threw it at Indra, yelling out: 'Death to you, O felon!' **3.** Unshaken by the sight of that weapon approaching through the sky like a planet or a brilliant meteor, Indra cut it with his thunderbolt weapon having innumerable joints *(sataparvana)*, as also one of Vritra's arms, stout and fleshy like the body of the king of serpents. **4.** Though bereft of one hand, Vritra charged furiously at Indra with an iron club in the remaining hand and struck at the cheek of Indra, the holder of the thunderbolt, and at his elephant-vehicle Airavata. Hit in this way, the thunderbolt weapon fell from the hands of Indra. **5.** All the celestial hosts, Devas, Asuras, Chāranas and Siddhas, acclaimed the wonderful skill of Vritra, but at the same time raised anxious cries at the predicament of Indra.

A Sermon on Time by Vritra (6-22)

6. Ashamed of himself, Indra hesitated to take up again the thunderbolt weapon that had fallen from his hand. Thereupon Vritra said: 'O Indra! Take up your thunderbolt weapon and kill me, your enemy. This is not the time for regrets. **7.** No

लोकाः सपाला यस्येमे श्वसन्ति विवशा वशे। द्विजा इव शिचा बद्धाः स काल इह कारणम् 8॥
ओजः सहो बलं प्राणममृतं मृत्युमेव च। तमज्ञाय जनो हेतुमात्मानं मन्यते जडम् ॥ 9॥
यथा दारुमयी नारी यथा यन्त्रमयो मृगः। एवं भूतानि मघवन्नीशतन्त्राणि विद्धि भोः 10॥
पुरुषः प्रकृतिर्व्यक्तमात्मा भूतेन्द्रियाशयाः। शक्नुवन्त्यस्य सर्गादौ न विना यदनुग्रहात् ॥11॥
अविद्वानेवमात्मानं मन्यतेऽनीशमीश्वरम्। भूतैः सृजति भूतानि ग्रसते तानि तैः स्वयम् ॥12॥
आयुः श्रीः कीर्तिरैश्वर्यमाशिषः पुरुषस्य याः। भवन्त्येव हि तत्काले यथानिच्छोर्विपर्ययाः 13॥
तस्मादकीर्तियशसोर्जयापजययोरपि। समः स्यात् सुखदुःखाभ्यां मृत्युजीवितयोस्तथा ॥
सत्त्वं रजस्तम इति प्रकृतेर्नात्मनो गुणाः। तत्र साक्षिणमात्मानं यो वेद न स बध्यते ॥15॥
पश्य मां निर्जितं शक्र वृक्णायुधभुजं मृधे। घटमानं यथाशक्ति तव प्राणजिहीर्षया ॥16॥
प्राणग्लहोऽयं समर इष्वक्षो वाहनासनः। अत्र न ज्ञायतेऽमुष्य जयोऽमुष्य पराजयः ॥17॥

श्रीशुक उवाच

इन्द्रो वृत्रवचः श्रुत्वा गतालीकमपूजयत्। गृहीतवज्रः प्रहसंस्तमाह गतविस्मयः ॥18॥

warrior fighting with weapons can expect victory always and never defeat; the fortunes of war vary, except in the case of the Infinite Being, the master of creation, perservation and dissolution. **8.** The ultimate cause of the success and failure of human effort is the Lord manifested as Time, within whose net all the worlds and their lords function in absolute subservience, like birds entangled in the fowler's net. **9.** The ignorant world without knowing the Lord functioning as Time, on whom the powers of the senses, mind and body depend, who manifests as energy, life, death and immortality, attributes success and failure to themselves, identifying with the physical body. **10.** O Indra! Know that just like a wooden doll figuring a woman or a mechanically worked animal, all creatures in this world are subject to the control of the Lord. **11.** Neither Prakriti nor Purusha, nor the Great Element (Mahattatva), nor egoity (Ahankara), nor elements (Bhutas), nor senses (Indriyas)—not one of them can project this universe without His grace and blessing. **12.** Man, ignorant of this, considers his little self as a master in himself. He is in truth only an instrument in the hands of the Lord. He makes him an instrument for procreating other beings and for destroying others too. **13.** When Time is favourable, man is blessed with longevity, prosperity, fame, plenty and the goodwill of all. And when Time is unfavourable, the opposite is the case, however much he may strive against it. **14.** Therefore one should remain unperturbed in all situations, whether in fame or in disrepute, in success or in failure, in life or in death. **15.** Sattva, Rajas and Tamas and all their effects pertain to Prakriti alone, and not to the Atman. He is free from bondage who realises that the Atman is only the witness of all the bodily and mental transformations, and is not involved in them. **16.** O Indra! Look at me who, though defeated and deprived of an arm and of weapons, am still standing facing you for battle, determined to do whatever I can to destroy you. **17.** This battle is a gamble, in which the stakes are the lives of the people; the arrows, the dice; and the vehicles of the fighters, the game-board. No one knows who will be victorious or who will be defeated in it.'

Sri Suka said: **18.** Indra acclaimed these words of Vritra, free from any touch of hypocrisy. Picking up the thunderbolt and without being too much surprised at Vritra's attitude, he said smiling. *Indra said:*

इन्द्र उवाच

अहो दानव सिद्धोऽसि यस्य ते मतिरीदृशी । भक्तः सर्वात्मनाऽऽत्मानं सुहृदं जगदीश्वरम् 19॥
भवानतार्षीन्मायां वै वैष्णवीं जनमोहिनीम् । यद् विहायासुरं भावं महापुरुषतां गतः ॥20॥
खल्विदं महदाश्चर्यं यद् रजःप्रकृतेस्तव । वासुदेवे भगवति सत्त्वात्मनि दृढा मतिः ॥21॥
यस्य भक्तिर्भगवति हरौ निःश्रेयसेश्वरे । विक्रीडतोऽमृताम्भोधौ किं क्षुद्रैः खातकोदकैः 22॥

श्रीशुक उवाच

इति ब्रुवाणावन्योन्यं धर्मजिज्ञासया नृप । युयुधाते महावीर्याविन्द्रवृत्रौ युधाम्पती ॥23॥
आविध्य परिघं वृत्रः कार्ष्णायसमरिन्दमः । इन्द्राय प्राहिणोद् घोरं वामहस्तेन मारिष ॥24॥
स तु वृत्रस्य परिघं करं च करभोपमम् । चिच्छेद युगपद्देवो वज्रेण शतपर्वणा ॥25॥
दोर्भ्यामुत्कृत्तमूलाभ्यां बभौ रक्तस्रवोऽसुरः । छिन्नपक्षो यथा गोत्रः खाद् भ्रष्टो वज्रिणा हतः ॥
कृत्वाधरां हनुं भूमौ दैत्यो दिव्युत्तरां हनुम् । नभोगम्भीरवक्त्रेण लेलिहोल्बणजिह्वया 27॥
दंष्ट्राभिः कालकल्पाभिर्ग्रसन्निव जगत्त्रयम् । अतिमात्रमहाकाय आक्षिपंस्तरसा गिरीन् ॥28॥
गिरिराट् पादचारीव पद्भ्यां निर्जरयन् महीम् । जग्रास स समासाद्य वज्रिणं सहवाहनम् ॥29॥
महाप्राणो महावीर्यो महासर्प इव द्विपम् । वृत्रग्रस्तं तमालक्ष्य सप्रजापतयः सुराः ।
हा कष्टमिति निर्विण्णाश्चुक्रुशुः समहर्षयः ॥30॥

19. 'O Dānava! Whoever has the outlook you have described, has certainly attained to great spiritual eminence. What a great good fortune it is that you have taken whole-hearted refuge at the feet of the Lord, who is the universal friend and master of all beings! **20.** You have indeed transcended the world-deluding Yogamaya of the Lord; for you have discarded your innate nature and attained to the state of an exalted sage. **21.** It is indeed most surprising that a person like you who is endowed with the Rajoguna of Prakriti, has developed firm and settled devotion for the worshipful Vāsudeva, the embodiment of pure Sattva and the Lord of all. **22.** What use is there for the dirty water of muddy pit for one who sports in the limitless ocean of Bliss, as a result of his having cultivated deep devotion for Vāsudeva, the Lord of all and the bestower of liberation?'

Vritra's final Charge and Death: (23-35)

Sri Suka said: **23.** Thus exchanging thoughts on spiritual matters, the warrior leaders Vritra and Indra of great prowess fought on. **24.** O great King! Vritra, the suppressor of enemies, now whirled a destructive iron club and hurled it at Indra with his left arm. **25.** Indra thereupon cut with one stroke of his thunderbolt weapon of a hundred joints, both the club and Vritra's other arm, which was stout and strong like the trunk of an elephant. **26.** The Asura, with both his arms cut at their base and bleeding profusely due to Indra's stroke, looked like a mountain hurled down after its wings were cut. **27-29.** Possessed of a huge body and fangs resembling Death itself, he looked as if he were going to swallow the three worlds. He moved like a mountain chief, causing tremors on hill tops and crushing the earth into powdery dust by the might of his strides. Opening his mouth so as to touch the heaven with the upper jaw and the earth with the lower one, he rushed at Indra, the wielder of the thunderbolt, and swallowed him and his vehicle Airavata by his mouth as wide as the sky and a tongue resembling that of a serpent. **30-31.** Great

निगीर्णोऽप्यसुरेन्द्रेण न ममारोदरं गतः । महापुरुषसन्नद्धो योगमायाबलेन च ॥31॥
भित्त्वा वज्रेण तत्कुक्षिं निष्क्रम्य बलभिद् विभुः । उच्चकर्त शिरः शत्रोर्गिरिशृङ्गमिवौजसा ॥32॥
वज्रस्तु तत्कन्धरमाशुवेगः कृन्तन् समन्तात् परिवर्तमानः ।
न्यपातयत् तावदहर्गणेन यो ज्योतिषामयने वार्त्रहत्ये ॥33॥
तदा च खे दुन्दुभयो विनेदुर्गन्धर्वसिद्धाः समहर्षिसङ्घाः ।
वार्त्रघ्नलिङ्गैस्तमभिष्टुवाना मन्त्रैर्मुदा कुसुमैरभ्यवर्षन् ॥34॥
वृत्रस्य देहान्निष्क्रान्तमात्मज्योतिररिन्दम । पश्यतां सर्वलोकानामलोकं समपद्यत ॥35॥

इति श्रीमद्भागवते महापुराणे पारमहंस्यां संहितायां षष्ठस्कन्धे वृत्रवधो नाम द्वादशोऽध्यायः ॥12॥

in strength and in powers, he swallowed Indra as a python swallows an elephant. Prajapatis, Maharshis and Devas raised a hue and cry and remained stunned with sorrow. Though swallowed by the Asura, Indra did not perish in his stomach, as he was protected by the Narayana-kavacha and his own Yogic power. **32.** The resourceful Indra cut open the abdomen of Vritra by force. Emerging from the Asura's body, he cut off his head, as if levelling the top of a mountain cliff. **33.** The thunderbolt weapon of tremendous speed whirled round and round the neck of Vritra for a period of one year, the time required for the sun to traverse through the zodiac, before it severed and hurled the head of Vritra at the appointed hour on the exhaustion of his Prarabdha. **34.** Thereupon kettle-drums sounded in the heavens. The heavenly choir consisting of Gandharvas, Siddhas and Chāranas extolled Indra with Mantras highlighting the prowess he showed in the destruction of Vritra, and showered a profuse rain of flowers on him. **35.** O valiant King! All witnessed a spiritual effulgence emerging from Vritra's body and entering the Realm that transcends all the manifested levels of existence.

अथ त्रयोदशोऽध्यायः

श्रीशुक उवाच

वृत्रे हते त्रयो लोका विना शक्रेण भूरिद । सपाला ह्यभवन् सद्यो विज्वरा निर्वृतेन्द्रियाः 1॥
देवर्षिपितृभूतानि दैत्या देवानुगाः स्वयम् । प्रतिजग्मुः स्वधिष्ण्यानि ब्रह्मेशेन्द्रादयस्ततः 2॥

राजोवाच

इन्द्रस्यानिर्वृतेर्हेतुं श्रोतुमिच्छामि भो मुने । येनासन् सुखिनो देवा हरेर्दुःखं कुतोऽभवत् ॥ 3॥

Skandha VI : Chapter 13
PURIFICATION OF INDRA

Indra's Apprehension (1-9)

Sri Suka said: **1.** O generous King! All in the three worlds felt freed from their woes and were filled with joy, with the sole exception of Indra. **2.** All of the assembled Devas, Rishis, Pitris, Bhūtas, Asuras and Gandharvas, besides Brahma, Parameswara and Indra himself, returned to their respective abodes.

The Rajah said: **3.** O sage! I am desirous of knowing why Indra failed to be happy.

श्रीशुक उवाच

वृत्रविक्रमसंविग्नाः सर्वे देवाः सहर्षिभिः। तद्वधायार्थयन्निन्द्रं नैच्छद् भीतो बृहद्वधात् ॥ 4॥

इन्द्र उवाच

स्त्रीभूजलद्रुमैरेनो विश्वरूपवधोद्भवम्। विभक्तमनुगृह्णद्भिर्वृत्रहत्यां क्व माज्र्म्यहम् 5॥

श्रीशुक उवाच

ऋषयस्तदुपाकर्ण्य महेन्द्रमिदमब्रुवन्। याजयिष्याम भद्रं ते हयमेधेन मा स्म भैः ॥ 6॥
हयमेधेन पुरुषं परमात्मानमीश्वरम्। इष्ट्वा नारायणं देवं मोक्ष्यसेऽपि जगद्वधात् ॥ 7॥
ब्रह्महा पितृहा गोघ्नो मातृहाऽऽचार्यहाघवान्। श्वादः पुल्कसको वापि शुद्ध्येरन् यस्य कीर्तनात् ॥
तमश्वमेधेन महामखेन श्रद्धान्वितोऽस्माभिरनुष्ठितेन।
हत्वापि सब्रह्म चराचरं त्वं न लिप्यसे किं खलनिग्रहेण ॥ 9॥

श्रीशुक उवाच

एवं सञ्चोदितो विप्रैर्मरुत्वानहनद् रिपुम्। ब्रह्महत्या हते तस्मिन्नाससाद वृषाकपिम् ॥10॥
तयेन्द्रः स्मासहत् तापं निर्वृतिर्नामुमाविशत्। ह्रीमन्तं वाच्यतां प्राप्तं सुखयन्त्यपि नो गुणाः ॥
तां ददर्शानुधावन्तीं चाण्डालीमिव रूपिणीम्। जरया वेपमानाङ्गीं यक्ष्मग्रस्तामसृक्पटाम् 12॥
विकीर्य पलितान् केशांस्तिष्ठ तिष्ठेति भाषिणीम् मीनगन्ध्यसुगन्धेन कुर्वतीं मार्गदूषणम् ॥13॥

While all the other celestials were happy, why was Indra alone unhappy?

Sri Suka said: **4.** Terrorised by the might of Vritra, all the Devas and Maharshis had appealed to Indra to destroy him. But Indra had been reluctant to do so because of the fear of Brahmahatya (or sin of killing a Brahmana). **5.** Indra said: 'In order to help me, women, earth, water and trees divided and appropriated among themselves the sin I derived from killing Viswarupa.'

Sri Suka said: **6.** Hearing these words of Indra, the Rishis said to him: 'May good fortune befall you! We shall help you to perform an Aswamedha sacrifice. Entertain no fear of the sin committed by you. **7.** If you adore the Supreme Being Narayana, the Lord and master of all, the soul of all souls, you will be free from the sin of slaughtering even the whole world. **8-9.** By chanting whose names and excellences even killers of holy men, of cows, of their fathers, of their mothers, of their teacher etc., as also those who eat dog's flesh and are most degenerate, are purified—by the devoted worship of Him, the Supreme Being, by means of a horse sacrifice that we propose to perform, you will be unaffected by the sin of killing even all beings in the world—beings who are none but expressions of the Lord Himself. What then to speak of the slaughter of this cruel one!'

Indra under Brahmahatya (10-16)

Sri Suka continued: **10.** Thus prompted by the Rishis, Indra had killed Vritra, and now the sin of Brahmahatya overtook him. **11.** He had to undergo very great suffering on account of this sin. For even virtue does not bring joy to one who has done something that makes him ashamed of himself and despicable in the eyes of others. **12.** He saw Brahmahatya following him in the form of an old shivering outcaste woman, infected with phthisis, and wearing a blood-stained cloth. **13.** She had grey dishevelled hair, and she was polluting the air everywhere with her

नभो गतो दिशः सर्वाः सहस्राक्षो विशाम्पते । प्रागुदीचीं दिशं तूर्णं प्रविष्टो नृप मानसम् ॥14॥
स आवसत् पुष्करनालतन्तूनलब्धभोगो यदिहाग्निदूतः ।
वर्षाणि साहस्रमलक्षितोऽन्तः स चिन्तयन् ब्रह्मवधाद्विमोक्षम् ॥15॥
तावत् त्रिणाकं नहुषः शशास विद्यातपोयोगबलानुभावः ।
स सम्पदैश्वर्यमदान्धबुद्धिर्नीतस्तिरश्चां गतिमिन्द्रपत्न्या ॥16॥
ततो गतो ब्रह्मगिरोपहूत ऋतम्भरध्याननिवारिताघः ।
पापस्तु दिग्देवतया हतौजास्तं नाभ्यभूदवितं विष्णुपत्न्या ॥17॥
तं च ब्रह्मर्षयोऽभ्येत्य हयमेधेन भारत । यथावद् दीक्षयाञ्चक्रुः पुरुषाराधनेन ह ॥18॥
अथेज्यमाने पुरुषे सर्वदेवमयात्मनि । अश्वमेधे महेन्द्रेण वितते ब्रह्मवादिभिः ॥19॥
स वै त्वाष्ट्रवधो भूयानपि पापचयो नृप । नीतस्तेनैव शून्याय नीहार इव भानुना ॥20॥
स वाजिमेधेन यथोदितेन वितायमानेन मरीचिमिश्रैः ।
इष्ट्वाधियज्ञं पुरुषं पुराणमिन्द्रो महानास विधूतपापः ॥21॥
इदं महाख्यानमशेषपाप्मनां प्रक्षालनं तीर्थपदानुकीर्तनम् ।
भक्त्युच्छ्रयं भक्तजनानुवर्णनं महेन्द्रमोक्षं विजयं मरुत्वतः ॥22॥

breath emitting the smell of rotten flesh. She followed Indra calling out to him to stop. **14.** O King! The hundred-eyed Indra rushed through the sky and all the quarters without getting peace anywhere. At last going in the northeastern direction he took shelter in the Manasa lake. **15.** Revolving in his mind on the ways of getting rid of the sin of Brahmahatya, he lived for a thousand years in water, hiding in the delicate fibre within the stalk of a lotus flower, without the enjoyment he usually derived from the sacrificial offerings. For, being hidden in water, fire who is the conveyor of such offerings, could not reach him. **16.** During this period of Indra's absence, Nahusha, who was endowed with the strength born of meditation, austerity and Yoga, ruled over heaven. But when out of infatuation resulting from wealth and power, he made indecent advances to Indra's wife, he was reduced to the state of a serpent.

Indra's Purification (17-23)

17. In the meantime the virulence of Indra's sin was mitigated by the influence of Rudra, the presiding deity of the region where Indra hid, and by the grace of the consort of Vishnu (dwelling in the lotuses in the Manasa lake). Further, purified by meditation on Mahavishnu, Indra was invited by great Maharshis to return to the heavenly region. **18.** O scion of Bharatas' house! The Brahmarshis then came and made Indra perform a horse sacrifice in adoration of the Supreme Being. **19-20.** When Indra, under the direction of the great Vedic scholars and ritualists, performed the Aswamedha sacrifice in adoration of Him who has assumed the forms of all the Deities (Devatas), the whole of the sin of Brahmahatya that had affected him dispersed like dew before the sun. **21.** Thus by that horse sacrifice, conducted by great Rishis like Marīchi according to the rules of the ritualistic code in adoration of the Supreme Being, the bestcwer of the fruits of all actions, Indra became cleansed of all his sins. **22.** This narrative concerning the victory and the redemption of Indra obliterates the sin of those who hear it. As it

पठेयुराख्यानमिदं सदा बुधाः शृण्वन्त्यथो पर्वणि पर्वणीन्द्रियम् ।
धन्यं यशस्यं निखिलाघमोचनं रिपुञ्जयं स्वस्त्ययनं तथाऽऽयुषम् ॥23॥

इति श्रीमद्भागवते महापुराणे पारमहंस्यां संहितायां षष्ठस्कन्धे इन्द्रविजयो नाम त्रयोदशोऽध्यायः ॥13॥

extols the Lord and describes the doings of His devotees, it enhances devotion in those hearing it. **23.** Let people read it time after time, and especially hear it read on days considered holy. Wise men will derive from the study of it a great strengthening of their faculties, as also prosperity, fame, longevity, and freedom from sins and enemies. It will bring them all that is auspicious.

अथ चतुर्दशोऽध्यायः

परीक्षिदुवाच

रजस्तमःस्वभावस्य ब्रह्मन् वृत्रस्य पाप्मनः । नारायणे भगवति कथमासीद् दृढा मतिः ॥ 1॥
देवानां शुद्धसत्त्वानामृषीणां चामलात्मनाम् । भक्तिर्मुकुन्दचरणे न प्रायेणोपजायते ॥ 2॥
रजोभिः समसंख्याताः पार्थिवैरिह जन्तवः । तेषां ये केचनेहन्ते श्रेयो वै मनुजादयः ॥ 3॥
प्रायो मुमुक्षवस्तेषां केचनैव द्विजोत्तम । मुमुक्षूणां सहस्रेषु कश्चिन्मुच्येत सिध्यति ॥ 4॥
मुक्तानामपि सिद्धानां नारायणपरायणः । सुदुर्लभः प्रशान्तात्मा कोटिष्वपि महामुने ॥ 5॥
वृत्रस्तु स कथं पापः सर्वलोकोपतापनः । इत्थं दृढमतिः कृष्ण आसीत् संग्राम उल्बणे ॥ 6॥
अत्र नः संशयो भूयाञ्छ्रोतुं कौतूहलं प्रभो । यः पौरुषेण समरे सहस्राक्षमतोषयत् ॥ 7॥

Skandha VI : Chapter 14

THE STORY OF CHITRAKETU

Further Question about Vritra (1-7)

Rajah Parikshit said: **1.** O illumined one! How did this Vritra, whose nature was rooted in Rajas and Tamas, and who was very sinful, obtain such firm devotion for the worshipful Narayana, the inner pervader of all beings? **2.** Even in Devas, who are endowed with the quality of Sattva, and in great Rishis, who have attained purity of mind, this kind of unalloyed devotion is not found. **3.** Living beings are countless in this world like grains of sand. Among them all, in the human species there are only a few here and there who aspire and strive for spiritual development. **4.** O holy one! even among them still fewer are aspirants for Mukti (liberation). And among such aspirants only a very limited number succeed in abandoning hearth and home and realising the Atman. **5.** O great soul! Among a crore of such liberated and spiritually illumined beings again, persons who have perfect equipoise and single-hearted, ecstatic love for Narayana, are extremely rare. **6.** How then did this Vritra, a sinful oppressor of all the worlds, come to have such firm devotion for Krishna, the Existence-Knowledge-Bliss-Absolute, even when engaged in a fierce battle? **7.** O revered Sir! We have great doubt in this matter, and we are therefore very much desirous of having a true understanding of it. This Vritra won the admiration of Indra by his prowess. His resigna-

सूत उवाच

परीक्षितोऽथ संप्रश्नं भगवान् बादरायणिः । निशम्य श्रद्दधानस्य प्रतिनन्द्य वचोऽब्रवीत् ।। 8।।

श्रीशुक उवाच

श‍ृणुष्वावहितो राजन्नितिहासमिमं यथा । श्रुतं द्वैपायनमुखान्नारदाद् देवलादपि ।। 9।।

आसीद् राजा सार्वभौमः शूरसेनेषु वै नृप । चित्रकेतुरिति ख्यातो यस्यासीत् कामधुङ्मही ।।

तस्य भार्यासहस्राणां सहस्राणि दशाभवन् । सान्तानिकश्चापि नृपो न लेभे तासु सन्ततिम् 11।।

रूपौदार्यवयोजन्मविद्यैश्वर्यश्रियादिभिः । सम्पन्नस्य गुणैः सर्वैश्चिन्ता वन्ध्यापतेरभूत् 12।।

न तस्य संपदः सर्वा महिष्यो वामलोचनाः । सार्वभौमस्य भूश्चेयमभवन् प्रीतिहेतवः ।।13।।

तस्यैकदा तु भवनमङ्गिरा भगवानृषिः । लोकाननुचरन्नेतानुपागच्छद् यदृच्छया ।।14।।

तं पूजयित्वा विधिवत् प्रत्युत्थानार्हणादिभिः । कृतातिथ्यमुपासीदत् सुखासीनं समाहितः 15।।

महर्षिस्तमुपासीनं प्रश्रयावनतं क्षितौ । प्रतिपूज्य महाराज समाभाष्येदमब्रवीत् ।।16।।

अङ्गिरा उवाच

अपि तेऽनामयं स्वस्ति प्रकृतीनां तथाऽऽत्मनः । यथा प्रकृतिभिर्गुप्तः पुमान् राजापि सप्तभिः 17।।

आत्मानं प्रकृतिष्वद्धा निधाय श्रेय आप्नुयात् । राज्ञा तथा प्रकृतयो नरदेवाहिताधयः ।।18।।

अपि दाराः प्रजामात्या भृत्याः श्रेण्योऽथ मन्त्रिणः । पौरा जानपदा भूपा आत्मजा वशवर्तिनः ।।19।।

tion to the Lord could not therefore have been caused by fear.

Chitraketu meeting Angiras (8-26)

Suta said: **8.** Sri Suka, the son of Bādarāyana, on hearing these sincere and earnest words of Parikshit, praised him for putting such a question, and began to answer it.

Sri Suka said: **9.** Listen, O King, to the traditional account on this subject, which I heard from Vedavyasa, Narada and Devala. **10.** In the land of Sūrasena (near Mathura), there was a famous emperor named Chitraketu, in whose region the earth yielded all the requirements of man. **11.** That king had many wives, but every one of them was barren, and the king was therefore without any issue. **12.** Though possessed of all desirable endowments like beauty, generosity, youth, high birth, learning, lordliness and wealth, he was very much worried over his wives being barren and he without issue. **13.** Neither wealth, nor his numerous beautiful wives, nor his vast empire could give him happiness under the above circumstances. **14.** Once the worshipful Rishi Angiras happened to arrive at the king's place in the course of his peregrinations all over the world. **15.** After receiving him standing and offering him an honoured seat and ceremonial worship, the king seated himself with a restrained mind near the Rishi. **16.** O King! Addressing King Chitraketu, who was seated near him on the floor in all humility, the Rishi returned the courtesies and said to him as follows: *The Rishi Angiras said:* **17.** 'I hope yourself and your subjects are healthy and happy. Just as man is protected by a defensive wall of seven aspects of Prakriti—namely Mahattattwa, Ahankara, and the five Tanmatras —, so also a king's defence consists of the seven constituents of the state—the preceptor, ministers, inhabited villages, fortresses, treasury, machinery of enforcement, and allies. **18.** The king thrives by putting confidence in these constituents of State, and they, by rallying round the king. **19.** I hope all your household and State

यस्यात्मानुवशश्चेत् स्यात् सर्वे तद्वशगा इमे । लोकाः सपाला यच्छन्ति सर्वे बलिमतन्द्रिताः 20॥
आत्मनः प्रीयते नात्मा परतः स्वत एव वा । लक्षयेऽलब्धकामं त्वां चिन्तया शबलं मुखम् 21॥
एवं विकल्पितो राजन् विदुषा मुनिनापि सः । प्रश्रयावनतोऽभ्याह प्रजाकामस्ततो मुनिम् 22॥

चित्रकेतुरुवाच

भगवन् किं न विदितं तपोज्ञानसमाधिभिः । योगिनां ध्वस्तपापानां बहिरन्तः शरीरिषु ॥23॥
तथापि पृच्छतो ब्रूयां ब्रह्मन्नात्मनि चिन्तितम् । भवतो विदुषश्चापि चोदितस्त्वदनुज्ञया ॥24॥
लोकपालैरपि प्रार्थ्याः साम्राज्यैश्वर्यसम्पदः । न नन्दयन्त्यप्रजं मां क्षुत्तृट्काममिवापरे ॥25॥
ततः पाहि महाभाग पूर्वैः सह गतं तमः । यथा तरेम दुस्तारं प्रजया तद्विधेहि नः ॥26॥

श्रीशुक उवाच

इत्यर्थितः स भगवान् कृपालुर्ब्रह्मणः सुतः । श्रपयित्वा चरुं त्वाष्ट्रं त्वष्टारमयजद्विभुः ॥27॥
ज्येष्ठा श्रेष्ठा च या राज्ञो महिषीणां च भारत । नाम्ना कृतद्युतिस्तस्यै यज्ञोच्छिष्टमदाद् द्विजः ॥
अथाह नृपतिं राजन् भवितैकस्तवात्मजः । हर्षशोकप्रदस्तुभ्यमिति ब्रह्मसुतो ययौ ॥29॥
सापि तत्प्राशनादेव चित्रकेतोरधारयत् । गर्भं कृतद्युतिर्देवी कृत्तिकाग्नेरिवात्मजम् ॥30॥
तस्या अनुदिनं गर्भः शुक्लपक्ष इवोडुपः । ववृधे शूरसेनेशतेजसा शनकैर्नृप ॥31॥

functionaries are obedient and faithful to you—your wives, subjects, ministers, executive officers, servants, vassals and children. **20.** He who has been able to control the mind, to him all the abovementioned are obedient. Not only that, all the worlds and their rulers come to him with tribute unfailingly. **21.** You do not seem to be happy within. Why is it so? Is it due to some internal worries, or due to some extraneous causes, that I see you as one with his cherished desires unfulfilled? Your face is overcast with worrying thoughts.' **22.** O King! Being thus questioned by the sage, who could, if he liked, intuit anything he wanted to know, Chitraketu in his eagerness for a son, replied to him as follows, making prostrations in all humility. *King Chitraketu said:* **23.** 'O all-knowing one! For Yogins who have overcome all evil tendencies through austerity, knowledge, and meditation, what is there unknown about a person's inside and outside? **24.** You know the minds of all; yet since you have now put the question, I shall give out the cause of my worry. **25.** Even though enjoying the power and plenty of an emperor, unattainable even by the world's overlords, none of these pleases me who am eager for an issue, just as a man hungry and thirsty is not satisfied with anything but food and drink. **26.** O great one! Being issueless, I along with my ancestors will be consigned to hell. By helping us to have an issue, deign to save us from this fate.'

Birth of a Son to Chitraketu (27-42)

Sri Suka said: **27.** The learned, merciful and all-knowing Angiras, the son of Brahma, made the king prepare some sacrificial food-offering and perform a sacrifice to Tvashta. **28.** O King! The Maharshi gave the sacrificial remnant to the seniormost of the king's wives named Kritadyuti to eat. **29.** Afterwards the Maharshi Angiras, the son of Brahma, told the king that he would have a son who could be the cause of both joy and sorrow to him, and departed. **30.** That queen Kritadyuti, by consuming that sacrificial remnant, bore a son from the seed of Chitraketu, as the goddess Krittika from the Fire-deity Agni. **31.** O King! The foetus that originated from the virility of

अथ काल उपावृत्ते कुमारः समजायत ।
जनयन् शूरसेनानां शृण्वतां परमां मुदम् ॥32॥
हृष्टो राजा कुमारस्य स्नातः शुचिरलङ्कृतः ।
वाचयित्वाऽऽशिषो विप्रैः कारयामास जातकम् ॥
तेभ्यो हिरण्यं रजतं वासांस्याभरणानि च ।
ग्रामान् हयान् गजान् प्रादाद् धेनूनामर्बुदानि षट् ॥
ववर्ष काममन्येषां पर्जन्य इव देहिनाम् ।
धन्यं यशस्यमायुष्यं कुमारस्य महामनाः ॥35॥
कृच्छ्रलब्धेऽथ राजर्षेस्तनयेऽनुदिनं पितुः ।
यथा निःस्वस्य कृच्छ्राप्ते धने स्नेहोऽन्ववर्धत 36॥
मातुस्त्वतितरां पुत्रे स्नेहो मोहसमुद्भवः ।
कृतद्युतेः सपत्नीनां प्रजाकामज्वरोऽभवत् ॥37॥
चित्रकेतोरतिप्रीतिर्यथा दारे प्रजावति ।
न तथान्येषु संजज्ञे बालं लालयतोऽन्वहम् ॥38॥
ताः पर्यतप्यन्नात्मानं गर्हयन्त्योऽभ्यसूयया ।
आनपत्येन दुःखेन राज्ञोऽनादरेण च ॥39॥
धिगप्रजां स्त्रियं पापां पत्युश्चागृहसम्मताम् ।
सुप्रजाभिः सपत्नीभिर्दासीमिव तिरस्कृताम् 40॥
दासीनां को नु सन्तापः स्वामिनः परिचर्यया ।
अभीक्ष्णं लब्धमानानां दास्या दासीव दुर्भगाः 41॥
एवं सन्दह्यमानानां सपत्न्याः पुत्रसम्पदा ।
राज्ञोऽसम्मतवृत्तीनां विद्वेषो बलवानभूत् ॥42॥
विद्वेषनष्टमतयः स्त्रियो दारुणचेतसः ।
गरं ददुः कुमाराय दुर्मर्षा नृपतिं प्रति ॥43॥

the king of Sūrasena developed in Kritadyuti as the disc of the moon in the bright fortnight.

32. When in due course the time for delivery arrived, a boy was born bringing great joy to all the inhabitants of Sūrasena who heard about the same. **33.** Rejoiced at it, Chitraketu took purificatory bath, put on decorations, got the blessings of holy men for the infant, and got its birth rituals (Jātakarma) performed. **34.** He presented them with gifts of gold, silver, clothes, ornaments, villages, horses, elephants and, above all, sixty crores of cows. **35.** As clouds shower rain, so the high-minded king made gifts very liberally to all for the prosperity, fame and longevity of his son. **36.** The king's attachment for the son, whom he had obtained with such great difficulty, grew day by day, as a miser's attachment for hard-earned wealth. **37.** The mother Kritadyuti, too, developed towards her son attachment that verged on infatuation, while the grief of her cowives for their childless condition also began to intensify.

38. Chitraketu now ceased to have for his childless wives the same degree of love that he developed for the one whose child he could now fondle with affection every day. **39.** These cowives suffered intensely from the combined effect of their envy towards Kritadyuti, their inferiority complex, their childlessness, and the king's neglect of them. **40.** 'Woe unto the woman who is childless, unfortunate, devoid of her husband's confidence, and looked down upon as a maid servant by her cowife who has become a mother! **41.** Maid servants, who receive the recognition of their masters again and again for service, have no cause to be aggrieved. But alas for us, unfortunate beings who are like maid servants of a maid servant!', so these cowives grieved. **42.** Great was the fire of anger and jealousy generated in them at the sight of their cowife's treasure of a child, while the indifference which the king developed towards them helped to fan the flame of that fire.

Poisoning of the Child (43-61)

43. Deprived of all goodness and discriminative intelligence due to jealousy and animosity, and prompted by their intolerant hatred for the faithless king, these cruel-hearted women administered

कृतद्युतिरजानन्ती सपत्नीनामघं महत् । सुप्त एवेति सञ्चिन्त्य निरीक्ष्य व्यचरद् गृहे ।।44।।
शयानं सुचिरं बालमुपधार्य मनीषिणी । पुत्रमानय मे भद्रे इति धात्रीमचोदयत् ।।45।।
सा शयानमुपव्रज्य दृष्ट्वा चोत्तारलोचनम् । प्राणेन्द्रियात्मभिस्त्यक्तं हतास्मीत्यपतद् भुवि ।।
तस्यास्तदाऽऽकर्ण्य भृशातुरं स्वरं घ्नन्त्याः कराभ्यामुर उच्चकैरपि ।
प्रविश्य राज्ञी त्वरयाऽऽत्मजान्तिकं ददर्श बालं सहसा मृतं सुतम् ।।47।।
पपात भूमौ परिवृद्धया शुचा मुमोह विभ्रष्टशिरोरुहाम्बरा ।।48।।
ततो नृपान्तःपुरवर्तिनो जना नराश्च नार्यश्च निशम्य रोदनम् ।
आगत्य तुल्यव्यसनाः सुदुःखितास्ताश्च व्यलीकं रुरुदुः कृतागसः ।।49।।
श्रुत्वा मृतं पुत्रमलक्षितान्तकं विनष्टदृष्टिः प्रपतन् स्खलन् पथि ।
स्नेहानुबन्धैधितया शुचा भृशं विमूर्च्छितोऽनुप्रकृतिर्द्विजैर्वृतः ।।50।।
पपात बालस्य स पादमूले मृतस्य विस्रस्तशिरोरुहाम्बरः ।
दीर्घं श्वसन् बाष्पकलोपरोधतो निरुद्धकण्ठो न शशाक भाषितुम् ।।51।।
पतिं निरीक्ष्योरुशुचार्पितं तदा मृतं च बालं सुतमेकसन्ततिम् ।
जनस्य राज्ञी प्रकृतेश्च हृद्रुजं सती दधाना विललाप चित्रधा ।।52।।
स्तनद्वयं कुङ्कुमगन्धमण्डितं निषिञ्चती साञ्जनबाष्पबिन्दुभिः ।
विकीर्य केशान् विगलत्स्रजः सुतं शुशोच चित्रं कुररीव सुस्वरम् ।।53।।

poison to the infant. **44.** Kritadyuti, unaware of the wicked act of her cowives, was under the impression that the child was sleeping and kept herself busy with domestic work. **45.** But later, the intelligent Kritadyuti felt that the child was asleep for too long a period and so called her maid to bring the child. **46.** On approaching the child on its bed, the maid was shocked to see the infant with pupils turned up and its vital forces, senses and mind not functioning. She fell down screaming: "Alas! Dead I am!" **47.** Hearing the loud and piteous cries of the woman, who was beating her breast, the queen Kritadyuti went to her side, only to be shocked to see her child most unexpectedly lying dead. **48.** Immediately she fell down and swooned out of overwhelming grief, her hair dishevelled and clothes in disarray. **49.** Hearing the cries, men and women living in the palace all came to the spot and joined the others in crying with an equal measure of anguish and sorrow. Those responsible for the dastardly act, also shed crocodile tears and joined the party of mourners.

50. Stunned with uncontrollable grief on hearing about the most unexpected and inexplicable death of his beloved son, the king, attended by his officers and advisers, came to the spot with great difficulty, almost blind with grief, and often stumbling and falling on the way. **51.** The king, whose locks and garments had become loose, fell at the feet of the dead child. He was sighing deeply and his voice was choked by sobs. **52.** Seeing her only child dead and her husband overwhelmed with grief on account of that, the queen began to lament variously, recounting her woes and causing great anguish in the hearts of the ministers and other people. **53.** The torrential flow of tears, mixed with the collyrium in her eyes, fell on her breasts and mingled with the red saffron applied thereon. With her hair dishevelled, the flower wreaths falling, and garments in disarray, she began to moan aloud in a voice like that of the

अहो विधातस्त्वमतीव बालिशो यस्त्वात्मसृष्टयप्रतिरूपमीहसे ।
परेऽनुजीवत्यपरस्य या मृतिर्विपर्ययश्चेत् त्वमसि ध्रुवः परः ॥54॥
न हि क्रमश्चेदिह मृत्युजन्मनोः शरीरिणामस्तु तदाऽऽत्मकर्मभिः ।
यः स्नेहपाशो निजसर्गवृद्धये स्वयं कृतस्ते तमिमं विवृश्चसि ॥55॥
त्वं तात नार्हसि च मां कृपणामनाथां त्यक्तुं विचक्ष्व पितरं तव शोकतप्तम् ।
अञ्जस्तरेम भवताप्रजदुस्तरं यद् ध्वान्तं न याह्यकरुणेन यमेन दूरम् ॥56॥
उत्तिष्ठ तात त इमे शिशवो वयस्यास्त्वामाह्वयन्ति नृपनन्दन संविहर्तुम् ।
सुप्तश्चिरं ह्यशनया च भवान् परीतो भुङ्क्ष्व स्तनं पिब शुचो हर नः स्वकानाम् ॥57॥
नाहं तनूज ददृशे हतमङ्गला ते मुग्धस्मितं मुदितवीक्षणमाननाब्जम् ।
किं वा गतोऽस्य पुनरन्वयमन्यलोकं नीतोऽघृणेन न शृणोमि कला गिरस्ते ॥58॥

श्रीशुक उवाच

विलपन्त्या मृतं पुत्रमिति चित्रविलापनैः । चित्रकेतुर्भृशं तप्तो मुक्तकण्ठो रुरोद ह ॥59॥
तयोर्विलपतोः सर्वे दम्पत्योस्तदनुव्रताः । रुरुदुः स्म नरा नार्यः सर्वमासीदचेतनम् ॥60॥
एवं कश्मलमापन्नं नष्टसंज्ञमनायकम् । ज्ञात्वाङ्गिरा नाम मुनिराजगाम सनारदः ॥61॥

इति श्रीमद्भागवते महापुराणे पारमहंस्यां संहितायां षष्ठस्कन्धे चित्रकेतुविलापो नाम चतुर्दशोऽध्यायः ॥14॥

bird Kuravi (osprey): **54.** 'O creator! You, who function contrary to your own creative activity, must indeed be unbelievably foolish. The death of a very young person, while old individuals are left behind, is an instance to the point. If you are doing this deliberately (and not out of foolishness as said before), you will be distinguishing yourself as an enemy of your own creatures. **55.** If it is said that in birth and in death there is no such rule based on the age of individuals, they being determined by the Karma of the Jivas, then you are cutting asunder the bond of affection which you have yourself generated for the multiplication of the species. For, people will abstain from having children, if such dire consequences attend on having them. **56.** O son! It does not befit you to desert me, your mother, afflicted and helpless. Look at your sorrow-stricken father also. With your help, we could have easily got over the hell which issueless people cannot cross. Do not go far away with the merciless Yama. **57.** O my dear child! Get up. Other children are calling you to play. You have been sleeping long and must be hungry now. So take food, have your feed at the breast, and comfort us, your near and dear ones! **58.** O son! My unfortunate self misses your face with its charming child-like and placid look. Have you been taken by pitiless Yama to that land from which there is no return? I am not able to hear your sweet indistinct speech.'

Sri Suka said: **59.** Sorrowing with his wife who was indulging in such words of lamentation, King Chitraketu burst forth into loud wails. **60.** All their relatives, men and women gathered there, joined the couple in their wailing. Everything bore the impress of death. **61.** Seeing that group of sorrowing people, leaderless and reduced to the state of inertness, the two sages Angiras and Narada appeared on the scene.

अथ पञ्चदशोऽध्यायः

श्रीशुक उवाच

ऊचतुर्मृतकोपान्ते पतितं मृतकोपमम् । शोकाभिभूतं राजानं बोधयन्तौ सदुक्तिभिः ॥ 1॥
कोऽयं स्यात् तव राजेन्द्र भवान् यमनुशोचति । त्वं चास्य कतमः सृष्टौ पुरेदानीमतः परम् ॥ 2॥
यथा प्रयान्ति संयान्ति स्रोतोवेगेन वालुकाः । संयुज्यन्ते वियुज्यन्ते तथा कालेन देहिनः ॥ 3॥
यथा धानासु वै धाना भवन्ति न भवन्ति च । एवं भूतेषु भूतानि चोदितानीशमायया ॥ 4॥
वयं च त्वं च ये चेमे तुल्यकालाश्चराचराः । जन्ममृत्योर्यथा पश्चात् प्राङ्नैवमधुनापि भोः 5॥
भूतैर्भूतानि भूतेशः सृजत्यवति हन्त्यजः । आत्मसृष्टैरस्वतन्त्रैरनपेक्षोऽपि बालवत् ॥ 6॥
देहेन देहिनो राजन् देहाद्देहोऽभिजायते । बीजादेव यथा बीजं देह्यर्थ इव शाश्वतः ॥ 7॥
देहदेहिविभागोऽयमविवेककृतः पुरा । जातिव्यक्तिविभागोऽयं यथा वस्तुनि कल्पितः 8॥

Skandha VI : Chapter 15

CONSOLATION OF CHITRAKETU BY THE SAGES

Transitoriness of Life (1-8)

Sri Suka said: **1.** Instructing the king, who was lying like a corpse by the side of the dead body of his son, the sages spoke to him the following words of wisdom. They said: **2.** 'O great King! He for whom you are mourning—what is he to you? In this flux of creation, how were you related to the dead child in the previous birth and what is to be the relation in future births? (The idea is that these relations are never the same in different births. There may be no relation or there may be the reverse relations also—the father being reborn as the son.) **3.** Just as grains of sand come together and separate in a current of water, so are living beings united and separated by the flow of Time. **4.** Just as sprouts may sometimes grow from seeds and sometimes not, so do offspring come sometimes out of parents, and sometimes do not, as dictated by the Lord's Maya. (Parental relation need not be taken more seriously than that between seeds and sprouts.) **5.** Just as I, you, and all these creatures did not exist before birth and will not exist after death, so they do not exist even now. **6.** The Lord of all, the Unoriginated Being, brought out of Himself the creative categories by the exercise of His inherent Power, and with these categories that are dependent on Him, He performs the work of creation, preservation and dissolution of all beings held absolutely under His control. In creation He has no object to gain, as a child in play. **7.** O King! A man is born to the body of a father through the body of the mother, just as a seed is grown from an earlier seed. Thus the body changes while the indwelling soul remains the same like the causal categories in objects. **8.** Just as the distinction made between the universal and the particular is an assumption, so also the distinction between the spirit and the body and their coming together is an assumption. The soul alone is the abiding reality. The concomitance between the two is no proof that the spirit dies with the body.'

Response of Chitraketu (9-16)

Sri Suka said: **9.** Thus comforted by the

श्रीशुक उवाच

एवमाश्वासितो राजा चित्रकेतुर्द्विजोक्तिभिः । प्रमृज्य पाणिना वक्त्रमाधिम्लानमभाषत ॥ 9॥

राजोवाच

कौ युवां ज्ञानसम्पन्नौ महिष्ठौ च महीयसाम् । अवधूतेन वेषेण गूढाविह समागतौ ॥10॥
चरन्ति ह्यवनौ कामं ब्राह्मणा भगवत्प्रियाः । मादृशां ग्राम्यबुद्धीनां बोधायोन्मत्तलिङ्गिनः 11॥
कुमारो नारद ऋभुरङ्गिरा देवलोऽसितः । अपान्तरतमो व्यासो मार्कण्डेयोऽथ गौतमः 12॥
वसिष्ठो भगवान् रामः कपिलो बादरायणिः । दुर्वासा याज्ञवल्क्यश्च जातूकर्ण्यस्तथाऽऽरुणिः 13॥
रोमशश्च्यवनो दत्त आसुरिः सपतञ्जलिः । ऋषिर्वेदशिरा बोध्यो मुनिः पञ्चशिरास्तथा 14॥
हिरण्यनाभः कौसल्यः श्रुतदेव ऋतध्वजः । एते परे च सिद्धेशाश्चरन्ति ज्ञानहेतवः ॥15॥
तस्माद् युवां ग्राम्यपशोर्मम मूढधियः प्रभू । अन्धे तमसि मग्नस्य ज्ञानदीप उदीर्यताम् ॥16॥

अङ्गिरा उवाच

अहं ते पुत्रकामस्य पुत्रदोऽस्म्यङ्गिरा नृप । एष ब्रह्मसुतः साक्षान्नारदो भगवानृषिः ॥17॥
इत्थं त्वां पुत्रशोकेन मग्नं तमसि दुस्तरे । अतदर्हमनुस्मृत्य महापुरुषगोचरम् ॥18॥
अनुग्रहाय भवतः प्राप्तावावामिह प्रभो । ब्रह्मण्यो भगवद्भक्तो नावसीदितुमर्हति ॥19॥
तदैव ते परं ज्ञानं ददामि गृहमागतः । ज्ञात्वान्याभिनिवेशं ते पुत्रमेव ददावहम् ॥20॥
अधुना पुत्रिणां तापो भवतैवानुभूयते । एवं दारा गृहा रायो विविधैश्वर्यसम्पदः ॥21॥
शब्दादयश्च विषयाश्चला राज्यविभूतयः । मही राज्यं बलं कोशो भृत्यामात्याः सुहृज्जनाः ॥
सर्वेऽपि शूरसेनेमे शोकमोहभयार्तिदाः । गन्धर्वनगरप्रख्याः स्वप्नमायामनोरथाः ॥23॥

sages, King Chitraketu wiped his sorrow-stricken face and said: **10.** 'Who may you be that have come here, disguised as bare-bodied wanderers (Avadhutas), but possessing the highest wisdom and deserving the first rank among those called great? **11.** Holy men, dear to the Lord, move about in the world, hiding their greatness under the veil of abnormal looks and ways, in order to bless worldly-minded persons like myself. **12-15.** Sanatkumāra and his group Nārada, Ribhu, Angiras, Devala, Asita, Apāntaratama, Vyāsa, Mārkandeya, Gautama, Vasishtha, Parasurāma, Kapila, Sri Suka, Durvāsas, Yājnavalkya, Jātukarnya, Āruni, Romasa, Chyavana, Dattātreya, Āsuri, Patanjali, Vedasiras, Bodhya, Panchasiras, Hiranyanābha, Kausalya, Srutadeva, Ritadhwaja—these and many other sages go about the world in order to bestow spiritual knowledge on others. **16.** Therefore it is befitting that you hold this lamp of wisdom and remove the darkness of one like me walking in ignorance like a village swine.'

Life bedevilled with Sorrow (17-28)

The Rishi Angiras said: **17.** O King! I am that Angiras who helped you to obtain a child. This is the all-knowing and worshipful sage Narada, the son of Brahma. **18-19.** We have arrived here thinking of you and to bless you, who are now submerged in grief arising from the loss of a son—a fate which a votary of holy men and a devotee of the Lord like you does not deserve. **20.** Even when I visited you earlier, I wanted to impart knowledge to you, but finding that you were then more intent on having an issue, I helped you to get one. **21-23.** You have now understood the kind of sorrow that people with children are likely to suffer

दृश्यमाना विनार्थेन न दृश्यन्ते मनोभवाः । कर्मभिर्ध्यायतो नानाकर्माणि मनसोऽभवन् 24।।
अयं हि देहिनो देहो द्रव्यज्ञानक्रियात्मकः । देहिनो विविधक्लेशसन्तापकृदुदाहृतः ।।25।।
तस्मात् स्वस्थेन मनसा विमृश्य गतिमात्मनः । द्वैते ध्रुवार्थविश्रम्भं त्यजोपशममाविश ।।26।।

नारद उवाच

एतां मन्त्रोपनिषदं प्रतीच्छ प्रयतो मम । यां धारयन् सप्तरात्राद् द्रष्टा सङ्कर्षणं प्रभुम् 27।।
यत्पादमूलमुपसृत्य नरेन्द्र पूर्वे शर्वादयो भ्रममिमं द्वितयं विसृज्य ।
सद्यस्तदीयमतुलानधिकं महित्वं प्रापुर्भवानपि परं नचिरादुपैति ।।28।।

इति श्रीमद्भागवते महापुराणे पारमहंस्यां संहितायां षष्ठस्कन्धे चित्रकेतुसान्त्वनं नाम पञ्चदशोऽध्यायः ।।15।।

from. All other kinds of worldly relationships and attainments, too—whether they be related to wife, houses, wealth, power, objects of enjoyment, land, kingdom and its majesties, army, treasury, servants, ministers and allies—are causes of sorrow, pride, fear and worry. They are fleeting phenomena like a castle in the air, and have no ultimacy as in the case of experiences caused by dream, magic and reverie. **24.** All these objects of enjoyment, which have no substantiality, are merely creations of the mind; for, they are experienced one moment and are gone in the next. It may be said that they are the products of one's meritorious and evil actions. No, it is from the mind engaged in the constant thoughts arising from the tendencies acquired from previous actions that various future actions and their results spring. **25.** This body of man, constituted of material substances, sense organs and organs of action is the cause of difficulties and sorrows of various kinds. **26.** Therefore meditate on the Atman with a peaceful mind, and get rid of the idea of permanency you have in regard to the world of duality.

Sri Narada said: **27.** Receive from me with one-pointed mind the Mantra that I shall impart to you. It brings about the highest good of man, and gives the experience of Sankarshana to those who meditate on it with concentration for a week. **28.** O King! It was by taking refuge at His feet, that a great one like Parameswara got over the ignorance-born identification with the body and attained to that state of spiritual power and glory, unequalled and unsurpassed, that is His. You too will attain to it if you worship Him with a devout heart.

अथ षोडशोऽध्यायः

श्रीशुक उवाच

अथ देवऋषी राजन् सम्परेतं नृपात्मजम् । दर्शयित्वेति होवाच ज्ञातीनामनुशोचताम् ।। 1।।

Skandha VI : Chapter 16
ENLIGHTENMENT OF CHITRAKETU

Chitraketu meeting his Son's Jiva (1-11)

Sri Suka said: **1.** Next Devarshi Narada, by the exercise of his Yogic powers, showed the subtle body of the dead child to the sorrowing relatives, and

नारद उवाच

जीवात्मन् पश्य भद्रं ते मातरं पितरं च ते। सुहृदो बान्धवास्तप्ताः शुचा त्वत्कृतया भृशम् 2॥
कलेवरं स्वमाविश्य शेषमायुः सुहृद्वृतः। भुङ्क्ष्व भोगान् पितृप्रत्तानधितिष्ठ नृपासनम् 3॥

जीव उवाच

कस्मिन् जन्मन्यमी मह्यं पितरो मातरोऽभवन्। कर्मभिर्भ्राम्यमाणस्य देवतिर्यङ्नृयोनिषु ॥ 4॥
बन्धुज्ञात्यरिमध्यस्थमित्रोदासीनविद्विषः। सर्व एव हि सर्वेषां भवन्ति क्रमशो मिथः ॥ 5॥
यथा वस्तूनि पण्यानि हेमादीनि ततस्ततः। पर्यटन्ति नरेष्वेवं जीवो योनिषु कर्तृषु ॥ 6॥
नित्यस्यार्थस्य सम्बन्धो ह्यनित्यो दृश्यते नृषु। यावद् यस्य हि सम्बन्धो ममत्वं तावदेव हि 7॥
एवं योनिगतो जीवः स नित्यो निरहङ्कृतः। यावद् यत्रोपलभ्येत तावत् स्वत्वं हि तस्य तत् 8॥
एष नित्योऽव्ययः सूक्ष्म एष सर्वाश्रयः स्वदृक्। आत्ममायागुणैर्विश्वमात्मानं सृजति प्रभुः ॥ 9॥
न ह्यस्यातिप्रियः कश्चिन्नाप्रियः स्वः परोऽपि वा। एकः सर्वधियां द्रष्टा कर्तॄणां गुणदोषयोः ॥10॥
नादत्त आत्मा हि गुणं न दोषं न क्रियाफलम्। उदासीनवदासीनः परावरदृगीश्वरः ॥11॥

श्रीशुक उवाच

इत्युदीर्य गतो जीवो ज्ञातयस्तस्य ते तदा। विस्मिता मुमुचुः शोकं छित्त्वाऽऽत्मस्नेहशृङ्खलाम्

said to it. **2.** *Sri Narada said:* 'O Jiva! May you be happy! See you not your father and mother and other relatives sorrowing for you? **3.** Assume your previous body, and succeed to the throne. Surrounded by your relatives, spend the rest of your life in enjoyments provided by your father.'

The Jiva said: **4.** I have been going from birth to birth in the transmigratory cycle among Devas, brute creations and men according to my Karma. In which birth of mine have these been my father and mother? **5.** In the succession of births, anyone might have been anyone's kinsman, consanguineous relation, enemy, unrelated neighbour, protector, or stranger. **6.** Just as objects of sale like gold and ornaments made of it pass from one hand to another in the course of transactions, so does the Jiva pass from one womb to another of individuals belonging to the species of Devas, men and brute creations. **7.** Relationship even with any living object, say with one's domestic animals, is found to be impermanent. So long as anything is considered one's own, there is relationship. When anyone's domestic animals are sold away, we do not look upon them as ours any more. **8.** Even in the embodied state the Jiva is the eternal and non-egoistic spirit. He has a continuous existence even after death, but has no continuous identification with its previous embodiment or his associates of that birth. Only as long as a Jiva is in a particular state of existence due to his Karma, only so long will the relationship pertaining to it subsist. **9.** In his real nature the Jiva is a part of Iswara, who is eternal, undecaying, subtle, the basis of all, and self-certifying awareness. **10.** In his real nature this Atman has none specially dear or inimical to him. None is "one's own", and none "another's". Without the attachments as a friend or a foe, He is the one Being that stands as the witness of all who do good and bad actions. **11.** He is an unconcerned witness of all that is high and low, everfree. He does not share any enjoyment or suffering, nor does he accept anything (even the sovereignty of a State) as the fruit of his actions.

Chitraketu's Transformation (12-17)

निर्हृत्य ज्ञातयो ज्ञातेर्देहं कृत्वोचिताः क्रियाः । तत्यजुर्दुस्त्यजं स्नेहं शोकमोहभयार्तिदम् ॥13॥
बालघ्न्यो व्रीडितास्तत्र बालहत्याहतप्रभाः । बालहत्याव्रतं चेरुर्ब्राह्मणैर्यन्निरूपितम् ।
यमुनायां महाराज स्मरन्त्यो द्विजभाषितम् ॥14॥
स इत्थं प्रतिबुद्धात्मा चित्रकेतुर्द्विजोक्तिभिः । गृहान्धकूपान्निष्क्रान्तः सरःपङ्कादिव द्विपः 15॥
कालिन्द्यां विधिवत्स्नात्वा कृतपुण्यजलक्रियः । मौनेन संयतप्राणो ब्रह्मपुत्राववन्दत ॥16॥
अथ तस्मै प्रपन्नाय भक्ताय प्रयतात्मने । भगवान् नारदः प्रीतो विद्यामेतामुवाच ह ॥17॥
ॐ नमस्तुभ्यं भगवते वासुदेवाय धीमहि । प्रद्युम्नायानिरुद्धाय नमः सङ्कर्षणाय च ॥18॥
नमो विज्ञानमात्राय परमानन्दमूर्तये । आत्मारामाय शान्ताय निवृत्तद्वैतदृष्टये ॥19॥
आत्मानन्दानुभूत्यैव न्यस्तशक्त्यूर्मये नमः । हृषीकेशाय महते नमस्ते विश्वमूर्तये ॥20॥
वचस्युपरतेऽप्राप्य य एको मनसा सह । अनामरूपश्चिन्मात्रः सोऽव्यान्नः सदसत्परः 21॥
यस्मिन्निदं यतश्चेदं तिष्ठत्यप्येति जायते । मृण्मयेष्विव मृज्जातिस्तस्मै ते ब्रह्मणे नमः 22॥

Sri Suka said: **12.** Saying so, the Jiva of the dead child departed. Then all its relatives were astounded, and cutting asunder the bond of attachment, they became free from grief. **13.** The relatives of the child then cremated the body and performed the prescribed obsequies. They somehow succeeded in abandoning attachment which is the prime cause of sorrow, infatuation, fear and worry.

14. O King! Those cruel women, who lost their lustre because of the sin of infanticide, became extremely ashamed of themselves. Remembering the words of the Rishis that all worldly entanglements like children are causes of sorrow, they abandoned jealousy and other vicious proclivities, and performed on the banks of the Yamuna the rites prescribed by priests as expiation for their sin. **15.** As for Chitraketu, the spiritual consciousness was roused by the words of the Rishis, and just as an elephant emerges from the mud and mire of a lake, he emerged from the dark well of household life. **16.** He took his bath in the Yamuna, performed the rites for the Pitris, controlled the senses through concentration on the Supreme Lord, and prostrated himself before the holy sages Narada and Angiras, both offspring of Brahma. **17.** Pleased with the devout king, who had surrendered his self and ingathered his mind, the sage Narada communicated to him the following meditation:

Meditation on Sankarshana (18-25)

18. Om! Salutations to Thee who hast manifested Thyself for worship by devotees as the four Vyuhas (epiphany)—Vāsudeva, Sankarshana, Pradyumna, and Aniruddha. **19.** O Thou of the form of Consciousness! O Thou of the form of Supreme Bliss! O Thou immersed in Thy inherent Bliss! O Thou the ever-peaceful! O Thou devoid of divisive consciousness! Salutations to Thee! **20.** He in whom Bliss-Consciousness has abolished all materiality, passions and activities arising from Maya, He who is the Great Being that directs the powers of all the senses, He of whom the universe is an expression—to Him our salutations! **21.** When mind and speech, failing to reach their source, relapse, He, the Pure Consciousness beyond name and form, shines. May He, the source of the dichotomy of cause and effect, protect us! **22.** He from whom all the universe is born, in whom it is established, in whom it dissolves, He whose presence persists in it through all these transformations, just as that of the

यन्न स्पृशन्ति न विदुर्मनोबुद्धीन्द्रियासवः । अन्तर्बहिश्च विततं व्योमवत्तन्नतोऽस्म्यहम् 23॥
देहेन्द्रियप्राणमनोधियोऽमी यदंशविद्धाः प्रचरन्ति कर्मसु ।
नैवान्यदा लोहमिवाप्रतप्तं स्थानेषु तद् द्रष्ट्रपदेशमेति ॥24॥

ॐ नमो भगवते महापुरुषाय महानुभावाय महाविभूतिपतये सकलसात्वतपरिवृढनिकरकर-
कमलकुड्मलोपलालितचरणारविन्दयुगल परमपरमेष्ठिन् नमस्ते ॥25॥

श्रीशुक उवाच

भक्तायैतां प्रपन्नाय विद्यामादिश्य नारदः । ययावङ्गिरसा साकं धाम स्वायम्भुवं प्रभो ॥26॥
चित्रकेतुस्तु विद्यां तां यथा नारदभाषिताम् । धारयामास सप्ताहमब्भक्षः सुसमाहितः ॥27॥
ततश्च सप्तरात्रान्ते विद्यया धार्यमाणया । विद्याधराधिपत्यं स लेभेऽप्रतिहतं नृपः ॥28॥
ततः कतिपयाहोभिर्विद्ययेद्धमनोगतिः । जगाम देवदेवस्य शेषस्य चरणान्तिकम् ॥29॥
मृणालगौरं शितिवाससं स्फुरत्किरीटकेयूरकटित्रकङ्कणम् ।
प्रसन्नवक्त्रारुणलोचनं वृतं ददर्श सिद्धेश्वरमण्डलैः प्रभुम् ॥30॥
तद्दर्शनध्वस्तसमस्तकिल्बिषः स्वच्छामलान्तःकरणोऽभ्ययान्मुनिः ।
प्रवृद्धभक्त्या प्रणयाश्रुलोचनः प्रहृष्टरोमानमदादिपूरुषम् ॥31॥

clay in objects made of clay, to that Brahman our salutations! **23.** He whom the mind, intellect, senses, and the organs of knowledge are unable to comprehend, whom Pranas and the organs of action are not able to contact—I salute that Being pervading inside and outside like Akasa. **24.** It is because of His penetration into them by a part of His that the body, senses, Prana, Manas and intelligence are able to function. Without His presence, these cannot function, just as iron cannot be moulded without being heated. In all the three states of consciousness, waking, dream and sleep, He is present as the witness of the Jiva, but the Jiva knows Him not. **25.** Om Salutations to Thee, O Bhagavan! O Thou the highest Being! O Thou the Lord of all! O Thou whose feet are served by the lotus buds of the hands of all devotees! Our salutations to Thee, the master of all Divine Majesties, the Lord of infinite glories and excellences!

Chitraketu's Vision (26-33)

Sri Suka said: **26.** O Monarch! After teaching this meditation to the devoted and resigned king, Narada went along with Angiras to the realm of Brahma. **27.** For seven days Chitraketu practised concentrated meditation on the Mantra communicated by Narada, taking in nothing but water. **28.** Afterwards he practised the same meditation for seven days more, as a subsidiary result of which he got the permanent leadership of the Vidyadharas. **29.** Again for seven days he practised meditation with very great ardour and, helped by a mind that had attained to a state of very great refinement, he approached the feet of the Lord Adisesha. **30.** He saw Adisesha of serene face and eyes of reddish tinge, white in colour like the inside fibre of lotus stalk, dressed in blue cloth, and wearing a brilliant crown, armlets, girdle, bracelets, etc. **31.** Freed from all his sins, Chitraketu's mind now attained to the state of extreme purity on account of His blessed vision. With devotion swelling in his heart, tears of spiritual joy flowing from his eyes, and horripilations all over, he took shelter in the Lord and made prostra-

स उत्तमश्लोकपदाब्जविष्टरं प्रेमाश्रुलेशैरुपमेहयन् मुहुः ।
प्रेमोपरुद्धाखिलवर्णनिर्गमो नैवाशकत् तं प्रसमीडितुं चिरम् ॥32॥
ततः समाधाय मनो मनीषया बभाष एतत् प्रतिलब्धवागसौ ।
नियम्य सर्वेन्द्रियबाह्यवर्तनं जगद्गुरुं सात्वतशास्त्रविग्रहम् ॥33॥

चित्रकेतुरुवाच

अजित जितः सममतिभिः साधुभिर्भवान् जितात्मभिर्भवता ।
विजितास्तेऽपि च भजतामकामात्मनां य आत्मदोऽतिकरुणः ॥34॥
तव विभवः खलु भगवन् जगदुदयस्थितिलयादीनि ।
विश्वसृजस्तेंऽशांशास्तत्र मृषा स्पर्धन्ते पृथगभिमत्या ॥35॥
परमाणुपरममहतोस्त्वमाद्यन्तान्तरवर्ती त्रयविधुरः ।
आदावन्तेऽपि च सत्त्वानां यद् ध्रुवं तदेवान्तरालेऽपि ॥36॥
क्षित्यादिभिरेष किलावृतः सप्तभिर्दशगुणोत्तरैराण्डकोशः ।
यत्र पतत्यणुकल्पः सहाण्डकोटिकोटिभिस्तदनन्तः ॥37॥
विषयतृषो नरपशवो य उपासते विभूतीर्न परं त्वाम् ।
तेषामाशिष ईश तदनु विनश्यन्ति यथा राजकुलम् ॥38॥

tions to Him. **32.** The tears of love flowing from his eyes moistened the Lord's footstool again and again, and for long he could not utter even a word in praise of Him, as his voice was choked by intense emotion. **33.** Soon he managed to control his emotions by the exercise of his intellect. Having recovered the power of speech, he ingathered all the outward-going tendencies of the senses, and concentrating all the powers of the mind on the Lord, addressed the following hymn to that manifestation of Him as the Adisesha, described in the texts on Bhakti.

Chitraketu's Hymn (34-48)

Chitraketu said: **34.** O Unconquerable One! Thou hast, however, been conquered by great devotees who have conquered their minds and are established in that unperturbed outlook resulting from seeing Thee in everything. And they, the desireless devotees, too, have been conquered by Thee who dost annex them to Thyself completely by giving Thy all-embracing Self to them in unitary consciousness. **35.** The creation, preservation and dissolution of the universe are expressions of Thy spiritual glory. Those deities concerned with such cosmic functions are only parts of Thy part. But not understanding this, and considering themselves independent entities, they struggle against one another in vain. **36.** Thou, the Being without a beginning, middle or end, art verily in the beginning, middle, and end of everything, of entities from atomic to cosmic dimension. What is persistently present in an entity at its beginning and at its end, is only what exists in the middle also. **37.** This cosmos is encased in seven sheaths of earth, water, fire, air, sky, I-sense (Ahankara), and the great element (Mahattattva), each succeeding sheath being ten times vaster than the earlier one. Amidst countless such world systems (Brahmandas), this cosmic shell or world system of ours is whirling about like an atom in the infinitude of Thyself—the Ananta or the Endless One. **38.** Men full of animality, and therefore thirsting for sensuous enjoyments, worship deities like

कामधियस्त्वयि रचिता न परम रोहन्ति यथा करम्भबीजानि ।
ज्ञानात्मन्यगुणमये गुणगणतोऽस्य द्वन्द्वजालानि ॥39॥
जितमजित तदा भवता यदाऽऽह भागवतं धर्ममनवद्यम् ।
निष्किञ्चना ये मुनय आत्मारामा यमुपासतेऽपवर्गाय ॥40॥
विषममतिर्न यत्र नृणां त्वमहमिति मम तवेति च यदन्यत्र ।
विषमधिया रचितो यः स ह्यविशुद्धः क्षयिष्णुरधर्मबहुलः ॥41॥
कः क्षेमो निजपरयोः कियानर्थः स्वपरद्रुहा धर्मेण ।
स्वद्रोहात् तव कोपः परसम्पीडया च तथाधर्मः ॥42॥
न व्यभिचरति तवेक्षा यया ह्यभिहितो भागवतो धर्मः ।
स्थिरचरसत्त्वकदम्बेष्वपृथग्धियो यमुपासते त्वार्याः ॥43॥
न हि भगवन्नघटितमिदं त्वद्दर्शनान्नृणामखिलपापक्षयः ।
यन्नामसकृच्छ्रवणात् पुल्कसकोऽपि विमुच्यते संसारात् ॥44॥
अथ भगवन् वयमधुना त्वदवलोकपरिमृष्टाशयमलाः ।
सुरऋषिणा यदुदितं तावकेन कथमन्यथा भवति ॥45॥

Indra who are the expressions of Thy glory, but not Thee, the Supreme Truth, in Thy fullness. The rewards that such persons get in the heavenly regions of these deities cease at the end of their period of supremacy, just as the dependants of a king lose everything, when the king loses his throne. **39.** O Supreme Being! If man directs his desire-nature to Thee, who art luminous Consciousness beyond the Gunas of Prakriti, he will not be affected by tendencies that create re-birth, just as fried seeds do not germinate. Desire-nature is burnt and transformed through communion with Thee. It is desire-nature turned to the sense objects that causes the bondage of duality. **40.** O Victorious One! When Thou didst promulgate the flawless Bhagavata Dharma, then didst Thou become truly victorious. For all the great sages like Sanatkumara and others, who have no possession but Thee and who delight only in the Spirit, follow that Dharma for the attainment of the spiritual *summum bonum*. **41.** Those who follow the Bhagavata Dharma are not self-centred and are therefore free from that partial outlook which makes such distinctions as 'I' and 'you', 'mine' and 'yours'. The desire-prompted works are vitiated by the passions of the mind. They are therefore impure, impermanent and full of moral defects. **42.** What good can come out, what achievement can there be, by practising Vedic ritualism, the performance of which causes sufferings to one's body and to others? By torturing one's body in the performance of rituals, they incur Thy displeasure, as Thou art residing in all. And by inflicting sufferings on others like the sacrificial animals, they become guilty of unrighteous actions. **43.** (It may be feared that the Bhagavata Dharma, consisting in disinterested and dedicated action is futile.) No, Thy law can never be futile. The noble ones who see Thy presence in all beings, moving and unmoving, follow this law of divine worship, the Bhagavata Dharma. **44.** It is not in the least impossible that by Thy vision, all the sins of aspirants are dissipated. For, even the most degraded man is liberated from Samsara by hearing Thy sacred name even once. (How then can Thy Dharma be futile?) **45.** O worshipful Lord! By Thy vision we have become extremely pure, as

विदितमनन्त समस्तं तव जगदात्मनो जनैरिहाचरितम् ।
विज्ञाप्यं परमगुरोः कियदिव सवितुरिव खद्योतैः ॥46॥
नमस्तुभ्यं भगवते सकलजगत्स्थितिलयोदयेशाय ।
दुरवसितात्मगतये कुयोगिनां भिदा परमहंसाय ॥47॥
यं वै श्वसन्तमनु विश्वसृजः श्वसन्ति यं चेकितानमनु चित्तय उच्चकन्ति ।
भूमण्डलं सर्षपायति यस्य मूर्ध्नि तस्मै नमो भगवतेऽस्तु सहस्रमूर्ध्ने ॥48॥

श्रीशुक उवाच

संस्तुतो भगवानेवमनन्तस्तमभाषत । विद्याधरपतिं प्रीतश्चित्रकेतुं कुरूद्वह ॥49॥

श्रीभगवानुवाच

यन्नारदाङ्गिरोभ्यां ते व्याहृतं मेऽनुशासनम् । संसिद्धोऽसि तया राजन् विद्यया दर्शनाच्च मे 50॥
अहं वै सर्वभूतानि भूतात्मा भूतभावनः । शब्दब्रह्म परं ब्रह्म ममोभे शाश्वती तनू ॥51॥
लोके विततमात्मानं लोकं चात्मनि संततम् । उभयं च मया व्याप्तं मयि चैवोभयं कृतम् ॥52॥
यथा सुषुप्तः पुरुषो विश्वं पश्यति चात्मनि । आत्मानमेकदेशस्थं मन्यते स्वप्न उत्थितः ॥53॥
एवं जागरणादीनि जीवस्थानानि चात्मनः । मायामात्राणि विज्ञाय तद्द्रष्टारं परं स्मरेत् 54॥

all the evil tendencies of our mind have been effaced by Thy vision. What has been said by Thy devotee Sri Narada, cannot but come to pass. **46.** Thou without a beginning or an end! To Thee who pervadest everything, the thoughts and actions of all beings are known. There is nothing that we need make known to Thee. It would be like fire-flies revealing things to the sun. **47.** Salutations to Thee, the worshipful Lord, who is the master of creation, preservation and dissolution of the universe—to Thee, the Transcendent Being who is beyond the understanding of perverse Yogis dominated by dualistic consciousness! **48.** He following whose will alone all the protecting deities of the universe make any move; He by whose functioning alone will the sense powers function; He on whose head the earth rests like a mustard seed—to Him, the worshipful Sankarshana, endowed with a thousand heads and with all the Divine powers, my salutations!

Instructions to Chitraketu (49-65)

Sri Suka said: **49.** O King of the Kurus! Extolled thus, the worshipful Lord Ananta was much pleased with Chitraketu, who had now become the head of the Vidyādharas, and said to him thus:

The Lord said: **50.** O King! By the practice of meditation communicated to you by Narada and Angiras, and by My vision thereby, you have become great in spiritual attainments. **51.** All the objects in the universe are Myself; within them all I am the witnessing self. I am also the cause of their origin. The Veda (Sabda-Brahman) and Prakriti (Param-Brahman) are my two eternal bodies. **52.** Know the Atman to be pervading the world as its experiencer, and the world to be spread in him as the object of experience. Both the world and the Atman are pervaded by Me, and both are established in Me. **53-54.** It happens that a dreamer dreams that he is fast asleep, and in that sleep, he dreams mountains, forest etc., within himself. Shortly he dreams he has awakened, and in that 'waking in dream' he perceives himself as lying in the corner of a room. To the sleeping man, all these dreams and that

येन प्रसुप्तः पुरुषः स्वापं वेदात्मनस्तदा । सुखं च निर्गुणं ब्रह्म तमात्मानमवेहि माम् ॥55॥
उभयं स्मरतः पुंसः प्रस्वापप्रतिबोधयोः । अन्वेति व्यतिरिच्येत तज्ज्ञानं ब्रह्म तत् परम् 56॥
यदेतद् विस्मृतं पुंसो मद्भावं भिन्नमात्मनः । ततः संसार एतस्य देहाद् देहो मृतेर्मृतिः ॥57॥
लब्ध्वेह मानुषीं योनिं ज्ञानविज्ञानसम्भवाम् । आत्मानं यो न बुद्ध्येत न क्वचिच्छममाप्नुयात् ॥
स्मृत्वेहायां परिक्लेशं ततः फलविपर्ययम् । अभयं चाप्यनीहायां सङ्कल्पाद् विरमेत् कविः 59॥
सुखाय दुःखमोक्षाय कुर्वाते दम्पती क्रियाः । ततोऽनिवृत्तिरप्राप्तिर्दुःखस्य च सुखस्य च ॥60॥
एवं विपर्ययं बुद्ध्वा नृणां विज्ञाभिमानिनाम् । आत्मनश्च गतिं सूक्ष्मां स्थानत्रयविलक्षणाम् 61॥
दृष्टश्रुताभिर्मात्राभिर्निर्मुक्तः स्वेन तेजसा । ज्ञानविज्ञानसन्तुष्टो मद्भक्तः पुरुषो भवेत् ॥62॥
एतावानेव मनुजैर्योगनैपुणबुद्धिभिः । स्वार्थः सर्वात्मना ज्ञेयो यत्परात्मैकदर्शनम् ॥63॥
त्वमेतच्छ्रद्धया राजन्नप्रमत्तो वचो मम । ज्ञानविज्ञानसम्पन्नो धारयन्नाशु सिध्यसि ॥64॥

'waking in dream' are mere projections of his own thought. So are the waking, dream, and sleep of everyday experience projections of the Lord's power or Maya. One should identify oneself as He who is the witness of these states, and not be their victim. **55.** That Consciousness, by which a man, who is fast asleep, knows himself to be asleep and experiences blissfulness and non-awareness of any object (of which he has a memory afterwards), know that to be Myself, the Brahman transcending the Gunas of Prakriti. **56.** When one reflects on both the waking and the sleep states, one is aware of the persistence of the same principle of Consciousness through both. From this one should draw the conclusion that this concomitant consciousness is the Witness, different from the states. It is identical with Brahman. **57.** When the Spirit forgets its identity with Me, and lapses into the state of separateness, he becomes subject to birth and death in the transmigratory cycle. **58.** No peace can be had by one who, having obtained a human body—a state in which one can have intellectual knowledge and spiritual intuition—fails to make any effort in that direction. **59.** Seeing on the one hand the prospect of pain in worldly desires and in work for their attainment as also the temporary nature of the satisfaction they give, and on the other, the way to peace and fearlessness in the renunciation of desires and desire-oriented works, man should abandon resolutions based on desires prompting him to work for the enjoyment of their fruits. **60.** Men and women undertake various kinds of work for the attainment of happiness and freedom from pain. But as a matter of fact they attain neither freedom from pain nor happiness. **61-62.** Observing the opposite results accruing to people who take pride in being wise and clever; knowing the subtle truth of the Atman as the witness of the three states of waking, dream and sleep; cultivating extreme detachment in respect of all experiences of the senses; and seeking satisfaction in the knowledge of the scripture and in the realisation of the truths they inculcate, man should cultivate supreme devotion to Me. **63.** The realisation of the Supreme Being as the one sole existence is the truth that should be known without any doubt by persons whose mind has attained to purity through spiritual communion. **64.** If you heed to these words of Mine with serious attention, then you would before long become endowed with knowledge and realisation.

श्रीशुक उवाच

आश्वास्य भगवानित्थं चित्रकेतुं जगद्गुरुः । पश्यतस्तस्य विश्वात्मा ततश्चान्तर्दधे हरिः ॥65॥

इति श्रीमद्भागवते महापुराणे पारमहंस्यां संहितायां षष्ठस्कन्धे चित्रकेतोः परमात्मदर्शनं नाम षोडशोऽध्यायः ॥16॥

Sri Suka said: **65.** Sri Hari, the soul of the world and the teacher of all, taught and consoled Chitraketu in this way, and disappeared as the latter looked on.

अथ सप्तदशोऽध्यायः

श्रीशुक उवाच

यतश्चान्तर्हितोऽनन्तस्तस्यै कृत्वा दिशे नमः । विद्याधरश्चित्रकेतुश्चचार गगनेचरः ॥ 1॥
स लक्षं वर्षलक्षाणामव्याहतबलेन्द्रियः । स्तूयमानो महायोगी मुनिभिः सिद्धचारणैः ॥ 2॥
कुलाचलेन्द्रद्रोणीषु नानासङ्कल्पसिद्धिषु । रेमे विद्याधरस्त्रीभिर्गापयन् हरिमीश्वरम् ॥ 3॥
एकदा स विमानेन विष्णुदत्तेन भास्वता । गिरिशं ददृशे गच्छन् परीतं सिद्धचारणैः ॥ 4॥
आलिङ्ग्याङ्कीकृतां देवीं बाहुना मुनिसंसदि । उवाच देव्याः शृण्वत्या जहासोच्चैस्तदन्तिके 5॥

चित्रकेतुरुवाच

एष लोकगुरुः साक्षाद्धर्मं वक्ता शरीरिणाम् । आस्ते मुख्यः सभायां वै मिथुनीभूय भार्यया 6॥
जटाधरस्तीव्रतपा ब्रह्मवादिसभापतिः । अङ्कीकृत्य स्त्रियं चास्ते गतह्रीः प्राकृतो यथा 7॥
प्रायशः प्राकृताश्चापि स्त्रियं रहसि बिभ्रति । अयं महाव्रतधरो बिभर्ति सदसि स्त्रियम् ॥ 8॥

Skandha VI : Chapter 17

HOW CHITRAKETU BECAME VRITRA

Parvati's Curse on Chitraketu (1-15)

Sri Suka said: **1.** Chitraketu, who had now become a Vidyadhara, travelled through the sky in the direction in which Adisesha disappeared, after making salutations in that direction. **2-3.** Endowed with inexhaustible power of the body and senses on account of his great Yogic attainments, and extolled by hosts of Munis, Siddhas and Charanas, Chitraketu the great Yogi sported for several lakhs of years in the wish-yielding valleys of the Mount Mahameru, making his Vidyadhara women sing hymns in praise of Sri Hari. **4.** Once in an aerial vehicle presented to him by Mahavishnu, he went to see Parameswara, the master of the mountain, accompanied by a vast host of Siddhas. **5.** There, seeing Siva sitting with his consort Parvati on his lap and embracing her, Chitraketu laughed aloud and said as follows in the hearing of the Devi: *Chitraketu said:* **6.** 'He, Sri Rudra, is the most important among embodied beings, and the teacher of the whole world. And yet he sits in public assembly in the embraces of his wife, while he explains Dharma to others. **7.** Wearing matted locks, reputed for great austerities, and the president of the assembly of learned theologians, he none the less sits with his wife on his lap shamelessly like a vulgar person. **8.** Even a vulgar person

श्रीशुक उवाच

भगवानपि तच्छ्रुत्वा प्रहस्यागाधधीर्नृप । तूष्णीं बभूव सदसि सभ्याश्च तदनुव्रताः ॥ 9॥
इत्यतद्वीर्यविदुषि ब्रुवाणे बह्वशोभनम् । रुषाऽऽह देवी धृष्टाय निर्जितात्माभिमानिने 10॥

पार्वत्युवाच

अयं किमधुना लोके शास्ता दण्डधरः प्रभुः । अस्मद्विधानां दुष्टानां निर्लज्जानां च विप्रकृत् 11
न वेद धर्मं किल पद्मयोनिर्न ब्रह्मपुत्रा भृगुनारदाद्याः ।
न वै कुमारः कपिलो मनुश्च ये नो निषेधन्त्यतिवर्तिनं हरम् ॥12॥
एषामनुध्येयपदाब्जयुग्मं जगद्गुरुं मङ्गलमङ्गलं स्वयम् ।
यः क्षत्रबन्धुः परिभूय सूरीन् प्रशास्ति धृष्टस्तदयं हि दण्ड्यः ॥13॥
नायमर्हति वैकुण्ठपादमूलोपसर्पणम् । सम्भावितमतिः स्तब्धः साधुभिः पर्युपासितम् ॥
अतः पापीयसीं योनिमासुरीं याहि दुर्मते । यथेह भूयो महतां न कर्ता पुत्र किल्बिषम् ॥15॥

श्रीशुक उवाच

एवं शप्तश्चित्रकेतुर्विमानादवरुह्य सः । प्रसादयामास सतीं मूर्ध्ना नम्रेण भारत ॥16॥

चित्रकेतुरुवाच

प्रतिगृह्णामि ते शापमात्मनोऽञ्जलिनाम्बिके । देवैर्मर्त्याय यत् प्रोक्तं पूर्वदिष्टं हि तस्य तत् 17॥

will hold a woman thus only in privacy, but this one, reputed for his great austerities, is doing so in public.'

Sri Suka said: **9.** O King! Lord Rudra, whose mind was deep and unperturbable, only smiled at this a little, but remained silent. The members of the assembly too sat silent, following the example of the Lord. **10.** When Chitraketu, ignorant of the Lord Siva's greatness, uttered these highly unbecoming remarks, Sri Parvati, roused to anger, spoke thus to that impertinent Vidyadhara who insolently prided himself upon his self-control. *Sri Parvati said:* **11.** 'Is this man the accredited authority to criticise, restrain and punish shameless and wicked beings like ourselves? He speaks as if he were. **12.** Is Brahma, the lotus-born, a stranger to Dharma? Are Bhrigu, Narada and other offspring of Brahma ignorant of it? Do not the Kumaras, Kapila and Manu understand its principles? Are they not all honouring Hara, the so-called transgressor of Dharma? Who then is this small fry to do so? **13.** This degenerate fellow of a Kshatriya who dares to over-ride the views of all great men and criticise Rudra in this way—Rudra whose feet are fit to be contemplated upon by Brahma and others, who is the teacher of the whole world and who is the holiest among holy beings—that impudent man deserves punishment. **14.** A man so conceited and arrogant does not deserve to go anywhere near the Lord of Vaikuntha, who is served only by persons of great holiness devoid of this kind of egotism. **15.** So, O arrogant one! You wanton child! May you have an evil embodiment as an Asura, in order that you may not do this kind of offence to great men.'

His unperturbed Reaction (16-24)

Sri Suka said: **16.** When cursed thus, Chitraketu descended from his aerial vehicle and humbly making prostrations to Sri Parvati, tried to pacify her. *Chitraketu said:* **17.** 'O Goddess! I accept your curse with both arms. Whatever divinities bestow on one, whether it be favourable or unfavourable, is all the result of one's

संसारचक्र एतस्मिञ्जन्तुरज्ञानमोहितः । भ्राम्यन् सुखं च दुःखं च भुङ्क्ते सर्वत्र सर्वदा 18॥
नैवात्मा न परश्चापि कर्ता स्यात् सुखदुःखयोः । कर्तारं मन्यतेऽप्राज्ञ आत्मानं परमेव च ॥19॥
गुणप्रवाह एतस्मिन् कः शापः को न्वनुग्रहः । कः स्वर्गो नरकः को वा किं सुखं दुःखमेव वा 20॥
एकः सृजति भूतानि भगवानात्ममायया । एषां बन्धं च मोक्षं च सुखं दुःखं च निष्कलः 21॥

न तस्य कश्चिद्दयितः प्रतीपो न ज्ञातिबन्धुर्न परो न च स्वः ।
समस्य सर्वत्र निरञ्जनस्य सुखे न रागः कुत एव रोषः ॥22॥
तथापि तच्छक्तिविसर्ग एषां सुखाय दुःखाय हिताहिताय ।
बन्धाय मोक्षाय च मृत्युजन्मनोः शरीरिणां संसृतयेऽवकल्पते ॥23॥

अथ प्रसादये न त्वां शापमोक्षाय भामिनि । यन्मन्यसे असाधूक्तं मम तत् क्षम्यतां सति 24॥

श्रीशुक उवाच

इति प्रसाद्य गिरिशौ चित्रकेतुररिन्दम । जगाम स्वविमानेन पश्यतोः स्मयतोस्तयोः 25॥
ततस्तु भगवान् रुद्रो रुद्राणीमिदमब्रवीत् । देवर्षिदैत्यसिद्धानां पार्षदानां च शृण्वताम् ॥26॥

श्रीरुद्र उवाच

दृष्टवत्यसि सुश्रोणि हरेरद्भुतकर्मणः । माहात्म्यं भृत्यभृत्यानां निःस्पृहाणां महात्मनाम् ॥
नारायणपराः सर्वे न कुतश्चन बिभ्यति । स्वर्गापवर्गनरकेष्वपि तुल्यार्थदर्शिनः ॥28॥

Karma. **18.** The Jiva overpowered by ignorance and moving about in this cycle of transmigratory existence, enjoys pleasurable and painful experiences wherever he may be born. **19.** Neither oneself nor others are responsible for one's happiness and misery. The ignorant man alone thinks that himself and others are the cause. **20.** In this perpetual movement of Prakriti, what is the place of a curse or a blessing, of pain or pleasure, of heaven or hell? They are all ephemeral. **21.** The impartible one, the Lord of all, creates everything with the power of His Maya and bestows on them joy and sorrow, liberation and bondage. **22.** No one is especially dear to Him, or inimical; none specially related or friendly; none His own or alien. For Him who is always unaffected and alike to all, there is no incentive for pleasure, much less for anger. **23.** Yet His Maya in the form of Karma makes for pleasure and pain, bondage and liberation, birth and death—in fact for the entire involvement of the Jiva in the cycle of transmigratory existence. **24.** Therefore, O angry One, I desire to pacify you. But it is not for release from the curse you have pronounced. O great lady! It is for asking pardon of you, if what I said was improper.'

Siva's Advice to Parvati (25-35)

Sri Suka said: **25.** O subduer of foes! Thus pacifying Parvati and Parameswara, Chitraketu went away in his aerial car, as all watched on in wonder. **26.** Then the worshipful Rudra said as follows to Sri Parvati in the hearing of all the Devas, Rishis, Asuras, Siddhas and attendants.

Sri Rudra said: **27.** O handsome one! Do you now see the greatness of even the servant of the servants of Sri Hari of wonderful deeds —of those men who are great in their devotion and in the absolutely desireless state of their mind? **28.** Whether it be in the enjoyments of heaven, the freedom of liberation, or the sufferings of the purgatory, these great devotees of Mahavishnu see Him and Him alone, and are free from every kind of

देहिनां देहसंयोगाद् द्वन्द्वानीश्वरलीलया। सुखं दुःखं मृतिर्जन्म शापोऽनुग्रह एव च ॥29॥
अविवेककृतः पुंसो ह्यर्थभेद इवात्मनि। गुणदोषविकल्पश्च भिदेव स्रजिवत् कृतः ॥30॥
वासुदेवे भगवति भक्तिमुद्वहतां नृणाम्। ज्ञानवैराग्यवीर्याणां नेह कश्चिद्व्यपाश्रयः ॥31॥
नाहं विरिञ्चो न कुमारनारदौ न ब्रह्मपुत्रा मुनयः सुरेशाः।
विदाम यस्येहितमंशकांशका न तत्स्वरूपं पृथगीशमानिनः ॥32॥
न ह्यस्यास्ति प्रियः कश्चिन्नाप्रियः स्वः परोऽपि वा। आत्मत्वात् सर्वभूतानां सर्वभूतप्रियो हरिः ॥33॥
तस्य चायं महाभागश्चित्रकेतुः प्रियोऽनुगः। सर्वत्र समदृक् शान्तो ह्यहं चैवाच्युतप्रियः 34॥
तस्मान्न विस्मयः कार्यः पुरुषेषु महात्मसु। महापुरुषभक्तेषु शान्तेषु समदर्शिषु ॥35॥

श्रीशुक उवाच

इति श्रुत्वा भगवतः शिवस्योमाभिभाषितम्। बभूव शान्तधी राजन् देवी विगतविस्मया ॥36॥
इति भागवतो देव्याः प्रतिशप्तुमलन्तमः। मूर्ध्ना सञ्जगृहे शापमेतावत् साधुलक्षणम् 37॥
जज्ञे त्वष्टुर्दक्षिणाग्नौ दानवीं योनिमाश्रितः। वृत्र इत्यभिविख्यातो ज्ञानविज्ञानसंयुतः ॥38॥
एतत् ते सर्वमाख्यातं यन्मां त्वं परिपृच्छसि। वृत्रस्यासुरजातेश्च कारणं भगवन्मतेः ॥39॥

fear. **29.** It is due to the sportive action of the Lord's power that the Jivas get bodies and all the contrary experiences of life like birth and death, happiness and misery, curse and blessing. **30.** The distinction of objects as good and bad, desirable and undesirable, is a kind of valuation made in our minds on the basis of our ignorance. It is like mistaking a flower wreath for a snake. **31.** For those who have supreme devotion to the worshipful Vāsudeva and are therefore endowed with the power of knowledge and renunciation, there is no need to depend upon anything in this world. The Lord is the support in all conditions. **32.** All of us including myself, Brahma, Sanatkumara, Narada and other offspring of Brahma, Indra and other Devas, are but parts of a part of Mahavishnu, the Divine Self, but being actuated by the feeling that we are by ourselves sovereign powers, we are not aware of His all-embracing will that is being worked out through us. Much less are we aware of His presence everywhere. **33.** For Him there is none who is specially dear, an enemy, or a stranger. Being the Self in all beings, Hari is dear to all alike. **34.** This great man Chitraketu is a devotee who loves the Lord intensely. He is even-sighted everywhere, ever peaceful. Being myself a devotee of Mahavishnu, I feel no displeasure towards Him. **35.** Therefore there is nothing to wonder at in any matter connected with the peaceful and even-sighted devotees of Mahavishnu, for they are beyond all our calculation.

Chitraketu becomes Vritra (36-41)

Sri Suka said: **36.** Hearing these words of the Lord Siva, the goddess Parvati was pacified, and no longer wondered at the conduct of Chitraketu. **37.** The great devotee Chitraketu, though capable of cursing the Devi in return, submitted himself to the curse without any reaction. Such conduct is the sign of holy men. **38.** Assuming the form of an Asura, but endowed with knowledge and devotion, this Chitraketu was born as Vritra in the Dakshināgni of Tvashta, who sacrificed in it for creating an agent for destroying Indra. **39.** I have now answered your question how Vritra, an Asura, could have constant remembrance and love of the

इतिहासमिमं पुण्यं चित्रकेतोर्महात्मनः । माहात्म्यं विष्णुभक्तानां श्रुत्वा बन्धाद्विमुच्यते ।।
य एतत् प्रातरुत्थाय श्रद्धया वाग्यतः पठेत् । इतिहासं हरिं स्मृत्वा स याति परमां गतिम् 41।।

इति श्रीमद्भागवते महापुराणे पारमहंस्यां संहितायां षष्ठस्कन्धे चित्रकेतुशापो नाम सप्तदशोऽध्यायः ।।17।।

Lord. **40.** By hearing the holy story of this great devotee Chitraketu and listening to the great excellences of Lord Vishnu's devotees, man is liberated from bondage. **41.** A man who gets up early in the morning and studies this narrative every day with faith, self-control, and constant remembrance of Sri Hari will attain to the highest spiritual state.

अथाष्टादशोऽध्यायः

श्रीशुक उवाच

पृश्निस्तु पत्नी सवितुः सावित्रीं व्याहृतिं त्रयीम् । अग्निहोत्रं पशुं सोमं चातुर्मास्यं महामखान् ।। 1।।
सिद्धिर्भगस्य भार्याङ्ग महिमानं विभुं प्रभुम् । आशिषं च वरारोहां कन्यां प्रासूत सुव्रताम् 2।।
धातुः कुहूः सिनीवाली राका चानुमतिस्तथा । सायं दर्शमथ प्रातः पूर्णमासमनुक्रमात् ।। 3।।
अग्नीन् पुरीष्यानाधत्त क्रियायां समनन्तरः । चर्षणी वरुणस्यासीद् यस्यां जातो भृगुः पुनः 4।।
वाल्मीकिश्च महायोगी वल्मीकादभवत् किल । अगस्त्यश्च वसिष्ठश्च मित्रावरुणयोर्ऋषी ।। 5।।
रेतः सिषिचतुः कुम्भे उर्वश्याः सन्निधौ द्रुतम् । रेवत्यां मित्र उत्सर्गमरिष्टं पिप्पलं व्यधात् 6।।

Skandha VI : Chapter 18

THE BIRTH OF THE MARUTS

Other Progeny of Aditi (1-9)

Sri Suka said: **1.** Prisni, the wife of Savita (the fifth son of Aditi), gave birth to three daughters who are the deities presiding over Gāyatri, Vyāhriti and Veda, and to nine sons who preside over the sacrifices known as Agnihotra, Pasu, Soma, Chaturmāsya, and the five daily obligatory Yajnas (Panchayajnas). **2.** O dear King! The wife of Bhaga named Siddhi gave birth to three sons, Mahima, Vibhu and Prabhu. She had also a daughter of great beauty and virtue named Āsis. **3.** Dhātā (the seventh son of Aditi) had four wives named Kuhu, Sinīvāli, Rāka, and Anumati, and in them he had four sons, Sāyam, Darsam, Prāta and Pūrnamāsa, respectively. **4.** Vidhātā, the eighth son of Aditi, begot by his wife Kriya the five presiding deities of the five fires known as Purīshyas. Varuna (the ninth son of Aditi) had Charshaṇī as his wife, and of her was born Bhrigu, the offspring of Brahma reincarnated. **5.** The great sage Vālmīki, reputed as having emerged from an ant hill, was also a son of Varuna. The sages Agastya and Vasishtha were sons of Mitra (the tenth son of Aditi) and Varuna. **6.** Mitra and Varuna happened to emit their seed due to sexual excitement in the presence of the heavenly nymph Urvasi, and they deposited it in a pot, wherefrom was born the sages Agastya and Vasishtha. Besides, Mitra begot by his wife Revati, three sons named Utsarga, Arishta and

पौलोम्यामिन्द्र आधत्त त्रीन् पुत्रानिति नः श्रुतम् । जयन्तमृषभं तात तृतीयं मीढुषं प्रभुः ॥ 7॥
उरुक्रमस्य देवस्य मायावामनरूपिणः । कीर्तौ पत्न्यां बृहच्छ्लोकस्तस्यासन् सौभगादयः ॥
तत्कर्मगुणवीर्याणि काश्यपस्य महात्मनः । पश्चाद् वक्ष्यामहेऽदित्यां यथा वावततार ह ॥ 9॥
अथ कश्यपदायादान् दैतेयान् कीर्तयामि ते । यत्र भागवतः श्रीमान् प्रह्लादो बलिरेव च ॥10॥
दितेर्द्वावेव दायादौ दैत्यदानववन्दितौ । हिरण्यकशिपुर्नाम हिरण्याक्षश्च कीर्तितौ ॥11॥
हिरण्यकशिपोर्भार्या कयाधुर्नाम दानवी । जम्भस्य तनया दत्ता सुषुवे चतुरः सुतान् ॥12॥
संह्लादं प्रागनुह्लादं ह्लादं प्रह्लादमेव च । तत्स्वसा सिंहिका नाम राहुं विप्रचितोऽग्रहीत् ॥
शिरोऽहरद्यस्य हरिश्चक्रेण पिबतोऽमृतम् । संह्लादस्य कृतिर्भार्यासूत पञ्चजनं ततः ॥14॥
ह्लादस्य धमनिर्भार्यासूत वातापिमिल्वलम् । योऽगस्त्याय त्वतिथये पेचे वातापिमिल्वलः 15॥
अनुह्लादस्य सूर्म्यायां बाष्कलो महिषस्तथा । विरोचनस्तु प्राह्लादिर्देव्यास्तस्याभवद् बलिः ॥
बाणज्येष्ठं पुत्रशतमशनायां ततोऽभवत् । तस्यानुभावः सुश्लोक्यः पश्चादेवाभिधास्यते 17॥
बाण आराध्य गिरिशं लेभे तद्गणमुख्यताम् । यत्पार्श्वे भगवानास्ते ह्यद्यापि पुरपालकः ॥18॥
मरुतश्च दितेः पुत्राश्चत्वारिंशन्नवाधिकाः । त आसन्नप्रजाः सर्वे नीता इन्द्रेण सात्मताम् 19॥

Pippala. **7.** We have heard that Indra (Aditi's eleventh son) had by his wife Sachi (daughter of Pauloma) three sons named Jayanta, Rishabha and Mīdhwān. **8.** The Lord in his incarnation in the assumed form of Vāmana (Aditi's twelfth and youngest son) had by his wife Kīrti, a son named Brihacchloka, who in turn had several sons like Saubhaga and others. **9.** About this incarnation, Vāmana, born as the son of Kasyapa and Aditi—of his actions, excellences and prowess—we shall describe in detail hereafter (in the 8th Skandha).

Issue of Diti, Mother of Asuras (10-19)

10. Now I shall tell you about the issue that Kasyapa had by his wife Diti. It is in one of these lines that the great devotees Prahlada and Bali were born. **11.** Diti had two sons Hiranyāksha and Hiranyakasipu, who were respected by all the Daityas and Danavas and who became famous. (In the third Skandha their story has been narrated.) **12-13.** Of these, Hiranyakasipu had by his wife Kayādhu, the daughter of Jambha, four sons named Samhlāda, Anuhlāda, Hlāda, and Prahlāda. They had a sister named Simhika who was married to Viprachitti, by whom she had a son named Rāhu. **14.** It was this Rāhu's head that Mahavishnu cut off when Rāhu slyly drank Amrita (immortal drink). Samhlāda had by his wife Kriti a son named Panchajana. **15.** Hlāda's wife Dhamani had two sons Vātāpi and Ilvala. Of these, Ilvala, it is said, cooked Vātāpi to feed their guest Agastya. **16.** Anuhlāda had by his wife Sūrmya two sons Bāshkala and Mahisha. Prahlāda's son was Virochana who had by his wife Devi, a son Bali. **17.** By his wife Asanāyā, Bali had a hundred children including Bāna. **18.** By worshipping Sri Parameswara, Bāna attained to a very high place among the devotees, and even to this day Sri Parameswara stands guard for the protection of his palace. **19.** Diti had in addition forty-nine sons who are well-known under a common appellation as the Maruts. They had no issue. Indra converted them into Devas.

Diti's Resolve to destroy Indra (20-37)

राजोवाच

कथं त आसुरं भावमपोह्यौत्पत्तिकं गुरो । इन्द्रेण प्रापिताः सात्म्यं किं तत्साधु कृतं हि तैः 20॥
इमे श्रद्दधते ब्रह्मन्नृषयो हि मया सह । परिज्ञानाय भगवंस्तन्नो व्याख्यातुमर्हसि ॥21॥

सूत उवाच

तद्विष्णुरातस्य स बादरायणिर्वचो निशम्यादृतमल्पमर्थवत् ।
सभाजयन् सन्निभृतेन चेतसा जगाद सत्रायण सर्वदर्शनः ॥22॥

श्रीशुक उवाच

हतपुत्रा दितिः शक्रपार्ष्णिग्राहेण विष्णुना । मन्युना शोकदीप्तेन ज्वलन्ती पर्यचिन्तयत् ॥23॥
कदा नु भ्रातृहन्तारमिन्द्रियाराममुल्बणम् । अक्लिन्नहृदयं पापं घातयित्वा शये सुखम् ॥24॥
कृमिविड्भस्मसंज्ञाऽऽसीद्यस्येशाभिहितस्य च । भूतध्रुक् तत्कृते स्वार्थं किं वेद निरयो यतः 25॥
आशासानस्य तस्येदं ध्रुवमुन्नद्धचेतसः । मदशोषक इन्द्रस्य भूयाद् येन सुतो हि मे ॥26॥
इति भावेन सा भर्तुराचचारासकृत्प्रियम् । शुश्रूषयानुरागेण प्रश्रयेण दमेन च ॥27॥
भक्त्या परमया राजन् मनोज्ञैर्वल्गुभाषितैः । मनो जग्राह भावज्ञा सुस्मितापाङ्गवीक्षणैः ॥28॥
एवं स्त्रिया जडीभूतो विद्वानपि विदग्धया । बाढमित्याह विवशो न तच्चित्रं हि योषिति 29॥
विलोक्यैकान्तभूतानि भूतान्यादौ प्रजापतिः । स्त्रियं चक्रे स्वदेहार्धं यया पुंसां मतिर्हृता ॥30॥
एवं शुश्रूषितस्तात भगवान् कश्यपः स्त्रिया । प्रहस्य परमप्रीतो दितिमाहाभिनन्द्य च ॥31॥

Rajah Parikshit said: **20.** O Teacher! How did Indra change the Maruts, born as Asuras, into Devas, transforming their nature? What merit had they to make themselves eligible for the same? **21.** O holy one! Like me, all these assembled Rishis too desire to be informed about this. So we request you to enlighten us on this theme.

The Suta said: **22.** O Sounaka, Thou the leader of the Satra! Hearing the request of the king, modest and brief, Sri Suka expressed his approval of it and spoke with his mind deeply concentrated.

Sri Suka said: **23.** On Diti's offspring, Hiranyāksha and Hiranyakasipu, being destroyed by Mahavishnu, the ally of Indra, she (Diti) thought as follows, burning with anger: **24.** 'When shall I sleep soundly after effecting the destruction of this Indra, sensuous, cruel, hard-hearted and guilty of fratricide? **25.** Even the body of a proud king is reduced on death to worms which feed on it, to the excreta of the animals that eat it, or to ashes when cremated. What can a person who oppresses others for the sake of such a body understand about his own real good? Only hell awaits him. **26.** How can I have a son who will be powerful enough to put an end to the overweening pride of this Indra whose ego is bloated because of his false notion that this body is something permanent?' **27.** With this end in view she did everything to please her husband by service, humility, love and sense control. **28.** O King! Quick in understanding the mind of man, she captivated her husband's mind by devotion to him and by her sweet speech and smiling looks. **29.** It is no wonder that Kasyapa Prajapati, though a wise man, became excited and overpowered by the charms of a woman, and agreed to satisfy her wishes. **30.** For, Brahma, the creator, found his creatures at first to have no worldly attractions or attachments. So he made one half of his body into that of a woman. Woman thus began to draw the mind of man powerfully.

31. O King! Pleased very much by Diti's

कश्यप उवाच

वरं वरय वामोरु प्रीतस्तेऽहमनिन्दिते । स्त्रिया भर्तरि सुप्रीते कः काम इह चागमः 32॥
पतिरेव हि नारीणां दैवतं परमं स्मृतम् । मानसः सर्वभूतानां वासुदेवः श्रियः पतिः ॥33॥
स एव देवतालिङ्गैर्नामरूपविकल्पितैः । इज्यते भगवान् पुम्भिः स्त्रीभिश्च पतिरूपधृक् ॥
तस्मात् पतिव्रता नार्यः श्रेयस्कामाः सुमध्यमे । यजन्तेऽनन्यभावेन पतिमात्मानमीश्वरम् ॥35॥
सोऽहं त्वयार्चितो भद्रे ईदृग्भावेन भक्तितः । तत्ते सम्पादये काममसतीनां सुदुर्लभम् ॥36॥

दितिरुवाच

वरदो यदि मे ब्रह्मन् पुत्रमिन्द्रहणं वृणे । अमृत्युं मृतपुत्राहं येन मे घातितौ सुतौ ॥37॥
निशम्य तद्वचो विप्रो विमनाः पर्यतप्यत । अहो अधर्मः सुमहानद्य मे समुपस्थितः ॥38॥
अहो अद्येन्द्रियारामो योषिन्मय्येह मायया । गृहीतचेताः कृपणः पतिष्ये नरके ध्रुवम् ॥39॥
कोऽतिक्रमोऽनुवर्तन्त्याः स्वभावमिह योषितः । धिङ्मां बताबुधं स्वार्थे यदहं त्वजितेन्द्रियः 40॥
शरत्पद्मोत्सवं वक्त्रं वचश्च श्रवणामृतम् । हृदयं क्षुरधाराभं स्त्रीणां को वेद चेष्टितम् 41॥
न हि कश्चित् प्रियः स्त्रीणामञ्जसा स्वाशिषात्मनाम् पतिं पुत्रं भ्रातरं वा घ्नन्त्यर्थे घातयन्ति च ॥42॥

faithful and devoted service, the worshipful Kasyapa appreciated her very much and said to her smiling: *Kasyapa said:* **32.** 'O handsome and noble lady, I am very much pleased with you. Seek whatever boon you want. When the husband is pleased, what is there, here or hereafter, that a woman cannot achieve? **33.** The husband has been declared as the Deity for women. Vāsudeva, the consort of Srī, resides in the heart of all beings (and it is therefore Him that a woman serves through the husband). **34.** It is Him Vāsudeva that men worship in images under different forms and names. It is Him alone that women worship through the form of husband. **35.** O handsome lady! Therefore devoted wives who aspire for blessedness worship the all-pervading Supreme Being through service of Him in the shape of the husband with unfailing devotion. **36.** O graceful lady! I have been served by you well in this spirit with great devotion. Therefore I shall grant you the boons you desire, which women without such devotion cannot obtain.' *Diti said:* **37.** 'Childless, as I am, I seek, if you are pleased to give me a boon, the birth of a son, free from death, who will be able to destroy Indra who has been the cause of the destruction of both my children.'

The Prajapati's Regret (38-44)

38. Hearing this, the Prajapati became very much repentant. He said to himself: 'Alas! I am guilty of a great transgression today. **39.** Alas, for allowing myself to be infatuated by Maya in the shape of a woman and for delighting in sensual pleasures, I shall be consigned to purgatory. **40.** In this matter, the woman, who is only following her nature, has no fault. It is I, who have been thoughtless about the great purpose of life, that deserve condemnation. For, I have become a slave of my senses. **41.** None can know the intention of a woman—her face may be smiling like an autumnal lotus, her words may be sweet to hear, but her heart can none the less be sharp as a razor's edge. **42.** For a woman who seeks her selfish ends, none is really dear, and love is a mere pretence. For her selfish purpose, she can kill or bring about the death of anyone, husband, son or brother.'

प्रतिश्रुतं ददामीति वचस्तन्न मृषा भवेत्। वधं नार्हति चेन्द्रोऽपि तत्रेदमुपकल्पते ॥43॥
इति संचिन्त्य भगवान् मारीचः कुरुनन्दन। उवाच किञ्चित्कुपित आत्मानं च विगर्हयन् 44॥

कश्यप उवाच

पुत्रस्ते भविता भद्रे इन्द्रहा देवबान्धवः। संवत्सरं व्रतमिदं यद्यञ्जो धारयिष्यसि ॥45॥

दितिरुवाच

धारयिष्ये व्रतं ब्रह्मन् ब्रूहि कार्याणि यानि मे। यानि चेह निषिद्धानि न व्रतं घ्नन्ति यानि तु 46॥

कश्यप उवाच

न हिंस्याद् भूतजातानि न शपेन्नानृतं वदेत्। न छिन्द्यान्नखरोमाणि न स्पृशेद् यदमङ्गलम् 47॥
नाप्सु स्नायान्न कुप्येत न सम्भाषेत दुर्जनैः। न वसीताधौतवासः स्रजं च विधृतां क्वचित् 48॥
नोच्छिष्टं चण्डिकान्नं च सामिषं वृषलाहृतम्। भुञ्जीतोदक्यया दृष्टं पिबेदञ्जलिना त्वपः 49॥
नोच्छिष्टास्पृष्टसलिला सन्ध्यायां मुक्तमूर्धजा। अनर्चितासंयतवाङ्नासंवीता बहिश्चरेत् ॥50॥
नाधौतपादाप्रयता नार्द्रपान्नो उदक्शिराः। शयीत नापराङ्नान्यैर्न नग्ना न च सन्ध्ययोः 51॥
धौतवासाः शुचिर्नित्यं सर्वमङ्गलसंयुता। पूजयेत् प्रातराशात् प्राग् गोविप्राञ् छ्रियमच्युतम् ॥

43-44. He further thought: 'My promise should not be falsified. Indra, too, should not be killed!' O King! Thinking thus, Kasyapa felt annoyed with himself and said a little angrily.

Instruction on Pumsavana (45-54)

Kasyapa said: **45.** 'O good lady! If you sincerely follow the practices and vows I give you for observance for one year, you will have a son capable of killing Indra. But if you break the vows, the son born will be a friend of Indra and the Devas.' **46.** *Diti said:* 'O learned one! I shall observe the vow. Please tell me what are allowed, what are prohibited during its observance, and what are neutral and therefore not leading to a break in the vow.' *Kasyapa said:* **47.** 'No injury should be done to living creatures. No curse should be uttered on anyone. No untruth should be spoken. Nails and hair should not be cut. No unclean thing should be touched. **48.** One should not take a dip in running water. One should not get angry. One should not speak with wicked people. Unbleached clothes should not be worn. A garland once worn and rejected should not be worn again. **49.** One should not eat the leavings of another. The offerings made to Chandika should not be eaten. Meat preparations and food brought by a low-born man should not be taken. Food seen by a woman in her periods should be avoided; water should not be drunk from palms cupped. **50.** The following rules must be observed especially when one goes out of the house: The mouth should not be unwashed after taking food; the hands and feet should be washed; the hair should not remain dishevelled in the evenings; one should wear jewelleries and the like; one should be controlled in speech; one should be properly dressed. **51.** One should not go to bed with feet unwashed and undried, with mind uncontrolled, naked, with another in bed, or with head towards the north or west. One should not be sleeping in the morning and evening twilight hours. **52.** The following must be practised: Wearing newly washed clothes, observing rules of cleanliness always, and adorning with auspicious substances like unguents and sandal paste, one should before breakfast offer worship to a cow, a

स्त्रियो वीरवतीश्चार्चेत् स्रग्गन्धबलिमण्डनैः । पतिं चार्च्योपतिष्ठेत ध्यायेत् कोष्ठगतं च तम् 53॥
सांवत्सरं पुंसवनं व्रतमेतदविप्लुतम् । धारयिष्यसि चेत् तुभ्यं शक्रहा भविता सुतः 54॥
बाढमित्यभिप्रेत्याथ दिती राजन् महामनाः । काश्यपं गर्भमाधत्त व्रतं चाञ्जो दधार सा 55॥
मातृष्वसुरभिप्रायमिन्द्र आज्ञाय मानद । शुश्रूषणेनाश्रमस्थां दितिं पर्यचरत् कविः ॥56॥
नित्यं वनात् सुमनसः फलमूलसमित्कुशान् । पत्राङ्कुरमृदोऽपश्च काले काल उपाहरत् ॥57॥
एवं तस्या व्रतस्थाया व्रतच्छिद्रं हरिर्नृप । प्रेप्सुः पर्यचरज्जिह्मो मृगहेव मृगाकृतिः ॥58॥
नाध्यगच्छद् व्रतच्छिद्रं तत्परोऽथ महीपते । चिन्तां तीव्रां गतः शक्रः केन मे स्याच्छिवं त्विह ॥
एकदा सा तु सन्ध्यायामुच्छिष्टा व्रतकर्शिता । अस्पृष्टवार्यधौताङ्घ्रिः सुष्वाप विधिमोहिता 60
लब्ध्वा तदन्तरं शक्रो निद्रापहृतचेतसः । दितेः प्रविष्ट उदरं योगेशो योगमायया ॥61॥
चकर्त सप्तधा गर्भं वज्रेण कनकप्रभम् । रुदन्तं सप्तधैकैकं मा रोदीरिति तान् पुनः ॥62॥
ते तमूचुः पाटयमानाः सर्वे प्राञ्जलयो नृप । नो जिघांससि किमिन्द्र भ्रातरो मरुतस्तव ॥63॥
मा भैष्ट भ्रातरो मह्यं यूयमित्याह कौशिकः । अनन्यभावान् पार्षदानात्मनो मरुतां गणान् 64॥
न ममार दितेर्गर्भः श्रीनिवासानुकम्पया । बहुधा कुलिशक्षुण्णो द्रौण्यस्त्रेण यथा भवान् 65॥

holy man, Sri Devi and Achyuta. **53.** One should offer worship to women who have husbands, with garland, sandal paste, food offerings, decorations etc. So one should worship one's own husband, praise him, and think that he has entered into one's womb. **54.** If this vow called Pumsavana (the observances leading to the birth of a son) is observed for one year, you will have a son capable of killing Indra.'

Birth of the Maruts (55-78)

55. O King! Agreeing to this, the high-souled Diti bore the seed of Kasyapa and then began to practise the vows of Pumsavana assiduously. **56.** Now Indra hearing soon about the resolution of his Aunt Diti, came to her hermitage and took upon himself the duty of serving her during the period of her vow. **57.** According to her need, he daily brought from the forest such requirements as flowers, fruits, roots, sacrificial fuel, leaves, sprouts, earth, water etc. **58.** The cruel-hearted Indra, who was intent on causing a breach of her vow, continued to serve her disguising his real intentions, just like a hunter who has put on an animal's form as a camouflage. **59.** O King! Indra was not able to bring about any break in Diti's vow, despite all his keen interest to effect it. So he began to think very seriously about the ways and means by which he could preserve himself.

60. In the meantime, as Destiny would have it, Diti, who was very much weakened by the observance of the vows, fell asleep one day at the evening twilight when her mouth, hands and feet were unwashed after meals. **61-62.** This was a breach of the vow, and taking advantage of it, Indra entered into the abdomen of the sleeping Diti by his Yogic power, and cut that golden coloured foetus with his thunder-bolt weapon into seven pieces. The seven pieces of the foetus then began to cry, whereupon Indra, as if he were going to pacify them, told them, 'Do not cry', and cut each of them into seven again. **63.** O King! All these cut pieces cried out to Indra in all humility: 'O Indra! Why do you want to kill us? We are Maruts, your brothers!' **64.** Indra thereupon told them, 'Do not be afraid, as all of you are indeed my brothers, and are to be my exclusive attendants.' **65.** Though they

सकृदिष्ट्वाऽऽदिपुरुषं पुरुषो याति साम्यताम्। संवत्सरं किञ्चिदूनं दित्या यद्धरिरर्चितः ॥66॥
सजूरिन्द्रेण पञ्चाशद् देवास्ते मरुतोऽभवन्। व्यपोह्य मातृदोषं ते हरिणा सोमपाः कृताः ॥67॥
दितिरुत्थाय ददृशे कुमाराननलप्रभान्। इन्द्रेण सहितान् देवी पर्यतुष्यदनिन्दिता ॥68॥
अथेन्द्रमाह ताताहमादित्यानां भयावहम्। अपत्यमिच्छन्त्यचरं व्रतमेतत् सुदुष्करम् ॥69॥
एकः सङ्कल्पितः पुत्रः सप्त सप्ताभवन् कथम्। यदि ते विदितं पुत्र सत्यं कथय मा मृषा ॥70॥

इन्द्र उवाच

अम्ब तेऽहं व्यवसितमुपधार्यागतोऽन्तिकम्। लब्धान्तरोऽच्छिदं गर्भमर्थबुद्धिर्न धर्मवित् 71॥
कृत्तो मे सप्तधा गर्भ आसन् सप्त कुमारकाः। तेऽपि चैकैकशो वृक्णाः सप्तधा नापि मम्रिरे 72॥
ततस्तत् परमाश्चर्यं वीक्ष्याध्यवसितं मया। महापुरुषपूजायाः सिद्धिः काप्यनुषङ्गिणी ॥73॥
आराधनं भगवत ईहमाना निराशिषः। ये तु नेच्छन्त्यपि परं ते स्वार्थकुशलाः स्मृताः 74॥
आराध्यात्मप्रदं देवं स्वात्मानं जगदीश्वरम्। को वृणीते गुणस्पर्शं बुधः स्यान्नरकेऽपि यत् 75॥
तदिदं मम दौर्जन्यं बालिशस्य महीयसि। क्षन्तुमर्हसि मातस्त्वं दिष्टया गर्भो मृतोत्थितः ॥

श्रीशुक उवाच

इन्द्रस्तयाभ्यनुज्ञातः शुद्धभावेन तुष्टया। मरुद्भिः सह तां नत्वा जगाम त्रिदिवं प्रभुः ॥77॥

were cut into pieces, the foetus in Diti's womb did not perish owing to the grace of Mahavishnu, the abode of Srī, just as you, Parikshit, were yourself saved by Him from the missile of Aswatthama while you were in your mother's womb. **66.** By adoring Him even once man attains salvation. Diti had, however, been worshipping Him for nearly one year. So she was bound to have His protection. **67.** These Maruts became fifty in number, including Indra. By the Lord's grace, their Asura nature derived from the mother was erased, and they were made fit to drink Soma like the Devas.

68. Purified by worshipping the Lord, Diti on awakening was very much pleased to find her children, firelike in splendour, in the company of Indra. **69.** She said to Indra: 'Dear one! I undertook this difficult vow desiring a son who will be a terror to all the offspring of Aditi. **70.** I desired for only one son. How is that I have now got forty nine of them? Please tell me the truth if you know it. Do not prevaricate.' **71.** Indra said: 'O Mother! Knowing your resolution, I got close to you, and in order to abort the pregnancy, I cut the foetus into pieces. I am not a follower of Dharma, but one who cares only for the achievement of my selfish purposes. **72.** I first cut the foetus into seven and they became seven children. Each of these I cut again into seven. Still they did not perish. **73.** I concluded that this astonishing phenomenon was only a subsidiary effect of the worship of the Supreme Being. **74.** Those who know their own real interest are persons who worship the Lord, entertaining desire for nothing, not even Mukti. **75.** Would any man with a modicum of intelligence ever desire for sense enjoyments, which could possibly be had even in purgatory, after being established in the adoration of the Supreme Mahavishnu who gives even Himself to a devotee, and who is the soul of one's own soul? **76.** O Mother! May you kindly excuse this offence I have foolishly done to a great personage. Your foetus which was destroyed, has fortunately come to life.'

Sri Suka said: **77.** Diti was pleased with Indra for his frank admission. He pros-

एवं ते सर्वमाख्यातं यन्मां त्वं परिपृच्छसि। मङ्गलं मरुतां जन्म किं भूयः कथयामि ते ॥78॥

इति श्रीमद्भागवते महापुराणे पारमहंस्यां संहितायां षष्ठस्कन्धे मरुदुत्पत्तिकथनं नामाष्टादशोऽध्यायः ॥18॥

trated himself before her, and taking her permission, returned to his heaven along with the Maruts. **78.** I have thus finished narrating to you the story of the birth of the Maruts. Is there anything more that you are interested to know?

अथैकोनविंशोऽध्यायः

राजोवाच

व्रतं पुंसवनं ब्रह्मन् भवता यदुदीरितम्। तस्य वेदितुमिच्छामि येन विष्णुः प्रसीदति ॥ 1॥

श्रीशुक उवाच

शुक्ले मार्गशिरे पक्षे योषिद् भर्तुरनुज्ञया। आरभेत व्रतमिदं सार्वकामिकमादितः ॥ 2॥
निशम्य मरुतां जन्म ब्राह्मणाननुमन्त्र्य च। स्नात्वा शुक्लदती शुक्ले वसीतालङ्कृताम्बरे।
पूजयेत् प्रातराशात् प्राग्भगवन्तं श्रिया सह ॥ 3॥
अलं ते निरपेक्षाय पूर्णकाम नमोऽस्तु ते। महाविभूतिपतये नमः सकलसिद्धये ॥ 4॥
यथा त्वां कृपया भूत्या तेजसा महिनौजसा। जुष्ट ईशगुणैः सर्वैस्ततोऽसि भगवान् प्रभुः ॥ 5॥
विष्णुपत्नि महामाये महापुरुषलक्षणे। प्रीयेथा मे महाभागे लोकमातर्नमोऽस्तु ते ॥ 6॥

ॐ नमो भगवते महापुरुषाय महानुभावाय महाविभूतिपतये सह महाविभूतिभिर्बलिमुपहराणीति

Skandha VI : Chapter 19

OBSERVANCE OF PUMSAVANA

Question on Pumsavana (1-6)

Rajah Parikshit said: **1.** O learned one! You spoke of the vow called Pumsavana by observing which Mahavishnu is propitiated. I wish to know more about it.

Sri Suka said: **2.** From the first day of the bright fortnight in the month of Māṛgasīrsha (December-January), a woman should begin the practice of this vow with the permission of her husband. **3.** After listening to this story of the birth of the Maruts, she should take the blessing of holy men, having beforehand cleaned her teeth, and taken bath, decorated herself, and put on clean clothes. Before breaking her fast in the morning, she should worship the Lord Mahavishnu along with His consort Srī. She should salute the Lord with the following Mantra: **4.** 'O Lord! Thou art self-fulfilled and without any wants. To Thee, the Independent, my salutations! Salutation to the consort of Srī, and the master of all powers! **5.** O Lord of all! Thou art possessed of all divine powers and attributes like mercy, lordliness, brilliance, greatness, vigour etc., and therefore Thou art the master of all and the object of worship for all. **6.** O Thou consort of Mahavishnu! O Thou great creative power! O Thou invested with all powers like the Lord Himself! O Thou great Mother of all! Be propitious unto me! My salutations to Thee!'

Mantra, Stotra for Pumsavana (7-14)

Mantra for worship: **7.** *Om namo bhaga-*

। अनेनाहरहर्मन्त्रेण विष्णोरावाहनार्घ्यपाद्योपस्पर्शनस्नानवासउपवीतविभूषणगन्धपुष्पधूपदीपोप-
हाराद्युपचारांश्च समाहित उपाहरेत् ॥7॥

हविःशेषं तु जुहुयादनले द्वादशाहुतीः ।
ॐ नमो भगवते महापुरुषाय महाविभूतिपतये स्वाहेति ॥ 8॥

श्रियं विष्णुं च वरदावाशिषां प्रभवावुभौ । भक्त्या सम्पूजयेन्नित्यं यदीच्छेत् सर्वसम्पदः 9॥
प्रणमेद् दण्डवद् भूमौ भक्तिप्रह्वेण चेतसा । दशवारं जपेन्मन्त्रं ततः स्तोत्रमुदीरयेत् ॥10॥
युवां तु विश्वस्य विभू जगतः कारणं परम् । इयं हि प्रकृतिः सूक्ष्मा मायाशक्तिर्दुरत्यया 11॥
तस्या अधीश्वरः साक्षात् त्वमेव पुरुषः परः । त्वं सर्वयज्ञ इज्येयं क्रियेयं फलभुग् भवान् 12॥
गुणव्यक्तिरियं देवी व्यञ्जको गुणभुग् भवान् । त्वं हि सर्वशरीर्यात्मा श्रीः शरीरेन्द्रियाशया ।
नामरूपे भगवती प्रत्ययस्त्वमपाश्रयः ॥13॥
यथा युवां त्रिलोकस्य वरदौ परमेष्ठिनौ । तथा म उत्तमश्लोक सन्तु सत्या महाशिषः 14॥
इत्यभिष्टूय वरदं श्रीनिवासं श्रिया सह । तन्निःसार्योपहरणं दत्त्वाऽऽचमनमर्चयेत् ॥15॥

vate mahāpurushāya mahānubhāvāya mahavibhūtipataye saha mahāvibhūtibhir balimupaharāni iti—'Om! Saluations to Thee the possessor of all the six majesties! Salutations to Thee the possessor of infinite prowess! Salutations to Thee attended by the Mahavibhutis (divine powers personified as attendants)! I make Thee this offering.' Uttering this Mantra with great devotion and concentration should one perform all items of worship like invocation; offering water for washing hands and feet, for sipping and bath; and presenting cloth, sacred thread, ornaments, sandal paste, flowers, incense, food offering etc. **8**. With the Mantra '*Om namo bhagavate mahāpurushāya mahāvibhūtipataye svāhā'*—with this Mantra oblations should be made twelve times in the sacrificial fire with the sanctified remnants of the food offerings made to the Deity in the worship mentioned earlier. **9.** If one is desirous of great wealth, one should adore every day with devotion both Lakshmi and Narayana, who can grant all boons and who are the cause of all prosperity and welfare. **10**. With a mind full of humility arising from an excess of devotion. one should make a full prostration, falling like a stick, repeat the Mantra at least ten times, and then recite the following verses in praise of Lakshmi and Narayana: **11.** 'You together (Lakshmi and Narayana) form the ultimate cause of the universe and the power that controls it. It is this Goddess, who is Thy Maya-Sakti, that operates as primordial Nature *(Sūkshma-prakriti)* of extreme subtlety whom none can overcome. **12.** Thou the Supreme One, art the master of this Power. Thou art of the form of all Yajnas, and the Goddess Srī is the 'will to perform' behind it. She is the sacrificial rite, and Thou art the enjoyer of the fruits. **13.** This Devi is manifested Nature, and Thou art its manifestor as Time and its enjoyer too. Thou art the Atman in all embodied creatures, and the Devi is their body, mind and senses. All name and form are the Devi, and Thou art their support and manifestor. **14**. Insofar as Thou art the master of the universe and the grantor of all their desires, may my prayer to Thee be fruitful.'

Other Details of Worship (15-24)

15. After thus extolling Mahavishnu, the abode of Srī and the grantor of all boons, as well as Srī Herself, the food offerings should be removed and the water

ततः स्तुवीत स्तोत्रेण भक्तिप्रह्वेण चेतसा । यज्ञोच्छिष्टमवघ्राय पुनरभ्यर्चयेद्धरिम् ॥16॥
पतिं च परया भक्त्या महापुरुषचेतसा । प्रियैस्तैस्तैरुपनमेत् प्रेमशीलः स्वयं पतिः ।
बिभृयात् सर्वकर्माणि पत्न्या उच्चावचानि च ॥17॥
कृतमेकतरेणापि दम्पत्योरुभयोरपि । पत्न्यां कुर्यादनर्हायां पतिरेतत् समाहितः ॥18॥
विष्णोर्व्रतमिदं बिभ्रन्न विहन्यात् कथञ्चन । विप्रान् स्त्रियो वीरवतीः स्रग्गन्धबलिमण्डनैः ।
अर्चेदहरहर्भक्त्या देवं नियममास्थितः ॥19॥
उद्वास्य देवं स्वे धाम्नि तन्निवेदितमग्रतः । अद्यादात्मविशुद्ध्यर्थं सर्वकामर्द्धये तथा ॥20॥
एतेन पूजाविधिना मासान् द्वादश हायनम् । नीत्वाथोपचरेत् साध्वी कार्तिके चरमेऽहनि 21॥
श्वोभूतेऽप उपस्पृश्य कृष्णमभ्यर्च्य पूर्ववत् । पयःशृतेन जुहुयाच्चरुणा सह सर्पिषा ।
पाकयज्ञविधानेन द्वादशैवाहुतीः पतिः ॥22॥
आशिषः शिरसाऽऽदाय द्विजैः प्रीतैः समीरिताः । प्रणम्य शिरसा भक्त्या भुञ्जीत तदनुज्ञया 23॥
आचार्यमग्रतः कृत्वा वाग्यतः सह बन्धुभिः । दद्यात् पत्न्यै चरोः शेषं सुप्रजस्त्वं सुसौभगम् ॥
एतच्चरित्वा विधिवद् व्रतं विभोरभीप्सितार्थं लभते पुमानिह ।
स्त्री त्वेतदास्थाय लभेत सौभगं श्रियं प्रजां जीवपतिं यशो गृहम् ॥25॥

for Āchamana (purificatory sip) be given. **16.** Next one should chant hymns extolling Sri Hari with great devotion and humility. Then partaking of the remnants of the food offerings by mere smell, one should continue the worship. **17.** The woman should also make offerings of pleasing things to her husband with great devotion and awareness that she is worshipping the Lord through him. The husband too should be loving towards her and be giving her co-operation and support in the performance of all the ordinary and special rites. **18.** Between couples, in what one does, the other becomes a sharer. So when the wife is incapacitated to do a rite, the husband should do it with great attention.

19. One who adopts this vow of worship of Vishnu, should perform it every day without break. That person observing it must offer daily with great devotion garland, sandal paste, food offerings and decorations to holy men, women with husbands, and to the Lord Himself. **20.** The Deity should then be put back into His abode, and afterwards one should partake of the food offered to Him along with others, for the purification of the mind, and the fulfilment of all prayers. **21.** A pious woman should adore the Lord in this way for full twelve months of a year (i.e. excluding intercalary months), and at the close, fast on the last day of Kartika. **22.** Early next morning after the fast, she should bathe and worship the Lord Krishna as before. Her husband should then make twelve oblations of rice cooked in milk and sprinkled with ghee according to the procedure described for *pāka-yajna* (cooked food offering). **23.** He should receive the blessings of highly pleased holy men, making humble prostrations to them, and take his food with their permission. **24.** Afterwards he should stand in silence with all relatives before the Acharya, and give the remnant of the sacrificial offerings to the wife to consume, for her happiness and the birth of worthy children.

Results of Worship (25-28)

25. By observing this vow properly a man will have the fulfilment of all his wants. A woman observing it will be

कन्या च विन्देत समग्रलक्षणं वरं त्ववीरा हतकिल्बिषा गतिम् ।
मृतप्रजा जीवसुता धनेश्वरी सुदुर्भगा सुभगा रूपमग्र्यम् ॥26॥
विन्देद् विरूपा विरुजा विमुच्यते य आमयावीन्द्रियकल्पदेहम् ।
एतत् पठन्नभ्युदये च कर्मण्यनन्ततृप्तिः पितृदेवतानाम् ॥27॥
तुष्टाः प्रयच्छन्ति समस्तकामान् होमावसाने हुतभुक् श्रीर्हरिश्च ।
राजन् महन्मरुतां जन्म पुण्यं दितेर्व्रतं चाभिहितं महत् ते ॥28॥

इति श्रीमद्भागवते महापुराणे वैयासिक्यामष्टादशसाहस्र्यां पारमहंस्यां संहितायां षष्ठस्कन्धे पुंसवनव्रतकथनं नामैकोनविंशोऽध्यायः ॥19॥

इति षष्ठः स्कन्धः समाप्तः

हरिः ॐ तत्सत्

blessed with good fortune, prosperity, progeny, good reputation, a comfortable home and a long-lived husband who would survive her. **26.** An unmarried girl will get a worthy husband. A childless widow will get over all her sins and attain Moksha. A woman whose children have died, will get long-lived issue. One wealthy but unfortunate will be attended by good fortune. An ugly woman can hope to have a seemly appearance. **27.** A sick man will be free from even a severe ailment and gain a healthy body with powerful senses. If one studies this account at the time of auspicious rites, he will have the blessing of the Pitris and the Devas. **28.** By reciting this at the end of the Homa, the sacred fire, Sri Devi and Sri Hari, will be pleased and grant all that one desires. O King! I have narrated to you now the sacred account of the birth of the Maruts and the austere discipline that Diti observed.

END OF THE SIXTH SKANDHA

Skandha Seven

PROLOGUE

The seventh Skandha consisting of fifteen chapters and seven hundred and fifty verses is said to deal with the topic *ūti* or how tendencies produced by Karma influence life. When by misbehaviour men provoke the displeasure of holy personages, that displeasure of theirs causes the downfall of these men, and contrariwise, when by service and humility men please holy personages, their goodwill can lead to their spiritual evolution. Two examples are given of this here. One is of Narada himself, the principal narrator in this Skandha. As a leader of Gandharva singers, he misbehaved, casting ridicule at sages who had assembled for a Brahmasatra. As a consequence, he was degraded to the condition of a servant boy in his next birth in the human species. Then he happened to serve some holy men during their Retreat in the rainy season (Chāturmāsya), and helped by their blessings, he took to asceticism and attained to the state of a Devarshi in a subsequent embodiment.

The second instance is of the attendants of Vaikuntha, Jaya and Vijaya, who, for their misbehaviour towards the group of sages known as the Kumaras, were cursed to become Asuras. In each of their three births as Asuras, they were born as innate enemies of Vishnu. Their attitude towards Mahavishnu in these births have made them exemplars of Vidwesha Bhakti, or devotion through confrontation. Mortal fear fixes one's mind on the enemy, in this case the Lord Himself, as much as affection and reverence do; and the mind being in both kinds of emotion fixed on God, it gets purified and elevated alike in the end. This concept is dealt with elaborately in the Prologue to the tenth Skandha.

In these three births, these attendants of Vishnu, Jaya and Vijaya, were born as Hiranyakasipu and Hiranyaksha, Ravana and Kumbhakarna, and Sisupala and Dantavaktra respectively. While the story of the redemption of all these is taken up separately in the other Skandhas, the case of Hiranyakasipu is specially treated here by Suka. The discourse on this topic is in the form of a quotation of a conversation of Narada with Yudhishthira, who at the campus of his Rajasuya sacrifice, was surprised to see the inveterate traducers of Krishna like Sisupala and Dantavaktra joining the spiritual aura of Krishna on being killed by him in battle.

The story of Hiranyakasipu's confrontation with Vishnu is identical with the Prahlada saga. Prahlada, Hiranya's son, is well known as the greatest exemplar of divine love, wherever the Indian devotional tradition is remembered or studied. It is through Prahlada's mouth that the *Bhagavata* propounds its famous dictum of the ninefold Bhakti discipline—Sravanam, Kirtanam etc. (Bh. VII. 5.23-24). The story of Prahlada is told in all detail as the main theme of the 7th Skandha. Care is taken in the course of the narrative to illustrate the main theme, *ūti* or how holy association and works lead to transformation of character and spiritual upliftment. Prahlada is himself taken as an example. Being the scion of an Asura family his natural tendency should have been towards a life of violence and sensual indulgences. But his inclinations were all transformed when he was in his mother's womb and happened to hear the spiritual discourses that the sage Narada gave to his mother. By the great spiritual power of the sage, the tendencies of the foetus changed, and Prahlada from birth grew up as a devotee par excellence. How his open devotional attitude was a red rag to his father Hiranya; how he tried to reform Prahlada through instruction; how in spite of all that, the boy not only continued to be entrenched in his devotional mood but even began to preach the devotional philosophy to all Asura children; how Hiranya subjected him to horrible persecutions and ordered him to be executed but failed to cause him the least injury on account of the protection offered to him by Mahavishnu; how he therefore attempted to behead him himself; how in order to fulfil the devotee Prahlada's declaration, given in reply to Hiranya's challenge, that the Lord was everywhere including the neighbouring pillar, He emerged from that pillar as the Manlion (Narasimha) and destroyed Hiranyakasipu—all these are graphically described in several chapters. It is specially pointed out that in this and other cases destruction at the hands of the Lord is really redemption. It is not an act of revenge, but His way of bestowing His grace on one who practises the devotional path of communion through confrontation (Vidwesha Bhakti).

The narration of these events is followed by the great hymn that Prahlada addresses to the Lord. It is one of the longest and noblest of the Hymns in the *Bhagavata*. It gathers into itself all the thoughts and sentiments included in the philosophy of Bhakti and Jnana and integrates them into a thrilling and uplifting Bhakti lyric in the form of a praise. The high-water mark of it is reached when Prahlada addressing the Lord says that liberation is significant for him only if all his fellow-sufferers in Samsara are also liberated. He says: "O Lord! Sages generally concern themselves only with their own salvation. They strive for it in solitude, without any thought for the salvation of others. But I do not desire salvation for myself alone, abandoning all the other creatures to their miserable fate. I find no shelter other than Thee for these creatures caught in the travails of Samsara" (Bh. VII.9.44). The same note is struck in Ranti Deva's prayer (Bh.IX.21.12-13), showing how Vaishnava devotionalism rose to the same level of self-abnegating universal love as embodied in the Bodhisattva ideal of Buddhism.

In five chapters starting from the 11th, a brief description is given of the ideals of the social system according to the Varnas and Ashramas. It is maintained that the system is meant to help man to develop his highest spiritual possibilities. A few important features of it, as described in the *Bhagavata* may be noted.

1. Though the Brahmana is given the highest place in the social scale, it is given in view of the high character ideal he is to set and the important part he has to play in the welfare of the society. He was the custodian of the Veda—who mastered it and transmitted it to the next generation, who lived according to its ideals, and practised the forms of worship and rituals inculcated by it. It was the belief of the times that the performance of the Vedic rites was very necessary for the society to be in harmony with the Divine agencies, and through this harmony, to attain general well-being and prosperity. The Brahmana was the master of these Vedic rites. Hence the Brahmana was of supreme importance for the general social good.

2. The Brahmana's importance stems only from his character and piety, and not from wealth or power or position. He is never a rich man. His livelihood is to be had from teaching, officiating at sacrifices, gifts that come unasked, and from fallen grain collected from fields and grain markets. The last is considered the most superior livelihood for him. In times of invasions, revolutions, and general social unsettlement, when his usual livelihood is not available, he can do agriculture or practise some trade, but never should he go for the 'livelihood of a dog'—namely, service under mean people. When good times return, he should again depend only on his ordained livelihood.

3. While the hereditary principle is recognised in determining the Varna of persons, it is also maintained (cf.Bh.VII. 11.35) that if the qualities of a particular Varna are not seen in one born in it, his Varna is to be changed. We thus get many examples of Kshatriyas becoming Brahmanas. The most conspicuous examples noticed in the *Bhagavata* are the sons of emperor Bharata. Many of them became Brahmanas, and the famous Navayogis, who appear in the eleventh Skandha and give a most impressive exposition of the Bhagavata Dharma, came from among them. This liberalisation of the hereditary principle takes the wind away from the sail of criticism directed against the Varna system that it was devised to preserve the vested interests of some sections of the society.

4. Though at a certain period the hereditary factor became the main objective consideration in determining the Varna, it is basically founded on the dominance of one or the other of the qualities of Prakriti—Sattva, Rajas and Tamas. And that is why change of Varna is sanctioned when the characteristics of an individual do not tally with those of the Varna in which he is born. In the moral consequences of actions also, variations are recognised according to the dominance of one or the other of the Gunas. The actions that are in line with one's nature form one's Svadharma or natural duty, and this is determined by one's dominant qualities. Any defect inherent in one's Svadharma will not cause sin or downfall to an individual, but to a person at higher levels of spiritual evolution, it can be morally harmful. Thus a kind of moral relativity is recognised according to the state of man's spiritual evolution. Moral susceptibility and moral downfall are more at the higher levels of spiritual evolution, than at the lower. This is illustrated by the analogy that a fall is possible only to one who is standing and not to one lying low.

5. None the less virtues indicating a very high standard of moral excellences are listed as common to all Varnas. These are thirty in number and they are listed as follows: Truth, kindliness, austerity, purity, forbearance, discrimination, control of the mind, control of the senses, avoiding infliction of pain on others; continence; charity; study of scriptures; straightforwardness; contentment; service of holy men; gradual withdrawal from works and rituals with selfish motives; preparedness to face failure of plans and accept disappointment; avoidance of too much of speech; self-criticism; giving food to other living beings; seeing the Lord in all beings; special perception of Divinity in man; and practice of the highest way of devotional life adopted by great men consisting in hearing, hymning, remembrance, service, worship, salutation, dedication of all action, friendship and complete self-surrender (Bh.VII.11.8-12). If all these virtues are common to all the four Varnas, one would feel that they must all alike be at a very high stage of moral and spiritual evolution, and the grading of any Varna as more Tamasika and therefore lower, may appear meaningless. It may, however, be interpreted that though the virtues are common, in their application to people at different stages of evolution, there can be gradation in the rigour of the disciplines, just as in regard to a topic in science like electricity, lessons of varying grades can be given to persons according to their standard and mental equipment.

6. The *Bhagavata* as a rule teaches uncompromising renunciation. In some places like Prahlada's Hymn the life in the household is criticised and condemned. But here in this section a very balanced view is taken, and all Ashramas are given equal importance. Though the Ashrama of the Sannyasins is held up as the crown of human life, it is maintained (cf. VII. 15.67) that if a person lives according to the ideal set forth for a householder, Moksha can be attained even while continuing to live at home.

श्रीमद्भागवतम्

सप्तमः स्कन्धः अथ प्रथमोऽध्यायः

राजोवाच

समः प्रियः सुहृद् ब्रह्मन् भूतानां भगवान् स्वयम् । इन्द्रस्यार्थे कथं दैत्यानवधीद् विषमो यथा 1॥
न ह्यस्यार्थः सुरगणैः साक्षान्निःश्रेयसात्मनः । नैवासुरेभ्यो विद्वेषो नोद्वेगश्चागुणस्य हि ॥ 2॥
इति नः सुमहाभाग नारायणगुणान् प्रति । संशयः सुमहाञ्जातस्तद् भवांश्छेत्तुमर्हति 3॥

श्रीशुक उवाच

साधु पृष्टं महाराज हरेश्चरितमद्भुतम् । यद् भागवतमाहात्म्यं भगवद्भक्तिवर्धनम् 4॥
गीयते परमं पुण्यमृषिभिर्नारदादिभिः । नत्वा कृष्णाय मुनये कथयिष्ये हरेः कथाम् 5॥
निर्गुणोऽपि ह्यजोऽव्यक्तो भगवान् प्रकृतेः परः । स्वमायागुणमाविश्य बाध्यबाधकतां गतः 6॥
सत्त्वं रजस्तम इति प्रकृतेर्नात्मनो गुणाः । न तेषां युगपद् राजन् ह्रास उल्लास एव वा 7॥
जयकाले तु सत्त्वस्य देवर्षीन् रजसोऽसुरान् । तमसो यक्षरक्षांसि तत्कालानुगुणोऽभजत् ॥ 8॥

Skandha VII : Chapter 1

THE LORD AS FREE FROM PARTIALITY

The Lord favours none (1-11)

Rajah Parikshit said: **1.** O learned one! The Lord is the same to all; he is the dear one and the friend of all. Then why did He act like a partial person? Why did he kill the Asuras in order to favour Indra? **2.** For the Lord who is ever blissful, there is nothing that is to be achieved through Indra and the Devas. He who transcends the Gunas of Prakriti has nothing to fear from Asuras, and cannot in any way be inimical to them. Love and hatred are to be found only in those who identify themselves with products of Prakriti (root matter). How can these be in one who is above Gunas? **3.** O great one! A grave doubt of this kind regarding the nature of the Lord Narayana is disturbing our mind. Please be gracious enough to clear this doubt.

Sri Suka said: **4-5.** O King! You have put a very relevant question about the Lord's wonderful sport; for, in it is involved the greatness of His devotees too. After making obeisance to sage Vyasa, I shall narrate to you these deeds of the Lord which bring out the greatness of devotees like Prahlada, extolled by Narada and other sages, and having the power of enhancing devotion in its listeners. **6.** It is true that the Lord, who transcends the Gunas, is birthless, free from all passions and partialities common to all embodied beings. But He assumes His Yogamaya or power of manifestation, with which He manifests as the two opposing forces, the attacker and the attacked (the thesis and the antithesis). **7.** Sattva, Rajas and Tamas are the qualities of Prakriti and not of the Atman. (And Prakriti, though she be His power, cannot affect Him by her transformation, He being the omnipotent Spirit.) So the Atman is not affected by the modification of the Gunas of Prakriti, O King! The dominance and decline of these two forces do not take place simultaneously but one after the other as regulated by Time. **8.** When Sattva is dominant, He is found

ज्योतिरादिरिवाभाति सङ्घातान्न विविच्यते। विदन्त्यात्मानमात्मस्थं मथित्वा कवयोऽन्ततः ॥

यदा सिसृक्षुः पुर आत्मनः परो रजः सृजत्येष पृथक् स्वमायया।
सत्त्वं विचित्रासु रिरंसुरीश्वरः शयिष्यमाणस्तम ईरयत्यसौ ॥10॥
कालं चरन्तं सृजतीश आश्रयं प्रधानपुम्भ्यां नरदेव सत्यकृत्।
य एष राजन्नपि काल ईशिता सत्त्वं सुरानीकमिवैधयत्यतः।
तत्प्रत्यनीकानसुरान् सुरप्रियो रजस्तमस्कान् प्रमिणोत्युरुश्रवाः ॥11॥

अत्रैवोदाहृतः पूर्वमितिहासः सुरर्षिणा। प्रीत्या महाक्रतौ राजन् पृच्छतेऽजातशत्रवे 12॥
दृष्ट्वा महाद्भुतं राजा राजसूये महाक्रतौ। वासुदेवे भगवति सायुज्यं चेदिभूभुजः ॥13॥
तत्रासीनं सुरर्षिं राजा पाण्डुसुतः क्रतौ। पप्रच्छ विस्मितमना मुनीनां शृण्वतामिदम् 14॥

युधिष्ठिर उवाच

अहो अत्यद्भुतं ह्येतद् दुर्लभैकान्तिनामपि। वासुदेवे परे तत्त्वे प्राप्तिश्चैद्यस्य विद्विषः ॥15॥

to favour the Devas and the Rishis; when Rajas is dominant, He is seen on the side of the Asuras; and when it is the turn of Tamas, He is with Yakshas and Rakshasas. **9.** Though the Lord transcends Prakriti, He is reflected in the medium of the attributes of Prakriti like the sun reflected in water and the fire appearing in the fuel. But this reflection of the Spirit is seen only in identification with the medium of Prakriti, namely the body in which it reflects. He is not apprehended in His distinctiveness by ordinary people. But wise men by churning, as it were, their whole being with the churning rod of discrimination, discover the Atman residing within themselves. **10.** When the Supreme Being desires to create bodies in order that Jivas may enjoy the fruits of their actions, then he augments the Rajas aspect by His Yogamaya. When He wants to sustain the creation and delight through playful manifestations, then he augments the Sattva. And when he goes into His cosmic slumber, He favours the domination of Tamas. Thus He is the master of the Gunas, not they of Him. **11.** O King! The Lord who, by a mere assertion of His will, can bring into being everything, creates through the instrumentality of Prakriti and Purusha, giving them as their ally and support His manifestation called Time (characterised by the experience of the present moment). When the process of Time favours the expansion of Sattva, then Mahavishnu also seems to promote the progress of Sattva by allying Himself with the Sattva-dominated Devas and destroying their enemies, the Asuras, who are full of Rajas and Tamas.

The Salvation of Enemies of God (12-20)

12. In connection with this, there is a traditional narrative, which was given out by Sri Narada at the Rajasuya sacrifice of Yudhishthira when the latter questioned him for the clarification of a doubt. **13-14.** When Yudhishthira, at the great Rajasuya sacrifice, saw with astonishment how the totally undeserving Sisupala, the king of the Chedis, gained union with Krishna, he questioned the divine Rishi Narada seated there as follows, in the hearing of the assembled sages:

Yudhishthira said: **15.** It is a wonder to me to see how this Sisupala, an arch-enemy of the divine Krishna, attained union with Him, the Supreme Being, Vāsudeva—a fulfilment which is difficult to obtain even

एतद् वेदितुमिच्छामः सर्व एव वयं मुने। भगवन्निन्दया वेनो द्विजैस्तमसि पातितः ॥16॥
दमघोषसुतः पाप आरभ्य कलभाषणात्। सम्प्रत्यमर्षी गोविन्दे दन्तवक्त्रश्च दुर्मतिः 17॥
शपतोरसकृद् विष्णुं यद् ब्रह्म परमव्ययम्। श्वित्रो न जातो जिह्वायां नान्धं विविशतुस्तमः ॥
कथं तस्मिन् भगवति दुरवग्राहधामनि। पश्यतां सर्वलोकानां लयमीयतुरञ्जसा ॥19॥
एतद् भ्राम्यति मे बुद्धिर्दीपार्चिरिव वायुना। ब्रूह्येतदद्भुततमं भगवांस्तत्र कारणम् ॥20॥

श्रीशुक उवाच

राज्ञस्तद् वच आकर्ण्य नारदो भगवानृषिः। तुष्टः प्राह तमाभाष्य शृण्वत्यास्तत्सदः कथाः 21॥

नारद उवाच

निन्दनस्तवसत्कारन्यक्कारार्थं कलेवरम्। प्रधानपरयो राजन्नविवेकेन कल्पितम् ॥22॥
हिंसा तदभिमानेन दण्डपारुष्ययोर्यथा। वैषम्यमिह भूतानां ममाहमिति पार्थिव ॥23॥
यन्निबद्धोऽभिमानोऽयं तद्वधात् प्राणिनां वधः। तथा न यस्य कैवल्यादभिमानोऽखिलात्मनः।
परस्य दमकर्तुर्हि हिंसा केनास्य कल्प्यते ॥24॥
तस्माद् वैरानुबन्धेन निर्वैरेण भयेन वा। स्नेहात् कामेन वा युञ्ज्यात् कथञ्चिन्नेक्षते पृथक् ॥

for men of whole-hearted devotion. **16.** All of us are eager to hear the explanation of this: how Vena, who insulted the Lord, was consigned to purgatory, while Sisupala, a traducer of the Lord deserving hell, attained salvation. **17.** The sinful Sisupala, the son of Damaghosha, and this Dantavaktra had said nothing but in vilification of the Lord Govinda ever since they began to lisp as infants. **18.** Those tongues of theirs, which indulged even in cursing Mahavishnu, the immaculate Brahman—how were they spared from white leprosy? How were those traducers of the Most High spared from hell? **19.** On the other hand, even while all were looking on, they got united with the Lord's Being—a consummation that is difficult for one to achieve. **20.** This is an intriguing doubt which puzzles me and agitates my mind as wind flickers a flame of light. Please explain the rationale of it.

Turning of Passions Godward (21-32)

Sri Suka said: **21.** Listening to those words of Yudhishthira, the worshipful Rishi Narada was very much pleased, and he said addressing him in the hearing of all assembled there.

Sri Narada said: **22.** The embodied state, which is the consequence of the inability to distinguish between Purusha and Prakriti (spirit and matter), is meant for the experience of such contrary conditions as insult and praise, welcome and rejection. **23-24.** O King! Living beings feel injured when subjected to physical sufferings or insults. They also feel killed when threatened with physical death. This is due to their identification with the physical body—the feeling that 'I am this body'. But the Supreme who is the one without a second, who transcends Prakriti and is the soul and controller of everything, can have no particular identification with anything or attachment to anybody. How then can cruelty and violence be attributed to Him when he chastises persons for disciplining them? **25.** Therefore what is important is that the mind is constantly fixed on Him—it does not matter whether it is due to antagonism or friendliness, fear or love, lust or any other passion. Through any of these one should cease to be aware of anything but

यथा वैरानुबन्धेन मर्त्यस्तन्मयतामियात् । न तथा भक्तियोगेन इति मे निश्चिता मतिः ॥26॥
कीटः पेशस्कृता रुद्धः कुड्यायां तमनुस्मरन् । संरम्भभययोगेन विन्दते तत्स्वरूपताम् ॥27॥
एवं कृष्णे भगवति मायामनुज ईश्वरे । वैरेण पूतपाप्मानस्तमापुरनुचिन्तया ॥28॥
कामाद् द्वेषाद् भयात् स्नेहाद् यथा भक्त्येश्वरे मनः । आवेश्य तदघं हित्वा बहवस्तद्गतिं गताः ॥29॥
गोप्यः कामाद् भयात् कंसो द्वेषाच्चैद्यादयो नृपाः । सम्बन्धाद् वृष्णयः स्नेहाद् यूयं भक्त्या वयं विभो ॥
कतमोऽपि न वेनः स्यात् पञ्चानां पुरुषं प्रति । तस्मात् केनाप्युपायेन मनः कृष्णे निवेशयेत् 31॥
मातृष्वस्रेयो वश्चैद्यो दन्तवक्त्रश्च पाण्डव । पार्षदप्रवरौ विष्णोर्विप्रशापात् पदाच्च्युतौ 32॥

युधिष्ठिर उवाच

कीदृशः कस्य वा शापो हरिदासाभिमर्शनः । अश्रद्धेय इवाभाति हरेरेकान्तिनां भवः ॥33॥
देहेन्द्रियासुहीनानां वैकुण्ठपुरवासिनाम् । देहसम्बन्धसम्बद्धमेतदाख्यातुमर्हसि ॥34॥

नारद उवाच

एकदा ब्रह्मणः पुत्रा विष्णोर्लोकं यदृच्छया । सनन्दनादयो जग्मुश्चरन्तो भुवनत्रयम् ॥35॥

Him. **26.** It is my view that through the ordinary communion of love, the mind does not get identified with Him to the extent that it does through constant antagonism. **27.** The worm confined to the mould on the wall by the wasp, and constantly made to think of it in anger and fear, becomes converted into the shape of the wasp itself. **28.** In the same way, their antagonism made persons like Sisupala constantly think of Krishna the Supreme Being who had assumed the shape of man through Maya. By such constant thought their minds were purified and they attained to Him. **29.** Being cleansed of all their impurities by fixing their minds on the Supreme Lord through lust, anger, fear, affection or Bhakti (devotion properly so called), many have attained to His being. **30.** The Gopis through lust, Kamsa through fear, Sisupala and other kings through hatred, the Vrishnis and other allies through kinship, you (Pandavas) through affection, and we (sages) through Bhakti—these, O great King, are examples of the above-mentioned doctrine. **31.** The example of Vena you mentioned does not come within the five forms of relationship possible for men as mentioned above. (His was the indifference of a sceptic and his mind was in no way fixed on the Lord.) **32.** O son of Pandu! This Sisupala and Dantavaktra, the sons of your mother's sisters, were originally the attendants of Mahavishnu in Vaikuntha, who happened to fall from their exalted place by the curse of sages.

Antecedents of Hiranya (33-47)

Yudhishthira said: **33.** Who gave this curse, and of what nature was it, that it should affect even the servants of Sri Hari? It is unbelievable that such devotees with whole-hearted devotion to Him can ever get involved in the transmigratory cycle. **34.** The residents of Vaikuntha have no material body, senses or Pranas. How then would they get embodiment? This requires explanation.

Narada said: **35.** Once the great sages Sanaka, Sanandana, Sanātana, and Sanatkumāra, the sons of Brahma, in the course of their peregrinations through all the spheres of the universe, happened to go to Vaikuntha, the divine realm of Maha-

पञ्चषड्ढायनार्भाभाः पूर्वेषामपि पूर्वजाः । दिग्वाससः शिशून् मत्वा द्वाःस्थौ तान् प्रत्यषेधताम्
अशपन् कुपिता एवं युवां वासं न चार्हथः । रजस्तमोभ्यां रहिते पादमूले मधुद्विषः ।
पापिष्ठामासुरीं योनिं बालिशौ यातमाश्वतः ॥37॥
एवं शप्तौ स्वभवनात् पतन्तौ तैः कृपालुभिः । प्रोक्तौ पुनर्जन्मभिर्वां त्रिभिर्लोकाय कल्पताम् 38॥
जज्ञाते तौ दितेः पुत्रौ दैत्यदानववन्दितौ । हिरण्यकशिपुर्ज्येष्ठो हिरण्याक्षोऽनुजस्ततः ॥39॥
हतो हिरण्यकशिपुर्हरिणा सिंहरूपिणा । हिरण्याक्षो धरोद्धारे बिभ्रता सौकरं वपुः ॥40॥
हिरण्यकशिपुः पुत्रं प्रह्लादं केशवप्रियम् । जिघांसुरकरोन्नाना यातना मृत्युहेतवे ॥41॥
सर्वभूतात्मभूतं तं प्रशान्तं समदर्शनम् । भगवत्तेजसा स्पृष्टं नाशक्नोद्धन्तुमुद्यमैः ॥42॥
ततस्तौ राक्षसौ जातौ केशिन्यां विश्रवःसुतौ । रावणः कुम्भकर्णश्च सर्वलोकोपतापनौ ॥43॥
तत्रापि राघवो भूत्वा न्यहनच्छापमुक्तये । रामवीर्यं श्रोष्यसि त्वं मार्कण्डेयमुखात् प्रभो 44॥
तावेव क्षत्रियौ जातौ मातृष्वस्रात्मजौ तव । अधुना शापनिर्मुक्तौ कृष्णचक्रहतांहसौ ॥45॥
वैरानुबन्धतीव्रेण ध्यानेनाच्युतसात्मताम् । नीतौ पुनर्हरेः पार्श्वं जग्मतुर्विष्णुपार्षदौ ॥46॥

vishnu. **36.** These sages, more ancient than the most ancient, looked like children five or six years old. They were sky-clad—absolutely nude. The gate-keepers of Vaikuntha did not let them in, taking them to be mere infants. **37.** Angry at this, the sages cursed them saying: 'You do not deserve to stay in this realm of Mahavishnu which is of pure Sattva, devoid of the touch of Rajas and Tamas. So you two will soon have a downfall and will be born in the species of Asuras.' **38.** But feeling pity on these attendants faced with degradation from that exalted place, the sages also gave them a blessing that they would be fit to come back to their original state, after three births in lower regions. **39.** They both were born as Asuras in the womb of Diti, the mother of the Asuras. The elder one was known as Hiranyakasipu and the younger as Hiranyāksha. They commanded great respect among all grades of Asuras. **40.** Hiranyakasipu was killed by the Lord, taking the form of the Man-lion, and Hiranyāksha, when He incarnated Himself as the Cosmic Boar to lift up the earth. **41.** Hiranyakasipu perpetrated many atrocities to kill his own son Prahlāda, who happened to be a great devotee of the Supreme Being. **42.** But he was not able by all his efforts to kill Prahlāda, who was established in the perception of Brahman in everything, who had become one with the soul of all beings, who was full of peace, and who was permeated by the power of the Lord. **43.** In their next birth they were born in the species of the Rakshasas as the sons of Visravas by Kesini, under the names of Ravana and Kumbhakarna, and became the terror of the worlds. **44.** Born as Rama in the line of Raghu, the Lord destroyed them for effecting their release from the curse. O King! You will hear about the prowess of Rama from the sage Mārkandeya. **45.** These same two have now been born among Kshatriyas as the sons of your mother's sisters under the names of Sisupāla and Dantavaktra. Meeting death with Krishna's discus they have been purified and freed from the effect of the curse. **46.** Concentrating their minds with great intensity on the Lord in the form of inveterate hatred of Him, they have got dissolved in Achyuta and regained their

युधिष्ठिर उवाच

विद्वेषो दयिते पुत्रे कथमासीन्महात्मनि । ब्रूहि मे भगवन् येन प्रह्लादस्याच्युतात्मता ॥47॥

इति श्रीमद्भागवते महापुराणे पारमहंस्यां संहितायां सप्तमस्कन्धे प्रह्लादचरितोपक्रमे प्रथमोऽध्यायः ॥1॥

place by Sri Hari's side as his attendants.

Yudhishthira said: **47.** O learned sage! It behoves you to tell me how Hiranyakasipu happened to entertain such intense antagonism to his dear son of great excellence, and how he, Prahlāda, came to have deep-rooted devotion to the Lord.

अथ द्वितीयोऽध्यायः

नारद उवाच

भ्रातर्येवं विनिहते हरिणा क्रोडमूर्तिना । हिरण्यकशिपू राजन् पर्यतप्यद् रुषा शुचा ॥ 1॥
आह चेदं रुषा घूर्णः सन्दष्टदशनच्छदः । कोपोज्ज्वलद्भ्यां चक्षुर्भ्यां निरीक्षन् धूम्रमम्बरम्
करालदंष्ट्रोग्रदृष्टचा दुष्प्रेक्ष्यभ्रुकुटीमुखः । शूलमुद्यम्य सदसि दानवानिदमब्रवीत् ॥ 3॥
भो भो दानवदैतेया द्विमूर्धंस्त्र्यक्ष शम्बर । शतबाहो हयग्रीव नमुचे पाक इल्वल ॥ 4॥
विप्रचित्ते मम वचः पुलोमन् शकुनादयः । शृणुतानन्तरं सर्वे क्रियतामाशु मा चिरम् ॥ 5॥
सपत्नैर्घातितः क्षुद्रैर्भ्राता मे दयितः सुहृत् । पार्ष्णिग्राहेण हरिणा समेनाप्युपधावनैः ॥ 6॥
तस्य त्यक्तस्वभावस्य घृणेर्मायावनौकसः । भजन्तं भजमानस्य बालस्येवास्थिरात्मनः ॥ 7॥
मच्छूलभिन्नग्रीवस्य भूरिणा रुधिरेण वै । रुधिरप्रियं तर्पयिष्ये भ्रातरं मे गतव्यथः ॥ 8॥

Skandha VII : Chapter 2
CONSOLATION OF DITI

Hiranyakasipu's Ire (1-16)

Narada said: **1**. O King! When his brother Hiranyāksha was destroyed by the Lord in His incarnation as the Cosmic Boar, Hiranyakasipu became agitated by both anger and sorrow. **2-3**. Trembling with anger, biting his lips, looking at the smoky sky with his eyes glittering with anger and his face too terrific to look at owing to its quivering brows, fierce eyes, and awe-inspiring fangs, Hiranyakasipu with his trident held aloft, said as follows, addressing the Danavas:

Hiranyakasipu said: **4-5**. O Dvimūrdhā! O Tryaksha! O Sambara! O Satabāhu! O Hayagrīva! O Namuchi! O Pāka! O Ilāvala! O Viprachitti! O Puloma! O Sakuni! Hear ye all with attention, O Daityas and Danavas, to what I say, and act upon it without delay. **6.** My unworthy enemies, the Devas, have brought about the slaughter of my dear and loving brother, with the help of Hari, who though in Himself impartial, has been placated and won over by these Devas by their prayers and offerings. **7-8**. Though he is called the Lord of all, he has like a fickle-minded child abandoned that status by taking sides and favouring those who flatter him. Besides, abandoning his naturally luminous nature, he has come to masquerade himself as an animal, a wild boar, following some crooked magical device. My sorrow will

तस्मिन् कूटेऽहिते नष्टे कृत्तमूले वनस्पतौ । विटपा इव शुष्यन्ति विष्णुप्राणा दिवौकसः 9॥
तावद् यात भुवं यूयं विप्रक्षत्रसमेधिताम् । सूदयध्वं तपोयज्ञस्वाध्यायव्रतदानिनः ॥10॥
विष्णुर्द्विजक्रियामूलो यज्ञो धर्ममयः पुमान् । देवर्षिपितृभूतानां धर्मस्य च परायणम् ॥11॥
यत्र यत्र द्विजा गावो वेदा वर्णाश्रमाः क्रियाः । तं तं जनपदं यात सन्दीपयत वृश्चत ॥12॥
इति ते भर्तृनिर्देशमादाय शिरसाऽऽदृताः । तथा प्रजानां कदनं विदधुः कदनप्रियाः ॥13॥
पुरग्रामव्रजोद्यानक्षेत्रारामाश्रमाकरान् । खेटखर्वटघोषांश्च ददहुः पत्तनानि च ॥14॥
केचित् खनित्रैर्बिभिदुः सेतुप्राकारगोपुरान् । आजीव्यांश्चिच्छिदुर्वृक्षान् केचित् परशुपाणयः ।
प्रादहन् शरणान्यन्ये प्रजानां ज्वलितोल्मुकैः ॥15॥
एवं विप्रकृते लोके दैत्येन्द्रानुचरैर्मुहुः । दिवं देवाः परित्यज्य भुवि चेरुरलक्षिताः ॥16॥
हिरण्यकशिपुर्भ्रातुः सम्परेतस्य दुःखितः । कृत्वा कटोदकादीनि भ्रातृपुत्रानसान्त्वयत् 17॥
शकुनिं शम्बरं धृष्टं भूतसन्तापनं वृकम् । कालनाभं महानाभं हरिश्मश्रुमथोत्कचम् 18॥
तन्मातरं रुषाभानुं दितिं च जननीं गिरा । श्लक्ष्णया देशकालज्ञ इदमाह जनेश्वर ॥19॥

not abate until I have offered my dead blood-thirsty brother libations with the abundant blood of this Hari's neck pierced with my trident. **9.** When this Hari, whose trade is deceit, is destroyed, the Devas, whose life-breath is constituted of Him, Vishnu, will also perish, like trees whose roots have been cut. **10.** You, Asuras, now go to the earth, whose prosperity depends on the proper functioning of the Brahmanas and Kshatriyas. You go and kill all of them and those who perform austerity, sacrifices, vows, Vedic studies, chanting, charities etc. **11.** Vishnu has his roots and his sustenance in the rites and rituals performed by the Brahmanas. His form is Dharma (Vedic ritualism). He is the institution of sacrifice (Yajna) itself. He is the refuge of the celestials, the seers, the manes and other living beings, and the final goal of the righteous. **12.** Wherever Brahmanas perform sacrifices, wherever there are cows, wherever the laws of Varnāshramas are observed—go to such villages and towns, set fire to everything you see, and cut down all trees and destroy all vegetation.

13. Accepting these directives of their master, these Asuras, who were always fond of oppressing others, began to harry people with their depredations. **14.** They started on a campaign of incendiarism, setting fire to towns, villages, and cowherd settlements; to flower gardens, cultivated lands, orchards, parks, and settlements of Rishis; to mines, hamlets of farmers, cowherds and forest tribes, and even palaces. **15.** With pick and spade they demolished the bunds of irrigation tanks, wells and city gates. Some cut down fruit-bearing trees forming the livelihood of people. Others set on fire with flaming torches buildings inhabited by men. **16.** Distressed repeatedly by these minions of the king of Daityas, the Devas abandoned their heavenly homes and wandered incognito on earth among men.

Consolation of Diti (17-26)

17. Hiranyakasipu, who was grief-stricken by his brother's bereavement, performed the obsequies for the dead, and comforted his nephews. **18-19.** To his dead brother's sons, Sakuni, Sambara, Dhrishta, Bhūtasantāpana, Vrika, Kālanābha, Mahānābha, Harismasru and Utkacha, and to their mother Rushābhānu and his own mother Diti, the Asura king Hiranyakasipu, who was a master of the art

हिरण्यकशिपुरुवाच

अम्बाम्ब हे वधूः पुत्रा वीरं मार्हथ शोचितुम् । रिपोरभिमुखे श्लाघ्यः शूराणां वध ईप्सितः 20॥
भूतानामिह संवासः प्रपायामिव सुव्रते । दैवेनैकत्र नीतानामुन्नीतानां स्वकर्मभिः ॥21॥
नित्य आत्माव्ययः शुद्धः सर्वगः सर्ववित्परः । धत्तेऽसावात्मनो लिङ्गं मायया विसृजन् गुणान् ॥
यथाम्भसा प्रचलता तरवोऽपि चला इव । चक्षुषा भ्राम्यमाणेन दृश्यते चलतीव भूः ॥23॥
एवं गुणैर्भ्राम्यमाणे मनस्यविकलः पुमान् । याति तत्साम्यतां भद्रे ह्यलिङ्गो लिङ्गवानिव 24॥
एष आत्मविपर्यासो ह्यलिङ्गे लिङ्गभावना । एष प्रियाप्रियैर्योगो वियोगः कर्मसंसृतिः ॥25॥
सम्भवश्च विनाशश्च शोकश्च विविधः स्मृतः । अविवेकश्च चिन्ता च विवेकास्मृतिरेव च ॥26॥
अत्राप्युदाहरन्तीममितिहासं पुरातनम् । यमस्य प्रेतबन्धूनां संवादं तं निबोधत ॥27॥
उशीनरेष्वभूद् राजा सुयज्ञ इति विश्रुतः । सपत्नैर्निहतो युद्धे ज्ञातयस्तमुपासत ॥28॥
विशीर्णरत्नकवचं विभ्रष्टाभरणस्रजम् । शरनिर्भिन्नहृदयं शयानमसृगाविलम् ॥29॥
प्रकीर्णकेशं ध्वस्ताक्षं रभसा दष्टदच्छदम् । रजःकुण्ठमुखाम्भोजं छिन्नायुधभुजं मृधे ॥30॥
उशीनरेन्द्रं विधिना तथा कृतं पतिं महिष्यः प्रसमीक्ष्य दुःखिताः ।
हताः स्म नाथेति करैरुरो भृशं घ्नन्त्यो मुहुस्तत्पदयोरुपापतन् ॥31॥

Hiranyakasipu said: **20.** O mother! O sister! O children! For heroic men, death in combat with an enemy is both fame-enhancing and self-satisfying. Sorrow not for the departed hero. **21.** The life of living beings in this world, brought together by Providence through their Karma, is like those of people gathering in, and dispersing from, a caravanserai. **22.** The Atman is eternal; he is changeless; he is pure, all-pervading and all-knowing. Through the power of Maya (ignorance), he projects bodies, and first comes to have the subtle body. **23.** In the extremely tremulous water surface, even trees seem to be moving; when the vision gets distorted, even the earth seems to whirl. **24.** In this way, when the Gunas of Prakriti create disturbances in the mind, the Purusha, who is in Himself perfect, gets identified with that mind and its movements, and then the Purusha, though he is really bodiless, appears to be one possessed of a body. **25.** This attribution of body for the bodiless Atman is a misapprehension. Because of this misapprehension, there is attachment to dear objects and revulsion to unfriendly ones; there is also the bondage of Karma and involvement in Samsara. **26.** It is again because of this misapprehension that there is birth and death, sorrows of various kind, the inability to distinguish the Atman from the body, obsession with wordly objects, and lapse of discrimination.

Story of Suyajna of Usīnara (27-34)

27. Hear an ancient legend in illustration of this in the form of a conversation between Yama and the relatives of a dead man. **28.** In the kingdom of Usīnara, there was a famous king called Suyajna. He was killed in battle by enemies. Many of his relatives came and gathered round his dead body. **29-30.** His body was lying in the battle-field, his jewel-studded armour shattered to pieces, his heart pierced through with an arrow, his ornaments and garlands all disarrayed, his hair dishevelled, his teeth pressing on the lower lip in anger, his eyes mutilated, his face covered with dust, and his arms holding weapons severed. **31.** Seeing the

रुदत्य उच्चैर्दयिताङ्‌घ्रिपङ्कजं सिञ्चन्त्य अस्रैः कुचकुङ्कुमारुणैः ।
विस्रस्तकेशाभरणाः शुचं नृणां सृजन्त्य आक्रन्दनया विलेपिरे ॥32॥
अहो विधात्राकरुणेन नः प्रभो भवान् प्रणीतो दृगगोचरां दशाम् ।
उशीनराणामसि वृत्तिदः पुरा कृतोऽधुना येन शुचां विवर्धनः ॥33॥
त्वया कृतज्ञेन वयं महीपते कथं विना स्याम सुहृत्तमेन ते ।
तत्रानुयानं तव बीर पादयोः शुश्रूषतीनां दिश यत्र यास्यसि ॥34॥
एवं विलपतीनां वै परिगृह्य मृतं पतिम् । अनिच्छतीनां निर्हारमर्कोऽस्तं संन्यवर्तत ॥35॥
तत्र ह प्रेतबन्धूनामाश्रुत्य परिदेवितम् । आह तान् बालको भूत्वा यमः स्वयमुपागतः 36॥

यम उवाच

अहो अमीषां वयसाधिकानां विपश्यतां लोकविधिं विमोहः ।
यत्रागतस्तत्र गतं मनुष्यं स्वयं सधर्मा अपि शोचन्त्यपार्थम् ॥37॥
अहो वयं धन्यतमा यदत्र त्यक्ताः पितृभ्यां न विचिन्तयामः ।
अभक्ष्यमाणा अबला वृकादिभिः स रक्षिता रक्षति यो हि गर्भे ॥38॥
य इच्छयेशः सृजतीदमव्ययो य एव रक्षत्यवलुम्पते च यः ।
तस्याबलाः क्रीडनमाहुरीशितुश्चराचरं निग्रहसंग्रहे प्रभुः ॥39॥

king of Usīnara brought to this plight by a cruel Providence, his sorrow-stricken wives came and fell at his feet, beating their breast and crying aloud, 'Alas! We are undone!' **32.** Weeping profusely, they washed the feet of their husband with their tears turned crimson by the saffron powder on their breasts. With their hair and ornaments in disarray, they wept and wailed aloud, stirring pity in the minds of men. **33.** They said: 'O lord of our lives! The merciless Brahma, the ordainer of the destiny of all, has chosen to take you away from our sight. You, who were till now the bestower of their livelihood to the people of Usīnara, have now become the giver of sorrow to them. **34.** O King! How can we live without you, who were the best of our well-wishers, and who appreciated our service with gratitude? O hero! Permit us to go with you, wherever you are, to be by your side as your servitors.'

Yama advises the sorrowing Women (35-49)

35. Holding their husband and mourning in this strain, they continued to sit there till it was sunset, without allowing the body to be cremated. **36.** Yama, the god of death, hearing the laments of these wives of the dead king, now appeared on the scene in the form of a boy and said as follows:

Yama said: **37.** Oh! how wonderful is the ignorance of these people! They are so much elder to me in years, and therefore must be well acquainted with the way of human life in this world. Futile is this mourning for those who have but returned to the unknown wherefrom they came, by others whose destination also will be the same very soon. **38.** We for our part are more blessed in this respect. For though we have been discarded by our parents, we are not in the least worried over it. Weak though we are, we have not been eaten by wolves. For, He who protects us in the mother's womb, is always there as our protector.

39. The Supreme Lord, the indestructible and unchanging Being, by His mere

पथि च्युतं तिष्ठति दिष्टरक्षितं गृहे स्थितं तद्विहतं विनश्यति ।
जीवत्यनाथोऽपि तदीक्षितो वने गृहेऽपि गुप्तोऽस्य हतो न जीवति ॥40॥
भूतानि तैस्तैर्निजयोनिकर्मभिर्भवन्ति काले न भवन्ति सर्वशः ।
न तत्र ह्यात्मा प्रकृतावपि स्थितस्तस्या गुणैरन्यतमो निबध्यते ॥41॥
इदं शरीरं पुरुषस्य मोहजं यथा पृथग् भौतिकमीयते गृहम् ।
यथौदकैः पार्थिवतैजसैर्जनः कालेन जातो विकृतो विनश्यति ॥42॥
यथानलो दारुषु भिन्न ईयते यथानिलो देहगतः पृथक् स्थितः ।
यथा नभः सर्वगतं न सज्जते तथा पुमान् सर्वगुणाश्रयः परः ॥43॥

सुयज्ञो नन्वयं शेते मूढा यमनुशोचथ । यः श्रोता योऽनुवक्तेह स न दृश्येत कर्हिचित् 44॥
न श्रोता नानुवक्तायं मुख्योऽप्यत्र महानसुः । यस्त्विहेन्द्रियवानात्मा स चान्यः प्राणदेहयोः 45॥
भूतेन्द्रियमनोलिङ्गान् देहानुच्चावचान् विभुः । भजत्युत्सृजति ह्यन्यस्तच्चापि स्वेन तेजसा ॥46॥
यावल्लिङ्गान्वितो ह्यात्मा तावत् कर्मनिबन्धनम् ततो विपर्ययः क्लेशो मायायोगोऽनुवर्तते ॥47॥

will creates, sustains and dissolves this universe. O ladies! This whole world with all its moving and unmoving beings provides only a sport for the Lord. He is the master of protection and destruction. **40.** Things fallen on the wayside are sometimes recovered intact if He favours it. Things preserved in the house are lost if the divine will is not favourable. Protected by Him one can live safely in the forest. And even well-protected in a home, man will only perish if that is His will. **41.** Guided by their Karma remaining latent in the Linga-sarira (subtle body), all Jivas get embodiment, and they perish too in course of time. In every birth, though the bodies partake of the nature of the species in which they are born, the spirit remains separate and unaffected by the bodily qualities. **42.** Just as a house one lives in is separate from oneself, so is the body of the Jiva which is born out of superimposition caused by ignorance, separate from the Jiva, it being an object of perception to him like a house. Just as bubbles, pots and ornaments formed of water, earth and gold respectively perish and dissolve into their elements, so will this body undergo dissolution into its elements. **43.** Just as fire in fuel, air in the body, and the all-pervading sky in objects remain distinct from the fields of their manifestation, so is the Atman distinct from all the vestments of Nature like the body, with which he is found associated.

44. O foolish women! This Suyajna, for whom you are mourning, lies here before you beyond the shadow of a doubt. When he heard you and replied, you saw this body alone doing it and not the real 'he' behind it. That body is still here before you. **45.** If you identify the principle Prana functioning in this body as the one who hears and replies, it is wrong, because the Prana and the Indiryas are as much unconscious entities as the body itself. It is the Spirit, the Atman, associating with the Indriyas, Prana, body etc., that makes them conscious entities, and he is distinct from them. **46.** The Spirit assumes high and low bodies formed of elements, senses, mind etc., and he throws them away also by the exercise of the superior power of discrimination. **47.** Only so long as the Atman is in association with the Linga-sarira (the subtle body), will he have the sufferings and the veiling by ignorance.

वितथाभिनिवेशोऽयं यद्गुणेष्वर्थदृग्वचः । यथा मनोरथः स्वप्नः सर्वमैन्द्रियकं मृषा ।।48।।
अथ नित्यमनित्यं वा नेह शोचन्ति तद्विदः । नान्यथा शक्यते कर्तुं स्वभावः शोचतामिति 49।।
लुब्धको विपिने कश्चित् पक्षिणां निर्मितोऽन्तकः । वितत्य जालं विदधे तत्र तत्र प्रलोभयन् ।।50।।
कुलिङ्गमिथुनं तत्र विचरत् समदृश्यत । तयोः कुलिङ्गी सहसा लुब्धकेन प्रलोभिता 51।।
सासज्जत शिचस्तन्त्यां महिषी कालयन्त्रिता । कुलिङ्गस्तां तथाऽऽपन्नां निरीक्ष्य भृशदुःखितः ।
स्नेहादकल्पः कृपणः कृपणां पर्यदेवयत् ।।52।।
अहो अकरुणो देवः स्त्रियाऽऽकरुणया विभुः । कृपणं मानुशोचन्त्या दीनया किं करिष्यति 53।।
कामं नयतु मां देवः किमर्धेनात्मनो हि मे । दीनेन जीवता दुःखमनेन विधुरायुषा ।।54।।
कथं त्वजातपक्षांस्तान् मातृहीनान् बिभर्म्यहम् । मन्दभाग्याः प्रतीक्षन्ते नीडे मे मातरं प्रजाः 55।।
एवं कुलिङ्गं विलपन्तमारात् प्रियावियोगातुरमश्रुकण्ठम् ।
स एव तं शाकुनिकः शरेण विव्याध कालप्रहितो विलीनः ।।56।।
एवं यूयमपश्यन्त्य आत्मापायमबुद्धयः । नैनं प्राप्स्यथ शोचन्त्यः पतिं वर्षशतैरपि ।।57।।

हिरण्यकशिपुरुवाच

बाल एवं प्रवदति सर्वे विस्मितचेतसः । ज्ञातयो मेनिरे सर्वमनित्यमयथोत्थितम् ।।58।।

48. The acceptance of the reality of the experience of joy and sorrow as well as of the sense objects that cause them, is as false a mental aberration as accepting the reality of castles in the air and dream experiences. Anything that is experienced as a sense object is false. **49.** So those who know the truth about what is permanent and what is impermanent never grieve for the eternal Self, or for the impermanent body! For, the nature of things cannot be changed by grief.

Story of the Kulinga Birds (50-61)

50. A hunter, a born killer of birds, once spread his net in the forest and caught several birds enticing them with baits. **51.** A couple of birds of the Kulinga species were moving about that place. The hunter was able to entice the female of that bird-couple. **52.** As ill luck would have it, the female was entangled in the meshes of the net. Seeing his helpmate sorrowing in that tragic situation, and himself helpless to come to her rescue, the male bird, out of love for the other, felt extremely afflicted and began to lament pitiably as follows: **53.** 'Alas! Providence is too cruel! What will he, who holds the destiny of all in his hands, get by depriving the life of a poor and pitiable female bird that is lamenting for me! **54.** Let the god of death take me away too. For why should I live on, deprived of my wife for the rest of my life and sorrowing for her with half of my body cut away, as it were, from me? **55.** How will I bring up my unfledged young ones, motherless as they are? Those hapless chicks of mine will be awaiting the arrival of their mother in the nests!' **56.** As the Kulinga male bird was thus bemoaning the separation from his wife, the hiding hunter, prompted by the spirit of time, shot an arrow from a distance and killed it. **57.** So without any awareness of your own end you are foolishly mourning over your dead husband. Even if you do so for a hundred years, it shall all be in vain.

Hiranyakasipu continued: **58.** When they heard the boy speaking like this, the king's relatives were astonished, and the awareness that everything in this world is fleeting and therefore unreal, dawned

यम एतदुपाख्याय तत्रैवान्तरधीयत। ज्ञातयोऽपि सुयज्ञस्य चक्रुर्यत् साम्परायिकम् 59॥
ततः शोचत मा यूयं परं चात्मानमेव च। क आत्मा कः परो वात्र स्वीयः पारक्य एव वा।
स्वपराभिनिवेशेन विनाज्ञानेन देहिनाम् ॥60॥

नारद उवाच

इति दैत्यपतेर्वाक्यं दितिराकर्ण्य सस्नुषा। पुत्रशोकं क्षणात् त्यक्त्वा तत्त्वे चित्तमधारयत् ॥

इति श्रीमद्भागवते महापुराणे पारमहंस्यां संहितायां सप्तमस्कन्धे दितिशोकापनयनं नाम द्वितीयोऽध्यायः ॥2॥

on their minds. **59.** After instructing them like this, Yama disappeared from sight. The relatives of King Suyajna then performed his funeral and the obsequies connected with it. **60.** Therefore you should entertain no sorrow about yourself and others. Apart from the ignorance-born sense of distinction made by creatures between self and others, who in reality is the self and who, the other—who is really *one's own,* and who, *of the others?*

Narada said: **61.** Hearing these words of the Daitya king Hiranyakasipu, Diti along with her daughter-in-law gave up grief for her dead son, and fixed her mind on spiritual verities.

अथ तृतीयोऽध्यायः

नारद उवाच

हिरण्यकशिपू राजन्नजेयमजरामरम्। आत्मानमप्रतिद्वन्द्वमेकराजं व्यधित्सत ॥ 1॥
स तेपे मन्दरद्रोण्यां तपः परमदारुणम्। ऊर्ध्वबाहुर्नभोदृष्टिः पादाङ्गुष्ठाश्रितावनिः 2॥
जटादीधितिभी रेजे संवर्तार्क इवांशुभिः। तस्मिंस्तपस्तप्यमाने देवाः स्थानानि भेजिरे 3॥
तस्य मूर्ध्नः समुद्भूतः सधूमोऽग्निस्तपोमयः। तिर्यगूर्ध्वमधोलोकानतपद्विष्वगीरितः ॥ 4॥
चुक्षुभुर्नद्युदन्वन्तः सद्वीपाद्रिश्चचाल भूः। निपेतुः सग्रहास्तारा जज्वलुश्च दिशो दश ॥ 5॥

Skandha VII : Chapter 3

FIERCE TAPAS OF HIRANYAKASIPU

Representation to Brahma (1-16)

Narada said: **1.** O King! Hiranyakasipu desired to make himself invincible, deathless and unaging, and the unchallenged sovereign over all the worlds. **2-3.** For this he performed the most terrible forms of austerity in the valley of the Mandara mountain. Holding his hands up, and with gaze fixed on the sky, he stood on his toes. The matted hair on the crown of his head sent forth gleams of light which made him look like the sun at the time of cosmic dissolution. While he was performing Tapas, the Devas, who had been expelled, used the chance to go back to their heavenly abodes. **4.** From his head emerged the fire of Tapas along with smoke which, spreading up, down, across and round about, burnt the worlds. **5.** The rivers and the oceans swelled up and became turbulent. The earth with its mountains and continents experienced tremors. Planets and stars seemed to fall down. All the ten directions seemed to be aglow with fire.

तेन तप्ता दिवं त्यक्त्वा ब्रह्मलोकं ययुः सुराः । धात्रे विज्ञापयामासुर्देवदेव जगत्पते ॥ 6॥
दैत्येन्द्रतपसा तप्ता दिवि स्थातुं न शक्नुमः । तस्य चोपशमं भूमन् विधेहि यदि मन्यसे ।
लोका न यावन्नङ्क्ष्यन्ति बलिहारास्तवाभिभूः ॥ 7॥
तस्यायं किल संकल्पश्चरतो दुश्चरं तपः । श्रूयतां किं न विदितस्तवाथापि निवेदितः ॥ 8॥
सृष्ट्वा चराचरमिदं तपोयोगसमाधिना । अध्यास्ते सर्वधिष्ण्येभ्यः परमेष्ठी निजासनम् 9॥
तदहं वर्धमानेन तपोयोगसमाधिना । कालात्मनोश्च नित्यत्वात् साधयिष्ये तथाऽऽत्मनः
अन्यथेदं विधास्येऽहमयथापूर्वमोजसा । किमन्यैः कालनिर्धूतैः कल्पान्ते वैष्णवादिभिः 11॥
इति शुश्रुम निर्बन्धं तपः परममास्थितः । विधत्स्वानन्तरं युक्तं स्वयं त्रिभुवनेश्वर ॥12॥
तवासनं द्विजगवां पारमेष्ठ्यं जगत्पते । भवाय श्रेयसे भूत्यै क्षेमाय विजयाय च ॥13॥
इति विज्ञापितो देवैर्भगवानात्मभूर्नृप । परीतो भृगुदक्षाद्यैर्ययौ दैत्येश्वराश्रमम् ॥14॥
न ददर्श प्रतिच्छन्नं वल्मीकतृणकीचकैः । पिपीलिकाभिराचीर्णमेदस्त्वङ्मांसशोणितम् 15॥
तपन्तं तपसा लोकान् यथाभ्रापिहितं रविम् । विलक्ष्य विस्मितः प्राह प्रहसन् हंसवाहनः ॥16॥

6-7. Scorched by the fire of his Tapas, the Devas left their heavenly abodes, resorted to the realm of Brahma, and represented to him thus: 'O Lord of Lords and protector of the worlds! The Tapas that is performed by the Asura is making it impossible for us to remain in the Swargaloka (Indra's heaven). If you want to save the worlds and its inhabitants who offer you tribute, be gracious enough to do so before it is too late, before they all perish in the fire of the Asura's Tapas. **8.** Why he is performing this kind of fierce and difficult form of Tapas, is not a matter unknown to your all-knowing self. Yet may you be pleased to hear the following representation of his object: **9.** "Having created this whole universe of moving and unmoving beings by his Tapas and spiritual power, Brahma is residing in the first and the most superior of the regions he has created, namely, Satyaloka. **10.** That region I will gain by the power of my Tapas, communion and concentration. It does not matter if my present body dies before this result is achieved. For time and the Atman have no end. I will therefore attain this goal through repeated births, if need be. **11.** By my power I will transform the whole world order from what it is today by making it topsy-turvy, making celestials into Asuras and Asuras into celestials, virtue into vice and vice into virtue. What is the use of attaining to perishable realms, like those of Dhruva, related to Vishnu, which will meet with dissolution at the end of the Kalpa?" **12.** We have heard that it is with such determination that he is performing this extreme form of Tapas. It is better that you, who are the lord of all the three worlds, take steps sufficiently early to meet this situation. **13.** It will indeed be a pity if he over-runs your realm of Satyaloka; for it is the refuge of all holy and innocent Jivas, a place where they can have happiness, prosperity, welfare and progress.'

14. On being supplicated thus by the Devas, the worshipful Brahma, the self-born, accompanied by sages like Bhrigu, Daksha and others, went to where the Asura was performing Tapas. **15-16.** At first the Asura, who was as it were burning the world by his Tapas, could not be seen, as his body, of which a great part of fat, skin, muscles and blood had already been eaten by ants, was hidden beneath a mould of ant-hills, grass and reeds. Catching sight of him on careful observation,

ब्रह्मोवाच

उत्तिष्ठोत्तिष्ठ भद्रं ते तपःसिद्धोऽसि काश्यप। वरदोऽहमनुप्राप्तो व्रियतामीप्सितो वरः ॥17॥
अद्राक्षमहमेतत् ते हृत्सारं महदद्भुतम्। दंशभक्षितदेहस्य प्राणा ह्यस्थिषु शेरते ॥18॥
नैतत् पूर्वर्षयश्चक्रुर्न करिष्यन्ति चापरे। निरम्बुर्धारयेत् प्राणान् को वै दिव्यसमाः शतम् ॥
व्यवसायेन तेऽनेन दुष्करेण मनस्विनाम्। तपोनिष्ठेन भवता जितोऽहं दितिनन्दन ॥20॥
ततस्त आशिषः सर्वा ददाम्यसुरपुङ्गव। मर्त्यस्य ते अमर्त्यस्य दर्शनं नाफलं मम ॥21॥

नारद उवाच

इत्युक्त्वाऽऽदिभवो देवो भक्षिताङ्गं पिपीलिकैः। कमण्डलुजलेनौक्षद् दिव्येनामोघराधसा ॥22॥
स तत्कीचकवल्मीकात् सहओजोबलान्वितः। सर्वावयवसम्पन्नो वज्रसंहननो युवा।
उत्थितस्तप्तहेमाभो विभावसुरिवैधसः ॥23॥
स निरीक्ष्याम्बरे देवं हंसवाहमवस्थितम्। ननाम शिरसा भूमौ तद्दर्शनमहोत्सवः ॥24॥
उत्थाय प्राञ्जलिः प्रह्व ईक्षमाणो दृशा विभुम्। हर्षाश्रुपुलकोद्भेदो गिरा गद्गदया‍गृणात् 25॥

हिरण्यकशिपुरुवाच

कल्पान्ते कालसृष्टेन योऽन्धेन तमसाऽऽवृतम्। अभिव्यनग् जगदिदं स्वयंज्योतिः स्वरोचिषा ॥
आत्मना त्रिवृता चेदं सृजत्यवति लुम्पति। रजःसत्त्वतमोधाम्ने पराय महते नमः ॥27॥

like the sun behind the clouds, Brahma, the swan-vehicled deity, was astounded, and said smiling.

Brahma's Revelation (17-25)

Brahma said: **17.** O son of Kasyapa! Your Tapas has come to its fulfilment. You may abandon your austere posture now. I have come here ready to give you whatever boon you ask for. Choose the boons you want. **18.** I am astonished at your wonderful determination because of which even when ants have eaten away all the flesh of your body, you are still sustaining your vitality (Prana) on your bony skeleton. **19.** No Rishi in the past practised such austerity, nor can anyone today. Who can retain life for a hundred divine years, without taking even a drop of water? **20.** I have been conquered by you on account of the tremendous determination you have displayed, which no sage of disciplined mind can rival. **21.** O leader of the Asuras! I am therefore ready to grant you everything you want. The vision of an immortal like me shall not be in vain for a person like you with a limited span of life.

Narada said: **22.** Saying so, Brahma, the first of all beings, who possessed powers that never fail, sprinkled the celestially potent water from his Kamandalu (water pot) on the ant-eaten frame of Hiranyakasipu. **23.** The Asura immediately rose up from the mould of earth—a young man in full mental and physical vigour, with all organs intact and the body as hard as adamant. Like fire emerging from fire-sticks, he emerged from the bush of reeds and earth with the glow of molten gold. **24.** When he saw Brahma in the sky seated on his swan-vehicle, he fell down in prostration before him in great joy. **25.** Shedding tears of joy and saluting him with folded hands, he began to extol Brahma in a hymn, with his voice faltering and hair standing on end.

Hiranya's Hymn to Brahma (26-38)

Hiranyakasipu said: **26-27**. When Time had engulfed everything in darkness at the end of the previous cosmic cycle, Thou, the self-luminous Consciousness, again manifested it by Thy light. With Thy three as-

नम आद्याय बीजाय ज्ञानविज्ञानमूर्तये। प्राणेन्द्रियमनोबुद्धिविकारैर्व्यक्तिमीयुषे ॥28॥

त्वमीशिषे जगतस्तस्थुषश्च प्राणेन मुख्येन पतिः प्रजानाम्।
चित्तस्य चित्तेर्मनइन्द्रियाणां पतिर्महान् भूतगुणाशयेशः ॥29॥

त्वं सप्ततन्तून् वितनोषि तन्वा त्रय्या चातुर्होत्रकविद्यया च।
त्वमेक आत्माऽऽत्मवतामनादिरनन्तपारः कविरन्तरात्मा ॥30॥

त्वमेव कालोऽनिमिषो जनानामायुर्लवाद्यावयवैः क्षिणोषि।
कूटस्थ आत्मा परमेष्ठ्यजो महांस्त्वं जीवलोकस्य च जीव आत्मा ॥31॥

त्वत्तः परं नापरमप्यनेजदेजच्च किञ्चिद् व्यतिरिक्तमस्ति।
विद्याः कलास्ते तनवश्च सर्वा हिरण्यगर्भोऽसि बृहत् त्रिपृष्ठः ॥32॥

व्यक्तं विभो स्थूलमिदं शरीरं येनेन्द्रियप्राणमनोगुणांस्त्वम्।
भुङ्क्षे स्थितो धामनि पारमेष्ठ्ये अव्यक्त आत्मा पुरुषः पुराणः ॥33॥

अनन्ताव्यक्तरूपेण येनेदमखिलं ततम्। चिदचिच्छक्तियुक्ताय तस्मै भगवते नमः ॥34॥

pects of Rajas, Sattva and Tamas, Thou createst, preservest, and destroyest this universe. Salutations to Thee, the support of the three Gunas of Sattva, Rajas and Tamas, and the Highest Being who infills everything. **28.** Salutations to the Primeval Seed! Salutations to Him who has the knowledge of the unity of existence and of the multiplicity as established in the unity. Salutation to Him who comes into clear manifestation as the Prana, Indriyas, mind, intellect and the like. **29.** As the Mukhyaprana (principal vital energy), otherwise known as Sūtratman (one pervading everything like a string through beads), Thou art the master and controller of all living and non-living beings. Thou art the master of their consciousness, life-force, mind and senses. Thou art the Great Being that controls and directs matter, external sense organs and the internal instrument of knowledge. **30.** Through the Veda, which constitutes Thy body, wherein sacrifices requiring four priests are expounded, Thou hast given to the world the seven types of sacrifices—Agnishtoma, Atyagnishtoma, Uktha, Shodasi, Atirātra, Āptoryāma and Vājapeya. Thou art the one soul of all living beings, the eternal and limitless one and the knower of all. **31.** Thou art the winkless Time, who, in the form of moments and longer measures, dost reduce the life-span of all beings and ultimately bring them to their death. Though Thou art the creator of everything, Thou art not in the least affected by Thy work of creation. Unmodified Spirit, Lord of all, and beginningless and partless Being, Thou vivifiest all with life.

32. There is nothing whatever as cause and effect, as the moving and the unmoving, that exists apart from Thee. All knowledge, sacred and secular (the Vedas and the arts) are Thy form. Thou art the vast All-comprehending Being who is beyond the Pradhana and who is described as the Hiranyagarbha, the mystic Golden Egg who holds the whole universe in seminal condition within Himself. **33.** O great one! This universe, with which Thou enjoyest the functions of the senses, Pranas and Manas, remaining at the same time in Thy transcendent Realm, is Thy gross body visible to the eye, while as the indweller in all and the eternal Being, Thou art the unseen. **34.** He who pervades all this by His limitless and imperceptible presence, to that Being having matter and spirit as His two powers—my salutation.

यदि दास्यस्यभिमतान् वरान् मे वरदोत्तम। भूतेभ्यस्त्वद्विसृष्टेभ्यो मृत्युर्मा भून्मम प्रभो 35॥
नान्तर्बहिर्दिवा नक्तमन्यस्मादपि चायुधैः। न भूमौ नाम्बरे मृत्युर्न नरैर्न मृगैरपि ॥36॥
व्यसुभिर्वासुमद्भिर्वा सुरासुरमहोरगैः। अप्रतिद्वन्द्वतां युद्धे ऐकपत्यं च देहिनाम् ॥37॥
सर्वेषां लोकपालानां महिमानं यथात्मनः। तपोयोगप्रभावाणां यन्न रिष्यति कर्हिचित् ॥38॥

इति श्रीमद्भागवते महापुराणे पारमहंस्यां संहितायां सप्तमस्कन्धे हिरण्यकशिपोर्वरयाचनं नाम तृतीयोऽध्यायः ॥3॥

35. O Thou the greatest among boon-givers! If it pleasest Thee to give me the boon that I desire, grant that none among Thy creations shall be able to kill me. **36.** It should be impossible to kill me during night or day, on the earth or in the sky, by man or animal. No weapon too should be capable of killing me. **37.** I should not meet with death from entities with life or without life, from Devas or Asuras including great serpents. Grant that no opponent will be able to face me in battle and that I shall be the emperor of all the worlds. **38.** May I have that imperishable glory and splendour which Thou and the protecting Deities possess naturally, and which great men acquire by Tapas and Yoga!

अथ चतुर्थोऽध्यायः

नारद उवाच

एवं वृतः शतधृतिर्हिरण्यकशिपोरथ। प्रादात् तत्तपसा प्रीतो वरांस्तस्य सुदुर्लभान् 1॥

ब्रह्मोवाच

तातेमे दुर्लभाः पुंसां यान् वृणीषे वरान् मम। तथापि वितराम्यङ्ग वरान् यदपि दुर्लभान् ॥ 2॥
ततो जगाम भगवानमोघानुग्रहो विभुः। पूजितोऽसुरवर्येण स्तूयमानः प्रजेश्वरैः ॥ 3॥
एवं लब्धवरो दैत्यो बिभ्रद्धेममयं वपुः। भगवत्यकरोद् द्वेषं भ्रातुर्वधमनुस्मरन् ॥ 4॥
स विजित्य दिशः सर्वा लोकांश्च त्रीन् महासुरः। देवासुरमनुष्येन्द्रान् गन्धर्वगरुडोरगान् ॥ 5॥
सिद्धचारणविद्याध्रानृषीन् पितृपतीन् मनून्। यक्षरक्षःपिशाचेशान् प्रेतभूतपतीनथ ॥ 6॥
सर्वसत्त्वपतीञ्जित्वा वशमानीय विश्वजित्। जहार लोकपालानां स्थानानि सह तेजसा ॥ 7॥

Skandha VII : Chapter 4

HIRANYAKASIPU AND HIS SON PRAHLADA

Oppressive Rule of Hiranya (1-18)

Narada said: **1.** When Hiranyakasipu prayed like this to Brahma, the latter, who was much pleased with him for his great austerity, granted him those extraordinary boons he prayed for. *Brahma said:* **2.** 'O dear one! It is not usual for people to be granted the type of boons you have asked for; for they are so extraordinary. Yet I am granting them to you.' **3.** After granting these boons, the worshipful Brahma, whose blessing will never fail in its effect, departed, receiving the praise and worship of the Asura and of the Prajapatis.

4. The Asura had now a body golden in complexion. Strengthened by the boon, he now resolved to wreak vengeance on Mahavishnu for killing his brother. **5-7.**

देवोद्यानश्रिया जुष्टमध्यास्ते स्म त्रिविष्टपम् । महेन्द्रभवनं साक्षान्निर्मितं विश्वकर्मणा ।
त्रैलोक्यलक्ष्म्यायतनमध्युवासाखिलर्द्धिमत् ॥ 8॥
यत्र विद्रुमसोपाना महामारकता भुवः । यत्र स्फाटिककुडयानि वैदूर्यस्तम्भपङ्क्तयः 9॥
यत्र चित्रवितानानि पद्मरागासनानि च । पयःफेननिभाः शय्या मुक्तादामपरिच्छदाः ॥10॥
कूजद्भिर्नूपुरैर्देव्यः शब्दयन्त्य इतस्ततः । रत्नस्थलीषु पश्यन्ति सुदतीः सुन्दरं मुखम् ॥11॥
तस्मिन् महेन्द्रभवने महाबलो महामना निर्जितलोक एकराट् ।
रेमेऽभिवन्द्याङ्घ्रियुगः सुरादिभिः प्रतापितैरूर्जितचण्डशासनः ॥12॥
तमङ्ग मत्तं मधुनोरुगन्धिना विवृत्तताम्राक्षमशेषधिष्ण्यपाः ।
उपासतोपायनपाणिभिर्विना त्रिभिस्तपोयोगबलौजसां पदम् ॥13॥
जगुर्महेन्द्रासनमोजसा स्थितं विश्वावसुस्तुम्बुरुरस्मदादयः ।
गन्धर्वसिद्धा ऋषयोऽस्तुवन् मुहुर्विद्याधरा अप्सरसश्च पाण्डव ॥14॥
स एव वर्णाश्रमिभिः क्रतुभिर्भूरिदक्षिणैः । इज्यमानो हविर्भागानग्रहीत् स्वेन तेजसा ॥15॥

The great Asura conquered all the three worlds and brought them under his control. The leaders of the Devas, Asuras and men; of the Gandharvas, Garudas and serpents; of the Siddhas, Chāranas and Vidyādharas; of the Rishis, Pitris and Manus; of the Yakshas, Pisāchas and demons; of the Pretas, goblins and other species of beings—all were conquered and brought under control by him. Appropriating to himself the power and the status of the guardian deities of the quarters also, he now claimed himself to be the conqueror of all the worlds. **8.** He moved his residence to the realm of Swarga (Indra's heaven), which was blazoned by the glory of the heavenly gardens of the celestials. There he stayed in the palace of Indra, which was built by the celestial craftsman Viswakarma, and which was the home of all beauty and prosperity in the universe. **9-11.** There could be seen terraces of emerald reached by flights of steps made of coral, as also walls of crystals and rows of pillars made of Vaidūrya (lapis lazuli). There could be seen canopies with artistic designs, seats made of ruby, beds as white and clean and soft as the foam of milk, festooned with strings of pearl. There went about handsome women of sparkling teeth, whose anklets tinkled as they moved and who saw their own faces reflected in the surfaces set with precious stones in several places.

12. The Asura, powerful in body and mind, was now the unchallenged and supreme ruler of all the worlds and enjoyed life in Indra's residence, served by all the Devas subdued by the rigours of his fiercely oppressive rule. **13.** O dear one! All the divinities except the Trimurti waited with presents on him, whose eyes were red under the influence of strong drink, and who possessed extraordinary vigour of body, senses and mind augmented by the power of Tapas and Yoga. **14.** O scion of Pandu's line! On him who had thus occupied the seat of Indra by virtue of his power, we sages, like Visvavasu, Tumburu and myself, sang panegyries. So did Gandharvas, Apsaras, Siddhas, Vidyādharas and other species of beings. **15.** He began to be worshipped by the followers of Varnāshrama-dharma (Vedic social system) by sacrifices in which great amounts were paid as Dakshina (sacrificial presents). By his power he appropriated for himself the sacrificial portions set apart for various deities.

अकृष्टपच्या तस्यासीत् सप्तद्वीपवती मही । तथा कामदुघा द्यौस्तु नानाश्चर्यपदं नभः ॥16॥
रत्नाकराश्च रत्नौघांस्तत्पत्न्यश्चोहुरूर्मिभिः । क्षारसीधुघृतक्षौद्रदधिक्षीरामृतोदकाः ॥17॥
शैला द्रोणीभिराक्रीडं सर्वर्तुषु गुणान् द्रुमाः । दधार लोकपालानामेक एव पृथग्गुणान् ॥18॥
स इत्थं निर्जितककुबेकराड् विषयान् प्रियान् । यथोपजोषं भुञ्जानो नातृप्यदजितेन्द्रियः ॥19॥
एवमैश्वर्यमत्तस्य दृप्तस्योच्छास्त्रवर्तिनः । कालो महान् व्यतीयाय ब्रह्मशापमुपेयुषः ॥20॥
तस्योग्रदण्डसंविग्नाः सर्वे लोकाः सपालकाः । अन्यत्रालब्धशरणाः शरणं ययुरच्युतम् ॥21॥
तस्यै नमोऽस्तु काष्ठायै यत्रात्मा हरिरीश्वरः । यद् गत्वा न निवर्तन्ते शान्ताः संन्यासिनोऽमलाः ॥
इति ते संयतात्मानः समाहितधियोऽमलाः । उपतस्थुर्हृषीकेशं विनिद्रा वायुभोजनाः ॥23॥
तेषामाविरभूद्वाणी अरूपा मेघनिस्वना । सन्नादयन्ती ककुभः साधूनामभयङ्करी ॥24॥
मा भैष्ट विबुधश्रेष्ठाः सर्वेषां भद्रमस्तु वः । मद्दर्शनं हि भूतानां सर्वश्रेयोपपत्तये ॥25॥
ज्ञातमेतस्य दौरात्म्यं दैतेयापसदस्य च । तस्य शान्तिं करिष्यामि कालं तावत् प्रतीक्षत 26
यदा देवेषु वेदेषु गोषु विप्रेषु साधुषु । धर्मे मयि च विद्वेषः स वा आशु विनश्यति 27॥

16. The earth with its seven continents began to yield him all her products without any agricultural operation. So also the heavens gave plentiful showers of highly desired rains, and the upper regions of air revealed many kinds of wonders. **17.** The rivers and the seven oceans of salt water, liquor, ghee, honey, curds, milk and pure water, all brought tributes of precious gems with their wavy arms. **18.** The mountains prepared their caves for his sports. The trees yielded flowers and fruits in all seasons. He took upon himself all the powers of the guardian deities of the quarters.

Devas in Quest of Relief (19-28)

19. Thus he conquered all the worlds and became the suzerain over them all, but he failed to conquer his own senses. Consequently though indulging in every form of pleasure, he felt no satisfaction. **20.** Infatuated with wealth and power, arrogant, and a law unto himself in complete transgression of all scriptural injunctions, he attracted on himself the curses of all holy men, but none the less ruled the world in this way for more than seventy-one Yugas. **21.** Writhing in agony under his oppressive rule, all the worlds with their rulers at last took refuge in Achyuta, the Indestructible Being, having failed to get relief from any other quarter. **22.** They prayed: Salutation to that Realm where the all-pervading Hari manifests in a form, and attaining which there is no return to Samsara for holy men of great purity and tranquillity! **23.** Praying like this with a pure and concentrated mind, with the senses under control, and giving up food and sleep, they invoked Mahavishnu, the master of the senses. **24.** While they were so hymning, they heard all of a sudden a disembodied voice, deep and reverberating like the sound of thunder, which evoked joy and confidence in the minds of all good people.

25. The voice said: 'O leaders of the celestials! Do not entertain any fear. May you be happy and prosperous! My communion, through sight or hearing, works for the all-round good of beings. **26.** I am already aware of the wickedness of this most degenerate Asura. I shall curb him, but you have to wait a little more. **27.** When anybody comes to entertain hatred towards celestials, Vedas, holy men, innocent creatures, Dharma, God etc., know his ruin to be near at hand.

निर्वैराय प्रशान्ताय स्वसुताय महात्मने । प्रह्लादाय यदा द्रुह्येद्धनिष्येऽपि वरोर्जितम् ॥28॥

नारद उवाच

इत्युक्ता लोकगुरुणा तं प्रणम्य दिवौकसः । न्यवर्तन्त गतोद्वेगा मेनिरे चासुरं हतम् ॥29॥
तस्य दैत्यपतेः पुत्राश्चत्वारः परमाद्भुताः । प्रह्लादोऽभून्महांस्तेषां गुणैर्महदुपासकः ॥30॥
ब्रह्मण्यः शीलसम्पन्नः सत्यसन्धो जितेन्द्रियः । आत्मवत् सर्वभूतानामेकः प्रियसुहृत्तमः ॥31॥
दासवत्संनतार्याङ्घ्रिः पितृवत् दीनवत्सलः । भ्रातृवत् सदृशे स्निग्धो गुरुष्वीश्वरभावनः ।
विद्यार्थरूपजन्माढ्यो मानस्तम्भविवर्जितः ॥32॥
नोद्विग्नचित्तो व्यसनेषु निःस्पृहः श्रुतेषु दृष्टेषु गुणेष्ववस्तुदृक् ।
दान्तेन्द्रियप्राणशरीरधीः सदा प्रशान्तकामो रहितासुरोऽसुरः ॥33॥
यस्मिन् महद्‌गुणा राजन् गृह्यन्ते कविभिर्मुहुः । न तेऽधुनापिधीयन्ते यथा भगवतीश्वरे ॥34॥
यं साधुगाथासदसि रिपवोऽपि सुरा नृप । प्रतिमानं प्रकुर्वन्ति किमुतान्ये भवादृशाः ॥35॥
गुणैरलमसंख्येयैर्माहात्म्यं तस्य सूच्यते । वासुदेवे भगवति यस्य नैसर्गिकी रतिः ॥36॥
न्यस्तक्रीडनको बालो जडवत् तन्मनस्तया । कृष्णग्रहगृहीतात्मा न वेद जगदीदृशम् ॥37॥

28. Though he is fortified in his strength by the boons he has received, I shall bring about his destruction when he persecutes his son Prahlada who is free from antagonisms, who is tranquil and high-souled.'

Character of Prahlada (29-46)

Narada said: **29.** After they had received the Lord's message through this disembodied voice, the celestials made prostrations and returned without any more fear, as they felt that the Asura was as good as dead now. **30-32.** This Hiranyakasipu had four sons of extraordinary nature. Of these, Prahlada was noted for his great virtues. Devoted to the holy and the learned, exemplary in his conduct, truthful, and having mastery of the senses, he was as dear to all beings as their own selves, and everyone found in him his closest friend. He attended on wise and holy men like a servant; he was loving to the poor and the afflicted like a parent; to his equals he was like a brother; and he viewed his teachers as God Himself. Though endowed with learning, wealth, beauty, noble birth etc., none of these swelled his ego or filled him with pride. **33.** Being intensely aware of the transitoriness and hollowness of all enjoyments, Prahlada could remain unmoved in difficulties, free from aspiration for any attainment in this world or the next, devoid of sexual desire, and established in the control of the senses, Prana, body and intellect. He was an Asura without any of the qualities of Asuras. **34.** O King! The great qualities of Prahlada are extolled again and again by wise men. Just like the excellence of the Supreme Being, his virtues are remembered even to this day. **35.** In assemblies for recitals on great and holy personages, even Devas, the natural enemies of Asuras, cite Prahlada, the Asura, as a glorious example of a great personage. That being the case, men like you will surely appreciate his greatness. **36.** All his numberless virtues noticed above do not exhaust his excellence, but are a mere indication of his indescribable greatness; for he was one whose mind naturally flowed towards the worshipful Vāsudeva. **37.** Even as a child, like one insensitive and dull, he evinced no interest in toys, as his mind was absorbed in the

आसीनः पर्यटन्नश्नन् शयानः प्रपिबन् ब्रुवन्। नानुसन्धत्त एतानि गोविन्दपरिरम्भितः ॥38॥
क्वचिद् रुदति वैकुण्ठचिन्ताशबलचेतनः। क्वचिद्धसति तच्चिन्ताह्लाद उद्गायति क्वचित् ॥
नदति क्वचिदुत्कण्ठो विलज्जो नृत्यति क्वचित्। क्वचित् तद्भावनायुक्तस्तन्मयोऽनुचकार ह ॥40॥
क्वचिदुत्पुलकस्तूष्णीमास्ते संस्पर्शनिर्वृतः। अस्पन्दप्रणयानन्दसलिलामीलितेक्षणः ॥41॥
स उत्तमश्लोकपदारविन्दयोर्निषेवयाकिञ्चनसङ्गलब्धया।
तन्वन् परां निर्वृतिमात्मनो मुहुर्दुःसङ्गदीनान्यमनःशमं व्यधात् ॥42॥
तस्मिन् महाभागवते महाभागे महात्मनि। हिरण्यकशिपू राजन्नकरोदघमात्मजे ॥43॥

युधिष्ठिर उवाच

देवर्ष एतदिच्छामो वेदितुं तव सुव्रत। यदात्मजाय शुद्धाय पितादात् साधवे ह्यघम् 44॥
पुत्रान् विप्रतिकूलान् स्वान् पितरःपुत्रवत्सलाः। उपालभन्ते शिक्षार्थं नैवाघमपरो यथा ॥45॥
किमुतानुवशान् साधूंस्तादृशान् गुरुदेवतान्। एतत् कौतूहलं ब्रह्मन्नस्माकं विधम प्रभो।
पितुः पुत्राय यद् द्वेषो मरणाय प्रयोजितः ॥46॥

इति श्रीमद्भागवते महापुराणे पारमहंस्यां संहितायां सप्तमस्कन्धे प्रह्लादचरिते चतुर्थोऽध्यायः ॥4॥

Lord. Like a man possessed by Krishna, his mind remained so absorbed in Him that he saw not the external world as as we do.

38. As he was ever in the embrace of Govinda, he was like an automaton unconscious of his own physical activities like sitting, walking, eating, drinking, lying etc. **39.** Sometimes he wept, his mind overpowered by the love of the Lord; sometimes he laughed, being reminded of His sportive actions; and sometimes he sang in great joy, his mind filled with the memory of His excellences. **40.** Sometimes he loudly chanted the names of the Lord; sometimes he danced about without any bashfulness; sometimes infilled with Him through imaginative identification, he would imitate the sportive actions of the Lord. **41.** Sometimes, being steeped in the thrilling joy of Divine contact, he remained speechless in complete absorption, his hair standing on end and his half-closed eyes shedding tears stimulated by the inward bliss of unshakable love for the Lord. **42.** He gave peace even to the minds of persons distressed on account of evil worldly associations by the spiritual joy he radiated—the joy which he derived from the service of the Lord, the same reward which he got for keeping the company of holy men devoid of any worldly possessions. **43.** O King! It was on this son of his, a devotee of the highest excellence and a truly great and fortunate soul, that Hiranyakasipu inflicted cruel tortures.

Yudhishthira said: **44**. O great ascetic! I would like to hear from you why Hiranyakasipu practised cruelty on a son so noted for his purity and holiness. **45.** Even loving parents are, no doubt, seen to threaten and reprimand their rebellious children to bring them round to the path of virtue, but no one behaves cruelly like an enemy even towards them. **46.** O learned one! It is needless to say therefore, that no parent will in the natural course practise such cruelty towards a son who is obedient, free from desire and hatred, and serves the parents as representatives of the Divine. How could a father, even though angry at his son, go to the extent of planning to kill him?'

अथ पञ्चमोऽध्यायः

नारद उवाच

पौरोहित्याय भगवान् वृतः काव्यः किलासुरैः । शण्डामर्कौ सुतौ तस्य दैत्यराजगृहान्तिके ॥ 1॥
तौ राज्ञा प्रापितं बालं प्रह्लादं नयकोविदम् । पाठयामासतुः पाठ्यानन्यांश्चासुरबालकान् ॥ 2॥
यत्तत्र गुरुणा प्रोक्तं शुश्रुवेऽनु पपाठ च । न साधु मनसा मेने स्वपरासद्ग्रहाश्रयम् ॥ 3॥
एकदासुरराट् पुत्रमङ्कमारोप्य पाण्डव । पप्रच्छ कथ्यतां वत्स मन्यते साधु यद् भवान् ॥ 4॥

प्रह्लाद उवाच

तत् साधु मन्येऽसुरवर्य देहिनां सदा समुद्विग्नधियामसद्ग्रहात् ।
हित्वाऽऽत्मपातं गृहमन्धकूपं वनं गतो यद्धरिमाश्रयेत ॥ 5॥

नारद उवाच

श्रुत्वा पुत्रगिरो दैत्यः परपक्षसमाहिताः । जहास बुद्धिर्बालानां भिद्यते परबुद्धिभिः ॥ 6॥
सम्यग् विधार्यतां बालो गुरुगेहे द्विजातिभिः । विष्णुपक्षैः प्रतिच्छन्नैर्न भिद्येतास्य धीर्यथा ॥ 7॥
गृहमानीतमाहूय प्रह्लादं दैत्ययाजकाः । प्रशस्य श्लक्ष्णया वाचा समपृच्छन्त सामभिः ॥ 8॥

Skandha VII : Chapter 5

PERSECUTION OF PRAHLADA

Hiranya examines his Son (1-7)

Narada said: **1.** It is well known that the Asuras had chosen the sage Sukra as their chief priest. Sukra's two sons, Sanda and Amarka, had their residence near the palace of Hiranyakasipu, the king of the Daityas. **2.** The Asura king put his son Prahlada of acute intelligence under these teachers for instruction in what he considered fit for him to learn along with the other Asura children. **3.** Whatever the teachers taught, he heard and learnt, but he did not accept the soundness of much of their teachings, which were based on the sense of difference between oneself and one's interests on the one hand, and others and their interests on the other. **4.** O scion of Pandu's line! One day the Asura king took his son on his lap and asked him: 'O dear one! Tell me what you consider to be the true and the good.' *Prahlada said:* **5.** 'O Lord of the Asuras! All embodied beings are overpowered by body-consciousness and are consequently subject to sorrow and suffering. I therefore deem that their ultimate good lies in abandoning their homes, which have caused their spiritual downfall by imprisoning them in the darkness of infatuation, like a discarded and dried-up well. Let them therefore abandon it and resort to some sequestered forest where they could take complete shelter in Sri Hari, the destroyer of all the sufferings of life.'

Narada said: **6.** When he heard these words of the boy conveying his unbounded faith in Sri Hari, his (Hiranya's) inveterate enemy, Hiranya laughed at first, thinking that the boy's mind had been perverted by the persuasions of some undesirable persons. **7.** And he warned the teachers to see particularly that devotees of Vishnu did not come incognito to their home and pervert the boy's mind.

Efforts to reform Prahlada (8-18)

8. When Prahlada was brought back to

वत्स प्रह्लाद भद्रं ते सत्यं कथय मा मृषा। बालानति कुतस्तुभ्यमेष बुद्धिविपर्ययः ॥ 9॥
बुद्धिभेदः परकृत उताहो ते स्वतोऽभवत्। भण्यतां श्रोतुकामानां गुरूणां कुलनन्दन ॥10॥

प्रह्लाद उवाच

स्वः परश्चेत्यसद्ग्राहः पुंसां यन्मायया कृतः। विमोहितधियां दृष्टस्तस्मै भगवते नमः ॥11॥
स यदानुव्रतः पुंसां पशुबुद्धिर्विभिद्यते। अन्य एष तथान्योऽहमिति भेदगतासती ॥12॥
स एष आत्मा स्वपरेत्यबुद्धिभिर्दुरत्ययानुक्रमणो निरूप्यते।
मुह्यन्ति यद्वर्त्मनि वेदवादिनो ब्रह्मादयो ह्येष भिनत्ति मे मतिम् ॥13॥
यथा भ्राम्यत्ययो ब्रह्मन् स्वयमाकर्षसन्निधौ। तथा मे भिद्यते चेतश्चक्रपाणेर्यदृच्छया ॥14॥

नारद उवाच

एतावद् ब्राह्मणायोक्त्वा विरराम महामतिः। तं निर्भर्त्स्याथ कुपितः स दीनो राजसेवकः 15॥
आनीयतामरे वेत्रमस्माकमयशस्करः। कुलाङ्गारस्य दुर्बुद्धेश्चतुर्थोऽस्योदितो दमः ॥16॥
दैतेयचन्दनवने जातोऽयं कण्टकद्रुमः। यन्मूलोन्मूलपरशोर्विष्णोर्नालायितोऽर्भकः ॥17॥
इति तं विविधोपायैर्भीषयंस्तर्जनादिभिः। प्रह्लादं ग्राहयामास त्रिवर्गस्योपपादनम् ॥18॥

their home, the teachers, Sanda and Amarka, called him to their side, and patting and praising him, asked him gently: **9.** 'Dear boy Prahlada! May you be happy! Tell us the truth: How did you get this outlook, which is quite alien to boys generally? **10.** Is this contrary way of thought inducted into you by someone or is it natural to you? O the delight of your tribe! Tell the truth about it to us, your teachers, who are keen to know the facts.'

Prahlada replied: **11.** Salutation to the worshipful Lord, by the working of whose Yogamaya men get the ignorance-born distinction between oneself and another—a distinction which only minds perverted by ignorance would make. **12.** When the Lord is propitious to you, then this vain, brutish distinction felt between one's interest and another's interest will disappear. **13.** It is He alone, the Supreme Being of inscrutable ways, that is distinguished by ignorant men as I and he, as friend and foe. There is nothing to wonder at in it. For, in trying to understand Him even Brahma and the knowers of the Veda fall into utter confusion. It is His grace that has erased in me this outlook of seeing a difference between myself and another! **14.** Just as before a magnet, iron pieces are naturally moved and attracted, so in the presence of the discus-armed Lord, my mind automatically runs to Him abandoning everything else.

Narada said: **15.** The high-minded Prahlada, having said this much to the teacher, remained silent. That pitiable teacher—pitiable because he had no freedom of thought as a servant of Hiranyakasipu—scolded the boy angrily and said: **16.** 'Who is there? Bring the cane! This boy is going to bring us disrepute. A dangerous fire-brand to our tribe, and evil-minded to the core, nothing but corporal punishment can do for him. **17.** In the sandalwood forest of this Asura race, this boy is a thorny tree. For Mahavishnu, the axe that cuts down the trees of the forest, this boy has become the veritable handle!' **18.** Brandishing threats of this kind, he taught Prahlada only subjects dealing with the three ends of life namely, Dharma, Artha and Kama.

Hiranya's second Examination (19-32)

तत एनं गुरुर्ज्ञात्वा ज्ञातज्ञेयचतुष्टयम् । दैत्येन्द्रं दर्शयामास मातृमृष्टमलङ्कृतम् ॥19॥
पादयोः पतितं बालं प्रतिनन्द्याशिषासुरः । परिष्वज्य चिरं दोर्भ्यां परमामाप निर्वृतिम् 20॥
आरोप्याङ्कमवघ्राय मूर्धन्यश्रुकलाम्बुभिः । आसिञ्चन् विकसद्वक्त्रमिदमाह युधिष्ठिर ॥21॥

हिरण्यकशिपुरुवाच

प्रह्लादानूच्यतां तात स्वधीतं किञ्चिदुत्तमम् । कालेनैतावताऽऽयुष्मन् यदशिक्षद् गुरोर्भवान् ॥

प्रह्लाद उवाच

श्रवणं कीर्तनं विष्णोः स्मरणं पादसेवनम् । अर्चनं वन्दनं दास्यं सख्यमात्मनिवेदनम् ॥23॥
इति पुंसार्पिता विष्णौ भक्तिश्चेन्नवलक्षणा । क्रियते भगवत्यद्धा तन्मन्येऽधीतमुत्तमम् ॥24॥
निशम्यैतत् सुतवचो हिरण्यकशिपुस्तदा । गुरुपुत्रमुवाचेदं रुषा प्रस्फुरिताधरः ॥25॥
ब्रह्मबन्धो किमेतत् ते विपक्षं श्रयतासता । असारं ग्राहितो बालो मामनादृत्य दुर्मते ॥26॥
सन्ति ह्यसाधवो लोके दुर्मैत्राश्छद्मवेषिणः । तेषामुदेत्यघं काले रोगः पातकिनामिव ॥27॥

गुरुपुत्र उवाच

न मत्प्रणीतं न परप्रणीतं सुतो वदत्येष तवेन्द्रशत्रो ।
नैसर्गिकीयं मतिरस्य राजन् नियच्छ मन्युं कददाः स्म मा नः ॥28॥

19. Sometime after, when the teacher was sure that the boy had mastered the four divisions of diplomacy—conciliation, subsidy, internal dissension, and force—he took him to Hiranyakasipu, bathed, well-dressed, and well-decorated by his mother. **20.** The Asura lifted the boy who prostrated himself at his feet, embraced him for long, and enjoyed the highest bliss thereby. **21.** O Yudhishthira! Seating the boy on his lap, kissing him on the crown of the head, and shedding tears over him, the Asura said with a blooming face. *Hiranyakasipu said:* **22.** 'O Prahlada, dear boy! May you be long-lived! You please tell me about the best lessons from the vast body of instructions you must have been receiving from your teachers during these days.'

Prahlada replied: **23-24.** Hearing about Vishnu, singing about Him, remembering Him, serving Him, worshipping Him, saluting Him, being His servant, being His comrade, and surrendering oneself and everything that is one's own to Him—these are the nine aspects of Bhakti or God-love. If man could be trained to practise devotion characterised by these nine features, that indeed would be the highest education he could have. That is what I have understood.

25. Hearing these words of his son, Hiranyakasipu said to his teacher's son in great anger, his lips trembling in emotion. *Hiranyakasipu said:* **26.** 'You unworthy and perverse teacher! How is it that taking the side of an enemy, you have totally discarded me and put absurd ideas into my boy's head? **27.** There are wicked men in this world who approach you in the disguise of friends. Just as disease takes time to afflict sinners as the wages of their sins, the evil wrought by enemies in the disguise of friends (like you) will take time to manifest clearly.' *The Preceptor's son said:* **28.** 'O Thou antagonist of Indra! What your son is saying has not been taught to him by me or anyone else. This bent of his mind, O King, is natural to him. Please be good enough to control your anger and not to charge us with this offence.'

नारद उवाच

गुरुणैवं प्रतिप्रोक्तो भूय आहासुरः सुतम् । न चेद् गुरुमुखीयं ते कुतोऽभद्रासती मतिः ॥29॥

प्रह्लाद उवाच

मतिर्न कृष्णे परतः स्वतो वा मिथोऽभिपद्येत गृहव्रतानाम् ।
अदान्तगोभिर्विशतां तमिस्रं पुनः पुनश्चर्वितचर्वणानाम् ॥30॥
न ते विदुः स्वार्थगतिं हि विष्णुं दुराशया ये बहिरर्थमानिनः ।
अन्धा यथान्धैरुपनीयमाना वाचीशतन्त्यामुरुदाम्नि बद्धाः ॥31॥
नैषां मतिस्तावदुरुक्रमाङ्घ्रिं स्पृशत्यनर्थापगमो यदर्थः ।
महीयसां पादरजोऽभिषेकं निष्किञ्चनानां न वृणीत यावत् ॥32॥

इत्युक्त्वोपरतं पुत्रं हिरण्यकशिपू रुषा । अन्धीकृतात्मा स्वोत्सङ्गान्निरस्यत महीतले 33॥
आहामर्षरुषाविष्टः कषायीभूतलोचनः । वध्यतामाश्वयं वध्यो निःसारयत नैर्ऋताः 34॥
अयं मे भ्रातृहा सोऽयं हित्वा स्वान् सुहृदोऽधमः । पितृव्यहन्तुर्यः पादौ विष्णोर्दासवदर्चति ॥35॥
विष्णोर्वा साध्वसौ किं नु करिष्यत्यसमञ्जसः । सौहृदं दुस्त्यजं पित्रोरहाद्यः पञ्चहायनः ॥36॥

Narada said: **29.** When the teacher said like this, the Asura asked his son again, 'O evil fellow! If it is not from the Guru's instruction, how did you come to have this perverse outlook?' *Prahlada replied:* **30.** 'For lack of control over the senses Jivas go round and round in the wheel of Samsara, chewing the cud of the same enjoyments and sufferings again and again without satiation. Their thoughts are ever confined to their homes, property and other domestic concerns. They can never develop this devotional proclivity of mind towards Krishna, the Supreme Being, either naturally, or through the teachings of others, or from mutual influence. **31.** People of impure nature, whose minds are always outward-going because of their domination by the notion that what is true and what is enjoyable lies outside, are never able to know Mahavishnu, who is apprehended only by the inward-going, introspective vision. Those extroverts immersed in Vedic ritualism are like a group of blind men led by another such group by a rope. This is the thick rope of Vedic ritualism to which these extroverts are bound by the several thin strings of practices, rituals, beliefs for the fulfilment of desires here and hereafter, as cattle are to the main rope of several tether ropes. **32.** So long as one is not able to bathe his head with the dust of the feet of His great devotees, who have no possession of any kind except Him, the mind of man does not take a serious turn towards the feet of the Lord. And the cessation of Samsara does not come about until the mind is thus turned towards Him.'

Persecution of Prahlada (33-47)

33. Saying thus, Prahlada stopped. Hiranyakasipu was mad with terrible anger on hearing these words of his son. Immediately he pushed him from his lap to the floor. **34.** Moved by irresistible anger, he exclaimed with blood-shot eyes: 'O you Rakshasa guards! He deserves to be executed. Take him away from here. Kill him without any delay. **35.** This fellow, who has rejected all of us, his own friends and well-wishers, and seeks to be a servant attending on Vishnu, the killer of his own uncle, must himself be considered that killer. **36.** Such an untrustworthy fel-

परोऽप्यपत्यं हितकृद् यथौषधं स्वदेहजोऽप्यामयवत् सुतोऽहितः ।
छिन्द्यात् तदङ्गं यदुतात्मनोऽहितं शेषं सुखं जीवति यद्विवर्जनात् ॥37॥
सर्वैरुपायैर्हन्तव्यः सम्भोजशयनासनैः । सुहृल्लिङ्गधरः शत्रुर्मुनेर्दुष्टमिवेन्द्रियम् ॥38॥
नैर्ऋतास्ते समादिष्टा भर्त्रा वै शूलपाणयः । तिग्मदंष्ट्रकरालास्यास्ताम्रश्मश्रुशिरोरुहाः ॥39॥
नदन्तो भैरवान् नादांश्छिन्धि भिन्धीति वादिनः । आसीनं चाहनन् शूलैः प्रह्लादं सर्वमर्मसु ॥40॥
परे ब्रह्मण्यनिर्देश्ये भगवत्यखिलात्मनि । युक्तात्मन्यफला आसन्नपुण्यस्येव सत्क्रियाः 41॥
प्रयासेऽपहते तस्मिन् दैत्येन्द्रः परिशङ्कितः । चकार तद्वधोपायान् निर्बन्धेन युधिष्ठिर 42॥
दिग्गजैर्दन्दशूकैश्च अभिचारावपातनैः । मायाभिः संनिरोधैश्च गरदानैरभोजनैः ॥43॥
हिमवाय्वग्निसलिलैः पर्वताक्रमणैरपि । न शशाक यदा हन्तुमपापमसुरः सुतम् ।
चिन्तां दीर्घतमां प्राप्तस्तत् कर्तुं नाभ्यपद्यत ॥44॥
एष मे बह्वसाधूक्तो वधोपायाश्च निर्मिताः । तैस्तैर्द्रोहैरसद्धर्मैर्मुक्तः स्वेनैव तेजसा ॥45॥
वर्तमानोऽविदूरे वै बालोऽप्यजडधीरयम् । न विस्मरति मेऽनार्यं शुनःशेप इव प्रभुः ॥46॥
अप्रमेयानुभावोऽयमकुतश्चिद्भयोऽमरः । नूनमेतद्विरोधेन मृत्युर्मे भविता न वा ॥47॥

low like him, who, even at the age of five, could break and throw overboard the natural and unbreakable affection for parents—of what good can he be even for Vishnu? **37.** Even an unrelated person can be considered as one's son, if like a medicine, he serves your interests well. One who does the opposite must be considered a disease, even if he be one's son, born of one's own body; and he has to be eradicated like a disease. When a limb of a body is diseased and becomes a threat to the whole body, that limb has to be cut off for the safety of the rest of the body. **38.** Therefore he deserves to be killed somehow or other—through poisoned food, or while sleeping, or while awake. For, as an attractive sensuous object is a danger to an ascetic, so is an enemy in the disguise of a friend.'

39-40. When the master ordered them thus, the Rakshasa guards, with sharp fangs, fierce faces and copper-coloured beard and hair, began to shout, 'Pierce, cut' etc., and struck Prahlada on his vital parts with their tridents. **41.** Just as all the pious rites done by unbelieving persons are fruitless, so were all the efforts of these Asuras to kill Prahlada, whose mind was ever immersed in the Supreme Lord, the centre of all power and excellences, the soul of all, the Indefinable Absolute.

42. O Yudhishthira! When all their efforts to kill Prahlada failed, Hiranyakasipu grew extremely anxious, and seriously began to think of some extraordinary means of killing him. **43-44.** He tried various measures such as having him trampled by elephants, bitten by serpents, attacked through black magic, rolled along the mountain side, imprisoned, poisoned, starved, and exposed to severely inclement weather and to fire, to storm and to water. When all these failed to kill his sinless son, Hiranyakasipu became extremely worried and perplexed. **45.** He thought: 'I have heaped abuses on him, and I have tried in many ways to kill him. All these persecutions and even the magical arts I tried, have all been set at naught by him by his own puissance. **46.** Though a mere boy and though standing in my presence, he is without the least fear or nervousness. This powerful chap, like Sunahsepa, is not likely to forget the atrocities I have committed on him. **47.** He seems to be of inscrutable nature,

इति तं चिन्तया किञ्चिन्म्लानश्रियमधोमुखम् । शण्डामर्कावौशनसौ विविक्त इति होचतुः 48॥

जितं त्वयैकेन जगत्त्रयं भ्रुवोर्विजृम्भणत्रस्तसमस्तधिष्ण्यपम् ।
न तस्य चिन्त्यं तव नाथ चक्ष्महे न वै शिशूनां गुणदोषयोः पदम् ॥49॥

इमं तु पाशैर्वरुणस्य बद्ध्वा निधेहि भीतो न पलायते यथा ।
बुद्धिश्च पुंसो वयसाऽऽर्यसेवया यावद् गुरुर्भार्गव आगमिष्यति ॥50॥

तथेति गुरुपुत्रोक्तमनुज्ञायेदमब्रवीत् । धर्मा ह्यस्योपदेष्टव्या राज्ञां ये गृहमेधिनाम् 51॥
धर्ममर्थं च कामं च नितरां चानुपूर्वशः । प्रह्लादायोचतू राजन् प्रश्रितावनताय च ॥52॥
यथा त्रिवर्गं गुरुभिरात्मने उपशिक्षितम् । न साधु मेने तच्छिक्षां द्वन्द्वारामोपवर्णिताम् ॥53॥
यदाऽऽचार्यः परावृत्तो गृहमेधीयकर्मसु । वयस्यैर्बालकैस्तत्र सोपहूतः कृतक्षणैः ॥54॥
अथ तान् श्लक्ष्णया वाचा प्रत्याहूय महाबुधः । उवाच विद्वांस्तन्निष्ठां कृपया प्रहसन्निव ॥55॥
ते तु तद्गौरवात् सर्वे त्यक्तक्रीडापरिच्छदाः । बाला नदूषितधियो द्वन्द्वारामेरितेहितैः ॥56॥
पर्युपासत राजेन्द्र तन्न्यस्तहृदयेक्षणाः । तानाह करुणो मैत्रो महाभागवतोऽसुरः ॥57॥

इति श्रीमद्भागवते महापुराणे पारमहंस्यां संहितायां सप्तमस्कन्धे प्रह्लादानुचरिते पञ्चमोऽध्यायः ॥ 5 ॥

fearless and deathless. Am I likely to meet with my death because of my enmity towards him? In no other way can I die.'

Further Efforts to reform him (48-57)

48. To Hiranyakasipu who sat brooding with his lack-lustre face turned down because of these depressing thoughts, Sanda and Amarka, the sons of Acharya Sukra, said as follows in private: **49.** 'By your own prowess, unaided by anyone else, you have conquered these three worlds. A mere quivering of your brow is enough to strike terror even into the hearts of the guardian deities of the quarters. O Master! To one such as you, we do not find anything to worry about. And as for Prahlada, he is yet a boy who has not reached the age of discretion. **50.** In order to prevent this Prahlada from running away out of fear, let us keep him tied up with Varuna's noose until the return of our teacher, Rishi Sukra. As one's age advances, and as one gets more chances of association with, and instruction from the wise, men gradually change in their character and outlook.'

51. Agreeing with the advice of his teacher's sons, Hiranyakasipu said to them: 'Instruct the boy in the Dharma of Kings and of householders.' **52.** O King! Accordingly they instructed the humble and obedient Prahlada in matters concerned with the pursuit of morality (Dharma), power (Artha), and pleasure (Kama). **53.** The instruction given to him by the teachers on the three ends of life, Dharma, Artha and Kama, was not considered by him as sound; for they were the teachings given by worldly-minded people for others of similar outlook. **54.** Whenever the teachers went out on their own household purposes, Prahlada's classmates, who then got time for play, would call him to join them. **55.** On one such occasion, this enlightened Prahlada spoke to them lovingly for their instruction, depicting the very pitiable condition of men steeped in worldly life. **56-57.** The boys, whose minds had not yet been corrupted by the words and examples of the extremely worldly-minded fellow Asuras, were powerfully attracted by the weight and seriousness of Prahlada's words. They threw away their playthings, and gathered round him, concentrating their looks and their hearts on him. To them the great devotee Prahlada spoke as follows with a mind full of love and pity.

अथ षष्ठोऽध्यायः

प्रह्लाद उवाच

कौमार आचरेत् प्राज्ञो धर्मान् भागवतानि । दुर्लभं मानुषं जन्म तदप्यध्रुवमर्थदम् ॥ 1॥
यथा हि पुरुषस्येह विष्णोः पादोपसर्पणम् । यदेष सर्वभूतानां प्रिय आत्मेश्वरः सुहृत् ॥ 2॥
सुखमैन्द्रियकं दैत्या देहयोगेन देहिनाम् । सर्वत्र लभ्यते दैवाद् यथा दुःखमयत्नतः ॥ 3॥
तत्प्रयासो न कर्तव्यो यत आयुर्व्ययः परम् । न तथा विन्दते क्षेमं मुकुन्दचरणाम्बुजम् ॥ 4॥
ततो यतेत कुशलः क्षेमाय भयमाश्रितः । शरीरं पौरुषं यावन्न विपद्येत पुष्कलम् ॥ 5॥
पुंसो वर्षशतं ह्यायुस्तदर्धं चाजितात्मनः । निष्फलं यदसौ रात्र्यां शेतेऽन्धं प्रापितस्तमः 6॥
मुग्धस्य बाल्ये कौमारे क्रीडतो याति विंशतिः । जरया ग्रस्तदेहस्य यात्यकल्पस्य विंशतिः ॥ 7॥
दुरापूरेण कामेन मोहेन च बलीयसा । शेषं गृहेषु सक्तस्य प्रमत्तस्यापयाति हि ॥ 8॥

Skandha VII : Chapter 6
PRAHLADA'S SERMON

Vanity of worldly Values (1-8)

Prahlada said: **1.** Wise men should begin the practice of devotional disciplines (Bhagavata-dharma) from their very boyhood. For, human birth in which alone devotional disciplines can be practised, is extremely rare, and it is uncertain how long life lasts. **2.** The highest and noblest act for a man to do in life is to surrender himself at the feet of the Lord. For He is the dear one, the soul, the master and the friend of all beings. **3.** Just as all creatures, having a body, experience naturally a measure of sorrow, happiness also accrues to them naturally without their effort. The Prarabdha or the Karma that has brought the body into being, yields them both these types of experience, and no special effort is required for them. **4.** Beyond exhausting life's span, nothing is achieved by efforts put forward for the attainment of pleasure and the avoidance of pain. A man full of desires never attains to that state of Bliss which one who serves the Lord attains.

5. Therefore one entangled in the fearful state of Samsara, if he is really intelligent, should in every way strive for the attainment of the Divine before the fall of this short-lived human body, even while it is in its full vigour and power. **6.** Man lives for a hundred years at the most. Of this span of life, if a man is of uncontrolled senses, half is wasted in sleep at night when he is in a state of darkness and inertia, almost like that of a dead body. **7.** Of the remaining half, the first twenty years are spent in the ignorance of childhood and the playfulness of early youth. Another twenty are spent in the decrepitude of old age, which reduces man to a helpless condition. **8.** Chained to domestic life, and oblivious of the ultimate purpose of his existence, the rest of man's life too is wasted in the

को गृहेषु पुमान् सक्तमात्मानमजितेन्द्रियः। स्नेहपाशैर्दृढैर्बद्धमुत्सहेत विमोचितुम् ॥ 9॥
को न्वर्थतृष्णां विसृजेत् प्राणेभ्योऽपि य ईप्सितः। यं क्रीणात्यसुभिः प्रेष्ठैस्तस्करः सेवको वणिक् 10
कथं प्रियाया अनुकम्पितायाः सङ्गं रहस्यं रुचिरांश्च मन्त्रान्।
सुहृत्सु च स्नेहसितः शिशूनां कलाक्षराणामनुरक्तचित्तः ॥11॥
पुत्रान् स्मरंस्ता दुहितॄर्हृदय्या भ्रातॄन् स्वसॄर्वा पितरौ च दीनौ।
गृहान् मनोज्ञोरुपरिच्छदांश्च वृत्तीश्च कुल्याः पशुभृत्यवर्गान् ॥12॥
त्यजेत कोशस्कृदिवेहमानः कर्माणि लोभादवितृप्तकामः।
औपस्थ्यजैह्व्यं बहु मन्यमानः कथं विरज्येत दुरन्तमोहः ॥13॥
कुटुम्बपोषाय वियन् निजायुर्न बुध्यतेऽर्थं विहतं प्रमत्तः।
सर्वत्र तापत्रयदुःखितात्मा निर्विद्यते न स्वकुटुम्बरामः ॥14॥
वित्तेषु नित्याभिनिविष्टचेता विद्वांश्च दोषं परवित्तहर्तुः।
प्रेत्येह चाथाप्यजितेन्द्रियस्तदशान्तकामो हरते कुटुम्बी ॥15॥
विद्वानपीत्थं दनुजाः कुटुम्बं पुष्णन् स्वलोकाय न कल्पते वै।
यः स्वीयपारक्यविभिन्नभावस्तमः प्रपद्येत यथा विमूढः ॥16॥

pursuit of insatiable sexual enjoyments and under the domination of overwhelming infatuation.

Exhortation to renounce (9-18)

9. Where is the man among those attached to their homes, enslaved by the senses and bound by the strong cords of affection to their near and dear ones, that can make even an effort to liberate himself? **10.** Who can give up the hankering for wealth which is dearer to man than his life itself—wealth for earning which thieves, servants, merchants and others pawn their very lives? **11.** How can a man renounce the intimacies he has been having with his dear wife in privacy as well as her loving prattle, his close friends and his lisping infants to whom he is bound by cords of affection? **12.** How can he renounce his sons, daughters, brothers, sisters, and sickly and pitiable parents—his attractive furniture and other household articles, houses, cattle, servants and hereditary vocations, when powerful memories of them are attracting his mind? **13.** Unsatisfied with enjoyments and imprisoned by greed in the cocoon of bondage-generating works, a man considers indulgence in sex and gluttony as the main purpose of life. How can a man in this condition, overpowered as he is by such an increasingly infatuated outlook, practise renunciation? (Therefore if a person is to tread the path of devotion, he must practise renunciation from early life, before all kinds of tendencies and entanglements have become finally established.) **14.** The heedless man who exhausts his whole lifetime for the maintenance of his family, fails to perceive that the ultimate purpose of his life is thereby getting defeated. He fails to cultivate renunciation even when afflicted by the three kinds of misery on all sides. For, such is his attachment for the family and the joy it gives. **15.** A householder, whose senses are uncontrolled and whose craving for pleasures is never satiated, will have unbounded greed for wealth too, and he will indulge in stealing and misappropriating others' properties in spite of being acquainted with the harm it will do to his life here and in the hereafter. **16.** O com-

यतो न कश्चित् क्व च कुत्रचिद् वा दीनः स्वमात्मानमलं समर्थः ।
विमोचितुं कामदृशां विहारक्रीडामृगो यन्निगडो विसर्गः ॥17॥
ततो विदूरात् परिहृत्य दैत्या दैत्येषु सङ्गं विषयात्मकेषु ।
उपेत नारायणमादिदेवं स मुक्तसङ्गैरिषितोऽपवर्गः ॥18॥

न ह्यच्युतं प्रीणयतो बह्वायासोऽसुरात्मजाः । आत्मत्वात् सर्वभूतानां सिद्धत्वादिह सर्वतः 19॥
परावरेषु भूतेषु ब्रह्मान्तस्थावरादिषु । भौतिकेषु विकारेषु भूतेष्वथ महत्सु च ॥20॥
गुणेषु गुणसाम्ये च गुणव्यतिकरे तथा । एक एव परो ह्यात्मा भगवानीश्वरोऽव्ययः 21॥
प्रत्यगात्मस्वरूपेण दृश्यरूपेण च स्वयम् । व्याप्यव्यापकनिर्देश्यो ह्यनिर्देश्योऽविकल्पितः ॥
केवलानुभवानन्दस्वरूपः परमेश्वरः । माययान्तर्हितैश्वर्य ईयते गुणसर्गया ॥23॥
तस्मात् सर्वेषु भूतेषु दयां कुरुत सौहृदम् । आसुरं भावमुन्मुच्य यया तुष्यत्यधोक्षजः ॥24॥

तुष्टे च तत्र किमलभ्यमनन्त आद्ये किं तैर्गुणव्यतिकरादिह ये स्वसिद्धाः ।
धर्मादयः किमगुणेन च काङ्क्षितेन सारंजुषां चरणयोरुपगायतां नः ॥25॥

rades! Even though a householder may be learned and know all this philosophy, still he is incapable of attaining the Atman. For he cannot get over the distinction between his self-interest and the interest of others, and therefore he continues to be in the darkness of transmigratory existence like any other ignorant person. **17-18.** Becoming the pet monkey of lustful women who hold him by the chain of progeny he has generated in them, the pitiable slave of the senses is never able to free his spirit from their clutches (unless he seeks shelter in the Lord, and the Lord helps him to break this chain). For this reason, O Asuras, you should shun association with such compatriots from early life and seek shelter in the primeval Being, Lord Narayana. For He is that beatitude sought after by people who have overcome worldly attachments.

God, our dearest and nearest (19-24)

19. O children of the Asuras! It is not at all difficult to please Achyuta. For He is the innermost spirit in all, and can be communed with anywhere. **20-24.** In all beings from immovable objects to Brahma the creator, in high and in low creatures, in the primordial elements, in Mahattattva and its evolutes, in the Gunas in a state of equilibrium and in Gunas in agitation—in all these entities and conditions is present that one Supreme Spirit, the all-powerful Divine Person, the Lord of all, the Unchangeable Substance. While baffling definition and remaining undifferentiated, He manifests as the indwelling spirit and as the objects of perception, as the pervader and as the pervaded. For this, He, the Supreme Lord and the undiluted fullness of Self-conscious Bliss, holds His transcendent supremacy in abeyance during creation, exercising His power of Yogamaya, and manifests Himself as the many. Therefore be kind to all creatures and extend your friendship to them abandoning your Asura nature. By this the Supreme Lord, who is beyond the purview of the senses, will be pleased.

Excellence of Bhagavata Dharma (25-30)

25. When the Lord, the infinite and the primeval being, is pleased with a devotee, what is there unattainable by him? But of what concern are such attainments to us—these material values of Dharma, Artha and Kama, which automatically fructify according to one's Karma? And pray, of what interest is even Moksha,

धर्मार्थकाम इति योऽभिहितस्त्रिवर्ग ईक्षा त्रयी नयदमौ विविधा च वार्ता ।
मन्ये तदेतदखिलं निगमस्य सत्यं स्वात्मार्पणं स्वसुहृदः परमस्य पुंसः 26॥
ज्ञानं तदेतदमलं दुरवापमाह नारायणो नरसखः किल नारदाय ।
एकान्तिनां भगवतस्तदकिञ्चनानां पादारविन्दरजसाऽऽप्लुतदेहिनां स्यात् ॥27॥
श्रुतमेतन्मया पूर्वं ज्ञानं विज्ञानसंयुतम् । धर्मं भागवतं शुद्धं नारदाद् देवदर्शनात् ॥28॥

दैत्यपुत्रा ऊचुः

प्रह्लाद त्वं वयं चापि नर्तेऽन्यं विद्महे गुरुम् । एताभ्यां गुरुपुत्राभ्यां बालानामपि हीश्वरौ 29॥
बालस्यान्तःपुरस्थस्य महत्सङ्गो दुरन्वयः । छिन्धि नः संशयं सौम्य स्याच्चेद् विश्रम्भकारणम्

इति श्रीमद्भागवते महापुराणे पारमहंस्यां संहितायां सप्तमस्कन्धे प्रह्लादानुचरिते षष्ठोऽध्यायः ॥ 6॥

which everyone aspires for, to us who serve His feet and who ever chant about His excellences and enjoy the bliss of His service? **26.** The Vedas do indeed deal with the three worldly values of morality, wealth and pleasure, with philosophy and ethics, with sacrificial rites, with statecraft and with various accomplishments useful for man. But I regard that the dedication of oneself to the Supreme Being, the friend and well-wisher of all, is their real teaching. (Or alternatively, the Vedas do indeed deal with the three worldly values of morality, wealth and pleasure; but they all become true Vedic teaching only to the extent they help man to make an absolute surrender of himself to the Supreme Being, the friend and well-wisher of all.) **27.** This doctrine of enlightenment, pure, pristine and unadulterated by any compromise with worldly values, was imparted by Rishi Narayana, the friend of Nara, to the sage Narada. It will shine in those who have the good fortune to be bathed in the dust of the sacred feet of those who have renounced worldly values absolutely, and cling to the Lord with undistracted devotion. **28.** From that Narada, who had the realisation of the Lord, I received this gospel of enlightenment in its theory and practice—which is the same as the nine-limbed doctrine of the practice of devotion to the Lord (Bhagavata Dharma).

The Asura boys said: **29.** O Prahlada! Neither you nor we have had any other instructors than these sons of the Guru of the Asuras. They are our sole masters and custodians, and we have no access to anyone else. **30.** It cannot also be that, when you were still in the women's quarters before coming here, you had contact with any great soul. O gentle comrade! If there is any convincing explanation for this, please tell us and solve our puzzle.

अथ सप्तमोऽध्यायः

नारद उवाच

एवं दैत्यसुतैः पृष्टो महाभागवतोऽसुरः । उवाच स्मयमानस्तान् स्मरन् मदनुभाषितम् ॥1॥

प्रह्लाद उवाच

पितरि प्रस्थितेऽस्माकं तपसे मन्दराचलम् । युद्धोद्यमं परं चक्रुर्विबुधा दानवान् प्रति ॥2॥

पिपीलिकैरहिरिव दिष्टचा लोकोपतापनः । पापेन पापोऽभक्षीति वादिनो वासवादयः ॥3॥

तेषामतिबलोद्योगं निशम्यासुरयूथपाः । वध्यमानाः सुरैर्भीता दुद्रुवुः सर्वतोदिशम् ॥4॥

कलत्रपुत्रमित्राप्तान् गृहान् पशुपरिच्छदान् । नावेक्षमाणास्त्वरिताः सर्वे प्राणपरीप्सवः ॥5॥

व्यलुम्पन् राजशिबिरममरा जयकाङ्क्षिणः । इन्द्रस्तु राजमहिषीं मातरं मम चाग्रहीत् ॥6॥

नीयमानां भयोद्विग्नां रुदतीं कुररीमिव । यदृच्छयाऽऽगतस्तत्र देवर्षिर्ददृशे पथि ॥7॥

प्राह मैनां सुरपते नेतुमर्हस्यनागसम् । मुञ्च मुञ्च महाभाग सतीं परपरिग्रहम् ॥8॥

इन्द्र उवाच

आस्तेऽस्या जठरे वीर्यमविषह्यं सुरद्विषः । आस्यतां यावत्प्रसवं मोक्ष्येऽर्थपदवीं गतः ॥9॥

नारद उवाच

अयं निष्किल्बिषः साक्षान्महाभागवतो महान् । त्वया न प्राप्स्यते संस्थामनन्तानुचरो बली ॥10॥

Skandha VII : Chapter 7

PRAHLADA'S LESSON ON SELF-KNOWLEDGE

Prahlada's previous History (1-16)

Narada said: **1.** Being thus questioned by the children of the Asuras, the great Asura devotee Prahlada recalled to memory what had been taught by me on the subject, and said with a smile to those curiously expectant children.

Prahlada said: **2-3.** When my father went away to Mandara mountain to perform Tapas, the Devas thought: 'By the Lord's grace this wretch is dead! As ants eat up a serpent, his own sins must have eaten him up.' Indra and other Devas therefore made extensive preparations for a war on the Asuras. **4.** Incapable of standing the massive attack of the huge army of the Devas, the Asuras ran away in all directions for fear of death. **5.** Afraid for their own lives, they fled in hot haste without any thought for the protection of their kith and kin or properties—their wives, children, relatives, friends, animals, household equipment and the like. **6.** In the flush of victory the Devas pillaged the royal palace, and Indra even took away my mother, the queen, as a captive. **7.** Trembling and weeping like a frightened Kuravi bird, she was being led off, when by chance the great Devarshi Narada met her on the way. **8.** *Narada said to Indra:* 'O noble-minded Indra! Release her, release her! This woman is guiltless. And she is the devoted wife of another person. It does not befit you to take her away as a captive.' **9.** *Indra said:* 'She has within her the most formidable embryo from the Asuras's seed. I shall release her after it is born and I have attained my objective (of killing the child).'

Narada said: **10.** This child to be born is sinless. He will be a great soul and a devotee and a servant of the Lord, equipped with the great power of the spirit. You

इत्युक्तस्तां विहायेन्द्रो देवर्षेर्मानयन् वचः । अनन्तप्रियभक्त्यैनां परिक्रम्य दिवं ययौ ।।11।।
ततो नो मातरमृषिः समानीय निजाश्रमम् । आश्वास्येहोष्यतां वत्से यावत् ते भर्तुरागमः 12।।
तथेत्यवात्सीद् देवर्षेरन्ति साप्यकुतोभया । यावद् दैत्यपतिर्घोरात् तपसा न न्यवर्तत ।।13।।
ऋषिं पर्यचरत् तत्र भक्त्या परमया सती । अन्तर्वत्नी स्वगर्भस्य क्षेमायेच्छाप्रसूतये ।।14।।
ऋषिः कारुणिकस्तस्याः प्रादादुभयमीश्वरः । धर्मस्य तत्त्वं ज्ञानं च मामप्युद्दिश्य निर्मलम् ।।15।।
तत् तु कालस्य दीर्घत्वात् स्त्रीत्वान्मातुस्तिरोदधे । ऋषिणानुगृहीतं मां नाधुनाप्यजहात् स्मृतिः 16।।
भवतामपि भूयान्मे यदि श्रद्दधते वचः । वैशारदी धीः श्रद्धातः स्त्रीबालानां च मे यथा 17।।
जन्माद्याः षडिमे भावा दृष्टा देहस्य नात्मनः । फलानामिव वृक्षस्य कालेनेश्वरमूर्तिना ।।18।।
आत्मा नित्योऽव्ययः शुद्ध एकः क्षेत्रज्ञ आश्रयः । अविक्रियः स्वदृग् हेतुर्व्यापकोऽसङ्ग्यनावृतः ।।19।।
एतैर्द्वादशभिर्विद्वानात्मनो लक्षणैः परैः । अहं ममेत्यसद्भावं देहादौ मोहजं त्यजेत् ।।20।।

will not be able to destroy him.'

11. Indra thereupon released my mother, honouring the words of the celestial Rishi. Out of his devotion to the Supreme Being, Indra circumambulated my mother, because, I, the Lord's devotee, was within her, and then departed to his heavenly abode. **12.** The Rishi then took my mother to his Ashrama, comforted her and said: 'Dear daughter! Until your husband returns, you may stay on here.' **13.** So, free from all fear, she stayed under Narada's protection till the return of the Lord of Asuras from his Tapas. **14.** That devoted wife spent this period of her sojourn there serving the Rishi with great devotion and praying in her heart for the health and welfare of the child in the womb and for its delivery only when she wished. **15.** Having me also in his mind, the merciful Rishi of great spiritual power imparted to her instructions regarding the flawless path of devotion and the enlightenment conveyed by it. **16.** My mother forgot those instructions, partly due to the lapse of a very long period of time and partly due to her inherent incapacity to retain them. But owing to the blessings of that Rishi, those teachings have ever remained green in my memory.

Separateness of Atman and Body (17-28)

17. If you listen to my words attentively, you too will gain that deep Faith that dawned on me by the Rishi's instructions. Faith will generate, even in women and children as in my case, that discriminative wisdom which puts an end to the travails of Samsara. **18.** By the action of the Supreme Being as Time, six kinds of transformations come to the body naturally, these being origination, existence, growth, maturity, decay and destruction. They affect only the body and not the spirit embodied in it, just as the changes undergone by a fruit do not affect the tree to which it is attached. **19.** In contrast, the Atman is eternal, undecaying, the one without a second, pure and unsullied by matter and its attributes, the one distinct from the body, for whom the body is an object and field of expression, the support of everything, pure consciousness without volition, the changeless being, self-conscious awareness, the cause of all, the pervasive, the unattached, and the uncircumscribed. **20.** Understanding these twelve unique characteristics of the Atman, one should give up the false feeling that I am the body or that the body is

स्वर्णं यथा ग्रावसु हेमकारः क्षेत्रेषु योगैस्तदभिज्ञ आप्नुयात् ।
क्षेत्रेषु देहेषु तथाऽऽत्मयोगैरध्यात्मविद् ब्रह्मगतिं लभेत ॥21॥

अष्टौ प्रकृतयः प्रोक्तास्त्रय एव हि तद्गुणाः । विकाराः षोडशाचार्यैः पुमानेकः समन्वयात् 22॥
देहस्तु सर्वसङ्घातो जगत् तस्थुरिति द्विधा । अत्रैव मृग्यः पुरुषो नेति नेतीत्यतत् त्यजन् ॥23॥
अन्वयव्यतिरेकेण विवेकेनोशताऽऽत्मना । सर्गस्थानसमाम्नायैर्विमृशद्भिरसत्वरैः ॥24॥
बुद्धेर्जागरणं स्वप्नः सुषुप्तिरिति वृत्तयः । ता येनैवानुभूयन्ते सोऽध्यक्षः पुरुषः परः ॥25॥
एभिस्त्रिवर्णैः पर्यस्तैर्बुद्धिभेदैः क्रियोद्भवैः । स्वरूपमात्मनो बुध्येद् गन्धैर्वायुमिवान्वयात् ॥26॥
एतद्द्वारो हि संसारो गुणकर्मनिबन्धनः । अज्ञानमूलोऽपार्थोऽपि पुंसः स्वप्न इवेष्यते ॥27॥
तस्माद्भवद्भिः कर्तव्यं कर्मणां त्रिगुणात्मनाम् । बीजनिर्हरणं योगः प्रवाहोपरमो धियः ॥28॥

mine—a feeling born of ignorance. **21.** Just as gold smelters extract gold from the ore through appropriate processes, so an expert in the science of the Spirit extracts, through spiritual communion, the gold of the Supreme Brahman from the mine of the body in which it is latent.

22. The Root Prakriti, Mahattattva, Ahankara and the five Tanmatras are spoken of as the eightfold Prakriti. Sattva, Rajas and Tamas are the three Gunas or constituent-attributes of Prakriti. The ten sense organs, the mind, the five gross elements—these sixteen categories are also spoken of by the Acharyas as the evolutes of Prakriti. From the body-mind, formed by the combination of these categories, the Purusha, who is the unitary principle, stands apart as their Witness without getting mixed with them, but at the same time forming the integrating principle that holds them together as a complex whole. **23.** The body is the complex of all the categories mentioned before. It is of two kinds—the unmoving like the trees, and the moving like other living beings. In this body, the non-Atman categories of Prakriti are to be rejected one after another as 'Not this, not this', and the Purusha or the Spirit arrived at, as the ultimate end of all negation. **24.** Observing the subsistence of the body when consciousness is present and its decay when consciousness departs, man should carefully investigate the truth of the Atman by discrimination, by purification of the mind, and by the scriptural texts on creation, preservation and dissolution. **25.** The states of waking, dream and sleep are the three modifications of the Buddhi (intellect). The awareness which stands aloof from these states as their witness is the Atman. **26.** These three states, born of the three Gunas of Prakriti and rejected as not pertaining to the Spirit, are the result of Karma. They do not contact or contaminate the Atman. As the Atman is seen to run through all these states, he is to be understood as the pervader distinct from them. He is just like the wind which carries odour, appearing to be one with that odour without being really so. **27.** Thus this Samsara is based on ignorance, producing the false identification of the Atman with these modifications of the Buddhi, which are a product of the Gunas of Prakriti, and with actions caused by them. Being based in ignorance, it is like the experiences of the dream state, without substantiality. (Direct or immediate experience through intuition is needed for this enlightenment, mere intellectual understanding will not do.) **28.** Therefore what you have to do is to destroy ignorance, the

तत्रोपायसहस्राणामयं भगवतोदितः। यदीश्वरे भगवति यथा यैरञ्जसा रतिः ॥29॥
गुरुशुश्रूषया भक्त्या सर्वलब्धार्पणेन च। सङ्गेन साधुभक्तानामीश्वराराधनेन च ॥30॥
श्रद्धया तत्कथायां च कीर्तनैर्गुणकर्मणाम्। तत्पादाम्बुरुहध्यानात् तल्लिङ्गेक्षार्हणादिभिः ॥
हरिः सर्वेषु भूतेषु भगवानास्त ईश्वरः। इति भूतानि मनसा कामैस्तैः साधु मानयेत् ॥32॥
एवं निर्जितषड्वर्गैः क्रियते भक्तिरीश्वरे। वासुदेवे भगवति यया संलभते रतिम् ॥33॥
निशम्य कर्माणि गुणानतुल्यान् वीर्याणि लीलातनुभिः कृतानि।
यदातिहर्षोत्पुलकाश्रुगद्गदं प्रोत्कण्ठ उद्गायति रौति नृत्यति ॥34॥
यदा ग्रहग्रस्त इव क्वचिद् हसत्याक्रन्दते ध्यायति वन्दते जनम्।
मुहुः श्वसन् वक्ति हरे जगत्पते नारायणेत्यात्ममतिर्गतत्रपः ॥35॥
तदा पुमान् मुक्तसमस्तबन्धनस्तद्भावभावानुकृताशयाकृतिः।
निर्दग्धबीजानुशयो महीयसा भक्तिप्रयोगेण समेत्यधोक्षजम् ॥36॥
अधोक्षजालम्भमिहाशुभात्मनः शरीरिणः संसृतिचक्रशातनम्।
तद् ब्रह्म निर्वाणसुखं विदुर्बुधास्ततो भजध्वं हृदये हृदीश्वरम् ॥37॥

seed which manifests as the multi-branched tree of Karma (actions). Yoga consists in destroying this seed of ignorance and thus calming the flow of the mental modifications.

Devotion as the easiest Path (29-40)

29. Of the numerous ways for achieving this, the easiest is the path prescribed by the Lord himself—the practice of virtues that stimulate deep devotion to Him. **30-32.** The path of devotion consists in the cultivation of these disciplines; practice of reverence to the Guru through devoted service of him; dedicating all one possesses to the Lord; keeping intimate contact with devotees leading a holy life; performing worship of the Supreme Being; having faith in the spiritual import of the accounts of His sportive manifestations; extolling His excellences and actions by recitals and hymns; practising meditation on his sacred form; seeing and adoring His divine emblems in the form of holy saints and holy images; and supplying all beings with their needs according to one's capacity, with the attitude that the Lord dwells in them all and that He is therefore the recipient through all His creatures.

33. Those who, through the practice of these devotional disciplines, succeed in conquering the senses and the passions, develop loving attachment (*rati*) to Vāsudeva, the Supreme Being. **34-36.** When, on hearing about the Lord's exploits in His Divine incarnations and about his unparalleled excellences, a devotee gets excessive joy resulting in horripilations all over, in tremulous voice, and in ecstatic singing, weeping and dancing; when like one possessed, he sometimes laughs, sometimes cries, sometimes meditates, sometimes salutes all as the Lord, crying aloud 'O Lord Hari! O Lord of all! O Narayana!' to the accompaniment of deep breath and utmost unconcern for what the world thinks of him—then is that man liberated from all bondage; then does he become identified with the Lord in mind and body in the state of ecstatic contemplation of His divine play; then does he, through the destruction of the subtle tendencies and their bases of ignorance by the power of Bhakti, attain to the Lord in truth and in reality. **37.** Wise men say that this embrace of the Supreme Being in consciousness is

कोऽतिप्रयासोऽसुरबालका हरेरुपासने स्वे हृदि छिद्रवत् सतः ।
स्वस्यात्मनः सख्युरशेषदेहिनां सामान्यतः किं विषयोपपादनैः ॥38॥
रायः कलत्रं पशवः सुतादयो गृहा मही कुञ्जरकोशभूतयः ।
सर्वेऽर्थकामाः क्षणभङ्गुरायुषः कुर्वन्ति मर्त्यस्य कियत् प्रियं चलाः ॥39॥
एवं हि लोकाः क्रतुभिः कृता अमी क्षयिष्णवः सातिशया न निर्मलाः ।
तस्माददृष्टश्रुतदूषणं परं भक्त्यैकयेशं भजतात्मलब्धये ॥40॥

यदध्यर्थ्येह कर्माणि विद्वान्मान्यसकृन्नरः ।
करोत्यतो विपर्यासममोघं विन्दते फलम् ॥41॥
सुखाय दुःखमोक्षाय सङ्कल्प इह कर्मिणः ।
सदाऽऽप्नोतीहया दुःखमनीहायाः सुखावृतः 42॥
कामान् कामयते काम्यैर्यदर्थमिह पूरुषः ।
स वै देहस्तु पारक्यो भङ्गुरो यात्युपैति च ॥43॥
किमु व्यवहितापत्यदारागारधनादयः ।
राज्यं कोशगजामात्यभृत्याप्ता ममतास्पदाः 44॥
किमेतैरात्मनस्तुच्छैः सह देहेन नश्वरैः ।
अनर्थैरर्थसंकाशैर्नित्यानन्दमहोदधेः ॥45॥
निरूप्यतामिह स्वार्थः कियान् देहभृतोऽसुराः ।
निषेकादिष्ववस्थासु क्लिश्यमानस्य कर्मभिः 46॥

what destroys the evil tendencies of the Jiva and saves him from involvement in transmigratory existence. This state is what is called the Bliss of oneness with Brahman. Therefore, meditate in your hearts on Him who is the Lord of the hearts of all.

38. What great difficulty is there in communing with Sri Hari, who like the sky, is pervading the hearts of all including yourselves, who is the soul of one's soul and who is the most genuine well-wisher and friend of all beings? And what special virtue is there in pursuing the vulgar enjoyments of the senses which can be had even in animal bodies? **39.** With his uncertain and short life-span, what real joy can a man have from such very temporary objects of possession and enjoyments like wealth, wife, sons, cattle, houses, lands, elephants, treasury and power? **40.** The same impermanence characterises the worlds that are attained through the performance of sacrifices. Not only are they perishable, but subject to evil passions, and to variations in the joy they provide according to the nature of the Karma. Therefore, for the attainment of your spiritual *summum bonum*, worship with single-hearted devotion the Supreme Lord who is free from any blemish, seen or heard of.

Fleeting worldly Values (41-48)

41. With whatever resolve a man with pretensions to wisdom might perform actions, they all become counter-productive, bringing him opposite results. **42.** All work with the idea of warding off pain and attaining happiness. But it is seen that he who has always been doing actions in order to ward off sufferings, lands himself actually in sufferings, whereas previously when he was doing no such works he had been happy. **43.** This body, for the satisfaction of which man goes after objects of enjoyments, is ultimately the food of dogs and jackals. It is extremely fragile and is seen to be here today, and gone tomorrow. **44.** How much more transitory are sons, wife, house, wealth, kingdom, treasury, elephants, ministers, servants, confidants etc., all that men consider as their possessions and as their own, but are none the less different from themselves, unlike the body, with which one is in identification as one's very self. **45.** For, of what use are all these fleeting, trifling and dangerous objects, including the body, to the eternally blissful Atman, in spite of their apparently enjoyable nature? **46.** O

कर्माण्यारभते देही देहेनात्मानुवर्तिना । कर्मभिस्तनुते देहमुभयं त्वविवेकतः ॥47॥

तस्मादर्थाश्च कामाश्च धर्माश्च यदपाश्रयाः । भजतानीहयाऽऽत्मानमनीहं हरिमीश्वरम् ॥48॥

सर्वेषामपि भूतानां हरिरात्मेश्वरः प्रियः । भूतैर्महद्भिः स्वकृतैः कृतानां जीवसंज्ञितः ॥49॥

देवोऽसुरो मनुष्यो वा यक्षो गन्धर्व एव च । भजन् मुकुन्दचरणं स्वस्तिमान् स्याद् यथा वयम् ॥

नालं द्विजत्वं देवत्वमृषित्वं वासुरात्मजाः । प्रीणनाय मुकुन्दस्य न वृत्तं न बहुज्ञता ॥51॥

न दानं न तपो नेज्या न शौचं न व्रतानि च । प्रीयतेऽमलया भक्त्या हरिरन्यद् विडम्बनम् 52॥

ततो हरौ भगवति भक्तिं कुरुत दानवाः । आत्मौपम्येन सर्वत्र सर्वभूतात्मनीश्वरे ॥53॥

दैतेया यक्षरक्षांसि स्त्रियः शूद्रा व्रजौकसः । खगा मृगाः पापजीवाः सन्ति ह्यच्युततां गताः 54॥

एतावानेव लोकेऽस्मिन् पुंसः स्वार्थः परः स्मृतः । एकान्तभक्तिर्गोविन्दे यत् सर्वत्र तदीक्षणम् ॥55॥

इति श्रीमद्भागवते महापुराणे पारमहंस्यां संहितायां सप्तमस्कन्धे प्रह्लादानुचरिते दैत्यपुत्रानुशासनं नाम सप्तमोऽध्यायः ॥7॥

children of Asuras! Just reflect what real joy can after all be derived through these so-called enjoyments by the Jiva who is suffering from the time of conception to death from the effects of his past Karmas. **47.** The Jiva engages himself in actions with the body that is now at his disposal. As a result of the works (Karma) he performs now, he gets a new body after death. Both the body and Karma are the effects of ignorance (Ajnana). (In that short span of time between birth and death, which is called life, how is enjoyment possible?) **48.** Sri Hari, no doubt, is the support of all worldly values like Dharma, Artha and Kama, and He will bestow them on votaries who desire them. But, pray, without caring for these worldly fulfilments, serve Him without any desire—Him the Self of all and the Lord of all.

Universality of Bhakti (49-55)

49. Sri Hari dwells as the Self, the Lord and Beloved, in the bodies of all beings formed with the primordial elements of His own creation. **50.** Blessedness is the reward for anyone—be he a Deva, Asura, man, Yaksha or Gandharva—who serves the feet of Mukunda, just as in the case of my humble self in spite of my being an Asura. **51.** O children of Asuras! Merely being a twice-born one or a Deva or a Rishi, one cannot win the favour of Achyuta. Nor is mere adherence to moral rules nor vast learning adequate. **52.** Neither charity nor austerity, neither sacrifices nor purificatory rites and vows are sufficient to please Him. He becomes pleased by pure Bhakti—by loving devotion without any ulterior motive. All other practices are an empty show. **53.** Therefore, O Asuras, practise devotion to Sri Hari, the soul of all and the Lord, seeing His equal presence in all others as in yourself. **54.** Asuras, Yakshas, disembodied spirits (Rakshas), women, Sudras, Gopas, birds, animals and sinful men have all attained Him through devotion. **55.** The supreme object of human life consists in cultivating exclusive and one-pointed devotion to Sri Hari and saluting His presence in all objects.

अथाष्टमोऽध्यायः

नारद उवाच

अथ दैत्यसुताः सर्वे श्रुत्वा तदनुवर्णितम् । जगृहुर्निरवद्यत्वान्नैव गुर्वनुशिक्षितम् ॥ 1॥
अथाचार्यसुतस्तेषां बुद्धिमेकान्तसंस्थिताम् । आलक्ष्य भीतस्त्वरितो राज्ञ आवेदयद् यथा ॥ 2॥
श्रुत्वा तदप्रियं दैत्यो दुःसहं तनयानयम् । कोपावेशचलद्गात्रः पुत्रं हन्तुं मनो दधे ॥ 3॥
क्षिप्त्वा परुषया वाचा प्रह्लादमतदर्हणम् । आहेक्षमाणः पापेन तिरश्चीनेन चक्षुषा ॥ 4॥
प्रश्रयावनतं दान्तं बद्धाञ्जलिमवस्थितम् । सर्पः पदाहत इव श्वसन् प्रकृतिदारुणः ॥ 5॥
हे दुर्विनीत मन्दात्मन् कुलभेदकराधम । स्तब्धं मच्छासनोद्धूतं नेष्ये त्वाद्य यमक्षयम् ॥ 6॥
क्रुद्धस्य यस्य कम्पन्ते त्रयो लोकाः सहेश्वराः । तस्य मेऽभीतवन्मूढ शासनं किम्बलोऽत्यगाः ॥ 7॥

प्रह्लाद उवाच

न केवलं मे भवतश्च राजन् स वै बलं बलिनां चापरेषाम् ।
परेऽवरेऽमी स्थिरजङ्गमा ये ब्रह्मादयो येन वशं प्रणीताः ॥ 8॥
स ईश्वरः काल उरुक्रमोऽसावोजःसहःसत्त्वबलेन्द्रियात्मा ।
स एव विश्वं परमः स्वशक्तिभिः सृजत्यवत्यत्ति गुणत्रयेशः ॥ 9॥

Skandha VII : Chapter 8

DESTRUCTION OF HIRANYAKASIPU

Hiranya's angry Reaction (1-7)

Narada said: **1.** Those Asura boys, being pure-minded, accepted the instructions given by Prahlada, and not those by the teachers. **2.** The teachers now saw how the minds of the boys were becoming more and more prone to contemplation in solitude. They were very much frightened to note this development, and to avoid blame falling on them, reported the whole matter to their ruler Hiranyakasipu. **3.** Hiranyakasipu's body trembled in violent rage on hearing of his son's unbearable misconduct, and he decided to kill the boy himself. **4-5.** Raining abusive words on Prahlada, who least deserved such harsh treatment, Hiranya, cruel by nature, looked at him with an angry side-long glance and, hissing like a trampled serpent, addressed the boy, who stood before him saluting in all humility and composure. **6.** He said: 'I shall immediately despatch you to the city of Yama, the god of death—you who are an audacious fool, a traitor to the family, a debased villain, and a defier of my authority! **7.** What is that source of strength depending on which you fearlessly flout the commands of one like me? My angry looks are sufficient to cause trepidation in the hearts of all the guardian deities and generate tremors in all the three worlds. How dare you flout me?'

Prahlada's Advice to Hiranya (8-11)

Prahlada said: **8.** O King! Not only for me but even for all considered strong, including yourself, the source of strength is He, the Supreme Being, who controls like His slaves all beings high and low, from Brahma down to a blade of grass. **9.** He, the Supreme Lord of world-measuring

जह्यासुरं भावमिमं त्वमात्मनः समं मनो धत्स्व न सन्ति विद्विषः ।
ऋतेऽजितादात्मन उत्पथस्थितात् तद्धि ह्यनन्तस्य महत् समर्हणम् ॥10॥
दस्यून् पुरा षण्ण विजित्य लुम्पतो मन्यन्त एके स्वजिता दिशो दश ।
जितात्मनो ज्ञस्य समस्य देहिनां साधोः स्वमोहप्रभवाः कुतः परे ॥11॥

हिरण्यकशिपुरुवाच

व्यक्तं त्वं मर्तुकामोऽसि योऽतिमात्रं विकत्थसे । मुमूर्षूणां हि मन्दात्मन् ननु स्युर्विप्लवा गिरः 12॥
यस्त्वया मन्दभाग्योक्तो मदन्यो जगदीश्वरः । क्वासौ यदि स सर्वत्र कस्मात् स्तम्भे न दृश्यते 13॥
सोऽहं विकत्थमानस्य शिरः कायाद्धरामि ते । गोपायेत हरिस्त्वाद्य यस्ते शरणमीप्सितम् ॥14॥
एवं दुरुक्तैर्मुहुरर्दयन् रुषा सुतं महाभागवतं महासुरः ।
खड्गं प्रगृह्योत्पतितो वरासनात् स्तम्भं तताडातिबलः स्वमुष्टिना ॥15॥
तदैव तस्मिन् निनदोऽतिभीषणो बभूव येनाण्डकटाहमस्फुटत् ।
यं वै स्वधिष्ण्योपगतं त्वजादयः श्रुत्वा स्वधामाप्ययमङ्ग मेनिरे ॥16॥
स विक्रमन् पुत्रवधेप्सुरोजसा निशम्य निर्ह्लादमपूर्वमद्भुतम् ।
अन्तःसभायां न ददर्श तत्पदं वितत्रसुर्येन सुरारियूथपाः ॥17॥

strides, is Time. He is the strength of the senses, of the mind, and of the body. It is verily He, the Lord Supreme and the master of the Gunas, that creates, preserves and destroys all beings. **10.** Please abandon your Asuric (monstrous) character. Have even-sightedness, abandoning the distinction between friend and foe. There is no enemy beyond one's own mind if it is uncontrolled and caught in the path of vice. The supreme worship of the Lord consists in keeping the mind even and unperturbed, seeing no difference between friend and foe. **11.** There are some who consider themselves as the victors of all the ten quarters, without first conquering the enemies within—the six senses which rob one of all one's real wealth. To a wise and good man who has conquered his lower self, who has an enlightened mind, who looks on all alike, there can be no enemy; for enemies are the creations of one's own ignorance.

Incarnation of Narasimha (12-23)

Hiranyakasipu said: **12.** 'O fool! You who indulge in such senseless and arrogant talk are facing imminent death. For none but those who are face to face with death will talk such unbridled nonsense.' **13.** Continuing, Hiranya asked, 'O hapless fellow! Where is that Lord of the worlds of whom you speak, if there is any such other than me?' 'Everywhere', replied Prahlada. 'Why? Is he in this pillar then?' questioned Hiranya. 'I see Him there too,' replied Prahlada looking at the pillar. **14.** 'I, the master of the universe, am now going to sever your head, O you impertinent prattler! Let Hari, of whom you speak as the shelter of all, protect you, if he can,' said Hiranya.

15. Castigating his highly pious son with such angry and abusive words, the powerful Hiranyakasipu jumped up from his throne, sword in hand, and delivered a blow with his very strong fist on the pillar wherein Prahlada had said he saw Sri Hari. **16.** Immediately a terrific sound arose from that pillar. That sound was so loud that it seemed to crack the Cosmic Shell. Hearing it, Brahma and other deities thought that the doomsday of the world, including their spheres, had come. **17.** Thus while Hiranyakasipu was making a determined effort to kill his son, he was

सत्यं विधातुं निजभृत्यभाषितं व्याप्तिं च भूतेष्वखिलेषु चात्मनः ।
अदृश्यतात्यद्भुतरूपमुद्वहन् स्तम्भे सभायां न मृगं न मानुषम् ।।18।।
स सत्त्वमेनं परितोऽपि पश्यन् स्तम्भस्य मध्यादनु निर्जिहानम् ।
नायं मृगो नापि नरो विचित्रमहो किमेतन्नृमृगेन्द्ररूपम् ।।19।।
मीमांसमानस्य समुत्थितोऽग्रतो नृसिंहरूपस्तदलं भयानकम् ।
प्रतप्तचामीकरचण्डलोचनं स्फुरत्सटाकेसरजृम्भिताननम् ।।20।।
करालदंष्ट्रं करवालचञ्चलक्षुरान्तजिह्वं भ्रुकुटीमुखोल्बणम् ।
स्तब्धोर्ध्वकर्णं गिरिकन्दराद्भुतव्यात्तास्यनासं हनुभेदभीषणम् ।।21।।
दिविस्पृशत्कायमदीर्घपीवरग्रीवोरुवक्षःस्थलमल्पमध्यमम् ।
चन्द्रांशुगौरैश्छुरितं तनूरुहैर्विष्वग्भुजानीकशतं नखायुधम् ।।22।।
दुरासदं सर्वनिजेतरायुधप्रवेकविद्रावितदैत्यदानवम् ।
प्रायेण मेऽयं हरिणोरुमायिना वधः स्मृतोऽनेन समुद्यतेन किम् ।।23।।
एवं ब्रुवंस्त्वभ्यपतद् गदायुधो नदन् नृसिंहं प्रति दैत्यकुञ्जरः ।
अलक्षितोऽग्नौ पतितः पतङ्गमो यथा नृसिंहौजसि सोऽसुरस्तदा ।।24।।

wonder-struck to hear the strange and terror-inspiring sound, whose source he could not trace anywhere in the assembly. **18.** In order to make true the words of His devotee that he saw Sri Hari in the pillar too, and also to demonstrate that He was immanent in everything, the Lord was seen as emerging into the assembly from the pillar, in a form that was neither of a beast nor of a man. **19.** The Asura, who was looking around for the source of that sound, now saw that form emerging from the pillar, a wonderful form which was neither a whole man nor a whole animal, but lo! a Manlion! **20.** While Hiranyakasipu was questioning himself anxiously within, there stood before him that very fierce form of the Man-lion, having glowing and fearful eyes resembling the colour of molten gold, and a face surrounded by brilliant matted locks and mane. **21.** His fangs were terror-inspiring. His tongue was sharp and quivering like a sword. His curved eyebrows gave a frightful look to His face. His ears stood erect and high. His open mouth and nostrils looked like strange mountain caves, while his cleft cheeks added ferocity to the face. **22.** His body touching the sky had a neck that was short and thick, a chest that was broad, and an abdomen that was slender. With hair resembling the rays of the moon covering His body, He had innumerable arms set on all sides with claws that looked like weapons. **23.** The form that stood before Hiranya was so formidable that none could approach Him, and the Daityas and Danavas all fled away in every direction before His special Sudarsana discus and other weapons. Then seeing Him, Hiranyakasipu thought: 'This is perhaps a stratagem thought out by that Hari, the master of all magical arts, to encompass my death. But let me see what this Hari can do against me.'

Destruction of Hiranya (24-39)

24. Soliloquising like this, the Asura, armed with a mace, rushed at the Man-lion, yelling. Like a moth rushing into a fire, the Asura was thereupon engulfed in the luminosity of the Man-lion and became

न तद् विचित्रं खलु सत्त्वधामनि स्वतेजसा यो नु पुरापिबत् तमः ।
ततोऽभिपद्याभ्यहनन्महासुरो रुषा नृसिंहं गदयोरुवेगया ॥25॥
तं विक्रमन्तं सगदं गदाधरो महोरगं तार्क्ष्यसुतो यथाग्रहीत् ।
स तस्य हस्तोत्कलितस्तदासुरो विक्रीडतो यद्वदहिर्गरुत्मतः ॥26॥
असाध्वमन्यन्त हृतौकसोऽमरा घनच्छदा भारत सर्वधिष्ण्यपाः ।
तं मन्यमानो निजवीर्यशङ्कितं यद्धस्तमुक्तो नृहरिं महासुरः ।
पुनस्तमासज्जत खड्गचर्मणी प्रगृह्य वेगेन जितश्रमो मृधे ॥27॥
तं श्येनवेगं शतचन्द्रवर्त्मभिश्चरन्तमच्छिद्रमुपर्यधो हरिः ।
कृत्वाट्टहासं खरमुत्स्वनोल्बणं निमीलिताक्षं जगृहे महाजवः ॥28॥
विष्वक् स्फुरन्तं ग्रहणातुरं हरिर्व्यालो यथाऽऽखुं कुलिशाक्षतत्वचम् ।
द्वार्यूर आपात्य ददार लीलया नखैर्यथाहिं गरुडो महाविषम् ॥29॥
संरम्भदुष्प्रेक्ष्यकराललोचनो व्यात्ताननान्तं विलिहन् स्वजिह्वया ।
असृग्लवाक्तारुणकेसराननो यथान्त्रमाली द्विपहत्यया हरिः ॥30॥
नखाङ्कुरोत्पाटितहृत्सरोरुहं विसृज्य तस्यानुचरानुदायुधान् ।
अहन् समन्तान्नखशस्त्रपार्ष्णिभिर्दोर्दण्डयूथोऽनुपथान् सहस्रशः ॥31॥

invisible. **25.** There is nothing extraordinary or astonishing about this in the case of Mahavishnu, the Pure Being of radiant Sattva, who at the end of the Pralaya neutralises that world-engulfing darkness of Tamas by His own brilliance. Approaching the Man-lion, the great Asura delivered a mighty blow on Him with his powerful mace. **26.** Just like Garuda catching a serpent, the Lord caught the attacking Asura in his claws; but the Asura freed himself from the hold of the sportive Man-lion, as a serpent from Garuda. **27.** O descendant of the Bharatas! The Devas and the lords of the quarters who had all been deprived of their realms by the Asuras, and who were now watching the scene from behind the clouds, considered it a calamity that the Asura had escaped from the hold of the Lord. The Asura too interpreted this episode as a proof of his opponent's fear of him. Soon without any sign of strain, he approached the Lord again for battle, sword and shield in hand. **28.** The fierce Asura whose eyes were dazzled by the brilliance of the Man-lion, was yelling and moving up and down with the speed of a falcon according to the tactics of combat in order to save himself from falling into the clutches of his opponent, but he was soon caught again by the Lord with a resounding roar.

29. Desperately struggling as the Asura was to free himself from the distressing hold of the Man-lion, as a mouse from that of a serpent, the Lord laid him on his thighs, sitting on the threshold of the Assembly Hall, and as Garuda tears apart a snake, He playfully tore open the Asura's body at the time of sunset—the body on which even a scratch could not be made by Indra's thunderbolt. **30-31.** The Man-lion form of the Lord then appeared forbidding to look at, because of the fury reflected in His eyes. With His tongue licking the two corners of His wide-open mouth, with the mane of his face and neck reddened by drops of blood, and with the loops of intestine hanging on His neck, the Lord as

सटावधूता जलदाः परापतन् ग्रहाश्च तद्दृष्टिविमुष्टरोचिषः ।
अम्भोधयः श्वासहता विचुक्षुभुर्निर्ह्रादभीता दिगिभा विचुक्रुशुः ॥32॥
द्यौस्तत्सटोत्क्षिप्तविमानसङ्कुला प्रोत्सर्पत क्ष्मा च पदातिपीडिता ।
शैलाः समुत्पेतुरमुष्य रंहसा तत्तेजसा खं ककुभो न रेजिरे ॥33॥
ततः सभायामुपविष्टमुत्तमे नृपासने संभृततेजसं विभुम् ।
अलक्षितद्वैरथमत्यमर्षणं प्रचण्डवक्त्रं न बभाज कश्चन ॥34॥
निशम्य लोकत्रयमस्तकज्वरं तमादिदैत्यं हरिणा हतं मृधे ।
प्रहर्षवेगोत्कलितानना मुहुः प्रसूनवर्षैर्ववृषुः सुरस्त्रियः ॥35॥
तदा विमानावलिभिर्नभस्तलं दिदृक्षतां सङ्कुलमास नाकिनाम् ।
सुरानका दुन्दुभयोऽथ जघ्निरे गन्धर्वमुख्या ननृतुर्जगुः स्त्रियः ॥36॥
तत्रोपव्रज्य विबुधा ब्रह्मेन्द्रगिरिशादयः । ऋषयः पितरः सिद्धा विद्याधरमहोरगाः ॥37॥
मनवः प्रजानां पतयो गन्धर्वाप्सरचारणाः । यक्षाः किम्पुरुषास्तात वेतालाः सिद्धकिन्नराः 38॥
ते विष्णुपार्षदाः सर्वे सुनन्दकुमुदादयः । मूर्ध्नि बद्धाञ्जलिपुटा आसीनं तीव्रतेजसम् ।
ईडिरे नरशार्दूलं नातिदूरचराः पृथक् ॥39॥

the Man-lion presented a formidable appearance, even as a lion that had slain an elephant. He now attacked the followers of Hiranyakasipu. Throwing aside the body of Hiranya with the heart torn out, the multi-armed Man-lion went around attacking and killing in hundreds with the stroke of his nails the numerous followers of the Asura who were standing with uplifted weapons in readiness to strike. **32.** The clouds were shattered by the movements of his manes. The luminaries in the sky like the sun lost their lustre in the abundant glory released from his eyes. His breath agitated the seas, and the elephants of the quarters trumpeted in fear, hearing His terrific roars. **33.** The heavens with the aerial cars of the celestials shattered by His mane, and the earth trembling under the tread of His feet, were both stirred to their depths. Under His powerful impact the mountains were tossed up, while the lustre emanating from Him drowned the brilliance of the sky and the quarters.

34. Afterwards he seated Himself on the royal throne in all his splendorous glory. None dared to approach that all-powerful being of terrific face, which bore marks of anger because there were no more opponents to be confronted. **35.** Hearing that the primeval Daitya (Titan), the headache of the worlds, had been slain by Sri Hari in battle, the celestial women with faces blooming in joy rained flowers. **36.** The sky was crowded with the aerial cars of celestials who gathered to see the happenings. The Devas then sounded their big drums and kettle-drums, while the leading Gandharvas danced and their women sang. **37-39.** Then, O dear ones, the assembled representatives of all species of beings—Brahma, Indra, Parameswara and other Divinities, Rishis, Pitris, Siddhas, Vidyādharas, great serpents, Manus, Prajapatis, Gandharvas, Asuras, Chāranas, Yakshas, Kimpurushas, Vetālas, Siddheswaras and Kinnaras, as well as the Lord's attendants like Sunanda and Kumuda—all these standing at a little distance away, with palms joined in reverential salutation, began to extol the Lord, one after another.

ब्रह्मोवाच

नतोऽस्म्यनन्ताय दुरन्तशक्तये विचित्रवीर्याय पवित्रकर्मणे ।
विश्वस्य सर्गस्थितिसंयमान् गुणैः स्वलीलया संदधतेऽव्ययात्मने ॥40॥

श्रीरुद्र उवाच

कोपकालो युगान्तस्ते हतोऽयमसुरोऽल्पकः । तत्सुतं पाह्युपसृतं भक्तं ते भक्तवत्सल ॥41॥

इन्द्र उवाच

प्रत्यानीताः परम भवता त्रायता नः स्वभागा दैत्याक्रान्तं हृदयकमलं त्वद्गृहं प्रत्यबोधि ।
कालग्रस्तं कियदिदमहो नाथ शुश्रूषतां ते मुक्तिस्तेषां न हि बहु मता नारसिंहापरैः किम् ॥42॥

ऋषय ऊचुः

त्वं नस्तपः परममात्थ यदात्मतेजो येनेदमादिपुरुषात्मगतं ससर्ज ।
तद् विप्रलुप्तममुनाद्य शरण्यपाल रक्षागृहीतवपुषा पुनरन्वमंस्थाः ॥43॥

पितर ऊचुः

श्राद्धानि नोऽधिबुभुजे प्रसभं तनूजैर्दत्तानि तीर्थसमयेऽप्यपिबत् तिलाम्बु ।
तस्योदरान्नखविदीर्णवपाद् य आर्च्छत् तस्मै नमो नृहरयेऽखिलधर्मगोप्त्रे ॥44॥

Hymns to Narasimha (40-56)

Brahma said: **40.** Salutation to Thee, the boundless Being, who art limitless in power, whose prowess is wonder-evoking, whose sportive actions are of such a sanctifying nature that those who hear accounts of them are purified immediately, and who sports in the creation, preservation and dissolution of limitless universes with Thy Prakriti (power), without however undergoing any change or diminution of Thyself as Sat-chit-ananda in the course of all the cosmic manifestations of Thy Nature!

Sri Rudra said: **41.** O friend of devotees! The time of cosmic dissolution is the time for Thy fury. Besides, this insignificant being of an Asura has already been killed. Therefore, deign to give shelter to Thy devotee Prahlada who is standing by Thy side.

Indra said: **42.** O Supreme Being! In affording us protection, Thou hast but recovered the sacrificial offerings due to Thee. For, the offerings offered to us apparently, are really to Thee, the resident of the hearts of all. The lotus of our hearts, which was Thy residence, and which was taken over by the Asura, has been reoccupied by Thee, and it has begun to bloom again. O Lord! For those who are engaged in Thy service—of what use are these felicities of the three worlds, liable to Time's depradation? They do not care even for Moksha (liberation)! What to speak then of other attainments!

The Rishis said: **43.** Thou hast imparted to us instructions about Tapas, which constitutes an expression of Thy glorious prowess. For, it is by Tapas that Thou didst bring out the vast and variegated universe into existence. But our practice of Tapas was obstructed by this Asura. O saviour of refugees! Thou who hast assumed a form for the protection of Dharma hast now again re-established the practice of Tapas.

The Pitris said: **44.** This Asura had forcibly appropriated to himself the offerings made by our descendants at the ancestral rites (Srāddha), as well as the libations of water with offerings of sesame seeds that are made while bathing in sacred waters on

सिद्धा ऊचुः

यो नो गतिं योगसिद्धामसाधुरहारषीद् योगतपोबलेन ।
नानादर्पं तं नखैर्निर्ददार तस्मै तुभ्यं प्रणताः स्मो नृसिंह ॥45॥

विद्याधरा ऊचुः

विद्यां पृथग्धारणयानुराद्धां न्यषेधदज्ञो बलवीर्यदृप्तः ।
स येन संख्ये पशुवद्धतस्तं मायानृसिंहं प्रणताः स्म नित्यम् ॥46॥

नागा ऊचुः

येन पापेन रत्नानि स्त्रीरत्नानि हृतानि नः । तद्वक्षःपाटनेनासां दत्तानन्द नमोऽस्तु ते ॥47॥

मनव ऊचुः

मनवो वयं तव निदेशकारिणो दितिजेन देव परिभूतसेतवः ।
भवता खलः स उपसंहृतः प्रभो करवाम ते किमनुशाधि किङ्करान् ॥48॥

प्रजापतय ऊचुः

प्रजेशा वयं ते परेशाभिसृष्टा न येन प्रजा वै सृजामो निषिद्धाः ।
स एष त्वया भिन्नवक्षा नु शेते जगन्मङ्गलं सत्त्वमूर्तेऽवतारः ॥49॥

गन्धर्वा ऊचुः

वयं विभो ते नटनाट्यगायका येनात्मसाद् वीर्यबलौजसा कृताः ।
स एष नीतो भवता दशामिमां किमुत्पथस्थः कुशलाय कल्पते ॥50॥

holy occasions. Thou hast recovered all that from his abdomen by tearing out the omentum with Thy claws. Salutations to the Lord as the Man-lion, the protector of all Dharma!

The Siddhas said: **45.** We salute the Supreme Being who tore open the trunk of this proud and oppressive Asura who had deprived us of our psychic powers through the strength of his concentration and austerities.

The Vidyādharas said: **46.** We always salute the Lord who has assumed the Man-lion form and has slain this Asura like an animal—the Asura who had grown so proud and haughty on account of his strength and courage, that he obstructed and prohibited our exercise of Yogic powers which we had acquired through practice of concentration on different objects in different ways.

The Nāgas said: **47.** The sinful Asura had deprived us of our crest jewels as also our jewels of women. Salutations to Thee, O Lord, who hast, by tearing open his chest, bestowed on these women continuing happiness through effecting their release.

The Manus said: **48.** O Lord! We, your servants, were helpless inasmuch as this Asura had broken all norms of virtue and good conduct by destroying the social order based on Varna and Ashrama. Now that he has been slain, order us, Thy servants, what we are to do in Thy service.

The Prajapatis said: **49.** O Supreme Ruler! We who have been created by Thee as the progenitors of living beings have ceased to function as such due to the obstruction caused by this Asura, who now lies dead with his chest torn by Thee. O embodiment of Sattva! Thy incarnation has brought about the good of all the worlds.

The Gandharvas said: **50.** We who are Thy dancers and musicians at entertainments have been enslaved by the courage, power and prowess of this Asura, who has

चारणा ऊचुः

हरे तवाङ्घ्रिपङ्कजं भवापवर्गमाश्रिताः । यदेष साधुहृच्छयस्त्वयासुरः समापितः ॥51॥

यक्षा ऊचुः

वयमनुचरमुख्याः कर्मभिस्ते मनोज्ञैस्त इह दितिसुतेन प्रापिता वाहकत्वम् ।
स तु जनपरितापं तत्कृतं जानता ते नरहर उपनीतः पञ्चतां पञ्चविंश ॥52॥

किम्पुरुषा ऊचुः

वयं किंपुरुषास्त्वं तु महापुरुष ईश्वरः । अयं कुपुरुषो नष्टो धिक्कृतः साधुभिर्यदा ॥53॥

वैतालिका ऊचुः

सभासु सत्रेषु तवामलं यशो गीत्वा सपर्यां महतीं लभामहे ।
यस्तां व्यनैषीद् भृशमेष दुर्जनो दिष्ट्या हतस्ते भगवन् यथाऽऽमयः ॥54॥

किन्नरा ऊचुः

वयमीश किन्नरगणास्तवानुगा दितिजेन विष्टिममुनानु कारिताः ।
भवता हरे स वृजिनोऽवसादितो नरसिंह नाथ विभवाय नो भव ॥55॥

विष्णुपार्षदा ऊचुः

अद्यैतद्धरिनररूपमद्भुतं ते दृष्टं नः शरणद सर्वलोकशर्म ।
सोऽयं ते विधिकर ईश विप्रशप्तस्तस्येदं निधनमनुग्रहाय विद्मः ॥56॥

इति श्रीमद्भागवते महापुराणे पारमहंस्यां संहितायां सप्तमस्कन्धे प्रह्लादानुचरिते दैत्यराजवधे नृसिंहस्तवो नामाष्टमोऽध्यायः ॥8॥

now been brought to this state at Thy hands. Can good ever befall a man of unrighteous conduct?

The Chāranas said: **51.** O worshipful Lord! We take refuge at Thy lotus feet which can save man from the transmigratory cycle. Thou hast now destroyed this Asura who had been an oppressor of holy men.

The Yakshas said: **52.** We who have become Thy principal servants by virtue of meritorious works, have been made his palanquin-bearers by this Asura. O Thou Lord in the form of Man-lion! Thou the Master of the twenty-four categories! Knowing, as Thou dost, his atrocities against the three worlds, Thou hast now been gracious enough to slaughter him.

The Kimpurushas said: **53.** We are only Kimpurushas, petty beings. Thou art the Lord of all—the Mahapurusha, or the Supreme Being. We are therefore incapable of extolling Thee adequately. The killing of this Asura is not the measure of Thy glory. For, this evil one had been killed the moment he earned the displeasure of holy men.

The Vaitālikas said: **54.** We used to receive great honour and presents by singing about Thy glory in assemblies and at holy sacrificial festivals. This wicked Asura had deprived us of all these opportunities. His destruction by Thee is for us a fortunate circumstance like the riddance of his disease for a sick man.

The Kinnaras said: **55.** O lord of all! We, Thy servants, were made by this Asura to work as his servants without any wages. O Hari! Thou our Master incarnate as Man-lion! That evil one has now been destroyed by Thee. May Thou bless us to prosper and to progress!

The attendants of Vishnu said: **56.** O Lord, our Master and Protector! Now hast Thou revealed Thy Man-lion form which is both wonderful and auspicious. Never has anyone seen it before. This Asura is none but a servant of Thine under the curse of Sanaka and other holy men. Thy sport of his destruction is only a blessing bestowed on Thy attendant.

अथ नवमोऽध्यायः

नारद उवाच

एवं सुरादयः सर्वे ब्रह्मरुद्रपुरःसराः । नोपैतुमशकन् मन्युसंरम्भं सुदुरासदम् ॥ 1॥
साक्षाच्छ्रीः प्रेषिता देवैर्दृष्ट्वा तन्महदद्भुतम् । अदृष्टाश्रुतपूर्वत्वात् सा नोपेयाय शङ्किता ॥ 2॥
प्रह्लादं प्रेषयामास ब्रह्मावस्थितमन्तिके । तात प्रशमयोपेहि स्वपित्रे कुपितं प्रभुम् ॥ 3॥
तथेति शनकै राजन् महाभागवतोऽर्भकः । उपेत्य भुवि कायेन ननाम विधृताञ्जलिः ॥ 4॥
स्वपादमूले पतितं तमर्भकं विलोक्य देवः कृपया परिप्लुतः ।
उत्थाप्य तच्छीर्ष्ण्यदधात कराम्बुजं कालाहिवित्रस्तधियां कृताभयम् ॥ 5॥
स तत्करस्पर्शधुताखिलाशुभः सपद्यभिव्यक्तपरात्मदर्शनः ।
तत्पादपद्मं हृदि निर्वृतो दधौ हृष्यत्तनुः क्लिन्नहृदश्रुलोचनः ॥ 6॥
अस्तौषीद्धरिमेकाग्रमनसा सुसमाहितः । प्रेमगद्गदया वाचा तन्न्यस्तहृदयेक्षणः ॥ 7॥

Skandha VII : Chapter 9

THE HYMN OF PRAHLADA

Prahlada assuaging the Lord's Wrath (1-7)

Narada said: **1.** None of the Divinities like Brahma or Rudra dared to go near the Lord in this wrathful mood which made Him unapproachable to them. **2.** Even Sri Devi, when requested by the Devas, feared to go near Him in that wrathful mood of His, unseen and unheard of at any time before. **3.** Thereupon Brahma told Prahlada standing nearby, 'O dear boy! Go near the Lord who has been angry at your father, and try to pacify him.'

4. Agreeing to do so, that great lover of the Lord, Prahlada, advanced slowly towards Him and with palms joined in salutation, prostrated full length on the ground before Him. **5.** When He saw the boy lying in prostration before Him, the Lord was bathed in an upsurge of tender feelings. He lifted him up and placed on his head those Divine palms of His which offer shelter to those who are frightened by the threat of the serpent of Time. **6.** The touch of the Lord's palms at once dissipated all traces of ignorance from Prahlada's heart and filled it with the clear Presence of the Lord. Overflowing with bliss within, his heart melted in love, his hairs stood on end, and tears streamed from his eyes. 7. His heart and eyes fixed on the Lord, his mind peaceful and concentrated, he now began to extol Sri Hari in a voice tremulous with love.

Birth no Inhibition to Lord's Grace (8-12)

प्रह्लाद उवाच

ब्रह्मादयः सुरगणा मुनयोऽथ सिद्धाः सत्त्वैकतानमतयो वचसां प्रवाहैः ।
नाराधितुं पुरुगुणैरधुनापि पिप्रुः किं तोष्टुमर्हति स मे हरिरुग्रजातेः ॥ 8॥
मन्ये धनाभिजनरूपतपःश्रुतौजस्तेजःप्रभावबलपौरुषबुद्धियोगाः ।
नाराधनाय हि भवन्ति परस्य पुंसो भक्त्या तुतोष भगवान् गजयूथपाय ॥ 9॥
विप्राद् द्विषड्गुणयुतादरविन्दनाभपादारविन्दविमुखाच्छ्वपचं वरिष्ठम् ।
मन्ये तदर्पितमनोवचनेहितार्थप्राणं पुनाति स कुलं न तु भूरिमानः ॥10॥
नैवात्मनः प्रभुरयं निजलाभपूर्णो मानं जनादविदुषः करुणो वृणीते ।
यद् यज्जनो भगवते विदधीत मानं तच्चात्मने प्रतिमुखस्य यथा मुखश्रीः ॥11॥
तस्मादहं विगतविक्लव ईश्वरस्य सर्वात्मना महि गृणामि यथामनीषम् ।
नीचोऽजया गुणविसर्गमनुप्रविष्टः पूयेत येन हि पुमाननुवर्णितेन ॥12॥
सर्वे ह्यमी विधिकरास्तव सत्त्वधाम्नो ब्रह्मादयो वयमिवेश न चोद्विजन्तः ।
क्षेमाय भूतय उतात्मसुखाय चास्य विक्रीडितं भगवतो रुचिरावतारैः ॥13॥

Prahlada said: **8.** Even Brahma, Munis and personages of high spiritual attainment, whose minds are naturally devoted to matters of a Sattvika nature exclusively, have not been able to adore Thee adequately and please Thee even till today, in spite of the flood of words proceeding from them about Thy excellences. Can I, born as I am in the race of Asuras with a fierce Tamasic nature, then ever hope to win Thy favour? **9.** I feel that none of these—wealth, high birth, beauty, austerity, scriptural study, vigour, impressiveness, prowess, strength of body, skill in action, intelligence, and practice of concentration—is adequate to please the Supreme Being. For, by mere devotion, The Lord was pleased with the lordly elephant who had none of these qualifications. **10.** I consider even a man of very low birth, a man born in the caste of dog-eaters, who has offered his mind, words, hopes, objects of desire, and vital energy to the Lord, as immensely superior to a Brahmana possessed of the twelve qualifications mentioned above (in verse 9), but is still indifferent to the Lord's holy feet. For the former purifies even his tribe, while the latter has only pride as his asset and not purity. **11.** The Lord, who is self-fulfilled by his own inherent bliss, does not solicit the worship of ignorant man for any purpose of his own. He accepts it only out of concern for the welfare of the worshipper. For, whatever offerings are made by people to the worshipful Lord, return as blessings to themselves, just as the beauty that a face derives from adornments only goes to beautify its reflection in the mirror. **12.** Since all can worship the Lord without any consideration of qualification, I, freed from all hesitation due to my low birth as an Asura, shall extol the Lord's majesty to the best of my capacity. Such praise of the Lord is itself the way for the purification of oneself caught in the transmigratory cycle created by the Lord's Maya.

I fear not this fearful Form (13-15)

13. All these, Brahma and the Devas, who stand there in utter fright of Thee, are Thy servants carrying out Thy will, unlike us Asuras. There is therefore no reason for them to fear Thee. All Thy incarnations are enchanting, as they are

तद् यच्छ मन्युमसुरश्च हतस्त्वयाद्य मोदेत साधुरपि वृश्चिकसर्पहत्या ।
लोकाश्च निर्वृतिमिताः प्रतियन्ति सर्वे रूपं नृसिंह विभयाय जनाः स्मरन्ति ॥14॥
नाहं बिभेम्यजित तेऽतिभयानकास्यजिह्वार्कनेत्रभ्रुकुटीरभसोग्रदंष्ट्रात् ।
आन्त्रस्रजः क्षतजकेसरशङ्कुकर्णान्निर्ह्रादभीतदिगिभादरिभिन्नखाग्रात् ॥15॥
त्रस्तोऽस्म्यहं कृपणवत्सल दुःसहोग्रसंसारचक्रकदनाद् ग्रसतां प्रणीतः ।
बद्धः स्वकर्मभिरुशत्तम तेऽङ्घ्रिमूलं प्रीतोऽपवर्गशरणं ह्वयसे कदा नु ॥16॥
यस्मात् प्रियाप्रियवियोगसयोगजन्मशोकाग्निना सकलयोनिषु दह्यमानः ।
दुःखौषधं तदपि दुःखमतद्धियाहं भूमन् भ्रमामि वद मे तव दास्ययोगम् ॥17॥
सोऽहं प्रियस्य सुहृदः परदेवताया लीलाकथास्तव नृसिंह विरिञ्चगीताः ।
अञ्जस्तितर्म्यनुगृणन् गुणविप्रमुक्तो दुर्गाणि ते पदयुगालयहंससङ्गः ॥18॥
बालस्य नेह शरणं पितरौ नृसिंह नार्तस्य चागदमुदन्वति मज्जतो नौः ।
तप्तस्य तत्प्रतिविधिर्य इहाञ्जसेष्टस्तावद् विभो तनुभृतां त्वदुपेक्षितानाम् ॥19॥

for the welfare of the world and for Thy sportive joy. They are never for causing fright. **14.** Therefore deign to defuse Thy wrath. The Asura is now dead, and there is no one here deserving Thy anger. Even pious men rejoice at the killing of harmful creatures like scorpions and serpents. Similarly the whole world feels relieved by the elimination of the Asura, and all are waiting to see Thy anger abate. O Thou of the Man-lion form! Henceforward men will contemplate on this form of Thine for freedom from fear. **15.** O Ever-victorious Lord! I am not frightened by this terror-inspiring form of Thine – Thy frightful face, tongue, sun-like eyes, quivering eyebrows, fierce molars, garlands of intestinal loops, blood-stained manes, bristling ears, fierce roars that startle even the elephants of the quarters, and claws that tore open the enemy's chest.

Involvement in Samsara (16-20)

16. But, O Thou friend of the lowly! I am afraid of the unbearable and frightful sufferings of this transmigratory cycle. Bound up by Karma, my lot has been cast in the midst of these Asuras given to violence and cruelty. When, O Thou Lord of abounding charms, shalt Thou be gracious to summon me to abide at Thy holy feet, granting me protection and freedom from the thraldom of ignorance! **17.** I am being burnt, in the fire of birth in successive wombs, involving experiences of pleasure and pain of union and separation. In this worldly existence all measures adopted for freedom from sufferings bring new sufferings in their turn. Not knowing this, I am in the grip of infatuation that makes one take the false for the real, the untrue for the true. Therefore grant me devotion and teach me to be Thy servant! **18.** O Lord! Thou of the Man-lion form! Thou being the dear one, the well-wisher and the Deity of all, I shall easily surmount the obstacles posed by body, mind and other limitations of material Nature by resorting to the recitals of Thy excellences and sportive manifestations, which have been glorified in songs even by Brahma, and by seeking the company of Thy great all-renouncing devotees—the Holy Swans (Paramahamsas) who always have their homes at Thy feet. **19.** No remedial measure sought as relief by sufferers in this world can be effective in the case of God-forsaken ones. They can at the

यस्मिन् यतो यर्हि येन च यस्य यस्माद् यस्मै यथा यदुत यस्त्वपरः परो वा ।
भावः करोति विकरोति पृथक्स्वभावः संचोदितस्तदखिलं भवतः स्वरूपम् ॥20॥
माया मनः सृजति कर्ममयं बलीयः कालेन चोदितगुणानुमतेन पुंसः ।
छन्दोमयं यदजयार्पितषोडशारं संसारचक्रमज कोऽतितरेत् त्वदन्यः ॥21॥
स त्वं हि नित्यविजितात्मगुणः स्वधाम्ना कालो वशीकृतविसृज्यविसर्गशक्तिः ।
चक्रे विसृष्टमजयेश्वर षोडशारे निष्पीडयमानमुपकर्ष विभो प्रपन्नम् ॥22॥
दृष्टा मया दिवि विभोऽखिलधिष्ण्यपानामायुः श्रियो विभव इच्छति याञ्जनोऽयम् ।
येऽस्मत्पितुः कुपितहासविजृम्भितभ्रूविस्फूर्जितेन लुलिताः स तु ते निरस्तः ॥23॥
तस्मादमूस्तनुभृतामहमाशिषो ज्ञ आयुः श्रियं विभवमैन्द्रियमाविरिञ्चात् ।
नेच्छामि ते विलुलितानुरुविक्रमेण कालात्मनोपनय मां निजभृत्यपार्श्वम् ॥24॥

most be a palliative of short duration, never an ultimate remedy. They have been deserted by Thee, while none but Thou can save them really. For, O Narasimha, Thou all-prevading one! a child cannot be protected by parents, a medicine cannot cure a patient, and a boat cannot save a drowning man, if they are all not supported by Thy will. **20.** Whatever agent high or low, be it one's own parents or the creator Brahma, constituted of the qualities of Sattva, Rajas and Tamas, brings into existence under Thy command anything new, or creates any modifications in anything old, that agent and what he accomplishes are in essence Thyself. Thou art the only existence and Thine the only will.

The Lord's Maya (21-22)

21. Thy Power Maya, when her triune Guna is stirred into activity by the prompting of Time, creates under the blessing of Thyself as Purusha, the Lingasarira or the subtle bodies of Jivas, which persist from birth to birth. They are the product of the latent effects of the Karmas of all the previous births. The hold of mind, the principal constituent of this subtle body, has its root in desires, which are confirmed and strengthened by Vedic ritualism. Mind is verily the wheel of Samsara, having for its spokes sixteen types of modifications generated by Maya. O Eternal One! None except those who seek refuge in Thee, can overcome it. **22.** O Lord of all! Thou omnipotent Being! Self-luminous Consciousness as Thou art, Thou transcendest all the Gunas of Prakriti and their products. Thou art manifest as Time, which controls and regulates all objects, entities and forces. Entangled by Maya, Thy Power, in the transmigratory wheel with sixteen spokes, I am being crushed like a piece of sugar cane. Deign to draw this refugee of Thine away from this wheel towards Thee.

Vanity of worldly Pleasures (23-25)

23. O Almighty Lord! What men usually aspire after—long life, wealth, and the resources of the guardian deities of the heavens—I have seen enough of these. All these attainments of theirs were dissipated before the mere movements of the brows of my father when he laughed aloud in anger at these deities. And that father of mine, surpassing all these deities in prowess, has been destroyed by Thee. Of what worth are these facilities and powers coveted by people? **24.** Therefore, I, who know these facts,

कुत्राशिषः श्रुतिसुखा मृगतृष्णिरूपाः क्वेदं कलेवरमशेषरुजां विरोहः ।
निर्विद्यते न तु जनो यदपीति विद्वान् कामानलं मधुलवैः शमयन् दुरापैः ॥25॥
क्वाहं रजःप्रभव ईश तमोऽधिकेऽस्मिन् जातः सुरेतरकुले क्व तवानुकम्पा ।
न ब्रह्मणो न तु भवस्य न वै रमाया यन्मेऽर्पितः शिरसि पद्मकरः प्रसादः ॥26॥
नैषा परावरमतिर्भवतो ननु स्याज्जन्तोर्यथाऽऽत्मसुहृदो जगतस्तथापि ।
संसेवया सुरतरोरिव ते प्रसादः सेवानुरूपमुदयो न परावरत्वम् ॥27॥
एवं जनं निपतितं प्रभवाहिकूपे कामाभिकाममनु यः प्रपतन् प्रसङ्गात् ।
कृत्वाऽऽत्मसात् सुरर्षिणा भगवन् गृहीतः सोऽहं कथं नु विसृजे तव भृत्यसेवाम् ॥28॥
मत्प्राणरक्षणमनन्त पितुर्वधश्च मन्ये स्वभृत्यऋषिवाक्यमृतं विधातुम् ।
खड्गं प्रगृह्य यदवोचदसद्विधित्सुस्त्वामीश्वरो मदपरोऽवतु कं हरामि ॥29॥

do not desire blessings like sensuous enjoyments, wealth, longevity, glory etc., after which all embodied beings from low creatures up to Brahma are mad. Not only these, I care not for any state or felicity that is subject to destruction by Thee as Time. I only pray that I may be led to the company of Thy devotees. **25.** Look at the nature of these worldly pleasures which are very attractive to hear about but insubstantial in actual experience like water in a mirage! Look at also these bodies through which the enjoyments are had—a hotbed of every kind of disease! And yet there are learned men, who know all this, but instead of feeling an abhorrence for such a life, vainly attempt to extinguish this flame of desire with the tiny honey drops of pleasure acquired with great difficulty!

The Lord as Kalpataru (26-29)

26. O Lord! Where am I, born in a family of Asuras having their origin in Rajas and dominated by Tamas? And where is Thy grace that prompted Thee to place Thy lotus-hands on my head in blessing—a condescension that could not be had by Brahma or Siva or Thy consort Ramā? **27.** Thou, who art the soul and the well-wisher of all beings in the world, dost not look upon anyone as high or as low unlike ordinary beings. Yet just as the heavenly wish-yielding Tree, the Kalpaka-vriksha, gives one's objects of desire only when one goes under it and prays for what one wants, so Thy grace too is bestowed on men through the service of Thee. Blessings come according to service, not on considerations of high and low.

28. Never shall I abandon the service of Thy devotees—I who, by contact with worldly people given to sensuous enjoyments, was about to fall into the pit of transmigratory existence infested by serpents in the shape of birth and death. It was Narada, a holy man, that took me as his own and lifted me up from that predicament. How can such a person like myself abandon the service of Thy devotees? **29.** O Infinite Being! I believe that it is in order to prove the truth of the words of Rishis like Sanaka, Sanandana and others, who are Thy devotees and servants, that Thou didst come forward to save me and destroy my father when the latter, with the evil intention of beheading me, took up the sword and challenged, saying: 'Let me see if there is any Power (Iswara) other than me to save you. I am going to take off your head.'

एकस्त्वमेव जगदेतदमुष्य यत् त्वमाद्यन्तयोः पृथगवस्यसि मध्यतश्च ।
सृष्ट्वा गुणव्यतिकरं निजमाययेदं नानेव तैरवसितस्तदनुप्रविष्टः ॥30॥
त्वं वा इदं सदसदीश भवांस्ततोऽन्यो माया यदात्मपरबुद्धिरियं ह्यपार्था ।
यद् यस्य जन्म निधनं स्थितिरीक्षणं च तद् वै तदेव वसुकालवदष्टितर्वोः ॥31॥
न्यस्येदमात्मनि जगद् विलयाम्बुमध्ये शेषेऽऽत्मना निजसुखानुभवो निरीहः ।
योगेन मीलितदृगात्मनिपीतनिद्रस्तुर्ये स्थितो न तु तमो न गुणांश्च युङ्क्षे ॥32॥
तस्यैव ते वपुरिदं निजकालशक्त्या सञ्चोदितप्रकृतिधर्मण आत्मगूढम् ।
अम्भस्यनन्तशयनाद् विरमत्समाधेर्नाभेरभूत् स्वकणिकावटवन्महाब्जम् ॥33॥
तत्सम्भवः कविरतोऽन्यदपश्यमानस्त्वां बीजमात्मनि ततं स्वबहिर्विचिन्त्य ।
नाविन्ददब्दशतमप्सु निमज्जमानो जातेऽङ्कुरे कथमु होपलभेत बीजम् ॥34॥

Divine Immanence and Transcendence (30-32)

30. It is Thou, the One Existence that hast manifested as the universe. Before its manifestation Thou wert, and at its dissolution also Thou wouldst exist as before. So in the middle, when the changeful universe is seen in the state of manifestation, Thou must have existed, uninvolved. By Thy inherent power Yoga-maya Thou manifestest this manifold universe through the transformation of the Gunas of Prakriti and abidest in it uninvolved and unaffected. **31.** O Lord! Thou art verily this universe both in its causal and manifested conditions. Thou art yet different from it insofar as Thou existest in Thy pristine condition at the end as Thou wert at the begining of this series of changes called creation. For one who sees this basic unity of existence, the opposition of interests between that of 'mine' and 'of another' is meaningless. He in whom the origin and the manifestation, subsistence and dissolution of the universe take place, must necessarily be one with Him. Just as in the case of a tree and its seed, the atoms of their constituent elements in their gross and subtle condition continue to be present unchanged in spite of the various combinations into which they enter, so is the Spirit present in all as their substance, without being affected in the least by all transformation. **32.** Withdrawing this whole universe into Thyself and established in Thy own inherent Bliss—actionless, eyes shut in inward communion, and dispelling the dullness of sleep in the bliss of Pure Self-consciousness—Thou liest in the Cosmic Waters in the state of Turiya, which is neither absorption in the oblivion of deep sleep, nor involvement in the objective movement of the waking and dream states.

Emergence of Universe from Lord (33-36)

33. This universe is verily Thy gross form. Like a huge banyan tree emerging from its latent condition in a seed, it emerges from Thee in the form of the Cosmic Lotus, when through Thy Power, the Time-Spirit, Thou spurrest Prakriti (Nature) into activity on awaking from Thy spiritual absorption (Samadhi), stretched on Thy bed of Infinity (Ananta) in cosmic waters. **34.** Brahma, who originated in that Lotus, could find nothing else existing except that Lotus whose source he could not discover. Though that source, the Supreme Lord, was latent in himself, he searched for Him for a hundred divine years in the cosmic waters, but could not discover Him. How could he? For lo!

स त्वात्मयोनिरतिविस्मित आस्थितोऽब्जं कालेन तीव्रतपसा परिशुद्धभावः ।
त्वामात्मनीश भुवि गन्धमिवातिसूक्ष्मं भूतेन्द्रियाशयमये विततं ददर्श ॥35॥
एवं सहस्रवदनाङ्घ्रिशिरःकरोरुनासास्यकर्णनयनाभरणायुधाढ्यम् ।
मायामयं सदुपलक्षितसन्निवेशं दृष्ट्वा महापुरुषमाप मुदं विरिञ्चः ॥36॥
तस्मै भवान् हयशिरस्तनुवं च बिभ्रद् वेदद्रुहावतिबलौ मधुकैटभाख्यौ ।
हत्वाऽऽनयच्छ्रुतिगणांस्तु रजस्तमश्च सत्त्वं तव प्रियतमां तनुमामनन्ति ॥37॥
इत्थं नृतिर्यगृषिदेवझषावतारैर्लोकान् विभावयसि हंसि जगत्प्रतीपान् ।
धर्मं महापुरुष पासि युगानुवृत्तं छन्नः कलौ यदभवस्त्रियुगोऽथ स त्वम् ॥38॥
नैतन्मनस्तव कथासु विकुण्ठनाथ सम्प्रीयते दुरितदुष्टमसाधु तीव्रम् ।
कामातुरं हर्षशोकभयैषणार्तं तस्मिन् कथं तव गतिं विमृशामि दीनः ॥39॥
जिह्वैकतोऽच्युत विकर्षति मावितृप्ता शिश्नोऽन्यतस्त्वगुदरं श्रवणं कुतश्चित् ।
घ्राणोऽन्यतश्चपलदृक् क्व च कर्मशक्तिर्बह्व्यः सपत्न्य इव गेहपतिं लुनन्ति ॥40॥

when the shoot has come out, how can its source, the seed, exist separate from it? **35.** Thereupon Brahma, the self-born, resumed his seat in the Lotus, being very much astonished and puzzled at his not being able to discover its source. Then he practised inward concentration for a very long time and gained purity of mind, which enabled him, O Lord, to experience Thy subtle presence in his own being constituted of the great elements, senses, mind, intellect etc., just as the presence of the quality of smell residing in the element earth is perceived by a Yogi. **36.** Brahma was delighted to see that Mahapurusha, the Cosmic Being, who had thousands of faces, feet, heads, hands, thighs, noses, mouths, eyes, ornaments, and weapons, who was the seat of all power and who was possessed of limbs that corresponded with the various regions of the universe.

Incarnations (37-38)

37. Incarnated as Hayagrīva (the Horse-headed), Thou didst destroy Madhu and Kaitabha, embodiments of Rajas and Tamas, and very powerful traducers of the Vedas, and retrieving the Vedas from them, Thou didst restore them to Brahma. This, Thy form as Hayagrīva constituted of pure Sattva, by which Rajas and Tamas represented by the Asuras were destroyed, is described by the wise as Thy favourite form, it being conducive to the development of Jnana. **38.** Thus, O All-powerful Lord! Incarnating Thyself as man, animal, fish, Rishi and celestial, in different Yugas (ages), Thou dost destroy the wicked and protect the worlds. Though Thou protectest the Dharma appropriate to every age, Thy presence is hidden in the age of Kali. Thou art therefore known as Triyuga, or one whose manifestations are confined to the three Yugas.

Prayer for Divine Grace (39-42)

39. O Lord of Vaikuntha! Evil tendencies corrupt my mind and make it outward-going. It is harassed by intense lust, by alternating feelings of joy and sorrow, by fear and the morbid craving for progeny, wealth and fame. As a consequence my mind is not able to feel delight in accounts of Thy deeds and excellences. Afflicted as I am with this shortcoming, how am I to persist in my quest of Thee? **40.** O Achyuta! My sense of taste, ever insatiate, drags me in one direction while lust draws me in another. So also hunger,

एवं स्वकर्मपतितं भववैतरण्यामन्योन्यजन्ममरणाशनभीतभीतम् ।
पश्यञ्जनं स्वपरविग्रहवैरमैत्रं हन्तेति पारचर पीपृहि मूढमद्य ॥41॥
को न्वत्र तेऽखिलगुरो भगवन् प्रयास उत्तारणेऽस्य भवसम्भवलोपहेतोः ।
मूढेषु वै महदनुग्रह आर्तबन्धो किं तेन ते प्रियजनाननुसेवतां नः ॥42॥
नैवोद्विजे पर दुरत्ययवैतरण्यास्त्वद्वीर्यगायनमहामृतमग्नचित्तः ।
शोचे ततो विमुखचेतस इन्द्रियार्थमायासुखाय भरमुद्वहतो विमूढान् ॥43॥
प्रायेण देव मुनयः स्वविमुक्तिकामा मौनं चरन्ति विजने न परार्थनिष्ठाः ।
नैतान् विहाय कृपणान् विमुमुक्ष एको नान्यं त्वदस्य शरणं भ्रमतोऽनुपश्ये ॥44॥
यन्मैथुनादि गृहमेधिसुखं हि तुच्छं कण्डूयनेन करयोरिव दुःखदुःखम् ।
तृप्यन्ति नेह कृपणा बहुदुःखभाजः कण्डूतिवन्मनसिजं विषहेत धीरः ॥45॥

hearing and smell drive me in certain directions while the fickle sense of sight and the vigorous organs of action drive me in still others. I am torn to pieces by their conflicting claims, as a husband by his several wives. Unfortunately there is none among these senses to drive me towards Thee! **41.** See us, the large number of Jivas fallen in this Vaitarini, the unfordable river of Samsara, by the force of our past actions, and struggling in it amidst the fear of life and death and of mutual competition for worldly enjoyments. See them engulfed in animosity and amity arising from the feeling of difference between oneself, one's friends and one's enemies. O Thou the resident on the bank of yonder river Vaitarani! Taking pity, save a fool like me from this predicament. **42.** O Father and Teacher of all! For Thee, who by Thy mere will art effortlessly carrying on the creation, sustentation and dissolution of this whole universe, what difficulty is there in lifting up Thy creatures from Samsara? Not only there is no difficulty, it is but proper, too. For, O friend of the afflicted! Thou art reputed to be very gracious to the ignorant. It is no good to say that this grace is confined to those of us who serve Thy dear devotees and tread the path of devotion shown by them. There is virtue in grace, only if it is bestowed on the least deserving.

Prayer for universal Salvation (43-44)

43. I do not mind, O Lord, even if I am consigned to the Vaitarani, the river of hell, as my mind is ever immersed in the ambrosial ocean of the recital of Thy divine attributes and sportive deeds. I am sorrowing for the ignorant persons who eschew the path of devotion, and for the sake of the petty and short-lived pleasures of the senses, shoulder the great burdens of worldly life. **44.** O Lord! Sages generally concern themselves only with their own salvation. They strive for it in solitude, without any thought for the salvation of others. But I do not desire salvation for myself alone, abandoning all other creatures to their miserable condition. I find no shelter other than Thee for these creatures caught in the travails of Samsara. (So if Thou art pleased to save me from Samsara, I am willing to accept it only on condition that all my fellow-sufferers too are saved.)

Mastery of Senses and Salvation (45-46)

45. The pleasures of sex life and other fulfilments available in household life are very petty. As relief sought by scratching an itching hand only adds a new form of

मौनव्रतश्रुततपोऽध्ययनस्वधर्मव्याख्यारहोजपसमाधय आपवर्ग्याः ।
प्रायः परं पुरुष ते त्वजितेन्द्रियाणां वार्ता भवन्त्युत न वात्र तु दाम्भिकानाम् ॥46॥
रूपे इमे सदसती तव वेदसृष्टे बीजाङ्कुराविव न चान्यदरूपकस्य ।
युक्ताः समक्षमुभयत्र विचिन्वते त्वां योगेन वह्निमिव दारुषु नान्यतः स्यात् ॥47॥
त्वं वायुरग्निरवनिर्वियदम्बुमात्राः प्राणेन्द्रियाणि हृदयं चिदनुग्रहश्च ।
सर्वं त्वमेव सगुणो विगुणश्च भूमन् नान्यत् त्वदस्त्यपि मनोवचसा निरुक्तम् ॥48॥
नैते गुण न गुणिनो महदादयो ये सर्वे मनःप्रभृतयः सहदेवमर्त्याः ।
आद्यन्तवन्त उरुगाय विदन्ति हि त्वामेवं विमृश्य सुधियो विरमन्ति शब्दात् ॥49॥
तत् तेऽर्हत्तम नमःस्तुतिकर्मपूजाः कर्म स्मृतिश्चरणयोः श्रवणं कथायाम् ।
संसेवया त्वयि विनेति षडङ्गया किं भक्तिं जनः परमहंसगतौ लभेत ॥50॥

suffering to the old one, these satisfactions only go to enhance the intensity of desire. Still these pitiable victims of sexual desire are never found to get satiation in spite of many sufferings arising from it. A wise man here or there may overcome sexuality, as a man sometimes escapes the temptation of the itch to scratch oneself; but that is achieved only through Thy grace. **46.** O Lord! For those who have no mastery of the senses, all the reputed means of spiritual attainment like silence, vows, scholarship, austerity, study of the Veda, discharge of duty, teaching, living in solitude, repetition of Mantras and practice of concentration, get reduced to a mere show for earning a livelihood. It is doubtful whether such hypocrites succeed even in this.

The Supremacy of Devotion (47-50)

47. The Vedas reveal Thee under two conceptions like the seed and the tree—the causal condition in which Thou art the source of the manifold, and the effect condition in which Thou art the indweller of the manifold. In no other way canst Thou, the formless, be comprehended. As one fire-stick is rubbed with another to bring out the fire latent in the sticks, so those who seek Thee practise communion with Thee in these causal and effect conditions through devotion and concentration. There is no other way. **48.** Thou art the fire, air, earth, sky, water, subtle elements (Tanmātras), vital energy, senses, mind, Chitta, Ahankara, and all the deities. All that is gross and subtle art Thou. Nothing that thought can think or words describe is outside Thee. **49.** O praiseworthy Lord! None included in Prakriti and its evolutes like intellect, mind and others, nor Devas, nor men are able to know Thee, because they are limited by a beginning and an end. Knowing this, the wise ones give up all self-centred efforts for knowing Thee like study of the Vedas and the philosophies (and practise pure resignation to attain Thy grace). **50.** O worshipful one! Without the practice of the six-limbed devotional discipline consisting of various forms of adoration of Thee like salutation, praise, dedication of all action, service, hearing and remembrance of Thy excellences and sportive manifestations—without the practice of these, how can that constant and deep-rooted love of Thee, the goal of the Paramahamsas, sprout in the mind of man? (Mere study of philosophy, works or concentration cannot generate the whole-hearted devotion, the one means for spiritual illumination.)

Prahlada tempted by Boons (51-55)

नारद उवाच

एतावद्वर्णितगुणो भक्त्या भक्तेन निर्गुणः। प्रह्लादं प्रणतं प्रीतो यतमन्युरभाषत ।।51।।

श्रीभगवानुवाच

प्रह्लाद भद्र भद्रं ते प्रीतोऽहं तेऽसुरोत्तम। वरं वृणीष्वाभिमतं कामपूरोऽस्म्यहं नृणाम् 52।।

मामप्रीणत आयुष्मन् दर्शनं दुर्लभं हि मे। दृष्ट्वा मां न पुनर्जन्तुरात्मानं तप्तुमर्हति ।।53।।

प्रीणन्ति ह्यथ मां धीराः सर्वभावेन साधवः। श्रेयस्कामा महाभागाः सर्वासामाशिषां पतिम् 54।।

एवं प्रलोभ्यमानोऽपि वरैर्लोकप्रलोभनैः। एकान्तित्वाद् भगवति नैच्छत् तानसुरोत्तमः 55।।

इति श्रीमद्भागवते महापुराणे पारमहंस्यां संहितायां सप्तमस्कन्धे प्रह्लादचरिते भगवत्स्तवो नाम नवमोऽध्यायः ।।9।।

Narada said: **51.** The Lord, who transcends the Gunas of Prakriti, whose excellences were thus extolled by the great devotee Prahlada lying prostrate at His feet, was now assuaged of His wrath, and being highly propitiated, said to Prahlada as follows. *The Lord said:* **52.** 'O Prahlada, virtuous boy! May all that is good and auspicious befall you! O the best of Asuras! I am highly pleased with you. Ask for whatever boons you want. I grant all that a devotee wants. **53.** I can never be seen by one who has not propitiated Me. One who has attained My vision shall have never afterwards any occasion to feel sorry that his wants have not been fulfilled. **54.** Therefore all virtuous men who have insight, and who aspire for higher evolution, seek to please Me who am the bestower of all that one aspires for.' **55.** Though thus tempted with rare boons that can overpower anyone else in the world however advanced, that noblest one among the Asuras did not go after any of them, as he was a person of unswerving devotion, seeking nothing but the Lord.

अथ दशमोऽध्यायः

नारद उवाच

भक्तियोगस्य तत् सर्वमन्तरायतयार्भकः। मन्यमानो हृषीकेशं स्मयमान उवाच ह ।। 1।।

प्रह्लाद उवाच

मा मां प्रलोभयोत्पत्त्याऽऽसक्तं कामेषु तैर्वरैः। तत्सङ्गभीतो निर्विण्णो मुमुक्षुस्त्वामुपाश्रितः 2।।

भृत्यलक्षणजिज्ञासुर्भक्तं कामेष्वचोदयत्। भवान् संसारबीजेषु हृदयग्रन्थिषु प्रभो ।। 3।।

Skandha VII : Chapter 10

SEQUEL TO THE STORY OF PRAHLADA

Prahlada and Boons (1-17)

Narada said: **1.** That boy, who knew that all these boons were obstacles in the practice of pure devotion to the Lord, said to Him smiling. *Prahlada said:* **2.** 'Deign not to tempt me with all these boons, as being an Asura, I am naturally prone to sense enjoyments. It is due to fear of getting involved in the pursuit of desires, that I have abandoned them, become an aspirant for release, and come to take refuge in Thee. **3.** O Lord! Thou must have offered to me these temptations of

नान्यथा तेऽखिलगुरो घटेत करुणात्मनः । यस्त आशिष आशास्ते न स भृत्यः स वै वणिक् 4॥
आशासानो न वै भृत्यः स्वामिन्याशिष आत्मनः । न स्वामी भृत्यतः स्वाम्यमिच्छन् यो राति चाशिषः
अहं त्वकामस्त्वद्भक्तस्त्वं च स्वाम्यनपाश्रयः । नान्यथेहावयोरर्थो राजसेवकयोरिव ॥ 6॥
यदि रासीश मे कामान् वरांस्त्वं वरदर्षभ । कामानां हृद्यसंरोहं भवतस्तु वृणे वरम् ॥ 7॥
इन्द्रियाणि मनः प्राण आत्मा धर्मो धृतिर्मतिः । ह्रीः श्रीस्तेजः स्मृतिः सत्यं यस्य नश्यन्ति जन्मना ॥
विमुञ्चति यदा कामान् मानवो मनसि स्थितान् । तर्ह्येव पुण्डरीकाक्ष भगवत्त्वाय कल्पते ॥ 9॥
नमो भगवते तुभ्यं पुरुषाय महात्मने । हरयेऽद्भुतसिंहाय ब्रह्मणे परमात्मने ॥10॥

नृसिंह उवाच

नैकान्तिनो मे मयि जात्विहाशिष आशासतेऽमुत्र च ये भवद्विधाः ।
अथापि मन्वन्तरमेतदत्र दैत्येश्वराणामनुभुङ्क्ष्व भोगान् ॥11॥
कथा मदीया जुषमाणः प्रियास्त्वमावेश्य मामात्मनि सन्तमेकम् ।
सर्वेषु भूतेष्वधियज्ञमीशं यजस्व योगेन च कर्म हिन्वन् ॥12॥

desirable enjoyments, which form the seed of Samsara and the knot of the heart, in order to show to the world the characteristic of a real devotee. **4.** O teacher of the worlds! Otherwise this attempt to tempt Thy devotee away from the right path is not compatible with Thy nature as the most merciful Lord. One who seeks favours and boons from Thee, is not a true servant, a true devotee. He is only a trader masquerading as a devotee. **5.** One who serves another with the idea of getting favours for himself, is not a true servant. So also he who bestows some favours on a servant with the idea of getting some service out of him, is not a true master. **6.** I am a devotee of Thine without any ulterior motive. And Thou art a master requiring the service of none to secure any objective. We both have no interdependent purpose to gain by coming together, unlike in the case of a king and his servants. **7.** O Lord! O the greatest of boon-givers! If Thou art very particular about giving a boon fulfilling any desire of mine, deign to grant the boon that no desire for any boon shall rise in my mind. **8.** The growth of desires in the mind causes the destruction of all the nobler faculties of man—the strength of his senses, of his mind, of his vital energy and of his body. With the sprouting of desires in the mind, man loses his sense of righteousness, determination, understanding, good fortune, modesty, prowess, memory, and adherence to truth. **9.** O Lotus-eyed one! When a man abandons all desires of the heart, then alone he becomes fit for liberation. **10.** Salutation to the worshipful Hari in this wonderful form of the Man-lion! Salutations to the Supreme Being, the possessor of all divine majesties, the indweller in everything, the high-souled, and the Brahman Supreme!'

Narasimha said: **11.** Whole-hearted devotees like you, do not long for any enjoyments here in this world or in the hereafter. Yet I bless you that for one Manvantara you be the head of the Asuras and enjoy the status and powers pertaining to that position. **12.** Practise the hearing of the delightful accounts of My sportive deeds. Install me in your mind—Me the one Lord of all, the indweller in all beings and the bestower of the fruits of all Yajnas—and worship Me by dedicating all your actions to Me. Karma thus loses its binding power, as a fried grain loses its

भोगेन पुण्यं कुशलेन पापं कलेवरं कालजवेन हित्वा।
कीर्तिं विशुद्धां सुरलोकगीतां विताय मामेष्यसि मुक्तबन्धः ॥13॥

य एतत् कीर्तयेन्मह्यं त्वया गीतमिदं नरः। त्वां च मां च स्मरन् काले कर्मबन्धात्प्रमुच्यते 14॥

प्रह्लाद उवाच

वरं वरय एतत् ते वरदेशान्महेश्वर। यदनिन्दत् पिता मे त्वामविद्वांस्तेज ऐश्वरम् ॥15॥
विद्धामर्षाशयः साक्षात् सर्वलोकगुरुं प्रभुम्। भ्रातृहेति मृषादृष्टिस्त्वद्भक्ते मयि चाघवान् 16॥
तस्मात् पिता मे पूयेत दुरन्ताद् दुस्तरादघात्। पूतस्तेऽपाङ्गसंदृष्टस्तदा कृपणवत्सल ॥17॥

श्रीभगवानुवाच

त्रिःसप्तभिः पिता पूतः पितृभिः सह तेऽनघ। यत् साधोऽस्य गृहे जातो भवान् वै कुलपावनः ॥
यत्र यत्र च मद्भक्ताः प्रशान्ताः समदर्शिनः। साधवः समुदाचारास्ते पूयन्त्यपि कीकटाः ॥19॥
सर्वात्मना न हिंसन्ति भूतग्रामेषु किञ्चन। उच्चावचेषु दैत्येन्द्र मद्भावेन गतस्पृहाः ॥20॥
भवन्ति पुरुषा लोके मद्भक्तास्त्वामनुव्रताः। भवान् मे खलु भक्तानां सर्वेषां प्रतिरूपधृक् ॥21॥
कुरु त्वं प्रेतकार्याणि पितुः पूतस्य सर्वशः। मदङ्गस्पर्शनेनाङ्ग लोकान् यास्यति सुप्रजाः 22॥
पित्र्यं च स्थानमातिष्ठ यथोक्तं ब्रह्मवादिभिः। मय्यावेश्य मनस्तात कुरु कर्माणि मत्परः ॥23॥

possibility of germinating. **13.** Work off your merits by enjoying their fruits, neutralise sin by doing good deeds, and let the passage of time consume your body. With your fame for holiness spreading even up to the celestial regions and all bondages and attachments broken, you will attain Me. **14.** Whoever recites this hymn of yours, remembering Me and you, that virtuous man will in the end attain freedom from the bondage of Karma.

Prahlada said: **15-17.** From Thee, grantor of boons, I seek but one favour. My father, without knowing Thee as the Lord of all, and looking upon Thee mistakenly as the killer of his brother, entertained antagonism towards Thee who art the father and the teacher of the whole universe, and persecuted me who am Thy devotee. By Thy grace may my father be purified from these gross sins that cannot be expiated in any other way. No doubt, when Thou didst cast Thy glance on him, even then he was purified. Yet as Thou art gracious to the humble and the lowly, I am making this request out of my anxiety.

Prahlada enthroned (18-34)

The Lord said: **18.** O pure and sinless one! Your father with twenty-one generations of his ancestors has been purified because of your birth in that line. **19.** Wherever my devotees, peaceful, even-sighted, holy and pure in conduct, stay, those families and those places get sanctified even if they are degraded and barbarous as the land of the Kikatas and its inhabitants. **20-21.** Those who do not persecute any being in any way, who have lost interest in everything in the world because of the absorption of their minds in Me, and who thus follow in your footsteps—they are my great devotees and they sanctify all the places they visit. You shall be the standard set for My devotees to follow. **22.** Do your father's cremation and other post-mortem rites according to custom, though, really speaking, he has been purified by My contact. A holy son like you is an assurance that he will attain higher regions. **23.** Ascend to the throne of your father and with your mind

नारद उवाच

प्रह्लादोऽपि तथा चक्रे पितुर्यत्साम्परायिकम् । यथाऽऽह भगवान् राजन्नभिषिक्तो द्विजोत्तमैः 24॥
प्रसादसुमुखं दृष्ट्वा ब्रह्मा नरहरिं हरिम् । स्तुत्वा वाग्भिः पवित्राभिः प्राह देवादिभिर्वृतः ॥

ब्रह्मोवाच

देवदेवाखिलाध्यक्ष भूतभावन पूर्वज । दिष्ट्या ते निहतः पापो लोकसंतापनोऽसुरः 26॥
योऽसौ लब्धवरो मत्तो न वध्यो मम सृष्टिभिः । तपोयोगबलोन्नद्धः समस्तनिगमानहन् ॥27॥
दिष्ट्यास्य तनयः साधुर्महाभागवतोऽर्भकः । त्वया विमोचितो मृत्योर्दिष्ट्या त्वां समितोऽधुना ॥
एतद् वपुस्ते भगवन् ध्यायतः प्रयतात्मनः । सर्वतो गोप्तृ संत्रासान्मृत्योरपि जिघांसतः ॥29॥

नृसिंह उवाच

मैवं वरोऽसुराणां ते प्रदेयः पद्मसम्भव । वरः क्रूरनिसर्गाणामहीनाममृतं यथा ॥30॥

नारद उवाच

इत्युक्त्वा भगवान् राजंस्तत्रैवान्तर्दधे हरिः । अदृश्यः सर्वभूतानां पूजितः परमेष्ठिना ॥31॥
ततः सम्पूज्य शिरसा ववन्दे परमेष्ठिनम् । भवं प्रजापतीन् देवान् प्रह्लादो भगवत्कलाः ॥32॥
ततः काव्यादिभिः सार्धं मुनिभिः कमलासनः । दैत्यानां दानवानां च प्रह्लादमकरोत् पतिम् ॥33॥
प्रतिनन्द्य ततो देवाः प्रयुज्य परमाशिषः । स्वधामानि ययू राजन् ब्रह्माद्याः प्रतिपूजिताः 34॥

resigned to Me, perform your duties as advised by wise and pious men who know the Vedas.

Narada said: **24.** O King! Prahlada performed all the funeral rites of his father, as directed by the Lord, and he was anointed king by learned and pious priests. **25.** Brahma, now seeing from the gracious look of the Lord in the Man-lion form that His wrath had been appeased, approached Him with a body of celestials, reciting hymns in His glorification and said:

Brahma said: **26.** O Lord! Thou master and origin of all! Thou whose existence precedes everything! It is the good fortune of all that this Asura, who was a mass of iniquity and a cause of misery to the world at large, has been destroyed by Thee. **27.** Obtaining boons from Me, this Asura became indestructible by anyone among my creations. Becoming inordinately proud and insolent because of the power he gained by austerity and concentration, he destroyed all the Vedic institutions for the maintenance of Dharma. **28.** Fortunate it is that his son, who is very good and pious by nature, has been saved by Thee from death, and he is now by Thy side free from all fear. **29.** O worshipful Lord! This form of Thine as the Man-lion would save a man, who meditates on it with concentration, from all difficulties, even from death that threatens to kill him.

Narasimha said: **30.** O lotus-born one! It behoves you not to give this kind of boons to Asuras. For, granting them to those who are basically cruel by nature is like feeding a snake with the immortal drink. It will only add to the world's woes.

Narada said: **31.** Saying so, Sri Hari, all-powerful and ordinarily imperceivable by any, disappeared from the vision of all, after receiving the worship of Brahma. **32.** Afterwards Prahlada made prostrations to all the Devas—Brahma, Bhava, the Prajapatis and the celestials who were all parts of Mahavishnu. **33.** Next Brahma, along with the Rishis like Sukra, proclaimed Prahlada to be the king of the Danavas and Daityas. **34.** They then pronounced blessings on Prahlada who in turn

एवं तौ पार्षदौ विष्णोः पुत्रत्वं प्रापितौ दितेः । हृदि स्थितेन हरिणा वैरभावेन तौ हतौ ॥35॥
पुनश्च विप्रशापेन राक्षसौ तौ बभूवतुः । कुम्भकर्णदशग्रीवौ हतौ तौ रामविक्रमैः ॥36॥
शयानौ युधि निर्भिन्नहृदयौ रामसायकैः । तच्चित्तौ जहतुर्देहं यथा प्राक्तनजन्मनि ॥37॥
ताविहाथ पुनर्जातौ शिशुपालकरूषजौ । हरौ वैरानुबन्धेन पश्यतस्ते समीयतुः ॥38॥
एनः पूर्वकृतं यत् तद् राजानः कृष्णवैरिणः । जहुस्त्वन्ते तदात्मानः कीटः पेशस्कृतो यथा 39॥
यथा यथा भगवतो भक्त्या परमयाभिदा । नृपाश्चैद्यादयः सात्म्यं हरेस्तच्चिन्तया ययुः ॥40॥
आख्यातं सर्वमेतत् ते यन्मां त्वं परिपृष्टवान् । दमघोषसुतादीनां हरेः सात्म्यमपि द्विषाम् 41॥
एषा ब्रह्मण्यदेवस्य कृष्णस्य च महात्मनः । अवतारकथा पुण्या वधो यत्रादिदैत्ययोः ॥42॥
प्रह्लादस्यानुचरितं महाभागवतस्य च । भक्तिर्ज्ञानं विरक्तिश्च याथात्म्यं चास्य वै हरेः 43॥
सर्गस्थित्यप्ययेशस्य गुणकर्मानुवर्णनम् । परावरेषां स्थानानां कालेन व्यत्ययो महान् ॥44॥
धर्मो भागवतानां च भगवान् येन गम्यते । आख्यानेऽस्मिन् समाम्नातमाध्यात्मिकमशेषतः ॥
य एतत् पुण्यमाख्यानं विष्णोर्वीर्योपबृंहितम् । कीर्तयेच्छ्रद्धया श्रुत्वा कर्मपाशैर्विमुच्यते 46॥

worshipped them all. All of them then repaired to their respective abodes.

The Secret of Divine Love (35-51)

35. Thus it was that the two attendants of Mahavishnu became Daityas on account of the curse of Sanaka and other sages. Hari who manifested in their hearts in a form appropriate to their attitude of confrontation, appeared before them and killed them. **36.** Later as the result of the same curse, they became the Rakshasas known as Kumbhakarna and the ten-headed Ravana, and they were killed by Rama. **37.** Fallen in the field of battle with their hearts pierced by the arrows of Rama, they died thinking of the Lord, as in the previous birth. **38.** They were again born as Sisupala and Dantavaktra, and you have seen how, through contemplation on the Lord as their enemy, they have attained to Him. **39.** Just as the worm, imprisoned by the wasp and contemplating on it, is transformed into a wasp through dread, so did many kings, inimical to Krishna, overcome their previous sins by concentration on Him through fear and enmity. **40.** Just as devotees attain to the state of seeing the Lord in everything through supreme and undivided Bhakti, in the same way, Sisupala and other enemy kings thought of Krishna with one-pointed concentration which hatred generated in them, and thinking so, attained to oneness with Sri Hari. **41.** I have now answered your question how haters of the Lord like Sisupala could gain oneness with Hari.

42. I have also finished narrating to you the sacred story of the worshipful Lord, the lover of holy ones, in his incarnation for the destruction of these primeval demons. **43-45.** In this story of Prahlada has been told all relevant matters connected with the salvation of man as conceived by the path of devotion of the Bhagavatas —Bhakti, Jnana, Virakti (dispassion), the unique power and glory of the Lord, the excellences and activities of Him who is the creator, preserver and the destroyer of the universe, and the change that Time brings about in the fortunes of Asuras and Devas. **46.** Whosoever hears and recites this holy account of Mahavishnu's glory with faith and devotion, he becomes liberated from all the bondages of Karma.

एतद् य आदिपुरुषस्य मृगेन्द्रलीलां दैत्येन्द्रयूथपवधं प्रयतः पठेत ।
दैत्यात्मजस्य च सतां प्रवरस्य पुण्यं श्रुत्वानुभावमकुतोभयमेति लोकम् ॥47॥
यूयं नृलोके बत भूरिभागा लोकं पुनाना मुनयोऽभियन्ति ।
येषां गृहानावसतीति साक्षाद् गूढं परं ब्रह्म मनुष्यलिङ्गम् ॥48॥
स वा अयं ब्रह्म महद्विमृग्यकैवल्यनिर्वाणसुखानुभूतिः ।
प्रियः सुहृद् वः खलु मातुलेय आत्मार्हणीयो विधिकृद् गुरुश्च ॥49॥
न यस्य साक्षाद् भवपद्मजादिभी रूपं धिया वस्तुतयोपवर्णितम् ।
मौनेन भक्त्योपशमेन पूजितः प्रसीदतामेष स सात्वतां पतिः ॥50॥
स एष भगवान् राजन् व्यतनोद् विहतं यशः । पुरा रुद्रस्य देवस्य मयेनानन्तमायिना ॥51॥

राजोवाच

कस्मिन् कर्मणि देवस्य मयोऽहञ्जगदीशितुः । यथा चोपचिता कीर्तिः कृष्णेनानेन कथ्यताम् 52॥

नारद उवाच

निर्जिता असुरा देवैर्युध्यनेनोपबृंहितैः । मायिनां परमाचार्यं मयं शरणमाययुः ॥53॥
स निर्माय पुरस्तिस्रो हैमीरौप्यायसीर्विभुः । दुर्लक्ष्यापायसंयोगा दुर्वितर्क्यपरिच्छदाः ॥54॥
ताभिस्तेऽसुरसेनान्यो लोकांस्त्रीन् सेश्वरान् नृप । स्मरन्तो नाशयाञ्चक्रुः पूर्ववैरमलक्षिताः ॥55॥

47. Man reaches the state beyond all fear if he hears this account of the Lord's sportive deeds as the Man-lion, His destruction of Hiranyakasipu and his Asura forces, and also the holy story of Prahlada, his son and prince among devotees. **48.** You, the sons of Pandu, are the most fortunate among men. For, the Supreme Brahman is Himself residing here with you under the guise of a human being, and sages, whose footsteps purify the places they tread, are flocking here from all sides in order to meet him. **49.** He, Krishna, is that very Brahman sought after by the greatest of sages, the Bliss of liberation intuited in unitive understanding. But wonder of wonders! He stays with you playing several parts with you as dear friend, well-wisher, uncle's son, worshipful teacher, servant and your very self. **50.** Even Brahma, Siva and others have not been able to determine by their intellect or describe by words the real form of Him, Krishna. May He be propitious to us through our observance of silence and other vows, the control of the senses and the cultivation of Bhakti. **51.** O King! It was the worshipful Lord Vishnu who restored and re-established the reputation of Lord Rudra, which was gravely affected by the nefarious practices of Maya, the Asura of great magical powers.

Destruction of the Tripuras (52-71)

Rajah Yudhishthira said: **52.** In what ways did Maya cause damage to the reputation of Rudra, and how did Krishna restore it once again? *Narada said:* **53.** When the Asuras were once defeated by the Devas, whose power had been enhanced by Mahavishnu, they took shelter with Maya, the master of all magical arts. **54.** The master-craftsman that He was, Maya built for them three large flying fortresses of gold, silver and iron which could move about invisibly, and had unique kinds of equipment inconceivable by anyone. **55.** O King! The Asura leaders, keeping their old antagonism in mind, moved about all over the world unseen, destroying everything that they

ततस्ते सेश्वरा लोका उपासाद्येश्वरं विभो । त्राहि नस्तावकान् देव विनष्टांस्त्रिपुरालयैः 56॥
अथानुगृह्य भगवान् मा भैष्टेति सुरान् विभुः । शरं धनुषि सन्धाय पुरेष्वस्त्रं व्यमुञ्चत ॥57॥
ततोऽग्निवर्णा इषव उत्पेतुः सूर्यमण्डलात् । यथा मयूखसंदोहा नादृश्यन्त पुरो यतः ॥58॥
तैः स्पृष्टा व्यसवः सर्वे निपेतुः स्म पुरौकसः । तानानीय महायोगी मयः कूपरसेऽक्षिपत् ॥59॥
सिद्धामृतरसस्पृष्टा वज्रसारा महौजसः । उत्तस्थुर्मेघदलना वैद्युता इव वह्नयः ॥60॥
विलोक्य भग्नसङ्कल्पं विमनस्कं वृषध्वजम् । तदायं भगवान् विष्णुस्तत्रोपायमकल्पयत् ॥61॥
वत्स आसीत्तदा ब्रह्मा स्वयं विष्णुरयं हि गौः । प्रविश्य त्रिपुरं काले रसकूपामृतं पपौ ॥62॥
तेऽसुरा ह्यपि पश्यन्तो न न्यषेधन् विमोहिताः । तद् विज्ञाय महायोगी रसपालानिदं जगौ ॥63॥
स्वयं विशोकः शोकार्तान् स्मरन् दैवगतिं च ताम् । देवोऽसुरो नरोऽन्यो वा नेश्वरोऽस्तीह कश्चन 64॥
आत्मनोऽन्यस्य वा दिष्टं दैवेनापोहितुं द्वयोः । अथासौ शक्तिभिः स्वाभिः शम्भोः प्राधनिकं व्यधात्
धर्मज्ञानविरक्त्यृद्धितपोविद्याक्रियादिभिः । रथं सूतं ध्वजं वाहान् धनुर्वर्म शरादि यत् ॥66॥
सन्नद्धो रथमास्थाय शरं धनुरुपाददे । शरं धनुषि सन्धाय मुहूर्तेऽभिजितीश्वरः ॥67॥
ददाह तेन दुर्भेद्या हरोऽथ त्रिपुरो नृप । दिवि दुन्दुभयो नेदुर्विमानशतसङ्कुलाः ॥68॥
देवर्षिपितृसिद्धेशा जयेति कुसुमोत्करैः । अवाकिरञ्जगुर्हृष्टा ननृतुश्चाप्सरोगणाः ॥69॥

came across. **56.** Thereupon the three worlds with their leader approached Sri Rudra and prayed: 'Omnipotent and worshipful one! The Tripuras (the masters of the three flying fortresses) have almost destroyed us, Thy dependants. Deign to protect us.'

57. The worshipful Lord Rudra gave them assurances of safety, and then took his bow and arrow, and shot at the vehicles of the Tripuras. **58.** Then from that arrow countless arrows, burning and brilliant like the sun's rays, went up into the sky and hid the fortresses of the air by their brilliance. **59.** Struck by these arrows of divine powers, all the Asuras occuping them fell down dead; but Maya took them all and revived them by putting them into the pond of Amrita (or ambrosia imparting immortality). **60.** Coming into contact with that ambrosia fortified with Mantras, all the dead Asuras became alive with bodies strong as iron, and rose up like flashes of lightning from the clouds.

61. Seeing Rudra despondent because of the failure of his plan, Mahavishnu adopted a stratagem to help him. **62.** Mahavishnu took up the form of a cow, and Brahma became its calf. One noon they went to the pond of ambrosia at the residence of the Asuras and drank up all its contents. **63-66.** These Asuras, though they saw it all, did not do anything to prevent it, as they fell under a spell cast by Mahavishnu. Coming to know all this, the great magician Maya addressed the protectors of that pond of ambrosia. Himself free from sorrow, because of his acceptance of Divine Will at the back of all happenings, he told those sorrow-stricken Asuras: 'Neither Devas, nor Asuras, nor men can alter the fate involving suffering and enjoyments which the Divine Will decrees.' Afterwards Mahavishnu Himself brought into existence by His power all the weapons and other equipment required by Siva to fight. By His divine excellences like righteousness, knowledge, renunciation, lordliness, austerity, learning, creative will etc., He brought into existence a chariot, charioteer, flagstaff, vehicles, bow, armour, arrows and all other equipment.

67-69. Rudra, now ready for fight, ascended the chariot, bow and arrow in

एवं दग्ध्वा पुरस्तिस्रो भगवान् पुरहा नृप । ब्रह्मादिभिः स्तूयमानः स्वधाम प्रत्यपद्यत ॥70॥
एवंविधान्यस्य हरेः स्वमायया विडम्बमानस्य नृलोकमात्मनः ।
वीर्याणि गीतान्यृषिभिर्जगद्गुरोर्लोकान् पुनानान्यपरं वदामि किम् ॥71॥

इति श्रीमद्भागवते महापुराणे पारमहंस्यां संहितायां सप्तमस्कन्धे युधिष्ठिरनारदसंवादे त्रिपुरविजयो नाम दशमोऽध्यायः ॥10॥

hand. O King! During the auspicious time at mid-noon, known as the Abhijit, Rudra shot his arrow and burnt up the three moving citadels of the Tripuras. Kettle-drums began to sound in the heavens. The large number of celestials who arrived in aerial vehicles cried 'hail!' and showered flowers and sang in great joy. Hosts of heavenly nymphs danced. **70.** Having thus destroyed the three moving fortresses, that Destroyer of Citadels, returned to His abode, amidst the hymns of praise sung by Brahma and others. **71.** The whole world is purified by the hymns and narratives composed by the Rishis extolling the sportive actions of the Lord in his incarnations as man, assuming His own Yogamaya. I have been narrating all these till now. What should I speak about next?

अथैकादशोऽध्यायः

श्रीशुक उवाच

श्रुत्वेहितं साधुसभासभाजितं महत्तमाग्रण्य उरुक्रमात्मनः ।
युधिष्ठिरो दैत्यपतेर्मुदा युतः पप्रच्छ भूयस्तनयं स्वयम्भुवः ॥ 1॥

युधिष्ठिर उवाच

भगवञ्छ्रोतुमिच्छामि नृणां धर्मं सनातनम् । वर्णाश्रमाचारयुतं यत् पुमान् विन्दते परम् ॥ 2॥
भवान् प्रजापतेः साक्षादात्मजः परमेष्ठिनः । सुतानां सम्मतो ब्रह्मंस्तपोयोगसमाधिभिः ॥ 3॥
नारायणपरा विप्रा धर्मं गुह्यं परं विदुः । करुणाः साधवः शान्तास्त्वद्विधा न तथापरे ॥ 4॥

Skandha VII : Chapter 11

VARNAS AND THEIR DHARMAS

The general Dharma of all Men (1-12)

Sri Suka said: **1.** Yudhishthira was delighted to hear the story of Prahlada, the prince among devotees and the pick among great men, a story that had received respectful recognition in the assemblies of holy men. He then put more questions to Narada.

Yudhishthira said: **2.** O worshipful one! I wish to know about the Eternal Religion of man, together with the practice of the way of life according to the laws of Varnas and Ashramas, by means of which man attains knowledge and devotion. **3**. You are the son of Brahma, and among his sons, the one noted for austerity, practice of concentration and perfection in spiritual communion. **4**. The saving truth is known only to holy personages like you who are devoted to Narayana and who are endowed with universal benevolence and

नारद उवाच

नत्वा भगवतेऽजाय लोकानां धर्महेतवे । वक्ष्ये सनातनं धर्मं नारायणमुखाच्छ्रुतम् ।। 5।।
योऽवतीर्यात्मनोंऽशेन दाक्षायण्यां तु धर्मतः । लोकानां स्वस्तयेऽध्यास्ते तपो बदरिकाश्रमे ।। 6।।
धर्ममूलं हि भगवान् सर्ववेदमयो हरिः । स्मृतं च तद्विदां राजन् येन चात्मा प्रसीदति ।। 7।।
सत्यं दया तपः शौचं तितिक्षेक्षा शमो दमः । अहिंसा ब्रह्मचर्यं च त्यागः स्वाध्याय आर्जवम् 8।।
सन्तोषः समदृक् सेवा ग्राम्येहोपरमः शनैः । नृणां विपर्ययेहेक्षा मौनमात्मविमर्शनम् ।। 9।।
अन्नाद्यादेः संविभागो भूतेभ्यश्च यथार्हतः । तेष्वात्मदेवताबुद्धिः सुतरां नृषु पाण्डव ।।10।।
श्रवणं कीर्तनं चास्य स्मरणं महतां गतेः । सेवेज्यावनतिर्दास्यं सख्यमात्मसमर्पणम् ।।11।।
नृणामयं परो धर्मः सर्वेषां समुदाहृतः । त्रिंशल्लक्षणवान् राजन् सर्वात्मा येन तुष्यति 12।।
संस्कारा यदविच्छिन्नाः स द्विजोऽजो जगाद यम् । इज्याध्ययनदानानि विहितानि द्विजन्मनाम् ।
जन्मकर्मावदातानां क्रियाश्चाश्रमचोदिताः ।।13।।

perfect tranquillity of mind.

Narada said: **5.** Saluting the Supreme Being, the birthless one and the teacher of the worlds, I shall expound to you the Eternal Religion of man as I heard it from the Lord Narayana Himself. **6.** Incarnating Himself by a part of His as the Nara-Narayana, the son of Dharma Prajapati by his wife Mūrti, He is to this day staying at Badarikashrama, performing austerities for the good of the world. **7.** The worshipful Hari, the supreme embodiment of all Divinities, is the source of Dharma. Also, what has been given out by men of spiritual illumination established in the Supreme Truth, is considered as authority. By the practice of this Dharma man attains peace.

8-12. The practice of the following thirty virtues and disciplines is the common Dharma of mankind, which brings on man the grace of the Supreme Divine. These are: Truth; compassion; austerity; purity; forbearance; discrimination; control of the mind; control of the senses; avoidance of infliction of pain on others; continence; Charity; scriptural study; integrity; contentment; service of holy men; gradual withdrawal from works and rituals with selfish motives; preparedness to meet failures of plans and face disappointment; avoidance of too much speech; self-criticism; giving food to other living beings according as they deserve; seeing the Lord in all beings; special perception of Divinity in man; and the practice of the highest way of life resorted to by devoted men consisting in hearing, hymning, remembrance, worship, salutation, dedication of all actions, friendship and complete self-surrender, all done with reference to the Supreme Being.

Duties and Livelihood of Varnas (13-24)

13. A Dwija or a twice-born, is a person for whom all the sixteen purificatory rites have been done without a break from the time of conception, and who is designated by that name in the Veda.[1] (By mere birth one does not become a member of that class.) On all the twice-born, who are pure by birth and work,

[1] From this it is to be understood that it is not mere birth that makes one a member of the Vedic Varnas of Brahmana, Kshatriya, Vaisya and Sudra. It is performance of the Samskaras or purificatory rites that makes one so. The rites are meant to make the body and mind of the individual fit for grasping and practising high ideals. As the Samskaras have been either given up, or reduced to an apology for them, Varna has disappeared as an organised and distinguishable social form. The modern caste system of India should never be identified with the Varna system, in which man's Guna (constituent nature) and Karma (work) are the clue to his Varna.

विप्रस्याध्ययनादीनि षडन्यस्याप्रतिग्रहः । राज्ञो वृत्तिः प्रजागोप्तुरविप्राद् वा करादिभिः 14॥
वैश्यस्तु वार्तावृत्तिश्च नित्यं ब्रह्मकुलानुगः । शूद्रस्य द्विजशुश्रूषा वृत्तिश्च स्वामिनो भवेत् 15॥
वार्ता विचित्रा शालीनयायावरशिलोञ्छनम् । विप्रवृत्तिश्चतुर्धेयं श्रेयसी चोत्तरोत्तरा ॥16॥
जघन्यो नोत्तमां वृत्तिमनापदि भजेन्नरः । ऋते राजन्यमापत्सु सर्वेषामपि सर्वशः ॥17॥
ऋतामृताभ्यां जीवेत मृतेन प्रमृतेन वा । सत्यानृताभ्यां जीवेत न श्ववृत्त्या कथञ्चन ॥18॥
ऋतमुञ्छशिलं प्रोक्तममृतं यदयाचितम् । मृतं तु नित्ययाच्ञा स्यात् प्रमृतं कर्षणं स्मृतम् 19॥
सत्यानृतं तु वाणिज्यं श्ववृत्तिर्नीचसेवनम् । वर्जयेत् तां सदा विप्रो राजन्यश्च जुगुप्सिताम् ।
सर्ववेदमयो विप्रः सर्वदेवमयो नृपः ॥20॥
शमो दमस्तपः शौचं सन्तोषः क्षान्तिरार्जवम् । ज्ञानं दयाच्युतात्मत्वं सत्यं च ब्रह्मलक्षणम् ॥21॥
शौर्यं वीर्यं धृतिस्तेजस्त्याग आत्मजयः क्षमा । ब्रह्मण्यता प्रसादश्च रक्षा च क्षत्रलक्षणम् ॥22॥

is enjoined the duty of performing Yajnas, studying the Veda, and giving gifts, as also the duties pertaining to the Ashramas (stages of life like Brahmacharya) that they belong to for the time being. **14.** A Brahmana has six duties—study of the Veda, teaching it, performing sacrifices, officiating at sacrifices, giving charity, and receiving gifts from those whose earnings are righteous. (Of these, teaching, officiating at sacrifices and receiving gifts are the means of livelihood.) The duties of the Kshatriya include all these, except receiving gifts. His chief duty, however, is the governance of the country and protection of the people. In the discharge of this work, he can collect taxes from all except the Brahmanas. That will form his livelihood. In times of danger, he can also adopt teaching and officiating as priest as a means of livelihood. **15.** The Vaisya's profession is agriculture and trade, and he is to live in obedience to the Brahmanas. The duty of the Sudra is service under the twice-born and his livelihood is to consist of the income he gets from his master by such service.

16. A Brahmana's livelihood is to be got from the following four occupations, the succeeding ones being superior to the preceding ones. These are: Agriculture, cow keeping etc.; unsought income; materials sought as alms; collection of grains and food stuffs fallen in the fields and bazaars. **17.** In normal times a man of the lower order should not take up the work of a man of the higher order. The Kshatriya is an exception, as he can take the duty of any other except receiving gifts. In times of danger anyone can take up any means of livelihood. **18.** In times of danger one can earn one's livelihood by Rita or Amrita, by Mrita or Pramrita or by Satyānrita, but never by Svavritti or the canine means of livelihood. **19.** Rita is food made by collections of fallen grains from the fields, called Unchasilam. Amrita is what is got without begging. Mrita consists of what is obtained every day as alms. Pramrita is the proceeds of agriculture. **20.** Satyānrita is the income from trade. Canine livelihood (Svavritti) is the service of mean persons of low origin and abominable ways. A Brahmana and a Kshatriya should avoid such a questionable way of livelihood. For a Brahmana is the repository of the whole Veda, and a Kshatriya, of all divinities. **21.** The mental traits of a Brahmana are restraint of the mind and senses, austerity, contentment, patience, absence of crookedness, knowledge, kindness, devotion to God and truth. **22.** A Kshatriya is characterised

देवगुर्वच्युते भक्तिस्त्रिवर्गपरिपोषणम् ।
आस्तिक्यमुद्यमो नित्यं नैपुणं वैश्यलक्षणम् ॥23॥
शूद्रस्य संनतिः शौचं सेवा स्वामिन्यमायया ।
अमन्त्रयज्ञो ह्यस्तेयं सत्यं गोविप्ररक्षणम् ॥24॥
स्त्रीणां च पतिदेवानां तच्छुश्रूषानुकूलता ।
तद्बन्धुष्वनुवृत्तिश्च नित्यं तद्व्रतधारणम् ॥25॥
सम्मार्जनोपलेपाभ्यां गृहमण्डलवर्तनैः ।
स्वयं च मण्डिता नित्यं परिमृष्टपरिच्छदा ॥26॥
कामैरुच्चावचैः साध्वी प्रश्रयेण दमेन च ।
वाक्यैः सत्यैः प्रियैः प्रेम्णा काले काले भजेत् पतिम्
संतुष्टालोलुपा दक्षा धर्मज्ञा प्रियसत्यवाक् ।
अप्रमत्ता शुचिः स्निग्धा पतिं त्वपतितं भजेत् 28॥
या पतिं हरिभावेन भजेच्छ्रीरिव तत्परा ।
हर्यात्मना हरेर्लोके पत्या श्रीरिव मोदते ॥29॥
वृत्तिः संकरजातीनां तत्तत्कुलकृता भवेत् ।
अचौराणामपापानामन्त्यजान्तेऽवसायिनाम् ॥30॥
प्रायः स्वभावविहितो नृणां धर्मो युगे युगे ।
वेददृग्भिः स्मृतो राजन् प्रेत्य चेह च शर्मकृत् 31॥

by heroism, valour, fortitude, impressiveness, spirit of sacrifice, self-control, patience, devotion to holy men, optimistic attitude, and readiness to offer protection to the weak. **23.** Devotion to Devas, teachers, and Achyuta; effort for fulfilment of duty and securing of wealth and pleasure; faith in God and the Veda; perseverance under all circumstances; and professional skill—these are the characteristics of a Vaisya. **24.** A Sudra's traits are humility, purity, straight-forwardness, service of his master, the five-fold sacrifice without the utterance of the Mantras but accompanied by prostrations only, avoidance of theft and misappropriation, truth, and care of Brahmanas and cows.

Duties of devoted Wives (25-29)

25. A devoted and pious wife (Pativrata) has the following duties: Service of the husband, doing everything in obedience to him, care of the husband's close relatives, and observance of the vows that the husband observes. **26.** A devoted wife should decorate herself well, clean and plaster the house, burnish utensils, put floral and powder designs in front of the house, and thus make life pleasing to the husband. **27.** She should please her husband with things of his liking, by modesty, self-control, truth, agreeable speech, and by love as occasion demands. **28.** Contented, free from greed, vigilant, well-established in the principle of Dharma, pure and loving, given to true and pleasing speech, and never careless, she should co-operate with her husband in all matters, except when he descends to sacrilegious and evil ways. **29.** A wife who looks upon and adores her husband as Hari, in the attitude of Srī, will in the Lord's realm attain to the bliss of Srī in the company of her husband, who is Sri Hari Himself.

Livelihood of Others (30)

30. The livelihood allowed for mixed castes outside the four Varnas and those living beyond the pale of civilization is determined by the practices of their families and tribes. This category includes all communities except those who are given to anti-social ways of life like robbery and commission of heinous sins.

Swadharma and Man's Evolution (31-35)

31. O King! Rishis who know the Veda well have declared that in all Yugas, for welfare in this life and in the hereafter, the pursuit of Swadharma (one's own duty) determined by the proportion of the qualities of Sattva, Rajas and Tamas

वृत्त्या स्वभावकृतया वर्तमानः स्वकर्मकृत्। हित्वा स्वभावजं कर्म शनैर्निर्गुणतामियात् ॥32॥
उप्यमानं मुहुः क्षेत्रं स्वयं निर्वीर्यतामियात्। न कल्पते पुनः सूत्यै उप्तं बीजं च नश्यति ॥33॥
एवं कामाशयं चित्तं कामानामतिसेवया। विरज्येत यथा राजन्नाग्निवत् कामबिन्दुभिः ॥34॥
यस्य यल्लक्षणं प्रोक्तं पुंसो वर्णाभिव्यञ्जकम्। यदन्यत्रापि दृश्येत तत् तेनैव विनिर्दिशेत् ॥35॥

इति श्रीमद्भागवते महापुराणे पारमहंस्यां संहितायां सप्तमस्कन्धे युधिष्ठिरनारदसंवादे सदाचारनिर्णयो नामैकादशोऽध्यायः ॥11॥

in him, is the best course for man. **32.** One who follows the duties dictated by one's natural disposition (Swabhava) will be free from the bondage of those actions, and will gradually reach the state of freedom from Gunas when Jnana and Bhakti are generated in him. **33.** In this respect man is like a field repeatedly ploughed and cultivated until it reaches a stage of absolute infertility when it becomes unfit for the growth of any crop. Seeds sown there perish. **34.** In this way the mind, which is the seat of desires, can gain dispassion through excessive enjoyments. Such enjoyment does not enhance desire unlike drops of ghee enhancing a fire.[1] **35.** If in members born in a certain Varna the qualities pertaining to another Varna are seen, they (the former) are to be classed as belonging to the latter Varna.

अथ द्वादशोऽध्यायः

नारद उवाच

ब्रह्मचारी गुरुकुले वसन् दान्तो गुरोर्हितम्। आचरन् दासवन्नीचो गुरौ सुदृढसौहृदः ॥ 1॥
सायं प्रातरुपासीत गुर्वग्न्यर्कसुरोत्तमान्। उभे सन्ध्ये च यतवाग् जपन् ब्रह्म समाहितः ॥ 2॥

Skandha VII : Chapter 12

DUTIES OF BRAHMACHARINS AND VANAPRASTHAS

Brahmacharin's Duties (1-16)

Narada said: **1.** A Brahmacharin should stay in the Guru's campus. He should practise control over the senses, remain obedient to the Guru, be humble before him like a servant and be loving towards him. Both morning and evening he should attend on the Guru. **2.** Repeating the Gayatri with a concentrated mind, he should, during the three Sandhyas (or junction times) of sunrise, noon and sunset, adore the teachers, fire, sun and important Divinities. During the morning and evening Sandhya rites he must observe silence and repeat and meditate on the

[1] This appears to contradict the view that like ghee poured in fire enjoyment enhances desire. This idea is mentioned in Prahlada's prayer and also in the 9th Skandha about king Yayati. Now it is pointed out that there is no contradiction, because these two doctrines are applicable to people at two different stages of spiritual evolution. In the verse under discussion here, people at very low levels of evolution with an intensely dominant desire-nature are meant. The intensity of passion makes reflection ineffective if not impossible in their case. Enjoyments together with sufferings incidental to them can also gradually bring them to some sort of satiation and sanity when they may be in a mood to have sense-control and renunciation. At this stage the other rule of abstinence and reflection begins to operate.

छन्दांस्यधीयीत गुरोराहूतश्चेत् सुयन्त्रितः । उपक्रमेऽवसाने च चरणौ शिरसा नमेत् ॥ 3॥
मेखलाजिनवासांसि जटादण्डकमण्डलून् । बिभृयादुपवीतं च दर्भपाणिर्यथोदितम् ॥ 4॥
सायं प्रातश्चरेद्भैक्षं गुरवे तन्निवेदयेत् । भुञ्जीत यद्यनुज्ञातो नो चेदुपवसेत् क्वचित् 5॥
सुशीलो मितभुग् दक्षः श्रद्दधानो जितेन्द्रियः । यावदर्थं व्यवहरेत् स्त्रीषु स्त्रीनिर्जितेषु च ॥ 6॥
वर्जयेत् प्रमदागाथामगृहस्थो बृहद्व्रतः । इन्द्रियाणि प्रमाथीनि हरन्त्यपि यतेर्मनः ॥ 7॥
केशप्रसाधनोन्मर्दस्नपनाभ्यञ्जनादिकम् । गुरुस्त्रीभिर्युवतिभिः कारयेन्नात्मनो युवा ॥ 8॥
नन्वग्निः प्रमदा नाम घृतकुम्भसमः पुमान् । सुतामपि रहो जह्यादन्यदा यावदर्थकृत् ॥ 9॥
कल्पयित्वाऽऽत्मना यावदाभासमिदमीश्वरः । द्वैतं तावन्न विरमेत् ततो ह्यस्य विपर्ययः ॥10॥
एतत् सर्वं गृहस्थस्य समाम्नातं यतेरपि । गुरुवृत्तिर्विकल्पेन गृहस्थस्यर्तुगामिनः ॥11॥
अञ्जनाभ्यञ्जनोन्मर्दस्त्र्यवलेखामिषं मधु । स्रग्गन्धलेपालङ्कारांस्त्यजेयुर्ये धृतव्रताः ॥12॥
उषित्वैवं गुरुकुले द्विजोऽधीत्यावबुध्य च । त्रयीं साङ्गोपनिषदं यावदर्थं यथाबलम् ॥13॥
दत्त्वा वरमनुज्ञातो गुरोः कामं यदीश्वरः । गृहं वनं वा प्रविशेत् प्रव्रजेत् तत्र वा वसेत् ॥14॥

Gayatri. **3.** When the Guru calls him for study, he should learn from him the Veda. At the beginning and end of the study, he should make full prostration before the Guru. **4.** He should hold Darbha grass in hand, besides staff and water vessel, and put on a girdle, deerskin garment, matted locks and sacred thread, as laid down in the scriptures. **5.** In the morning and evening he can collect food as alms. He should offer what is thus got to the Guru. If ordered by the Guru, he can eat what he likes of that food. On days when the Guru withholds permission, he will have to fast. **6.** He must be of good conduct, moderate in eating, skilful, full of faith and endued with control of the senses. Only under compelling circumstances should he speak or have dealings with women or men under the domination of women. **7.** Excepting the householder, the members of the other states of life (Ashramas) who observe continence, should avoid songs and poems dealing with the affairs of females. For, the senses which can cause agitation to the mind, can carry away the mind of even a self-controlled ascetic. **8.** He should not allow the Guru's wife or any young woman to do intimate services to him like dressing the hair, massaging the body, bathing, anointing etc. **9.** For, woman is like fire, and man resembles a pot of ghee. Just as there is danger of ignition when they come too close, there is danger if men and women come too close. So one should not meet even a daughter in solitude. Even in other situations, their contacts must be few, and that only when absolutely necessary. **10.** Although a man may be clever and learned, so long as his mind conceives this reflection, the body, as his self, the distinction between the sexes would remain, and the threat of a spiritual fall is a reality before him.

11. Good conduct and other virtues and disciplines of mind with reference to the Brahmacharin apply to the householders and Sannyasins, too, with the following difference in regard to the householders: He need serve the teacher only occasionally; and he may live with his wife at regulated times. **12.** Those who are observing the vow of celibacy, should avoid oil bath, massage of the body, company of women, drawing or observing the figures of women, taking meat and intoxicants, applying unguents or collyrium and putting on garlands and other decorations. **13-14.** Living thus in the

अग्नौ गुरावात्मनि च सर्वभूतेष्वधोक्षजम् । भूतैः स्वधामभिः पश्येदप्रविष्टं प्रविष्टवत् ॥15॥
एवंविधो ब्रह्मचारी वानप्रस्थो यतिर्गृही । चरन् विदितविज्ञानः परं ब्रह्माधिगच्छति ॥16॥
वानप्रस्थस्य वक्ष्यामि नियमान् मुनिसम्मतान् । यानातिष्ठन् मुनिर्गच्छेदृषिलोकमिहाञ्जसा 17॥
न कृष्टपच्यमश्नीयादकृष्टं चाप्यकालतः । अग्निपक्वमथामं वा अर्कपक्वमुताहरेत् ॥18॥
वन्यैश्चरुपुरोडाशान् निर्वपेत् कालचोदितान् । लब्धे नवे नवेऽन्नाद्ये पुराणं तु परित्यजेत् ॥19॥
अग्न्यर्थमेव शरणमुटजं वाद्रिकन्दराम् । श्रयेत हिमवाय्वग्निवर्षार्कातपषाट् स्वयम् ॥20॥
केशरोमनखश्मश्रुमलानि जटिलो दधत् । कमण्डल्वजिने दण्डवल्कलाग्निपरिच्छदान् ॥21॥
चरेद् वने द्वादशाब्दानष्टौ वा चतुरो मुनिः । द्वावेकं वा यथाबुद्धिर्न विपद्येत कृच्छ्रतः ॥22॥
यदाकल्पः स्वक्रियायां व्याधिभिर्जरयाथवा । आन्वीक्षिक्यां वा विद्यायां कुर्यादनशनादिकम् 23॥
आत्मन्यग्नीन् समारोप्य संन्यस्याहंममात्मताम् । कारणेषु न्यसेत् सम्यक् संघातं तु यथार्हतः ॥24॥

Guru's household the Brahmacharin has to study and reflect on the meaning of the Vedas with its auxiliaries and the Upanishads according to his capacity and competence. Then he has to give the parting gifts to the Guru, if he has the means, and take to the life of a householder, or of a Vanaprastha (forest-dwelling recluse or anchorite), or, if he is endowed with perfect renunciation, of a Sannyasin. He can also continue to stay as a life-long Brahmacharin at the Guru's house. **15.** Though the Lord transcends everything and cannot be spoken of as contained in anything, He should be still looked upon as having entered into, and indwelling, the fire, the teacher, oneself, and all beings. **16.** One who lives like this, whether he is a Brahmacharin, a Vanaprastha (anchorite) or a Sannyasin, becomes enlightened and attains Brahman.

Vanaprastha's Duties (17-22)

17. I am now going to tell you the duties of the life of a Vanaprastha as ordained by great sages. Following these duties of the Vanaprastha one easily attains to Maharloka. **18.** The Vanaprastha should not subsist on cereals produced by cultivation. He should not also pluck and eat before they become ripe, the fruits of plants and trees that have grown uncultivated. He should not eat things burnt in fire or raw in the natural condition. He can eat fruits ripened in the heat of the sun. **19.** He should perform the daily Yajnas with Charu and Purodāsa (sacrificial offerings) made of naturally grown cereals of the forest. As he gets new fruits, the old ones gathered should be thrown away. **20.** Physically withstanding the inclemencies due to wind, fire, rain, sun etc. he should maintain a hermitage in a mountain cave with the sole purpose of preserving the sacred fire. **21-22.** He should have matted hair, beard and nails uncut, and physical appearance unattended to. He should carry with him a water pot, skin, staff, bark garment and accessories of fire-worship. He should live in the forest for twelve or eight or four or two or one year in a way that would not impair the strength of his mind.

How Vanaprastha should face Death (23-31)

23. When, due to old age or disease, he becomes incapable of performing the rites that form his ordained duty, or of pursuing the discipline of knowledge, he should fast unto death. **24.** He should prepare himself for that in the following way: He should withdraw the three fires

खे खानि वायौ निःश्वासांस्तेजस्यूष्माणमात्मवान् । अप्स्वसृक्श्लेष्मपूयानि क्षितौ शेषं यथोद्भवम् 25॥
वाचमग्नौ सवक्तव्यामिन्द्रे शिल्पं करावपि । पदानि गत्या वयसि रत्योपस्थं प्रजापतौ ॥26॥
मृत्यौ पायुं विसर्गं च यथास्थानं विनिर्दिशेत् । दिक्षु श्रोत्रं सनादेन स्पर्शमध्यात्मनि त्वचम् ॥27॥
रूपाणि चक्षुषा राजन् ज्योतिष्यभिनिवेशयेत् । अप्सु प्रचेतसा जिह्वां घ्रेयैर्घ्राणं क्षितौ न्यसेत् 28॥
मनो मनोरथैश्चन्द्रे बुद्धिं बोध्यैः कवौ परे । कर्माण्यध्यात्मना रुद्रे यदहंममताक्रिया ।
सत्त्वेन चित्तं क्षेत्रज्ञे गुणैर्वैकारिकं परे ॥29॥
अप्सु क्षितिमपो ज्योतिष्यदो वायौ नभस्यमुम् । कूटस्थे तच्च महति तदव्यक्तेऽक्षरे च तत् ॥30॥
इत्यक्षरतयाऽऽत्मानं चिन्मात्रमवशेषितम् । ज्ञात्वाद्वयोऽथ विरमेद् दग्धयोनिरिवानलः ॥31॥

इति श्रीमद्भागवते महापुराणे पारमहंस्यां संहितायां सप्तमस्कन्धे युधिष्ठिरनारदसंवादे सदाचारनिर्णयो नाम द्वादशोऽध्यायः ॥12॥

beginning with Ahavaniya into his inner self, abandon his feeling of identification with the body, and dissolve this psycho-physical combination called the body into the causal substances of which it is formed—the gross elements into Tanmatras, the senses into Rājasikāhankara, and the mind into Sāttvikāhankara. **25.** A wise man should dissolve the space contained in bodily orifices like ears and nose in Akasa; the breath in the air; the digestive power in fire; the fluid substances like blood, phlegm and urine in water; and the rest of the bodily substances in earth. Everything is thus restored to its own source. **26.** The organ of speech and its function should be dissolved in its deity Agni; hand and its function in Indra; leg and its function of movement in Vishnu; and generative organ and its function in Prajapati. **27.** The anus and its function should be dissolved in the deity Mrityu (death); ears and their function sound, in the deity Diti; and skin and its function touch, in the deity Vayu. **28.** O King! The eye with its function, perception of forms, is to be dissolved in the deity Aditya. The sense of taste together with its deity Varuna should be dissolved in water having the property of taste. The sense of smell with its deity of Asvinīdevas should be dissoved in the element earth. **29.** The mind with its functions of imagination and doubt should be dissolved in the deity moon; the Buddhi (intellect) with the determinative faculty, in Brahma; the Ahankara with I-sense, in Rudra; the Chitta (mind stuff) with consciousness, in Kshetrajna (Jiva or individual soul); and that Kshetrajna, released from the entanglements of the Gunas, in the Supreme Being. **30.** Earth (Prithvi) must be dissolved in Apah (water); Apah, in Tejas (fire); Tejas, in Vayu (air); Vayu, in Akasa (sky); Akasa, in Ahankara (I-sense); Ahankara, in Mahattattva (the 'Cosmic I'); and Mahattattva, in Pradhana (root matter); and Pradhana in the Supreme Being. **31.** The residue is only the Self which is Pure Consciousness. Knowing Him to be the Immortal and the Non-dual, let there be cessation of enquiry, like that of the flame of the fire that has burnt its fuel.

अथ त्रयोदशोऽध्यायः

नारद उवाच

कल्पस्त्वेवं परिव्रज्य देहमात्रावशेषितः । ग्रामैकरात्रविधिना निरपेक्षश्चरेन्महीम् ॥ 1॥
बिभृयाद् यद्यसौ वासः कौपीनाच्छादनं परम् । त्यक्तं न दण्डलिङ्गादेरन्यत् किञ्चिदनापदि ॥ 2॥
एक एव चरेद् भिक्षुरात्मारामोऽनपाश्रयः । सर्वभूतसुहृच्छान्तो नारायणपरायणः ॥ 3॥
पश्येदात्मन्यदो विश्वं परे सदसतोऽव्यये । आत्मानं च परं ब्रह्म सर्वत्र सदसन्मये ॥ 4॥
सुप्तप्रबोधयोः सन्धावात्मनो गतिमात्मदृक् । पश्यन् बन्धं च मोक्षं च मायामात्रं न वस्तुतः ॥ 5॥
नाभिनन्देद् ध्रुवं मृत्युमध्रुवं वास्य जीवितम् । कालं परं प्रतीक्षेत भूतानां प्रभवाप्ययम् ॥ 6॥
नासच्छास्त्रेषु सज्जेत नोपजीवेत जीविकाम् । वादवादांस्त्यजेत् तर्कान् पक्षं कं च न संश्रयेत् 7॥

Skandha VII : Chapter 13

THE ASCETIC'S WAY OF LIFE

Mode of Sannyasin's Life (1-10)

Narada said: **1.** (If he has become physically disabled by old age and disease and is incapable of following the Sannyasin's way of life, the Vanaprastha may starve himself to death, meditating as mentioned above.) But if he is physically and mentally fit for a Sannyasin's life, he should, after resolving everything in the Atman, wander forth over the world without any special destination. He should carry the body alone with him, stop in no village for more than a day, and depend on no one for anything. **2.** If he is particular about wearing anything, he can have a Kaupina (codpiece covering the private parts) and nothing more. Except in times of danger, he shall not resume anything that he has abandoned on becoming a Sannyasin. He can have only the Sannyasin's emblems of a staff and water pot made of shell. **3.** He should move about alone, absorbed in the Atman, depending on nothing external, friendly to all living beings and completely resigned to the Lord Narayana, the support of all beings.

4. He should view this world as subsisting in the Supreme Spirit, who is none the less uninvolved in the cause and effect relation, and unaffected by any change or transformation. In everything that is bound by cause and effect relation, one should see the Self, inseparable from the Supreme Brahman, as the indwelling principle. **5.** Between waking and sleep, there is a junction in which there is neither the unconscious dullness of sleep, nor the form-taking tendency of the mind. A close observer of this Pure Self-awareness will realise the true Self as also the apparency of both bondage and freedom. **6.** He should not think of the death of this body, which is certain to come whether one thinks of it or not. Nor should he think of the continuance of this life, which is by nature impermanent. Let him be indifferent to both. Let him think of Time, which is the Supreme Being Himself in the process of bringing out and swallowing everything.

7. A Sannyasin should not interest himself with the study of subjects that are not concerned with spiritual realisation; nor should he take up any occupation merely for his livelihood. He should avoid sophistry and those who indulge in vain argumentation, which

न शिष्याननुबध्नीत ग्रन्थान्नैवाभ्यसेद् बहून् । न व्याख्यामुपयुञ्जीत नारम्भानारभेत् क्वचित् ॥
न यतेराश्रमः प्रायो धर्महेतुर्महात्मनः । शान्तस्य समचित्तस्य बिभृयादुत वा त्यजेत् ॥ 9॥
अव्यक्तलिङ्गो व्यक्तार्थो मनीष्युन्मत्तबालवत् । कविर्मूकवदात्मानं स दृष्टचा दर्शयेन्नृणाम् ॥10॥
अत्राप्युदाहरन्तीममितिहासं पुरातनम् । प्रह्लादस्य च संवादं मुनेराजगरस्य च ॥11॥
तं शयानं धरोपस्थे कावेर्यां सह्यसानुनि । रजस्वलैस्तनूदेशैर्निगूढामलतेजसम् ॥12॥
ददर्श लोकान् विचरंल्लोकतत्त्वविवित्सया । वृतोऽमात्यैः कतिपयैः प्रह्लादो भगवत्प्रियः ॥13॥
कर्मणाऽऽकृतिभिर्वाचा लिङ्गैर्वर्णाश्रमादिभिः । न विदन्ति जना यं वै सोऽसाविति न वेति च ॥14॥
तं नत्वाभ्यर्च्य विधिवत् पादयोः शिरसा स्पृशन् । विवित्सुरिदमप्राक्षीन्महाभागवतोऽसुरः ॥15॥
बिभर्षि कायं पीवानं सोद्यमो भोगवान् यथा । वित्तं चैवोद्यमवतां भोगो वित्तवतामिह ।
भोगिनां खलु देहोऽयं पीवा भवति नान्यथा ॥16॥
न ते शयानस्य निरुद्यमस्य ब्रह्मन् नु हार्थो यत एव भोगः ।
अभोगिनोऽयं तव विप्र देहः पीवा यतस्तद्वद नः क्षमं चेत् ॥17॥

serves no other purpose than logic-chopping. He should not take sides in controversies. **8.** He should not strive to attract disciples and followers. Study of many books is not for him. He should not go about giving discourses merely for gaining popularity; nor should he initiate new ventures (like starting monasteries etc.).

9. In the case of a great ascetic who has attained tranquillity and equability through spiritual realisation, adherence to the rules and insignia of an Ashrama (state of life) ceases to be a means for attaining any great end. He may stick to them or abandon them. **10.** He may appear to others as one without any distinguishing insignia but with his spiritual aura manifest; he will have wisdom but look like a child or one intoxicated; he will be full of inspiration but appear dumb.

Prahlada with an Avadhuta (11-18)

11. In clarification of the Paramahamsa ideal there is the following old story in the form of a conversation between Prahlada and an ascetic (Dattātreya) who followed the mode of life of a python. **12-13.** Prahlada, the beloved of the Lord, was once moving about in the land with some of his advisers in the valleys of the Western Ghats in order to have a first-hand knowledge of the affairs of the country, when he came across an ascetic on the banks of the Cauvery, lying on the ground with his body covered with dust that hid his natural aura. **14-15.** None could recognise who he was from his actions, appearance, or words. Nor did he bear the insignia of any Varna or Ashrama. The great devotee Prahlada prostrated himself before him, touched his feet with his head, offered him worship and entered into conversation with him, inspired by his eagerness to know the truth. **16.** He said: 'You, Sir, have a fat body like a man given to work and enjoyments, though you are neither of these. Only those who work will have money; only men with money in hand can have enjoyments; and only those who enjoy the blessings of life have a fat body. **17.** You, who simply lie in a place without doing anything, cannot have any money which alone can bring enjoyments for man. How is it then that your body, without any objects of enjoyments, has become

कविः कल्पो निपुणदृक् चित्रप्रियकथः समः। लोकस्य कुर्वतः कर्म शेषे तद्वीक्षितापि वा ॥18॥

नारद उवाच

स इत्थं दैत्यपतिना परिपृष्टो महामुनिः। स्मयमानस्तमभ्याह तद्वागमृतयन्त्रितः ॥19॥

ब्राह्मण उवाच

वेदेदमसुरश्रेष्ठ भवान् नन्वार्यसम्मतः। ईहोपरमयोर्नृणां पदान्यध्यात्मचक्षुषा ॥20॥

यस्य नारायणो देवो भगवान् हृद्गतः सदा। भक्त्या केवलयाज्ञानं धुनोति ध्वान्तमर्कवत् ॥21॥

अथापि ब्रूमहे प्रश्नांस्तव राजन् यथाश्रुतम्। सम्भावनीयो हि भवानात्मनः शुद्धिमिच्छताम् ॥

तृष्णया भववाहिन्या योग्यैः कामैरपूरया। कर्माणि कार्यमाणोऽहं नानायोनिषु योजितः 23॥

यदृच्छया लोकमिमं प्रापितः कर्मभिर्भ्रमन्। स्वर्गापवर्गयोर्द्वारं तिरश्चां पुनरस्य च ॥24॥

अत्रापि दम्पतीनां च सुखायान्यापनुत्तये। कर्माणि कुर्वतां दृष्ट्वा निवृत्तोऽस्मि विपर्ययम् 25॥

सुखमस्यात्मनो रूपं सर्वेहोपरतिस्तनुः। मनःसंस्पर्शजान् दृष्ट्वा भोगान् स्वप्स्यामि संविशन्

इत्येतदात्मनः स्वार्थं सन्तं विस्मृत्य वै पुमान्। विचित्रामसति द्वैते घोरामाप्नोति संसृतिम् 27॥

so fat? If it is not improper, we want to know the truth about it. **18.** You are learned, capable, clever and endowed with astonishing power of speech. You see all the world working hard, and yet you keep quiet, lying down in spite of your many capacities.'

Avadhuta's Mode of Life (19-24)

Narada said: **19.** Thus questioned by the king of the Asuras, the great sage, who was very much pleased by his nectarine words, replied with a smile.

The Avadhuta said: **20.** O great Asura! You know all about this by your spiritual insight. You are one who has the recognition of all good men. You know what are the respective consequences of following the path of desire and the path of renunciation. **21.** For, in your heart Narayana, the Lord of All-inclusive Self-consciousness, dwells for ever, drawn by unswerving devotion and dispelling the darkness of ignorance like the sun. **22.** O honoured one! Still, I shall answer your questions from what I have learnt from my teacher. For, you are respected by all who care for their spiritual evolution. **23.** Desire, which remains unsatiated in spite of repeated experiences of highly exciting pleasures, entangled me in transmigratory cycles and took me to innumerable embodiments. **24.** After being driven to several embodiments in diverse species of beings by my Karma, I have at last got this human body, which can once again be the gateway to heavenly regions or to liberation, to the status of a brute or to a human embodiment, according as it is made use of.

Withdrawal as a Way of Life (25-29)

25. Observing how householders in this world perform work for attainment of happiness and avoidance of unhappiness but happen to get only contrary results, I have withdrawn from all work. **26.** Joy is the nature of the Atman. Abstinence from every work is what makes that nature manifest. As enjoyments are largely projections of the mind and quite temporary, I rest quietly, undergoing the effects of my Prārabdha but making no new efforts of any kind. **27.** Though the bliss of the Atman is present in man, he is forgetful of it and wanders in search of it through the various travails of trans-

जलं तदुद्भवैश्छन्नं हित्वाज्ञो जलकाम्यया । मृगतृष्णामुपाधावेद् यथान्यत्रार्थदृक् स्वतः ॥28॥
देहादिभिर्दैवतन्त्रैरात्मनः सुखमीहतः । दुःखात्ययं चानीशस्य क्रिया मोघाः कृताः कृताः ॥
आध्यात्मिकादिभिर्दुःखैरविमुक्तस्य कर्हिचित् । मर्त्यस्य कृच्छ्रोपनतैरर्थैः कामैः क्रियेत किम् ॥30॥
पश्यामि धनिनां क्लेशं लुब्धानामजितात्मनाम् । भयादलब्धनिद्राणां सर्वतोऽभिविशङ्किनाम् 31॥
राजतश्चौरतः शत्रोः स्वजनात् पशुपक्षितः । अर्थिभ्यः कालतः स्वस्मान्नित्यं प्राणार्थवद्भयम् ॥
शोकमोहभयक्रोधरागक्लैब्यश्रमादयः । यन्मूलाः स्युर्नृणां जह्यात् स्पृहां प्राणार्थयोर्बुधः 33
मधुकारमहासर्पौ लोकेऽस्मिन्नो गुरूत्तमौ । वैराग्यं परितोषं च प्राप्ता यच्छिक्षया वयम् ॥34॥
विरागः सर्वकामेभ्यः शिक्षितो मे मधुव्रतात् । कृच्छ्राप्तं मधुवद् वित्तं हत्वाप्यन्यो हरेत् पतिम् ॥
अनीहः परितुष्टात्मा यदृच्छोपनतादहम् । नो चेच्छये बह्वहानि महाहिरिव सत्त्ववान् ॥36॥
क्वचिदल्पं क्वचिद् भूरि भुञ्जेऽन्नं स्वाद्वस्वादु वा । क्वचिद् भूरिगुणोपेतं गुणहीनमुत क्वचित् ॥37॥

migratory existence. **28.** It is like a man running foolishly after the illusory water seen at a distance in the mirage, not recognising the real water in the lake by his side under the cover of the grass growing from it. **29.** People without any faith in God or in the spiritual destiny of man, who are ignorant of the fact that their present body and mind are the result of their past Karma, engage themselves in actions calculated to bring about happiness and ward off unhappiness. But their repeated efforts in this respect will be of little avail (succeeding or failing according to what past Karma would allow).

Ways of the Bee and the Python (30-36)

30. Of what avail will be the wealth and the objects of enjoyment gained by great effort for man who is naturally subject to the three types of sufferings caused by his own body and mind (Ādhyātmika), by external natural forces (Ādhibhautika), and by extra-human agencies (Ādhidaivika)? **31.** I find how wealthy men, who are miserly and slaves of their senses, are ever subject to sufferings. Out of fear they get no sleep, and suspicion of others becomes second nature with them. **32.** Men who want to preserve their life and their wealth are both subject to fear from a variety of sources—from the ruling power, robbers, enemies, one's own relatives, birds and animals, suppliants, time, and even from oneself (through exhaustion of wealth and one's energies by enjoyment). **33.** A wise man should therefore abandon love of sense enjoyments and the desire for wealth, both of which are productive of grief, infatuation, fear, anger, attachment, helplessness and exhaustion. **34.** In this world, I have two teachers—the honey-bee and the python. It is from them that I learnt the lesson of renunciation and contentment. **35.** The honey-bee taught me renunciation. Just as the honey gathered by the bee through hard labour, is taken away by others who do not hesitate even to kill it, so the hard-earned wealth of a rich man is robbed by others, killing him if need be. **36.** Like the python I make no effort for food, but am satisfied with what chance brings. If nothing comes for many days, I lie all the time like the python without food, but with my strength undiminished.

Taking Life as it comes (37-42)

37. I eat whatever I get, sometimes a small quantity and sometimes large, some-

श्रद्धयोपाहृतं क्वापि कदाचिन्मानवर्जितम् । भुञ्जे भुक्त्वाथ कस्मिंश्चिद् दिवा नक्तं यदृच्छया ॥
क्षौमं दुकूलमजिनं चीरं वल्कलमेव वा । वसेऽन्यदपि सम्प्राप्तं दिष्टभुक् तुष्टधीरहम् 39॥
क्वचिच्छये धरोपस्थे तृणपर्णाश्मभस्मसु । क्वचित् प्रासादपर्यङ्के कशिपौ वा परेच्छया ॥40॥
क्वचित् स्नातोऽनुलिप्ताङ्गः सुवासाः स्रग्व्यलङ्कृतः रथेभाश्वैश्चरे क्वापि दिग्वासा ग्रहवद् विभो ॥41॥
नाहं निन्दे न च स्तौमि स्वभावविषमं जनम् । एतेषां श्रेय आशासे उतैकात्म्यं महात्मनि ॥42॥
विकल्पं जुहुयाच्चित्तौ तां मनस्यर्थविभ्रमे । मनो वैकारिके हुत्वा तन्मायायां जुहोत्यनु ॥43॥
आत्मानुभूतौ तां मायां जुहुयात् सत्यदृङ्मुनिः । ततो निरीहो विरमेत् स्वानुभूत्याऽऽत्मनि स्थितः ॥
स्वात्मवृत्तं मयेत्थं ते सुगुप्तमपि वर्णितम् । व्यपेतं लोकशास्त्राभ्यां भवान् हि भगवत्परः ॥45॥

नारद उवाच

धर्मं पारमहंस्यं वै मुनेः श्रुत्वासुरेश्वरः । पूजयित्वा ततः प्रीत आमन्त्र्य प्रययौ गृहम् ॥46॥

इति श्रीमद्भागवते महापुराणे पारमहंस्यां संहितायां सप्तमस्कन्धे युधिष्ठिरनारदसंवादे यतिधर्मे त्रयोदशोऽध्यायः ॥13॥

times well-cooked and sometimes ill-cooked, sometimes with condiments and sometimes without them. **38.** Sometimes I eat food that is given with reverence, and sometimes food given without it. Sometimes I take food only at night, sometimes only during day, and sometimes at night too, as chance would bring it. **39.** I, who am exhausting my Prarabdha, wear with satisfaction whatever I get—be it a silk, skin, torn cloth, or bark. **40.** If the kindness of others makes it available, I may lie on a soft bed on the top floor of a house, or otherwise I may sleep in any place like an ash heap, stones, leaves, grass, or bare ground. **41.** O great one! Sometimes I may move about accompanied by chariots, elephants and horses, bathed, well-dressed in silk and well-decorated with unguents and garlands; sometimes I may be going about naked like a ghost. **42.** I never praise or criticise people who vary so widely in their nature. Irrespective of their nature, I only pray that they may all gain devotion to Him, and the knowledge of their unity with Him.

Establishment in the Self (43-46)

43-44. Diversity of perception should be dissolved in the mental mode that grasps it. These modes must be dissolved in Manas (inner perceptive mechanism or Antahkarana), which causes the distortion of perceptions through its modes. The mind should be dissolved in its cause, the Sattva aspect of Ahankara (I-sense); and that I-sense, in Mahattattva (inchoate all-inclusive self-awareness). The Mahattattva should be dissolved in Maya, the power of the Lord. The Truth-seeking sage should dissolve Maya in the Universal Self, the Supreme Being. Then without any desire or expression of will, he should retreat into the Atman which is Pure Consciousness. **45.** Different from all codes of conduct recognised in worldly behaviour, a secret unknown, is this, the way of my life. I have communicated this to you only because you are whole-heartedly devoted to the Lord.

Narada said: **46.** Having thus heard the Dharma of the Paramahamsa from this sage, Prahlada offered him worship with a joyful heart, took his leave, and went home.

अथ चतुर्दशोऽध्यायः

युधिष्ठिर उवाच

गृहस्थ एतां पदवीं विधिना येन चाञ्जसा। याति देवऋषे ब्रूहि मादृशो गृहमूढधीः ॥ 1॥

नारद उवाच

गृहेष्ववस्थितो राजन् क्रियाः कुर्वन् गृहोचिताः। वासुदेवार्पणं साक्षादुपासीत महामुनीन् ॥ 2॥
शृण्वन् भगवतोऽभीक्ष्णमवतारकथामृतम्। श्रद्दधानो यथाकालमुपशान्तजनावृतः ॥ 3॥
सत्सङ्गाच्छनकैः सङ्गमात्मजायात्मजादिषु। विमुच्येन्मुच्यमानेषु स्वयं स्वप्नवदुत्थितः ॥ 4॥
यावदर्थमुपासीनो देहे गेहे च पण्डितः। विरक्तो रक्तवत् तत्र नृलोके नरतां न्यसेत् ॥ 5॥
ज्ञातयः पितरौ पुत्रा भ्रातरः सुहृदोऽपरे। यद् वदन्ति यदिच्छन्ति चानुमोदेत निर्ममः ॥ 6॥
दिव्यं भौमं चान्तरिक्षं वित्तमच्युतनिर्मितम्। तत् सर्वमुपभुञ्जान एतत् कुर्यात् स्वतो बुधः ॥ 7॥
यावद् भ्रियेत जठरं तावत् स्वत्वं हि देहिनाम्। अधिकं योऽभिमन्येत स स्तेनो दण्डमर्हति ॥ 8॥
मृगोष्ट्रखरमर्काखुसरीसृप्खगमक्षिकाः। आत्मनः पुत्रवत् पश्येत् तैरेषामन्तरं कियत् ॥ 9॥

Skandha VII : Chapter 14

THE IDEAL OF A HOUSEHOLDER

Life of Non-attachment (1-6)

Yudhishthira said: **1.** O divine sage! How can a person like me, engrossed as I am with the affairs of household life, attain to this state of beatitude easily?

Narada said: **2.** A householder should perform all the duties pertaining to his state as an offering to Vāsudeva and attend on spiritually illumined personages. **3-4.** After attending to his duties in this world, he should spend the rest of his time in the company of men who have attained peace and engage himself in hearing the excellences of Divine Incarnations with full faith in the teachings. Just as one abandons all thoughts and objects seen in dream, one should gradually learn to detach oneself from body, wife, children etc., all of which are bound to slip away in course of time. **5.** Though satisfied with what is required for the bare maintenance of physical life, and though endowed with renunciation, a learned householder should make all manly effort externally like one attached to the world. **6.** One should give assent to the advice and suggestions of parents, sons, brothers, friends and relatives, without any personal attachment for the matters concerned.

Attitude to Wealth and Sex (7-13)

7. One should consider all the wealth one gets to be the gifts of Achyuta—be it grains produced by cultivation with the help of rains that come from the skies, or be it got as a treasure trove from the earth, or be it what chance brings. Enjoying wealth with this attitude of mind, he should discharge all his duties. **8.** An embodied being is entitled to possess what is required as food to fill his stomach. One who claims more than that, is a thief and deserves punishment. **9.** Deer, camels, asses, monkeys, rats, serpents, birds, flies etc., must be looked upon as one's own children. What difference is there between

त्रिवर्गं नातिकृच्छ्रेण भजेत गृहमेध्यपि । यथादेशं यथाकालं यावद्दैवोपपादितम् ॥10॥
आश्वाघान्तेऽवसायिभ्यः कामान् संविभजेद् यथा । अप्येकामात्मनो दारां नृणां स्वत्वग्रहो यतः ॥11॥
जह्याद् यदर्थे स्वप्राणान् हन्याद् वा पितरं गुरुम् । तस्यां स्वत्वं स्त्रियां जह्याद् यस्तेन ह्यजितो जितः ॥
कृमिविड्भस्मनिष्ठान्तं क्वेदं तुच्छं कलेवरम् । क्व तदीयरतिर्भार्या क्वायमात्मा नभश्छदिः ॥13॥
सिद्धैर्यज्ञावशिष्टार्थैः कल्पयेद् वृत्तिमात्मनः । शेषे स्वत्वं त्यजन् प्राज्ञः पदवीं महतामियात् ॥14॥
देवानृषीन् नृभूतानि पितॄनात्मानमन्वहम् । स्ववृत्त्यागतवित्तेन यजेत पुरुषं पृथक् ॥15॥
यर्ह्यात्मनोऽधिकाराद्याः सर्वाः स्युर्यज्ञसम्पदः । वैतानिकेन विधिना अग्निहोत्रादिना यजेत् 16॥
न ह्यग्निमुखतोऽयं वै भगवान् सर्वयज्ञभुक् । इज्येत हविषा राजन् यथा विप्रमुखे हुतैः ॥17॥
तस्माद् ब्राह्मणदेवेषु मर्त्यादिषु यथार्हतः । तैस्तैः कामैर्यजस्वैनं क्षेत्रज्ञं ब्राह्मणाननु ॥18॥
कुर्यादापरपक्षीयं मासि प्रौष्ठपदे द्विजः । श्राद्धं पित्रोर्यथावित्तं तद्बन्धूनां च वित्तवान् ॥19॥

these creatures and one's own issue? **10.** A householder should not make undue effort to secure the three worldly values of Dharma, Artha and Kama (merits, wealth and pleasure). Honouring the regulations of time and place, one should be satisfied with what one's previous Karma brings. **11.** All the objects of enjoyment one possesses should be divided among dogs, vagabonds and out-castes. One should not have a sense of possession even with regard to one's own wedded wife who is generally guarded very jealously by men. **12.** For the sake of woman, it is found that man does not hesitate to put an end to the life of his father or teacher or even himself. If one is able to overcome the sense of possession in regard to her (woman), one would have conquered even the invincible Lord Himself. **13.** Oh! How worthless is this body which is reducible to dirt and ashes, or into food for worms! How absurd is the idea of a wife for giving enjoyment to this worthless thing of a body! And by the side of these, how overpowering is the grandeur of the Atman which can cover up by its brilliance even the all-pervading sky!

Attitude to Yajnas (14-18)

14. A pious householder should do his five-fold Yajna with substances easily collected and subsist on the remnant of the Yajna. He should give up the sense of possessiveness regarding all other things. A wise man of the type will thus be treading towards the goal of those who have taken to a life of renunciation. **15.** Panchamahāyajna consists in worshipping with righteously got materials the Supreme Being manifest as the five objects of worship—Devas, Rishis, men, Pitris and brute creations. **16.** If one has competency, skill and the necessary ingredients, one can perform the Agnihotra sacrifice according to the rules laid down for sacrifices. **17.** The worshipful Lord, who is the recipient of Yajnas, is never so satisfied with offerings made in fire as with the food offered to Him through the mouth of holy men. **18.** So the Supreme Being who indwells everything should be worshipped through all beings, from Devas and holy men down to all men, according to their status and need.

Srāddha and auspicious Rites (19-26)

19. If the person is wealthy enough, he should perform Srāddha to the dead parents and their relatives in the dark

अयने विषुवे कुर्याद् व्यतीपाते दिनक्षये। चन्द्रादित्योपरागे च द्वादशीश्रवणेषु च ।।20।।
तृतीयायां शुक्लपक्षे नवम्यामथ कार्तिके। चतसृष्वप्यष्टकासु हेमन्ते शिशिरे तथा ।।21।।
माघे च सितसप्तम्यां मघाराकासमागमे। राकया चानुमत्या वा मासर्क्षाणि युतान्यपि ।।22।।
द्वादश्यामनुराधा स्याच्छ्रवणस्तिस्र उत्तराः। तिसृष्वेकादशी वाऽऽसु जन्मर्क्षश्रोणयोगयुक् 23।।
त एते श्रेयसः काला नृणां श्रेयोविवर्धनाः। कुर्यात् सर्वात्मनैतेषु श्रेयोऽमोघं तदायुषः ।।24।।
एषु स्नानं जपो होमो व्रतं देवद्विजार्चनम्। पितृदेवनृभूतेभ्यो यद् दत्तं तद्ध्यनश्वरम् ।।25।।
संस्कारकालो जायाया अपत्यस्यात्मनस्तथा। प्रेतसंस्था मृताहश्च कर्मण्यभ्युदये नृप ।।26।।
अथ देशान् प्रवक्ष्यामि धर्मादिश्रेयआवहान्। स वै पुण्यतमो देशः सत्पात्रं यत्र लभ्यते ।।27।।
बिम्बं भगवतो यत्र सर्वमेतच्चराचरम्। यत्र ह ब्राह्मणकुलं तपोविद्यादयान्वितम् ।।28।।

fortnight called Mahālaya in the month of Bhādra. **20-23.** He should perform their Srāddha also at the time of the summer and winter solstices and the vernal and the autumnal equinoxes; during the astronomical division of time called Vyatīpāta; on the day when a lunar day begins and ends without the sunrise or between two sunrises; during the lunar or solar eclipses; on a twelfth lunar day as well as during the period when the constellations known by the name of Srāvana, Dhanishtha, and Satabhisha are ascendant; on the third lunar day of the bright half of Vaishākha as well as on the ninth lunar day of the bright half of Kārtika; or the four Ashtakas during the seasons known as Hemanta and Sisira; on the seventh lunar day of Māgha; on the full-moon day of Māgha when the constellation called Māgha is in the ascendant; when the constellations associated with other lunar months also appear on the full moon day; or even when the moon rises one digit less than the full; on any twelfth lunar day when the constellations of Anurādha, Srāvana, and any of the three constellations associated with the name of Uttara (Uttaraphalguni, Uttarāshādha and Uttarabhadrapāda) are ascendant; or when the eleventh lunar day is conjoined with any of these constellations; and lastly, on any day when the constellation under which one was born or the constellation of Srāvana is ascendant. **24.** All these days are auspicious times, conducive to good fortune, and therefore suited not only for Srāddhas but also for all good works which make one's life fruitful. **25.** Holy acts like ritual ablutions, repetition of Mantra, sacrifice in fire, observance of vows, worship of Devas and holy men, making gifts in the name of ancestors, men, Devas etc.,—all such holy and altruistic acts become infinitely fruitful when done at such times. **26.** O King! During the purificatory rite for the wife called Pumsavana, the birth rites for the son, sacraments for oneself, funeral rites, the rites on the anniversary of a death—at all such times holy works conducive to welfare should be done.

Value of Holy Places (27-33)

27. Now I shall tell you what are the places that augment the results of good acts done at those places. The best of such places is where one gets a holy man who has been the object of the Lord's grace. **28.** Wherever the image of the Supreme Being in whom all the worlds reside, is installed and worshipped, and where holy men who practise austerity, knowledge, benevolence and other virtues

यत्र यत्र हरेरर्चा स देशः श्रेयसां पदम् । यत्र गङ्गादयो नद्यः पुराणेषु च विश्रुताः ॥29॥
सरांसि पुष्करादीनि क्षेत्राण्यर्हाश्रितान्युत । कुरुक्षेत्रं गयशिरः प्रयागः पुलहाश्रमः ॥30॥
नैमिषं फाल्गुनं सेतुः प्रभासोऽथ कुशस्थली । वाराणसी मधुपुरी पम्पा बिन्दुसरस्तथा ॥31॥
नारायणाश्रमो नन्दा सीतारामाश्रमादयः । सर्वे कुलाचला राजन् महेन्द्रमलयादयः ॥32॥
एते पुण्यतमा देशा हरेरर्चाश्रिताश्च ये । एतान् देशान् निषेवेत श्रेयस्कामो ह्यभीक्ष्णशः ।
धर्मो ह्यत्रेहितः पुंसां सहस्राधिफलोदयः ॥33॥
पात्रं त्वत्र निरुक्तं वै कविभिः पात्रवित्तमैः । हरिरेवैक उर्वीश यन्मयं वै चराचरम् ॥34॥
देवर्ष्यर्हत्सु वै सत्सु तत्र ब्रह्मात्मजादिषु । राजन् यदग्रपूजायां मतः पात्रतयाच्युतः ॥35॥
जीवराशिभिराकीर्ण आण्डकोशाङ्घ्रिपो महान् । तन्मूलत्वादच्युतेज्या सर्वजीवात्मतर्पणम् ॥36॥
पुराण्यनेन सृष्टानि नृतिर्यगृषिदेवताः । शेते जीवेन रूपेण पुरेषु पुरुषो ह्यसौ ॥37॥
तेष्वेषु भगवान् राजंस्तारतम्येन वर्तते । तस्मात् पात्रं हि पुरुषो यावानात्मा यथेयते ॥38॥
दृष्ट्वा तेषां मिथो नृणामवज्ञानात्मतां नृप । त्रेतादिषु हरेरर्चा क्रियायै कविभिः कृता ॥39॥

reside—these places also are holy. **29.** Where the worship of Hari is carried on, and where rivers like Ganga, specially sung about in the Puranas, flow—they are all holy places. **30.** The localities where sacred lakes like Pushkara and holy pilgrimage spots like Kurukshetra, Gaya Prayāga, Pulahāshrama etc., are situated, and where great devotees had stayed in the past—they are all holy places. **31-33.** Naimishāranya, Phālguna, Srīrāmasetu, Prabhāsa, Kusasthali, Vārānasi, Mathura, Lake Pampa, Bindusaras, Badaryāshrama, banks of Alakananda, Chitrakūta, Panchavati etc., where Rama and Sita stayed, great mountains like Mahendra and Malaya—all these are very sacred places, and so are others where Sri Hari's images are permanently installed and worshipped. Spiritual aspirants should visit such places often; for, spiritual practices and good acts done there are a thousandfold effective.

True Worship (34-42)

34. O King! Those who have thought deeply on the question of who constitutes the best recipient, have come to the conclusion that the only one fit to receive worship is the Supreme Bhagavan, of whom this whole world is a gross manifestation. **35.** For, in your Rajasuya sacrifice, where Devas, Rishis, Siddhas, and sages like Sanaka were present, it was Sri Krishna alone that was selected as the fit recipient to be adored as the greatest personage present at the sacrifice. **36.** This all-inclusive cosmic shell (Brahmanda) is like a tree, of which all the worlds of living beings constitute the spreading branches. Achyuta being the root of that tree, His worship results in satisfying all beings included in the universe. **37.** After creating men, animals and all other creatures, He, the all-pervading one, resides in all bodies as the indwelling Self and as the Jiva. As He lives in the city of this body, He is called Purusha (the resident of this city). **38.** His manifestation in some bodies is greater, and in some others less. Therefore, man is the fit recipient, and among men, he in whom the Spirit is more manifest. He is a better recipient than others.

39. O King! But men became mutually disrespectful and antagonistic due to the perception of each other's defects and therefore incapable of seeing the Lord

ततोऽर्चायां हरिं केचित् संश्रद्धाय सपर्यया । उपासत उपास्तापि नार्थदा पुरुषद्विषाम् ॥40॥
पुरुषेष्वपि राजेन्द्र सुपात्रं ब्राह्मणं विदुः । तपसा विद्यया तुष्ट्या धत्ते वेदं हरेस्तनुम् ॥41॥
नन्वस्य ब्राह्मणा राजन् कृष्णस्य जगदात्मनः । पुनन्तः पादरजसा त्रिलोकीं दैवतं महत् ॥42॥

इति श्रीमद्भागवते महापुराणे पारमहंस्यां संहितायां सप्तमस्कन्धे सदाचारनिर्णयो नाम चतुर्दशोऽध्यायः ॥14॥

within. Hence in the Treta Yuga great sages brought into being the system of worshipping Him in holy images (to which none can attribute evil). **40.** So some serve Hari by worshipping Him with utmost faith and attention in holy images. But it is of no benefit to one who persecutes and oppresses one's fellow beings. **41.** O King! Among men, a holy man is considered the best recipient. For he takes care of the Veda, the body of Hari, through his austerity, knowledge and equanimity. **42.** O King! Krishna, the soul of the universe, reckons such holy men, who purify the whole world by the touch of their feet, as the Deity for Himself to worship. Imagine therefore their greatness!

अथ पञ्चदशोऽध्यायः

नारद उवाच

कर्मनिष्ठा द्विजाः केचित् तपोनिष्ठा नृपापरे । स्वाध्यायेऽन्ये प्रवचने ये केचिज्ज्ञानयोगयोः ॥ 1॥
ज्ञाननिष्ठाय देयानि कव्यान्यानन्त्यमिच्छता । दैवे च तदभावे स्यादितरेभ्यो यथार्हतः ॥ 2॥
द्वौ दैवे पितृकार्ये त्रीनेकैकमुभयत्र वा । भोजयेत् सुसमृद्धोऽपि श्राद्धे कुर्यान्न विस्तरम् 3॥
देशकालोचितश्रद्धाद्रव्यपात्रार्हणानि च । सम्यग् भवन्ति नैतानि विस्तरात् स्वजनार्पणात् ॥
देशे काले च सम्प्राप्ते मुन्यन्नं हरिदैवतम् । श्रद्धया विधिवत् पात्रे न्यस्तं कामधुगक्षयम् 5॥

Skandha VII : Chapter 15

LIBERATION AS THE IDEAL OF ALL ASHRAMAS

Food Offering to Devas and Pitris (1-11)

Narada said: **1.** Some Dwijas are devoted to ritualistic works, some to the practice of austerity, some to chanting of the Veda, some to discoursing on learned topics, and a few to the disciplines of Jnana and Yoga. **2.** Those who hope for high results should offer the different food offerings prepared for the Pitris and the Devas to one who is established in knowledge. If such a one is not available, it can be given to lesser persons according to their qualification. **3.** Feeding of two in the rites connected with the Devas and of three in the rites of the Pitris may be done. Or, in both, a holy one may be fed. Especially in a Srāddha (the rites of the Pitris), too much elaboration of feeding should be avoided, however rich a person might be. **4.** For, in the midst of making elaborate arrangements for feasting a large number of invited relatives, it will be impossible to ensure proper attention to all the other aspects of the rite like place, time, worthiness of the guest, careful performance, materials, vessels, ingredients of worship etc., all of which are immediate and essential requirements of the rite. **5.** If fruits and roots, offered to Sri Hari

देवर्षिपितृभूतेभ्य आत्मने स्वजनाय च।
अन्नं संविभजन् पश्येत् सर्वं तत् पुरुषात्मकम् ॥ 6॥
न दद्यादामिषं श्राद्धे न चाद्याद् धर्मतत्त्ववित्।
मुन्यन्नैः स्यात् परा प्रीतिर्यथा न पशुहिंसया ॥ 7॥
नैतादृशः परो धर्मो नृणां सद्धर्ममिच्छताम्।
न्यासो दण्डस्य भूतेषु मनोवाक्कायजस्य यः ॥ 8॥
एके कर्ममयान् यज्ञान् ज्ञानिनो यज्ञवित्तमाः।
आत्मसंयमनेऽनीहा जुह्वति ज्ञानदीपिते ॥ 9॥
द्रव्ययज्ञैर्यक्ष्यमाणं दृष्ट्वा भूतानि बिभ्यति।
एष माकरुणो हन्यादतज्ज्ञो ह्यसुतृब् ध्रुवम् ॥10॥
तस्माद् दैवोपपन्नेन मुन्यन्नेनापि धर्मवित्।
सन्तुष्टोऽहरहः कुर्यान्नित्यनैमित्तिकीः क्रियाः ॥11॥
विधर्मः परधर्मश्च आभास उपमा छलः।
अधर्मशाखाः पञ्चेमा धर्मज्ञोऽधर्मवत् त्यजेत् ॥12॥
धर्मबाधो विधर्मः स्यात् परधर्मोऽन्यचोदितः।
उपधर्मस्तु पाखण्डो दम्भो वा शब्दभिच्छलः ॥13॥
यस्त्विच्छया कृतः पुम्भिराभासो ह्याश्रमात् पृथक्।
स्वभावविहितो धर्मः कस्य नेष्टः प्रशान्तये ॥14॥
धर्मार्थमपि नेहेत यात्रार्थं वाधनो धनम्।
अनीहानीहमानस्य महाहेरिव वृत्तिदा ॥15॥

at the proper time and place, are given to a fit recipient, that will be really effective in fulfilling one's prayers and giving lasting results. **6.** When food is separately offered to Devas, Rishis, Pitris, relatives and brute creations, as also to oneself and one's relatives, they should all be viewed as manifestations of the Divine.

7. A man who knows the real intention of the Sacred Law should not offer or eat meat at Srāddha. The offering of roots and fruits, free from the taint of violence, is more pleasing to the Pitris than the slaughter of animals. **8.** For those who aspire for spiritual advancement, there is no rule more important than the avoidance of all injury to living beings by thought, word or action. **9.** So these wise ones who know the true import of Yajna and are free from desires, reduce ritualistic sacrifice into the sacrifice of knowledge, consisting of enlightenment-born self-control. **10.** On seeing a person who practises external sacrificial rituals, all living creatures run away frightened, remarking, 'This man, who is without any spiritual enlightenment, who wants only to satisfy his passions and his senses, and who is devoid of even an atom of pity, is sure to kill me.' **11.** Therefore a righteous man should be satisfied with the food of ascetics consisting of cereals, fruits and roots got without much effort, and with these he should do his duty and occasional rites.

Perversions of Dharma (12-14)

12. A knower of Dharma should abandon, as Adharma, the following five aspects of Adharma which may look like Dharma. These are known as Vidharma, Paradharma, Ābhāsa, Upamā, and Cchala. **13.** Vidharma is that by performing which one's Dharma (duty) can be adversely affected in spite of the work appearing good. Paradharma means the Dharma meant for another. Upadharma is the way of unbelievers or of people who make a mere show of observing Dharma. Cchala means interpreting scriptural passages regarding conduct in whatever way one likes. **14.** The works which men do disregarding what is prescribed for their Ashrama or station in life, is called Ābhāsa or perversion. Work that is in accordance with one's nature only is conducive to peace.

Contentment and Happiness (15-25)

15. Neither for the discharge of his religious duties nor for his livelihood need a desireless man of poor means struggle. For, in the case of the desireless man, his giving up all work and activity will

सन्तुष्टस्य निरीहस्य स्वात्मारामस्य यत् सुखम् । कुतस्तत् कामलोभेन धावतोऽर्थेहया दिशः ॥16॥
सदा सन्तुष्टमनसः सर्वाः सुखमया दिशः । शर्कराकण्टकादिभ्यो यथोपानत्पदः शिवम् 17॥
सन्तुष्टः केन वा राजन् न वर्तेतापि वारिणा । औपस्थ्यजैह्व्यकार्पण्याद् गृहपालायते जनः 18॥
असन्तुष्टस्य विप्रस्य तेजो विद्या तपो यशः । स्रवन्तीन्द्रियलौल्येन ज्ञानं चैवावकीर्यते ॥19॥
कामस्यान्तं च क्षुत्तृड्भ्यां क्रोधस्यैतत्फलोदयात् । जनो याति न लोभस्य जित्वा भुक्त्वा दिशो भुवः ॥
पण्डिता बहवो राजन् बहुज्ञाः संशयच्छिदः । सदसस्पतयोऽप्येके असन्तोषात् पतन्त्यधः ॥21॥
असङ्कल्पाज्जयेत् कामं क्रोधं कामविवर्जनात् । अर्थानर्थेक्षया लोभं भयं तत्त्वावमर्शनात् ॥22॥
आन्वीक्षिक्या शोकमोहौ दम्भं महदुपासया । योगान्तरायान् मौनेन हिंसां कायाद्यनीहया ॥23॥
कृपया भूतजं दुःखं दैवं जह्यात् समाधिना । आत्मजं योगवीर्येण निद्रां सत्त्वनिषेवया ॥24॥
रजस्तमश्च सत्त्वेन सत्त्वं चोपशमेन च । एतत् सर्वं गुरौ भक्त्या पुरुषो ह्यञ्जसा जयेत् 25॥

itself procure him food, as in the case of a python. **16.** How can a man running hither and thither for the acquisition of money out of his desire for objects of enjoyment, have the bliss of that one who is ever enraptured in the Self, actionless and ever-satisfied? **17.** Just as the feet protected by a pair of shoes can walk fearlessly over stones and thorns, so also a man who is at peace within finds happiness in all places. **18.** If a person is happy within, he would surely be happy even with some liquid food to imbibe once. But those who are not happy within, run about like dogs on account of their abominable desire to satisfy their sex instinct and gluttony. **19.** In the case of one who has no feeling of happiness and contentment within, all higher qualities like impressiveness, learning, austerity, reputation etc., will ebb away through his sensuous indulgences. Whatever higher understanding he has, perishes. **20.** Hunger and thirst are appeased with food and drink. Anger abates when the victim has been suppressed or killed. But greed does not subside even if one conquers all the quarters and enjoys the whole earth. **21.** Many scholars noted for their learning and capacity to clear doubts of others, who can preside even over learned assemblies, become degenerate because of their lack of contentment and inner joy. **22.** Sexuality has to be conquered by abandoning the will to enjoy (Sankalpa); anger by abandoning desire; greed by reflecting on the risks in being wealthy; and fear by meditation on the Supreme Truth. **23.** Grief and infatuation are to be overcome by discrimination between the Atman and the Anātman, the Self and the Not-Self; pride in one's greatness, by association with the wise; obstacles to concentration, by practice of silence; proneness to violence, by controlling attachment to body and possessions. **24.** The painful experiences from other living creatures are to be overcome by kindness towards them; those arising from past Karma, by practising equanimity; those from body, by Pranayama; and those from sleep, by consumption of Sattvika food. **25.** Rajas and Tamas are to be conquered by Sattva; and Sattva by proper discrimination.[1] An aspirant will succeed in all this easily if he has true devotion to the Guru.

[1] Though Sattva is a desirable experience, even that has to be controlled and regulated, so that one is not diverted from the main path. Even a virtue misapplied can prove to be a danger. The story of Jada Bharata, who happened to be born as a deer, because of his being over-kind, is quoted as an example. There are certain things which one can do, and certain others which one cannot, however good they may be.

यस्य साक्षाद् भगवति ज्ञानदीपप्रदे गुरौ । मर्त्यासद्धीः श्रुतं तस्य सर्वं कुञ्जरशौचवत् ॥26॥
एष वै भगवान् साक्षात् प्रधानपुरुषेश्वरः । योगेश्वरैर्विमृग्याङ्घ्रिर्लोको यं मन्यते नरम् ॥27॥
षड्वर्गसंयमैकान्ताः सर्वा नियमचोदनाः । तदन्ता यदि नो योगानावहेयुः श्रमावहाः ॥28॥
यथा वार्तादयो ह्यर्था योगस्यार्थं न बिभ्रति । अनर्थाय भवेयुस्ते पूर्तमिष्टं तथासतः ॥29॥
यश्चित्तविजये यत्तः स्यान्निःसङ्गोऽपरिग्रहः । एको विविक्तशरणो भिक्षुर्भिक्षामिताशनः 30॥
देशे शुचौ समे राजन् संस्थाप्यासनमात्मनः । स्थिरं समं सुखं तस्मिन्नासीतर्ज्वङ्ग ओमिति 31॥
प्राणापानौ सन्निरुन्ध्यात् पूरकुम्भकरेचकैः । यावन्मनस्त्यजेत् कामान् स्वनासाग्रनिरीक्षणः ॥
यतो यतो निःसरति मनः कामहतं भ्रमत् । ततस्तत उपाहृत्य हृदि रुन्ध्याच्छनैर्बुधः ॥33॥
एवमभ्यसतश्चित्तं कालेनाल्पीयसा यतेः । अनिशं तस्य निर्वाणं यात्यनिन्धनवह्निवत् ॥34॥

Faith in the Guru (26-27)

26. If a disciple thinks of his Guru as a mere man, instead of as a manifestation of the Lord Himself bringing the light of wisdom, the scriptural study and the knowledge he has gained will have all failed in their purpose, as a bath given to an elephant.[1] **27.** If it is said that the Guru is looked upon only as a man by all his friends and acquaintances, and so it will be irrational to look upon him as divine, the answer is: Look, here is Krishna, who in reality is the Master of Prakriti and the Jivas, the Supreme Lord whose feet are sought even by masters of Yoga. Even He is considered by most people as a man; his divinity is not recognised by ordinary people. (Hence the humanity of the Guru is no argument against his being recognised as the light of the Lord illumining the disciple.)

Control of Mind (28-35)

28. All the Vedic injunctions regarding rites and charities have the control of the senses as their ultimate purpose. But if these practices, while helping the control of the senses, happen to obstruct the practice of concentration and Samadhi, they are to be considered merely as purposeless hardship. **29.** Just as agriculture, trade etc., do not help one to attain to the goal of spiritual communion but become obstructing factors, so can the charitable works and sacrificial offerings of a man be, if he is an Asat, an extrovert devoid of any higher idea about life.

30. A man who is intent on the control of the mind, if he finds obstruction in home life, should become non-attached, give up the idea of possession, become a mendicant and live alone in solitude, subsisting on a spare meal obtained as alms. **31.** O King! Taking a seat on clean and level ground, he should sit there with his body, neck and head erect, and repeat the Mantra 'Om'. **32.** Until the mind is free from desires, he should sit with eyes half-closed, as if looking on the nose, and regulate Prana and Apana by Pranayama, consisting of Pūraka, Kumbhaka and Rechaka. **33.** Whenever the mind runs away under the stress of desires, a discriminating person should draw it towards the heart again and again, and concentrate it there. **34.** The mind of an aspirant who practises like this without break, will soon subside in calmness, as the fire that has

[1] It is the elephant's habit to sprinkle mud over its body even immediately after its bath, so that bathing serves no purpose.

कामादिभिरनाविद्धं प्रशान्ताखिलवृत्ति यत् । चित्तं ब्रह्मसुखस्पृष्टं नैवोत्तिष्ठेत कर्हिचित् ।।35।।
यः प्रव्रज्य गृहात् पूर्वं त्रिवर्गावपनात् पुनः । यदि सेवेत तान् भिक्षुः स वै वान्ताश्यपत्रपः ।।36।।
यैःस्वदेहःस्मृतो नात्मा मर्त्यो विट्कृमिभस्मसात् । त एनमात्मसात्कृत्वा श्लाघयन्ति ह्यसत्तमाः 37।।
गृहस्थस्य क्रियात्यागो व्रतत्यागो वटोरपि । तपस्विनो ग्रामसेवा भिक्षोरिन्द्रियलोलता ।।38।।
आश्रमापसदा ह्येते खल्वाश्रमविडम्बकाः । देवमायाविमूढांस्तानुपेक्षेतानुकम्पया ।।39।।
आत्मानं चेद् विजानीयात् परं ज्ञानधुताशयः । किमिच्छन् कस्य वा हेतोर्देहं पुष्णाति लम्पटः 40।।

आहुः शरीरं रथमिन्द्रियाणि हयानभीषून् मन इन्द्रियेशम् ।
वर्त्मानि मात्रा धिषणां च सूतं सत्त्वं बृहद् बन्धुरमीशसृष्टम् ।।41।।
अक्षं दशप्राणमधर्मधर्मौ चक्रेऽभिमानं रथिनं च जीवम् ।
धनुर्हि तस्य प्रणवं पठन्ति शरं तु जीवं परमेव लक्ष्यम् ।।42।।

रागो द्वेषश्च लोभश्च शोकमोहौ भयं मदः । मानोऽवमानोऽसूया च माया हिंसा च मत्सरः 43।।
रजः प्रमादः क्षुन्निद्रा शत्रवस्त्वेवमादयः । रजस्तमःप्रकृतयः सत्त्वप्रकृतयः क्वचित् ।।44।।

consumed the fuel. **35.** The mind that is not agitated by sexuality and other passions, and has been calmed by the cessation of all modes, and is enjoying the bliss of Brahman, will never again become outward-going.

Self-control, Ideal of Ashramas (36-46)

36. A person who has once left the state of a householder, which is the field for the acquisition of Dharma, Artha and Kama, to become a Sannyasin, but again goes after those threefold worldly values, is a shameless man, an eater of his own vomit. **37.** There are certainly people who at first declare that this body, which is perishable and will be reduced to faeces, worms, ashes etc., can never be the Atman, but afterwards under the influence of evil tendencies again make their dependants and disciples praise this very body. **38-39.** A householder's abandonment of the prescribed rites and duties, a Brahmacharin's violation of his vow of celibacy, a Vanaprastha's fondness to live in towns and villages, a Sannyasin's addiction to sensuous indulgences—such conduct marks them as mere pretenders and as the meanest followers of their respective Ashramas. Victims of the Lord's Maya, they are to be pitied and avoided. **40.** When a person has come to understand that the Atman is one with the Existence-Knowledge-Bliss, why should that knowing one, who must have already swept away all his tendencies for sensuous indulgence from the mind, again get engrossed in such indulgences and fatten his body?

41. The body is compared to a chariot; the senses to horses; the mind to the controlling reins; the sense objects to the roads to be traversed; the intellect to the charioteer; and the Chitta or the mind-stuff, which is the repository of all affections, to the big binding cord. **42.** The knowing ones speak of the ten Prāṇās as the axle-tree; Dharma and Adharma as the wheels; the Jiva bound by the I-sense as the master of the chariot; the Pranava (the symbol Om) as his bow; the purified Jiva as the arrow; and Brahman as the target. **43-44.** Attachment, anger, greed, grief, infatuation, fear, conceit, pride, feeling of insult, jealousy, dacoitry, violence, rivalry, passionate involvement, heedlessness, hunger, sleep—these are all manifestations of Rajas and Tamas, and are enemies of a spiritual aspirant. Sometimes for advanced as-

यावन्नृकायरथमात्मवशोपकल्पं धत्ते गरिष्ठचरणार्चनया निशातम् ।
ज्ञानासिमच्युतबलो दधदस्तशत्रुः स्वाराज्यतुष्ट उपशान्त इदं विजह्यात् ॥45॥
नो चेत् प्रमत्तमसदिन्द्रियवाजिसूता नीत्वोत्पथं विषयदस्युषु निक्षिपन्ति ।
ते दस्यवः सहयसूतममुं तमोऽन्धे संसारकूप उरुमृत्युभये क्षिपन्ति ॥46॥

प्रवृत्तं च निवृत्तं च द्विविधं कर्म वैदिकम् । आवर्तेत प्रवृत्तेन निवृत्तेनाश्नुतेऽमृतम् ॥47॥
हिंस्रं द्रव्यमयं काम्यमग्निहोत्राद्यशान्तिदम् । दर्शश्च पूर्णमासश्च चातुर्मास्यं पशुः सुतः ॥48॥
एतदिष्टं प्रवृत्ताख्यं हुतं प्रहुतमेव च । पूर्तं सुरालयारामकूपाजीव्यादिलक्षणम् ॥49॥
द्रव्यसूक्ष्मविपाकश्च धूमो रात्रिरपक्षयः । अयनं दक्षिणं सोमो दर्श ओषधिवीरुधः ॥50॥
अन्नं रेत इति क्ष्मेश पितृयानं पुनर्भवः । एकैकश्येनानुपूर्वं भूत्वा भूत्वेह जायते ॥51॥

pirants, even Sattva, which is usually helpful in spiritual development, can become an obstruction, as kindness became in the case of Jada-bharata. Ultimately all the three Gunas have to be transcended. **45.** When the chariot of the human body has been mastered by the complete subdual of the senses, then the sword of knowledge, sharpened by the service of great men, should be taken in hand, and all the enemies mentioned above should be killed with the strength derived from Achyuta. Having thus attained one's pristine state, the bliss of the Atman, one should abandon this chariot of a body. **46.** If one does not follow the path described, the horses of senses, which always gallop forward directed by the charioteer of intellect (Buddhi), will land the heedless man in the midst of the robbers of sense objects. These robbers will haul the master of the chariot (the Jiva), along with the horses and the charioteer, into the dilapidated well of Samsara, which is characterised by the dense darkness of ignorance and the constant fear of death.

Pravritti, Nivritti and Yānas (47-56)

47. The works described in the Vedas are of two kinds—those that relate to Pravritti and those that lead to Nivritti. By following the path of Pravritti one gets repeated births, whereas by Nivritti one overcomes rebirth and attains to immortality. **48-49.** All sacrifices, involving slaughter of animals or requiring an abundance of materials, such as Agnihotra, Darsa, Pūrnamāsa, Chāturmāsya, Pasuyāga, Somayāga, Vaisvedeva rites, offering of Bali—all these forms of sacrifice are called Ishta. Building of temples, of public gardens, wells, tanks etc., arranging for distribution of water—all such charitable works stand for Pūrta. If all these are done with desire for their fruits, and are consequently contributive to mental disquiet, they all fall within Pravritti, or acts leading to rebirths. (If done without desire, as offering to the Supreme Being, they take the character of Nivritti or liberation.)

50-51. (The following is the Pitriyāna, or the Path of the Fathers, the post-mortem states that await one who is involved in Pravritti or works with desire.) The subtle effects of the sacrificial offerings generating an ethereal body, ascent through the deities associated with smoke, night, dark fortnight, southern solstice etc., to the sphere of the lunar heaven, the dissolution of the heavenly body due to grief, and the descent through rain to vegetation, food and semen, ending with birth in the world—these, O King, constitute the Pitriyāna, the Path of the Fathers. Passing through stage after stage

निषेकादिश्मशानान्तैः संस्कारैः संस्कृतो द्विजः । इन्द्रियेषु क्रियायज्ञान् ज्ञानदीपेषु जुह्वति ॥52॥
इन्द्रयाणि मनस्यूर्मौ वाचि वैकारिकं मनः । वाचं वर्णसमाम्नाये तमोङ्कारे स्वरे न्यसेत् ।
ओङ्कारं बिन्दौ नादे तं तं तु प्राणे महत्यमुम् ॥53॥
अग्निः सूर्यो दिवा प्राह्णः शुक्लो राकोत्तरं स्वराट् । विश्वश्च तैजसः प्राज्ञस्तुर्य आत्मा समन्वयात् 54॥
देवयानमिदं प्राहुर्भूत्वा भूत्वानुपूर्वशः । आत्मयाज्युपशान्तात्मा ह्यात्मस्थो न निवर्तते ॥
य एते पितृदेवानामयने वेदनिर्मिते । शास्त्रेण चक्षुषा वेद जनस्थोऽपि न मुह्यति ॥56॥
आदावन्ते जनानां सद् बहिरन्तः परावरम् । ज्ञानं ज्ञेयं वचो वाच्यं तमो ज्योतिस्त्वयं स्वयम् 57
आबाधितोऽपि ह्याभासो यथा वस्तुतया स्मृतः । दुर्घटत्वादैन्द्रियकं तद्वदर्थविकल्पितम् ॥58॥
क्षित्यादीनामिहार्थानां छाया न कतमापि हि । न संघातो विकारोऽपि न पृथङ् नान्वितो मृषा 59॥

as described above, one is re-born. **52.** It is only a Dwija, or a twice-born one, who has undergone all the purificatory rites from conception to cremation, and has performed the Vedic rites described earlier that becomes eligible to tread this Path of the Fathers. But one who is devoted to Nivritti, i.e., liberation, sacrifices in the senses rendered blazing by knowledge, all their functions (consisting in Ishta and Pūrta) as oblations by the process of meditation. **53.** The senses should be dissolved in the mind characterised by imaginative and doubting functions; the mind and all its modes, in speech; and the speech, in the collectivity of articulate sounds that is in Omkara; Omkara in Bindu; Bindu in Nāda; Nāda in the Indwelling Spirit; and the Indwelling Spirit in the Supreme Spirit. **54.** The aspirant to Nivritti (liberation) passes through the deities representing fire, sun, day, forenoon, the bright fortnight as well as its end, the full moon, and northern solstice, and reaches Brahmaloka. Then he becomes identified with Viswa, Taijasa and Prājna and dissolves the bodies associated with these states, namely, the gross body, the subtle body and the causal body, and becomes established in the Transcendental Fourth, the Turiya. He is then one with the all-pervading Atman. **55.** Great men call this Devayāna, the path of the Divine. He who meditates on the Atman in peace, becomes established in that consciousness as the Spirit, and is not reborn again and again, unlike one engrossed in Karma. **56.** One who has a true understanding of these two paths, the Pitriyāna and the Devayāna, with the help of the Vedic teaching, will not get infatuated even when he is in the body.

Knowledge of Non-duality (57-65)

57. That which was before the origin of the body and remains as it was, unsublated at its dissolution; which manifests both as the enjoyer and the enjoyed, the high and the low, knowledge and the object of knowledge, word and its significance, light and darkness—all these are the knowing one himself. (Where there is nothing as the 'other', different from the Self, there is no question of infatuation or fear.) **58.** The reflection of an object is actually observed as existing, though in the eye of logic it is not there where it is seen. In the same way, the objects experienced are not existences independent in themselves, as it is contrary to fact. (They are the expression of the will of the Supreme Being appearing to be independent existences so long as the Jiva does not realise his oneness with the Supreme.) **59.** In the being of the Lord, there is not the shadow even of earth

धातवोऽवयवित्वाच्च तन्मात्रावयवैर्विना ।
स्यात् सादृश्यभ्रमस्तावद् विकल्पे सति वस्तुनः ।
भावाद्वैतं क्रियाद्वैतं द्रव्याद्वैतं तथाऽऽत्मनः ।
न स्युर्ह्यसत्यवयविन्यसन्नवयवोऽन्ततः ॥60॥
जाग्रत्स्वापौ यथा स्वप्ने तथा विधिनिषेधता ॥61॥
वर्तयन् स्वानुभूत्येह त्रीन् स्वप्नान् धुनुते मुनिः ॥

and other material elements, neither as a collection of parts, nor as a development, nor as a transformation. They are not in separation from Him, nor in union with Him in a way that affects His entity. They form a Mithya—an experience without ultimacy.[1] **60.** Even primordial elements, which are 'wholes' formed by collocations of their subtle ingredients called Tanmatras, do not really exist apart from these ingredients. The 'whole' is only something imagined to explain the combinations of parts. Now if the 'whole' is imaginary and unreal, the parts that are supposed to form them also must be unreal. **61.** Even though there is no difference in the Atman, the sense of recognition based on difference would persist so long as there is Ajnana. Then the question will arise whether the scriptural prohibitions and injunctions based on the sense of difference will not be unreal and not binding. The answer is that they are binding only so long as there is the spell of ignorance. It is just like sleeping and waking experienced in the course of a dream. After the basic dream breaks, they have no relevance. Such is the case with the Vedic injunctions and prohibitions.

62. By the practice of Bhāvādvaita, Kriyādvaita and Dravyādvaita in regard to

[1] This passage and earlier ones are very obscure, and different commentators can interpret it differently according to their respective metaphysics. The one central idea is that the Lord is the sole existence, including in Himself the relative subject, the Jiva, and the relative object, the world. But the unity or integrity of the Lord is not in the least affected by the Jiva and the Jagat. This is said to be the function of the mysterious power of the Lord (Maya)—to manifest without being affected. Others try to give a kind of logical explanation for it by describing it as Mithya—an appearance which is felt but is not actually there, a phenomenon that is experienced but has no ultimacy.

But the question arises: who experiences these apparent phenomena? One will have to say it is the Lord Himself, or an experiencing subject, the Jiva which is under delusion. As pure Advaitins accept the identity of the Jiva and Iswara, the question posed is irrelevant to them, they will say that the world is the result of delusion, and this delusion is in whoever experiences it. This answer will not satisfy many, as its implication is solipsism (Drishti-srishti-vada).

Others therefore maintain that the Supreme Being has an inherent Power or Will called by various names—as Maya, Prakriti, Sakti etc; for, He is both Being and Will. Both the subject (the Jiva) and the object (the world) are expressions of His Will, the Sakti, while He is Himself the uninvolved witness of both, of the involved consciousness or the Jiva, and of the changeful world of objectivity. The Jiva, being a centre of consciousness, can by the grace of that Divine will or Shakti that brought about its sense of separation, recognise his oneness with the Divine also. He then ceases to be an individual as a drop of water ceases to be a drop when it gets into the ocean.

The question will now crop up: What happens to all the other Jivas and the world when one Jiva overcomes ignorance and attains salvation? The answer varies. The Drishti-srishti-vadins or solipsists, who find the basis of the world in the individual's ignorance, would maintain that the question will cease to have any relevancy as the whole of duality vanishes with the cessation of ignorance, just as all the persons and things included in a dream vanish when the dream vanishes. Individuality and multiplicity are bound up with the state of ignorance whose locus is the individual. The subject-objectless Reality alone is.

The second school of Vedanta, designated by pure Advaitins as a school of compromise, would consider this view as solipsistic. The individual's ignorance springs from Maya, the will or the power of Brahman, and all involved beings are subject to it. The individual's ignorance is only a distorted expression of the Divine Maya in him. The Maya of Iswara is Cosmic Power, whereas its distorted expression in the Jiva as ignorance, is a disvalue hiding the truth. So when a Jiva breaks the spell of ignorance, that centre gets identified with the Supreme, but the others continue in separateness without the awareness of their basic oneness with Him. If, however, a Jiva's individuality is retained even after illumination, he shares the world-awareness with the Divine, the Lord. Maya, the Divine Will that projects the world, is no longer a factor of bondage and suffering for him but a Divine Leela or sport in which he is a participant. Such a Jiva appears as a world Teacher, a Supreme Lover and playmate of God, through whom the Jivas in bondage are redeemed. The *Bhagavata* seems to highlight this ideal, even while expounding the solipsistic idea of Vedanta.

कार्यकारणवस्त्वैक्यमर्शनं पटतन्तुवत् । अवस्तुत्वाद् विकल्पस्य भावाद्वैतं तदुच्यते ॥63॥
यद् ब्रह्मणि परे साक्षात् सर्वकर्मसमर्पणम् । मनोवाक्तनुभिः पार्थ क्रियाद्वैतं तदुच्यते ॥64॥
आत्मजायासुतादीनामन्येषां सर्वदेहिनाम् । यत् स्वार्थकामयोरैक्यं द्रव्याद्वैतं तदुच्यते ॥65॥
यद् यस्य वानिषिद्धं स्याद् येन यत्र यतो नृप । स तेनेहेत कर्माणि नरो नान्यैरनापदि ॥66॥
एतैरन्यैश्च वेदोक्तैर्वर्तमानः स्वकर्मभिः । गृहेऽप्यस्य गतिं यायाद् राजंस्तद्भक्तिभाङ्नरः ॥
यथा हि यूयं नृपदेव दुस्त्यजादापद्गणादुत्तरतात्मनः प्रभोः ।
यत्पादपङ्केरुहसेवया भवानहार्षीन्निर्जितदिग्गजः क्रतून् ॥68॥
अहं पुराभवं कश्चिद्गन्धर्व उपबर्हणः । नाम्नातीते महाकल्पे गन्धर्वाणां सुसम्मतः ॥69॥
रूपपेशलमाधुर्यसौगन्ध्यप्रियदर्शनः । स्त्रीणां प्रियतमो नित्यं मत्तस्तु पुरुलम्पटः ॥70॥
एकदा देवसत्रे तु गन्धर्वाप्सरसां गणाः । उपहूता विश्वसृग्भिर्हरिगाथोपगायने ॥71॥
अहं च गायंस्तद्विद्वान् स्त्रीभिः परिवृतो गतः । ज्ञात्वा विश्वसृजस्तन्मे हेलनं शेपुरोजसा ।
याहि त्वं शूद्रतामाशु नष्टश्रीः कृतहेलनः ॥72॥

the Atman, the aspirant can overcome the three dreams—the state of waking, the dream proper, and sleep (or the difference of objects, of rites according to competency, and claim to the fruits of actions). **63.** Duality is only imaginary and not real in itself. The reality of an effect lies in its cause, as of cotton fabrics in cotton. Cotton, the causal substance is real, and the fabrics are one with it. To cognise in that way the unity of all existence in the One Supreme Cause is Bhāvādvaita. **64.** Kriyādvaita is the offering of all one's actions by body, speech and mind in the Supreme Brahman. **65.** The recognition that the need for wealth and other means of physical life is the same for oneself and one's close kith and kin, on the one hand, and for strangers, on the other, is Dravyādvaita.

Salvation through Surrender (66-68)

66. O King! Except in times of danger, a pious householder should perform his duties sacred and secular with unprohibited wealth got by means sanctioned by the scriptures, at the proper place and time. **67.** A man living as a householder, performing his duties and other Vedic rites in the manner described above, can attain to the Supreme Being even while he is a householder, provided he has deep-rooted Bhakti (devotion) to the Lord. **68.** He, the Supreme Master, by whose grace you, the king, and your brothers were saved from insuperable difficulties, He by the service of whose feet you were able to conquer the whole world and perform the Aswamedha sacrifice without obstruction—by surrendering yourselves to Him, may you attain liberation!

Narada's Past (69-73)

69. In the past Kalpa (cosmic cycle) I was a Gandharva named Upabarhana, held in high esteem by all Gandharvas. **70.** Endowed with a charming form, sweet speech and fragrant odour, I was very dear to women, and lived a life of drunkenness and pleasure-seeking. **71.** Once in a sacrificial festival of the Devas, the Prajapatis summoned all the Gandharvas and Apsaras to sing about the sportive activities of the Lord. **72.** Though aware of this, I went there surrounded by women and singing love songs. The Prajapatis, noting my insolent conduct, cursed me by their power of Tapas, saying: May

तावद्दास्यामहं जज्ञे तत्रापि ब्रह्मवादिनाम् । शुश्रूषयानुषङ्गेण प्राप्तोऽहं ब्रह्मपुत्रताम् ॥73॥
धर्मस्ते गृहमेधीयो वर्णितः पापनाशनः । गृहस्थो येन पदवीमञ्जसा न्यासिनामियात् 74॥
यूयं नृलोके बत भूरिभागा लोकं पुनाना मुनयोऽभियन्ति ।
येषां गृहानावसतीति साक्षाद् गूढं परं ब्रह्म मनुष्यलिङ्गम् ॥75॥
स वा अयं ब्रह्म महद्विमृग्यं कैवल्यनिर्वाणसुखानुभूतिः ।
प्रियः सुहृद् वः खलु मातुलेय आत्मार्हणीयो विधिकृद् गुरुश्च ॥76॥
न यस्य साक्षाद् भवपद्मजादिभी रूपं धिया वस्तुतयोपवर्णितम् ।
मौनेन भक्त्योपशमेन पूजितः प्रसीदतामेष स सात्वतां पतिः ॥77॥

श्रीशुक उवाच

इति देवर्षिणा प्रोक्तं निशम्य भरतर्षभः । पूजयामास सुप्रीतः कृष्णं च प्रेमविह्वलः ॥78॥
कृष्णपार्थावुपामन्त्र्य पूजितः प्रययौ मुनिः । श्रुत्वा कृष्णं परं ब्रह्म पार्थः परमविस्मितः ॥79॥
इति दाक्षायणीनां ते पृथग् वंशाः प्रकीर्तिताः । देवासुरमनुष्याद्या लोका यत्र चराचराः ॥80॥

इति श्रीमद्भागवते महापुराणे वैयासिक्यामष्टादशसाहस्र्यां पारमहंस्यां संहितायां सप्तमस्कन्धे प्रह्लादानुचरिते युधिष्ठिरनारदसंवादे सदाचारनिर्णयो नाम पञ्चदशोऽध्यायः ॥15॥

इति सप्तमः स्कन्धः समाप्तः

हरिः ॐ तत्सत्

you, who insulted all of us, become immediately a low-born one deprived of all your power and beauty. **73.** After that I was born as the son of a maid-servant. In that birth as I had association with, and served, holy men established in the thought of Brahman, I became in a later Kalpa the mind-born son of Brahma.

Devotion to Krishna (74-80)

74. I have now described to you the sin-redeeming duties of the state of a householder, by which he will reach the same supreme goal as the Sannyasins. **75.** Indeed, you are the most fortunate people in the world, because holy sages, whose tread is said to sanctify places, are flocking to your house, knowing that the Supreme Being Krishna is staying at your house, hiding his identity under a human form. **76.** Lo! this Krishna, who is for you your dear friend, well-wisher, uncle's son, Atman, worshipful one, servant and teacher, is verily the Supreme Brahman, who is sought after by great men and who is the immediate experience of transcendent bliss. **77.** He whose form could not be described by Siva and Brahma, and whose worship is done through devotion, silence, and tranquillity—may He be propitious to us!

Sri Suka said: **78.** Yudhishthira, the great leader of the Bhāratas, was delighted to hear these words of the divine Rishi Narada. Overcome with devotion he adored both Krishna and the Rishi. **79.** Receiving Yudhishthira's worship, Narada took leave of both the king and the Lord. And Yudhishthira was wonderstruck to learn that Krishna was none but the Supreme Brahman. **80.** I have thus described to you separately many generations and families descended from the daughters of Daksha, in which have appeared all species of beings, like the Devas, Asuras and men.

END OF THE SEVENTH SKANDHA

Skandha Eight

PROLOGUE

The eighth Skandha, divided into twenty-four chapters, consists of 931 verses. The first chapter deals principally with the Manvantaras and the Lord's sportive manifestations in some of them for the establishment of Dharma and the redemption of devotees. Manvantara is one of the ten themes of the Puranas. A Manvantara means the epoch of a Manu. A Manu is a patriarch endowed with divine powers, who is the instrument of the Divinity for directing the orderly progress of the world during a long period of about 30.8 crores of human years. There are fourteen Manus during a Brahma's day-time of a thousand divine years. The theory of the Manvantaras and Kalpas has been discussed in detail in the General Introduction in Volume I, pp. xxxvi to xxxviii, as also in chapters 13 and 14 of this Skandha. The important incidents that took place in the first three Manvantaras were described in the earlier Skandhas. Here, the 4th Manvantara, namely that of Tāmasa, is referred to, and the Lord's manifestations in it are described in chapters two to four. The most important incident described is the well-known story of the liberation of the elephant king or Gajendra from a curse. Gajendra's redemption is an example of how the Lord saves one who takes refuge in Him absolutely, forlorn and helpless, every kind of self-effort and the effort of others having failed to save. The narration is also remarkable for the great hymn on the Divine as the Impersonal that occurs in it.

From chapter five to chapter twelve the great event of the churning of the milk ocean along with the incidents preceding it is described. Before the story is taken up, the fifth and the sixth Manvantaras, those of Raivata and Chākshusha, are referred to. It was in the sixth Manvantara of Chākshusha that the above event took place. The outline of the story is this: As a result of the curse of sage Durvasas, the Devas lost their prowess and celestial glory and were overcome and expelled from heaven by the Asuras headed by Bali. To recover it, a strategy was suggested to them. They were to make a truce and be reconciled with the Asuras for the time being, and make a joint effort with them to churn the milk ocean and obtain Amrita, the immortal drink, from it. When their joint effort succeeded and they obtained the immortal drink, the Devas were to deprive the Asuras of it and consume the whole of it themselves. The plan succeeded. Rendered invincible by consuming the immortal drink, the Devas were able to defeat the Asuras and recover their old glory and status. The infuriated Asuras declared war on the Devas. A fierce battle ensued in which the Asuras were decimated by the rejuvenated Devas. The narrative is noted for the very highly poetical description of the emergence of Srī, otherwise called Ramā, from the milk ocean. Two incarnations of Mahavishnu took place in connection with these incidents—those as Tortoise, and as Mohini, the world-bewitching maiden.

In chapters thirteen and fourteen the epochs of the later seven of the fourteen Manus are described. The part of the Manus in world governance, and the relation between the fourteen Manvantaras and a day-time of Brahma are discussed. A day-time of Brahma, known as a Kalpa, is four hundred and thirty-two million human years. This long period of time is divided into fourteen Manvantaras or periods of fourteen Manus.

Next from chapter fourteen to chapter twenty-three, is described a great event that took place in the seventh Manvantara, the rule of the Manu known as Vaivaswata. The incident is the wresting of the three worlds from Mahabali by Mahavishnu in His incarnation as the Vamana in order to help the Devas whose fortunes had again declined under a fresh attack by Mahabali, who had been revived and made invincible by the sacrificial rites which his teacher Sukra made him perform. The Devas took refuge again at the feet of Mahavishnu who incarnated Himself as the Vamana, the dwarf Brahmacharin. The famous story of how he measured the three worlds with two steps, and for the third had to place his foot on Mahabali's head, is described. Many instructive lessons on morality and spiritual life are expounded in the narratives and the hymns of these chapters. The lesson is inculcated that before the Lord truly blesses a devotee, He puts Him to severe trials to efface his pride of wealth and position. Mahabali, though generous and truthful by nature, was proud of his wealth and generosity, forgetting that all the wealth of the world belongs to the Lord. He scoffed at the Lord for asking for a ridiculous pittance of three feet of land. He soon realised that before the infinite puissance of the Lord, his own power and prosperity were almost insignificant entities. After he was chastened by defeat and humiliation, he was rewarded by being made the master of a paradise of the nether world, with the prospect of being made the Indra of the eighth Manvantara headed by Sāvarni.

It is pointed out that in helping the Devas against the Asuras, Mahavishnu is not showing any partiality to his devotees as against his opponents. He is the same to all. But there is what is called the ebb and flow of the Time-spirit in the life of living beings. When a favourable time comes, it appears to observers that Mahavishnu is helping one section against the other.

In the twenty-fourth and last chapter of the Skandha, a Naimitttika Pralaya (intermediary Deluge) that occured at the end of a day-time of Brahma in the previous Kalpa is described. Satyavrata, a pious king, found a fish in his hands while keeping them cupped for holding water during his evening prayer. The fish was Mahavishnu Himself. The Incarnate Fish, which was Vedic wisdom embodied, offered to guide Satyavrata through the Pralaya waters. He imparted wisdom to Satyavrata, as He tugged Satyavrata's boat through the waters of the Deluge. This Satyavrata was destined to become the seventh Manu Vaivaswata in the new Kalpa that began with the incarnation as the Fish. The age in which we are living falls in the epoch of Vaivaswata, the seventh Manu.

श्रीमद्भागवतम्

अष्टमः स्कन्धः अथ प्रथमोऽध्यायः

राजोवाच

स्वायम्भुवस्येह गुरो वंशोऽयं विस्तराच्छ्रुतः । यत्र विश्वसृजां सर्गो मनूनन्यान् वदस्व नः ॥ 1॥
यत्र यत्र हरेर्जन्म कर्माणि च महीयसः । गृणन्ति कवयो ब्रह्मंस्तानि नो वद शृण्वताम् ॥ 2॥
यद् यस्मिन्नन्तरे ब्रह्मन् भगवान् विश्वभावनः । कृतवान् कुरुते कर्ता ह्यतीतेऽनागतेऽद्य वा ॥ 3॥

ऋषिरुवाच

मनवोऽस्मिन् व्यतीताः षट् कल्पे स्वायम्भुवादयः । आद्यस्ते कथितो यत्र देवादीनां च सम्भवः ॥ 4॥
आकूत्यां देवहूत्यां च दुहित्रोस्तस्य वै मनोः । धर्मज्ञानोपदेशार्थं भगवान् पुत्रतां गतः ॥ 5॥
कृतं पुरा भगवतः कपिलस्यानुवर्णितम् । आख्यास्ये भगवान् यज्ञो यच्चकार कुरूद्वह ॥ 6॥
विरक्तः कामभोगेषु शतरूपापतिः प्रभुः । विसृज्य राज्यं तपसे सभार्यो वनमाविशत् ॥ 7॥
सुनन्दायां वर्षशतं पदैकेन भुवं स्पृशन् । तप्यमानस्तपो घोरमिदमन्वाह भारत ॥ 8॥

मनुरुवाच

येन चेतयते विश्वं विश्वं चेतयते न यम् । यो जागर्ति शयानेऽस्मिन्नायं तं वेद वेद सः ॥ 9॥

Skandha VIII : Chapter 1
THE FIRST FOUR MANVANTARAS

Swāyambhuva, the first Manu (1-18)

Rajah Parikshit said: **1.** We have heard from you about the line of Swāyambhuva Manu in detail. We have also heard how in the course of his Manvantara the various Prajapatis like Marīchi multiplied the species by begetting sons and grandsons by the daughters of the Manus. Now tell us about the periods of the other Manus (Manvantaras). **2.** O great one! Describe to us, intent on listening, all those periods of Manus in which had occured many incarnations of the almighty Sri Hari, which have been glorified by sages. **3.** Describe what Sri Hari, the originator of the whole universe, did in earlier Manvantaras, is doing in the current one, and will do in the Manvantaras to come.

Sri Suka said: **4.** In this Kalpa (cosmic cycle) six Manvantaras beginning with that of Swāyambhuva are over. Among these, I have described to you the period of Swāyambhuva, wherein took place, the origin of the Devas and other species of beings. **5.** In order to strengthen the cause of righteous life (Dharma) and of divine knowledge (Jnana), the Lord incarnated Himself in the two daughters of the Manu, named Ākūti and Devahūti, as Yajna and Kapila respectively. **6.** I have already described to you the doings of the Lord as Kapila. I shall now describe to you, O great King, what the worshipful Yajna did. **7.** Swāyambhuva, the husband of Satarūpa, growing averse to all worldly enjoyments, retired to the forest with his wife, adopting the austere life of Vanaprastha. **8.** On the banks of the Sunanda, he performed severe austerities, standing on a single leg for a hundred years, and chanted as follows:

9. He the Supreme Consciousness, by

आत्मावास्यमिदं विश्वं यत् किञ्चिज्जगत्यां जगत् । तेन त्यक्तेन भुञ्जीथा मा गृधः कस्यस्विद्धनम् ॥10॥
यं न पश्यति पश्यन्तं चक्षुर्यस्य न रिष्यति । तं भूतनिलयं देवं सुपर्णमुपधावत ॥11॥
न यस्याद्यन्तौ मध्यं च स्वः परो नान्तरं बहिः । विश्वस्यामूनि यद् यस्माद विश्वं च तदृतं महत् 12॥
स विश्वकायः पुरुहूत ईशः सत्यः स्वयंज्योतिरजः पुराणः ।
धत्तेऽस्य जन्माद्यजयाऽऽत्मशक्त्या तां विद्ययोदस्य निरीह आस्ते ॥13॥
अथाग्रे ऋषयः कर्माणीहन्तेऽकर्महेतवे । ईहमानो हि पुरुषः प्रायोऽनीहां प्रपद्यते ॥14॥
ईहते भगवानीशो न हि तत्र विषज्जते । आत्मलाभेन पूर्णार्थो नावसीदन्ति येऽनु तम् ॥15॥
तमीहमानं निरहङ्कृतं बुधं निराशिषं पूर्णमनन्यचोदितम् ।
नॄञ्छिक्षयन्तं निजवर्त्मसंस्थितं प्रभुं प्रपद्येऽखिलधर्मभावनम् ॥16॥

virtue of whom there is consciousness in the world, but whom the world does not, and cannot, make conscious, as He is Swayamprakāsa, the universal Self-luminous Awareness, with the world for His object; He who is awake even when all this world is asleep—Him the world does not know but He knows the world. **10.** All things of this world of moving and unmoving objects are pervaded by the Lord. Everything in this world therefore belongs to Him. So offering everything to Him, enjoy what is left with you by Him. Do not covet the wealth of others. Who else but He is the possessor of all the wealth of this world? **11.** He the universal subject, who sees everything but whom none can see; He whose Consciousness is ever unfailing even when the individual modes of consciousness arising in it subside—in Him the support of all, the unaffected Being who is described as the bird of beautiful plumage in the Veda, we seek shelter. **12.** He for whom there is no beginning, middle or end, neither anything to be reckoned as one's 'own' nor as alien, neither as inside nor as outside, but who none the less is the source from which the universe has derived all these features, and who stands forth as the universe—that Paramatman is the Truth, the all-inclusive Being. **13.** He, the Lord of all, is the inner pervader having the whole universe as his body, the possessor of infinite names, the truth, the self-revealing consciousness, the Being without birth or death but ever-existing. By His inherent power of Maya He originates, protects and dissolves countless world systems. But at the same time, by His power of knowledge, He transcends Maya and remains unchanged and unaffected. **14.** So the Rishis, for attaining to that bliss of worklessness (that is, the state transcending all changes like Iswara Himself), at first do work as an offering to Iswara. Through such dedicated action, man gradually attains to transcendence of work. **15.** Though the Supreme Lord is working always, He is not bound by it, because He is ever satisfied with His inherent bliss. He has no want to be satisfied through work. Those who follow the example of the Lord, will also not fall into bondage. **16.** I take refuge in the Lord, who performs works according to the purpose and nature of His incarnations, who is all-knowing, who has no particularised ego-sense, who is self-satisfied and free from all desires, who has mastery over all, who is not under the command or prompting of any other agency, who is the teacher and pathfinder for all, and who is the source of all Dharma.

श्रीशुक उवाच

इति मन्त्रोपनिषदं व्याहरन्तं समाहितम्।
दृष्ट्वासुरा यातुधाना जग्धुमभ्यद्रवन् क्षुधा ॥17॥
तांस्तथावसितान् वीक्ष्य यज्ञः सर्वगतो हरिः।
यामैः परिवृतो देवैर्हत्वाशासत् त्रिविष्टपम् ॥18॥
स्वारोचिषो द्वितीयस्तु मनुरग्नेः सुतोऽभवत्।
द्युमत्सुषेणरोचिष्मत्प्रमुखास्तस्य चात्मजाः ॥19॥
तत्रेन्द्रो रोचनस्त्वासीद् देवाश्च तुषितादयः।
ऊर्जस्तम्भादयः सप्त ऋषयो ब्रह्मवादिनः ॥20॥
ऋषेस्तु वेदशिरसस्तुषिता नाम पत्न्यभूत्।
तस्यां जज्ञे ततो देवो विभुरित्यभिविश्रुतः ॥21॥
अष्टाशीतिसहस्राणि मुनयो ये धृतव्रताः।
अन्वशिक्षन् व्रतं तस्य कौमारब्रह्मचारिणः ॥22॥
तृतीय उत्तमो नाम प्रियव्रतसुतो मनुः।
पवनः सृञ्जयो यज्ञहोत्राद्यास्तत्सुता नृप ॥23॥
वसिष्ठतनयाः सप्त ऋषयः प्रमदादयः।
सत्या वेदश्रुता भद्रा देवा इन्द्रस्तु सत्यजित् ॥24॥
धर्मस्य सूनृतायां तु भगवान् पुरुषोत्तमः।
सत्यसेन इति ख्यातो जातः सत्यव्रतैः सह ॥25॥
सोऽनृतव्रतदुःशीलानसतो यक्षराक्षसान्।
भूतद्रुहो भूतगणांस्त्ववधीत् सत्यजित्सखः ॥26॥
चतुर्थ उत्तमभ्राता मनुर्नाम्ना च तामसः।
पृथुः ख्यातिर्नरः केतुरित्याद्या दश तत्सुताः ॥27॥
सत्यका हरयो वीरा देवास्त्रिशिख ईश्वरः।
ज्योतिर्धामादयः सप्त ऋषयस्तामसेऽन्तरे ॥28॥

Sri Suka said: **17.** While he was in this way uttering these sacred Mantras with a concentrated mind, hungry Asuras and Rakshasas saw him and came running to eat him up. **18.** Seeing them so resolved, the all-pervading Hari, embodied as Yajna and accompanied by his sons, the celestials known as Yamas, destroyed these demoniacal beings and protected the heavens.[1]

Svārochisha, the second Manu (19-22)

19. The second Manu was Svārochisha, the son of Agni. The sons of that Manu were Dyumān, Sushena, Rochishmān and others. **20.** Rochana was the Indra then. Tushita and others were the Devas. Ūrjastambha and others, who were knowers of Brahman, constituted the Saptarshis. **21.** The Rishi Vedasiras had as wife Tushitā. Of them the Lord incarnated as Vibhu. **22.** Vibhu, who remained a celibate (Brahmacharin) all through life, got as followers, eighty-eight thousand youths who followed the discipline of celibacy.

Uttama and Tāmasa (23-33)

23. The third Manu was Uttama, the the son of Priyavrata. O King! Pavana, Srinjaya, Yajnahotra and others were his seven sons. **24.** Pramada and other sons of Vasishtha, were the Saptarshis; and Satyas, Vedasrutas and Bhadras were the Devas of this period. The Indra was Satyajit. **25.** The worshipful Lord then incarnated as Satyasena, the son of Dharma by his wife Sūnrita, along with the Devas known as Satyavratas. **26.** As the friend of Satyajit, the Indra of that age, he destroyed a number of untruthful and wicked Yakshas, Rakshasas and goblins.

27. Tāmasa, the brother of Uttama, was the fourth Manu. He had ten sons—Prithu, Khyāti, Nara, Ketu etc. **28.** The

[1] Here it must be understood that each Manvantara (rule of a Manu) has its own Manu, Devas, Saptarshis, Manuputras, Indra and Avatara. Swāyambhuva's is the first Manvantara in the present Kalpa, and Yamas are the Devas of this period. The Manuputras (sons of Manus) are Priyavrata and Uttānapāda, and both the Indra and the Avatara is Yajna. There are fourteen such Manus in a day-time of Brahma (432 crores of human years) the period of each Manu being about 30·8 crores of human years.

देवा वैधृतयो नाम विधृतेस्तनया नृप। नष्टाः कालेन यैर्वेदा विधृताः स्वेन तेजसा ॥29॥
तत्रापि जज्ञे भगवान् हरिण्यां हरिमेधसः। हरिरित्याहृतो येन गजेन्द्रो मोचितो ग्रहात् ॥30॥

राजोवाच

बादरायण एतत् ते श्रोतुमिच्छामहे वयम्। हरिर्यथा गजपतिं ग्राहग्रस्तममूमुचत् ॥31॥
तत्कथा सुमहत् पुण्यं धन्यं स्वस्त्ययनं शुभम्। यत्र यत्रोत्तमश्लोको भगवान् गीयते हरिः ॥32॥

सूत उवाच

परीक्षितैवं स तु बादरायणिः प्रायोपविष्टेन कथासु चोदितः।
उवाच विप्राः प्रतिनन्द्य पार्थिवं मुदा मुनीनां सदसि स्म शृण्वताम् ॥33॥

इति श्रीमद्भागवते महापुराणे पारमहंस्यां संहितायामष्टमस्कन्धे मन्वन्तरानुचरिते प्रथमोऽध्यायः ॥ 1॥

Devas in that Manvantara were the groups known as Satyakas, Haris and Viras, while Trisikha was the Indra. In the Manvantara of Tāmasa, the Saptarshis were Jyotidharma and others. **29.** O King! The famous sons of Vidhriti called Vaidhritas were the Devas in this Manvantara. The Vedas, which were practically forgotten in the course of time, were recovered by their power of memory. **30.** In that Manvantara the Lord incarnated Himself as Hari in Harinī, the wife of Harimedhas. By him the lordly elephant was released from the jaws of the crocodile.

Rajah Parikshit said: **31.** O son of Vyasa! I would like to know from you how Hari saved the lordly elephant who was in the grip of a crocodile. **32.** Among descriptions of men and things, those wherein the Lord of holy fame is extolled are the most attractive, sanctifying, rewarding and auspicious.

Suta said: **33.** O holy one! Suka, the son of Bādarāyana, being prompted in this way by Parikshit to expound the glorious deeds of the Lord, said joyously as follows in that assembly of sages.

अथ द्वितीयोऽध्यायः

श्रीशुक उवाच

आसीद् गिरिवरो राजंस्त्रिकूट इति विश्रुतः। क्षीरोदेनावृतः श्रीमान् योजनायुतमुच्छ्रितः ॥ 1॥
तावता विस्तृतः पर्यक् त्रिभिः शृङ्गैः पयोनिधिम्। दिशः खं रोचयन्नास्ते रौप्यायसहिरण्मयैः ॥ 2॥
अन्यैश्च ककुभः सर्वा रत्नधातुविचित्रितैः। नानाद्रुमलतागुल्मैर्निर्घोषैर्निर्झराम्भसाम् ॥ 3॥

Skandha VIII : Chapter 2

THE LORDLY ELEPHANT ENDANGERED

Beauty of Trikūta Mountain (1-19)

Sri Suka said: **1.** O King! There was a famous mountain called Trikūta, ten thousand Yojanas in height, full of precious things and girt by an ocean of milk. **2.** Ten thousand Yojanas wide, it had three peaks of silver, steel and gold having in them such a profusion of metals that they illuminated the ocean and the quarters with their glitter. **3.** It stood as an ornament to all the quarters, with

स चावनिज्यमानाङ्घ्रिः समन्तात् पयऊर्मिभिः । करोति श्यामलां भूमिं हरिन्मरकताश्मभिः ।। 4।।
सिद्धचारणगन्धर्वविद्याधरमहोरगैः । किन्नरैरप्सरोभिश्च क्रीडद्भिर्जुष्टकन्दरः ।। 5।।
यत्र सङ्गीतसन्नादैर्नदद्गुहममर्षया । अभिगर्जन्ति हरयः श्लाघिनः परशङ्कया ।। 6।।
नानारण्यपशुव्रातसङ्कुलद्रोण्यलङ्कृतः । चित्रद्रुमसुरोद्यानकलकण्ठविहङ्गमः ।। 7।।
सरित्सरोभिरच्छोदैः पुलिनैर्मणिवालुकैः । देवस्त्रीमज्जनामोदसौरभाम्ब्वनिलैर्युतः ।। 8।।
तस्य द्रोण्यां भगवतो वरुणस्य महात्मनः । उद्यानमृतुमन्नाम आक्रीडं सुरयोषिताम् ।। 9।।
सर्वतोऽलङ्कृतं दिव्यैर्नित्यं पुष्पफलद्रुमैः । मन्दारैः पारिजातैश्च पाटलाशोकचम्पकैः ।।10।।
चूतैः प्रियालैः पनसैराम्रैराम्रातकैरपि । क्रमुकैर्नालिकेरैश्च खर्जूरैर्बीजपूरकैः ।।11।।
मधूकैः सालतालैश्च तमालैरसनार्जुनैः । अरिष्टोदुम्बरप्लक्षैर्वटैः किंशुकचन्दनैः ।।12।।
पिचुमन्दैः कोविदारैः सरलैः सुरदारुभिः । द्राक्षेक्षुरम्भाजम्बूभिर्बदर्यक्षाभयामलैः ।।13।।
बिल्वैः कपित्थैर्जम्बीरैर्वृतो भल्लातकादिभिः । तस्मिन् सरः सुविपुलं लसत्काञ्चनपङ्कजम् ।।14।।
कुमुदोत्पलकह्लारशतपत्रश्रियोर्जितम् । मत्तषट्पदनिर्घुष्टं शकुन्तैश्च कलस्वनैः ।।15।।
हंसकारण्डवाकीर्णं चक्राह्वैः सारसैरपि । जलकुक्कुटकोयष्टिदात्यूहकुलकूजितम् ।।16।।

its precious stones and metals, with its abundance of various types of trees and creepers, and with its waterfalls spreading their sound on all sides. **4.** Washed by the waves of the milk ocean, its base was rendered green by the multitude of emeralds and other stones of greenish hue. **5.** It had many caves that were used for their sports by various species of beings like Siddhas, Chāranas, Candharvas, Vidyādharas, great serpents, Kinnaras, Apsaras and others. **6.** The echo of the music of the Kinnaras coming from the caves there often provoked the proud lions to roar under the mistaken impression of the presence of other lions in the neighbourhood. **7.** It was made attractive by its numerous valleys full of wild animals of various species, and by woodlands abounding in trees that were the resort of numerous warbling birds. **8.** That region had many rivers and lakes of pellucid water, bordered by sand dunes with pearl-like sand. The water and the atmosphere there were charged with the fragrance from the bodies of celestial damsels who had their ablutions in the lakes.

9-14. In one of the valleys of that mountain was a garden belonging to the high-souled and worshipful Varuna named Ritumān, which was a field of sports for celestial women. That garden was full of heavenly trees having an abundance of flowers and fruits. The mountain round about it abounded in trees like Mandāra, Pārijāta, Pātala, Asoka, Champaka, mango, Priyāla, jackfruit, Āmra, hog-plum, arecanut, coconut, date-palm, Bījapooraka, Madhuka, Sāla, palmyra, Tamāla, Rasana, Arjuna, Arishta, Udumbara, Plaksha, Vata, Kimsuka, Chandana, Pichumanda, Kovidāra, Sarala, Devadāru, Drāksha, sugar-cane, Rambha, Jambu, Badari, Aksha, Abhaya, Āmala, Bilwa, Kapittha, Jambīra, Bhallātaka and many others. In their midst was an extensive lake with golden lotuses. **15-16.** The lake in that region was beautified by the wealth of aquatic flowers like Kumuda, Utpala, Saugandhika and Satapatra, and the atmosphere was filled with the buzzing of inebriated honey-bees and the sweet sounds of birds. The lake was also full of water-birds like Hamsas, Kārandakas, Chakravākas and Sārasas, while the crooning of Jalakukkutas, Ko-

मत्स्यकच्छपसञ्चारचलत्पद्मरजःपयः । कदम्बवेतसनलनीपवञ्जुलकैर्वृतम् ॥17॥
कुन्दैः कुरबकाशोकैः शिरीषैः कुटजेङ्गुदैः । कुब्जकैः स्वर्णयूथीभिर्नागपुन्नागजातिभिः ॥18॥
मल्लिकाशतपत्रैश्च माधवीजालकादिभिः । शोभितं तीरजैश्चान्यैर्नित्यर्तुभिरलं द्रुमैः ॥19॥

तत्रैकदा तद्गिरिकाननाश्रयः करेणुभिर्वारणयूथपश्चरन् ।
सकण्टकान् कीचकवेणुवेत्रवद्विशालगुल्मं प्ररुजन् वनस्पतीन् ॥20॥
यद्गन्धमात्राद्धरयो गजेन्द्रा व्याघ्रादयो व्यालमृगाः सखड्गाः ।
महोरगाश्चापि भयाद् द्रवन्ति सगौरकृष्णाः शरभाश्चमर्यः ॥21॥
वृका वराहा महिषर्क्षशल्या गोपुच्छशालावृकमर्कटाश्च ।
अन्यत्र क्षुद्रा हरिणाः शशादयश्चरन्त्यभीता यदनुग्रहेण ॥22॥
स घर्मतप्तः करिभिः करेणुभिर्वृतो मदच्युत्कलभैरनुद्रुतः ।
गिरिं गरिम्णा परितः प्रकम्पयन् निषेव्यमाणोऽलिकुलैर्मदाशनैः ॥23॥
सरोऽनिलं पङ्कजरेणुरूषितं जिघ्रन् विदूरान्मदविह्वलेक्षणः ।
वृतः स्वयूथेन तृषार्दितेन तत्सरोवराभ्याशमथागमद् द्रुतम् ॥24॥
विगाह्य तस्मिन्नमृताम्बु निर्मलं हेमारविन्दोत्पलरेणुवासितम् ।
पपौ निकामं निजपुष्करोद्धृतमात्मानमद्भिः स्नपयन् गतक्लमः ॥25॥

yashtis and Dātyoohas, could be heard everywhere. **17.** Shaken by the movements of fish, turtle and other aquatic creatures, the blooming lotus flowers shed their pollen into the water of the lake, giving it an agreeable fragrance. Its banks were lined with trees like Kadamba, Vetasa, Nala, Nīpa, and Vanjulaka. **18-19.** Its banks were thick with trees and creepers that bore flowers and fruits during all seasons—trees and creepers like Kunda, Kurabaka, Asoka, Sirīsha, Kutaja, Inguda, Kubjaka, Svarna-yūthi, Nāga, Punnāga, Jāti, Mallika, Satapatra and Mādhavi.

Lordly Elephant in Danger (20-33)

20. Once a lordly elephant, the leader of his herd, arrived on the banks of this lake with his cows, ranging through the forest and, in the course of it, breaking into bits the branches of thorny trees and bushes of bamboos, as also groves of creepers clustering over canes and other kinds of reeds. **21.** The very smell of him was sufficient to frighten and put to flight all kinds of wild beasts—lions, tuskers, tigers, rhinoceroses, serpents, white-faced and black-faced monkeys, Chāmari deer and others. **22.** While other animals like wolves, wild boars, bisons, bears and porcupines, ran away in fear of him, there were smaller and less conspicuous creatures fearlessly moving about, as he took no notice of them. **23-24.** Scorched by the heat of the sun, that lordly elephant, surrounded by other bulls and cows and followed by calves, moved forward shaking the earth by his weight. He was pursued by swarms of black bees inebriated by feeding on the ichor flowing from him, and he was himself in a mood of inebriation that was reflected in his rolling eyes. Drawn by the fragrance of the lotus pollen spreading through the air, the thirsty pachyderms with their leader approached the lake quickly. **25.** The lordly elephant submerged himself in water to get relief from heat. Then with his trunk, he drank to his fill the clear water of the lake, which was rendered fragrant with the pollen of

स्वपुष्करेणोद्धृतशीकराम्बुभिर्निपाययन् संस्नपयन् यथा गृही ।
घृणी करेणूः कलभांश्च दुर्मदो नाचष्ट कृच्छ्रं कृपणोऽजमायया ॥26॥
तं तत्र कश्चिन्नृप दैवचोदितो ग्राहो बलीयांश्चरणे रुषाग्रहीत् ।
यदृच्छयैवं व्यसनं गतो गजो यथाबलं सोऽतिबलो विचक्रमे ॥27॥
तथाऽऽतुरं यूथपतिं करेणवो विकृष्यमाणं तरसा बलीयसा ।
विचुक्रुशुर्दीनधियोऽपरे गजाः पार्ष्णिग्रहास्तारयितुं न चाशकन् ॥28॥
नियुध्यतोरेवमिभेन्द्रनक्रयोर्विकर्षतोरन्तरतो बहिर्मिथः ।
समाः सहस्रं व्यगमन् महीपते सप्राणयोश्चित्रममंसतामराः ॥29॥
ततो गजेन्द्रस्य मनोबलौजसां कालेन दीर्घेण महानभूद् व्ययः ।
विकृष्यमाणस्य जलेऽवसीदतो विपर्ययोऽभूत् सकलं जलौकसः ॥30॥
इत्थं गजेन्द्रः स यदाऽऽप सङ्कटं प्राणस्य देही विवशो यदृच्छया ।
अपारयन्नात्मविमोक्षणे चिरं दध्याविमां बुद्धिमथाभ्यपद्यत ॥31॥
न मामिमे ज्ञातय आतुरं गजाः कुतः करिण्यः प्रभवन्ति मोचितुम् ।
ग्राहेण पाशेन विधातुरावृतोऽप्यहं च तं यामि परं परायणम् ॥32॥
यः कश्चनेशो बलिनोऽन्तकोरगात् प्रचण्डवेगादभिधावतो भृशम् ।
भीतं प्रपन्नं परिपाति यद्भयान्मृत्युः प्रधावत्यरणं तमीमहि ॥33॥

इति श्रीमद्भागवते महापुराणे पारमहंस्यां संहितायामष्टमस्कन्धे मन्वन्तरानुवर्णने गजेन्द्रोपाख्याने द्वितीयोऽध्यायः ॥ 2॥

the golden lotuses and lilies in it. **26.** Deluded by the Lord's Maya, he was unaware, like a pitiable and foolish family man, of the imminent danger lurking, as he bathed and fed the cows and the calves with the water he drew in his trunk. **27.** O King! As Providence would have it, he found all on a sudden that his foot was in the grip of an infuriated crocodile stronger than himself. The powerful elephant tried as best as he could to release himself from its hold. **28.** As the exhausted elephant-king was thus being pulled away by that strong crocodile, the cow elephants stood around crying loudly in distress, while the males of the herd tried their best from behind to save him, but with no success. **29.** In that tug-of-war from within and from without the water, the elephant and the crocodile spent a thousand years with unimpeded strength, to the astonishment of the onlooking celestials. **30.** Submerged in water and pulled by the leg for such a long and protracted period, the lordly elephant became exhausted in body and weak in his mental resolution, while the contrary was the case with the crocodile who was operating from his own watery home.

31. The lordly elephant, who identified himself with his huge body, now found himself weak and shut off from all chance of escape from that unforeseen danger. As he thought deeply in that state of utter distress, there arose in him an awakening which made him resolve thus: **32.** These, the sorrowing friends of my species, are not able to release me. The cow-elephants are still more helpless. Though I am in the grip of this crocodile, the stranglehold of destiny, I take shelter in Him, the Lord and the refuge of even Brahma and others. **33.** He who gives shelter to all who seek refuge in Him from the fear of the powerful serpent of Death that is irresistibly encircling them; He for fear of whom even Death operates on all —in Him I seek refuge.

अथ तृतीयोऽध्यायः

श्रीशुक उवाच

एवं व्यवसितो बुद्ध्या समाधाय मनो हृदि । जजाप परमं जाप्यं प्राग्जन्मन्यनुशिक्षितम् ॥ 1॥

गजेन्द्र उवाच

ॐ नमो भगवते तस्मै यत एतच्चिदात्मकम् । पुरुषायादिबीजाय परेशायाभिधीमहि ॥ 2॥
यस्मिन्निदं यतश्चेदं येनेदं य इदं स्वयम् । योऽस्मात् परस्माच्च परस्तं प्रपद्ये स्वयम्भुवम् 3॥

यः स्वात्मनीदं निजमाययार्पितं क्वचिद् विभातं क्व च तत् तिरोहितम् ।
अविद्धदृक् साक्ष्युभयं तदीक्षते स आत्ममूलोऽवतु मां परात्परः ॥ 4॥
कालेन पञ्चत्वमितेषु कृत्स्नशो लोकेषु पालेषु च सर्वहेतुषु ।
तमस्तदाऽऽसीद् गहनं गभीरं यस्तस्य पारेऽभिविराजते विभुः ॥ 5॥
न यस्य देवा ऋषयः पदं विदुर्जन्तुः पुनः कोऽर्हति गन्तुमीरितुम् ।
यथा नटस्याकृतिभिर्विचेष्टतो दुरत्ययानुक्रमणः स मावतु ॥ 6॥

Skandha VIII : Chapter 3

THE HYMN OF THE LORDLY ELEPHANT

A Hymn on the Impersonal (1-29)

Sri Suka said: **1.** Resolving in this way, and concentrating his mind, the lordly elephant began to utter the great Mantra that he had practised in his previous births. *The lordly elephant said:* **2.** Om! My salutation to that Worshipful One, who bestows consciousness to inert nature; who is both Prakriti and Purusha as also their controller; who is pervading everything; and who is the source of all. **3.** I seek shelter in that eternally existent One from whom this universe has come, in whom it subsists, who is its instrumental cause, of whom it is a manifestation, and who at the same time transcends that world-manifestation both in the causal and the effect conditions. **4.** He is the unimpeded Awareness and the Witness of all, who by his own Maya (Power) has established in Himself this universe, which is seen in its manifested condition and unseen in its causal state by others, but is witnessed by Himself in both these conditions. He is the basic Self-conscious Awareness, from whom all other centres of self-conscious awareness (Jivas) arise. I seek refuge in that Being transcending all the highest human conceptions of Him.

5. When all the worlds and their protectors and all causal agencies had been dissolved in their primeval condition by the inexorable power of Time, and only the darkness of dissolution, abysmal in depth and endless in extent, remained, He the Supreme Light of Consciousness, shone undimmed over that darkness. **6.** The ordinary people in an audience do not understand the identity of an actor from his make-up and movements on the stage. In the same way, neither the Rishis nor the Devas are able to grasp His being in the disguise provided by His own Yoga-maya. How then can an ordinary man understand or describe anything about His inscrutable ways? May that Lord whom none knows in truth and in reality,

दिदृक्षवो यस्य पदं सुमङ्गलं विमुक्तसङ्गा मुनयः सुसाधवः ।
चरन्त्यलोकव्रतमव्रणं वने भूतात्मभूताः सुहृदः स मे गतिः ॥ 7॥
न विद्यते यस्य च जन्म कर्म वा न नामरूपे गुणदोष एव वा ।
तथापि लोकाप्ययसम्भवाय यः स्वमायया तान्यनुकालमृच्छति ॥ 8॥
तस्मै नमः परेशाय ब्रह्मणेऽनन्तशक्तये । अरूपायोरुरूपाय नम आश्चर्यकर्मणे ॥ 9॥
नम आत्मप्रदीपाय साक्षिणे परमात्मने । नमो गिरां विदूराय मनसश्चेतसामपि ॥10॥
सत्त्वेन प्रतिलभ्याय नैष्कर्म्येण विपश्चिता । नमः कैवल्यनाथाय निर्वाणसुखसंविदे ॥11॥
नमः शान्ताय घोराय मूढाय गुणधर्मिणे । निर्विशेषाय साम्याय नमो ज्ञानघनाय च ॥12॥
क्षेत्रज्ञाय नमस्तुभ्यं सर्वाध्यक्षाय साक्षिणे । पुरुषायात्ममूलाय मूलप्रकृतये नमः ॥13॥
सर्वेन्द्रियगुणद्रष्ट्रे सर्वप्रत्ययहेतवे । असताच्छाययोक्ताय सदाभासाय ते नमः ॥14॥
नमो नमस्तेऽखिलकारणाय निष्कारणायाद्भुतकारणाय ।
सर्वागमाम्नायमहार्णवाय नमोऽपवर्गाय परायणाय ॥15॥

protect me! **7.** He, the most Auspicious Being, to have an intuitive knowledge of whom sages, free from attachments, practise the sense of oneness and friendship with all beings, observe the vow of unbroken Brahmacharya and live in the solitude of forests—may He, the Lord of all, be my refuge! **8.** He who has neither birth nor activity, who has neither name, form, nor subjection to the Gunas of Prakriti, yet assumes all these through His inherent power of Maya from time to time for the creation, preservation, and dissolution of the universe—to that Supreme Being my salutation! **9.** He, the Brahman, the formless, who yet assumes infinite forms and performs astounding deeds—to Him the Lord of all, my salutation! **10.** He who is self-luminous consciousness, the witness of all, the Supreme Self, the One beyond the grasp of mind, words and every kind of mental mode—to Him my salutation! **11.** He who is none the less attained as the indwelling Self by those purified by absolute renunciation, who is the dispenser of absolute consciousness and is of the nature of absolute bliss—to Him my salutation! **12.** Salutations to Him who through the assumption of the Gunas of Prakriti appears as the calm, the terrible, and the inert—who is also the one without modifications, the same always and everywhere, and the condensation of Pure Consciousness!

13. To Thee the knower within the body, to Thee the Lord of all, to Thee the witness of all, to Thee the Original Being, the source of both Atman (spirit) and Prakriti (matter)—my salutations! **14.** To Thee the seer of the functions of all the senses; to Thee who makest all concepts and percepts possible; to Thee whose truth-nature is made known through its reflection in the shape of the impermanent I-sense, as an image does in regard to its object; to Thee who art the substance behind this shadowy world—my salutations!

15. Salutations to Thee who art the cause of all causes and who therefore art without any cause; to Thee who art the unique First or Absolute Cause, who, in becoming the multiplicity of effects, art unaffected in the least unlike all relative causes; to Thee the limitless ocean into which all scriptures like the Vedas and Agamas flow and find fulfilment; to Thee who art the bliss of salvation and the one

गुणारणिच्छन्नचिदूष्मपाय तत्क्षोभविस्फूर्जितमानसाय ।
नैष्कर्म्यभावेन विवर्जितागमस्वयंप्रकाशाय नमस्करोमि ॥16॥
मादृक्प्रपन्नपशुपाशविमोक्षणाय मुक्ताय भूरिकरुणाय नमोऽलयाय ।
स्वांशेन सर्वतनुभृन्मनसि प्रतीतप्रत्यग्दृशे भगवते बृहते नमस्ते ॥17॥
आत्मात्मजाप्तगृहवित्तजनेषु सक्तैर्दुष्प्रापणाय गुणसङ्गविवर्जिताय ।
मुक्तात्मभिः स्वहृदये परिभाविताय ज्ञानात्मने भगवते नम ईश्वराय ॥18॥
यं धर्मकामार्थविमुक्तिकामा भजन्त इष्टां गतिमाप्नुवन्ति ।
किं त्वाशिषो रात्यपि देहमव्ययं करोतु मेऽदभ्रदयो विमोक्षणम् ॥19॥
एकान्तिनो यस्य न कञ्चनार्थं वाञ्छन्ति ये वै भगवत्प्रपन्नाः ।
अत्यद्भुतं तच्चरितं सुमङ्गलं गायन्त आनन्दसमुद्रमग्नाः ॥20॥
तमक्षरं ब्रह्म परं परेशमव्यक्तमाध्यात्मिकयोगगम्यम् ।
अतीन्द्रियं सूक्ष्ममिवातिदूरमनन्तमाद्यं परिपूर्णमीडे ॥21॥
यस्य ब्रह्मादयो देवा वेदा लोकाश्चराचराः । नामरूपविभेदेन फल्व्या च कलया कृताः ॥22॥

resort for all spiritual aspirants! **16.** To Thee who art the spiritual fire hidden in the fire-sticks of Prakriti's Gunas; to Thee who willest to create when those Gunas of Prakriti get agitated; to Thee who art self-manifested in those who are established in the Atman-consciousness beyond the purview of the injunctions and prohibitions of the Vedas—to Thee my salutation!

17. Salutation to Thee who blessest ignorant creatures like me by cutting off our binding cords of nescience; who art ever-free Thyself and ever-vigilant in exercising Thy mercy to save devotees; and who by a particle of Thyself shinest in all embodied beings as individualised self-consciousness without any impairment to Thyself as the Absolute Being and the Absolute Will! **18.** Salutations to Thee the embodiment of Pure Consciousness (*Jnānātmane*) and the Lord of all who, though the indweller within all, art difficult of approach by those who are attached to their own body, to relations like wife, children, kith and kin, and to possessions like properties, wealth, etc.; who art Thyself without any involvement with the Gunas of Prakriti though functioning through them; and who art immediately intuited in their hearts by those who are free from ignorance!

19. May He, by adoring whom the seekers of Dharma, Artha, Kama and Moksha (morality, prosperity, pleasures and liberation) attain their objects; who even rewards His votaries with something more than they pray for, as also with an imperishable divine body—may He be gracious enough to release me (from the grip of the crocodile as well as of Samsara)! **20-21.** I sing the praise of Him, whose unique and glorious deeds his surrendered devotees hymn about in a mood of whole-hearted and blissful abandon to the exclusion of desire for every fulfilment including Moksha—of Him, the imperishable, the Brahman, the Lord of lords, the Unclear to the senses and to the mind, the one that can be gained by the inward communion of devotion, the subtle, the infinite one, the primeval and perfect Being, and the one who though the closest to all, is far off to those of unregenerate mind. **22-24.** He, from a very minor particle of whom all the Devas, the Vedas and the mighty universe of living and

यथार्चिषोऽग्नेः सवितुर्गभस्तयो निर्यान्ति संयान्त्यसकृत् स्वरोचिषः ।
तथा यतोऽयं गुणसम्प्रवाहो बुद्धिर्मनः खानि शरीरसर्गाः ॥23॥
स वै न देवासुरमर्त्यतिर्यङ् न स्त्री न षण्ढो न पुमान् न जन्तुः ।
नायं गुणः कर्म न सन्न चासन् निषेधशेषो जयतादशेषः ॥24॥
जिजीविषे नाहमिहामुया किमन्तर्बहिश्चावृतयेभयोन्या ।
इच्छामि कालेन न यस्य विप्लवस्तस्यात्मलोकावरणस्य मोक्षम् ॥25॥
सोऽहं विश्वसृजं विश्वमविश्वं विश्ववेदसम् । विश्वात्मानमजं ब्रह्म प्रणतोऽस्मि परं पदम् ॥26॥
योगरन्धितकर्माणो हृदि योगविभाविते । योगिनो यं प्रपश्यन्ति योगेशं तं नतोऽस्म्यहम् ॥27॥
नमो नमस्तुभ्यमसह्यवेगशक्तित्रयायाखिलधीगुणाय ।
प्रपन्नपालाय दुरन्तशक्तये कदिन्द्रियाणामनवाप्यवर्त्मने ॥28॥
नायं वेद स्वमात्मानं यच्छक्त्याहंधिया हतम् । तं दुरत्ययमाहात्म्यं भगवन्तमितोऽस्म्यहम् ॥29॥

श्रीशुक उवाच

एवं गजेन्द्रमुपवर्णितनिर्विशेषं ब्रह्मादयो विविधलिङ्गभिदाभिमानाः ।
नैते यदोपससृपुर्निखिलात्मकत्वात् तत्राखिलामरमयो हरिराविरासीत् ॥30॥

non-living beings were given shape with name and form; He out of whom, as sparks from fire and rays from the sun, the evolutes of Prakriti like the intellect, the mind, senses and bodies emerge and into whom they dissolve; He who is neither Deva nor Asura, nor man nor brute, nor woman nor neuter; who is neither an attribute nor a product; neither being (Sat) nor non-being (Asat); who is the residue left after total negation but who is also the all-inclusive One—to Him I sing.

25. I have no desire to live on in this world. Of what use is life in this elephant body wherein veils of ignorance hide the spiritual vision both from within and without? It is not from the crocodile threatening my life that I pray for release, but from this obstructive screen of ignorance, hiding the awareness of my spiritual self—an obstructive screen that Time cannot undo but only illumination can. For, Time will put an end to this physical body but not to ignorance, which persists until Thy grace removes it.

26. I prostrate myself before Him who is the creator of the worlds; who is of the form of the world; who is none the less not affected by the world; for whom the world is a toy, an object of sport; who is the soul of the universe; who is birthless, all-pervading and the Supreme Status. **27.** I salute Him who is the master and the reward of all Yogic disciplines, and who is perceived by Yogis who have been freed from the effects of their past Karma by the observance of the Bhagavata Dharma and whose hearts are purified by constant meditation on Him. **28.** I do homage again and again to Thee who art endowed with the threefold Sakti of irresistible might, who art infinite in power, who makest Thyself visible through all objects of the senses and understanding, who art ever ready to protect the devotees who take shelter in Thee, but who art not accessible to those who do not care to control their senses. **29.** I seek refuge in that worshipful Lord by whose Yogamaya is generated the 'I-sense' which hides the real Self from all in this world, and whose glory and power are endless.

Release of the lordly Elephant (30-33)

Sri Suka said: **30.** When the lordly

तं तद्वदार्तमुपलभ्य जगन्निवासः स्तोत्रं निशम्य दिविजैः सह संस्तुवद्भिः।
छन्दोमयेन गरुडेन समुह्यमानश्चक्रायुधोऽभ्यगमदाशु यतो गजेन्द्रः ॥31॥
सोऽन्तः सरस्युरुबलेन गृहीत आर्तो दृष्ट्वा गरुत्मति हरिं ख उपात्तचक्रम्।
उत्क्षिप्य साम्बुजकरं गिरमाह कृच्छ्रान्नारायणाखिलगुरो भगवन् नमस्ते ॥32॥
तं वीक्ष्य पीडितमजः सहसावतीर्य सग्राहमाशु सरसः कृपयोज्जहार।
ग्राहाद् विपाटितमुखादरिणा गजेन्द्रं सम्पश्यतां हरिरमूमुचदुस्त्रियाणाम् ॥33॥

इति श्रीमद्भागवते महापुराणे पारमहंस्यां संहितायामष्टमस्कन्धे गजेन्द्रमोक्षणे तृतीयोऽध्यायः ॥ 3॥

elephant thus invoked the Divine without any particularising attributes, none of the Deities like Brahma, who are characterised by such attributes, appeared. It was Hari, who is the soul of all, and who therefore includes in Himself all the Deities, that came to the scene. **31.** Quickly did the discus-armed Lord Hari, the indweller in all beings, arrive by the side of the distressed elephant, seated on His (the Lord's) Veda-formed eagle-vehicle and accompanied by a large company of Devas who were singing the praise of the Lord. **32.** Caught in the powerful jaws of the crocodile and suffering to the extreme limit, that lordly elephant, on seeing Sri Hari arrive on his eagle-vehicle with the Sudarsana discus upraised, lifted his trunk with a lotus in it by way of worship and said with great difficulty: 'O Narayana! O Teacher of all! O Bhagavan, Thou endowed with all powers and excellences! Salutations!" **33.** Seeing him in an agonising situation, Sri Hari got down from Garuda in haste and, out of his mercy, pulled out the elephant along with the crocodile from the water; cutting open the mouth of the crocodile with his discus, He released the lordly elephant in the presence of all the Devas.

अथ चतुर्थोऽध्यायः

श्रीशुक उवाच

तदा देवर्षिगन्धर्वा ब्रह्मेशानपुरोगमाः। मुमुचुः कुसुमासारं शंसन्तः कर्म तद्धरेः ॥ 1॥
नेदुर्दुन्दुभयो दिव्या गन्धर्वा ननृतुर्जगुः। ऋषयश्चारणाः सिद्धास्तुष्टुवुः पुरुषोत्तमम् ॥ 2॥
योऽसौ ग्राहः स वै सद्यः परमाश्चर्यरूपधृक्। मुक्तो देवलशापेन हूहूर्गन्धर्वसत्तमः ॥ 3॥

Skandha VIII : Chapter 4

ANTECEDENTS OF THE LORDLY ELEPHANT

Transformation of Crocodile (1-5)

Sri Suka said: **1.** In acclamation of the Lord's deed revealing His redeeming love for devotees, Brahma, Parameswara, the celestials, Rishis and Gandharvas rained a shower of flowers. **2.** Kettle-drums sounded. The Gandharvas sang and danced. The Rishis, Chāranas and Siddhas sang in praise of the Supreme Person. **3.** The crocodile, who was none but a leading Gandharva by name Hūhū, turned into that form under the curse of Rishi Devala, now attained freedom from the

प्रणम्य शिरसाधीशमुत्तमश्लोकमव्ययम् । अगायत यशोधाम कीर्तन्यगुणसत्कथम् ॥ 4॥
सोऽनुकम्पित ईशेन परिक्रम्य प्रणम्य तम् । लोकस्य पश्यतो लोकं स्वमगान्मुक्तकिल्बिषः ॥ 5॥
गजेन्द्रो भगवत्स्पर्शाद् विमुक्तोऽज्ञानबन्धनात् । प्राप्तो भगवतो रूपं पीतवासाश्चतुर्भुजः ॥ 6॥
स वै पूर्वमभूद् राजा पाण्ड्यो द्रविडसत्तमः । इन्द्रद्युम्न इति ख्यातो विष्णुव्रतपरायणः ॥ 7॥
स एकदाऽऽराधनकाल आत्मवान् गृहीतमौनव्रत ईश्वरं हरिम् ।
जटाधरस्तापस आप्लुतोऽच्युतं समर्चयामास कुलाचलाश्रमः ॥ 8॥
यदृच्छया तत्र महायशा मुनिः समागमच्छिष्यगणैः परिश्रितः ।
तं वीक्ष्य तूष्णीमकृतार्हणादिकं रहस्युपासीनमृषिश्चुकोप ह ॥ 9॥
तस्मा इमं शापमदादसाधुरयं दुरात्माकृतबुद्धिरद्य ।
विप्रावमन्ता विशतां तमोऽन्धं यथा गजः स्तब्धमतिः स एव ॥10॥

श्रीशुक उवाच

एवं शप्त्वा गतोऽगस्त्यो भगवान् नृप सानुगः । इन्द्रद्युम्नोऽपि राजर्षिर्दिष्टं तदुपधारयन् ॥11॥
आपन्नः कौञ्जरीं योनिमात्मस्मृतिविनाशिनीम् । हर्यर्चनानुभावेन यद्गजत्वेऽप्यनुस्मृतिः ॥12॥

curse all of a sudden by the Lord's touch and assumed a uniquely wonderful form. **4.** Prostrating, he sang hymns in praise of the Lord, the imperishable, the most famous, renowned as the Supreme, and noted for qualities and deeds for which no extolling is too much. **5.** Blessed by the Lord, he circumambulated Him and prostrated at His feet. He was freed from all his sins, and as others looked on, he departed to his abode in the sphere of Gandharvas.

Antecedents of the lordly Elephant (6-12)

6. And as for the lordly elephant, he was freed from the bondage of ignorance by the touch of the Lord, and he got a form resembling that of the Lord Himself, having four arms and yellow wearing cloth. **7.** He was in his previous birth Indradyumna, the well-known king of the Pāndyas, in the Dravida country. He was devoted to all observances connected with the worship of Mahavishnu. **8.** While staying at an Ashrama on the Kulāchala (Malaya mountain) as an ascetic wearing matted hair, observing silence and practising control of mind, he was, after his bath, engaged one day in devout worship of Sri Hari, the Undecaying Being. **9.** Just at that time the great sage Agastya surrounded by numerous disciples happened to visit his Ashrama. The king who was sitting silently in solitude for his worship, did not do any obeisance or give any reception to the sage, whose anger was provoked by this conduct of his. **10.** He thereupon cursed the king thus: 'May this evil-minded fellow of undisciplined intellect, who has insulted holy personages in this way, sink into the blinding darkness of ignorance! He has shown himself to be stupid like an elephant. I curse him to become in truth like that—an elephant immersed in the dullness of ignorance.' **11.** Having cursed him in this way, the sage Agastya went away with his followers. And the Rajarshi Indradyumna consoled himself with the thought that this was the dictate of destiny. **12.** Indradyumna was soon born as an elephant, a birth in which there was complete forgetfulness of his spiritual nature. But as a result of his worship of Sri Hari, he had his memory of the Lord restored at the last moment in spite of his elephant-consciousness.

एवं विमोक्ष्य गजयूथपमब्जनाभस्तेनापि पार्षदगतिं गमितेन युक्तः ।
गन्धर्वसिद्धविबुधैरुपगीयमानकर्माद्भुतं स्वभवनं गरुडासनोऽगात् ॥13॥
एतन्महाराज तवेरितो मया कृष्णानुभावो गजराजमोक्षणम् ।
स्वर्ग्यं यशस्यं कलिकल्मषापहं दुःस्वप्ननाशं कुरुवर्य शृण्वताम् ॥14॥
यथानुकीर्तयन्त्येतच्छ्रेयस्कामा द्विजातयः । शुचयः प्रातरुत्थाय दुःस्वप्नाद्युपशान्तये ॥15॥
इदमाह हरिः प्रीतो गजेन्द्रं कुरुसत्तम । शृण्वतां सर्वभूतानां सर्वभूतमयो विभुः ॥16॥

श्रीभगवानुवाच

ये मां त्वां च सरश्चेदं गिरिकन्दरकाननम् । वेत्रकीचकवेणूनां गुल्मानि सुरपादपान् ॥17॥
शृङ्गाणीमानि धिष्ण्यानि ब्रह्मणो मे शिवस्य च । क्षीरोदं मे प्रियं धाम श्वेतद्वीपं च भास्वरम् ॥18॥
श्रीवत्सं कौस्तुभं मालां गदां कौमोदकीं मम । सुदर्शनं पाञ्चजन्यं सुपर्णं पतगेश्वरम् ॥19॥
शेषं च मत्कलां सूक्ष्मां श्रियं देवीं मदाश्रयाम् । ब्रह्माणं नारदमृषिं भवं प्रह्लादमेव च ॥20॥
मत्स्यकूर्मवराहाद्यैरवतारैः कृतानि मे । कर्माण्यनन्तपुण्यानि सूर्यं सोमं हुताशनम् ॥21॥
प्रणवं सत्यमव्यक्तं गोविप्रान् धर्ममव्ययम् । दाक्षायणीर्धर्मपत्नीः सोमकश्यपयोरपि ॥22॥
गङ्गां सरस्वतीं नन्दां कालिन्दीं सितवारणम् । ध्रुवं ब्रह्मऋषीन् सप्त पुण्यश्लोकांश्च मानवान् ।23॥
उत्थायापररात्रान्ते प्रयताः सुसमाहिताः । स्मरन्ति मम रूपाणि मुच्यन्ते ह्येनसोऽखिलात् 24॥

Greatness of the Episode (13-26)

13-14. Thus was the lordly elephant released and given a place among the Lord's attendants. Then, accompanied by him and extolled by the Devas and Gandharvas for his wonderful deeds, Sri Hari went on his eagle-vehicle to his unique abode. I have with this finished narrating to you, O great King, the glory of the Lord revealed through the story of the release of the lordly elephant. O leader of the Kurus! Those who hear it will be spiritually elevated; the adverse influence of Kali will have no hold on them; and they will be freed from the evil dream of worldly existence. **15.** The twice-born ones who care for their spiritual good and want the elimination of evil dreams, recite this account early in the morning after purifying themselves. **16.** Highly pleased, Sri Hari, the all-comprehensive and all-pervading Being, declared as follows in the hearing of all.

The worshipful Lord said: **17**. Those who in their morning prayers remind themselves of Me, of you, this lake and this forest with its caves, trees and thickets of bamboo and cane—will be freed from all sins. **18-24.** One should remember these mountains. Also worthy of remembrance for the purification of one's mind are the following: these mountain peaks constituting the stations of Brahma, Siva and Myself; the milk Ocean where I have my abode; the luminous continent of Swetadweepa so dear to Me; Srīvatsa the mark on My chest; Kaustubha My neck-jewel; Vanamāla My floral wreath; Kaumodaki My mace; Sudarsana My discus; Pānchajanya My conch; Garuda My vehicle; Sesha My subtle part; and Srīdevi My Power inseparable from me. My son Brahma, My devotee Rishi Narada, My part Bhava, and the greatest of the the Bhāgavatas Prahlada; My incarnations like fish, tortoise, boar and others and the countless acts of spiritual glory performed by these incarnate divinities; and My manifestations consisting of the sun, moon and fire; the Mantra Om, truth, the Pradhāna or root-matter, cows,

ये मां स्तुवन्त्यनेनाङ्ग प्रतिबुध्य निशात्यये। तेषां प्राणात्यये चाहं ददामि विमलां मतिम् ॥25॥

श्रीशुक उवाच

इत्यादिश्य हृषीकेशः प्रध्माय जलजोत्तमम्। हर्षयन् विबुधानीकमारुरोह खगाधिपम् ॥26॥

इति श्रीमद्भागवते महापुराणे पारमहंस्यां संहितायामष्टमस्कन्धे गजेन्द्रमोक्षणं नाम चतुर्थोऽध्यायः ॥ 4॥

holy men, and the eternal Dharma; the daughters of Daksha who married the Rishi Dharma, Chandra and Rishi Kasyapa; the rivers Ganga, Saraswati, Nanda and Kālindi and the white elephant Airavata; Dhruva, the Saptarshis, the Brahmarshis and other holy men—if all the above-mentioned places, objects and personages are remembered in the mornings with the firm conviction that they are My parts, those who do so will be freed from all their sins. **25.** To those who extol me at the close of night with this hymn, I grant a pure understanding before the end of their lives.

Sri Suka said: **26.** With these words, Mahavishnu, the Prime Mover of all the senses, sounded his divine conch to the great delight of the Devas and then ascended his eagle-vehicle to depart.

अथ पञ्चमोऽध्यायः

श्रीशुक उवाच

राजन्नुदितमेतत् ते हरेः कर्माघनाशनम्। गजेन्द्रमोक्षणं पुण्यं रैवतं त्वन्तरं शृणु ॥ 1॥

पञ्चमो रैवतो नाम मनुस्तामससोदरः। बलिविन्ध्यादयस्तस्य सुता अर्जुनपूर्वकाः ॥ 2॥

विभुरिन्द्रः सुरगणा राजन् भूतरयादयः। हिरण्यरोमा वेदशिरा ऊर्ध्वबाह्वादयो द्विजाः 3॥

पत्नी विकुण्ठा शुभ्रस्य वैकुण्ठैः सुरसत्तमैः। तयोः स्वकलया जज्ञे वैकुण्ठो भगवान् स्वयम् ॥ 4॥

वैकुण्ठः कल्पितो येन लोको लोकनमस्कृतः। रमया प्रार्थ्य मानेन देव्या तत्प्रियकाम्यया ॥ 5॥

तस्यानुभावः कथितो गुणाश्च परमोदयाः। भौमान् रेणून् स विममे यो विष्णोर्वर्णयेद् गुणान् 6॥

Skandha VIII : Chapter 5

PRELUDE TO CHURNING OF THE MILK OCEAN

Fifth and sixth Manvantaras (1-10)

Sri Suka said: **1.** O King! I have now finished narrating to you Sri Hari's bestowal of grace on the lordly elephant, an episode that is very holy and destructive of the sins of those listening to it. Now you hear from me about the Manvantara known as Raivata. **2.** The Manu of the fifth Manvantara was Raivata, the brother of Tāmasa, the Manu of the fourth Manvantara. His sons were Arjuna, Vindhya, Bali and others. **3.** O King! Vibhu was the Indra in that Manvantara. Bhūtarayas were the Devas, and the Saptarshis consisted of Hiranyaromā, Vedasiras, Urdhvabāhu and others. **4.** Subhra had Vikuntha for his wife. In this couple the Lord incarnated as Vaikuntha along with the group of Devas known as Vaikunthas. **5.** In answer to the prayer of His consort Ramā, He created by His will his Abode known as the Vaikuntha, which is superior to all the worlds. **6.** The divine powers and excellences of it have been described in the account

षष्ठश्च चक्षुषः पुत्रश्चाक्षुषो नाम वै मनुः । पूरुपूरुषसुद्युम्नप्रमुखाश्चाक्षुषात्मजाः ॥ 7॥
इन्द्रो मन्त्रद्रुमस्तत्र देवा आप्यादयो गणाः । मुनयस्तत्र वै राजन् हविष्मद्वीरकादयः ॥ 8॥
तत्रापि देवः सम्भूत्यां वैराजस्याभवत् सुतः । अजितो नाम भगवानंशेन जगतः पतिः ॥ 9॥
पयोधिं येन निर्मथ्य सुराणां साधिता सुधा । भ्रममाणोऽम्भसि धृतः कूर्मरूपेण मन्दरः ॥10॥

राजोवाच

यथा भगवता ब्रह्मन् मथितः क्षीरसागरः । यदर्थं वा यतश्चाद्रिं दधाराम्बुचरात्मना ॥11॥
यथामृतं सुरैः प्राप्तं किञ्चान्यदभवत् ततः । एतद् भगवतः कर्म वदस्व परमाद्भुतम् ॥12॥
त्वया संकथ्यमानेन महिम्ना सात्वतां पतेः । नातितृप्यति मे चित्तं सुचिरं तापतापितम् ॥13॥

सूत उवाच

सम्पृष्टो भगवानेवं द्वैपायनसुतो द्विजाः । अभिनन्द्य हरेर्वीर्यमभ्याचष्टुं प्रचक्रमे ॥14॥

श्रीशुक उवाच

यदा युद्धेऽसुरैर्देवा बाध्यमानाः शितायुधैः । गतासवो निपतिता नोत्तिष्ठेरन् स्म भूयशः ॥15॥
यदा दुर्वाससः शापात् सेन्द्रा लोकास्त्रयो नृप । निःश्रीकाश्चाभवंस्तत्र नेशुरिज्यादयः क्रियाः ॥16॥
निशाम्यैतत् सुरगणा महेन्द्रवरुणादयः । नाध्यगच्छन् स्वयं मन्त्रैर्मन्त्रयन्तो विनिश्चयम् 17॥

given of the visit of Sanaka and other sages to Vaikuntha. Such descriptions of divine glory are extremely inadequate. For one may hope to exhaust counting the particles of dust on the earth, but not the powers and glories of the Lord. **7.** Chākshusha, the son of Chakshusha, was the sixth Manu. His sons were Pūru, Purusha, and Sudyumna. **8.** The Indra in that Manvantara was Mantradruma; Āpya and others were the Devas; and the Saptarshis were Havishman, Vīraka and others.

9. In that age the worshipful Lord incarnated by a part of Himself as Ajita in Sambhūti, the wife of Vairāja. **10.** The Lord then helped the Devas to get Amrita, the immortal drink, by churning the milk ocean, and as the Divine Tortoise he bore on Himself the Mandara mountain as it whirled while the ocean was being churned with it.

Curse of Durvasas and after (11-23)

The Rajah said: **11.** O learned one! How did the Lord churn the milk ocean and why? For what reason did He support the Mandara mountain as the Divine Tortoise? **12.** How did the Devas obtain the Amrita? What other things were got? Please narrate to me all the wonderful sports of the Lord relating to these questions. **13.** My mind that was being burnt in the fire of Samsara is never satiated by hearing about the excellences of the Lord that are being described by you.

The Suta said: **14.** O sages! Being thus questioned, the worshipful Suka, the son of Dwaipāyana, greatly appreciated the king's question, and once more began to describe the Lord's glories.

Sri Suka said: **15-16.** Once Indra was cursed by the Rishi Durvasas, and as a consequence he and all the three worlds lost their luck and lustre. None of the rituals like sacrifices were able to remedy their state. Besides, the Devas were attacked by the Asuras who killed them in large numbers with their sharp arrows. **17.** Indra, Varuna and the other Devas held council to decide what they should do in that situation, but were unable to

ततो ब्रह्मसभां जग्मुर्मेरोर्मूर्धनि सर्वशः । सर्वं विज्ञापयाञ्चक्रुः प्रणताः परमेष्ठिने ॥18॥
स विलोक्येन्द्रवाय्वादीन् निःसत्त्वान् विगतप्रभान् । लोकानमङ्गलप्रायानसुरानयथा विभुः ॥19॥
समाहितेन मनसा संस्मरन् पुरुषं परम् । उवाचोत्फुल्लवदनो देवान् स भगवान् परः ॥20॥

अहं भवो यूयमथोऽसुरादयो मनुष्यतिर्यग्द्रुमघर्मजातयः ।
यस्यावतारांशकलाविसर्जिता व्रजाम सर्वे शरणं तमव्ययम् ॥21॥
न यस्य वध्यो न च रक्षणीयो नोपेक्षणीयादरणीयपक्षः ।
अथापि सर्गस्थितिसंयमार्थं धत्ते रजःसत्त्वतमांसि काले ॥22॥
अयं च तस्य स्थितिपालनक्षणः सत्त्वं जुषाणस्य भवाय देहिनाम् ।
तस्माद् व्रजामः शरणं जगद्गुरुं स्वानां स नो धास्यति शं सुरप्रियः ॥23॥

श्रीशुक उवाच

इत्याभाष्य सुरान् वेधाः सह देवैररिन्दम । अजितस्य पदं साक्षाज्जगाम तमसः परम् ॥24॥
तत्रादृष्टस्वरूपाय श्रुतपूर्वाय वै विभो । स्तुतिमब्रूत दैवीभिर्गीर्भिस्त्ववहितेन्द्रियः ॥25॥

ब्रह्मोवाच

अविक्रियं सत्यमनन्तमाद्यं गुहाशयं निष्कलमप्रतर्क्यम् ।
मनोऽग्रयानं वचसानिरुक्तं नमामहे देववरं वरेण्यम् ॥26॥

decide on a plan of action. **18.** Thereupon they all resorted to the assembly of Brahma at the top of Mount Meru, and after prostrating themselves before that Divinity, represented the state of affairs to him. **19-20.** Seeing Indra, Vayu and other celestials without any strength or freshness, and seeing also the world caught up in a spell of gloom while the power of the Asuras on the contrary was waxing, Brahma began to meditate on the Supreme Being with a concentrated mind. Then with a face brightened, he said to the Devas: **21.** 'We shall all take shelter in that Supreme Being who first manifested as the Purusha, the first Avatara or Divine descent. I, Brahma, and Bhava form fractions of that Purusha, the first incarnation of His. And as emanations of a fraction (Kala, here Brahma himself) have come into being the Prajapatis like Marīchi and others who populated the worlds with various species of beings like Devas and Asuras and others that are born of the womb, or egg, or sweat, or by germination from seeds. **22.** There is none whom He specially cares to destroy or to protect, to neglect or to welcome. Still He assumes the qualities of Sattva, Rajas and Tamas, as the times require, for the preservation, creation and dissolution of the universe. **23.** This is the time when He has assumed the Guna of Sattva for the protection and prosperity of beings. So let us seek shelter in that Father of the worlds. This being the time for exercising his function of protection, He will be favourable to us Devas, His own people, and do what is good for us.'

Hymn of Brahma (24-50)

Sri Suka said: **24.** O great King! Saying so, Brahma along with the Devas went to the Lord's abode, which is free from the taint of ignorance. **25.** There making his senses controlled and indrawn, and reciting a hymn based on Vedic Mantras, Brahma extolled the Lord, who is beyond the power of physical eyes to see but can be understood only through scriptural dicta.

Brahma said: **26.** We salute Thee, the

विपश्चितं प्राणमनोधियात्मनामर्थेन्द्रियाभासमनिद्रमव्रणम् ।
छायातपौ यत्र न गृध्रपक्षौ तमक्षरं खं त्रियुगं व्रजामहे ॥27॥
अजस्य चक्रं त्वजयेर्यमाणं मनोमयं पञ्चदशारमाशु ।
त्रिणाभि विद्युच्चलमष्टनेमि यदक्षमाहुस्तमृतं प्रपद्ये ॥28॥
य एकवर्णं तमसः परं तदलोकमव्यक्तमनन्तपारम् ।
आसाञ्चकारोपसुपर्णमेनमुपासते योगरथेन धीराः ॥29॥
न यस्य कश्चातितितर्ति मायां यया जनो मुह्यति वेद नार्थम् ।
तं निर्जितात्मात्मगुणं परेशं नमाम भूतेषु समं चरन्तम् ॥30॥
इमे वयं यत्प्रिययैव तन्वा सत्त्वेन सृष्टा बहिरन्तराविः ।
गतिं न सूक्ष्मामृषयश्च विद्महे कुतोऽसुराद्या इतरप्रधानाः ॥31॥
पादौ महीयं स्वकृतैव यस्य चतुर्विधो यत्र हि भूतसर्गः ।
स वै महापूरुष आत्मतन्त्रः प्रसीदतां ब्रह्म महाविभूतिः ॥32॥

Highest and most adorable Being, the one without a beginning or an end, the undecaying, the True, the one beyond words and thought and therefore beyond argument as well, the one faster than the mind, the partless, and the resident in the recess of the heart. **27.** We take refuge in Him, who is the witness of the Pranas, mind, intellect and 'I-sense'; who is manifest both as the senses and their objects; who is free from corporeality and its functions like sleep, as also from Vidya (knowledge) and Avidya (ignorance) characteristic of Jivas; who is all-pervading like the sky; and who incarnates Himself in the three Yugas. **28.** I seek shelter in Him who is the Truth and the axle supporting the wheel of the Jiva's body-mind in his transmigratory existence. Fleeting like the glow of lightning, the wheel of the Jiva's body-mind is largely mental in constitution and is being speeded up by the Lord's Maya. The wheel has got fifteen spokes consisting of the ten Indriyas and the five Pranas; three naves consisting of the three Gunas of Prakriti; and eight fellies constituted of Prakriti, Mahattattva, Ahankara and the five Tanmatras. **29.** Very close to the Jivas stands the Lord as their most intimate well-wisher—the Lord who is the embodiment of Pure Consciousness, the one untouched by ignorance, the unseen and the subtle, the vast all-inclusive Being whom time and space do not limit. We seek refuge in Him whom the wise seek to reach in their chariot of concentration.

30. His inherent power Yogamaya has infatuated all beings, hiding from them the truth that they are the spirit and not the body. None can overcome that omnipotent power. He alone has mastery over her, who is His own inherent attribute. We prostrate before Him, the Lord and master of all, who though unaffected pervades everything. **31.** Even Divinities like us constituted of Sattva, a quality so close to Him, are not able of knowing the subtle nature of Him as the Spirit, though He is clearly presenting Himself as existence outside and consciouness within. How could the Asuras and men dominated by Rajas and Tamas then know Him? Our salutations to that Supreme Being!

32. He created this earth, which forms His feet, having its four forms of life —the womb-born, egg-born, sweat-born and seed-born. May He, the Brahman Supreme, the great Being of unrestricted

अम्भस्तु यद्रेत उदारवीर्यं सिध्यन्ति जीवन्त्युत वर्धमानाः ।
लोकास्त्रयोऽथाखिललोकपालाः प्रसीदतां ब्रह्म महाविभूतिः ॥33॥
सोमं मनो यस्य समामनन्ति दिवौकसां वै बलमन्ध आयुः ।
ईशो नगानां प्रजनः प्रजानां प्रसीदतां नः स महाविभूतिः ॥34॥
अग्निर्मुखं यस्य तु जातवेदा जातः क्रियाकाण्डनिमित्तजन्मा ।
अन्तःसमुद्रेऽनुपचन् स्वधातून् प्रसीदतां नः स महाविभूतिः ॥35॥
यच्चक्षुरासीत् तरणिर्देवयानं त्रयीमयो ब्रह्मण एष धिष्ण्यम् ।
द्वारं च मुक्तेरमृतं च मृत्युः प्रसीदतां नः स महाविभूतिः ॥36॥
प्राणादभूद् यस्य चराचराणां प्राणः सहो बलमोजश्च वायुः ।
अन्वास्म सम्राजमिवानुगा वयं प्रसीदतां नः स महाविभूतिः ॥37॥
श्रोत्राद् दिशो यस्य हृदश्च खानि प्रजज्ञिरे खं पुरुषस्य नाभ्याः ।
प्राणेन्द्रियात्मासुशरीरकेतं प्रसीदतां नः स महाविभूतिः ॥38॥
बलान्महेन्द्रस्त्रिदशाः प्रसादान्मन्योर्गिरीशो धिषणाद् विरिञ्चः ।
खेभ्यश्च छन्दांस्यृषयो मेढ्रतः कः प्रसीदतां नः स महाविभूतिः ॥39॥
श्रीर्वक्षसः पितरश्छाययाऽऽसन् धर्मः स्तनादितरः पृष्ठतोऽभूत् ।
द्यौर्यस्य शीर्ष्णोऽप्सरसो विहारात् प्रसीदतां नः स महाविभूतिः ॥40॥

freedom and infinite glories, be propitious unto us! **33**. He whose seminal fluid is constituted of the Cosmic Waters, from whose potency all the World-Lords and the three worlds were generated and continue to live and flourish—may He, Brahman of infinite glories, be propitious unto us! **34.** He whose mind is described by the Vedas as Soma (the moon), which constitutes the food, strength and life-span of the celestials; who is the ruler of all vegetation and the factor contributing to the growth of all creatures—may He, Brahman of infinite glories, be propitious unto us! **35.** He whose face is Agni (fire), who is the bestower of wealth, who enables the performance of Vedic sacrifices, who digests with the stomach the food congenial to the body—may He, Brahman of infinite glories, be propitious unto us! **36.** He whose eye is the Sun, who is the master of Devayāna or the path of spiritual ascent, who is the symbol for the adoration of Brahman, who is the gateway to liberation, who is immortality as also the dealer of death as Time—may He, Brahman of infinite glories, be propitious unto us! **37.** He who is the Prana, the Cosmic Energy, whom all of us obey and follow as the subjects obey and follow an emperor, from whom is derived that Vayu, the individual Prana, which gives strength to the body, senses and mind—may He, Brahman of infinite glories, be propitious unto us. **38.** He from whose power of hearing the quarters arose; from whose heart the cavities in the body originated; from whose navel came out the element Sky (Akasa) which is the support of Prana, senses, mind, life, body etc.—may He, Brahman of infinite glories, be propitious unto us! **39.** He from whose strength arose Indra; from whose graciousness, the Devas; from whose anger, Rudra; from whose intellect, Brahma; from whose bodily orifices, the Vedic metres and the Rishis; from whose sex-organ, the Prajapatis—may He, Brahman of infinite glories, be propitious unto us! **40.** He from whose bosom

विप्रो मुखं ब्रह्म च यस्य गुह्यं राजन्य आसीद् भुजयोर्बलं च ।
ऊर्वोर्विडोजोऽङ्घ्रिरवेदशूद्रौ प्रसीदतां नः स महाविभूतिः ॥41॥
लोभोऽधरात् प्रीतिरुपर्यभूद् द्युतिर्नस्तः पशव्यः स्पर्शेन कामः ।
भ्रुवोर्यमः पक्ष्मभवस्तु कालः प्रसीदतां नः स महाविभूतिः ॥42॥
द्रव्यं वयः कर्म गुणान् विशेषं यद्योगमायाविहितान् वदन्ति ।
यद् दुर्विभाव्यं प्रबुधापबाधं प्रसीदतां नः स महाविभूतिः ॥43॥
नमोऽस्तु तस्मा उपशान्तशक्तये स्वाराज्यलाभप्रतिपूरितात्मने ।
गुणेषु मायारचितेषु वृत्तिभिर्न सज्जमानाय नभस्वदूतये ॥44॥
स त्वं नो दर्शयात्मानमस्मत्करणगोचरम् । प्रपन्नानां दिदृक्षूणां सस्मितं ते मुखाम्बुजम् ॥45॥
तैस्तैः स्वेच्छाधृतै रूपैः काले काले स्वयं विभो । कर्म दुर्विषहं यन्नो भगवांस्तत् करोति हि ॥46॥
क्लेशभूर्यल्पसाराणि कर्माणि विफलानि वा । देहिनां विषयार्तानां न तथैवार्पितं त्वयि ॥47॥
नावमः कर्मकल्पोऽपि विफलायेश्वरार्पितः । कल्पते पुरुषस्यैष स ह्यात्मा दयितो हितः ॥48॥
यथा हि स्कन्धशाखानां तरोर्मूलावसेचनम् । एवमाराधनं विष्णोः सर्वेषामात्मनश्च हि ॥49॥

arose Srī; from whose shadow, the Pitris; from whose chest, Dharma; from whose back, Adharma; from whose head, heaven; from whose play, the Apsaras—may He, Brahman of infinite glories, be propitious unto us! **41.** He from whose face arose the Brahmana and the holy Veda; from whose arms, the Kshatriya and strength; from whose thigh, the Vaisya and dexterity; from whose feet, the Sudra and the secular services—may He, Brahman of infinite glories, be propitious unto us. **42.** He from whose upper lip arose greed; from whose lower lip, satisfaction; from whose nose, lustre; from whose touch, animal satisfactions; from whose brows, Yama the lord of death; from whose eyelids, Time—may He, Brahman of infinite glories, be propitious unto us. **43.** He whose Yogamaya or inherent power has brought into existence the five elements, Time, Karma, the three Gunas of Prakriti, in fact, the whole of this unimaginably vast universe—Yogamaya whom none but the enlightened can overcome—may He, Brahman of infinite glories, be propitious unto us.

44. Salutations to the One who transcends His own powers of manifestation; who is self-fulfilled in His inherent bliss and freedom; who is unaffected by the contacts of the senses created by His Maya; whose sportive activities in the world leave no pollution in Him even as the atmosphere is unsullied by its own movements everywhere. **45.** May Thou deign to reveal to us, who have taken refuge in Thee and are eager for Thy vision, that smiling divine form of Thine in a manner that is perceptible to our senses. **46.** O omnipotent one! From time to time Thou dost assume different forms out of Thy own will, and accomplish works that are difficult for us to perform. **47.** The works done by desire-prompted persons secure for them some good together with a great deal of trouble; or sometimes it may bring no results at all. But this is not the case with the works of those who dedicate them to Thee. **48.** Even if an act is insignificant and imperfect, it does not become fruitless when it is dedicated to the Lord. For He, the Lord, is the very soul and dearest well-wisher of the Jiva. **49.** The adoration of Vishnu is adoration to all beings, just as pouring water at the root of a tree is like

नमस्तुभ्यमनन्ताय दुर्वितर्क्यात्मकर्मणे । निर्गुणाय गुणेशाय सत्त्वस्थाय च साम्प्रतम् ॥50॥

इति श्रीमद्भागवते महापुराणे पारमहंस्यां संहितायामष्टमस्कन्धेऽमृतमथने पञ्चमोऽध्यायः ॥ 5॥

watering all its branches and leaves too. **50.** Obeisance to Thee, the Infinite Being whose essence and actions cannot be understood through our limited intellectual processes, and who, though now manifesting in a form of Sattva, remainest none the less essentially untouched by the Gunas, as their director.

अथ षष्ठोऽध्यायः

श्रीशुक उवाच

एवं स्तुतः सुरगणैर्भगवान् हरिरीश्वरः । तेषामाविरभूद् राजन् सहस्रार्कोदयद्युतिः ॥ 1॥
तेनैव महसा सर्वे देवाः प्रतिहतेक्षणाः । नापश्यन् खं दिशः क्षोणिमात्मानं च कुतो विभुम् 2
विरिञ्चो भगवान् दृष्ट्वा सहशर्वेण तां तनुम् । स्वच्छां मरकतश्यामां कञ्जगर्भारुणेक्षणाम् ॥ 3॥
तप्तहेमावदातेन लसत्कौशेयवाससा । प्रसन्नचारुसर्वाङ्गीं सुमुखीं सुन्दरभ्रुवम् ॥ 4॥
महामणिकिरीटेन केयूराभ्यां च भूषिताम् । कर्णाभरणनिर्भातकपोलश्रीमुखाम्बुजाम् ॥ 5॥
काञ्चीकलापवलयहारनूपुरशोभिताम् । कौस्तुभाभरणां लक्ष्मीं बिभ्रतीं वनमालिनीम् 6॥
सुदर्शनादिभिः स्वास्त्रैर्मूर्तिमद्भिरुपासिताम् । तुष्टाव देवप्रवरः सशर्वः पुरुषं परम् ।
सर्वामरगणैः साकं सर्वाङ्गैरवनिं गतैः ॥ 7॥

ब्रह्मोवाच

अजातजन्मस्थितिसंयमायागुणाय निर्वाणसुखार्णवाय ।
अणोरणिम्नेऽपरिगण्यधाम्ने महानुभावाय नमो नमस्ते ॥ 8॥

Skandha VIII : Chapter 6

THE CHURNING OF THE OCEAN

Brahma's subsequent Hymn (1-15)

1. O King! Being thus extolled by the Devas, the worshipful Hari, the Lord of all, appeared before them brilliant like the light of a thousand suns. **2.** Dazzled by that brilliance, the Devas could not perceive the sky, the quarters, the ground or themselves. How then could they see the Lord? **3-7.** Brahma and Siva saw before them that Divine form—deep blue in complexion like an emerald; eyes crimson-tinged, like the inside of a lotus; wearing a pure yellow silk brilliant and stainless like molten gold; having well-formed and attractive limbs, face and forehead; bedecked with a bright gem-studded crown, and ornaments like bracelets, girdle, necklaces, anklets and the neck-jewel Kaustubha; with cheeks that reflected the glow of the ear-rings adding to the loveliness of the lotus-like face; having Srīdevi on the chest along with floral wreaths; and attended by His weapons like Sudarsana that had taken form. Seeing this form, all the celestials prostrated themselves on the floor, and Brahma and Siva recited a hymn extolling the Lord.

Brahma said: **8.** Salutations again and

रूपं तवैतत् पुरुषर्षभेज्यं श्रेयोऽर्थिभिर्वैदिकतान्त्रिकेण ।
योगेन धातः सह नस्त्रिलोकान् पश्याम्यमुष्मिन् नु ह विश्वमूर्तौ ।। 9।।
त्वय्यग्र आसीत् त्वयि मध्य आसीत् त्वय्यन्त आसीदिदमात्मतन्त्रे ।
त्वमादिरन्तो जगतोऽस्य मध्यं घटस्य मृत्स्नेव परः परस्मात् ।।10।।
त्वं माययाऽऽत्माश्रयया स्वयेदं निर्माय विश्वं तदनुप्रविष्टः ।
पश्यन्ति युक्ता मनसा मनीषिणो गुणव्यवायेऽप्यगुणं विपश्चितः ।।11।।
यथाग्निमेधस्यमृतं च गोषु भुव्यन्नमम्बूद्यमने च वृत्तिम् ।
योगैर्मनुष्या अधियन्ति हि त्वां गुणेषु बुद्ध्या कवयो वदन्ति ।।12।।
तं त्वां वयं नाथ समुज्जिहानं सरोजनाभातिचिरेप्सितार्थम् ।
दृष्ट्वा गता निर्वृतिमद्य सर्वे गजा दवार्ता इव गाङ्गमम्भः ।।13।।
स त्वं विधत्स्वाखिललोकपाला वयं यदर्थास्तव पादमूलम् ।
समागतास्ते बहिरन्तरात्मन् किं वान्यविज्ञाप्यमशेषसाक्षिणः ।।14।।

again to Thee, the great Being, who, though himself birthless, art the cause of the origin, sustentation and dissolution of the Universe; who art the ocean of Bliss untouched by the transformations of Prakriti and its Gunas; who though subtler than the subtlest atom, art infinite existence unlimited by time and space. **9.** O Supreme Being! O Creator! This form of Thine is suitable to be worshipped by all who aspire for their own material and spiritual welfare, following the paths of communion described in the Vedas and the Tantras. Though it is seen as a limited form, I perceive in this all-inclusive form the three worlds including ourselves. **10.** The whole universe existed in Thee, the one free being, in its origin, it exists in Thee in its middle, and it dissolves in Thee at its end, just as a pot does with reference to the mud. Thou the one that transcendest even Pradhana, constitutest the Substance in the beginning, in the middle, and at the end of the universe. **11.** Creating this universe through Thy Maya or Cosmic Power, which is always subservient to Thee, Thou hast entered into the entities created by Thee. But those who have the power of introspection and discrimination, discern that Thou, in spite of Thy entrance into the whole creation, art not in the least affected or involved in the process of the evolutionary changes that matter undergoes. **12.** Just as fire is sought and found in fire-sticks, milk in cows, cereals in the soil, water under the ground, and livelihood through toil—so, say the wise, the spiritual aspirants seek and find Thee, the Spirit permeating everything, in the body-mind combination and in the other products of Prakriti, through discriminative intelligence and introspection, and proclaim their finding to the world. **13.** O Lord! Thou in whose navel stands the lotus holding the worlds! Today we have attained great relief by the fulfilment of our long-standing desire to have Thy direct vision, just as elephants scorched by forest fire are happy on reaching the cool waters of the Ganga. **14.** May thou be pleased to fulfil the object with which we, together with all the protecting deities of the quarters, have sought shelter at Thy lotus feet! Where is the need to represent that object further to Thee who dwellest both within and without all beings, and therefore knowest the innermost thought of

अहं गिरित्रश्च सुरादयो ये दक्षादयोऽग्नेरिव केतवस्ते ।
किं वा विदामेश पृथग्विभाता विधत्स्व शं नो द्विजदेवमन्त्रम् ॥15॥

श्रीशुक उवाच

एवं विरिञ्चादिभिरीडितस्तद् विज्ञाय तेषां हृदयं तथैव ।
जगाद जीमूतगभीरया गिरा बद्धाञ्जलीन् संवृतसर्वकारकान् ॥16॥

एक एवेश्वरस्तस्मिन् सुरकार्ये सुरेश्वरः । विहर्तुकामस्तानाह समुद्रोन्मथनादिभिः ॥17॥

श्रीभगवानुवाच

हन्त ब्रह्मन्नहो शम्भो हे देवा मम भाषितम् । शृणुतावहिताः सर्वे श्रेयो वः स्याद् यथा सुराः ॥18॥
यात दानवदैतेयैस्तावत् सन्धिर्विधीयताम् । कालेनानुगृहीतैस्तैर्यावद् वो भव आत्मनः ॥19॥
अरयोऽपि हि सन्धेयाः सति कार्यार्थगौरवे । अहिमूषकवद् देवा ह्यर्थस्य पदवीं गतैः ॥20॥
अमृतोत्पादने यत्नः क्रियतामविलम्बितम् । यस्य पीतस्य वै जन्तुर्मृत्युग्रस्तोऽमरो भवेत् ॥21॥
क्षिप्त्वा क्षीरोदधौ सर्वा वीरुत्तृणलतौषधीः । मन्थानं मन्दरं कृत्वा नेत्रं कृत्वा तु वासुकिम् ॥22॥
सहायेन मया देवा निर्मन्थध्वमतन्द्रिताः । क्लेशभाजो भविष्यन्ति दैत्या यूयं फलग्रहाः ॥23॥
यूयं तदनुमोदध्वं यदिच्छन्त्यसुराः सुराः । न संरम्भेण सिध्यन्ति सर्वेऽर्थाः सान्त्वया यथा 24॥

all? **15.** We, including Siva, the Devas and myself, are maintaining a separate existence from Thee, as sparks from fire. What power of understanding have we, limited beings? Therefore do Thou decide and do what will be good for the worlds, the Devas and the holy men.

The Lord's Instructions (16-25)

Sri Suka said: **16.** Extolled in this way by Brahma, the Lord, who understood the hearts of His votaries, spoke in a voice as deep as the roll of thunder to those celestials who stood before Him with palms joined in salutation and all their sense powers drawn inward. **17.** Though He, the Lord of all the divinities, was by Himself capable of solving that problem of the Devas, He, being desirous of enacting the play of churning the ocean, said to them as follows: *The Lord said:* **18.** 'O Brahma! O Sambhu! O Celestials! Hear ye all what I say for your welfare. **19.** You now go and make peace with the Asuras, your enemies. For, the present time is favourable to the Asuras. You have therefore got to wait until time turns in your favour. **20.** Even mutual enemies have to come to terms for the achievement of important objectives. After the objective is gained, they can again relapse into their mutual enmity like the mouse and the snake.[1] **21.** Do not delay in arranging for the production of Amrita, the immortal drink. One who drinks it, even if he be in the jaws of Death, will be turned immortal. **22.** Consign to the milk ocean various kinds of shrubs, grasses, creepers and medicinal plants; and get Mandara mountain for the churning rod, and the serpent Vāsuki for the churning string. **23.** O Devas! With My help you will be able to churn the ocean without fatigue. The Asuras will have to stand the hard labour of churning while the fruits will go to you. **24.** You agree to whatever terms the Asuras propose. Conciliatory methods are far more successful than those of confrontation.

[1] In order to get out of the basket of the snake-charmer, the snake makes friends with a mouse who cuts an opening in the basket with its teeth. After this objective is gained, the snake and the mouse become enemies again as before.

न भेतव्यं कालकूटाद् विषाज्जलधिसम्भवात् । लोभः कार्यो न वो जातु रोषः कामस्तु वस्तुषु ॥25॥

श्रीशुक उवाच

इति देवान् समादिश्य भगवान् पुरुषोत्तमः । तेषामन्तर्दधे राजन् स्वच्छन्दगतिरीश्वरः ॥26॥
अथ तस्मै भगवते नमस्कृत्य पितामहः । भवश्च जग्मतुः स्वं स्वं धामोपेयुर्बलिं सुराः ॥27॥
दृष्ट्वारीनप्यसंयत्ताञ्जातक्षोभान् स्वनायकान् । न्यषेधद् दैत्यराट् श्लोक्यः सन्धिविग्रहकालवित् 28॥
ते वैरोचनिमासीनं गुप्तं चासुरयूथपैः । श्रिया परमया जुष्टं जिताशेषमुपागमन् ॥29॥
महेन्द्रः श्लक्ष्णया वाचा सान्त्वयित्वा महामतिः । अभ्यभाषत तत् सर्वं शिक्षितं पुरुषोत्तमात् ॥30॥
तदरोचत दैत्यस्य तत्रान्ये येऽसुराधिपाः । शम्बरोऽरिष्टनेमिश्च ये च त्रिपुरवासिनः ॥31॥
ततो देवासुराः कृत्वा संविदं कृतसौहृदाः । उद्यमं परमं चक्रुरमृतार्थे परंतप ॥32॥
ततस्ते मन्दरगिरिमोजसोत्पाट्य दुर्मदाः । नदन्त उदधिं निन्युः शक्ताः परिघबाहवः ॥33॥
दूरभारोद्वहश्रान्ताः शक्रवैरोचनादयः । अपारयन्तस्तं वोढुं विवशा विजहुः पथि ॥34॥
निपतन् स गिरिस्तत्र बहूनमरदानवान् । चूर्णयामास महता भारेण कनकाचलः ॥35॥
तांस्तथा भग्नमनसो भग्नबाहूरुकन्धरान् । विज्ञाय भगवांस्तत्र बभूव गरुडध्वजः ॥36॥

25. When the ocean is churned the poison called Kālakūta will come out. You should not be afraid of it. Many objects will come out of the ocean when churned. You should not have any attraction for, or desire to possess, them. Nor should you feel angry if you are prevented from possessing them.'

Lifting the Mandara Mountain (26-39)

Sri Suka said: **26.** O King! The worshipful Lord, whose will is free and who is endowed with the six majesties, disappeared from their vision after giving the above instruction. **27.** Having made prostrations to the Lord, Brahma and Siva departed to their abodes while the Devas repaired to the region of the Asura leader, Bali. **28.** The leaders of the Asuras saw their enemies, the Devas, approaching without any military equipment. They got excited and made themselves ready for battle. But noble Bali, a master of the arts of both conciliation and combat, restrained them. **29.** The Devas now approached Bali, the son of Virochana and the conqueror of the three worlds. He was surrounded by his splendorous majesty and by his body-guards consisting of the leaders of the Asura army. **30.** The highly intelligent Indra conciliated Bali by sweet words, and after that, told him all that the Lord had instructed him to say. **31.** Indra's proposals were very welcome to the Daitya king as well as to Sambara, Arishtanemi, and the other leaders residing in Tripura.

32. The Devas and Asuras now came to terms and became friends. They jointly put forth all their energies for obtaining Amrita, the immortal drink. **33.** With perverse confidence in their own strength and shouting aloud, they lifted the Mandara mountain from its base with their powerful club-like arms, and started taking it to the sea. **34.** Tired by carrying its heavy weight for a long distance, Bali, Indra and others found themselves thoroughly helpless, and dropped it on the way unable to move it further. **35.** While falling down, that golden mountain pulverised many Devas and Asuras under its weight. **36.** In this situation, Sri Hari, who knew how the arms, thighs and necks of the Devas and Asuras were bruised and broken, made His appearance there,

गिरिपातविनिष्पिष्टान् विलोक्यामरदानवान् । ईक्षया जीवयामास निर्जरान् निर्व्रणान् यथा ।।37।।
गिरिं चारोप्य गरुडे हस्तेनैकेन लीलया । आरुह्य प्रययावब्धिं सुरासुरगणैर्वृतः ।।38।।
अवरोप्य गिरिं स्कन्धात् सुपर्णः पततां वरः । ययौ जलान्त उत्सृज्य हरिणा स विसर्जितः ।।39।।

इति श्रीमद्भागवते महापुराणे पारमहंस्यां संहितायामष्टमस्कन्धेऽमृतमथने मन्दराचलानयनं नाम षष्ठोऽध्यायः ।। 6।।

riding his eagle-vehicle. **37.** By a look of His, he healed the wounds of the Devas and revived them from the effects of the fall of the mountain. **38.** With a single hand He lifted up the mountain as a mere play, and put it on Garuda, and Himself mounting him, He carried it to the sea, surrounded by the Devas and Asuras. **39.** On arrival, Garuda, the king of the birds, unloaded the mountain from his shoulders on the seashore, and flew away with the permission of Sri Hari.

अथ सप्तमोऽध्यायः

श्रीशुक उवाच

ते नागराजमामन्त्र्य फलभागेन वासुकिम् । परिवीय गिरौ तस्मिन् नेत्रमब्धिं मुदान्विताः ।। 1।।
आरेभिरे सुसंयत्ता अमृतार्थं कुरूद्वह । हरिः पुरस्ताज्जगृहे पूर्वं देवास्ततोऽभवन् ।। 2।।
तन्नैच्छन् दैत्यपतयो महापुरुषचेष्टितम् । न गृह्णीमो वयं पुच्छमहेरङ्गममङ्गलम् ।। 3।।
स्वाध्यायश्रुतसम्पन्नाः प्रख्याता जन्मकर्मभिः । इति तूष्णीं स्थितान् दैत्यान् विलोक्य पुरुषोत्तमः ।
स्मयमानो विसृज्याग्रं पुच्छं जग्राह सामरः ।। 4।।
कृतस्थानविभागास्त एवं कश्यपनन्दनाः । ममन्थुः परमायत्ता अमृतार्थं पयोनिधिम् ।। 5।।
मथ्यमानेऽर्णवे सोऽद्रिरनाधारो ह्यपोऽविशत् । ध्रियमाणोऽपि बलिभिर्गौरवात् पाण्डुनन्दन ।। 6।।
ते सुनिर्विण्णमनसः परिम्लानमुखश्रियः । आसन् स्वपौरुषे नष्टे दैवेनातिबलीयसा ।। 7।।

Skandha VIII : Chapter 7

EMERGENCE OF THE POISON KĀLAKŪTA

Incarnation as Tortoise (1-12)

Sri Suka said: **1-2.** Then they requested Vāsuki,. the lord of serpents, to act as the churning-rope on the understanding that he too would get a share of Amrita, the fruit of the enterprise. With great joy they wound the serpent round the mountain and began churning. Sri Hari held the head of the serpent-rope, and the Devas lined up after him. **3-6.** The leaders of the Asuras refused to approve this act of Hari. 'We who are famous by the nobility of our birth and by our actions, and who are well-instructed in the Vedas, shall not hold the tail, an inferior part of the serpent,' thought the Daityas. The Lord saw that the Daityas stood still and silent after cogitating thus. Smiling at this, Sri Hari along with the Devas, left the head of the serpent. Their sides being thus determined, the Devas and Asuras, the offspring of Kasyapa, began to churn the ocean with all their might. In the process, the Mandara mountain, the churning rod, began to sink in the water, as it was not supported by anything. **7.** O scion of Pandu's line! Though those powerful

विलोक्य विघ्नेशविधिं तदेश्वरो दुरन्तवीर्योऽवितथाभिसन्धिः ।
कृत्वा वपुः काच्छपमद्भुतं महत् प्रविश्य तोयं गिरिमुज्जहार ॥ 8॥
तमुत्थितं वीक्ष्य कुलाचलं पुनः समुत्थिता निर्मथितुं सुरासुराः ।
दधार पृष्ठेन स लक्षयोजनप्रस्तारिणा द्वीप इवापरो महान् ॥ 9॥
सुरासुरेन्द्रैर्भुजवीर्यवेपितं परिभ्रमन्तं गिरिमङ्ग पृष्ठतः ।
बिभ्रत् तदावर्तनमादिकच्छपो मेनेऽङ्गकण्डूयनमप्रमेयः ॥10॥
तथासुरानाविशदासुरेण रूपेण तेषां बलवीर्यमीरयन् ।
उद्दीपयन् देवगणांश्च विष्णुर्दैवेन नागेन्द्रमबोधरूपः ॥11॥
उपर्यगेन्द्रं गिरिराडिवान्य आक्रम्य हस्तेन सहस्रबाहुः ।
तस्थौ दिवि ब्रह्मभवेन्द्रमुख्यैरभिष्टुवद्भिः सुमनोऽभिवृष्टः ॥12॥
उपर्यधश्चात्मनि गोत्रनेत्रयोः परेण ते प्राविशता समेधिताः ।
ममन्थुरब्धिं तरसा मदोत्कटा महाद्रिणा क्षोभितनक्रचक्रम् ॥13॥
अहीन्द्रसाहस्रकठोरदृङ्मुखश्वासाग्निधूमाहतवर्चसोऽसुराः ।
पौलोमकालेयबलील्वलादयो दवाग्निदग्धाः सरला इवाभवन् ॥14॥

beings held up the mountain with all their strength, it sank by its sheer weight. Very much disappointed to see that their effort was of no avail against Providence, their faces drooped in utter dejection. **8.** When confronted with this Providential obstacle, the Lord, whose power is limitless and whose will always becomes true, assumed the form of a wonderful Tortoise of huge proportions and entered into the water and jacked up the mountain. **9.** The mountain being thus lifted, the Devas and the Asuras resumed the churning, while that Divine Tortoise of a thousand Yojanas expanse supported the mountain like another island in the sea. **10.** The Primeval Tortoise of infinite strength bore the mountain on its back and felt its whirling movement as mere scratching, as the Devas and Asuras churned with all the strength of their arms. **11.** In the ranks of the Devas and the Asuras, Mahavishnu appeared in the form of a Deva and Asura respectively in order to encourage and embolden them to continue the churning. He also entered into the serpent Vāsuki as anaesthesia in order to shield it from the torture of the churning. **12.** When the movement of churning seemed to upset the balance of the mountain, Mahavishnu stood on its top assuming a form as huge as another mountain, and with one of His thousand arms, pressed down the mountain to its proper place. The celestials headed by Brahma showered flowers on Him as they stood above and viewed the scene.

Appearance of Kālakūta (13-20)

13. The Lord strengthened the resolve of all by this manifestation of His in many ways—above the mountain pressing it down, and underneath, supporting it as tortoise, in the hearts of Asuras and Devas as strength, and in Vāsuki as insensitiveness. So with the furious abandon of drunkards, they churned the ocean with the mountain with all their might and main, causing wild consternation among the aquatic creatures. **14.** Now the Asuras, who were holding the head of Vāsuki—the Paulomas, Kāleyas, Mahabali, Ilvala and others, in course of time became scor-

देवांश्च तच्छ्वासशिखाहतप्रभान् धूम्राम्बरस्रग्वरकञ्चुकाननान् ।
समभ्यवर्षन् भगवद्वशा घना ववुः समुद्रोर्म्युपगूढवायवः ॥15॥
मथ्यमानात् तथा सिन्धोर्देवासुरवरूथपैः । यदा सुधा न जायेत निर्ममन्थाजितः स्वयम् ॥16॥
मेघश्यामः कनकपरिधिः कर्णविद्योतविद्युन्मूर्ध्नि भ्राजद्विलुलितकचः स्रग्धरो रक्तनेत्रः ।
जैत्रैर्दोर्भिर्जगदभयदैर्दन्दशूकं गृहीत्वा मथ्नन् मथ्ना प्रतिगिरिरिवाशोभताथोद्धृताद्रिः ॥17॥
निर्मथ्यमानादुदधेरभूद्विषं महोल्बणं हालहलाह्वमग्रतः ।
सम्भ्रान्तमीनोन्मकराहिकच्छपात् तिमिद्विपग्राहतिमिङ्गिलाकुलात् ॥18॥
तदुग्रवेगं दिशि दिश्युपर्यधो विसर्पदुत्सर्पदसह्यमप्रति ।
भीताः प्रजा दुद्रुवुरङ्ग सेश्वरा अरक्ष्यमाणाः शरणं सदाशिवम् ॥19॥
विलोक्य तं देववरं त्रिलोक्या भवाय देव्याभिमतं मुनीनाम् ।
आसीनमद्रावपवर्गहेतोस्तपो जुषाणं स्तुतिभिः प्रणेमुः ॥20॥

प्रजापतय ऊचुः

देवदेव महादेव भूतात्मन् भूतभावन । त्राहि नः शरणापन्नांस्त्रैलोक्यदहनाद् विषात् 21॥
त्वमेकः सर्वजगत ईश्वरो बन्धमोक्षयोः । तं त्वामर्चन्ति कुशलाः प्रपन्नार्तिहरं गुरुम् ॥22॥

ched and faded like the Sarala tree in a forest fire, on being exposed to the unbearable heat and smoke issuing from the eyes, face, and breath of the serpent Vāsuki. **15.** The Devas too had their lustre effaced by the flaming breath of the serpent, and their face, clothes, wreaths and coats all turned grey with smoke. Just then the clouds, which were under the Lord's control, rained a shower over them while a breeze cooled by the waves of the ocean fanned them.

16. When no Amrita appeared in spite of churning by the Devas and Asuras, the Lord himself began to churn it very powerfully. **17.** Blue in colour like a rain cloud; wearing garments that shone like gold and ear-rings that glowed like lightning; with locks of attractive hair all scattered; wearing the floral wreath on the chest; and having eyes slightly reddish in tinge—the Lord shone like another mountain, as he churned with the churning rod of Mount Mandara, holding the serpent-cord of Vāsuki with his four victorious arms. **18.** From the sea full of aquatic creatures like Timi, sea-elephants, alligators and whales, the violent churning threw up various kinds of fish and amphibians until the virulent and notorious poision Hālāhala, called also Kālakūta, emerged. **19.** Its fiercely penetrating and fatal fumes spread everywhere quickly —above, below and on all the sides. O King! Terror-stricken and defenceless, the Prajapatis and all the celestials hurried to take shelter at the feet of the Lord Sadasiva. **20.** They found Him established on the Kailasa along with the Devi for the good of the world. He was dear to the sages because of His practising meditation conducive to bestowing the bliss of salvation on all contemplatives. They prostrated themselves before Him and recited the following hymn.

Hymn to Siva (21-35)

The Prajapatis said: **21.** O Lord of Lords! Thou great Divinity, soul and protector of the worlds! Save us from this poison that threatens the life of the three worlds. **22**. Thou art the master of the destinies of all beings, of their

गुणमय्या स्वशक्त्यास्य सर्गस्थित्यप्ययान् विभो। धत्से यदा स्वदृग् भूमन् ब्रह्मविष्णुशिवाभिधाम् 23
त्वं ब्रह्म परमं गुह्यं सदसद्भावभावनः। नानाशक्तिभिराभातस्त्वमात्मा जगदीश्वरः ॥24॥
त्वं शब्दयोनिर्जगदादिरात्मा प्राणेन्द्रियद्रव्यगुणस्वभावः।
कालः क्रतुः सत्यमृतं च धर्मस्त्वय्यक्षरं यत् त्रिवृदामनन्ति ॥25॥
अग्निर्मुखं तेऽखिलदेवतात्मा क्षितिं विदुर्लोकभवाङ्घ्रिपङ्कजम्।
कालं गतिं तेऽखिलदेवतात्मनो दिशश्च कर्णौ रसनं जलेशम् ॥26॥
नाभिर्नभस्ते श्वसनं नभस्वान् सूर्यश्च चक्षूंषि जलं स्म रेतः।
परावरात्माश्रयणं तवात्मा सोमो मनो द्यौर्भगवञ्छिरस्ते ॥27॥
कुक्षिः समुद्रा गिरयोऽस्थिसङ्घा रोमाणि सर्वौषधिवीरुधस्ते।
छन्दांसि साक्षात् तव सप्त धातवस्त्रयीमयात्मन् हृदयं सर्वधर्मः ॥28॥
मुखानि पञ्चोपनिषदस्तवेश यैस्त्रिंशदष्टोत्तरमन्त्रवर्गः।
यत् तच्छिवाख्यं परमार्थतत्त्वं देव स्वयंज्योतिरवस्थितिस्ते ॥29॥
छाया त्वधर्मोर्मिषु यैर्विसर्गो नेत्रत्रयं सत्त्वरजस्तमांसि।
सांख्यात्मनः शास्त्रकृतस्तवेक्षा छन्दोमयो देव ऋषिः पुराणः ॥30॥

bondage and liberation. Wise men worship Thee as the teacher and remover of the sufferings of those who seek shelter in Thee. **23.** All-pervading Being! When Thou, who art pure Self-awareness, dost will to create, preserve and dissolve this universe, Thou dost then assume Thy power Maya with its threefold aspect of Sattva, Rajas and Tamas, in association with which Thou comest to be known as Vishnu, Brahma and Siva. **24.** Thou art the subtle truth of Brahman, the Lord and the soul of the worlds, out of whom has originated the universe in its unmanifested causal and its manifested gross conditions. **25.** Thou art the source of the Vedas constituted of sounds as also of the worlds. Thou manifestest as Prana, sense organs, substances and qualities; Thou art the I-sense, Time, sacrifices, truth and righteousness; Prakriti with its three Gunas of Sattva, Rajas and Tamas are said to exist in Thee.

26. Of Thee who art the embodiment of all Divinities, fire is the face; the earth, the lotus feet; time, movement; the quarters, the ears; and the ocean, the tongue. **27.** O worshipful Lord! The sky is Thy navel; the wind, Thy breath; the sun, Thy eyes; water, Thy semen; the power supporting everything high and low, Thy ego; the moon, Thy mind; and the heaven, Thy head. **28.** O Embodiment of the Vedas! The oceans form Thy abdomen; the mountains, Thy bones; the plants and creepers, Thy hair; the Vedic metres (Gāyatri, Trishtubh, Anushtubh, Brihati, Pankti, Jagati and Ushnik), Thy seven bodily constituents (Dhātus); and all Dharmas, Thy heart. **29.** O Lord! The five secret Mantras (Tatpurusha, Aghora, Sadyojāta, Vāmadeva and Īsāna) from which the other thirty-eight Mantras arose, are Thy five faces. The supreme Truth called Siva is verily the Self-effulgent Being-Consciousness. **30.** The waves of the sea of Adharma like pride and the rest are Thy shadow; Sattva, Rajas and Tamas, the constituents of Prakriti forming the basis of creation, are Thy eyes; and the primordial Veda of metrical composition is the illumining glance of Thine, the source of all knowledge and scriptures.

न ते गिरित्राखिललोकपालविरिञ्चवैकुण्ठसुरेन्द्रगम्यम् ।
ज्योतिः परं यत्र रजस्तमश्च सत्त्वं न यद् ब्रह्म निरस्तभेदम् ॥31॥
कामाध्वरत्रिपुरकालगराद्यनेकभूतद्रुहः क्षपयतः स्तुतये न तत् ते ।
यस्त्वन्तकाल इदमात्मकृतं स्वनेत्रवह्निस्फुलिङ्गशिखया भसितं न वेद ॥32॥
ये त्वात्मरामगुरुभिर्हृदि चिन्तिताङ्घ्रिद्वन्द्वं चरन्तमुमया तपसाभितप्तम् ।
कत्थन्त उग्रपरुषं निरतं श्मशाने ते नूनमूतिमविदंस्तव हातलज्जाः ॥33॥
तत् तस्य ते सदसतोः परतः परस्य नाञ्जः स्वरूपगमने प्रभवन्ति भूम्नः ।
ब्रह्मादयः किमुत संस्तवने वयं तु तत्सर्गसर्गविषया अपि शक्तिमात्रम् ॥34॥
एतत् परं प्रपश्यामो न परं ते महेश्वर । मृडनाय हि लोकस्य व्यक्तिस्तेऽव्यक्तकर्मणः ॥35॥

श्रीशुक उवाच

तद् वीक्ष्य व्यसनं तासां कृपया भृशपीडितः । सर्वभूतसुहृद् देव इदमाह सतीं प्रियाम् ॥36॥

शिव उवाच

अहो बत भवान्येतत् प्रजानां पश्य वैशसम् । क्षीरोदमथनोद्भूतात् कालकूटादुपस्थितम् ॥37॥
आसां प्राणपरीप्सूनां विधेयमभयं हि मे । एतावान् हि प्रभोरर्थो यद् दीनपरिपालनम् ॥38॥

31. O Sadasiva! That Light Supernal, which constitutes Thy real form, is what is called Non-dual Brahman. As non-dual Brahman Thou art not accessible to Brahma, Vishnu, Indra and other Divinities; for in that supreme state of Thine, there is no touch of the Gunas of Prakriti. **32.** For Thee, who could view with indifference even the reduction to ashes of the whole universe of Thy own creation by a spark of fire coming out of Thy eyes at the time of dissolution, it is no matter of praise to be extolled by reference to acts of Thine calculated to eliminate evil, such as the destruction of Cupid, of the Tripuras, of Yama the angel of death, of Daksha's sacrifice, and of the poison Kālakūta.

33. There are some who indulge in meaningless criticism of Thee, that because Thou art always seen with Uma, Thou art intensely attached to her, and that because Thou movest about in cremation ground, Thou art fierce and uncouth. Those who speak like that about Thee, who art ever immersed in Samadhi and whose feet constitute the object of contemplation even for the greatest teachers absorbed in the bliss of Atman, are shameless persons who know nothing about Thy cosmic sport! **34.** Even a Divinity like Brahma is not able to grasp the true nature of Thy transcendent Self, which is beyond the cause and effect relation and the states of grossness and subtlety. How can we, the creatures of Thy creature Brahma, hope to extol Thee adequately? Our inadequate praise is only an expression of our very limited powers. **35.** O Great God! We see only this form of Thine that Thou revealest. We are totally unaware of Thy transcendent state. But we know that Thou, who art of inscrutable ways, hast assumed this form for the good of the world.

Siva drinking Kālakūta (36-46)

Sri Suka said: **36.** Seeing the miserable condition of the Devas, the merciful Lord Siva, the friend and well-wisher of all, felt extremely pained and said as follows to his consort Sati. *Siva said:* **37.** 'O Bhavāni! See the pitiable plight of beings

प्राणैः स्वैः प्राणिनः पान्ति साधवः क्षणभङ्गुरैः । बद्धवैरेषु भूतेषु मोहितेष्वात्ममायया ॥39॥
पुंसः कृपयतो भद्रे सर्वात्मा प्रीयते हरिः । प्रीते हरौ भगवति प्रीयेऽहं सचराचरः ।
तस्मादिदं गरं भुञ्जे प्रजानां स्वस्तिरस्तु मे ॥40॥

श्रीशुक उवाच

एवमामन्त्र्य भगवान् भवानीं विश्वभावनः । तद् विषं जग्धुमारेभे प्रभावज्ञान्वमोदत ॥41॥
ततः करतलीकृत्य व्यापि हालाहलं विषम् । अभक्षयन्महादेवः कृपया भूतभावनः ॥42॥
तस्यापि दर्शयामास स्ववीर्यं जलकल्मषः । यच्चकार गले नीलं तच्च साधोर्विभूषणम् ॥43॥
तप्यन्ते लोकतापेन साधवः प्रायशो जनाः । परमाराधनं तद्धि पुरुषस्याखिलात्मनः ॥44॥
निशम्य कर्म तच्छम्भोर्देवदेवस्य मीढुषः । प्रजा दाक्षायणी ब्रह्मा वैकुण्ठश्च शशंसिरे ॥45॥
प्रस्कन्नं पिबतः पाणेर्यत् किञ्चिज्जगृहुः स्म तत् । वृश्चिकाहिविषौषध्यो दन्दशूकाश्च येऽपरे ॥46॥

इति श्रीमद्भागवते महापुराणे पारमहंस्यां संहितायामष्टमस्कन्धेऽमृतमथने सप्तमोऽध्यायः ॥ 7॥

harassed by the poison Kālakūta produced at the churning of the milk ocean. **38.** I have to give shelter to them in their effort to save themselves. Affording protection for the weak and the suffering is the only object and justification of lordship. **39.** While beings under the infatuating power of the Lord are ordinarily at discord with one another and are bent on mutual destruction, the enlightened holy men, who have realised the transitoriness of life, seek to give protection to other creatures even at the expense of their own lives. **40.** O noble lady! Sri Hari, the soul of all, is pleased with the person who shows kindness to beings. When Hari is pleased, I, along with all moving and unmoving beings, feel pleased. So I am going to drink the poison. May all beings be saved by it!'

Sri Suka said: **41.** Speaking thus to Devi Bhavāni, the Lord, who is the protector of the worlds, got ready to drink that poison with the approval of the Devi, who knew the Lord's power. **42.** Then Mahadeva, the protector of the worlds, collected the spreading poison of Kālakūta in his palms and drank it with a heart full of love and pity for all beings. **43.** The poison born of the ocean showed its destructive power even on this Divine Being, the Lord of the worlds. It turned his throat blue. But it remained there only as a decoration proclaiming his zeal in the welfare of others. **44.** Devoted good men generally feel the sufferings of others as their own. Such fellow-feeling for others is the highest form of worship of the Supreme Being, who is the soul of all. **45.** On hearing about it, high encomiums were bestowed on this act of worshipful Sambhu, the Lord of Lords, by all beings, by Sati Devi the daughter of Daksha, by Brahma and by Narayana the lord of Vaikuntha. **46.** The small portion of the poison which happened to fall from the Lord's hand while drinking, was appropriated by scorpions, serpents, poisonous plants and other poisonous creatures.

अथाष्टमोऽध्यायः

श्रीशुक उवाच

पीते गरे वृषाङ्केण प्रीतास्तेऽमरदानवाः । ममन्थुस्तरसा सिन्धुं हविर्धानी ततोऽभवत् ॥ 1॥
तामग्निहोत्रीमृषयो , जगृहुर्ब्रह्मवादिनः । यज्ञस्य देवयानस्य मेध्याय हविषे नृप ॥ 2॥
तत उच्चैःश्रवा नाम हयोऽभूच्चन्द्रपाण्डुरः । तस्मिन् बलिः स्पृहां चक्रे नेन्द्र ईश्वरशिक्षया ॥ 3॥
तत ऐरावतो नाम वारणेन्द्रो विनिर्गतः । दन्तैश्चतुर्भिः श्वेताद्रेर्हरन् भगवतो महिम् ॥ 4॥
कौस्तुभाख्यमभूद् रत्नं पद्मरागो महोदधेः । तस्मिन् हरिः स्पृहां चक्रे वक्षोऽलङ्करणे मणौ ॥ 5॥
ततोऽभवत् पारिजातः सुरलोकविभूषणम् । पूरयत्यर्थिनो योऽर्थैः शश्वद् भुवि यथा भवान् ॥ 6॥
ततश्चाप्सरसो जाता निष्ककण्ठ्यः सुवाससः । रमण्यः स्वर्गिणां वल्गुगतिलीलावलोकनैः ॥ 7॥
ततश्चाविरभूत् साक्षाच्छ्री रमा भगवत्परा । रञ्जयन्ती दिशः कान्त्या विद्युत् सौदामनी यथा 8॥
तस्यां चक्रुः स्पृहां सर्वे ससुरासुरमानवाः । रूपौदार्यवयोवर्णमहिमाक्षिप्तचेतसः ॥ 9॥
तस्या आसनमानिन्ये महेन्द्रो महदद्भुतम् । मूर्तिमत्यः सरिच्छ्रेष्ठा हेमकुम्भैर्जलं शुचि ॥10॥

Skandha VIII : Chapter 8

EMERGENCE OF RAMĀ, AMRITA AND MOHINI

Gifts of the Ocean (1-7)

Sri Suka said: **1.** After Lord Siva, who had the emblem of a bull for his standard, had drunk the poison, the Devas and Asuras were again cheerful and began to churn the ocean with great enthusiasm. Now came out from the ocean Kāmadhenu, the heavenly cow that yields all that one wants. **2.** The Rishis, who are specialists in the Veda and the rituals inculcated by it, appropriated this cow, so useful for Agnihotra and other Vedic Yajnas which enable one to gain the heavenly realm; for the cow yields milk and butter, required for the preparation of pure Havis, the offerings to the Devas made in the sacred fire. **3.** Next came out the horse known as Ucchaisravas, white like the moon. The Asura Bali liked to have it. On the Lord's advice, Indra did not entertain any desire for it. **4.** This was followed by the emergence of Airāvata, the white four-tusked elephant that excelled the greatness of even Mount Kailasa, the snow-covered mountain, which constitutes the abode of Siva. **5.** Now the Kaustubha, a gem of the species of Padmarāga, came out of the sea. Hari desired to have it as an ornament for his neck. **6.** Next came the celestial tree known as the Pārijāta, an ornament of the heavenly region. It fulfils the wants of those who approach it for anything, just as you, King Parikshit, have been doing in this world. **7.** The heavenly nymphs known as Apsaras came next. Adorned with necklaces and dressed impeccably, they were the attraction of the whole celestial realm with their gaiety, looks and movements.

Emergence of Ramā (8-22)

8. Next took place the emergence of Ramā who was Srī embodied and devoted to Mahavishnu By her brilliance like that of lightning, she illumined the quarters. **9.** Attracted by her beauty, sweetness, tender age, complexion and sublimity, all species of beings, Devas, Asuras and men, lost their hearts to her. **10.** Mahendra brought her a most marvel-

आभिषेचनिका भूमिराहरत् सकलौषधीः । गावः पञ्च पवित्राणि वसन्तो मधुमाधवौ ॥11॥
ऋषयः कल्पयाञ्चक्रुरभिषेकं यथाविधि । जगुर्भद्राणि गन्धर्वा नटयश्च ननृतुर्जगुः ॥12॥
मेघा मृदङ्गपणवमुरजानकगोमुखान् । व्यनादयञ्छङ्खवेणुवीणास्तुमुलनिःस्वनान् ॥13॥
ततोऽभिषिषिचुर्देवीं श्रियं पद्मकरां सतीम् । दिगिभाः पूर्णकलशैः सूक्तवाक्यैर्द्विजेरितैः ॥14॥
समुद्रः पीतकौशेयवाससी समुपाहरत् । वरुणः स्रजं वैजयन्तीं मधुना मत्तषट्पदाम् ॥15॥
भूषणानि विचित्राणि विश्वकर्मा प्रजापतिः । हारं सरस्वती पद्ममजो नागाश्च कुण्डले ॥16॥

ततः कृतस्वस्त्ययनोत्पलस्रजं नदद्द्विरेफां परिगृह्य पाणिना ।
चचाल वक्त्रं सुकपोलकुण्डलं सव्रीडहासं दधती सुशोभनम् ॥17॥
स्तनद्वयं चातिकृशोदरी समं निरन्तरं चन्दनकुङ्कुमोक्षितम् ।
ततस्ततो नूपुरवल्गुशिञ्जितैर्विसर्पती हेमलतेव सा बभौ ॥18॥
विलोकयन्ती निरवद्यमात्मनः पदं ध्रुवं चाव्यभिचारिसद्गुणम् ।
गन्धर्वयक्षासुरसिद्धचारणत्रैविष्टपेयादिषु नान्वविन्दत ॥19॥
नूनं तपो यस्य न मन्युनिर्जयो ज्ञानं क्वचित् तच्च न सङ्गवर्जितम् ।
कश्चिन्महांस्तस्य न कामनिर्जयः स ईश्वरः किं परतोव्यपाश्रयः ॥20॥

lous seat; Gangā and other sacred streams offered that embodiment of Beauty their pure waters in bright golden vessels. **11.** The earth brought all the herbs and medicinal plants required for the consecration ceremony, while the cows contributed their five sacred products *(Panchagavya)*, and the spring season, the flowers special to the months of Chaitra and Vaisākha. **12.** The Rishis made all arrangements for the bath of consecration. The Gandharvas sang auspicious songs and danseuses danced to the accompaniment of music. **13.** From the region of the clouds came the music of a variety of instruments—Mridanga, drum, cymbal, tabor, trumpet, conch, flute, and Vina. **14.** The Elephants of the Quarters now poured potfuls of holy water over the Devi, sporting a lotus in her hand, for her ceremonial bath of consecration, while holy men chanted the Vedas. **15.** The ocean offered her a pair of yellow silks, while Varuna presented the floral wreath Vaijayanti, round which intoxicated honey-beetles hovered. **16.** Prajapati Viswakarma offered various ornaments; Devi Saraswati, a necklace; Brahma, a lotus; and serpents, ear-rings studded with precious stones. **17.** With the floral wreath surrounded by honey-beetles in her hand, and her ear-pendants reflecting their glow from her cheeks, the Devi got up with a bashful countenance, seeking a worthy person on whom she could put the garland. **18.** Endowed with well-formed and well-proportioned breasts that were decorated with saffron powder and sandal paste, and an abdomen tender and deep-set, she moved about here and there like a creeper of gold producing a delightful murmuring sound from her anklets. **19.** For long did she look for one fit to be her partner—one who was without any imperfection, who was free from decay and death, who possessed everlasting virtues. But she could find none such among Gandharvas, Yakshas, Asuras, Siddhas, Chāranas and Devas.

She cogitated: **20.** One who has much of austerity to his credit is seen not to have subdued anger (as in the case of Durvāsas); others having much knowledge are found to be victims of personal

धर्मः क्वचित् तत्र न भूतसौहृदं त्यागः क्वचित् तत्र न मुक्तिकारणम् ।
वीर्यं न पुंसोऽस्त्यजवेगनिष्कृतं न हि द्वितीयो गुणसङ्गवर्जितः ॥21॥
क्वचिच्चिरायुर्न हि शीलमङ्गलं क्वचित् तदप्यस्ति न वेद्यमायुषः ।
यत्रोभयं कुत्र च सोऽप्यमङ्गलः सुमङ्गलः कश्च न काङ्क्षते हि माम् ॥22॥
एवं विमृश्याव्यभिचारिसद्गुणैर्वरं निजैकाश्रयतयागुणाश्रयम् ।
वव्रे वरं सर्वगुणैरपेक्षितं रमा मुकुन्दं निरपेक्षमीप्सितम् ॥23॥
तस्यांसदेश उशतीं नवकञ्जमालां माद्यन्मधुव्रतवरूथगिरोपघुष्टाम् ।
तस्थौ निधाय निकटे तदुरः स्वधाम सव्रीडहासविकसन्नयनेन याता ॥24॥
तस्याः श्रियस्त्रिजगतो जनको जनन्या वक्षो निवासमकरोत् परमं विभूतेः ।
श्रीः स्वाः प्रजाः सकरुणेन निरीक्षणेन यत्र स्थितैधयत साधिपतींस्त्रिलोकान् ॥25॥
शङ्खतूर्यमृदङ्गानां वादित्राणां पृथुः स्वनः । देवानुगानां सस्त्रीणां नृत्यतां गायतामभूत् ॥26॥

attachments (as in the case of Sukra). There are still others who are dubbed great, but they have no control over the sex instinct (as in the case of Brahma and Chandra). How can anyone dependant on another (like Indra) be called Iswara, the Lord of all at all? **21.** Some follow Dharma but are heartless (as Parasurama). Others have renunciation, but it might not bring them liberation (as in the case of Sibi). Some have prowess, like Kārtavīrya, but being subject to the destructive speed of Time, it is purely illusory. There are still others who are absolutely detached from life and are pure ascetics (like Sanaka). Surely such could not be a fitting partner to me. **22.** Some have long life, but are not attractive by nature (as Mārkandeya). Some are attractive but their life may be short (as in the case of Hiranyāksha). Some who have both attractiveness and longevity follow ways of life that are repulsive (as in the case of Sri Rudra). But there is one who combines all these—attractiveness, longevity and auspicious way of life, and that is Mahavishnu. But He is immersed in His Self (*Ātmārāma*), and may not care for me.

Ramā chooses Mahavishnu (23-29)

23. Cogitating in this way, Ramā chose as partner Mukunda (Mahavishnu) who alone was according to her heart. For she found Him the centre of unabating virtues; supreme over all as being the only independent person; unaffected by the impure Gunas of Prakriti, but endowed with all auspicious Gunas or attributes. Though free from every form of desire Himself, she chose Him in the conviction that He would not desert one who resigns oneself to Him in complete trust. **24.** She then put round the neck of Mahavishnu the most attractive garland made of choice fresh lotuses surrounded by humming honey-beetles, and stood looking at Him with her eyes blooming by her bashful smile, as if asking for the chest of Him to be offered as her residence. **25.** The worshipful Lord, the Father of the worlds, assigned his chest, the most sublime of regions, as the residence for Srīdevi, the Mother of the universe and the source of all power, glory and prosperity. Casting her benign glance from her residence there on all her children in the three worlds, including the presiding divinities, she brought about their progress and prosperity. **26.** Then the loud sound produced by the music, dance, trumpets, Mridangas and conch shells of the celestial attendants of the

ब्रह्मरुद्राङ्गिरोमुख्याः सर्वे विश्वसृजो विभुम् । ईडिरेऽवितथैर्मन्त्रैस्तल्लिङ्गैः पुष्पवर्षिणः ॥27॥
श्रिया विलोकिता देवाः सप्रजापतयः प्रजाः । शीलादिगुणसम्पन्ना लेभिरे निर्वृतिं पराम् ॥28॥
निःसत्त्वा लोलुपा राजन् निरुद्योगा गतत्रपाः । यदा चोपेक्षिता लक्ष्म्या बभूवुर्दैत्यदानवाः ॥29॥
अथासीद् वारुणी देवी कन्या कमललोचना । असुरा जगृहुस्तां वै हरेरनुमतेन ते ॥30॥
अथोदधेर्मथ्यमानात् काश्यपैरमृतार्थिभिः । उदतिष्ठन्महाराज पुरुषः परमाद्भुतः ॥31॥
दीर्घपीवरदोर्दण्डः कम्बुग्रीवोऽरुणेक्षणः । श्यामलस्तरुणः स्रग्वी सर्वाभरणभूषितः ॥32॥
पीतवासा महोरस्कः सुमृष्टमणिकुण्डलः । स्निग्धकुञ्चितकेशान्त सुभगः सिंहविक्रमः ॥33॥
अमृतापूर्णकलशं बिभ्रद् वलयभूषितः । स वै भगवतः साक्षाद्विष्णोरंशांशसम्भवः ॥34॥
धन्वन्तरिरिति ख्यात आयुर्वेददृगिज्यभाक् । तमालोक्यासुराः सर्वे कलशं चामृताभृतम् ॥35॥
लिप्सन्तः सर्ववस्तूनि कलशं तरसाहरन् । नीयमानेऽसुरैस्तस्मिन् कलशेऽमृतभाजने ॥36॥
विषण्णमनसो देवा हरिं शरणमाययुः । इति तद्दैन्यमालोक्य भगवान् भृत्यकामकृत् ।
मा खिद्यत मिथोऽर्थं वः साधयिष्ये स्वमायया ॥37॥
मिथः कलिरभूत्तेषां तदर्थे तर्षचेतसाम् । अहं पूर्वमहं पूर्वं न त्वं न त्वमिति प्रभो ॥38॥

assembled Divinities, swelled forth everywhere in the air. **27.** The Prajapatis like Brahma, Rudra and Angiras, showered flowers and extolled the Lord with Vedic Mantras dealing with the supreme truth and the attributes of Mahavishnu. **28.** By the gracious glances of Srīdevi, all virtues were perfected in the celestials, the Prajapatis and all other beings and they were established in perfect joy. **29.** The Daityas and Danavas, abandoned by Srī, lost all higher qualities like courage, modesty and enthusiasm, and propensities like greed gained the upper hand in them.

Emergence of Vāruni and Amrita (30-39)

30. Next appeared Vāruni, the presiding deity of liquors, in the form of a lotus-eyed and handsome girl. Permitted by Hari, the Asuras took possession of her. **31.** On the Devas and the Asuras, the issue of Kasyapa, churning the ocean further in their quest for Amrita, the immortal drink, there arose from the sea a man with a unique and astounding form. **32.** His hands were long and stout; and his eyes, reddish in tinge. His neck resembled a conch shell. Blue in complexion and young in appearance, he was bedecked with garlands and various kinds of ornaments. **33.** Having smooth and curly hair, broad-chested, and handsome, he wore a yellow cloth, and his strides resembled those of a lion. **34-35.** In his arm decorated with bracelets, he carried the pot of Amrita. He was Dhanvantari, an incarnation of a part of Vishnu, who is noted for promulgating Ayurveda, the science of health, and who is entitled to a share in the sacrificial offerings. Seeing him emerge, the Asuras, who entertained desire for all things, took away from him all of a sudden the pot containing the Amrita. **36.** When the Asuras thus carried away the vessel of Amrita, the Devas in great distress took refuge in Sri Hari. **37.** On seeing the forlorn condition of the Devas, the Lord, the grantor of the prayers of devotees, said to them: 'Do not be sad; by my Maya I shall achieve your end without anyone knowing about it.'

38. Meanwhile, O King, there arose a quarrel among these Asuras, all of whom desired to have the Amrita. So each one of them claimed, 'I shall have it first, not

देवाः स्व भागमर्हन्ति ये तुल्यायासहेतवः । सत्रयाग इवैतस्मिन्नेष धर्मः सनातनः ॥39॥
इति स्वान् प्रत्यषेधन् वै दैतेया जातमत्सराः । दुर्बलाः प्रबलान् राजन् गृहीतकलशान् मुहुः ॥40॥
एतस्मिन्नन्तरे विष्णुः सर्वोपायविदीश्वरः । योषिद्रूपमनिर्देश्यं दधार परमाद्भुतम् ॥41॥
प्रेक्षणीयोत्पलश्यामं सर्वावयवसुन्दरम् । समानकर्णाभरणं सुकपोलोन्नसाननम् ॥42॥
नवयौवननिर्वृत्तस्तनभारकृशोदरम् । मुखामोदानुरक्तालिझङ्कारोद्विग्नलोचनम् ॥43॥
बिभ्रत् स्वकेशभारेण मालामुत्फुल्लमल्लिकाम् । सुग्रीवकण्ठाभरणं सुभुजाङ्गदभूषितम् ॥44॥
विरजाम्बरसंवीतनितम्बद्वीपशोभया । काञ्च्या प्रविलसद्वल्गुचलच्चरणनूपुरम् ॥45॥
सव्रीडस्मितविक्षिप्तभ्रूविलासावलोकनैः । दैत्ययूथपचेतःसु काममुद्दीपयन् मुहुः ॥46॥

इति श्रीमद्भागवते महापुराणे पारमहंस्यां संहितायामष्टमस्कन्धे भगवन्मायोपलम्भनं नामाष्टमोऽध्यायः ॥ 8॥

you', and they began to quarrel among themselves over this question. **39-40.** The weaker among the Asuras, who feared that they might not get any share of the Amrita, felt jealous of the stronger ones holding the pot, and remonstrated, saying, 'The Devas whose labour in the enterprise is equal to ours, are entitled to an equal share of Amrita, just as the master of the sacrifice and all priests participating in a Satra-Yaga get their due rewards. This is the law eternal.'

The Lord incarnates as Mohini (41-46)

41. While matters stood thus, the all-powerful Mahavishnu, who was a master of the art of devising means for achieving any end however difficult, assumed the form of a woman so wonderful that it defies description. **42.** Her complexion was like the colour of an extremely attractive blue lotus. Every limb of hers was handsome. Her ears, with appropriate ornaments, were exactly alike in formation. She had shining cheeks and a high nose. **43.** Her breasts indicative of her blooming youth, were well-rounded and proportionate, and her abdomen in contrast seemed very thin. The humming bees, which were attracted to her face by the fragrance of her breath, often made her eyes shrink in fear. **44.** Her luxuriant braids were decorated with blooming jasmine wreaths, while necklaces adorned her handsome neck, and armlets, her attractive arms. **45.** Her hips, extensive like an island, were draped with a silk cloth, over which there was an encircling girdle of great brilliance, while well-fashioned anklets added to the beauty of the slow and attractive movements of her feet. **46.** By her frequent glances, accompanied by the movements of the brows caused by her bashful smile, she roused gusts of passion in the minds of the Asura leaders.

अथ नवमोऽध्यायः

श्रीशुक उवाच

तेऽन्योन्यतोऽसुराः पात्रं हरन्तस्त्यक्तसौहृदाः । क्षिपन्तो दस्युधर्माण आयान्तीं ददृशुः स्त्रियम् ॥ 1॥
अहो रूपमहो धाम अहो अस्या नवं वयः । इति ते तामभिद्रुत्य पप्रच्छुर्जातहृच्छयाः ॥ 2॥
का त्वं कञ्जपलाशाक्षि कुतो वा किं चिकीर्षसि । कस्यासि वद वामोरु मथ्नन्तीव मनांसि नः ॥ 3॥
न वयं त्वामरैर्दैत्यैः सिद्धगन्धर्वचारणैः । नास्पृष्टपूर्वां जानीमो लोकेशैश्च कुतो नृभिः ॥ 4॥
नूनं त्वं विधिना सुभ्रूः प्रेषितासि शरीरिणाम् । सर्वेन्द्रियमनः प्रीतिं विधातुं सघृणेन किम् ॥ 5॥
सा त्वं नः स्पर्धमानानामेकवस्तुनि मानिनि । ज्ञातीनां बद्धवैराणां शं विधत्स्व सुमध्यमे ॥ 6॥
वयं कश्यपदायादा भ्रातरः कृतपौरुषाः । विभजस्व यथान्यायं नैव भेदो यथा भवेत् ॥ 7॥
इत्युपामन्त्रितो दैत्यैर्मायायोषिद्वपुर्हरिः । प्रहस्य रुचिरापाङ्गैर्निरीक्षन्निदमब्रवीत् ॥ 8॥

श्रीभगवानुवाच

कथं कश्यपदायादाः पुंश्चल्यां मयि सङ्गताः । विश्वासं पण्डितो जातु कामिनीषु न याति हि ॥ 9॥
सालावृकाणां स्त्रीणां च स्वैरिणीनां सुरद्विषः । सख्यान्याहुरनित्यानि नूत्नं नूत्नं विचिन्वताम् ॥ 10॥

Skandha VIII : Chapter 9

ASURAS DEPRIVED OF AMRITA

Mohini accepted as Distributor (1-16)

Sri Suka said: **1.** While the Asuras, abandoning all ties of friendship and adopting the ways of robbers, were engaged in a mutual wrangle for wresting the vessel of Amrita, they saw the handsome maiden approaching them. **2.** Agitated by lust at her sight, the Asuras rushed towards her exclaiming: 'Ah, what a beauty! What a complexion! What a blooming youth!' **3.** They addressed her saying: 'O lotus-eyed beauty! Tell us who you are, whence you come, and why. Whose daughter are you, O lass of handsome thighs? Your charm seems to churn our heart by excitement. **4.** We know for certain that you are still a maiden untouched by anyone from among the Devas, Asuras, Siddhas, Gandharvas, Chāranas, or the world-lords, not to speak of men. **5.** O girl of attractive eyes! Is it that the merciful creator has sent you here to enthral the minds and senses of all beings? **6.** O slender-waisted beauty! All of us, who are mutually related, have now become bitter enemies because of a competition to get possession of a common object. Settle that quarrel and bring peace among us. **7.** We are all the descendants of Kasyapa, and therefore brothers. We have worked alike for churning the ocean and getting Amrita. Now be pleased to divide the Amrita among us in a way that would look just and avoid later disputes.'

8. On being thus requested, the Lord Hari, who had assumed this maiden's form, replied as follows casting bewitching glances from the corners of her lovely eyes. *The Lord said:* **9.** 'O descendants of Kasyapa! How is it that you approach me putting so much trust in one who is but a harlot soliciting men? Wise men never trust wanton women. **10.** It is said that no lasting relationship can be forged with women who are ever in quest of new sex

श्रीशुक उवाच

इति ते क्ष्वेलितैस्तस्या आश्वस्तमनसोऽसुराः । जहसुर्भावगम्भीरं ददुश्चामृतभाजनम् ॥11॥
ततो गृहीत्वामृतभाजनं हरिर्बभाष ईषत्स्मितशोभया गिरा ।
यद्यभ्युपेतं क्व च साध्वसाधु वा कृतं मया वो विभजे सुधामिमाम् ॥12॥
इत्यभिव्याहृतं तस्या आकर्ण्यासुरपुङ्गवाः । अप्रमाणविदस्तस्यास्तत् तथेत्यन्वमंसत ॥13॥
अथोपोष्य कृतस्नाना हुत्वा च हविषानलम् । दत्त्वा गोविप्रभूतेभ्यः कृतस्वस्त्ययना द्विजैः ॥14॥
यथोपजोषं वासांसि परिधायाहतानि ते । कुशेषु प्राविशन् सर्वे प्रागग्रेष्वभिभूषिताः ॥15॥
प्राङ्मुखेषूपविष्टेषु सुरेषु दितिजेषु च । धूपामोदितशालायां जुष्टायां माल्यदीपकैः ॥16॥
तस्यां नरेन्द्र करभोरुरुशद्दुकूलश्रोणीतटालसगतिर्मदविह्वलाक्षी ।
सा कूजती कनकनूपुरशिञ्जितेन कुम्भस्तनी कलशपाणिरथाविवेश ॥17॥
तां श्रीसखीं कनककुण्डलचारुकर्णनासाकपोलवदनां परदेवताख्याम् ।
संवीक्ष्य सम्मुमुहुरुत्स्मितवीक्षणेन देवासुरा विगलितस्तनपट्टिकान्ताम् ॥18॥
असुराणां सुधादानं सर्पाणामिव दुर्नयम् । मत्वा जातिनृशंसानां न तां व्यभजदच्युतः ॥19॥
कल्पयित्वा पृथक् पङ्क्तीरुभयेषां जगत्पतिः । तांश्चोपवेशयामास स्वेषु स्वेषु च पङ्क्तिषु ॥20॥

experiences, and with wolves that are ever hungry.'

Sri Suka said: **11.** Their faith in her being reinforced by these teasing words, the Asuras laughed as a token of their deep confidence in her and handed over the Amrita to her. **12.** Hari received the vessel of Amrita and said with a smile: 'If you undertake to abide by my actions, irrespective of whether you consider them right or wrong, I shall agree to divide the Amrita among you.' **13.** Without realizing the implications, the Asuras agreed to the proposal of the charming maiden. **14-15.** As preparation for the sacred act of taking Amrita, the Asuras fasted for a day. Next morning they performed their oblations in the fire, fed all living beings high and low, received the blessings of holy men, put on new dress and ornaments, and sat on seats of Kusa grass arranged with the blade tips directed eastward. **16.** Both the Asuras and Devas sat facing eastward in readiness in a hall decorated with lights and flowers, and rendered fragrant by burning incense.

Asuras befooled (17-29)

17. O King! Into the hall now entered that handsome woman with vase-like breasts, holding the Amrita jar in hand. A brilliant cloth of silk draped the lower part of her body. Her tread was slow, and her eyes unsteady as if under inebriation, and the sweet sounds of her tinkling anklets announced her slow movement. **18.** As the Devas and Asuras smiled and looked carefully at that female form assumed by the Deity to match Srī Herself, they were stupefied with excitement to see her face illumined by ear ornaments and beautified by her handsome cheeks, ears and nose, and her torso from which the end of her clothes covering the breasts had slipped down.

19. It will be as unwise a policy to give Amrita to, and confer immortality on, the Asuras as on the cobras, who are both naturally cruel-hearted. So the Lord did not distribute the Amrita among these naturally depraved Asuras. **20.** The Lord made different seating arrangements for

दैत्यान् गृहीतकलशो वञ्चयन्नुपसञ्चरैः । दूरस्थान् पाययामास जरामृत्युहरां सुधाम् ॥21॥
ते पालयन्तः समयमसुराः स्वकृतं नृप । तूष्णीमासन् कृतस्नेहाः स्त्रीविवादजुगुप्सया ॥22॥
तस्यां कृतातिप्रणयाः प्रणयापायकातराः । बहुमानेन चाबद्धा नोचुः किञ्चन विप्रियम् ॥23॥
देवलिङ्गप्रतिच्छन्नः स्वर्भानुर्देवसंसदि । प्रविष्टः सोममपिबच्चन्द्रार्काभ्यां च सूचितः ॥24॥
चक्रेण क्षुरधारेण जहार पिबतः शिरः । हरिस्तस्य कबन्धस्तु सुधयाप्लावितोऽपतत् ॥25॥
शिरस्त्वमरतां नीतमजो ग्रहमचीक्लृपत् । यस्तु पर्वणि चन्द्रार्कावभिधावति वैरधीः ॥26॥
पीतप्रायेऽमृते देवैर्भगवाँल्लोकभावनः । पश्यतामसुरेन्द्राणां स्वं रूपं जगृहे हरिः ॥27॥

एवं सुरासुरगणाः समदेशकालहेत्वर्थकर्ममतयोऽपि फले विकल्पाः ।
तत्रामृतं सुरगणाः फलमञ्जसाऽऽपुर्यत्पादपङ्कजरजःश्रयणान्न दैत्याः ॥28॥
यद् युज्यतेऽसुवसुकर्ममनोवचोभिर्देहात्मजादिषु नृभिस्तदसत् पृथक्त्वात् ।
तैरेव सद् भवति यत् क्रियतेऽपृथक्त्वात् सर्वस्य तद् भवति मूलनिषेचनं यत् ॥29॥

इति श्रीमद्भागवते महापुराणे पारमहंस्यां संहितायामष्टमस्कन्धेऽमृतमथने नवमोऽध्यायः ॥ 9॥

the two parties and assigned to them seats in their respective rows. **21.** In order to hoodwink the Asuras, the Lord moved about in the rows of the Asuras with the Amrita vessel in hand and sweet words in His mouth, while he arranged to actually distribute that rejuvenating drink among the Devas who were sitting at a distance. **22.** O King! All the while the Asuras sat silently, honouring their agreement not to raise any dispute. Besides, their minds were fully taken up with infatuation for the maiden, and they also disliked to get the opprobrium of quarreling with a woman. **23.** Their lustful attachment to her was so great that they were afraid to do anything that might cause a breach in their relationship. Their respect for her was also a restraining factor. So they remained silent without making any adverse remarks.

24. But an Asura named Swarbhānu (otherwise known as Rāhu) went into the midst of the Devas disguised as one of them, and drank a share of Amrita. But his identity was soon discovered and revealed by the sun and the moon deities between whom he had sat. **25.** At once Hari cut off his head with his sharp discus. As the Amrita had gone only up to the neck above and not come into contact with the trunk, this lower portion of his body fell dead while the head remained immortal. **26.** The head, which thus gained eternal life, was converted by the Lord into a planet. Rāhu, who entertains antagonism to the moon and the sun deities for betraying him, assails them as eclipse on certain full-moon and new-moon days.

27. After the Devas had finished drinking the Amrita, the wonderful Lord, the protector of the worlds, assumed His real form in the view of the Asuras. **28.** In this way though the Devas and the Daityas started on a common enterprise, at the same time and place, and with the same motive, plan and objective, they got divergent results in the end, the Devas getting the Amrita to consume, and the Asuras nothing of it. By resignation to the Lord and devotion to Him, the Devas achieved this easily, but the Asuras failed in the final result (because they had no reliance on Him). **29.** Whatever service or sacrifice men perform with their life, wealth, work, mind and words for the sake of themselves and their dear ones—all these will be in vain in the last resort, because all such efforts are directed towards entities separate from the Divine. But all that becomes immensely fruitful, if the service is done to Him (or to others with the knowledge that those served are all the Lord's manifestation). It is like pouring water at the root of a tree, which is equal to watering the whole tree. Watering the leaves and branches serves no purpose.

अथ दशमोऽध्यायः

श्रीशुक उवाच

इति दानवदैतेया नाविन्दन्नमृतं नृप । युक्ताः कर्मणि यत्ताश्च वासुदेवपराङ्मुखाः ॥ 1॥
साधयित्वामृतं राजन् पाययित्वा स्वकान् सुरान् । पश्यतां सर्वभूतानां ययौ गरुडवाहनः ॥ 2॥
सपत्नानां परामृद्धिं दृष्ट्वा ते दितिनन्दनाः । अमृष्यमाणा उत्पेतुर्देवान् प्रत्युद्यतायुधाः ॥ 3॥
ततः सुरगणाः सर्वे सुधया पीतयैधिताः । प्रतिसंयुयुधुः शस्त्रैर्नारायणपदाश्रयाः ॥ 4॥
तत्र दैवासुरो नाम रणः परमदारुणः । रोधस्युदन्वतो राजंस्तुमुलो रोमहर्षणः ॥ 5॥
तत्रान्योन्यं सपत्नास्ते संरब्धमनसो रणे । समासाद्यासिभिर्बाणैर्निजघ्नुर्विविधायुधैः ॥ 6॥
शङ्खतूर्यमृदङ्गानां भेरीडमरिणां महान् । हस्त्यश्वरथपत्तीनां नदतां निस्वनोऽभवत् ॥ 7॥
रथिनो रथिभिस्तत्र पत्तिभिः सह पत्तयः । हया हयैरिभाश्चेभैः समसज्जन्त संयुगे ॥ 8॥
उष्ट्रैः केचिदिभैः केचिदपरे युयुधुः खरैः । केचिद् गौरमृगैर्ऋक्षैर्द्वीपिभिर्हरिभिर्भटाः ॥ 9॥

Skandha VIII : Chapter 10

WAR BETWEEN THE DEVAS AND THE ASURAS

Battle Scene described (1-15)

Sri Suka said: **1.** In this way, O King, the Daityas and the Danavas, in spite of their putting forth effort peacefully and enthusiastically, failed to achieve their object, because they had no devotion to Vāsudeva. **2.** After churning out the Amrita and enabling the Devas, His own devotees, to consume it, the Lord departed on his eagle-vehicle in the presence of all.

3. Now seeing the prosperity of the Devas, their enemies, the sons of Diti (the Asuras) became jealous beyond the point of control, and went to war with them. **4.** Thereupon all the Devas, who were resigned to the Lord Narayana and whose strength had been augmented by taking Amrita, took up arms and put up a defence against the attack of the Asuras. **5.** A fierce battle, tumultuous and hair-raising, took place between the Devas and the Asuras on the shore of the ocean. **6.** The ranks of the two enemies closed together in battle, and the warriors struck fiercely at one another with swords, arrows and various other kinds of weapons. **7.** The sound of martial music with instruments like conch shell, trumpets, Mridangas, drums and Damarus, augmented by the roar of the regiments of elephants, horses, chariots, and foot-soldiers—all together produced a terrific din. **8.** In the battle, chariots closed on chariots, elephants on elephants, horses on horses, and infantry on infantry. **9.** They fought sitting on various kinds of vehicles and mounts—some on camels, some on elephants, some on

गृध्रैः कङ्कैर्बकैरन्ये श्येनभासैस्तिमिङ्गिलैः । शरभैर्महिषैः खड्गैर्गोवृषैर्गवयारुणैः ॥10॥
शिवाभिराखुभिः केचित् कृकलासैः शशैर्नरैः । बस्तैरेके कृष्णसारैर्हंसैरन्ये च सूकरैः ॥11॥
अन्ये जलस्थलखगैः सत्त्वैर्विकृतविग्रहैः । सेनयोरुभयो राजन् विविशुस्तेऽग्रतोऽग्रतः ॥12॥
चित्रध्वजपटै राजन्नातपत्रैः सितामलैः । महाधनैर्वज्रदण्डैर्व्यजनैर्बार्हचामरैः ॥13॥
वातोद्धूतोत्तरोष्णीषैरर्चिर्भिर्वर्मभूषणैः । स्फुरद्भिर्विशदैः शस्त्रैः सुतरां सूर्यरश्मिभिः ॥14॥
देवदानववीराणां ध्वजिन्यौ पाण्डुनन्दन । रेजतुर्वीरमालाभिर्यादसामिव सागरौ ॥15॥
वैरोचनो बलिः संख्ये सोऽसुराणां चमूपतिः । यानं वैहायसं नाम कामगं मयनिर्मितम् ॥16॥
सर्वसांग्रामिकोपेतं सर्वाश्चर्यमयं प्रभो । अप्रतर्क्यमनिर्देश्यं दृश्यमानमदर्शनम् ॥17॥
आस्थितस्तद् विमानाग्र्यं सर्वानीकाधिपैर्वृतः । वालव्यजनछत्राग्र्यै रेजे चन्द्र इवोदये ॥18॥
तस्यासन् सर्वतो यानैर्यूथानां पतयोऽसुराः । नमुचिः शम्बरो बाणो विप्रचित्तिरयोमुखः ॥19॥
द्विमूर्धा कालनाभोऽथ प्रहेतिर्हेतिरिल्वलः । शकुनिर्भूतसन्तापो वज्रदंष्ट्रो विरोचनः ॥20॥
हयग्रीवः शङ्कुशिराः कपिलो मेघदुन्दुभिः । तारकश्चक्रदृक् शुम्भो निशुम्भो जम्भ उत्कलः 21॥
अरिष्टोऽरिष्टनेमिश्च मयश्च त्रिपुराधिपः । अन्ये पौलोमकालेया निवातकवचादयः ॥22॥
अलब्धभागाः सोमस्य केवलं क्लेशभागिनः । सर्व एते रणमुखे बहुशो निर्जितामराः ॥23॥

donkeys, some on Gours, some on bears, some on tigers, and some on lions. **10.** Some others had vultures, herons, cranes and falcons as vehicles; still others rode on whales, Sarabhas, buffaloes, rhinoceros, oxen, Gavayas and Arunas. **11.** Still others were riding on jackals, rats, chameleons, hares, men, goats, Krishnasāras, swans, and horses. **12.** Both sides closed up on the battle front—those described above and several others sitting on various kinds of birds living on land and waters, and on creatures shaped in curious ways. **13.** The battlefield was picturesque with clean and white royal umbrellas, banners of various designs, ceremonial fans of peacock feathers, and fly-whisks having handles studded with precious gems. **14.** It was impressive also by such features as the fluttering clothes and turbans of the warriors exposed to wind, the lustre of armours and ornaments and the sheen of weapons in the brilliant sun. **15.** O son of Pandu! The two armies of the Devas and Asuras looked like two oceans with rows and rows of aquatic creatures arrayed in confrontation.

Combats and Duels (16-40)

16-18. Bali, the son of Virochana and the leader of the Asuras, was seated in a unique aerial vehicle called Vaihāyasa, made by Maya. The vehicle was equipped with every kind of weapon and was possessed of features that are unimaginable and difficult to describe. It moved as one wanted; its movements could sometimes be seen and sometimes not seen. Surrounded by the commanders of the army and amidst an array of peacock feather fans and fly-whisks, he shone like the moon arising in the horizon. **19-23.** Among the Asura leaders who stood by Mahabali in their respective vehicles were the following: Namuchi, Sambara, Bāna, Viprachitti, Ayomukha, Dwimūrdhā, Kālanābha, Praheti, Heti, Ilvala, Sakuni, Bhūtasantāpa, Vajradamshtra, Virochana, Hayagrīva, Sankusiras, Kapila, Meghadundubhi, Tāraka, Chakradrik, Sumbha, Nisumbha, Jambha, Ulkala, Arishta, Arishtanemi, Maya the master of Tripura, Nivātakavachas, Kālakeyas and Paulomas. Being deprived of their share of Amrita,

सिंहनादान् विमुञ्चन्तः शङ्खान् दध्मुर्महारवान् । दृष्ट्वा सपत्नानुत्सिक्तान् बलभित् कुपितो भृशम् ।24
ऐरावतं दिक्करिणमारूढः शुशुभे स्वराट् । यथा स्रवत्प्रस्रवणमुदयाद्रिमहर्पतिः ।।25।।
तस्यासन् सर्वतो देवा नानावाहध्वजायुधाः । लोकपालाः सह गणैर्वाय्वग्निवरुणादयः ।।26।।
तेऽन्योन्यमभिसंसृत्य क्षिपन्तो मर्मभिर्मिथः । आह्वयन्तो विशन्तोऽग्रे युयुधुर्द्वन्द्वयोधिनः ।।27।।
युयोध बलिरिन्द्रेण तारकेण गुहोऽस्यत । वरुणो हेतिनायुध्यन्मित्रो राजन् प्रहेतिना ।।28।।
यमस्तु कालनाभेन विश्वकर्मा मयेन वै । शम्बरो युयुधे त्वष्ट्रा सवित्रा तु विरोचनः ।।29।।
अपराजितेन नमुचिरश्विनौ वृषपर्वणा । सूर्यो बलिसुतैर्देवो बाणज्येष्ठैः शतेन च ।।30।।
राहुणा च तथा सोमः पुलोम्ना युयुधेऽनिलः । निशुम्भशुम्भयोर्देवी भद्रकाली तरस्विनी ।।31।।
वृषाकपिस्तु जम्भेन महिषेण विभावसुः । इल्वलः सह वातापिर्ब्रह्मपुत्रैररिन्दम ।।32।।
कामदेवेन दुर्मर्ष उत्कलो मातृभिः सह । बृहस्पतिश्चोशनसा नरकेण शनैश्चरः ।।33।।
मरुतो निवातकवचैः कालेयैर्वसवोऽमराः । विश्वेदेवास्तु पौलोमै रुद्राः क्रोधवशैः सह ।।34।।

त एवमाजावसुराः सुरेन्द्रा द्वन्द्वेन संहत्य च युध्यमानाः ।
अन्योन्यमासाद्य निजघ्नुरोजसा जिगीषवस्तीक्ष्णशरासितोमरैः ।।35।।
भुशुण्डिभिश्चक्रगदर्ष्टिपट्टिशैः शक्त्युल्मुकैः प्रासपरश्वधैरपि ।
निस्त्रिंशभल्लैः परिघैः समुद्गरैः सभिन्दिपालैश्च शिरांसि चिच्छिदुः ।।36।।

and condemned to share only the trouble, these had all come to the battle, filled with the idea of defeating the Devas as they had done many times before.

24. Indra, the slayer of Bala, was all wrath to see these enemies inebriated with war lust, roaring like lions and lustily blowing their loud conch shells. **25.** Just as the morning sun ascends the Mountain of Sun-rise with rivers flowing on the sides, Indra mounted his white elephant Irāvata, which belonged to the species of the elephants of the quarters. **26.** Equipped with various weapons and seated in many kinds of vehicles, the Devas and the various guardian deities of the quarters like Vāyu, Agni and Varuna, stood by the side of Indra. **27.** On closing up they began at first to send at one another shafts of virulent abuse that cleaved vulnerable parts of one's being. The individuals from both parties, calling contestants by name, began to challenge one another for duels, and such warriors now came forward and engaged themselves in fight. **28.** Indra fought with Bali; Guha with Tāraka; Varuna with Heti; and Mitra with Praheti. **29.** Yama fought with Kālanābha, Viswakarma with Maya; Twashta with Sambara, and Savita with Virochana. **30.** Namuchi fought with Aparājita; the Aswins with Vrishaparva; and Sūrya with the hundred sons of Bali having Bāna as the eldest. **31.** Soma fought with Rāhu; Vāyu with Puloma; and the powerful Devi Bhadrakāli with Sumbha and Nisumbha. **32.** Siva fought with Jambha; Agni with Mahisha; the Marīchis, the sons of Brahma, with Ilvala and Vātāpi. **33.** Kāmadeva fought with Durmarsha; the Saptamātris with Ulkala; Sukra with Brihaspati; and Sani with Narakāsura. **34.** The Maruts fought with Nivātakavachas; the eight Vasus with Kālakeyas; Visvedevas with Paulomas; and the Rudras with Krodhavasas.

35. With their hearts fixed on victory in the duel, the Asuras and the leaders of the Devas closed in combat, and struck fiercely at one another with sharp arrows, swords and javelins. **36.** They chopped off the heads of opponents with various weap-

गजास्तुरङ्गाः सरथाः पदातयः सारोहवाहा विविधा विखण्डिताः ।
निकृत्तबाहूरुशिरोधराङ्घ्रयश्छिन्नध्वजेष्वासतनुत्रभूषणाः ॥37॥
तेषां पदाघातरथाङ्गचूर्णितादायोधनादुल्बण उत्थितस्तदा ।
रेणुर्दिशः खं द्युमणिं च छादयन् न्यवर्ततासृक्स्रुतिभिः परिप्लुतात् ॥38॥
शिरोभिरुद्धूतकिरीटकुण्डलैः संरम्भदृग्भिः परिदष्टदच्छदैः ।
महाभुजैः साभरणैः सहायुधैः सा प्रास्तृता भूः करभोरुभिर्बभौ ॥39॥

कबन्धास्तत्र चोत्पेतुः पतितस्वशिरोऽक्षिभिः । उद्यतायुधदोर्दण्डैराधावन्तो भटान् मृधे ॥40॥
बलिर्महेन्द्रं दशभिस्त्रिभिरैरावतं शरैः । चतुर्भिश्चतुरो वाहानेकेनारोहमार्च्छयत् ॥41॥
स तानापततः शक्रस्तावद्भिः शीघ्रविक्रमः । चिच्छेद निशितैर्भल्लैरसम्प्राप्तान् हसन्निव ॥42॥
तस्य कर्मोत्तमं वीक्ष्य दुर्मर्षः शक्तिमाददे । तां ज्वलन्तीं महोल्काभां हस्तस्थामच्छिनद्धरिः 43
ततः शूलं ततः प्रासं ततस्तोमरमृष्टयः । यद् यच्छस्त्रं समादद्यात् सर्वं तदच्छिनद् विभुः 44॥
ससर्जाथासुरीं मायामन्तर्धानगतोऽसुरः । ततः प्रादुरभूच्छैलः सुरानीकोपरि प्रभो ॥45॥
ततो निपेतुस्तरवो दह्यमाना दवाग्निना । शिलाः सटङ्कशिखराश्चूर्णयन्त्यो द्विषद्बलम् ॥46॥
महोरगाः समुत्पेतुर्दन्दशूकाः सवृश्चिकाः । सिंहव्याघ्रवराहाश्च मर्दयन्तो महागजान् ॥47॥

ons like Bhusundis, discuses, maces, lances, spears, javelins, fire-brands, tridents, axes, scimitars, Bhallas, iron clubs, hammers and Bhindipālas (catapults). **37**. The armies constituted of elephant regiments, chariot regiments, cavalry and infantry as also of men riding other kinds of mounts, gradually came to present a scene of warriors with limbs cut off and bodies mutilated, and with flagstaff, bows, armours and ornaments shattered to pieces. **38.** The clouds of dust raised by their tread and the rolling of the chariot wheels covered the skies, the quarters and the sun, but soon settled down on the earth, being wetted by the jets of blood that were being sprayed into the sky. **39.** That battle field was covered with scattered crowns and ear ornaments, with heads showing angry-looking eyes and bitten lips, with severed arms of huge size having ornaments and weapons, and with thighs resembling the trunks of elephants. **40.** Headless trunks seemed in their last struggle to continue rushing at enemies for attack with upraised arms, as if spotting them with the eyes that were still in their fallen heads!

Bali's magical Warfare (41-51)

41. Bali sought to strike Indra with ten arrows, his elephant Irāvata with three, the guards protecting the elephant's legs with four, and its keeper with one. **42.** Laughing,–Indra of abounding skill and courage, cut off all those arrows with counter-missiles even before they came anywhere near him. **43.** Unable to brook this superb feat of Indra, Bali now took a powerful javelin, shining like a fire-brand but Indra cut it to pieces even when it was still in Bali's hands. **44.** Bali then struck with several kinds of weapons one after another—trident, spear, javelin, Tomara (iron club) and Rishtis (double-edged swords)—but the highly skilled Indra shattered them all to pieces. **45.** O powerful King! Bali now took to the magical warfare of Asuras, and disappeared from sight. Soon a mountain appeared above the ranks of the Devas. **46.** From that mountain, trees set ablaze by the forest fire and rocks with sharp edges began to fall and pulverize the Deva army. **47.** Also

यातुधान्यश्च शतशः शूलहस्ता विवाससः । छिन्धि भिन्धीति वादिन्यस्तथा रक्षोगणाः प्रभो 48
ततो महाघना व्योम्नि गम्भीरपरुषस्वनाः । अङ्गारान् मुमुचुर्वातैराहताः स्तनयित्नवः ॥49॥
सृष्टो दैत्येन सुमहान् वह्निः श्वसनसारथिः । सांवर्तक इवात्युग्रो विबुधध्वजिनीमधाक् ॥50॥
ततः समुद्र उद्वेलः सर्वतः प्रत्यदृश्यत । प्रचण्डवातैरुद्धूततरङ्गावर्तभीषणः ॥51॥
एवं दैत्यैर्महामायैरलक्ष्यगतिभीषणैः । सृज्यमानासु मायासु विषेदुः सुरसैनिकाः ॥52॥
न तत्प्रतिविधिं यत्र विदुरिन्द्रादयो नृप । ध्यातः प्रादुरभूत् तत्र भगवान् विश्वभावनः ॥53॥

ततः सुपर्णांसकृताङ्घ्रिपल्लवः पिशङ्गवासा नवकञ्जलोचनः ।
अदृश्यताष्टायुधबाहुरुल्लसच्छ्रीकौस्तुभानर्घ्यकिरीटकुण्डलः ॥54॥
तस्मिन् प्रविष्टेऽसुरकूटकर्मजा माया विनेशुर्महिना महीयसः ।
स्वप्नो यथा हि प्रतिबोध आगते हरिस्मृतिः सर्वविपद्विमोक्षणम् ॥55॥
दृष्ट्वा मृधे गरुडवाहमिभारिवाह आविध्य शूलमहिनोदथ कालनेमिः ।
तल्लीलया गरुडमूर्ध्नि पतद् गृहीत्वा तेनाहनन्नृप सवाहमरिं त्र्यधीशः ॥56॥
माली सुमाल्यतिबलौ युधि पेततुर्यच्चक्रेण कृत्तशिरसावथ माल्यवांस्तम् ।
आहत्य तिग्मगदयाहनदण्डजेन्द्रं तावच्छिरोऽच्छिनदरेर्नदतोऽरिणाऽऽद्यः ॥57॥

इति श्रीमद्भागवते महापुराणे पारमहंस्यां संहितायामष्टमस्कन्धे देवासुरसङ्ग्रामे दशमोऽध्यायः ॥10॥

began a rain of pythons, fanged vipers, scorpions, lions and tigers and wild boars that caused devastation among the elephants. **48.** Rakshasa women, stark naked and carrying tridents, appeared in hundreds, while Rakshasas came in waves, crying, 'Cut, pierce' etc. **49.** Powerful winds brought in extensive clouds producing the deep roll of thunder and the brilliance of lightning and pouring rains of flaming cinder. **50.** The fire created by the magic of the Asura, fanned by powerful winds, became as fierce as the fire at the cosmic dissolution and threatened to burn up the whole army of the Devas. **51.** Next was seen everywhere the terror-inspiring ocean in spate, stirred by fierce winds into raging waves and deep whirlpools.

The Lord's Appearance (52-57)

52. When the Asuras, experts in magical devices and in concealed movement, released their magical skill as described, the leaders of the Devas felt utterly distressed. **53.** O King! Indra and others did not know how to ward off these magical attacks. So they meditated on Mahavishnu, the protector of all the worlds, and the worshipful Lord made His appearance there. **54.** The Devas saw Him arrive riding on His vehicle Garuda, with His feet attractive like tender shoots of leaves resting on Garuda's shoulders. Wearing a yellow cloth, with eyes like fresh lotus petals, and armed with weapons in His eight arms, He shone in the lustre of Srī situated on the chest, the jewel Kaustubha on His neck, the pendants on His ears, and the priceless diadem on His head. **55.** When the Lord came to the spot, all the magical phenomena produced by the black art of the Asuras vanished immediately, as phantoms of dream disappear when a person wakes up. Remembrance of Hari is the means of freedom from all dangers. **56.** When the Asura Kālanemi riding a lion saw the Lord Mahavishnu on the back of Garuda, he whirled the trident and threw it at Him. The Lord, who saw it falling on Garuda's head, caught hold of the trident with the utmost ease, and striking with it, He killed the Asura and his mount. **57.** Next He cut off the heads of two powerful Asuras, Māli and Sumāli, with His discus. Immediately Mālyavān came forward and aimed a mighty blow with his mace at the head of Garuda. But before the mace descended, the Lord decapitated this Asura too.

अथैकादशोऽध्याय:

श्रीशुक उवाच

अथो सुराः प्रत्युपलब्धचेतसः परस्य पुंसः परयानुकम्पया ।
जघ्नुर्भृशं शक्रसमीरणादयस्तांस्तान् रणे यैरभिसंहताः पुरा ॥ 1॥

वैरोचनाय संरब्धो भगवान् पाकशासनः । उदयच्छद् यदा वज्रं प्रजा हाहेति चुक्रुशुः ॥ 2॥
वज्रपाणिस्तमाहेदं तिरस्कृत्य पुरःस्थितम् । मनस्विनं सुसम्पन्नं विचरन्तं महामृधे ॥ 3॥
नटवन्मूढ मायाभिर्मायेशान् नो जिगीषसि । जित्वा बालान् निबद्धाक्षान् नटो हरति तद्धनम् 4॥
आरुरुक्षन्ति मायाभिरुत्सिसृप्सन्ति ये दिवम् । तान् दस्यून् विधुनोम्यज्ञान् पूर्वस्माच्च पदादधः 5।
सोऽहं दुर्मायिनस्तेऽद्य वज्रेण शतपर्वणा । शिरो हरिष्ये मन्दात्मन् घटस्व ज्ञातिभिः सह ॥ 6॥

बलिरुवाच

संग्रामे वर्तमानानां कालचोदितकर्मणाम् । कीर्तिर्जयोऽजयो मृत्युः सर्वेषां स्युरनुक्रमात् ॥ 7॥
तदिदं कालरशनं जनाः पश्यन्ति सूरयः । न हृष्यन्ति न शोचन्ति तत्र यूयमपण्डिताः ॥ 8॥

Skandha VIII : Chapter 11

TRIUMPH OF THE DEVAS

Contest of Indra and Bali (1-12)

Sri Suka said: **1.** By the infinite grace of the Lord, Indra, Vāyu and the other Devas recovered their mental and physical power and struck their opponents again with volleys of arrows. **2.** The powerful Indra, now enraged, raised his thunderbolt weapon against Bali, the son of Virochana. Seeing that, all people raised the cry of alarm 'Ah! Ah!'. **3.** In derision of the bold and well equipped Bali, who was moving about in the battle front, Indra said with the thunderbolt weapon in hand: **4.** 'O fool! Did you think that by your jugglery you could defeat us, the masters of illusory devices, just as a trickster plunders children after blindfolding them? **5.** I shall hurl still further down from their present situation those foolish persons who attempt to capture and surpass the heavenly region by their magical tricks. **6.** You fool of a perverse sorcerer! I shall have your head cut off today with my thunderbolt weapon of a hundred joints. If you can, defend yourself with all your tribes.'

Bali replied: **7.** People engage themselves in war under the prompting of their collective Karma, brought together by the power of Time, and to everyone so engaged, fame, success, defeat and death can occur by turns according to that Karma. Therefore, neither victory nor defeat is permanent with any party. **8.** Wise men find the regulating influence

न वयं मन्यमानानामात्मानं तत्र साधनम् । गिरो वः साधुशोच्यानां गृह्णीमो मर्मताडनाः ॥ 9॥

श्रीशुक उवाच

इत्याक्षिप्य विभुं वीरो नाराचैर्वीरमर्दनः । आकर्णपूर्णैरहनदाक्षेपैराहतं पुनः ॥10॥
एवं निराकृतो देवो वैरिणा तथ्यवादिना । नामृष्यत् तदधिक्षेपं तोत्राहत इव द्विपः ॥11॥
प्राहरत् कुलिशं तस्मा अमोघं परमर्दनः । सयानो न्यपतद् भूमौ छिन्नपक्ष इवाचलः ॥12॥
सखायं पतितं दृष्ट्वा जम्भो बलिसखः सुहृत् । अभ्ययात् सौहृदं सख्युर्हतस्यापि समाचरन् ॥13॥
स सिंहवाह आसाद्य गदामुद्यम्य रंहसा । जत्रावताडयच्छक्रं गजं च सुमहाबलः ॥14॥
गदाप्रहारव्यथितो भृशं विह्वलितो गजः । जानुभ्यां धरणीं स्पृष्ट्वा कश्मलं परमं ययौ ॥15॥
ततो रथो मातलिना हरिभिर्दशशतैर्वृतः । आनीतो द्विपमुत्सृज्य रथमारुरुहे विभुः ॥16॥
तस्य तत् पूजयन् कर्म यन्तुर्दानवसत्तमः । शूलेन ज्वलता तं तु स्मयमानोऽहनन्मृधे ॥17॥
सेहे रुजं सुदुर्मर्षां सत्त्वमालम्ब्य मातलिः । इन्द्रो जम्भस्य संक्रुद्धो वज्रेणापाहरच्छिरः ॥18॥
जम्भं श्रुत्वा हतं तस्य ज्ञातयो नारदादृषेः । नमुचिश्च बलः पाकस्तत्रापेतुस्त्वरान्विताः ॥19॥
वचोभिः परुषैरिन्द्रमर्दयन्तोऽस्य मर्मसु । शरैरवाकिरन् मेघा धाराभिरिव पर्वतम् ॥20॥

of Time in all these matters. They, therefore, are not elated or depressed in success or failure. You seem to be ignorant of all this. **9.** We do not therefore attach much importance to your piercing words of abuse. You who think yourself to be the master of your destiny without taking the factor of Time into consideration will be the object of pity for wise men.

Sri Suka said: **10.** Having thus rebuked the powerful Indra with piercing and deadly words, Bali, who was equal to any heroic warrior, followed his speech with a volley of arrows drawn up to the ear. **11.** This rebuff given by the truth-speaking Bali, was too much for Indra to bear, as the application of the goad is to an elephant. **12.** Indra, the destroyer of foes, now struck Bali with his never-failing thunderbolt weapon, whereupon Bali fell on the ground along with his aerial vehicle, like a mountain whose wings have been clipped.

Attack and Fall of Jambha (13-18)

13. Jambha, a friend and well-wisher of Bali, now rushed to the aid of his fallen friend to do whatever service he could to him. **14.** Seated on a lion, he rushed to Indra with a mace in hand, and delivered a powerful blow on Indra and on his elephant-mount Irāvata below its neck. **15.** The elephant Irāvata sustained severe injuries by the stroke of the mace, and fell down on its knees in utter distress. **16.** Thereupon, Mātali, the charioteer of Indra, brought his chariot to which a thousand horses were attached. Indra now left the elephant and got into this chariot. **17.** Jambha, the great Asura leader, while appreciating with a smile the timely action of Mātali in bringing the chariot, none the less darted a flaming spear at him. **18.** The weapon caused unbearable pain to Mātali, which he somehow stood with the help of all the fortitude at his command. Roused to great anger, Indra now cut off the head of Jambha with his thunderbolt weapon.

Attack of Namuchi, Bala, Pāka (19-36)

19. Hearing about the death of Jambha from the sage Narada, his relatives Namuchi, Bala and Pāka arrived at the spot immediately. **20.** After subjecting

हरीन् दशशतान्याजौ हर्यश्वस्य बलः शरैः । तावद्भिरर्दयामास युगपल्लघुहस्तवान् ॥21॥
शताभ्यां मातलिं पाको रथं सावयवं पृथक् । सकृत्सन्धानमोक्षेण तदद्भुतमभूद् रणे ॥22॥
नमुचिः पञ्चदशभिः स्वर्णपुङ्खैर्महेषुभिः । आहत्य व्यनदत् संख्ये सतोय इव तोयदः ॥23॥
सर्वतः शरकूटेन शक्रं सरथसारथिम् । छादयामासुरसुराः प्रावृट्सूर्यमिवाम्बुदाः ॥24॥
अलक्षयन्तस्तमतीव विह्वला विचुक्रुशुर्देवगणाः सहानुगाः ।
अनायकाः शत्रुबलेन निर्जिता वणिक्पथा भिन्ननवो यथार्णवे ॥25॥
ततस्तुराषाडिषुबद्धपञ्जराद् विनिर्गतः साश्वरथध्वजाग्रणीः ।
बभौ दिशः खं पृथिवीं च रोचयन् स्वतेजसा सूर्य इव क्षपात्यये ॥26॥
निरीक्ष्य पृतनां देवः परैरभ्यर्दितां रणे । उदयच्छद् रिपुं हन्तुं वज्रं वज्रधरो रुषा ॥27॥
स तेनैवाष्टधारेण शिरसी बलपाकयोः । ज्ञातीनां पश्यतां राजञ्जहार जनयन् भयम् ॥28॥
नमुचिस्तद्वधं दृष्ट्वा शोकामर्षरुषान्वितः । जिघांसुरिन्द्रं नृपते चकार परमोद्यमम् ॥29॥
अश्मसारमयं शूलं घण्टावद्धेमभूषणम् । प्रगृह्याभ्यद्रवत् क्रुद्धो हतोऽसीति वितर्जयन् ।
प्राहिणोद् देवराजाय निनदन् मृगराडिव ॥30॥
तदापतद् गगनतले महाजवं विचिच्छिदे हरिरिषुभिः सहस्रधा ।
तमाहनन्नृप कुलिशेन कन्धरे रुषान्वितस्त्रिदशपतिः शिरो हरन् ॥31॥

Indra to a volley of abusive words, they showered on him arrows as clouds rain on mountains. **21.** Bala swiftly attacked and wounded at one stroke the thousand horses of Indra's chariot. **22.** The Asura Pāka simultaneously released numerous arrows at Mātali and at the chariot with its several parts. He aimed all these arrows at the same moment, which was the most wonderful feat in that battle. **23.** Namuchi shot at Indra fifteen powerful arrows with golden shafts, and raised a howl that resembled the rumbling of a rain-laden cloud. **24.** All the Asuras together hid Indra, his charioteer and chariot in a thick veil of arrows, making them invisible like the sun covered by the clouds in the rainy season. **25.** Thereupon, attacked by the enemy to the point of defeat, leaderless, and distressed in the extreme, the Devas and their following began to cry aloud like a company of merchants on board a wrecked ship. **26.** But soon enough, Indra came out of that cage of arrows together with his chariot, its charioteer, flag staff and the horses, and like the sun at the end of night, illumined the sky, the earth and all the quarters by his brilliance. **27.** Seeing that his army was being harassed on all sides by the enemy, Indra in great wrath took the thunderbolt weapon to kill them. **28.** With that weapon, having eight sharp edges, Indra cut off the heads of Bala and Pāka, creating great fear in the minds of their friends and relatives who witnessed the scene.

29. Namuchi was very much inflamed with anger and sorrow at the death of the above Asura leaders and now made an all-out effort to kill Indra. **30.** Armed with a lance of very hard iron embellished with gold decorations and bells, he charged, roaring out in great wrath like a lion, 'You are dead!' **31.** That weapon released by him and advancing rapidly, was cut in the sky itself into innumerable bits by Indra with his arrows. Then he struck at Namuchi's neck with his Vajra, the thunderbolt weapon, with a view to

न तस्य हि त्वचमपि वज्र ऊर्जितो बिभेद यः सुरपतिनौजसेरितः ।
तदद्भुतं परमतिवीर्यवृत्रभित् तिरस्कृतो नमुचिशिरोधरत्वचा ॥32॥

तस्मादिन्द्रोऽबिभेच्छत्रोर्वज्रः प्रतिहतो यतः । किमिदं दैवयोगेन भूतं लोकविमोहनम् ॥33॥
येन मे पूर्वमद्रीणां पक्षच्छेदः प्रजात्यये । कृतो निविशतां भारैः पतत्त्रैः पततां भुवि ॥34॥
तपःसारमयं त्वाष्ट्रं वृत्रो येन विपाटितः । अन्ये चापि बलोपेताः सर्वास्त्रैरक्षतत्वचः ॥35॥
सोऽयं प्रतिहतो वज्रो मया मुक्तोऽसुरेऽल्पके । नाहं तदाददे दण्डं ब्रह्मतेजोऽप्यकारणम् ॥36॥
इति शक्रं विषीदन्तमाह वागशरीरिणी । नायं शुष्कैरथो नार्द्रैर्वधमर्हति दानवः ॥37॥
मयास्मै यद् वरो दत्तो मृत्युर्नैवार्द्रशुष्कयोः । अतोऽन्यश्चिन्तनीयस्ते उपायो मघवन् रिपोः ॥38॥
तां दैवीं गिरमाकर्ण्य मघवान् सुसमाहितः । ध्यायन् फेनमथापश्यदुपायमुभयात्मकम् ॥39॥
न शुष्केण न चार्द्रेण जहार नमुचेः शिरः । तं तुष्टुवुर्मुनिगणा माल्यैश्चावाकिरन् विभुम् ॥40॥
गन्धर्वमुख्यौ जगतुर्विश्वावसुपरावसू । देवदुन्दुभयो नेदुर्नर्तक्यो ननृतुर्मुदा ॥41॥
अन्येऽप्येवं प्रतिद्वन्द्वान् वाय्वग्निवरुणादयः । सूदयामासुरस्त्रौघैर्मृगान् केसरिणो यथा ॥42॥

put an end to him. **32.** But lo! Though struck by Indra with all his force, the weapon could not hurt even the skin. It was indeed a wonder that the powerful Vajra, which killed even the mighty Vritra, was rebuffed by the mere skin of Namuchi's neck. **33.** When the thunderbolt weapon was thus repelled by the enemy, Indra was filled with great fear, and thought: 'The power of Prarabdha (the operative Karma) is indeed very great! Otherwise how could this astounding phenomenon, the failure of the thunderbolt weapon, take place? **34.** It was with this weapon that I once clipped off the wings of the mountains which used to move about on their wings and fall down here and there due to their weight, causing destruction in human settlements. **35.** It was with this weapon that I destroyed Vritra, who was the embodiment of the power of Twashta's austerities, as also other powerful Asuras whose skin even could not be scratched by other powerful missiles. **36.** That thunderbolt weapon has now been found ineffective when used by me against this most insignificant fellow of an Asura. Even the superior Brahmic power of Rishi Dadhīchi (which this weapon is) has proved to be worthless. It is a mere stick, which I shall not touch hereafter!'

Victory of Indra (37-48)

37. When Indra was thus lamenting grief-stricken, he heard a divine disembodied voice telling: 'This Asura cannot be killed by anything that is dry or anything that is moist. **38.** I had given this Asura the boon that he could not be killed by any weapon made of dry or moist substance. So, O Indra, think of some other means of dealing with this enemy.' **39.** After hearing this divine voice, Indra meditated with a concentrated mind, and came to find in foam a suitable weapon that is both dry and moist. **40.** It was thus with foam, which cannot be called exclusively dry nor exclusively watery, that the powerful Indra finally cut off the head of Namuchi, drawing the praise of Munis and the rain of flowers they showered on him. **41.** The chiefs and Gandharvas named Viswāvasu and Parāvasu sang. The kettle-drums of the celestials sounded and the Apsara women danced in great joy. **42.** Meanwhile, the other Deva leaders like Vāyu, Agni and

ब्रह्मणा प्रेषितो देवान् देवर्षिर्नारदो नृप । वारयामास विबुधान् दृष्ट्वा दानवसंक्षयम् ॥43॥

नारद उवाच

भवद्भिरमृतं प्राप्तं नारायणभुजाश्रयैः । श्रिया समेधिताः सर्व उपारमत विग्रहात् ॥44॥

श्रीशुक उवाच

संयम्य मन्युसंरम्भं मानयन्तो मुनेर्वचः । उपगीयमानानुचरैर्ययुः सर्वे त्रिविष्टपम् ॥45॥
येऽवशिष्टा रणे तस्मिन् नारदानुमतेन ते । बलिं विपन्नमादाय अस्तं गिरिमुपागमन् ॥46॥
तत्राविनष्टावयवान् विद्यमानशिरोधरान् । उशना जीवयामास संजीविन्या स्वविद्यया ॥47॥
बलिश्चोशनसा स्पृष्टः प्रत्यापन्नेन्द्रियस्मृतिः । पराजितोऽपि नाखिद्यल्लोकतत्त्वविचक्षणः ॥48॥

इति श्रीमद्भागवते महापुराणे पारमहंस्यां संहितायामष्टमस्कन्धे देवासुरसंग्रामे एकादशोऽध्यायः ॥11॥

Varuna killed their opponents with showers of arrows, as the lion kills deer. **43.** Seeing that the whole tribe of Asuras was about to perish, Brahma now sent the sage Narada to intervene, and the sage stopped the Devas from continuing that destructive war. *Narada said*: **44.** 'By depending on the protective arms of Narayana, you have got the Amrita. And by the gracious glance of Sri Hari, you have been blessed with plenty and prosperity. Now stop the battle.'

Sri Suka said: **45.** Honouring the words of the Rishi, the Devas controlled their anger, and stopped the battle. To the accompaniment of the panegyrics sung by their camp followers, all the Devas returned to their heavenly abode. **46.** With the permission of Narada, the remaining Asuras went to the western Mountain of Sunset, carrying with them Bali who was in a precarious condition from the impact of the thunderbolt weapon. **47.** Then all the Asuras whose bodies had not lost the head and limbs, were revived by the Acharya Sukra who had knowledge of that art. **48.** Touched by Sukra, Bali too got back the power of the senses and memory. Though defeated, he did not grieve, as he was a philosopher knowing the evanescent nature of the world and the life in it.

अथ द्वादशोऽध्यायः

श्रीबादरायणिरुवाच

वृषध्वजो निशम्येदं योषिद्रूपेण दानवान् । मोहयित्वासुरगणान् हरिः सोममपाययत् ॥ 1॥
वृषमारुह्य गिरिशः सर्वभूतगणैर्वृतः । सह देव्या ययौ द्रष्टुं यत्रास्ते मधुसूदनः ॥ 2॥

Skandha VIII : Chapter 12

INCARNATION AS THE MOHINI

Siva's Curiosity about Mohini (1-3)

Sri Suka said: **1-2.** Sri Parameswara, who has a bull as his vehicle, heard that assuming the form of a woman, Mahavishnu deluded the Asuras and helped the Devas to consume Amrita. Desirous of meeting Him, Lord Siva started on his bull to the spot where Madhusūdana was. He was accompanied by the Devi and

सभाजितो भगवता सादरं सोमया भवः। सूपविष्ट उवाचेदं प्रतिपूज्य स्मयन् हरिम् ॥ 3॥

श्रीमहादेव उवाच

देवदेव जगद्व्यापिञ्जगदीश जगन्मय। सर्वेषामपि भावानां त्वमात्मा हेतुरीश्वरः ॥ 4॥
आद्यन्तावस्य यन्मध्यमिदमन्यदहं बहिः। यतोऽव्ययस्य नैतानि तत् सत्यं ब्रह्म चिद् भवान् 5॥
तवैव चरणाम्भोजं श्रेयस्कामा निराशिषः। विसृज्योभयतः सङ्गं मुनयः समुपासते ॥ 6॥
त्वं ब्रह्म पूर्णममृतं विगुणं विशोकमानन्दमात्रमविकारमनन्यदन्यत्।
विश्वस्य हेतुरुदयस्थितिसंयमानामात्मेश्वरश्च तदपेक्षतयानपेक्षः ॥ 7॥
एकस्त्वमेव सदसद् द्वयमद्वयं च स्वर्णं कृताकृतमिवेह न वस्तुभेदः।
अज्ञानतस्त्वयि जनैर्विहितो विकल्पो यस्माद् गुणैर्व्यतिकरो निरुपाधिकस्य ॥ 8॥
त्वां ब्रह्म केचिदवयन्त्युत धर्ममेके एके परं सदसतोः पुरुषं परेशम्।
अन्येऽवयन्ति नवशक्तियुतं परं त्वां केचिन्महापुरुषमव्ययमात्मतन्त्रम् ॥ 9॥

surrounded by his retinue of goblins. **3.** Bhava, along with Uma, was warmly welcomed and worshipped by the Lord and was seated on a worthy seat. Parameswara also honoured him in return, and then addressed Hari with a smile expressive of wonder.

The Hymn by Siva (4-11)

Sri Mahadeva said: **4.** O Lord of all Devas! Thou all-pervading Being, Lord of all, and the world embodied! Thou art the source and the soul of all beings as also their controller. **5.** He who is the origin, the middle and the finale of this manifested universe; He who is also the changeless Being to whom such states as origination, continuation and end are inapplicable; He who is both the subject 'I' and the object 'this', both the enjoyer and the enjoyed—that Brahman, the Truth, the Pure Consciousness, Thou art. **6.** The sages who have no desire for enjoyment and care only for liberation, abandoning attachments for everything in this world and in the hereafter, devote themselves to the contemplation of Thy feet. **7.** Thou art the full, the immortal, the immaterial, the sorrowless, and the changeless Being. Thou art pure Bliss, the Being that is all-inclusive yet transcendent. Though Thou art thus the Absolute, Thou art also relational—the cause of the universe, that in which it arises, subsists and dissolves, the soul of all beings and their Lord. All beings depend on Thee, but Thou on none. **8.** Thou art the one without a second, manifesting at the same time as the world of cause and effect and remaining as the non-dual unrelated Substance. It is like the one gold, manifesting as various objects made of it, and as their cause, the substance gold. There is no difference as far as the causal substance is concerned in both its conditions. It is due to ignorance that people speak of the substance and the forms taking shape from it as different. In the same way the duality attributed to Thee, who art really without any limitation, is due to ignorance born of the play of the Gunas.

9. The Vedantins speak of Thee as Brahman, the all-inclusive Absolute Being, and the Mīmāmsakas as Dharma. The Sānkhyas look upon Thee as the Supreme Being transcending Prakriti and Purusha. The Pāncharātrins call Thee the Purushottama, the transcendent Divine Person with nine powers; and the Yogins look upon Thee as the Great Purusha, eternally free and independent.

नाहं परायुर्ऋषयो न मरीचिमुख्या जानन्ति यद्विरचितं खलु सत्त्वसर्गाः ।
यन्मायया मुषितचेतस ईश दैत्यमर्त्यादयः किमुत शश्वदभद्रवृत्ताः ॥10॥
स त्वं समीहितमदःस्थितिजन्मनाशं भूतेहितं च जगतो भवबन्धमोक्षौ ।
वायुर्यथा विशति खं च चराचराख्यं सर्वं तदात्मकतयावगमोऽवरुन्त्से ॥11॥
अवतारा मया दृष्टा रममाणस्य ते गुणैः । सोऽहं तद् द्रष्टुमिच्छामि यत् ते योषिद्वपुर्धृतम् 12॥
येन सम्मोहिता दैत्याः पायिताश्चामृतं सुराः । तद् दिदृक्षव आयाताः परं कौतूहलं हि नः ॥13॥

श्रीशुक उवाच

एवमभ्यर्थितो विष्णुर्भगवान् शूलपाणिना । प्रहस्य भावगम्भीरं गिरिशं प्रत्यभाषत ॥14॥

श्रीभगवानुवाच

कौतूहलाय दैत्यानां योषिद्वेषो मया कृतः । पश्यता सुरकार्याणि गते पीयूषभाजने ॥15॥
तत्तेऽहं दर्शयिष्यामि दिदृक्षोः सुरसत्तम । कामिनां बहु मन्तव्यं सङ्कल्पप्रभवोदयम् ॥16॥

श्रीशुक उवाच

इति ब्रुवाणो भगवांस्तत्रैवान्तरधीयत । सर्वतश्चारयंश्चक्षुर्भव आस्ते सहोमया ॥17॥
ततो ददर्शोपवने वरस्त्रियं विचित्रपुष्पारुणपल्लवद्रुमे ।
विक्रीडतीं कन्दुकलीलया लसद्दुकूलपर्यस्तनितम्बमेखलाम् ॥18॥

10. Neither I nor Brahma nor the Sattva-born sages like Marīchi, who are all under the spell of Thy Maya, are able to know much even about Thy creation. There is no need then to speak about the state of Asuras and men who are given to impure ways of life. **11.** Only Thou, being pure intelligence and the soul of all, are endowed with the knowledge of Thy own works of creation, preservation and dissolution of the worlds, and of the working of all creatures and the problem of their bondage and liberation. For just as air has entered into all moving and unmoving bodies and into all space, even so Thou indwellest everything as the all-pervading Spirit.

Siva's Vision of Mohini (12-21)

12-13. I have had occasions to see many incarnations of Thine in which Thou didst manifest assuming qualities like love of devotees. But now I wish to see Thee in that womanly form, with which Thou didst charm the Asuras and enable the Devas to consume the Amrita. I have a great desire to see that form, and I have come here for that purpose.

Sri Suka said: **14.** On being so requested by the trident-armed Parameswara, the Supreme Lord Mahavishnu replied with a deeply meaningful smile to that Lord of the Mountains. *The worshipful Lord said:* **15.** 'When the pot of Amrita was lost, I had to help the Devas to get it back by exciting the Asuras into a mood of delusion. **16.** O the greatest of Divinities! I shall show you that form which has excited sex passion in people and commanded the respect of those who are inclined in this direction.'

Sri Suka said: **17.** Saying this much, the Lord disappeared and Parameswara stood there with Uma, casting his glances in the four directions. **18.** Presently he saw before him a garden full of trees in blossom and with shoots of tender leaves of pink colour, and in the midst of it an attractive lady playing ball. She had the noble appearance of a high-born lady, was dressed in silk, and had a golden girdle round her

आवर्तनोद्वर्तनकम्पितस्तनप्रकृष्टहारोरुभरैः पदे पदे ।
प्रभज्यमानामिव मध्यतश्चलत्पदप्रवालं नयतीं ततस्ततः ॥19॥
दिक्षु भ्रमत्कन्दुकचापलैर्भृशं प्रोद्विग्नतारायतलोललोचनाम् ।
स्वकर्णविभ्राजितकुण्डलोल्लसत्कपोलनीलालकमण्डिताननाम् ॥20॥
श्लथद् दुकूलं कबरीं च विच्युतां सन्नह्यतीं वामकरेण वल्गुना ।
विनिघ्नतीमन्यकरेण कन्दुकं विमोहयन्तीं जगदात्ममायया ॥21॥
तां वीक्ष्य देव इति कन्दुकलीलयेषद्व्रीडास्फुटस्मितविसृष्टकटाक्षमुष्टः ।
स्त्रीप्रेक्षणप्रतिसमीक्षणविह्वलात्मा नात्मानमन्तिक उमां स्वगणांश्च वेद ॥22॥
तस्याः कराग्रात् स तु कन्दुको यदा गतो विदूरं तमनुव्रजत्स्त्रियाः ।
वासः ससूत्रं लघु मारुतोऽहरद् भवस्य देवस्य किलानुपश्यतः ॥23॥
एवं तां रुचिरापाङ्गीं दर्शनीयां मनोरमाम् । दृष्ट्वा तस्यां मनश्चक्रे विषज्जन्त्यां भवः किल ॥24॥
तयापहृतविज्ञानस्तत्कृतस्मरविह्वलः । भवान्या अपि पश्यन्त्या गतह्रीस्तत्पदं ययौ ॥25॥
सा तमायान्तमालोक्य विवस्त्रा व्रीडिता भृशम् । निलीयमाना वृक्षेषु हसन्ती नान्वतिष्ठत ॥26॥
तामन्वगच्छद् भगवान् भवः प्रमुषितेन्द्रियः । कामस्य च वशं नीतः करेणुमिव यूथपः ॥27॥

waist. **19.** As she took each step with her tender legs while pursuing the up and down movements of the ball, now stooping, now lifting up her body, it appeared that her slender middle region would break under the weight of her tremulous breasts and the precious pearl necklaces on her neck. **20.** The pupils of her long and quivering eyes moved excitedly and fast in pursuit of the unpredictable ball straying in different directions and the beauty of her face was enhanced by her bluish curls and by the luminous reflection of her ear-pendant on her smooth cheeks. **21.** The inherent charm she displayed as she held her loosening cloth and braids with her handsome left hand while striking the ball with the other, was sufficient to blind the whole world with excitement.

Siva under Infatuation (22-36)

22. That Divinity was completely carried away as the damsel cast at him a glance accompanied by a bashful smile, soft yet clearly visible, on being watched while at her game of ball. Agitated in mind by the woman's side-long glance and his own return look at her, he forgot himself, his consort Uma standing by, and his followers, the goblins. **23.** Now the ball sped away to some distance from her hand, and as she was following it, the wind, it seems, carried away her light wearing cloth along with the decorative girdle she had over it, thus exposing her to the view of Sri Rudra.

24. Seeing her attractive glances and enchanting beauty, Sri Rudra is said to have gazed at her with extreme longing, especially seeing that she was requiting his attention. **25.** His discriminative power plundered by her, and his sex passion distressingly stimulated, he ran shamelessly towards that charming damsel, in spite of his consort Uma watching him. **26.** Seeing him approaching, the damsel felt all the more bashful in her nakedness, and flitted about laughing, from tree to tree to take cover behind them. **27.** But Sri Rudra pursued her as a bull elephant its cow, being enslaved by Cupid and

सोऽनुव्रज्यातिवेगेन गृहीत्वानिच्छतीं स्त्रियम् । केशबन्ध उपानीय बाहुभ्यां परिषस्वजे ॥28॥
सोपगूढा भगवता करिणा करिणी यथा । इतस्ततः प्रसर्पन्ती विप्रकीर्णशिरोरुहा ॥29॥
आत्मानं मोचयित्वाङ्ग सुरर्षभभुजान्तरात् । प्राद्रवत् सा पृथुश्रोणी माया देवविनिर्मिता ॥30॥
तस्यासौ पदवीं रुद्रो विष्णोरद्भुतकर्मणः । प्रत्यपद्यत कामेन वैरिणेव विनिर्जितः ॥31॥
तस्यानुधावतो रेतश्चस्कन्दामोघरेतसः । शुष्मिणो यूथपस्येव वासितामनु धावतः ॥32॥
यत्र यत्रापतन्मह्यां रेतस्तस्य महात्मनः । तानि रूप्यस्य हेम्नश्च क्षेत्राण्यासन् महीपते ॥33॥
सरित्सरस्सु शैलेषु वनेषूपवनेषु च । यत्र क्व चासन्नृषयस्तत्र संनिहितो हरः ॥34॥
स्कन्ने रेतसि सोऽपश्यदात्मानं देवमायया । जडीकृतं नृपश्रेष्ठ संन्यवर्तत कश्मलात् ॥35॥
अथावगतमाहात्म्य आत्मनो जगदात्मनः । अपरिज्ञेयवीर्यस्य न मेने तदु हाद्भुतम् ॥36॥
तमविक्लवमव्रीडमालक्ष्य मधुसूदनः । उवाच परमप्रीतो बिभ्रत् स्वां पौरुषीं तनुम् ॥37॥

श्रीभगवानुवाच

दिष्टया त्वं विबुधश्रेष्ठ स्वां निष्ठामात्मना स्थितः । यन्मे स्त्रीरूपया स्वैरं मोहितोऽप्यङ्ग मायया ॥38॥
को नु मेऽतितरेन्मायां विषक्तस्त्वदृते पुमान् । तांस्तान् विसृजतीं भावान् दुस्तरामकृतात्मभिः 39
सेयं गुणमयी माया न त्वामभिभविष्यति । मया समेता कालेन कालरूपेण भागशः ॥40॥

deprived of all control over his senses. **28.** Chasing her, Rudra caught hold of her hair, and embraced her even without her consent. **29-30.** Caught in Siva's embrace like a cow elephant in the bull's, she, who was none but the Lord's Maya embodied, struggled in his arms and released herself by force. In spite of her heavy hips, she ran here and there quickly with dishevelled hair. **31.** Rudra now closely followed the footsteps of the running Mahavishnu of wonderful deeds. It looked as if Rudra, who was already under the Cupid's influence, was now routed and completely under the enemy's domination. **32.** As he followed her as an excited bull elephant does a cow in heat, his potent semen dropped on the ground. **33.** O King! Wherever on the earth the semen of the great divinity dropped, those places became silver and gold mines. **34.** Siva thus pursued her wherever Rishis were staying—on the banks of rivers and lakes, in woodlands, forests and mountains, as if to demonstrate to them by example of the need for guarding against exposure to sexual charms. **35.** When his semen was ejaculated, he realised how the Lords's Maya had completely stupefied him. He now recovered from that infatuation. **36.** Siva was not at all struck with wonder at the unusual events. For he well understood the unique power of Mahavishnu, the soul of the world, and that of his own in relation to Him—how He, the Lord, is the director, and himself only the directed.

Reflections on the Incident (37-47)

37. Seeing Siva serene, free from any shock of sin, Mahavishnu, who now assumed His real form, was very much pleased and spoke to Him. *The Lord said*: **38.** 'O great divinity and my dear friend! It is a very fortunate circumstance that in spite of being completely infatuated by my deluding power in the form of the charming damsel, you have by your own discrimination been able to overcome it and recover your natural state of desirelessness. **39.** Who except you is there among those of subdued senses that can, after having once come under its spell, overcome My Maya, which generates various passions like desire, anger, greed etc. in the heart? **40.** This Maya of mine

श्रीशुक उवाच

एवं भगवता राजन् श्रीवत्साङ्केन सत्कृतः। आमन्त्र्य तं परिक्रम्य सगणः स्वालयं ययौ ॥41॥
आत्मांशभूतां तां मायां भवानीं भगवान् भवः। शंसतामृषिमुख्यानां प्रीत्याऽऽचष्टाथ भारत ॥42॥
अपि व्यपश्यस्त्वमजस्य मायां परस्य पुंसः परदेवतायाः।
अहं कलानामृषभो विमुह्ये ययावशोऽन्ये किमुतास्वतन्त्राः ॥43॥
यं मामपृच्छस्त्वमुपेत्य योगात् समासहस्रान्त उपारतं वै।
स एष साक्षात् पुरुषः पुराणो न यत्र कालो विशते न वेदः ॥44॥

श्रीशुक उवाच

इति तेऽभिहितस्तात विक्रमः शार्ङ्गधन्वनः। सिन्धोर्निर्मथने येन धृतः पृष्ठे महाचलः ॥45॥
एतन्मुहुः कीर्तयतोऽनुशृण्वतो न रिष्यते जातु समुद्यमः क्वचित्।
यदुत्तमश्लोकगुणानुवर्णनं समस्तसंसारपरिश्रमापहम् ॥46॥
असदविषयमङ्घ्रिं भावगम्यं प्रपन्नानमृतममरवर्यानाशयत् सिन्धुमथ्यम्।
कपटयुवतिवेषो मोहयन् यः सुरारींस्तमहमुपसृतानां कामपूरं नतोऽस्मि ॥47॥

इति श्रीमद्भागवते महापुराणे पारमहंस्यां संहितायामष्टमस्कन्धे शङ्करमोहनं नाम द्वादशोऽध्यायः ॥12॥

constituted of the three Gunas, which I, as Purusha, assume partially under the stimulation of Time, shall never more overpower you.'

Sri Suka said: **41.** Being thus blessed by the Lord, who has the decorative mark of Srivatsa on his chest, Sri Rudra along with his following circumambulated the Lord, and departed to his abode. **42.** O scion of Bharata's line! When Siva reached his abode and while many Rishis hymned his praise, he turned to Bhavāni, his consort, who had become a part of his being, and said to her: **43.** 'Did you observe the power of the Maya of the birthless one, the Supreme Lord? I am the master of all arts and free. Yet I was enslaved and infatuated by His Maya. What then will be the condition of ordinary Jivas bound by their Karmas! **44.** On my coming to normal consciousness after a thousand years of Samadhi, you asked me the question on whom I had been meditating. Now that one is this Primeval Being. Time has no place in Him, and Vedic ritualism cannot take one to Him.'

Sri Suka said: **45.** I have now finished describing to you the might of Mahavishnu who supported the Mandara mountain on his back on the occasion of the churning of the ocean. **46.** No efforts of one who repeats or hears again and again this account of the Lord's deeds and excellences will ever go in vain. He will be released from the vicious cycle of birth and death. **47.** I salute the Lord who fulfils the prayers of devotees that take refuge in Him, who, assuming a false female form, filled the Asuras with infatuation and enabled the Devas to consume the ocean-born Amrita—the Devas who sought refuge at His feet which only Bhakti can reveal, and which the faithless and the impious men can never reach.

अथ त्रयोदशोऽध्यायः

श्रीशुक उवाच

मनुर्विवस्वतः पुत्रः श्राद्धदेव इति श्रुतः । सप्तमो वर्तमानो यस्तदपत्यानि मे शृणु ॥ 1॥
इक्ष्वाकुर्नभगश्चैव धृष्टः शर्यातिरेव च । नरिष्यन्तोऽथ नाभागः सप्तमो दिष्ट उच्यते ॥ 2॥
करूषश्च पृषध्रश्च दशमो वसुमान् स्मृतः । मनोर्वैवस्वतस्यैते दश पुत्राः परन्तप ॥ 3॥
आदित्या वसवो रुद्रा विश्वेदेवा मरुद्गणाः । अश्विनावृभवो राजन्निन्द्रस्तेषां पुरन्दरः ॥ 4॥
कश्यपोऽत्रिर्वसिष्ठश्च विश्वामित्रोऽथ गौतमः । जमदग्निर्भरद्वाज इति सप्तर्षयः स्मृताः ॥ 5॥
अत्रापि भगवज्जन्म कश्यपाददितेरभूत् । आदित्यानामवरजो विष्णुर्वामनरूपधृक् ॥ 6॥
सङ्क्षेपतो मयोक्तानि सप्त मन्वन्तराणि ते । भविष्याण्यथ वक्ष्यामि विष्णोः शक्त्यान्वितानि च 7
विवस्वतश्च द्वे जाये विश्वकर्मसुते उभे । संज्ञा छाया च राजेन्द्र ये प्रागभिहिते तव ॥ 8॥
तृतीयां वडवामेके तासां संज्ञासुतास्त्रयः । यमो यमी श्राद्धदेवश्छायायाश्च सुताञ्छृणु ॥ 9॥
सावर्णिस्तपती कन्या भार्या संवरणस्य या । शनैश्चरस्तृतीयोऽभूदश्विनौ वडवात्मजौ ॥10॥
अष्टमेऽन्तर आयाते सावर्णिर्भविता मनुः । निर्मोकविरजस्काद्याः सावर्णितनया नृप ॥11॥

Skandha VIII: Chapter 13

THE LAST SEVEN MANVANTARAS

Vaivaswata Manvantara (1-10)

Sri Suka said: **1.** Hear now from me about the offspring of the present Manu, the son of Vivaswān or sun, and famous under the name Srāddhadeva. He is the seventh Manu (and is popularly known as Vaivaswata Manu, after the name of his father Vivaswān). **2-3.** O great warrior! He had ten sons, their names being Ikshvāku, Nabhaga, Dhrishta, Saryāti, Narishyanta, Nābhāga, Dishta, Karūsha, Prishadhra and Vasumān. **4.** The Devas of his rule are the Ādityas, Vasus, Rudras, Visvedevas, Maruts, Aswinidevas and Ribhus. Purandara, the leader of them all, is the Indra. **5.** The Saptarshis of this period are Kasyapa, Atri, Vasishtha, Viswāmitra, Gautama, Jamadagni and Bharadwāja. **6**. The Lord then incarnated Himself in the form of Vāmana as the son of Kasyapa and Aditi—as the youngest of the Ādityas.

7. I have given you (with this) a brief description of the seven Manvantaras that have taken place. I shall now describe to you the future Manvantaras along with the Divine Incarnations that are to take place then. **8.** Two daughters of Viswakarma by name Samjna and Cchāya were the wives of Vivaswān. I have told you about this earlier (in the sixth Skandha). **9.** Some say he had a third wife named Badava. (Some others think that Badava is only another name for Samjna.) Vivaswān had three sons by Samjnā—Yama, Yamī and Srāddhadeva. Now hear the names of his issue by Cchāya. **10.** They had a son Sāvarni, a daughter named Tapatī who became the wife of Samvarana, and another son Sanaischara. The Aswins are his sons by Badava.

Sāvarni the eighth Manu (11-17)

11. O King! When the time for the eighth Manvantara comes, this Sāvarni, the son of Vivaswān, will be the Manu.

तत्र देवाः सुतपसो विरजा अमृतप्रभाः ।
तेषां विरोचनसुतो बलिरिन्द्रो भविष्यति ॥12॥
दत्त्वेमां याचमानाय विष्णवे यः पदत्रयम् ।
राद्धमिन्द्रपदं हित्वा ततः सिद्धिमवाप्स्यति ॥13॥
योऽसौ भगवता बद्धः प्रीतेन सुतले पुनः ।
निवेशितोऽधिके स्वर्गादधुनाऽऽस्ते स्वराडिव ॥14॥
गालवो दीप्तिमान् रामो द्रोणपुत्रः कृपस्तथा ।
ऋष्यश्रृङ्गः पितास्माकं भगवान् बादरायणः ॥15॥
इमे सप्तर्षयस्तत्र भविष्यन्ति स्वयोगतः ।
इदानीमासते राजन् स्वे स्व आश्रममण्डले ॥16॥
देवगुह्यात् सरस्वत्यां सार्वभौम इति प्रभुः ।
स्थानं पुरन्दराद्धृत्वा बलये दास्यतीश्वरः ॥17॥
नवमो दक्षसावर्णिर्मनुर्वरुणसम्भवः ।
भूतकेतुर्दीप्तकेतुरित्याद्यास्तत्सुता नृप ॥18॥
पारा मरीचिगर्भाद्या देवा इन्द्रोऽद्भुतः स्मृतः ।
द्युतिमत्प्रमुखास्तत्र भविष्यन्त्यृषयस्ततः ॥19॥
आयुष्मतोऽम्बुधारायामृषभो भगवत्कला ।
भविता येन संराद्धां त्रिलोकीं भोक्ष्यतेऽद्भुतः ॥20॥
दशमो ब्रह्मसावर्णिरुपश्लोकसुतो महान् ।
तत्सुता भूरिषेणाद्या हविष्मत्प्रमुखा द्विजाः ॥21॥
हविष्मान् सुकृतिः सत्यो जयो मूर्तिस्तदा द्विजाः ।
सुवासनविरुद्धाद्या देवाः शम्भुः सुरेश्वरः ॥22॥
विष्वक्सेनो विषूच्यां तु शम्भोः सख्यं करिष्यति ।
जातः स्वांशेन भगवान् गृहे विश्वसृजो विभुः ॥23॥
मनुर्वै धर्मसावर्णिरेकादशम आत्मवान् ।
अनागतास्तत्सुताश्च सत्यधर्मादयो दश ॥24॥

He will have as sons Nirmoka, Virajaska etc. **12.** In this Manvantara, Sutapasa, Viraja and Amritaprabha will be the Devas, and Virochana's son Bali will become Indra. **13.** In the seventh Manvantara, Bali gave the whole of this earth as gift to Mahavishnu, who begged of him for three strides of earth. As a reward for this Mahabali will become Indra in the eighth Manvantara. In the end he will abandon the state of Indra and attain oneness with the Lord. **14.** Though at first bound as a prisoner by the Lord, he was, out of the Lord's love and appreciation of him, sent to Sutala, a region more splendid than heaven, and is living there even now with all the glory of Indra, the master of heaven. **15-16.** During this eighth Manvantara, Gālava, Dīptimān, Parasurāma, Asvatthāma, Kripa, Rishyasringa, and my father Vedavyasa, will be the Saptarshis. All of them are now engaged in austerities in their own Ashramas in different places. **17.** The all-powerful Lord will then incarnate Himself as Sārvabhauma, the son of Devaguhya by his wife Saraswati, and will take away the heavenly region from the then Indra Purandara, and bestow it on Mahabali.

9th to the 14th Manvantaras (18-36)

18. The ninth Manu will be Dakshasāvarni, the son of Varuna. Bhūtaketu, Dīptaketu and others will be his sons. **19.** Pāra, Marīchigarbha etc., will be the Devas then. Adbhuta will be the Indra, and the Saptarshis will consist of Dyutimān and others. **20.** The Lord will incarnate by a part of Himself as Rishabha, the son of Āyushmān by Ambhudhāra. Adbhuta, under the protection of the Lord, will become Indra over the three worlds.

21-22. Upasloka's son will be the tenth Manu, the great Brahma-sāvarni. Bhūrishena and others will be his sons. Havishmān, Sukriti, Satya, Jaya, Mūrti etc., will be the Saptarshis; Suvāsana, Viruddha etc., the Devas; and Sambhu, the Indra. **23.** The Lord will then incarnate as Vishvaksena in the house of Visvasrik by his wife Vishūchi, and will help Sambhu the Indra of that age.

24. Dharma-sāvarni, possessed of great mental powers, will be the eleventh Manu. He will be having ten sons beginning with

विहङ्गमाः कामगमा निर्वाणरुचयः सुराः । इन्द्रश्च वैधृतस्तेषामृषयश्चारुणादयः ॥25॥
आर्यकस्य सुतस्तत्र धर्मसेतुरिति स्मृतः । वैधृतायां हरेरंशस्त्रिलोकीं धारयिष्यति ॥26॥
भविता रुद्रसावर्णी राजन् द्वादशमो मनुः । देववानुपदेवश्च देवश्रेष्ठादयः सुताः ॥27॥
ऋतधामा च तत्रेन्द्रो देवाश्च हरितादयः । ऋषयश्च तपोमूर्तिस्तपस्व्याग्नीध्रकादयः ॥28॥
स्वधामाख्यो हरेरंशः साधयिष्यति तन्मनोः । अन्तरं सत्यसहसः सूनृतायाः सुतो विभुः ॥29॥
मनुस्त्रयोदशो भाव्यो देवसावर्णिरात्मवान् । चित्रसेनविचित्राद्या देवसावर्णिदेहजाः ॥30॥
देवाः सुकर्मसुत्रामसंज्ञा इन्द्रो दिवस्पतिः । निर्मोकतत्त्वदर्शाद्या भविष्यन्त्यृषयस्तदा ॥31॥
देवहोत्रस्य तनय उपहर्ता दिवस्पतेः । योगेश्वरो हरेरंशो बृहत्यां सम्भविष्यति ॥32॥
मनुर्वा इन्द्रसावर्णिश्चतुर्दशम एष्यति । उरुगम्भीरबुद्ध्याद्या इन्द्रसावर्णिवीर्यजाः ॥33॥
पवित्राश्चाक्षुषा देवाः शुचिरिन्द्रो भविष्यति । अग्निर्बाहुः शुचिः शुद्धो मागधाद्यास्तपस्विनः ॥34॥
सत्रायणस्य तनयो बृहद्भानुस्तदा हरिः । वितानायां महाराज क्रियातन्तून् वितायिता ॥35॥
राजंश्चतुर्दशैतानि त्रिकालानुगतानि ते । प्रोक्तान्येभिर्मितः कल्पो युगसाहस्रपर्ययः ॥36॥

इति श्रीमद्भागवते महापुराणे पारमहंस्यां संहितायामष्टमस्कन्धे मन्वन्तरानुवर्णनं नाम त्रयोदशोऽध्यायः ॥13॥

Satyadharma. **25.** The Vihangamas, Kāmagamas and Nirvānaruchayas will be the gods; Vaidhrita will be the Indra and the Chārunas and others will be the Saptarshis. **26.** In that age the Lord will incarnate Himself under the name Dharmasetu, the son of Āryaka and his wife Vaidhritā, and will protect the three worlds.

27. O King! The twelfth Manu will be Rudra-sāvarni, and he will be having ten sons, the first three being Devavān, Upadeva and Devasreshtha. **28.** In that age Ritadhāma will be the Indra; Harita and others the Devas; and Tapomūrti, Tapasvi, Agnīdhraka and others, the Saptarshis. **29.** Incarnating by a part of His under the name Svadhāma as the son of Satyasahas and his wife Sunritā, the Lord will protect the worlds during this Manvantara.

30. Deva-sāvarni will be the thirteenth Manu, and Chitrasena, Vichitra and others will be his sons. **31.** Sukarma, Sutrāma and others will be the Devas; Divaspati will be the Indra; and Nirmoka, Tattvadarsa and others will be the Saptarshis. **32.** Under the name Yogeswara, a part of the Lord will then incarnate as the son of Devahotra by Brihatī, and help the Indra of the age, Divaspati.

33. Indra-sāvarni will be the fourteenth Manu. Urugambhīra, Buddhi etc., will be his sons. **34.** Pavitras, Chākshushas etc., will be the Devas; Suchi will be the Indra; and Agni, Bāhu, Suchi, Suddha, Māgadha etc., will be the Saptarshis. **35.** Sri Hari will then incarnate as Brihadbhānu, the son of Satrāyana by Vitāna, and encourage the sacrificial cult.

36. O King! I have now described to you the fourteen Manvantaras including those of the past, the present and the future, all of which put together will be a thousand Chaturyugas (a unit of four ages). This is one Kalpa, constituting one day-time of Brahma.

अथ चतुर्दशोऽध्यायः

राजोवाच

मन्वन्तरेषु भगवन् यथा मन्वादयस्त्विमे । यस्मिन् कर्मणि ये येन नियुक्तास्तद् वदस्व मे ॥ 1॥

ऋषिरुवाच

मनवो मनुपुत्राश्च मुनयश्च महीपते । इन्द्राः सुरगणाश्चैव सर्वे पुरुषशासनाः ॥ 2॥
यज्ञादयो याः कथिताः पौरुष्यस्तनवो नृप । मन्वादयो जगद्यात्रां नयन्त्याभिः प्रचोदिताः ॥ 3॥
चतुर्युगान्ते कालेन ग्रस्ताञ्छ्रुतिगणान् यथा । तपसा ऋषयोऽपश्यन् यतो धर्मः सनातनः ॥ 4॥
ततो धर्मं चतुष्पादं मनवो हरिणोदिताः । युक्ताः सञ्चारयन्त्यद्धा स्वे स्वे काले महीं नृप ॥ 5॥
पालयन्ति प्रजापाला यावदन्तं विभागशः । यज्ञभागभुजो देवा ये च तत्रान्विताश्च तैः ॥ 6॥
इन्द्रो भगवता दत्तां त्रैलोक्यश्रियमूर्जिताम् । भुञ्जानः पाति लोकांस्त्रीन् कामं लोके प्रवर्षति 7॥
ज्ञानं चानुयुगं ब्रूते हरिः सिद्धस्वरूपधृक् । ऋषिरूपधरः कर्म योगं योगेशरूपधृक् ॥ 8॥
सर्गं प्रजेशरूपेण दस्यून् हन्यात् स्वराड्वपुः । कालरूपेण सर्वेषामभावाय पृथग्गुणः ॥ 9॥
स्तूयमानो जनैरेभिर्मायया नामरूपया । विमोहितात्मभिर्नानादर्शनैर्न च दृश्यते ॥10॥

Skandha VIII : Chapter 14

WHAT IS A MANVANTARA

Functions of Manus (1-11)

The Rajah asked: **1.** O holy one! Please tell me on what works or duties were these Manus commissioned by the Lord during the periods of their supremacy.

Sri Suka said: **2.** O King! The Manus, the sons of Manus, the Saptarshis, Indras, Devas etc., all function subordinate to the commands of the Lord. **3.** The function of the Manus and others is to maintain the world order and its progress under the direction of divine incarnations like Yajna and others of whom I have spoken to you earlier. **4.** At the end of a period of four Yugas (Chaturyuga), the Saptarshis by their Tapas would re-discover the Vedas, most of which would have gradually been swallowed by Time by the end of that period. By the revival of the Veda, the eternal Dharma would be kept up. **5.** O King! The Manus, inspired and directed by Mahavishnu, and endowed with great powers of self-control, would in their time set Dharma in motion on all its four feet. **6.** The sons of Manus followed by their descendants, as also by the Devas receiving the Yajna offerings, and their associates, join in this work of maintaining the world order. **7.** Indra who could be in the enjoyment of the vast resources of all the three worlds assigned to him by the Lord, would protect these worlds and give them an abundance of rain. **8.** Sri Hari in all these ages would impart spiritual wisdom by assuming the form of enlightened ones, ritualistic duties by assuming the role of masters of them, and the path of Yoga by appearing as great master-yogis. **9.** In the form of Prajeswara He created this universe, as Indra He slew the Dasyus, and as Time, brings all things and beings to an end. **10.** Though the Lord is described and praised by various scriptures and philosophies, man with the perceptive power of his mind dulled and

एतत् कल्पविकल्पस्य प्रमाणं परिकीर्तितम् । यत्र मन्वन्तराण्याहुश्चतुर्दश पुराविदः ॥11॥

इति श्रीमद्भागवते महापुराणे पारमहंस्यां संहितायामष्टमस्कन्धे चतुर्दशोऽध्यायः ॥14॥

destroyed by Maya, is not able to perceive Him directly. **11.** A Mahakalpa is the full life-span of Brahma lasting for two Parārdhas. In that there are divisions called intermediary Kalpas (Vikalpa), each of which stands for a day of Brahma. What has been said relates to the Vikalpas each of which, wise men say, has fourteen Manvantaras (periods of supremacy of Manus).

अथ पञ्चदशोऽध्यायः

राजोवाच

बलेः पदत्रयं भूमेः कस्माद्धरिरयाचत । भूत्वेश्वरः कृपणवल्लब्धार्थोऽपि बबन्ध तम् ॥ 1॥
एतद् वेदितुमिच्छामो महत् कौतूहलं हि नः । यज्ञेश्वरस्य पूर्णस्य बन्धनं चाप्यनागसः ॥ 2॥

श्रीशुक उवाच

पराजितश्रीरसुभिश्च हापितो हीन्द्रेण राजन् भृगुभिः स जीवितः ।
सर्वात्मना तानभजद् भृगून् बलिः शिष्यो महात्मार्थनिवेदनेन ॥ 3॥
तं ब्राह्मणा भृगवः प्रीयमाणा अयाजयन् विश्वजिता त्रिणाकम् ।
जिगीषमाणं विधिनाभिषिच्य महाभिषेकेण महानुभावाः ॥ 4॥
ततो रथः काञ्चनपट्टनद्धो हयाश्च हर्यश्वतुरङ्गवर्णाः ।
ध्वजश्च सिंहेन विराजमानो हुताशनादास हविर्भिरिष्टात् ॥ 5॥
धनुश्च दिव्यं पुरटोपनद्धं तूणावरिक्तौ कवचं च दिव्यम् ।
पितामहस्तस्य ददौ च मालामम्लानपुष्पां जलजं च शुक्रः ॥ 6॥

Skandha VIII : Chapter 15

MAHABALI'S ASCENT

Bali invades Indra's Heaven (1-11)

The Rajah said: **1.** Why did Sri Hari, the Lord of all, ask Mahabali for three feet of earth like a miserable beggar? And why, after getting what he wanted, did the Lord bind him with cords as a prisoner? **2.** I desire to know how the one who is self-fulfilled and without any wants, who is the recipient of all sacrifices, could take to begging, and also how he could put fetters on an innocent person like Bali.

Sri Suka said: **3.** O King! Mahabali, who was killed and deprived of all his prosperous realm by Indra, was revived by his teachers the Bhrigus including Sukra. In return Bali served those teachers with great sincerity and liberality. **4.** The Bhrigus, the clan of eminent Brahmanas headed by Sukra, were very much pleased with Bali, who was desirous of conquering the heavenly region. These great Rishis administered to him the consecratory bath and made him perform the Yajna known as Viswajit, in which one must give away all one's possessions. **5.** Out of the sacrificial fire came out a divine chariot inlaid with gold and yoked to horses which vied with Indra's steeds in colour, and having a flag with the emblem of a lion. **6.** Also

एवं स विप्राजितयोधनार्थस्तैः कल्पितस्वस्त्ययनोऽथ विप्रान् ।
प्रदक्षिणीकृत्य कृतप्रणामः प्रह्लादमामन्त्र्य नमश्चकार ॥ 7॥

अथारुह्य रथं दिव्यं भृगुदत्तं महारथः । सुस्रग्धरोऽथ संनह्य धन्वी खड्गी धृतेषुधिः ॥ 8॥
हेमाङ्गदलसद्बाहुः स्फुरन्मकरकुण्डलः । रराज रथमारूढो धिष्ण्यस्थ इव हव्यवाट् ॥ 9॥
तुल्यैश्वर्यबलश्रीभिः स्वयूथैर्दैत्ययूथपैः । पिबद्भिरिव खं दृग्भिर्दहद्भिः परिधीनिव ॥10॥
वृतो विकर्षन् महतीमासुरीं ध्वजिनीं विभुः । ययाविन्द्रपुरीं स्वृद्धां कम्पयन्निव रोदसी ॥11॥
रम्यामुपवनोद्यानैः श्रीमद्भिर्नन्दनादिभिः । कूजद्विहङ्गमिथुनैर्गायन्मत्तमधुव्रतैः ॥12॥
प्रवालफलपुष्पोरुभारशाखामरद्रुमैः । हंससारसचक्राह्वकारण्डवकुलाकुलाः ।
नलिन्यो यत्र क्रीडन्ति प्रमदाः सुरसेविताः ॥13॥

आकाशगङ्गया देव्या वृतां परिखभूतया । प्राकारेणाग्निवर्णेन साट्टालेनोन्नतेन च ॥14॥
रुक्मपट्टकपाटैश्च द्वारैः स्फटिकगोपुरैः । जुष्टां विभक्तप्रपथां विश्वकर्मविनिर्मिताम् ॥15॥
सभाचत्वररथ्याढ्यां विमानैर्न्यर्बुदैर्युताम् । शृङ्गाटकैर्मणिमयैर्वज्रविद्रुमवेदिभिः ॥16॥
यत्र नित्यवयोरूपाः श्यामा विरजवाससः । भ्राजन्ते रूपवन्नार्यो ह्यर्चिर्भिरिव वह्नयः ॥17॥

came out a never-exhaustible quiver and an armour of heavenly workmanship. Bali was presented with an unfading garland of flowers by his grandfather Prahlada, and a conch by the Rishi Sukra.

7. Being thus equipped with all armaments with the help of these Rishis, Bali circumambulated them and made obeisance to them and also to Prahlada, and then took his leave. **8-9.** He now shone like the Āhavanīyāgni, the Vedic sacrificial fire of the household, as he seated himself in his chariot given by Rishi Sukra of Bhrigu's line with all equipment like bow, quiver, sword and armour, and with his personal decorations like garlands, shining armlets of gold and sparkling ear-rings. **10-11.** Bali, bent on the conquest of the most splendorous heavenly region of Indra, led his big Asura army whose march caused tremors on the earth and the intermediary regions. That army was full of Asura chiefs who were equal to him in wealth and power, and who were so heroic that they seemed ready to drink up the sky with their mouths, and to burn the quarters with their looks.

Description of Heaven (12-22)

12-13. The heaven of Indra was so full of attractive features that it made the very deity of splendour lustreless. It had famous gardens and parks like Nandana, great centres of natural beauty, wherein were celestial trees whose branches bent under the weight of tender leaves, flowers and fruits, and which harboured numerous birds warbling with their consorts, and humming bees inebriated with honey. It had lotus lakes abounding in many kinds of water birds like swans, cranes, Chakravākas and Kārandavas and providing facility for water sports for hilarious celestial women attended by their male companions. **14-15.** That city built by Viswakarma was surrounded like a moat by the holy Ganga of heaven and by high walls resplendent like fire and having on their tops battlements for use in times of war. It had doors with shutters of plated gold, towers of crystal, and highways well laid with proper alignment—all planned by the celestial architect, Viswakarma.

16. It had many assembly halls, courtyards and subsidiary roads, and its several cross roads were lined by high mansions with balconies and sit-outs made of coral and studded with diamonds. **17.** Resplen-

सुरस्त्रीकेशविभ्रष्टनवसौगन्धिकस्रजाम् । यत्रामोदमुपादाय मार्ग आवाति मारुतः ॥18॥
हेमजालाक्षनिर्गच्छद्धूमेनागुरुगन्धिना । पाण्डुरेण प्रतिच्छन्नमार्गे यान्ति सुरप्रियाः ॥19॥
मुक्तावितानैर्मणिहेमकेतुभिर्नानापताकावलभीभिरावृताम् ।
शिखण्डिपारावतभृङ्गनादितां वैमानिकस्त्रीकलगीतमङ्गलाम् ॥20॥
मृदङ्गशङ्खानकदुन्दुभिस्वनैः सतालवीणामुरजर्ष्टिवेणुभिः ।
नृत्यैः सवाद्यैरुपदेवगीतकैर्मनोरमां स्वप्रभया जितप्रभाम् ॥21॥
यां न व्रजन्त्यधर्मिष्ठाः खला भूतद्रुहः शठाः । मानिनः कामिनो लुब्धा एभिर्हीना व्रजन्ति यत् 22॥
तां देवधानीं स वरूथिनीपतिर्बहिः समन्ताद् रुरुधे पृतन्यया ।
आचार्यदत्तं जलजं महास्वनं दध्मौ प्रयुञ्जन् भयमिन्द्रयोषिताम् ॥23॥
मघवांस्तमभिप्रेत्य बलेः परममुद्यमम् । सर्वदेवगणोपेतो गुरुमेतदुवाच ह ॥24॥
भगवन्नुद्यमो भूयान् बलेर्नः पूर्ववैरिणः । अविषह्यमिमं मन्ये केनासीत्तेजसोर्जितः ॥25॥
नैनं कश्चित् कुतो वापि प्रतिव्योढुमधीश्वरः । पिबन्निव मुखेनेदं लिहन्निव दिशो दश ।
दहन्निव दिशो दृग्भिः संवर्ताग्निरिवोत्थितः ॥26॥

dent like rays of fire, girls with perpetual youth and beauty, and dressed in spotless garments, moved about everywhere. **18.** There the wind-deity is ever present, to welcome visitors, as it were, with a gentle breeze rendered fragrant with the sweet smell of fresh Saugandhika flowers fallen from the braids of celestial women. **19.** Through the gold-inlaid windows of the mansions, through which celestial women were seen to pass up and down, came out thick and grey clouds of smoke from burning frankincense, spreading on to the roads. **20.** Everywhere there were decorations of pearl strings, flagstaffs inlaid with gold and studded with precious stones, many banners of variegated colours and sizes, and balconies decorated with buntings. The atmosphere was filled with the sound of peacocks, doves and humming bees mingled with the sweet and auspicious music of celestial women occupying the mansions of the city. **21.** Every other attraction was overpowered by the sonorous heavenly music, in which was combined the booming sounds of various instruments like Mridanga, conch, drums and time-keeping cymbals with the sweet strains of Veena, Muraja, Rishti and flute and with the songs of the demigods accompanying the dances of heavenly danseuses. **22.** This realm is never attained by persons who are violators of the moral law, evil doers, oppressors of others, and persons who are cruel, conceited, licentious or greedy.

Siege of Heaven: Indra's Retreat (23-36)

23. Mahabali, the commander of the Asura forces, now besieged the city of Indra with his army. He blew his mighty conch presented to him by his Acharya (teacher), generating fear in the minds of the women of the heavenly realm. **24.** Seeing all these military preparations of Mahabali, Indra with all the Devas approached their teacher and said: **25.** 'O Honoured Sir! Our old enemy Mahabali is making another effort to conquer us. It is impossible for me to bear with his conduct. How has he become powerful again? **26.** No one will now be powerful enough to meet him in battle. It looks as if he is going to swallow the whole world, lick up the regions, and burn up everything by his look. He is as fierce as

ब्रूहि कारणमेतस्य दुर्धर्षत्वस्य मद्रिपोः । ओजः सहो बलं तेजो यत एतत्समुद्यमः ॥27॥

गुरुरुवाच

जानामि मघवञ्छत्रोरुन्नतेरस्य कारणम् । शिष्यायोपभृतं तेजो भृगुभिर्ब्रह्मवादिभिः ॥28॥
भवद्विधो भवान् वापि वर्जयित्वेश्वरं हरिम् । नास्य शक्तः पुरः स्थातुं कृतान्तस्य यथा जनाः ॥29॥
तस्मान्निलयमुत्सृज्य यूयं सर्वे त्रिविष्टपम् । यात कालं प्रतीक्षन्तो यतः शत्रोर्विपर्ययः ॥30॥
एष विप्रबलोदर्कः सम्प्रत्यूर्जितविक्रमः । तेषामेवापमानेन सानुबन्धो विनङ्क्ष्यति ॥31॥
एवं सुमन्त्रितार्थास्ते गुरुणार्थानुदर्शिना । हित्वा त्रिविष्टपं जग्मुर्गीर्वाणाः कामरूपिणः ॥32॥
देवेष्वथ निलीनेषु बलिर्वैरोचनः पुरीम् । देवधानीमधिष्ठाय वशं निन्ये जगत्त्रयम् ॥33॥
तं विश्वजयिनं शिष्यं भृगवः शिष्यवत्सलाः । शतेन हयमेधानामनुव्रतमयाजयन् ॥34॥
ततस्तदनुभावेन भुवनत्रयविश्रुताम् । कीर्तिं दिक्षु वितन्वानः स रेज उडुराडिव ॥35॥
बुभुजे च श्रियं स्वृद्धां द्विजदेवोपलम्भिताम् । कृतकृत्यमिवात्मानं मन्यमानो महामनाः ॥36॥

इति श्रीमद्भागवते महापुराणे पारमहंस्यां संहितायामष्टमस्कन्धे पञ्चदशोऽध्यायः ॥15॥

the fire that comes out of the mouth of Sankarshana at the time of the cosmic deluge. **27.** Please tell me how our enemy has acquired this irresistible might. How did he get this power of body and mind and the courage that have emboldened him to attack us?

The Teacher said: **28.** O Indra! I know that the cause of the enhancement of the powers of your enemy is that the Bhrigus, his teacher Sukra and his disciples, who are great experts in the Vedic lore, have imparted their own Brahmic power to him. **29.** Neither your nor other celestials like you can stand before him, as men cannot before Yama, the deity of Death. Only Sri Hari can face Him. **30.** Therefore you all abandon the heavenly region now, and go into hiding until the time turns against the enemy and tends to his downfall. **31.** Now, because of the power of holy men behind him, he has benefited immensely, and his power is at its zenith. In course of time, disrespect shown to these men will in itself be the cause of his downfall as well as of all his followers.

32. Thus after the deliberation with their wise teacher of great insight, the Devas left their heavenly regions disguised in different forms and disappeared from there. **33.** When the Devas thus disappeared, Bali, the son of Virochana, took possesion of the heavenly citadel of the Devas, and making it his capital, controlled all the three worlds. **34.** Sukra, who loved his obedient and victorious disciple Bali, made him perform a hundred horse sacrifices for the retention of the power and status he had gained. **35.** By the efficacy of these horse sacrifices, Bali's reputation spread everywhere in all the three worlds, and he shone like the moon everywhere. **36.** With a complete sense of fulfilment, Bali enjoyed the power and opulence he had gained through the power of holy men.

अथ षोडशोऽध्यायः

श्रीशुक उवाच

एवं पुत्रेषु नष्टेषु देवमातादितिस्तदा । हृते त्रिविष्टपे दैत्यैः पर्यतप्यदनाथवत् ॥ 1॥
एकदा कश्यपस्तस्या आश्रमं भगवानगात् । निरुत्सवं निरानन्दं समाधेर्विरतश्चिरात् ॥ 2॥
स पत्नीं दीनवदनां कृतासनपरिग्रहः । सभाजितो यथान्यायमिदमाह कुरूद्वह ॥ 3॥
अप्यभद्रं न विप्राणां भद्रे लोकेऽधुनाऽऽगतम् । न धर्मस्य न लोकस्य मृत्योश्छन्दानुवर्तिनः ॥ 4॥
अपि वाकुशलं किञ्चिद् गृहेषु गृहमेधिनि । धर्मस्यार्थस्य कामस्य यत्र योगो ह्ययोगिनाम् ॥ 5॥
अपि वातिथयोऽभ्येत्य कुटुम्बासक्तया त्वया । गृहादपूजिता याताः प्रत्युत्थानेन वा क्वचित् ॥ 6॥
गृहेषु येष्वतिथयो नार्चिताः सलिलैरपि । यदि निर्यान्ति ते नूनं फेरुराजगृहोपमाः ॥ 7॥
अप्यग्नयस्तु वेलायां न हुता हविषा सति । त्वयोद्विग्नधिया भद्रे प्रोषिते मयि कर्हिचित् ॥ 8॥
यत्पूजया कामदुघान् याति लोकान् गृहान्वितः । ब्राह्मणोऽग्निश्च वै विष्णोः सर्वदेवात्मनो मुखम् 9॥
अपि सर्वे कुशलिनस्तव पुत्रा मनस्विनि । लक्षयेऽस्वस्थमात्मानं भवत्या लक्षणैरहम् ॥10॥

Skandha VIII : Chapter 16

KASYAPA'S INSTRUCTIONS ON PAYOVRATA

Aditi's Petition to Kasyapa (1-21)

Sri Suka said: **1.** Aditi, the mother of the Devas, was very much afflicted and felt helpless, when her children had all to desert her, as their abode the heavenly region was wrested from them by the Asuras. **2.** Once Kasyapa, the great patriarch, came to her Ashrama after a very long interval spent in the state of Samadhi. He found that his wife Aditi and the whole Ashrama was without any trace of joy. **3.** After being worshipped and honoured, he took his seat, and addressed his sorrow-stricken wife as follows: **4.** 'I hope nothing evil has happened to holy men. I hope the path of Dharma has not been adversely affected. I hope the world, though subject to death, is free from calamities. **5.** O mistress of my household! The household is the institution that yields the fruits of Yoga even to persons who do not follow the path of Yoga. Has anything adverse overtaken the pursuit of the ideals it provides—Dharma (religion), Artha (wealth) and Kama (desire)? **6.** Or have at any time guests gone away from your home without being properly received and attended to by you on account of your pre-occupation with household affairs? **7.** A house from which guests have to go away without being offered even water, is verily a fox-hole and nothing more than that. **8.** O noble lady! During my absence, had you at any time under the stress of some excitement or diversion, forgotten to make the daily oblations in the sacred fires? **9.** For, the holy man and the sacred fire, which the householder is expected to tend and worship, are the faces of the Supreme Lord, Vishnu, who has manifested Himself as the various deities. **10.** Are all your sons doing well, O lady of courageous mind? For, I infer from the signs about you that you are in an unhappy state of mind.'

अदितिरुवाच

भद्रं द्विजगवां ब्रह्मन् धर्मस्यास्य जनस्य च। त्रिवर्गस्य परं क्षेत्रं गृहमेधिन् गृहा इमे ॥11॥
अग्नयोऽतिथयो भृत्या भिक्षवो ये च लिप्सवः। सर्वं भगवतो ब्रह्मन्ननुध्यानान्न रिष्यति ॥12॥
को नु मे भगवन् कामो न सम्पद्येत मानसः। यस्या भवान् प्रजाध्यक्ष एवं धर्मान् प्रभाषते ॥13॥
तवैव मारीच मनःशरीरजाः प्रजा इमाः सत्त्वरजस्तमोजुषः।
समो भवांस्तास्वसुरादिषु प्रभो तथापि भक्तं भजते महेश्वरः ॥14॥
तस्मादीश भजन्त्या मे श्रेयश्चिन्तय सुव्रत। हृतश्रियोहृतस्थानान् सपत्नैः पाहि नः प्रभो ॥15॥
परैर्विवासिता साहं मग्ना व्यसनसागरे। ऐश्वर्यं श्रीर्यशः स्थानं हृतानि प्रबलैर्मम ॥16॥
यथा तानि पुनः साधो प्रपद्येरन् ममात्मजाः। तथा विधेहि कल्याणं धिया कल्याणकृत्तम ॥17॥

श्रीशुक उवाच

एवमभ्यर्थितोऽदित्या कस्तामाह स्मयन्निव। अहो मायाबलं विष्णोः स्नेहबद्धमिदं जगत् ॥18॥
क्व देहो भौतिकोऽनात्मा क्व चात्मा प्रकृतेः परः। कस्य के पतिपुत्राद्या मोह एव हि कारणम् ॥19॥
उपतिष्ठस्व पुरुषं भगवन्तं जनार्दनम्। सर्वभूतगुहावासं वासुदेवं जगद्गुरुम् ॥20॥
स विधास्यति ते कामान् हरिर्दीनानुकम्पनः। अमोघा भगवद्भक्तिर्नेतरेति मतिर्मम ॥21॥

Aditi said: **11.** O Lord! The holy men and others including myself are all happy, and the rules of Dharma are in force. The homes are serving the threefold purpose of acquiring religious merits, wealth and happiness. **12.** By the greatness of your name, all the sacred fires, guests, servants, mendicants etc., are properly served and satisfied. **13.** O worshipful one! How can there be any dissatisfaction for me when you, a lord of creation, are there at hand to advise me on questions of Dharma? **14.** O son of Marīchi! All these creatures with dominance of Sattva, Rajas or Tamas are your offspring, born of your mind and body. O mighty one! You who are all-powerful through your austerity are alike to all, including the Asuras. You are, however, bound to support those who show special veneration to you. **15.** Therefore, O master who is endowed with great power born of vows, deign to think of the welfare of one like me who has been serving you. We, including the Devas, my children, have been deprived of our position and wealth by our enemies. We seek your protection. **16.** Powerful enemies have expelled me from my residence in heaven (after depriving me of my wealth and status) and I am submerged in the ocean of sorrow. **17.** O holy one and bestower of happiness! Deign to think of ways and means by which my children, the Devas, will be restored to their power and prosperity, and our welfare reassured.

Sri Suka said: **18.** On being so petitioned by Aditi, the sage Kasyapa smiled and said in wonder: 'Oh, wonderful is the power of Mahavishnu's Maya! This world is bound by ties of affection. **19.** Where is this material body which is not the Atman but on which the Atman-consciousness is superimposed! And where is the Atman that transcends material nature! Who and whose are husbands, sons or relatives? Such ideas of relationship are pure delusion. **20.** Seek refuge in Vāsudeva, the Supreme Being, the pervader of everything, the repository of all divine majesties, the one approachable to all, and the Lord of all. **21.** The Lord, who is merciful to the afflicted, will fulfil your desires. Devotion to Sri Hari will

अदितिरुवाच

केनाहं विधिना ब्रह्मन्नुपस्थास्ये जगत्पतिम् । यथा मे सत्यसङ्कल्पो विदध्यात् स मनोरथम् ॥22॥
आदिश त्वं द्विजश्रेष्ठ विधिं तदुपधावनम् । आशु तुष्यति मे देवः सीदन्त्याः सह पुत्रकैः ॥23॥

कश्यप उवाच

एतन्मे भगवान् पृष्टः प्रजाकामस्य पद्मजः । यदाह ते प्रवक्ष्यामि व्रतं केशवतोषणम् ॥24॥
फाल्गुनस्यामले पक्षे द्वादशाहं पयोव्रतः । अर्चयेदरविन्दाक्षं भक्त्या परमयान्वितः ॥25॥
सिनीवाल्यां मृदाऽऽलिप्य स्नायात् क्रोडविदीर्णया । यदि लभ्येत वै स्रोतस्येतं मन्त्रमुदीरयेत् ॥26॥
त्वं देव्यादिवराहेण रसायाः स्थानमिच्छता । उद्धृतासि नमस्तुभ्यं पाप्मानं मे प्रणाशय ॥27॥
निर्वर्तितात्मनियमो देवमर्चेत् समाहितः । अर्चायां स्थण्डिले सूर्ये जले वह्नौ गुरावपि ॥28॥
नमस्तुभ्यं भगवते पुरुषाय महीयसे । सर्वभूतनिवासाय वासुदेवाय साक्षिणे ॥29॥
नमोऽव्यक्ताय सूक्ष्माय प्रधानपुरुषाय च । चतुर्विंशद्गुणज्ञाय गुणसंख्यानहेतवे ॥30॥
नमो द्विशीर्ष्णे त्रिपदे चतुःश्रृङ्गाय तन्तवे । सप्तहस्ताय यज्ञाय त्रयीविद्यात्मने नमः ॥31॥

bring all-round good and welfare. Not so the worship of other Divinities.'

Description of Payovrata (22-25)

Aditi said: **22.** O great one! What form of worship of the Lord of the universe should I adopt? In what ways would my prayer be granted by Him whose will always comes true? **23.** Instruct me in that form of service by which the Lord will be quickly pleased with me, who along with my children am extremely grief-stricken.

Kasyapa replied: **24.** Once when I was eager to do the work of creation, I put this identical question to Brahma. The instruction that Brahma then gave me about the observance for winning the favour of Kesava—that I shall make known to you. **25.** A person should observe Payovrata, the vow of subsisting only on milk for twelve days in the bright fortnight of the month of Phalguna and worship the lotus-eyed Lord with supreme devotion.

Preliminary Worship (26-43)

26. On the fourteenth day of the dark fortnight (i.e. the day previous to the commencement of the vow), a person should, if available, get mud that has been dug up by a wild boar, and applying it all over the body, take bath in a river. He should also utter the following Mantra: **27.** 'O Earth-goddess! Thou wert lifted from Rasātala by the Lord as the Primeval Boar for providing a stable residence for all creatures. Salutation to Thee, O goddess! Destroy my sins.' **28.** After performing one's daily and contingent rituals, one should worship the Lord either in the image or on consecrated ground with ritualistic design, or in sun, water, fire, or one's teacher.

29. The following Mantra of invocation should be uttered: 'Salutation to Thee, the worshipful Vāsudeva, the inner pervader of all, the great radiance, the resident in all beings, the witness of everything! **30.** Salutations to Thee who art the gross and the subtle, Purusha (spirit) and Pradhana (matter), the knower of the twenty-four evolutes of Pradhana, and the promulgator of the Sankhya doctrine! **31.** Salutations to Thee who art the bestower of the fruits of Yajna and also of the form of Yajna as described in the Vedas, having

नमः शिवाय रुद्राय नमः शक्तिधराय च । सर्वविद्याधिपतये भूतानां पतये नमः ॥32॥
नमो हिरण्यगर्भाय प्राणाय जगदात्मने । योगैश्वर्यशरीराय नमस्ते योगहेतवे ॥33॥
नमस्त आदिदेवाय साक्षिभूताय ते नमः । नारायणाय ऋषये नराय हरये नमः ॥34॥
नमो मरकतश्यामवपुषेऽधिगतश्रिये । केशवाय नमस्तुभ्यं नमस्ते पीतवाससे ॥35॥
त्वं सर्ववरदः पुंसां वरेण्य वरदर्षभ । अतस्ते श्रेयसे धीराः पादरेणुमुपासते ॥36॥
अन्ववर्तन्त यं देवाः श्रीश्च तत्पादपद्मयोः । स्पृहयन्त इवामोदं भगवान् मे प्रसीदताम् ॥37॥
एतैर्मन्त्रैर्हृषीकेशमावाहनपुरस्कृतम् । अर्चयेच्छ्रद्धया युक्तः पाद्योपस्पर्शनादिभिः ॥38॥
अर्चित्वा गन्धमाल्याद्यैः पयसा स्नपयेद् विभुम् । वस्त्रोपवीताभरणपाद्योपस्पर्शनैस्ततः ।
गन्धधूपादिभिश्चार्चेद् द्वादशाक्षरविद्यया ॥39॥
शृतं पयसि नैवेद्यं शाल्यन्नं विभवे सति । ससर्पिः सगुडं दत्त्वा जुहुयान्मूलविद्यया ॥40॥
निवेदितं तद् भक्ताय दद्याद् भुञ्जीत वा स्वयम् । दत्त्वाऽऽचमनमर्चित्वा ताम्बूलं च निवेदयेत् ॥41॥
जपेदष्टोत्तरशतं स्तुवीत स्तुतिभिः प्रभुम् । कृत्वा प्रदक्षिणं भूमौ प्रणमेद् दण्डवन्मुदा ॥42॥
कृत्वा शिरसि तच्छेषां देवमुद्वासयेत् ततः । द्व्यवरान् भोजयेद् विप्रान् पायसेन यथोचितम् 43॥

the two bricks Prāyadīya and Udayanīya as the head, the three Savanas as legs, the four Vedas as horns, and the seven metres as hands! **32.** Salutation to Thee who art both Siva (the good) and Rudra (the fierce), who holdest the Sakti, who art the master of all arts and learning, and who art the lord of all elements! **33.** Salutations to Thee, the Hiranyagarbha, the Prana, the soul of the universe! Salutations to Thee, the one with power of Yoga as His form, who is the promulgator of the Yoga discipline! **34.** Salutations to Thee, Hari, who art the primeval Divinity, who art the witness of all, and who art the Rishi Nara-Narayana! **35.** Salutations to Thee whose form is of a blue complexion like an emerald, who art accompanied by Sri Devi, who art the Lord of the Trimurti, and who art dressed in yellow raiment. **36.** Thou art the best of boon givers, Thou art the one whom everyone should choose. All men of steady intellect, desirous of the ultimate good, worship Thee. **37.** May He, whom the Devas and Srī adore desirous of enjoying the fragrance of His lotus feet—may that worshipful Lord be propitious to me!'

38. Invoking Sri Hari, the controller and director of all the senses, with this Mantra, He, the Lord, should be honoured and worshipped with water for washing etc. **39.** After offering sandal paste and garlands, the all-pervading Lord should be bathed with milk. Next He should be offered clothes, sacred thread, decorations, Arghya and Pādya, sandal paste, incense, light etc., accompanied with the utterance of the twelve-lettered Mantra *Om Namo Bhagavate Vāsudevāya*. **40.** If a person has sufficient means, he should make an offering of rice cooked in milk with ghee and jaggery, and offer the same in fire uttering the above Mantra. **41.** Next water offering should be made, and betels presented. The food offerings made to the Lord, should be given to some devotees or one may eat it oneself. **42.** Afterwards the twelve-lettered Mantra should be uttered a hundred and eight times. Then one should do circumambulation and prostration. **43.** The worshipper should place the offered flowers etc., on his own head and put the Deity to rest. At least two holy men should be fed with the offered Payasa.

भुञ्जीत तैरनुज्ञातः शेषं सेष्टः सभाजितैः । ब्रह्मचार्यथ तद्रात्र्यां श्वोभूते प्रथमेऽहनि ॥44॥
स्नातः शुचिर्यथोक्तेन विधिना सुसमाहितः । पयसा स्नापयित्वार्चेद् यावद्व्रतसमापनम् ॥45॥
पयोभक्षो व्रतमिदं चरेद् विष्ण्वर्चनादृतः । पूर्ववज्जुहुयादग्निं ब्राह्मणांश्चापि भोजयेत् ॥46॥
एवं त्वहरहः कुर्याद् द्वादशाहं पयोव्रतः । हरेराराधनं होममर्हणं द्विजतर्पणम् ॥47॥
प्रतिपद्दिनमारभ्य यावच्छुक्लत्रयोदशी । ब्रह्मचर्यमधःस्वप्नं स्नानं त्रिषवणं चरेत् ॥48॥
वर्जयेदसदालापं भोगानुच्चावचांस्तथा । अहिंस्रः सर्वभूतानां वासुदेवपरायणः ॥49॥
त्रयोदश्यामथो विष्णोः स्नपनं पञ्चकैर्विभोः । कारयेच्छास्त्रदृष्टेन विधिना विधिकोविदैः ॥50॥
पूजां च महतीं कुर्याद् वित्तशाठ्यविवर्जितः । चरुं निरूप्य पयसि शिपिविष्टाय विष्णवे ॥51॥
श्रृतेन तेन पुरुषं यजेत सुसमाहितः । नैवेद्यं चातिगुणवद् दद्यात् पुरुषतुष्टिदम् ॥52॥
आचार्यं ज्ञानसम्पन्नं वस्त्राभरणधेनुभिः । तोषयेदृत्विजश्चैव तद् विद्ध्याराधनं हरेः ॥53॥
भोजयेत् तान् गुणवता सदन्नेन शुचिस्मिते । अन्यांश्च ब्राह्मणाञ्छक्त्या ये च तत्र समागताः 54॥
दक्षिणां गुरवे दद्यादृत्विग्भ्यश्च यथार्हतः । अन्नाद्येनाश्वपाकांश्च प्रीणयेत्समुपागतान् ॥55॥
भुक्तवत्सु च सर्वेषु दीनान्धकृपणेषु च । विष्णोस्तत्प्रीणनं विद्वान् भुञ्जीत सह बन्धुभिः 56

The Principles of Worship (44-62)

44-45. Permitted by those guests he can take what is left of the offered food in the company of his friends and relatives. He should observe continence that night, and from the next day, that is, the first day of the vow, he should, till the end of it, get up early in the morning, bathe, and with concentration perform the ceremonial milk bath for the Deity in His image as described earlier, and offer worship. **46.** The devotee who is intent on worshipping the Lord in this way, should subsist only on milk, make oblations in the fire, and feed the holy men every day. **47.** The observer of Payovrata should daily follow this routine of worship, Homa and feeding for twelve days. **48.** For these twelve days of the bright fortnight, the worshipper should be continent, avoid luxuries like sleeping on a cot, and bathe at the three Sandhyas (dawn, noon and sunset) of the day. **49.** He should avoid all talk except about the Lord and give up all sensuous indulgences, whether they be petty pleasures or rare luxuries. He should not injure creatures, and should practise intense devotion to the Lord.

50. Next on the thirteenth day of the bright fortnight, he should arrange for the performance of the bath of the Deity with Panchāmrita by experts in rituals, as laid down in the scriptures. **51.** Without stinting money, he should prepare offering of rice boiled in milk and arrange for grand and elaborate worship of the Lord sitting on the back of Garuda. **52.** With great concentration of mind that food offering cooked in milk should be made to the Lord, and afterwards one should partake of the remnant, which is very holy and attracts the grace of the Lord. **53.** The learned, the Acharyas (teachers) and the officiating priests should be honoured and rendered happy with presents of silk, ornaments and cows. Pleasing them is equal to the worship of Sri Hari Himself. **54.** Pure and well-prepared food must be given to the Acharya, the priests and other Brahmanas, who might have assembled there. **55.** Proper Dakshina (ceremonial parting gifts) must be given to the Acharya and the priests. All assembled on the occasion, down to the lowest outcaste, must be fed to satisfaction. **56.** When food

नृत्यवादित्रगीतैश्च स्तुतिभिः स्वस्तिवाचकैः । कारयेत्तत्कथाभिश्च पूजां भगवतोऽन्वहम् ॥57॥
एतत्पयोव्रतं नाम पुरुषाराधनं परम् । पितामहेनाभिहितं मया ते समुदाहृतम् ॥58॥
त्वं चानेन महाभागे सम्यक् चीर्णेन केशवम् । आत्मनाशुद्धभावेन नियतात्मा भजाव्ययम् ॥59॥
अयं वै सर्वयज्ञाख्यः सर्वव्रतमिति स्मृतम् । तपःसारमिदं भद्रे दानं चेश्वरतर्पणम् ॥60॥
त एव नियमाः साक्षात्त एव च यमोत्तमाः । तपो दानं व्रतं यज्ञो येन तुष्यत्यधोक्षजः ॥61॥
तस्मादेतद्व्रतं भद्रे प्रयता श्रद्धया चर । भगवान् परितुष्टस्ते वरानाशु विधास्यति ॥62॥

इति श्रीमद्भागवते महापुराणे पारमहंस्यां संहितायामष्टमस्कन्धेऽदितिपयोव्रतकथनं नाम षोडशोऽध्यायः ॥16॥

is served and eaten by the sick, the blind, the beggars etc., one should understand that it is the veritable worship of the Lord. After all are thus fed, one may take food with one's relatives. **57.** In the daily worship of the Lord, there must be a place for dance, songs, instrumental music, hymns, etc.

58. I have now described to you the way of divine service called Payovrata, in which I was instructed by Brahma. **59.** O fortunate lady! You too worship the Lord Kesava with a concentrated mind, full of pure devotion acquired through the observance of Payovrata. **60.** This is called comprehensive Yajna and comprehensive vow (*sarvayajna and sarvavrata)*. It is the essence of all austerity and of all charity, because it is pleasing to the Lord. **61.** That by which the Lord is pleased is verily austerity; it is charity and self-restraint. That alone is Jnana and the famous Yoga disciplines of Yama and Niyama (control of the senses and the mind). (For, to please the Lord is the end of all spiritual disciplines.) **62.** So, O noble lady, observe this discipline of Payovrata with faith and concentration. The Lord will soon be pleased with you and grant you the desired boons.

अथ सप्तदशोऽध्यायः

श्रीशुक उवाच

इत्युक्ता सादिती राजन् स्वभर्त्रा कश्यपेन वै । अन्वतिष्ठद् व्रतमिदं द्वादशाहमतन्द्रिता ॥ 1॥
चिन्तयन्त्येकया बुद्ध्या महापुरुषमीश्वरम् । प्रगृह्येन्द्रियदुष्टाश्वान् मनसा बुद्धिसारथिः ॥ 2॥
मनश्चैकाग्रया बुद्ध्या भगवत्यखिलात्मनि । वासुदेवे समाधाय चचार ह पयोव्रतम् ॥ 3॥
तस्याः प्रादुरभूत् तात भगवानादिपूरुषः । पीतवासाश्चतुर्बाहुः शङ्खचक्रगदाधरः ॥ 4॥

Skandha VIII : Chapter 17

ADITI'S VISION OF MAHAVISHNU

Mahavishnu appears to Aditi (1-6)

Sri Suka said: **1.** O King! As advised by her husband Kasyapa, Aditi observed this vow of Payovrata for a period of twelve days without any slackening of attention. **2.** She practised meditation on the Supreme Being with a concentrated intellect. With the intellect as the chariot and the mind for the reins, she controlled the restive horses of the senses. **3.** Fixing the mind one-pointed in Vāsudeva, the worshipful Lord and the soul of all, she observed the Payovrata. **4.** O dear one!

तं नेत्रगोचरं वीक्ष्य सहसोत्थाय सादरम् । ननाम भुवि कायेन दण्डवत् प्रीतिविह्वला ॥ 5॥
सोत्थाय बद्धाञ्जलिरीडितुं स्थिता नोत्सेह आनन्दजलाकुलेक्षणा ।
बभूव तूष्णीं पुलकाकुलाकृतिस्तद्दर्शनात्युत्सवगात्रवेपथुः ॥ 6॥
प्रीत्या शनैर्गद्गदया गिरा हरिं तुष्टाव सा देव्यदितिः कुरूद्वह ।
उद्वीक्षती सा पिबतीव चक्षुषा रमापतिं यज्ञपतिं जगत्पतिम् ॥ 7॥

अदितिरुवाच

यज्ञेश यज्ञपुरुषाच्युत तीर्थपाद तीर्थश्रवः श्रवणमङ्गलनामधेय ।
आपन्नलोकवृजिनोपशमोदयाद्य शं नः कृधीश भगवन्नसि दीननाथः ॥ 8॥
विश्वाय विश्वभवनस्थितिसंयमाय स्वैरं गृहीतपुरुशक्तिगुणाय भूम्ने ।
स्वस्थाय शश्वदुपबृंहितपूर्णबोधव्यापादितात्मतमसे हरये नमस्ते ॥ 9॥
आयुः परं वपुरभीष्टमतुल्यलक्ष्मीर्द्योर्भूरसाः सकलयोगगुणास्त्रिवर्गः ।
ज्ञानं च केवलमनन्त भवन्ति तुष्टात् त्वत्तो नृणां किमु सपत्नजयादिराशीः ॥10॥

श्रीशुक उवाच

अदित्यैवं स्तुतो राजन् भगवान् पुष्करेक्षणः । क्षेत्रज्ञः सर्वभूतानामिति होवाच भारत ॥11॥

The worshipful Lord, the origin of all, soon appeared before her in a form dressed in yellow cloth, and having four arms sporting the conch, discus, and mace. **5.** Seeing Him before her, she got up from her seat in great joy and made a respectful prostration before Him, stretching her body at full length on the ground. **6.** Trembling with emotion born of His vision, with horripilation all over the body, and with eyes brimming with tears of joy, she stood silent with joined plams, unable to praise Him with a hymn.

Aditi's Hymn (7-10)

7. That Devi Aditi stood there silently for some time, as if she was absorbed in drinking through her eyes that form of the Lord, the master of all Yajnas and of all that exists. Afterwards, O the noblest among the Kurus, she somehow controlled her mind, and began to praise the Lord in a voice choked with emotion.

Aditi said: **8.** O Thou bestower of the fruits of all Yajnas! O Thou who art in the form of Yajna! O Thou undecaying Being! O Thou of holy feet! O Thou about whom it is sanctifying to hear! O Thou whose names are the most auspicious things to hear! O Thou who hast embodied Thyself to save Thy surrendered devotees from all evil! Deign to do what is good to us. Thou art the protector of all stricken with sorrow and suffering. **9.** Salutations to Thee who art of the form of the world; who hast assumed the three Gunas out of Thy own will for the creation, preservation and dissolution of the universe; who by Thy limitless effulgence of consciousness hast scattered the darkness of ignorance; who art ever immersed in Thy own spiritual essence; and who destroyest all the obstacles and sorrows of devotees. **10.** Longevity, beauty of form, endless wealth, realms like heaven, earth and Patala, all the great powers that the practice of Yoga brings, the attainment of Dharma, Artha and Kama, the realisation of the state of non-duality—all these, O Infinite Being, accrue to one towards whom Thou art pleased. What to speak then of minor blessings like conquest of enemies!

Bestowal of Boon on Aditi (11-24)

Sri Suka said: **11.** O King! On being

श्रीभगवानुवाच

देवमातर्भवत्या मे विज्ञातं चिरकाङ्क्षितम् । यत् सपत्नैर्हृतश्रीणां च्यावितानां स्वधामतः ॥12॥
तान् विनिर्जित्य समरे दुर्मदानसुरर्षभान् । प्रतिलब्धजयश्रीभिः पुत्रैरिच्छस्युपासितुम् ॥13॥
इन्द्रज्येष्ठैः स्वतनयैर्हतानां युधि विद्विषाम् । स्त्रियो रुदन्तीरासाद्य द्रष्टुमिच्छसि दुःखिताः 14॥
आत्मजान् सुसमृद्धांस्त्वं प्रत्याहृतयशःश्रियः । नाकपृष्ठमधिष्ठाय क्रीडतो द्रष्टुमिच्छसि ॥15॥

प्रायोऽधुना तेऽसुरयूथनाथा अपारणीया इति देवि मे मतिः ।
यत्तेऽनुकूलेश्वरविप्रगुप्ता न विक्रमस्तत्र सुखं ददाति ॥16॥
अथाप्युपायो मम देवि चिन्त्यः संतोषितस्य व्रतचर्यया ते ।
ममार्चनं नार्हति गन्तुमन्यथा श्रद्धानुरूपं फलहेतुकत्वात् ॥17॥
त्वयार्चितश्चाहमपत्यगुप्तये पयोव्रतेनानुगुणं समीडितः ।
स्वांशेन पुत्रत्वमुपेत्य ते सुतान् गोप्तास्मि मारीचतपस्यधिष्ठितः ॥18॥

उपधाव पतिं भद्रे प्रजापतिमकल्मषम् । मां च भावयती पत्यावेवंरूपमवस्थितम् ॥19॥
नैतत् परस्मा आख्येयं पृष्टयापि कथंचन । सर्वं सम्पद्यते देवि देवगुह्यं सुसंवृतम् ॥20॥

श्रीशुक उवाच

एतावदुक्त्वा भगवांस्तत्रैवान्तरधीयत । अदितिर्दुर्लभं लब्ध्वा हरेर्जन्मात्मनि प्रभोः ॥21॥
उपाधावत् पतिं भक्त्या परया कृतकृत्यवत् । स वै समाधियोगेन कश्यपस्तदबुध्यत ॥22॥
प्रविष्टमात्मनि हरेरंशं ह्यवितथेक्षणः । सोऽदित्यां वीर्यमाधत्त तपसा चिरसम्भृतम् ।
समाहितमना राजन् दारुण्यग्निं यथानिलः ॥23॥

extolled by Aditi thus, the lotus-eyed Lord, who is the possessor of all majesties and who indwells the hearts of all, said to her as follows:

The Lord said: **12.** O mother of the celestials! I am very well aware of your long-standing prayer for the restoration of your sons to their rightful position and prosperity, of which they have been deprived by the Asuras. **13.** Your desire is to see that these proud and evil-minded Asura leaders are defeated in battle and to find yourself amidst your victorious sons. **14.** You desire also to see the grief-stricken wives of the warriors of the opposite camp weeping by the side of their husbands dead at the hands of your sons headed by Indra. **15.** You desire to see your sons relaxing in sports in heaven after having recovered their lost fame, wealth and prosperity. **16.** O lady! Those Asura leaders are now almost invincible, because they are now protected by holy men, who are endowed with great divine powers and are very favourably disposed towards them. **17.** Still I shall think of some way of fulfilling your desire. For My worship done with faith must yield the result due to it. **18.** Desirous of the protection of your children's interests, you observed the Payovrata in adoration of Me, and you have invoked Me by a hymn. Residing in the power of austerity of Kasyapa, I shall be born by a part of Mine as your son. **19.** O good-natured lady! Meditating on this form of Mine as dwelling in your husband, the Prajapati, live with him. **20.** You should not reveal these matters to others even if questioned. Matters of divine significance have to be protected from publicity, if they are to fructify.

Sri Suka said: **21-23.** Saying so, the Lord disappeared then and there. And

अदितेर्धिष्ठितं गर्भं भगवन्तं सनातनम् । हिरण्यगर्भो विज्ञाय समीडे गुह्यनामभिः ॥24॥

ब्रह्मोवाच

जयोरुगाय भगवन्नुरुक्रम नमोऽस्तु ते । नमो ब्रह्मण्यदेवाय त्रिगुणाय नमो नमः ॥25॥

नमस्ते पृश्निगर्भाय वेदगर्भाय वेधसे । त्रिनाभाय त्रिपृष्ठाय शिपिविष्टाय विष्णवे ॥26॥

त्वमादिरन्तो भुवनस्य मध्यमनन्तशक्तिं पुरुषं यमाहुः ।
कालो भवानाक्षिपतीश विश्वं स्रोतो यथान्तःपतितं गभीरम् ॥27॥
त्वं वै प्रजानां स्थिरजङ्गमानां प्रजापतीनामसि सम्भविष्णुः ।
दिवौकसां देव दिवश्च्युतानां परायणं नौरिव मज्जतोऽप्सु ॥28॥

इति श्रीमद्भागवते महापुराणे पारमहंस्यां संहितायामष्टमस्कन्धे वामनप्रादुर्भावे सप्तदशोऽध्यायः ॥17॥

Aditi, feeling highly satisfied that she would have such a rare blessing as the birth of Hari as her son, returned to her husband with a sense of fulfilment. Kasyapa had already come to know through Samadhi what had happened to Aditi. The seer of truth that he was, Kasyapa felt simultaneously in his Samadhi that a part of Sri Hari had entered into him. He transmitted into Aditi that virility of his acquired through a long period of austerity, as the wind transmits its energy into forest trees to produce fire by friction. **24.** Knowing that the foetus in Aditi's womb was none but the Supreme Lord, Brahma extolled him by a divine hymn full of his esoteric names.

Brahma's Hymn (25-28)

Brahma said: **25.** O worshipful Lord! O Thou of mighty strides! Salutations to Thee. Salutations again and again to Thee who art devoted to devotees, and who manifestest in the Gunas of Prakriti in Thy creative activity. **26.** Salutation to Thee who wert born in the womb of Prisni, who was this very Aditi in a previous birth! Salutation to Thee who holdest the Vedas within Thyself! Salutations to Thee who art the creator of all! Salutations to Thee who holdest the three worlds in Thy navel-lotus! Salutations to Thee who shinest, transcending the three worlds! Salutations to Thee who indwellest all beings, including brute creations! Salutations to Thee Vishnu, the all-pervading one! **27.** Thou art the origin of the universe, Thou art its middle when it is manifested, and Thou art its end too. Thou art spoken of as the Supreme Being, the repository of infinite powers. Just as a mighty river carries away every kind of object in the sweep of its current, so dost Thou as Time draw everything to their end. **28.** Thou art the source of both this world of moving and unmoving beings, and also of the Prajapatis. O Lord! For us Devas, who have been deprived of our position, Thou art the only support, just as the boat is to one who is being drowned in water.

अथाष्टादशोऽध्यायः

श्रीशुक उवाच

इत्थं विरिञ्चस्तुतकर्मवीर्यः प्रादुर्बभूवामृतभूरदित्याम् ।
चतुर्भुजः शङ्खगदाब्जचक्रः पिशङ्गवासा नलिनायतेक्षणः ॥ 1॥
श्यामावदातो झषराजकुण्डलत्विषोल्लसच्छ्रीवदनाम्बुजः पुमान् ।
श्रीवत्सवक्षा वलयाङ्गदोल्लसत्किरीटकाञ्चीगुणचारुनूपुरः ॥ 2॥
मधुव्रतव्रातविघुष्टया स्वया विराजितः श्रीवनमालया हरिः ।
प्रजापतेर्वेश्मतमः स्वरोचिषा विनाशयन् कण्ठनिविष्टकौस्तुभः ॥ 3॥
दिशः प्रसेदुः सलिलाशयास्तदा प्रजाः प्रहृष्टा ऋतवो गुणान्विताः ।
द्यौरन्तरिक्षं क्षितिरग्निजिह्वा गावो द्विजाः संजहृषुर्नगाश्च ॥ 4॥
श्रोणायां श्रवणद्वादश्यां मुहूर्तेऽभिजिति प्रभुः । सर्वे नक्षत्रताराद्याश्चक्रुस्तज्जन्म दक्षिणम् ॥ 5॥
द्वादश्यां सवितातिष्ठन्मध्यंदिनगतो नृप । विजया नाम सा प्रोक्ता यस्यां जन्म विदुर्हरेः ॥ 6॥
शङ्खदुन्दुभयो नेदुर्मृदङ्गपणवानकाः । चित्रवादित्रतूर्याणां निर्घोषस्तुमुलोऽभवत् ॥ 7॥
प्रीताश्चाप्सरसोऽनृत्यन् गन्धर्वप्रवरा जगुः । तुष्टुवुर्मुनयो देवा मनवः पितरोऽग्नयः ॥ 8॥
सिद्धविद्याधरगणाः सकिम्पुरुषकिन्नराः । चारणा यक्षरक्षांसि सुपर्णा भुजगोत्तमाः ॥ 9॥
गायन्तोऽतिप्रशंसन्तो नृत्यन्तो विबुधानुगाः । अदित्या आश्रमपदं कुसुमैः समवाकिरन् ॥10॥

Skandha VIII : Chapter 18

VĀMANA AT BALI'S SACRIFICIAL HALL

Incarnation of Vāmana (1-19)

Sri Suka said: **1.** The Lord, whose deeds and prowess were thus extolled by Brahma, again manifested Himself through Aditi with a form characterised by lotus eyes, yellow wearing cloth, and four arms holding conch, mace, lotus and discus. **2.** He was of pure blue complexion. His hallowed lotus-like face shone in the brilliance of the fish-marked ear-rings he wore. The Srivatsa mark on his chest, bracelets, armlets, brilliant diadem, girdle and anklets were his other decorations. **3.** Beautified by the floral wreath thronged by buzzing honey-bees and by the Kaustubha gem on his neck, Sri Hari scattered away all darkness from the Prajapati's Ashrama by His brilliance. **4.** Then the quarters and the oceans became serene. All men rejoiced while all the seasons turned simultaneously favourable. In the heaven, on the earth, in the intermediate region, on mountain tops, among animals, and among holy men, there was jubilation everywhere. **5.** The Lord was born at an auspicious time called Abhijit, on the holy day called Srāvana-Dwādasi, during which the moon dwelt in the constellation called Srāvana. The position of all the planets and the Nakshatras declared the exalted future of that birth. **6.** O King! It was midday of the Dwādasi (twelfth day of the fortnight) when the Lord was born, so say wise men. That Dwādasi is known as Vijaya-Dwādasi. **7.** The boom of conch, Panava, Mridanga and drums of various kinds filled the air, mingling with the swelling harmony of Tūrya and a variety of musical instruments. **8-10.** The Apsara women danced in joy while the Gandharvas sang.

दृष्ट्वादितिस्तं निजगर्भसम्भवं परं पुमांसं मुदमाप विस्मिता ।
गृहीतदेहं निजयोगमायया प्रजापतिश्चाह जयेति विस्मितः ॥11॥
यत् तद् वपुर्भातिविभूषणायुधैरव्यक्तचिद् व्यक्तमधारयद्धरिः ।
बभूव तेनैव स वामनो वटुः सम्पश्यतोर्दिव्यगतिर्यथा नटः ॥12॥

तं वटुं वामनं दृष्ट्वा मोदमाना महर्षयः । कर्माणि कारयामासुः पुरस्कृत्य प्रजापतिम् ॥13॥
तस्योपनीयमानस्य सावित्रीं सविताब्रवीत् । बृहस्पतिर्ब्रह्मसूत्रं मेखलां कश्यपोऽददात् ॥14॥
ददौ कृष्णाजिनं भूमिर्दण्डं सोमो वनस्पतिः । कौपीनाच्छादनं माता द्यौश्छत्रं जगतः पतेः ॥15॥
कमण्डलुं वेदगर्भः कुशान् सप्तर्षयो ददुः । अक्षमालां महाराज सरस्वत्यव्ययात्मनः ॥16॥
तस्मा इत्युपनीताय यक्षराट् पात्रिकामदात् । भिक्षां भगवती साक्षादुमादादम्बिका सती ॥17॥
स ब्रह्मवर्चसेनैवं सभां सम्भावितो वटुः । ब्रह्मर्षिगणसंजुष्टामत्यरोचत मारिषः ॥18॥
समिद्धमाहितं वह्निं कृत्वा परिसमूहनम् । परिस्तीर्य समभ्यर्च्य समिद्भिरजुहोद् द्विजः ॥19॥

श्रुत्वाश्वमेधैर्यजमानमूर्जितं बलिं भृगूणामुपकल्पितैस्ततः ।
जगाम तत्राखिलसारसम्भृतो भारेण गां सन्नमयन् पदे पदे ॥20॥

Beings of all species—Devas, Manus, Pitris, Agnis, Siddhas, Vidyādharas, Kimpurushas, Kinnaras, Chāranas, Yakshas, Rākshasas, Garuda and other birds, and serpents—all showered flowers over the Ashrama of Aditi.

11. Aditi was wonderstruck and filled with joy to see the Supreme Person born of her womb. The Prajapati too was filled with joy and wonder to see Him embodied as his own son through His mysterious power of Maya. **12.** Hari, who is Pure Consciousness not perceptible to the senses, had assumed a divine form characterised by brilliance, special decorations, weapons etc., in order that His divine identity might be recognised by his parents and others. Having accomplished this, all of a sudden, before the very eyes of His parents, He now transformed the divine form into that of a short-statured Brahmacharin (Vāmana), just as a stage actor changes his impersonation. **13.** Seeing the Lord in the form of the Vāmana, the sages were delighted, and with Kasyapa Prajapati as their leader, they had his post-natal ceremonies conducted. **14.** After his Upanayana was performed, the sun-deity (Savitā) initiated him into the Gāyatrī-mantra, while Brihaspati invested him with the sacred thread and Kasyapa with the grass girdle. **15.** The earth-deity gave him the skin of a black deer; Soma, the master of forests, the staff; mother Aditi, his loin cloth; and the sky-deity, an umbrella. **16.** Brahma gave him the water vessel; the Saptarshis, Kusa grass; and Goddess Saraswati, O great King, a string of beads for Japa. **17.** To him whose Upanayana was thus completed, Kubera gave a begging bowl; and the supreme Goddess and the mother of the universe, Sati Umā, gave him Bhiksha (holy alms). **18.** That Brahmacharin, who was honoured in this way by all, outshone by his Brahmic brilliance even that assembly of Brahmarshis. **19.** He heaped the fuel, lit the fire according to rites, placed twigs around it, worshipped the fire, and offered sacred twigs into it.

Vāmana at sacrificial hall: (20-25)

20. He now heard that the powerful Mahabali was engaged in the performance of an Aswamedha sacrifice under the

तं नर्मदायास्तट उत्तरे बलेर्य ऋत्विजस्ते भृगुकच्छसंज्ञके ।
प्रवर्तयन्तो भृगवः क्रतूत्तमं व्यचक्षतारादुदितं यथा रविम् ॥21॥
तं ऋत्विजो यजमानः सदस्या हततत्विषो वामनतेजसा नृप ।
सूर्यः किलायात्युत वा विभावसुः सनत्कुमारोऽथ दिदृक्षया क्रतोः ॥22॥
इत्थं सशिष्येषु भृगुष्वनेकधा वितर्क्यमाणो भगवान् स वामनः ।
छत्रं सदण्डं सजलं कमण्डलुं विवेश बिभ्रद्धयमेधवाटम् ॥23॥
मौञ्ज्या मेखलया वीतमुपवीताजिनोत्तरम् । जटिलं वामनं विप्रं मायामाणवकं हरिम् ॥24॥
प्रविष्टं वीक्ष्य भृगवः सशिष्यास्ते सहाग्निभिः । प्रत्यगृह्णन् समुत्थाय संक्षिप्तास्तस्य तेजसा ॥25॥
यजमानः प्रमुदितो दर्शनीयं मनोरमम् । रूपानुरूपावयवं तस्मा आसनमाहरत् ॥26॥
स्वागतेनाभिनन्द्याथ पादौ भगवतो बलिः । अवनिज्यार्चयामास मुक्तसङ्गमनोरमम् ॥27॥
तत्पादशौचं जनकल्मषापहं स धर्मविन्मूर्ध्न्यदधात् सुमङ्गलम् ।
यद् देवदेवो गिरिशश्चन्द्रमौलिर्दधार मूर्ध्ना परया च भक्त्या ॥28॥

बलिरुवाच

स्वागतं ते नमस्तुभ्यं ब्रह्मन् किं करवाम ते । ब्रह्मर्षीणां तपः साक्षान्मन्ये त्वाऽऽर्यवपुर्धरम् ॥29॥

direction of the Rishis of the Bhrigu family headed by Sukra. The Vāmana, who was endowed with all majesties, therefore started for the sacrificial campus of Mahabali. As he walked, the earth seemed to get tremors at every step he took. **21.** Bhrigu and the other priests conducting the sacrifice on the northern bank of the Narmada at a place called Bhrigūkaccha saw the Lord come up close to them like the rising sun at dawn. **22.** O King! Before the brilliance of Vāmana, the master of the sacrifice and the assembled Rishis paled into a mere shadow, and they began to wonder whether the august visitor was the sun-deity, or the fire-deity, or the sage Sanatkumara come to witness the sacrifice. **23.** When the Bhrigus and their disciple (Bali) were thus cogitating in their mind, the worshipful Lord Vāmana entered the sacrificial hall holding in his hands an umbrella, a water vessel full of water, and a staff. **24-25.** Hari in the assumed form of the Brahmacharin had a girdle of Munja grass, an upper garment of the black antelope's skin worn in the fashion of Yajnopavīta, and matted locks on the head. As he entered, the Bhrigus and their disciples and the fire-deity, overwhelmed by the radiating glory of Vāmana, stood up automatically to receive him.

Bali's Reception of Vāmana (26-32)

26. The master of the sacrifice, Mahabali, offered him a seat, delighted to see that handsome and attractive visitor whose limbs and body were well-formed and proportionate. **27.** Then he welcomed him with all courtesy, honoured him, washed his feet and worshipped him, who sports in the hearts of those who are devoid of all attachments. **28.** Bali, who was well-versed in the rules of Dharma, poured on his own head the water with which he had washed the Vāmana's feet. For, so sacred is that water from His feet that even Maheswara carries it on his head with deep devotion in the form of the holy Ganga.

Bali said: **29**. Welcome to you, O holy one, and my salutations! I look upon you, honoured sir, as the special embodiment of Tapas (austerity) which forms the

अद्य नः पितरस्तृप्ता अद्य नः पावितं कुलम् । अद्य स्विष्टः क्रतुरयं यद् भवानागतो गृहान् ।।30।।
अद्याग्नयो मे सुहुता यथाविधि द्विजात्मज त्वच्चरणावनेजनैः ।
हतांहसो वार्भिरियं च भूरहो तथा पुनीता तनुभिः पदैस्तव ।।31।।
यद् यद् वटो वाञ्छसि तत् प्रतीच्छ मे त्वामर्थिनं विप्रसुतानुतर्कये ।
गां काञ्चनं गुणवद् धाम मृष्टं तथान्नपेयमुत वा विप्र कन्याम् ।
ग्रामान् समृद्धांस्तुरगान् गजान् वा रथांस्तथार्हत्तम सम्प्रतीच्छ ।।32।।

इति श्रीमद्भागवते महापुराणे पारमहंस्यां संहितायामष्टमस्कन्धे वामनप्रादुर्भावे बलिवामनसंवादेऽष्टादशोऽध्यायः ।।18।।

glory of Brahmarshis. **30.** Your arrival at my house today has brought satisfaction to my ancestors and purification to my dynasty, and this sacrifice that I have undertaken has become perfect in all its limbs. **31.** O holy one! The sacrificial offerings that I make in the sacred fires will be true and perfect, because I, the sacrificer, has been freed from all my impurities by the water from your feet. This part of the earth too has been sanctified by the contact of your handsome limbs and the tread of your feet. **32.** O Brahmacharin! I presume that you have come here seeking something. Whatever you want, ask that of me, and it shall be yours. I shall grant you anything you ask for—whether it be cows, gold, house, hearty meal and drink, a damsel to wed, prosperous villages, horses, chariots or anything else you fancy.

अथैकोनविंशोऽध्यायः

श्रीशुक उवाच

इति वैरोचनेर्वाक्यं धर्मयुक्तं ससूनृतम् । निशम्य भगवान् प्रीतः प्रतिनन्द्येदमब्रवीत् ।। 1।।

श्रीभगवानुवाच

वचस्तवैतज्जनदेव सूनृतं कुलोचितं धर्मयुतं यशस्करम् ।
यस्य प्रमाणं भृगवः साम्पराये पितामहः कुलवृद्धः प्रशान्तः ।। 2।।

न ह्येतस्मिन् कुले कश्चिन्निःसत्त्वः कृपणः पुमान् । प्रत्याख्याता प्रतिश्रुत्य यो वादाता द्विजातये ।। 3।।

Skandha VIII : Chapter 19

VĀMANA'S SUPPLICATION

Vāmana's Eulogy of Mahabali (1-15)

Sri Suka said: **1.** Hearing this cordial and righteous speech of Mahabali, the son of Virochana, the Lord was very much pleased and he replied:

The worshipful Lord said: **2.** Those cordial and righteous words truly befit the tradition of one like you who has, as adviser in matters spiritual, a teacher like Sukra of Bhrigu's line, and an ancestor like Prahlada, noted for his devotion and poise of mind. **3.** In this line of yours there has never been a man undignified enough to refuse the request of a holy man, or miserly enough to fail to honour

न सन्ति तीर्थे युधि चार्थिनार्थिताः पराङ्मुखा ये स्वमनस्विनो नृपाः ।
युष्मत्कुले यद्यशसामलेन प्रह्लाद उद्भाति यथोडुपः खे ॥ 4॥
यतो जातो हिरण्याक्षश्चरन्नेक इमां महीम् । प्रतिवीरं दिग्विजये नाविन्दत गदायुधः ॥ 5॥
यं विनिर्जित्य कृच्छ्रेण विष्णुः क्ष्मोद्धार आगतम् । नात्मानं जयिनं मेने तद्वीर्यं भूर्यनुस्मरन् ॥ 6॥
निशम्य तद्वधं भ्राता हिरण्यकशिपुः पुरा । हन्तुं भ्रातृहणं क्रुद्धो जगाम निलयं हरेः ॥ 7॥
तमायान्तं समालोक्य शूलपाणिं कृतान्तवत् । चिन्तयामास कालज्ञो विष्णुर्मायाविनां वरः ॥ 8॥
यतो यतोऽहं तत्रासौ मृत्युः प्राणभृतामिव । अतोऽहमस्य हृदयं प्रवेक्ष्यामि पराग्दृशः ॥ 9॥
एवं स निश्चित्य रिपोः शरीरमाधावतो निर्विविशेऽसुरेन्द्र ।
श्वासानिलान्तर्हितसूक्ष्मदेहस्तत्प्राणरन्ध्रेण विविग्नचेताः ॥10॥
स तन्निकेतं परिमृश्य शून्यमपश्यमानः कुपितो ननाद ।
क्ष्मां द्यां दिशः खं विवरान् समुद्रान् विष्णुं विचिन्वन् न ददर्श वीरः ॥11॥
अपश्यन्निति होवाच मयान्विष्टमिदं जगत् । भ्रातृहा मे गतो नूनं यतो नावर्तते पुमान् ॥12॥
वैरानुबन्ध एतावानामृत्योरिह देहिनाम् । अज्ञानप्रभवो मन्युरहंमानोपबृंहितः ॥13॥
पिता प्रह्लादपुत्रस्ते तद्विद्वान् द्विजवत्सलः । स्वमायुर्द्विजलिङ्गेभ्यो देवेभ्योऽदात् स याचितः 14

the promise of a gift. **4.** Your royal family had never in it a member who showed reluctance to give a suppliant what he wanted, or one who tucked tail in the field of battle. Just like the moon in the sky, Prahlada shines in your house in his matchless and stainless glory. **5.** Hiranyaksha, who was born in this family, could not get an opponent worthy of his steel when he traversed this whole earth, mace in hand, challenging everyone. **6.** Even Mahavishnu who had to face Hiranyaksha when he undertook to lift up the earth, overcame him only with such great difficulty that He hardly considered Himself the victor.

7. Hearing of Hiranyaksha's destruction, his brother Hiranyakasipu was roused to great anger and went up to Vaikuntha, Vishnu's abode, to avenge his brother's death by destroying his killer. **8.** Seeing him advancing like Yama, the god of death, with a three-pronged trident in hand, Mahavishnu, the arch-strategist and dissembler, thought thus: **9.** 'Wherever I go, he comes pursuing Me, as the god of death follows creatures. So in order to avoid him, I shall enter into his heart; for being a thorough extrovert, he is not likely to look within.' **10.** O chief of Asuras! Deciding like this, with trepidation in his heart, Mahavishnu made His form subtle enough to be sucked in by the Asura's breath, and entered into him through his nose. **11.** So when he failed to find Vishnu in spite of a vigorous search of the whole of the empty Vaikuntha, he yelled in fierce anger and ranged all the universe—the earth, the heaven, the sky, the quarters, the oceans, the fourteen worlds high and low—in search of Vishnu, but could not find Him anywhere. **12.** Not seeing Him anywhere, he said to himself: 'I have searched the whole world, but my brother's killer is not to be seen. He must have gone the way of no return.' **13.** Death is the limit of animosity between embodied beings. For, anger thrives on the ignorance-born 'I-sense' which we maintain with regard to the body, and when the body of a person is destroyed, there is no longer any relevancy for anger towards that person. **14.** And your father, the son of Prahlada,

भवानाचरितान् धर्मानास्थितो गृहमेधिभिः । ब्राह्मणैः पूर्वजैः शूरैरन्यैश्चोद्दामकीर्तिभिः ॥15॥
तस्मात् त्वत्तो महीमीषद् वृणेऽहं वरदर्षभात् । पदानि त्रीणि दैत्येन्द्र संमितानि पदा मम ॥16॥
नान्यत् ते कामये राजन् वदान्याज्जगदीश्वरात् । नैनः प्राप्नोति वै विद्वान् यावदर्थप्रतिग्रहः ॥17॥

बलिरुवाच

अहो ब्राह्मणदायाद वाचस्ते वृद्धसम्मताः । त्वं बालो बालिशमतिः स्वार्थं प्रत्यबुधो यथा ॥18॥
मां वचोभिः समाराध्य लोकानामेकमीश्वरम् । पदत्रयं वृणीते योऽबुद्धिमान् द्वीपदाशुषम् ॥19॥
न पुमान् मामुपव्रज्य भूयो याचितुमर्हति । तस्माद् वृत्तिकरीं भूमिं वटो कामं प्रतीच्छ मे ॥20॥

श्रीभगवानुवाच

यावन्तो विषयाः प्रेष्ठास्त्रिलोक्यामजितेन्द्रियम् । न शक्नुवन्ति ते सर्वे प्रतिपूरयितुं नृप ॥21॥
त्रिभिः क्रमैरसन्तुष्टो द्वीपेनापि न पूर्यते । नववर्षसमेतेन सप्तद्वीपवरेच्छया ॥22॥
सप्तद्वीपाधिपतयो नृपा वैन्यगयादयः । अर्थैः कामैर्गता नान्तं तृष्णाया इति नः श्रुतम् ॥23॥
यदृच्छयोपपन्नेन सन्तुष्टो वर्तते सुखम् । नासन्तुष्टस्त्रिभिर्लोकैरजितात्मोपसादितैः ॥24॥
पुंसोऽयं संसृतेर्हेतुरसन्तोषोऽर्थकामयोः । यदृच्छयोपपन्नेन सन्तोषो मुक्तये स्मृतः ॥25॥

being endowed with great reverence for holy men, gave up his life to the Devas who went to him begging in the guise of holy men, though he knew these were Devas and not holy men. **15.** You too are following the Dharma shown by householder Rishis like Sukra and by your own heroic ancestors.

The three Feet of Earth (16-28)

16. Therefore, O King of Asuras, from you, the most noted among generous persons, I seek a small strip of land—just what is measured by three paces of mine. **17.** O King! I do not seek anything more than this from you, who are noted for your generosity and who are the master of all the worlds. For one should receive as gifts only what is absolutely necessary; he acquires no sin thereby.

Bali said: **18.** O you stripling of a Brahmana boy! Your words are, no doubt, noble enough to get the approval of wise men. So meaningful and dignified they are. But you still show signs of immaturity, a childishness in outlook. For, you do not seem to know your own interest. **19.** After having extolled and pleased me by words—I who am the master of the whole world and have got the resources to make a gift of a whole continent—you ask of me a mere pittance of three feet of earth! Such a person must indeed be stupid! **20.** It is my principle that one who comes to me for a favour, should have no occasion to depend upon another in the future. Therefore, O boy, ask of me land sufficient to maintain you for life.

The worshipful Lord said: **21.** O King! Even all the pleasing objects of the universe will not be enough to satisfy a man who has no mastery over the senses. **22.** A person who is not satisfied with three feet of earth, will not be satisfied by getting the whole of Jambu-dweepa with its nine regions. He will afterwards aspire to get all the seven Dweepas (continents). **23.** We have heard that even emperors like Prithu and Gaya, who were the masters of the seven continents, were not satisfied with the wealth and pleasure which their power and position made available to them. **24.** A man who is satisfied with what chance gives him lives happily. But a man who has no mastery of his mind is dissatisfied even if he gets all the three worlds. **25.** The chief cause of man's entanglement in Samsara is his

यदृच्छालाभतुष्टस्य तेजो विप्रस्य वर्धते । तत् प्रशाम्यत्यसन्तोषादम्भसेवाशुशुक्षणिः ॥26॥
तस्मात् त्रीणि पदान्येव वृणे त्वद् वरदर्षभात् । एतावतैव सिद्धोऽहं वित्तं यावत्प्रयोजनम् ॥27॥

श्रीशुक उवाच

इत्युक्तः स हसन्नाह वाञ्छातः प्रतिगृह्यताम् । वामनाय महीं दातुं जग्राह जलभाजनम् ॥28॥
विष्णवे क्ष्मां प्रदास्यन्तमुशना असुरेश्वरम् । जानंश्चिकीर्षितं विष्णोः शिष्यं प्राह विदां वरः 29॥

शुक्र उवाच

एष वैरोचने साक्षाद् भगवान् विष्णुरव्ययः । कश्यपाददितेर्जातो देवानां कार्यसाधकः ॥30॥
प्रतिश्रुतं त्वयैतस्मै यदनर्थमजानता । न साधु मन्ये दैत्यानां महानुपगतोऽनयः ॥31॥
एष ते स्थानमैश्वर्यं श्रियं तेजो यशः श्रुतम् । दास्यत्याच्छिद्य शक्राय मायामाणवको हरिः ॥32॥
त्रिभिः क्रमैरिमाँल्लोकान् विश्वकायः क्रमिष्यति । सर्वस्वं विष्णवे दत्त्वा मूढ वर्तिष्यसे कथम् ॥33॥
क्रमतो गां पदैकेन द्वितीयेन दिवं विभोः । खं च कायेन महता तार्तीयस्य कुतो गतिः ॥34॥
निष्ठां ते नरके मन्ये ह्यप्रदातुः प्रतिश्रुतम् । प्रतिश्रुतस्य योऽनीशः प्रतिपादयितुं भवान् ॥35॥

insatiable longing for wealth and pleasure. It is contentment with what comes by chance that helps the attainment of liberation. **26.** The spiritual aura of a holy man is enhanced in its radiance if he lives satisfied with what chance brings. On the contrary dissatisfaction with possessions and enjoyments stifles it as water damps fire. **27.** Therefore I shall take only three feet of earth from you, who are the most noted of generous men and capable of granting all the desires of a suppliant. With this three feet of earth I shall feel fully satisfied. Wealth becomes a cause of happiness when it is just enough to meet one's bare needs—neither less nor more.

Sri Suka said: **28.** Hearing this, Mahabali laughed, and deciding to give what Vāmana wanted, he took his water vessel and said: 'You may take what you have asked for.'

Sukra's Remonstrance (29-37)

29. But now the sage Sukra, the most learned among men, coming to guess the plan of Vishnu, said as follows to his disciple Mahabali, who was just about to make a gift of land to the Lord. *Sukra said*: **30.** 'O son of Virochana! This is none but the Eternal Being, the worshipful Mahavishnu. He has incarnated as the offspring of Aditi and Kasyapa for achieving the purpose of the Devas. **31.** I do not consider it correct for you to have promised to give him three feet of land without any awareness of the adverse consequences of it. The Asuras are on the verge of a great catastrophe as a result. **32.** Hari, who has come in the disguise of a Brahmacharin, is going to deprive you of, and present to Indra, all that you have—your position, sovereignty, wealth, splendour, fame and the merits of Vedic study. **33.** This Brahmacharin can assume a cosmic form, and can measure the whole universe with three strides of his. O fool! Having thus given away all your possessions to Vishnu, how will you manage to get on? **34.** With one stride he will cover the earth and with the second the heaven, while his body will fill the interspace. Where will there be space for a third step? **35.** It will thus be impossible for you to give what you have promised, and you will get the due for one breaking his promise, namely prolonged consignment

न तद् दानं प्रशंसन्ति येन वृत्तिर्विपद्यते । दानं यज्ञस्तपः कर्म लोके वृत्तिमतो यतः ॥36॥
धर्माय यशसेऽर्थाय कामाय स्वजनाय च । पञ्चधा विभजन् वित्तमिहामुत्र च मोदते ॥37॥
अत्रापि बह्वृचैर्गीतं शृणु मेऽसुरसत्तम । सत्यमोमिति यत् प्रोक्तं यन्नेत्याहानृतं हि तत् ॥38॥
सत्यं पुष्पफलं विद्यादात्मवृक्षस्य गीयते । वृक्षेऽजीवति तन्न स्यादनृतं मूलमात्मनः ॥39॥
तद् यथा वृक्ष उन्मूलः शुष्यत्युद्वर्ततेऽचिरात् । एवं नष्टानृतः सद्य आत्मा शुष्येन्न संशयः ॥40॥
पराग् रिक्तमपूर्णं वा अक्षरं यत् तदोमिति । यत् किञ्चिदोमिति ब्रूयात् तेन रिच्येत वै पुमान् ।
भिक्षवे सर्वमोङ्कुर्वन्नालं कामेन चात्मने ॥41॥
अथैतत् पूर्णमभ्यात्मं यच्च नेत्यनृतं वचः । सर्वं नेत्यनृतं ब्रूयात् स दुष्कीर्तिः श्वसन् मृतः ॥42॥
स्त्रीषु नर्मविवाहे च वृत्त्यर्थे प्राणसङ्कटे । गोब्राह्मणार्थे हिंसायां नानृतं स्याज्जुगुप्सितम् 43॥

इति श्रीमद्भागवते महापुराणे पारमहंस्यां संहितायामष्टमस्कन्धे वामनप्रादुर्भावे एकोनविंशोऽध्यायः ॥19॥

to hell. **36.** Charity that will jeopardise one's livelihood is not praiseworthy. For all disciplines like gifts, Yajna, austerity, and other duties are prescribed for one who has the means to live in this world. **37.** He is a happy man in this world and the next who allots his wealth for the following five purposes, namely, for the discharge of one's religious and altruistic duties, for spreading one's name and fame, for augmenting one's income, for pleasure, and for helping one's friends and relatives.

Falsehood in worldly Life (38-43)

38. O king of Asuras! Hear from me what many Vedic passages have to say on this question of truth and untruth. What one accepts solemnly, saying 'yes', is truth. What is rejected, saying 'no', is untruth. **39-40.** Truth is the flower and fruit of the plant of an embodied being. When the plant is alive only, it can bear fruits and flowers on it, not when it is dead. The root of the body is untruth (i.e. its origin and sustenance are through human passion); so will this body perish when it is completely disconnected from untruth. There is no doubt about it. (And therefore it has to be concluded that what the Veda condemns is untruth that is superfluous for the maintenance of life.) **41.** The syllable 'Om', indicating 'I give', means that one's wealth flows out of oneself, and to that extent, one gets deprived. Now if one says 'Om', or gives away only a little of one's possessions, he will become poor by that much only. With the remaining he can somehow support himself. But if he says 'Om' to a suppliant in regard to all his possessions, that is, gives a blank cheque to a person in need, then he will have nothing left to fulfil his own needs. Life will become impossible for him. **42.** So to stick to untruth, that is, to refuse to give away everything, is the way to preserve one's existing wealth and to draw that of others to oneself. But one should not stick to this way always, because it will bring the disrepute of being a miser or a greedy man, and a man who is subject to ill-fame is as good as dead even if he is breathing. Gifts have therefore to be given, but very discriminatingly. **43.** Besides, it is said that to tell an untruth under the following circumstances is not sinful. These conditions are: to please and attract a woman; in jest; for the purpose of finalising a marriage; for preserving one's livelihood; to save oneself from death; to save a holy man or a helpless creature; and to save another from death or great danger.

अथ विंशोऽध्यायः

श्रीशुक उवाच

बलिरेवं गृहपतिः कुलाचार्येण भाषितः । तूष्णीं भूत्वा क्षणं राजन्नुवाचावहितो गुरुम् ॥ 1॥

बलिरुवाच

सत्यं भगवता प्रोक्तं धर्मोऽयं गृहमेधिनाम् । अर्थं कामं यशो वृत्तिं यो न बाधेत कर्हिचित् ॥ 2॥
स चाहं वित्तलोभेन प्रत्याचक्षे कथं द्विजम् । प्रतिश्रुत्य ददामीति प्राह्लादिः कितवो यथा ॥ 3॥
न ह्यसत्यात् परोऽधर्म इति होवाच भूरियम् । सर्वं सोढुमलं मन्ये ऋतेऽलीकपरं नरम् ॥ 4॥
नाहं बिभेमि निरयान्नाधन्यादसुखार्णवात् । न स्थानच्च्यवनान्मृत्योर्यथा विप्रप्रलम्भनात् ॥ 5॥
यद् यद्धास्यति लोकेऽस्मिन् सम्परेतं धनादिकम् । तस्य त्यागे निमित्तं किं विप्रस्तुष्येन्न तेन चेत् ॥ 6॥
श्रेयः कुर्वन्ति भूतानां साधवो दुस्त्यजासुभिः । दध्यङ्शिबिप्रभृतयः को विकल्पो धरादिषु ॥ 7॥
यैरियं बुभुजे ब्रह्मन् दैत्येन्द्रैरनिवर्तिभिः । तेषां कालोऽग्रसील्लोकान् न यशोऽधिगतं भुवि 8॥
सुलभा युधि विप्रर्षे ह्यनिवृत्तास्तनुत्यजः । न तथा तीर्थ आयाते श्रद्धया ये धनत्यजः ॥ 9॥

Skandha VIII : Chapter 20

THE REVELATION OF VĀMANA

Sukra's Advice rejected (1-18)

Sri Suka said: **1.** O King! Hearing the speech of Rishi Sukra, his family teacher, Mahabali, the master of the sacrifice, sat quiet for a moment, and then said with determination. **2.** He said: 'What you, worshipful Sir, said about the Dharma of the householder, that his actions should not adversely affect his worldly interests, happiness, name and livelihood, is no doubt right. **3.** But how can I, a grandson of Prahlada, behave like a cheat and refuse to give this holy Brahmacharin what I have promised? **4.** The earth-deity has declared: Save a liar, I can put up with any one else. So according to the earth-deity there is no Adharma greater than lying. **5.** Nothing is more frightening to me than disappointing a holy man—neither poverty, nor loss of position and power, nor death, nor even hell. **6.** In this world wealth and such other earthly acquisitions are all lost to one at death. Then what harm is there in giving them up for a good cause even when one is alive? (Then give a portion and retain the rest of your wealth for comfortable living —if such a suggestion is made, my answer is:) Of what use, too, is a partial gift, if it is not going to satisfy a holy man? **7.** For the benefit of the world at large, great personages like Dadhīchi and Sibi gave up their very lives. Then why should one feel any hesitation to give up such small things like the earth and other possessions? **8.** O learned one! Time might consume this earth, the possession that the Asuras have been enjoying by virtue of their valour which has made them strangers to anything like retreat in battle. But Time shall not so consume the reputation in which they are held everywhere. **9.** O holy sage! There are quite many in this world who give up their bodies in the field of battle without retreating. But those who are ready to give their wealth to worthy persons or causes, with genuine

मनस्विनः कारुणिकस्य शोभनं यदर्थिकामोपनयेन दुर्गतिः ।
कुतः पुनर्ब्रह्मविदां भवादृशां ततो वटोरस्य ददामि वाञ्छितम् ॥10॥
यजन्ति यज्ञक्रतुभिर्यमादृता भवन्त आम्नायविधानकोविदाः ।
स एव विष्णुर्वरदोऽस्तु वा परो दास्याम्यमुष्मै क्षितिमीप्सितां मुने ॥11॥
यद्यप्यसावधर्मेण मां बध्नीयादनागसम् । तथाप्येनं न हिंसिष्ये भीतं ब्रह्मतनुं रिपुम् ॥12॥
एष वा उत्तमश्लोको न जिहासति यद् यशः । हत्वा मैनां हरेद् युद्धे शयीत निहतो मया ॥13॥

श्रीशुक उवाच

एवमश्रद्धितं शिष्यमनादेशकरं गुरुः । शशाप दैवप्रहितः सत्यसन्धं मनस्विनम् ॥14॥
दृढं पण्डितमान्यज्ञः स्तब्धोऽस्यस्मदुपेक्षया । मच्छासनातिगो यस्त्वमचिराद् भ्रश्यसे श्रियः 15॥
एवं शप्तः स्वगुरुणा सत्यान्न चलितो महान् । वामनाय ददावेनामर्चित्वोदकपूर्वकम् ॥16॥
विन्ध्यावलिस्तदाऽऽगत्य पत्नी जालकमालिनी । आनिन्ये कलशं हैममवनेजन्यपां भृतम् ॥17॥
यजमानः स्वयं तस्य श्रीमत् पादयुगं मुदा । अवनिज्यावहन्मूर्ध्नि तदपो विश्वपावनीः ॥18॥

faith and unselfish dedication, are few and far between in this world. **10.** For an enlightened man with a kind heart, the suffering involved in satisfying the needs of even an ordinary suppliant is an embellishment. That being so, how much more glorious it is to satisfy illumined personages like you by providing for your wants. So I shall give this Brahmacharin what he has asked for. **11.** O sage! In Yagas and Yajnas, you, who are experts in those rites, make sacrificial offerings to Mahavishnu with great reverence and devotion. That being so, if, as you say, this Brahmacharin is that Vishnu, irrespective of whether He has come as a benefactor to give us boon or as an enemy to destroy us, I shall certainly give Him whatever He has asked for, not barring the whole earth even. **12.** Even if by adopting some improper and unrighteous means He were to tie me up—me who am absolutely innocent—even then I shall not injure Him, as he has come assuming a garb of holiness out of fear. **13.** If He is really Mahavishnu, the one of extensive fame for holiness, and He wants to add to that fame by conquering me, then He will kill me in battle and take over the earth. If on the contrary, he be an imposter, he will be killed by me in the battle field.

Sri Suka said: **14.** Thereupon, by the prompting of the Lord within, Rishi Sukra, the teacher of the Asuras, cursed his truthful and courageous disciple Bali who rejected his advice without attaching much seriousness to it. **15.** The curse ran thus: 'You, who consider yourself very learned, but are really ignorant and arrogant, and have disobeyed my order, shall soon be deprived of all your wealth and glory.' **16.** The high-souled Bali, however, did not swerve from truth even under the threat of his teacher's curse. He worshipped Vāmana according to rites and offered him the earth with libations of water. **17.** Bali's wife Vindhyāvali, bedecked with necklaces of pearls, now came forward and placed there a golden jar full of consecrated water for the rites connected with the gift. **18.** Mahabali, the master of the sacrifice, took the water vessel, washed the feet of Vāmana in great joy, and sprinkled on his own head that world-sanctifying water with which the Lord's feet had been washed.

Revelation of Cosmic Form (19-29)

तदासुरेन्द्रं दिवि देवतागणा गन्धर्वविद्याधरसिद्धचारणाः ।
तत्कर्म सर्वेऽपि गृणन्त आर्जवं प्रसूनवर्षैर्ववृषुर्मुदान्विताः ॥19॥
नेदुर्मुहुर्दुन्दुभयः सहस्रशो गन्धर्वकिम्पूरुषकिन्नरा जगुः ।
मनस्विनानेन कृतं सुदुष्करं विद्वानदाद् यद् रिपवे जगत्त्रयम् ॥20॥
तद् वामनं रूपमवर्धताद्भुतं हरेरनन्तस्य गुणत्रयात्मकम् ।
भूः खं दिशो द्यौर्विवराः पयोधयस्तिर्यङ्नृदेवा ऋषयो यदासत ॥21॥
काये बलिस्तस्य महाविभूतेः सहर्त्विगाचार्यसदस्य एतत् ।
ददर्श विश्वं त्रिगुणं गुणात्मके भूतेन्द्रियार्थाशयजीवयुक्तम् ॥22॥
रसामचष्टाङ्घ्रितलेऽथ पादयोर्महीं महीध्रान् पुरुषस्य जङ्घयोः ।
पतत्त्रिणो जानुनि विश्वमूर्तेरूर्वोर्गणं मारुतमिन्द्रसेनः ॥23॥
सन्ध्यां विभोर्वाससि गुह्य ऐक्षत् प्रजापतीञ्जघने आत्ममुख्यान् ।
नाभ्यां नभः कुक्षिषु सप्तसिन्धूनुरुक्रमस्योरसि चर्क्षमालाम् ॥24॥
हृद्यङ्ग धर्मं स्तनयोर्मुरारेर्ऋतं च सत्यं च मनस्यथेन्दुम् ।
श्रियं च वक्षस्यरविन्दहस्तां कण्ठे च सामानि समस्तरेफान् ॥25॥
इन्द्रप्रधानानमरान् भुजेषु तत्कर्णयोः ककुभो द्यौश्च मूर्ध्नि ।
केशेषु मेघाञ्छ्वसनं नासिकायामक्ष्णोश्च सूर्यं वदने च वह्निम् ॥26॥

19. Then in appreciation of the absolute integrity and straightforwardness of Mahabali in fulfilling his promise, a rain of flowers was showered on Bali, the Asura king, from heaven by a host of jubiliant celestials—Devas, Gandharvas, Vidhyādharas, Siddhas, Chāranas and others. **20.** Kettle-drums and other instruments were sounded again and again. Gandharvas, Kinnaras and Kimpurushas sang, praising Bali thus: 'Even knowing that he will lose his all, this great hero has accomplished the impossible task of making an offering of all the three worlds to his enemy.'

21. That form of Vāmana which included in itself the whole of Prakriti, now expanded in a wonderful manner, revealing within it all that exits—the earth, sky, quarters, heaven, the fourteen worlds, oceans, brute creations, men, celestials, Rishis and everything else. **22.** In that most glorious divine form of the Lord, Bali along with his priests and members of the sacrificial assembly saw the whole universe included in this manifestation of the Gunas (constituents) of Prakriti like the gross elements, Indriyas, objects, mind, and the embodied beings. **23.** Mahabali saw in that Cosmic Form of the Lord, the nether worlds in the undersurface of His feet, the earth in His foot, the mountains in His ankles, the birds in His knee and the wind in His thigh. **24.** In that all-comprehending form of His, Bali saw Sandhya in His garments, the Prajapatis in His genitals, the Asuras, including himself, in His lips, the sky in His navel, the seven seas in His abdomen, and the stars in His chest. **25.** O dear one! He saw Dharma in His heart; Rita (cosmic order) and Satya (truth) in His breasts; the moon in His mind; the goddess Srī with a play-lotus in His chest; and the Vedic metres and all sounds in His neck. **26.** He saw Indra and the Devas in His arms; the quarters in His ears; the heaven in the crown of His head; the clouds in

वाण्यां च छन्दांसि रसे जलेशं भ्रुवोर्निषेधं च विधिं च पक्ष्मसु ।
अहश्च रात्रिं च परस्य पुंसो मन्युं ललाटेऽधर एव लोभम् ॥27॥
स्पर्शे च कामं नृप रेतसोऽम्भः पृष्ठे त्वधर्मं क्रमणेषु यज्ञम् ।
छायासु मृत्युं हसिते च मायां तनूरुहेष्वोषधिजातयश्च ॥28॥
नदीश्च नाडीषु शिला नखेषु बुद्धावजं देवगणानृषींश्च ।
प्राणेषु गात्रे स्थिरजङ्गमानि सर्वाणि भूतानि ददर्श वीरः ॥29॥
सर्वात्मनीदं भुवनं निरीक्ष्य सर्वेऽसुराः कश्मलमापुरङ्ग ।
सुदर्शनं चक्रमसह्यतेजो धनुश्च शार्ङ्गं स्तनयित्नुघोषम् ॥30॥
पर्जन्यघोषो जलजः पाञ्चजन्यः कौमोदकी विष्णुगदा तरस्विनी ।
विद्याधरोऽसिः शतचन्द्रयुक्तस्तूणोत्तमावक्षयसायकौ च ॥31॥
सुनन्दमुख्या उपतस्थुरीशं पार्षदमुख्याः सहलोकपालाः ।
स्फुरत्किरीटाङ्गदमीनकुण्डलश्रीवत्सरत्नोत्तममेखलाम्बरैः ॥32॥
मधुव्रतस्रग्वनमालया वृतो रराज राजन् भगवानुरुक्रमः ।
क्षितिं पदैकेन बलेर्विचक्रमे नभः शरीरेण दिशश्च बाहुभिः ॥33॥
पदं द्वितीयं क्रमतस्त्रिविष्टपं न वै तृतीयाय तदीयमण्वपि ।
उरुक्रमस्याङ्घ्रिरुपर्युपर्यथो महर्जनाभ्यां तपसः परं गतः ॥34॥

इति श्रीमद्भागवते महापुराणे पारमहंस्यां संहितायामष्टमस्कन्धे विश्वरूपदर्शनं नाम विंशोऽध्यायः ॥20॥

His hair; the air in His nose; the sun in His eyes; and the fire in His face. **27.** He saw the Vedas in the speech of that Supreme One; the deity Varuna in His tongue; the Vedic commandments and prohibitions in His eyebrows; day and night in His eyelids; anger in His forehead; and greed in His lips. **28.** He saw lust in His sense of touch; water in His semen; Adharma in His back; Yajna in His strides; death in His shadow; Maya in His laughter; and plants in His hair. **29.** That hero saw rivers in his blood vessels; rocks in His nails; Brahma in His intellect; and the Devas and Rishis in His senses. Thus he saw in this universal form everything moving and unmoving in the universe.

Worlds measured in two Paces (30-34)

30-33. Seeing this whole universe in the Cosmic Form of the Lord, the support of all, the Asuras felt much depressed and dispirited. Along with that form of the Lord were visible Sudarsana, the discus of irresistible might; the bow Sārnga with its twanging sound like a thunderclap; the sea-born conch Pānchajanya whose blare resembled the roll of thunder; the powerful mace of Vishnu called Kaumodaki; the sword called Vidyādhara in its moon-marked scabbard; the quiver that never got empty of arrows; and Sunanda and other principal attendants of His, besides the guardian deities of the quarters waiting upon Him. Waited on by all these, there stood the Lord, shining in the brilliance of His sparkling diadem, armlet, and fish-marked ear rings, as also of the Srivatsa mark, Kaustubha jewel, superb girdle, yellow garment, and fragrant flower wreath that attracted large numbers of honey-bees—ready to measure and take over the three worlds by his three steps. He measured the whole of Bali's earth with one step, and He occupied the skies with his body and the quarters by stretching his arms. **34.** The heaven was hardly sufficient for his second stride, and for the third stride, there was nothing left of Mahabali's possessions. For, the second step that the Lord took extended byeond the Swarga to all the higher realms like Maharloka, Janaloka and Tapoloka, and reached up to the Satyaloka. There was nothing more to measure.

अथैकविंशोऽध्यायः

श्रीशुक उवाच

सत्यं समीक्ष्याब्जभवो नखेन्दुभिर्हतस्वधामद्युतिरावृतोऽभ्यगात् ।
मरीचिमिश्रा ऋषयो बृहद्व्रताः सनन्दनाद्या नरदेव योगिनः ॥ 1॥
वेदोपवेदा नियमान्विता यमास्तर्केतिहासाङ्गपुराणसंहिताः ।
ये चापरे योगसमीरदीपितज्ञानाग्निना रन्धितकर्मकल्मषाः ।
ववन्दिरे यत्स्मरणानुभावतः स्वायम्भुवं धाम गता अकर्मकम् ॥ 2॥
अथाङ्घ्रये प्रोन्नमिताय विष्णोरुपाहरत् पद्मभवोऽर्हणोदकम् ।
समर्च्य भक्त्याभ्यगृणाच्छुचिश्रवा यन्नाभिपङ्केरुहसम्भवः स्वयम् ॥ 3॥
धातुः कमण्डलुजलं तदुरुक्रमस्य पादावनेजनपवित्रतया नरेन्द्र ।
स्वर्धुन्यभून्नभसि सा पतती निमार्ष्टि लोकत्रयं भगवतो विशदेव कीर्तिः ॥ 4॥
ब्रह्मादयो लोकनाथाः स्वनाथाय समादृताः । सानुगा बलिमाजह्रुः संक्षिप्तात्मविभूतये ॥ 5॥

Skandha VIII : Chapter 21

BALI IN BONDAGE

Brahma's Worship of Vāmana (1-8)

Sri Suka said: **1-2.** Brahma now saw the lustre of the toe nails of the Lord, whose feet had touched the Satyaloka, submerging the brilliance of that realm of his. So Brahma went forward to do honour to those feet of the Lord, accompanied by Rishis like Marichi, life-long Brahmacharins like Sanandana, and Yogis and other sages who have burnt up the dirt of Karmic tendencies in themselves by the fire of knowledge ignited by Yoga; by devotees who by the contemplation of the Lord's feet through Bhakti have attained to Satyaloka; and by the presiding deities of the Vedas and Upavedas, law codes, faculties like logic, the Puranas, Ithihasas and Samhitas. In that worship all joined who by virtue of their devotion to the Lord had attained to Brahmaloka—a realm to which ritualistic worship alone cannot elevate one. **3.** Then Brahma, who was born of the navel-lotus of the Lord, worshipped His feet with flowers, as they (the feet) came higher and higher upto his realm. **4.** O King! The water that Brahma poured from his water pot on the measuring feet of the Lord, became the heavenly Ganga by virtue of the purity it attained by the contact of the Lord's feet. Falling down through the skies, it sanctifies all the three worlds, just like the Lord's holy fame itself. **5.** Brahma and other divinities now offered ingredients of worship at the feet of Vāmana who had by this time withdrawn His cosmic form which revealed his Divine

तोयैः समर्हणैः स्रग्भिर्दिव्यगन्धानुलेपनैः ।
धूपैर्दीपैः सुरभिभिर्लाजाक्षतफलाङ्कुरैः ॥ 6॥
स्तवनैर्जयशब्दैश्च तद्वीर्यमहिमाङ्कितैः ।
नृत्यवादित्रगीतैश्च शङ्खदुन्दुभिनिःस्वनैः ॥ 7॥
जाम्बवानृक्षराजस्तु भेरीशब्दैर्मनोजवः ।
विजयं दिक्षु सर्वासु महोत्सवमघोषयत् ॥ 8॥
महीं सर्वां हृतां दृष्ट्वा त्रिपदव्याजयाच्ञया ।
ऊचुः स्वभर्तुरसुरा दीक्षितस्यात्यमर्षिताः ॥ 9॥
न वा अयं ब्रह्मबन्धुर्विष्णुर्मायाविनां वरः ।
द्विजरूपप्रतिच्छन्नो देवकार्यं चिकीर्षति ॥10॥
अनेन याचमानेन शत्रुणा वटुरूपिणा ।
सर्वस्वं नो हृतं भर्तुर्न्यस्तदण्डस्य बर्हिषि ॥11॥
सत्यव्रतस्य सततं दीक्षितस्य विशेषतः ।
नानृतं भाषितुं शक्यं ब्रह्मण्यस्य दयावतः ॥12॥
तस्मादस्य वधो धर्मो भर्तुः शुश्रूषणं च नः ।
इत्यायुधानि जगृहुर्बलेरनुचरासुराः ॥13॥
ते सर्वे वामनं हन्तुं शूलपट्टिशपाणयः ।
अनिच्छतो बले राजन् प्राद्रवञ्जातमन्यवः ॥14॥
तानभिद्रवतो दृष्ट्वा दितिजानीकपान् नृप ।
प्रहस्यानुचरा विष्णोः प्रत्यषेधन्नुदायुधाः ॥15॥
नन्दः सुनन्दोऽथ जयो विजयः प्रबलो बलः ।
कुमुदः कुमुदाक्षश्च विष्वक्सेनः पतत्रिराट् ॥16॥
जयन्तः श्रुतदेवश्च पुष्पदन्तोऽथ सात्वतः ।
सर्वे नागायुतप्राणाश्चमूं ते जघ्नुरासुरीम् ॥17॥
हन्यमानान् स्वकान् दृष्ट्वा पुरुषानुचरैर्बलिः ।
वारयामास संरब्धान् काव्यशापमनुस्मरन् ॥18॥

majesty. **6.** They offered Him scented water to wash His feet, wreaths of sweet-smelling flowers, unguents like specially prepared sandal paste, fragrant incense, light, rice, Yava, Durva grass etc. **7.** They celebrated the occasion with the singing of hymns and lyrics, extolling the Lord's doings and excellences, as also by joyous exclamations and the sounding of various musical instruments like kettle-drums and conchs. **8.** The king of the bears Jāmbavān, who was noted for his speed, celebrated this occasion of the Lord's triumph by announcing the joyous news all over the universe by beat of drums.

Discomfiture of Asura Army (9-24)

9. Seeing that under the guise of measuring three paces of earth, all the possessions of their master had been taken away, and that at a time he was observing the vows of sacrifice, the Asuras became furious and began to say: **10.** 'This pretender is not a holy man. He is none other than Vishnu, the master of all artifices and dissembling, presenting himself here in the disguise of a Brahmacharin for the achievement of the purpose of the Devas. **11.** This enemy of ours, come as a suppliant in the guise of a Brahmacharin, has managed to wrest all the possessions of our master, who on account of this sacrifice, has abandoned all violence. **12.** A firm adherent of truth, a respecter of holy men, and very kind and merciful by nature, it is impossible for our master to tell an untruth even ordinarily, and more so when he has been consecrated for the performance of a holy rite like this sacrifice. **13.** So it is our duty now to serve our master by killing this enemy. Saying so, the Asura following of Bali took up arms to fight Vāmana.

14. Without Bali's direction or permission, these Asuras, armed with tridents and spears, rushed at Vāmana to kill him. **15.** Laughing at these Asura leaders rushing for an attack, the attendants of Vishnu stopped them with weapons in hand. **16-17.** The attendants of Vishnu—Nanda, Sunanda, Jaya, Vijaya, Prabala, Bala, Kumuda, Kumudāksha, Vishvaksena, Garuda, Jayanta, Srutadeva, Pushpadanta, Sātvata and others, who had each the strength of ten thousand elephants, began to decimate these Asuras.

18. Remembering the curse of his pre-

हे विप्रचित्ते हे राहो हे नेमे श्रूयतां वचः ।
मा युध्यत निवर्तध्वं न नः कालोऽयमर्थकृत् ।।19।।
यः प्रभुः सर्वभूतानां सुखदुःखोपपत्तये ।
तं नातिवर्तितुं दैत्याः पौरुषैरीश्वरः पुमान् ।।20।।
यो नो भवाय प्रागासीदभवाय दिवौकसाम् ।
स एव भगवानद्य वर्तते तद्विपर्ययम् ।।21।।
बलेन सचिवैर्बुद्ध्या दुर्गैर्मन्त्रौषधादिभिः ।
सामादिभिरुपायैश्च कालं नात्येति वै जनः ।।22।।
भवद्भिर्निर्जिता ह्येते बहुशोऽनुचरा हरेः ।
दैवेनर्द्धैस्त एवाद्य युधि जित्वा नदन्ति नः ।।23।।
एतान् वयं विजेष्यामो यदि दैवं प्रसीदति ।
तस्मात् कालं प्रतीक्षध्वं यो नोऽर्थत्वाय कल्पते ।24।

श्रीशुक उवाच

पत्युर्निगदितं श्रुत्वा दैत्यदानवयूथपाः ।
रसां निर्विविशू राजन् विष्णुपार्षदताडिताः ।।25।।
अथ तार्क्ष्यसुतो ज्ञात्वा विराट्प्रभुचिकीर्षितम् ।
बबन्ध वारुणैः पाशैर्बलिं सौत्येऽहनि क्रतौ ।।26।।
हाहाकारो महानासीद् रोदस्योः सर्वतोदिशम् ।
गृह्यमाणेऽसुरपतौ विष्णुना प्रभविष्णुना ।।27।।
तं बद्धं वारुणैः पाशैर्भगवानाह वामनः ।
नष्टश्रियं स्थिरप्रज्ञमुदारयशसं नृप ।।28।।
पदानि त्रीणि दत्तानि भूमेर्मह्यं त्वयासुर ।
द्वाभ्यां क्रान्ता मही सर्वा तृतीयमुपकल्पय ।।29।।

ceptor, and seeing the great slaughter among his followers at the hands of the emissaries of Vishnu, Mahabali stopped his agitated followers from fighting. **19.** He said: 'O Rāhu! O Nemi! Hear what I say! Stop fighting and retreat. Times are not now propitious for us. **20.** Besides, no effort can overcome Him, who determines the destinies of all beings, and distributes enjoyments and sufferings to all creatures according to their deserts. **21.** That same Bhagavan, the Supreme Being Mahavishnu, who favoured us in the past and wrought the downfall of the Devas, has now reversed His attitude. At present the cause of the Devas attracts His favour, and ours His disfavour. **22.** Man cannot overcome or defeat Time by any of these means—army, competent ministers, intelligence, fortifications, medicinal drugs and Mantras, or by the four techniques of diplomacy. **23.** In the past when Time was in your favour you had defeated these followers of Hari many a time. The very same men are now raising cries of victory after defeating us in battle. **24.** When Time is again in our favour, we shall conquer these very people. Therefore wait patiently for the coming of that favourable Time.'

Binding of Bali (25-34)

Sri Suka said: **25.** O King! Thus admonished by their master, the leaders of the Asuras, who were under the attack of Vishnu's attendants, left the field of battle and fled to Rasātala, the nether world. **26.** Then on the day when the rite with the Soma juice was to be performed at the sacrifice, Garuda, the king of all species of birds, bound up Bali with the celestial cord of Varuna, knowing the intention of his master Lord Vāmana that His great devotee Bali should gain everlasting fame thereby. **27.** When Bali was thus bound up by the all-powerful Mahavishnu, loud cries of 'alas' rose from the earth and the skies and from all directions.

28. O King! To Bali, who was thus deprived of his possessions and put in bondage, but who had none the less not lost his presence of mind and his world-wide reputation, the Lord Vāmana said: **29.** ' O Asura! You promised to give me earth measured by my three paces. With two paces I have measured all the worlds.

यावत् तपत्यसौ गोभिर्यावदिन्दुः सहोडुभिः । यावद् वर्षति पर्जन्यस्तावती भूरियं तव ॥30॥
पदैकेन मया क्रान्तो भूर्लोकः खं दिशस्तनोः । स्वर्लोकस्तु द्वितीयेन पश्यतस्ते स्वमात्मना ॥31॥
प्रतिश्रुतमदातुस्ते निरये वास इष्यते । विश त्वं निरयं तस्माद् गुरुणा चानुमोदितः ॥32॥
वृथा मनोरथस्तस्य दूरे स्वर्गः पतत्यधः । प्रतिश्रुतस्यादानेन योऽर्थिनं विप्रलम्भते ॥33॥
विप्रलब्धो ददामीति त्वयाहं चाढ्यमानिना । तद्व्यलीकफलं भुङ्क्ष्व निरयं कतिचित् समाः ।34॥

इति श्रीमद्भागवते महापुराणे पारमहंस्यां संहितायामष्टमस्कन्धे वामनप्रादुर्भावे बलिनिग्रहो नामैकविंशोऽध्यायः ॥21॥

Show me the space for the third pace. **30.** Your possessions extend up to the limits that the sun and the moon with the stars illumine, and up to where the clouds shower rain. **31.** In your very presence, I, the all-pervading being, have measured the whole of the earth with one pace and filled the sky and the quarters with My body; and with the second pace I have measured the heavens. Thus all your possessions have been measured. **32.** For you who cannot give what you have promised, the proper place is evidently hell. For this reason you have now to enter hell with the congratulations of your Guru, who has condemned you to this fate. **33.** For one who deceives a suppliant by refusing to give what is promised, all his hopes go in vain; heaven is far away for him; only downfall is near at hand. **34.** Now for a long number of years enjoy the fruits of hell—the fruit of the deception you practised in the pride of your wealth and power.'

अथ द्वाविंशोऽध्यायः

श्रीशुक उवाच

एवं विप्रकृतो राजन् बलिर्भगवतासुरः । भिद्यमानोऽप्यभिन्नात्मा प्रत्याहाविक्लवं वचः । 1।

बलिरुवाच

यद्युत्तमश्लोक भवान् ममेरितं वचो व्यलीकं सुरवर्य मन्यते ।
करोम्यृतं तन्न भवेत् प्रलम्भनं पदं तृतीयं कुरु शीर्ष्णि मे निजम् ॥ 2॥
बिभेमि नाहं निरयात् पदच्युतो न पाशबन्धाद् व्यसनाद् दुरत्ययात् ।
नैवार्थकृच्छ्राद् भवतो विनिग्रहादसाधुवादाद् भृशमुद्विजे यथा ॥ 3॥

Skandha VIII : Chapter 22

BESTOWAL OF GRACE ON BALI

Bali stands Tests unmoved (1-11)

Sri Suka said: **1.** O King! Even though thus deceived and in many ways induced to climb down from his ideal of truth and generosity by the Lord, the Asura Bali remained unmoved in the resolution to stick to truth, and replied without any trace of mental dejection. *Bali said*: **2.** 'O Divinity of worldwide fame for holiness! If Thy idea is to make my plighted words to be false, I am equally resolved to make them true. My speech shall never end in deception (of the kind Thou hast practised). Be pleased to place Thy third step on my head. **3.** The disrepute of being a

पुंसां श्लाघ्यतमं मन्ये दण्डमर्हत्तमार्पितम् । यं न माता पिता भ्राता सुहृदश्चादिशन्ति हि ॥ 4॥
त्वं नूनमसुराणां नः पारोक्ष्यः परमो गुरुः । यो नोऽनेकमदान्धानां विभ्रंशं चक्षुरादिशत् ॥ 5॥
यस्मिन् वैरानुबन्धेन रूढेन विबुधेतराः । बहवो लेभिरे सिद्धिं यामु हैकान्तयोगिनः ॥ 6॥
तेनाहं निगृहीतोऽस्मि भवता भूरिकर्मणा । बद्धश्च वारुणैः पाशैर्नातिव्रीडे न च व्यथे ॥ 7॥
पितामहो मे भवदीयसम्मतः प्रह्लाद आविष्कृतसाधुवादः ।
भवद्विपक्षेण विचित्रवैशसं सम्प्रापितस्त्वत्परमः स्वपित्रा ॥ 8॥
किमात्मनानेन जहाति योऽन्ततः किं रिक्थहारैः स्वजनाख्यदस्युभिः ।
किं जायया संसृतिहेतुभूतया मर्त्यस्य गेहैः किमिहायुषो व्ययः ॥ 9॥
इत्थं स निश्चित्य पितामहो महानगाधबोधो भवतः पादपद्मम् ।
ध्रुवं प्रपेदे ह्यकुतोभयं जनाद् भीतः स्वपक्षक्षपणस्य सत्तमः ॥10॥
अथाहमप्यात्मरिपोस्तवान्तिकं दैवेन नीतः प्रसभं त्याजितश्रीः ।
इदं कृतान्तान्तिकवर्ति जीवितं ययाध्रुवं स्तब्धमतिर्न बुध्यते ॥11॥

liar and a dissembler is more of a terror for me than hell, downfall, bondage, insurmountable sorrow, poverty or any torture of a more intense kind that Thou mightest inflict on me. **4.** I consider that a punishment inflicted by a most venerable personage like Thee is to be welcomed more than shunned, as it leads to the supreme welfare of the individual concerned in the long run. The punishment that parents and other well-wishers give cannot achieve the purpose of Thy punishment, which consists in one's spiritual elevation. **5.** Thou art the supreme teacher of us Asuras, too, indirectly. For Thou hast given us enlightenment through downfall—us who otherwise would ever have been under the blinding infatuation caused by prosperity. **6.** By the concentration produced by deep-rooted antagonism to Thee, many an Asura has obtained the same goal reached by Yogis who concentrate on Thee through exclusive devotion. **7.** I am not very much ashamed or aggrieved by the fact that I have been subdued and tied up with Varuna's cords by Thee of many great and glorious deeds. **8.** My grandfather Prahlada, who was completely dedicated to Thee, who had established his reputation for devotion, and whom Thy devotees considered a great soul, was subjected to many ordeals by his own father who was moved by antagonism to Thee. **9.** My grandfather thought in this way: What is the good of keeping up this body which has to die in the end in spite of all care one takes of it? Of what good are sons who are only plunderers of your wealth and of relatives who are only enemies in friendly guise? Of what use is a wife who is the cause of greater and greater involvement in Samsara? Of what use is a home for one who is threatened with death at any time? All these preoccupations only help the ebbing away of the short span of one's life. **10.** Thinking thus, my grandfather, a saintly personage of exceeding greatness and vast knowledge, abandoned association with his own people for fear of spiritual degeneration, and took refuge at Thy feet—a firm shelter free from all fear, in spite of Thy being the destroyer of Asuras. **11.** It is a fortunate circumstance that Providence has brought me close to Thee, the natural enemy of Asuras, after depriving me of my prosperous state. For it is wealth and

श्रीशुक उवाच

तस्येत्थं भाषमाणस्य प्रह्लादो भगवत्प्रियः । आजगाम कुरुश्रेष्ठ राकापतिरिवोत्थितः ॥12॥
तमिन्द्रसेनः स्वपितामहं श्रिया विराजमानं नलिनायतेक्षणम् ।
प्रांशुं पिशङ्गाम्बरमञ्जनत्विषं प्रलम्बबाहुं सुभगं समैक्षत ॥13॥
तस्मै बलिर्वारुणपाशयन्त्रितः समर्हणं नोपजहार पूर्ववत् ।
ननाम मूर्ध्नाश्रुविलोललोचनः सव्रीडनीचीनमुखो बभूव ह ॥14॥
स तत्र हासीनमुदीक्ष्य सत्पतिं सुनन्दनन्दाद्यनुगैरुपासितम् ।
उपेत्य भूमौ शिरसा महामना ननाम मूर्ध्ना पुलकाश्रुविक्लवः ॥15॥

प्रह्लाद उवाच

त्वयैव दत्तं पदमैन्द्रमूर्जितं हृतं तदेवाद्य तथैव शोभनम् ।
मन्ये महानस्य कृतो ह्यनुग्रहो विभ्रंशितो यच्छ्रिय आत्ममोहनात् ॥16॥
यया हि विद्वानपि मुह्यते यतस्तत् को विचष्टे गतिमात्मनो यथा ।
तस्मै नमस्ते जगदीश्वराय वै नारायणायाखिललोकसाक्षिणे ॥17॥

श्रीशुक उवाच

तस्यानुशृण्वतो राजन् प्रह्लादस्य कृताञ्जलेः । हिरण्यगर्भो भगवानुवाच मधुसूदनम् ॥18॥
बद्धं वीक्ष्य पतिं साध्वी तत्पत्नी भयविह्वला । प्राञ्जलिः प्रणतोपेन्द्रं बभाषेऽवाङ्मुखी नृप ॥19॥

prosperity that stupefy the mind of man and make him forget the truth that he is ever in the jaws of death.'

Prahlada's Arrival and Plea (12-17)

Sri Suka said: **12.** While Bali was speaking thus, his grandfather Prahlada, the darling of the Lord, arrived at the spot, shining like the newly risen full moon. **13.** Bali now saw before him his own grandfather—resplendent with auspicious glory, lotus-eyed, tall, dressed in yellow robes, brilliantly black like antimony, long-armed, and very handsome in appearance. **14.** Being bound by Varuna's cords, Bali could not do full obeisance to his grandfather as usual. So he bent down his head in salutation, with tears in his eyes and his face downcast. **15.** On seeing the Lord Mahavishnu, waited upon by his attendants like Sunanda and Nanda, the high-souled Prahlada approached Him with head bowed in devotion, and fell down prostrate at His feet with tears in His eyes and horripilation all over his body.

Prahlada said: **16.** The glory of Indrahood was bestowed on him by Thee alone. Thou hast now deprived him of it. This will be for his good in the long run. It is a great blessing bestowed on him. For, he has now been bereft of prosperity which often infatuates a man and brings about spiritual insensitivity. **17.** The blindness of pride consequent on prosperity affects even a man learned and established in self-control. Who is the man that can keep level-headed in prosperity and stick to the spiritual path! Salutations to Thee Narayana, the witness and Lord of all the worlds!

Brahma's Plea (18-23)

Sri Suka said: **18.** O King! Brahma was now about to speak to the Lord, the destroyer of Madhu, in the hearing of Prahlada, who was standing there with joined palms. **19.** But he was interrupted by Vindhyāvali, the faithful wife of Bali, who was in the throes of fear to see her husband bound up. Bowing down before

विन्ध्यावलिरुवाच

क्रीडार्थमात्मन इदं त्रिजगत् कृतं ते स्वाम्यं तु तत्र कुधियोऽपर ईश कुर्युः।
कर्तुः प्रभोस्तव किमस्यत आवहन्ति त्यक्तह्रियस्त्वदवरोपितकर्तृवादाः ॥20॥

ब्रह्मोवाच

भूतभावन भूतेश देवदेव जगन्मय। मुञ्चैनं हृतसर्वस्वं नायमर्हति निग्रहम् ॥21॥
कृत्स्ना तेऽनेन दत्ता भूर्लोकाः कर्मार्जिताश्च ये। निवेदितं च सर्वस्वमात्माविक्लवया धिया ॥22॥
यत्पादयोरशठधीः सलिलं प्रदाय दूर्वाङ्कुरैरपि विधाय सतीं सपर्याम्।
अप्युत्तमां गतिमसौ भजते त्रिलोकीं दाश्वानविक्लवमनाः कथमार्तिमृच्छेत् ॥23॥

श्रीभगवानुवाच

ब्रह्मन् यमनुगृह्णामि तद्विशो विधुनोम्यहम्। यन्मदः पुरुषः स्तब्धो लोकं मां चावमन्यते ॥24॥
यदा कदाचिज्जीवात्मा संसरन् निजकर्मभिः। नानायोनिष्वनीशोऽयं पौरुषीं गतिमाव्रजेत् ॥25॥
जन्मकर्मवयोरूपविद्यैश्वर्यधनादिभिः। यद्यस्य न भवेत् स्तम्भस्तत्रायं मदनुग्रहः ॥26॥
मानस्तम्भनिमित्तानां जन्मादीनां समन्ततः। सर्वश्रेयःप्रतीपानां हन्त मुह्येन्न मत्परः ॥27॥

Lord Vāmana and with face downcast, she spoke to the Lord. *Vindhyāvali said:* **20.** 'O Lord! For Thy sport Thou hast created these three worlds. Men of perverted intelligence consider themselves masters in this world which belongs to Thee. Such people who shamelessly consider themselves masters and free agents—what have they got as their own to offer Thee, who art the one agent, the one Lord, and the one destroyer of this whole universe?'

21. *Brahma said*: O creator and Lord of all! O Supreme Being who indwells everything! All the possessions of Bali have been taken away. He does not deserve to be bound. Deign to release him from fetters. **22.** The whole of this earth, the higher worlds attained through Karma, all his wealth and power and his own body,—all these he has offered to Thee as gift without any regret. **23.** By making an offering of water followed by some tender shoots of Durva grass with faith and purity of mind, devotees attain to the highest state, the Vaikuntha. How then can he (Bali), who has made an offering of all the three worlds at Thy feet without the least hesitation, deserve this suffering and humiliation?

On Bali's Greatness (24-36)

The Lord said: **24.** O Brahma! Whomever I really wish to bless, I first take off his wealth. For wealth makes a man proud and arrogant, as a result of which he is led to insult the world and Myself. **25.** Subject as the Jiva is to his own Karma, he transmigrates by the compulsion of Karma from species to species and from body to body, until at some distant date he gets a human body (by My grace). **26.** If you find a man free from pride and arrogance in spite of being in favourable circumstances, in respect of birth, works, age, beauty of form, learning and wealth, know that it is only by My grace. **27.** However, a person who is devoted to Me never gets infatuated even when favoured by high birth, prosperity etc., which generally generate pride and arrogance in others and block all their spiritual progress. (Such was the case with great devotees like Dhruva, Prahlada and others.)

एष दानवदैत्यानामग्रणीः कीर्तिवर्धनः । अजैषीदजयां मायां सीदन्नपि न मुह्यति ।।28।।
क्षीणरिक्थश्च्युतः स्थानात् क्षिप्तो बद्धश्च शत्रुभिः । ज्ञातिभिश्च परित्यक्तो यातनामनुयापितः ।।29।।
गुरुणा भर्त्सितः शप्तो जहौ सत्यं न सुव्रतः । छलैरुक्तो मया धर्मो नायं त्यजति सत्यवाक् ।।30।।
एष मे प्रापितः स्थानं दुष्प्रापममरैरपि । सावर्णेरन्तरस्यायं भवितेन्द्रो मदाश्रयः ।।31।।
तावत् सुतलमध्यास्तां विश्वकर्मविनिर्मितम् । यन्नाधयो व्याधयश्च क्लमस्तन्द्रा पराभवः ।
नोपसर्गा निवसतां सम्भवन्ति ममेक्षया ।।32।।
इन्द्रसेन महाराज याहि भो भद्रमस्तु ते । सुतलं स्वर्गिभिः प्रार्थ्यं ज्ञातिभिः परिवारितः ।।33।।
न त्वामभिभविष्यन्ति लोकेशाः किमुतापरे । त्वच्छासनातिगान् दैत्यांश्चक्रं मे सूदयिष्यति ।।34।।
रक्षिष्ये सर्वतोऽहं त्वां सानुगं सपरिच्छदम् । सदा सन्निहितं वीर तत्र मां द्रक्ष्यते भवान् ।।35।।
तत्र दानवदैत्यानां सङ्गात् ते भाव आसुरः । दृष्ट्वा मदनुभावं वै सद्यः कुण्ठो विनङ्क्ष्यति ।।36।।

इति श्रीमद्भागवते महापुराणे पारमहंस्यां संहितायामष्टमस्कन्धे वामनप्रादुर्भावे बलिवामनसंवादो नाम द्वाविंशोऽध्यायः ।।22।।

28. This Mahabali, who is the leader of the Daityas and Danavas and an ornament enhancing the reputation of his people, has conquered even My Maya which is difficult for anyone to overcome. For he has remained absolutely unruffled and unconcerned even in the face of total downfall and persecution. **29-30.** Even though reduced to poverty, expelled from his position, put in fetters by the enemy, deserted by friends and scolded and cursed by his preceptor, Mahabali, firm in his vow of Truth, did not break his promise. Even the false interpretation of Dharma given by Me could not budge him an inch away from the righteous path.

31. I am giving him, who is entirely resigned to Me, a boon which is difficult to get by even a celestial; He will become the Indra in the age of Manu Sāvarni. **32.** Till then let him live in the realm called Sutala, in which there are many handiworks of the heavenly architect Viswakarma. Those who live there shall, due to My gracious concern for them, be free from every kind of difficulty—worry, disease, weakness, lethargy, defeat and the like. **33.** So, O Mahabali, great ruler! May you prosper! Along with all your friends, relatives and dependants go to Sutala which even the residents of Swarga long to reach. **34.** None will be able to overpower you there, not even the guardian deities of the worlds. And if any Asura dares to challenge you, that person will be destroyed by My divine discus, Sudarsana. **35.** I shall be affording protection to you and your people residing at Sutala. You will ever feel My presence there. **36.** Residing there amidst Daityas and Danavas, whatever Asuric tendency you may happen to contract from them, will all be weakened and obliterated immediately by the consciousness of My divine majesty.

अथ त्रयोविंशोऽध्यायः

श्रीशुक उवाच

इत्युक्तवन्तं पुरुषं पुरातनं महानुभावोऽखिलसाधुसम्मतः ।
बद्धाञ्जलिर्बाष्पकलाकुलेक्षणो भक्त्युद्गलो गद्गदया गिराब्रवीत् ॥ 1॥

बलिरुवाच

अहो प्रणामाय कृतः समुद्यमः प्रपन्नभक्तार्थविधौ समाहितः ।
यल्लोकपालैस्त्वदनुग्रहोऽमरैरलब्धपूर्वोऽपसदेऽसुरेऽर्पितः ॥ 2॥

श्रीशुक उवाच

इत्युक्त्वा हरिमानम्य ब्रह्माणं सभवं ततः । विवेश सुतलं प्रीतो बलिर्मुक्तः सहासुरैः ॥ 3॥
एवमिन्द्राय भगवान् प्रत्यानीय त्रिविष्टपम् । पूरयित्वादितेः काममशासत् सकलं जगत् ॥ 4॥
लब्धप्रसादं निर्मुक्तं पौत्रं वंशधरं बलिम् । निशाम्य भक्तिप्रवणः प्रह्लाद इदमब्रवीत् ॥ 5॥

प्रह्लाद उवाच

नेमं विरिञ्चो लभते प्रसादं न श्रीर्न शर्वः किमुतापरे ते ।
यन्नोऽसुराणामसि दुर्गपालो विश्वाभिवन्द्यैरपि वन्दिताङ्घ्रिः ॥ 6॥

Skandha VIII : Chapter 23

BALI'S EXIT AND AFTER

Hymns of Bali and Prahlada (1-10)

Sri Suka said: **1.** To the Supreme Being who spoke thus, the high-souled Bali, the object of admiration for all good and righteous people, replied in choked voice and in a mood of surging emotion of Bhakti, with his palms joined in adoration and his eyelids dropping with the heavy downpour of blissful tears.

Bali said: **2.** Thy grace is generally bestowed on those who surrender themselves to Thee. But lo! Thou hast been pleased to bestow on me that grace, although I have hardly taken the first step of self-surrender, namely making a devoted prostration to Thee. By merely taking a resolve to make Thee a prostration, I, an Asura and the meanest of them, have been vouchsafed a blessing which even the guardian deities have never had till now.

Sri Suka said: **3.** Saying so, Bali, who was now free from bondage, made prostrations to Hari, Brahma and Parameswara, and went joyfully to Sutala with his followers. **4.** In this way the worshipful Lord restored the heavenly region to Indra and fulfilled the prayer of Aditi. And as the brother of Indra (Upendra) he protected the three worlds.

5. Seeing Bali, his grandson and the preserver of the continuity of his line, freed from bondages and favoured by the Lord, Prahlada said as follows with fervent devotion. *Prahlada said*: **6.** 'A blessing of this kind has never been the privilege of Brahma, nor of Srī, nor of Siva, nor of any others. For Thou, who art the object of adoration of Divinities like Brahma whom the whole world reveres, hast undertaken to be the gate-keeper of us, Asuras, offering us protection from all others.

यत्पादपद्ममकरन्दनिषेवणेन ब्रह्मादयः शरणदाश्नुवते विभूतीः ।
कस्माद् वयं कुसृतयः खलयोनयस्ते दाक्षिण्यदृष्टिपदवीं भवतः प्रणीताः ॥ 7॥
चित्रं तवेहितमहोऽमितयोगमायालीलाविसृष्टभुवनस्य विशारदस्य ।
सर्वात्मनः समदृशो विषमः स्वभावो भक्तप्रियो यदसि कल्पतरुस्वभावः ॥ 8॥

श्रीभगवानुवाच

वत्स प्रह्लाद भद्रं ते प्रयाहि सुतलालयम् । मोदमानः स्वपौत्रेण ज्ञातीनां सुखमावह ॥ 9॥
नित्यं द्रष्टासि मां तत्र गदापाणिमवस्थितम् । मद्दर्शनमहाह्लादध्वस्तकर्मनिबन्धनः ॥10॥

श्रीशुक उवाच

आज्ञां भगवतो राजन् प्रह्लादो बलिना सह । बाढमित्यमलप्रज्ञो मूर्ध्न्याधाय कृताञ्जलिः ॥11॥
परिक्रम्यादिपुरुषं सर्वासुरचमूपतिः । प्रणतस्तदनुज्ञातः प्रविवेश महाबिलम् ॥12॥
अथाहोशनसं राजन् हरिर्नारायणोऽन्तिके । आसीनमृत्विजां मध्ये सदसि ब्रह्मवादिनाम् ॥13॥
ब्रह्मन् संतनु शिष्यस्य कर्मच्छिद्रं वितन्वतः । यत् तत् कर्मसु वैषम्यं ब्रह्मदृष्टं समं भवेत् ॥14॥

शुक्र उवाच

कुतस्तत्कर्मवैषम्यं यस्य कर्मेश्वरो भवान् । यज्ञेशो यज्ञपुरुषः सर्वभावेन पूजितः ॥15॥

7. O grantor of protection! Brahma and other Divinities enjoy the rulership of the worlds by virtue of the power they have gained through the service of Thy lotus feet. But it is a wonder that even we Asuras, born of evil wombs and given to evil ways, have become the objects of Thy condescension. Thy mercy is indeed unconditioned and limitless. **8.** Wonderful is Thy play consisting in the manifestation of this infinitely vast universe through the sportive functioning of Thy Yogamaya! So too is it a mystery how Thou, the saviour of the whole universe and even-sighted towards all, could have a nature favouring some called Thy devotees, and some others who are said to be antagonistic and who disregard Thee. This is not partiality. For thou art like the Kalpataru, the wish-yielding heavenly tree, in Thy love of devotees.' (For the Kalpataru is open to all to resort to and get its favour. If some do not do so, the Kalpataru cannot be blamed as partial to those who resort to it and get its favour. It is equally open for others also to do so.)

The Lord said: **9.** Prahlada dear! May you be happy and prosperous. You too go to Sutala. There you can be happy with this grandson of yours, and benefit all your relatives. **10.** There you will see Me every day, with mace in My hand, guarding the place. The bliss arising from this vision of Me will shatter your bondage of ignorance.

Vāmana crowned as Upendra (11-27)

Sri Suka said: **11-12.** Endowed as he was with pure knowledge, Prahlada, the leader of the Asura forces, accepted the Lord's order with complete submission. Along with Bali he then worshipped and circumambulated the Lord, and left for Sutala with His consent. **13.** Then Hari, known also as Narayana, addressed Sri Sukra, who was seated among the sacrificial priests.

The Lord said: **14.** O holy one! Please perform what is required to expiate the breach of ritual that has taken place in your disciple's Yajna by these incidents. Even the look of a holy one is sufficient to rectify such faults in rites.

The sage Sukra said: **15.** O Lord! How can there be any flaw in the rite when

मन्त्रतस्तन्त्रतश्छिद्रं देशकालार्हवस्तुतः । सर्वं करोति निश्छिद्रं नामसङ्कीर्तनं तव ।।16।।
तथापि वदतो भूमन् करिष्याम्यनुशासनम् । एतच्छ्रेयः परं पुंसां यत् तवाज्ञानुपालनम् ।।17।।

श्रीशुक उवाच

अभिनन्द्य हरेराज्ञामुशना भगवानिति । यज्ञच्छिद्रं समाधत्त बलेर्विप्रर्षिभिः सह ।।18।।
एवं बलेर्महीं राजन् भिक्षित्वा वामनो हरिः । ददौ भ्रात्रे महेन्द्राय त्रिदिवं यत् परैर्हृतम् ।।19।।
प्रजापतिपतिर्ब्रह्मा देवर्षिपितृभूमिपैः । दक्षभृग्वङ्गिरोमुख्यैः कुमारेण भवेन च ।।20।।
कश्यपस्यादितेः प्रीत्यै सर्वभूतभवाय च । लोकानां लोकपालानामकरोद् वामनं पतिम् ।।21।।
वेदानां सर्वदेवानां धर्मस्य यशसः श्रियः । मङ्गलानां व्रतानां च कल्पं स्वर्गापवर्गयोः ।।22।।
उपेन्द्रं कल्पयाञ्चक्रे पतिं सर्वविभूतये । तदा सर्वाणि भूतानि भृशं मुमुदिरे नृप ।।23।।
ततस्त्विन्द्रः पुरस्कृत्य देवयानेन वामनम् । लोकपालैर्दिवं निन्ये ब्रह्मणा चानुमोदितः ।।24।।
प्राप्य त्रिभुवनं चेन्द्र उपेन्द्रभुजपालितः । श्रिया परमया जुष्टो मुमुदे गतसाध्वसः ।।25।।
ब्रह्मा शर्वः कुमारश्च भृग्वाद्या मुनयो नृप । पितरः सर्वभूतानि सिद्धा वैमानिकाश्च ये ।।26।।
सुमहत् कर्म तद् विष्णोर्गायन्तः परमाद्भुतम् । धिष्ण्यानि स्वानि ते जग्मुरदितिं च शशंसिरे ।।27।।

Thou, the operator of all sacrifices, the bestower of the fruits of all sacrifices, and the embodiment of all sacrifices, hast been devoutly worshipped and propitiated by the offering of all his possessions by Bali, the master of this sacrifice? **16.** Whatever defects arise in a rite out of the Mantras uttered, rituals followed, time, place, recipients of gifts etc., it is all corrected by the recital of Thy names. What then to speak of the perfection that would be effected by a worship consisting in the total offering of all one's possessions to Thee! **17.** O all-powerful one! Still I shall certainly carry out the the command that Thou hast given. For the highest good of man consists in carrying out Thy commands.

Sri Suka said: **18.** Accepting the command of Hari, the learned Rishi Sukra with the help of other Rishis did the rites necessary to complete the obstructed sacrifice of Bali. **19.** Thus, O King, Hari restored the heavenly region to Indra, His brother, by begging it of the enemies of Indra who had captured it from him. **20-21.** All the divine personages assembled there—Brahma the Lord of all Prajapatis, the Devas, Rishis, Pitris, Manus, Daksha, Bhrigu, Angiras, Sanaka and his group, Sri Parameswara etc.,—all together crowned Vāmana, who had incarnated for fulfilling the wishes of Kasyapa and Aditi as also for the good of the whole world, as the over-lord of all the worlds and of the guardian deities of different regions. **22-23.** For the welfare of all beings, they made Vāmana, known also as Upendra or the brother of Indra, the over-lord, as he had the power to protect and espouse the cause of spiritual values and institutions like the Vedas, the Devas, Dharma, holiness, welfare, auspicious vows and rites, Swarga and liberation. O King! All creatures alike were full of joy on this occasion. **24.** Along the path of the Devas (Devayāna), Indra now entered heaven preceded by the august Vāmana, blessed by Brahma, and accompanied by the guardian deities of the regions.

25. Recovering the three worlds, now under the protection of Upendra's arms, Indra attained to unending wealth and prosperity, and enjoyed them without any fear. **26-27.** All the visiting divinities, Brahma, Parameswara, Sanaka and his

सर्वमेतन्मयाऽऽख्यातं भवतः कुलनन्दन । उरुक्रमस्य चरितं श्रोतॄणामघमोचनम् ॥28॥
पारं महिम्न उरु विक्रमतो गृणानो यः पार्थिवानि विममे स रजांसि मर्त्यः ।
किं जायमान उत जात उपैति मर्त्य इत्याह मन्त्रदृगृषिः पुरुषस्य यस्य ॥29॥
य इदं देवदेवस्य हरेरद्भुतकर्मणः । अवतारानुचरितं शृण्वन् याति परां गतिम् ॥30॥
क्रियमाणे कर्मणीदं दैवे पित्र्येऽथ मानुषे । यत्र यत्रानुकीर्त्येत तत् तेषां सुकृतं विदुः ॥31॥

इति श्रीमद्भागवते महापुराणे पारमहंस्यां संहितायामष्टमस्कन्धे वामनावतारचरिते त्रयोविंशोऽध्यायः ॥23॥

group, Bhrigu and other Rishis, Pitris, Siddhas, and the Devas in their chariots—returned to their respective abodes, singing on the way with great devotion about the glory of the Lord as revealed in these wonderful achievements of His, and also expressing their great regard and admiration for Aditi, the mother of Vāmana.

The Lord's Greatness (28-31)

28. O Parikshit, the delight of your clan! I have narrated to you in full the incidents connected with the Lord's incarnation as Vāmana, which erases the sins of those listening to their recital. **29.** Infinite is His glory. He who seeks to find out the limits of it should have first exhausted counting the particles of dust constituting the earth! Of such inconceivable might and excellences is He! Rightly has Vasishtha, endowed with the insight for discovering spiritual truths, declared: 'Where is the man born till now that has sounded the depth of His greatness? And surely there is none that will be able to do so in the future too.' **30.** He who hears the account of this Incarnation of Hari, the Lord of all Divinities, and one of wonder-evoking deeds, will attain to the highest goal open to the Jiva. **31.** If at whatever rite or work devoted to the Devas or Pitris or men, this account of the Lord's incarnation is expounded or recited, that rite or action will become complete and perfect, its defects, if any, being made good by the spiritual efficacy of the Lord's name and deeds.

अथ चतुर्विंशोऽध्यायः

राजोवाच

भगवञ्छ्रोतुमिच्छामि हरेरद्भुतकर्मणः । अवतारकथामाद्यां मायामत्स्यविडम्बनम् ॥ 1॥
यदर्थमदधाद् रूपं मात्स्यं लोकजुगुप्सितम् । तमःप्रकृति दुर्मर्षं कर्मग्रस्त इवेश्वरः ॥ 2॥
एतन्नो भगवन् सर्वं यथावद् वक्तुमर्हसि । उत्तमश्लोकचरितं सर्वलोकसुखावहम् ॥ 3॥

Skandha VIII : Chapter 24

THE INCARNATION AS FISH

Brahma loses the Veda (1-9)

The Rajah said: **1.** O worshipful one! I would like to hear about the first of the incarnations of Hari of wonderful deeds, assuming the form of the Mystic Fish. **2-3.** Why did the Supreme Lord assume, as if He were under the bondage of Karma, such a Tamas-dominated form as that of a fish, looked down upon in the world as

सूत उवाच

इत्युक्तो विष्णुरातेन भगवान् बादरायणिः । उवाच चरितं विष्णोर्मत्स्यरूपेण यत् कृतम् ॥ 4॥

श्रीशुक उवाच

गोविप्रसुरसाधूनां छन्दसामपि चेश्वरः । रक्षामिच्छंस्तनूर्धत्ते धर्मस्यार्थस्य चैव हि ॥ 5॥
उच्चावचेषु भूतेषु चरन् वायुरिवेश्वरः । नोच्चावचत्वं भजते निर्गुणत्वाद्धियो गुणैः ॥ 6॥
आसीदतीतकल्पान्ते ब्राह्मो नैमित्तिको लयः । समुद्रोपप्लुतास्तत्र लोका भूरादयो नृप ॥ 7॥
कालेनागतनिद्रस्य धातुः शिशयिषोर्बली । मुखतो निःसृतान् वेदान् हयग्रीवोऽन्तिकेऽहरत् 8
ज्ञात्वा तद् दानवेन्द्रस्य हयग्रीवस्य चेष्टितम् । दधार शफरीरूपं भगवान् हरिरीश्वरः ॥ 9॥
तत्र राजऋषिः कश्चिन्नाम्ना सत्यव्रतो महान् । नारायणपरोऽतप्यत् तपः स सलिलाशनः ॥10॥
योऽसावस्मिन् महाकल्पे तनयः स विवस्वतः । श्राद्धदेव इति ख्यातो मनुत्वे हरिणार्पितः ॥11॥
एकदा कृतमालायां कुर्वतो जलतर्पणम् । तस्याञ्जल्युदके काचिच्छफर्येकाभ्यपद्यत ॥12॥
सत्यव्रतोऽञ्जलिगतां सह तोयेन भारत । उत्ससर्ज नदीतोये शफरीं द्रविडेश्वरः ॥13॥
तमाह सातिकरुणं महाकारुणिकं नृपम् । यादोभ्यो ज्ञातिघातिभ्यो दीनां मां दीनवत्सल ।
कथं विसृजसे राजन् भीतामस्मिन् सरिज्जले ॥14॥

low and repulsive?

Suta said: **4.** When King Parikshit said as above to Suka, the son of Bādarāyana, the latter narrated to him the story of the Lord's incarnation in the form of a Fish.

Sri Suka said: **5.** The Lord assumes a form and incarnates Himself for the all-round good of helpless ones, of holy men, of Devas, of righteous people, and of the Vedas, as also for safeguarding the four ends of life—Dharma, Artha, Kama, Moksha. **6.** Though like the air the Lord pervades all beings considered high or low according to their stage of evolution, He, being non-material, is not affected by the qualities of the minds and bodies of the objects He pervades.

7. Towards the close of the previous Kalpa, there was a Naimittika-pralaya (periodical deluge) caused by Brahma's sleep at the close of his day. During that Pralaya all the three worlds were flooded by water. **8.** This being his night, Brahma was sleepy and was about to retire when the Vedas dropped out of his mouth. An Asura named Hayagrīva, who was standing nearby, snatched away the Vedas. **9.** Coming to know about this high-handedness of Hayagrīva, the all-powerful Lord took the form of a Fish.

Satyavrata and the mysterious Fish (10-24)

10. In that Kalpa there was a pious king named Satyavrata, who was deeply devoted to Narayana and was performing austerity, subsisting only on water. **11.** It was this Satyavrata who was born as the son of Vivaswān and made a Manu in this Kalpa under the well-known names Srāddha Deva and Vaivaswata. **12.** Once when this Satyavrata was performing rites with water (*Jalatarpana*) in the river Kritamāla, an unusual kind of tiny fish was found in the water he held in his cupped palms. **13.** Thereupon Satyavrata, the king of the Dravida country, let down the water he held in his palms, and together with it, the fish too. **14.** The fish then appealed to that merciful king in the most piteous manner: 'O King! You who are noted for your mercy towards the poor and the suffering—why are you consigning

तमात्मनोऽनुग्रहार्थं प्रीत्या मत्स्यवपुर्धरम् ।
अजानन् रक्षणार्थाय शफर्याः स मनो दधे ॥15॥
तस्या दीनतरं वाक्यमाश्रुत्य स महीपतिः ।
कलशाप्सु निधायैनां दयालुर्निन्य आश्रमम् ॥16॥
सा तु तत्रैकरात्रेण वर्धमाना कमण्डलौ ।
अलब्ध्वाऽऽत्मावकाशं वा इदमाह महीपतिम् ॥17॥
नाहं कमण्डलावस्मिन् कृच्छ्रं वस्तुमिहोत्सहे ।
कल्पयौकः सुविपुलं यत्राहं निवसे सुखम् ॥18॥
स एनां तत आदाय न्यधादौदञ्चनोदके ।
तत्र क्षिप्ता मुहूर्तेन हस्तत्रयमवर्धत ॥19॥
न म एतदलं राजन् सुखं वस्तुमुदञ्चनम् ।
पृथु देहि पदं मह्यं यत् त्वाहं शरणं गता ॥20॥
तत आदाय सा राज्ञा क्षिप्ता राजन् सरोवरे ।
तदावृत्यात्मना सोऽयं महामीनोऽन्ववर्धत ॥21॥
नैतन्मे स्वस्तये राजन्नुदकं सलिलौकसः ।
निधेहि रक्षायोगेन ह्रदे मामविदासिनि ॥22॥
इत्युक्तः सोऽनयन्मत्स्यं तत्र तत्राविदासिनि ।
जलाशये सम्मितं तं समुद्रे प्राक्षिपज्झषम् ॥23॥
क्षिप्यमाणस्तमाहेदमिह मां मकरादयः ।
अदन्त्यतिबला वीर मां नेहोत्स्रष्टुमर्हसि ॥24॥
एवं विमोहितस्तेन वदता वल्गुभारतीम् ।
तमाह को भवानस्मान् मत्स्यरूपेण मोहयन् ॥25॥
नैवंवीर्यो जलचरो दृष्टोऽस्माभिः श्रुतोऽपि च ।
यो भवान् योजनशतमह्नाभिव्यानशे सरः ॥26॥
नूनं त्वं भगवान् साक्षाद्धरिर्नारायणोऽव्ययः ।
अनुग्रहाय भूतानां धत्से रूपं जलौकसाम् ॥27॥

a poor creature like myself into this water, where I have to be in constant dread of other aquatic creatures who subsist on their own kind?' **15.** The king then decided to give protection to that fish without any inkling that it was the Lord come in the form of a Fish to bless him.

16. Touched by the piteous appeal that the Fish made, the merciful king brought it to his Ashrama, putting it in his water vessel. **17.** Within one night the fish grew too big to be accommodated in the water vessel. Unable to remain there, it said to the king: **18.** 'It is impossible for me to put up with the difficulty of staying in this water vessel. So please give me a spacious water receptacle in which I can stay in comfort.' **19.** So the king removed it from there and put it in a big vessel. But within a few seconds after being consigned there, it grew to a size of three cubits. **20.** The Fish thereupon said: 'Even this, O King, is not sufficient for me to be comfortable. I have taken refuge with you. Give me a much bigger place.' **21.** O King! Satyavrata now consigned it to a pond. But this Fish of unending growth soon filled the pond with its body. **22.** The Fish therefore said: 'For me, a creature requiring a wide expanse of water, the very limited water area of a pond is insufficient to stay comfortably. Put me into a big lake where the water will not dry and where I am protected from the attentions of alligators and other denizens of the water.' **23.** Being so requested, the king transferred the fish from one lake of perennial water to another, as it filled up every lake in a short time. Finally he put it into the sea. **24.** When the Fish was put in the ocean, it said to the king: 'O heroic King! It behoves you not to put me in the ocean where I am likely to be eaten up by whales and other powerful creatures. So please do not let me down in the ocean'.

The Fish reveals its Identity (25-30)

25. To the Fish who was thus mystifying him with fine words, the King said: 'Who are you in this form of a Fish giving us so many surprises? **26.** We have never seen or heard of an aquatic creature with such divine powers as you seem to possess. You have filled up a lake of a hundred Yojanas in one day! **27.** Surely you must

नमस्ते पुरुषश्रेष्ठ स्थित्युत्पत्त्यप्ययेश्वर । भक्तानां नः प्रपन्नानां मुख्यो ह्यात्मगतिर्विभो ॥28॥
सर्वे लीलावतारास्ते भूतानां भूतिहेतवः । ज्ञातुमिच्छाम्यदो रूपं यदर्थं भवता धृतम् ॥29॥
न तेऽरविन्दाक्ष पदोपसर्पणं मृषा भवेत् सर्वसुहृत्प्रियात्मनः ।
यथेतरेषां पृथगात्मनां सतामदीदृशो यद्वपुरद्भुतं हि नः ॥30॥

श्रीशुक उवाच

इति ब्रुवाणं नृपतिं जगत्पतिः सत्यव्रतं मत्स्यवपुर्युगक्षये ।
विहर्तुकामः प्रलयार्णवेऽब्रवीच्चिकीर्षुरेकान्तजनप्रियः प्रियम् ॥31॥

श्रीभगवानुवाच

सप्तमेऽद्यतनादूर्ध्वमहन्येतदरिन्दम । निमङ्क्ष्यत्यप्ययाम्भोधौ त्रैलोक्यं भूर्भुवादिकम् 32
त्रिलोक्यां लीयमानायां संवर्ताम्भसि वै तदा । उपस्थास्यति नौः काचिद् विशाला त्वां मयेरिता 33
त्वं तावदोषधीः सर्वा बीजान्युच्चावचानि च । सप्तर्षिभिः परिवृतः सर्वसत्त्वोपबृंहितः ॥34॥
आरुह्य बृहतीं नावं विचरिष्यस्यविक्लवः । एकार्णवे निरालोके ऋषीणामेव वर्चसा ॥35॥
दोधूयमानां तां नावं समीरेण बलीयसा । उपस्थितस्य मे शृङ्गे निबध्नीहि महाहिना ॥36॥
अहं त्वामृषिभिः साकं सहनावमुदन्वति । विकर्षन् विचरिष्यामि यावद् ब्राह्मी निशा प्रभो 37

be the worshipful Hari, the Lord Narayana, who has assumed the form of a Fish for the good of the worlds. **28.** O Thou the Supreme Spirit! Salutation to the master of creation, preservation and dissolution! Thou art the soul and the goal of us who have taken refuge in Thee. **29.** All the forms that Thou hast taken as incarnations are for the good of the worlds. Pray, what is the special object of taking this form in the present incarnation? I would like to understand that. **30.** O Lotus-eyed one! The service rendered to Thee, the soul and friend of all, will never go in vain unlike dependence on limited beings with the consciousness of their physical individuality. For, as a fruit of my devotion to Thee, Thou hast now revealed this most wonderful form of Thine to me.'

Announcement of the Deluge (31-45)

Sri Suka said: **31.** The Lord of the universe, who is ever loving to His whole-hearted devotees, and who had now assumed the form of the Fish in order to sport in the water of the deluge as also to bless His devotees, said as follows to the Rajarshi Satyavrata. *The Lord said*: **32.** 'O King! On the seventh day from today all the three worlds, the earth, the intermediary region and the heaven, will get submerged in the water of the periodical deluge (Naimittika-pralaya). **33.** When the worlds have got submerged in the waters of the Pralaya, a ship sent by Me will come near you. **34-35.** You will then get into that ship with all the seeds of trees and vegetation collected earlier and with representatives of all species of creatures, and also accompanied by the Saptarshis. Without any difficulty you will be able to navigate in that darkness of Pralaya guided by the brilliance of the Saptarshis. **36.** When the boat will be rolling heavily in the stormy sea, I shall be appearing there, and to my antenna, the boat may be tied, the rope to be used for the purpose being the serpent Vāsuki. **37.** O pious King! With you and the Rishis in it, I shall pilot this ship through the Pralaya waters until Brahma's night is over and

मदीयं महिमानं च परं ब्रह्मेति शब्दितम् । वेत्स्यस्यनुगृहीतं मे सम्प्रश्नैर्विवृतं हृदि ॥38॥
इत्थमादिश्य राजानं हरिरन्तरधीयत । सोऽन्ववैक्षत तं कालं यं हृषीकेश आदिशत् ॥39॥
आस्तीर्य दर्भान् प्राक्कूलान् राजर्षिः प्रागुदङ्मुखः । निषसाद हरेः पादौ चिन्तयन् मत्स्यरूपिणः ॥40॥
ततः समुद्र उद्वेलः सर्वतः प्लावयन् महीम् । वर्धमानो महामेघैर्वर्षद्भिः समदृश्यत ॥41॥
ध्यायन् भगवदादेशं ददृशे नावमागताम् । तामारुरोह विप्रेन्द्रैरादायौषधिवीरुधः ॥42॥
तमूचुर्मुनयः प्रीता राजन् ध्यायस्व केशवम् । स वै नः संकटादस्मादविता शं विधास्यति ॥43॥
सोऽनुध्यातस्ततो राज्ञा प्रादुरासीन्महार्णवे । एकश्रृङ्गधरो मत्स्यो हैमो नियुतयोजनः ॥44॥
निबध्य नावं तच्छृङ्गे यथोक्तो हरिणा पुरा । वरत्रेणाहिना तुष्टस्तुष्टाव मधुसूदनम् ॥45॥

राजोवाच

अनाद्यविद्योपहतात्मसंविदस्तन्मूलसंसारपरिश्रमातुराः ।
यदृच्छयेहोपसृता यमाप्नुयुर्विमुक्तिदो नः परमो गुरुर्भवान् ॥46॥
जनोऽबुधोऽयं निजकर्मबन्धनः सुखेच्छया कर्म समीहतेऽसुखम् ।
यत्सेवया तां विधुनोत्यसन्मतिं ग्रन्थिं स भिन्द्याद्धृदयं स नो गुरुः ॥47॥

the Naimittika-pralaya ends. **38.** During that time, as answers given to questions, I shall reveal the truth of my all-comprehending essence or glory known as the Transcendent Brahman. Thus instructed, and with my blessings besides, you shall realise the Truth of Brahman in your heart.'

39. Saying this to Satyavrata, Hari disappeared from view. And Satyavrata for his part waited for the time of the deluge mentioned to him by the Lord. **40.** Making a seat of Durva grass with the pointed ends of the grass turned eastwards, Satyavrata sat on it facing north-east and meditated on the feet of Sri Hari incarnated as the Fish. **41.** Now appeared heavy rain clouds sending torrential rains, helped by which the oceans swelled and deluged the whole earth. **42.** As King Satyavrata thought of the Lord's words, the ship appeared on the scene. The king carrying all the seeds of plants and animals and accompanied by the Saptarshis, boarded the ship.

43. The Rishis now told the king with a joyous heart: 'O King! Meditate on Kesava, the Lord Mahavishnu. He will save us from all difficulties and work for our welfare.' **44.** As the king meditated, Mahavishnu now appeared as the Fish of golden colour, having only one antenna, and endowed with a body a lakh of Yojanas in size. **45.** As directed by Sri Hari earlier, the king had the ship attached to the antenna of the Fish using the serpent Vāsuki as the cord for tying. With great joy in his heart, he began to sing the praise of the Lord in a hymn.

Satyavrata's Hymn (46-53)

Rajah Satyavrata said: **46.** Men whose knowledge of the Atman has been effaced by the beginningless nescience, and who, as a consequence, are subject to intense suffering in Samsara, sometimes surrender themselves to Thee by Thy grace alone, and thereby attain to Thee. May Thou, that grantor of liberation, be our Teacher! **47.** Bound by the impressions of his past Karma, the ignorant man continues to perform Karma with the idea of gaining more and more enjoyments, but the ultimate result of all such self-centred work is more misery. This self-centredness, the

यत्सेवयाग्नेरिव रुद्ररोदनं पुमान् विजह्यान्मलमात्मनस्तमः ।
भजेत वर्णं निजमेष सोऽव्ययो भूयात् स ईशः परमो गुरोर्गुरुः ॥48॥
न यत्प्रसादायुतभागलेशमन्ये च देवा गुरवो जनाः स्वयम् ।
कर्तुं समेताः प्रभवन्ति पुंसस्तमीश्वरं त्वां शरणं प्रपद्ये ॥49॥
अचक्षुरन्धस्य यथाग्रणीः कृतस्तथा जनस्याविदुषोऽबुधो गुरुः ।
त्वमर्कदृक् सर्वदृशां समीक्षणो वृतो गुरुर्नः स्वगतिं बुभुत्सताम् ॥50॥
जनो जनस्यादिशतेऽसतीं मतिं यया प्रपद्येत दुरत्ययं तमः ।
त्वं त्वव्ययं ज्ञानममोघमञ्जसा प्रपद्यते येन जनो निजं पदम् ॥51॥
त्वं सर्वलोकस्य सुहृत् प्रियेश्वरो ह्यात्मा गुरुर्ज्ञानमभीष्टसिद्धिः ।
तथापि लोको न भवन्तमन्धधीर्जानाति सन्तं हृदि बद्धकामः ॥52॥
तं त्वामहं देववरं वरेण्यं प्रपद्य ईशं प्रतिबोधनाय ।
छिन्ध्यर्थदीपैर्भगवन् वचोभिर्ग्रन्थीन् हृदय्यान् विवृणु स्वमोकः ॥53॥

canker within, can be overcome only through the service of Thee, the world-teacher. May He be pleased to destroy in us that knot of the heart, namely, the identification of the self with the body. **48.** Gold and silver cannot be purified by merely washing, but only by being heated in fire. So also Karmas by themselves cannot purify one's being. Thy service alone can be the fire for burning up that darkness of corruption that has entered the soul of man, and for restoring its luminosity. Work can form only a limb of that devotional service. May He, the eternal one and the Lord of all, greater than all other teachers, by whose service the impurity of the mind is erased and the spirit restored to its natural condition, bring us enlightement. **49.** I take refuge in Thee, the Supreme Being, whose abounding grace bestowed on devotees is of such potency that even an infinitesimal fraction of it cannot be matched by the combined help that may be offered by all the deities, teachers and other competent persons put together. **50.** Ignorant men accepting other ignorant men as Guru is like one blind man taking another blind man to guide him. Desirous of attaining to our spiritual goal we have adopted as our Guru Thyself, the self-luminous Awareness which like the sun reveals everything else, and also endows the senses with self-consciousness and luminosity. **51.** Inferior teachers give instructions for the attainment of worldly good, by pursuing which men continue to be endlessly entangled in the cycle of births and deaths. Thou, however, instructest one in the knowledge of the Spirit that is eternal and incorruptible and helps one to attain to one's original state without difficulty. **52.** Thou art the friend of all the worlds, their well-wisher, their dear Lord, their soul and the grantor of their prayers. Yet the blind worlds, full of worldly desires, do not know Thee who art residing in their very heart. **53.** I take shelter in Thee, the Supreme Deity, the Lord of all, and the noblest one to be resorted to, for being instructed in the knowledge of the Atman which would shatter the darkness of ignorance in me by the light of Thy words. Cut asunder the knot of ignorance which binds the body with the Spirit! Reveal to me Thy true form!

Satyavrata made Manu (54-61)

श्रीशुक उवाच

इत्युक्तवन्तं नृपतिं भगवानादिपूरुषः । मत्स्यरूपी महाम्भोधौ विहरंस्तत्त्वमब्रवीत् ॥54॥
पुराणसंहितां दिव्यां सांख्ययोगक्रियावतीम् । सत्यव्रतस्य राजर्षेरात्मगुह्यमशेषतः ॥55॥
अश्रौषीदृषिभिः साकमात्मतत्त्वमसंशयम् । नाव्यासीनो भगवता प्रोक्तं ब्रह्म सनातनम् ॥56॥
अतीतप्रलयापाय उत्थिताय स वेधसे । हत्वासुरं हयग्रीवं वेदान् प्रत्याहरद्धरिः ॥57॥
स तु सत्यव्रतो राजा ज्ञानविज्ञानसंयुतः । विष्णोः प्रसादात् कल्पेऽस्मिन्नासीद् वैवस्वतो मनुः
सत्यव्रतस्य राजर्षेर्मायामत्स्यस्य शार्ङ्गिणः । संवादं महदाख्यानं श्रुत्वा मुच्येत किल्बिषात् ॥59॥
अवतारो हरेर्योऽयं कीर्तयेदन्वहं नरः । सङ्कल्पास्तस्य सिध्यन्ति स याति परमां गतिम् 60॥

प्रलयपयसि धातुः सुप्तशक्तेर्मुखेभ्यः श्रुतिगणमपनीतं प्रत्युपादत्त हत्वा ।
दितिजमकथयद् यो ब्रह्म सत्यव्रतानां तमहमखिलहेतुं जिह्ममीनं नतोऽस्मि ॥61॥

इति श्रीमद्भागवते महापुराणे वैयासिक्यामष्टादशसाहस्र्यां पारमहंस्यां संहितायामष्टमस्कन्धे मत्स्यावतारचरितानुवर्णनं नाम चतुर्विंशोऽध्यायः ॥24॥

इत्यष्टमस्कन्धः समाप्तः

हरिः ॐ तत्सत्

Sri Suka said: **54.** To the king who spoke thus, the Lord, the Primeval One in the form of a Fish, gave spiritual instruction while sporting in the waters of Pralaya. **55.** He imparted the subtle truth of the Atman in its fullness to the royal sage Satyavrata, in the shape of the sacred Purana-Samhita known as Matsyapurana, in which doctrines of Jnana, Bhakti and Karma are discussed. **56.** Seated in the ship constituted of the earth, the king along with the Rishis heard the exposition of the truth of the Atman and of the eternal Brahman, which drove away all doubt from his heart. **57.** When that Pralaya ended and Brahma awoke from sleep, Sri Hari gave him the Veda, having destroyed Hayagrīva and recovered the Veda from him. **58.** It is this King Satyavrata, endowed with knowledge and experience of Truth, who has become Vaivaswata Manu in the present Kalpa, out of Mahavishnu's grace. **59.** Those who hear this great narrative dealing with the conversation between King Satyavrata and Mahavishnu incarnated as Fish will be freed from sins. **60.** A devotee who daily adores the Lord with the recital of the account of this incarnation of His will have the fulfilment of all his wishes, and he will ultimately attain the supreme goal. **61.** I salute Him who is the ultimate cause of all in the guise of the Incarnate Fish, who restored the Veda to Brahma,—killing the Asura who had taken it away when it fell into the Pralaya waters from the mouth of Brahma who had become weak by the onset of sleep at the start of the Pralaya,—and who instructed the king Satyavrata in the truth of Brahman.

END OF THE EIGHTH SKANDHA

Skandha Nine

PROLOGUE

The Ninth Skandha with 24 chapters and 964 verses deals with Vamsa and Vamsānucharita—the genealogy of the great kingly and priestly lines and accounts of some of the eminent ones among them. It is one of the ten themes to be treated in all Puranas. More of this will come in the 12th Skandha also.

From the point of view of the modern reader, this Skandha forms the most dreary of all the sections of the *Bhagavata* —a parched desert occasionally brightened by an oasis here and there of very inspiring accounts of some eminent devotees like Ambarīsha, Parasurama, Khatvānga, Ranti Deva, Bhagīratha, etc., and of the Rama incarnation. The rest of it, apart from brief dissertations on some more persons, consists of long and endless lists of kings in their order of succession with some details about a few of them. There is no way of understanding from these descriptions anything about their dates beyond a vague idea of the Yuga in which they lived, about where most of them ruled, whether they ruled at all or what type of persons they were. Perhaps it is impossible to give all this information because their number is so vast. The cumulative effect of it on the reader is not an enrichment of his information of the past, but the promotion of a hazy sense of the vastness of the bygone times.

And this perhaps is the main object of the author of a Purana like the *Bhagavata* which claims that not a word is said in it which is not related to the Lord and the cultivation of devotion towards him. This is made plain in the following verses of the text (XII.3.14-15): "I have narrated to you the stories of these great men who have spread their names in the three worlds, and then passed away. All this literary effort is only to generate in you discrimination and knowledge (by bringing home to you the very transitoriness of human greatness and worldly achievements). They have no relation to any abiding reality."

Attempts are being made today by some modern Indian historians to reconstruct a sort of India's ancient history from these bewildering genealogical lists of the Puranas and the brief accounts of certain kings they give. British historians in the past recognised Indian history proper as starting from the time of Alexander's invasion (325 B.C.) and left all the ancient past of India as a blank. This, however, is a very undesirable position, as it gives a very imperfect background of India and its culture. So, to utilise the Pauranika material to fill up the lacuna is very desirable, provided one keeps its limitation also in mind. That material is vague, imperfect in chronology, mostly bare lists without details, devoid of evidence by contemporary records, archaeology, historical concordance, etc., which are insisted on by history in the modern sense. They are traditions where no other source of information of an exact nature exists. It is valuable in spite of its imperfections, as even to have some vague information is better than having none.

A very creditable attempt has been made to work in this field, on what may be called the proto-history of India, in the book *History of the Pre-Kaliyuga of India by* R. Siddhanta Sastri, published by the Inter-India Publications, Delhi. Pre-Kaliyuga means the time anterior to the demise of Sri Krishna, which took place in 3102 B.C. The author should be given great credit for the original study he has made. He has collated the genealogies of princely lines given in the *Bhagavata, Vishnupurana, Matsyapurana* and *Mahabharata*, and tried to arrive at a consensus of rulers from the time of Swāyambhuva Manu, the first of the Manus, to that of Vaivaswata, the seventh and the current Manu. He has, however, used much imagination in the process and discarded the Pauranika conception of time, in order to accommodate these lists of kings into the pattern of modern history.

The Pauranika history of the present Kalpa, called Swetavarāha Kalpa and also Padma Kalpa, begins with Swāyambhuva Manu. His two sons Uttānapāda and Priyavrata became the lords of the world. Uttānapāda's line produced some distinguished rulers like the famous Dhruva, the tyrant Vena, the great emperor Prithu, Sisti, Ripu, and Chakshusha, the last of whom became, much later, the sixth Manu. Priyavrata's line was of much longer duration. Some of the noted kings of his line were Nābhi, Rishabha, Bharata, Gaya, etc. Some forty-two kings are listed in Sri Siddhanta Sastri's work. It is to be noted that if we take the Pauranika chronology, obviously all these kings are supposed to have ruled during six Manvantras, that is from that of Swāyambhuva to the end of Chākshusha, which will cover a period of 25,920,000 years. Prof. Sastri chooses to ignore the Pauranika time scale, but does not show into what other system of chronology he fits the rule of all these ancient kings. This is an unavoidable difficulty that all who distil history from the Puranas have to face. All these form the subject matter of earlier Skandhas.

The 9th Skandha, however, is concerned only with the kings who ruled during the supremacy of the seventh Manu Vaivaswata, who in the previous Kalpa was King Satyavrata of the Dravida Country, to whom the Lord appeared as the Cosmic Fish (VIII.16.10-24), and who was born in his next birth as the son of Vivaswān, the Sun-deity, under the name Srāddha Deva, known also as Vaivaswata after his father's name. The whole of the ninth Skandha is an attempt to trace the two famous royal dynasties of ancient India, the Solar Dynasty (Surya-Vamsa) to Vaivaswata Manu, the son of the Sun-deity, and the Lunar Dynasty (Chandra-Vamsa) to Soma the Moon-deity. Vaivaswata Manu had ten sons—Ikshvāku, Nriga, Saryāti, Dishti, Karūshaka, Narishya, Prishadhra, Nabhaga and Kavi. Of these Ikshvāku was the ancestor of the kings of the Solar Dynasty, whose number as given in the *Bhagavata,* is listed by Prof. Sastri as eighty-four. Among these are some kings very famous in the Indian tradition—kings like Kākutstha, Māndhāta, Ambarīsha, Harischandra, Dilīpa, Raghu, Aja, Dasaratha and, above all, Sri Rama, classified as a Divine Incarnation who has exercised an abiding influence on Indian culture. The dynasty ended with Brihadbala who died in the Mahabharata War. There were also other subsidiary families of the Solar Dynasty, all descended from the Manu and his sons. Some of them were the Mithila kings known as Videhas, the dynasty ruling at Vaisāli, the Saryāti family, the Nabhaga family, the Nriga family and the Narishyanta family.

The second great kingly line, the Lunar Dynasty (Soma-Vamsa), was descended from the Moon-Deity who had Budha for his son. The Moon-Deity himself was born of the tears of Bliss flowing from the eyes of Rishi Atri, a mind-born offspring of Brahma.

Whether the Solar and Lunar Dynasties were parallel kingly lines is not clear from the Purana, but Prof. Sastri thinks that the Lunar Dynasty came into prominence after the Solar line had become decadent. But it is however known from the Purana that the last king of the Solar Dynasty, Brihadbala, was killed in the Mahabharata War.

The Lunar Dynasty is of special importance to the *Bhagavata*, because in that dynasty was born Sri Krishna, the description of whose glory forms the special theme of this Purana. Some of the illustrious kings of this line, famous in the Indian tradition, are Purūravas, Nahusha, Yayāti, Puru, Dushyanta, Bharata, Hastin, Kuru, Santanu, Vichitravīrya, Pāndu and Yudhishthira. Seventy-six kings of this dynasty are listed. The line continued into Kali Yuga also until it decayed with the march of Kali.

The Lunar Dynasty had many branches, important among them being the Kshatravriddha family at Kasi, the kings of the Pānchāla descended from Haryaswa, the rulers of Ahicchatra family, the kings of Kāmpilya, etc.

But the most important branch for the *Bhagavata* is the one containing the descendants of King Yayāti belonging to the main Lunar Dynasty. Yayāti had five sons Yadu, Turvasu, Druhyu, Anu and Puru. As Puru alone was dutiful enough to the father to assume the father's old age and give him his own youth, Yayāti, when he retired, made Puru the emperor and the other brothers as subordinate governors without title to royal insignia. Of the brothers, Puru and Yadu are of special importance, because from the former (Puru) descended the Pandavas and Kauravas of Mahabharata fame, and from the latter (Yadu), the clans of Yādavas, Sāttvatas, Srinjayas, etc. to whom Sri Krishna belonged. In the last two chapters of the Skandha, the details of the descendants of Yadu up to Sri Krishna are given.

While all the genealogical details given in the 24 chapters of this Skandha may be of interest to historical researchers, the general reader will find them tedious and will be prone to skip them. But here and there, there are chapters of high devotional and ethical import which the reader should not miss. We are therefore giving below references to such important sections for selective reading: Chaps. 4 and 5 on the great devotee Ambarīsha; Chaps. 8 and 9 on Sagara's Yajna and Bhagīratha's bringing of the Ganga to the earth; Chaps. 10 and 11 on Sri Rama's incarnation; Chaps. 15 and 16 for the story of Parasurama; Chaps. 18 and 19 on King Yayāti and his doings; Chap. 20 on Dushyanta and Bharata; and Chap. 21 on Ranti Deva.

श्रीमद्भागवतम्

नवमः स्कन्धः अथ प्रथमोऽध्यायः

राजोवाच

मन्वन्तराणि सर्वाणि त्वयोक्तानि श्रुतानि मे। वीर्याण्यनन्तवीर्यस्य हरेस्तत्र कृतानि च ॥ 1॥
योऽसौ सत्यव्रतो नाम राजर्षिर्द्रविडेश्वरः। ज्ञानं योऽतीतकल्पान्ते लेभे पुरुषसेवया ॥ 2॥
स वै विवस्वतः पुत्रो मनुरासीदिति श्रुतम्। त्वत्तस्तस्य सुताश्चोक्ता इक्ष्वाकुप्रमुखा नृपाः ॥ 3॥
तेषां वंशं पृथग् ब्रह्मन् वंश्यानुचरितानि च। कीर्तयस्व महाभाग नित्यं शुश्रूषतां हि नः ॥ 4॥
ये भूता ये भविष्याश्च भवन्त्यद्यतनाश्च ये। तेषां नः पुण्यकीर्तीनां सर्वेषां वद विक्रमान् ॥ 5॥

सूत उवाच

एवं परीक्षिता राज्ञा सदसि ब्रह्मवादिनाम्। पृष्टः प्रोवाच भगवञ्छुकः परमधर्मवित् ॥ 6॥

श्रीशुक उवाच

श्रूयतां मानवो वंशः प्राचुर्येण परंतप। न शक्यते विस्तरतो वक्तुं वर्षशतैरपि ॥ 7॥
परावरेषां भूतानामात्मा यः पुरुषः परः। स एवासीदिदं विश्वं कल्पान्तेऽन्यन्न किञ्चन ॥ 8॥
तस्य नाभेः समभवत् पद्मकोशो हिरण्मयः। तस्मिञ्जज्ञे महाराज स्वयम्भूश्चतुराननः ॥ 9॥

Skandha IX : Chapter 1

THE STORY OF SUDYUMNA

Manu Srāddha Deva and his Issue (1-12)

Rajah Parikshit said: **1.** I have listened to the descriptions of the various Manvantaras you gave, as also of the exploits of Sri Hari of infinite prowess in those periods. **2-3.** I heard from you that the royal sage Satyavrata, the king of the Dravida country, obtained spiritual illumination through the service of the Supreme Being in the previous Kalpa; that he became the Vaivaswata Manu, the son of Vivaswān, in the present Kalpa; and that Ikshavāku and some others were his sons. **4.** O holy one! I wish to hear about the line of Ikshavāku and other sons of the Manu and the life-stories of great devotee kings born in their families. Narrate, O blessed one, the accounts of those great ones to us, who are always eager to listen to such narratives. **5.** Tell me about the great doings of the members of these families famous for their piety—of members who are past, who are now alive, and who are to come in the future.

Suta said: **6.** When thus questioned by Rajah Parikshit in that assembly of Vedic savants, the worshipful Suka, who had an understanding of Dharma in all its phases including the highest, said as follows.

Sri Suka said: **7.** O hero! I shall tell you about the important families of the Manu's line. To narrate it all exhaustively is not possible even in a hundred years. **8.** The Supreme Purusha, who is the indweller of all beings, high and low, alone existed at the end of the Kalpa, this whole universe having dissolved in His being. Nothing besides Him existed. **9.** From his navel came out a golden lotus in which appeared

मरीचिर्मनसस्तस्य जज्ञे तस्यापि कश्यपः । दाक्षायण्यां ततोऽदित्यां विवस्वानभवत् सुतः ॥10॥
ततो मनुः श्राद्धदेवः संज्ञायामास भारत । श्रद्धायां जनयामास दश पुत्रान् स आत्मवान् ॥11॥
इक्ष्वाकुनृगशर्यातिदिष्टधृष्टकरूषकान् । नरिष्यन्तं पृषध्रं च नभगं च कविं विभुः ॥12॥
अप्रजस्य मनोः पूर्वं वसिष्ठो भगवान् किल । मित्रावरुणयोरिष्टिं प्रजार्थमकरोत् प्रभुः ॥13॥
तत्र श्रद्धा मनोः पत्नी होतारं समयाचत । दुहित्रर्थमुपागम्य प्रणिपत्य पयोव्रता ॥14॥
प्रेषितोऽध्वर्युणा होता ध्यायंस्तत् सुसमाहितः । हविषि व्यचरत् तेन वषट्कारं गृणन् द्विजः ॥15॥
होतुस्तद्व्यभिचारेण कन्येला नाम साभवत् । तां विलोक्य मनुः प्राह नातिहृष्टमना गुरुम् ॥16॥
भगवन् किमिदं जातं कर्म वो ब्रह्मवादिनाम् । विपर्ययमहो कष्टं मैवं स्याद् ब्रह्मविक्रिया ॥17॥
यूयं मन्त्रविदो युक्तास्तपसा दग्धकिल्बिषाः । कुतः संकल्पवैषम्यमनृतं विबुधेष्विव ॥18॥
तन्निशम्य वचस्तस्य भगवान् प्रपितामहः । होतुर्व्यतिक्रमं ज्ञात्वा बभाषे रविनन्दनम् ॥19॥
एतत् संकल्पवैषम्यं होतुस्ते व्यभिचारतः । तथापि साधयिष्ये ते सुप्रजास्त्वं स्वतेजसा ॥20॥

the self-created and four-faced Brahma. **10.** From Brahma's mind was born Marīchi; and from him, Kasyapa was born. To him Vivasvān was born of Daksha's daughter, Aditi. **11.** Vivasvān had by his wife Samjnā a son named Srāddha Deva, who became the Manu. That self-controlled one, also known as Vaivaswata Manu, begot ten sons by his wife Sraddhā. **12.** They were Ikshvāku, Nriga, Saryāti, Dishta, Dhrishta, Karushaka, Narishyanta, Prishadhra, Nabhaga, and Kavi.

Daughter Ila becoming Son Sudyumna (13-22)

13. Before the birth of Ikshvāku and others, the Manu Srāddha Deva was without offspring. The holy sage Vasishtha, endowed with great powers, had a sacrifice to Mitra and Varuna performed by the Manu for the sake of offspring. **14.** The Manu's wife Sraddhā, who was observing Payovrata, approached the sacrificial priest and prayed that she would like to have a daughter born to her. **15.** Directed by the Adhvaryu priest, the Hota or the sacrificing priest, meditating with a concentrated mind, made an offering with the Mantra '*vashat*' for the fulfilment of the wish of the Manu's wife. **16.** Though the Manu was performing his sacrifice desiring a son, the difference in the Hota's prayer resulted in the birth of a daughter who came to be well-known as Ila in later times. But the Manu was not happy to have a daughter, and so said to his teacher Vasishtha in none-too-pleased a mood: **17.** 'O worshipful one! How did it happen like this? It is a tragedy indeed that rites done by Vedic savants like you all should produce contrary results. How can this aberration take place in regard to a Mantra? **18.** You are all experts in the knowledge and application of Mantras. You have also the qualification of having mastery over the senses, and also of austerity and freedom from sins. How then can results contrary to the desired one come about as if the Devas have begun to be untruthful?'

19. Hearing these words of the Manu, our grandfather Vasishtha, came to know about the change in the prayer-resolution (Sankalpa) made by the sacrificing priest. He said as follows to him, the son of Ravi: **20.** 'This difficult situation has arisen because of the deviation of your sacrificing priest. But I shall, by virtue of my power gained through austerity, see

एवं व्यवसितो राजन् भगवान् स महायशाः । अस्तौषीदादिपुरुषमिलायाः पुंस्त्वकाम्यया ॥21॥
तस्मै कामवरं तुष्टो भगवान् हरिरीश्वरः । ददाविलाभवत् तेन सुद्युम्नः पुरुषर्षभः ॥22॥
स एकदा महाराज विचरन् मृगयां वने । वृतः कतिपयामात्यैरश्वमारुह्य सैन्धवम् ॥23॥
प्रगृह्य रुचिरं चापं शरांश्च परमाद्भुतान् । दंशितोऽनुमृगं वीरो जगाम दिशमुत्तराम् ॥24॥
स कुमारो वनं मेरोरधस्तात् प्रविवेश ह । यत्रास्ते भगवाञ्छर्वो रममाणः सहोमया ॥25॥
तस्मिन् प्रविष्ट एवासौ सुद्युम्नः परवीरहा । अपश्यत् स्त्रियमात्मानमश्वं च वडवां नृप ॥26॥
तथा तदनुगाः सर्वे आत्मलिङ्गविपर्ययम् । दृष्ट्वा विमनसोऽभूवन् वीक्षमाणाः परस्परम् ॥27॥

राजोवाच

कथमेवंगुणो देशः केन वा भगवन् कृतः । प्रश्नमेनं समाचक्ष्व परं कौतूहलं हि नः ॥28॥

श्रीशुक उवाच

एकदा गिरिशं द्रष्टुमृषयस्तत्र सुव्रताः । दिशो वितिमिराभासाः कुर्वन्तः समुपागमन् ॥29॥
तान् विलोक्याम्बिका देवी विवासा व्रीडिता भृशम् भर्तुरङ्कात् समुत्थाय नीवीमाश्वथ पर्यधात् ॥30॥
ऋषयोऽपि तयोर्वीक्ष्य प्रसङ्गं रममाणयोः । निवृत्ताः प्रययुस्तस्मान्नरनारायणाश्रमम् ॥31॥
तदिदं भगवानाह प्रियायाः प्रियकाम्यया । स्थानं यः प्रविशेदेतत् स वै योषिद् भवेदिति ॥32॥
तत ऊर्ध्वं वनं तद् वै पुरुषा वर्जयन्ति हि । सा चानुचरसंयुक्ता विचचार वनाद् वनम् ॥33॥

that you get a male issue according to your wish.' **21.** O King, deciding like this, Vasishtha, the far-famed and powerful Rishi, invoked Narayana, the primordial Being, with hymns and prayers in order that Ila might become a man. **22.** Being propitiated, Hari the all-powerful Lord, the master of all, gave him the desired boon by converting the female Ila into a strong and noble male named Sudyumna.

Sudyumna's Reconversion into a Woman (23-33)

23. O King! One day attended by some of his high officers, Sudyumna got upon a horse of Sindhu breed and went to the forest on a hunt. **24.** Equipped with his attractive bow and unique shafts, and protected by his mail, he went northwards pursuing a deer. **25.** That prince entered into the forest in the valleys of Meru where the all-powerful Siva was sporting with Uma. **26.** As soon as he entered that region the accomplished warrior Sudyumna found himself transformed into a woman and his horse into a mare. **27.** All his followers too found a similar sex transformation in themselves also, and much puzzled and distressed at this, began to look at each other.

Rajah Parikshit said: **28.** O worshipful one! How did a region with such properties come into existence? Who was responsible for this arrangement? Please tell me all about it, as I feel very curious to know all the details.

Sri Suka said: **29.** Once some very austere Rishis, whose radiance dispelled the darkness in the quarters and also drowned the brightness of all other bodies, went to this region for meeting Siva, the master of the mountain. **30.** Seeing them, Ambika, who was then sitting without any dress in the lap of Siva, got up in great bashfulness and put on her dress. **31.** The Rishis, too, seeing the engrossment of the divine couple in sexual enjoyment, turned away and went to the Ashrama of Nara-Narayana at Badari. **32.** Thereupon, in order to please his consort, Siva declared that any man who entered that forest would be converted into a woman. **33.**

अथ तामाश्रमाभ्याशे चरन्तीं प्रमदोत्तमाम् । स्त्रीभिःपरिवृतां वीक्ष्य चकमे भगवान् बुधः ॥34॥
सापि तं चकमे सुभ्रूः सोमराजसुतं पतिम् । स तस्यां जनयामास पुरूरवसमात्मजम् ॥35॥
एवं स्त्रीत्वमनुप्राप्तः सुद्युम्नो मानवो नृपः । सस्मार स्वकुलाचार्यं वसिष्ठमिति शुश्रुम ॥36॥
स तस्य तां दशां दृष्ट्वा कृपया भृशपीडितः । सुद्युम्नस्याशयन् पुंस्त्वमुपाधावत शङ्करम् ॥37॥
तुष्टस्तस्मै स भगवानृषये प्रियमावहन् । स्वां च वाचमृतां कुर्वन्निदमाह विशाम्पते ॥38॥
मासं पुमान् स भविता मासं स्त्री तव गोत्रजः । इत्थं व्यवस्थया कामं सुद्युम्नोऽवतु मेदिनीम् ॥39॥
आचार्यानुग्रहात् कामं लब्ध्वा पुंस्त्वं व्यवस्थया । पालयामास जगतीं नाभ्यनन्दन् स्म तं प्रजाः ॥40॥
तस्योत्कलो गयो राजन् विमलश्च सुतास्त्रयः । दक्षिणापथराजानो बभूवुर्धर्मवत्सलाः ॥41॥
ततः परिणते काले प्रतिष्ठानपतिः प्रभुः । पुरूरवस उत्सृज्य गां पुत्राय गतो वनम् ॥42॥

इति श्रीमद्भागवते महापुराणे पारमहंस्यां संहितायां नवमस्कन्धे इलोपाख्याने प्रथमोऽध्यायः ॥ 1॥

From that time onwards men avoided that forest. So Sudyumna and his followers now moved from forest to forest in the form of women.

Birth of Purūravas and his Ascension (34-42)

34. In the course of his wanderings in the forest along with the other women, Sudyumna, now a very handsome lady, was noticed by the august Budha, as she moved about his Ashrama with the other ladies, Budha fell in love with her. **35.** That handsome lady also longed to have Budha, the son of Chandra (moon-deity), as her husband. They had a son named Purūravas.

36. We have heard that this Sudyumna, the son of the Manu, thought of his family teacher Vasishtha for help while he was thus in the state of a woman. **37.** Vasishtha felt great pity at the fate of Sudyumna, and to restore his manhood to him, prayed to Lord Siva. **38.** Being propitiated, Lord Siva was anxious to do what was pleasing to the Rishi and what would be fulfilling his own words also. **39.** He therefore said as follows: 'Your protege Sudyumna, who is as dear to you as a son, will be a man for a month and a woman in the next. Under this arrangement, let him rule the earth.'

40. Having got back his manhood partially at least, Sudyumna continued to rule the earth, but his subjects were not reconciled to the idea of a king who changed sex periodically. **41.** His three sons, Utkal, Gaya, and Vimala, who were very virtuous, became kings of countries in the south. **42.** After a long rule, Sudyumna, who was the ruler of Pratishthāna, entrusted the rule of his kingdom to his eldest son Purūravas and went to dwell in the forest as an ascetic.

अथ द्वितीयोऽध्यायः

श्रीशुक उवाच

एवं गतेऽथ सुद्युम्ने मनुर्वैवस्वतः सुते। पुत्रकामस्तपस्तेपे यमुनायां शतं समाः ॥ 1॥
ततोऽयजन्मनुर्देवमपत्यार्थं हरिं प्रभुम्। इक्ष्वाकुपूर्वजान् पुत्राँल्लेभे स्वसदृशान् दश ॥ 2॥
पृषध्रस्तु मनोः पुत्रो गोपालो गुरुणा कृतः। पालयामास गा यत्तो रात्र्यां वीरासनव्रतः ॥ 3॥
एकदा प्राविशद् गोष्ठं शार्दूलो निशि वर्षति। शयाना गाव उत्थाय भीतास्ता बभ्रमुर्व्रजे ॥ 4॥
एकां जग्राह बलवान् सा चुक्रोश भयातुरा। तस्यास्तत् क्रन्दितं श्रुत्वा पृषध्रोऽभिससार ह ॥ 5॥
खड्गमादाय तरसा प्रलीनोडुगणे निशि। अजानन्नहनद् बभ्रोः शिरः शार्दूलशङ्कया ॥ 6॥
व्याघ्रोऽपि वृक्णश्रवणो निस्त्रिंशाग्राहतस्ततः। निश्चक्राम भृशं भीतो रक्तं पथि समुत्सृजन् ॥ 7॥
मन्यमानो हतं व्याघ्रं पृषध्रः परवीरहा। अद्राक्षीत् स्वहतां बभ्रुं व्युष्टायां निशि दुःखितः ॥ 8॥
तं शशाप कुलाचार्यः कृतागसमकामतः। न क्षत्रबन्धुः शूद्रस्त्वं कर्मणा भवितामुना ॥ 9॥
एवं शप्तस्तु गुरुणा प्रत्यगृह्णात् कृताञ्जलिः। अधारयद् व्रतं वीर ऊर्ध्वरेता मुनिप्रियम् ॥10॥
वासुदेवे भगवति सर्वात्मनि परेऽमले। एकान्तित्वं गतो भक्त्या सर्वभूतसुहृत् समः ॥11॥

Skandha IX : Chapter 2

THE LINES OF THE OTHER SONS OF THE MANU

Story of Prishadhra and Kavi (1-15)

Sri Suka said: 1. When his son Sudyumna retired to the forest, Manu Vaivaswata (identical with Srāddha Deva) took to the practice of austerities on the banks of the Yamuna for a hundred years for having more progeny. **2.** Afterwards he adored Sri Hari with a sacrifice for progeny, and got ten worthy sons with Ikshvāku as the eldest. **3.** Prishadhra, one of the Manu's sons, was appointed by his father as the guardian of cattle. He spent his nights awake, sword in hand, guarding the cattle against wild beasts.

4. One rainy night a tiger entered the cow-pen, and the cows, which were lying down, got up and began to run about here and there in fear. **5.** The powerful tiger caught hold of one of the cows which began to low aloud in pain and fright. Hearing its cries, Prishadhra came running. **6.** He took his sword and slashed at the neck of the tiger. But as it was pitch dark and even the stars were invisible, he beheaded the red-hued cow mistaking it for the tiger. **7.** The end of the sword had wounded the tiger's ear also, and the animal, frightened by it, ran away shedding blood all the way.

8. In the morning heroic Prishadhra, who had thought that he had killed the tiger, discovered to his great sorrow that it was the red-hued cow that he had slaughtered. **9.** His Acharya now cursed him that for the sin of killing the cow, though it be unawares, he would become a Sudra—much lower than even a fallen Kshatriya. **10.** Prishadhra accepted the curse with palms joined in salutation. He observed the vow of continence for life, a state dear to ascetics. **11.** Friendly to all and aware of Divinity in all, he attained to the state of an Ekāntin, one for whom the Supreme Being Vāsudeva, the worshipful, the soul of all, the one

विमुक्तसङ्गः शान्तात्मा संयताक्षोऽपरिग्रहः । यदृच्छयोपपन्नेन कल्पयन् वृत्तिमात्मनः ॥12॥
आत्मन्यात्मानमाधाय ज्ञानतृप्तः समाहितः । विचचार महीमेतां जडान्धबधिराकृतिः ॥13॥
एवंवृत्तो वनं गत्वा दृष्ट्वा दावाग्निमुत्थितम् । तेनोपयुक्तकरणो ब्रह्म प्राप परं मुनिः ॥14॥
कविः कनीयान् विषयेषु निःस्पृहो विसृज्य राज्यं सह बन्धुभिर्वनम् ।
निवेश्य चित्ते पुरुषं स्वरोचिषं विवेश कैशोरवयाः परं गतः ॥15॥
करूषान्मानवादासन् कारूषाः क्षत्रजातयः । उत्तरापथगोप्तारो ब्रह्मण्या धर्मवत्सलाः ॥16॥
धृष्टाद् धार्ष्टमभूत् क्षत्रं ब्रह्मभूयं गतं क्षितौ । नृगस्य वंशः सुमतिर्भूतज्योतिस्ततो वसुः ॥17॥
वसोः प्रतीकस्तत्पुत्र ओघवानोघवत्पिता । कन्या चौघवती नाम सुदर्शन उवाह ताम् ॥18॥
चित्रसेनो नरिष्यन्तादृक्षस्तस्य सुतोऽभवत् । तस्य मीढ्वांस्ततः कूर्च इन्द्रसेनस्तु तत्सुतः ॥19॥
वीतिहोत्रस्त्विन्द्रसेनात् तस्य सत्यश्रवा अभूत् । उरुश्रवाः सुतस्तस्य देवदत्तस्ततोऽभवत् ॥20॥
ततोऽग्निवेश्यो भगवानग्निः स्वयमभूत् सुतः । कानीन इति विख्यातो जातूकर्ण्यो महानृषिः ॥21॥
ततो ब्रह्मकुलं जातमाग्निवेश्यायनं नृप । नरिष्यन्तान्वयः प्रोक्तो दिष्टवंशमतः शृणु ॥22॥

without any stain, was the only object of love. **12.** He was without any attachments, serene in mind, established in the control of all senses, without any possession, and habituated to maintain his body with whatever he got by chance. **13.** Resembling a senseless man or a blind man or a deaf man, he wandered all over the country, with his mind always established in the Supreme Being and satisfied with the knowledge of Him, and ever steeped in His bliss. **14.** While travelling like this, he entered a forest one day. He saw there a fierce forest fire raging. He threw his body into it and attained to the Supreme Brahman. (He had no issue.) **15.** Kavi, the youngest of Manu's sons, showed signs of renunciation of all worldly enjoyments from his very boyhood. He renounced all relatives and kingdom very early in life, went to the forest, meditated on the effulgent Purusha in the heart, and attained to the Supreme state of the Divine. (He too had therefore no issue.)

Lines of Karūsha and Dhrishta (16-18)

16. From Karūsha, another son of the Manu, came into existence a race of Kshatriyas called Kārūshas, who ruled over the northern regions, and who were devoted to holy men and Dharma. **17.** From another son of the Manu named Dhrishta, a race of Kshatriyas called Dhrāshtas arose. They, however, became transformed into Brahmanas because of their noble qualities. Nriga had a son Sumati; his son was Bhūtajyotis; and his, Vasu. **18.** To Vasu, Pratīka was born; and to him, Oghavān. Oghavān had a son of the same name and a daughter named Oghavati who was married to Sudarsana.

Line of Narishyanta (19-22)

19. Narishyanta's son was Chitrasena; his son was Driksha; his son, Mīdhvān; his son, Kūrcha; and his son, Indrasena. **20.** From Indrasena was born Vītihotra; from him, Satyasravas; from him, Urusrava; and from him, Devadatta. **21.** From Devadatta was born Agnivesya who was an incarnation of the deity Agni, and who became famous also under the names Kānīna and Jātūkarnya. **22.** From him arose a line of famous Brahmanas named Agnivesyas. O King! With this I have finished the line of Narishyanta, and I shall now deal with that of Dishta.

नाभागो दिष्टपुत्रोऽन्यः कर्मणा वैश्यतां गतः । भलन्दनः सुतस्तस्य वत्सप्रीतिर्भलन्दनात् ॥23॥
वत्सप्रीतेः सुतः प्रांशुस्तत्सुतं प्रमतिं विदुः । खनित्रः प्रमतेस्तस्माच्चाक्षुषोऽथ विविंशतिः ॥24॥
विविंशतिसुतो रम्भः खनिनेत्रोऽस्य धार्मिकः । करन्धमो महाराज तस्यासीदात्मजो नृप ॥25॥
तस्यावीक्षित् सुतो यस्य मरुत्तश्चक्रवर्त्यभूत् । संवर्तोऽयाजयद् यं वै महायोग्यङ्गिरःसुतः ॥26॥
मरुत्तस्य यथा यज्ञो न तथान्यस्य कश्चन । सर्वं हिरण्मयं त्वासीद् यत् किञ्चिच्चास्य शोभनम्
अमाद्यदिन्द्रः सोमेन दक्षिणाभिर्द्विजातयः । मरुतः परिवेष्टारो विश्वेदेवाः सभासदः ॥28॥
मरुत्तस्य दमः पुत्रस्तस्यासीद् राज्यवर्धनः । सुधृतिस्तत्सुतो जज्ञे सौधृतेयो नरः सुतः ॥29॥
तत्सुतः केवलस्तस्माद् बन्धुमान् वेगवांस्ततः । बन्धुस्तस्याभवद् यस्य तृणबिन्दुर्महीपतिः ॥30॥
तं भेजेऽलम्बुषा देवी भजनीयगुणालयम् । वराप्सरा यतः पुत्राः कन्या चेडविडाभवत् ॥31॥
तस्यामुत्पादयामास विश्रवा धनदं सुतम् । प्रादाय विद्यां परमामृषिर्योगेश्वरात् पितुः ॥32॥
विशालः शून्यबन्धुश्च धूम्रकेतुश्च तत्सुताः । विशालो वंशकृद् राजा वैशालीं निर्ममे पुरीम् ॥33॥
हेमचन्द्रः सुतस्तस्य धूम्राक्षस्तस्य चात्मजः । तत्पुत्रात् संयमादासीत् कृशाश्वः सहदेवजः ॥34॥
कृशाश्वात् सोमदत्तोऽभूद् योऽश्वमेधैरिडस्पतिम् । इष्ट्वा पुरुषमापाग्र्यां गतिं योगेश्वराश्रितः ॥35॥
सौमदत्तिस्तु सुमतिस्तत्सुतो जनमेजयः । एते वैशालभूपालास्तृणबिन्दोर्यशोधराः ॥36॥

इति श्रीमद्भागवते महापुराणे पारमहंस्यां संहितायां नवमस्कन्धे द्वितीयोऽध्यायः ॥ 2॥

Line of Dishta (23-36)

23. As the son of Dishta was born a Nābhāga different from the famous man of the same name. He became a Vaisya by profession. His son was Bhalandana, and from him Vatsaprīti was born. **24.** Vatsaprīti's son was Prāmsu; his son, Pramati; his son, Khānitra; his son; Chākshusha; and his son, Vivimsati. **25.** From Vivimsati was born Rambha whose son was Khaninetra noted for his adherence to Dharma. His son was Karandhama. **26.** Avīkshit was his son; and his son was Marutta, who became an emperor. It was at the Yajna of this Marutta that Samvarta, the son of Angiras and a famous Yogi, officiated as priest. **27.** Never has there been a Yajna as grand as Marutta's. All the utensils and outfits used in those rites were made of gold and looked brilliant. **28.** Indra had the juice of Soma to drink to inebriation. The priests too got Dakshinas to their satisfaction. The celestials called Maruts served food, and the sacrificial assembly consisted of Viswedevas.

29. Marutta's son was Dama; his son, Rājyavardhana; his son, Sudhriti; and his son Nara, who was also known as Saudhriteya. **30.** Nara's son was Kevala; his son Bandhumān; his son, Vegavān; his son, Bandhu; and his son, Trinabindu. **31.** Trinabindu, who possessed various praiseworthy qualities, married a noted Apsara woman named Alambushā. By that woman he had many sons and a daughter named Idavida. **32.** Idavida married the sage Visravas, who was highly intelligent and had learnt from his father the way of making oneself invisible. They had a son named Dhanada (Kubera). **33.** Trinabindu had as sons Visāla. Sūnyabandhu and Dhūmraketu. Of them, Visāla, who propagated his line, founded the city of Vaisāli. **34.** Visāla's son was Hemachandra; his son, Dhūmrāksha; his son, Samyama who had two sons Devaja and Krisāsva. **35.** Krisāsva's son was Somadatta. By adoring the Supreme Lord with Asvamedha sacrifices, he attained to the highest state and became adored of even the masters of

Yoga. **36.** Somadatta had a son Sumati; and he, Janamejaya. These kings ruled at Vaisāli, and continued to maintain the fame and traditions of Trinabindu.

अथ तृतीयोऽध्यायः

श्रीशुक उवाच

शर्यातिर्मानवो राजा ब्रह्मिष्ठः स बभूव ह। यो वा अङ्गिरसां सत्रे द्वितीयमह ऊचिवान् ॥ 1॥
सुकन्या नाम तस्यासीत् कन्या कमललोचना। तया सार्धं वनगतो ह्यगमच्च्यवनाश्रमम् ॥ 2॥
सा सखीभिः परिवृता विचिन्वत्यङ्घ्रिपान् वने। वल्मीकरन्ध्रे ददृशे खद्योते इव ज्योतिषी ॥ 3॥
ते दैवचोदिता बाला ज्योतिषी कण्टकेन वै। अविध्यन्मुग्धभावेन सुस्रावासृक् ततो बहु ॥ 4॥
शकृन्मूत्रनिरोधोऽभूत् सैनिकानां च तत्क्षणात्। राजर्षिस्तमुपालक्ष्य पुरुषान् विस्मितोऽब्रवीत् 5॥
अप्यभद्रं न युष्माभिर्भार्गवस्य विचेष्टितम्। व्यक्तं केनापि नस्तस्य कृतमाश्रमदूषणम् ॥ 6॥
सुकन्या प्राह पितरं भीता किञ्चित् कृतं मया। द्वे ज्योतिषी अजानन्त्या निर्भिन्ने कण्टकेन वै ॥ 7॥
दुहितुस्तद्वचः श्रुत्वा शर्यातिर्जातसाध्वसः। मुनिं प्रसादयामास वल्मीकान्तर्हितं शनैः ॥ 8॥
तदभिप्रायमाज्ञाय प्रादाद् दुहितरं मुनेः। कृच्छ्रान्मुक्तस्तमामन्त्र्य पुरं प्रायात् समाहितः ॥ 9॥

Skandha IX : Chapter 3

THE LINE OF SARYĀTI

Saryāti at Chyavana's Ashrama (1-9)

Sri Suka said: **1.** Saryāti, the son of Vaivaswata Manu, was one who was versed in the Veda and its real purport. It was he who explained all their rites and all the Mantras on the rituals that were to be performed on the second day of the Satra conducted by members of the clan of Angiras. **2.** He had a daughter named Sukanya with eyes beautiful like the lotus. One day he went into the forest with her and visited the Ashrama of Chyavana. **3.** While moving about in the forest with attendant maids, viewing the trees, she came across a white ant-hill in which she saw two gleaming points of light like glow worms. **4.** Prompted by fate, that girl in her childish curiosity took a thorn and poked at the brilliant spots in the ant-hill. At once much blood began to flow out.

5. Immediately after this incident all the troops and the rest of the royal retinue found their excretory functions obstructed. In great astonishment the royal sage Saryāti said to his men: **6.** 'Have any of you done anything harmful to sage Chyavana of Bhrigu's line? It is clear from this experience of ours that someone in our party has committed something violating the sanctity of this Ashrama.' **7.** Sukanya thereupon confessed to her father how unknowingly she had pricked two points of light with a thorn. **8.** The words of his daughter alarmed Saryāti very much. With considerable effort, he pacified the Rishi Chyavana who had been covered over by the white ant-hill. **9.** Divining the mind of the Rishi, the king offered his daughter in marriage to him. Thus freeing himself from a dangerous situation, he took leave of the sage and returned to his capital with a peaceful mind.

सुकन्या च्यवनं प्राप्य पतिं परमकोपनम् । प्रीणयामास चित्तज्ञा अप्रमत्तानुवृत्तिभिः ॥10॥
कस्यचित् त्वथ कालस्य नासत्यावाश्रमागतौ । तौ पूजयित्वा प्रोवाच वयो मे दत्तमीश्वरौ ॥11॥
ग्रहं ग्रहीष्ये सोमस्य यज्ञे वामप्यसोमपोः । क्रियतां मे वयो रूपं प्रमदानां यदीप्सितम् ॥12॥
बाढमित्यूचतुर्विप्रमभिनन्द्य भिषक्तमौ । निमज्जतां भवानस्मिन् ह्रदे सिद्धविनिर्मिते ॥13॥
इत्युक्त्वा जरया ग्रस्तदेहो धमनिसंततः । ह्रदं प्रवेशितोऽश्विभ्यां वलीपलितविप्रियः ॥14॥
पुरुषास्त्रय उत्तस्थुरपीच्या वनिताप्रियाः । पद्मस्रजः कुण्डलिनस्तुल्यरूपाः सुवाससः ॥15॥
तान् निरीक्ष्य वरारोहा सरूपान् सूर्यवर्चसः । अजानती पतिं साध्वी अश्विनौ शरणं ययौ ॥16॥
दर्शयित्वा पतिं तस्यै पातिव्रत्येन तोषितौ । ऋषिमामन्त्र्य ययतुर्विमानेन त्रिविष्टपम् ॥17॥
यक्ष्यमाणोऽथ शर्यातिश्च्यवनस्याश्रमं गतः । ददर्श दुहितुः पार्श्वे पुरुषं सूर्यवर्चसम् ॥18॥
राजा दुहितरं प्राह कृतपादाभिवन्दनाम् । आशिषश्चाप्रयुञ्जानो नातिप्रीतमना इव ॥19॥
चिकीर्षितं ते किमिदं पतिस्त्वया प्रलम्भितो लोकनमस्कृतो मुनिः ।
यत् त्वं जराग्रस्तमसत्यसम्मतं विहाय जारं भजसेऽमुमध्वगम् ॥20॥

Chyavana's Rejuvenation (10-17)

10. Sage Chyavana, who became Sukanya's husband, was a person with a highly choleric temperament. The intelligent Sukanya, through her insight into the working of his mind and her alertness, was able to please him by her devoted and careful service. **11.** Some time after, Nāsatyas, the physicians of the heavenly region, visited the Ashrama of Chyavana. After properly honouring them, the sage said to them: 'You are physicians of great knowledge and power. Can you make me a youth? **12.** You are not now offered Soma juice in Yajnas. I shall arrange for your getting it, if you can transform me into a youth of attractive appearance pleasing to young women.' **13.** The celestial physicians agreed to the proposal and said to the sage: ' Please plunge into this lake made by the Siddhas.' **14.** Saying so, the Aswins dipped themselves in that lake, taking with them that decrepit and old sage whose body was disfigured by folds, grey hairs, and protruding bones and patent blood vessels. **15.** Soon after, three persons emerged from that lake. All the three were alike—young, decorated with lotus garlands and ear rings, dressed in shining attire, and in every way attractive to the eyes of women. **16.** Looking at the three, luminous like the sun and looking alike, Sukanya was not able to distinguish her husband Chyavana from among the three. She therefore sought the grace of the Aswins. **17.** Pleased at the lady's faithfulness to the husband, the Aswins helped her to pick out her husband, and then bidding farewell to the sage, went away in their aerial car to the heavenly regions.

A Surprise for King Saryāti (18-26)

18. Some time after, Saryāti went to Chyavana's Ashrama in connection with a sacrifice, and was astonished to find with his daughter a person luminous like the sun. **19.** On his daughter doing obeisance to him, he not only uttered no word of blessing, but spoke as follows in a mood of annoyance and displeasure: **20.** 'Your conduct is a surprise to me. Have you deceived your husband, the sage Chyavana who commands the respect of the whole world? Wretch! Dissatisfied with that aged sage as your husband, you seem to have taken a stray traveller as your lover.

कथं मतिस्तेऽवगतायथा सतां कुलप्रसूते कुलदूषणं त्विदम् ।
बिभर्षि जारं यदपत्रपा कुलं पितुश्च भर्तुश्च नयस्यधस्तमः ॥21॥

एवं ब्रुवाणं पितरं स्मयमाना शुचिस्मिता । उवाच तात जामाता तवैष भृगुनन्दनः ॥22॥
शशंस पित्रे तत् सर्वं वयोरूपाभिलम्भनम् । विस्मितः परमप्रीतस्तनयां परिषस्वजे ॥23॥
सोमेन याजयन् वीरं ग्रहं सोमस्य चाग्रहीत् । असोमपोरप्यश्विनोश्च्यवनः स्वेन तेजसा ॥24॥
हन्तुं तमाददे वज्रं सद्योमन्युरमर्षितः । सवज्रं स्तम्भयामास भुजमिन्द्रस्य भार्गवः ॥25॥
अन्वजानंस्ततः सर्वे ग्रहं सोमस्य चाश्विनोः । भिषजाविति यत् पूर्वं सोमाहुत्या बहिष्कृतौ ॥26॥
उत्तानबर्हिरानर्तो भूरिषेण इति त्रयः । शर्यातेरभवन् पुत्रा आनर्ताद् रेवतोऽभवत् ॥27॥
सोऽन्तःसमुद्रे नगरीं विनिर्माय कुशस्थलीम् । आस्थितोऽभुङ्क्त विषयानानर्तादीनरिन्दम ॥28॥
तस्य पुत्रशतं जज्ञे ककुद्मिज्येष्ठमुत्तमम् । ककुद्मी रेवतीं कन्यां स्वामादय विभुं गतः ॥29॥
कन्यावरं परिप्रष्टुं ब्रह्मलोकमपावृतम् । आवर्तमाने गान्धर्वे स्थितोऽलब्धक्षणः क्षणम् ॥30॥
तदन्त आद्यमानम्य स्वाभिप्रायं न्यवेदयत् । तच्छ्रुत्वा भगवान् ब्रह्मा प्रहस्य तमुवाच ह ॥31॥
अहो राजन् निरुद्धास्ते कालेन हृदि ये कृताः । तत्पुत्रपौत्रनप्तॄणां गोत्राणि च न शृण्महे ॥32॥

21. O you who are born in a noble family! How is it that your mind has gone in this ignoble direction opposed to your family traditions? Your conduct is a matter of disgrace for our whole ancestry. For, deserting your husband, you have taken to a lover! You have degraded the families of your father and husband to the level of the sinful.' **22.** To her father who was speaking thus, she replied smiling in a very pleasing mood: 'O father! This person is none other than your son-in-law the scion of the family of the Bhrigus.' **23.** She then told her father everything about how and from whom her husband attained to youth and physical beauty. And the king, astonished and delighted on hearing the story, embraced his daughter with great affection.

24. The sage Chyavana made the heroic king Saryāti perform a Somayaga, in which, on the authority of his inherent strength, he broke tradition and made an offering of Soma to the Aswins who were not eligible for it. **25.** Excited with anger at this honour shown to Aswins against all rules and customs, Indra raised his thunderbolt weapon to slay Chyavana, but Chyavana of Bhrigu's line caused Indra's hand holding the Vajra to be paralysed. **26.** Thereafter all began to offer the cup of Soma to the Aswins who were hitherto denied the Soma offering on the ground that they were physicians.

Kakudmi Grandson of Saryāti (27-36)

27. The King Saryāti had three sons—Uttānabarhis, Ānarta, and Bhūrishena. Of these, Ānarta had a son named Revata. **28.** O queller of foes! He built the city of Kusasthali, in an island in the sea and from there he governed Ānarta and other countries. **29-30.** He had a hundred sons, the eldest of whom was Kakudmi. Kakudmi went to the assembly of Brahma together with his daughter Revati in order to ascertain to whom he was to give this daughter in marriage. Though he could get free access to Brahma's assembly, he could not get an early opportunity to consult Brahma on this point, as a music programme was on at that time. **31.** When that item was over, he saluted Brahma and informed him of the object of his visit. Brahma thereupon said to him smiling: **32.** 'O King! All those whom you have in mind, have been effaced by Time long ago.

कालोऽभियातस्त्रिणवचतुर्युगविकल्पितः । तद् गच्छ देवदेवांशो बलदेवो महाबलः ॥33॥
कन्यारत्नमिदं राजन् नररत्नाय देहि भोः । भुवो भारावताराय भगवान् भूतभावनः ॥34॥
अवतीर्णो निजांशेन पुण्यश्रवणकीर्तनः । इत्यादिष्टोऽभिवन्द्याजं नृपः स्वपुरमागतः ।
त्यक्तं पुण्यजनत्रासाद् भ्रातृभिर्दिक्ष्ववस्थितैः ॥35॥
सुतां दत्त्वानवद्याङ्गीं बलाय बलशालिने । बदर्याख्यं गतो राजा तप्तुं नारायणाश्रमम् ॥36॥

इति श्रीमद्भागवते महापुराणे पारमहंस्यां संहितायां नवमस्कन्धे तृतीयोऽध्यायः ॥ 3॥

No one hears now-a-days even of their descendants—their sons, grandsons, and great grandsons. **33-35.** Since your coming here, a period of twenty seven Chaturyugas have passed. Now there lives on earth Baladeva, who is Mahavishnu incarnated as a personage of great prowess. You may give this jewel of a girl in marriage to that illustrious personage. He is a partial incarnation of the Lord who, through his name and sportive actions, works for the welfare of all, and whose mission it is to rid the world of its unbearable burdens.' Being so commanded by Brahma, the king went back to his capital after offering his worshipful obeisance to him. **36.** When he reached his capital, he found that it had been abandoned by his brothers who had fled in different directions on account of the fear of Yakshas. The king, after bestowing his daughter on Balarama of great prowess, went to Narayanāshrama at Badari for engaging himself in austerities.

अथ चतुर्थोऽध्यायः

श्रीशुक उवाच

नाभागो नभगापत्यं यं ततं भ्रातरः कविम् । यविष्ठं व्यभजन् दायं ब्रह्मचारिणमागतम् ॥ 1॥
भ्रातरोऽभाङ्क्त किं मह्यं भजाम पितरं तव । त्वां ममार्यास्तताभाङ्क्षुर्मा पुत्रक तदादृथाः ॥ 2॥
इमे अङ्गिरसः सत्रमासतेऽद्य सुमेधसः । षष्ठं षष्ठमुपेत्याहः कवे मुह्यन्ति कर्मणि ॥ 3॥

Skandha IX : Chapter 4

STORY OF AMBARISHA

Nābhāga claiming Patrimony (1-13)

Sri Suka said: **1-2**. Nabhaga, a son of the Manu, had Nābhāga as his son. Nabhaga's other sons partitioned all the ancestral property while Nābhāga, the youngest and the most learned of the brothers, was still in the Guru's house undergoing education for an unusually long period. They therefore thought that he would be a lifelong Brahmacharin and would never come to claim his share. (But he eventually returned and claimed his share, whereupon, since nothing was left undivided, his brothers gave him their father as his share.) He asked: 'O brothers! Where is my share?' The brothers replied: 'We forgot you when partitioning. You may therefore take our father as your share.' But the father told him: 'O son! Don't accept this offer. They are deceiving you. For I am not a property to be enjoyed. **3.** Now the wise group of sages known as Angiras have started a Satra (a long-drawn

तांस्त्वं शंसय सूक्ते द्वे वैश्वदेवे महात्मनः । ते स्वर्यन्तो धनं सत्रपरिशेषितमात्मनः ।। 4।।
दास्यन्ति तेऽथ तान् गच्छ तथा स कृतवान् यथा । तस्मै दत्त्वा ययुः स्वर्गं ते सत्रपरिशेषितम् ।। 5।।
तं कश्चित् स्वीकरिष्यन्तं पुरुषः कृष्णदर्शनः । उवाचोत्तरतोऽभ्येत्य ममेदं वास्तुकं वसु ।। 6।।
ममेदमृषिभिर्दत्तमिति तर्हि स्म मानवः । स्यान्नौ ते पितरि प्रश्नः पृष्टवान् पितरं तथा 7।।
यज्ञवास्तुगतं सर्वमुच्छिष्टमृषयः क्वचित् । चक्रुर्विभागं रुद्राय स देवः सर्वमर्हति ।। 8।।
नाभागस्तं प्रणम्याह तवेश किल वास्तुकम् । इत्याह मे पिता ब्रह्मञ्छिरसा त्वां प्रसादये ।। 9।।
यत् ते पितावदद् धर्मं त्वं च सत्यं प्रभाषसे । ददामि ते मन्त्रदृशे ज्ञानं ब्रह्म सनातनम् ।।10।।
गृहाण द्रविणं दत्तं मत्सत्रे परिशेषितम् । इत्युक्त्वान्तर्हितो रुद्रो भगवान् सत्यवत्सलः ।।11।।
य एतत् संस्मरेत् प्रातः सायं च सुसमाहितः । कविर्भवति मन्त्रज्ञो गतिं चैव तथाऽऽत्मनः ।।12।।
नाभागादम्बरीषोऽभून्महाभागवतः कृती । नास्पृशद् ब्रह्मशापोऽपि यं न प्रतिहतः क्वचित् 13।।

राजोवाच

भगवञ्छ्रोतुमिच्छामि राजर्षेस्तस्य धीमतः । न प्राभूद् यत्र निर्मुक्तो ब्रह्मदण्डो दुरत्ययः ।।14।।

sacrifice). O my learned son! Though they are men of learning, they are put to great anxiety because they do not know the Mantras to be chanted at the close of every six days in connection with the rites pertaining to Viswedevas. **4-5.** Though they be great men, you go and help them by chanting the two Suktas connected with Viswedevas. When at the end of the Satra, they ascend to heaven, they will give you all the wealth remaining after the Satra.' Hearing this, the son did accordingly. Those sacrificers, before being transported to heaven, gave him (Nābhāga) all the remaining wealth at the site of the Satra.

6. When he was about to take possession of that wealth, a man of dark complexion (Rudra), coming from the north, claimed as his own whatever wealth remained on the sacrificial campus. **7.** Nābhāga the grandson of Manu, thereupon told him that the Rishis had gifted that wealth to him. To settle the dispute Rudra said that they could refer the matter to Nābhāga's father himself. **8.** On enquiry Nabhaga, the father, said: 'The Rishis had once made the arrangement that whatever is left in the campus of a Yajna belongs to Rudra. So this too has to go to him.' **9.** Nābhāga thereupon made prostration to Rudra and said: 'My father said that all that is left in the sacrificial field really belongs to you. So I prostrate to you, requesting you to forgive me for my transgression.' **10.** Then Rudra said: 'As your father spoke according to Dharma, and as you have spoken the truth, I am pleased to instruct you, a knower of the Veda, in the knowledge regarding the eternal Brahman. **11.** Besides, I am giving you all this, my rightful possession consisting of the residuary wealth of the sacrificial field. Please accept it!' Saying so, Sri Rudra disappeared from sight. **12.** Whoever studies this account with faith and concentration in the mornings and evenings, will become learned and become a knower of the Vedas. He will attain to his spiritual destiny. **13.** Of Nābhāga was born Ambarīsha, the noted devotee and holy personage, who could not be affected even in the least by the curse of Durvāsas, which none can ordinarily resist.

Ambarīsha's Devotion (14-28)

Rajah Parikshit said: **14.** O worshipful one! I desire to hear the story of that high-minded royal sage Ambarīsha whom even the weapon of an ogre released by

श्रीशुक उवाच

अम्बरीषो महाभागः सप्तद्वीपवतीं महीम्। अव्ययां च श्रियं लब्ध्वा विभवं चातुलं भुवि ॥15॥
मेनेऽतिदुर्लभं पुंसां सर्वं तत् स्वप्नसंस्तुतम्। विद्वान् विभवनिर्वाणं तमो विशति यत् पुमान् ॥16॥
वासुदेवे भगवति तद्भक्तेषु च साधुषु। प्राप्तो भावं परं विश्वं येनेदं लोष्टवत् स्मृतम् ॥17॥

स वै मनः कृष्णपदारविन्दयोर्वचांसि वैकुण्ठगुणानुवर्णने।
करौ हरेर्मन्दिरमार्जनादिषु श्रुतिं चकाराच्युतसत्कथोदये ॥18॥
मुकुन्दलिङ्गालयदर्शने दृशौ तद्भृत्यगात्रस्पर्शेऽङ्गसङ्गमम्।
घ्राणं च तत्पादसरोजसौरभे श्रीमत्तुलस्या रसनां तदर्पिते ॥19॥
पादौ हरेः क्षेत्रपदानुसर्पणे शिरो हृषीकेशपदाभिवन्दने।
कामं च दास्ये न तु कामकाम्यया यथोत्तमश्लोकजनाश्रया रतिः ॥20॥
एवं सदा कर्मकलापमात्मनः परेऽधियज्ञे भगवत्यधोक्षजे।
सर्वात्मभावं विदधन्महीमिमां तन्निष्ठविप्राभिहितः शशास ह ॥21॥
ईजेऽश्वमेधैरधियज्ञमीश्वरं महाविभूत्योपचिताङ्गदक्षिणैः।
ततैर्वसिष्ठासितगौतमादिभिर्धन्वन्यभिस्रोतमसौ सरस्वतीम् ॥22॥

यस्य क्रतुषु गीर्वाणैः सदस्या ऋत्विजो जनाः। तुल्यरूपाश्चानिमिषा व्यदृश्यन्त सुवाससः ॥23॥

Durvāsas could not affect in the least.

Sri Suka said: **15-16.** Ambarīsha was the master of the whole earth with its seven continents, with inexhaustible wealth, and of incomparable prowess. But he knew that all this worldly wealth is shortlived and dream-like in nature, and also that it leads only to spiritual blindness. **17.** As he had the highest devotion for Vāsudeva and to holy men devoted to Him, he could regard this whole universe, representing all wealth, as nothing but a clod of earth. **18.** He trained his mind to be ever engrossed in the thought of Krishna's feet; his words in recounting the excellences of Krishna; his hands in cleaning His places of worship; and his ears in listening to the sacred accounts dealing with Krishna's actions. **19.** He devoted his eyes to looking at the holy images of Mukunda; his sense of touch to contacting His great devotees; his sense of smell to imbibing the fragrance of Tulasi leaves enhanced by the contact of the Lord's lotus feet; and his sense of taste in the consumption of food left after offering to Him. **20.** With his feet he ever circumambulated the holy temples of the Lord; and with his head, he constantly bowed down to Him present everywhere. He partook of the delicious offerings made to the Lord, not for satisfying the cravings of his desire-nature, but as a part of his devotional service, calculated to enhance his attachment to the Lord. **21.** Thus practising His presence in everything, he offered all his actions to that Supreme Being, the bestower of the fruits of all Yajnas and the controller of all the senses. Cultivating this attitude of mind and following the advice of ministers who were established in this devotional ideal, he governed the whole earth.

22. In the desert region facing the flow of the river Saraswati, he adored the Supreme Being with several Asvamedha sacrifices, conducted by priests like Vasishtha, Asita, Gautama and others, and performed with an elaboration of all ancillary rites and of liberal gifts, made possible by his enormous resources. **23.** In Ambarīsha's sacrifice all the sacrificial

स्वर्गो न प्रार्थितो यस्य मनुजैरमरप्रियः। शृण्वद्भिरुपगायद्भिरुत्तमश्लोकचेष्टितम् ॥24॥
समर्द्धयन्ति तान् कामाः स्वाराज्यपरिभाविताः। दुर्लभा नापि सिद्धानां मुकुन्दं हृदि पश्यतः ॥25॥
स इत्थं भक्तियोगेन तपोयुक्तेन पार्थिवः। स्वधर्मेण हरिं प्रीणन् सङ्गान् सर्वाञ्छनैर्जहौ ॥26॥
गृहेषु दारेषु सुतेषु बन्धुषु द्विपोत्तमस्यन्दनवाजिपत्तिषु।
अक्षय्यरत्नाभरणायुधादिष्वनन्तकोशेष्वकरोदसन्मतिम् ॥27॥
तस्मा अदाद्धरिश्चक्रं प्रत्यनीकभयावहम्। एकान्तभक्तिभावेन प्रीतो भृत्याभिरक्षणम् ॥28॥
आरिराधयिषुः कृष्णं महिष्या तुल्यशीलया। युक्तः सांवत्सरं वीरो दधार द्वादशीव्रतम् ॥29॥
व्रतान्ते कार्तिके मासि त्रिरात्रं समुपोषितः। स्नातः कदाचित् कालिन्द्यां हरिं मधुवनेऽर्चयत् 30॥
महाभिषेकविधिना सर्वोपस्करसम्पदा। अभिषिच्याम्बराकल्पैर्गन्धमाल्यार्हणादिभिः ॥31॥
तद्गतान्तरभावेन पूजयामास केशवम्। ब्राह्मणांश्च महाभागान् सिद्धार्थानपि भक्तितः 32॥
गवां रुक्मविषाणीनां रूप्याङ्घ्रीणां सुवाससाम्। पयःशीलवयोरूपवत्सोपस्करसम्पदाम् ॥33॥
प्राहिणोत् साधुविप्रेभ्यो गृहेषु न्यर्बुदानि षट्। भोजयित्वा द्विजानग्रे स्वाद्वन्नं गुणवत्तमम् ॥34॥
लब्धकामैरनुज्ञातः पारणायोपचक्रमे। तस्य तर्ह्यतिथिः साक्षाद् दुर्वासा भगवानभूत् ॥35॥

priests and members of the sacrificial assembly were dressed in splendid raiments and resembled celestials with eyes unwinking because of the wondrous display before them. (But he had no desire for the heavenly felicities which sacrifices bring.) **24.** Not only he, but even his attendants and associates, who were always hearing and reciting hymns on the Lord's sportive activities and were steeped in the bliss of it, cared not for heavenly regions, which the celestials long for. **25.** For, those who have the intuition of the Lord within, feel no attraction even for objects desired by Siddhas, as all such external attainments are made insipid by the side of the bliss of the Self.

26. By practising devotion, by performing his ordained duties with perfect detachment, and by austerities, the king propitiated Sri Hari, and by His grace overcame all attachments to the world. **27.** He therefore attached no importance to home, comforts, sons, relatives, army consisting of regiments of elephants, chariots, horses and foot soldiers, to the unending wealth of ornaments, gems and weapons, and a treasury with inexhaustible resources. **28.** Sri Hari, being pleased with his unswerving devotion, offered him his own weapon of Sudarsana which gives protection to devotees like him always and is a terror to hostile armies.

Ambarīsha's Vow of Dwādasi (29-35)

29. Being desirous of adoring Krishna, the king along with the queen, who was well-matched with him in devotional spirit, observed the Dwādasi vow, characterised by the breaking of the full day's fast. **30.** Towards the close of the period of vow they observed fast for three days in the month of Kartika. During this period, they bathed in the Yamuna and worshipped Hari in Madhuvana. **31-32.** They adored Hari with the highest devotional exaltation and intense concentration, performing the great ceremony of holy bath (Mahābhisheka) in accordance with the ordained rules and procedures, accompanied with a wealth of materials and utensils. They offered Him and His desireless devotees worship with sandal paste, flowers, Arghya etc., costly clothes and jewellery. **33-35.** He sent as gifts to the

तमानर्चातिथिं भूपः प्रत्युत्थानासनार्हणैः । ययाचेऽभ्यवहाराय पादमूलमुपागतः ॥36॥
प्रतिनन्द्य स तद्याच्ञां कर्तुमावश्यकं गतः । निममज्ज बृहद् ध्यायन् कालिन्दीसलिले शुभे 37॥
मुहूर्तार्धावशिष्टायां द्वादश्यां पारणं प्रति । चिन्तयामास धर्मज्ञो द्विजैस्तद्धर्मसङ्कटे ॥38॥
ब्राह्मणातिक्रमे दोषो द्वादश्यां यदपारणे । यत् कृत्वा साधु मे भूयादधर्मो वा न मां स्पृशेत् 39॥
अम्भसा केवलेनाथ करिष्ये व्रतपारणम् । प्राहुरब्भक्षणं विप्रा ह्यशितं नाशितं च तत् ॥40॥
इत्यपः प्राश्य राजर्षिश्चिन्तयन् मनसाच्युतम् । प्रत्यचष्ट कुरुश्रेष्ठ द्विजागमनमेव सः ॥41॥
दुर्वासा यमुनाकूलात् कृतावश्यक आगतः । राज्ञाभिनन्दितस्तस्य बुबुधे चेष्टितं धिया ॥42॥
मन्युना प्रचलद्गात्रो भ्रुकुटीकुटिलाननः । बुभुक्षितश्च सुतरां कृताञ्जलिमभाषत ॥43॥
अहो अस्य नृशंसस्य श्रियोन्मत्तस्य पश्यत । धर्मव्यतिक्रमं विष्णोरभक्तस्येशमानिनः ॥44॥
यो मामतिथिमायातमातिथ्येन निमन्त्र्य च । अदत्त्वा भुक्तवांस्तस्य सद्यस्ते दर्शये फलम् ॥45॥

abodes of holy men sixty crores of cows young in age, gentle by nature, beautiful in appearance and great in milking quality, all decorated with wrappings of costly cloths and provided with golden encasements for horn and silver shoes for hooves. Then after feeding holy men with delicious food and getting their blessings and permission to break his fast, he was about to do so when there arrived as guest no less a personage than the worshipful sage Durvāsas.

The Threat of Durvāsas (36-48)

36. After honouring the guest by a cordial welcome, offering of seat, presentation of Arghya etc., the king prostrated himself before him, and requested him to have his midday meal there. **37.** The sage accepted the invitation joyfully, and went to the Yamuna for his noonday rites. He immersed himself in the water of the Yamuna meditating on the Supreme Being. **38.** The king waited for the return of the sage till only half a Muhurta (a few minutes) was left for the twelfth day of the fortnight (Dwādasi) to elapse, before which he was to break his fast according to the rules of the vow he was observing. Caught in this dilemma in respect of a sacred duty, he conferred with some learned persons as to what he should do. **39.** He asked them: 'If I break my fast now, I shall be violating the rules of hospitality to a holy man by eating before feeding him; if I do not take food now, I shall be violating the rule requiring the breaking of the fast on the twelfth day itself. What shall I do in this situation for my good and avoiding sin?' Then he concluded: **40.** 'I shall break my fast by drinking mere water. Learned men say that drinking water can be considered both as taking food and not taking it too.' **41.** O leader of the Kurus! Thus after drinking some water and dwelling on the Lord mentally, King Ambarīsha stood there awaiting the arrival of Durvāsas.

42. Now Durvāsas returned after his noonday rites from the banks of the Yamuna, and was respectfully welcomed by the king. The sage was, however, able to know through his mental power that the king had already broken his fast by drinking water. **43.** To the king, who was standing before him with joined palms, Durvāsas, who was as angry as he was hungry, said with his body shivering and his face distorted by the arching of his brows in extreme anger: **44.** 'Atrocious! Look at the transgression of this man, who is cruel, unbalanced by pride of wealth, without an atom of real devotion to Vishnu, and behaving as if he were a law unto himself. **45.** You invited me to come as your guest. But without feeding

एवं ब्रुवाण उत्कृत्य जटां रोषविदीपितः । तया स निर्ममे तस्मै कृत्यां कालानलोपमाम् ॥46॥
तामापतन्तीं ज्वलतीमसिहस्तां पदा भुवम् । वेपयन्तीं समुद्वीक्ष्य न चचाल पदान्नृपः ॥47॥
प्राग्दिष्टं भृत्यरक्षायां पुरुषेण महात्मना । ददाह कृत्यां तां चक्रं क्रुद्धाहिमिव पावकः ॥48॥
तदभिद्रवदुद्वीक्ष्य स्वप्रयासं च निष्फलम् । दुर्वासा दुद्रुवे भीतो दिक्षु प्राणपरीप्सया ॥49॥

तमन्वधावद् भगवद्रथाङ्गं दावाग्निरुद्धूतशिखो यथाहिम् ।
तथानुषक्तं मुनिरीक्षमाणो गुहां विविक्षुः प्रससार मेरोः ॥50॥
दिशो नभः क्ष्मां विवरान् समुद्राँल्लोकान् सपालांस्त्रिदिवं गतः सः ।
यतो यतो धावति तत्र तत्र सुदर्शनं दुष्प्रसहं ददर्श ॥51॥
अलब्धनाथः स यदा कुतश्चित् संत्रस्तचित्तोऽरणमेषमाणः ।
देवं विरिञ्चं समगाद्विधातस्त्राह्यात्मयोनेऽजिततेजसो माम् ॥52॥

ब्रह्मोवाच

स्थानं मदीयं सहविश्वमेतत् क्रीडावसाने द्विपरार्धसंज्ञे ।
भ्रूभङ्गमात्रेण हि सन्दिधक्षोः कालात्मनो यस्य तिरोभविष्यति ॥53॥
अहं भवो दक्षभृगुप्रधानाः प्रजेशभूतेशसुरेशमुख्याः ।
सर्वे वयं यन्नियमं प्रपन्ना मूर्ध्न्यर्पितं लोकहितं वहामः ॥54॥

प्रत्याख्यातो विरिञ्चेन विष्णुचक्रोपतापितः । दुर्वासाः शरणं यातः शर्वं कैलासवासिनम् ॥55॥

me, you have taken food. I shall show you the consequences of it immediately.' **46.** So saying, Durvāsas, who was burning with anger, pulled out a lock of his matted hair and generated out of it a fiend (Kritya), as fierce as the fire at the time of cosmic dissolution. **47.** Even seeing that fiery spirit rushing at him, sword in hand and causing tremors on the earth, Ambarīsha did not budge a step from where he stood. **48.** Sudarsana, the discus of the Lord that had already been appointed as the protector of His devotee by Him, now burnt up the threatening Kritya, as the forest fire consumes a serpent.

The flight of Durvāsas (49-62)

49. Frightened by the failure of his effort and by the apparition of the Sudarsana rushing towards him, Durvāsas now began to run in all directions for his own safety. **50.** The spreading flames of the fire coming from Sudarsana pursued the sage as a forest fire does a snake, compelling the sage to take shelter in a cave of Mount Mahameru. **51.** But the Sudarsana of irresistible might pursued him wherever he rushed for safety—the quarters, the sky, the heaven, the ocean, the earth, and the fourteen Lokas. **52.** When he failed to get shelter anywhere, he went to Brahma the creator, and prayed for protection, saying: 'O Master, O creator! Save me from Sri Hari's power, the Sudarsana.'

Brahma said: **53-54.** He is the Time-spirit, by a mere vibration of whose brows this whole universe including my realm of Satyaloka passes into dissolution at the close of the Dviparārdhas when His divine play closes. How can we protect you, who have offended a devotee of that Being? He is the One whose commandments we all, including myself, Bhava, Daksha, Bhrigu, the Prajapatis, the Lord of Bhūtas, and Devas, accept with bent head and implement for the good of the world. How can we protect you, who have offended a devotee of that Being?

55. Thus abandoned by Brahma, Dur-

श्रीरुद्र उवाच

वयं न तात प्रभवाम भूम्नि यस्मिन् परेऽन्येऽप्यजजीवकोशाः ।
भवन्ति काले न भवन्ति हीदृशाः सहस्रशो यत्र वयं भ्रमामः ॥56॥
अहं सनत्कुमारश्च नारदो भगवानजः । कपिलोऽपान्तरतमो देवलो धर्म आसुरिः ॥57॥
मरीचिप्रमुखाश्चान्ये सिद्धेशाः पारदर्शनाः । विदाम न वयं सर्वे यन्मायां माययाऽऽवृताः ॥58॥
तस्य विश्वेश्वरस्येदं शस्त्रं दुर्विषहं हि नः । तमेव शरणं याहि हरिस्ते शं विधास्यति ॥59॥
ततो निराशो दुर्वासाः पदं भगवतो ययौ । वैकुण्ठाख्यं यदध्यास्ते श्रीनिवासः श्रिया सह ॥60॥
सन्दह्यमानोऽजितशस्त्रवह्निना तत्पादमूले पतितः सवेपथुः ।
आहाच्युतानन्त सदीप्सित प्रभो कृतागसं माव हि विश्वभावन ॥61॥
अजानता ते परमानुभावं कृतं मयाघं भवतः प्रियाणाम् ।
विधेहि तस्यापचितिं विधातर्मुच्येत यन्नाम्न्युदिते नारकोऽपि ॥62॥

श्रीभगवानुवाच

अहं भक्तपराधीनो ह्यस्वतन्त्र इव द्विज । साधुभिर्ग्रस्तहृदयो भक्तैर्भक्तजनप्रियः ॥63॥
नाहमात्मानमाशासे मद्भक्तैः साधुभिर्विना । श्रियं चात्यन्तिकीं ब्रह्मन् येषां गतिरहं परा ॥64॥
ये दारागारपुत्राप्तान् प्राणान् वित्तमिमं परम् । हित्वा मां शरणं याताः कथं तांस्त्यक्तुमुत्सहे ॥65॥
मयि निर्बद्धहृदयाः साधवः समदर्शनाः । वशीकुर्वन्ति मां भक्त्या सत्स्त्रियः सत्पतिं यथा 66॥
मत्सेवया प्रतीतं च सालोक्यादिचतुष्टयम् । नेच्छन्ति सेवया पूर्णाः कुतोऽन्यत् कालविद्रुतम् 67॥

vāsas, who was being constantly threatened by the Sudarsana, next went to Kailasa and took shelter at the feet of Sri Rudra. *Sri Rudra said:* **56.** 'He by whose will innumerable universes (Brahmandas) like the one in which we are involved, emerge and get dissolved continuously,—against Him, we are not capable of doing anything. **57-59.** I, Sanatkumāra, Nārada, Brahma, Kapila, Saubhari, Devala, Dharma, Āsuri, Marīchi and other men of knowledge and perfection are all subject to His Maya and are without any understanding of the nature of that Maya. His weapon Sudarsana is beyond my power to control. So you go for shelter to Sri Hari, who alone can help you in your present predicament.' **60.** Filled with despair, Durvāsas then proceeded to the Realm of Vaikuntha where the Lord Srīnivasa along with Srī has His abode. **61.** Scorched by the heat of Sudarsana, he fell down trembling at the feet of the Lord and said: 'O Achyuta! O Ananta! O lover of devotees! O Lord of all! O protector of the worlds! Deign to save me, even though I am a grave transgressor. **62.** Without knowing Thy powers, I did wrong to a devotee of Thine. Deign to order what atonement I should do for the same. For, Thou canst certainly save me, as even those undergoing suffering in hell are saved by the utterance of Thy name.'

The Lord's Advice (63-71)

The blessed Lord said: **63.** O sage! It is as if I am not free, subject as I am to My devotees. Being fond of my devotees, My heart is under their sway. **64.** I do not value myself or even Srī, who is ever associated with Me, as I do these holy men who have accepted Me as their supreme goal. **65.** How can I abandon these men who have sought refuge in Me, abandoning their wives, children, relatives, house, wealth, this world and the next? **66.** The holy men who have deep-rooted affection for Me and respect My presence in all

साधवो हृदयं मह्यं साधूनां हृदयं त्वहम् । मदन्यत् ते न जानन्ति नाहं तेभ्यो मनागपि ॥68॥
उपायं कथयिष्यामि तव विप्र शृणुष्व तत् । अयं ह्यात्माभिचारस्ते यतस्तं यातु वै भवान् ।
साधुषु प्रहितं तेजः प्रहर्तुः कुरुतेऽशिवम् ॥69॥
तपो विद्या च विप्राणां निःश्रेयसकरे उभे । ते एव दुर्विनीतस्य कल्पेते कर्तुरन्यथा ॥70॥
ब्रह्मंस्तद् गच्छ भद्रं ते नाभागतनयं नृपम् । क्षमापय महाभागं ततः शान्तिर्भविष्यति ॥71॥

इति श्रीमद्भागवते महापुराणे पारमहंस्यां संहितायां नवमस्कन्धेऽम्बरीषचरिते चतुर्थोऽध्यायः ॥ 4॥

alike, win Me over as a faithful wife does a dutiful husband. **67.** Having attained to life's fulfilment through My service, they do not care for the four forms of Mukti—Sālokya (attaining to His realm), Sāmīpya (being near Him), Sārūpya (having His form) and Sāyūjya (being one with him)—which are theirs by virtue of their service of Me. How little would they then care for the perishable attainments of the world? **68.** Holy men are verily My heart, and I verily am the heart of holy men. They do not know anything but Me and I, of anything but them.

69. O learned one! I shall tell you a way out. Listen to it. Go for help to Ambarīsha himself, against whom you used black magic. The black magic done against a saintly person would cause the ruin of the person who resorts to such practices. **70.** Austerity and learning are beneficial to spiritual aspirants. But in the hands of a haughty and perverse person, they can prove to be the contrary. **71.** So, O learned one, you return to Ambarīsha, the son of Nābhāga, and seek his pardon, You will then be at peace.

अथ पञ्चमोऽध्यायः

श्रीशुक उवाच

एवं भगवताऽऽदिष्टो दुर्वासाश्चक्रतापितः । अम्बरीषमुपावृत्य तत्पादौ दुःखितोऽग्रहीत् ॥ 1॥
तस्य सोद्यमनं वीक्ष्य पादस्पर्शविलज्जितः । अस्तावीत् तद्धरेरस्त्रं कृपया पीडितो भृशम् ॥ 2॥

अम्बरीष उवाच

त्वमग्निर्भगवान् सूर्यस्त्वं सोमो ज्योतिषां पतिः । त्वमापस्त्वं क्षितिर्व्योम वायुर्मात्रेन्द्रियाणि च ॥ 3॥
सुदर्शन नमस्तुभ्यं सहस्राराच्युतप्रिय । सर्वास्त्रघातिन् विप्राय स्वस्ति भूया इडस्पते ॥ 4॥

Skandha IX : Chapter 5

DURVĀSAS SUBMITS TO AMBARĪSHA

Ambarīsha's Prayer for Durvāsas (1-11)

Sri Suka said: **1.** Thus instructed by the Lord, Durvāsas, who was extremely distressed by the threat of the discus, now went to Ambarīsha and held his feet seeking protection. **2.** Ambarīsha was shocked at a Rishi holding his feet. Extremely bashful and pained at heart, he began to recite a hymn in praise of Sudarsana.

Ambarīsha said: **3.** Thou art the power manifesting in the fire, the worshipful sun and the moon who is the lord of all the stars. Thou art all these categories—water and earth, sky and air, the subtle elements (the Tanmatras) and the senses. **4.** O Thou Sudarsana! Thou the thousand-

त्वं धर्मस्त्वमृतं सत्यं त्वं यज्ञोऽखिलयज्ञभुक् । त्वं लोकपालः सर्वात्मा त्वं तेजः पौरुषं परम ॥ 5॥
नमः सुनाभाखिलधर्मसेतवे ह्यधर्मशीलासुरधूमकेतवे ।
त्रैलोक्यगोपाय विशुद्धवर्चसे मनोजवायाद्भुतकर्मणे गृणे ॥ 6॥
त्वत्तेजसा धर्ममयेन संहृतं तमः प्रकाशश्च धृतो महात्मनाम् ।
दुरत्ययस्ते महिमा गिरां पते त्वद्रूपमेतत् सदसत् परावरम् ॥ 7॥
यदा विसृष्टस्त्वमनञ्जनेन वै बलं प्रविष्टोऽजित दैत्यदानवम् ।
बाहूदरोर्वङ्घ्रिशिरोधराणि वृक्णन्नजस्रं प्रधने विराजसे ॥ 8॥
स त्वं जगत्त्राण खलप्रहाणये निरूपितः सर्वसहो गदाभृता ।
विप्रस्य चास्मत्कुलदैवहेतवे विधेहि भद्रं तदनुग्रहो हि नः ॥ 9॥
यद्यस्ति दत्तमिष्टं वा स्वधर्मो वा स्वनुष्ठितः । कुलं नो विप्रदैवं चेद् द्विजो भवतु विज्वरः ॥10॥
यदि नो भगवान् प्रीत एकः सर्वगुणाश्रयः । सर्वभूतात्मभावेन द्विजो भवतु विज्वरः ॥11॥

श्रीशुक उवाच

इति संस्तुवतो राज्ञो विष्णुचक्रं सुदर्शनम् । अशाम्यत् सर्वतो विप्रं प्रदहद् राजयाच्ञया ॥12॥
स मुक्तोऽस्त्राग्नितापेन दुर्वासाः स्वस्तिमांस्ततः । प्रशशंस तमुर्वीशं युञ्जानः परमाशिषः ॥13॥

spoked! Thou the favourite weapon of Achyuta! Thou the power that consumes the efficacy of all other weapons! Thou the master of the earth! I salute Thee! May Thou be propitious to the sage! **5.** Thou the puissance of the Supreme and the Soul of all, art verily Dharma, Rita, and Satya as also the sacrifice and the One adored through all sacrifices. **6.** O Thou of auspicious nave! Salutations to Thee the protector of Dharma and the terror of Asuras who follow the path of Adharma! Salutations to Thee that art pure radiance; to Thee mind-like in speed and astounding in Thy works! **7.** By Thy spiritual radiance the darkness of ignorance is dispelled and the minds of great men are illumined. O Lord of speech! None can excel Thee in greatness! For, the whole universe in its subtle and gross conditions is Thy manifestation. **8.** O unconquerable one! When Thou art released by the Lord, who is free from all stain, Thou shinest in the field of battle cutting off the limbs and heads of Asuras. **9.** O world's protector! Thou art given to pardoning the offences of those who have sought refuge in Thee. Thou hast been deputed by the Most High to punish the wicked only. It will be a blessing to me if Thou sparest this holy man; for, it will bring good fortune to our family. It would be a great condescension on Thy part. **10.** If I have done any charities, if I have done the meritorious rites prescribed in the Veda and the Sacred Law, if I have done my ordained duties properly, if my family has honoured holy men as divine, then may this holy man be free from his predicament. **11.** If the worshipful Lord, who is one without a second and the repository of all auspicious qualities, is pleased with our service of Him in His capacity as the soul of all beings, may this holy man be free from fear!

Durvāsas praises Ambarīsha (12-27)

Sri Suka said: **12.** The hymn addressed by Ambarīsha calmed Sudarsana, the discus of Mahavishnu, that was till then harassing Durvāsas. **13.** Freed from the fierce and burning aura of Sudarsana, Durvāsas was again at peace. Pronouncing blessings on Ambarīsha, he now

दुर्वासा उवाच

अहो अनन्तदासानां महत्त्वं दृष्टमद्य मे । कृतागसोऽपि यद् राजन् मङ्गलानि समीहसे ॥14॥
दुष्करः को नु साधूनां दुस्त्यजो वा महात्मनाम् । यैः संगृहीतो भगवान् सात्वतामृषभो हरिः ॥15॥
यन्नामश्रुतिमात्रेण पुमान् भवति निर्मलः । तस्य तीर्थपदः किं वा दासानामवशिष्यते ॥16॥
राजन्ननुगृहीतोऽहं त्वयातिकरुणात्मना । मदघं पृष्ठतः कृत्वा प्राणा यन्मेऽभिरक्षिताः ॥17॥
राजा तमकृताहारः प्रत्यागमनकाङ्क्षया । चरणावुपसंगृह्य प्रसाद्य समभोजयत् ॥18॥
सोऽशित्वाऽऽदृतमानीतमातिथ्यं सार्वकामिकम् । तृप्तात्मा नृपतिं प्राह भुज्यतामिति सादरम् ॥19॥
प्रीतोऽस्म्यनुगृहीतोऽस्मि तव भागवतस्य वै । दर्शनस्पर्शनालापैरातिथ्येनात्ममेधसा ॥20॥
कर्मावदातमेतत् ते गायन्ति स्वःस्त्रियो मुहुः । कीर्तिं परमपुण्यां च कीर्तयिष्यति भूरियम् ॥21॥

श्रीशुक उवाच

एवं संकीर्त्य राजानं दुर्वासाः परितोषितः । ययौ विहायसाऽऽमन्त्र्य ब्रह्मलोकमहैतुकम् ॥22॥
संवत्सरोऽत्यगात् तावद् यावता नागतो गतः । मुनिस्तद्दर्शनाकाङ्क्षो राजाब्भक्षो बभूव ह ॥23॥
गते च दुर्वाससि सोऽम्बरीषो द्विजोपयोगातिपवित्रमाहरत् ।
ऋषेर्विमोक्षं व्यसनं च बुद्ध्वा मेने स्ववीर्यं च परानुभावम् ॥24॥

spoke in prasise of him. *Durvāsas said:* **14.** 'Today I have experienced the inconceivable greatness of the servants of the Infinite One. For, O King, you, His devotee, are doing good in return to one like me who has done you evil. **15.** What is there impossible of achievement for these pious men, who have by their devotion won over as their own the worshipful Sri Hari, the master and protector of all devotees? And for the good and the magnanimous, what is there impossible to renounce? **16.** What unfulfilled longing there can be for the devotees of Him, whose very name purifies one by its hearing and whose feet can make one holy by their touch? **17.** O King! I have been blessed by you of abounding mercy. For you have pardoned my offence and saved my life.'

Sri Suka said: **18.** King Ambarīsha who had not yet taken his food awaiting the return of Durvāsas, now prostrated himself before the sage, cheered him up, and fed him. **19.** With great satisfaction, the sage partook of that delicious meal, providing varieties of dishes with all the six flavours. He then requested the king to take his meal. **20.** Durvāsas then said: 'I feel pleased, I feel blessed by what I have received from a great devotee like you—from your sight, speech, touch and hospitality in the spirit of divine service. **21.** The celestial damsels shall constantly extol this action of yours in songs. And on the earth too your holy fame shall be glorified by all.'

Sri Suka said: **22.** Thus praising the king, Durvāsas left the place in a joyous mood and went to Brahmaloka, which none can obtain by Karma. **23.** But now one year had passed since Durvāsas had taken to his heels for fear of the discus Sudarsana. All the time Ambarīsha had waited for his arrival to feed himself, taking nothing more than the water with which he had broken his fast. **24.** When Durvāsas had gone, Ambarīsha took his food considering it specially sacred because it was what was left after feeding a holy man. He saw the hand of the Divine in all that had happened—in the sufferings of the sage and in the relief he got afterwards as well as in the courageous way

एवंविधानेकगुणः स राजा परात्मनि ब्रह्मणि वासुदेवे ।
क्रियाकलापैः समुवाह भक्तिं ययाऽऽविरिञ्च्यान् निरयांश्चकार ॥25॥
अथाम्बरीषस्तनयेषु राज्यं समानशीलेषु विसृज्य धीरः ।
वनं विवेशात्मनि वासुदेवे मनो दधद् ध्वस्तगुणप्रवाहः ॥26॥
इत्येतत् पुण्यमाख्यानमम्बरीषस्य भूपतेः । संकीर्तयन्ननुध्यायन् भक्तो भगवतो भवेत् ॥27॥

इति श्रीमद्भागवते महापुराणे पारमहंस्यां संहितायां नवमस्कन्धेऽम्बरीषचरितं नाम पञ्चमोऽध्यायः ॥ 5॥

in which he himself could stand the trials. **25.** In this way King Ambarīsha, who was endowed with many a great virtue, attained to the highest form of Bhakti consisting in the consecration and offering of all the fruits of work and sense of agency to Vāsudeva, the soul of all and the universal Being (Brahman). Devotion filled him with such intense renunciation that made him feel all heavens with their enjoyments up to Brahmaloka as mere hells. **26.** Afterwards high-souled Ambarīsha entrusted the kingdom to his sons who were equal to him in virtue, and took to the life of a forest-dwelling ascetic. He gave his mind entirely to Vāsudeva, the soul of all, and transcended the play of the forces of Prakriti (Nature). **27.** One who devoutly recites and reflects on this great narrative concerning King Ambarīsha will become a devotee of the Lord.

अथ षष्ठोऽध्यायः

श्रीशुक उवाच

विरूपः केतुमाञ्छम्भुरम्बरीषसुतास्त्रयः । विरूपात् पृषदश्वोऽभूत् तत्पुत्रस्तु रथीतरः ॥ 1॥
रथीतरस्याप्रजस्य भार्यायां तन्तवेऽर्थितः । अङ्गिरा जनयामास ब्रह्मवर्चस्विनः सुतान् ॥ 2॥
एते क्षेत्रे प्रसूता वै पुनस्त्वाङ्गिरसाः स्मृताः । रथीतराणां प्रवराः क्षत्रोपेता द्विजातयः ॥ 3॥
क्षुवतस्तु मनोर्जज्ञे इक्ष्वाकुर्घ्राणतः सुतः । तस्य पुत्रशतज्येष्ठा विकुक्षिनिमिदण्डकाः ॥ 4॥

Skandha IX : Chapter 6
FROM AMBARISHA TO MĀNDHĀTA

Ambarīsha's Sons (1-3)

Sri Suka said: **1.** Ambarīsha had three sons—Virūpa, Ketumān and Sambhu. Virūpa's son was Prishadasva, and his son Rathītara. **2.** Rathītara being incapable of having an offspring, his wife approached for progeny the sage Angiras who begot by her sons with Brahmic splendour. **3.** As they were born in the wife of Rathītara, and as they were also the sons of Angiras, they were considered as belonging to the lines of both Rathītara and Angiras and they were endowed with both Brahmanical and royal qualities.

Ikshvāku and his Sons (4-11)

4. Ikshvāku was born from the nose of the Manu Vaivaswata when he sneezed. Ikshvāku had a hundred sons, of whom the important were the three—Vikukshi,

तेषां पुरस्तादभवन्नार्यावर्ते नृपा नृप ।
पञ्चविंशतिः पश्चाच्च त्रयो मध्ये परेऽन्यतः ॥ 5॥
स एकदाष्टकाश्राद्धे इक्ष्वाकुः सुतमादिशत् ।
मांसमानीयतां मेध्यं विकुक्षे गच्छ माचिरम् ॥ 6॥
तथेति स वनं गत्वा मृगान् हत्वा क्रियार्हणान् ।
श्रान्तो बुभुक्षितो वीरः शशं चाददपस्मृतिः ॥ 7॥
शेषं निवेदयामास पित्रे तेन च तद्गुरुः ।
चोदितः प्रोक्षणायाह दुष्टमेतदकर्मकम् ॥ 8॥
ज्ञात्वा पुत्रस्य तत् कर्म गुरुणाभिहितं नृपः ।
देशान्निःसारयामास सुतं त्यक्तविधिं रुषा ॥ 9॥
स तु विप्रेण संवादं जापकेन समाचरन् ।
त्यक्त्वा कलेवरं योगी स तेनावाप यत्परम् ॥10॥
पितर्युपरतेऽभ्येत्य विकुक्षिः पृथिवीमिमाम् ।
शासदीजे हरिं यज्ञैः शशाद इति विश्रुतः ॥11॥
पुरञ्जयस्तस्य सुत इन्द्रवाह इतीरितः ।
ककुत्स्थ इति चाप्युक्तः शृणु नामानि कर्मभिः ॥12॥
कृतान्त आसीत् समरो देवानां सह दानवैः ।
पार्ष्णिग्राहो वृतो वीरो देवैर्दैत्यपराजितैः ॥13॥
वचनाद् देवदेवस्य विष्णोर्विश्वात्मनः प्रभोः ।
वाहनत्वे वृतस्तस्य बभूवेन्द्रो महावृषः ॥14॥
स संनद्धो धनुर्दिव्यमादाय विशिखाञ्छितान् ।
स्तूयमानः समारुह्य युयुत्सुः ककुदि स्थितः ॥15॥
तेजसाऽऽप्यायितो विष्णोः पुरुषस्य परात्मनः ।
प्रतीच्यां दिशि दैत्यानां न्यरुणत् त्रिदशैः पुरम् ॥16॥

Nimi, and Dandaka. **5.** O King! Of these hundred, twentyfive became kings in the eastern regions of Aryavarta; another twenty five, in the western region; three in the middle region; and the remaining in the northern and the southern regions.

6. Once Ikshvāku was performing Ashtakāsrāddha. He called his son and said: 'O Vikukshi! Go to the forest and get the flesh of animals that are considered fit for offering at sacrifices. Do not delay.' **7.** Agreeing to this, that bold warrior went to the forest and slaughtered many animals that were fit for use in sacrifices. But very much tired as he was after all that exertion, he by oversight had his meal prepared with a hare from among the slaughtered animals. **8.** He brought the rest of the hunted animals and gave them to his father. His preceptor Vasishtha, on being asked to consecrate the flesh of the animals for sacrifice, declared it to be defiled by being already used and therefore unfit for use in sacrificial rites. **9.** Informed by the preceptor, King Ikshvāku came to understand the nature of his sons's transgression of Dharma, and in great anger, expelled him from the country. **10.** Ikshvāku then held discussions on matters spiritual with Vasishtha and took to the practice of Yoga. Eventually he gave up his body in Yoga and attained the Supreme State. **11.** On his father's death Vikukshi returned to the country to rule over the whole earth under the name Sasāda and to adore the Supreme Being with many sacrifices.

Indravāha (12-19)

12. Sasāda had a famous son Indravāha, who was also known as Kakutstha and Puranjaya. Hear from me how he earned these names by his deeds. **13.** There was a very destructive war between the Asuras and the Devas. Being defeated, the Devas sought heroic Indravāha as their ally. **14.** As directed by the all-powerful Mahavishnu, the Lord of lords and the soul of all beings, Indra converted himself into a huge bull and became the mount of King Indravāha. **15.** Equipped with armour, an excellent bow and arrows, and extolled by all the celestials, he sat on the hump (Kakut) of that Indra bull, ready for battle.

16. With his powers augmented by the energy of Mahavishnu, the Supreme Person and the Supreme Spirit, Indravāha along with the Devas attacked the

तैस्तस्य चाभूत् प्रधनं तुमुलं लोमहर्षणम् । यमाय भल्लैरनयद् दैत्यान् येऽभिययुर्मृधे ॥17॥
तस्येषुपाताभिमुखं युगान्ताग्निमिवोल्बणम् । विसृज्य दुद्रुवुर्दैत्या हन्यमानाः स्वमालयम् ॥18॥
जित्वा पुरं धनं सर्वं सश्रीकं वज्रपाणये । प्रत्ययच्छत् स राजर्षिरिति नामभिराहृतः ॥19॥
पुरञ्जयस्य पुत्रोऽभूदनेनास्तत्सुतः पृथुः । विश्वरन्धिस्ततश्चन्द्रो युवनाश्वश्च तत्सुतः ॥20॥
शाबस्तस्तत्सुतो येन शाबस्ती निर्ममे पुरी । बृहदश्वस्तु शाबस्तिस्ततः कुवलयाश्वकः ॥21॥
यः प्रियार्थमुतङ्कस्य धुन्धुनामासुरं बली । सुतानामेकविंशत्या सहस्रैरहनद् वृतः ॥22॥
धुन्धुमार इति ख्यातस्तत्सुतास्ते च जज्वलुः । धुन्धोर्मुखाग्निना सर्वे त्रय एवावशेषिताः ॥23॥
दृढाश्वः कपिलाश्वश्च भद्राश्व इति भारत । दृढाश्वपुत्रो हर्यश्वो निकुम्भस्तत्सुतः स्मृतः ॥24॥
बर्हणाश्वो निकुम्भस्य कृशाश्वोऽथास्य सेनजित् । युवनाश्वोऽभवत् तस्य सोऽनपत्यो वनं गतः ॥25॥
भार्याशतेन निर्विण्ण ऋषयोऽस्य कृपालवः । इष्टिं स्म वर्तयाञ्चक्रुरैन्द्रीं ते सुसमाहिताः ॥26॥
राजा तद् यज्ञसदनं प्रविष्टो निशि तर्षितः । दृष्ट्वा शयानान् विप्रांस्तान् पपौ मन्त्रजलं स्वयम् 27
उत्थितास्ते निशाम्याथ व्युदकं कलशं प्रभो । पप्रच्छुः कस्य कर्मेदं पीतं पुंसवनं जलम् ॥28॥

city of the Asuras in the west. **17.** A fierce and thrilling battle now followed between him and the Asuras. Whichever Asura faced him, he transported him to the realm of Yama with his arrows. **18.** Impossible to stand before his arrows that were fierce like the fire at the time of deluge, the remaining Asuras fled away from the battle field to their abode in the Pātāla. **19.** Because this king conquered the realm of the Asuras and transferred it with all its wealth and splendour to Indra, he got the name Puranjaya added to his other names. (For the reason he used Indra as his mount he was called Indravāha; for sitting on the Kakut or hump of the bull, he came to be known as Kakutstha also).

From Puranjaya to Yuvanāsva (20-29)

20. Puranjaya (alias Indravāha) had a son named Anenas. His son was Prithu; his son, Viswarandhi; his son, Chandra; and his son, Yuvanāsva. **21.** His son was Sābasta, who built the city named Sābasti. Sābasta's son was Brihadaswa, and his son, Kuvalayāswaka. **22.** This last very powerful king, in order to please sage Utanka, destroyed the Asura named Dhundhu, assisted by an army of his own sons numbering twenty one thousand. **23.** He came to be famous as Dhundhumāra. But most of his sons perished in the fire emerging from the mouth of the Asura Dhundhu. Only three survived. **24.** The names of those who survived were: Dhridhāsva, Kapilāsva, and Bhadrāsva. Dhridhāsva's son was named Haryasva; and his son, Nikumbha. **25.** Nikumbaha's son was Barhanāsva; his son, Krisāsva; his son, Senajit; and his son, Yuvanāsva. This last king had no issue when he left for the forest to practise austerities. **26.** For lack of progeny he had become indifferent to everything and took to the forest life with his hundred wives. It is said that some merciful sages therefore made him perform a special sacrifice to Indra with great concentration. **27.** At night that king entered the sacrificial hall in a very thirsty condition. He found all the sacrificial priests sleeping. So he himself took some water, which happened to have been consecrated by Mantras. **28.** O King! On awakening, those priests, finding the water-pot empty, exclaimed: 'Ah! Who has done this! Someone has drunk the consecrated water

राज्ञा पीतं विदित्वाथ ईश्वरप्रहितेन ते। ईश्वराय नमश्चक्रुरहो दैवबलं बलम् ॥29॥
ततः काल उपावृत्ते कुक्षिं निर्भिद्य दक्षिणम्। युवनाश्वस्य तनयश्चक्रवर्ती जजान ह ॥30॥
कं धास्यति कुमारोऽयं स्तन्यं रोरूयते भृशम्। मां धाता वत्स मा रोदीरितीन्द्रो देशिनीमदात् ।31॥
न ममार पिता तस्य विप्रदेवप्रसादतः। युवनाश्वोऽथ तत्रैव तपसा सिद्धिमन्वगात् ॥32॥
त्रसद्दस्युरितीन्द्रोऽङ्ग विदधे नाम तस्य वै। यस्मात् त्रसन्ति ह्युद्विग्ना दस्यवो रावणादयः ॥33॥
यौवनाश्वोऽथ मान्धाता चक्रवर्त्यवनीं प्रभुः। सप्तद्वीपवतीमेकः शशासाच्युततेजसा ॥34॥
ईजे च यज्ञं क्रतुभिरात्मविद् भूरिदक्षिणैः। सर्वदेवमयं देवं सर्वात्मकमतीन्द्रियम् ॥35॥
द्रव्यं मन्त्रो विधिर्यज्ञो यजमानस्तथर्त्विजः। धर्मो देशश्च कालश्च सर्वमेतद् यदात्मकम् ॥36॥
यावत् सूर्य उदेति स्म यावच्च प्रतितिष्ठति। सर्वं तद्यौवनाश्वस्य मान्धातुः क्षेत्रमुच्यते ॥37॥
शशबिन्दोर्दुहितरि बिन्दुमत्यामधान्नृपः। पुरुकुत्समम्बरीषं मुचुकुन्दं च योगिनम्।
तेषां स्वसारः पञ्चाशत् सौभरिं वव्रिरे पतिम् ॥38॥
यमुनान्तर्जले मग्नस्तप्यमानः परन्तपः। निर्वृतिं मीनराजस्य वीक्ष्य मैथुनधर्मिणः ॥39॥
जातस्पृहो नृपं विप्रः कन्यामेकामयाचत। सोऽप्याह गृह्यतां ब्रह्मन् कामं कन्या स्वयंवरे ॥40॥

that has the power of producing progeny!' **29.** Learning that it was done by the king, prompted as it were by the Lord, the priests bowed down to Him and declared: 'It is only the Divine will that prevails; man's efforts count for little.'

Māndhātā (30-38)

30. The king Yuvanāsva became pregnant, and when the time for delivery came, the right side of his abdomen burst, bringing forth a child, who grew to be an emperor. **31.** 'This child is crying aloud to be suckled. How shall we feed him?' so exclaimed the priests. Thereupon Indra said: 'Dear baby! Do not cry. Drink of me (*mām dhātā*)', and gave it his thumb to suck, which yielded Amrita, the immortal drink. The child therefore came to be known as Māndhātā. **32.** The father of the infant, king Yuvanāsva, in spite of his abdomen being rent, providentially survived. He continued to observe austere practices in that forest until his end. **33-34.** Dear Parikshit! As even powerful enemies like Rāvana trembled with fear before him, Indra gave Māndhātā the title Trasaddasyu, 'the terror of evil ones'. This son of Yuvanāsva, by virtue of the power bestowed on Him by Achyuta, became the famous Emperor Māndhātā holding sway over all the seven continents of the earth. **35.** Though he had the highest Self-knowledge, he none the less adored the Supreme Being, the embodiment of all deities, the sould of all and the one incomprehensible to the senses, with many sacrifices characterised by an abundance of gifts. **36.** By these Yajnas he only adored Him who has Himself become all the parts of the sacrifice—the substances used, the Mantras chanted, the procedures followed, the sacrifice itself, the performer of the sacrifice, the officiating priests, Dharma, and time and place. **37.** All the land included within the horizons between which the sun rises and sets, was included in the empire of Māndhātā, the son of Yuvanāsva. **38.** Māndhātā had by Indumati, the daughter of Sasabindu, three sons—Purukutsa, Ambarīsha, and the great Yogi Muchukunda. They had fifty sisters, all of whom married the Rishi Saubhari.

The Story of Saubhari (39-55)

39-40. The Rishi Saubhari, who was

स विचिन्त्याप्रियं स्त्रीणां जरठोऽयमसम्मतः । वलीपलित एजत्क इत्यहं प्रत्युदाहृतः ॥41॥
साधयिष्ये तथाऽऽत्मानं सुरस्त्रीणामपीप्सितम् । किं पुनर्मनुजेन्द्राणामिति व्यवसितः प्रभुः ॥42॥
मुनिः प्रवेशितः क्षत्त्रा कन्यान्तःपुरमृद्धिमत् । वृतश्च राजकन्याभिरेकः पञ्चाशता वरः ॥43॥
तासां कलिरभूद् भूयांस्तदर्थेऽपोह्य सौहृदम् । ममानुरूपो नायं व इति तद्गतचेतसाम् ॥44॥

स बह्वृचस्ताभिरपारणीयतपःश्रियानर्घ्यपरिच्छदेषु ।
गृहेषु नानोपवनामलाम्भःसरस्सु सौगन्धिककाननेषु ॥45॥
महार्हशय्यासनवस्त्रभूषणस्नानानुलेपाभ्यवहारमाल्यकैः ।
स्वलङ्कृतस्त्रीपुरुषेषु नित्यदा रेमेऽनुगायद्द्विजभृङ्गवन्दिषु ॥46॥

यद्गार्हस्थ्यं तु संवीक्ष्य सप्तद्वीपवतीपतिः । विस्मितः स्तम्भमजहात् सार्वभौमश्रियान्वितम् 47।
एवं गृहेष्वभिरतो विषयान् विविधैः सुखैः । सेवमानो न चातुष्यदाज्यस्तोकैरिवानलः ॥48॥
स कदाचिदुपासीन आत्मापह्नवमात्मनः । ददर्श बह्वृचाचार्यो मीनसङ्गसमुत्थितम् ॥49॥

observing severe austerities submerged under the waters of Kālindi, saw once the great pleasure that a king of fish derived from sexual intercourse. This generated a longing for such pleasure in himself, and he begged King Māndhātā to give one of his daughters to him. The king stipulated that he would arrange a function of bridal choice, at which a daughter of his would be free to choose him. **41-42.** The Rishi thereupon thought: 'Under the guise of a bridal choice, the king is out to deceive me. Thinking that an old man like me, dilapidated with infirmities and trembling in movements, will not be to the liking of women, the king has planned to deceive me by this proposal of a bridal choice. Therefore with the great powers derived from austerity, I shall make my body attractive even for celestial women, not to speak of the princesses in view.' **43.** When the Rishi was led to the splendid quarters of women by the guards for the bridal choice, each of the king's fifty daughters chose him as her husband. **44.** These girls, whose minds were passionately drawn towards him, started quarrelling among themselves over him, each claiming that he was more suited to her than to the others.

45-46. The sage, who was a master of the Rig Veda, by virtue of his unlimited power of austerity, created facilities for enjoyments and sported with these women amidst a variety of objects of luxury like high-class beddings, seats, dress, decorations, unguents, wreaths and food, in palatial buildings provided also with costly outfits, decors and liveried attendants of both sexes, as well as in wooded parks enlivened by sets of continuously singing minstrels in the shape of warbling birds and intoxicated and buzzing honey-bees, and in lakes with a plentiful supply of water in them. **47.** Seeing the splendour of the household life of Saubhari surpassing that of an emperor, king Māndhātā, who was in fact the emperor of the earth with its seven continents, gave up pride in his own riches and glory.

48. But Saubhari soon found that by enjoying every kind of pleasure of household life with great avidity, he could obtain no peace and satisfaction. On the other hand, he found his desire-nature only augmented by it, just like fire on which 'ghee is sprinkled'. **49.** One day while Saubhari, the master of the Vedas, was sitting in his house in a reflective mood, the thought came to him how degeneration had overtaken him by wit-

अहो इमं पश्यत मे विनाशं तपस्विनः सच्चरितव्रतस्य ।
अन्तर्जले वारिचरप्रसङ्गात् प्रच्यावितं ब्रह्म चिरं धृतं यत् ॥50॥
सङ्गं त्यजेत मिथुनव्रतिनां मुमुक्षुः सर्वात्मना न विसृजेद् बहिरिन्द्रियाणि ।
एकश्चरन् रहसि चित्तमनन्त ईशे युञ्जीत तद्व्रतिषु साधुषु चेत् प्रसङ्गः ॥51॥
एकस्तपस्व्यहमथाम्भसि मत्स्यसङ्गात् पञ्चाशदासमुत पञ्चसहस्रसर्गः ।
नान्तं व्रजाम्युभयकृत्यमनोरथानां मायागुणैर्हृतमतिर्विषयेऽर्थभावः ॥52॥
एवं वसन् गृहे कालं विरक्तो न्यासमास्थितः । वनं जगामानुययुस्तत्पत्न्यः पतिदेवताः ॥53॥
तत्र तप्त्वा तपस्तीक्ष्णमात्मकर्शनमात्मवान् । सहैवाग्निभिरात्मानं युयोज परमात्मनि ॥54॥
ताः स्वपत्युर्महाराज निरीक्ष्याध्यात्मिकीं गतिम् । अन्वीयुस्तत्प्रभावेण अग्निं शान्तमिवार्चिषः ॥55॥

इति श्रीमद्भागवते महापुराणे पारमहंस्यां संहितायां नवमस्कन्धे सौभर्याख्याने षष्ठोऽध्यायः ॥ 6॥

nessing with an uncontrolled mind the mating of fish. **50.** He thought: 'Alas! Look at this, my degradation, in spite of my great austerity, holy living and observance of vows! The attraction I felt while living submerged in water, for the sexual pleasures of the fish, has ended in complete dissipation of the Brahmic glory I acquired by long effort. **51.** Therefore a seeker after liberation should completely eschew the company of those who revel in sexual indulgences. They should never allow the senses to wander uncontrolled among sense objects. Let them move about alone, uniting their mind with the Supreme Lord, the Infinite Being. If they seek company, let it be only of those virtuous persons who follow the spiritual path. **52.** First I was an ascetic living alone. Afterwards by my association with fish, I came to be united with fifty wives and thus became fifty. Still later, through children and grandchildren, I have become five thousand. Still attracted by the powers of Maya, I am sticking on to the objects of senses as the be-all and the end-all of life, and am involved deeply in works that will promote my interest in this life and the next.'

53. *Sri Suka said:* After continuing for long in the householder's life, he became full of the spirit of renunciation, and at last went away into the woods to pursue the life of a Vanaprastha. His wives, to whom the husband was the manifest Deity, followed him to the forest. **54.** There he observed severe austere practices that reduced him to bones. Finally as the symbol of his attaining enlightenment, he offered the sacred fires he maintained as a householder into the Atman, which he dissolved in the Supreme Atman in complete non-difference. **55.** O King! His wives, who witnessed the supreme attainment of their husband, felt strengthened and inspired by his example and followed him, as the shooting tongues of flames sink in a subsiding fire.

अथ सप्तमोऽध्यायः

श्रीशुक उवाच

मान्धातुः पुत्रप्रवरो योऽम्बरीषः प्रकीर्तितः । पितामहेन प्रवृतो यौवनाश्वश्च तत्सुतः ।
हारीतस्तस्य पुत्रोऽभून्मान्धातृप्रवरा इमे ॥ 1॥
नर्मदा भ्रातृभिर्दत्ता पुरुकुत्साय योरगैः । तया रसातलं नीतो भुजगेन्द्रप्रयुक्तया ॥ 2॥
गन्धर्वानवधीत्तत्र वध्यान् वै विष्णुशक्तिधृक् । नागाल्लब्धवरः सर्पादभयं स्मरतामिदम् ॥ 3॥
त्रसद्दस्युः पौरुकुत्सो योऽनरण्यस्य देहकृत् । हर्यश्वस्तत्सुतस्तस्मादरुणोऽथ त्रिबन्धनः ॥ 4॥
तस्य सत्यव्रतः पुत्रस्त्रिशङ्कुरिति विश्रुतः । प्राप्तश्चाण्डालतां शापाद् गुरोः कौशिकतेजसा 5॥
सशरीरो गतः स्वर्गमद्यापि दिवि दृश्यते । पातितोऽवाक्शिरा देवैस्तेनैव स्तम्भितो बलात् 6॥
त्रैशङ्कवो हरिश्चन्द्रो विश्वामित्रवसिष्ठयोः । यन्निमित्तमभूद् युद्धं पक्षिणोर्बहुवार्षिकम् ॥ 7॥
सोऽनपत्यो विषण्णात्मा नारदस्योपदेशतः । वरुणं शरणं यातः पुत्रो मे जायतां प्रभो ॥ 8॥
यदि वीरो महाराज तेनैव त्वां यजे इति । तथेति वरुणेनास्य पुत्रो जातस्तु रोहितः ॥ 9॥
जातः सुतो ह्यनेनाङ्ग मां यजस्वेति सोऽब्रवीत् । यदा पशुर्निर्दशः स्यादथ मेध्यो भवेदिति ॥10॥

Skandha IX : Chapter 7
THE LINE OF MĀNDHĀTĀ

Purukutsa to Trisanku (1-6)

Sri Suka said: **1.** Ambarīsha, mentioned earlier as the son of Māndhātā, was adopted by his grandfather Yuvanāsva as his son. To Ambarīsha was born a son who too was named Yuvanāsva, and to him Hārīta. From these two arose branches in the line of Māndhātā.

2. Purukutsa was offered as wife Narmada a serpent princess, by her brother serpents. At the prompting of the serpents, Narmada persuaded Purukutsa to go to Rasātala, the abode of the serpents. **3.** Possessed as he was of a part of Vishnu's prowess, Purukutsa destroyed there some Gandharvas who were a menance to that place and therefore deserved elimination. The serpents in gratitude gave him the boon that those who remember this episode will be free from fear of serpent-bite. **4.** Purukutsa's son was Trasaddasyu; his son, Anaranya; his son, Haryasva; his son, Aruna; and his son, Tribandhana. **5-6.** The last had a son named Satyavrata who became famous under another name Trisanku. By the curse of his preceptor Vasishtha, he became an out-caste. But by the prowess of Viswamitra, he was bodily elevated to heaven. But the Devas hurled him down headlong, and Viswamitra stopped him midway. Even today he is seen in the sky as a star.

Harischandra and Rohita (7-27)

7. Trisanku's son was Harischandra. Centring on him, a quarrel arose between Viswamitra and Vasishtha, who cursed each other to become birds. A long drawn fight ensued between them as birds. **8.** Having no sons, Harischandra in deep sorrow took refuge in Varuna for relief, under the instruction of Narada. **9.** He prayed to Varuna: 'O Lord! If I have a heroic son born, I shall offer him in sacrifice to you.' Varuna blessed him to have a son, and he had one accordingly, named Rohita. **10.** Varuna said to him:

निर्दशे च स आगत्य यजस्वेत्याह सोऽब्रवीत् ।
जाता दन्ता यजस्वेति स प्रत्याहाथ सोऽब्रवीत् ।
पशोर्निपतिता दन्ता यजस्वेत्याह सोऽब्रवीत् ।
पुनर्जाता यजस्वेति स प्रत्याहाथ सोऽब्रवीत् ।
इति पुत्रानुरागेण स्नेहयन्त्रितचेतसा ।
रोहितस्तदभिज्ञाय पितुः कर्म चिकीर्षितम् ।
पितरं वरुणग्रस्तं श्रुत्वा जातमहोदरम् ।
भूमेः पर्यटनं पुण्यं तीर्थक्षेत्रनिषेवणैः ।
एवं द्वितीये तृतीये चतुर्थे पञ्चमे तथा ।
षष्ठं संवत्सरं तत्र चरित्वा रोहितः पुरीम् ।
शुनःशेपं पशुं पित्रे प्रदाय समवन्दत ।
मुक्तोदरोऽयजद् देवान् वरुणादीन् महत्कथः ।
जमदग्निरभूत् ब्रह्मा वसिष्ठोऽयास्यसामगः ।

दन्ताः पशोर्यज्जायेरन्नथ मेध्यो भवेदिति ॥11॥
यदा पतन्त्यस्य दन्ता अथ मेध्यो भवेदिति ॥12॥
यदा पशोः पुनर्दन्ता जायन्तेऽथ पशुः शुचिः ॥13॥
सांनाह्निको यदा राजन् राजन्योऽथ पशुः शुचिः 14॥
कालं वञ्चयता तं तमुक्तो देवस्तमैक्षत ॥15॥
प्राणप्रेप्सुर्धनुष्पाणिररण्यं प्रत्यपद्यत ॥16॥
रोहितो ग्राममेयाय तमिन्द्रः प्रत्यषेधत ॥17॥
रोहितायादिशच्छक्रः सोऽप्यरण्येऽवसत् समाम् 18
अभ्येत्याभ्येत्य स्थविरो विप्रो भूत्वाऽऽह वृत्रहा 19॥
उपव्रजन्नजीगर्तादक्रीणान्मध्यमं सुतम् ॥20॥
ततः पुरुषमेधेन हरिश्चन्द्रो महायशाः ॥21॥
विश्वामित्रोऽभवत् तस्मिन् होता चाध्वर्युरात्मवान् ।
तस्मै तुष्टो ददाविन्द्रः शातकौम्भमयं रथम् ॥23॥

'Now you have got a son. Offer him in sacrifice to me!' To this the king replied: 'Let ten days pass. Then only he will be fit for sacrifice.' **11.** Ten days later Varuna came again and demanded his offering. The king then said: 'Let the sacrificial animal teethe, and then only he will be fit for sacrifice.' **12.** 'The child has now developed teeth. Why not sacrifice it?' said Varuna afterwards. 'Only when these teeth fall will he be fit for sacrifice,' said the king. **13.** 'The sacrificial animal has shed its teeth now. Why not sacrifice it now?' asked Varuna. 'No' it is only after all the teeth have reappeared, he will be fit for sacrifice,' replied the king. **14.** 'Now the teeth have grown again. Sacrifice him now', said Varuna. The king replied: 'Being a Kshatriya, this animal is fit for sacrifice only when he is fully trained for battle.'

15. Thus prompted by love of his son, the king deceptively put off the time for sacrifice, and Varuna kept on waiting all the time. **16.** Now Rohita, coming to know of his father's desire to perform the sacrifice, went away into the forest with bow in hand in order to save his life. **17.** The angry Varuna now possessed the king and produced in him the disease called dropsy. Hearing about this, Rohita was about to return to the country, but was prevented by Indra. **18.** Indra advised him that his father would recover, if he, Rohita, went as a wandering pilgrim to holy spots and streams in the land. Accordingly Rohita spent one more year in the forest. **19.** Year after year Indra would visit Rohita in the guise of an old Brahmana and advise him to prolong his stay in the forest. This went on for five years.

20. After staying in the forest for five years, Rohita returned in the sixth year to his own city. On his way back, he purchased from Ajīgarta his middle son named Sunassepa. **21-23.** He presented to his father Sunassepa as the sacrificial victim, and did his obeisance. Afterwards Harischandra of great fame performed a human sacrifice for the propitiation of Varuna and other Devas, and got relief from his ailment of dropsy. In that Yajna, Viswamitra, the sage of mighty prowess, was the Hota; Jamadagni of great self-control, the Adhvaryu; Vasishtha, Brah-

शुनःशेपस्य माहात्म्यमुपरिष्टात्प्रचक्ष्यते। सत्यसारां धृतिं दृष्ट्वा सभार्यस्य च भूपतेः ॥24॥
विश्वामित्रो भृशं प्रीतो ददावविहतां गतिम्। मनः पृथिव्यां तामद्भिस्तेजसापोऽनिलेन तत् ॥25॥
खे वायुं धारयंस्तच्च भूतादौ तं महात्मनि। तस्मिञ्ज्ञानकलां ध्यात्वा तयाज्ञानं विनिर्दहन् ॥26॥
हित्वा तां स्वेन भावेन निर्वाणसुखसंविदा। अनिर्देश्याप्रतर्क्येण तस्थौ विध्वस्तबन्धनः ॥27॥

इति श्रीमद्भागवते महापुराणे पारमहंस्यां संहितायां नवमस्कन्धे हरिश्चन्द्रोपाख्यानं नाम सप्तमोऽध्यायः ॥ 7॥

ma; and Ayāsya, the singer of Sama chants. Indra, being highly pleased, presented Harischandra with a chariot of gold.

24-27. Sunassepa's greatness will be discussed later along with the account of Viswamitra's sons. Viswamitra was very much pleased with the king and his wife for their devotion to truth and imparted to him the knowledge of the Atman that leads one unobstructed to liberation. He dissolved the body-centred mind in the earth element; that in its cause, the water element; that in the fire element; that in the air element; that in the sky element; that in the I-sense; and that in the universal I (Mahattattva). Rejecting the objective side of it, he meditated on its subjective (intellectual) side as his own Self. By the illumination thus derived, he destroyed the obstruction of ignorance, and then dissolved even that knowledge, producing a mental mode, in the self-luminous, subject-objectless Bliss, the true nature of the Self, which is beyond thought and words.

अथाष्टमोऽध्यायः

श्रीशुक उवाच

हरितो रोहितसुतश्चम्पस्तस्माद्विनिर्मिता। चम्पापुरी सुदेवोऽतो विजयो यस्य चात्मजः ॥ 1॥
भरुकस्तत्सुतस्तस्माद् वृकस्तस्यापि बाहुकः। सोऽरिभिर्हृतभू राजा सभार्यो वनमाविशत् ॥ 2॥
वृद्धं तं पञ्चतां प्राप्तं महिष्यनु मरिष्यती। और्वेण जानताऽऽत्मानं प्रजावन्तं निवारिता ॥ 3॥
आज्ञायास्यै सपत्नीभिर्गरो दत्तोऽन्धसा सह। सह तेनैव संजातः सगराख्यो महायशाः ॥ 4॥

Skandha IX : Chapter 8
THE STORY OF SAGARA

Sagara and his Exploits (1-6)

Sri Suka said: **1.** Rohita had as his son Harita; and he, Champa. This Champa built the city known as Champāpuri. His son was Sudeva; and his, Vijaya. **2.** His son was Bharuka; his, Vrika; and his, Bāhuka. Being defeated by enemies and deprived of his kingdom, Bāhuka went to the forest with his queen. **3.** When he died of old age his queen wanted to immolate herself and follow him. But sage Aurva prevented her, as she was carrying within her the only issue that was to sustain the line. **4.** Knowing her to be with child, her co-wives gave her poison with her food. But none the less the child was born intact along with the poison. In due time, he became a famous king under the name Sagara, mean-

सगरश्चक्रवर्त्यासीत् सागरो यत्सुतैः कृतः । यस्तालजङ्घान् यवनाञ्छकान् हैहयबर्बरान् ॥ 5॥
नावधीद् गुरुवाक्येन चक्रे विकृतवेषिणः । मुण्डाञ्छ्मश्रुधरान् कांश्चिन्मुक्तकेशार्धमुण्डितान् 6
अनन्तर्वाससः कांश्चिदबहिर्वाससोऽपरान् । सोऽश्वमेधैरयजत सर्ववेदसुरात्मकम् ॥ 7॥
और्वोपदिष्टयोगेन हरिमात्मानमीश्वरम् । तस्योत्सृष्टं पशुं यज्ञे जहाराश्वं पुरंदरः ॥ 8॥
सुमत्यास्तनया दृप्ताः पितुरादेशकारिणः । हयमन्वेषमाणास्ते समन्तान्न्यखनन्महीम् ॥ 9॥
प्रागुदीच्यां दिशि हयं ददृशुः कपिलान्तिके । एष वाजिहरश्चौर आस्ते मीलितलोचनः ॥10॥
हन्यतां हन्यतां पाप इति षष्टिसहस्रिणः । उदायुधा अभिययुरुन्मिमेष तदा मुनिः ॥11॥
स्वशरीराग्निना तावन्महेन्द्रहृतचेतसः । महद्व्यतिक्रमहता भस्मसादभवन् क्षणात् ॥12॥

न साधुवादो मुनिकोपभर्जिता नृपेन्द्रपुत्रा इति सत्त्वधामनि ।
कथं तमो रोषमयं विभाव्यते जगत्पवित्रात्मनि खे रजो भुवः ॥13॥
यस्येरिता सांख्यमयी दृढेह नौर्यया मुमुक्षुस्तरते दुरत्ययम् ।
भवार्णवं मृत्युपथं विपश्चितः परात्मभूतस्य कथं पृथङ्मतिः ॥14॥

योऽसमञ्जस इत्युक्तः स केशिन्या नृपात्मजः । तस्य पुत्रोंऽशुमान् नाम पितामहहिते रतः ॥15॥

ing 'one born with poison'. **5-6.** It was his sons that dug up the ocean, which therefore came to be known as Sāgara. He defeated Tālajanghas, Yavanas, Sakas, Haihayas, and Barbaras. But on the advice of his teacher he spared their lives. He, however, deformed them, shaving the head and face of some, the head or the face only of some, and half the face and half the scalp of still others. Some he made to wear the underwear only and some the outer one alone.

Sagara's Aswamedha (7-14)

7-8. Following the instruction of his preceptor Aurva, Sagara performed Aswamedha sacrifices as adoration of the Supreme Being, of whom the Veda and the Divinities are embodiments. To obstruct this Yajna, Indra stole away the horse meant for the sacrifice, when it was let loose for grazing. **9.** Sagara had two queens Sumati and Kesini. The sons of Sumati, proud of their strength, went searching for the horse at their father's command and dug up all around the earth in the course of their quest. **10-11.** In the north eastern direction, they saw the sage Kapila in the state of meditation, with the horse standing by his side. 'Here is the horse-lifter, here he sits with eyes closed, as if he were in Samadhi. Kill him,' so cried out the princes with their weapons uplifted when the sage opened his eyes. **12.** Deprived of their intelligence by Indra, they sought to insult a great sage, and as a consequence, they perished in the fire that came out of their own evil-possessed bodies.

13. The common belief that Sagara's sons died in the fire of the anger of Kapila is wrong. How can you attribute anger, a product of Tamas, to a personage who was all Sattva and who could sanctify the whole world? It would be like attributing the dust, which is of the earth, to the sky. **14.** How can there be distinction between friend and foe for the all-knowing sage, who had become one with the Supreme Being and who set in motion that firm boat of the path of knowledge (Sankhya) by which man could easily go across the ocean of Samsara, the playground of death, which is so difficult to cross otherwise?

Search for Horse By Amsumān (15-21)

15. (When the sons of Sumati thus

असमञ्जस आत्मानं दर्शयन्नसमञ्जसम् । जातिस्मरः पुरा सङ्गाद् योगी योगाद् विचालितः 16
आचरन् गर्हितं लोके ज्ञातीनां कर्म विप्रियम् । सरय्वां क्रीडतो बालान् प्रास्यदुद्वेजयञ्जनम् ।।17।।
एवंवृत्तः परित्यक्तः पित्रा स्नेहमपोह्य वै । योगैश्वर्येण बालांस्तान् दर्शयित्वा ततो ययौ ।।18।।
अयोध्यावासिनः सर्वे बालकान् पुनरागतान् । दृष्ट्वा विसिस्मिरे राजन् राजा चाप्यन्वतप्यत ।।19।।
अंशुमांश्चोदितो राज्ञा तुरङ्गान्वेषणे ययौ । पितृव्यखातानुपथं भस्मान्ति ददृशे हयम् ।।20।।
तत्रासीनं मुनिं वीक्ष्य कपिलाख्यमधोक्षजम् । अस्तौत् समाहितमनाः प्राञ्जलिः प्रणतो महान् 21

अंशुमानुवाच

न पश्यति त्वां परमात्मनोऽजनो न बुध्यतेऽद्यापि समाधियुक्तिभिः ।
कुतोऽपरे तस्य मनःशरीरधीविसर्गसृष्टा वयमप्रकाशाः ।।22।।
ये देहभाजस्त्रिगुणप्रधाना गुणान् विपश्यन्त्युत वा तमश्च ।
यन्मायया मोहितचेतसस्ते विदुः स्वसंस्थं न बहिःप्रकाशाः ।।23।।

perished, the progeny of the second wife Kesini came forward to do the task.) The king had by his second wife Kesini a son whom people called Asamanjasa. His son was Amsumān, who wanted to work for the redemption of his granduncles. **16-17.** Asamanjasa was in his previous birth a great Yogi, but due to attachment he happened to have a downfall in his spiritual life. He had, however, the memory of his last birth, and so to avoid the same bondage of attachment now also, he behaved like an insane man doing things that displeased the relatives and caused revulsion in the minds of others. One such act was his consigning to the Sarayu river children who were playing on the river bank. **18.** Because of such conduct, his father lost all his affection for him and abandoned him. Asamanjasa, on his part, brought back all those children by his Yogic power and then left hearth and home to take to the life of a nonattached ascetic. **19.** O King! All the inhabitants of Ayodhya were wonder-struck to see all the children return, and the King too, susbsequently felt repentant for having abandoned his great son.

20. Directed by the King, Amsumān, the son of Asamanjasa, started in search of the sacrificial horse. He went through the subterranean path his paternal uncles had made, and came across the horse standing by the side of the ash-heap to which they had been reduced. **21.** There he also saw the great sage Kapila sitting in concentrated meditation. He made obeisance to the sage, and stood before him with his mind controlled and palms joined in adoration.

Hymn to Kapila (22-31)

Amsumān said: **22.** Even Brahma has not been able to realise Thee, who transcendest Him, though he has been striving for it through concentration and ratiocination. How then can these beings, and specially ignorant persons like me, know Thee, being only creatures born of the body, mind and intellect of that Brahma who is himself ignorant of Thee? **23.** All these living beings, who are dominated by the three Gunas of Prakriti, Sattva, Rajas and Tamas, are under the infatuation of Thy Maya. Consequently their mind goes only outward, and fails to perceive Thee within, present there as the inner pervader of everything. They are aware of modifications of Gunas as sense objects in waking and dream, and in sleep only the

तं त्वामहं ज्ञानघनं स्वभावप्रध्वस्तमायागुणभेदमोहैः ।
सनन्दनाद्यैर्मुनिभिर्विभाव्यं कथं हि मूढः परिभावयामि ॥24॥
प्रशान्तमायागुणकर्मलिङ्गमनामरूपं सदसद्विमुक्तम् ।
ज्ञानोपदेशाय गृहीतदेहं नमामहे त्वां पुरुषं पुराणम् ॥25॥
त्वन्मायारचिते लोके वस्तुबुद्धया गृहादिषु । भ्रमन्ति कामलोभेर्ष्यामोहविभ्रान्तचेतसः ॥26॥
अद्य नः सर्वभूतात्मन् कामकर्मेन्द्रियाशयः । मोहपाशो दृढश्छिन्नो भगवंस्तव दर्शनात् ॥27॥

श्रीशुक उवाच

इत्थंगीतानुभावस्तं भगवान् कपिलो मुनिः । अंशुमन्तमुवाचेदमनुगृह्य धिया नृप ॥28॥

श्रीभगवानुवाच

अश्वोऽयं नीयतां वत्स पितामहपशुस्तव । इमे च पितरो दग्धा गङ्गाम्भोऽर्हन्ति नेतरत् ॥29॥
तं परिक्रम्य शिरसा प्रसाद्य हयमानयत् । सगरस्तेन पशुना क्रतुशेषं समापयत् ॥30॥
राज्यमंशुमति न्यस्य निःस्पृहो मुक्तबन्धनः । और्वोपदिष्टमार्गेण लेभे गतिमनुत्तमाम् ॥31॥

इति श्रीमद्भागवते महापुराणे पारमहंस्यां संहितायां नवमस्कन्धे सगरोपाख्यानेऽष्टमोऽध्यायः ॥ 8॥

darkness of ignorance. **24.** How can an ignorant person grasp the truth of Thee, who art the condensation of Pure Consciousness and conceivable only to sages like Sanandana having natural freedom from the infatuation of dualistic understanding arising from the influence of the Gunas of Maya. **25.** O Tranquillity personified! Though Thou art in reality without any particular name and form, and beyond cause and effect relation, Thou hast assumed the attributes, activities and forms based on Thy Maya, and taken a body for imparting knowledge to aspirants. My obeisance to Thee, the most ancient being. **26.** Men, infatuated by greed and passion and thereby confused in thought, consider impermanent and ephemeral objects like house and properties belonging to Thy realm of Maya as real, and get entangled. **27.** O All-pervading Being! Thy contact today has cut asunder the bondage of deep-rooted ignorance in Me—ignorance which is the cause of desire, action and addiction to the senses.

Sri Suka said: **28.** O King! Being thus extolled, that powerful sage Kapila blessed Amsumān mentally and said: *Lord Kapila said:* **29.** 'Dear one! You may take away this sacrificial horse of your grandfather. As for your granduncles who have been reduced to ashes, nothing but the holy water of the Ganga can purify them.' **30**. Circumambulating the sage and making prostrations, Amsumān led away the sacrificial horse, and helped his grandfather to complete the sacrifice. **31.** In the end Sagara, freed from desires and the bondages arising from them, entrusted the kingdom to his grandson Amsumān, and as instructed by his teacher Aurva, practised spiritual disciplines and attained to the highest spiritual fulfilment.

अथ नवमोऽध्यायः

श्रीशुक उवाच

अंशुमांश्च तपस्तेपे गङ्गानयनकाम्यया । कालं महान्तं नाशक्नोत् ततः कालेन संस्थितः ॥1॥
दिलीपस्तत्सुतस्तद्वदशक्तः कालमेयिवान् । भगीरथस्तस्य पुत्रस्तेपे स सुमहत् तपः ॥ 2॥
दर्शयामास तं देवी प्रसन्ना वरदास्मि ते । इत्युक्तः स्वमभिप्रायं शशंसावनतो नृपः ॥ 3॥
कोऽपि धारयिता वेगं पतन्त्या मे महीतले । अन्यथा भूतलं भित्त्वा नृप यास्ये रसातलम् ॥ 4॥
किं चाहं न भुवं यास्ये नरा मय्यामृजन्त्यघम् । मृजामि तदघं कुत्र राजंस्तत्र विचिन्त्यताम् ॥ 5॥

भगीरथ उवाच

साधवो न्यासिनः शान्ता ब्रह्मिष्ठा लोकपावनाः । हरन्त्यघं तेऽङ्गसङ्गात् तेष्वास्ते ह्यघभिद्धरिः ॥ 6॥
धारयिष्यति ते वेगं रुद्रस्त्वात्मा शरीरिणाम् । यस्मिन्नोतमिदं प्रोतं विश्वं शाटीव तन्तुषु ॥ 7॥
इत्युक्त्वा स नृपो देवं तपसातोषयच्छिवम् । कालेनाल्पीयसा राजंस्तस्येशः समतुष्यत ॥ 8॥
तथेति राज्ञाभिहितं सर्वलोकहितः शिवः । दधारावहितो गङ्गां पादपूतजलां हरेः ॥ 9॥
भगीरथः स राजर्षिर्निन्ये भुवनपावनीम् । यत्र स्वपितॄणां देहा भस्मीभूताः स्म शेरते ॥10॥

Skandha IX : Chapter 9

FROM AMSUMĀN TO KHATVĀNGA

Bhagīratha bringing Ganga (1-15)

Sri Suka said: **1.** Amsumān performed Tapas for a very long time in order to bring the holy Ganga for the purification of his ancestors. But he could not succeed and had to die with his object unfulfilled. **2.** His son Dilīpa also tried to accomplish this, but failed. In spite of this his son the famous Bhagīratha took up the task, and performed great Tapas for its accomplishment. **3.** Mother Ganga revealed herself to him and said: 'I am pleased with you and offer you the boon you seek.' In great humility he informed her of his desire to redeem his ancestors. **4.** (Mother Ganga said:) 'Who is there to bear my impact, as I flow down to the earth? Otherwise I may penetrate through the earth to Rasātala. **5.** Besides, I do not like to come to the earth, because men will wash off their sins in me. Where shall I deposit all that sin? How can this difficulty be solved?'

Bhagīratha said: **6.** Men of renunciation, tranquil, immersed in Brahman and capable of purifying the whole world, will come to you under the guise of pilgrimage, and purify you of all sins by their contact with your water during their ablutions. For, Sri Hari, the destroyer of all sins, clearly manifests Himself in these holy men. **7.** Rudra, in whom all the worlds rest as a piece of cloth does in the warp and woof, and who is the innermost essence of all beings, will bear your impact.

8. Next Bhagīratha proceeded to win the grace of that luminous being, Rudra, through Tapas, and before long succeeded in pleasing him. **9.** Siva, the benefactor of all the worlds, acceded to the request of the king, and bore on his head the water of the Ganga, purified by the feet of Hari, as she flowed down to the earth. **10.** Bhagīratha now led the

रथेन वायुवेगेन प्रयान्तमनुधावती । देशान् पुनन्ती निर्दग्धानासिञ्चत् सगरात्मजान् ।।11।।
यज्जलस्पर्शमात्रेण ब्रह्मदण्डहता अपि । सगरात्मजा दिवं जग्मुः केवलं देहभस्मभिः ।।12।।
भस्मीभूताङ्गसङ्गेन स्वर्याताः सगरात्मजाः । किं पुनः श्रद्धया देवीं ये सेवन्ते धृतव्रताः ।।13।।
न ह्येतत् परमाश्चर्यं स्वर्धुन्या यदिहोदितम् । अनन्तचरणाम्भोजप्रसूताया भवच्छिदः ।।14।।
सन्निवेश्य मनो यस्मिञ्छ्रद्धया मुनयोऽमलाः । त्रैगुण्यं दुस्त्यजं हित्वा सद्यो यातास्तदात्मताम् ।।15।।
श्रुतो भगीरथाज्जज्ञे तस्य नाभोऽपरोऽभवत् । सिन्धुद्वीपस्ततस्तस्मादयुतायुस्ततोऽभवत् ।।16।।
ऋतुपर्णो नलसखो योऽश्वविद्यामयान्नलात् । दत्त्वाक्षहृदयं चास्मै सर्वकामस्तु तत्सुतः ।।17।।
ततः सुदासस्तत्पुत्रो मदयन्तीपतिर्नृप । आहुर्मित्रसहं यं वै कल्माषाङ्घ्रिमुत क्वचित् ।
वसिष्ठशापाद् रक्षोऽभूदनपत्यः स्वकर्मणा ।।18।।

राजोवाच

किंनिमित्तो गुरोः शापः सौदासस्य महात्मनः । एतद् वेदितुमिच्छामः कथ्यतां न रहो यदि ।।19।।

श्रीशुक उवाच

सौदासो मृगयां किञ्चिच्चरन् रक्षो जघान ह । मुमोच भ्रातरं सोऽथ गतः प्रतिचिकीर्षया ।।20।।

world-sanctifying Ganga to the place where the ashes of his ancestors lay. **11.** As Bhagīratha drove in his chariot of wind-like speed, the Ganga flowed following him, purifying everything on the way until she drenched the ash-heap of Sagara's sons. **12.** In spite of their sin of insulting holy ones, those sons of Sagara attained to heaven immediately they contacted the Ganga through their ashes. **13.** When the sons of Sagara could attain heaven thus by mere indirect contact of the Ganga through their ashes, it is needless to speak of the glorious fruits accruing to persons who adore her with faith and observance of vows.

14. There is nothing to wonder at in what has been said above about the greatness of the heavenly stream Ganga—about its power of purifying the degraded and of assuaging the pains of worldly life, seeing that it has its origin at the lotus-feet of the Supreme Being Mahavishnu. **15.** For, numerous have been the sages who, by directing their mind with faith and concentration on Him, have achieved the otherwise impossible task of overcoming the sense of identification with the body, the product of the Gunas, and attaining union with Him.

Bhagīratha to Mitrasaha (16-24)

16. Bhagīratha's son was Sruta; his son, Nābha; his son, Sindhudweepa; and his son, Ayutāyus. **17.** His son was the well-known Rituparna who was a friend of Nala. Nala learnt from him the secrets of the game of dice, and in return taught him the science regarding the management of horses. Rituparna's son was Sarvakāma. **18.** Sarvakāma had Sudāsa as his son. His son was Saudāsa also known as Mitrasaha, the husband of Madayanti. Mitrasaha was also sometimes known as Kalmāshānghri. Due to the curse of Vasishtha, he became a Rakshasa. Due to his own bad Karma, he had no issue also.

The Rajah said: **19.** What was the occasion for his preceptor to curse the high-souled Mitrasaha? I would like to know it, provided it is not anything secret.

Sri Suka said: **20.** Mitrasaha once went to the forest hunting. In the course of the hunt, he killed a Rakshasa but allowed

स चिन्तयन्नघं राज्ञः सूदरूपधरो गृहे । गुरवे भोक्तुकामाय पक्त्वा निन्ये नरामिषम् ।।21।।
परिवेक्ष्यमाणं भगवान् विलोक्याभक्ष्यमञ्जसा । राजानमशपत् क्रुद्धो रक्षो ह्येवं भविष्यसि ।।22।।
रक्षःकृतं तद्विदित्वा चक्रे द्वादशवार्षिकम् । सोऽप्यपोऽञ्जलिनाऽऽदाय गुरुं शप्तुं समुद्यतः ।।23।।
वारितो मदयन्त्यापो रुशतीः पादयोर्जहौ । दिशः खमवनीं सर्वं पश्यञ्जीवमयं नृपः ।।24।।
राक्षसं भावमापन्नः पादे कल्माषतां गतः । व्यवायकाले ददृशे वनौकोदम्पती द्विजौ ।।25।।
क्षुधार्तो जगृहे विप्रं तत्पत्न्याहाकृतार्थवत् । न भवान् राक्षसः साक्षादिक्ष्वाकूणां महारथः ।।26।।
मदयन्त्याः पतिर्वीर नाधर्मं कर्तुमर्हसि । देहि मेऽपत्यकामाया अकृतार्थं पतिं द्विजम् ।।27।।
देहोऽयं मानुषो राजन् पुरुषस्याखिलार्थदः । तस्मादस्य वधो वीर सर्वार्थवध उच्यते ।।28।।
एष हि ब्राह्मणो विद्वांस्तपःशीलगुणान्वितः । आरिराधयिषुर्ब्रह्म महापुरुषसंज्ञितम् ।
सर्वभूतात्मभावेन भूतेष्वन्तर्हितं गुणैः ।।29।।
सोऽयं ब्रह्मर्षिवर्यस्ते राजर्षिप्रवराद् विभो । कथमर्हति धर्मज्ञ वधं पितुरिवात्मजः ।।30।।
तस्य साधोरपापस्य भ्रूणस्य ब्रह्मवादिनः । कथं वधं यथा बभ्रोर्मन्यते सन्मतो भवान् ।।31।।

his brother to go unhurt. This Rakshasa, whose life was spared, went away with the resolve to wreak vengeance on Mitrasaha. **21.** Desirous of doing harm to the king, he got employed as a cook in the king's palace, and when one day the king's preceptor was very hungry, he brought cooked human flesh for him to eat. **22.** Sensing that the food about to be served was prohibited meat, the preceptor Vasishtha became angry at once and cursed the king that he would become a Rakshasa. **23.** On knowing that this was the work of the Rakshasa, the preceptor reduced the term of the curse for a mere twelve years. The King also wanted to pronounce a curse on the preceptor, and took water in hand for the purpose. **24.** But he was prevented from doing so by his wife Madayanti. As he found living beings everywhere, he could not throw away anywhere the water he had taken in hand for cursing; for it would injure them. So he poured it on his own legs.

Mitrasaha as Rakshasa (25-36)

25. When he became a Rakshasa, his legs were found discoloured owing to the water he had himself poured on them. So he came to be known as Kalmāshānghri. While moving about as a Rakshasa with his discoloured legs, he came across a forest-dwelling Brahmana couple in the act of sexual intercourse. **26.** Being distressed by hunger, he caught hold of that Brahmana to eat him, but his wife piteously cried out to him: 'O hero! You are not a Rakshasa really. You are a great car-warrior of the line of Ikshvāku. **27.** You are the husband of Madayanti. It behoves you not to do this unrighteous act. I, who long for an issue, want back my husband who has not yet fulfilled his desire. **28.** O King! It is with this body that man can attain to all the desirable ends of life. So its destruction means the denial of all human fulfilments. **29.** He is a learned Brahmana of virtuous character and noble disposition, given to austere living. He is striving to adore Mahavishnu as the Spirit forming the essence in all, hidden by the qualities of Prakriti. **30.** O noble one! A Brahmarshi like him does not deserve to be killed by a Rajarshi like you, as a father does not by a son. **31.** A virtuous man like you cannot but consider the slaughter of a sinless, holy and learned Brahmana as in no way less heinous than the killing of a

यद्ययं क्रियते भक्षस्तर्हि मां खाद पूर्वतः ।
न जीविष्ये विना येन क्षणं च मृतकं यथा ॥32॥
एवं करुणभाषिण्या विलपन्त्या अनाथवत् ।
व्याघ्रः पशुमिवाखादत् सौदासः शापमोहितः ॥33॥
ब्राह्मणी वीक्ष्य दिधिषुं पुरुषादेन भक्षितम् ।
शोचन्त्यात्मानमुर्वीशमशपत् कुपिता सती ॥34॥
यस्मान्मे भक्षितः पाप कामार्तायाः पतिस्त्वया ।
तवापि मृत्युराधानादकृतप्रज्ञ दर्शितः ॥35॥
एवं मित्रसहं शप्त्वा पतिलोकपरायणा ।
तदस्थीनि समिद्धेऽग्नौ प्रास्य भर्तुर्गतिं गता ॥36॥
विशापो द्वादशाब्दान्ते मैथुनाय समुद्यतः ।
विज्ञाय ब्राह्मणीशापं महिष्या स निवारितः ॥37॥
तत ऊर्ध्वं स तत्याज स्त्रीसुखं कर्मणाप्रजाः ।
वसिष्ठस्तदनुज्ञातो मदयन्त्यां प्रजामधात् ॥38॥
सा वै सप्त समा गर्भमबिभ्रन्न व्यजायत ।
जघ्नेऽश्मनोदरं तस्याः सोऽश्मकस्तेन कथ्यते ॥39॥
अश्मकान्मूलको जज्ञे यः स्त्रीभिः परिरक्षितः ।
नारीकवच इत्युक्तो निःक्षत्रे मूलकोऽभवत् ॥40॥
ततो दशरथस्तस्मात् पुत्र ऐडविडस्ततः ।
राजा विश्वसहो यस्य खट्वाङ्गश्चक्रवर्त्यभूत् ॥41॥
यो देवैरर्थितो दैत्यानवधीद् युधि दुर्जयः ।
मुहूर्तमायुर्ज्ञात्वैत्य स्वपुरं संदधे मनः ॥42॥

cow. **32.** If you are going to eat him up, do eat me beforehand. For without him, I shall not live for even a moment more.'

33. While she was thus piteously bemoaning her fate in a helpless manner, Mitrasaha, now a Rakshasa under a curse, ate up the Brahmana as a tiger eats a cow. **34.** Roused to anger at the sight of her husband being eaten by the Rakshasa, the Brahmana woman cursed him in a mood of self-pity saying: **35.** 'Just as you have eaten my husband while he was stricken with sexual passion, so shall you die when satisfying your sexual appetite.' **36.** Next, desirous as she was of following her husband to the other world, she made a fire into which she consigned her husband's bones as well as herself.

Mitrasaha to Khatvānga (37-41)

37. Afterwards, at the end of twelve years, Mitrasaha, being free from the curse of the preceptor, returned to his kingdom. When, on his return, he wanted to have sexual intercourse with his wife, she made him desist from it, reminding him of the curse of the Brahmana woman on him. **38.** Afterwards he gave up living with women, and thus due to his Karma, was without an issue of his own. At his request, Vasishtha begot an issue for him by his wife Madayanti. **39.** It is said that she did not deliver the child for seven years, and so the sage Vasishtha had to open her abdomen with a stone implement. The child born was for this reason called Asmaka. **40.** Asmaka's son was Mūlaka. When Parasurama destroyed the whole race of Kshatriyas, Mūlaka was protected by women under the guise of one of them. For this reason he came to be known also as Nārīkavacha (one with women as the protecting mail). He became the regenerator of the line of Kshatriyas destroyed by Parasurama. **41.** From him Dasaratha was born, and from him Aidavida. His son was Viswasaha, to whom was born Khatvānga.

Story of devoted Khatvānga (42-49)

42. Because he was invincible by any one, his help was sought by the Devas in their war against the Asuras. Khatvānga destroyed all the Asuras in battle, but by that time he was informed by the Devas that he had only one Muhurta more of life. So he hastened to his capital and tried to make his mind one-pointed in the

न मे ब्रह्मकुलात् प्राणाः कुलदैवान्न चात्मजाः । न श्रियो न मही राज्यं न दाराश्चातिवल्लभाः ॥43॥
न बाल्येऽपि मतिर्मह्यमधर्मे रमते क्वचित् । नापश्यमुत्तमश्लोकादन्यत् किंचन वस्त्वहम् ॥44॥
देवैः कामवरो दत्तो मह्यं त्रिभुवनेश्वरैः । न वृणे तमहं कामं भूतभावनभावनः ॥45॥
ये विक्षिप्तेन्द्रियधियो देवास्ते स्वहृदि स्थितम् । न विन्दन्ति प्रियं शश्वदात्मानं किमुतापरे ॥46॥
अथेशमायारचितेषु सङ्गं गुणेषु गन्धर्वपुरोपमेषु ।
रूढं प्रकृत्याऽऽत्मनि विश्वकर्तुर्भावेन हित्वा तमहं प्रपद्ये ॥47॥
इति व्यवसितो बुद्धया नारायणगृहीतया । हित्वान्यभावमज्ञानं ततः स्वं भावमाश्रितः ॥48॥
यत् तद् ब्रह्म परं सूक्ष्ममशून्यं शून्यकल्पितम् । भगवान् वासुदेवेति यं गृणन्ति हि सात्वताः ॥49॥

इति श्रीमद्भागवते महापुराणे पारमहंस्यां संहितायां नवमस्कन्धे सूर्यवंशानुवर्णने नवमोऽध्यायः ॥ 9॥

Lord. **43.** He meditated thus: 'My family deity is the community of holy men, who are dearer to me than my life-breath. Neither son, nor wealth, nor lands, nor kingdoms, nor wife is dearer to me than they. **44.** Even in my boyhood my mind has never been drawn towards, or found delight in, evil ways. I have never looked upon anything other than the Lord of the holy fame as reality. **45.** The Devas, who rule the three worlds, offered to me the boon of my choice, but I accepted them not, because my mind was constantly centred on the Supreme Being alone. **46.** He is present in the hearts of all, but still even Devas, possessed of mind and senses that are always outward-going and involved in sense objects, fail to understand that Atman within, who is what makes anything dear. The condition of others is even worse. **47.** I take refuge in Him, the great Creator, having abandoned through devotion to Him, the naturally rooted attachment of my mind for sense objects, which His mysterious power Maya has brought into existence like castles in the air.' **48.** Deciding like this in his mind, which was entirely dominated by the thought of the Lord Narayana, he abandoned the body-based ignorance and became established in the nature of the Atman, one's own higher Self. **49.** That state is the Supreme Brahman, extremely subtle, but positively existent. Though considered a nihil by gross-minded people because of the impossibility of knowing Him through the senses, He is what the Bhāgavatas call Vāsudeva.

अथ दशमोऽध्यायः

श्रीशुक उवाच

खट्वाङ्गाद् दीर्घबाहुश्च रघुस्तस्मात् पृथुश्रवाः । अजस्ततो महाराजस्तस्माद् दशरथोऽभवत् ॥ 1॥
तस्यापि भगवानेष साक्षाद् ब्रह्ममयो हरिः । अंशांशेन चतुर्धागात् पुत्रत्वं प्रार्थितः सुरैः ।
रामलक्ष्मणभरतशत्रुघ्ना इति संज्ञया ॥ 2॥
तस्यानुचरितं राजन्नृषिभिस्तत्त्वदर्शिभिः । श्रुतं हि वर्णितं भूरि त्वया सीतापतेर्मुहुः ॥ 3॥
गुर्वर्थे त्यक्तराज्यो व्यचरदनुवनं पद्मपद्भ्यां प्रियायाः
पाणिस्पर्शाक्षमाभ्यां मृजितपथरुजो यो हरीन्द्रानुजाभ्याम् ।
वैरूप्याच्छूर्पणख्याः प्रियविरहरुषाऽऽरोपितभ्रूविजृम्भ-
त्रस्ताब्धिर्बद्धसेतुः खलदवदहनः कोसलेन्द्रोऽवतान्नः ॥ 4॥
विश्वामित्राध्वरे येन मारीचाद्या निशाचराः । पश्यतो लक्ष्मणस्यैव हता नैर्ऋतपुङ्गवाः ॥ 5॥
यो लोकवीरसमितौ धनुरैशमुग्रं सीतास्वयंवरगृहे त्रिशतोपनीतम् ।
आदाय बालगजलील इवेक्षुयष्टिं सज्जीकृतं नृप विकृष्य बभञ्ज मध्ये ॥ 6॥

Skandha IX : Chapter 10
THE INCARNATION OF RAMA

Rama's Greatness (1-4)

Sri Suka said: **1.** Khatvānga's son was Dīrghabāhu. From him was born the world-famous Raghu; from, him, Aja; and from him, Dasaratha. **2.** The Lord of all excellences, the Supreme Hari, the very Brahman, being invoked and prayed to by the celestials, was born by a fraction of Himself divided into four parts as the four sons of Dasaratha. **3.** He was born as his four sons, Rama, Lakshmana, Bharata and Satrughna. Enlightened personages have given elaborate accounts of the story of Rama, the consort of Sita, and you must have heard these recited again and again. **4.** He who gave up a kingdom to keep his father's plighted words; whose feet, though too soft to stand even the touch of his consort, nevertheless trudged through forest after forest along paths cleared by his brother and the monkey king; who frightened the deity of the seas by an angry frown and arching brows, consequent on the abduction of his wife Sita by Ravana who was earlier incensed by Rama's mutilation of his sister Sūrpanakha; who built the bridge across the sea to Lanka where he raged like a forest fire destroying the tribe of evil-doers—may that Rama, the king of Kosala, be our refuge.

Early Life (5-8)

5. At the sacrificial ceremony of Viswamitra, he destroyed the Rakshasa chiefs like Mārīcha with the utmost ease, as if it were a play, while his brother Lakshmana merely looked on. **6.** In the gathering of heroic men seated in the assembly hall of Sita's marriage, he pulled and broke, with the ease with which an elephant breaks a sugarcane, the mighty bow of Siva, which required three hundred

जित्वानुरूपगुणशीलवयोऽङ्गरूपां सीताभिधां श्रियमुरस्यभिलब्धमानाम् ।
मार्गे व्रजन् भृगुपतेर्व्यनयत् प्ररूढं दर्पं महीमकृत यस्त्रिरराजबीजाम् :। 7॥
यः सत्यपाशपरिवीतपितुर्निदेशं स्त्रैणस्य चापि शिरसा जगृहे सभार्यः ।
राज्यं श्रियं प्रणयिनःसुहृदो निवासं त्यक्त्वा ययौ वनमसूनिव मुक्तसङ्गः ॥ 8॥
रक्षःस्वसुर्व्यकृत रूपमशुद्धबुद्धेस्तस्याः खरत्रिशिरदूषणमुख्यबन्धून् ।
जघ्ने चतुर्दशसहस्रमपारणीयकोदण्डपाणिरटमान उवास कृच्छ्रम् ॥ 9॥
सीताकथाश्रवणदीपितहृच्छयेन सृष्टं विलोक्य नृपते दशकन्धरेण ।
जघ्नेऽद्भुतैणवपुषाऽऽश्रमतोऽपकृष्टो मारीचमाशु विशिखेन यथा कमुग्रः ॥10॥
रक्षोऽधमेन वृकवद् विपिनेऽसमक्षं वैदेहराजदुहितर्यपयापितायाम् ।
भ्रात्रा वने कृपणवत् प्रियया वियुक्तः स्त्रीसङ्गिनां गतिमिति प्रथयंश्चचार ॥11॥
दग्ध्वाऽऽत्मकृत्यहतकृत्यमहन् कबन्धं सख्यं विधाय कपिभिर्दयितागतिं तैः ।
बुद्ध्वाथ वालिनि हते प्लवगेन्द्रसैन्यैर्वेलामगात् स मनुजोऽजभवार्चिताङ्घ्रिः ॥12॥

persons for its transport. **7.** Sita, who was none but Srī, honoured by being made the resident of the Lord's chest, thereby became his wife, well-matched with him in point of virtues, conduct, age, form, beauty and the like. On his way back after the marriage, he came into confrontation with Parasurama, the chief of the Bhrigus, and humbled his pride of having erased the ruling class of Kshatriyas in his twenty one campaigns. **8.** Submitting willingly to the command of his helpless father who, being under the domination of his wife Kaikeyi, was compelled by the bond of his plighted word to exile him, he (Rama) abandoned the country, wealth, house, relations and friends with utmost gladness as a Yogi gives up his body, and went to the forest accompanied by his wife. May that Rama protect us!

Abduction of Sita (9-12)

9. He mutilated the lustful Sūrpanakha who attempted to kill Sita. He decimated the Asura army of fourteen thousand led by her relatives Khara, Dūshana and Trisiras, with utmost ease as in a play. Himself carrying his bow too formidable for any one else to handle, he wandered from forest to forest, and took his residence there, standing every form of difficulty. **10.** O King! Ravana became lovelorn on hearing about the beauty of Sita, and sent Mārīcha to draw Rama away from his forest residence. Attracted by Mārīcha in the form of a wonderful deer, he went far away into the forest in pursuit of him, and in the end killed the deer with a sharp arrow as Rudra killed Daksha. **11.** As a wolf carries away a lamb at the opportune moment, Ravana carried away Sita during Rama's absence from his forest dwelling. Afterwards Rama wandered through the forest in great sorrow and distress, along with his brother, in quest of Sita, in order to show to the world that this is the miserable fate of persons intensely attached to women. **12.** Next he, whose feet are worshipped by Siva and Brahma, cremated Jatāyu who had courted death in his service, with the affection of a son, then destroyed Kabandha, made friendship with monkeys, came to know about the whereabouts of Sita through the search of those monkeys, killed Vāli, and marched to the ocean shore with that army of monkeys.

यद्रोषविभ्रमविवृत्तकटाक्षपातसम्भ्रान्तनक्रमकरो भयगीर्णघोषः ।
सिन्धुः शिरस्यर्हणं परिगृह्य रूपी पादारविन्दमुपगम्य बभाष एतत् ॥13॥
न त्वां वयं जडधियो नु विदाम भूमन् कूटस्थमादिपुरुषं जगतामधीशम् ।
यत्सत्त्वतः सुरगणा रजसः प्रजेशा मन्योश्च भूतपतयः स भवान् गुणेशः ॥14॥
कामं प्रयाहि जहि विश्रवसोऽवमेहं त्रैलोक्यरावणमवाप्नुहि वीर पत्नीम् ।
बध्नीहि सेतुमिह ते यशसो वितत्यै गायन्ति दिग्विजयिनो यमुपेत्य भूपाः ॥15॥
बद्ध्वोदधौ रघुपतिर्विविधाद्रिकूटैः सेतुं कपीन्द्रकरकम्पितभूरुहाङ्गैः ।
सुग्रीवनीलहनुमत्प्रमुखैरनीकैर्लङ्कां विभीषणदृशाऽऽविशदग्रदग्धाम् ॥16॥
सा वानरेन्द्रबलरुद्धविहारकोष्ठश्रीद्वारगोपुरसदोवलभीविटङ्का ।
निर्भज्यमानधिषणध्वजहेमकुम्भशृङ्गाटका गजकुलैर्ह्रदिनीव घूर्णा ॥17॥
रक्षःपतिस्तदवलोक्य निकुम्भकुम्भधूम्राक्षदुर्मुखसुरान्तनरान्तकादीन् ।
पुत्रं प्रहस्तमतिकायविकम्पनादीन् सर्वानुगान् समहिनोदथ कुम्भकर्णम् ॥18॥
तां यातुधानपृतनामसिशूलचापप्रासर्ष्टिशक्तिशरतोमरखड्गदुर्गाम् ।
सुग्रीवलक्ष्मणमरुत्सुतगन्धमादनीलाङ्गदर्क्षपनसादिभिरन्वितोऽगात् ॥19॥

Crossing the Sea (13-16)

13. As the angry look of Rama's wide open eyes fell on him, the sea-deity got into a fright, resulting in the subsidence of the roar of his wavy voice and in the consternation of the aquatic residents within him. His form emerged from the sea carrying a load of articles for worshipful presentation and he sought shelter at his feet and said: **14.** 'O Almighty One! Dull-witted creatures that we are, we have little understanding of Thee, the undecaying and all-powerful Being controlling the whole universe. Now we have come to know Thee and understand that Thou art the ruler of Prakriti, from whose qualities of Sattva, Rajas and Tamas are produced the Devas, Prajapatis and Rudras. **15.** O hero! Thou art free to go across the sea. Destroy the monstrous Ravana, born of the dirt of Visravas—a veritable Ravana or bully who makes all the three worlds weep and wail—and recover Thy spouse Sita. Build across the sea a bridge that will spread Thy fame everywhere. The world-conquering heroes who come to see Thy bridge will extol Thee in songs.' **16.** Building the bridge with thickly forested mountain peaks that were manually plucked and brought by the monkeys, he, under the guidance of Vibhīshana and accompanied by leading monkey chiefs like Sugrīva, Nīla and Hanumān, crossed over to Lanka, to which Hanumān had already set fire earlier.

Attack on Lanka (17-20)

17. Like a lake that has been ravaged by a herd of elephants, the city of Lanka, besieged by the army of monkey chiefs, was soon in shambles, its pleasure gardens, granaries, treasuries, gate towers, assembly halls and terraces were under the occupation of the monkey forces, and its altars, flag-staffs, golden domes, road-crossings etc., were all wrecked by them. **18.** The Rakshasa chief Ravana thereupon dispatched one after another all his great warriors to the battle front—warriors like Nikumbha, Kumbha, Dhūmrāksha, Durmukha, Surānta, Narāntaka, his son Indrajit, Prahasta, Atikāya, Vikampana, and finally Kumbhakarna. **19.** Rama along with Sugrīva, Lakshmana, Ha-

तेऽनीकपा रघुपतेरभिपत्य सर्वे द्वन्द्वं वरूथमिभपत्तिरथाश्वयोधैः ।
जघ्नुर्द्रुमैर्गिरिगदेषुभिरङ्गदाद्या सीताभिमर्शहतमङ्गलरावणेशान् ॥20॥
रक्षःपतिः स्वबलनष्टिमवेक्ष्य रुष्ट आरुह्य यानकमथाभिससार रामम् ।
स्वःस्यन्दने द्युमति मातलिनोपनीते विभ्राजमानमहनन्निशितैः क्षुरप्रैः ॥21॥
रामस्तमाह पुरुषादपुरीष यन्नः कान्तासमक्षमसताहृता श्ववत् ते ।
त्यक्तत्रपस्य फलमद्य जुगुप्सितस्य यच्छामि काल इव कर्तुरलङ्घ्यवीर्यः ॥22॥
एवं क्षिपन् धनुषि सन्धितमुत्ससर्ज बाणं स वज्रमिव तद्धृदयं बिभेद ।
सोऽसृग् वमन् दशमुखैर्न्यपतद् विमानाद्धाहेति जल्पति जने सुकृतीव रिक्तः ॥23॥

ततो निष्क्रम्य लङ्कााया यातुधान्यः सहस्रशः । मन्दोदर्या समं तस्मिन् प्ररुदत्य उपाद्रवन् ॥24॥
स्वान् स्वान् बन्धून् परिष्वज्य लक्ष्मणेषुभिरर्दितान् । रुरुदुः सुस्वरं दीना घ्नन्त्य आत्मानमात्मना ॥25॥
हा हताः स्म वयं नाथ लोकरावण रावण । कं यायाच्छरणं लङ्का त्वद्विहीना परार्दिता ॥26॥
नैवं वेद महाभाग भवान् कामवशं गतः । तेजोऽनुभावं सीताया येन नीतो दशामिमाम् ॥27॥
कृतैषा विधवा लङ्का वयं च कुलनन्दन । देहः कृतोऽन्नं गृध्राणामात्मा नरकहेतवे ॥28॥

numān, Gandhamāda, Nīla, Angada, Jāmbavān, Panasa and other monkey chiefs faced that army of Rakshasas, which was formidable and well-equipped with weapons, like swords, tridents, bows and arrows,—darts, double-edged swords, javelin, lances and scimitars. **20.** The leaders of Rama's army like Angada and others joined in combats with well-matched opponents on the opposite side, consisting of elephant regiments, infantry, cavalry and chariots. With trees, mountain tops, maces and arrows the monkey forces of Rama destroyed that army of Rakshasas mobilised by Ravana, who had lost his luck and good fortune because of his laying violent hands on holy Sita.

Death of Ravana and After (21-33)

21. The king of the Rakshasas, infuriated at the destruction of his forces, now ascended a chariot and charged at Rama, who was seated in the luminous chariot of Indra brought by his charioteer Mātali, and showered sharp arrows on him. **22.** Rama said to him: 'O wretch of a Rakshasa, you mean fellow! Like a pilfering dog you have stolen away my wife during my absence. The consequences of this shameless and despicable act will soon fall on you from my hands like the irresistible doom of Time.' **23.** Berating Ravana in this way, Rama shot a powerful arrow at him. Like the thunderbolt it pierced Ravana's heart, and vomitting blood through all his ten mouths, Ravana fell down, as an individual drops from the heavenly regions when his merits are exhausted. All the world cried 'Alas!' at this. **24.** Now hundreds of Rakshasa women headed by Mandodari came out of the city weeping and wailing. **25.** They cried aloud, beating their breasts, as they clung to the bodies of their husbands and other relatives who met with death from the arrows of Lakshmana. **26.** They wailed: 'O Ravana, the terror of all the worlds! Alas! We are half dead. Without you what will be the fate of Lanka, now under the attack of enemies? **27.** O great one! Under the influence of lust, you failed to recognise the unique power of Sita's spiritual glory. It was ignorance of this that has brought you to this predicament. **28.** By your death

श्रीशुक उवाच

स्वानां विभीषणश्चक्रे कोसलेन्द्रानुमोदितः । पितृमेधविधानेन यदुक्तं साम्परायिकम् ॥29॥
ततो ददर्श भगवानशोकवनिकाश्रमे । क्षामां स्वविरहव्याधिं शिंशपामूलमास्थिताम् 30॥
रामः प्रियतमां भार्यां दीनां वीक्ष्यान्वकम्पत । आत्मसंदर्शनाह्लादविकसन्मुखपङ्कजाम् ॥31॥
आरोप्यारुरुहे यानं भ्रातृभ्यां हनुमद्युतः । विभीषणाय भगवान् दत्त्वा रक्षोगणेशताम् ॥32॥
लङ्कामायुश्च कल्पान्तं ययौ चीर्णव्रतः पुरीम् । अवकीर्यमाणः कुसुमैर्लोकपालार्पितैः पथि ॥33॥
उपगीयमानचरितः शतधृत्यादिभिर्मुदा । गोमूत्रयावकं श्रुत्वा भ्रातरं वल्कलाम्बरम् ॥34॥
महाकारुणिकोऽतप्यज्जटिलं स्थण्डिलेशयम् । भरतः प्राप्तमाकर्ण्य पौरामात्यपुरोहितैः ॥35॥
पादुके शिरसि न्यस्य रामं प्रत्युद्यतोऽग्रजम् । नन्दिग्रामात् स्वशिबिराद् गीतवादित्रनिःस्वनैः 36
ब्रह्मघोषेण च मुहुः पठद्भिर्ब्रह्मवादिभिः । स्वर्णकक्षपताकाभिर्हैमैश्चित्रध्वजै रथैः ॥37॥
सदश्वै रुक्मसन्नाहैर्भटैः पुरटवर्मभिः । श्रेणीभिर्वारमुख्याभिर्भृत्यैश्चैव पदानुगैः ॥38॥
पारमेष्ठ्यान्युपादाय पण्यान्युच्चावचानि च । पादयोर्न्यपतत् प्रेम्णा प्रक्लिन्नहृदयेक्षणः ॥39॥
पादुके न्यस्य पुरतः प्राञ्जलिर्बाष्पलोचनः । तमाश्लिष्य चिरं दोर्भ्यां स्नापयन् नेत्रजैर्जलैः ॥40॥

this city of Lanka has been widowed just as we have been. Your body has become the food for vultures, and your soul is heading for the tortures of hell.'

Sri Suka said: **29.** As advised by Rama, Vibhīshana now performed the obsequies of all the dead according to the injunctions. **30.** Next the Lord met Sita under a Simsapa tree in the Asoka grove, almost reduced to skin and bones by the sorrow of separation from him. **31.** Rama felt great compassion for his most miserably placed wife, whose face now bloomed with joy at the sight of him. **32-33.** Installing Vibhīshana as the king of the Rakshasas in Lanka, Rama along with Sita, Lakshmana, Sugrīva and Hanumān got into the aerial car called Pushpaka. He gave to Vibhīshana as gift the land of Lanka and a span of a long life lasting till the end of the Kalpa. Thus completing his vow of forest life for fourteen years, he returned to Ayodhya, worshipped with rains of flowers from above by the Devas.

Reception by Bharata (34-41)

34-36. Hearing on the way the hymns of praise sung by Indra and others, he reached his country to receive the sad report that his brother Bharata, out of sorrow for his expulsion, was living on a diet of mere barley cooked in cow's urine, wearing only the bark of trees, and sleeping on a bare floor. Now on hearing of his brother's arrival, Bharata started from his residence in Nandigrama to receive him fittingly. Accompanied by ministers, leading citizens, and elders, and amidst the auspicious sound of music, vocal and instrumental, he approached, carrying his brother's sandals on his own head. **37-39.** Accompanied by a long train consisting of expert Vedic scholars chanting the Vedic Mantras aloud, of banners with gilted fringes, of gold-inlaid chariots yoked to excellent horses and carrying gold flag-staff and equipments, and of guards with golden liveries, artistes, leading dancing girls and other retainers, he advanced towards Rama, presented to him the royal insignias like ceremonial umbrella and chowris, and fell down at his feet. **40.** He placed the sandals before Rama and with palms joined in salutation fell pro-

रामो लक्ष्मणसीताभ्यां विप्रेभ्यो येऽर्हसत्तमाः । तेभ्यः स्वयं नमश्चक्रे प्रजाभिश्च नमस्कृतः ॥41॥
धुन्वन्त उत्तरासङ्गान् पतिं वीक्ष्य चिरागतम् । उत्तराः कोसला माल्यैः किरन्तो ननृतुर्मुदा ॥42॥
पादुके भरतोऽगृह्णाच्चामरव्यजनोत्तमे । विभीषणः ससुग्रीवः श्वेतच्छत्रं मरुत्सुतः ॥43॥
धनुर्निषङ्गाञ्छत्रुघ्नः सीता तीर्थकमण्डलुम् । अबिभ्रदङ्गदः खड्गं हैमं चर्मर्क्षराण्नृप ॥44॥
पुष्पकस्थोऽन्वितः स्त्रीभिः स्तूयमानश्च वन्दिभिः । विरेजे भगवान् राजन् ग्रहैश्चन्द्र इवोदितः ॥45॥
भ्रातृभिर्नन्दितः सोऽपि सोत्सवां प्राविशत् पुरीम् । प्रविश्य राजभवनं गुरुपत्नीः स्वमातरम् ॥46॥
गुरून् वयस्यावरजान् पूजितः प्रत्यपूजयत् । वैदेही लक्ष्मणश्चैव यथावत् समुपेयतुः ॥47॥
पुत्रान् स्वमातरस्तास्तु प्राणांस्तन्व इवोत्थिताः । आरोप्याङ्केऽभिषिञ्चन्त्यो बाष्पौघैर्विजहुः शुचः 48
जटा निर्मुच्य विधिवत् कुलवृद्धैः समं गुरुः । अभ्यषिञ्चद् यथैवेन्द्रं चतुःसिन्धुजलादिभिः ॥49॥
एवं कृतशिरःस्नानः सुवासाः स्रग्व्यलङ्कृतः । स्वलङ्कृतैः सुवासोभिर्भ्रातृभिर्भार्यया बभौ ॥50॥
अग्रहीदासनं भ्रात्रा प्रणिपत्य प्रसादितः । प्रजाः स्वधर्मनिरता वर्णाश्रमगुणान्विताः ।
जुगोप पितृवद् रामो मेनिरे पितरं च तम् ॥51॥
त्रेतायां वर्तमानायां कालः कृतसमोऽभवत् । रामे राजनि धर्मज्ञे सर्वभूतसुखावहे ॥52॥

strate in front of him, his heart melting in love and eyes swimming in tears. And Rama embraced him tight and long, enfolding him with both hands and drenching him with a stream of tears. **41.** Along with Sita and Lakshmana, Rama made prostrations to holy men, and in turn received the obeisance of the subjects.

Coronation of Rama (42-56)

42. Seeing the Lord returned after fourteen years of absence, the residents of Uttarakosala were caught in a paroxysm of joy, and rained flowers and garlands and danced wildly, fluttering their upper garments. **43.** As he entered Ayodhya, Bharata bore his sandals, Sugrīva and Vibhīshana held the chowris on both sides, and Hanumān held the white royal umbrella. **44.** Satrughna carried his bow and arrows; Sita, his water vessel; Angada, his sword; and Jāmbavān, the leader of the bears, his gold-inlaid shield. **45.** As he sat in the Pushpaka vehicle, surrounded by women and extolling panegyrists, he looked like the rising moon whose beauty is enhanced by the surrounding galaxy of stars. **46-47.** After being greeted by all his brothers, he entered the palace with its festive decorations, saluted his mother, step-mothers and other elders, and was in turn greeted by juniors. Sita and Lakshmana too did likewise on entering the palace. **48.** Getting back their sons, their mothers sprang up with a new upsurge of energy, as the senses do when the Prana returns. They seated them in their laps and bathed them in tears of joy. **49.** Their preceptor removed the matted locks of Rama according to injunctions, and with the waters brought from the four oceans and the holy rivers, performed the ceremonial bath for the coronation with the help of the elders of the clan, as the celestial teacher Brihaspati did for Indra. **50.** Bathed, dressed in silk, and decorated with wreaths, he shone amidst his consort and brothers, who were also similarly bedecked. **51.** Prostrating before him, Bharata invited him to the royal throne and he accepted it. Like a father he ruled over his subjects who followed the rules of Dharma and the ways of life prescribed for the Varnas and the Ashramas. His subjects too looked upon him as a father. **52.** When Rama, the knower of

वनानि नद्यो गिरयो वर्षाणि द्वीपसिन्धवः । सर्वे कामदुघा आसन् प्रजानां भरतर्षभ ॥53॥
नाधिव्याधिजराग्लानिदुःखशोकभयक्लमाः । मृत्युश्चानिच्छतां नासीद् रामे राजन्यधोक्षजे ॥54॥
एकपत्नीव्रतधरो राजर्षिचरितः शुचिः । स्वधर्मं गृहमेधीयं शिक्षयन् स्वयमाचरत् ॥55॥
प्रेम्णानुवृत्त्या शीलेन प्रश्रयावनता सती । धिया ह्रिया च भावज्ञा भर्तुः सीताहरन्मनः ॥56॥

इति श्रीमद्भागवते महापुराणे पारमहंस्यां संहितायां नवमस्कन्धे रामचरिते दशमोऽध्यायः ॥10॥

all Dharma and the bestower of joy on all, ruled, it looked as if it was Kritayuga (golden age), though actually it was Treta (the next age, less perfect than the Krita). **53.** O leader of the Bharatas! Forests, rivers, mountains, regions, continents, oceans, all yielded the needs of his subjects when Rama ruled. **54.** While he was the king there were no worries, diseases, decrepitude, sorrow, fear, or depression for his subjects. Death came only when one wished. **55.** He lived observing the vow of having only a single consort, following all the sacred traditions of Rajarshis, and teaching men how to observe the scripture-ordained duties both by precept and example. **56.** And Sita by her humility, her skill in divining her husband's mind, her loving behaviour, ungrudging service, discrimination, good behaviour and modesty won the heart of her husband in every way.

अथैकादशोऽध्यायः

श्रीशुक उवाच

भगवानात्मनाऽऽत्मानं राम उत्तमकल्पकैः । सर्वदेवमयं देवमीज आचार्यवान् मखैः ॥ 1॥
होत्रेऽददाद् दिशं प्राचीं ब्रह्मणे दक्षिणां प्रभुः । अध्वर्यवे प्रतीचीं च उदीचीं सामगाय सः ॥ 2॥
आचार्याय ददौ शेषां यावती भूस्तदन्तरा । मन्यमान इदं कृत्स्नं ब्राह्मणोऽर्हति निःस्पृहः ॥ 3॥
इत्ययं तदलङ्कारवासोभ्यामवशेषितः । तथा राज्ञ्यपि वैदेही सौमङ्गल्यावशेषिता ॥ 4॥
ते तु ब्रह्मण्यदेवस्य वात्सल्यं वीक्ष्य संस्तुतम् । प्रीताः क्लिन्नधियस्तस्मै प्रत्यर्प्येदं बभाषिरे ॥ 5॥

Skandha IX : Chapter 11

SUBSEQUENT LIFE OF SRI RAMA AT AYODHYA

Rama's Sacrifice (1-7)

Sri Suka said: **1.** The worshipful Rama with the help of his preceptor performed many grand sacrifices adoring the Supreme Being who is the embodiment of all Divinities and identical with his own Self. **2.** In the sacrifice he gave as gift the eastern region of his kingdom to the priest Hotā, the southern regions to the priest Brahmā, the western parts to Adhvaryu, and the northern countries to the chanter of the Sāman (Udgātā). **3.** The remaining part of the land, which lay in the middle of the regions gifted, he wanted to give to one who had no desire or attachments, and he found a suitable recipient of that description in his own preceptor. **4.** After these gifts were made, the sole possessions left for him were his dress and decorations, and for his queen, her auspicious wedding necklace indicative of the married state. **5.** Seeing the magnitude of his devotion to holy

अप्रत्तं नस्त्वया किं नु भगवन् भुवनेश्वर । यन्नोऽन्तर्हृदयं विश्य तमो हंसि स्वरोचिषा ॥ 6॥
नमो ब्रह्मण्यदेवाय रामायाकुण्ठमेधसे । उत्तमश्लोकधुर्याय न्यस्तदण्डार्पिताङ्घ्रये ॥ 7॥
कदाचिल्लोकजिज्ञासुर्गूढो रात्र्यामलक्षितः । चरन् वाचोऽश्रृणोद् रामो भार्यामुद्दिश्य कस्यचित् 8
नाहं बिभर्मि त्वां दुष्टामसतीं परवेश्मगाम् । स्त्रीलोभी बिभृयात् सीतां रामो नाहं भजे पुनः 9॥
इति लोकाद् बहुमुखाद् दुराराध्यादसंविदः । पत्या भीतेन सा त्यक्ता प्राप्ता प्राचेतसाश्रमम् ॥10॥
अन्तर्वत्न्यागते काले यमौ सा सुषुवे सुतौ । कुशो लव इति ख्यातौ तयोश्चक्रे क्रिया मुनिः ॥11॥
अङ्गदश्चित्रकेतुश्च लक्ष्मणस्यात्मजौ स्मृतौ । तक्षः पुष्कल इत्यास्तां भरतस्य महीपते ॥12॥
सुबाहुः श्रुतसेनश्च शत्रुघ्नस्य बभूवतुः । गन्धर्वान् कोटिशो जघ्ने भरतो विजये दिशाम् 13॥
तदीयं धनमानीय सर्वं राज्ञे न्यवेदयत् । शत्रुघ्नश्च मधोः पुत्रं लवणं नाम राक्षसम् ।
हत्वा मधुवने चक्रे मथुरां नाम वै पुरीम् ॥14॥
मुनौ निक्षिप्य तनयौ सीता भर्त्रा विवासिता । ध्यायन्ती रामचरणौ विवरं प्रविवेश ह ॥15॥
तच्छ्रुत्वा भगवान् रामो रुन्धन्नपि धिया शुचः । स्मरंस्तस्या गुणांस्तांस्तान्नाशक्नोद् रोद्धुमीश्वरः

men, the heart of the recipients of his gifts melted out of respect and love, and they gave all those countries back to Rama and said: **6.** 'O worshipful one!, O Lord of all! What blessings are there that have not already been granted to us by Thee! For, entering into our heart, Thou hast dispelled even the darkness of ignorance from there. **7.** Salutation to Thee, the Supreme Being in the form of Sri Rama, who always honours devotees, whose light of knowledge never fades, who is most noted for his holy fame, and whose feet reside for ever in the hearts of those who have abandoned hatred.

Last Phase of Rama's Life (8-19)

8. Once when Rama was moving about incognito at night unknown to any in order to ascertain the real views of his people, he happened to hear by chance the following talk of some one about his wife Sita. **9.** 'I shall not,' he said, ' any more entertain you in my house—you who have lived in another's residence, who is unchaste and of evil nature. I am not going to follow the example of the uxorious Rama, who is still living with Sita.' **10.** Frightened, as it were, by this kind of irresponsible criticism of the ignorant who are difficult to satisfy or placate, Rama abandoned Sita. Thereupon she took shelter in the Ashrama of Valmiki. **11.** Sita was in the family way at the time of her abandonment, and in due time she gave birth to twins, who became famous under the names of Lava and Kusa. The sage Valmiki performed all their post-natal ceremonies.

12. O King, Lakshmana had two sons named Angada and Chitraketu, and Bharata also two whose names were Taksha and Pushkala. **13.** Satrughna too had two sons named Subāhu and Srutasena. In his conquest of the quarters Bharata destroyed a very large number of Gandharvas. **14.** He brought large booties from his conquests and presented it all to Rama. Satrughna defeated and killed in battle the Rakshasa known as Lavana, the son of Madhu, and established the famous city of Mathura in Madhuvana.

15. Sita entrusted her sons to the sage Valmiki. Unable to bear separation from Rama, she it seems entered into the bowels of the earth, contemplating on him. **16.** Hearing this, Rama, though he was the Lord incarnate, could not control

स्त्रीपुंप्रसङ्ग एतादृक् सर्वत्र त्रासमावहः । अपीश्वराणां किमुत ग्राम्यस्य गृहचेतसः ॥17॥
तत ऊर्ध्वं ब्रह्मचर्यं धारयन्नजुहोत् प्रभुः । त्रयोदशाब्दसाहस्रमग्निहोत्रमखण्डितम् ॥18॥
स्मरतां हृदि विन्यस्य विद्धं दण्डककण्टकैः । स्वपादपल्लवं राम आत्मज्योतिरगात् ततः ॥19॥

नेदं यशो रघुपतेः सुरयाच्ञयाऽऽत्तलीलातनोरधिकसाम्यविमुक्तधाम्नः ।
रक्षोवधो जलधिबन्धनमस्त्रपूगैः किं तस्य शत्रुहनने कपयः सहायाः ॥20॥
यस्यामलं नृपसदस्सु यशोऽधुनापि गायन्त्यघघ्नमृषयो दिगिभेन्द्रपट्टम् ।
तं नाकपालवसुपालकिरीटजुष्टपादाम्बुजं रघुपतिं शरणं प्रपद्ये ॥21॥

स यैः स्पृष्टोऽभिदृष्टो वा संविष्टोऽनुगतोऽपि वा । कोसलास्ते ययुः स्थानं यत्र गच्छन्ति योगिनः ॥22॥
पुरुषो रामचरितं श्रवणैरुपधारयन् । आनृशंस्यपरो राजन् कर्मबन्धैर्विमुच्यते ॥23॥

राजोवाच

कथं स भगवान् रामो भ्रातॄन् वा स्वयमात्मनः । तस्मिन् वा तेऽन्ववर्तन्त प्रजाः पौराश्च ईश्वरे ॥24॥

श्रीशुक उवाच

अथादिशद् दिग्विजये भ्रातॄंस्त्रिभुवनेश्वरः । आत्मानं दर्शयन् स्वानां पुरीमैक्षत सानुगः ॥25॥

his sorrow in spite of his best efforts, remembering all the great qualities of Sita. **17.** The intensity of attachment between man and woman is of this order, even in the case of those with mastery over their minds. Needless then to say what it would be like, in the case of an ordinary householder with worldly attachments. **18.** Since Sita's depature, Rama, even while observing the vow of strict celibacy, performed Agnihotra for the thirteen thousand years of his life (without the aid of a wife). **19.** After that, Rama entered that Supreme State of his, leaving behind his feet lacerated with thorns in his Dandakāranya days in the heart of devotees to contemplate upon.

The Greatness of Rama (20-23)

20. For Rama, the Supreme Being who assumed a sportive body at the earnest prayer of the Devas, whose prowess is unequalled and unexcelled, it is not a high achievement but a trifle to have crossed the sea bridging it, and destroyed the hosts of Asuras with his arrows, though poets have described them as wonderful achievements adding to his glory. What need is there for him to seek the help of monkeys to destroy his enemies! **21.** I seek refuge at the feet of Rama whose feet are ever contacted by the crowns of kings and divinities, whose pure and sin-destroying fame, extending to the very quarters, adds lustre to the frontal plates of the elephants guarding the cardinal points, and who is constantly hymned by sages in the royal assemblies. **22.** Among these residents of Kosala, whoever touched him, saw him, sat with him, followed him—all of them attained to that state which great Yogis attain. **23.** O King! By hearing Rama's story and thinking over it, man is established in the peaceful state of devotion and becomes free from the bondage of Karma.

Rama at Ayodhya (24-36)

The Rajah asked: **24.** How did worshipful Rama spend his life? How did he deal with his brothers, who were his own parts? How did his brothers, subjects, and citizens, in turn, deal with that divine personage?

Sri Suka replied: **25.** After he ascended

आसिक्तमार्गां गन्धोदैः करिणां मदशीकरैः । स्वामिनं प्राप्तमालोक्य मत्तां वा सुतरामिव ॥26॥
प्रासादगोपुरसभाचैत्यदेवगृहादिषु । विन्यस्तहेमकलशैः पताकाभिश्च मण्डिताम् ॥27॥
पूगैः सवृन्तै रम्भाभिः पट्टिकाभिः सुवाससाम् । आदर्शैरंशुकैः स्रग्भिः कृतकौतुकतोरणाम् ॥28॥
तमुपेयुस्तत्र तत्र पौरा अर्हणपाणयः । आशिषो युयुजुर्देव पाहीमां प्राक् त्वयोद्धृताम् 29॥
ततः प्रजा वीक्ष्य पतिं चिरागतं दिदृक्षयोत्सृष्टगृहाः स्त्रियो नराः ।
आरुह्य हर्म्याण्यरविन्दलोचनमतृप्तनेत्राः कुसुमैरवाकिरन् ॥30॥
अथ प्रविष्टः स्वगृहं जुष्टं स्वैः पूर्वराजभिः । अनन्ताखिलकोशाढ्यमनर्घ्योरुपरिच्छदम् ॥31॥
विद्रुमोदुम्बरद्वारैर्वैदूर्यस्तम्भपङ्क्तिभिः । स्थलैर्मारकतैः स्वच्छैर्भ्राजत्स्फटिकभित्तिभिः ॥32॥
चित्रस्रग्भिः पट्टिकाभिर्वासोमणिगणांशुकैः । मुक्ताफलैश्चिदुल्लासैः कान्तकामोपपत्तिभिः ॥33॥
धूपदीपैः सुरभिभिर्मण्डितं पुष्पमण्डनैः । स्त्रीपुम्भिः सुरसंकाशैर्जुष्टं भूषणभूषणैः ॥34॥
तस्मिन् स भगवान् रामः स्निग्धया प्रिययेष्टया । रेमे स्वाराममधीराणामृषभः सीतया किल ॥35॥
बुभुजे च यथाकालं कामान् धर्ममपीडयन् । वर्षपूगान् बहून् नृणामभिध्याताङ्घ्रिपल्लवः 36॥

इति श्रीमद्भागवते महापुराणे पारमहंस्यां संहितायां नवमस्कन्धे श्रीरामोपाख्याने एकादशोऽध्यायः ॥11॥

the throne, he sent his brothers on Digvijaya or expeditions for the establishment of his supremacy over all the surrounding countries. And he went with followers all over his kingdom, enabling all his subjects to have a sight of his auspicious form. **26.** He saw the city, with its roads moistened by fragrant water and ichor of elephants in rut, gazing at him, like an inebriated woman, as it were, at its master on his return after a lapse of fourteen years. **27-28.** He went around the city seeing its terraced houses, gate-towers, assembly halls, and places of worship covered with golden domes and banners, as well as other places decorated with arecanut palms, fruit-laden banana plants, flags of superior cloth, mirrors, draperies and garlands. **29.** Wherever he went, the citizens approached him with presents and glorified him, saying, 'O Lord! Deign to protect this earth which Thou didst once save in Thy incarnation as the Cosmic Boar.' **30.** Seeing their Lord and master come after a long time, the people, both men and women, left their homes and ascended balconies of wayside houses, and looked at that lotus-eyed one from there with unsatiated looks, and showered flowers on him.

31. Afterwards he entered the palace of his ancestors, which had treasuries with countless number of gems and numerous fittings and furniture of inestimable value. **32-34.** It had doorways of coral; lines of pillars made of cat's eye (Vaidūrya); clean floors of emeralds; and shining walls studded with crystals. It was decorated with garlands of many kinds, draperies, shining gems, pearl strings, and all kinds of attractive and enjoyable objects. The inside of the palace was well lighted and filled with the fragrance of incense, and was occupied by celestial-like and well-bedecked men and women who by their beauty were an ornament to the very ornaments they wore. **35.** Rama, who was the greatest among the self-controlled ones, lived happily in that palace with Sita who was full of love for him and for whom he was in turn full of love. **36.** Worshipped by all, he lived there for several hundred years, having such enjoyments of life as are permitted by Dharma.

अथ द्वादशोऽध्यायः

श्रीशुक उवाच

कुशस्य चातिथिस्तस्मान्निषधस्तत्सुतो नभः । पुण्डरीकोऽथ तत्पुत्रः क्षेमधन्वाभवत्ततः ॥ 1॥
देवानीकस्ततोऽनीहः पारियात्रोऽथ तत्सुतः । ततो बलस्थलस्तस्माद्वज्रनाभोऽर्कसम्भवः ॥ 2॥
खगणस्तत्सुतस्तस्माद् विधृतिश्चाभवत् सुतः । ततो हिरण्यनाभोऽभूद्योगाचार्यस्तु जैमिनेः ॥ 3॥
शिष्यः कौसल्य आध्यात्मं याज्ञवल्क्योऽध्यगाद् यतः । योगं महोदयमृषिर्हृदयग्रन्थिभेदकम् ॥ 4॥
पुष्यो हिरण्यनाभस्य ध्रुवसन्धिस्ततोऽभवत् । सुदर्शनोऽथाग्निवर्णः शीघ्रस्तस्य मरुः सुतः ॥ 5॥
योऽसावास्ते योगसिद्धः कलापग्राममाश्रितः । कलेरन्ते सूर्यवंशं नष्टं भावयिता पुनः ॥ 6॥
तस्मात् प्रसुश्रुतस्तस्य सन्धिस्तस्याप्यमर्षणः । महस्वांस्तत्सुतस्तस्माद् विश्वसाह्वोऽन्वजायत 7॥
ततः प्रसेनजित् तस्मात् तक्षको भविता पुनः । ततो बृहद्बलो यस्तु पित्रा ते समरे हतः ॥ 8॥
एते हीक्ष्वाकुभूपाला अतीताः शृण्वनागतान् । बृहद्बलस्य भविता पुत्रो नाम बृहद्रणः ॥ 9॥
उरुक्रियस्ततस्तस्य वत्सवृद्धो भविष्यति । प्रतिव्योमस्ततो भानुर्दिवाको वाहिनीपतिः ॥10॥
सहदेवस्ततो वीरो बृहदश्वोऽथ भानुमान् । प्रतीकाश्वो भानुमतः सुप्रतीकोऽथ तत्सुतः ॥11॥
भविता मरुदेवोऽथ सुनक्षत्रोऽथ पुष्करः । तस्यान्तरिक्षस्तत्पुत्रः सुतपास्तदमित्रजित् ॥12॥

Skandha IX : Chapter 12

KUSA AND HIS SUCCESSORS

From Kusa to Brihadbala (1-8)

Sri Suka said: **1.** Rama's son Kusa had Atithi as his son; he, Nishadha; he, Nabha; he, Pundarīka, and he, Kshemadhanvā. **2.** To Kshemadhanvā was born Devānīka; to him, Anīha; to him, Pāriyātra; to him, Balasthala; and to him Vajranābha who was a part of the sun-deity. **3-4.** His son was Khagana; his, Vidhriti; and his, Hiranyanābha who was the disciple of Jaimini and a teacher of Yoga. It was from him that Yājnavalkya of Kosala learnt the science of the Self which enables one to overcome ignorance and attain great illumination.

5. Hiranyanābha's son was Pushya; his son, Dhruvasandhi; his son, Sudarsana; his son, Agnivarna; his son, Sīghra; and his son, Maru. **6.** That Maru, who is perfect in Yoga, stays in Kalāpagrāma. At the end of the age of Kali he will revive the solar dynasty that would have perished by that time. **7.** From him Prasusruta was born; from him, Sandhi; from him, Amarshana; from him, Mahasvā; and from him, Viswasāhva; **8.** From him Prasenajit was born; from him, Takshaka; and from him, Brihadbala. This Brihadbala was slain in battle by your father (Abhimanyu).

End of the Solar Dynasty (9-16)

9. These are the past rulers of the Solar Dynasty. Now hear of the future kings. Brihadbala will have a son Brihadrana. **10.** His son will be Urukriya; his son, Vatsavriddha; his son, Prativyoma; his son, Bhānu; and his son, Divāka a leader of vast hosts. **11.** From Divāka will be born Sahadeva; from him, heroic Brihadasva; from him, Bhānumān; from him, Pratīkāswa; and from him, Supratīka. **12.** From Supratīka will be born Marudeva; from him, Sunakshatra; from him, Pushkara; from him, Antariksha; from

बृहद्राजस्तु तस्यापि बर्हिस्तस्मात् कृतञ्जयः । रणञ्जयस्तस्य सुतः सञ्जयो भविता ततः ॥13॥
तस्माच्छाक्योऽथ शुद्धोदो लाङ्गलस्तत्सुतः स्मृतः । ततः प्रसेनजित् तस्मात् क्षुद्रको भविता ततः ॥14॥
रणको भविता तस्मात् सुरथस्तनयस्ततः । सुमित्रो नाम निष्ठान्त एते बार्हद्बलान्वयाः ॥15॥
इक्ष्वाकूणामयं वंशः सुमित्रान्तो भविष्यति । यतस्तं प्राप्य राजानं संस्थां प्राप्स्यति वै कलौ ॥16॥

इति श्रीमद्भागवते महापुराणे पारमहंस्यां संहितायां नवमस्कन्धे इक्ष्वाकुवंशवर्णनं नाम द्वादशोऽध्यायः ॥12॥

him, Sutapas; and from him, Amitrajit. **13.** From Amitrajit will be born Brihadrāja; from him, Barhis; from him, Kritanjaya; from him, Rananjaya; and from him, Sanjaya. **14.** From him will be born Sākya; from him, Suddhoda; from him, Lāngala; from him, Prasenajit; and from him, Kshudraka. **15.** From him will be born Ranaka; from him, Suratha; and from him, Sumitra, the last of this dynasty. All these are of the line of Brihadbala. **16.** The line of Ikshvāku ends with Sumitra. For, with this king this dynasty will perish in the age of Kali.

अथ त्रयोदशोऽध्यायः

श्रीशुक उवाच

निमिरिक्ष्वाकुतनयो वसिष्ठमवृतर्त्विजम् । आरभ्य सत्रं सोऽप्याह शक्रेण प्राग्वृतोऽस्मि भोः 1॥
तं निर्वर्त्यागमिष्यामि तावन्मां प्रतिपालय । तूष्णीमासीद् गृहपतिः सोऽपीन्द्रस्याकरोन्मखम् 2॥
निमिश्चलमिदं विद्वान् सत्रमारभतात्मवान् । ऋत्विग्भिरपरैस्तावन्नागमद् यावता गुरुः ॥ 3॥
शिष्यव्यतिक्रमं वीक्ष्य निर्वर्त्य गुरुरागतः । अशपत् पतताद् देहो निमेः पण्डितमानिनः ॥ 4॥
निमिः प्रतिददौ शापं गुरवेऽधर्मवर्तिने । तवापि पतताद् देहो लोभाद् धर्ममजानतः ॥ 5॥
इत्युत्ससर्ज स्वं देहं निमिरध्यात्मकोविदः । मित्रावरुणयोर्जज्ञे उर्वश्यां प्रपितामहः ॥ 6॥

Skandha IX : Chapter 13

LINE OF NIMI THE SON OF IKSHVĀKU

Nimi and Vasishtha (1-11)

Sri Suka said: **1-2.** Nimi, the son of Ikshvāku, chose Vasishtha as his sacrificial priest when he started the performance of a Satra. Vasishtha, however, told him: 'I have already been chosen as sacrificial priest by Indra. I shall finish that duty and come. Please wait till then.' Nimi kept silent and Vasishtha went for conducting the sacrifice of Indra. **3.** Being a wise and self-controlled man, Nimi knew that the duration of life is very uncertain. So he started the sacrifice, even before the preceptor Vasishtha's return, with the help of some other sacrificial priests. **4.** Returning after Indra's Yajna, the preceptor came to know of the audacious act of his disciple in contravening his behest. He therefore cursed him, saying, 'You who arrogantly consider yourself to be so learned—may your body fall down dead!' **5.** Nimi also pronounced a counter-curse on the preceptor who had cursed him contrary to the principles of Dharma. He declared, 'May you, who out of greed have forgotten Dharma, also fall down dead.'

6. Saying so, Nimi, who was a knower of the Self, abandoned his body. And

गन्धवस्तुषु तद्देहं निधाय मुनिसत्तमाः। समाप्ते सत्रयागेऽथ देवानूचुः समागतान् ॥ 7॥
राज्ञो जीवतु देहोऽयं प्रसन्नाः प्रभवो यदि। तथेत्युक्ते निमिः प्राह मा भून्मे देहबन्धनम् ॥ 8॥
यस्य योगं न वाञ्छन्ति वियोगभयकातराः। भजन्ति चरणाम्भोजं मुनयो हरिमेधसः ॥ 9॥
देहं नावरुरुत्सेऽहं दुःखशोकभयावहम्। सर्वत्रास्य यतो मृत्युर्मत्स्यानामुदके यथा ॥10॥

देवा ऊचुः

विदेह उष्यतां कामं लोचनेषु शरीरिणाम्। उन्मेषणनिमेषाभ्यां लक्षितोऽध्यात्मसंस्थितः ॥11॥
अराजकभयं नृणां मन्यमाना महर्षयः। देहं ममन्थुः स्म निमेः कुमारः समजायत ॥12॥
जन्मना जनकः सोऽभूद् वैदेहस्तु विदेहजः। मिथिलो मथनाज्जातो मिथिला येन निर्मिता ॥13॥
तस्मादुदावसुस्तस्य पुत्रोऽभून्नन्दिवर्धनः। ततः सुकेतुस्तस्यापि देवरातो महीपते ॥14॥
तस्माद् बृहद्रथस्तस्य महावीर्यः सुधृत्पिता। सुधृतेर्धृष्टकेतुर्वै हर्यश्वोऽथ मरुस्ततः ॥15॥
मरोः प्रतीपकस्तस्माज्जातः कृतिरथो यतः। देवमीढस्तस्य सुतो विश्रुतोऽथ महाधृतिः ॥16॥
कृतिरातस्ततस्तस्मान्महारोमाथ तत्सुतः। स्वर्णरोमा सुतस्तस्य ह्रस्वरोमा व्यजायत ॥17॥
ततः सीरध्वजो जज्ञे यज्ञार्थं कर्षतो महीम्। सीता सीराग्रतो जाता तस्मात् सीरध्वजः स्मृतः 18
कुशध्वजस्तस्य पुत्रस्ततो धर्मध्वजो नृपः। धर्मध्वजस्य द्वौ पुत्रौ कृतध्वजमितध्वजौ ॥19॥

Vasishtha, leaving the present body was born as a son of Mitra and Varuna by Urvasi. **7.** The sages preserved the body of Nimi by embalming it in oil made fragrant with medications. In the presence of the embalmed body, they continued the sacrifice, and at the close of it, said to the Devas present. **8.** 'If you are powerful and if you are pleased with the sacrifice, may the body of king Nimi become alive.' **9.** When the Devas granted this prayer, Nimi (disembodied) said: 'I do not need this imprisonment in the body any more. **10.** Wise ones do not desire to have a body, knowing that they will have to leave it also. They therefore adore the feet of Hari, by whose adoration they get freedom from the cycle of births and deaths.' *The Devas thereupon said:* **11.** 'Even without any body, may you reside on the eyelids of living beings.' Residing there, he is supposed to function as the opening and closing of the eyelids of creatures when they wink.

Nimi's son Janaka, the Videha (12-27)

12. Afraid of anarchy among men, the sages churned the body of Nimi, and a child was born by that process. **13.** He came to be known by three names. Because of his unusual birth he was known as Janaka. As he was born of one who had abandoned his body he got the name of Vaideha. And as his birth took place by Mathana, churning, he came to be known as Mithila. It was he who founded the city of Mithilā.

14. His son was Udāvasu: his, Nandivardhana; his, Suketu; and his, Devarāta. **15.** From him was born Brihadratha; from him, Mahāvīrya; from him, Sudhriti; from him, Dhrishtaketu; from him, Haryasva; and from him, Maru. **16.** From Maru was born Pratīpaka; from him, Kritiratha; from him, Devamīdha; from him, Visruta; and from him, Mahādhriti. **17.** Mahādhriti's son was Kritirāta; his son, Mahāromā; his son, Svarnaromā; and his son, Hrasvaromā. **18.** Of Hrasvaromā was born Sīradhwaja. It was when he was ploughing the land to grow cereals for Yajna that Sita was recovered from the furrow cut by the plough. So he came to be known as Sīradhwaja (plough-bannered). **19.** His son was Ku-

कृतध्वजात् केशिध्वजः खाण्डिक्यस्तु मितध्वजात् । कृतध्वजसुतो राजन्नात्मविद्याविशारदः ॥20॥
खाण्डिक्यःकर्मतत्त्वज्ञो भीतःकेशिध्वजाद् द्रुतः । भानुमांस्तस्य पुत्रोऽभूच्छतद्युम्नस्तु तत्सुतः ॥21॥
शुचिस्तत्तनयस्तस्मात् सनद्वाजस्ततोऽभवत् । ऊर्ध्वकेतुः सनद्वाजादजोऽथ पुरुजित्सुतः ॥22॥
अरिष्टनेमिस्तस्यापि श्रुतायुस्तत्सुपार्श्वकः । ततश्चित्ररथो यस्य क्षेमधिर्मिथिलाधिपः ॥23॥
तस्मात् समरथस्तस्य सुतः सत्यरथस्ततः । आसीदुपगुरुस्तस्मादुपगुप्तोऽग्निसम्भवः ॥24॥
वस्वनन्तोऽथ तत्पुत्रो युयुधो यत्सुभाषणः । श्रुतस्ततो जयस्तस्माद् विजयोऽस्मादृतःसुतः ॥25॥
शुनकस्तत्सुतो जज्ञे वीतहव्यो धृतिस्ततः । बहुलाश्वो धृतेस्तस्य कृतिरस्य महावशी ॥26॥
एते वै मैथिला राजन्नात्मविद्याविशारदाः । योगेश्वरप्रसादेन द्वन्द्वैर्मुक्ता गृहेष्वपि ॥27॥

इति श्रीमद्भागवते महापुराणे पारमहंस्यां संहितायां नवमस्कन्धे निमिवंशानुवर्णनं नाम त्रयोदशोऽध्यायः ॥13॥

sadhwaja; and from him king Dharmadhwaja was born. Dharmadhwaja had two sons named Kritadhwaja and Mitadhwaja. **20.** From Kritadhwaja was born Kesidhwaja; and from Mitadhwaja, Khāndikya. O King! Of these, the son of Kritadhwaja named Kesidhwaja became an adept in the science of the Self (Atma Vidya) **21.** Khāndikya who was versed in the science of rituals was afraid of Kesidhwaja, the expert in Atma Vidya, and ran away from fear of him! Kesidhwaja's son was Bhānumān; and his son Satadyumna. **22.** His son was Suchi; his son, Sanadwāja; and his son, Ūrdvaketu. He had a son Aja to whom was born Purujit as son. **23.** From Purujit was born Arishtanemi; from him, Srutāyus; from him, Supārsvaka; from him, Chitraratha; and from him, Kshemadhi. All these were kings of Mithilā. **24.** To Kshemadhi was born Samaratha; to him, Satyaratha; to him, Upaguru; and to him, Upagupta, who was a part of the fire-deity. **25.** His son was Vasvananta; his son, Yuyudha; his son, Subhāshana; his son, Sruta; his son, Jaya; his son, Vijaya, and his son, Rita. **26.** His son was Sunaka; his son, Vītahavya; his son, Dhriti; his son, Bahulāsva; his son, Kriti; and his son Mahāvasī. **27.** O King! These kings of Mithilā were versed in the knowledge of the Atman, and remained free from attachments even while living as householders, owing to the grace of great Yoga teachers like Yājnavalkya.

अथ चतुर्दशोऽध्यायः

श्रीशुक उवाच

अथातः श्रूयतां राजन् वंशः सोमस्य पावनः । यस्मिन्नैलादयो भूपाः कीर्त्यन्ते पुण्यकीर्तयः ॥ 1॥
सहस्रशिरसः पुंसो नाभिह्रदसरोरुहात् । जातस्यासीत् सुतां धातुरत्रिः पितृसमो गुणैः ॥ 2॥

Skandha IX : Chapter 14

PURŪRAVAS OF THE LUNAR DYNASTY

Soma the First of the Dynasty (1-7)

Sri Suka said: **1.** O King! Now hear about the holy Lunar Dynasty. In that dynasty were born kings of holy fame like Aila otherwise known as Purūravas. **2.**

तस्य दृग्भ्योऽभवत् पुत्रः सोमोऽमृतमयः किल। विप्रौषध्युडुगणानां ब्रह्मणा कल्पितः पतिः ॥ 3॥
सोऽयजद् राजसूयेन विजित्य भुवनत्रयम्। पत्नीं बृहस्पतेर्दर्पात् तारां नामाहरद्बलात् ॥ 4॥
यदा स देवगुरुणा याचितोऽभीक्ष्णशो मदात्। नात्यजत् तत्कृते जज्ञे सुरदानवविग्रहः ॥ 5॥
शुक्रो बृहस्पतेर्द्वेषादग्रहीत् सासुरोडुपम्। हरो गुरुसुतं स्नेहात् सर्वभूतगणावृतः ॥ 6॥
सर्वदेवगणोपेतो महेन्द्रो गुरुमन्वयात्। सुरासुरविनाशोऽभूत् समरस्तारकामयः ॥ 7॥
निवेदितोऽथाङ्गिरसा सोमं निर्भर्त्स्य विश्वकृत्। तारां स्वभर्त्रे प्रायच्छदन्तर्वत्नीमवैत् पतिः ॥ 8॥
त्यज त्यजाशु दुष्प्रज्ञे मत्क्षेत्रादाहितं परैः। नाहं त्वां भस्मसात् कुर्यां स्त्रियं सान्तानिकः सति ॥
तत्याज व्रीडिता तारा कुमारं कनकप्रभम्। स्पृहामाङ्गिरसश्चक्रे कुमारे सोम एव च ॥10॥
ममायं न तवेत्युच्चैस्तस्मिन् विवदमानयोः। पप्रच्छुर्ऋषयो देवा नैवोचे व्रीडिता तु सा ॥11॥
कुमारो मातरं प्राह कुपितोऽलीकलज्जया। किं न वोचस्यसद्वृत्ते आत्मावद्यं वदाशु मे ॥12॥
ब्रह्मा तां रह आहूय समप्राक्षीच्च सान्त्वयन्। सोमस्येत्याह शनकैः सोमस्तं तावदग्रहीत् ॥13॥
तस्यात्मयोनिरकृत बुध इत्यभिधां नृप। बुद्ध्या गम्भीरया येन पुत्रेणापोडुराण्मुदम् ॥14॥

From the navel-lotus of the thousand-headed Cosmic Being, Brahma was born, and to him was born Atri, a sage equal to his father in meritorious qualities. **3.** From the tears of bliss that flowed from Atri's eyes was born Soma (moon-deity) who is of the nature of nectar (Amrita). Brahma made him the master of Brahmanas, herbage, and the stars. **4.** Conquering all the three worlds, he performed several Rajasuyas. Out of his inordinate arrogance he abducted Brihaspati's wife Tārā. **5.** In spite of Brihaspati's repeated requests to him for the release of Tārā, Soma heeded not, out of his pride and infatuation. As a sequel a fierce war broke out between the Devas and Asuras. **6.** Owing to his enmity towards Brihaspati, Sukra, the preceptor of the Asuras, took the side of Soma, the moon-deity, along with his Asura following. And Rudra, because of his love for his own preceptor Angiras whose son Brihaspati was, took the side of the latter along with all his host of spirits and elementals. **7.** Indra joined the side of his preceptor Brihaspati along with all the Devas. Thus on account of Tārā arose a war between Devas and Asuras, highly destructive to both sides.

Budha the Son of Soma (8-14)

8. Requested by the sage Angiras, Brahma reprimanded Soma and made him restore Tārā to Brihaspati. But Brihaspati found her big with child. **9.** Thereupon Brihaspati said: 'O evil one! Throw out, throw out the foetus planted by others in your womb, which is my field. Do not however be afraid that I shall reduce you to ashes, my good lady. For I am myself most eager for an issue.' **10.** Tārā thereupon bashfully ejected the foetus, which turned out to be a boy luminous like gold. Both Brihaspati and Soma developed interest in that infant. **11.** While Brihaspati and Soma were disputing about the ownership of the child, the Devas and the Rishis asked Tārā to declare whose it was. She only remained silent bashfully. **12.** At this the child became angry and said to his mother: 'O evil woman! Why do you cover up your sin with false bashfulness? Speak out!' **13.** Brahma thereupon consoled her with gentle words and questioned her in privacy. She reluctantly admitted that Soma was the father of the child. So Soma took possession of that child. **14.** O King! Brahma named him Budha.

ततः पुरूरवा जज्ञे इलायां य उदाहृतः। तस्य रूपगुणौदार्यशीलद्रविणविक्रमान् ॥15॥
श्रुत्वोर्वशीन्द्रभवने गीयमानान् सुरर्षिणा। तदन्तिकमुपेयाय देवी स्मरशरार्दिता ॥16॥
मित्रावरुणयोः शापादापन्ना नरलोकताम्। निशम्य पुरुषश्रेष्ठं कन्दर्पमिव रूपिणम्।
धृतिं विष्टभ्य ललना उपतस्थे तदन्तिके ॥17॥
स तां विलोक्य नृपतिर्हर्षेणोत्फुल्ललोचनः। उवाच श्लक्ष्णया वाचा देवीं हृष्टतनूरुहः ॥18॥

राजोवाच

स्वागतं ते वरारोहे आस्यतां करवाम किम्। संरमस्व मया साकं रतिर्नौ शाश्वतीः समाः ॥19॥

उर्वश्युवाच

कस्यास्त्वयि न सज्जेत मनो दृष्टिश्च सुन्दर। यदङ्गान्तरमासाद्य च्यवते ह रिरंसया ॥20॥
एतावुरणकौ राजन् न्यासौ रक्षस्व मानद। संरंस्ये भवता साकं श्लाघ्यः स्त्रीणां वरः स्मृतः ॥21॥
घृतं मे वीर भक्ष्यं स्यान्नेक्षे त्वान्यत्र मैथुनात्। विवाससं तत् तथेति प्रतिपेदे महामनाः ॥22॥
अहो रूपमहो भावो नरलोकविमोहनम्। को न सेवेत मनुजो देवीं त्वां स्वयमागताम् ॥23॥
तया स पुरुषश्रेष्ठो रमयन्त्या यथार्हतः। रेमे सुरविहारेषु कामं चैत्ररथादिषु ॥24॥
रममाणस्तया देव्या पद्मकिञ्जल्कगन्धया। तन्मुखामोदमुषितो मुमुदेऽहर्गणान् बहून् ॥25॥

Soma, the king of the stars, was rejoiced to find him highly intelligent.

Purūravas unites with Urvasi (15-25)

15-16. As stated earlier (IX.1.35) King Purūravas was born as the son of Budha by Ila. Hearing from Narada about the form, virtues, wealth, courage and other attractive features of Purūravas, the heavenly beauty Urvasi fell in love with him and approached him. **17-18.** Owing to a curse by Mitra and Varuna, Urvasi was consigned to earth. Hearing about Purūravas, who was in beauty like Cupid embodied, Urvasi mustered courage to appear before him. That king was delighted to see her, and with eyes wide open and horripilations all over, he spoke to her softly. *The Rajah said:* **19.** 'Welcome to you, O beauty! Please be seated. What can I do for you? Enjoy life with me for long years to come.' *Urvasi replied:* **20.** 'O handsome one! There is no woman whose eyes and mind would not get stuck to you. Desirous of the delight of your embrace, my mind and my eyes refuse to part from your limbs. **21.** I shall enjoy life with you, O King, who has done me this honour! Protect like a treasure these two rams of mine that I entrust to you. I shall certainly enjoy life with one like you. For on praiseworthy men fall the choice of women. **22.** I should be fed with ghee which forms my diet. I should also never see you naked except at the time of love-making.' Purūravas, intelligent as he was, agreed to these conditions. (He said:) **23.** 'O what a form! what a form! What a loving demeanour! All the world would get infatuated by it. Where is the man that will not oblige a woman of this kind, who has approached him of her own accord?' **24.** Purūravas now sported as he pleased in the heavenly gardens like Chaitraratha in the company of Urvasi who was an expert in purveying pleasure. **25.** Inebriated with the sweet flavour of her mouth, he sported for long years with her, whose body emitted the fragrance of lotus.

Purūravas separated from Urvasi (26-39)

अपश्यन्नुर्वशीमिन्द्रो गन्धर्वान् समचोदयत् । उर्वशीरहितं मह्यमास्थानं नातिशोभते ।।26।।
ते उपेत्य महारात्रे तमसि प्रत्युपस्थिते । उर्वश्या उरणौ जह्रुर्न्यस्तौ राजनि जायया ।।27।।
निशम्याक्रन्दितं देवी पुत्रयोर्नीयमानयोः । हतास्म्यहं कुनाथेन नपुंसा वीरमानिना ।।28।।
यद्विश्रम्भादहं नष्टा हृतापत्या च दस्युभिः । यः शेते निशि संत्रस्तो यथा नारी दिवा पुमान् ।।29।।
इति वाक्सायकैर्विद्धः प्रतोत्त्रैरिव कुञ्जरः । निशि निस्त्रिंशमादाय विवस्त्रोऽभ्यद्रवद् रुषा ।30।।
ते विसृज्योरणौ तत्र व्यद्योतन्त स्म विद्युतः । आदाय मेषावायान्तं नग्नमैक्षत सा पतिम् ।।31।।
ऐलोऽपि शयने जायामपश्यन् विमना इव । तच्चित्तो विह्वलः शोचन् बभ्रामोन्मत्तवन्महीम् 32
स तां वीक्ष्य कुरुक्षेत्रे सरस्वत्यां च तत्सखीः । पञ्च प्रहृष्टवदनाः प्राह सूक्तं पुरूरवाः ।।33।।
अहो जाये तिष्ठ तिष्ठ घोरे न त्यक्तुमर्हसि । मां त्वमद्याप्यनिर्वृत्य वचांसि कृणवावहै ।।34।।
सुदेहोऽयं पतत्यत्र देवि दूरं हृतस्त्वया । खादन्त्येनं वृका गृध्रास्त्वत्प्रसादस्य नास्पदम् ।।35।।

उर्वश्युवाच

मा मृथाः पुरुषोऽसि त्वं स्म त्वाद्युर्वृका इमे । क्वापि सख्यं न वै स्त्रीणां वृकाणां हृदयं यथा ।।36।।
स्त्रियो ह्यकरुणाः क्रूरा दुर्मर्षाः प्रियसाहसाः । घ्नन्त्यल्पार्थेऽपि विश्रब्धं पतिं भ्रातरमप्युत ।।37।।
विधायालीकविश्रम्भमज्ञेषु त्यक्तसौहृदाः । नवं नवमभीप्सन्त्यः पुंश्चल्यः स्वैरवृत्तयः ।।38।।

26. Now Indra, failing to see Urvasi any longer in the heavenly region, felt that heaven was not worth living in without her, and despatched Gandharvas to bring her back. **27.** At the dead of night when it was pitch dark, the Gandharvas stole away the pair of rams entrusted to the king by Urvasi. **28.** When she heard the bleating of the rams as they were being led away, Urvasi, who loved them as her children, cried out in alarm, 'Oh, I am lost! This eunuch of a husband has failed me! A worthless fellow, he pretends to be a hero! **29.** On account of the faith I put in him, I have been undone. The rams, which are to me like my own children, are being taken away by thieves. It looks that at night he lies in a place like a frightened woman; only during daytime he is a man.'

30. Like an elephant assailed with a goad, Purūravas felt hit by these verbal arrows, and without caring even to dress himself, rushed out naked in the night, sword in hand, in a mood of extreme anger. **31.** The Gandharvas left the rams there, and illumined the place with lightning. Now Urvasi saw her husband coming undressed, with the rams. **32.** On returning, Purūravas did not find his wife in the bed. He became dejected with sorrow, was grief-stricken and was lost in thought of her. He searched for her all the world over like a demented man.

33. Purūravas discovered her at last at Kurukshetra beside the Saraswati river, with five of her friends, all in a gay mood. He thereupon said to her, appealing: **34.** 'O dear one! Stop, stop. O angry one!. You cannot go away from here without satisfying me. Let us chat for a while. **35.** O lady! This excellent body of mine, which you have attracted to this distance, will now fall down dead and become food for wolves and vultures.' *Urvasi said:* **36.** 'Don't die, please. Are you not a powerful man? Allow not these wolves of women to eat you up! Women like wolves have no enduring friendship or kindness. **37.** Women are pitiless, cruel, impatient, and ready to risk anything to gain what they have set their hearts on. Even for petty ends they may murder a husband or a brother who had put trust in them. **38.** Pretending to be very faithful to those who have not yet seen through

संवत्सरान्ते हि भवानेकरात्रं मयेश्वर । वत्स्यत्यपत्यानि च ते भविष्यन्त्यपराणि भोः ॥39॥
अन्तर्वत्नीमुपालक्ष्य देवीं स प्रययौ पुरम् । पुनस्तत्र गतोऽब्दान्ते उर्वशीं वीरमातरम् ॥40॥
उपलभ्य मुदा युक्तः समुवास तया निशाम् । अथैनमुर्वशी प्राह कृपणं विरहातुरम् ॥41॥
गन्धर्वानुपधावेमांस्तुभ्यं दास्यन्ति मामिति । तस्य संस्तुवतस्तुष्टा अग्निस्थालीं ददुर्नृप ।
उर्वशीं मन्यमानस्तां सोऽबुध्यत चरन् वने ॥42॥
स्थालीं न्यस्य वने गत्वा गृहानाध्यायतो निशि । त्रेतायां सम्प्रवृत्तायां मनसि त्रय्यवर्तत ॥43॥
स्थालीस्थानं गतोऽश्वत्थं शमीगर्भं विलक्ष्य सः । तेन द्वे अरणी कृत्वा उर्वशीलोककाम्यया ॥44॥
उर्वशीं मन्त्रतो ध्यायन्नधरारणिमुत्तराम् । आत्मानमुभयोर्मध्ये यत् तत् प्रजननं प्रभुः ॥45॥
तस्य निर्मन्थनाज्जातो जातवेदा विभावसुः । त्रय्या स विद्यया राज्ञा पुत्रत्वे कल्पितस्त्रिवृत् ॥46॥
तेनायजत यज्ञेशं भगवन्तमधोक्षजम् । उर्वशीलोकमन्विच्छन् सर्वदेवमयं हरिम् ॥47॥
एक एव पुरा वेदः प्रणवः सर्ववाङ्मयः । देवो नारायणो नान्य एकोऽग्निर्वर्ण एव च ॥48॥

their deceit, they go about freely in quest of newer and newer lovers. **39.** At the end of each year, my lord, you can spend a night with me, and you will have another issue, besides the one I am now bearing.'

Subsequent History of Purūravas (40-49)

40-41. Seeing Urvasi expectant, Purūravas returned to his city. One year after, he returned to Kurukshetra and was delighted to see Urvasi coming back to him with a splendid child. He lived with her that night. Finding him extremely grief-stricken at the prospect of separation from her, Urvasi said as follows to that pitiable king: **42.** 'Seek to propitiate the Gandharvas. They will give me to you.' On the king extolling them, the Gandharvas were pleased, and they gave him a fire-pot, wherein he could keep the fire for performing the ritual for obtaining Urvasi. He travelled with it in hand identifying it with Urvasi, but soon realised it was only a fire-pot and not Urvasi. **43.** He then kept that fire-pot in the forest and went home. Every night he spent meditating on her. In his mind so meditating, the Trayī, the three Vedas dealing with rituals, dawned at the start of the Tretāyuga. **44-45.** He now went to the place where he had kept the fire-pot, and saw nearby an Aswattha tree growing as a graft from the bottom of a Sami tree. Desirous of attaining to the realms of Urvasi, he made two fire sticks with that Aswattha for lighting a sacrificial fire. Meditating on the lower fire stick as Urvasi, on the upper one as himself, and on a piece of wood kept between as their son expected to be born, he rubbed the sticks, to the accompaniment of proper Mantras. **46.** From this rubbing of the fire sticks came the sacrificial fire or Jātaveda, called so because it helps one gain heavenly enjoyments. It became the threefold fire of Āhavanīya, Gārhapatya, and Dakshina by the power of meditation prescribed in the Veda. The Rajah adopted the fire as his son. **47.** In that fire, he offered sacrifice to Hari, the embodiment of all deities, the all-powerful and the sense-transcending one, desiring the realm of Urvasi.

48. In the Kritayuga, the Pranava (Om), which includes in it every possible sound, alone was the Veda. And the Deity too was one only, and that was Narayana. So also Agni or sacred fire, and Varna or human community, were

पुरूरवस एवासीत् त्रयी त्रेतामुखे नृप । अग्निना प्रजया राजा लोकं गान्धर्वमेयिवान् ॥49॥

इति श्रीमद्भागवते महापुराणे पारमहंस्यां संहितायां नवमस्कन्धे ऐलोपाख्याने चतुर्दशोऽध्यायः ॥14॥

all single. **49.** It was at the beginning of Tretāyuga only that the one Veda became three by the action of Purūravas. With the help of Agni, his son, he attained to the world of Gandharvas.

अथ पञ्चदशोऽध्यायः

श्रीशुक उवाच

ऐलस्य चोर्वशीगर्भात् षडासन्नात्मजा नृप । आयुः श्रुतायुः सत्यायू रयोऽथ विजयो जयः ॥ 1॥

श्रुतायोर्वसुमान् पुत्रः सत्यायोश्च श्रुतञ्जयः । रयस्य सुत एकश्च जयस्य तनयोऽमितः ॥ 2॥

भीमस्तु विजयस्याथ काञ्चनो होत्रकस्ततः । तस्य जह्नुः सुतो गङ्गां गण्डूषीकृत्य योऽपिबत् ।

जह्नोस्तु पुरुस्तत्पुत्रो बलाकश्चात्मजोऽजकः ॥ 3॥

ततः कुशः कुशस्यापि कुशाम्बुस्तनयो वसुः । कुशनाभश्च चत्वारो गाधिरासीत् कुशाम्बुजः ॥ 4॥

तस्य सत्यवतीं कन्यामृचीकोऽयाचत द्विजः । वरं विसदृशं मत्वा गाधिर्भार्गवमब्रवीत् ॥ 5॥

एकतः श्यामकर्णानां हयानां चन्द्रवर्चसाम् । सहस्रं दीयतां शुल्कं कन्यायाः कुशिका वयम् ॥ 6॥

इत्युक्तस्तन्मतं ज्ञात्वा गतः स वरुणान्तिकम् । आनीय दत्त्वा तानश्वानुपयेमे वराननाम् ॥ 7॥

स ऋषिः प्रार्थितः पत्न्या श्वश्र्वा चापत्यकाम्यया । श्रपयित्वोभयैर्मन्त्रैश्चरुं स्नातुं गतो मुनिः ॥ 8॥

Skandha IX : Chapter 15

ADVENT OF PARASURAMA

Birth of Parasurama (1-15)

Sri Suka said: **1.** O King! Purūravas, the son of Ila, had by Urvasi six sons—Āyus, Srutāyus, Satyāyus, Raya, Vijaya, and Jaya. **2.** Of these, Srutāyus had Vasumān as son; Satyāyus, Srutanjaya; Raya, Eka; and Jaya, Amita. **3.** Vijaya had as son Bhīma; he, Kānchana; and he, Hotraka. Hotraka had as son Jahnu who happened to sip the whole of Ganga in doing the Āchamana rite. Jahnu's son was Pūru; his son, Balāka, and his son, Ajaka. **4.** From Ajaka was born Kusa; and from him, four sons—Kusāmbu, Mūrtaya, Vasu and Kusanābha. Kusāmbu had a son named Gādhi. **5.** A Rishi named Richīka approached Gādhi, praying for the hand of his daughter Satyavati. Thinking that the bridegroom was not a suitable person, Gādhi said to the Rishi: **6.** 'Give me a bridal money of a thousand horses white in colour like the moon, but having one ear blue. This is not too high a demand at all, as we belong to the highly aristocratic clan of Kausikas.' **7.** Divining the mind of the king, the Rishi Richīka approached Varuna, got from him the kind of horses required, and married the handsome Satyavati.

8. Being pressed for issue both by his wife and by the wife's mother, the Rishi arranged two dishes of Charu (sacrificial food offering) consecrated with two different sets of Mantras, one for his wife and the other for his mother-in-law, and went

तावत् सत्यवती मात्रा स्वचरुं याचिता सती। श्रेष्ठं मत्वा तयायच्छन्मात्रे मातुरदत् स्वयम् ॥ 9॥
तद् विज्ञाय मुनिः प्राह पत्नीं कष्टमकारषीः। घोरो दण्डधरः पुत्रो भ्राता ते ब्रह्मवित्तमः ॥10॥
प्रसादितः सत्यवत्या मैवं भूदिति भार्गवः। अथ तर्हि भवेत् पौत्रो जमदग्निस्ततोऽभवत् ॥11॥
सा चाभूत् सुमहापुण्या कौशिकी लोकपावनी। रेणोः सुतां रेणुकां वै जमदग्निरुवाह याम् ॥12॥
तस्यां वै भार्गवऋषेः सुता वसुमदादयः। यवीयाञ्जज्ञ एतेषां राम इत्यभिविश्रुतः ॥13॥
यमाहुर्वासुदेवांशं हैहयानां कुलान्तकम्। त्रिःसप्तकृत्वो य इमां चक्रे निःक्षत्रियां महीम् ॥14॥
दुष्टं क्षत्रं भुवो भारमब्रह्मण्यमनीनशत्। रजस्तमोवृतमहन् फल्गुन्यपि कृतेंऽहसि ॥15॥

राजोवाच

किं तदंहो भगवतो राजन्यैरजितात्मभिः। कृतं येन कुलं नष्टं क्षत्रियाणामभीक्ष्णशः ॥16॥

श्रीशुक उवाच

हैहयानामधिपतिरर्जुनः क्षत्रियर्षभः। दत्तं नारायणस्यांशमाराध्य परिकर्मभिः ॥17॥
बाहून् दशशतं लेभे दुर्धर्षत्वमरातिषु। अव्याहतेन्द्रियौजःश्रीतेजोवीर्ययशोबलम् ॥18॥
योगेश्वरत्वमैश्वर्यं गुणा यत्राणिमादयः। चचाराव्याहतगतिर्लोकेषु पवनो यथा ॥19॥

for bath. **9.** Before the Rishi returned after bath, Satyavati, on being asked by her mother for Charu, gave her the one meant for herself, thinking it would be the superior of the two, and she ate the Charu that was prepared for the mother. **10.** Coming to know of it, the Rishi Richīka said to his wife: 'You have done a great wrong. You are going to have a son very stern in nature, a terrific chastiser of evil ones! The son to be born to your mother, that is, your brother, on the other hand, will be a great knower of Brahman.' **11.** Satyavati now prayed to Richīka that it should not happen like that. The sage, pitying her, said: 'All right. In place of your son, your grandson will be a terror.' In due course the gentle sage Jamadagni was born to her.

12. Satyavati now became converted into the sacred river Kausiki, which purifies the whole world. Her son Jamadagni married Renuka, the daughter of Renu. **13.** Jamadagni had by Renuka several sons, beginning with Vasumān. The youngest of them was the famous Parasurama. **14.** Great men speak of him, the destroyer of the tribe of Haihayas, as a part of Vāsudeva. He rid this land of Kshatriyas in twenty-one campaigns. **15.** He destroyed these Kshatriyas, who were dominated by Rajas and Tamas, who were persecutors of holy men, and who had become a burden to the earth. Some of them were not, however, that perverse, but Parasurama spared none.

High-handedness of Kārtavīrya Arjuna (16-26)

The Rajah said: **16.** What was that offence that the Kshatriyas of uncontrolled senses did to Parasurama that he should efface them in repeated campaigns?

Sri Suka said: **17-19.** Arjuna, the king of the Haihayas and a leading Kshatriya, adored Dattātreya, who was a partial incarnation of Narayana, and pleased him by his devout services. Through Dattātreya's grace he came to have a thousand arms, strength that could never be overcome by any enemy, unfailing power of the senses, vigour, lustre, prosperity, courage, fame, strength, mastery of Yoga, and the eightfold Yogic powers. He travelled all over the world unrestricted like air.

स्त्रीरत्नैरावृतः क्रीडन् रेवाम्भसि मदोत्कटः । वैजयन्तीं स्रजं बिभ्रद् रुरोध सरितं भुजैः ॥20॥
विप्लावितं स्वशिबिरं प्रतिस्रोतःसरिज्जलैः । नामृष्यत् तस्य तद् वीर्यं वीरमानी दशाननः ॥21॥
गृहीतो लीलया स्त्रीणां समक्षं कृतकिल्बिषः । माहिष्मत्यां संनिरुद्धो मुक्तो येन कपिर्यथा ॥22॥
स एकदा तु मृगयां विचरन् विपिने वने । यदृच्छयाऽऽश्रमपदं जमदग्नेरुपाविशत् ॥23॥
तस्मै स नरदेवाय मुनिरर्हणमाहरत् । ससैन्यामात्यवाहाय हविष्मत्या तपोधनः ॥24॥
स वीरस्तत्र तद् दृष्ट्वा आत्मैश्वर्यातिशायनम् । तन्नाद्रियताग्निहोत्र्यां साभिलाषः सहैहयः ॥25॥
हविर्धानीमृषेर्दर्पान्नरान् हर्तुमचोदयत् । ते च माहिष्मतीं निन्युः सवत्सां क्रन्दतीं बलात् ॥26॥
अथ राजनि निर्याते राम आश्रम आगतः । श्रुत्वा तत् तस्य दौरात्म्यं चुक्रोधाहिरिवाहतः ॥27॥
घोरमादाय परशुं सतूणं चर्म कार्मुकम् । अन्वधावत दुर्धर्षो मृगेन्द्र इव यूथपम् ॥28॥
तमापतन्तं भृगुवर्यमोजसा धनुर्धरं बाणपरश्वधायुधम् ।
ऐणेयचर्माम्बरमर्कधामभिर्युतं जटाभिर्ददृशे पुरीं विशन् ॥29॥

20. Once while inebriated and bedecked with a garland of Vaijayanti flowers, he was indulging in water sports with numerous women in the sacred river Narmada. He stopped the flow of water in the river with his thousand arms. **21.** The water thereupon changed its course, flooding the upper banks of the river, where Ravana, then on his world-conquering campaign, was camping. That flood water carried away Ravana's camp while he was engaged in his daily worship. The ten-headed Ravana, who was proud of his own unusual powers, could not brook this expression of Arjuna's strength. **22.** Ravana therefore went to attack him, but was captured by Arjuna as in play, in the presence of women, and shut up in his prison at Māhishmati. Afterwards, out of pity he released him from prison, like a monkey from a cage.

23. Once when he was moving about hunting in a forest far away from human habitations, Arjuna came across Jamadagni's Ashrama by chance. **24.** With the help of the wish-yielding cow Kāmadhenu, that sage, whose wealth was his Tapas, did hospitality to the king and all his retinue consisting of troops, ministers and vehicles. **25.** Struck by the abundance which characterised that hospitality far beyond what his own wealth would allow, the king of the Haihayas set his heart on that Kāmadhenu who made that abundance possible. Out of jealousy he had not the heart even to accept the sage's hospitality. **26.** On his return, the arrogant king sent his men to capture that Kāmadhenu which yielded the requisites for the sacrificial rites of the sage. They led away the cow and its calf, lowing in fear, to Māhishmati by force.

Parasurama destroying Arjuna (27-41)

27. Rama, who was the youngest of the sons of the sage, returned to his father's Ashrama shortly after the king's emissaries had departed with the Kāmadhenu, and was much excited and incensed to hear of the depredation of those evil-doers. He reacted like a serpent that has been trampled upon. **28.** Taking his terrible weapon of a battle-axe, his bow, quiver and shield, he mounted an irresistible attack on the emissaries of the king, as a lion at an elephant. **29.** While just entering his city, Arjuna saw the pursuing Parasurama equipped with bow, arrows, and battle-axe, dressed in deer skin, and

अचोदयद्धस्तिरथाश्वपत्तिभिर्गदासिबाणर्ष्टिशतघ्निशक्तिभिः ।
अक्षौहिणीः सप्तदशातिभीषणास्ता राम एको भगवानसूदयत् ॥30॥
यतो यतोऽसौ प्रहरत्परश्वधो मनोऽनिलौजाः परचक्रसूदनः ।
ततस्ततश्छिन्नभुजोरुकन्धरा निपेतुरुर्व्यां हतसूतवाहनाः ॥31॥
दृष्ट्वा स्वसैन्यं रुधिरौघकर्दमे रणाजिरे रामकुठारसायकैः ।
विवृक्णचर्मध्वजचापविग्रहं निपातितं हैहय आपतद् रुषा ॥32॥
अथार्जुनः पञ्चशतेषु बाहुभिर्धनुःषु बाणान् युगपत् स सन्दधे ।
रामाय रामोऽस्त्रभृतां समग्रणीस्तान्येकधन्वेषुभिराच्छिनत् समम् ॥33॥
पुनः स्वहस्तैरचलान् मृधेऽङ्घ्रिपानुत्क्षिप्य वेगादभिधावतो युधि ।
भुजान् कुठारेण कठोरनेमिना चिच्छेद रामः प्रसभं त्वहेरिव ॥34॥
कृत्तबाहोः शिरस्तस्य गिरेः शृङ्गमिवाहरत् । हते पितरि तत्पुत्रा अयुतं दुद्रुवुर्भयात् ॥35॥
अग्निहोत्रीमुपावर्त्य सवत्सां परवीरहा । समुपेत्याश्रमं पित्रे परिक्लिष्टां समर्पयत् ॥36॥
स्वकर्म तत्कृतं रामः पित्रे भ्रातृभ्य एव च । वर्णयामास तच्छ्रुत्वा जमदग्निरभाषत ॥37॥
राम राम महाबाहो भवान् पापमकारषीत् । अवधीन्नरदेवं यत् सर्वदेवमयं वृथा ॥38॥
वयं हि ब्राह्मणास्तात क्षमयार्हणतां गताः । यया लोकगुरुर्देवः पारमेष्ठ्यमगात् पदम् ॥39॥

possessed of matted hair which shone like the rays of the sun. **30.** Against him Arjuna sent an army of seventeen formidable Akshouhinis (battalions) consisting of regiments of elephants, cavalry, chariots and foot-soldiers, and equipped with all kinds of weapons like maces, swords, arrows, double-edged swords, Sataghnis, javelins etc. Single-handed, the worshipful Rama destroyed the whole force. **31.** Wherever Rama, with his axe in hand, moved about with the speed of the mind or air destroying the enemy forces, there the earth was covered with the severed arms, legs, and heads of men and with broken chariots with their charioteers killed.

32. Seeing his whole army now strewn on the ground with severed bodies and shattered weapons and chariots, and the battle field boggy with the blood of slain warriors, Arjuna now rushed forward in a fit of fury. **33.** Holding five hundred bows in his hands, Arjuna showered arrows at Rama with all of them; but Rama, the superb archer that he was, cut to pieces all these arrows shot at him with a single bow of his. **34.** Next Arjuna rushed at him with trees and mountains in his hands, but Rama, as in play, cut those arms with his sharp battle-axe as if they were so many hoods of a serpent. **35.** After cutting all his hands, he severed Arjuna's head also like chipping the peak of a mountain. When their father was thus killed, his ten thousand sons fled away in fear. **36.** Rama, the destroyer of foes, now recovered the ill-treated Kāmadhenu and its calf, and presented them to his father.

37. Rama narrated to his father and brothers the story of his attack on Arjuna. On hearing it Jamadagni said: **38.** 'O Rama, O heroic one! You have committed a sin. For no purpose you have killed a king, in whose body live all the Divinities. **39.** We are Brahmanas. It is by virtue of patience that we have got a place of preeminence. It is because of his infinite patience that Brahma, the father of the worlds, has attained to the state of Brahmahood. **40.** Patience is what generates

क्षमया रोचते लक्ष्मीर्ब्राह्मी सौरी यथा प्रभा। क्षमिणामाशु भगवांस्तुष्यते हरिरीश्वरः ॥40॥
राज्ञो मूर्धाभिषिक्तस्य वधो ब्रह्मवधाद् गुरुः। तीर्थसंसेवया चांहो जह्यङ्गाच्युतचेतनः ॥41॥

इति श्रीमद्भागवते महापुराणे पारमहंस्यां संहितायां नवमस्कन्धे पञ्चदशोऽध्यायः ॥15॥

that Brahmic aura, which shines like the brilliance of the sun; for Lord Hari is pleased with those that are forbearing. **41.** The killing of a king, on whose head consecrated water had been poured making him an emperor, is even more heinous than the killing of a Brahmana. So, O dear son, do expiation for this sin through pilgrimage to holy places, by practice of Yoga, and by concentrating your mind on Achyuta.

अथ षोडशोऽध्यायः

श्रीशुक उवाच

पित्रोपशिक्षितो रामस्तथेति कुरुनन्दन। संवत्सरं तीर्थयात्रां चरित्वाऽऽश्रममाव्रजत् ॥ 1॥
कदाचिद् रेणुका याता गङ्गायां पद्ममालिनम्। गन्धर्वराजं क्रीडन्तमप्सरोभिरपश्यत ॥ 2॥
विलोकयन्ती क्रीडन्तमुदकार्थं नदीं गता। होमवेलां न सस्मार किञ्चिच्चित्ररथस्पृहा ॥ 3॥
कालात्ययं तं विलोक्य मुनेः शापविशङ्किता। आगत्य कलशं तस्थौ पुरोधाय कृताञ्जलिः ॥ 4॥
व्यभिचारं मुनिर्ज्ञात्वा पत्न्याः प्रकुपितोऽब्रवीत्। घ्नतैनां पुत्रकाः पापामित्युक्तास्ते न चक्रिरे ॥ 5॥
रामः सञ्चोदितः पित्रा भ्रातॄन् मात्रा सहावधीत्। प्रभावज्ञो मुनेः सम्यक् समाधेस्तपसश्च सः ॥ 6॥
वरेणच्छन्दयामास प्रीतः सत्यवतीसुतः। वव्रे हतानां रामोऽपि जीवितं चास्मृतिं वधे ॥ 7॥

Skandha IX : Chapter 16

PARASURAMA'S EXTIRPATION OF KSHATRIYAS

Renuka's Mishap (1-8)

Sri Suka said: **1.** O King! Respecting fully the father's command, Rama spent one year in pilgrimage and returned to the Ashrama. **2.** One of those days when Renuka had gone to the Ganga, she happened to see there the Gandharva Chitraratha, decorated with a garland of lotuses, sporting with Apsara women. **3.** She had gone to the river to fetch water; but seeing Chitraratha sporting, she was a bit attracted to him, and forgot that it was time for the Rishi's Homa (fire sacrifice). **4.** When she became conscious of her delay, she got frightened by the prospect of incurring the sage's curse. She returned post-haste with the water, and placing it before her husband, stood there with palms joined in a worshipful pose. **5.** The Muni divined her mental adultery, and ordered in great anger: 'O sons! Kill this sinful woman.' But none of the sons ventured to obey him. **6.** When, however, Rama was ordered to do so, knowing as he did the great powers acquired by his father through austerity and concentration, he killed the mother along with her other disobedient sons. **7.** When the highly pleased Jamadagni, the son of Satyavati, asked him to choose any boon, he chose that those dead persons should come back to life and that they should have no memory of what

उत्तस्थुस्ते कुशलिनो निद्रापाय इवाञ्जसा ।
पितुर्विद्वांस्तपोवीर्यं रामश्चक्रे सुहृद्वधम् ॥ 8॥
येऽर्जुनस्य सुता राजन् स्मरन्तः स्वपितुर्वधम् ।
रामवीर्यपराभूता लेभिरे शर्म न क्वचित् ॥ 9॥
एकदाऽऽश्रमतो रामे सभ्रातरि वनं गते ।
वैरं सिसाधयिषवो लब्धच्छिद्रा उपागमन् ॥10॥
दृष्ट्वाग्न्यगार आसीनमावेशितधियं मुनिम् ।
भगवत्युत्तमश्लोके जघ्नुस्ते पापनिश्चयाः ॥11॥
याच्यमानाः कृपणया राममात्रातिदारुणाः ।
प्रसह्य शिर उत्कृत्य निन्युस्ते क्षत्रबन्धवः ॥12॥
रेणुका दुःखशोकार्ता निघ्नन्त्यात्मानमात्मना ।
राम रामेहि तातेति विचुक्रोशोच्चकैः सती ॥13॥
तदुपश्रुत्य दूरस्थो हा रामेत्यार्तवत् स्वनम् ।
त्वरयाऽऽश्रममासाद्य ददृशे पितरं हतम् ॥14॥
तद्दुःखरोषामर्षार्तिशोकवेगविमोहितः ।
हा तात साधो धर्मिष्ठ त्यक्त्वास्मान् स्वर्गतो भवान् ।
विलप्यैवं पितुर्देहं निधाय भ्रातृषु स्वयम् ।
प्रगृह्य परशुं रामः क्षत्रान्ताय मनो दधे ॥16॥
गत्वा माहिष्मतीं रामो ब्रह्मघ्नविहतश्रियम् ।
तेषां स शीर्षभी राजन् मध्ये चक्रे महागिरिम् ॥17॥
तद्रक्तेन नदीं घोरामब्रह्मण्यभयावहाम् ।
हेतुं कृत्वा पितृवधं क्षत्रेऽमङ्गलकारिणि ॥18॥
त्रिःसप्तकृत्वः पृथिवीं कृत्वा निःक्षत्रियां प्रभुः ।
समन्तपञ्चके चक्रे शोणितोदान् ह्रदान् नृप ॥19॥
पितुः कायेन सन्धाय शिर आदाय बर्हिषि ।
सर्वदेवमयं देवमात्मानमयजन्मखैः ॥20॥

took place. **8.** Immediately they all got up in full health like persons awakening from sleep. Rama did this heinous act of killing his own near and dear ones, only because he was sure of his father's great powers of Tapas, by which he could get them revived.

Avenging Jamadagni's Murder (9-27)

9. Now the sons of Arjuna could never have any peace of mind, thinking over the slaughter of their father and their defeat at the hands of Rama. **10.** Once when Rama with his brothers had gone to the forest, the sons of Arjuna went there, deeming it an opportune moment to wreak vengeance. **11.** Finding Jamadagni sitting in his sacrificial chamber, with his mind concentrated on the Lord, those evil ones murdered him. **12.** In spite of the very earnest and pitiable appeals of Renuka, the mother of Rama, those extremely cruel-hearted Kshatriya warriors decapitated Jamadagni and carried away the head with them. **13.** Overcome with grief, the virtuous lady Renuka now began to beat her breast in grief and cry aloud, 'O Rama! O Rama! Dear one! come quickly.' **14.** Rama, who was then away at some distance from the Ashrama, heard these distressing cries, and hastened back to see his father lying murdered. **15.** He was stunned with agonising grief and blinding anger at the sight, and cried aloud, 'O father! O holy one! O righteous one! How is it that you have gone to your heavenly abode, leaving us all here!'

16. After bemoaning his father's death in this way, he entrusted the body to his brothers, and started, battle-axe in hand, on a campaign of extirpation of the tribe of Kshatriyas. **17.** O King! He first went to Māhishmati, a city accursed due to the murder of a holy man, and he made in the middle of the city a hillock of the heads of the Kshatriyas he killed. **18-19.** Making his father's murder the occasion, he let flow there a stream of blood by the slaughter of those evil Kshatriyas, to stand as a warning to those indulging in the persecution of holy ones. He launched twenty-one such campaigns, almost effacing the whole tribe of Kshatriyas from the earth, and created five pools of blood at the place called Samanta-panchaka.

20. Then recovering his father's head, he united it with his trunk at a Yajna,

ददौ प्राचीं दिशं होत्रे ब्रह्मणे दक्षिणां दिशम् ।
अध्वर्यवे प्रतीचीं वै उद्गात्रे उत्तरां दिशम् ॥21॥
अन्येभ्योऽवान्तरदिशः कश्यपाय च मध्यतः ।
आर्यावर्तमुपद्रष्ट्रे सदस्येभ्यस्ततः परम् ॥22॥
ततश्चावभृथस्नानविधूताशेषकिल्बिषः ।
सरस्वत्यां ब्रह्मनद्यां रेजे व्यभ्र इवांशुमान् ॥23॥
स्वदेहं जमदग्निस्तु लब्ध्वा संज्ञानलक्षणम् ।
ऋषीणां मण्डले सोऽभूत् सप्तमो रामपूजितः ॥24॥
जामदग्न्योऽपि भगवान् रामः कमललोचनः ।
आगामिन्यन्तरे राजन् वर्तयिष्यति वै बृहत् ॥25॥
आस्तेऽद्यापि महेन्द्राद्रौ न्यस्तदण्डः प्रशान्तधीः ।
उपगीयमानचरितः सिद्धगन्धर्वचारणैः ॥26॥
एवं भृगुषु विश्वात्मा भगवान् हरिरीश्वरः ।
अवतीर्य परं भारं भुवोऽहन् बहुशो नृपान् ॥27॥
गाधेरभून्महातेजाः समिद्ध इव पावकः ।
तपसा क्षात्रमुत्सृज्य यो लेभे ब्रह्मवर्चसम् ॥28॥
विश्वामित्रस्य चैवासन् पुत्रा एकशतं नृप ।
मध्यमस्तु मधुच्छन्दा मधुच्छन्दस एव ते ॥29॥
पुत्रं कृत्वा शुनःशेपं देवरातं च भार्गवम् ।
आजीगर्तं सुतानाह ज्येष्ठ एष प्रकल्प्यताम् ॥30॥
यो वै हरिश्चन्द्रमखे विक्रीतः पुरुषः पशुः ।
स्तुत्वा देवान् प्रजेशादीन् मुमुचे पाशबन्धनात् ॥31॥
यो रातो देवयजने देवैर्गाधिषु तापसः ।
देवरात इति ख्यातः शुनःशेपः स भार्गवः ॥32॥

and worshipped the Supreme Being, the embodiment of all Divinities, through the performance of several Yajnas. **21.** He gifted the country to the east to the Hota, the sacrificing priest; that to the south, to the priest Brahmā; that to the west, to the priest Adhvaryu; and that to the north, to Udgātā. **22.** The countries between, he gave to the other sacrificial priests; and the middle region to Kasyapa Prajapati. He gave Aryavarta to the priest Upadrashta, and whatever remained, to the members of the sacrificial assembly. **23.** Then he took the final ceremonial bath (Avabhrithasnāna) in the Saraswati, the holy river. Liberated from all sins, he now shone like the sun freed from the clouds. **24.** And Jamadagni, adored by Rama, was restored to life with a body characterised by a continuity of consciousness from the earlier body and became the seventh among the Saptarshis. **25.** The lotus-eyed Rama, the worshipful son of Jamadagni, will be the propagator of the Veda in the next Manvantara. **26.** Extolled by Siddhas, Chāranas and Gandharwas, he lives even today in the Mahendra mountain as a peaceful contemplative, having given up his fighting propensities. **27.** In this way Hari, the Supreme Lord and the indweller of all, incarnated Himself in the line of the Bhrigus and several times detroyed the rulers who had become a burden to the earth.

The Line of Kausikas (28-37)

28. Gādhi had a son Viswamitra, who was born with the splendour of a well-lit fire. By Tapas he got himself elevated from the state of a Kshatriya to that of a Brahmana. **29.** Viswamitra had a hundred and one sons. The middle one among them was named Madhuchchandas. So all the brothers were known collectively by the common name of Madhuchchandas. **30.** But Viswamitra adopted Sunassepa who was of Bhrigu's line and a son of Ajīgarta, whose life had been saved by the Devas. Viswamitra commanded his sons to recognise him as the eldest among them. **31.** Sunassepa, being the middle son of his parents, was sold by them to Harischandra's son as a sacrificial victim for Harischandra's Yajna. But he was saved by his prayers to Devas and Prajapatis as directed by Viswamitra. **32.** This Sunassepa, who was saved from immolation in the Yajna by the Devas, though belonging by birth to the line of

ये मधुच्छन्दसो ज्येष्ठाः कुशलं मेनिरे न तत्। अशपत् तान् मुनिः क्रुद्धो म्लेच्छा भवत दुर्जनाः ॥33॥
स होवाच मधुच्छन्दाः सार्धं पञ्चाशता ततः। यन्नो भवान् संजानीते तस्मिंस्तिष्ठामहे वयम् ॥34॥
ज्येष्ठं मन्त्रदृशं चक्रुस्त्वामन्वञ्चो वयं स्म हि। विश्वामित्रः सुतानाह वीरवन्तो भविष्यथ।
ये मानं मेऽनुगृह्णन्तो वीरवन्तमकर्त माम् ॥35॥
एष वः कुशिका वीरो देवरातस्तमन्वित। अन्ये चाष्टकहारीतजयक्रतुमदादयः ॥36॥
एवं कौशिकगोत्रं तु विश्वामित्रैः पृथग्विधम्। प्रवरान्तरमापन्नं तद्धि चैवं प्रकल्पितम् ॥37॥

इति श्रीमद्भागवते महापुराणे पारमहंस्यां संहितायां नवमस्कन्धे षोडशोऽध्यायः ॥16॥

Bhrigu, became a famous ascetic among the descendants of Gādhi because of his being adopted by Viswamitra (the son of Gādhi). He came to be well known under the name of Devarāta. **33.** Of Viswamitra's own sons, the first fifty Madhuchchandas, did not look upon this adoption as a commendable act. Viswamitra became angry at this, and cursed them that they would become heinous Mlechchas (barbarians outside the Vedic pale). **34.** At this the middle one among the Madhuchchandas, along with the remaining fifty of his brothers, said: 'We shall obey whatever you order.' Thus agreeing to obey him, these fifty brothers accepted Sunassepa, who was a knower of Mantras, as their eldest. **35.** Thereupon Viswamitra said to his sons: 'Those of you who have obeyed me and made me a father of virtuous children, will yourself become blessed with noble sons. **36.** O members of Kusika's line! This Devarāta (alias Sunassepa) is one of your line. Therefore obey him!' He had also other sons like Ashtaka, Hārīta, Jaya and Kratumān. **37.** Thus the family of Kusikas came to have many lines sprung from the different sons of Viswamitra. By giving seniority to Devarāta, this line has got a distinct Pravara.

अथ सप्तदशोऽध्यायः

श्रीशुक उवाच

यः पुरूरवसः पुत्र आयुस्तस्याभवन् सुताः। नहुषः क्षत्रवृद्धश्च रजी रम्भश्च वीर्यवान् ॥ 1॥
अनेना इति राजेन्द्र शृणु क्षत्रवृधोऽन्वयम्। क्षत्रवृद्धसुतस्यासन् सुहोत्रस्यात्मजास्त्रयः ॥ 2॥
काश्यः कुशो गृत्समद इति गृत्समदादभूत्। शुनकः शौनको यस्य बह्वृचप्रवरो मुनिः ॥ 3॥
काश्यस्य काशिस्तत्पुत्रो राष्ट्रो दीर्घतमः पिता। धन्वन्तरिर्दैर्घतम आयुर्वेदप्रवर्तकः ॥ 4॥

Skandha IX : Chapter 17

OTHER SUCCESSORS OF PURŪRAVAS

Decendants of Kshatravriddha (1-9)

Sri Suka said: **1-3.** O King! Āyus, the son of Purūravas, had five sons—Nahusha, Kshatravriddha, Rajī, Rambha and Anenas. Of these, hear now about the descendants by Kshatravriddha. Kshatravriddha's son was Suhotra, and he had three sons—Kāsya, Kusa and Gritsamada. From the last Gritsamada was born Sunaka, and from him, Saunaka, a sage of great fame and an expert in the Rig Veda. **4.** Kāsya's son was Kāsi; his son, Rāshtra; and his son, Dīrghatamas. Dīrghatamas

यज्ञभुग्वासुदेवांशः स्मृतमात्रार्तिनाशनः । तत्पुत्रः केतुमानस्य जज्ञे भीमरथस्ततः ॥ 5॥
दिवोदासो द्युमांस्तस्मात् प्रतर्दन इति स्मृतः । स एव शत्रुजिद् वत्स ऋतध्वज इतीरितः ।
तथा कुवलयाश्वेति प्रोक्तोऽलर्कादयस्ततः ॥ 6॥
षष्टिवर्षसहस्राणि षष्टिवर्षशतानि च । नालर्कादपरो राजन् मेदिनीं बुभुजे युवा ॥ 7॥
अलर्कात् सन्ततिस्तस्मात् सुनीथोऽथ सुकेतनः । धर्मकेतुः सुतस्तस्मात् सत्यकेतुरजायत ॥ 8॥
धृष्टकेतुः सुतस्तस्मात् सुकुमारः क्षितीश्वरः । वीतिहोत्रस्य भर्गोऽतो भार्गभूमिरभून्नृप: ॥ 9॥
इतीमे काशयो भूपाः क्षत्रवृद्धान्वयायिनः । रम्भस्य रभसः पुत्रो गम्भीरश्चाक्रियस्ततः ॥10॥
तस्य क्षेत्रे ब्रह्म जज्ञे शृणु वंशमनेनसः । शुद्धस्ततः शुचिस्तस्मात् त्रिककुद् धर्मसारथिः ॥11॥
ततः शान्तरयो जज्ञे कृतकृत्यः स आत्मवान् । रजेः पञ्चशतान्यासन् पुत्राणाममितौजसाम् ॥12॥
देवैरभ्यर्थितो दैत्यान् हत्वेन्द्रायाददाद् दिवम् । इन्द्रस्तस्मै पुनर्दत्त्वा गृहीत्वा चरणौ रजेः ॥13॥
आत्मानमर्पयामास प्रह्लादाद्यरिशङ्कितः । पितर्युपरते पुत्रा याचमानाय नो ददुः ॥14॥
त्रिविष्टपं महेन्द्राय यज्ञभागान् समाददुः । गुरुणा हूयमानेऽग्नौ बलभित् तनयान् रजेः ॥15॥
अवधीद् भ्रंशितान् मार्गान्न कश्चिदवशेषितः । कुशात् प्रतिः क्षात्रवृद्धात् सञ्जयस्तत्सुतो जयः 16॥

had a son named Dhanvantari, who promulgated the system of medicine called Āyurveda. **5.** He was born of a part of Vāsudeva, and has a share in Yajna offerings. By the very remembrance of him, diseases are cured. His son was Ketumān, and his son Bhīmaratha. **6.** His son was Divodāsa and his son Dyumān, known by several other names as Pratardana, Satrujit, Vatsa, Ritadhvaja, and Kuvalayāsva. He (Dyumān) had as sons Alarka and others. **7.** O King! He (Alarka) ruled the earth for sixty-six thousand years, retaining the freshness of youth all along. None but he had ever achieved this. **8.** From Alarka was born Santati; from him, Sunītha; from him, Suketana; from him, Dharmaketu; and from him, Satyaketu. **9.** Satyaketu's son was Dhrishtaketu; his son, Sukumara; his son, Vītihotra; his son, Bharga; and his son, Bhārgabhūmi.

Rambha and Anenas (10-12)

10. What has been narrated is the list of kings descended from Kāsya belonging to the line of Kshatravriddha. Now follows the line of Rambha, the son of Āyu. Rabhasa and Gambhīra were the sons of Rambha. From Rabhasa was born Akriya. **11.** From the wife of Akriya, a line of Brahmanas originated. Now hear about the line of Anenas. From Anenas was born Suddha; from him, Suchi; from him, Dharmasārathi, who was also known under the famous name Trikakut. **12.** To Trikakut was born Sāntaraya, who became an ascetic and a knower of the Self without any worldly desires. Rajī had five hundred sons of great prowess.

Rajī and Kshatradharmā (13-18)

13-16. Requested by Indra, Rajī fought against the Asuras and restored the Swarga to Indra. But being afraid of attack from Prahlada and other Asuras, Indra entrusted his realm of Swarga and himself, too, to the protection of Rajī. But when Indra wanted his realm back after the death of Rajī, his sons refused to restore the same to him. They also appropriated to themselves the portions of the Yajna due to Indra. So in order to sidetrack them from the Vedic Dharma and then weaken them, Brihaspati, the preceptor of the Devas, performed black magic. After that Indra destroyed these

ततः कृतः कृतस्यापि जज्ञे हर्यवनो नृपः। सहदेवस्ततो हीनो जयसेनस्तु तत्सुतः ॥17॥
सङ्कृतिस्तस्य च जयः क्षत्रधर्मा महारथः। क्षत्रवृद्धान्वया भूपाः शृणु वंशं च नाहुषात् ॥18॥

इति श्रीमद्भागवते महापुराणे पारमहंस्यां संहितायां नवमस्कन्धे चन्द्रवंशानुवर्णने सप्तदशोऽध्यायः ॥17॥

sons of Rajī. None of them survived. Kshatravriddha had a grandson named Kusa; from him Prati was born; from him, Sanjaya; and from him, Jaya. **17.** From him Krita was born; from him, Haryavana; from him, Sahadeva; from him, Hīna; and from him, Jayasena. **18.** From him was born Sankriti; from him, another Jaya; and from him, the great car-warrior Kshatradharma. All these belong to the line of Kshatravriddha. Now hear about the line of Nahusha.

अथाष्टादशोऽध्यायः

श्रीशुक उवाच

यतिर्ययातिः संयातिरायतिर्वियतिः कृतिः। षडिमे नहुषस्यासन्निन्द्रियाणीव देहिनः ॥ 1॥
राज्यं नैच्छद् यतिः पित्रा दत्तं तत्परिणामवित्। यत्र प्रविष्टः पुरुष आत्मानं नावबुध्यते ॥ 2॥
पितरि भ्रंशिते स्थानादिन्द्राण्या धर्षणाद् द्विजैः। प्रापितेऽजगरत्वं वै ययातिरभवन्नृपः ॥ 3॥
चतसृष्वादिशद् दिक्षु भ्रातॄन् भ्राता यवीयसः। कृतदारो जुगोपोर्वीं काव्यस्य वृषपर्वणः ॥ 4॥

राजोवाच

ब्रह्मर्षिर्भगवान् काव्यः क्षत्रबन्धुश्च नाहुषः। राजन्यविप्रयोः कस्माद् विवाहः प्रतिलोमकः ॥ 5॥

श्रीशुक उवाच

एकदा दानवेन्द्रस्य शर्मिष्ठा नाम कन्यका। सखीसहस्रसंयुक्ता गुरुपुत्र्या च भामिनी ॥ 6॥
देवयान्या पुरोद्याने पुष्पितद्रुमसङ्कुले। व्यचरत् कलगीतालिनलिनीपुलिनेऽबला ॥ 7॥

Skandha IX : Chapter 18

STORY OF YAYĀTI AND DEVAYĀNI

Yayāti as King (1-4)

Sri Suka said: **1.** Just as embodied beings have six senses, Nahusha had six sons—Yati, Yayāti, Samyāti, Āyati, Viyati, and Kriti. **2.** Of these, Yati did not accept the kingdom that his father offered him as his successor, because he was aware of the evil consequences that would follow. For, one who has entered into the affairs of State will totally forget the Self. **3.** When Nahusha was expelled from heaven for his attempt on Indra's wife, and cursed to become a python by the sages, Yayāti became the king. **4.** Yayāti appointed his four younger brothers as governors of the four quarters. He governed the country, having married the daughters of the Maharshi Sukra and of King Vrishaparva.

Quarrel between Devayāni and Sarmishtha (5-14)

The Rajah said: **5.** Sukra is a Brahmarshi, and Yayāti, the son of Nahusha, was only an ordinary Kshatriya. How was it that a *pratiloma* marriage, in which a man of a lower Varna (Kshatriya) marries a woman of a higher Varna (Brahmana), took place?

Sri Suka said: **6-7.** Once Sarmishtha, the daughter of the king of the Asuras, who

ता जलाशयमासाद्य कन्याः कमललोचनाः । तीरे न्यस्य दुकूलानि विजह्रुः सिञ्चतीर्मिथः ॥ 8॥
वीक्ष्य व्रजन्तं गिरिशं सह देव्या वृषस्थितम् । सहसोत्तीर्य वासांसि पर्यधुर्व्रीडिताः स्त्रियः ॥ 9॥
शर्मिष्ठाजानती वासो गुरुपुत्र्याः समव्ययत् । स्वीयं मत्वा प्रकुपिता देवयानीदमब्रवीत् ॥10॥
अहो निरीक्ष्यतामस्या दास्याः कर्म ह्यसाम्प्रतम् । अस्मद्धार्यं धृतवती शुनीव हविरध्वरे ॥11॥
यैरिदं तपसा सृष्टं मुखं पुंसः परस्य ये । धार्यते यैरिह ज्योतिः शिवः पन्थाश्च दर्शितः ॥12॥
यान् वन्दन्त्युपतिष्ठन्ते लोकनाथाः सुरेश्वराः । भगवानपि विश्वात्मा पावनः श्रीनिकेतनः ॥13॥
वयं तत्रापि भृगवः शिष्योऽस्या नः पितासुरः । अस्मद्धार्यं धृतवती शूद्रो वेदमिवासती ॥14॥
एवं शपन्तीं शर्मिष्ठा गुरुपुत्रीमभाषत । रुषा श्वसन्त्युरङ्गीव धर्षिता दष्टदच्छदा ॥15॥
आत्मवृत्तमविज्ञाय कत्थसे बहु भिक्षुकि । किं न प्रतीक्षसेऽस्माकं गृहान् बलिभुजो यथा ॥16॥
एवंविधैः सुपरुषैः क्षिप्त्वाऽऽचार्यसुतां सतीम् । शर्मिष्ठा प्राक्षिपत् कूपे वास आदाय मन्युना ॥17॥
तस्यां गतायां स्वगृहं ययातिर्मृगयां चरन् । प्राप्तो यदृच्छया कूपे जलार्थी तां ददर्श ह ॥18॥
दत्त्वा स्वमुत्तरं वासस्तस्यै राजा विवाससे । गृहीत्वा पाणिना पाणिमुज्जहार दयापरः ॥19॥

was well-known for her beauty, along with many of her companions including Devayāni, the daughter of the Asura preceptor Sukra, was walking about in a pleasure garden full of trees and sandy embankments of lakes covered with lotuses, over which buzzing honey-suckers hovered. **8.** Reaching the banks of a lake, those handsome girls put aside their garments on the shore and began to sport in water splashing water on one another. **9.** They now saw Parameswara riding on his ox-mount with Pārvati. Feeling abashed, they rushed up and put on their garments. **10.** Now Sarmishtha unwittingly put on the garments of Devayāni, the preceptor's daughter. Devayāni was terribly annoyed at this and said: **11.** 'Look at the audacity of this servant maid! Like a dog eating up the offerings made ready for a Yajna, she has put on the dress that I should have worn. **12.** We are Brahmanas, by whose austerity the universe itself was created, who represent the face of the Supreme Being, who exhibit Brahmic splendour in this world, and who teach and practise the beneficent way of the Vedas. **13.** We belong to that great community of Brahmanas, who are respected even by the Divinities, nay, who even the Supreme Lord salutes and serves! **14.** Not only that, among the Brahmanas we belong to the highly superior line of Bhrigus. Besides, the Asura, her father, is our disciple. She has put on my cloth, as a Sudra learns the Veda! What audacity on her part!'

Yayāti marries Devayāni (15-23)

15. To the preceptor's daughter, who was railing at her like this, Sarmishtha, now infuriated like a trampled snake, said, biting her lips and releasing long breaths. **16.** 'O beggar girl! Think of your condition before you talk in this fashion. You are like a watchdog in our house, eating the crumbs we give.' **17.** After hurling such scandalously abusive words at the good daughter of the preceptor, she disrobed her and pushed her into a well out of burning anger.

18. After Sarmishtha and party had gone home, Yayāti, who was on a hunting expedition, approached that well by chance in search of water, and he happened to see Devayāni in the well. **19.** The merciful Yayāti threw down his upper cloth to her to cover her nakedness, and then lifted her up, holding her by the

तं वीरमाहौशनसी प्रेमनिर्भरया गिरा । राजंस्त्वया गृहीतो मे पाणिः परपुरञ्जय ॥20॥
हस्तग्राहोऽपरो मा भूद् गृहीतायास्त्वया हि मे । एष ईशकृतो वीर सम्बन्धो नौ न पौरुषः ।
यदिदं कूपलग्नाया भवतो दर्शनं मम ॥21॥
न ब्राह्मणो मे भविता हस्तग्राहो महाभुज । कचस्य बार्हस्पत्यस्य शापाद् यमशपं पुरा ॥22॥
ययातिरनभिप्रेतं दैवोपहृतमात्मनः । मनस्तु तद्गतं बुद्ध्वा प्रतिजग्राह तद्वचः ॥23॥
गते राजनि सा वीरे तत्र स्म रुदती पितुः । न्यवेदयत् ततः सर्वमुक्तं शर्मिष्ठया कृतम् ॥24॥
दुर्मना भगवान् काव्यः पौरोहित्यं विगर्हयन् । स्तुवन् वृत्तिं च कापोतीं दुहित्रा स ययौ पुरात् ॥25॥
वृषपर्वा तमाज्ञाय प्रत्यनीकविवक्षितम् । गुरुं प्रसादयन् मूर्ध्ना पादयोः पतितः पथि ॥26॥
क्षणार्धमन्युर्भगवान् शिष्यं व्याचष्ट भार्गवः । कामोऽस्याः क्रियतां राजन् नैनां त्यक्तुमिहोत्सहे ॥
तथेत्यवस्थिते प्राह देवयानी मनोगतम् । पित्रा दत्ता यतो यास्ये सानुगा यातु मामनु ॥28॥
स्वानां तत् सङ्कटं वीक्ष्य तदर्थस्य च गौरवम् । देवयानीं पर्यचरत् स्त्रीसहस्रेण दासवत् ॥29॥
नाहुषाय सुतां दत्त्वा सह शर्मिष्ठयोशना । तमाह राजञ्छर्मिष्ठामाधास्तल्पे न कर्हिचित् ॥30॥
विलोक्यौशनसीं राजञ्छर्मिष्ठा सप्रजां क्वचित् । तमेव वव्रे रहसि सख्याः पतिमृतौ सती ॥31॥

hand. **20.** Devayāni, the daughter of Usanas (Sukra), now spoke to that heroic king in a way expressive of her love for him. She said: 'O King! You have held my hand in yours. **21.** Let there not be another man to hold my hand which you have held in yours! O great king! This union between us is not made by man but by the very Divine. **22.** It is by the will of Providence that you happened to meet me clinging to the sides of the well. Besides, no Brahmana can possibly become my husband, because of the curse of Kacha, the son of Brihaspati, that I had incurred in olden days.' **23.** Though Yayāti did not like that marriage alliance because of it being not sanctioned by scriptures, he however submitted to it, as he believed it was ordained by the Lord and as he felt his mind was fascinated by her.

Sarmishtha's Humiliation (24-33)

24. After king Yayāti had gone, Devayāni went to her father, sage Sukra, weeping, and informed him of all that Sarmishtha had said and done. **25.** The worshipful Rishi Sukra felt very sad on hearing about it. He went away with his daughter from that palace, condemning the priestly occupation and praising the excellence of Ūnjhavritti, a livelihood gained by the collection of fallen grains from fields and grain markets. **26.** On knowing this, the Asura king Vrishaparva, afraid that his enemies might take the sage into their service, went after him and propitiated him with prostrations. **27.** The sage whose rage was only momentary, said to his disciple: 'Do what my daughter wants. I cannot abandon her.' **28.** When the Asura king had agreed to this, Devayāni gave out her mind as follows: 'Wherever I go after my father gives me in marriage, let this Sarmishtha follow me with her attendant maids.'

29. Realising the critical condition of his people, and the advantage that they would gain by the presence of Sukra in their midst, it was arranged that Sarmishtha should attend on Devayāni along with a thousand others. **30.** When the sage next sent his daughter away as Yayāti's wife with Sarmishtha attending on her, he especially instructed the king that he should never share the bed with the latter. **31.** O

राजपुत्र्यार्थितोऽपत्ये धर्मं चावेक्ष्य धर्मवित् । स्मरञ्छुक्रवचः काले दिष्टमेवाभ्यपद्यत ॥32॥
यदुं च तुर्वसुं चैव देवयानी व्यजायत । द्रुह्युं चानुं च पूरुं च शर्मिष्ठा वार्षपर्वणी ॥33॥
गर्भसम्भवमासुर्या भर्तुर्विज्ञाय मानिनी । देवयानी पितुर्गेहं ययौ क्रोधविमूर्च्छिता ॥34॥
प्रियामनुगतः कामी वचोभिरुपमन्त्रयन् । न प्रसादयितुं शेके पादसंवाहनादिभिः ॥35॥
शुक्रस्तमाह कुपितः स्त्रीकामानृतपूरुष । त्वां जरा विशतां मन्द विरूपकरणी नृणाम् ॥36॥

ययातिरुवाच

अतृप्तोऽस्म्यद्य कामानां ब्रह्मन् दुहितरि स्म ते । व्यत्यस्यतां यथाकामं वयसा योऽभिधास्यति ॥37॥
इति लब्धव्यवस्थानः पुत्रं ज्येष्ठमवोचत । यदो तात प्रतीच्छेमां जरां देहि निजं वयः ॥38॥
मातामहकृतां वत्स न तृप्तो विषयेष्वहम् । वयसा भवदीयेन रंस्ये कतिपयाः समाः ॥39॥

यदुरुवाच

नोत्सहे जरसा स्थातुमन्तरा प्राप्तया तव । अविदित्वा सुखं ग्राम्यं वैतृष्ण्यं नैति पूरुषः ॥40॥
तुर्वसुश्चोदितः पित्रा द्रुह्युश्चानुश्च भारत । प्रत्याचख्युरधर्मज्ञा ह्यनित्ये नित्यबुद्धयः ॥41॥
अपृच्छत् तनयं पूरुं वयसोनं गुणाधिकम् । न त्वमग्रजवद् वत्स मां प्रत्याख्यातुमर्हसि ॥42॥

King! The virtuous Sarmishtha soon saw Devayāni big with issue. Herself desirous of issue, Sarmishtha approached the king, the husband of her mistress, in privacy during her fertile period, and chose him as her husband too. **32.** The Rajah knew that according to Dharmasastra, the solicitation of a woman in that condition should not be rejected, and so agreed to her request as ordained by Providence, though he remembered Sukra's prohibition. **33.** Devayāni gave birth to Yadu and Turvasu; and Sarmishtha, the daughter of Vrishaparva, bore three sons, Druhyu, Anu and Pūru.

Sukra's Curse and After (34-51)

34. On coming to know that her husband, the king, had children by Sarmishtha, the proud Devayāni was moved to great anger and went away to her father Sukra's house. **35.** The love-infatuated Yayāti went after her and tried to pacify her with sweet words and personal endearments, but failed. **36.** Angry Sukra now cursed the king: 'O you liar and a slave of lust! Old age which makes the human form ugly shall now set on you!' *Yayati said:* **37.** 'I have not yet been satisfied with life with your daughter.' So Sukra replied: 'If any person is willing to take over your old age, may you be capable of transferring it to him and yourself receiving his youth.'

38. Under this settlement the king called his eldest son Yadu and said: 'O dear son Yadu! You take over for the time being this old age of mine and let me have your youth. **39.** It is your maternal grandfather who conferred this old age on me. I have not yet been satisfied with worldly enjoyments. Let me enjoy the pleasures of life for some time more with the help of your youth.' *Yadu said:* **40.** 'I am not ready to take on the old age that has overtaken you in the middle of my own life. For, I have only just started enjoying life's pleasures, and without sufficient enjoyments of them, a man cannot get a distaste for them.' **41.** In spite of their father's pleading, the other sons Turvasu, Druhyu and Anu also refused to accept the proposal, being ignorant of Dharma and being under the mistaken notion that their fleeting youth was perpetual.

42. Next he made the same request to

पूरुरुवाच

को नु लोके मनुष्येन्द्र पितुरात्मकृतः पुमान् । प्रतिकर्तुं क्षमो यस्य प्रसादाद् विन्दते परम् ॥43॥
उत्तमश्चिन्तितं कुर्यात् प्रोक्तकारी तु मध्यमः । अधमोऽश्रद्धया कुर्यादकर्तोच्चरितं पितुः ॥44॥
इति प्रमुदितः पूरुः प्रत्यगृह्णाज्जरां पितुः । सोऽपि तद्वयसा कामान् यथावज्जुजुषे नृप ॥45॥
सप्तद्वीपपतिः सम्यक् पितृवत् पालयन् प्रजाः । यथोपजोषं विषयाञ्जुजुषेऽव्याहतेन्द्रियः ॥46॥
देवयान्यप्यनुदिनं मनोवाग्देहवस्तुभिः । प्रेयसः परमां प्रीतिमुवाह प्रेयसी रहः ॥47॥
अयजद् यज्ञपुरुषं क्रतुभिर्भूरिदक्षिणैः । सर्वदेवमयं देवं सर्ववेदमयं हरिम् ॥48॥
यस्मिन्निदं विरचितं व्योम्नीव जलदावलिः । नानेव भाति नाभाति स्वप्नमायामनोरथः ॥49॥
तमेव हृदि विन्यस्य वासुदेवं गुहाशयम् । नारायणमणीयांसं निराशीरयजत् प्रभुम् ॥50॥
एवं वर्षसहस्राणि मनःषष्ठैर्मनःसुखम् । विदधानोऽपि नातृप्यत् सार्वभौमः कदिन्द्रियैः ॥51॥

इति श्रीमद्भागवते महापुराणे पारमहंस्यां संहितायां नवमस्कन्धेऽष्टादशोऽध्यायः ॥18॥

his last son Pūru, who was young in years but advanced in virtue. He said: 'Dear one! Do not refuse my request like your elder brothers.' *Pūru replied:* **43.** 'O best of men, who can make an adequate return to one's father for the gift of this body, which is the means for attaining the highest values? The father's grace helps us to realise our highest destiny. **44.** The best son is the one who performs the father's wish even without telling. The one who does what is asked, is the middling. The bad one is he who executes the father's command in a careless and imperfect way. And he who totally refuses to do anything even when asked by the father, cannot be called the father's son, but only his excreta.' **45.** So saying, Pūru took over his father's old age on himself with joy, and Yayāti, assuming his youth, enjoyed the pleasures of life to his heart's content. **46.** The king ruled over the seven continents of the earth like a father to his subjects, and enjoyed the good things of life with unfading vigour of the senses. **47.** And his beloved wife Devayāni gave him the most intense joy in privacy with all the endowments of her mind, word and body. **48.** By the performance of several Yajnas, accompanied with plentiful Dakshinas, he adored the Supreme Being Hari, the recipient of all Yajnas, the embodiment of all Vedas and of all deities and the eraser of all miseries. **49-50.** Establishing in his heart Vāsudeva, the indweller, the subtlest of the subtle—based on whom this universe shines like clouds in the sky or like objects seen in dream, magical show, or reverie, and in whom it subsides when the mind has become calm—establishing Him, known also as Narayana, in the heart, he adored Him with Yajnas giving up all selfish motives. **51.** Thus for a thousand years the emperor enjoyed by means of the five roguish senses and the mind the pleasures which are really mental. Yet he found no satiety.

अथैकोनविंशोऽध्यायः

श्रीशुक उवाच

स इत्थमाचरन् कामान् स्त्रैणोऽपह्नवमात्मनः । बुद्ध्वा प्रियायै निर्विण्णो गाथामेतामगायत ।। 1।।
शृणु भार्गव्यमूं गाथां मद्विधाचरितां भुवि । धीरा यस्यानुशोचन्ति वने ग्रामनिवासिनः ।। 2।।
बस्त एको वने कश्चिद् विचिन्वन् प्रियमात्मनः । ददर्श कूपे पतितां स्वकर्मवशगामजाम् ।। 3।।
तस्या उद्धरणोपायं बस्तः कामी विचिन्तयन् । व्यधत्त तीर्थमुद्धृत्य विषाणाग्रेण रोधसी ।। 4।।
सोत्तीर्य कूपात् सुश्रोणी तमेव चकमे किल । तया वृतं समुद्वीक्ष्य बह्व्योऽजाः कान्तकामिनीः 5।।
पीवानं श्मश्रुलं प्रेष्ठं मीढ्वांसं याभकोविदम् । स एकोऽजवृषस्तासां बह्वीनां रतिवर्धनः ।
रेमे कामग्रहग्रस्त आत्मानं नावबुध्यत ।। 6।।
तमेव प्रेष्ठतमया रममाणमजान्यया । विलोक्य कूपसंविग्ना नामृष्यद् बस्तकर्म तत् ।। 7।।
तं दुर्हृदं सुहृद्रूपं कामिनं क्षणसौहृदम् । इन्द्रियाराममुत्सृज्य स्वामिनं दुःखिता ययौ ।। 8।।
सोऽपि चानुगतः स्त्रैणः कृपणस्तां प्रसादितुम् । कुर्वन्निडविडाकारं नाशक्नोत् पथि संधितुम् ।। 9।।
तस्यास्तत्र द्विजः कश्चिदजास्वाम्यच्छिनद् रुषा । लम्बन्तं वृषणं भूयः सन्दधेऽर्थाय योगवित् ।।10।।

Skandha IX : Chapter 19
YAYĀTI'S RENUNCIATION

The Parable of the Goats (1-11)

Sri Suka said: **1.** Immersed in sensual indulgences, uxorious Yayāti became aware after some time of his steep spiritual fall. He then developed a revulsion for sensuality, and narrated the following story to his wife: **2.** 'O daughter of sage Sukra! Hear a story that is parallel to mine—in which story some sages living in the forest bemoan the fate of one who had given himself up to sensuous indulgences. **3.** A he-goat was once moving about in the forest eating whatever he liked. He came across a she-goat that had fallen in a well owing to the force of its past Karmas. **4.** The sex-intoxicated he-goat, on seeing the female in the well, began to think of the ways and means of lifting her out. Digging the sides of the well with his horns, he made a passage for the she-goat to come out of the well. **5-6.** On coming out of the well, that beautiful she-goat desired to have that he-goat as her mate. Seeing him mated with her, many other she-goats, seeking mates, also sought him, seeing him so plump, hairy, lusty and tireless in mating. A slave to lust, the he-goat never thought of his own true nature. **7.** But the she-goat that was rescued from the well could not bear the sight of her husband mating with another she-goat. **8.** Thus seeing her husband unfaithful, hypocritical, lascivious and bent on enjoyment only, she went away to her master's place in great grief. **9.** But that pitiable he-goat, addicted to female company, ran after her bleating in many ways, to cajole and please her, but in vain. **10.** In great anger the owner of the she-goat, a Brahmana, now cut off the hanging testicles of the he-goat. But through his occult powers, he later united the testicles with the body of the he-goat, so that his she-goat might continue to

सम्बद्धवृषणः सोऽपि ह्यजया कूपलब्धया । कालं बहुतिथं भद्रे कामैर्नाद्यापि तुष्यति ॥११॥
तथाहं कृपणः सुभ्रु भवत्याः प्रेमयन्त्रितः । आत्मानं नाभिजानामि मोहितस्तव मायया ॥१२॥
यत् पृथिव्यां व्रीहियवं हिरण्यं पशवः स्त्रियः । न दुह्यन्ति मनःप्रीतिं पुंसः कामहतस्य ते ॥१३॥
न जातु कामः कामानामुपभोगेन शाम्यति । हविषा कृष्णवर्त्मेव भूय एवाभिवर्धते ॥१४॥
यदा न कुरुते भावं सर्वभूतेष्वमङ्गलम् । समदृष्टेस्तदा पुंसः सर्वाः सुखमया दिशः ॥१५॥
या दुस्त्यजा दुर्मतिभिर्जीर्यतो या न जीर्यते । तां तृष्णां दुःखनिवहां शर्मकामो द्रुतं त्यजेत् ॥१६॥
मात्रा स्वस्रा दुहित्रा वा नाविविक्तासनो भवेत् । बलवानिन्द्रियग्रामो विद्वांसमपि कर्षति ॥१७॥
पूर्णं वर्षसहस्रं मे विषयान् सेवतोऽसकृत् । तथापि चानुसवनं तृष्णा तेषूपजायते ॥१८॥
तस्मादेतामहं त्यक्त्वा ब्रह्मण्याधाय मानसम् । निर्द्वन्द्वो निरहंकारश्चरिष्यामि मृगैः सह ॥१९॥
दृष्टं श्रुतमसद् बुद्ध्वा नानुध्यायेन्न संविशेत् । संसृतिं चात्मनाशं च तत्र विद्वान् स आत्मदृक् ॥२०॥
इत्युक्त्वा नाहुषो जायां तदीयं पूरवे वयः । दत्त्वा स्वां जरसं तस्मादाददे विगतस्पृहः ॥२१॥
दिशि दक्षिणपूर्वस्यां द्रुह्युं दक्षिणतो यदुम् । प्रतीच्यां तुर्वसुं चक्र उदीच्यामनुमीश्वरम् ॥२२॥

mate with him! **11.** That he-goat, after the restoration of his virility, has been indulging in several pleasures with its mate, the she-goat from the well, but he has not reached the satiation point yet.

Yayāti's Sermon on Renunciation (12-20)

12. 'O handsome lady! I too have been like that—a pitiable creature, bound by love of you and infatuated by your charms, going about without any understanding of my spiritual self. **13.** All foods in the world, all animals, all wealth, and all women cannot bring satiety to a man whose mind is a victim of inordinate desire. **14.** Desire is never satisfied by the enjoyment of its objects. Like fire fed with ghee, it only flames up all the more. **15.** When a man's mind, established in same-sightedness, ceases to be moved by vile attachment and antagonism to others, then he finds happiness in all situations. **16.** A man who seeks his own good, should at once abandon his hankering for sense-enjoyments, which evil-minded men find difficult to do. It does not decay even when he himself decays through old age. **17.** A person should not sit on the same seat in solitude even with a mother, a sister, or a daughter. For, the senses are strong, and even a wise man cannot resist their pull. **18.** For a full thousand years I have been having every kind of sensuous enjoyments, but in place of subsiding, the craving for them comes with added force whenever situations arise. **19.** Therefore, I shall now abandon hankering for everything, and then giving over my mind entirely to Him, I shall wander with the animals in the forest without caring for the extremes of weather and abandoning every trace of self-esteem.

20. 'Realising the ephemerality of all objects of the senses, one should not longingly think of them or actually enjoy them. He who is able to recognise bondage and destruction in the thought and enjoyment of objects delighting the senses, he is the learned man, he is the spiritually enlightened person.'

The End of Yayāti's Story (21-29)

21. Saying so to his wife, Yayāti gave back to Pūru the youth he had taken from him and resumed his own old age. He was now without any desire for enjoyments. **22.** Regarding his sons, he appointed Druhyu as ruler of the south-eastern parts of his empire; Yadu, of the

भूमण्डलस्य सर्वस्य पूरुमर्हत्तमं विशाम् । अभिषिच्याग्रजांस्तस्य वशे स्थाप्य वनं ययौ ॥23॥
आसेवितं वर्षपूगान् षड्वर्गं विषयेषु सः । क्षणेन मुमुचे नीडं जातपक्ष इव द्विजः ॥24॥
स तत्र निर्मुक्तसमस्तसङ्ग आत्मानुभूत्या विधुतत्रिलिङ्गः ।
परेऽमले ब्रह्मणि वासुदेवे लेभे गतिं भागवतीं प्रतीतः ॥25॥
श्रुत्वा गाथां देवयानी मेने प्रस्तोभमात्मनः । स्त्रीपुंसोः स्नेहवैक्लव्यात् परिहासमिवेरितम् 26॥
सा संनिवासं सुहृदां प्रपायामिव गच्छताम् । विज्ञायेश्वरतन्त्राणां मायाविरचितं प्रभोः ॥27॥
सर्वत्र सङ्गमुत्सृज्य स्वप्नौपम्येन भार्गवी । कृष्णे मनः समावेश्य व्यधुनोल्लिङ्गमात्मनः ॥28॥
नमस्तुभ्यं भगवते वासुदेवाय वेधसे । सर्वभूताधिवासाय शान्ताय बृहते नमः ॥29॥

इति श्रीमद्भागवते महापुराणे पारमहंस्यां संहितायां नवमस्कन्धे एकोनविंशोऽध्यायः ॥19॥

southern parts; Turvasu, of the western parts; and Anu, of the northern parts. **23.** When he finally departed to the forest as an ascetic, he made the noble Pūru the emperor over the whole earth and its peoples, his elder brothers being only subordinate rulers under him. **24.** Just as fledglings leave their nests immediately they develop wings, so did Yayāti in an instant abandon the senses after having all kinds of indulgences through them for the past several thousand years. **25.** That famous king abandoned there itself all attachments and material objects catering to sense life, established himself in the Atman, the spiritual Self, and through that Self-intuition attained to Brahman, the Supreme Vāsudeva—ever-pure, the transcendent, the support of all.

26. Devayāni, who had listened to the story of the goats, understood that it was meant to prompt her to the path of renunciation through a satire on the flimsy nature of the sexual relation between man and woman. **27-28.** Now she realised that the life of loving association with relatives and friends who are all but mere puppets of the Divine will, is like the gathering of travellers in a wayside rest-house, extremely temporary and fleeting like a dream, brought about by the Maya of the Lord. So she abandoned attachment for everything in life, made her mind fully absorbed in the Lord, and dissolved even her subtle body. **29.** (And Suka concluded:) Salutation to Thee the worshipful Vāsudeva, endowed with the fullness of all divine excellences, the creator of all, the indweller of all, the infinite Being, and the source of all peace!

अथ विंशोऽध्यायः

श्रीशुक उवाच

पूरोर्वंशं प्रवक्ष्यामि यत्र जातोऽसि भारत। यत्र राजर्षयो वंश्या ब्रह्मवंश्याश्च जज्ञिरे ॥ 1॥

जनमेजयो ह्यभूत् पूरोः प्रचिन्वांस्तत्सुतस्ततः। प्रवीरोऽथ नमस्युर्वै तस्माच्चारुपदोऽभवत् ॥ 2॥

तस्य सुद्युरभूत् पुत्रस्तस्माद् बहुगवस्ततः। संयातिस्तस्याहंयाती रौद्राश्वस्तत्सुतः स्मृतः ॥ 3॥

ऋतेयुस्तस्य कुक्षेयुः स्थण्डिलेयुः कृतेयुकः। जलेयुः सन्ततेयुश्च धर्मसत्यव्रतेयवः ॥ 4॥

दशैतेऽप्सरसः पुत्रा वनेयुश्चावमः स्मृतः। घृताच्यामिन्द्रियाणीव मुख्यस्य जगदात्मनः ॥ 5॥

ऋतेयो रन्तिभारोऽभूत् त्रयस्तस्यात्मजा नृप। सुमतिर्ध्रुवोऽप्रतिरथः कण्वोऽप्रतिरथात्मजः ॥ 6॥

तस्य मेधातिथिस्तस्मात् प्रस्कण्वाद्या द्विजातयः। पुत्रोऽभूत् सुमते रैभ्यो दुष्यन्तस्तत्सुतो मतः ॥ 7॥

दुष्यन्तो मृगयां यातः कण्वाश्रमपदं गतः। तत्रासीनां स्वप्रभया मण्डयन्तीं रमामिव ॥ 8॥

विलोक्य सद्यो मुमुहे देवमायामिव स्त्रियम्। बभाषे तां वरारोहां भटैः कतिपयैर्वृतः ॥ 9॥

तद्दर्शनप्रमुदितः संनिवृत्तपरिश्रमः। पप्रच्छ कामसंतप्तः प्रहसञ्श्लक्ष्णया गिरा ॥10॥

का त्वं कमलपत्राक्षि कस्यासि हृदयङ्गमे। किं वा चिकीर्षितं त्वत्र भवत्या निर्जने वने ॥11॥

व्यक्तं राजन्यतनयां वेद्म्यहं त्वां सुमध्यमे। न हि चेतः पौरवाणामधर्मे रमते क्वचित् ॥12॥

Skandha IX : Chapter 20

DUSHYANTA AND BHARATA

From Pūru to Dushyanta (1-7)

Sri Suka said: **1.** Now I shall tell you about the line of Pūru, to which you yourself belong, and which was augmented by the birth of several Rajarshis and Brahmarshis in it. **2.** From Pūru was born Janamejaya; from him, Prachinvān; from him, Pravīra; from him, Namasyu; and from him, Chārupada. **3.** Of Chārupada was born Sudyu; of him, Bahugava; of him, Samyāti; of him, Ahamyāti; and of him, Raudrāsva. **4-5.** Raudrāsva had by his Apsara wife Ghritāchi ten sons—Riteyu, Kuksheyu, Sthandileyu, Kriteyu, Jaleyu, Santateyu, Dharmeyu, Sateyu, Vrateyu, and Vaneyu. These were to their father as the ten Indiryas are to Prana. **6.** Riteyu had as son Rantibhāra. He had three sons named Sumati, Dhruva and Apratiratha. The son of Apratiratha was Kanva. **7.** Kanva's son was Medhātithi. From him were born Praskanva and others, who were Brahmanas. Sumati had Raibhya as son; and from Raibhya was born Dushyanta, according to tradition.

Dushyanta and Sakuntala (8-22)

8-9. Dushyanta accompanied by a few troops went into the forest for a hunt. There he entered the precincts of the Ashrama of Kanva, where he saw a lady who illumined that place with her brilliant aura, as if she were Ramā herself, the enchanting power of the Lord. He fell in love with her instantly. **10.** Her sight filled him with joy and relieved him of the exhaustion from hunting. Excited with love, he addressed her in sweet words: **11.** 'Who are you, lotus-eyed beauty? Whose daughter are you? Why are you here in the solitude of this forest? **12.** O handsome girl! I can clearly see that you are the daughter of some royal house and not of any of these Brahmarshis here.

शकुन्तलोवाच

विश्वामित्रात्मजैवाहं त्यक्ता मेनकया वने । वेदैतद् भगवान् कण्वो वीर किं करवाम ते ॥13॥
आस्यतां ह्यरविन्दाक्ष गृह्यतामर्हणं च नः । भुज्यतां सन्ति नीवारा उष्यतां यदि रोचते ॥14॥

दुष्यन्त उवाच

उपपन्नमिदं सुभ्रु जातायाः कुशिकान्वये । स्वयं हि वृणते राज्ञां कन्यकाः सदृशं वरम् ॥15॥
ओमित्युक्ते यथाधर्ममुपयेमे शकुन्तलाम् । गान्धर्वविधिना राजा देशकालविधानवित् ॥16॥
अमोघवीर्यो राजर्षिर्महिष्यां वीर्यमादधे । श्वोभूते स्वपुरं यातः कालेनासूत सा सुतम् ॥17॥
कण्वः कुमारस्य वने चक्रे समुचिताः क्रियाः । बद्ध्वा मृगेन्द्रांस्तरसा क्रीडति स्म स बालकः ॥18॥
तं दुरत्ययविक्रान्तमादाय प्रमदोत्तमा । हरेरंशांशसम्भूतं भर्तुरन्तिकमागमत् ॥19॥
यदा न जगृहे राजा भार्यापुत्रावनिन्दितौ । शृण्वतां सर्वभूतानां खे वागाहाशरीरिणी ॥20॥
माता भस्त्रा पितुः पुत्रो येन जातः स एव सः । भरस्व पुत्रं दुष्यन्त मावमंस्थाः शकुन्तलाम् ॥21॥
रेतोधाः पुत्रो नयति नरदेव यमक्षयात् । त्वं चास्य धाता गर्भस्य सत्यमाह शकुन्तला ॥22॥
पितर्युपरते सोऽपि चक्रवर्ती महायशाः । महिमा गीयते तस्य हरेरंशभुवो भुवि ॥23॥
चक्रं दक्षिणहस्तेऽस्य पद्मकोशोऽस्य पादयोः । ईजे महाभिषेकेण सोऽभिषिक्तोऽधिराड् विभुः ॥24॥

For, I find that my mind is fascinated by you, and it is a truth that the mind of the kings of Pūru's line will never go after anything unrighteous.' *Sakuntala said:* **13.** 'I am the daughter of Viswāmitra by Menaka, who abandoned me in the forest. This is known to the sage Kanva. Now what service are we to do for you? **14.** O one of prepossessing appearance! Please take your seat here. We have food made of wild rice (*nīvāra*). You can take it, and you may stay here, if you like.' *Dushyanta replied:* **15.** 'O handsome one! Your words are befitting one born in the line of Kausika. For, the daughters of royal houses have the right to choose their husbands themselves privately, according to the Gāndharva rite.' **16.** When Sakuntala agreed to this, the king, who knew very well how to behave according to time, place and circumstance, married her according to the Gāndharva rite.

17. After living with her for the night, the king returned to his capital, and in due course Sakuntala delivered a son. **18.** The Maharshi Kanva himself did all the post-natal ceremonies for the baby in his forest Ashrama. It was found that as he grew up, the child by himself captured lions and played with them. **19.** In due course Sakuntala went to the palace of her husband, along with her son of unbridled prowess who had an element of divinity in him. **20.** When the king refused to accept Sakuntala and her son, all heard a disembodied voice say from the sky: **21.** 'The mother is a mere vessel of skin. The child belongs to the father. The issue that a man begets, is the man himself. O Dushyanta! Take charge of your son, and do not disgrace Sakuntala. **22.** A son who continues the ancestral line can lift his father from the sphere of Yama. You have begotten this boy. Sakuntala has spoken the truth.'

From Bharata to Bharadwāja (23-39)

23. After the death of Dushyanta, this boy Bharata became the emperor and attained to great renown. Endowed as he was with a spark of the Divine Spirit, many are the people who extol him in songs. **24.** On his right palm there was

पञ्चपञ्चाशता मेध्यैर्गङ्गायामनु वाजिभिः । मामतेयं पुरोधाय यमुनायामनु प्रभुः ।।25।।
अष्टसप्ततिमेध्याश्वान् बबन्ध प्रददद् वसु । भरतस्य हि दौष्यन्तेरग्निः साचीगुणे चितः ।
सहस्रं बद्वशो यस्मिन् ब्राह्मणा गा बिभेजिरे ।।26।।
त्रयस्त्रिंशच्छतं ह्यश्वान् बद्ध्वा विस्मापयन् नृपान् । दौष्यन्तिरत्यगान्मायां देवानां गुरुमाययौ ।।27।।
मृगाञ्छुक्लदतः कृष्णान् हिरण्येन परीवृतान् । अदात् कर्मणि मष्णारे नियुतानि चतुर्दश ।।28।।
भरतस्य महत् कर्म न पूर्वे नापरे नृपाः । नैवापुर्नैव प्राप्स्यन्ति बाहुभ्यां त्रिदिवं यथा ।।29।।
किरातहूणान् यवनानन्ध्रान् कङ्कान् खशाञ्छकान् । अब्रह्मण्यान्नृपांश्चाहन्म्लेच्छान्दिग्विजयेऽखिलान् ।।
जित्वा पुरासुरा देवान् ये रसौकांसि भेजिरे । देवस्त्रियो रसां नीताः प्राणिभिः पुनराहरत् ।।31।।
सर्वकामान् दुदुहतुः प्रजानां तस्य रोदसी । समास्त्रिणवसाहस्रीर्दिक्षु चक्रमवर्तयत् ।।32।।
स सम्राड् लोकपालाख्यमैश्वर्यमधिराड्श्रियम् । चक्रं चास्खलितं प्राणान् मृषेत्युपरराम ह ।।33।।
तस्यासन् नृप वैदर्भ्यः पत्न्यस्तिस्रः सुसम्मताः । जघ्नुस्त्यागभयात् पुत्रान् नानुरूपा इतीरिते ।।34।।
तस्यैवं वितथे वंशे तदर्थं यजतः सुतम् । मरुत्स्तोमेन मरुतो भरद्वाजमुपाददुः ।।35।।

the sign of the discus, and on the soles of his feet, the marks of lotus flowers. He was enthroned as emperor to the accompaniment of grand coronation rituals, and he adored the Lord with several Yajnas. **25-26.** Along the course of the Ganges he performed sacrifices with fifty-five horses of great excellence and along the course of the Yamuna, with seventy eight. Dīrghatamas, the son of Mamata, was the officiating priest. The sacrifices of Bharata were performed in every holy place. The enormous number of cows he gifted to thousand Brahmanas was taken by each in lots of thirteen thousand and eighty-four. **27.** In total he conducted one hundred and thirty three horse sacrifices to the great astonishment of all rulers. He surpassed the glory and excellences of all Devas, and he attained to the Supreme Being. **28.** On the occasion of various holy rites, he gave as gift fourteen lakhs of elephants with very white tusks, dark body and golden decorations. **29.** These great devotional acts of Bharata were never matched by anything done by any king in the past, nor will any king in the future be able to do so. It is as futile for anyone to attempt it as trying to catch the heaven with one's hands. **30.** In his campaign for the conquest of all the four regions, he suppressed many tribes of barbarians antagonistic to Vedic culture—tribes like Kirātas, Hūnas, Yavanas, Andhras, Kankas, Khasas, and Sakas. **31.** He rescued all those celestial women whom powerful Asuras had carried with them to Rasātala, which they had wrested from the Devas after defeating them in battle. **32.** Heaven and earth yielded all their requirements to his subjects. In this way he ruled for twenty-seven thousand years, extending his unchallenged sway over all the regions. **33.** Bharata, the emperor of all the worlds, in the end retired from rulership, realising the ephemerality of everything—wealth, prosperity, unquestioned power, and even life.

34. Bharata had as wives three daughters of the king of Vidarbha. When the king complained that none of the children they had borne him were worthy of him, they managed to kill them all, fearing that the king might discard them for not having worthy issue. **35.** When his line was thus threatened with extinction, he performed a Yajna known as Marutstoma, and as a consequence the Maruts presented to him a son named Bharadwāja.

अन्तर्वत्न्यां भ्रातृपत्न्यां मैथुनाय बृहस्पतिः । प्रवृत्तो वारितो गर्भं शप्त्वा वीर्यमवासृजत् ॥36॥
तं त्यक्तुकामां ममतां भर्तृत्यागविशङ्किताम् । नामनिर्वचनं तस्य श्लोकमेनं सुरा जगुः ॥37॥
मूढे भर द्वाजमिमं भर द्वाजं बृहस्पते । यातौ यदुक्त्वा पितरौ भरद्वाजस्ततस्त्वयम् ॥38॥
चोद्यमाना सुरैरेवं मत्वा वितथमात्मजम् । व्यसृजन् मरुतोऽबिभ्रन् दत्तोऽयं वितथेऽन्वये ॥39॥

इति श्रीमद्भागवते महापुराणे पारमहंस्यां संहितायां नवमस्कन्धे विंशोऽध्यायः ॥20॥

36. (How Bharadwāja was obtained by the Maruts is explained.) Brihaspati sought sexual intercourse with the already pregnant wife of his brother Uthya. Thereupon the child in the womb protested, but Brihaspati performed the act by force, cursing the child in the womb. **37.** Afraid that her husband might discard her for this transgression, Mamata, the woman concerned, wanted to discard the child of Brihaspati (who was instantly born), but the Devas made her abstain from it, declaring through Brihaspati: **38.** 'O foolish woman! As he is born of both of us (of Brihaspati and his brother Uthya), you take care of him (*bhara dwājam imam*)'. Mamata replied: 'O Brihaspati! You better protect him who is born of both of us'. The mother and the father said like this to each other and abandoned the child there. He became famous as Bharadwāja. **39.** Mamata thus abandoned the child as of no use for her in spite of being asked by the Devas not to do so. So the Maruts brought up that child, and when Bharata's line was threatened with extinction, they gave him to Bharata as his son.

अथैकविंशोऽध्यायः

श्रीशुक उवाच

वितथस्य सुतो मन्युर्बृहत्क्षत्रो जयस्ततः । महावीर्यो नरो गर्गः सङ्कृतिस्तु नरात्मजः ॥ 1॥
गुरुश्च रन्तिदेवश्च सङ्कृतेः पाण्डुनन्दन । रन्तिदेवस्य हि यश इहामुत्र च गीयते ॥ 2॥
वियद्वित्तस्य ददतो लब्धं लब्धं बुभुक्षतः । निष्किञ्चनस्य धीरस्य सकुटुम्बस्य सीदतः ॥ 3॥
व्यतीयुरष्टचत्वारिंशदहान्यपिबतः किल । घृतपायससंयावं तोयं प्रातरुपस्थितम् ॥ 4॥

Skandha IX : Chapter 21

RANTI DEVA THE COMPASSIONATE

Bharadwāja to Ranti Deva (1-10)

Sri Suka said: **1.** Bharadwāja, also known as Vitatha, (because he was gifted to Bharata when his line was 'vitatha' or about to be extinguished) had Manyu as his son, and Manyu had five sons—Brihadkshatra, Jaya, Mahāvīrya, Nara and Garga. Of these, Nara had Sankriti as son. **2.** O joy of Pāndu's line! Sankriti had two sons—Guru, and Ranti Deva whose fame is a theme for song both in this and in the other worlds. **3.** He lived satisfied with what chance brought him. Even when he was hungry in the extreme, he gave away to others whatever food he happened to get. A man of steady mind, he suffered with his family from privations, as he was without any possessions. **4.** He has once to spend forty-eight days

कृच्छ्रप्राप्तकुटुम्बस्य क्षुत्तृड्भ्यां जातवेपथोः । अतिथिर्ब्राह्मणः काले भोक्तुकामस्य चागमत् ॥ 5॥
तस्मै संव्यभजत् सोऽन्नमादृत्य श्रद्धयान्वितः । हरिं सर्वत्र संपश्यन् स भुक्त्वा प्रययौ द्विजः ॥ 6॥
अथान्यो भोक्ष्यमाणस्य विभक्तस्य महीपते । विभक्तं व्यभजत् तस्मै वृषलाय हरिं स्मरन् ॥ 7॥
याते शूद्रे तमन्योऽगादतिथिः श्वभिरावृतः । राजन् मे दीयतामन्नं सगणाय बुभुक्षते ॥ 8॥
स आदृत्यावशिष्टं यद् बहुमानपुरस्कृतम् । तच्च दत्त्वा नमश्चक्रे श्वभ्यः श्वपतये विभुः ॥ 9॥
पानीयमात्रमुच्छेषं तच्चैकपरितर्पणम् । पास्यतः पुल्कसोऽभ्यागादपो देह्यशुभस्य मे ॥10॥
तस्य तां करुणां वाचं निशम्य विपुलश्रमाम् । कृपया भृशसन्तप्त इदमाहामृतं वचः ॥11॥

न कामयेऽहं गतिमीश्वरात् परामष्टर्द्धियुक्तामपुनर्भवं वा ।
आर्तिं प्रपद्येऽखिलदेहभाजामन्तःस्थितो येन भवन्त्यदुःखाः ॥12॥

क्षुत्तृट्श्रमो गात्रपरिश्रमश्च दैन्यं क्लमः शोकविषादमोहाः ।
सर्वे निवृत्ताः कृपणस्य जन्तोर्जिजीविषोर्जीवजलार्पणान्मे ॥13॥

इति प्रभाष्य पानीयं म्रियमाणः पिपासया । पुल्कसायाददाद्धीरो निसर्गकरुणो नृपः ॥14॥
तस्य त्रिभुवनाधीशाः फलदाः फलमिच्छताम् । आत्मानं दर्शयाञ्चक्रुर्माया विष्णुविनिर्मिताः ॥15॥

without any food or drink. At the end of it he chanced to get some Payasa with ghee, cooked wheat and water. **5.** The members of his family had been reduced to the utmost strait, and he himself was trembling with hunger and thirst. When they were about to eat that food got by chance, a Brahmana guest arrived. **6.** Ranti Deva gave him a good share of that food with great cordiality and sincere reverence; for he saw Hari residing in all. That Brahmana took his meal and went away highly satisfied. **7.** O King! Next when he was dividing the remaining food among the hungry members of his family, a labourer arrived there as guest. Seeing Sri Hari in him too, Ranti Deva gave away to him even that remaining food which he was about to divide. **8.** When that guest was gone, a hunter with a pack of dogs arrived, and said: 'O Master! give some food to me and my dogs. We are very hungry.' **9.** So the great Ranti Deva gave away whatever food remained to the dogs and their master, and prostrated himself before them, seeing the Lord residing in them. **10.** All that remained now was only water enough for one person to drink. When he was about to drink it, an outcaste came and cried: 'For this wretch, give at least some water to drink.'

Ranti Deva's Sermon (11-18)

11. Hearing his heart-rending appeal, Ranti Deva was moved to great pity, and spoke to him in the following sweet words of great import: **12.** 'I do not pray to the Lord for a state in which I shall be endowed with the eightfold powers, nor even for the state of liberation from the cycle of birth and death. I desire only to abide within all beings and undergo the sufferings that accrue to them. By my taking over their sufferings, they will be free from misery. **13.** By supplying the life-giving water to a man panting for it in great distress, I have been freed of all sufferings—hunger, thirst, exhaustion, physical ailment, misery, sorrow and mental confusion.' (For true happiness lies in suffering for others.)

14. So saying, Ranti Deva, the kind-hearted and heroic, gave whatever water there was to that outcaste guest, although he was himself dying of thirst. **15.** At this point Brahma, Vishnu and Maheswara, who bestow the fruits of

स वै तेभ्यो नमस्कृत्य निःसङ्गो विगतस्पृहः । वासुदेवे भगवति भक्त्या चक्रे मनः परम् ॥16॥
ईश्वरालम्बनं चित्तं कुर्वतोऽनन्यराधसः । माया गुणमयी राजन् स्वप्नवत् प्रत्यलीयत ॥17॥
तत्प्रसङ्गानुभावेन रन्तिदेवानुवर्तिनः । अभवन् योगिनः सर्वे नारायणपरायणाः ॥18॥
गर्गाच्छिनिस्ततो गार्ग्यः क्षत्राद् ब्रह्म ह्यवर्तत । दुरितक्षयो महावीर्यात् तस्य त्रय्यारुणिः कविः ॥19॥
पुष्करारुणिरित्यत्र ये ब्राह्मणगतिं गताः । बृहत्क्षत्रस्य पुत्रोऽभूद्धस्ती यद्धस्तिनापुरम् ॥20॥
अजमीढो द्विमीढश्च पुरुमीढश्च हस्तिनः । अजमीढस्य वंश्याः स्युः प्रियमेधादयो द्विजाः ॥21॥
अजमीढाद् बृहदिषुस्तस्य पुत्रो बृहद्धनुः । बृहत्कायस्ततस्तस्य पुत्र आसीज्जयद्रथः ॥22॥
तत्सुतो विशदस्तस्य सेनजित् समजायत । रुचिराश्वो दृढहनुः काश्यो वत्सश्च तत्सुताः ॥23॥
रुचिराश्वसुतः पारः पृथुसेनस्तदात्मजः । पारस्य तनयो नीपस्तस्य पुत्रशतं त्वभूत् ॥24॥
स कृत्व्यां शुककन्यायां ब्रह्मदत्तमजीजनत् । स योगी गवि भार्यायां विष्वक्सेनमधात् सुतम् 25॥
जैगीषव्योपदेशेन योगतन्त्रं चकार ह । उदक्स्वनस्ततस्तस्माद् भल्लादो बार्हदीषवाः ॥26॥
यवीनरो द्विमीढस्य कृतिमांस्तत्सुतः स्मृतः । नाम्ना सत्यधृतिर्यस्य दृढनेमिः सुपार्श्वकृत् ॥27॥

action to their desire-prompted votaries, revealed themselves before him, discarding the false forms of the Brahmana, the labourer, the hunter and the outcaste in which they had clothed themselves by the power of Maya. **16.** Ranti Deva made prostrations before them. Unattached and desireless, he only surrendered himself to the worshipful Lord Vāsudeva but prayed for no boons, in spite of his most trying worldly situation. **17.** As the dream phenomena dissolve on waking, the bondage of body and mind created by Maya dissipated itself before Ranti Deva, who had made the Lord the sole support of his being, discarding every form of desire. **18.** By their association with him all persons in Ranti Deva's establishment also became Yogis highly devoted to Lord Narayana.

Lines of Garga and Others (19-26)

19-21. Garga's son was Sini, and Sini's son, Gārgya. Though Gārgya was a Kshatriya, his sons were recognised as Brahmanas. Manyu's son Mahāvīrya had as son Duritakshaya; and he had three sons named Trayyāruni, Kavi, and Pushkarāruni. These, though Kshatriyas by birth, became Brahmanas. Brihatkshatra, Manyu's eldest son, had a son named Hastī, who was the founder of Hastināpura. Hastī had three sons, Ajamedha, Dvimīdha and Purumīdha. Priyamīdha and other issue of Ajamīdha became Brahmanas.

22. Ajamīdha had another son named Brihadishu. His son was Brihaddhanu; his son, Brihatkāya; and his, Jayadratha. **23.** Jayadratha's son was Visada; his son, Senajit; and his sons, Ruchirāsva, Dridhahanu, Kāsya, and Vatsa. **24.** Ruchirāsva had as son Pāra; he, Prithusena and another son, Nīpa. Nīpa had a hundred sons. **25.** Nīpa also begot Brahmadatta by Kritvi, the daughter of Suka. Brahmadatta, who was a Yogi begot by his wife Saraswati, the goddess of speech, a son named Vishvaksena. **26**. Brahmadatta created the Yogatantra on the advice of Jaigīshavya. From Vishvaksena was born Udaksvana, and from him, Bhallāda. These constitute the line of Brihadishu.

Lines of Dvimīdha and Others (27-36)

27. Dvimīdha, another son of Hasti, had Yavīnara as son. His son was Kritimān. He had as son Satyadhriti; he,

सुपार्श्वात् सुमतिस्तस्य पुत्रः सन्नतिमांस्ततः । कृतिर्हिरण्यनाभाद् यो योगं प्राप्य जगौ स्म षट् 28॥
संहिताः प्राच्यसाम्नां वै नीपो ह्युग्रायुधस्ततः । तस्य क्षेम्यः सुवीरोऽथ सुवीरस्य रिपुञ्जयः ॥29॥
ततो बहुरथो नाम पुरमीढोऽप्रजोऽभवत् । नलिन्यामजमीढस्य नीलः शान्तिः सुतस्ततः ॥30॥
शान्तेः सुशान्तिस्तत्पुत्रः पुरुजोऽर्कस्ततोऽभवत् । भर्म्यार्श्वस्तनयस्तस्य पञ्चासन्मुद्गलादयः ॥31॥
यवीनरो बृहदिषुः काम्पिल्यः संजयः सुताः । भर्म्यार्श्वः प्राह पुत्रा मे पञ्चानां रक्षणाय हि ॥32॥
विषयाणामलमिमे इति पञ्चालसंज्ञिताः । मुद्गलाद् ब्रह्म निर्वृत्तं गोत्रं मौद्गल्यसंज्ञितम् 33॥
मिथुनं मुद्गलाद् भार्म्याद् दिवोदासः पुमानभूत् । अहल्या कन्यका यस्यां शतानन्दस्तु गौतमात् ॥34॥
तस्य सत्यधृतिः पुत्रो धनुर्वेदविशारदः । शरद्वांस्तत्सुतो यस्मादुर्वशीदर्शनात् किल ॥35॥
शरस्तम्बेऽपतद् रेतो मिथुनं तदभूच्छुभम् । तद् दृष्ट्वा कृपयागृह्णाच्छन्तनुर्मृगयां चरन् ।
कृपः कुमारः कन्या च द्रोणपत्न्यभवत् कृपी ॥36॥

इति श्रीमद्भागवते महापुराणे पारमहंस्यां संहितायां नवमस्कन्धे एकविंशोऽध्यायः ॥21॥

Dridhanemi; and he, Supārsva. **28-29**. Supārsva's son was Sumati; his son, Sannatimān; and his son, Kriti. Kriti learnt the Yogasastra from Hiranyanābha, and gained efficiency in the six collections of Prāchyasāmas. From Kriti was born Nīpa; from him, Ugrāyudha; from him, Kshemya; from him, Suvīra; and from him Ripunjaya. **30.** From Ripunjaya was born Bahuratha. Purumīdha was without issue. But Ajamīdha had by his wife Nalini a son named Nīla, and from him was born Sānti. **31.** Sānti had as son Susānti; he, Puruja; he, Arka; and he, Bharmyāsva. Bharmyāsva had five sons beginning with Mudgala. **32-33.** Bharmyāsva's five sons were Mudgala, Yavīnara; Brihadishu, Kāmpilya and Sanjaya. Bharmyāsva said to his sons: 'You are capable of protecting my five provinces like my five senses!' So they came to be known under the group name Panchālas. From Mudgala a line of Brahmanas known as Maudgalyas arose. **34.** To Bharmyāsva's son Mudgala was born a son Divodāsa and a daughter Ahalya. From that Ahalya was born Satānanda as the son of the sage Gautama. **35-36.** He had a son named Satyadhriti, an expert in the science of arms. His son was Saradvān. Owing to infatuation caused by the sight of the heavenly beauty Urvasi, his virility fell on a clump of Munja grass. It became a boy and a girl of auspicious deportment. While King Santanu was hunting in the forest, he saw this couple and took them under his care. The boy came to be known as the Acharya Kripa, and the female child, known as Kripī, grew to be the wife of Dronāchārya.

अथ द्वाविंशोऽध्यायः

श्रीशुक उवाच

मित्रेयुश्च दिवोदासाच्च्यवनस्तत्सुतो नृप । सुदासः सहदेवोऽथ सोमको जन्तुजन्मकृत् ॥ 1॥
तस्य पुत्रशतं तेषां यवीयान् पृषतः सुतः । द्रुपदो द्रौपदी तस्य धृष्टद्युम्नादयः सुताः ॥ 2॥
धृष्टद्युम्नाद् धृष्टकेतुर्भार्म्याः पञ्चालका इमे । योऽजमीढसुतो ह्यन्य ऋक्षः संवरणस्ततः ॥ 3॥
तपत्यां सूर्यकन्यायां कुरुक्षेत्रपतिः कुरुः परीक्षित् सुधनुर्जह्नुर्निषधाश्वः कुरोः सुताः ॥ 4॥
सुहोत्रोऽभूत् सुधनुषश्च्यवनोऽथ ततः कृती । वसुस्तस्योपरिचरो बृहद्रथमुखास्ततः ॥ 5॥
कुशाम्बमत्स्यप्रत्यग्रचेदिपाद्याश्च चेदिपाः । बृहद्रथात् कुशाग्रोऽभूदृषभस्तस्य तत्सुतः ॥ 6॥
जज्ञे सत्यहितोऽपत्यं पुष्पवांस्तत्सुतो जहुः । अन्यस्यां चापि भार्यायां सकले द्वे बृहद्रथात् ॥ 7॥
ते मात्रा बहिरुत्सृष्टे जरया चाभिसन्धिते । जीव जीवेति क्रीडन्त्या जरासन्धोऽभवत् सुतः 8॥
ततश्च सहदेवोऽभूत् सोमापिर्यच्छ्रुतश्रवाः । परीक्षिदनपत्योऽभूत् सुरथो नाम जाह्नवः ॥ 9॥
ततो विदूरथस्तस्मात् सार्वभौमस्ततोऽभवत् । जयसेनस्तत्तनयो राधिकोऽतोऽयुतो ह्यभूत् ॥10॥

Skandha IX : Chapter 22

BHĪSHMA, KURU, PĀNDAVAS AND OTHERS

Drupada, Kuru etc. (1 6)

Sri Suka said: **1.** O King! Divodāsa had a son named Mitreyu. He had four sons named Chyavana, Sudāsa, Sahadeva and Somaka. Somaka had a son named Jantu. **2.** Besides him, Somaka had a hundred sons, of whom the youngest was Prishata. His son was Drupada, whose daughter was Draupadi and sons, Dhrishtadyumna and others. **3.** From Dhrishtadyumna was born Dhrishtaketu. As they were born in the line of Panchālas connected with Bharmyāsva, they came to be known as Panchālas. Another son of Ajamīdha was Riksha. To him was born Samvarana. **4.** Samvarana had by his wife Tapati, the daughter of the sun-deity, a son named Kuru, the ruler of Kurukshetra. Kuru's sons were Parīkshit, Sudhanu, Jahnu and Nishadhāsva. **5.** From among them, Sudhanu had a son named Suhotra; he, Chyavana; he, Kriti; he, Vasu who could travel through the sky, and he, Brihadratha and others. **6.** Vasu had also sons who became the rulers of Kusāmbas, Matsyas, Pratyagras and Chedipas. All of them ruled parts of the region called Chedi. From Brihadratha, Kusāgra was born, and from him, Rishabha.

Jarāsandha (7-10)

7. Rishabha's son was Satyahita; his son, Pushpavān; and his son, Jahu. By another wife, Brihadratha had a child who was born with a body split into two. **8**. The split halves of the body were thrown out by the mother. But a demoness named Jarā, who was sporting there, united the halves, exhorting the child to become alive. This child therefore came to be known as Jarāsandha. **9.** From Jarāsandha was born Sahadeva; from him, Somāpi and Srutasravas. Parīkshit, the son of Kuru, had no issue; but Jahnu, another son, had Suratha as his offspring. **10.** From him was born Vidūratha; from him, Sārvabhauma; from him, Jayasena; from him, Rādhika; and from him, Ayuta.

ततश्च क्रोधनस्तस्माद् देवातिथिरमुष्य च । ऋष्यस्तस्य दिलीपोऽभूत् प्रतीपस्तस्य चात्मजः 11
देवापिः शन्तनुस्तस्य बाह्लीक इति चात्मजाः । पितृराज्यं परित्यज्य देवापिस्तु वनं गतः ॥12॥
अभवच्छन्तनू राजा प्राङ्महाभिषसंज्ञितः । यं यं कराभ्यां स्पृशति जीर्णं यौवनमेति सः ॥13॥
शान्तिमाप्नोति चैवाग्र्यां कर्मणा तेन शन्तनुः । समा द्वादश तद्राज्ये न ववर्ष यदा विभुः ॥14॥
शन्तनुर्ब्राह्मणैरुक्तः परिवेत्तायमग्रभुक् । राज्यं देह्यग्रजायाशु पुरराष्ट्रविवृद्धये ॥15॥
एवमुक्तो द्विजैर्ज्येष्ठं छन्दयामास सोऽब्रवीत् । तन्मन्त्रिप्रहितैर्विप्रैर्वेदाद् विभ्रंशितो गिरा ॥16॥
वेदवादातिवादान् वै तदा देवो ववर्ष ह । देवापिर्योगमास्थाय कलापग्राममाश्रितः ॥17॥
सोमवंशे कलौ नष्टे कृतादौ स्थापयिष्यति । बाह्लीकात् सोमदत्तोऽभूद् भूरिर्भूरिश्रवास्ततः 18॥
शलश्च शन्तनोरासीद् गङ्गायां भीष्म आत्मवान् । सर्वधर्मविदां श्रेष्ठो महाभागवतः कविः ॥19॥
वीरयूथाग्रणीर्येन रामोऽपि युधि तोषितः । शन्तनोर्दाशकन्यायां जज्ञे चित्राङ्गदः सुतः ॥20॥
विचित्रवीर्यश्चावरजो नाम्ना चित्राङ्गदो हतः । यस्यां पराशरात् साक्षादवतीर्णो हरेः कला ॥21॥

Santanu (11-18)

11. From Ayuta was born Krodhana; from him, Devātithi; from him, Rishya; from him Dilīpa; and from him, Pratīpa. **12.** Pratīpa had as sons Devāpi, Santanu, and Bāhlīka. Devāpi left the kingdom for the woods to take to the ascetic way of life. **13.** So Santanu, who was known in his previous life as Mahābhishak, became king. Whatever old object he touched, that became young. **14-15.** He became widely known as Santanu, because his touch brought peace (Sānti) everywhere. For twelve years, Indra did not send rain to his country. So he consulted learned Brahmanas to know the cause of it. They said: 'By enjoying the land while your elder brother is alive, you have become a *Parivettā*. So for the good and prosperity of the country, entrust it to your brother.' **16-17.** When the Brahmanas gave this ruling, he requested his brother Devāpi to take charge of the kingdom. But his ministers (who did not want this change) had sent some Brahmanas to lead Devāpi astray from the Vedas and thus make him unfit to become the ruler. Under their instruction Devāpi spoke criticising and condemning the Vedas. When he thus ceased to be qualified any more for leadership, Indra released rain at once over the country. Devāpi continues to stay in the village of Kalāpa, practising Yoga. **18.** After the Lunar dynasty perishes in the Kali Yuga, this Devāpi will resuscitate it at the beginning of Satya Yuga. Bāhlīka, the youngest brother, had a son named Somadatta. He had as sons Bhūri, Bhūrisravas, and Sala.

Bhīshma and Pāndavas (19-33)

19. Santanu had by Ganga Devi a son—the great Bhīshma, who was established in the Self, who was a devotee of the highest order, who was learned and who knew all about the codes of Dharma. **20.** Even heroic Parasurama was highly pleased with Bhīshma for his heroism in battle. Santanu had by the fisherwoman Satyavati another son named Chitrāngada, who died early in life at the hands of a Gandharva. **21.** Santanu had also a younger son named Vichitravīrya. Now before her marriage with Santanu, the fisherwoman Satyavati had a son by the sage Parāsara, who was a partial incarna-

वेदगुप्तो मुनिः कृष्णो यतोऽहमिदमध्यगाम् । हित्वा स्वशिष्यान् पैलादीन् भगवान् बादरायणः 22
मह्यं पुत्राय शान्ताय परं गुह्यमिदं जगौ । विचित्रवीर्योऽथोवाह काशिराजसुते बलात् ।।23।।
स्वयंवरादुपानीते अम्बिकाम्बालिके उभे । तयोरासक्तहृदयो गृहीतो यक्ष्मणा मृतः ।।24।।
क्षेत्रेऽप्रजस्य वै भ्रातुर्मात्रोक्तो बादरायणः । धृतराष्ट्रं च पाण्डुं च विदुरं चाप्यजीजनत् ।।25।।
गान्धार्यां धृतराष्ट्रस्य जज्ञे पुत्रशतं नृप । तत्र दुर्योधनो ज्येष्ठो दुःशला चापि कन्यका ।।26।।
शापान्मैथुनरुद्धस्य पाण्डोः कुन्त्यां महारथाः । जाता धर्मानिलेन्द्रेभ्यो युधिष्ठिरमुखास्त्रयः ।।27।।
नकुलः सहदेवश्च माद्र्यां नासत्यदस्रयोः । द्रौपद्यां पञ्च पञ्चभ्यः पुत्रास्ते पितरोऽभवन् ।।28।।
युधिष्ठिरात् प्रतिविन्ध्यः श्रुतसेनो वृकोदरात् । अर्जुनाच्छ्रुतकीर्तिस्तु शतानीकस्तु नाकुलिः ।।29।।
सहदेवसुतो राजञ्छ्रुतकर्मा तथापरे । युधिष्ठिरात् तु पौरव्यां देवकोऽथ घटोत्कचः ।।30।।
भीमसेनाद्धिडिम्बायां काल्यां सर्वगतस्ततः । सहदेवात् सुहोत्रं तु विजयासूत पार्वती ।।31।।
करेणुमत्यां नकुलो निरमित्रं तथार्जुनः । इरावन्तमुलूप्यां वै सुतायां बभ्रुवाहनम् ।
मणिपूरपतेः सोऽपि तत्पुत्रः पुत्रिकासुतः ।।32।।
तव तातः सुभद्रायामभिमन्युरजायत । सर्वातिरथजिद् वीर उत्तरायां ततो भवान् ।।33।।

tion of Sri Hari. **22-24.** That son was the sage Krishna-Dwaipāyana also known as Bādarāyana, who became the saviour of the Veda. It was from him that I (Suka) was born. Discarding the claims of his disciples like Paila, he imparted the great esoteric gospel of the *Bhagavata* to me, his son, given to serenity. Vichitravīrya was married to two daughters of the Rajah of Kāsi, named Ambika and Ambālika, who were brought by force (by Bhīshma) on the occasion of their Swayamvara or marriage by the bride's choice. With his heart absorbed in them, he died early a victim to consumption. **25.** At the order of his mother Satyavati, Bādarāyana raised issue in the widows of his brother Vichitravīrya who had died childless. These were Dhritarāshtra, Pāndu and Vidura. **26.** O King! Of these, Dhritarāshtra had, by his wife Gāndhāri, a hundred sons headed by Duryodhana. He had also a daughter by name Dussala. **27.** As his brother, King Pāndu, could not have intercourse with his wife Kunti owing to a sage's curse, the great car-warriors Yudhishthira, Bhīma and Arjuna were begotten in her by Yama, Vāyu and Indra respectively. **28.** Mādri, another wife of Pāndu, had Nakula and Sahadeva as sons begotten by the Aswini-Devas. Draupadi had five sons by her five husbands, the sons of Pāndu, but the sons died in their boyhood and left no issue. **29-31.** The issue of Draupadi born to Yudhishthira was Prativindhya; to Bhīmasena, Srutasena; to Arjuna, Srutakīrti; to Nakula, Satānīka; and to Sahadeva, Srutakarma. From other wives they had other issue: Devaka for Yudhishthira in Pauravi; Ghatotkacha and Sarvagata for Bhīma in Hidimbī and Kālī respectively. And Vijaya, the daughter of the mountain, brought forth Suhotra as the son son of Sahadeva. **32.** Nakula begot Niramitra by Karenumati, Arjuna begot Irāvan by the Nāga lady Ulūpi and Babhruvāhana by the daughter of the king of Manipūra. Babhruvāhana remained as the son of the king of Manipūra following the rules of marriage according to Putrikādharma. **33.** Abhimanyu, the heroic, who was victorious over all super-warriors, was Arjuna's son by Subhadra.

परिक्षीणेषु कुरुषु द्रौणेर्ब्रह्मास्त्रतेजसा । त्वं च कृष्णानुभावेन सजीवो मोचितोऽन्तकात् ॥34॥
तवेमे तनयास्तात जनमेजयपूर्वकाः । श्रुतसेनो भीमसेन उग्रसेनश्च वीर्यवान् ॥35॥
जनमेजयस्त्वां विदित्वा तक्षकान्निधनं गतम् । सर्पान् वै सर्पयागाग्नौ स होष्यति रुषान्वितः ॥36॥
कावषेयं पुरोधाय तुरं तुरगमेधयाट् । समन्तात् पृथिवीं सर्वां जित्वा यक्ष्यति चाध्वरैः ॥37॥
तस्य पुत्रः शतानीको याज्ञवल्क्यात् त्रयीं पठन् । अस्त्रज्ञानं क्रियाज्ञानं शौनकात् परमेष्यति ॥38॥
सहस्रानीकस्तत्पुत्रस्ततश्चैवाश्वमेधजः । असीमकृष्णस्तस्यापि नेमिचक्रस्तु तत्सुतः ॥39॥
गजाह्वये हृते नद्या कौशाम्ब्यां साधु वत्स्यति । उक्तस्ततश्चित्ररथस्तस्मात् कविरथः सुतः ॥40॥
तस्माच्च वृष्टिमांस्तस्य सुषेणोऽथ महीपतिः । सुनीथस्तस्य भविता नृचक्षुर्यत्सुखीनलः ॥41॥
परिप्लवः सुतस्तस्मान्मेधावी सुनयात्मजः । नृपञ्जयस्ततो दूर्वस्तिमिस्तस्माज्जनिष्यति ॥42॥
तिमेर्बृहद्रथस्तस्माच्छतानीकः सुदासजः । शतानीकाद् दुर्दमनस्तस्यापत्यं वहीनरः ॥43॥
दण्डपाणिर्निमिस्तस्य क्षेमको भविता नृपः । ब्रह्मक्षत्रस्य वै प्रोक्तो वंशो देवर्षिसत्कृतः ॥44॥
क्षेमकं प्राप्य राजानं संस्थां प्राप्स्यति वै कलौ । अथ मागधराजानो भवितारो वदामि ते ॥45॥
भविता सहदेवस्य मार्जारिर्यच्छ्रुतश्रवाः । ततो युतायुस्तस्यापि निरमित्रोऽथ तत्सुतः ॥46॥

From that Abhimanyu, you (Parikshit) were born in Uttara.

Parikshit and Successors (34-44)

34. After all the Kurus headed by Duryodhana had died in battle, Aswatthama, the son of Drona, released the Brahma missile, and you in the mother's womb were scorched by it, but by Krishna's grace you were revived and rescued from the hands of death. **35.** O dear one! With Janamejaya as the eldest, Srutasena, Bhīmasena and Ugrasena are your sons. **36.** Knowing about your death by the bite of the serpent Takshaka, Janamejaya will perform a sacrifice in which he will put all the serpents as offerings in the sacrificial fire. **37.** After conquering the whole world, Janamejaya will adore the Supreme Being by performing an Aswamedha and other sacrifices, taking as his officiating priest Tura belonging to the line of Kavasha. **38.** His son Satānīka will learn the Veda from Yājnavalkya, the science of arms from Kripa, and the knowledge of rituals and of Supreme Brahman from Saunaka. **39.** He will have as son Sahasrānīka; he, Asvamedhaja; he, Asīmakrishna; and he, Nemichakra. **40.** When Hastināpura will be swallowed by the river, he will go to reside in Kausāmbi. To Nemichakra would be born Utka; to him, Chitraratha, and to him, Kavirattha. **41.** To Kaviratha will be born Vrishtimān; to him, Sushena; to him, Sunītha; to him, Nrichakshus; and to him, Sukhīnala. **42.** Of Sukhīnala will be born Pariplava; of him, Sunaya; of him, Medhāvī; of him, Nripanjaya; of him, Dūrva; and of him, Timi. **43.** To Timi will be born Brihadratha; to him, Sudāsa; to him, Satānīka; to him, Durdamana; and to him, Vahīnara. **44.** To him will be born Dandapāni; to him, Nimi; and to him, Kshemaka. I have now described to you this line of Brahmanas and Kshatriyas who have been honoured by Devas and Rishis. **45.** This line will cease with Kshemaka in the age of Kali. Next I shall speak to you of those who will become kings of Magadha.

Kings of Magadha (46-49)

46. Sahadeva will have a son Mārjari

सुनक्षत्रः सुनक्षत्राद् बृहत्सेनोऽथ कर्मजित् । ततः सृतञ्जयाद् विप्रः शुचिस्तस्य भविष्यति ।47॥
क्षेमोऽथ सुव्रतस्तस्माद् धर्मसूत्रः शमस्ततः । द्युमत्सेनोऽथ सुमतिः सुबलो जनिता ततः ॥48॥
सुनीथः सत्यजिदथ विश्वजिद् यद् रिपुञ्जयः । बार्हद्रथाश्च नृपाला भाव्याः साहस्रवत्सरम् ॥49॥

इति श्रीमद्भागवते महापुराणे पारमहंस्यां संहितायां नवमस्कन्धे द्वाविंशोऽध्यायः ॥22।

known also as Somapi. His son will be Srutasravas; his, Ayutāyus; and his, Niramitra. **47.** His son will be Sunakshatra; his son, Brihatsena; his son, Karmajit; his son, Sritanjaya; his son, Vipra; and his son, Suchi. **48.** Suchi's son will be Kshema; his son, Suvrata; his son, Dharmasūtra; his son, Sama; his son, Dyumatsena; his son, Sumati; and his son, Subala. **49.** Subala will have as son Sunītha; he Satyajit; he, Viswajit; and he, Ripunjaya. All these belonging to the line of Brihadratha, will rule for a thousand years.

अथ त्रयोविंशोऽध्यायः

श्रीशुक उवाच

अनोः सभानरश्चक्षुः परोक्षश्च त्रयः सुताः । सभानरात् कालनरः सृञ्जयस्तत्सुतस्ततः ॥ 1॥
जनमेजयस्तस्य पुत्रो महाशीलो महामनाः । उशीनरस्तितिक्षुश्च महामनस आत्मजौ ॥ 2॥
शिबिर्वनः शमिर्दक्षश्चत्वारोशीनरात्मजाः । वृषादर्भः सुवीरश्च मद्रः कैकेय आत्मजाः ॥ 3॥
शिबेश्चत्वार एवासंस्तितिक्षोश्च रुशद्रथः । ततो हेमोऽथ सुतपा बलिः सुतपसोऽभवत् ॥ 4॥
अङ्गवङ्गकलिङ्गाद्याः सुह्मपुण्ड्रान्ध्रसंज्ञिताः । जज्ञिरे दीर्घतमसो बलेः क्षेत्रे महीक्षितः ॥ 5॥
चक्रुः स्वनाम्ना विषयान् षडिमान् प्राच्यकांश्च ते । खनपानोऽङ्गतो जज्ञे तस्माद् दिविरथस्ततः ॥ 6॥
सुतो धर्मरथो यस्य जज्ञे चित्ररथोऽप्रजाः । रोमपाद इति ख्यातस्तस्मै दशरथः सखा ॥ 7॥
शान्तां स्वकन्यां प्रायच्छदृष्यशृङ्ग उवाह ताम् । देवेऽवर्षति यं रामा आनिन्युर्हरिणीसुतम् ॥ 8॥

Skandha IX : Chapter 23

DESCENDANTS OF YAYĀTI'S SONS

Descendants of Anu and Druhya (1-17)

Sri Suka said: **1.** Anu, a son of Yayāti, had as sons Sabhānara, Chakshu, and Paroksha. Sabhānara's son was Kālanara; and his son, Srinjaya. **2.** From Srinjaya was born Janamejaya; from him, Mahāsīla; from him, Mahāmanas; and from him, Usīnara and Titikshu. **3-4.** From among these, Usīnara had four sons named Sibi, Vana, Sami and Daksha. Sibi had four sons Vrishādarbha, Suvīra, Madra and Kaikeya. Titikshu, another son of Mahāmanas, had a son named Rusadratha. From him was born Hema; from him, Sutapas; and from him, Bali.

5. By Bali's wife, Dīrghatamas begot as sons Anga, Vanga, Kalinga, Suhma, Pundra and Āndhra. **6.** They ruled over six provinces on the eastern side of Bhārata known after their names. From among these, Anga had a son named Khanapāna, and from him was born Diviratha. **7-8.** He had a son named Dharmaratha. His son Chitraratha, more widely known as Romapāda, was childless. His

नाट्यसङ्गीतवादित्रैर्विभ्रमालिङ्गनार्हणैः । स तु राज्ञोऽनपत्यस्य निरूप्येष्टिं मरुत्वतः ॥ 9॥
प्रजामदाद् दशरथो येन लेभेऽप्रजाः प्रजाः । चतुरङ्गो रोमपादात् पृथुलाक्षस्तु तत्सुतः ॥10॥
बृहद्रथो बृहत्कर्मा बृहद्भानुश्च तत्सुताः । आद्याद् बृहन्मनास्तस्माज्जयद्रथ उदाहृतः ॥11॥
विजयस्तस्य सम्भूत्यां ततो धृतिरजायत । ततो धृतव्रतस्तस्य सत्कर्माधिरथस्ततः ॥12॥
योऽसौ गङ्गातटे क्रीडन् मञ्जूषान्तर्गतं शिशुम् । कुन्त्यापविद्धं कानीनमनपत्योऽकरोत् सुतम् ॥13॥
वृषसेनः सुतस्तस्य कर्णस्य जगतीपतेः । द्रुह्योश्च तनयो बभ्रुः सेतुस्तस्यात्मजस्ततः ॥14॥
आरब्धस्तस्य गान्धारस्तस्य धर्मस्ततो धृतः । धृतस्य दुर्मनास्तस्मात् प्रचेताः प्राचेतसं शतम् ॥15॥
म्लेच्छाधिपतयोऽभूवन्नुदीचीं दिशमाश्रिताः । तुर्वसोश्च सुतो वह्निर्वह्नेर्भर्गोऽथ भानुमान् ॥16॥
त्रिभानुस्तत्सुतोऽस्यापि करन्धम उदारधीः । मरुतस्तत्सुतोऽपुत्रः पुत्रं पौरवमन्वभूत् ॥17॥
दुष्यन्तः स पुनर्भेजे स्वं वंशं राज्यकामुकः । ययातेर्ज्येष्ठपुत्रस्य यदोर्वंशं नरर्षभ ॥18॥
वर्णयामि महापुण्यं सर्वपापहरं नृणाम् । यदोर्वंशं नरः श्रुत्वा सर्वपापैः प्रमुच्यते ॥19॥
यत्रावतीर्णो भगवान् परमात्मा नराकृतिः । यदोः सहस्रजित् क्रोष्टा नलो रिपुरिति श्रुताः ॥20॥
चत्वारः सूनवस्तत्र शतजित् प्रथमात्मजः । महाहयो वेणुहयो हैहयश्चेति तत्सुताः ॥21॥

friend Dasaratha gave his daughter Sāntā to Romapāda as daughter. The sage Rishyasringa married her. This happened because they had to bring Rishyasringa to perform rites for remedying the causes that led to the absence of rain for a long time, by attracting him through the song and dance of handsome women. **9-10.** Brought to the city by women through the attraction they offered by their song, dances, poses, presents and embraces, Rishyasringa arranged for king Dasaratha's performance of Putrakāmeshti by which Dasaratha got issue. Romapāda had Chaturanga as son, and he, Prithulāksha. **11.** Prithulāksha's sons were Brihadratha, Brihadkarma and Brihadbhānu. To Brihadratha was born Brihanmanas, and to him, Jayadratha. **12.** Jayadratha had by Sambhūti a son Vijaya; and Vijaya's son was Dhriti. His son was Dhritavrata; his son, Satkarma; and his son, Adhiratha. **13.** Adhiratha was without issue. One day when he was sporting on the Ganga's shore, he got a box with a child within, It was the infant born to Kunti when she was unmarried and therefore deserted by her. Adhiratha took up the baby and brought it up as his own child.

14. He became King Karna. His son was Vrishasena. Druhyu, the third son of Yayāti, had as son Babhru; and he, Setu. **15.** From Setu was born Ārabdha; from him, Gāndhāra; from him, Dharma; from him, Dhrita; from him, Durmanas; and from him, Prachetas. Prachetas had a hundred sons. **16.** Going northwards they became the rulers of barbarians (Mlechchas). Turvasu, the second son of Yayāti, had as son Vahni; he, Bharga; and he, Bhānumān. **17.** His son was Tribhānu; his son, the generous Karandhama; and his son, Maruta, who left no issue. He adopted Dushyanta as his son.

The Line of Yadus (18-23)

18-19. Though thus adopted by Maruta, Dushyanta, being desirous of kingship, went back to his own ancestral family. I shall now describe to you the very holy line of Yadu, the eldest son of Yayāti. Listening to the narration of his line, man is liberated from sins. **20-21.** For, it was in that line of Yadu that the Supreme

धर्मस्तु हैहयसुतो नेत्रः कुन्तेः पिता ततः । सोहञ्जिरभवत् कुन्तेर्महिष्मान् भद्रसेनकः ॥22॥
दुर्मदो भद्रसेनस्य धनकः कृतवीर्यसूः । कृताग्निः कृतवर्मा च कृतौजा धनकात्मजाः ॥23॥
अर्जुनः कृतवीर्यस्य सप्तद्वीपेश्वरोऽभवत् । दत्तात्रेयाद्धरेरंशात् प्राप्तयोगमहागुणः ॥24॥
न नूनं कार्तवीर्यस्य गतिं यास्यन्ति पार्थिवाः । यज्ञदानतपोयोगश्रुतवीर्यजयादिभिः ॥25॥
पञ्चाशीतिसहस्राणि ह्यव्याहतबलः समाः । अनष्टवित्तस्मरणो बुभुजेऽक्षय्यषड्वसु ॥26॥
तस्य पुत्रसहस्रेषु पञ्चैवोर्वरिता मृधे । जयध्वजः शूरसेनो वृषभो मधुरूर्जितः ॥27॥
जयध्वजात् तालजङ्घस्तस्य पुत्रशतं त्वभूत् । क्षत्रं यत् तालजङ्घाख्यमौर्वतेजोपसंहृतम् ॥28॥
तेषां ज्येष्ठो वीतिहोत्रो वृष्णिः पुत्रो मधोः स्मृतः । तस्य पुत्रशतं त्वासीद् वृष्णिज्येष्ठं यतः कुलम् ॥29॥
माधवा वृष्णयो राजन् यादवाश्चेति संज्ञिताः । यदुपुत्रस्य च क्रोष्टोः पुत्रो वृजिनवांस्ततः ॥30॥
श्वाहिस्ततो रुशेकुर्वै तस्य चित्ररथस्ततः । शशबिन्दुर्महायोगी महाभोजो महानभूत् ॥31॥
चतुर्दशमहारत्नश्चक्रवर्त्यपराजितः । तस्य पत्नीसहस्राणां दशानां सुमहायशाः ॥32॥
दशलक्षसहस्राणि पुत्राणां तास्वजीजनत् । तेषां तु षट्प्रधानानां पृथुश्रवस आत्मजः ॥33॥

Lord was incarnated as man. Yadu had four famous sons by name Sahasrajit, Kroshtā, Nala and Ripu. Of these, the eldest Sahasrajit had as son Satajit; his sons were Mahāhaya, Venuhaya, and Haihaya. **22.** Haihaya had a son Dharma; he, Kunti's father Netra. Kunti's son was Sohanjit; his son was Mahishmān; and his son, Bhadrasena. **23.** Bhadrasena had as sons Durmada, and Dhanaka whose son was Kritavīrya. Dhanaka's other sons were Kritāgni, Kritavarma, and Kritaujas.

Arjuna (24-27)

24. Of those, Kritavīrya had a son named Arjuna (otherwise known as Kārtavīryārjuna) who became king over the whole earth girt by the seven oceans. He was a disciple of Dattātreya, an incarnation of the Lord, who possessed great Yogic powers. **25.** No king has come or will ever come anywhere near Kārtavīryārjuna in respect of Yajna, charity, Tapas, Yoga, sacrificial study, prowess and victory. **26.** He lived a full life of worldly power and enjoyment for eighty five thousand years. His might was irresistible by any other, and his wealth inexhaustible. He always kept up the remembrance of the Lord. **27.** In his conflict with Parasurama, all his numerous sons perished except five, these being Jayadhwaja, Sūrasena, Vrishabha, Madhu and Ūrjita.

The Yadus (28-39)

28. Jayadhwaja had Tālajangha as son. He in turn had a hundred sons, who were all destroyed by Sagara helped by the power he received from Aurva. **29.** Among those sons of Tālajangha, the eldest son was Vītihotra. His son was Madhu who in turn had a hundred sons, of whom Vrishni was the eldest. Because of Vrishni, Madhu and Yadu, this line became famous. **30.** For, the kings born in the line came to be called after them as Mādhavas, Vrishnis and Yādavas. **31.** Kroshtā, the second son of Yadu, had as son Vrijinavān; his son was Svāhi; his, Ruseku; his, Chitraratha; and his, Sasabindu, who was great in his powers of Yoga and of enjoyment.

32-33. He was an emperor of invincible might possessing the fourteen rare gems consisting of elephant regiments, cavalry etc. He had ten thousand wives, and by each of them a lakh of sons. Of these sons six were important, one of these being Pri-

धर्मो नामोशना तस्य हयमेधशतस्य याट् । तत्सुतो रुचकस्तस्य पञ्चासन्नात्मजाः शृणु ।।34।।
पुरुजिद्रुक्मरुक्मेषुपृथुज्यामघसंज्ञिताः । ज्यामघस्त्वप्रजोऽप्यन्यां भार्यां शैब्यापतिर्भयात् 35
नाविन्दच्छत्रुभवनाद् भोज्यां कन्यामहारषीत् । रथस्थां तां निरीक्ष्याह शैब्या पतिमर्मर्षिता ।।36।।
केयं कुहक मत्स्थानं रथमारोपितेति वै । स्नुषा तवेत्यभिहिते स्मयन्ती पतिमब्रवीत् ।।37।।
अहं वन्ध्यासपत्नी च स्नुषा मे युज्यते कथम् । जनयिष्यसि यं राज्ञि तस्येयमुपयुज्यते ।।38।।
अन्वमोदन्त तद्विश्वेदेवाः पितर एव च । शैब्या गर्भमधात् काले कुमारं सुषुवे शुभम् ।
स विदर्भ इति प्रोक्त उपयेमे स्नुषां सतीम् ।।39।।

इति श्रीमद्भागवते महापुराणे पारमहंस्यां संहितायां नवमस्कन्धे यदुवंशानुवर्णने त्रयोविंशोऽध्यायः ।।23।।

thusravas whose son was Dharma. **34.** He got a son named Usanas who performed a hundred sacrifices. His son was Ruchaka. Ruchaka had five sons whose names were as follows: **35.** They were Purujit, Rukma, Rukmeshu, Prithu and Jyāmagha. Jyāmagha had no issue by his wife Saibyā, but for fear of Saibyā he did not take another wife. **36.** Once on return from a campaign he brought with him a daughter of a conquered king to be kept as a concubine. Saibyā saw her sitting in the chariot and became very much annoyed with her husband and said to him: **37.** 'O unfaithful one! Who is that woman you are keeping at my place by your side?' He replied: 'This is your daughter-in-law.' Thereupon she said smiling to her husband: **38.** 'I am sterile and I have no co-wife. How can I then have a daughter-in-law?' He replied: 'O queen! When you come to have a son, this girl will be available for him as wife.' **39.** His words were heard with acclamation by Viswedevas and Pitris, whom he had been worshipping. By their grace, Saibyā became pregnant and had a beautiful child. That child became famous as Vidarbha. He married the girl who had been brought by his father to be the daughter-in-law.

अथ चतुर्विंशोऽध्यायः

श्रीशुक उवाच

तस्यां विदर्भोऽजनयत् पुत्रौ नाम्ना कुशक्रथौ । तृतीयं रोमपादं च विदर्भकुलनन्दनम् ।। 1।।
रोमपादसुतो बभ्रुर्बभ्रोः कृतिरजायत । उशिकस्तत्सुतस्तस्माच्चेदिश्चैद्यादयो नृप ।। 2।।
क्रथस्य कुन्तिः पुत्रोऽभूद् धृष्टिस्तस्याथ निर्वृतिः । ततो दशार्हो नाम्नाभूत्तस्य व्योमः सुतस्ततः ।। 3।।

Skandha IX : Chapter 24

THE GENEALOGICAL BACKGROUND OF SRI KRISHNA

Other Yādavas (1-25)

Sri Suka said: **1.** Vidarbha begot three sons—Kusa, Kratha, and Romapāda, the delight of the Vidarbha family. **2.** Romapāda's son was Babhru; his son, Kriti; his son, Usika; and his son, Chedi. His sons were Damaghosha and others known as the Chaidyas. **3.** Kratha had as son Kunti; he, Dhrishti; he, Nirvriti; he,

जीमूतो विकृतिस्तस्य यस्य भीमरथः सुतः । ततो नवरथः पुत्रो जातो दशरथस्ततः ॥ 4॥
करम्भिः शकुनेः पुत्रो देवरातस्तदात्मजः । देवक्षत्रस्ततस्तस्य मधुः कुरुवशादनुः ॥ 5॥
पुरुहोत्रस्त्वनोः पुत्रस्तस्यायुः सात्वतस्ततः । भजमानो भजिर्दिव्यो वृष्णिर्देवावृधोऽन्धकः ॥ 6॥
सात्वतस्य सुताः सप्त महाभोजश्च मारिष । भजमानस्य निम्लोचिः किङ्किणो धृष्टिरेव च 7॥
एकस्यामात्मजाः पत्न्यामन्यस्यां च त्रयः सुताः । शताजिच्च सहस्राजिदयुताजिदिति प्रभो ॥ 8॥
बभ्रुर्देवावृधसुतस्तयोः श्लोकौ पठन्त्यमू । यथैव शृणुमो दूरात् सम्पश्यामस्तथान्तिकात् 9॥
बभ्रुः श्रेष्ठो मनुष्याणां देवैर्देवावृधः समः । पुरुषाः पञ्चषष्टिश्च षट् सहस्राणि चाष्ट च ॥10॥
येऽमृतत्वमनुप्राप्ता बभ्रोर्देवावृधादपि । महाभोजोऽपि धर्मात्मा भोजा आसंस्तदन्वये ॥11॥
वृष्णेः सुमित्रः पुत्रोऽभूद् युधाजिच्च परंतप । शिनिस्तस्यानमित्रश्च निम्नोऽभूदनमित्रतः ॥12॥
सत्राजितः प्रसेनश्च निम्नस्याप्यासतुः सुतौ । अनमित्रसुतो योऽन्यः शिनिस्तस्याथ सत्यकः ॥13॥
युयुधानः सात्यकिर्वै जयस्तस्य कुणिस्ततः । युगन्धरोऽनमित्रस्य वृष्णिः पुत्रोऽपरस्ततः ॥14॥
श्वफल्कश्चित्ररथश्च गान्दिन्यां च श्वफल्कतः । अक्रूरप्रमुखा आसन् पुत्रा द्वादश विश्रुताः ॥15॥
आसङ्गः सारमेयश्च मृदुरो मृदुविद् गिरिः । धर्मवृद्धः सुकर्मा च क्षेत्रोपेक्षोऽरिमर्दनः ॥16॥
शत्रुघ्नो गन्धमादश्च प्रतिबाहुश्च द्वादश । तेषां स्वसा सुचीराख्या द्वावक्रूरसुतावपि ॥17॥
देववानुपदेवश्च तथा चित्ररथात्मजाः । पृथुर्विदूरथाद्याश्च बहवो वृष्णिनन्दनाः ॥18॥

Dasārha; and he, Vyoma. **4.** His son was Jīmūta; his, Vikriti; his, Bhīmaratha; his, Navaratha; and his, Dasaratha. **5.** His son was Sakuni; his son, Karambhi; his son, Devarāta; his son, Devakshatra; his son, Madhu; his son, Kuruvasa; and his son, Anu. **6-7.** Anu's son was Puruhotra, his son, Āyus; and his son, Sātvata. Sātvata had seven sons named Bhajamāna, Bhaji, Divya, Vrishni, Devāvridha, Andhaka and Mahābhoja. Bhajamāna had by one wife Nimlochi, Kinkina and Dhrishti. **8.** By another wife, he had three sons, Satājit, Sahasrājit, Ayutājit. **9-11.** Great men recite the two following verses in praise of Devāvridha and his son Babhru: 'On knowing them at close quarters we find them as wonderful as the reports we had of them from a distance. Babhru is the noblest among men, while Devāvridha is equal to a divinity. Fourteen thousand and sixty-five persons got liberated on account of these two, Babhru and Devāvridha.' Mahābhoja, the son of Sātvata, was also a strict follower of Dharma. The famous Bhojas sprang from his line.

12. Vrishni had two sons named Sumitra and Yudhājit. Of these Yudhājit had Sini and Anamitra as sons. Of Anamitra, Nimna was born. **13.** Nimna had two sons, Satrājit and Prasena. Anamitra had also another son named Sini and he had a son Satyaka by name. **14.** Satyaka's son was Yuyudhāna. He had Jaya as son; he, Kuni; and he, Yugandhara. Anamitra had another Vrishni as son.

15. He, Vrishni, had as sons Svaphalka and Chitraratha. Svaphalka had by his wife Gāndini twelve famous sons, besides Akrūra. **16-18.** These sons of Svaphalka were Āsanga, Sārameya, Mridura, Mriduvit, Giri, Dharmavriddha, Sukarma, Kshetropeksha, Arimardana, Satrughna, Gandhamāda, and Pratibāhu. They had also a sister Suchīrā. Akrūra had two sons Devavān and Upadeva. Many sons beginning with Prithu and Vidūratha were born to Chitraratha. All these belonged to the clan of Vrishnis.

कुकुरो भजमानश्च शुचिः कम्बलबर्हिषः ।
कुकुरस्य सुतो वह्निर्विलोमा तनयस्ततः ॥19॥
कपोतरोमा तस्यानुः सखा यस्य च तुम्बुरुः ।
अन्धको दुन्दुभिस्तस्मादरिद्योतः पुनर्वसुः ॥20॥
तस्याहुकश्चाहुकी च कन्या चैवाहुकात्मजौ ।
देवकश्चोग्रसेनश्च चत्वारो देवकात्मजाः ॥21॥
देववानुपदेवश्च सुदेवो देववर्धनः ।
तेषां स्वसारः सप्तासन् धृतदेवादयो नृप ॥22॥
शान्तिदेवोपदेवा च श्रीदेवा देवरक्षिता ।
सहदेवा देवकी च वसुदेव उवाह ताः ॥23॥
कंसः सुनामा न्यग्रोधः कङ्कः शङ्कुः सुहूस्तथा ।
राष्ट्रपालोऽथ सृष्टिश्च तुष्टिमानौग्रसेनयः ॥24॥
कंसा कंसवती कङ्का शूरभू राष्ट्रपालिका ।
उग्रसेनदुहितरो वसुदेवानुजस्त्रियः ॥25॥
शूरो विदूरथादासीद् भजमानः सुतस्ततः ।
शिनिस्तस्मात् स्वयम्भोजो हृदीकस्तत्सुतो मतः 26
देवबाहुः शतधनुः कृतवर्मेति तत्सुताः ।
देवमीढस्य शूरस्य मारिषा नाम पत्न्यभूत् ॥27॥
तस्यां स जनयामास दश पुत्रानकल्मषान् ।
वसुदेवं देवभागं देवश्रवसमानकम् ॥28॥
सृञ्जयं श्यामकं कङ्कं शमीकं वत्सकं वृकम् ।
देवदुन्दुभयो नेदुरानका यस्य जन्मनि ॥29॥
वसुदेवं हरेः स्थानं वदन्त्यानकदुन्दुभिम् ।
पृथा च श्रुतदेवा च श्रुतकीर्तिः श्रुतश्रवाः ॥30॥
राजाधिदेवी चैतेषां भगिन्यः पञ्च कन्यकाः ।
कुन्तेः सख्युः पिता शूरो ह्यपुत्रस्य पृथामदात् ॥31॥
साऽऽप दुर्वाससो विद्यां देवहूतीं प्रतोषितात् ।
तस्या वीर्यपरीक्षार्थमाजुहाव रविं शुचिम् ॥32॥

19. Andhaka had as sons Kukura, Bhajamāna, Suchi, and Kambalabarhisha. Among them Kukura had Vahni as son; and he, Vilomā. **20.** Of Vilomā was born Kapotaroma; and of him, Anu, having Tumburu as friend. Anu's son was Andhaka; his, Dundubhi; his, Aridyota; and his, Punarvasu. **21-23.** He had Āhuka as son and Āhukī as daughter. Āhuka's sons were Devaka and Ugrasena. Devaka had four sons named Devavān, Upadeva, Sudeva, Devavardhana, besides, as their sisters, seven daughters named Dhritadevā, Sāntidevā, Upadevā, Devarakshitā, Sahadevā, and Devakī. Vasudeva married them all.

24. Ugrasena had nine sons, Kamsa, Sunāma, Nyagrodha, Kanka, Sanku, Suhū, Rāshtrapāla, Srishti and Tushtimān. **25.** Vasudeva's younger brothers married the daughters of Ugrasena named Kamsā, Kamsavatī, Kankā, Sūrabhū and Rāshtrapālikā.

Vasudeva, Krishna's father, and Prithā (26-36)

26. From Sūra, the son of Vidūratha, was born Bhajamāna; from him, Sini; from him, Swayambhoja; and from him, Hridīka. **27-31.** He had as sons Devabāhu, Satadhanus and Kritavarmā. Sūra, the son of Devamīdha, had as wife Mārishā. He, Sūra, begot by this wife Mārishā ten sons, they being Vasudeva, Devabhāga, Devasravas, Ānaka, Srinjaya, Syāmaka, Kanka, Samīka, Vatsaka, and Vrika. Vasudeva, at whose birth the Devas sounded their percussion instruments called Ānaka and Dundubhi, came to be known also as Ānakadundubhi; he was to be the vehicle for the manifestation of Hari on earth as Sri Krishna. Prithā, Srutadevā, Srutakīrti, Srutasravā, and Rājādhidevi were the five sisters of Sūra's sons. Sūra, the father of Prithā, allowed his friend Kuntibhoja, to adopt Prithā as his daughter. Henceforth she came to be called Kunti. **32.** Prithā pleased the sage Durvāsas very much by service, and he imparted to her the esoteric technique known as Devahūtī by which one could call the Devas to one's side. And she, in order to test the efficacy of the Vidya, used it to invoke Ravi, the sun-deity.

तदैवोपगतं देवं वीक्ष्य विस्मितमानसा । प्रत्ययार्थं प्रयुक्ता मे याहि देव क्षमस्व मे ॥33॥
अमोघं दर्शनं देवि आधित्से त्वयि चात्मजम् । योनिर्यथा न दुष्येत कर्ताहं ते सुमध्यमे ॥34॥
इति तस्यां स आधाय गर्भं सूर्यो दिवं गतः । सद्यः कुमारः संजज्ञे द्वितीय इव भास्करः ॥35॥
तं सात्यजन्नदीतोये कृच्छ्राल्लोकस्य बिभ्यती । प्रपितामहस्तामुवाह पाण्डुर्वै सत्यविक्रमः ॥36॥
श्रुतदेवां तु कारूषो वृद्धशर्मा समग्रहीत् । यस्यामभूद् दन्तवक्त्र ऋषिशप्तो दितेः सुतः ॥37॥
कैकेयो धृष्टकेतुश्च श्रुतकीर्तिमविन्दत । सन्तर्दनादयस्तस्य पञ्चासन् कैकयाः सुताः ॥38॥
राजाधिदेव्यामावन्त्यौ जयसेनोऽजनिष्ट ह । दमघोषश्चेदिराजः श्रुतश्रवसमग्रहीत् ॥39॥
शिशुपालः सुतस्तस्याः कथितस्तस्य सम्भवः । देवभागस्य कंसायां चित्रकेतुबृहद्बलौ ॥40॥
कंसवत्यां देवश्रवसः सुवीर इषुमांस्तथा । कङ्कायामानकाज्जातः सत्यजित् पुरुजित्तथा ॥41॥
सृञ्जयो राष्ट्रपाल्यां च वृषदुर्मर्षणादिकान् । हरिकेशहिरण्याक्षौ शूरभूम्यां च श्यामकः ॥42॥
मिश्रकेश्यामप्सरसि वृकादीन् वत्सकस्तथा । तक्षपुष्करशालादीन् दुर्वाक्ष्यां वृक आदधे ॥43॥
सुमित्रार्जुनपालादीञ्छमीकात्तु सुदामिनी । कङ्कश्च कर्णिकायां वै ऋतधामजयावपि ॥44॥
पौरवी रोहिणी भद्रा मदिरा रोचना इला । देवकीप्रमुखा आसन् पत्न्य आनकदुन्दुभेः ॥45॥

33. She was astonished to find the sun-deity immediately by her side, and she said to him: 'Lord, I used the Vidya only for testing. You may therefore go, pardoning me.' **34.** Thereupon the sun-deity said: 'O Devi! My visit cannot go fruitless. I shall impregnate you, I shall do it without breaking your maidenhood.' **35.** So saying, the deity impregnated her, and went away to his celestial abode in the sky. Immediately after, a divine child, looking like another sun, was born. **36.** Afraid of public criticism, she drifted the child down a stream. Afterwards she was married to Pāndu, your truth-abiding paternal grandfather.

Dantavaktra, Sisupāla etc. (37-44)

37. Vriddhasarma, the king of Karūsha married Srutadevā. Vijaya, who had been cursed by Sanaka and the other Kumaras, and who had as a consequence been born as the Asura Hiranyāksha in an earlier birth, now got embodiment as Dantavaktra in Srutadevā. **38.** Dhrishtaketu, the king of the Kekayas, married Srutakirti. The king had five sons by her, famous as Kaikayas. **39.** Jayasena begot by Rājādhidevi, Vinda and Anuvinda, who became kings of Avanti. Damaghosha, the king of Chedi, married Srutasravā. **40.** To them was born Sisupāla, the circumstances of whose birth have already been described. Devabhāga begot by his wife Kamsā two sons Chitraketu and Brihadbala. **41.** Devasravas had by his wife Kamsavatī two sons, Suvīra and Ishumān. In the same way Ānaka had by his wife Kankā two sons Satyajit and Purujit. **42.** Srinjaya begot by Rāshtrapālī, Vrisha, Durmarshana and other sons, while Syāmaka begot Harikesa and Hiranyāksha by Sūrabhūmi. **43.** Vatsaka begot Vrika and others by the Apsaras named Misrakesi, and Vrika had by his wife Durvākshi several sons beginning with Taksha, Pushkara and Sāla. **44.** Sudāmini bore to Samīka, Sumitra, Arjuna, Pāla and others. Kanka begot Ritadhāma and Jaya by Karnikā.

Vasudeva and his Issue (45-53)

45. Vasudeva the son of Sūra, had as wives Devaki, Pauravi, Rohini, Bhadra,

बलं गदं सारणं च दुर्मदं विपुलं ध्रुवम् । वसुदेवस्तु रोहिण्यां कृतादीनुदपादयत् ॥46॥
सुभद्रो भद्रवाहश्च दुर्मदो भद्र एव च । पौरव्यास्तनया ह्येते भूताद्या द्वादशाभवन् ॥47॥
नन्दोपनन्दकृतकशूराद्या मदिरात्मजाः । कौसल्या केशिनं त्वेकमसूत कुलनन्दनम् ॥48॥
रोचनायामतो जाता हस्तहेमाङ्गदादयः । इलायामुरुवल्कादीन् यदुमुख्यानजीजनत् ॥49॥
विपृष्ठो धृतदेवायामेक आनकदुन्दुभेः । शान्तिदेवात्मजा राजञ्छ्रमप्रतिश्रुतादयः ॥50॥
राजानः कल्पवर्षाद्या उपदेवासुता दश । वसुहंससुवंशाद्याः श्रीदेवायास्तु षट् सुताः ॥51॥
देवरक्षितया लब्धा नव चात्र गदादयः । वसुदेवः सुतानष्टावादधे सहदेवया ॥52॥
पुरुविश्रुतमुख्यांस्तु साक्षाद् धर्मो वसूनिव । वसुदेवस्तु देवक्यामष्ट पुत्रानजीजनत् ॥53॥
कीर्तिमन्तं सुषेणं च भद्रसेनमुदारधीः । ऋजुं सम्मर्दनं भद्रं सङ्कर्षणमहीश्वरम् ॥54॥
अष्टमस्तु तयोरासीत् स्वयमेव हरिः किल । सुभद्रा च महाभागा तव राजन् पितामही ॥55॥
यदा यदेह धर्मस्य क्षयो वृद्धिश्च पाप्मनः । तदा तु भगवानीश आत्मानं सृजते हरिः ॥56॥
न ह्यस्य जन्मनो हेतुः कर्मणो वा महीपते । आत्ममायां विनेशस्य परस्य द्रष्टुरात्मनः ॥57॥
यन्मायाचेष्टितं पुंसः स्थित्युत्पत्त्यप्ययाय हि । अनुग्रहस्तन्निवृत्तेरात्मलाभाय चेष्यते ॥58॥
अक्षौहिणीनां पतिभिरसुरैर्नृपलाञ्छनैः । भुव आक्रम्यमाणाया अभाराय कृतोद्यमः ॥59॥

Madira, Rochana and Ila. **46.** He begot by Rohini the following sons: Bala, Gada, Sārana, Durmada, Vipula, Dhruva and Krita. **47.** By Pauravi he begot twelve sons, some of them being Bhūta, Subhadra, Bhadravāhan, Durmada and Bhadra. **48.** Nanda, Upananda, Kritaka, Sūra and others were his sons by Madira. Kausalya had only one son Kesi who was the delight of his family. **49.** Vasudeva had sons like Hasta and Hemāngada by Rochana, and noted Yādava chiefs like Uruvalka by Ila. **50.** Viprishtha was the only son Vasudeva had by Dhritadevā. Srama and Pratisruta were the sons of Sāntidevā. **51.** Ten sons including Kalpavarsha were born of Upadevā, and six sons beginning with Vasuhamsa and Suvamsa were born to Sridevā. **52-53.** Devarakshitā brought forth for Vasudeva nine sons beginning with Gada; and Sahadevā brought forth begotten by him, eight sons beginning with Puruvisruta as Dharma begot the eight Vasus. And by Devaki, Vasudeva had eight sons.

Sri Krishna (54-67)

54. The seven sons of noble Vasudeva by Devaki were Kīrtimān, Sushena, Bhadrasena, Riju, Sammardana, Bhadra, and Sankarshana. **55.** As the eighth son of Vasudeva and Devaki, the supreme Hari Himself appeared as the perfect incarnation Sri Krishna. Your grandmother Subhadrā also was born of them. **56.** Whenever there is decline of Dharma and ascendency of Adharma, the Supreme Lord Himself bodies forth. **57.** Except His own Yoga Maya (the Divine will), no other reason can be found for His incarnating; for He is the controller of Maya, the unattached, the all-pervading, and the ultimate witness. **58.** O King! He whose activity is only for the blessing of the Jivas—how can His birth be accounted for by Karma and other factors? His sportive activity has a twofold aspect—to maintain the order of creation, sustentation and dissolution on the one hand and, on the other, to redeem Jivas from this cycle of worldly existence caused by Himself, and establish them in the bliss of their Atmanhood. **59-60.** In this incarnation, along with Balarama, He, the worshipful

कर्माण्यपरिमेयाणि मनसापि सुरेश्वरैः । सहसङ्कर्षणश्चक्रे भगवान् मधुसूदनः ॥60॥
कलौ जनिष्यमाणानां दुःखशोकतमोनुदम् । अनुग्रहाय भक्तानां सुपुण्यं व्यतनोद् यशः ॥61॥
यस्मिन् सत्कर्णपीयूषे यशस्तीर्थवरे सकृत् । श्रोत्राञ्जलिरुपस्पृश्य धुनुते कर्मवासनाम् ॥62॥
भोजवृष्ण्यन्धकमधुशूरसेनदशार्हकैः । श्लाघनीयेहितः शश्वत् कुरुसृञ्जयपाण्डुभिः ॥63॥
स्निग्धस्मितेक्षितोदारैर्वाक्यैर्विक्रमलीलया । नृलोकं रमयामास मूर्त्या सर्वाङ्गरम्यया ॥64॥

यस्याननं मकरकुण्डलचारुकर्णभ्राजत्कपोलसुभगं सविलासहासम् ।
नित्योत्सवं न ततृपुर्दृशिभिः पिबन्त्यो नार्यो नराश्च मुदिताः कुपिता निमेश्च ॥65॥
जातो गतः पितृगृहाद् व्रजमेधितार्थो हत्वा रिपून् सुतशतानि कृतोरुदारः ।
उत्पाद्य तेषु पुरुषः क्रतुभिः समीजे आत्मानमात्मनिगमं प्रथयञ्जनेषु ॥66॥
पृथ्व्याः स वै गुरुभरं क्षपयन् कुरूणामन्तःसमुत्थकलिना युधि भूपचम्वः ।
दृष्टचा विधूय विजये जयमुद्विघोष्य प्रोच्योद्धवाय च परं समगात् स्वधाम ॥67॥

इति श्रीमद्भागवते महापुराणे वैयासिक्यामष्टादशसाहस्र्यां पारमहंस्यां संहितायां नवमस्कन्धे श्रीसूर्यसोमवंशानुकीर्तने यदुवंशानुकीर्तनं नाम चतुर्विंशोऽध्यायः ॥24॥

इति नवमः स्कन्धः समाप्तः

हरिः ॐ तत्सत्

Lord Madhusūdana, accomplished a task impossible even for great Divinities to do—the task of relieving the earth of the onslaught and burden of numerous Asuras in the guise of kings with limitless armies. **61.** As an antidote to the spiritual blindness and the consequent sorrow and sufferings of the people living in the evil age of Kali, He spread everywhere His sanctifying fame which is a great blessing to the devotees. **62.** Man overcomes the bondage of tendencies generated by Karma, if he but once imbibes with his ears even a handful of the waters of the river of His holy fame, which is a veritable ambrosia to the ears of men with good instinct. **63-64.** The Lord delighted the whole world including the Bhojas, Vrishnis, Andhakas, Madhus, Sūrasenas, Dāsārhas, Kauravas, Srinjayas, and Pāndavas with that form of His, of which every limb was a piece of thrilling beauty—with His charming smile and looks and gracious speech and with His sportive actions which were cast in a heroic mould. **65.** Great was the annoyance among men and women against their eyelids which by their winking, were causing obstruction to the continuous drinking of the ambrosia of His face, beautified by His shining cheeks, by His ears resplendent with fish-marked ear-rings, by His charming and playful smile, and by His blissful face which thrilled one the more one looked at it. **66.** Revealing His real form at birth but next assuming the form of a human infant, He departed to Vraja from His father's place, fulfilled all the longings of the inhabitants of Vraja, destroyed numerous enemies, married many wives, had several sons in them, and performed many Yajnas, in which He had to worship only Himself in order to exemplify before others the Vedic way of life promulgated by Himself. **67.** Relieving the earth's burden of the large body of Kauravas by creating internecine conflict among themselves and by causing the destruction of their hosts by His very looks, conferring victory on Yudhishthira, and revealing the Supreme Truth to Uddhava, He accomplished the object of His incarnation and then resumed His transcendent state.

END OF THE NINTH SKANDHA